Windows® 7 Resource Kit

Mitch Tulloch, Tony Northrup, Jerry Honeycutt,
and Ed Wilson, with the Windows 7 Team at Microsoft

PUBLISHED BY
Microsoft Press
A Division of Microsoft Corporation
One Microsoft Way
Redmond, Washington 98052-6399

Library of Congress Control Number: 2009935674

Printed and bound in the United States of America.

1 2 3 4 5 6 7 8 9 QWT 4 3 2 1 0 9

Distributed in Canada by H.B. Fenn and Company Ltd.

A CIP catalogue record for this book is available from the British Library.

Microsoft Press books are available through booksellers and distributors worldwide. For further information about international editions, contact your local Microsoft Corporation office or contact Microsoft Press International directly at fax (425) 936-7329. Visit our Web site at www.microsoft.com/mspress. Send comments to rkinput@microsoft.com.

Acquisitions Editor: Juliana Aldous
Developmental Editor: Karen Szall
Project Editor: Melissa von Tschudi-Sutton
Editorial Production: Custom Editorial Productions, Inc.
Technical Reviewers: Mitch Tulloch and Bob Dean; Technical Review services provided by Content Master, a member of CM Group, Ltd.
Cover: Tom Draper Design

Body Part No. X15-66448

Contents at a Glance

Contents

PART III DESKTOP MANAGEMENT

Chapter 13 Overview of Management Tools 383

Chapter 16 Managing Disks and File Systems 611

PART IV DESKTOP MAINTENANCE

Chapter 21 Maintaining Desktop Health 935

PART VI TROUBLESHOOTING

Chapter 31 Troubleshooting Network Issues 1521

Acknowledgments

The authors of the Windows 7 Resource Kit would like to thank the numerous product team members and other experts at Microsoft who contributed hundreds of hours of their valuable time to this project by helping us plan the scope of coverage, providing access to product specifications, reviewing chapters for technical accuracy, writing sidebars that provide valuable insights, and offering their advice, encouragement, and support as we worked on this project. We would particularly like to express our thanks to the following individuals who work at Microsoft:

Aanand Ramachandran, Aaron Smith, Abhishek Tiwari, Adrian Lannin, Alan Morris, Alex Balcanquall, Alwin Vyhmeister, Andy Myers, Anirban Paul, Anjli Chaudhry, Anton Kucer, Ayesha Mascarenhas, Baldwin Ng, Bill Mell, Brent Goodpaster, Brian Lich, Chandra Nukala, Chris Clark, Connie Rock, Crispin Cowan, Darren Baker, Dave Bishop, Denny Gursky, Desmond Lee, Devrim Iyigun, George Roussos, Gerardo Diaz Cuellar, Gov Maharaj, James Kahle, James O'Neill, Jason Grieves, Jason Popp, Jez Sadler, Jim Martin, Joe Sherman, John Thekkethala, Jon Kay, Joseph Davies, Judith Herman, Katharine O'Doherty, Kathleen Carey, Kevin Woley, Kim Griffiths, Kukjin Lee, Kyle Beck, Lilia Gutnik, Lyon Wong, Mark Gray, Michael Murgolo, Michael Niehaus, Michael Novak, Mike Lewis, Mike Owen, Mike Stephens, Narendra Acharya, Nazia Zaman, Nils Dussart, Pat Stemen, Ramprabhu Rathnam, Richie Fang, Rick Kingslan, Scott Roberts, Sean Gilmour, Sean Siler, Sharad Kylasam, Steve Campbell, Thomas Willingham, Tim Mintner, Troy Funk, Varun Bahl, Vikram Singh, and Wole Moses.

Thanks also to Bill Noonan, Mark Kitris, and the CTS Global Technical Readiness (GTR) team at Microsoft for contributing their expertise to this project. The GTR team develops readiness training for Microsoft Commercial Technical Support (CTS) engineers in all product clusters, including Platforms, Messaging, Office Worker, and Developer. GTR creates deep technical content "by engineers, for engineers" with the help of top Subject Matter Experts (SMEs) who are real support engineers from the CTS product clusters.

Finally, special thanks to our outstanding editorial team at Microsoft Press, including Juliana Aldous, Karen Szall, and Melissa von Tschudi-Sutton, for their unflagging energy and tireless commitment to working with us on this challenging project and making it a success. Thanks also to Jean Findley at Custom Editorial Productions, Inc. (CEP), who handled the production aspects of this book, and to Susan McClung and Julie Hotchkiss, our copy editors, who showed wonderful attention to detail. And thanks to Bob Dean, our tireless technical reviewer.

Thanks everyone!

—*The Authors*

Introduction

Welcome to the *Windows 7 Resource Kit* from Microsoft Press! The *Windows 7 Resource Kit* is a comprehensive technical resource for deploying, maintaining, and troubleshooting Windows 7. The target audience for this resource kit is experienced IT professionals who work in medium-size and large organizations, but anyone who wants to learn how to deploy, configure, support, and troubleshoot Windows 7 in Active Directory Domain Services (AD DS) environments will find this resource kit invaluable.

Within this resource kit, you'll find in-depth information and task-based guidance on managing all aspects of Windows 7, including automated deployment, desktop management, search and organization, software update management, client protection, networking, remote access, and systematic troubleshooting techniques. You'll also find numerous sidebars contributed by members of the Windows team at Microsoft that provide deep insight into how Windows 7 works, best practices for managing the platform, and invaluable troubleshooting tips. Finally, the companion media includes the *Windows 7 Resource Kit PowerShell Pack* and sample Windows PowerShell scripts that you can customize to help you automate various aspects of managing Windows 7 clients in enterprise environments.

Overview of the Book

The six parts of this book cover the following topics:

- **Part I—Overview** Provides an introduction to the features of Windows 7 and an overview of security enhancements for the platform.
- **Part II—Deployment** Provides in-depth information and guidance on deploying Windows 7 in enterprise environments, with particular focus on using the Microsoft Deployment Toolkit 2010 (MDT 2010).
- **Part III—Desktop Management** Describes how to use Group Policy to manage the desktop environment for users of computers running Windows 7 and how to manage specific features such as disks and file systems, devices and services, printing, search, and Windows Internet Explorer.
- **Part IV—Desktop Maintenance** Describes how to maintain the health of computers running Windows 7 by using the eventing infrastructure, monitoring performance, managing software updates, managing client protection, and using Remote Assistance.

- **Part V—Networking** Provides in-depth information concerning core networking, wireless networking, Windows Firewall, Internet Protocol Security (IPsec), remote connectivity using virtual private networking (VPN), Remote Desktop, and Internet Protocol version 6 (IPv6).
- **Part VI—Troubleshooting** Describes how to troubleshoot startup, hardware, and networking issues, as well as how to interpret Stop messages.

Document Conventions

The following conventions are used in this book to highlight special features or usage.

Readeraids

The following readeraids are used throughout this book to point out useful details:

READERAID	MEANING
Note	Underscores the importance of a specific concept or highlights a special case that might not apply to every situation
Important	Calls attention to essential information that should not be disregarded
Warning	Warns you that failure to take or avoid a specified action can cause serious problems for users, systems, data integrity, and so on
On the Companion Media	Calls attention to a related script, tool, template, or job aid on the book's companion media that helps you perform a task described in the text

Sidebars

The following sidebars are used throughout this book to provide added insight, tips, and advice concerning different features of Windows 7:

SIDEBAR	MEANING
Direct from the Source	Contributed by experts at Microsoft to provide "from-the-source" insight into how Windows 7 works, best practices for managing clients, and troubleshooting tips.
How It Works	Provides unique glimpses of Windows 7 features and how they work.

Command-Line Examples

The following style conventions are used in documenting command-line examples throughout this book:

STYLE	MEANING
Bold font	Used to indicate user input (characters that you type exactly as shown)
Italic font	Used to indicate variables for which you need to supply a specific value (for example, *file_name* can refer to any valid file name)
`Monospace font`	Used for code samples and command-line output
%SystemRoot%	Used for environment variables

On the Companion Media

The companion media is a valuable addition to this book and includes the following:

- **Windows 7 Resource Kit PowerShell Pack** A collection of Windows PowerShell modules you can install on Windows 7 to provide additional functionality for scripting Windows administration tasks using Windows PowerShell. For more information, see the section titled "Using the Windows 7 Resource Kit PowerShell Pack" later in this introduction.
- **Sample Windows PowerShell scripts** Almost two hundred sample Windows PowerShell scripts are included to demonstrate how you can administer different aspects of Windows 7 using Windows PowerShell. For more information, see the section titled "Using the Sample Windows PowerShell Scripts" later in this introduction.
- **Additional documentation and files** Additional documentation and supporting files for several chapters are included on the companion media.
- **Additional reading** Sample chapters from other Microsoft Press titles are included on the book's companion media.
- **Windows 7 Training Portal** A link to Windows 7–related products presented by Microsoft Learning.
- **Author links** A page that has links to each author's Web site, where you can find out more about each author and his accomplishments.
- **eBook** An electronic version of the entire *Windows 7 Resource Kit* is also included on the companion media.

Additional information concerning the contents of the companion media can be found in Readme.txt files in various folders.

FIND ADDITIONAL CONTENT ONLINE **As new or updated material becomes available that complements your book, it will be posted online on the Microsoft Press Online Windows Server and Client Web site. The type of material you might find includes updates to book content, articles, links to companion content, errata, sample chapters, and more. This Web site is available at *http://microsoftpresssrv.libredigital.com/serverclient/* and is updated periodically.**

Digital Content for Digital Book Readers: If you bought a digital-only edition of this book, you can enjoy select content from the print edition's companion CD. Visit *http://go.microsoft.com/fwlink/?LinkId=161993* to get your downloadable content. This content is always up-to-date and available to all readers.

Using the Windows 7 Resource Kit PowerShell Pack

The Windows 7 Resource Kit PowerShell Pack is a collection of Windows PowerShell modules that you can install on Windows 7 to provide additional functionality for scripting Windows administration tasks using Windows PowerShell. *Modules*—a new feature of Windows PowerShell 2.0—allow Windows PowerShell scripts and functions to be organized into independent, self-contained units. For example, a single module can package together multiple cmdlets, providers, scripts, functions, and other files that can be distributed to users. See the section titled "Disclaimer Concerning Windows PowerShell CD Content" later in this introduction for more information.

The PowerShell Pack contains ten modules that can be installed to add additional scripting capabilities to your Windows PowerShell environment. The additional functionalities provided by these modules are as follows:

- **WPK** Creates rich user interfaces quickly and easily from Windows PowerShell. Features over 600 scripts to help you build quick user interfaces. Think HTML Applications (HTAs), but easy.
- **FileSystem** Monitors files and folders, checks for duplicate files, and checks disk space.
- **IsePack** Supercharge your scripting in the Integrated Scripting Environment (ISE) with more than thirty-five shortcuts.

- **DotNet** Explores loaded types, finds commands that can work with a type, and describes how you can use Windows PowerShell, DotNet, and COM together.
- **PSImageTools** Converts, rotates, scales, and crops images and gets image metadata.
- **PSRSS** Harnesses the FeedStore from Windows PowerShell.
- **PSSystemTools** Gets operating system or hardware information.
- **PSUserTools** Gets the users on a system, checks for elevation, and starts a process as administrator.
- **PSCodeGen** Generates Windows PowerShell scripts, C# code, and Pinvoke.
- **TaskScheduler** Lists scheduled tasks and creates and deletes tasks.

For information on how to install the PowerShell Pack on Windows 7, see the ReadmePP.txt file in the \PowerShellPack folder on the companion media.

Note that the modules and accompanying documentation included in the PowerShell Pack are presented as is, with no warranty, and are entirely unsupported by Microsoft. Do not use these modules in your production environment without testing them first in a nonproduction environment. See the section titled "Disclaimer Concerning Windows PowerShell CD Content" later in this introduction for more information.

Using the Sample Windows PowerShell Scripts

Included on the companion media are almost two hundred sample scripts that demonstrate how you can administer different aspects of Windows 7 using Windows PowerShell. These sample scripts are presented as is, with no warranty, and are entirely unsupported by Microsoft. Do not use these scripts in your production environment without testing them first in a nonproduction environment. You may need to customize some scripts to make them work properly in a production environment. See the section titled "Disclaimer Concerning Windows PowerShell CD Content" later in this introduction for more information.

Before you use these scripts, you must understand how Windows PowerShell execution policy controls how scripts are run on a computer. Windows PowerShell can have five possible values for the script execution policy on a computer:

- **Restricted** This is the default setting and allows no scripts to run.
- **AllSigned** This setting means that scripts need a digital signature before they can be run.

- **RemoteSigned** This setting means that only scripts run from file shares, downloaded using Internet Explorer, or received as e-mail attachments must be signed.
- **Unrestricted** This setting means that all scripts can be run.
- **Bypass** This setting means that nothing is blocked and there are no prompts or warnings.

To view the current script execution policy, open a Windows PowerShell command prompt and type **Get-ExecutionPolicy**. The current execution policy for your system can be changed by typing **Set-ExecutionPolicy <*value*>,** where <*value*> is one of the five values listed previously. Changing the execution policy requires that Windows PowerShell be run as an administrator. Note, however, that if your script execution policy is set by your network administrator using Group Policy, you will not be permitted to change the execution policy on your computer.

Microsoft recommends that the execution policy be configured as *Remote-Signed* within a production environment, unless you have a compelling reason for either a stricter or a less strict setting. For information on how to sign PowerShell scripts, see *http://technet.microsoft.com/en-us/magazine/2008.04.powershell.aspx*. You can also type **Get-Help about_signing** at the Windows PowerShell command prompt for further information about signing scripts.

Remoting, a new feature of Windows PowerShell 2.0, uses the WS-Management protocol to allow you to run Windows PowerShell commands on one or many remote computers. This means that many of the scripts included on the companion media will work on remote computers even though they may not have the *–computer* parameter that allows you to specify a remote computer name. For Windows PowerShell remoting to work, you must have Windows PowerShell 2.0 installed and configured on both the local computer and the targeted remote computer. You must also enable remoting on the targeted remote computers by running the **Enable-PSRemoting** command on them, which configures these computers to receive remote commands. The **Enable-PSRemoting** command must be run with administrative rights. For more information about Windows PowerShell remoting technology, type **Get-Help about_remoting** at the Windows PowerShell command prompt.

Some of these sample scripts use Windows Management Instrumentation (WMI), Active Directory Services Interface (ADSI), or the Microsoft .NET Framework application programming interfaces (APIs) to connect to remote computers. These scripts may work on remote computers even if Windows PowerShell is not installed on those computers. Before some of these scripts can work remotely, however, you may need to enable remote administration through Windows Firewall on both the host computer and the target computer on the appropriate network connection. You will also need to be a member of the local administrators group on the remote computer.

You can use the *EnableDisableRemoteAdmin.ps1* script to enable remote administration through Windows Firewall. Note that the actions performed by this script are not appropriate for edge-connected machines and may not be appropriate for some enterprise customers. Before you run **EnableDisableRemoteAdmin.ps1** in a production environment, you should evaluate the changes being made by this script to determine if they are appropriate for your environment. For more information about how WMI works through the Windows Firewall, see *http://msdn.microsoft.com/en-us/library/aa389286.aspx*.

All the sample scripts include command-line help. To obtain basic information about a script, type **Get-Help *script_name.ps1*,** where *script_name.ps1* is the name of the script. To see sample syntax for using the script, as well as detailed help information, type **Get-Help *script_name.ps1* –Full**. If you only want to see examples of how to use the script, type **Get-Help *script_name.ps1* –Examples.**

Disclaimer Concerning Windows PowerShell CD Content

The Windows PowerShell scripts included on the companion media are only samples and are not finished tools. These scripts are provided as proof-of-concept examples of how to administer Windows 7 clients using Windows PowerShell. Although every effort has been made to ensure that these sample scripts work properly, Microsoft disclaims any responsibility for any and all liability or responsibility for any damages that may result from using these scripts. The sample scripts are provided to you as is, with no warranty or guarantee concerning their functionality, and Microsoft does not provide any support for them.

The Windows 7 Resource Kit PowerShell Pack included on the companion media is also unsupported by Microsoft and is provided to you as is, with no warranty or guarantee concerning its functionality. For the latest news and usage tips concerning this PowerShell Pack, see the Windows PowerShell Team Blog at *http://blogs.msdn.com/powershell/*.

Be sure to thoroughly familiarize yourself with using these Windows PowerShell scripts and modules in a test environment before attempting to use them in your production environment. Because these sample scripts are provided as proof-of-concept samples only, you may need to customize them if you intend to use them in your production environment. For example, the scripts as provided include only minimal error handling and assume that the clients they are being run against exist and are configured appropriately. The authors therefore encourage readers to customize these scripts to meet their particular needs.

Resource Kit Support Policy

Every effort has been made to ensure the accuracy of this book and the companion media content. Microsoft Press provides corrections to this book through the Internet at the following location:

http://www.microsoft.com/mspress/support/search.aspx

If you have comments, questions, or ideas regarding the book or companion media content, or if you have questions that are not answered by querying the Knowledge Base, please send them to Microsoft Press by using either of the following methods:

E-mail:

rkinput@microsoft.com

Postal Mail:

Microsoft Press
Attn: Windows 7 Resource Kit Editor
One Microsoft Way
Redmond, WA 98052-6399

Please note that product support is not offered through the preceding mail addresses. For product support information, please visit the Microsoft Product Support Web site at the following address:

http://support.microsoft.com

PART I

Overview

CHAPTER 1

Overview of Windows 7 Improvements

Windows 7 is a complex operating system with thousands of features. Understanding it thoroughly can require years of study. Fortunately, most IT professionals have experience with the earlier versions of Windows that the Windows 7 operating system is based on, such as Windows XP and Windows Vista. This chapter, which assumes that you have basic familiarity with the features of Windows Vista, describes the most significant improvements that are not security related and are not discussed elsewhere in this book, the different editions of Windows 7, and the hardware requirements for Windows 7.

> ***NOTE*** **This high-level chapter is designed to quickly give IT professionals a broad view of changes in Windows 7. However, it is also suitable for less-technical executive staff who need to understand the new technologies.**

For an overview of Windows 7 security improvements, read Chapter 2, "Security in Windows 7."

Windows 7 Improvements by Chapter

Windows 7 has hundreds of improvements over earlier Windows client operating systems. This chapter provides a very high-level overview of those features, focusing on features that are not discussed in depth elsewhere in this resource kit. Table 1-1 lists some of the key improvements to Windows 7 that will be of interest to IT professionals and indicates the chapters in this book that provide detailed information about each improvement.

TABLE 1-1 Windows 7 Improvements

IMPROVEMENT	CHAPTER
Security improvements	2
Deployment improvements	3 through 12
Application compatibility	4
Windows PowerShell 2.0	13
Group Policy preferences	14
Starter Group Policy Objects (GPOs)	14
Group Policy PowerShell cmdlets	14
Libraries	15
Offline Files improvements	15
Windows BitLocker improvements	16
Windows ReadyBoost improvements	16
Device Stage and other device experience improvements	17
Trigger Start services	17
Using Powercfg to evaluate energy efficiency	17
Print experience improvements	18
Location-Aware Printing	18
Printer driver isolation	18
Search improvements	19
Internet Explorer Protected Mode	20
Performance Monitor	21
Windows System Assessment (WinSAT)	21
Diagnostics	21, 30, 31
Remote Assistance Easy Connect	22
Windows AppLocker	24
User Account Control (UAC)	24
Networking improvements	25
Uniform Resource Locator (URL)–based Quality of Service (QoS)	25
Domain Name System security (DNSsec)	25
Multiple active firewall profiles	26
Internet Protocol security (IPsec) improvements	26

IMPROVEMENT	CHAPTER
BranchCache	27
Virtual private network (VPN) Reconnect	27
DirectAccess	27
Remote Desktop Protocol 7.0	27
IPv6 changes	28
Windows Troubleshooting Platform	30
Resource Monitor	30, 31
Windows PowerShell remote troubleshooting	30
Advanced and customized troubleshooting	30, 31
Reliability Monitor	30
Problem Steps Recorder	31, 31

NOTE **Windows Vista and Windows 7 include significant security improvements compared with previous versions of Windows. The changes are so numerous that this resource kit dedicates a separate chapter (Chapter 2) to describing them.**

This book does not cover features that are primarily used in home environments, such as parental controls, games, Windows Media Player, Windows Media Center, and so on.

User Interactions

For users, the most important improvements to Windows 7 will be the visible changes to the user interface. This section discusses how the Windows 7 user interface has changed. As you read this section, consider which changes will require end-user training or changes to your desktop management settings prior to deployment.

Taskbar

As shown in Figure 1-1, the Windows 7 taskbar has changed significantly. First, the taskbar is taller, although this default setting can be configured differently if you want. Second, Windows 7 displays large icons for running applications instead of the small application icons and the window's title used in previous versions of Windows. This setting is also configurable; users can choose to display window titles along with the icon.

FIGURE 1-1 The new taskbar displays icons instead of application titles and supports pinning applications.

The Quick Launch toolbar has been removed. Instead, users can now pin applications directly to the taskbar. When an application is pinned to the taskbar, its icon always appears on the taskbar as if the application were running. Users can start the application by clicking the icon.

A new feature called Aero Peek in Windows 7 allows users to hover their cursor over the far-right side of the Windows Taskbar to make all open windows transparent so that users can see their desktop. This feature makes gadgets, which can now be placed anywhere on the desktop, more useful. Users can also preview an open window or running application by hovering over a taskbar item to display a thumbnail image of the item and then hovering over the thumbnail image.

Jump Lists

Users can now open a Jump List by right-clicking an application icon on the taskbar or by selecting an application icon on the Start menu. As shown in Figure 1-2, Jump Lists provide access to frequently used functions within an application. If you right-clicked an application in previous versions of Windows, you typically would see only the standard menu items, including Maximize, Restore, Minimize, and Move. In Windows 7, applications can add application-specific tasks to the window's shortcut menu.

For example, the Windows Media Player Jump List allows users to play all music or resume the last playlist without first opening Windows Media Player. Any application designed for Windows 7 can take advantage of Jump Lists, so the feature will become more useful over time.

FIGURE 1-2 Jump Lists provide access to frequently used applications and files.

Notification Area

In versions of Windows prior to Windows 7, the notification area (the portion of the taskbar closest to the clock) could become crowded with unwanted icons added by different applications. In Windows 7, only Network, Action Center (which replaces the Security Center found in Windows Vista), and battery (on mobile computers) icons appear unless users specifically allow other icons to appear. Figure 1-3 shows the new notification area with the Action Center icon selected.

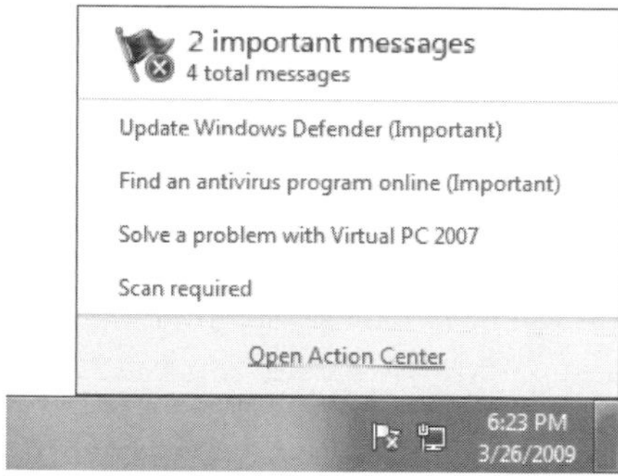

FIGURE 1-3 The notification area is simplified.

Mouse Gestures

To improve user productivity, Windows 7 includes two new mouse gestures:

- **Aero Snap** Users can drag windows to the top of the screen to maximize them or to the left or right of the screen to size the window to take up half the screen. The title bar still includes buttons for Minimize, Maximize, and Close. Resizing the window by dragging a corner of it to the top or bottom of the screen automatically increases the vertical size of the window to full screen.
- **Aero Shake** To reduce distraction and clutter caused by background applications, users can minimize all other windows by shaking a window with the mouse. Shaking the window again restores background windows to their previous position.

Despite the names, both gestures work whether or not Aero is enabled.

Improved Alt+Tab

Switching between applications is a common, but often confusing, user task. In previous versions of Windows, the Alt+Tab combination allows the user to switch between applications. If the user holds the Alt key and repeatedly presses the Tab key, Windows cycles through multiple applications, allowing the user to select any application.

Windows 7 continues to support Alt+Tab. In addition, when the Aero interface is enabled, the Alt+Tab display will show a thumbnail version of each application, as shown in Figure 1-4. If the user pauses while flipping through the applications, it will briefly display the window.

FIGURE 1-4 When Aero is enabled, the Alt+Tab display shows thumbnails of each window.

Keyboard Shortcuts

To reduce the time required to complete common tasks, Windows 7 supports the keyboard shortcuts listed in Table 1-2.

TABLE 1-2 New Windows 7 Keyboard Shortcuts

KEYBOARD SHORTCUT	ACTION
⊞+up arrow	Maximizes the current window.
⊞+down arrow	Restores or minimizes the current window.
⊞+left arrow	Snaps the current window to the left half of your screen.
⊞+right arrow	Snaps the current window to the right half of your screen.
⊞+Shift+left arrow	Moves the current windows to the left screen when running dual monitors.
⊞+Shift+right arrow	Moves the current windows to the right screen when running dual monitors.
⊞+Home	Minimizes or restores all but the current window.
⊞+T	Focuses on the taskbar so you can then use the arrow keys and Enter to select an item. Pressing this shortcut again will cycle through items. Windows Key+Shift+T cycles backward.
⊞+Tab	Cycles through your open applications in 3D.
Alt+Tab	Cycles through your open applications in 2D.
⊞+spacebar (hold keys)	Peeks at the desktop.
⊞+D	Shows the desktop.
⊞+M	Minimizes the current windows.
⊞+G	Brings your gadgets to the top of your applications.
⊞+P	Shows presentation and external display options.
⊞+U	Opens the Ease Of Access Center.
⊞+X	Opens the Mobility Center, enabling quick access to features like WiFi.
⊞+[a number key 1–5]	Starts the program from the taskbar that corresponds to that number key. For example, pressing ⊞+1 starts the first application on the taskbar.
⊞++	Zooms in.
⊞+-	Zooms out.
⊞+L	Locks your PC back to the logon screen.

Tablet PC Improvements

Tablet PCs are portable computers that enable input using a special pen. With this pen, users can write (or draw) directly on the Tablet PC display. Before Windows Vista, Microsoft provided Tablet PC features only with Windows XP Tablet PC Edition. With Windows 7, Tablet PC features are included with the Windows 7 Home Premium, Windows 7 Professional, Windows 7 Enterprise, and Windows 7 Ultimate operating systems.

Windows 7 includes several improvements to the pen interface used by Tablet PCs. Handwriting recognition is improved. The new Math Input Panel allows users to enter mathematical expressions, which can then be used by applications. Text prediction improves text entry when using the soft keyboard, and it learns your vocabulary over time. Windows 7 supports handwriting recognition in more languages, including Swedish, Danish, Norwegian, Finnish, Portuguese (Portugal), Polish, Russian, Romanian, Catalan, Serbian Latin, Croatian, Serbian-Cyrillic, and Czech. As with Windows Vista, Windows 7 continues to support English (U.S.), English (U.K.), German, French, Spanish, Italian, Dutch, Portuguese (Brazil), Chinese Simplified, Chinese Traditional, Japanese, and Korean.

To configure or disable Tablet PC features, use the Group Policy settings located within both Computer Configuration and User Configuration under Policies\Administrative Templates \Windows Components\Tablet PC.

Touch Interface

Windows 7 includes an improved touch interface for computers with touch screens. While Tablet PCs use a pen for input, the touch interface uses a finger for input. Initial capabilities include:

- Selecting text by dragging your finger across it.
- Scrolling up and down by dragging the screen or scrolling in any direction by dragging the screen with two fingers.
- Right-clicking by either holding one finger on an icon for a moment or by holding a finger and tapping with a second finger.
- Zooming by using two fingers to pinch the screen.
- Rotating pictures by moving two fingers in a rotating motion.
- Flipping pages by flicking a finger across the screen.
- Dragging up on the taskbar to get a Jump List.

With appropriate hardware, these new features will make Windows 7 more intuitive to use. They have the potential to improve user productivity on mobile computers by reducing the need to use a keyboard.

Libraries

Libraries function like folders but display files of a specific type from multiple computers. For example, you might create a library to store all employee training videos from multiple servers within your organization. Users can then open the library and access the videos without knowing which server stores the individual files. Libraries can be accessed from the Start menu, Windows Explorer, and the Open and Save dialog boxes.

Libraries in Windows 7 are similar to search folders in Windows Vista. However, users can save files to a library, whereas search folders are read-only. Files saved to a library are stored in a configurable physical folder. Windows 7 automatically indexes libraries for faster viewing and searching.

For example, the default Windows Explorer view shows the Documents library instead of the user's Documents folder. As the Documents Properties dialog box shows in Figure 1-5, the Documents library includes both the user's Documents folder and the Public Documents folder. The user's Documents folder is configured as the save location, so any new files will be placed in the user's Documents folder. By clicking the Include A Folder button, users can add more folders in the Documents library.

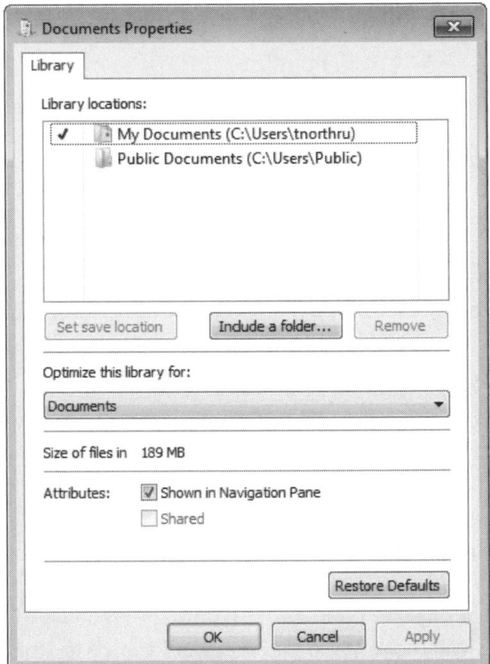

FIGURE 1-5 The Documents library properties

Search Improvements

Windows 7 includes improved search capabilities that use a more intelligent algorithm to sort search results. Search results show portions of the document and highlight words in the search, as shown in Figure 1-6. These highlights help users find the documents, messages, and images they are looking for more quickly. Windows 7 also makes it easier to add filters, enabling users to search specific folders easily.

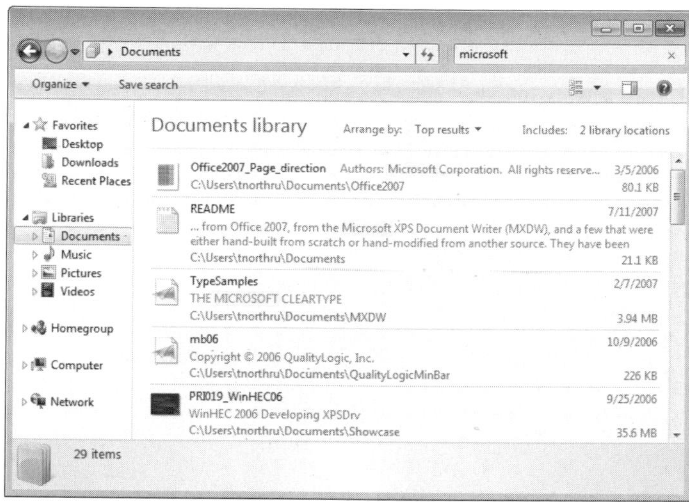

FIGURE 1-6 The Search function now highlights keywords in the results.

Search Federation

Search Federation enables users to search computers across their network and the Internet easily, including Microsoft SharePoint sites. Search Federation supports open-source Search Federation providers that use the OpenSearch standard. This enables users (or IT professionals via Group Policy) to add search connectors that connect to Web sites on an intranet or the Internet. As of the time of this writing, searching the Internet for "Windows 7 Search Federation providers" returns pages that allow users to install search connectors for many popular Web sites quickly. Figure 1-7 shows three search connectors installed for MSDN Channel 9, MSDN, and Microsoft TechNet and displays results for searching the TechNet Web site.

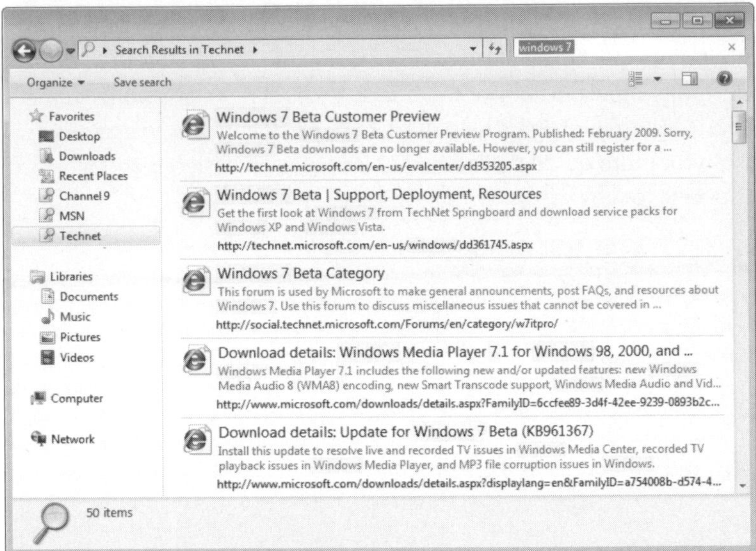

FIGURE 1-7 Search connectors enable users to search Web sites from Windows Explorer.

Action Center

Windows Vista includes the Security Center, which provides users with information about actions they might need to take to keep their computer protected. For example, Windows Vista uses the Security Center to warn the user that Windows Defender or Windows Firewall is disabled.

Windows 7 replaces the Security Center with the Action Center, as shown in Figure 1-8. The Action Center notifies the user of the same types of security issues as the Security Center. In addition, the Action Center notifies users of issues that are not security related, such as a problem performing a scheduled backup.

The Action Center consolidates alerts from the following Windows features:

- Security Center
- Problem Reports and Solutions
- Windows Defender
- Windows Update
- Diagnostics
- Network Access Protection (NAP)
- Backup and Restore
- Recovery
- User Account Control (UAC)

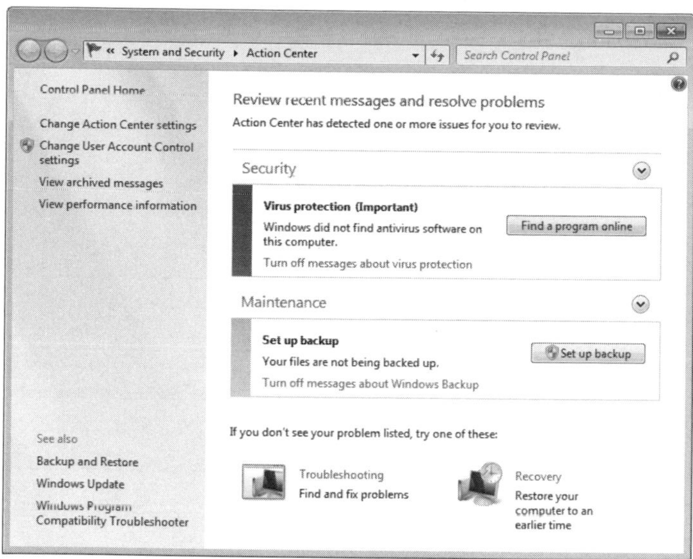

FIGURE 1-8 The Action Center consolidates system messages.

XML Paper Specification

Windows Vista and Windows 7 include built-in support for the new XML Paper Specification (XPS). XPS is a document format that can be created from any printable document and then easily shared with almost any platform. XPS provides similar capabilities to the Adobe PDF format, but XPS has the advantage of being built into the operating system.

Windows 7 includes an improved version of the XPS Viewer, as shown in Figure 1-9, to enable you to open and read XPS-based documents without the tool that was used to create the document. Users can also use the improved XPS Viewer to sign XPS documents digitally. If an organization deploys Windows Rights Management Services (RMS), users can also limit access to who can open and edit XPS documents using the improved XPS Viewer.

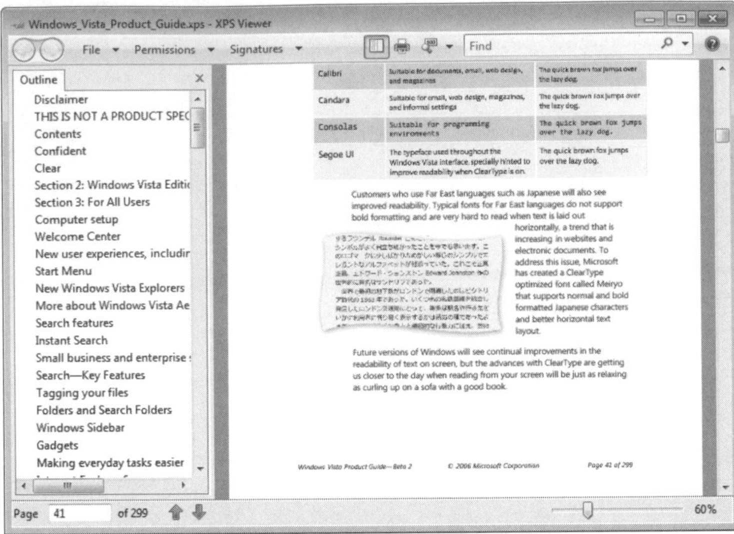

FIGURE 1-9 The XPS Viewer

Windows Internet Explorer 8

Windows 7 includes Windows Internet Explorer 8, a high-performance Web browser designed to help protect the user from Internet security threats. Although Internet Explorer 8 can be installed on Windows XP and Windows Server 2003, it includes an important security improvement called Protected Mode that works only on Windows Vista, Windows 7, and Windows Server 2008. Protected Mode runs Internet Explorer with minimal privileges, helping to prevent malicious Web sites from making permanent changes to a computer's configuration.

Performance

Although some features of Windows 7, such as Aero, require high-performance hardware, Windows 7 is designed to perform similarly to earlier versions of Windows when run on the same hardware and can frequently outperform earlier versions of Windows. The following sections describe technologies designed to improve Windows 7 performance.

ReadyBoost

Windows ReadyBoost, originally introduced with Windows Vista, uses a universal serial bus (USB) flash drive or a secure digital (SD) memory card to cache data that would otherwise need to be read from the much slower hard disk. Windows Vista uses SuperFetch technology to determine which data to cache automatically.

After you insert a USB flash drive or SD card greater than 256 megabytes (MB) in size, Windows Vista checks the performance to determine whether the device is fast enough to work with ReadyBoost. (Flash devices designed for ReadyBoost display the phrase "Enhanced for Windows ReadyBoost" on the package, but other devices can also work.) If the device is fast enough, Windows Vista gives the user the option to enable ReadyBoost. Alternatively, users can enable ReadyBoost manually on compatible devices by viewing the drive's properties.

Windows 7 improves on ReadyBoost by adding support for using up to eight flash devices simultaneously. For example, you can enable ReadyBoost on both a USB key and an SD card, and Windows 7 will cache to both devices. Although Windows Vista can create a cache of 4 gigabytes (GB) or less, Windows 7 can create larger caches.

If you remove the flash memory, ReadyBoost will be disabled, but the computer's stability will not be affected because the files stored on the flash memory are only temporary copies. Data on the flash memory is encrypted to protect privacy.

BranchCache

BranchCache stores local copies of files on an organization's intranet and transfers them to other computers in the local branch so they do not have to be transferred across the wide area network (WAN). In this way, BranchCache can reduce WAN utilization and increase the responsiveness of network applications. BranchCache can cache files from shared folders and Web servers, but only if the server is running Windows Server 2008 R2.

BranchCache can work in two different modes: Hosted Cache (which requires a computer running Windows Server 2008 R2 at each branch office) and Distributed Cache (in which clients within a branch office use peer-to-peer networking to exchange cached files). Hosted Cache provides better performance, but branches that do not have a computer running Windows Server 2008 R2 can use Distributed Cache.

Solid-State Drives

Windows 7 includes several improvements to performance with solid-state drives (SSDs), such as flash drives:

- Disk defragmentation is disabled because it is unnecessary in SSDs.
- Windows 7 uses the SSD *TRIM* command to erase data that is no longer used, which reduces the time required to reuse the same location.
- Windows 7 formats the SSD differently.

RemoteApp and Desktop Connections

After connecting to Terminal Servers running Windows Server 2008 R2, Windows 7 users have a much more integrated experience. Not only is the user interface more full featured, but remote applications can be launched directly from the Start menu. When they run, they are practically indistinguishable from local applications, and this makes centralized application management and thin client architectures easier to enable and use.

Remote Desktop in Windows 7 supports using the Aero user interface and multiple monitors, which provides an experience more like working on the local computer. Multimedia works better in Remote Desktop, too, because Windows Media Player can now play video better across remote desktop connections, and Remote Desktop includes support for microphones. Users can print to a local printer without the need to install printer drivers on the server.

New PowerCfg –energy Option

The Powercfg utility has been enhanced in Windows 7 with a new command-line option (–energy) to enable the detection of common energy-efficiency problems. These problems can include excessive processor utilization, increased timer resolution, inefficient power policy settings, ineffective use of suspend by USB devices, and battery capacity degradation. This new Powercfg option can help IT professionals validate a system prior to deployment, provide support to users who encounter battery life or power consumption issues, and more. In addition, Power users can use this option to diagnose energy-efficiency problems on their own systems.

Process Reflection

When applications failed in Windows Vista (and earlier versions of Windows), users waited while diagnostics collected information about the failure. This delay made the failure even more frustrating to users by reducing their productivity further. In Windows 7, Process Reflection enables Windows to recover a failed process and continue running while diagnostics collects information about the state of the failed application.

Mobility

More and more new computers are laptops or Tablet PCs, which are used very differently from desktop computers. Mobile PCs must manage their power effectively, and the user should be able to easily monitor power usage and battery levels. Mobile PCs are also often used in meetings, which requires them to be able to easily connect to wireless networks and then find and use network resources. The following sections provide a high-level overview of Windows 7 mobility improvements.

Improved Battery Life

In Windows Vista and earlier versions of Windows, services could be configured to start automatically, in which case they started at the same time as the operating system or with a delayed start. In Windows 7, these options are still available. In addition, services can be started or stopped via triggers.

In earlier versions of Windows, after services are started, they need to schedule processor time based on the system clock. In other words, a service needs to be activated after a specific number of milliseconds have passed, even if the service doesn't have any work to do. In Windows 7, services can be activated by a variety of different trigger events, including an incoming network communication or a user event. This allows a computer's processor to be in an idle state more often, which increases battery life.

Windows 7 is more efficient when playing standard-definition video DVDs by using less processing power and spinning the disk more efficiently. When travelling, mobile users will be more likely to watch an entire DVD on a single battery charge.

Adaptive Display Brightness

Windows 7 automatically dims the display brightness after a period of inactivity. This enables Windows 7 to reduce battery consumption without the full impact of going into Sleep mode. Adaptive Display Brightness intelligently responds to user activity, too. For example, if Adaptive Display Brightness dims the display after 30 seconds of inactivity and the user immediately moves the mouse to brighten the display, Adaptive Display Brightness will wait 60 seconds before again dimming the display.

View Available Networks

Mobile users frequently need to connect to WiFi, mobile broadband, virtual private network (VPN), and dial-up networks. In Windows 7, users can connect to wireless networks with two clicks—one click on the network icon in the notification area and a second click on the network. Figure 1-10 shows the View Available Networks (VAN) list.

FIGURE 1-10 The View Available Networks list

Smart Network Power

Wired network connections use power when they're enabled, even if a network cable isn't connected. Windows 7 offers the ability to turn off power to the network adapter automatically when the cable is disconnected. When the user connects a cable, power is restored automatically. This feature offers the power-saving benefits of disabling a wired network connection while still allowing users to connect easily to wired networks.

VPN Reconnect

Internet connectivity for mobile users is often unreliable. For example, wireless broadband users who take a train from Boston to New York can have Internet connectivity for most of the trip. However, they might lose their Internet connection when passing through tunnels or rural areas.

This intermittent connectivity is especially frustrating when the user is connected to a VPN. In Windows Vista and earlier versions of Windows, users had to reconnect to the VPN manually when their Internet connection returned. With VPN Reconnect, Windows 7 will detect that it is once again connected to the Internet and automatically reconnect a VPN server running Windows Server 2008 R2.

DirectAccess

VPN Reconnect makes VPN connections easier to maintain, but users still need to establish the initial VPN connection. Typically, this process requires the user to provide a user name and password and then wait several seconds (or even minutes) while the VPN connection is established and the health of the computer is checked. Because of this nuisance, mobile users often skip connecting to the VPN and instead use only resources available on the public Internet.

However, mobile users who do not connect to their internal network are not taking advantage of their internal resources. As such, they are not as productive as they could be. In addition, their computers will not receive security or Group Policy updates, which can make the computers vulnerable to attack and allow them to fall out of compliance.

DirectAccess automatically connects Windows 7 to the internal network whenever the mobile computer has Internet access. It is very similar to a VPN in function. However, DirectAccess does not prompt the user in any way—the connection is entirely automatic. To the user, internal resources are always available. To IT professionals, mobile computers can be managed as long as they have an Internet connection, without ever requiring the user to connect to a VPN.

DirectAccess has other benefits, including the ability to work through firewalls that restrict VPN access and the ability to provide end-to-end authentication and encryption between client computers and destination servers on the internal network. DirectAccess requires a server running Windows Server 2008 R2.

Wake on Wireless LAN

Users can save energy by putting computers into Sleep mode when they're not in use. With earlier versions of Windows, users and IT professionals could use Wake on LAN (WOL) to wake the computer so that it could be managed across the network. However, WOL works only when computers are connected to wired networks. Wireless computers in Sleep mode cannot be started or managed across the network, allowing them to fall behind on configuration changes, software updates, and other management tasks.

Windows 7 adds support for Wake on Wireless LAN (WoWLAN). With WoWLAN, Windows 7 can reduce electricity consumption by enabling users and IT professionals to wake computers connected to wireless networks from Sleep mode remotely. Because users can wake computers to access them across the network, IT professionals can configure them to enter the low-power Sleep mode when not in use.

Reliability and Supportability

Although end users tend to focus on changes to the user interface, IT professionals benefit most from improvements to reliability and supportability. These types of improvements can reduce the number of support center calls and improve the efficiency of IT departments significantly. In addition, Windows 7 can improve users' satisfaction with their IT departments by reducing the time spent solving computer problems. The following sections describe important reliability and supportability improvements to Windows 7.

Starter Group Policy Objects

Starter Group Policy Objects (GPOs) in Windows 7 are collections of preconfigured administrative templates that IT professionals can use as standard baseline configurations to create a live GPO. They encapsulate Microsoft best practices, containing recommended policy settings and values for key enterprise scenarios. IT professionals also can create and share their own Starter GPOs based on internal or industry regulatory requirements.

Group Policy Preferences

Group Policy preferences extend the reach of what Group Policy can manage and how settings are applied. With Group Policy preferences, system administrators can manage Windows features that are not Group Policy aware, such as mapped network drives and desktop shortcuts.

Windows 7 and Windows Server 2008 R2 now include Group Policy preferences by default. (In Windows Vista and Windows Server 2008, you had to separately download this feature to use it.) Windows 7 and Windows Server 2008 R2 also contain new Group Policy preferences for flexible power management and more advanced task scheduling. Group Policy preferences can also be used to deploy registry settings for managing applications. System administrators can even create custom Group Policy preference extensions.

Unlike traditional Group Policy settings, Group Policy preferences are not enforced. Rather, they are treated as defaults that users might be able to change. Preferences can be configured to reapply preferred settings every time standard Group Policies are applied (if the user has made a change) or to use the preferred setting as a baseline configuration that the user can permanently change. This gives IT professionals the flexibility to strike an optimal balance between control and user productivity. Group Policy preferences provide additional flexibility by enabling system administrators to configure unique settings for different groups of users or PCs within a single GPO without requiring Windows Management Instrumentation (WMI) filters.

URL-Based Quality of Service

System administrators today prioritize network traffic based on application, port number, and IP address. However, new initiatives such as software-as-a-service introduce the need to prioritize network traffic in new ways. Windows 7 provides the ability to implement Quality of Service (QoS) based on a URL. URL-based QoS is configurable through Group Policy, giving IT professionals the capabilities they need to tune their networks more finely.

Resource Monitor

Windows 7 includes an enhanced version of Resource Monitor that displays processor, memory, disk, and network performance data in a format that provides rapid access to a great deal of information that you can use to easily delve into process-specific details. As shown in Figure 1-11, Resource Monitor is a powerful tool for identifying which applications, services, and other processes are consuming resources. During the troubleshooting process, IT professionals can use this information to quickly identify the root cause of problems related to unresponsive computers and applications.

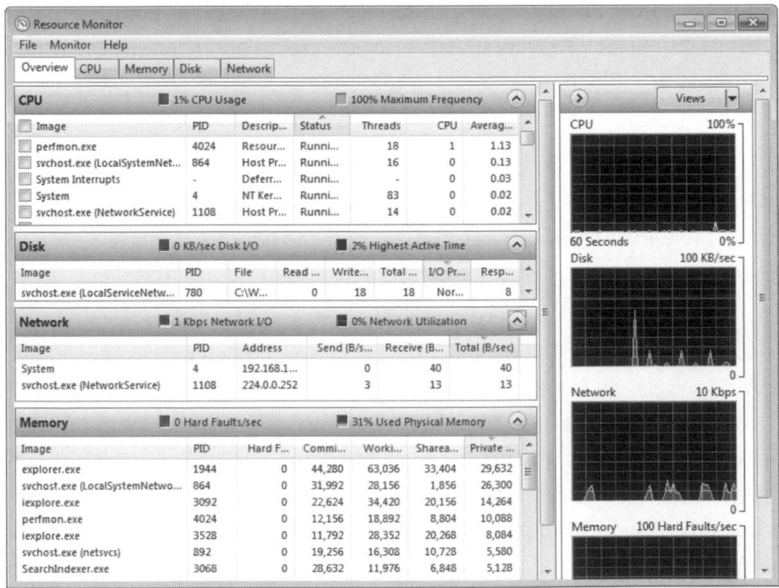

FIGURE 1-11 Resource Monitor provides detailed information into application activities.

Windows PowerShell 2.0

To enable IT professionals to automate complex or monotonous tasks, Windows 7 includes an improved version of the Windows scripting environment—Windows PowerShell 2.0. Unlike traditional programming languages designed for full-time developers, Windows PowerShell is a scripting language designed to be used by systems administrators. Because Windows PowerShell can use WMI, scripts can perform almost any management task an IT professional would want to automate.

Some of the tasks for which IT professionals use Windows PowerShell 2.0 with Windows 7 include:

- Creating a System Restore point remotely prior to troubleshooting.
- Restoring a computer to a System Restore point remotely to resolve a problem that cannot be easily fixed.
- Querying for installed updates remotely.
- Editing the registry using transactions, which ensures that a group of changes are implemented.
- Remotely examining system stability data from the reliability database.

Windows 7 includes the Windows PowerShell Integrated Scripting Environment (ISE), as shown in Figure 1-12. The Windows PowerShell ISE enables IT professionals to develop scripts without installing additional tools.

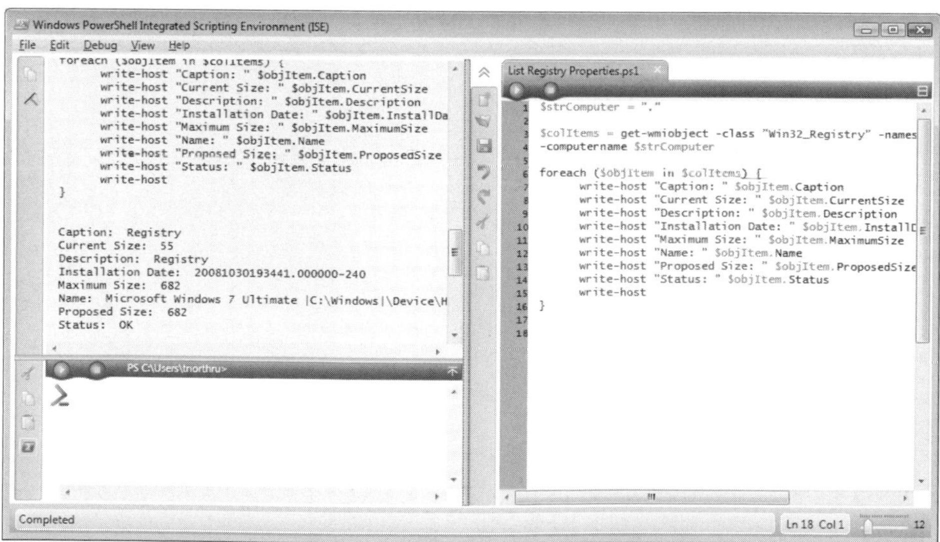

FIGURE 1-12 The Windows PowerShell 2.0 ISE

Fault-Tolerant Heap

Many application failures are caused by memory mismanagement on the part of the application. Although these failures are the application's responsibility, Windows 7 includes a fault-tolerant heap. The *heap* is the portion of memory that applications use to store data temporarily while the application is running, typically in the form of variables. The fault-tolerant heap in Windows 7 minimizes the most common causes of heap corruption and can significantly reduce the number of application failures.

Troubleshooting

Built-in diagnostics and failure-recovery mechanisms in Windows Vista minimize user impact when problems occur, reducing support costs and improving productivity for users and support professionals. The following sections describe improvements to Windows Vista that will make it easier for users to solve their own problems and for IT departments to troubleshoot the more challenging problems that still require IT support.

Windows Troubleshooting Platform

Windows Vista includes several advanced diagnostic and troubleshooting tools designed to allow users to resolve many common problems without calling the IT support center. Windows 7 expands these tools by introducing the Windows Troubleshooting Platform. The Windows Troubleshooting Platform includes user-friendly tools that can diagnose and often resolve problems automatically in the following categories:

- Aero
- DirectAccess
- Hardware and devices
- HomeGroup networking
- Incoming connections
- Internet connections
- Internet Explorer performance
- Internet Explorer safety
- Network adapters
- Performance
- Playing audio
- Power
- Printers
- Program compatibility
- Recording audio
- Search and indexing

- Shared folders
- System maintenance
- Windows Media Player DVD
- Windows Media Player library
- Windows Media Player settings
- Windows Update

Figure 1-13 shows how the Search And Indexing troubleshooting pack is able to diagnose a problem finding files that had multiple root causes.

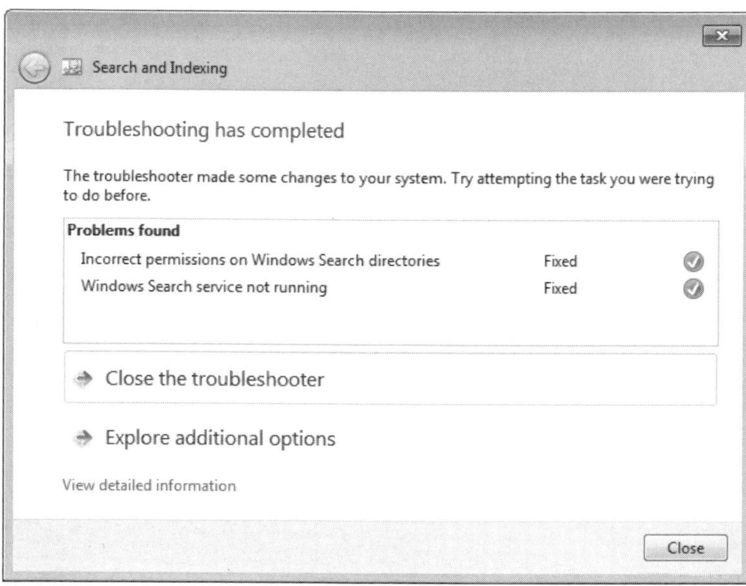

FIGURE 1-13 A troubleshooting pack resolving a complex problem automatically

The Windows Troubleshooting Platform is based on Windows PowerShell, so IT departments can create their own troubleshooting packs for internal applications. Besides simplifying troubleshooting for users, administrators can use troubleshooting tools to speed complex diagnostic and testing procedures. To enable this, administrators can run troubleshooting tools interactively from a command prompt, or silently, using an answer file. Administrators can run troubleshooting packs locally or remotely.

Problem Steps Recorder

One of the biggest challenges with troubleshooting is reproducing the problem. If IT professionals cannot duplicate the problem, they can't diagnose it. Problem Steps Recorder, as shown in Figure 1-14, is a tool that users can run to document thoroughly the circumstances leading to a problem. Users begin recording, recreate the problem, and then send the resulting HTML report to the IT professional.

FIGURE 1-14 The Problem Steps Recorder

The HTML report contains a series of screenshots showing exactly what the user did, including each keypress and mouse click. In addition, users can add comments to describe a step in further detail. Figure 1-15 shows one step from a sample Problem Steps Recorder report. Notice that the top of the page describes exactly where the user is clicking.

Problem Step 40: User left click on "litware (text)" in "View Available Networks"

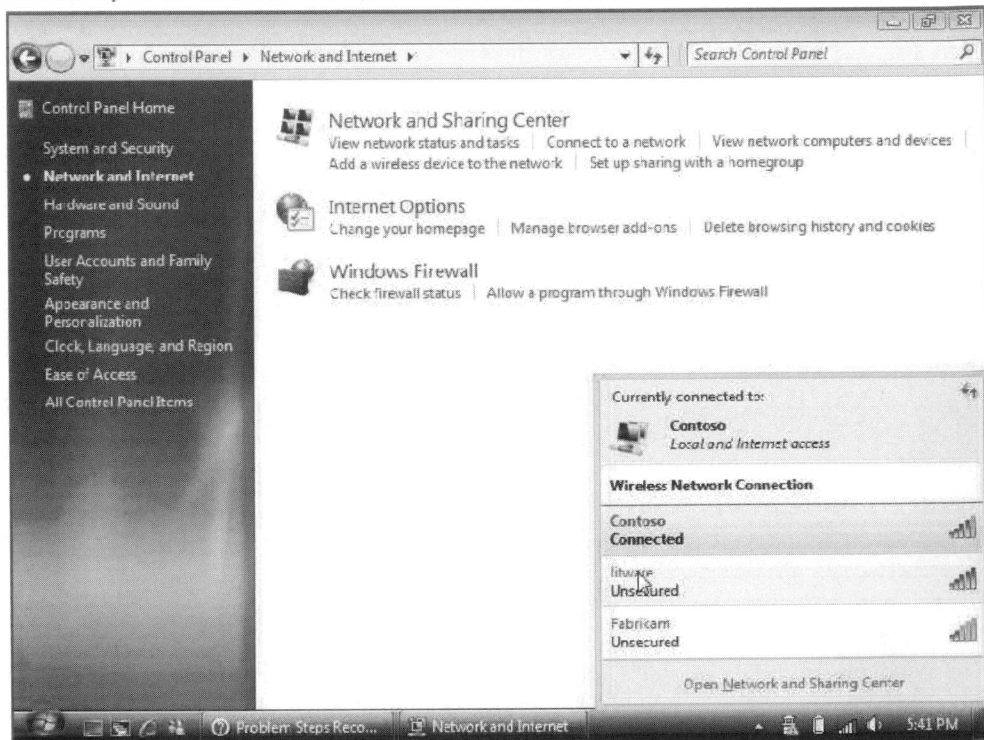

FIGURE 1-15 A step from a sample Problem Steps Recorder

Program Compatibility Troubleshooter

Windows 7 improves on the application compatibility features in Windows Vista. If an application fails to install because it does not recognize the version of Windows, Windows 7 prompts the user to attempt to reinstall the application. During the next attempt, Windows 7 will provide a different version number that might allow the application to install properly. In this way, Windows 7 is even more compatible with applications created for earlier versions of Windows, minimizing the time IT professionals need to put into planning and troubleshooting applications.

Folder Redirection and Offline Files

Folder Redirection and Offline Files provide a convenient way for users to access files stored on a central server when not connected to the corporate network. Windows 7 reduces the initial wait times when connecting to offline folders and enables IT professionals to manage Folder Redirection and Offline Files more effectively.

With Windows 7, IT professionals can use Group Policy to prevent specific types of files (such as music files) from being synchronized to the server. In addition, because Offline Files operates in a "usually offline" mode when users are not connected to the same LAN as the central server, performance is improved for branch office and remote access scenarios. IT professionals can also control when offline files are synchronized with the server, set up specific time intervals for synchronization, block out other times for purposes of bandwidth management, and configure a maximum "stale" time after which files must be resynchronized.

Roaming User Profiles

In Windows Vista and earlier versions of Windows, roaming user profiles were synchronized from the client computer to the server only when the user logged off. In this scenario, users who disconnected from the network without logging off (a common technique for mobile users) would not have their roaming user profile synchronized.

In Windows 7, roaming user profiles can be synchronized from the client to the server while the user is still logged on. As a result, a user can stay logged on to a computer, log on to a second computer, and have recent changes to their user profile reflected on the second computer.

System Restore

Administrators can use System Restore to return Windows to an earlier configuration. System Restore is vital for resolving complex problems such as malware installations, but restoring configuration settings to an earlier state can cause applications that were installed since the restore point was made to fail.

In Windows 7, System Restore has been improved to display a list of applications that might be affected by returning to an earlier restore point. This list enables administrators to assess the potential problems before performing the restoration. After the restoration, the administrator can test the potentially affected applications and reinstall them if required to return the user to a fully functional state.

Windows Recovery Environment

During setup, Windows 7 automatically creates a second partition and installs Windows Recovery Environment (Windows RE) on it. If Windows 7 is unable to start, the user can open Windows RE and attempt to use the included troubleshooting tools to resolve the problem. Often, Startup Repair (one of the troubleshooting tools included with WinRE) can automatically fix the problem preventing Windows from starting, allowing the user to fix the problem quickly without reinstalling Windows or restoring a backup.

Unified Tracing

Unified Tracing provides a single tool for isolating problems in the Windows 7 networking stack. It collects event logs and captures packets across all layers of the networking stack and groups the data into activities.

Deployment

Like Windows Vista, Windows 7 supports image-based deployment without the need for third-party tools. IT professionals can completely automate deployment, inject custom drivers into images, install applications and operating system updates prior to deployment, and support multiple languages and hardware configurations. Windows 7 includes several new deployment features, which are described in the sections that follow. In addition to these changes, Windows Setup now automatically creates a partition for BitLocker (as described in Chapter 2) and for Windows RE (as described in Chapter 29, "Configuring Startup and Troubleshooting Startup Issues").

Microsoft Deployment Toolkit 2010

MDT 2010, the next version of the Microsoft Deployment Toolkit solution accelerator, will enable rapid deployment of the Windows 7, Windows Server 2008 R2, Windows Vista Service Pack 1 (SP1), Windows Server 2008, Windows XP SP3, and Windows 2003 SP2 operating systems. MDT provides unified tools, scripts, and documentation for desktop and server deployment using an integrated deployment console called the Deployment Workbench. Using MDT to deploy Windows can help reduce your deployment time, facilitate the creation and management of standardized desktop and server images, provide improved security, and facilitate ongoing configuration management.

Windows Automated Installation Kit 2.0

The Windows AIK 2.0, the next version of the Windows Automated Installation Kit, includes new deployment tools and updated documentation for building custom solutions for deploying Windows 7, Windows Server 2008 R2, Windows Vista SP1, and Windows Server 2008. The Windows AIK 2.0 also forms the foundation for MDT 2010 to simplify automating the task of Windows deployment. Some of the new tools included in the Windows AIK 2.0 include:

- Deployment Image Servicing and Management (DISM) tool.
- User State Migration Tool (USMT) 4.0.
- Windows Preinstallation Environment (Windows PE) 3.0.
- Volume Activation Management Tool (VAMT) 1.2.

Windows PE 3.0

The updated version of Windows PE is based on the Windows 7 kernel rather than the Windows Vista kernel. A new tool, DISM, replaces Pkgmgr, PEImg, and Intlcfg. Windows PE 3.0 also inherits support for user interface elements, such as Aero Snap, from Windows 7 as described in the mouse gesture section.

Deployment Image Servicing and Management Tool

The new Deployment Image Servicing and Management (DISM) tool provides a central place for IT professionals to build and service Windows images offline. DISM combines the functionality of many different Windows Vista tools, including International Settings Configuration (IntlCfg.exe), PEImg, and Package Manager (Pkgmgr.exe). With DISM, IT professionals can update operating system images; add optional features; add, enumerate, and remove third-party device drivers; add language packs and apply international settings; and maintain an inventory of offline images that includes drivers, packages, features, and software updates. You can also use DISM to upgrade a Windows image during deployment, such as from the Windows 7 Professional to the Windows 7 Ultimate Edition, which can help reduce the number of separate images you need to maintain for your organization.

For example, your organization might create a custom Windows image file using the .wim format. You could use the DISM tool to mount the custom image, examine the drivers included with the image, add custom files, save the updated state of the image, and then unmount the image.

User State Migration Tool

The User State Migration Tool (USMT) has been updated to add a hard-link migration feature that migrates files from one operating system to another on the same PC without physically moving those files on the disk, providing significant performance gains compared with previous methods that move files. In addition, the USMT for Windows 7 enables offline migrations and provides support for Volume Shadow Copy so that IT professionals can migrate files that are being used by an application at the time of file capture. You can also migrate domain accounts without a domain controller being available, which will simplify many upgrade scenarios.

> ***NOTE*** **For consumers, small offices, and one-off upgrades, Windows Easy Transfer provides a simple way for users to transfer files and settings from an earlier version of Windows to a new computer running Windows 7. Windows 7 improves the performance of Windows Easy Transfer by not stopping the transfer to prompt the user to handle problems copying files. As with Windows Vista and earlier versions of Windows, users need to reinstall applications on the new computer. However, Windows 7 makes the process of reinstalling applications easier by inventorying installed programs on the old computer and presenting that information in a post-migration report that includes links provided by independent software vendors to product information, software updates, and support.**

VHD Boot

You can configure the Windows 7 bootloader to start Windows from a virtual hard disk (VHD) file exactly as if the VHD file were a standard partition. Simply copy the VHD file to the local computer and then use BCDEdit.exe to add an entry to the boot menu for the VHD file. Windows 7 can also mount VHD files in the Disk Management console as if they were native partitions.

Dynamic Driver Provisioning

Dynamic Driver Provisioning stores drivers in a central location, which saves IT professionals time by not requiring operating system images to be updated when new drivers are required (for example, when the IT department buys different hardware). Drivers can be installed dynamically based on the Plug and Play IDs of a PC's hardware or as predetermined sets based on information contained in the basic input/output system (BIOS).

Multicast Multiple Stream Transfer

Multicast Multiple Stream Transfer in Windows 7 enables you to more efficiently deploy images to multiple computers across a network. Instead of requiring separate direct connections between deployment servers and each client, it enables deployment servers to send image data to multiple clients simultaneously. Windows 7 includes an improvement that allows servers to group clients with similar network bandwidth and to stream at different rates to each group so that total throughput is not limited by the slowest client.

Windows 7 Editions

As with earlier versions of Windows, Microsoft has released several different versions (also known as Stock Keeping Units, or SKUs) of Windows 7 to meet the needs of different types of customers, as detailed in Table 1-3.

TABLE 1-3 Windows 7 Offerings by Customer Segment

FOR CONSUMERS	FOR SMALL BUSINESSES	FOR MEDIUM TO LARGE BUSINESSES	FOR EMERGING MARKETS
Windows 7 Home Premium	Windows 7 Professional	Windows 7 Professional	Windows 7 Starter
Windows 7 Ultimate	Windows 7 Ultimate	Windows 7 Enterprise	Windows 7 Home Basic

Although several different editions of Windows 7 are available, the Windows 7 product media contains every version. The specific edition installed is determined by the product key used to install the software. Users have the option of upgrading to a higher edition using

Windows Anytime Upgrade. For example, if a Windows 7 Home Basic user decides she wants Media Center capabilities, she can use Windows Anytime Upgrade to upgrade to the Windows 7 Home Premium or Windows 7 Ultimate Edition.

Table 1-4 summarizes the differences among the editions of Windows 7 (excluding Windows 7 Starter Edition, which is discussed later in this section). The following sections describe each edition in more detail.

TABLE 1-4 Features of Windows 7 Editions

FEATURE	HOME BASIC	HOME PREMIUM	PROFESSIONAL	ENTERPRISE	ULTIMATE
Create HomeGroups	Join only	X	X	X	X
Multi-touch		X	X	X	X
Location-Aware Printing			X	X	X
Remote Desktop host			X	X	X
Presentation mode			X	X	X
BranchCache				X	X
DirectAccess				X	X
VHD booting				X	X
Joining domains			X	X	X
AppLocker				X	X
Scheduled backups		X	X	X	X
Complete PC Backup			X	X	X
Aero user interface	Partial	X	X	X	X
Support for dual processors (not counting individual processor cores)			X	X	X
Years of product support	5	5	10	10	5
Windows Media Center		X	X	X	X
Windows DVD Maker		X			X
Parental controls	X	X			X

FEATURE	HOME BASIC	HOME PREMIUM	PROFESSIONAL	ENTERPRISE	ULTIMATE
Windows Fax And Scan			X	X	X
Network And Sharing Center			X	X	X
Wireless network provisioning			X	X	X
Incoming file and printer sharing connections	5	10	10	10	10
Tablet PC		X	X	X	X
Encrypting File System			X	X	X
Desktop deployment tools			X	X	X
Policy-based QoS for networking			X	X	X
Control over driver installations			X	X	X
Network Access Protection client			X	X	X
Windows BitLocker Drive Encryption				X	X
Simultaneous installation of multiple user interface languages				X	X
Subsystem for UNIX-based applications				X	X

Windows 7 Starter

Although Windows Vista Starter was available only in emerging markets, Windows 7 Starter is available worldwide. This edition of Windows 7 provides a basic feature set and is only offered preinstalled by an Original Equipment Manufacturer (OEM). Users can take advantage of improvements to security, search, and organization. However, the Windows 7 Aero interface is not available, and Windows 7 Starter is available only in 32-bit versions; it is not available in a 64-bit version. All other editions of Windows 7 are available in both 32-bit and 64-bit versions.

Windows 7 Home Basic

Windows 7 Home Basic, available only in emerging markets, is designed to meet the needs of home users seeking a lower-cost operating system. Windows 7 Home Basic is sufficient for users who use their computers primarily for e-mail, instant messaging, and browsing the Web. Features include:

- Instant Search
- Internet Explorer 8
- Windows Defender
- Windows Photo Gallery
- Windows Easy Transfer

Like Windows 7 Starter, Windows 7 Home Basic does not include the Aero user interface.

Windows 7 Home Premium

The preferred edition for consumers worldwide, Windows 7 Home Premium includes all the features of Windows 7 Home Basic, plus the following:

- Aero user interface
- Windows Media Center
- Tablet PC support
- Windows DVD Maker
- Scheduled Backup
- Windows SideShow support

Windows 7 Professional

Windows 7 Professional will suit the needs of most business users, including small- and medium-size businesses and enterprises. Windows 7 Professional includes all of the features included with Windows 7 Home Basic, plus the following:

- Aero user interface
- Tablet PC support
- Backup and restore capabilities (including Complete PC Backup, Automatic File Backup, and ShadowCopy Backup)
- Core business features, including joining domains, Group Policy support, and Encrypting File System (EFS)
- Fax And Scan
- Small Business resources

Like the Windows Vista Business Edition that it replaces, Windows 7 Professional is available through volume licensing.

Windows 7 Enterprise

Windows 7 Enterprise builds on the Windows 7 Professional feature set, adding the following features:

- **Windows BitLocker Drive Encryption** Encrypts all files on your system disk to help protect you from data theft if an attacker gains physical access to your hard disk
- **All worldwide interface languages** Makes deployment easier in enterprises with offices in different countries and cultures
- **Licensing rights to four virtual operating systems** Makes it possible to run multiple versions of Windows within virtual machines—perfect for testing software or for running applications that require earlier versions of Windows
- **Subsystem for UNIX-based Applications (SUA)** Can be used to compile and run Portable Operating System Interface for UNIX (POSIX) applications in Windows

Like Windows Vista Enterprise, Windows 7 Enterprise is available through the Software Assurance and Enterprise Advantage volume licensing programs from Microsoft.

Windows 7 Ultimate

Windows 7 Ultimate includes every feature provided with all other versions of Windows, including both Windows 7 Home Premium and Windows 7 Enterprise. Users who might use their computers both for work and personal use should choose Windows 7 Ultimate. Similarly, users who never want to find themselves missing a Windows feature in the future should choose Windows 7 Ultimate.

Business customers who choose Windows 7 Ultimate will encounter several drawbacks:

- **Deployment** Volume licensing keys are not available for Windows 7 Ultimate. Its deployment and manageability in an enterprise scenario are not efficient for IT professionals to carry out because each install requires manual and single-handled implementation. Furthermore, if customers acquire Windows 7 Ultimate through an OEM, they won't have access to reimaging rights, which allow customers to install a standard corporate image instead of using the OEM's preinstalled operating system.
- **Manageability** Windows 7 Ultimate contains consumer features, such as Windows Media Center, that cannot be easily managed via Group Policy.
- **Support** Windows 7 Ultimate is not covered under Premier support. Companies that have installed Windows 7 Ultimate need to get their support directly from their hardware manufacturers. In addition, the servicing policy for a consumer operating system such as Ultimate is limited to five years rather than the 10 years for a business servicing policy, as is applicable to Windows 7 Enterprise.

Despite these drawbacks, Windows 7 Ultimate is available through Software Assurance at no additional charge. Business customers should choose Windows 7 Enterprise for most computers and install Windows 7 Ultimate only on specific computers that require media or home features.

Choosing Software and Hardware

Windows 7 is designed to work with computer hardware that supports Windows Vista and can even outperform Windows Vista on the same hardware. Windows 7 is also designed to take advantage of modern hardware capabilities. The following sections describe the different Windows 7 logos and hardware requirements, which can help you choose hardware capable of providing the Windows 7 features you need.

Windows 7 Software Logo

Microsoft provides Windows 7 logos for hardware and software vendors to show that the product has been tested to work with Windows 7. For an application to qualify for the Windows 7 Logo Program, it must meet the following criteria:

- Comply with Anti-Spyware Coalition Guidelines
- Do not try to circumvent Windows Resource Protection
- Ensure ongoing quality
- Clean, reversible installation
- Install to the correct folders by default
- Sign files and drivers digitally
- Support x64 versions of Windows
- Do not block installation or application launch based on an operating system version check
- Follow UAC guidelines
- Adhere to Restart Manager messages
- Do not load services and drivers in safe mode
- Support multiuser sessions

For more information, read "The Windows 7 Client Software Logo Program," which is available from the Microsoft Download Center at *www.microsoft.com/downloads/*.

Hardware Requirements

Windows 7 has the same hardware requirements as Windows Vista. For the Windows 7 basic experience, a computer requires the following:

- A modern processor (at least 800 MHz)
- 512 MB of system memory
- A graphics processor that is DirectX 9 capable

For the Windows 7 premium experience, a computer requires the following:

- A 1-GHz 32-bit (x86) or 64-bit (x64) processor

- 1 GB of system memory
- Support for DirectX 9 graphics with a Windows Display Driver Model (WDDM) driver, 128 MB of graphics memory (minimum), Pixel Shader 2.0, and 32 bits per pixel
- 40 GB of hard drive capacity with 15 GB of free space
- DVD-ROM drive
- Audio output capability
- Internet access capability

Figure 1-16 shows the Windows 7 hardware logo, which signifies that a computer has been tested with Windows 7. Software and hardware without the logo will probably work with your Windows 7 computers. However, setup might be more difficult—you might need to locate drivers manually, and applications might have compatibility problems. A separate Windows Touch logo is used for computers that have been certified to work with the Windows Touch interface.

FIGURE 1-16 The Windows 7 hardware logo

Summary

Windows 7 includes many significant improvements from previous versions of Windows. Users will immediately notice the improved user interface, which is designed specifically to enhance user productivity. Performance improvements will help reduce annoying delays and make the most of older computer hardware. Mobile users will find it much easier to manage power and wireless networking capabilities, and users with Tablet PCs will benefit from the improved pen behavior and handwriting recognition.

Most Windows 7 improvements are designed to improve the efficiency of IT departments, however. Windows 7 deployment offers the efficiency of image-based deployment without requiring the use of third-party tools. Improved reliability, supportability, and troubleshooting capabilities can reduce the number of Support Center calls and allow IT professionals to resolve problems that must still be escalated more quickly.

Windows 7 is available in several different editions; however, most IT professionals will choose Windows 7 Professional or Windows 7 Enterprise. You can probably deploy Windows 7 using your existing computer hardware without upgrades. If you do need to purchase additional computers, you must understand the varying hardware requirements for different Windows 7 features.

This chapter provides only an overview of significant improvements. The remainder of this resource kit discusses improvements in depth and provides detailed information about how to manage Windows 7 in enterprise environments.

Additional Resources

These resources contain additional information and tools related to this chapter.

Related Information

- The Windows 7 home page on Microsoft.com at *http://www.microsoft.com/windows/windows-7/default.aspx*.
- "What's New for IT Pros in Windows 7 Release Candidate" in the Windows Client TechCenter on Microsoft TechNet at *http://technet.microsoft.com/en-us/library/dd349334.aspx*.

On the Companion Media

- Get-ProcessorArchitecture.ps1
- Get-WindowsEdition.ps1
- DisplayProcessor.ps1
- ListOperatingSystem.ps1
- Test-64bit.ps1
- Get-OSVersion.ps1

CHAPTER 2

Security in Windows 7

Windows Vista dramatically changed Windows operating system security. Most significantly, Windows Vista used lesser-privileged standard user accounts for most tasks by default. Implemented as part of User Account Control (UAC) and Windows Internet Explorer Protected Mode, the effect was to decrease malware infections by limiting the changes an application can make to the operating system without the user approving the changes.

Windows 7 refines the improvements to Windows Vista. UAC is now less intrusive by default. Windows BitLocker is more flexible and has been extended to work with removable storage. Windows AppLocker provides more flexibility when restricting which applications a user can run. Windows Firewall now supports separate profiles for a physical network and a virtual private network (VPN). Although Windows Vista dramatically changed Windows client operating system security, Windows 7 focuses on making the most of the security foundation established in Windows Vista.

This chapter provides an overview of the most important Windows Vista and Windows 7 security improvements, explains how they can improve common security scenarios, and offers information about how you can use these security improvements to meet your organization's security requirements. In most cases, you will find more detailed information about each security feature in other chapters of this resource kit. This chapter cross-references the more detailed chapters.

Addressing Specific Security Concerns

Windows 7 includes many new and improved security technologies. Although understanding security technologies often requires more detailed knowledge, the security scenarios that these technologies serve are practical and straightforward. The sections that follow describe how Windows Vista and Windows 7 security features work together to improve security in regard to three major, common concerns: wireless networks, spyware and other kinds of malware, and network worms. Each security technology is discussed in more detail later in this chapter and elsewhere in this resource kit.

Help Desk Calls Related to Malware

Security threats have constantly changed to adapt to each new generation of operating system. In the past several years, the prevalence of *malware* (a broad term that encompasses viruses, worms, Trojan horses, and rootkits, as well as spyware and other potentially unwanted software) has soared.

> **NOTE** **Microsoft uses the term *spyware and potentially unwanted software* to refer to software that is unwanted but not unambiguously harmful. In this book, the definition of *malware* includes both clearly malicious viruses and worms and the more ambiguous spyware and potentially unwanted software.**

Viruses, worms, and Trojan horses can spread from computer to computer by exploiting software vulnerabilities, guessing user credentials, or tricking users with social engineering techniques. Spyware and potentially unwanted software spread via these techniques and also by legitimate installations initiated by users. Users can install an application, unaware of the undesired functionality of the program or of a program that is bundled with the application.

Because of the challenges in identifying malware, it might be impossible to eliminate the threat completely. However, Windows Vista and Windows 7 have many new security features to help protect computers from malware.

Many malware infections can be prevented by installing updates on a mobile computer or by adjusting the security configuration. Group Policy, Windows Server Update Services (WSUS), and other management technologies have greatly simplified the task of rapidly distributing updates and security changes. However, these changes take effect only when client computers connect to the internal network. When users travel, mobile computers might go days, weeks, or months without connecting to the internal network. DirectAccess, a new technology introduced with Windows 7 and Windows Server 2008 R2, automatically connects computers to the internal network any time they have an Internet connection. Therefore, DirectAccess can keep Windows 7 mobile client computers up to date more regularly than earlier versions of Windows, giving IT the control they need to mitigate newly discovered vulnerabilities by distributing updates or configuration changes.

Originally introduced with Windows Vista, UAC limits the ability of malware to install by enabling IT professionals to deploy users as standard users rather than as administrators. This helps prevent users from making potentially dangerous changes to their computers without limiting their ability to control other aspects on their computers, such as time zone or power settings. For anyone who does log on as an administrator, UAC makes it more difficult for malware to have a computer-wide impact. Windows 7 includes improvements to UAC by reducing the number of prompts that users experience. Additionally, administrators can adjust consent prompt behavior. By making UAC more usable, Windows 7 reduces the cost of deploying Windows using a protected desktop environment.

Similarly, the Protected Mode of Internet Explorer runs it without the necessary privileges to install software (or even write files outside of the Temporary Internet Files directory), thereby reducing the risk that Internet Explorer can be abused to install malware without the user's consent.

Windows Defender detects many types of spyware and other potentially unwanted software and prompts the user before applications can make potentially malicious changes. In Windows 7, Windows Defender includes significantly improved performance for real-time monitoring. By reducing the performance penalty of real-time monitoring, more IT departments can leave real-time monitoring enabled, thus realizing the security benefits. Additionally, Windows Defender uses the Action Center to notify users of potential problems.

Windows Service Hardening limits the damage attackers can do in the event that they are able to successfully compromise a service, thereby reducing the risk of attackers making permanent changes to the operating system or attacking other computers on the network. Although Windows 7 cannot eliminate malware, these new technologies can significantly reduce the impact of malware.

Windows 7 is designed to block many types of common malware installation techniques. The sections that follow describe how Windows Vista and Windows 7 protect against malware that attempts to install without the user's knowledge through bundling and social engineering, browser exploits, and network worms.

Protecting Against Bundling and Social Engineering

Two of the most common ways that malware becomes installed on a computer are bundling and social engineering. With bundling, malware is packaged with useful software. Often the user is not aware of the negative aspects of the bundled software. With social engineering, the user is tricked into installing the software. Typically, the user receives a misleading e-mail or browser pop-up containing instructions to open an attachment or visit a Web site.

Windows Vista and Windows 7 offer significantly improved protection against both bundling and social engineering. With the default settings, malware that attempts to install via bundling or social engineering must circumvent two levels of protection: UAC and Windows Defender.

UAC either prompts the user to confirm the installation of the software (if the user is logged on with an administrative account) or prompts the user for administrative credentials (if the user is logged on with a Standard account). This feature makes users aware that a process is trying to make significant changes and allows them to stop the process. Standard users are required to contact an administrator to continue the installation. For more information, see the section titled "User Account Control" later in this chapter.

Windows Defender real-time protection blocks applications that are identified as malicious. Windows Defender also detects and stops changes the malware might attempt to make, such as configuring the malware to run automatically upon a reboot. Windows Defender notifies the user that an application has attempted to make a change and gives the user the opportunity to block or proceed with the installation. For more information, see the section titled "Windows Defender" later in this chapter.

NOTE **Windows Defender adds events to the System Event Log. Combined with event subscriptions or a tool such as Microsoft Systems Center Operations Manager (SCOM), you can easily aggregate and analyze Windows Defender events for your organization.**

These levels of protection are illustrated in Figure 2-1.

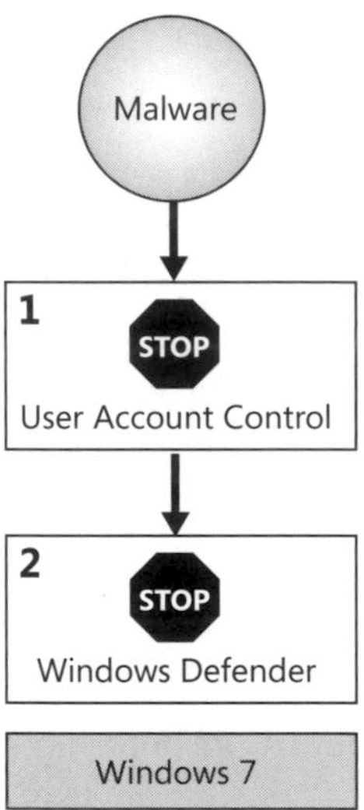

FIGURE 2-1 Windows Vista and Windows 7 use defense-in-depth to protect against bundling and social engineering malware attacks.

With Windows XP and earlier versions of Windows, bundling and social engineering malware installations were likely to succeed because none of these protections was included with the operating system or service packs.

Defense-in-Depth

Defense-in-depth is a proven technique of layered protection that reduces the exposure of vulnerabilities. For example, you might design a network with three layers of packet filtering: a packet-filtering router, a hardware firewall, and software firewalls on each of the hosts (such as Internet Connection Firewall). If an attacker manages to bypass one or two of the layers of protection, the hosts are still protected.

The real benefit of defense-in-depth is its ability to protect against human error. Whereas a single layer of defense is sufficient to protect you under normal circumstances, an administrator who disables the defense during troubleshooting, an accidental misconfiguration, or a newly discovered vulnerability can disable that single layer of defense. Defense-in-depth provides protection even when a single vulnerability exists.

Although most new Windows security features are preventive countermeasures that focus on directly mitigating risk by blocking vulnerabilities from being exploited, your defense-in-depth strategy should also include detective and reactive countermeasures. Auditing and third-party intrusion-detection systems can help to analyze an attack after the fact, enabling administrators to block future attacks and possibly identify the attacker. Backups and a disaster recovery plan enable you to react to an attack and limit the potential data lost.

Protecting Against Browser Exploit Malware Installations

Historically, many malware installations occurred because the user visited a malicious Web site, and the Web site exploited a vulnerability in the Web browser to install the malware. In some cases, users received no warning that software was being installed. In other cases, users were prompted to confirm the installation, but the prompt might have been misleading or incomplete.

Windows 7 provides four layers of protection against this type of malware installation:

- Automatic Updates, enabled by default, helps keep Internet Explorer and the rest of the operating system up to date with security updates that can fix many security vulnerabilities. Automatic Updates can obtain security updates from either Microsoft.com or from an internal WSUS server. For more information, read Chapter 23, "Managing Software Updates."
- Internet Explorer Protected Mode provides only extremely limited rights to processes launched by Internet Explorer, even if the user is logged on as an administrator. Any process launched from Internet Explorer has access only to the Temporary Internet Files directory. Any file written to that directory cannot be executed.

- For administrators, UAC prompts the user to confirm before computer-wide configuration changes are made. For standard users, the limited privileges block most permanent per-computer changes unless the user can provide administrative credentials.
- Windows Defender notifies the user if malware attempts to install itself as a browser helper object, start itself automatically after a reboot, or modify another monitored aspect of the operating system.

These levels of protection are illustrated in Figure 2-2.

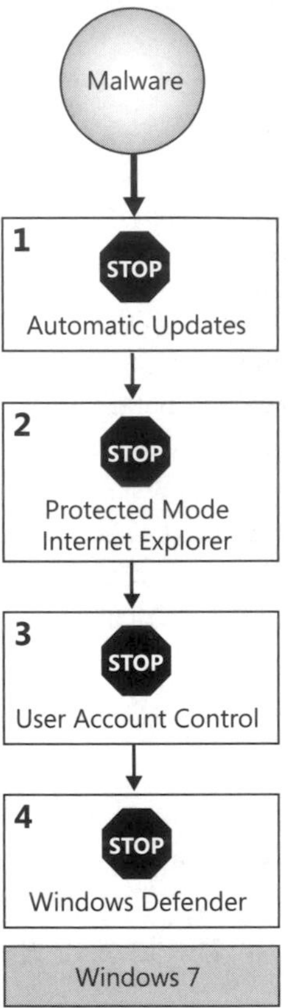

FIGURE 2-2 Windows 7 uses defense-in-depth to protect against browser exploit malware installations.

Protecting Against Network Worms

Bundling, social engineering, and browser exploits all rely on the user to initiate a connection to a site that hosts malware, but worms can infect a computer without any interaction from the user. Network worms spread by sending network communications across a network to exploit a vulnerability in remote computers and install the worm. After it is installed, the worm continues looking for new computers to infect.

If the worm attacks a Windows Vista or Windows 7 computer, Windows offers four levels of protection:

- Windows Firewall blocks all incoming traffic that has not been explicitly permitted (plus a few exceptions for core networking functionality in the domain and private profiles). This feature blocks the majority of all current worm attacks.
- If the worm attacks an updated vulnerability in a Microsoft feature, Automatic Updates—which is enabled by default—might have already addressed the security vulnerability.
- If the worm exploits a vulnerability in a service that uses Windows Service Hardening and attempts to take an action that the service profile does not allow (such as saving a file or adding the worm to the startup group), Windows will block the worm.
- If the worm exploits a vulnerability in a user application, limited privileges enabled by UAC block system-wide configuration changes.

These levels of protection are illustrated in Figure 2-3.

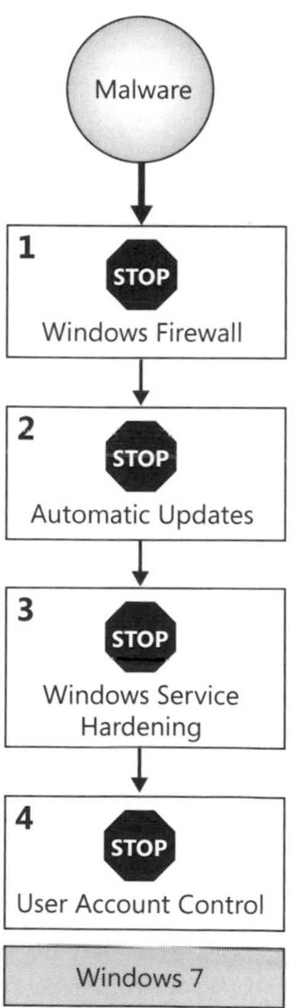

FIGURE 2-3 Windows Vista and Windows 7 use defense-in-depth to protect against network worms.

The original release of Windows XP lacked all of these levels of protection. With Windows XP Service Pack 2 (SP2), Windows Firewall and Automatic Updates are enabled, but the other levels of protection offered by Windows Vista and Windows 7 are unavailable.

Data Theft

As mobile computers, network connectivity, and removable media have become more common, so has data theft. Many businesses and government organizations store extremely valuable data on their computers, and the cost of having the data fall into the wrong hands can be devastating.

Today, many organizations mitigate the risk of data theft by limiting access to data. For example, applications might not allow confidential files to be stored on mobile computers. Or, users simply might not be allowed to remove computers from the office. These limitations do successfully reduce the risk, but they also reduce employee productivity by not allowing the staff to benefit from mobile computing.

Windows Vista and Windows 7 provide data protection technologies designed to meet stricter security requirements while still allowing users to work with confidential data in a variety of locations. Consider the following common data theft scenarios and how Windows mitigates the risks of each.

Physical Theft of a Mobile Computer or a Hard Disk, or Recovering Data from a Recycled or Discarded Hard Disk

Operating systems can provide active protection for the data stored on your hard disk only while the operating system is running. In other words, file access control lists (ACLs), such as those provided by the New Technology File System (NTFS), cannot protect data if an attacker can physically access a computer or hard disk. In recent years, there have been many cases of stolen mobile computers whose confidential data was extracted from the hard disk. Data is often recovered from computers that are recycled (by assigning an existing computer to a new user) or discarded (at the end of a computer's life), even if the hard disk has been formatted.

Windows Vista and Windows 7 reduce the risk of this type of data theft by allowing administrators to encrypt files stored on the disk. As with Windows XP, Windows Vista and Windows 7 support *Encrypting File System (EFS)*. EFS enables administrators and users to selectively encrypt files or to mark an entire folder to encrypt all files it contains. In addition to the capabilities offered by Windows XP, Windows Vista and Windows 7 enable you to configure EFS using Group Policy settings so that you can centrally protect an entire domain without requiring users to understand encryption.

EFS cannot protect Windows system files, however. Protecting Windows from offline attack (booting from removable media to access the file system directly or moving the hard disk to a different computer) helps ensure the integrity of the operating system even if a computer is stolen. BitLocker Drive Encryption in Windows Vista provides encryption for the entire system volume—thus protecting not only the operating system but also any data stored on the same volume (drive letter). In Windows 7, administrators can use BitLocker to protect both system and non-system volumes (as well as removable media, described in the next section). BitLocker can work transparently with supported hardware, or it can require multifactor authentication by requiring users to enter a password before allowing the volume to be decrypted. Depending on your security requirements, you can use BitLocker with existing computer hardware by storing the decryption keys on removable media or even by having users type a personal identification number (PIN) or password before Windows boots. For more information, read Chapter 16, "Managing Disks and File Systems."

Copying Confidential Files to Removable Media

Organizations with strict security requirements often limit access to confidential data to computers on the local network and then do not allow those computers to be removed from the facility. Historically, these organizations would remove floppy drives from the computers to prevent users from saving confidential files. Recently, however, there has been a huge increase in the types of removable media available. Specifically, mobile phones, PDAs, portable audio players, and USB drives often have several gigabytes of storage capacity. Because they are small and extremely common, they might be overlooked even if a facility has security staff available to search employees entering or leaving a building.

Windows Vista and Windows 7 enable you to use Group Policy settings to limit the risk of removable media. Using the Group Policy settings in Computer Configuration\Policies\Administrative Templates\System\Device Installation\Device Installation Restrictions, administrators can:

- Allow installation of entire classes of devices (such as printers) using the Allow Installation Of Devices Using Drivers That Match These Device Setup Classes setting.
- Disallow all unsupported or unauthorized devices using the Prevent Installation Of Devices That Match Any Of These Device IDs setting.
- Disallow any kind of removable storage device using the Prevent Installation Of Removable Devices setting.
- Override these policies if necessary for troubleshooting or management purposes using the Allow Administrators To Override Device Installation Policy setting.

While Windows Vista focused on providing administrators with the control they needed to prevent users from saving files to removable media, Windows 7 includes technology to protect files when they are copied to removable media: BitLocker To Go. BitLocker To Go provides volume-level encryption for removable media. To decrypt the contents of removable media, a user must type a password or insert a smart card. Without the password or smart card, the contents of the BitLocker To Go–encrypted media are almost impossible to access.

For more information on managing devices and on BitLocker, see Chapter 16. For more information on using Group Policy to manage Windows 7 computers, see Chapter 14, "Managing the Desktop Environment."

Accidentally Printing, Copying, or Forwarding Confidential Documents

Often, users need to share confidential documents to collaborate efficiently. For example, a user might e-mail a document to another user for review. However, when the document is copied from your protected shared folder or intranet, you lose control of the document. Users might accidentally copy, forward, or print the document, where it can be found by a user who shouldn't have access.

There's no perfect solution to protect electronic documents from copying. However, the Windows *Rights Management Services (RMS)* client, built into Windows Vista and Windows 7, enables computers to open RMS-encrypted documents and enforce the restrictions applied to the document. With an RMS infrastructure and an application that supports RMS, such as Microsoft Office, you can:

- Allow a user to view a document but not save a copy of it, print it, or forward it.
- Restrict users from copying and pasting text within a document.
- Make it very difficult to open the document using a client that does not enforce RMS protection.

Windows 7 provides built-in support for using RMS to protect XML Paper Specification (XPS) documents. To use RMS, you need an RMS infrastructure and supported applications in addition to Windows Vista or Windows 7. For more information about RMS, see the section titled "Rights Management Services" later in this chapter.

Security Features Previously Introduced in Windows Vista

This section describes the most visible and tangible Windows Vista security improvements that have not been substantially changed in Windows 7, which are listed in Table 2-1. Each of these improvements is also included in Windows 7. Architectural and internal improvements—as well as improvements that require additional applications or infrastructure—are described later in this chapter. Security improvements new to Windows 7 and Windows Vista features that are significantly improved in Windows 7 also are discussed later in this chapter.

TABLE 2-1 Security Improvements Previously Introduced In Windows Vista

IMPROVEMENT	DESCRIPTION
Windows Defender	Attempts to detect and block unwanted software.
Windows Firewall	Filters incoming and outgoing network traffic. New improvements provide greater flexibility and manageability.
Encrypting File System	Encrypts files and folders other than system files. Improvements provide greater flexibility and manageability.
Credential Manager enhancements	Enable users to perform common credential management security tasks, such as resetting PINs.

The sections that follow describe these features in more detail. For detailed recommendations on how to configure Windows Vista security settings, refer to the *Windows Vista Security Guide*, available at *http://www.microsoft.com*. For an interesting description of how Windows Vista security changes have led to real-world improvements, read "Windows Vista Security One Year Later" at *http://blogs.msdn.com/windowsvistasecurity/archive/2008/01/23/windows-vista-security-one-year-later.aspx*.

Windows Defender

Windows Defender is a feature of Windows Vista and Windows 7 that provides protection from spyware and other potentially unwanted software. Windows Defender is signature based, using descriptions that uniquely identify spyware and other potentially unwanted software to detect and remove known applications. Windows Defender regularly retrieves new signatures from Microsoft so that it can identify and remove newly created spyware and other potentially unwanted software. Microsoft does not charge for signature updates.

Additionally, Windows Defender real-time protection monitors critical touchpoints in the operating system for changes usually made by spyware. Real-time protection scans every file as it is opened and also monitors the Startup folder, Run keys in the registry, Windows add-ons, and other areas of the operating system for changes. If an application attempts to make a change to one of the protected areas of the operating system, Windows Defender prompts the user to take appropriate action.

As shown in Figure 2-4, Windows Defender can also run a scan on demand to detect and remove known spyware. By default, Windows Defender will scan Windows Vista computers daily at 2:00 A.M. for malware infections; however, you can configure this behavior. Although Windows Defender real-time protection attempts to prevent most infections, nightly scanning allows Windows Defender to detect and remove newly discovered malware that might have circumvented the defenses of real-time protection.

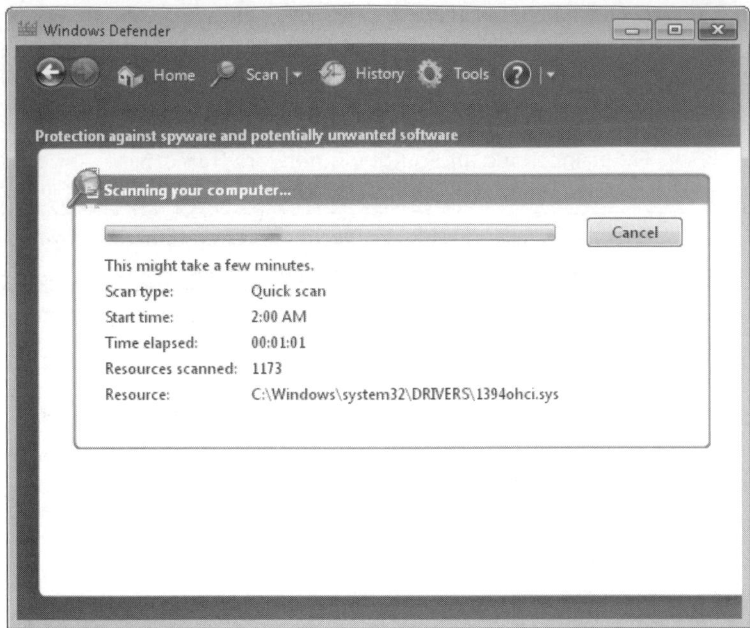

FIGURE 2-4 Users who suspect malware has infected their computer can run a Windows Defender scan on demand.

The Microsoft SpyNet Community enables Windows Defender to communicate discoveries about new applications and whether users identify applications as malware or legitimate. Depending on how you configure Windows Defender, it can provide feedback to the SpyNet Community about new applications and whether users choose to allow the application to be installed. Feedback from the SpyNet Community helps Microsoft and users distinguish malware from legitimate software, enabling Windows Defender to more accurately identify malware and reduce the number of false alarms. Providing private feedback to the SpyNet Community is optional; however, all users can benefit from the information gathered by the community.

In addition to these features, Windows Defender includes Software Explorer. Software Explorer provides users with control over many different types of applications, including applications that install themselves into the browser and into applications that start automatically. Software Explorer is primarily intended for users who manage their own computers. In enterprise environments, IT departments will typically handle software removal.

Windows Defender can also be installed on Windows XP with SP2. For more information about Windows Defender, see Chapter 24, "Managing Client Protection."

Windows Firewall

Windows Vista and Windows 7 have an enhanced version of the Windows Firewall that was first included in Windows XP SP2. The Windows Firewall combines the functionality of a bidirectional host firewall and Internet Protocol security (IPsec) into a single, unified utility with a consistent user interface. Unlike a perimeter firewall, the Windows Firewall runs on each computer running Windows Vista or Windows 7 and provides local protection from network attacks that might pass through your perimeter network or originate inside your organization. It also provides computer-to-computer connection security that allows you to require authentication and data protection for all communications.

The Windows Firewall is a stateful firewall, so it inspects and filters all TCP/IP version 4 (IPv4) and TCP/IP version 6 (IPv6) traffic. Unsolicited incoming traffic is dropped unless it is a response to a request by the host (solicited traffic) or it is specifically allowed (that is, it has been added to the exceptions list or is permitted by an inbound rule). Outgoing traffic from interactive applications is allowed by default, but outgoing traffic from services is limited by the firewall to that which is required according to each service's profile in Windows Service Hardening. You can specify traffic to be added to the exceptions list and create inbound and outbound rules according to application name, service name, port number, destination network, domain membership, or other criteria by configuring Windows Firewall with Advanced Security settings.

For traffic that is allowed, the Windows Firewall also allows you to request or require that computers authenticate each other before communicating and to use data integrity and data encryption while exchanging traffic.

In Windows Vista, the Windows Firewall has many new features, including the following:

- **Management integration with IPsec** Windows XP and earlier operating systems used two separate interfaces, even though the Windows Firewall and IPsec had a significant amount of feature overlap. Now, as Figure 2-5 shows, you can manage both using a single interface.

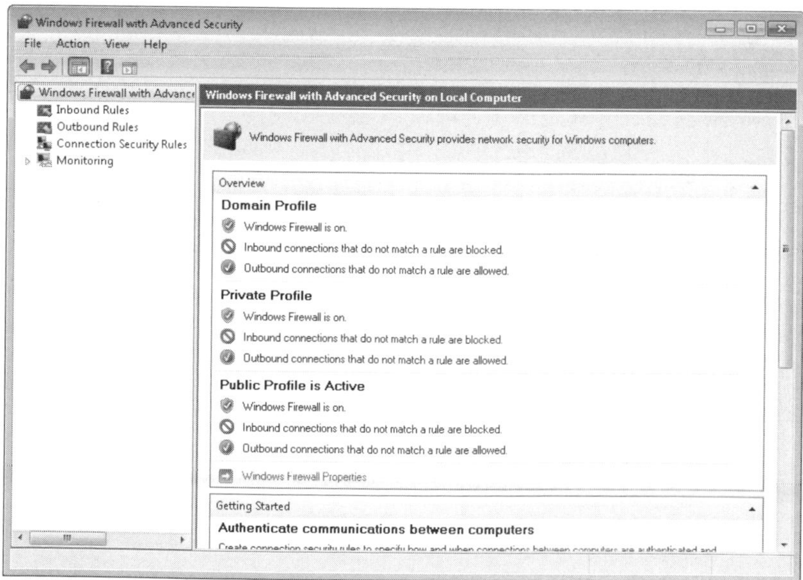

FIGURE 2-5 You can use a single tool to manage both Windows Firewall and IPsec.

- **New user and command-line interfaces** Improved interfaces simplify management and enable automated, scripted control over firewall settings.
- **Full IPv6 support** If your organization uses IPv6, you can now take advantage of Windows Firewall.
- **Outbound filtering** You can filter traffic being sent from a client computer as well as traffic being received by the computer. This enables you to restrict which applications can send traffic and where they can send it. For example, you might filter management alerts so that they can be sent only to your internal network. The outbound filtering feature in the Windows Firewall is not intended to prevent an infected computer from communicating, which is generally not possible (the malware might simply disable the firewall). Rather, outbound filtering allows administrators to assign policies to machines to prohibit known behavior, such as preventing unauthorized peer-to-peer software from communicating.
- **Windows Service Hardening** This feature limits the actions a service can take and also limits how the service communicates on the network, reducing the damage caused during a security compromise.
- **Full Group Policy integration** This feature enables you to centrally configure the Windows Firewall on all computers in your Active Directory Domain Services (AD DS) domain.
- **Filtering traffic by new properties** The Windows Firewall can filter traffic by using the following:
    - AD DS groups (authorized users and authorized computers)
    - Internet Control Message Protocol (ICMP) extensions
    - IP address lists
    - Port lists
    - Service names
    - Authenticated by IPsec
    - Encrypted by IPsec
    - Interface type
- **IP address authentication** The Windows Firewall supports IP address authentication with the ability to have two rounds of authentication with different credentials in each, including user credentials if desired.
- **Application-based IPsec policies** The Windows Firewall now supports application-based IPsec policies.

- **Simplified IPsec policy** This type of policy makes it much easier to deploy Server and Domain Isolation. When configured with a simplified policy, client computers make two connections to a destination: one unprotected connection and one connection with IPsec. The client computer will drop whichever connection does not receive a reply. With a single rule, then, client computers can adapt themselves to communicate with IPsec or in clear-text, whichever the destination supports.

For detailed information about the Windows Firewall, see Chapter 26, "Configuring Windows Firewall and IPsec."

> ***NOTE*** **One of the biggest challenges of protecting computers is that security settings can degrade over time. For example, support desk personnel might change a security setting while troubleshooting a problem and forget to correct it. Even if you enable Automatic Updates, a mobile computer might fail to download updates while disconnected from the network. To help you detect security vulnerabilities, use the Microsoft Baseline Security Analyzer (MBSA), available at *http://www.microsoft.com/mbsa*. MBSA can audit security settings on multiple computers on your network. MBSA is also a great way to verify security settings on new computers before deploying them.**

Encrypting File System

Encrypting File System (EFS) is a file encryption technology (supported only on NTFS volumes) that protects files from offline attacks, such as hard-disk theft. EFS is entirely transparent to end users because encrypted files behave exactly like unencrypted files. However, if a user does not have the correct decryption key, the file is impossible to open, even if an attacker bypasses the operating system security.

EFS is especially useful for securing sensitive data on portable PCs or on computers that several users share. Both kinds of systems are susceptible to attack by techniques that circumvent the restrictions of ACLs. An attacker can steal a computer, remove the hard disk drives, place the drives in another system, and gain access to the stored files. Files encrypted by EFS, however, appear as unintelligible characters when the attacker does not have the decryption key.

Windows Vista and Windows 7 include the following new features for EFS:

- Storing both user and recovery keys on smart cards. If smart cards are used for logon, EFS operates in a Single Sign-On mode in which it uses the logon smart card for file encryption without further prompting for the PIN. New wizards guide users through the process of creating and selecting smart card keys, as well as the process of migrating their encryption keys from an old smart card to a new one. The command-line utilities for smart cards have also been enhanced to include these features. Storing encryption keys on smart cards provides especially strong protection for mobile and shared computer scenarios.
- Encrypting the system page file.

For more information about EFS, see Chapter 16.

Credential Manager Enhancements

Windows Vista and Windows 7 include new tools to enable administrators to better support credential management for roaming users, including the Digital Identity Management Services (DIMS) and a new certificate enrollment process. Among other improvements, users can now reset their own smart card PINs without calling the support center. Additionally, users can now back up and restore credentials stored in the Stored User Names And Passwords key ring.

To improve the security of Task Scheduler, Windows Vista and Windows 7 can use Service-for-User (S4U) Kerberos extensions to store credentials for scheduled tasks instead of storing the credentials locally, where they might be compromised. This has the added benefit of preventing scheduled tasks from being affected by password expiration policies.

Architectural and Internal Security Improvements

Whenever possible, Windows Vista and Windows 7 security features have been designed to be transparent to end users and to require no administration time. Nonetheless, administrators and developers can benefit from understanding the architectural improvements. This section describes these architectural and internal improvements, as well as improvements that require additional applications or infrastructure. Table 2-2 describes these features originally introduced in Windows Vista and also included in Windows 7.

TABLE 2-2 Architectural and Internal Security Improvements in Windows Vista and Windows 7

IMPROVEMENT	DESCRIPTION
Code Integrity	Detects malicious modifications to kernel files at startup.
Windows Resource Protection	Prevents potentially dangerous changes to system resources.
Kernel Patch Protection	Blocks potentially malicious changes that might compromise the integrity of the kernel on 64-bit systems.
Required Driver Signing	Requires drivers to be signed, which improves reliability and makes it more difficult to add malicious drivers. Mandatory on 64-bit systems.
Windows Service Hardening	Allows system services to access only those resources they normally need to access, reducing the impact of a compromised service.
Network Access Protection client	When used together with Windows Server 2008, helps to protect your network from clients who do not meet your security requirements.
Web Services for Management	Reduces risks associated with remote management by supporting encryption and authentication.

IMPROVEMENT	DESCRIPTION
Crypto Next Generation services	Allows the addition of custom cryptographic algorithms to meet government requirements.
Data Execution Prevention	Reduces the risk of buffer overflow attacks by marking data sections of memory as nonexecutable.
Address Space Layout Randomization	Reduces the risk of buffer overflow attacks by assigning executable code to random memory locations.
New Logon Architecture	Simplifies development of custom logon mechanisms.
Rights Management Services client	Provides support for opening Rights Management Services protected documents when the proper applications are installed and the necessary infrastructure is in place.
Multiple Local Group Policy Objects	Allows administrators to apply multiple Local Group Policy Objects to a single computer, simplifying security configuration management for workgroup computers.

The sections that follow describe these features in more detail.

Code Integrity

When Windows starts up, Code Integrity (CI) verifies that system files haven't been maliciously modified and ensures that there are no unsigned drivers running in Kernel Mode. The bootloader checks the integrity of the kernel, the Hardware Abstraction Layer (HAL), and the boot-start drivers. After those files are verified, CI verifies the digital signatures of any binaries that are loaded into the kernel's memory space. Additionally, CI verifies binaries loaded into protected processes and the cryptography dynamic-link libraries (DLLs).

CI works automatically and does not require management.

> ***NOTE*** **CI is an example of a detective countermeasure because it can identify that the computer was compromised after the fact. Although it is always preferable to prevent attacks, detective countermeasures such as CI enable you to limit the damage caused by the attack by detecting the compromise so that you can repair the computer. You should also have a response plan in place to enable you to quickly repair a system that has had critical files compromised.**

Windows Resource Protection

Any code that runs in Kernel Mode, including many types of drivers, can potentially corrupt kernel data in ways that surface later. Diagnosing and fixing these bugs can be difficult and time consuming. Corruption of the registry tends to have a disproportionate impact on overall reliability because this corruption can persist across reboots.

Windows Vista and Windows 7 protect system settings from corruption or inadvertent changes that can cause the system to run incorrectly or to not run at all. Windows Resource Protection (WRP), the follow-up to the Windows File Protection (WFP) feature found in previous Windows platforms, sets tight ACLs on critical system settings, files, and folders to protect them from changes by any source (including administrators) except a trusted installer. This prevents users from accidentally changing critical system settings that can render systems inoperable.

Windows Vista and Windows 7 also prevent poorly written drivers from corrupting the registry. This protection enables the memory-management feature to achieve protection the vast majority of the time, with low overhead. Protected resources include:

- Executable files, libraries, and other critical files installed by Windows.
- Critical folders.
- Essential registry keys installed by Windows.

WRP does not allow you to modify protected resources, even if you provide administrative credentials.

Kernel Patch Protection

64-bit versions of Windows Vista and Windows 7, like the 64-bit versions of Windows XP and Windows Server 2003, support *Kernel Patch Protection* technology. Kernel Patch Protection prevents unauthorized programs from patching the Windows kernel, giving you greater control over core aspects of the system that can affect overall performance, security, and reliability. Kernel Patch Protection detects changes to critical portions of kernel memory. If a change is made in an unsupported way (for example, a user-mode application does not call the proper operating system functions), Kernel Patch Protection creates a Stop error to halt the operating system. This prevents kernel-mode drivers from extending or replacing other kernel services and prevents third-party software from updating any part of the kernel.

Specifically, to prevent Kernel Patch Protection from generating a Stop error, 64-bit drivers must avoid the following practices:

- Modifying system service tables
- Modifying the interrupt descriptor table (IDT)
- Modifying the global descriptor table (GDT)
- Using kernel stacks that are not allocated by the kernel
- Updating any part of the kernel on AMD64-based systems

In practice, these factors are primarily significant to driver developers. No 64-bit driver should ever be released that can cause problems with Kernel Patch Protection, so administrators should never need to manage or troubleshoot Kernel Patch Protection. For detailed information, read "An Introduction to Kernel Patch Protection" at *http://blogs.msdn.com/windowsvistasecurity/archive/2006/08/11/695993.aspx*.

NOTE Kernel Patch Protection, hardware-based Data Execution Prevention (DEP), and required driver signing are the primary reasons that 64-bit systems can be more secure than 32-bit systems.

Required Driver Signing

Drivers typically run as part of the kernel, which gives them almost unprotected access to system resources. As a result, drivers that have bugs or are poorly written, or malware drivers specifically written to abuse these privileges, can significantly affect a computer's reliability and security.

To help reduce the impact of drivers, Microsoft introduced driver signing beginning with Microsoft Windows 2000. Signed drivers have a digital signature that indicates they have been approved by Microsoft and are likely to be free from major weaknesses that might affect system reliability. Administrators can configure Windows 2000 and later operating systems to block all unsigned drivers, which can dramatically decrease the risk of driver-related problems.

However, the large number of unsigned 32-bit drivers has made blocking unsigned drivers impractical for most organizations. As a result, most existing Windows computers allow unsigned drivers to be installed.

With 64-bit versions of Windows Vista and Windows 7, all kernel-mode drivers must be digitally signed. A kernel module that is corrupt or has been subject to tampering will not load. Any driver that is not properly signed cannot enter the kernel space and will fail to load. Although a signed driver is not a guarantee of security, it does help identify and prevent many malicious attacks while allowing Microsoft to help developers improve the overall quality of drivers and reduce the number of driver-related crashes.

Mandatory driver signing also helps improve the reliability of Windows Vista and Windows 7 because many system crashes result from vulnerabilities in kernel-mode drivers. Requiring the authors of these drivers to identify themselves makes it easier for Microsoft to determine the cause of system crashes and work with the responsible vendor to resolve the issue. System administrators also benefit from digitally signed and identified drivers because they get additional visibility into software inventory and install state on client computers. From a compatibility perspective, existing Windows Hardware Quality Labs–certified x64 kernel drivers are considered validly signed in Windows Vista and Windows 7.

Windows Service Hardening

Historically, many Windows network compromises (especially worms) resulted from attackers exploiting vulnerabilities in Windows services. Because many Windows services listen for incoming connections and often have system-level privileges, a vulnerability can allow an attacker to perform administrative tasks on a remote computer.

Windows Service Hardening, a feature of Windows Vista and Windows 7, restricts all Windows services from performing abnormal activities in the file system, registry, network, or other resources that can be used to allow malware to install itself or attack other computers. For example, the Remote Procedure Call (RPC) service is restricted to performing network communications on defined ports only, eliminating the possibility of abusing it to, for instance, replace system files or modify the registry (which is what the Blaster worm did). Essentially, Windows Service Hardening enforces the security concept of least privilege on services, granting them only enough permission to perform their required tasks.

> ***NOTE*** **Windows Service Hardening provides an additional layer of protection for services based on the security principle of defense-in-depth. Windows Service Hardening cannot prevent a vulnerable service from being compromised—a task Windows Firewall and Automatic Updates supports. Instead, Windows Service Hardening limits how much damage an attacker can do in the event the attacker is able to identify and exploit a vulnerable service.**

Windows Service Hardening reduces the damage potential of a compromised service by:

- Introducing a per-service security identifier (SID) to uniquely identify services, which subsequently enables access control partitioning through the existing Windows access control model covering all objects and resource managers that use ACLs. Services can now apply explicit ACLs to resources that are private to the service, which prevents other services, as well as the user, from accessing the resource.
- Moving services from LocalSystem to a lesser-privileged account, such as LocalService or NetworkService, to reduce the privilege level of the service.
- Stripping unnecessary Windows privileges on a per-service basis—for example, the ability to perform debugging.
- Applying a write-restricted token to services that access a limited set of files and other resources so that the service cannot update other aspects of the system.
- Assigning a network firewall policy to services to prevent network access outside the normal bounds of the service program. The firewall policy is linked directly to the per-service SID and cannot be overridden or relaxed by user- or administrator-defined exceptions or rules.

A specific goal of Windows Service Hardening is to avoid introducing management complexity for users and system administrators. Every service included in Windows Vista and Windows 7 has been through a rigorous process to define its Windows Service Hardening profile, which is applied automatically during Windows setup and requires no ongoing administration, maintenance, or interaction from the end user. For these reasons, there is no administrative interface for managing Windows Service Hardening. For more information about Windows Service Hardening, see Chapter 26.

NOTE Third-party software developers can also take advantage of the Windows Service Hardening security benefits by providing profiles for custom services.

Network Access Protection Client

Most networks have perimeter firewalls to help protect the internal network from worms, viruses, and other attackers. However, attackers can penetrate your network through remote access connections (such as a VPN) or by infecting a mobile PC and then spreading to other internal computers after the mobile PC connects to your LAN.

Windows Vista and Windows 7, when connecting to a Windows Server 2008 infrastructure, support Network Access Protection (NAP) to reduce the risk of attackers entering through remote access and LAN connections using the built-in NAP client software of Windows Vista. If a Windows client computer lacks current security updates or antivirus signatures or otherwise fails to meet your requirements for a healthy computer, NAP can block the computer from reaching your internal network.

However, if a computer fails to meet the requirements to join your network, the user doesn't have to remain frustrated. Client computers can be directed to an isolated quarantine network to download the updates, antivirus signatures, or configuration settings required to comply with your health requirements policy. Within minutes, a potentially vulnerable computer can be protected and once again allowed to connect to your network.

NAP is an extensible platform that provides an infrastructure and an application programming interface (API) for health policy enforcement. Independent hardware and software vendors can plug their security solutions into NAP so that IT administrators can choose the security solutions that meet their unique needs. NAP helps to ensure that every machine on the network makes full use of those custom solutions.

Microsoft will also release NAP client support with Windows XP SP3. For more information about NAP, see *http://www.microsoft.com/nap/*.

Web Services for Management

Web Services for Management (WS-Management) makes Windows Vista and Windows 7 easier to manage remotely. An industry-standard Web services protocol for protected remote management of hardware and software, WS-Management—along with the proper software tools—allows administrators to run scripts and perform other management tasks remotely. In Windows Vista and Windows 7, communications can be both encrypted and authenticated, limiting security risks. Microsoft management tools, such as Systems Center Configuration Manager 2007, use WS-Management to provide safe and secure management of both hardware and software.

Crypto Next Generation Services

Cryptography is a critical feature of Windows authentication and authorization services, which use cryptography for encryption, hashing, and digital signatures. Windows Vista and Windows 7 deliver Crypto Next Generation (CNG) services, which are requested by many governments and organizations. CNG allows new algorithms to be added to Windows for use in Secure Sockets Layer/Transport Layer Security (SSL/TLS) and IPsec. Windows Vista and Windows 7 also include a new security processor to enable trust decisions for services, such as rights management.

For organizations that are required to use specific cryptography algorithms and approved libraries, CNG is an absolute requirement.

Data Execution Prevention

One of the most commonly used techniques for exploiting vulnerabilities in software is the buffer overflow attack. A buffer overflow occurs when an application attempts to store too much data in a buffer, and memory not allocated to the buffer is overwritten. An attacker might be able to intentionally induce a buffer overflow by entering more data than the application expects. A particularly crafty attacker can even enter data that instructs the operating system to run the attacker's malicious code with the application's privileges.

One well-known buffer overflow exploit is the CodeRed worm, which exploited a vulnerability in an Index Server Internet Server Application Programming Interface (ISAPI) application shipped as part of an earlier version of Microsoft Internet Information Services (IIS) to run malicious software. The impact of the CodeRed worm was tremendous, and it could have been prevented by the presence of Data Execution Prevention (DEP).

DEP marks sections of memory as containing either data or application code. The operating system will not run code contained in memory marked for data. User input—and data received across a network—should always be stored as data and is therefore not eligible to run as an application.

The 32-bit versions of Windows Vista and Windows 7 include a software implementation of DEP that can prevent memory not marked for execution from running. The 64-bit versions of Windows Vista and Windows 7 work with the 64-bit processor's built-in DEP capabilities to enforce this security at the hardware layer, where it is very difficult for an attacker to circumvent it.

> ***NOTE*** **DEP provides an important layer of security for protection from malicious software. However, it must be used alongside other technologies, such as Windows Defender, to provide sufficient protection to meet business requirements.**

As Figure 2-6 shows, DEP is enabled by default in both 32- and 64-bit versions of Windows Vista and Windows 7. By default, DEP protects only essential Windows programs and services to provide optimal compatibility. For additional security, you can protect all programs and services.

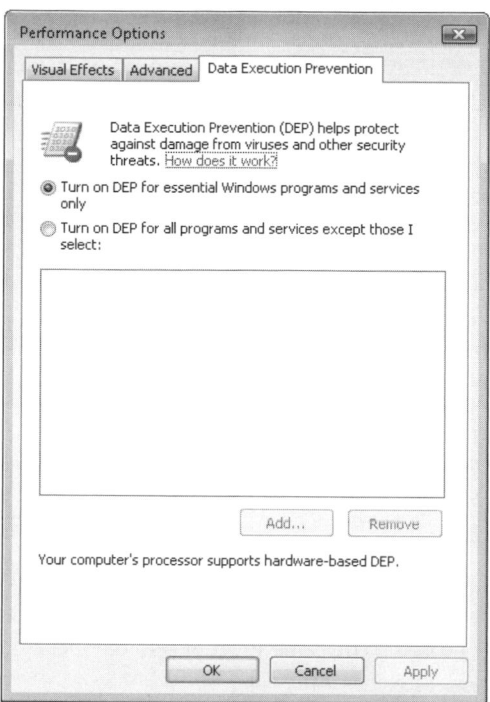

FIGURE 2-6 You can enable or disable DEP from the Performance Options dialog box or from Group Policy settings.

Address Space Layout Randomization

Address Space Layout Randomization (ASLR) is another defense capability in Windows Vista and Windows 7 that makes it harder for malicious code to exploit a system function. Whenever a Windows Vista or Windows 7 computer is rebooted, ASLR randomly assigns executable images (.dll and .exe files) included as part of the operating system to one of multiple possible locations in memory. This makes it harder for exploitative code to locate and therefore take advantage of functionality inside the executables.

Windows Vista and Windows 7 also introduce improvements in heap buffer overrun detection that are even more rigorous than those introduced in Windows XP SP2. When signs of heap buffer tampering are detected, the operating system can immediately terminate the affected program, limiting damage that might result from the tampering. This protection technology is enabled for operating system features, including built-in system services, and can also be leveraged by Independent Software Vendors (ISVs) through a single API call.

New Logon Architecture

Logging on to Windows provides access to local resources (including EFS-encrypted files) and, in AD DS environments, protected network resources. Many organizations require more than a user name and password to authenticate users. For example, they might require multifactor authentication using both a password and biometric identification or a one-time password token.

In Windows XP and earlier versions of Windows, implementing custom authentication methods required developers to completely rewrite the Graphical Identification and Authentication (GINA) interface. Often, the effort required did not justify the benefits provided by strong authentication, and the project was abandoned. Additionally, Windows XP supported only a single GINA.

With Windows Vista and Windows 7, developers can now provide custom authentication methods by creating a new credential provider. This requires significantly less development effort, allowing more organizations to offer custom authentication methods.

The new architecture also enables credential providers to be event driven and integrated throughout the user experience. For example, the same code used to implement a fingerprint authentication scheme at the Windows logon screen can be used to prompt the user for a fingerprint when accessing a particular corporate resource. The same prompt also can be used by applications that use the new credential user interface API.

Additionally, the Windows logon user interface can use multiple credential providers simultaneously, providing greater flexibility for environments that might have different authentication requirements for different users.

Rights Management Services

Windows Rights Management Services (RMS) is an information-protection technology that works with RMS-enabled applications to help safeguard digital information from unauthorized use both inside and outside your private network. RMS provides persistent usage policies (also known as usage rights and conditions) that remain with a file no matter where it goes. RMS persistently protects any binary format of data, so the usage rights remain with the information—even in transport—rather than merely residing on an organization's network.

RMS works by encrypting documents and then providing decryption keys only to authorized users with an approved RMS client. To be approved, the RMS client must enforce the usage rights assigned to a document. For example, if the document owner has specified that the contents of the document should not be copied, forwarded, or printed, the RMS client will not allow the user to take these actions.

In Windows Vista and Windows 7, RMS is now integrated with the XPS format. XPS is an open, cross-platform document format that helps customers effortlessly create, share, print, archive, and protect rich digital documents. With a print driver that outputs XPS, any application can produce XPS documents that can be protected with RMS. This basic functionality significantly broadens the range of information that can be protected by RMS.

The 2007 Microsoft Office system provides even deeper integration with RMS through new developments in Microsoft SharePoint. SharePoint administrators can set access policies for the SharePoint document libraries on a per-user basis that will be inherited by RMS policies. This means that users who have "view-only" rights to access the content will have that "view-only" access (no print, copy, or paste) enforced by RMS, even when the document has been removed from the SharePoint site. Enterprise customers can set usage policies that are enforced not only when the document is at rest, but also when the information is outside the direct control of the enterprise.

Although the RMS features are built into Windows Vista and Windows 7, they can be used only with a rights management infrastructure and an application that supports RMS, such as Microsoft Office. The RMS client can also be installed on Windows 2000 and later operating systems. For more information about how to use RMS, visit *http://www.microsoft.com/rms*.

Multiple Local Group Policy Objects

As an administrator, you can now apply multiple Local Group Policy Objects to a single computer. This simplifies configuration management because you can create separate Group Policy Objects for different roles and apply them individually, just as you can with AD DS Group Policy Objects. For example, you might have a Group Policy Object for computers that are members of the Marketing group and a separate Group Policy Object for mobile computers. If you need to configure a mobile computer for a member of the Marketing group, you can simply apply both local Group Policy Objects rather than creating a single Local Group Policy Object that combines all of the settings.

New and Improved Security Features of Windows 7

This section describes the most visible and tangible Windows 7 security improvements, which are listed in Table 2-3. Architectural and internal improvements—as well as improvements that require additional applications or infrastructure—are described later in this chapter.

TABLE 2-3 Windows 7 Security Improvements

IMPROVEMENT	DESCRIPTION
BitLocker and BitLocker To Go	Encrypts entire volumes, including system volumes, non-system volumes, and removable drives.
AppLocker	Provides flexible control over which applications users can run.
Multiple active firewall profiles	Provides different firewall profiles for the physical network adapter and virtual network adapters used by VPNs.

IMPROVEMENT	DESCRIPTION
User Account Control	Gives standard users the opportunity to provide administrative credentials when the operating system requires them. For administrators, it runs processes with standard privileges by default and prompts the administrator to confirm before granting administrative privileges to a process.
Internet Explorer security features	Reduces the risk of phishing and malware attacks when users browse the Web.
Auditing enhancements	Provide more granular control over which events are audited.
Safe unlinking in the kernel pool	Reduces the risk of overrun attacks.
Windows Biometric Framework	Provides a uniform interface for fingerprint scanners.
Smart cards	Provides a standard smart card driver interface.
Service accounts	Enables administrators to create accounts for services without needing to manage service account passwords.

The sections that follow describe these features in more detail.

BitLocker and BitLocker To Go

Using BitLocker Drive Encryption, organizations can reduce the risk of confidential data being lost when a user's mobile PC is stolen. Its full-volume encryption seals the symmetric encryption key in a Trusted Platform Module (TPM) 1.2 chip (available in some newer computers) or a USB flash drive. BitLocker has four TPM modes:

- **TPM only** This is transparent to the user, and the user logon experience is unchanged. However, if the TPM is missing or changed, BitLocker will enter recovery mode, and you will need a recovery key or PIN to regain access to the data. This provides protection from hard-disk theft with no user training necessary.
- **TPM with startup key** The user will also need a startup key to start Windows. A startup key can be either physical (a USB flash drive with a computer-readable key written to it) or personal (a password set by the user). This provides protection from both hard-disk theft and stolen computers (assuming the computer was shut down or locked); however, it requires some effort from the user.
- **TPM with PIN** The user will need to type a PIN to start Windows. Like requiring a startup key, this provides protection from both hard-disk theft and stolen computers (assuming the computer was shut down or locked); however, it requires some effort from the user.
- **TPM with PIN and startup key** The user will need to type a PIN and insert the startup key to start Windows.

NOTE To manage TPM chips, Windows 7 includes the TPM Management snap-in.

BitLocker works by storing measurements of various parts of the computer and operating system in the TPM chip. In its default configuration, BitLocker instructs the TPM to measure the master boot record, the active boot partition, the boot sector, the Windows Boot Manager, and the BitLocker storage root key. Each time the computer is booted, the TPM computes the SHA-1 hash of the measured code and compares this to the hash stored in the TPM from the previous boot. If the hashes match, the boot process continues; if the hashes do not match, the boot process halts. At the conclusion of a successful boot process, the TPM releases the storage root key to BitLocker; BitLocker decrypts data as Windows reads it from the protected volume.

BitLocker protects Windows from offline attacks. An offline attack is a scenario in which an attacker starts an alternate operating system to gain control of the computer. The TPM releases the storage root key only when instructed to by BitLocker running within the instance of Windows that initially created the key. Because no other operating system can do this (even an alternate instance of Windows), the TPM never releases the key, and therefore the volume remains a useless encrypted blob. Any attempts to modify the protected volume will render it unbootable.

NOTE **Prior to SP1, BitLocker Drive Encryption could protect only the Windows partition. To protect other partitions before SP1, you could use EFS. After installing SP1, you can use BitLocker Drive Encryption to encrypt any partition. However, you should still use EFS to protect data when multiple users use the same computer.**

As shown in Figure 2-7, individual users can enable BitLocker from Control Panel. Most enterprises should use AD DS to manage keys, however.

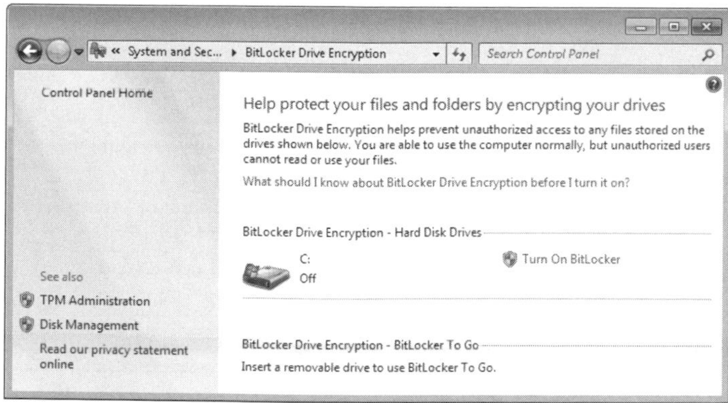

FIGURE 2-7 You can enable BitLocker from Control Panel.

Key management and data recovery requirements are the primary reasons that BitLocker is targeted toward enterprises. As with any type of encryption, if you lose the key, you also lose access to your data. Just as if you were a malicious attacker, the entire Windows partition will be inaccessible without the key. The most effective way to manage keys is to leverage an enterprise's existing AD DS infrastructure to escrow recovery keys remotely. BitLocker also has a disaster recovery console integrated into the early boot features to provide for in-the-field data retrieval. Individual users can use the BitLocker key-management tools to create a recovery key or an additional startup key and store the key on removable media (or any location besides the encrypted volume). Administrators can create scripts to automate key creation and recovery.

BitLocker provides an important layer of protection, but it is only one part of Windows data protection. BitLocker:

- DOES make it very difficult for an attacker to gain access to your data from a stolen computer or hard disk.
- DOES encrypt the entire Windows volume, including the hibernation file, page file, and temporary files (unless they are moved to some other volume).
- DOES allow you to easily recycle or reuse drives by simply deleting the encryption keys.
- DOES NOT protect data from network attacks.
- DOES NOT protect data while Windows is running.

Other security technologies, such as EFS, Windows Firewall, and NTFS file permissions, provide data protection while Windows is running. For more information about BitLocker, see Chapter 16.

The Three Pillars of Information Security

The three pillars of information security are known as the CIA triad:

- **Confidentiality** Let people who should see your data access it, but nobody else.
- **Integrity** Know who has created, viewed, and modified your data, and prevent unauthorized changes and impersonations of legitimate users.
- **Availability** Allow users to access data when they need it, even when attacks and natural disasters occur.

BitLocker provides confidentiality by encrypting data and making it more difficult for an attacker who has physical access to a hard drive to access that data. BitLocker can also provide integrity by detecting changes to critical system files. It does not improve availability, however. In fact, if you don't plan to quickly recover systems with lost keys, BitLocker might reduce availability.

DIRECT FROM THE SOURCE

Trustworthy Administrators

Steve Riley, Senior Security Strategist
Microsoft Corporation, Trustworthy Computing Group

Do you trust your administrators? It's a serious question, and it deserves serious thought. I asked this question in a packed seminar room of nearly 1,000 attendees listening to my presentation on security policies and, astonishingly, no one raised a hand. That frightened me and even left me speechless for a few moments—and those who know me will admit this is an uncommon occurrence! If we can't trust the very people we hire to build and manage the mission-critical networks on which our business successes depend, we might as well unplug it all and revert to the days of stone knives and bearskins.

Administrators have nearly or absolutely unfettered access to everything in your network. That's a lot of power concentrated in a few people—power that can be used for good or abused for bad. What are you doing to help ensure that the people you entrust with such power will use it only for good?

To put it boldly: You must trust your administrators. You need a process for interviewing, investigating, hiring, monitoring, and terminating these employees. I know that many of you reading this book are administrators and might be getting a bit incensed at what I'm writing. You're probably thinking, "Who is he to assume I'm malicious?" But recall my TechEd experiment: In an audience composed of (presumably) mostly administrators, 0 percent said they trusted other administrators. That's got to mean something. Technical measures can make it more difficult for malicious administrators to carry out their ill will, but sufficiently motivated people will find ways around the protection. Administrators who can't be trusted really must be replaced; there's no other alternative.

In Windows Vista, administrators could enable BitLocker protection to encrypt the entire system volume. This made it very difficult for an attacker to remove a computer's hard disk and access the contents of the system volume.

Windows 7 continues to support using BitLocker to encrypt the system volume. Additionally, administrators can encrypt any fixed volume with BitLocker, a feature introduced with Windows Vista SP1. Windows 7 setup automatically partitions the system disk to provide the extra partition required by BitLocker. In Windows Vista, administrators needed to repartition the system disk before enabling BitLocker, which could be very difficult depending on the fullness of the existing volumes.

BitLocker To Go can encrypt removable drives, such as USB flash drives. Because users frequently carry confidential documents using these drives, they are at a high risk of loss and theft. BitLocker To Go protects the contents of the removable drive even if an attacker has access to them. Whereas BitLocker typically protects the system volume using a key stored on a TPM chip, BitLocker To Go protects removable volumes using a password specified by the user, as Figure 2-8 shows.

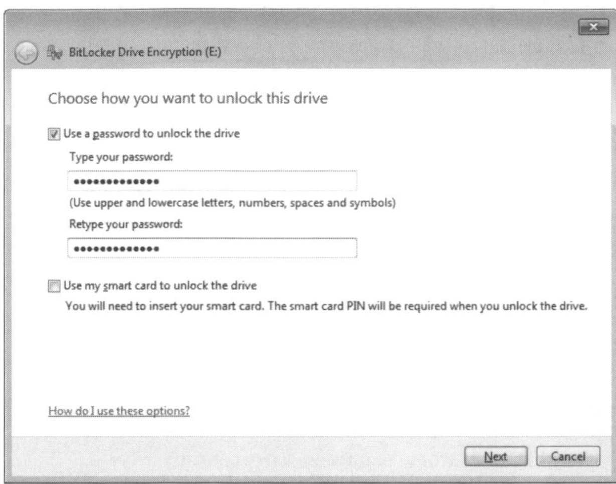

FIGURE 2-8 BitLocker To Go protects removable volumes with a password.

When a user connects a BitLocker To Go drive to a computer running Windows XP with SP3, Windows Vista with SP1, or Windows 7, the AutoPlay capability opens a tool that prompts the user for a password and allows the user to copy the unencrypted files. On Windows 7, users can choose to unlock a BitLocker To Go–encrypted volume automatically. If users do not know the password, they are unable to access the contents of the removable drive. If the user connects a BitLocker To Go–encrypted drive into an earlier version of Windows, the drive appears to be an unformatted device, and the user will be unable to access the data. The user who protects the removable drive with BitLocker To Go must save or print a recovery key that can be used to access the contents of the drive if the password is lost.

IT professionals can use Group Policy settings to require BitLocker To Go encryption on removable drives. For more information about BitLocker To Go, read Chapter 16.

AppLocker

AppLocker is a new feature in Windows 7 and Windows Server 2008 R2 that replaces Software Restriction Policies in earlier versions of Windows. Like Software Restriction Policies, AppLocker gives administrators control over which applications standard users can run. Restricting the applications that users can run not only gives greater control over the desktop environment, but it is one of the best ways to reduce the risk of malware infections, limit the possibility of running unlicensed software, and prevent users from running software that IT has not verified as meeting security compliance requirements.

Compared with Software Restriction Policies, AppLocker provides the following benefits:

- Defines rules based on attributes in the digital signature, such as the publisher, filename, and version. This is a tremendously useful feature because it can allow administrators to let users run any version of a signed application, including future versions. For example, consider an IT department that develops and signs a custom application that users should be able to run. In earlier versions of Windows, administrators could create a rule based on the hash of the file, allowing users to run that specific version of the application. If the IT department released an update to the executable file, administrators would need to create a new rule for the update. With Windows 7, administrators can create a rule that applies to current and future versions, allowing updates to be quickly deployed without waiting for rule changes.
- Assigns rules to security groups or individual users.
- Creates exceptions for .exe files. For example, administrators can create a rule that allows any application to run except a specific .exe file.
- Imports and exports rules, which allow administrators to copy and edit rules easily.
- Identifies files that cannot be allowed to run if a policy is applied by using the audit-only mode.

For more information about AppLocker, refer to Chapter 24.

Multiple Active Firewall Profiles

Many computers, especially portable computers, have multiple network adapters. For example, a laptop computer might have a wired Ethernet connection and a wireless WiFi connection. This can lead to computers being connected to private and public networks simultaneously—for example, a portable computer might be docked at the user's desk and connected to the private LAN, while the WiFi network adapter maintains a connection to the public WiFi network at the coffee shop next door. Even with only a single network adapter, a user might connect to a corporate VPN across a public wireless network.

In Windows Vista and earlier versions of Windows, a single firewall profile was applied to all network adapters. In the previous example, this would lead to the portable computer applying a public firewall profile to the private LAN or VPN connection, which might block important management traffic. Windows 7 supports multiple active firewall profiles, which allows it to apply a public firewall profile to the WiFi network while applying a private or domain firewall profile to the VPN connection. Figure 2-9 illustrates how Windows Vista clients use a single firewall profile and Windows 7 clients can use multiple firewall profiles.

For more information about this enhancement, refer to Chapter 26.

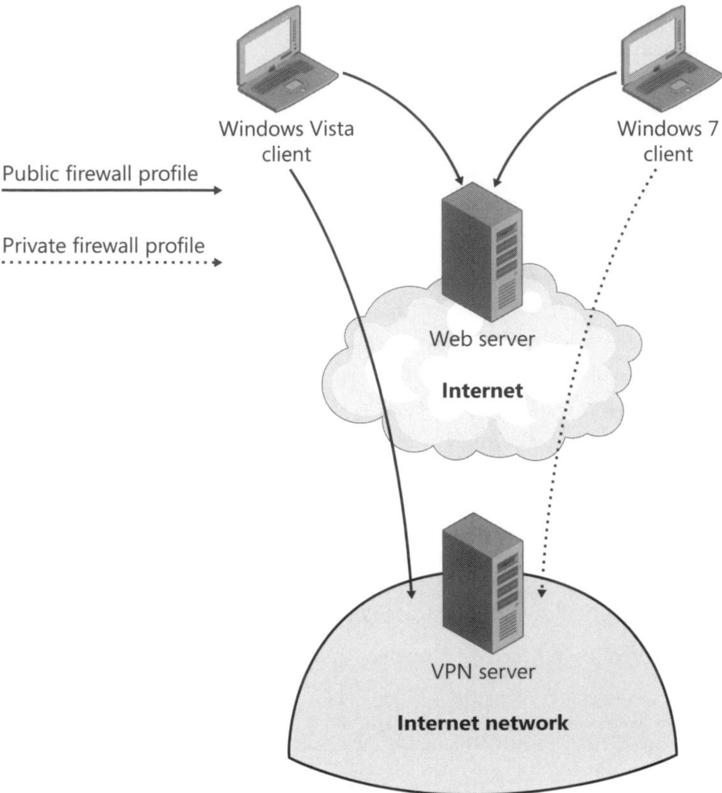

FIGURE 2-9 Windows 7 supports using different firewall profiles for standard and VPN network connections on a single network adapter.

User Account Control

Over the years, the most common security threats have changed from viruses to worms and, most recently, to spyware and Trojan horses. To help protect users from these types of malicious software, Microsoft recommends using accounts with limited privileges (known as standard user accounts in Windows Vista or Limited user accounts in Windows XP). Standard user accounts help prevent malware from making system-wide changes, such as installing software that affects multiple users—if a user lacks permission to install a new application to a shared location, such as %SystemRoot%\Program Files, any malware the user accidentally runs is also prevented from making those changes. In other words, malware run in the context of the user account has the same security restrictions as the user.

Although standard user accounts do improve security, using standard user accounts with Windows XP and earlier versions of Windows results in two major problems:

- Users cannot install software, change the system time or time zone, install printers, change power settings, add a WEP key for wireless settings, or perform other common tasks that require elevated privileges.

- Many poorly written applications require administrative privileges and do not run correctly with limited privileges.

Although logging on to your computer as a standard user offers better protection from malware, working with this type of account has been so difficult in the past that many organizations choose to give users administrative privileges on their computers. User Account Control (UAC) is a set of features first introduced in Windows Vista that offers the benefits of standard user accounts without the unnecessary limitations. First, all users (including administrators) run with limited privileges by default. Second, Windows Vista allows standard user accounts to change the time zone (but not the time) and perform other common tasks without providing administrative credentials, which enables organizations to configure more users with Standard accounts. Third, UAC enables most applications—even those that require administrative privileges on Windows XP—to run correctly in standard user accounts.

DIRECT FROM THE SOURCE

How Users Are Prompted when Permission Is Denied

Steve Hiskey, Lead Program Manager
Windows Security Core

Many enterprises are starting to lock down their users even on Windows XP in an attempt to improve security and to comply with various regulations. Windows Vista allows you to lock down these users to a greater degree by giving the users an Access Denied By Policy message box when they attempt an action that requires elevated privileges. You can configure this by defining the User Account Control: Behavior Of The Elevation Prompt For Standard Users Group Policy setting as No Prompt.

When Windows Vista was first released, many users struggled with the application compatibility and with the frequency of UAC prompts generated by applications. Over time, application developers have modified their applications so that they run correctly with standard user privileges and thus do not require a UAC prompt. This was one of the original goals of UAC—to motivate application developers to comply with security best practices.

Admin Approval Mode

With Windows XP and earlier versions of Windows, any process started by a user logged on as an administrator would be run with administrative privileges. This situation was troublesome because malware could make system-wide changes, such as installing software, without confirmation from the user. In Windows Vista and Windows 7, members of the Administrators group run in *Admin Approval Mode*, which (by default) prompts administrators to confirm actions that require more than Standard privileges. For example, even though a user might log on as an administrator, Windows Messenger and Windows Mail will run only with standard user privileges.

To do this, Admin Approval Mode creates two access tokens when a member of the Administrators local group logs on: one token with full permissions and a second, restricted token that mimics the token of a standard user. The lower-privilege token is used for non-administrative tasks, and the privileged token is used only after the user's explicit consent. As shown in Figure 2-10, Windows Vista prompts the user for consent before allowing an application to complete an action that requires administrative privileges.

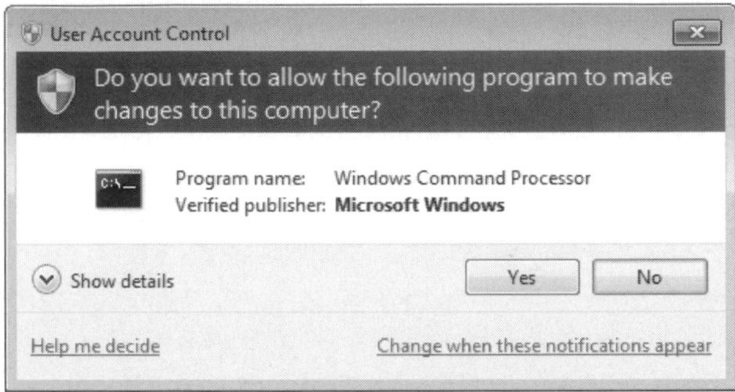

FIGURE 2-10 UAC prompts administrators to confirm administrative actions.

Many organizations use the benefits of UAC to create Standard, rather than Administrator, user accounts. Admin Approval Mode offers some protection for those users who need administrator privileges—such as developers—by requiring confirmation before an application makes any potentially malicious changes. Like most Windows 7 security improvements, the consent prompt is enabled by default but can be disabled using Group Policy settings. Additionally, the consent prompt can require users to type an administrative password or, for standard users, simply inform them that access is not permitted.

DIRECT FROM THE SOURCE

Developers Should Run as Standard Users

Chris Corio, Program Manager
Windows Security

One of my favorite aspects of Windows Vista and Windows 7 is the trend toward reducing the privilege that applications run with by default. This protects users from damaging their computers unknowingly and further allows for trust in the fidelity of the operating system. Unfortunately, many developers make a common mistake that prevents their code from running well in a lesser-privileged environment: They run as administrators! If you are writing a new application for Windows Vista or Windows 7, you should be designing and running your application as a standard user. This is the easiest way for you as a developer to understand the impact of User Account Control and the other technologies that will affect your code.

Enabling Non-Administrators to Make Configuration Changes

Standard user accounts in Windows Vista can make configuration changes that don't compromise the computer's security. For example, standard user accounts in Windows Vista have the right to change the time zone on their computers, an important setting for users who travel. In Windows XP, ordinary user accounts do not have this right by default, an inconvenience that causes many IT professionals to deploy accounts for mobile users as administrators and sacrifice the security benefits of using ordinary user accounts. Additionally, standard users can now connect to encrypted wireless networks and add VPN connections—two tasks commonly required by enterprises.

However, standard user accounts in Windows Vista do not have the right to change the system time because many applications and services rely on an accurate system clock. As shown in Figure 2-11, a user who attempts to change the time is prompted for administrative credentials.

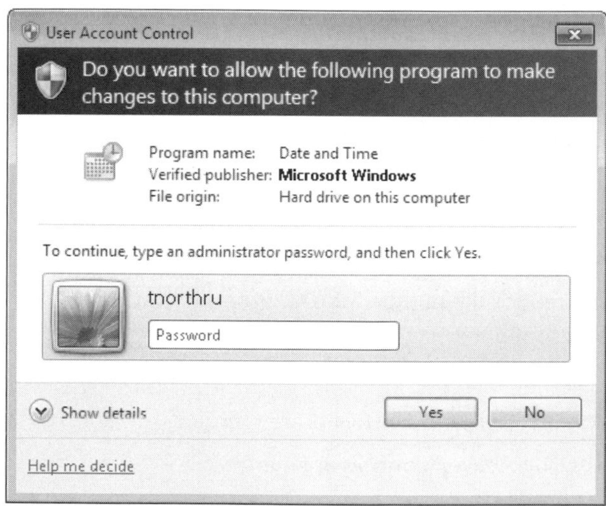

FIGURE 2-11 UAC prompts standard users for administrator credentials.

Some applications do not run in Windows XP without administrative privileges because these applications attempt to make changes to file and registry locations that affect the entire computer (for example, C:\Program Files, C:\Windows, HKEY_LOCAL_MACHINE), and standard user accounts lack the necessary privileges. Registry and file virtualization in Windows Vista redirects many of these per-machine file and registry writes to per-user locations. This feature enables applications to be run by a standard user, whereas on previous operating systems, these applications would have failed as standard user. Ultimately, this will enable more organizations to use standard user accounts because applications that would otherwise require administrative privileges can run successfully without any changes to the application.

NOTE Do not confuse file and registry virtualization with operating system virtualization products, such as Microsoft Virtual PC or Microsoft Virtual Server. File and registry virtualization virtualizes just those operating system features, not the computer's hardware.

For more information about UAC, see Chapter 24.

HOW IT WORKS

File Virtualization

Steve Hiskey, Lead Program Manager
Windows Security Core

Windows Vista includes a filter driver extension to the file system that intercepts access-denied errors before the file operation can be returned to the application. If the file location that generated the access-denied error is in a place where the operating system is configured to virtualize data, a new file path is generated and retried without the application knowing that this has occurred.

UAC Improvements in Windows 7

Windows 7 and Windows Server 2008 R2 reduce the number of UAC prompts that local administrators and standard users must respond to:

- File operation prompts are merged.
- Internet Explorer prompts for running application installers are merged.
- Internet Explorer prompts for installing ActiveX controls are merged.

The default UAC setting allows a standard user to perform the following tasks without receiving a UAC prompt:

- Install updates from Windows Update.
- Install drivers that are downloaded from Windows Update or included with the operating system.
- View Windows settings. Changing settings still requires a UAC prompt.
- Pair Bluetooth devices to the computer.
- Reset the network adapter and perform other network diagnostic and repair tasks.

Additionally, the default UAC setting allows administrators to perform administrative tasks using operating system features without a UAC prompt. For example, an administrator can change the system time or restart a service without receiving a UAC prompt. However, administrators will still receive a UAC prompt if an application requires administrative privileges.

Windows Vista offers two levels of UAC protection to the user: on or off. Additionally, an administrator can change a Group Policy setting to prevent the screen from being dimmed (a feature known as the secure desktop) when prompting the user for consent.

Windows 7 and Windows Server 2008 R2 introduce two additional UAC prompt levels. If you are logged on as a local administrator, you can enable or disable UAC prompts, or you can choose when to be notified about changes to the computer. Administrators can choose from three levels of notification, with an additional option to disable the secure desktop:

- **Always Notify Me** Users are notified when they make changes to Windows settings and when programs attempt to make changes to the computer. This is the default setting for standard users.
- **Notify Me Only When Programs Try To Make Changes To My Computer** Users are not notified when they make changes to Windows settings, but they do receive notification when a program attempts to make changes to the computer. This is the default setting for administrators.
- **Never Notify Me** Users are not notified of any changes made to Windows settings or when software is installed.

Figure 2-12 shows the UAC control settings Control Panel tool. The tool displays a fourth option with the condition Do Not Dim My Desktop that disables the secure desktop to make the UAC prompt less intrusive.

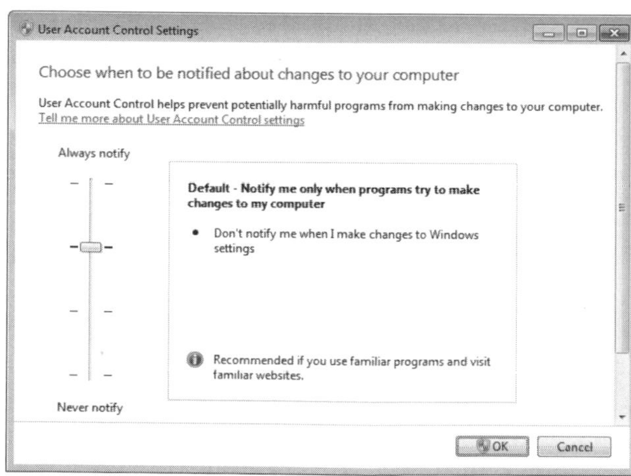

FIGURE 2-12 Setting the UAC prompt level

Table 2-4 compares the number of UAC prompts for user actions in Windows 7 and Windows Server 2008 R2 with the number of UAC prompts in Windows Vista SP1.

TABLE 2-4 Windows 7 UAC Prompting Default Behaviors

ACTIONS	WINDOWS 7 DEFAULT
Change personalization settings	No prompts
Manage your desktop	No prompts
Set up and troubleshoot your network	No prompts
Use Windows Easy Transfer	Fewer prompts
Install ActiveX controls through Internet Explorer	Fewer prompts
Connect devices	No prompts
Use Windows Update	No prompts
Set up backups	No prompts
Install or remove software	No prompts

Using Group Policy settings, administrators can configure different behaviors for administrators and non-administrators. For more information about UAC, refer to Chapter 24.

Internet Explorer Security Features

Windows Internet Explorer 8, included with Windows 7, offers incremental security improvements over Internet Explorer 7. These improvements provide dynamic protection against data theft, fraudulent Web sites, and malicious and hidden software. Microsoft made architectural enhancements to Internet Explorer 7, and has carried those enhancements over to Internet Explorer 8, to make the Web browser less of a target for attackers and other malicious people, which will help users browse with better peace of mind. However, as security is tightened, compatibility and extensibility tend to suffer. With Internet Explorer 8, Microsoft is working hard to ensure that this balance is met effectively so that users can have the safest and best possible browsing experience.

Internet Explorer 8 includes the following security features (some of which are also included with Internet Explorer 7):

- **SmartScreen filter** Internet Explorer 8 uses an Internet service to check Uniform Resource Locators (URLs) that a user visits and warns users when they attempt to visit a site that might be unsafe. The SmartScreen filter can also warn users when they attempt to download software that is potentially unsafe. Users still have the ability to complete an action, even if SmartScreen warns them of a risk. In this way, SmartScreen reduces the risk of users visiting phishing sites or downloading malware without limiting what a user can do.
- **Cross-Site Scripting (XSS) filter** Sometimes attackers exploit vulnerabilities in a Web site and then use the Web site to extract private information from users who visit the site. This can make a site that is normally safe a security risk—without the site owner's knowledge. Internet Explorer 8 can detect malicious code running on compro-

mised Web sites, helping to protect users from exploits that can lead to information disclosure, cookie stealing, identity theft, and other risks.

- **Domain Highlighting** Attackers often use carefully structured URLs to trick users into thinking they are visiting a legitimate Web site. For example, a Web site owner might use the hostname *www.microsoft.com.contoso.com* to make a user think they are visiting the *www.microsoft.com* site—even though *contoso.com* controls the domain. Domain Highlighting helps users more easily interpret URLs to avoid deceptive Web sites that attempt to trick users with misleading addresses. It does this by highlighting the domain name in the address bar in black, as shown in Figure 2-13, with the remainder of the URL string in gray, making for easier identification of the site's true identity.

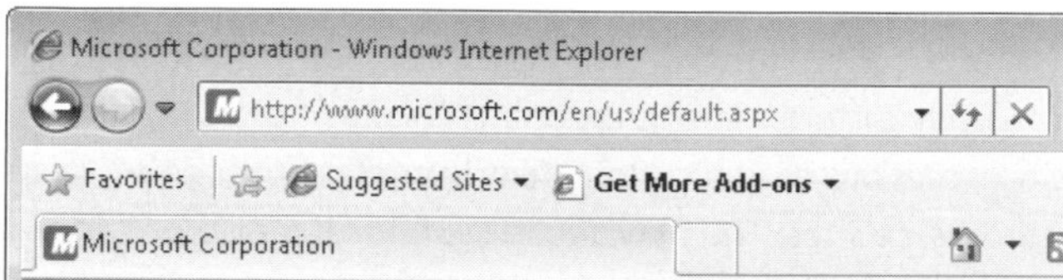

FIGURE 2-13 Domain Highlighting makes it easier to identify the domain name within a URL.

- **Data Execution Prevention** DEP is a security feature that can help prevent compromises from viruses and other security threats by preventing certain types of code from writing to executable memory space. Although DEP is an operating system feature included with Windows Vista and Windows 7, Internet Explorer 8 makes use of it to minimize the risk of exploits for Web sites in the Internet zone. DEP is not enabled for Web sites in the intranet zone.
- **Internet Explorer Protected Mode** In Protected Mode, Internet Explorer 8 runs with reduced permissions to help prevent user or system files or settings from changing without the user's explicit permission. The new browser architecture, introduced with Internet Explorer 7, users a "broker" process that helps to enable existing applications to elevate out of Protected Mode in a more secure way. This additional defense helps verify that scripted actions or automatic processes are prevented from downloading data outside of the low-rights directories, such as the Temporary Internet Files folder. Protected Mode is available only when using Internet Explorer 8 with Windows Vista or Windows 7 when UAC is enabled. Protected Mode is not available in Windows XP.
- **ActiveX Opt-In** ActiveX Opt-In automatically disables all controls that the developer has not explicitly identified for use on the Internet. This mitigates the potential misuse of preinstalled controls. In Windows Vista and Windows 7, users are prompted by the Information Bar before they can access a previously installed ActiveX control that has not yet been used on the Internet but has been designed to be used on the Internet. This notification mechanism enables the user to permit or deny access on a control-by-control basis, further reducing available surface area for attacks. Web sites that attempt automated attacks can no longer secretly attempt to exploit ActiveX controls that were never intended to be used on the Internet.

- **Fix My Settings** Most users install and operate applications using the default configuration, so Internet Explorer 7 and Internet Explorer 8 ship with security settings that provide the maximum level of usability while maintaining controlled security. In rare instances, a custom application might legitimately require a user to lower security settings from the default, but it is critical that the user reverse those changes when the custom settings are no longer needed. The Fix My Settings feature warns users with an Information Bar when current security settings might put them at risk. Clicking the Fix My Settings option in the Information Bar instantly resets Internet Explorer security settings to the Medium-High default level. In AD DS environments, you can configure the required permissions for internal applications so that security restrictions do not need to be a concern.
- **Security Status Bar** The Security Status Bar in Internet Explorer 7 and Internet Explorer 8 helps users quickly differentiate authentic Web sites from suspicious or malicious ones by enhancing access to digital certificate information that helps validate the trustworthiness of e-commerce sites. The new Security Status Bar also provides users with clearer, more prominent visual cues indicating the safety and trustworthiness of a site, and it supports information about High Assurance certificates for stronger identification of secure sites (such as banking sites).
- **URL handling protections** Internet Explorer 7 and Internet Explorer 8 have a single function to process URL data, significantly reducing the internal attack surface. This new data handler ensures greater reliability while providing more features and increased flexibility to address the changing nature of the Internet as well as the globalization of URLs, international character sets, and domain names.

Additionally, each of these features is configurable by using Group Policy, enabling centralized control over Internet Explorer security. Windows 7 includes Internet Explorer 8, which includes all of these features. Internet Explorer 8 can also be installed on Windows Vista. For more information about Internet Explorer, refer to Chapter 20, "Managing Windows Internet Explorer."

Auditing Enhancements

Auditing in Windows Vista and Windows 7 is very granular, allowing you to enable auditing for very specific events. This reduces the number of irrelevant events, potentially reducing the "noise" generated by false-positive auditing events. This, in turn, can enable operations staff to more easily detect significant events. Combined with the new Windows Event Collector service, you can build a system to aggregate only the most important security events in your organization.

To view the new categories, run the following command from an administrative command prompt. Lines in bold show categories that are new in Windows 7 and thus are not included in Windows Vista.

```
Auditpol /get /category:*
System audit policy
Category/Subcategory                      Setting
System
  Security System Extension               No Auditing
  System Integrity                        Success and Failure
  IPsec Driver                            No Auditing
  Other System Events                     Success and Failure
  Security State Change                   Success
Logon/Logoff
  Logon                                   Success
  Logoff                                  Success
  Account Lockout                         Success
  IPsec Main Mode                         No Auditing
  IPsec Quick Mode                        No Auditing
  IPsec Extended Mode                     No Auditing
  Special Logon                           Success
  Other Logon/Logoff Events               No Auditing
  Network Policy Server                   Success and Failure
Object Access
  File System                             No Auditing
  Registry                                No Auditing
  Kernel Object                           No Auditing
  SAM                                     No Auditing
  Certification Services                  No Auditing
  Application Generated                   No Auditing
  Handle Manipulation                     No Auditing
  File Share                              No Auditing
  Filtering Platform Packet Drop          No Auditing
  Filtering Platform Connection           No Auditing
  Other Object Access Events              No Auditing
  Detailed File Share                     No Auditing
Privilege Use
  Sensitive Privilege Use                 No Auditing
  Non Sensitive Privilege Use             No Auditing
  Other Privilege Use Events              No Auditing
Detailed Tracking
  Process Termination                     No Auditing
  DPAPI Activity                          No Auditing
  RPC Events                              No Auditing
  Process Creation                        No Auditing
Policy Change
  Audit Policy Change                     Success
  Authentication Policy Change            Success
  Authorization Policy Change             No Auditing
  MPSSVC Rule-Level Policy Change         No Auditing
```

```
  Filtering Platform Policy Change        No Auditing
  Other Policy Change Events              No Auditing
Account Management
  User Account Management                 Success
  Computer Account Management             No Auditing
  Security Group Management               Success
  Distribution Group Management           No Auditing
  Application Group Management            No Auditing
  Other Account Management Events         No Auditing
DS Access
  Directory Service Changes               No Auditing
  Directory Service Replication           No Auditing
  Detailed Directory Service Replication  No Auditing
  Directory Service Access                No Auditing
Account Logon
  Kerberos Service Ticket Operations      No Auditing
  Other Account Logon Events              No Auditing
  Kerberos Authentication Service         No Auditing
  Credential Validation                   No Auditing
```

Similarly, you can use the *Auditpol /set* command to enable granular auditing. The most straightforward way to enable granular auditing is to enable or disable the Group Policy settings located in Computer Configuration\Windows Settings\Security Settings\Advanced Audit Policy Configuration. Managing granular auditing using Group Policy is a feature new to Windows 7 and Windows Server 2008 R2.

Windows 7 also supports Global Object Access Auditing, which you can use to configure file or registry auditing on computers using Group Policy settings. To do this, define the File System or Registry policies in Computer Configuration\Windows Settings\Security Settings\Advanced Audit Policy Configuration\System Audit Policies\Global Object Access Auditing. Then click the Configure button to specify the objects to audit.

For more information about Windows event logs and event log collection, see Chapter 21, "Maintaining Desktop Health."

Safe Unlinking in the Kernel Pool

Windows 7 includes low-level integrity checks not included with earlier versions of Windows to reduce the risk of overruns. Malware frequently uses different types of overruns to run elevated privileges and code without the user's consent. Essentially, Windows 7 double-checks the contents of memory in the pool—a portion of memory that applications use temporarily but which is managed by the operating system. If the pool has been modified or corrupted, Windows 7 initiates a bug check that prevents more code from running.

According to internal Microsoft testing, the additional memory checking does not have a measurable performance impact. For more information, read "Safe Unlinking in the Kernel Pool" at *http://blogs.technet.com/srd/archive/2009/05/26/safe-unlinking-in-the-kernel-pool.aspx*.

Windows Biometric Framework

Before Windows 7, fingerprint biometric device manufacturers had to provide their own technology stack, including drivers, software development kits (SDKs), and applications. Unfortunately, because different manufacturers created their own solutions, they lacked a consistent user interface and management platform.

The Windows Biometric Framework (WBF) enables biometric manufacturers to better integrate fingerprint scanners, iris scanners, and other biometric devices into Windows. Now, biometric devices can use the same Control Panel tools for configuration, regardless of the hardware vendor. Users can search for biometric capabilities by clicking Start and then typing **biometrics, fingerprint** or other related phrases to start the Biometric Devices Control Panel. IT professionals benefit because they no longer need to manage different software for each type of biometric device. Additionally, fingerprint scanners can now be used to respond to UAC credential prompts and to log on to AD DS domains.

Applications can use an API built into Windows 7 to interface with any type of biometric device. In the past, applications needed to use device-specific APIs, making it difficult for developers to integrate different types of biometric devices. Therefore, application developers also benefit because they can use a well-defined API and support biometric devices from any vendor.

Administrators can use Group Policy settings to prevent biometric devices from being used to log on to the local computer or domain, or they can completely disable biometrics. In Windows 7, fingerprint scanners are the only supported biometric device type.

Smart Cards

For many organizations, the risk that a password will be stolen or guessed is not acceptable. To supplement password security, organizations implement multifactor authentication that requires both a password and a second form of identification. Often, that second form of identification is a smart card, which contains a digital certificate that uniquely identifies the card holder and a private key for use in authentication.

Like fingerprint biometric devices, previous versions of Windows lacked a standardized framework for smart cards. In Windows 7, smart cards can use conventional drivers. This means that users can access smart cards from vendors who have published their drivers through Windows Update without requiring additional software. Users simply insert a Personal Identity Verification (PIV)–compliant smart card, and Windows 7 attempts to download a driver from Windows Update or use the PIV-compliant minidriver that is included with Windows 7.

The new smart card support options in Windows 7 include the following, all of which can be accomplished without additional software:

- Unlocking BitLocker-encrypted drives with a smart card.
- Logging on to the domain with a smart card.

- Signing XPS documents and e-mail messages.
- Using smart cards with custom applications that use CNG or Crypto API to enable the application to use certificates.

Service Accounts

Services are background processes. For example, the Server service accepts incoming file-sharing connections, and the Workstation service manages outgoing file-sharing connections.

Each service must run in the context of a service account. The permissions of the service account largely define what the service can and cannot do, just like a user account defines what a user can do. In early versions of Windows, security vulnerabilities in services were often exploited to make changes to the computer. To minimize this risk, service accounts should have the most restrictive permissions possible.

Windows Vista provided three types of service accounts: Local Service, Network Service, and Local System. These accounts were simple for administrators to configure, but they were often shared between multiple services and could not be managed at the domain level.

Administrators can also create domain user accounts and configure them to act as a service account. This gives administrators complete control over the permissions assigned to the service, but it requires administrators to manually manage passwords and service principal names (SPNs). This management overhead can become very time consuming in an enterprise environment.

Windows 7 introduces two new types of service accounts:

- Managed service accounts provide services with the isolation of a domain account while eliminating the need for administrators to manage the account credentials.
- Virtual service accounts act like managed service accounts, but they operate at the local computer level rather than at the domain level. Virtual service accounts can use a computer's credentials to access network resources.

Both types of accounts have passwords that reset automatically so that administrators do not need to manually reset the passwords. Either type of account can be used for multiple services on a single computer. However, they cannot be used for services on different computers, including computers in a cluster.

For more information on how services are implemented and managed in Windows 7, see Chapter 17, "Managing Devices and Services."

Summary

Windows 7 security improvements touch almost every aspect of the operating system. The details of the security features are discussed throughout this resource kit, but this chapter has provided an overview of key security improvements to enable you to create a comprehensive security plan and better understand how Windows Vista will impact the security of your organization.

Windows 7 security improvements align with several different security principles:

- **Assign least privilege** Users, applications, and services should have only the minimum privileges they absolutely need. For example, users should not have administrator permissions on their desktop computer because a virus or Trojan horse could misuse those permissions. AppLocker, UAC, Internet Explorer Protected Mode, and service accounts enforce least privilege for users, Internet Explorer, and services.
- **Protect data in storage and transit** Although you might consider computer files and communications safe within a physically secure facility, the increase in mobile communications means that your data requires additional protection. Windows 7 improves BitLocker, allowing both system and non-system volumes to be encrypted. Windows 7 also adds BitLocker To Go, enabling users to encrypt the entire contents of removable drives. Even if an attacker steals a BitLocker To Go–protected removable drive, they will not be able to access the contents without the password.
- **Reduce the attack surface** Any application, service, or operating system feature might contain vulnerabilities. The more services and applications that are enabled by default in an operating system, the greater the risk of a vulnerability being exploited. Windows 7 minimizes the network attack surface without blocking important management traffic by assigning different firewall profiles to different virtual network adapters. For example, a physical network adapter can have the public firewall profile assigned to it, thus protecting it from many network attacks. A VPN network adapter can have the domain firewall profile assigned to it, thus allowing administrators on the internal network to connect to and manage the remote computer.

Combined with the improved security infrastructure of the WBF and standardized smart card drivers, these improvements offer multiple layers of protection that you can use to limit your organization's security risks.

Additional Resources

These resources contain additional information and tools related to this chapter.

Related Information

- "Windows 7 Security Enhancements" in the Windows Client TechCenter on Microsoft TechNet at *http://technet.microsoft.com/en-us/library/dd548337.aspx.*
- "An Introduction to Security in Windows 7" in TechNet Magazine at *http://technet.microsoft.com/en-us/magazine/2009.05.win7.aspx.*
- "Windows 7—The Security Story" on-demand webcast at *http://msevents.microsoft.com/CUI/WebCastEventDetails.aspx?culture=en-AU&EventID=1032407883&CountryCode=AU.*

- Download the latest version of the *Windows Vista Security Guide* at *http://www.microsoft.com/downloads/details.aspx?FamilyID=a3d1bbed-7f35-4e72-bfb5-b84a526c1565&DisplayLang=en*. It provides detailed information about how to best configure Windows Vista security for your organization.
- "Windows 7 Security Compliance Management Toolkit" at *http://go.microsoft.com/fwlink/?LinkId=156033*.

On the Companion Media

- Get-FileAcl.ps1
- Get-LocalAdministrators.ps1
- UnlockLockedOutUsers.ps1
- UserToSid.ps1
- WhoIs.ps1

PART II

Deployment

CHAPTER 3

Deployment Platform

Building on technology that the Windows Vista operating system introduced, Windows 7 deployment technology has evolved significantly since Windows XP Professional. For example, it supports file-based disk imaging to make high-volume deployments quicker, more efficient, and more cost effective. The Windows 7 operating system also provides more robust deployment tools through the Windows Automated Installation Kit 2.0 (Windows AIK 2.0), including Windows System Image Manager (Windows SIM) and Windows Preinstallation Environment (Windows PE).

This chapter helps you get started with the Windows 7 deployment platform. It introduces these tools, describing how they relate to each other and providing you with a basic understanding of why and when to use each tool. The remaining chapters in Part II, "Deployment," describe in detail the tools introduced in this chapter. The *Windows Automated Installation Kit User's Guide* in the Windows AIK 2.0 also details each tool described in this chapter.

Tools Introduction

Compared to Windows XP, Windows 7 introduces numerous changes to the technology you use for deployment. Additionally, Windows 7 improves and consolidates many of the tools you used for Windows Vista deployment. The Windows AIK 2.0 includes most of these tools. Others are built into the operating system. The Windows AIK 2.0 fully documents all of the tools this chapter describes, including command-line options for using them, how they work on a detailed level, and so on.

> ***NOTE*** **The Windows AIK 2.0 is not included in the Windows 7 media. (By comparison, Windows XP has a file called Deploy.cab that includes its deployment tools.) Instead, the Windows AIK 2.0 is a free download from the Microsoft Download Center at *http://www.microsoft.com/downloads*.**

The following features are new for Windows 7 deployment:

- **Windows System Image Manager** Windows System Image Manager (Windows SIM) is a tool for creating distribution shares and editing answer files (Unattend.xml). It exposes all configurable settings in Windows 7; you use it to save customizations in Unattend.xml. The Windows AIK 2.0 includes the Windows SIM.
- **Windows Setup** Setup for Windows 7 installs the Windows image (.wim) file and uses the new Unattend.xml answer file to automate installation. Unattend.xml replaces the set of answer files used in earlier versions of Windows (Unattend.txt, Sysprep.inf, and so on). Because image-based setup (IBS) is faster, you can use it in high-volume deployments and for automating image maintenance. Microsoft made numerous improvements to Windows Setup (now called Setup.exe instead of Winnt.exe or Winnt32.exe), such as a completely graphical user interface, use of a single answer file (Unattend.xml) for configuration, and support for configuration passes (phases).
- **Sysprep** The System Preparation (Sysprep) tool prepares an installation of Windows 7 for imaging, auditing, and deployment. You use imaging to capture a customized Windows 7 image that you can deploy throughout your organization. You use audit mode to add additional device drivers and applications to a Windows 7 installation and test the integrity of the installation before handing off the computer to the end user. You can also use Sysprep to prepare an image for deployment. When the end user starts Windows 7, Windows Welcome starts. Unlike earlier versions of Windows, Windows 7 includes Sysprep natively—you no longer have to download the current version.
- **Windows Preinstallation Environment** Windows Preinstallation Environment 3.0 (Windows PE 3.0) provides operating system features for installing, troubleshooting, and recovering Windows 7. Windows PE 3.0 is the latest release of Windows PE based on Windows 7. With Windows PE, you can start a computer from a network or removable media. Windows PE provides the network and other resources necessary to install and troubleshoot Windows 7. Windows Setup, Windows Deployment Services, Microsoft System Center Configuration Manager 2007 R2, and Microsoft Deployment Toolkit 2010 (MDT 2010) all use Windows PE to start computers. The Windows AIK 2.0 includes Windows PE 3.0.

- **Deployment Image Servicing and Management** Deployment Image Servicing and Management (DISM) is a new command-line tool that you can use to service a Windows 7 image or prepare a Windows PE image. DISM consolidates the functionality of the Package Manager (Pkgmgr.exe), PEImg, and Intlcfg tools from Windows Vista. You can use DISM to service packages, device drivers, Windows 7 features, and international settings in Windows 7 images. Additionally, DISM provides rich enumeration features that you can use to determine the contents of Windows 7 images.
- **ImageX** ImageX is a command-line tool that you can use to capture, modify, and apply file-based images for deployment. Windows Setup, Windows Deployment Services, System Center Configuration Manager 2007, and MDT 2010 all use ImageX to capture, edit, and deploy Windows 7 images. Windows 7 improves ImageX over Windows Vista by enabling it to mount multiple images simultaneously and support interim saves (you must still service each mounted image individually by using DISM). Additionally, the Windows 7 version of ImageX has a new architecture for mounting and servicing images that is more robust than in Windows Vista. The Windows AIK 2.0 includes ImageX. You can also mount images in Windows PE, and Windows 7 includes the device driver inbox.
- **Windows Imaging** Microsoft delivers Windows 7 on product media as a highly compressed Windows Imaging (.wim) file. You can install Windows 7 directly from the Windows 7 media or customize the image for deployment. Windows 7 images are file based, allowing you to edit them nondestructively. You can also store multiple operating system images in a single .wim file.
- **DiskPart** Using DiskPart, you can mount a virtual hard disk (.vhd) file offline and service it just like a Windows image file.
- **User State Migration Tool** You can use the User State Migration Tool 4.0 (USMT 4.0) to migrate user settings from the previous operating system to Windows 7. Preserving user settings helps ensure that users can get back to work quickly after deployment. USMT 4.0 provides new features that improve its flexibility and performance over USMT 3.0. Hard-link migration improves performance in refresh scenarios, offline migration enables you to capture user state from within Windows PE, and the document finder reduces the need for you to create custom migration Extensible Markup Language (XML) files when capturing all user documents. The Windows AIK 2.0 includes USMT 4.0.

Windows 7 Deployment Terminology

The following terms are unique to Windows 7 deployment and MDT 2010. Understanding this terminology will help you better understand the deployment content in this book and the resources it refers to:

- **Answer file** An XML file that scripts the setup experience and installation settings for Windows 7. The answer file for Windows Setup is usually Unattend.xml or

Autounattend.xml. You can use Windows SIM to create and modify this answer file. MDT 2010 builds answer files automatically, which you can customize if necessary.

- **Catalog file** A binary file that contains the state of all the settings and packages in a Windows 7 image. When you use Windows SIM to create a catalog file, it enumerates the Windows 7 image for a list of all settings in that image as well as the current list of features and their current states. Because the contents of a Windows 7 image can change over time, it is important that you re-create the catalog file whenever you update an image.
- **Feature** A part of the Windows 7 operating system that specifies the files, resources, and settings for a specific Windows 7 feature or part of a Windows 7 feature. Some features include unattended installation settings, which you can customize by using Windows SIM.
- **Configuration pass** A phase of Windows 7 installation. Windows Setup installs and configures different parts of the operating system in different configuration passes. You can apply Windows 7 unattended installation settings in one or more configuration passes. For more information about configuration passes, see the *Windows Automated Installation Kit User's Guide* in the Windows AIK 2.0.
- **Configuration set** A file and folder structure that contains files that control the preinstallation process and define customizations for the Windows 7 installation.
- **Destination computer** The computer on which you install Windows 7 during deployment. You can either run Windows Setup on the destination computer or copy a master installation onto a destination computer. The term *target computer* is also commonly used to refer to this.
- **Deployment share** A folder that contains the source files for Windows products that you install. It may also contain additional device drivers and application files. You can create this folder manually or by using Windows SIM. In MDT 2010, the *deployment share*, called a distribution share in previous versions of MDT, contains operating system, device driver, application, and other source files that you configure with task sequences.
- **Image-based setup** A setup process based on applying an image of an operating system to the computer.
- **Master computer** A fully assembled computer containing a master installation of Windows 7 that you capture to a master image and deploy to destination computers. The term *source computer* is also commonly used to refer to this.
- **Master image** A collection of files and folders (usually compressed into one file) captured from a master installation. This image contains the base operating system as well as additional applications, configurations, and files.
- **Master installation** A Windows 7 installation on a master computer that you can capture as a master image. You can create the master installation using automation to ensure a consistent and repeatable configuration each time.

- **Package** A group of files that Microsoft provides to modify Windows 7 features. Package types include service packs, security updates, language packs, and hotfixes.
- **Task sequence** A sequence of tasks that runs on a destination computer to install Windows 7 and applications and then configures the destination computer. In MDT 2010, task sequences drive the installation routine.
- **Task Sequencer** The MDT 2010 component that runs the task sequence when installing a build.
- **Technician computer** The computer on which you install and use MDT 2010 or Windows AIK 2.0. This computer is typically located in a lab environment, separate from the production network. It can be a workstation- or a server-class computer.
- **Unattend.xml** The generic name for the Windows 7 answer file. Unattend.xml replaces all the answer files in earlier versions of Windows, including Unattend.txt, Winbom.ini, and others.
- **.wim** A file name extension that identifies Windows image files created by ImageX.
- **Windows 7 feature** An optional feature of Windows 7 that you can enable or disable by using Unattend.xml or DISM.
- **Windows image file** A single compressed file containing a collection of files and folders that duplicate a Windows installation on a disk volume. Windows image files have the .wim file extension.

Platform Components

Understanding the new deployment tools and how they interconnect is the first step in beginning a Windows 7 deployment project. Figure 3-1 illustrates the Windows 7 deployment platform. At the lowest tier are Windows Imaging (.wim) files, which are highly compressed, file-based operating system images.

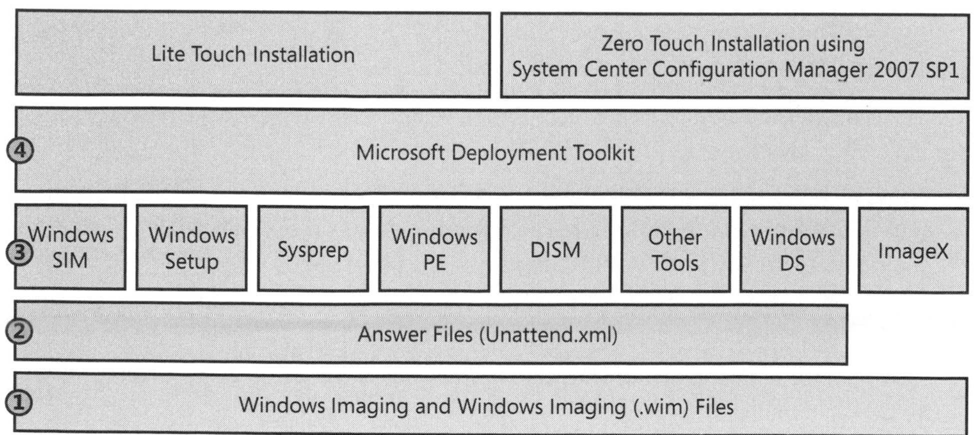

FIGURE 3-1 Windows 7 deployment platform components

At the second tier are answer files. Versions of Windows earlier than Windows Vista had numerous answer files, including Unattend.txt and Sysprep.inf, to drive the deployment process. Windows 7 uses a single XML-based answer file, Unattend.xml, to drive all its *configuration passes*. (A configuration pass is an installation phase.) This improvement makes configuration more consistent and simplifies engineering.

At the third tier are the various deployment tools for Windows 7. The Windows 7 distribution media includes some of these tools, including Sysprep, DISM, and other command-line tools—they aren't on the media in a separate file such as Deploy.cab. The Windows AIK 2.0 includes the bigger tools, such as Windows SIM, Windows PE, and ImageX. These are the basic tools necessary to create, customize, and deploy Windows 7 images. They are standalone tools that don't provide a deployment framework or add business intelligence and best practice to the process.

The fourth tier, MDT 2010, provides the framework, business intelligence, and best practices. MDT 2010 is a process and technology framework that uses all the tools in the third tier, potentially saving your organization hundreds of hours of planning, developing, testing, and deployment. MDT 2010 is based on best practices developed by Microsoft, its customers, and its partners. It includes time-proven management and technology guidance as well as thousands of lines of thoroughly tested script code that you can use as is or customize to suit your organization's requirements.

Using MDT 2010, you can perform both Lite Touch Installation (LTI) and Zero Touch Installation (ZTI) deployment. LTI requires very little infrastructure and is suitable for most small and medium businesses. ZTI requires a System Center Configuration Manager 2007 R2 infrastructure and is suitable for organizations that already have the infrastructure in place.

The following sections provide more information about the components shown in Figure 3-1. For more information about the deployment process using the components in the first three tiers, see the section titled "Basic Deployment Process" later in this chapter. For more information about the deployment process using MDT 2010, see the section titled "Microsoft Deployment Toolkit Process" later in this chapter.

Windows Imaging

Windows 7 is distributed in .wim files, which use the Windows Imaging file format. This format has the following advantages:

- Windows Imaging files are a file-based image format that lets you store multiple images in one file. You can perform partial volume captures by excluding files, such as paging files, that you don't want to deploy using the image.
- This format reduces file sizes significantly by using a compressed file format and single-instance storage techniques: The image file contains one physical copy of a file for each instance of it in the image file, which significantly reduces the size of image files that contain multiple images.

- You can service the image contained in the .wim file—adding and deleting packages, software updates, and device drivers, for example—without re-creating a new image by applying it, customizing it again, and recapturing it.
- You can mount .wim files as folders, making it easier to update files in images they contain.
- Windows Imaging files allow you to apply an image nondestructively to the destination computer's hard disk. You can also apply an image to different-sized destination drives because .wim files don't require the destination hard disk to be the same size or larger than the source hard disk.
- Windows Imaging files can span media so that you can use CD-ROMs to distribute large .wim files.
- Windows PE .wim files are bootable. For example, you can start Windows PE from a .wim file. In fact, Windows Setup and Windows Deployment Services start Windows PE from the .wim file Boot.wim, which you can customize by adding items such as device drivers and scripts.

> ***NOTE*** **ImageX is the tool you use to manage .wim files. For more information about ImageX, see the section titled "ImageX" later in this chapter, and Chapter 6, "Developing Disk Images."**

Answer Files

An answer file is an XML-based file that contains settings to use during a Windows 7 installation. An answer file can fully automate all or part of the installation process. In an answer file, you provide settings such as how to partition disks, the location of the Windows 7 image to install, and the product key to apply. You can also customize the Windows 7 installation, including adding user accounts, changing display settings, and updating Windows Internet Explorer favorites. Windows 7 answer files are commonly called Unattend.xml.

You use Windows SIM (see the section titled "Windows SIM" later in this chapter) to create an answer file and associate it with a particular Windows 7 image. This association allows you to validate the settings in the answer file against the settings available in the Windows 7 image. However, because you can use any answer file to install any Windows 7 image, Windows Setup ignores settings in the answer file for features that do not exist in the Windows image.

The features section of an answer file contains all the feature settings that Windows Setup applies. Answer files organize features into different configuration passes: windowsPE, offlineServicing, generalize, specialize, auditSystem, auditUser, and oobeSystem. (See the sidebar titled "How It Works: Configuration Passes" later in this chapter.) Each configuration pass represents a different installation phase, and not all passes run during the normal Windows 7 setup process. You can apply settings during one or more passes. If a setting is available in more than one configuration pass, you can choose the pass in which to apply the setting.

MORE INFO The *Windows Automated Installation Kit User's Guide* in the Windows AIK 2.0 fully documents the features you can configure using Windows SIM and the settings available for each feature.

Microsoft uses packages to distribute software updates, service packs, and language packs. Packages can also contain Windows features. By using Windows SIM, you can add packages to a Windows 7 image, remove them from a Windows 7 image, or change the settings for features within a package.

The Windows Foundation Package, included in all Windows 7 images, includes all core Windows 7 features such as Media Player, Games, and Windows Backup. Features are either enabled or disabled in Windows 7. If a Windows 7 feature is enabled, the resources, executable files, and settings for that feature are available to users on the system. If a Windows 7 feature is disabled, the package resources are not available, but the resources are not removed from the system.

Windows SIM

Windows SIM is the tool you use to create and configure Windows 7 answer files. You can configure features, packages, and answer file settings. Windows Setup uses Unattend.xml to configure and customize the default Windows 7 installation for all configuration passes. For instance, you can customize Internet Explorer, configure Windows Firewall, and specify the hard drive configuration. You can use Windows SIM to customize Windows 7 in many ways, including the following:

- Install third-party applications during installation.
- Customize Windows 7 by creating answer files (Unattend.xml).
- Apply language packs, service packs, and updates to an image during installation.
- Add device drivers to an image during installation.

With versions of Windows earlier than Windows Vista, you had to edit answer file settings manually using a text editor, even after initially creating an answer file by using Windows Setup Manager. The Windows 7 answer file (Unattend.xml) is based on XML and is far too complex to edit manually, however. So you must use Windows SIM to edit Windows 7 answer files. Figure 3-2 shows Windows SIM.

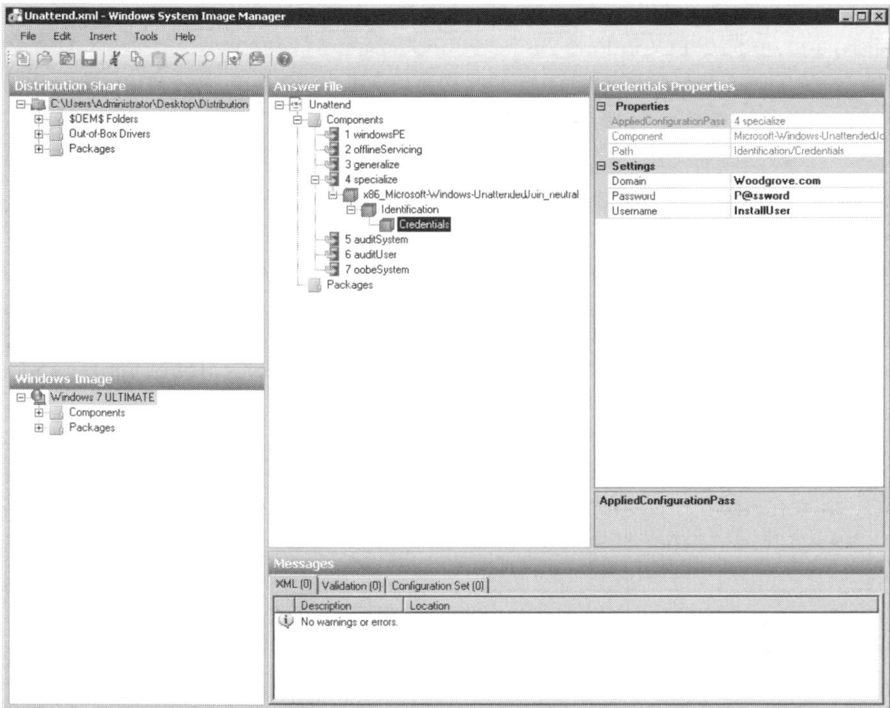

FIGURE 3-2 Windows SIM

Windows Setup

Windows Setup (Setup.exe) is the program that installs Windows 7. It uses image-based setup (IBS) to provide a single, unified process with which all customers can install Windows. IBS performs clean installations and upgrades of Windows. Windows Setup and IBS allow you to deploy Windows 7 in your organization easily and cost effectively.

Windows Setup includes several new features that facilitate installations that are faster and more consistent than Windows XP, including the following:

- **Improved image management** Windows 7 images are stored in a single .wim file. A .wim file can store multiple instances of the operating system in a single, highly compressed file. The install file, Install.wim, is located in the Sources folder on the Windows 7 media.
- **Streamlined installation** Windows Setup is optimized to enable the deployment scenarios used by most organizations. Installation takes less time and provides a more consistent configuration and deployment process, resulting in lower deployment costs.

- **Faster installations and upgrades** Because Windows Setup is now image based, installing and upgrading Windows 7 is faster and easier. You can perform clean installations of Windows 7 by deploying the Windows image to destination computers; you perform upgrades by installing a new image onto an existing installation of Windows. Windows Setup protects the previous Windows settings during the installation.

Windows Setup improves the installation experience over Windows Vista. For example, Windows Setup moves the license key to the Windows Welcome page, allowing users to type a product key after completing installation. Windows Setup also automatically creates a small, hidden partition for BitLocker Drive Encryption. This makes it easier to enable BitLocker Drive Encryption later, because users don't have to prepare the drive. Additionally, the last phase of Windows Setup, Windows Welcome, is faster and gives more feedback on the progress of the setup process.

Sysprep

You use Sysprep to prepare a master installation for imaging and deployment. Sysprep does the following:

- **Removes computer-specific and operating system–specific installation data from Windows 7** Sysprep can remove all computer-specific information from an installed Windows 7 image, including the computer security identifier (SID). You can then capture and install the Windows installation throughout your organization.
- **Configures Windows 7 to boot in audit mode** You can use audit mode to install third-party applications and device drivers, as well as to test the functionality of the computer, before delivering the computer to the user.
- **Configures Windows 7 to boot to Windows Welcome** Sysprep configures a Windows 7 installation to boot to Windows Welcome the next time the computer starts. Generally, you configure a system to boot to Windows Welcome as a final step before delivering the computer to the user.
- **Resets Windows Product Activation** Sysprep can rearm (reset) Windows Product Activation up to three times.

Sysprep.exe is located in the %WinDir%\System32\Sysprep directory on all Windows 7 installations. (You do not have to install Sysprep separately, as in earlier versions of Windows, because it's a native part of the installation.) You must always run Sysprep from the %WinDir%\System32\Sysprep directory on the version of Windows 7 with which it was installed. For more information about Sysprep, see the *Windows Automated Installation Kit User's Guide* in the Windows AIK 2.0.

Windows PE

Prior to Windows PE, organizations often had to use MS-DOS boot floppies to start destination computers and then start Windows Setup from a network share or other distribution media. MS-DOS boot floppies had numerous limitations, however, including that they offered no support for the NTFS file system and no native networking support. In addition, they needed to locate 16-bit device drivers that worked in MS-DOS.

Now Windows PE 3.0 provides a minimal Win32 or Win64 operating system with limited services—built on the Windows 7 kernel—that you use to prepare a computer for Windows 7 installation, copy images to and from a network file server, and start Windows Setup. Windows PE 3.0 is a stand-alone preinstallation environment and an integral component of other setup and recovery technologies, such as Windows Setup, Windows Deployment Services, System Center Configuration Manager 2007 R2, and MDT 2010. Unlike earlier versions of Windows PE, which were available only as a Software Assurance (SA) benefit, Windows PE 3.0 is now publicly available in the Windows AIK 2.0.

Windows PE provides the following features and capabilities:

- Native support for NTFS 5.x file system, including dynamic volume creation and management
- Native support for Transmission Control Protocol/Internet Protocol (TCP/IP) networking and file sharing (client only)
- Native support for 32-bit (or 64-bit) Windows device drivers
- Native support for a subset of the Win32 Application Programming Interface (API); optional support for Windows Management Instrumentation (WMI) and Windows Script Host (WSH)
- Can be started from multiple media, including CD, DVD, USB Flash drive (UFD), and Windows Deployment Services

Windows PE runs every time you install Windows 7, whether you install the operating system by booting the computer with the Windows 7 DVD or deploying Windows 7 from Windows Deployment Services. The graphical tools that collect configuration information during the windowsPE configuration pass run within Windows PE. In addition, you can customize and extend Windows PE to meet specific deployment needs. For example, MDT 2010 customizes Windows PE for LTI by adding device drivers, deployment scripts, and so on.

For Windows 7, Windows PE 3.0 includes improvements that make it easier to customize. First, the functionality of PEImg is now included in DISM, providing a single tool you can use to service images whether they're Windows 7 images or Windows PE images. Second, Windows PE 3.0 uses a new package model. Instead of the base image including all the feature packages from which you remove the disabled features, the base image doesn't include these feature packages, and you add the features that you want to include in the image. For more information about Windows PE, see Chapter 9, "Preparing Windows PE."

NOTE Because Windows PE is only a subset of Windows 7, it has limitations. For example, Windows PE automatically stops running the shell and reboots after 72 hours of continuous use to prevent piracy. You cannot configure Windows PE as a file server, terminal server, or embedded operating system. Moreover, mapped driver letters and changes to the registry are not persistent between sessions. For more information about the limitations of Windows PE, see the *Windows Preinstallation Environment User's Guide* in the Windows AIK 2.0.

Deployment Image Servicing and Management

Deployment Image Servicing and Management (DISM) is a new command-line tool that you can use to service Windows 7 images offline before deployment. With DISM, you can install, remove, configure, and update Windows features, packages, device drivers, and international settings. You can use some DISM commands to service online Windows 7 images.

You can use DISM to:

- Add, remove, and enumerate packages.
- Add, remove, and enumerate drivers.
- Enable or disable Windows features.
- Apply changes based on the offlineServicing section of an Unattend.xml answer file.
- Configure international settings.
- Upgrade a Windows image to a different edition.
- Prepare a Windows PE image.
- Take advantage of better logging.
- Service earlier versions of Windows.
- Service all platforms (32-bit, 64-bit, and Itanium).
- Service a 32-bit image from a 64-bit host, and vice versa.
- Use old Package Manager scripts.

DISM consolidates the functionality of the Package Manager (Pkgmgr.exe), PEImg, and Intlcfg tools from Windows Vista. It provides one tool to use for servicing Windows 7 and Windows PE images.

Other Tools

Windows 7 and the Windows AIK 2.0 also provide various command-line tools that are useful during deployment:

- **BCDboot** BCDboot can set up a system partition or repair the boot environment on a system partition quickly. It copies a small set of boot environment files from the installed Windows 7 image to the system partition. It also creates a boot configuration data (BCD) store on the system partition, which includes a new boot entry that enables the Windows image to boot.

- **Bootsect** Bootsect.exe updates the master boot code for hard-disk partitions to switch between BOOTMGR and NTLDR. You can use this tool to restore the boot sector on your computer. This tool replaces FixFAT and FixNTFS.
- **DiskPart** DiskPart is a text-mode command interpreter in Windows 7. You can use DiskPart to manage disks, partitions, or volumes by using scripts or direct input at a command prompt. In Windows 7, DiskPart can also mount .vhd files. Mounting a .vhd file allows you to service it or make other offline changes.
- **Drvload** The Drvload tool adds out-of-box drivers to a booted Windows PE image. It takes one or more driver .inf files as inputs. To add a driver to an offline Windows PE image, use the DISM tool. If the driver .inf file requires a reboot, Windows PE will ignore the request. If the driver .sys file requires a reboot, you cannot add the driver with Drvload.
- **Expand** The Expand tool expands one or more compressed update files. Expand.exe supports opening updates for Windows 7 as well as previous versions of Windows. By using Expand, you can open and examine updates for Windows 7 on a Windows XP or Microsoft Windows Server 2003 operating system.
- **Lpksetup** You can use Lpksetup to perform unattended or silent-mode language pack operations. Lpksetup runs only on an online Windows 7 operating system.
- **Oscdimg** Oscdimg is a command-line tool for creating an image (.iso) file of a customized 32-bit or 64-bit version of Windows PE. You can then burn an .iso file to a CD-ROM or DVD-ROM or copy its contents to a bootable UFD.
- **Powercfg** You can use the Powercfg tool to control power settings and configure computers to default to Hibernate or Standby modes. In Windows 7, Powercfg provides troubleshooting help for diagnosing energy consumption problems.
- **Winpeshl** Winpeshl.ini controls whether a custom shell is loaded in Windows PE instead of the default Command Prompt window.
- **Wpeinit** Wpeinit is a command-line tool that initializes Windows PE each time it boots. When Windows PE starts, Winpeshl.exe executes Startnet.cmd, which starts Wpeinit.exe. Wpeinit.exe specifically installs Plug and Play (PnP) devices, processes Unattend.xml settings, and loads network resources. Wpeinit replaces the initialization function previously supported using the Factory.exe –*winpe* command. Wpeinit outputs log messages to C:\Windows\System32\Wpeinit.log.
- **Wpeutil** The Windows PE utility (Wpeutil) is a command-line tool that you can use to run various commands in a Windows PE session. For example, you can shut down or reboot Windows PE, enable or disable Windows Firewall, set language settings, and initialize a network.

Windows Deployment Services

Windows Deployment Services is the updated and redesigned version of Remote Installation Services (RIS) in Windows Server 2008. Windows Deployment Services helps organizations rapidly deploy Windows operating systems, particularly Windows 7. Using Windows Deployment Services, you can deploy Windows operating systems over a network without having to be physically present at the destination computer and without using the media.

Windows Deployment Services delivers a better in-box deployment solution than RIS. It provides platform components that enable you to use custom solutions, including remote boot capabilities; a plug-in model for Pre-Boot Execution Environment (PXE) server extensibility; and a client-server communication protocol for diagnostics, logging, and image enumeration. Also, Windows Deployment Services unifies on a single image format (.wim) and provides a greatly improved management experience through the Microsoft Management Console (MMC) and scriptable command-line tools.

Windows Deployment Services uses the Trivial File Transfer Protocol (TFTP) to download network boot programs and images. TFTP uses a configurable windowing mechanism that reduces the number of packets network boot clients send, improving performance. Also, Windows Deployment Services now logs detailed information about clients to the Windows Server 2008 logging feature. You can export and process these logs by using Microsoft Office InfoPath or other data mining tools. The most significant new feature, and possibly the most anticipated, is multicast. Multicast deployment allows you to deploy Windows 7 to many computers simultaneously, conserving network bandwidth.

In Windows 7 and Windows Server 2008 R2, Windows Deployment Services includes the following new features:

- **Multicast Multiple Stream Transfer** Allows you to set performance thresholds on multicast clients. Slower clients can move to slower streams so that they don't slow down faster clients, which was a limitation in the original multicast feature.
- **Dynamic Driver Provisioning** Allows Windows Setup to choose device drivers stored on Windows Deployment Services servers dynamically during deployment. This makes updating Windows images with new device drivers less important because you can just add them to the driver store, reducing image size and maintenance costs. You can also insert device drivers into Windows PE images directly from the driver store.

For more information about Windows Deployment Services, see Chapter 10, "Configuring Windows Deployment Services."

ImageX

ImageX is the Windows 7 tool that you use to work with .wim image files. ImageX is an easy-to-use command-line utility. You use ImageX to create and manage .wim image files. With ImageX, you can capture images and apply them to destination computers' hard drives. You can mount .wim image files as folders and thereby edit images offline. ImageX addresses the challenges that organizations faced when using sector-based imaging formats or the MS-DOS

XCopy command to copy an installation of Windows onto new hardware. For example, sector-based imaging:

- Destroys the existing contents of the destination computer's hard drive, complicating migration scenarios.
- Duplicates the hard drive exactly; therefore, the image can deploy only to partitions that are the same type and at least as large as the source partition on the master computer.
- Does not allow for direct modification of image file contents.

The limitations of sector-based imaging led Microsoft to develop ImageX and the accompanying .wim image file format. You can use ImageX to create an image, modify the image without going through the extraction and re-creation process, and deploy the image to your environment—all using the same tool.

Because ImageX works at the file level, it provides numerous benefits. It provides more flexibility and control over your images. For example, you can mount an image onto a folder and then add files to, copy files from, and delete files from the image using a file-management tool such as Windows Explorer. ImageX allows for quicker deployment of images and more rapid installations. With the file-based image format, you can also deploy images nondestructively so that ImageX does not erase the destination computer's hard drive.

ImageX also supports highly compressed images. First, .wim files support single instancing: File data is stored separately from path information so .wim files can store duplicate files that exist in multiple paths at one time. Second, .wim files support two compression algorithms—fast and maximum—that give you control over the size of your images and the time required to capture and deploy them.

Deployment Scenarios

In general, you will perform automated Windows 7 deployments in four scenarios: Upgrade Computer (in-place upgrade), New Computer (wipe-and-load), Refresh Computer, and Replace Computer. The following sections provide an overview of each scenario.

Upgrade Computer Scenario

You can upgrade from Windows Vista Service Pack 1 (SP1) to Windows 7 in place, which means you can install Windows 7 and retain your applications, files, and settings as they were in your previous version of Windows Vista. If you want to upgrade from Windows XP to Windows 7, however, you will need to use the Refresh Computer scenario, which preserves files and settings but not applications. For more information, see the section titled "Refresh Computer Scenario" later in this chapter.

Although upgrading might be the simplest way to deploy Windows 7, you run the risk of preserving misconfigurations and unauthorized software or settings. In many cases, the existing system configuration is difficult to assess and change-control processes are more difficult to implement. Upgrading from Windows Vista with Service Pack 1 computers in an unknown state to Windows 7 does not change the computer's status—its state is still unknown. A better scenario for managed environments is to use the New Computer scenario with user state migration to preserve settings selectively (that is, the Refresh Computer scenario).

New Computer Scenario

In the New Computer scenario, you install a clean copy of Windows 7 on a clean (freshly partitioned and formatted) hard drive. This scenario has the most consistent results, creating a configuration in a known state. Installing a known configuration on a clean computer is the foundation of good configuration management. You can use established change-control processes to manage any subsequent changes closely.

Refresh Computer Scenario

The Refresh Computer scenario is similar to the New Computer scenario. The differences are that the destination computer contains a Windows operating system, and this scenario preserves users' existing files and settings, as shown in Figure 3-3.

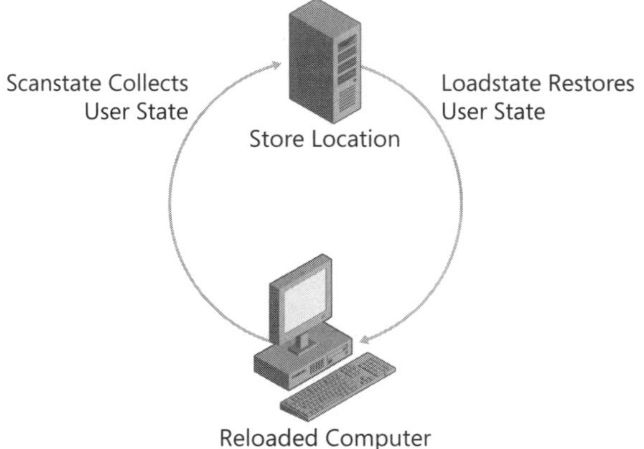

FIGURE 3-3 Preserving user state during migration

You can use migration technologies, such as USMT 4.0, to migrate users' files and settings from the previous version of Windows to Windows 7. This helps ensure that no data is lost while still establishing the best possible system configuration. For more information about using USMT 4.0, see Chapter 7, "Migrating User State Data." You can think of the Refresh Computer scenario as combining the benefits of a new installation that the New Computer scenario provides with the benefits of preserving files and settings.

Replace Computer Scenario

Windows migration technologies such as the Windows Easy Transfer tool and USMT 4.0 allow side-by-side data migration between an old computer running Windows XP or Windows Vista and a new computer running Windows 7. This scenario, which is called Replace Computer, allows you to perform a clean installation on the new computer and simply migrate files and settings from the old one. Figure 3-4 shows an overview of this scenario.

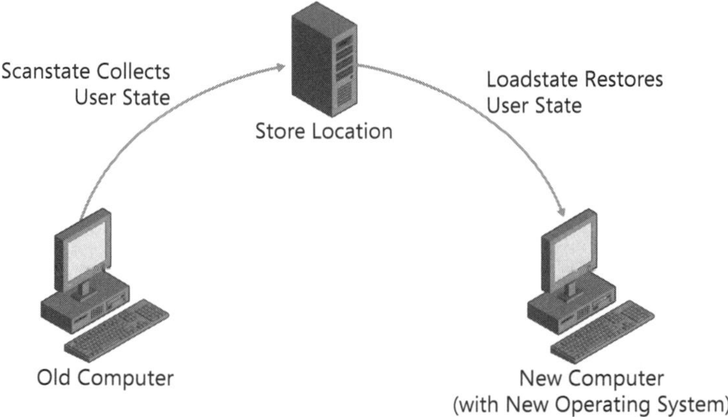

FIGURE 3-4 Side-by-side upgrades begin with a clean, new system.

Understanding Setup

To automate Windows Setup, you must first understand the installation process. Knowing the underlying process will help you understand the decisions you must make when developing Windows 7 for deployment.

The Windows 7 installation process is simple. All editions of Windows 7 use the same installation image (Install.wim in the Sources folder of the installation media), but Microsoft is shipping edition-specific media. As a result, you can install only one edition of Windows 7 through the user interface, but you can use an Unattend.xml file to install a different edition. The installation process is divided into three phases: Windows PE, Online Configuration, and Windows Welcome.

Windows Setup runs in *phases*, which the following sections describe. These phases—Preinstallation Phase, Online Configuration Phase, and Windows Welcome Phase—occur in order and simply designate a point in the installation process. Windows Setup also has configuration *passes*. Each configuration pass performs a specific function and applies related settings from the Unattend.xml answer file.

ON THE COMPANION MEDIA **The *Windows Automated Installation Kit User's Guide* (Waik.chm), which is in the Windows AIK 2.0, fully describes the command-line options for running Windows Setup (Setup.exe).**

You can customize the setup process at many phases through the use of answer files. The following list describes the answer files you use to customize the Windows 7 installation experience:

- **Unattend.xml** The generic name given to an answer file that controls most unattended installation actions and settings for most phases. When named Autounattend.xml and placed in the appropriate folder, such as the root of a UFD, this file can fully automate installations from the original Windows 7 media.
- **Oobe.xml** Oobe.xml is a content file you use to customize the out-of-box experience: Windows Welcome and Welcome Center.

Preinstallation Phase

During the Preinstallation phase, Windows Setup loads and prepares the target system for installation. Figure 3-5 illustrates where this phase fits in the installation process.

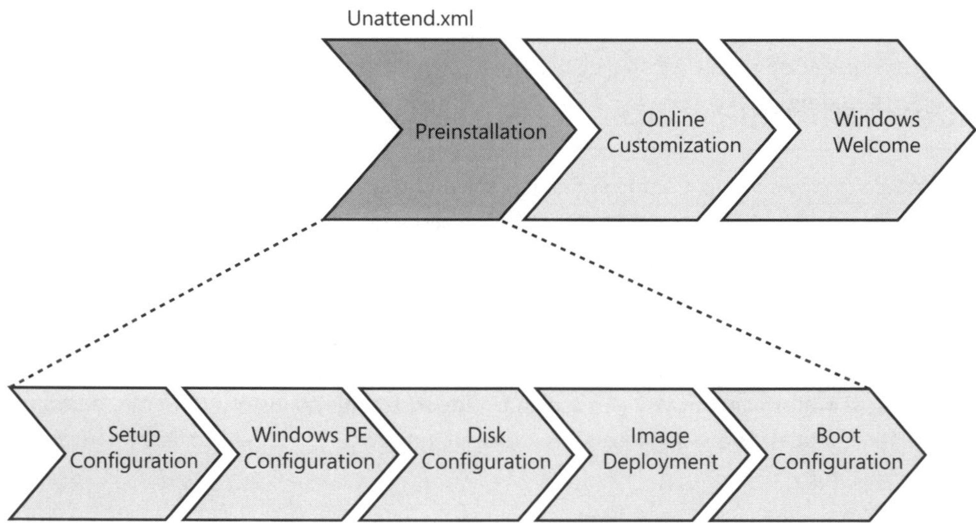

FIGURE 3-5 Preinstallation phase

Tasks performed during the Preinstallation phase include:

- **Windows Setup configuration** Windows Setup is configured by using either the Windows Setup dialog boxes (interactive) or an answer file (unattended). Windows Setup configurations include configuring a disk or language settings.

- **Windows PE configuration** Answer file settings are applied during the Windows PE configuration pass.
- **Disk configuration** The hard disk is prepared for image deployment. This might include partitioning and formatting the disk.
- **Windows image file copy** The Windows 7 image is copied to the disk from the distribution media or a network share. By default, the image is contained in Sources\Install.wim on the product media or distribution share.
- **Prepare boot information** The Windows 7 boot configuration is finalized. This includes configuring single- or multiboot configuration settings.
- **Process answer file settings in the offlineServicing configuration pass** Updates and packages are applied to the Windows 7 image, including software fixes, language packs, and other security updates.

> ***MORE INFO*** **Windows Setup produces numerous log files that are useful for troubleshooting installation. For more information about these log files, see "Windows Setup Log File Locations," at *http://support.microsoft.com/default.aspx/kb/927521*.**

Online Configuration Phase

During the Online Configuration phase, Windows 7 performs customization tasks related to the computer's identity. Figure 3-6 shows where this phase fits into the overall process.

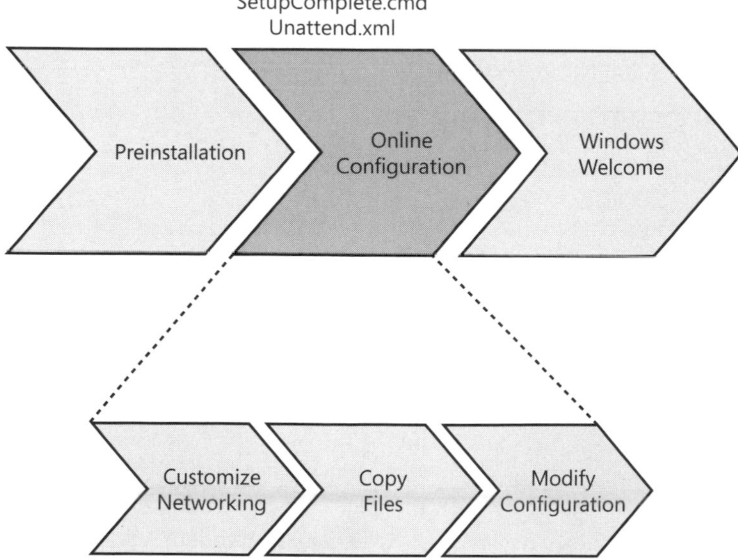

FIGURE 3-6 Online Configuration phase

The Specialize pass, which runs during this phase, creates and applies computer-specific information. For example, you can use an unattended setup answer file (Unattend.xml) to configure network settings, international settings, and domain information, as well as run installation programs.

During the Online Configuration phase, you can use scripts to configure the destination computer. However, a task sequencer, which enables you to filter tasks based on conditions, such as whether a particular device is installed, is better suited to this purpose. A task sequencer also provides advanced features such as the ability to wait until a certain condition arises before continuing, and grouping tasks into folders and then filtering the entire group.

ON THE COMPANION MEDIA **The companion media includes a script-based task sequencer, Taskseq.wsf, that provides all of these advanced features, among others. It reads tasks sequences from .xml files and then executes them. The file Sample_Task_Sequences.zip includes sample task sequences that demonstrate how to build .xml files for Taskseq.wsf. Do not run these sample task sequences on production computers. Read the documentation included in the source code for more information about using Taskseq.wsf.**

Windows Welcome Phase

In the Windows Welcome phase, shown in Figure 3-7, the installation is finalized, and any first-use customizations you want to apply are presented. Additionally, Windows 7 prompts for the product key during this phase. You can customize the Windows Welcome screens and messages and store these customizations in an Oobe.xml file.

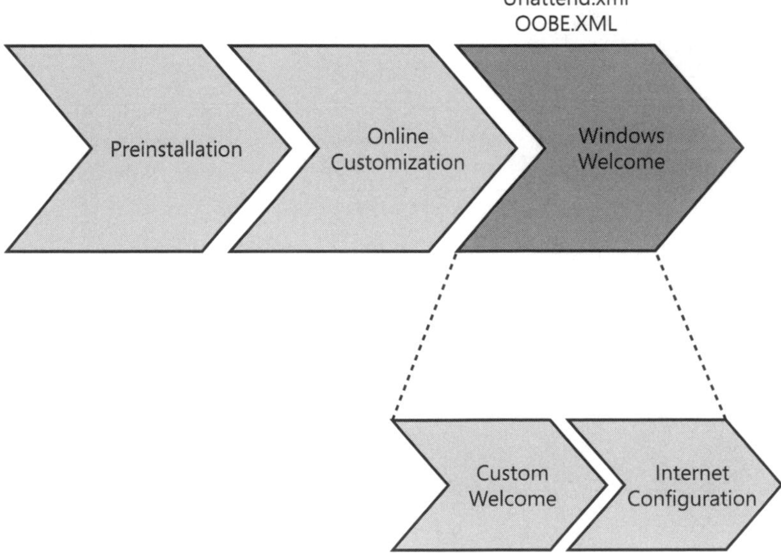

FIGURE 3-7 Windows Welcome phase

DIRECT FROM THE SOURCE

Text-Mode Setup Is Gone

Michael Niehaus, Systems Design Engineer
Microsoft Deployment Toolkit

The basic process used to install Windows XP has been unchanged since the earliest days of Microsoft Windows NT. This time-consuming procedure involved an initial text-mode installation step in which every operating system file was decompressed and installed, all registry entries were created, and all security was applied. Beginning with Windows Vista, this text-mode installation phase is completely gone. Instead, a new setup program performs the installation, applying a Windows image to a computer.

After this image is applied, it needs to be customized for the computer. This customization takes the place of what was called mini-setup in Windows XP and Microsoft Windows 2000. The purpose is the same: the operating system picks the necessary settings and configuration for the specific computer to which it was deployed.

The image preparation process has also changed. With Windows XP, you would Sysprep a computer to prepare the reference operating system for deployment. Beginning with Windows Vista, you'll still run Sysprep.exe, but it's installed by default in C:\Windows\System32\Sysprep.

Beginning with Windows Vista, the Windows operating system is provided on the DVD as an already-installed, generalized (Sysprepped) image, ready to deploy to any computer. Some customers may choose to deploy this image as is (possibly injecting fixes or drivers using the servicing capabilities provided by the deployment tools).

Basic Deployment Process

Figure 3-8 illustrates the basic deployment process using only the Windows 7 deployment tools to build images for high-volume deployments. Although this is useful background information, direct use of these tools isn't recommended. Using a framework like MDT 2010 is the best way to deploy Windows 7.

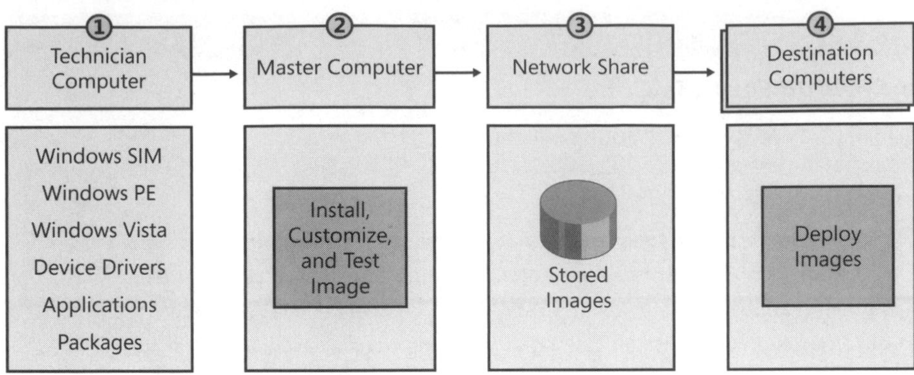

FIGURE 3-8 Basic deployment process

The following list describes the steps in Figure 3-8:

- **Technician Computer** You build a distribution share on a technician computer. The distribution share includes the Windows 7 source files, applications, device drivers, and packages. You use Windows SIM to configure the distribution share by adding source files to it. You also use Windows SIM to create and customize the Windows 7 answer file to use for installation.
- **Master Computer** On a master computer, you create a master installation by running Windows Setup from the distribution share, using an answer file you created with Windows SIM. The installation should be automated fully to ensure a consistent, repeatable process from one build to the next. After creating the master installation, run Sysprep to prepare it for duplication. In low-volume deployments, you can skip this step and deploy to desktop computers directly from the volume license or retail Windows 7 media that Microsoft provides and then customize the installation during deployment.
- **Network Share** You use ImageX to capture an image of the master installation from the master computer. Then you store the image on a network share accessible to the destination computers to which you're deploying the image. Alternatives to deploying from a network share include deploying the image from a DVD, a UFD, or Windows Deployment Services.
- **Destination Computers** On the destination computers, run Windows Setup to install Windows 7. Windows Setup accepts the image file and answer file to use as command-line options. Using Windows Setup to apply an image to destination computers is preferable to using ImageX to apply the image. Windows Setup includes logic that ImageX does not include, such as properly preparing the BCD.

HOW IT WORKS

Configuration Passes

Windows Setup uses configuration passes to configure systems. The following list describes each configuration pass that Windows Setup runs:

- **windowsPE** Configures Windows PE options as well as basic Windows Setup options. These options can include configuring a disk or language settings.
- **offlineServicing** Applies updates to a Windows 7 image. Also applies packages, including software fixes, language packs, and other security updates.
- **generalize** The generalize pass runs only if you run sysprep /generalize. In this pass, you can minimally configure Windows 7 as well as configure other settings that must persist on your master image. The sysprep /generalize command removes system-specific information. For example, the unique SID and other hardware-specific settings are removed from the image.
- **specialize** Creates and applies system-specific information. For example, you can configure network settings, international settings, and domain information.
- **auditSystem** Processes unattended Setup settings while Windows 7 is running in system context, before a user logs on to the computer in audit mode. The auditSystem pass runs only if you boot in audit mode.
- **auditUser** Processes unattended Setup settings after a user logs on to the computer in audit mode. The auditUser pass runs only if you boot in audit mode.
- **oobeSystem** Applies settings to Windows 7 before Windows Welcome starts.

Microsoft Deployment Toolkit Process

Microsoft Deployment Toolkit 2010 (MDT 2010) is a holistic approach to desktop deployment, bringing together the people, processes, and technology required to perform highly successful, repeatable, and consistent deployment projects. Because of its strong focus on methodology and best practices, MDT 2010 is much more valuable than the sum of its parts. Not only does it have the benefit of decreasing the time required to develop a desktop-deployment project, but it also reduces errors and helps you create a higher-quality desktop-deployment project.

Microsoft recommends that you use MDT 2010 to deploy Windows 7 instead of using the basic deployment tools directly. All the deployment tools in Windows 7 and the Windows AIK 2.0 are huge improvements over the deployment tools for earlier versions of Windows. However, they are simply tools without a framework, without any business logic. They have no "glue" to bind them into an end-to-end process. MDT 2010 provides this glue in the form of a complete technology framework. Internally, MDT 2010 is an extremely complex solution. It provides solutions for the problems facing most customers during deployment, including preinstallation phases (disk partitioning, formatting, and so on), installation (disk imaging), and postinstallation phases (user state migration, application installation, customization, and so on). Even though MDT 2010 is complex internally, the solution makes building, customizing, and deploying Windows 7 images easier by masking the details.

DIRECT FROM THE SOURCE

Microsoft Deployment Toolkit

Manu Namboodiri
Windows Product Management

Microsoft has invested a lot to provide innovative technologies that help customers deploy desktops effectively, especially the new capabilities around file-based imaging, feature-based architectures, hardware independence, and so on. These have significant benefits in reducing image count, costs, and complexity.

However, where we have heard a lot of feedback from our customers and partners is regarding the best practices and methodology to use these tools most effectively. We also hear from industry analysts that most of the migration challenges that customers face center around building teams, schedules, project plans, business cases, and the right set of images as well as process and methodology. Technology, in itself, plays a smaller role than we would think in successful deployments.

The challenges our customers face are the following:

- No standard set of deployment guidelines, which results in widely varying results and costs for desktop deployments
- More focus on technology and less on methodology, which has caused varying types of solutions and, therefore, varying results
- Customer perception of cost/complexity because of the lack of repeatable and consistent processes around the technology
- Unclear guidance about which of our many new tools to use and when

Discovering these concerns has made us extremely focused on enhancing our guidance around deployments. The result is the significantly improved MDT methodology for desktop deployment. We are working with industry experts, system integrators, and deployment/management software providers to enhance this guidance so that it captures best practices from throughout the industry.

Figure 3-9 describes the typical process for using MDT 2010 to deploy Windows 7. The process is the same whether you're capturing an image in the lab or deploying images in a production environment. Additionally, MDT 2010 provides a user interface to configure all of its processes. Behind the scenes, thousands of lines of code work to implement your choices during deployment.

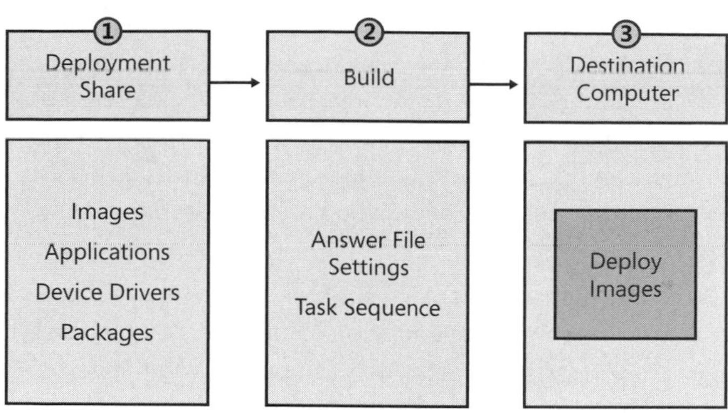

FIGURE 3-9 Microsoft Deployment Toolkit process

The following list describes each part of the MDT 2010 process. (See Chapter 6 and Chapter 12, "Deploying with Microsoft Deployment Toolkit," for more information.)

- **Deployment share** After installing MDT 2010 on a build server in a lab environment, you use the Deployment Workbench to stock the deployment share with source files. Source files include Windows 7 images, applications, device drivers, and packages. The Deployment Workbench provides a user interface for adding all source files to the deployment share. The user interface also provides intelligence, such as error checking and building a device driver database for device driver injection during deployment.

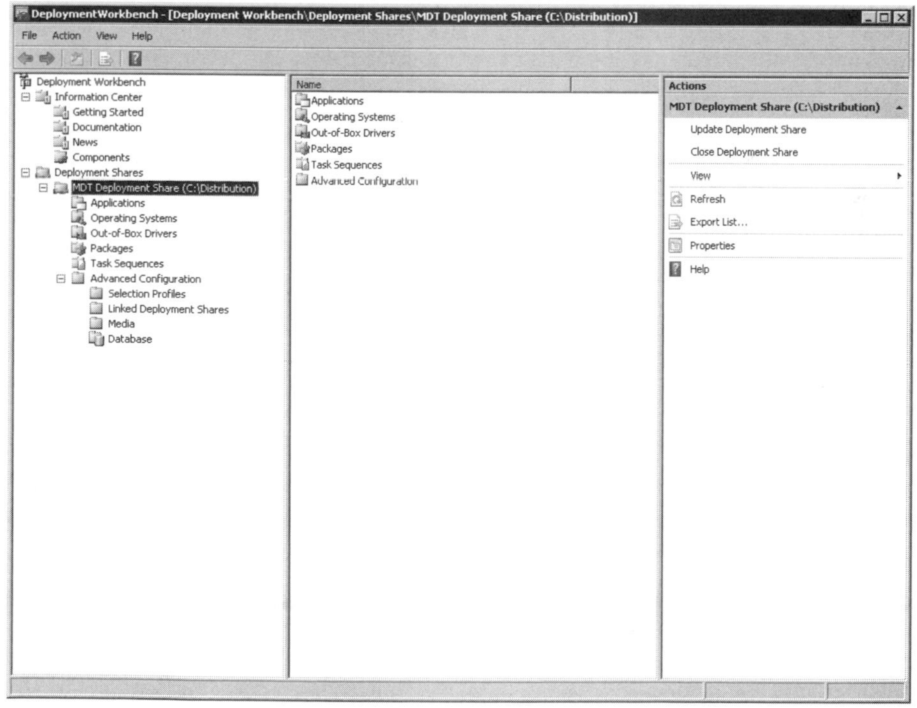

- **Task sequence** After the deployment share is fully stocked, you use the Deployment Workbench to create a task sequence. A task sequence associates source files from the deployment share with a list of steps to take during installation. The task sequence specifies when to take each step and when to skip it (filtering). The task sequence supports reboots during installation, and data collected during the task sequence persists between reboots. The task sequence represents one of the primary customization points for MDT 2010.
- **Destination computer** With a fully stocked deployment share and a task sequence, you can use MDT 2010 to deploy Windows 7 to destination computers. You can use LTI to deploy Windows 7. To use LTI, you start the destination computer using the deployment share's Windows PE boot image. You can put the boot image on removable media (DVD, UFD, and so on) or add it to a Windows Deployment Services server. Either way, you start the destination computer using the Windows PE boot image provided by the deployment share to begin the Windows Deployment Wizard. The wizard displays several pages to collect data from you (computer name, domain membership, applications to install, and so on), and then installs the operating system without any further interaction.

You can also use ZTI to deploy Windows 7. MDT 2010 integrates directly in System Center Configuration Manager 2007. For more information about using ZTI, see the MDT 2010 documentation.

Note that Figure 3-9 makes no reference to creating a master installation and capturing an image. In MDT 2010, creating and capturing an image is an LTI process. You can configure any deployment share to capture an image of an installation and store the image in the deployment share automatically. After you make this choice, the imaging process is fully automated. You don't have to run Sysprep or ImageX—the Windows Deployment Wizard automatically runs Sysprep and then runs ImageX to capture the image and store it in the deployment share. Then you can simply add the image to the deployment share using Deployment Workbench.

NOTE You can download MDT 2010 from *http://technet.microsoft.com/en-us/desktopdeployment/default.aspx.*

Summary

The Windows 7 deployment platform and tools will make deploying the operating system in your organization easier than deploying earlier versions of Windows. The .wim file format makes it possible to deploy highly compressed image files. Windows 7 helps reduce image count by removing hardware dependencies from the image. Modularization in Windows 7 makes servicing images easier than legacy methods so that you no longer have to apply, customize, and recapture an image to update it. The answer file format, Unattend.xml, provides a more flexible and consistent configuration. Finally, the deployment tools, DISM, ImageX, and Windows SIM, provide a robust way to create, customize, and manage Windows 7 images.

Although the Windows AIK 2.0 provides the basic tools for customizing and deploying Windows 7, MDT 2010 provides a more flexible framework for deploying Windows 7 in organizations. With MDT 2010, you can create and customize multiple image builds. The framework includes automation common to most organizations and is highly extensible to suit any requirements.

Additional Resources

These resources contain additional information and tools related to this chapter.

Related Information

- *Windows Automated Installation Kit User's Guide* in the Windows AIK 2.0 includes detailed information about each of the tools described in this chapter.
- Chapter 6, "Developing Disk Images," includes more information about using MDT 2010 to create deployment shares, create builds, and capture images.
- Chapter 9, "Preparing Windows PE," includes more information about customizing Windows PE for Windows 7 deployment.
- Chapter 10, "Configuring Windows Deployment Services," includes more information about installing, configuring, and using Windows Deployment Services to deploy Windows 7.
- Chapter 12, "Deploying with Microsoft Deployment Toolkit," includes more information about using the Microsoft Deployment Toolkit to deploy Windows 7 images.
- *http://technet.microsoft.com/en-us/desktopdeployment/default.aspx* contains the latest information about using the Microsoft Deployment Toolkit to deploy Windows 7.
- Deployment Forum at *http://www.deploymentforum.com/* is a member-driven community for IT professionals deploying Windows 7.
- Download the Windows Automated Installation Kit 2.0 (Windows AIK 2.0) and the Microsoft Deployment Toolkit 2010 (MDT 2010) from the Microsoft Download Center at *http://www.microsoft.com/downloads*.

On the Companion Media

- Taskseq.wsf
- Sample_Task_Sequences.zip

CHAPTER 4

Planning Deployment

This chapter helps you plan the deployment of the Windows 7 operating system in your organization. Deploying an operating system requires careful planning. Application compatibility, user state migration, automation, and other issues complicate the process—making deployment more than just installing a new operating system on a handful of desktop computers. This chapter helps you use the best planning tools available and discover issues that require planning so that you can make informed decisions early in the process.

Using the Microsoft Deployment Toolkit

Microsoft Development Toolkit 2010 (MDT 2010) is Microsoft's best solution for high-volume Windows 7 deployment projects. It reduces complexity and increases standardization by allowing you to deploy a hardware and software baseline to all users and computers. With standard baselines, you can manage the computing environment more easily, spend less time managing and deploying computers, and spend more time on mission-critical tasks.

MDT 2010 provides automation tools and guidance that help reduce labor and increase reliability by producing standardized configurations. It provides fully developed processes for you to do the following:

- Determine which applications can be redeployed on new systems and start a process for packaging or scripting those applications so that you can reinstall them quickly and consistently without user intervention.
- Create an imaging process to produce a standard enterprise image of Windows 7 to aid in configuration management and to speed deployments.
- Establish a process for capturing user state from existing computers and for restoring user state on the newly deployed computers.
- Provide a method for backing up the current computer before deploying Windows 7.
- Provide an end-to-end process for the actual deployment of the new computers. The guidance includes Lite Touch and Zero Touch Installations.

Although you can certainly undertake a high-volume deployment project without MDT 2010, that approach is discouraged. This is because without MDT 2010, you must develop your own development and deployment processes. You also must define your own best practices and develop your own automation. By using MDT 2010 as your deployment framework, you save potentially hundreds of hours that you would otherwise spend writing scripts, writing answer files, developing images, and so on. MDT 2010 handles most scenarios intrinsically, and you can easily extend MDT 2010 for additional scenarios. You can even use MDT 2010 with most third-party deployment technologies. This chapter assumes you'll be using MDT 2010.

MDT 2010 has two major components: the documentation and the solution framework. The following sections describe these components in more detail. Earlier versions of MDT provided detailed planning guidance and job aids. However, due to the overwhelming size of the documentation in MDT, Microsoft has reduced the documentation in MDT to essential technical guidance only. Additionally, MDT now includes quick-start guides that provide end-to-end instructions for Lite Touch Installation (LTI) and Zero Touch Installation (ZTI) deployment. The section titled "Planning High-Volume Deployment" later in this chapter describes how to plan high-volume deployment projects in lieu of the MDT planning documentation.

> ***NOTE*** **Install MDT 2010 to view its documentation as compiled help (.chm) files. After installing MDT 2010, click Start, point to All Programs, select Microsoft Deployment Toolkit, and then click Microsoft Deployment Help. To learn how to install MDT 2010, see the section titled "Installing the Microsoft Deployment Toolkit," later in this chapter. You can download printer-ready documentation from the Microsoft Download Center at *http://www.microsoft.com/downloads*.**

Documentation

MDT 2010 includes three types of documentation. The technical guides provide detailed information about specific technical areas, such as application packaging or image engineering. The reference guides contain content formatted as lists and tables so readers can find information quickly and easily. For example, MDT 2010 provides a reference for the properties that it supports. Finally, the quick-start guides provide end-to-end instructions for scenarios such as LTI and ZTI deployment. The following sections describe these guides.

Technical Guides

The following list describes the technical guides in MDT 2010:

- **Application Packaging Guide** Provides guidance for repackaging applications.
- **Deployment Customization Guide** Describes how to customize LTI and ZTI deployments.
- **Microsoft Deployment Toolkit 2010 Samples Guide** Identifies deployment scenarios and corresponding configuration settings when deploying target computers using LTI and ZTI deployment. You can use the sample configuration files in this guide as a starting point for your own project.
- **Microsoft Deployment Toolkit 2010 Management Pack** Describes the installation and configuration of the management pack. The MDT 2010 Management Pack can provide detailed information about the MDT 2010 deployment process to IT professionals involved in the deployment and operations processes.
- **Image Customization Guide** Describes how to customize reference images by setting the task sequence, developing custom scripts, revising existing MDT 2010 scripts, and so on. It includes information about customizing actions, such as disk, network, and role configuration.
- **Preparing for LTI Tools** Describes how to create a default installation of MDT 2010 for LTI deployment.
- **Preparing for Microsoft Systems Center Configuration Manager 2007** Describes how to create a default installation of MDT 2010 for ZTI deployment by using Microsoft Systems Center Configuration Manager.
- **Microsoft System Center Configuration Manager 2007 Imaging Guide** Describes how to use the Configuration Manager to prepare for image creation and deployment.
- **User State Migration Guide** Describes key concepts and decisions regarding the use of the User State Migration Tool (USMT) to migrate user state data from the previous configuration to the new configuration.
- **Workbench Imaging Guide** Describes how to use Deployment Workbench to prepare for image creation and deployment.

Reference Guides

The following list describes the reference guides in MDT 2010:

- **Toolkit Reference** Describes all customizable task sequence steps; properties that you can configure, use in scripts, or use in the Task Sequencer; each script contained in the task sequence; and customization points.
- **Troubleshooting Reference** Describes common error codes and failures. Where available, it provides resolutions for certain issues.

Quick Start Guides

The following list describes the quick-start guides in MDT 2010:

- **Quick-Start Guide for Lite Touch Installation** Helps you evaluate MDT 2010 quickly by providing condensed, step-by-step instructions for using MDT 2010 to install Windows operating systems by using LTI
- **Quick-Start Guide for Microsoft Systems Center Configuration Manager 2007** Helps you evaluate MDT 2010 quickly by providing condensed, step-by-step instructions for using MDT 2010 to install Windows operating systems by using Configuration Manager

Solution Framework

You use the solution framework (technology files) to set up the imaging and deployment servers. This framework helps you create standard desktop configurations. It includes tools to build and deploy custom Windows 7 images with a variety of special needs, such as backing up the destination computer prior to deployment, capturing and restoring user state, enabling Windows BitLocker Drive Encryption, and so on. By using the solution framework as your starting point, you can take advantage of the deployment best practices that Microsoft and its customers have developed over several years, most of which are manifested in the framework's script code.

> ***NOTE*** The solution framework does not contain copies of Windows 7 or the 2007 Microsoft Office system. To use MDT 2010, you must acquire licensed copies of this software and other hardware-specific software such as DVD-player software and CD-creation software. Each technical guide in MDT 2010 describes requirements for using the guidance as well as the tools.

Planning High-Volume Deployment

MDT 2008 and earlier versions included detailed planning guidance and job aids that helped you set up project teams, synchronize their work, and manage milestones. However, Microsoft condensed the documentation in MDT 2008 Update 1 and MDT 2010 to eliminate much of the planning guidance. This move helped reduce an overwhelming amount of documentation, making it easier for people who just want technical guidance to use it.

Microsoft still provides excellent planning and management guidance for high-volume deployment projects, however. In fact, it's better: The Microsoft Operations Framework (MOF) 4.0, available at *http://technet.microsoft.com/en-us/library/cc506049.aspx*, provides project management guidance and job aids based on the original *Planning Guide* in MDT 2008. In MOF 4.0, the Deliver phase uses familiar terminology, such as *envisioning, planning, building, stabilizing,* and *deploying*. [These were phases in previous MDT documentation but are Service Management Functions (SMFs) in MOF 4.0 guidance.] This guidance maps out a workflow, including inputs, responsibilities, activities, deliverables, and reviews for each step. Figure 4-1 is an example of the types of workflow that MOF 4.0 provides for high-volume deployment.

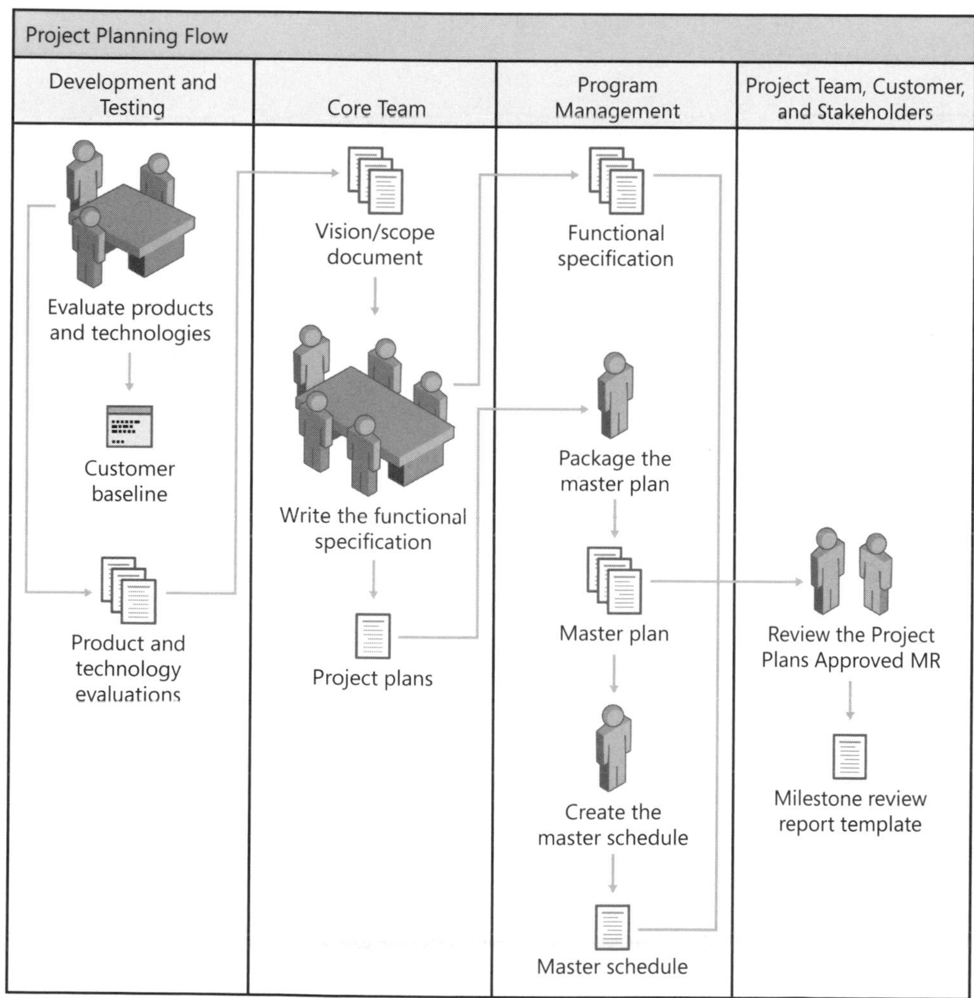

FIGURE 4-1 MOF 4.0 Project Planning SMF

This guidance helps you to do the following:

- Capture the business needs and requirements prior to planning a solution
- Prepare a functional specification and solution design
- Develop work plans, cost estimates, and schedules for the deliverables
- Build the solution to the customer's specification so that all features are complete and the solution is ready for external testing and stabilization
- Release the highest-quality solution by performing thorough testing and release-candidate piloting
- Deploy a stable solution to the production environment and stabilize the solution in production
- Prepare the operations and support teams to manage and provide customer service for the solution

> ***NOTE*** **MDT 2010 no longer includes job aids for writing vision documents, functional specifications, and so on. MOF 4.0 now includes these job aids. You can download the job aids from the Microsoft Download Center at *http://go.microsoft.com/fwlink/?LinkId=116390*.**

The following sections describe each MOF 4.0 Deliver SMF. Because MOF 4.0 is generic, they relate each SMF specifically to performing a high-volume deployment by using MDT 2010.

Envision

The Envision SMF involves envisioning the deployment project and determining goals and expected outcomes. The Envision SMF is largely a management exercise; you don't assemble full project teams until this phase is complete. The Envision SMF includes the following key steps:

- **Set up core teams** The initial task is to define the teams that will plan, design, and perform the deployment.
- **Perform a current assessment** This step includes identifying existing systems and applications, determining existing operating systems, and identifying deficiencies in the current environment that the Windows 7 deployment will address.
- **Define business goals** Concrete, quantifiable business goals should drive your need for the deployment. Rather than simply planning to deploy the latest technology for technology's sake, identify key deficiencies in the existing system that Windows 7 will address, as well as process and productivity gains that the deployment will make possible.
- **Create a vision statement and define the scope** Create a vision statement that defines how planned technology changes (including the Windows 7 deployment) will meet the defined business goals. The scope determines the extent of the vision that can be accomplished through the deployment of Windows 7.

- **Create user profiles** Develop an accurate and complete picture of users' functions, needs, and wants. Refine these into user profiles that accurately identify the types of users in the organization. Understanding users and what they need is the first step in determining how to structure the deployment to benefit the most users.
- **Develop a solution concept** Create a high-level document to define how the team will meet the requirements of the project.
- **Create risk-assessment documents** In this step, evaluate the overall deployment with the intent to anticipate, address, mitigate, and prevent risks associated with the deployment. Documentation of risk assessment is an ongoing task throughout the project.
- **Write a project structure** This document describes how the team manages and supports the project and describes the administrative structure for the project team. This document should define standards that the team will use, including methods of communication, documentation standards, and change-control standards.
- **Approve milestones** When you complete the initial planning and documentation, identify and schedule key milestones for the deployment.

NOTE **MOF 4.0 provides job aids to help complete many of these envisioning steps.**

Project Planning

The Envision SMF creates the framework for the Windows 7 deployment. The Project Planning SMF serves as a transition between vision and implementation, laying the groundwork for the actual deployment. The Project Planning SMF uses the documents and processes created in the Envision SMF to add structure and content to the deployment plan. Key steps in this phase include the following tasks:

- **Create the development and testing environment** Build a testing lab that adequately embodies the target deployment environment, using virtualization to reduce the cost of creating labs. In addition to resources such as servers and sample target systems used to develop and test the deployment, the labs should also include the resources that the project team will use to prepare and accomplish the final deployment.
- **Develop the solution design** The solution design builds on the solution concept, project structure, and other documents created by the Envision SMF to define the conceptual, logical, and physical solution designs for the planned deployment. This document serves as a road map for the project team to begin building the deployment.
- **Create the functional specification** The functional specification defines the requirements of all stakeholders targeted by the deployment and serves as a contract between the customer and the project team. It should clearly define the goals, scope, and outcomes of the deployment.

- **Develop the project plan** The project plan is actually a collection of plans that address the tasks the project team will perform to carry out the project, as defined by the functional specification. Each plan in this document covers a particular area, such as facilities and hardware, testing, training, and communication.
- **Create the project schedule** The project schedule compiles individual schedules created by team members for the purpose of planning deployment activities.
- **Complete a computer inventory** In the Project Planning SMF, a complete computer inventory must be made to identify existing systems and applications that the deployment will affect. In addition, the server resources to be used for deployment must also be identified and evaluated for suitability.
- **Perform a network analysis** Diagram network topology and identify and inventory network devices.

NOTE MOF 4.0 includes job aids for many of these planning tasks.

Build

The Build SMF is the period during which the team builds and unit-tests the solution. The Build SMF includes six key tasks:

- **Start the development cycle** In this initial step, the team creates a lab server for development work and begins the process of creating images, installation scripts, and application packages. The team should also create an issue-tracking system so that team members can communicate about and coordinate solutions to issues.
- **Prepare the computing environment** In this key task, the teams build a deployment environment with facilities such as servers, networking, system backup, and data repositories (such as Microsoft Visual SourceSafe) with separate workspaces (that is, computers and network shares) for each team role. This environment provides the infrastructure for teams to work both independently and jointly as necessary to complete their development tasks.
- **Develop the solution scripts** In this step, the teams begin the process of packaging applications, creating computer images, and developing remediation steps for application-compatibility issues. The teams also plan how and what user data will be retained and migrated during the deployment and validate that network infrastructure (that is, shares, credentials, and other components) is in place and functioning properly prior to deployment.
- **Develop deployment procedures** Using the documents, processes, and other resources created up to this point, begin creating the documents that the teams will use to accomplish the deployment and post-deployment tasks. These documents include training materials for users, administrators, and others who will maintain systems and applications after deployment; a plan for communicating with users about the upcoming

changes; and site-deployment procedures to simplify and standardize the deployment of solutions across sites.

- **Develop operations procedures** Create a document that describes the operations procedures to support, maintain, and carry out the solution following deployment. Key processes to describe include maintenance, disaster recovery, new-site installation, performance and fault monitoring, and support and troubleshooting.
- **Test the solution** Perform test deployments and remedy any issues that arise using the issue-tracking framework created by the Project Planning SMF to monitor and address these issues.

Stabilize

The Stabilize SMF addresses the testing of a solution that is feature-complete. This phase usually occurs when pilots are conducted, with an emphasis on real-world testing and with the goal of identifying, prioritizing, and fixing bugs. Key tasks in this phase include the following:

- **Conducting the pilot** At this stage, the teams use a small pilot deployment to test the deployment and identify any remaining issues. Procedures, resources, and personnel should be in place to assist in addressing any user issues that arise during the pilot deployment. This key task should also include obtaining user feedback as well as review and remediation of issues identified during the pilot.
- **Operational-readiness review** All teams at this stage perform a complete operational-readiness review to determine that the deployment plan is ready to move forward to full-scale deployment. The solution is frozen at this stage, and any remaining issues are addressed.
- **Final release** This task incorporates all fixes and issue resolutions to create the final release of the solution, which should now be ready for full deployment.

Deploy

In the Deploy SMF, the team implements the solution and ensures that it is stable and usable. The key tasks involved in the Deploy SMF include the following:

- **Deploying core technology** Based on the plans and procedures developed in the Project Planning SMF, install, configure, and test deployment servers at each site. Also train administration staff in preparation for deployment.
- **Deploying sites** Teams perform the deployment of Windows 7 at each site using the procedures and resources developed by the Project Planning and Build SMFs. Team members remain on site to stabilize each site deployment, ensuring that users can move forward with reliable systems and applications and that the goals of the deployment plan for the site have been met.
- **Stabilizing the deployment** In this key step, the project team ensures stabilization across all sites and addresses any remaining deployment issues.

- **Completing the deployment** This step marks the transition from deployment to operations and support. Ongoing operations are transferred from the project team to permanent staff. Reporting systems are activated, and support processes are fully operational.

Planning Low-Volume Deployment

In low-volume deployment projects, such as in a small or medium-sized business, the planning guidance in MOF 4.0 can be overwhelming. Regardless, the MDT 2010 technology framework is well suited to low-volume deployment projects. In fact, a small business can prepare MDT 2010 to deploy Windows 7 in as little as a few hours, and a medium-sized business can accomplish it in a few days. This section describes some of the planning steps you should take in this scaled-down scenario. (Even though you can use the MDT 2010 technology framework without using the planning guidance available in MOF 4.0, you should still put some effort into planning your deployment, along the lines of what is outlined here.)

The first step in the deployment process is to assess your business needs so that you can define the project scope and objectives. Next, decide how best to use Windows 7 to meet those needs. Then assess your current network and desktop configurations, determine whether you need to upgrade your hardware or software, and choose the tools for your deployment. Having made these decisions, you are ready to plan your deployment. An effective plan typically includes the following:

- **A schedule for the deployment** Build a simple schedule by using Microsoft Office Excel 2007, or use a more formal tool like Microsoft Office Project 2007.
- **All the details for customizing Windows 7 to suit your requirements** Document the applications, device drivers, updates, and settings that you want to customize.
- **An assessment of your current configuration, including information about users, organizational structure, network infrastructure, and hardware and software** Create a test environment in which you can deploy Windows 7 by using the features and options in your plan. Have your test environment mirror your production network as closely as possible, including hardware, network architecture, and business applications.
- **Test and pilot plans** When you're satisfied with the results in your test environment, roll out your deployment to a specific group of users to test the results in a controlled production environment. This is your pilot test.
- **A rollout plan** Finally, roll out Windows 7 to your entire organization.

Creating the deployment plan is a cyclical process. As you move through each phase, modify the plan based on your experiences.

NOTE Even if you choose not to use the deployment guidance in MOF 4.0, you can still use the job aids it includes, which provide templates for planning a deployment project more quickly and more thoroughly.

Scope and Objectives

The scope is the baseline for creating a specification for your deployment project. The scope of your deployment project is defined largely by your answers to the following questions:

- What business needs do you want to address with Windows 7?
- What are the long-term goals for the deployment project?
- How will your Windows 7 client computers interact with your IT infrastructure?
- What parts of your IT infrastructure will the project touch, and how will this happen?

The scope is simply a statement of what you are trying to accomplish and how you plan to accomplish it. Your statement of scope need only be a few paragraphs long and should not be longer than a page.

Current Environment

Document your existing computing environment, looking at your organization's structure and how it supports users. Use this assessment to determine your readiness for desktop deployment of Windows 7. The three major areas of your computing environment to assess include your hardware, software, and network.

- **Hardware** Do your desktop and laptop computers meet the minimum hardware requirements for Windows 7? In addition to meeting these requirements, all hardware must be compatible with Windows 7. For more information, see Chapter 1, "Overview of Windows 7 Improvements."
- **Software** Are your applications compatible with Windows 7? Make sure that all of your applications, including line-of-business (LOB) applications, work with computers running Windows 7. For more information about application compatibility, see Chapter 8, "Deploying Applications."
- **Network** Document your network architecture, including topology, size, and traffic patterns. Also, determine which users need access to various applications and data, and describe how they obtain access.

NOTE Where appropriate, create diagrams to include in your project plan. Diagrams convey more information than words alone. A good tool for creating these diagrams is Microsoft Office Visio 2007. See *http://www.microsoft.com/office* for more information.

Configuration Plan

Determine which features to include in your configuration and how to implement these features to simplify the management of users and computers in your organization. An important means of simplification is standardization. Standardizing desktop configurations makes it easier to install, update, manage, support, and replace computers that run Windows 7. Standardizing users' configuration settings, software, hardware, and preferences simplifies deploying operating system and application upgrades, and configuration changes can be guaranteed to work on all computers.

When users install their own operating system upgrades, applications, device drivers, settings, preferences, and hardware devices, a simple problem can become complex. Establishing standards for desktop configurations prevents many problems and makes it easier for you to identify and resolve problems. Having a standard configuration that you can install on any computer minimizes downtime by ensuring that user settings, applications, drivers, and preferences are the same as before the problem occurred. The following list provides an overview of some of the features that you must plan to use:

- **Management** Desktop management features allow you to reduce the total cost of ownership in your organization by making it easier to install, configure, and manage clients. For more information about Windows 7 management features, see Part III of this book, "Desktop Management."
- **Networking** You can configure computers that run Windows 7 to participate in a variety of network environments. For more information about Windows 7 networking features, see Part V of this book, "Networking."
- **Security** Windows 7 includes features to help you secure your network and computers by controlling authentication and access to resources and by encrypting data stored on computers. These features include BitLocker Drive Encryption, Windows Firewall with Advanced Security, and so on. For more information about Windows 7 security features, see Chapter 2, "Security in Windows 7."

Testing and Piloting

Before rolling out your deployment project, you need to test it for functionality in a controlled environment. Before you begin testing your deployment project, create a test plan that describes the tests you will run, who will run each test, a schedule for performing tests, and the expected results. The test plan must specify the criteria and priority for each test. Prioritizing your tests can help you avoid slowing down your deployment because of minor failures that you can easily correct later; it can also help you identify larger problems that might require redesigning your plan.

The testing phase is essential because a single error can be replicated to all computers in your environment if it is not corrected before you deploy the image. Create a test lab that is not connected to your network but that mirrors your organization's network and hardware configurations as closely as possible. Set up your hardware, software, and network services as they are in your production environment. Perform comprehensive testing on each hardware platform, testing both application installation and operation. These steps can greatly increase the confidence of the project teams and the business-decision makers, resulting in a higher-quality deployment.

Microsoft recommends that you pilot the project (that is, roll out the deployment) to a small group of users after you test the project. Piloting the installation allows you to assess the success of the deployment project in a production environment before rolling it out to all users. The primary purpose of pilot projects is not to test Windows 7, but to get user feedback. This feedback will help to determine the features that you must enable or disable in Windows 7. For pilots, you might choose a user population that represents a cross-section of your business in terms of job function and computer proficiency. Install pilot systems by using the same method that you plan to use for the final rollout.

The pilot process provides a small-scale test of the eventual full-scale rollout: You can use the results of the pilot, including any problems encountered, to create your final rollout plan. Compile the pilot results and use the data to estimate upgrade times, the number of concurrent upgrades you can sustain, and peak loads on the user-support functions.

Rolling Out

After you thoroughly test your deployment plan, pilot the deployment to smaller groups of users, and are satisfied with the results, begin rolling out Windows 7 to the rest of your organization. To create your final rollout plan, you need to determine the following:

- The number of computers to include in each phase of the rollout
- The time needed to upgrade or perform a clean installation for each computer that you include
- The personnel and other resources needed to complete the rollout
- The time frame during which you plan to roll out the installations to different groups
- The training needed for users throughout the organization

Throughout the rollout, gather feedback from users and modify the deployment plan as appropriate.

Windows 7 Requirements

To plan deployment, you must understand the deployment requirements for Windows 7. The following sections describe the minimum hardware requirements and the migration paths for Windows 7. For more information about Windows 7 hardware requirements and editions, see Chapter 1.

Hardware Requirements

Table 4-1 describes the minimum hardware requirements for installing Windows 7. Part of the Project Planning SMF is collecting a hardware inventory. Compare the hardware requirements in Table 4-1 to your hardware inventory to identify any computers that require upgrades or replacements.

TABLE 4-1 Minimum Hardware Requirements for Windows 7 Computers

HARDWARE	MINIMUM REQUIREMENT
Processor	1 GHz or faster 32-bit or 64-bit processor
Memory	1 GB for 32-bit computers, or 2 GB for 64-bit computers
Graphics Processor	DirectX 9 graphics processor with Windows Display Driver Model (WDDM) 1.0 or later driver
Free Hard Disk Drive Space	16 GB

NOTE **The minimum requirements for Windows 7 are the same across all editions.**

Upgrade Paths

Table 4-2 describes the Windows 7 upgrade and migration paths. As shown in the table, performing an in-place upgrade from Windows Vista with Service Pack 1 (SP1) or later to Windows 7 is supported. This means you can install Windows 7 on a computer running Windows Vista with SP1 and retain your applications, files, and settings. Using Windows Easy Transfer or the USMT to migrate user states from Windows XP to Windows 7 is also supported.

TABLE 4-2 Windows 7 Migration Paths

FROM	UPGRADE TO WINDOWS 7?	MIGRATE TO WINDOWS 7 USING WINDOWS EASY TRANSFER?	MIGRATE TO WINDOWS 7 USING THE USMT?
Windows XP with SP2 or later	No	Yes	Yes
Windows Vista with SP1 or later	Yes	Yes	Yes
Windows 7	Yes (higher SKU)	Yes	Yes

NOTE To assess the readiness of client computers for Windows 7, you can use the Microsoft Assessment and Planning Solution Accelerator, a centralized and agentless tool that can remotely inventory computers, identify their supported Windows 7 experience, and recommend specific hardware upgrades where appropriate. For more information on this tool, see "Microsoft Assessment and Planning (MAP) Toolkit" found at *http://technet.microsoft.com/en-us/solutionaccelerators/dd537566.aspx*.

Preparing for Development

Whether your organization uses MDT 2010 or not, it will likely require multiple teams to develop high-volume deployment projects. Most teams need a lab environment. Although each team can construct a separate lab, most organizations create a single lab that shares facilities such as servers, networks, system backup, and source control with separate workspaces (computers and network shares) for each team. Within this environment, teams can work separately when necessary and jointly when appropriate. It also helps minimize the number of computers and servers required.

The remaining chapters in Part II of this book, "Deployment," describe specific lab requirements for each team working on a high-volume deployment project. The Project Planning SMF is the best time to begin preparing the development environment, however. The process includes installing MDT 2010, stocking the lab environment with the files necessary to perform each team's job, locating application media, and so on. The following sections describe steps to complete during the Project Planning SMF to expedite the development process.

Application Management

Application management is the process of repackaging applications or automating their installation and configuration. Organizations can have hundreds or thousands of applications. Often, users install each application differently on each computer, leading to inconsistency across computers and resulting in support and management issues.

Repackaging or automating an application's installation has many benefits. Most obviously, it allows applications to install without user intervention, which is especially desirable when deploying applications as part of a disk image or during disk image deployment. In addition, repackaging or automating leads to consistency that lowers deployment and ownership costs by reducing support issues and enhancing management. Chapter 8 describes a process for repackaging and automating application installations.

Before migrating from your current version of Windows to Windows 7, the project team must also test applications to ensure that they are compatible with Windows 7. You might have several thousand applications installed across distributed networks. Compatibility problems with one or many of these applications can disrupt productivity and damage the user experience and satisfaction with the project. Testing applications and solving compatibility problems saves time and money for the organization. It also prevents roadblocks to future deployment projects based on perceived pain.

Although most applications developed for earlier versions of Windows will probably perform well on Windows 7, some applications might behave differently because of new technologies in it. Test the following applications to ensure compatibility:

- Custom tools, such as logon scripts
- Core applications that are part of the standard desktop configurations, such as office productivity suites
- LOB applications, such as Enterprise Resource Planning (ERP) suites
- Administrative tools, such as antivirus, compression, backup, and remote-control applications

Chapter 5, "Testing Application Compatibility," describes how to build an application compatibility test lab and how application compatibility integrates into the overall deployment process. The following list describes steps that you can take in the Project Planning SMF to begin building the lab environment for application packaging and compatibility testing:

- **Installation media** For each application you test, repackage, and automate, you must have a copy of the application's installation media, any configuration documentation, and product keys. If your IT department doesn't have the media or other information, check with the subject matter expert (SME) for each application.
- **Destination computers** Within the lab, the project team requires destination computers that resemble computers found in the production environment. Each destination computer should have Windows 7 installed on it to test applications' compatibility with the operating system and application installation.
- **Application Compatibility Toolkit** For more information on the Application Compatibility Toolkit (ACT), see Chapter 5.
- **SQL Server** Install Microsoft SQL Server in the lab environment. The ACT stores the application inventory using SQL Server, which is available on volume-licensed media.
- **Host computer with network shares** You must have a computer on which to host the application installations. Shares on this computer hold the original installation sources and completed packages. You can install the ACT and SQL Server on the host computer.
- **Application packaging software** The project team needs software with which to repackage applications. Chapter 8 describes this software. The application packaging software will be installed on each team member's development computer.
- **Deployment mechanism** The project team requires a mechanism for deploying ACT and application packages. This can be through logon scripts, a local Web site, or another deployment mechanism.

Image Engineering

You're probably already familiar with disk imaging tools such as Symantec Ghost or ImageX (which was introduced by Windows Vista). Using imaging tools effectively is a significant challenge, however, and this challenge is the reason that Microsoft developed MDT 2010. With MDT 2010, you do not have to engineer the entire imaging process; the framework provides most of the code for you already. All you need to do is customize it to suit your organization's requirements. Using MDT 2010 to build Windows 7 images involves the following steps:

- **Create a build server** The build server is the host for MDT 2010 and its distribution share.
- **Configure a deployment share** The deployment share contains the source files (Windows 7, applications, device drivers, and so on) from which you build operating system images.
- **Create and customize task sequences** After stocking the deployment share, you create task sequences. Task sequences associate source files from the deployment share with the steps necessary to install and configure them. For more information about answer files and task sequences, refer to Chapter 3, "Deployment Platform."
- **Build initial operating system images** With MDT 2010, building a custom Windows 7 image is as simple as installing the operating system from a deployment share by using the Windows Deployment Wizard. This is an LTI Installation process that requires minimal user interaction; it automatically captures a Windows 7 image and stores it back in the deployment share.

Chapter 6, "Developing Disk Images," describes how to use MDT 2010 to build custom Windows 7 images. In preparation for the development process, you can begin building the lab during the Project Planning SMF, using the items in the following list:

- **Windows 7 media** You will need media and volume license keys for Windows 7.
- **Destination computers** You will need computers on which to create, install, and test Windows 7 images.
- **A build computer for MDT 2010** You must have a computer on which to host MDT 2010 and the deployment share. The build computer should have a DVD-RW drive and should be networked with the destination computers. You can install MDT 2010 on a desktop or server computer.
- **Windows Deployment Services** The lab environment should contain a server running Windows Deployment Services. Using Windows Deployment Services to boot destination computers is much faster than burning DVDs and starting computers with them.
- **Additional source files** Early in the Project Planning SMF, the project team can begin assembling the source files required to stock the distribution share. Source files include device drivers and hardware-specific applications for each computer in the production environment. Additionally, the team should begin assembling any security updates and operating system packages that must be added to the distribution share.

NOTE **The Project Planning SMF is the best time to install MDT 2010 in the lab environment and begin familiarizing yourself with it. The section titled "Installing the Microsoft Deployment Toolkit" later in this chapter describes the requirements for installing MDT 2010 and how to install MDT 2010 in the lab environment.**

Deployment

Deployment is an intense, time-consuming process during any high-volume deployment. MDT 2010 provides technical guidance and tools that help streamline the following processes:

- Choosing server placement
- Evaluating server and network capacity
- Installing the distribution shares and tools
- Deploying the client computers

Chapter 12, "Deploying with Microsoft Deployment Toolkit," describes how to use MDT 2010 to deploy Windows 7 using the LTI process. During the Project Planning SMF, the project team should begin preparing the lab environment using the items in the following list:

- **Production replica** The project team needs a replica of the production environment to unit-test the combined efforts of all the other teams. Destination computers should be running the versions of Windows found in the production environment with user data loaded. These computers are used for the unit-test deployment, including user state migration.
- **Network shares on a host computer** Two types of network shares are required: one for the MDT 2010 deployment share and a second for the data server share. These shares could be all on the same physical server or on separate servers. Also, it's useful to store images of the production computers on the host computer to restore them quickly and easily after each test pass.
- **Windows Deployment Services** The lab environment should contain a server running Windows Deployment Services. Using Windows Deployment Services to boot destination computers is much faster than burning DVDs and starting computers with them. Team members can use the same Windows Deployment Services server for image engineering and deployment testing.

Infrastructure Remediation

Understanding the network environment is critical with any project that introduces changes. To plan and prepare to incorporate these changes, first understand the current status of the organization's environment, identify other sources of change that may affect this project, perform a risk-mitigation approach to the changes, and then incorporate the proposed changes. Organizations can solve and possibly avoid most networking problems by creating and maintaining adequate network documentation. Using a networking tool, the team can do the following:

- Gather information necessary to help understand a network as it exists today.
- Plan for growth.
- Diagnose problems when they occur.
- Update the information with network changes.
- Work with the information to manage network assets. (Often, an apparently simple configuration change can result in an unexpected outage.)
- Present information visually so that the network structure appears in as much detail as necessary for each task.

The project team must have access to SQL Server. The team uses SQL Server to create hardware inventory reports against the application compatibility database. This could be the same installation that the team uses for application management. The team must also have access to current network topology diagrams and network device inventory information.

Operations Readiness

The project team is responsible for a smooth and successful handoff of the deployed solution to the operations staff. This aspect of the overall project is important, because the success of the handoff directly reflects the success of the deployment project. To ensure success, the activities of the team must be integrated with the ongoing management and operating functions of the operations staff. The project team can facilitate deployment by completing the following tasks:

- Confirm that the workstation roles identified in the functional specification are valid.
- Analyze and evaluate the management tools currently in use.
- Assess the maturity of the operations environment in key operational areas.
- Establish effective management processes and tools in deficient key areas.
- Develop a training program for operations and support staff.
- Prepare the operations staff for the pilot.

The project team does not initially have any additional lab requirements for operations readiness.

Security

Security is important to the overall success of the deployment project. Security is a primary concern in all organizations, and a goal of the project team is to secure the organization's data. Inadequate security in an organization can result in lost or corrupted data, network downtime, lost productivity, frustrated employees, overworked IT employees, and possibly stolen proprietary information that results in lost revenue. Additionally, many organizations are subject to compliance regulations that carry significant penalties for security breaches, such as exposing customer data. To ensure that adequate security measures are in place, the project team should do the following:

- Analyze and determine the existing security level of the organization.
- Identify vulnerabilities caused by software upgrades and update network security specifications accordingly.
- Ensure that security measures are current.

The project team does not initially have any additional lab requirements for security. For more information about Windows 7 security features, see Chapter 2.

Migration

One of the most tedious and time-consuming tasks during deployment is identifying data files and settings on users' current computers (known as the *user state*), saving them, and then restoring them. Users spend significant time restoring items such as wallpaper, screen savers, and other customizable features. And most users don't remember how to restore these settings. Migrating user state can increase user productivity and satisfaction. The project team can perform the following steps to plan for user state migration:

- Inventory existing production client computer applications.
- Identify applications with data or preference migration requirements.
- Prioritize the application list to be addressed.
- Identify SMEs for each application.
- Identify data file requirements for each application.

The following list describes actions that you can take in the Project Planning SMF to begin building the lab environment for migration. Team members working on migration can share resources with team members working on application management.

- **Installation media** For each application containing settings to migrate, you must have a copy of the application's installation media, any configuration documentation, and product keys. If your IT department doesn't have the media or other information, check with the SME for each application.
- **Destination computers** The project team requires computers in the lab on which to test user state migration solutions. Destination computers should be running the versions of Windows found in the production environment with applications and user data loaded. These computers are used for the unit-test user state migration.
- **Host computer** You must have a computer on which to host application source files and migration solutions. It's useful to store images of the destination computers on the host computer to restore them quickly and easily after each test pass.

- **Data store** The data store is a network share on which you can put user state data during testing. You can create the data store on the host computer, or you can optionally create the data store on each destination computer.
- **USMT** MDT 2010 uses the USMT to migrate the user state. The functionality is already built into the MDT 2010 framework. The team must download and prepare the distribution share with the USMT executables, however. Chapter 7, "Migrating User State Data," describes where to place these files.

Installing the Microsoft Deployment Toolkit

MDT 2010 requires Windows PowerShell 2.0. If you're installing MDT 2010 on Windows Server 2008 or Windows Server 2008 R2, you must also add the Windows PowerShell feature by using the Add Features Wizard.

If you're installing MDT 2010 on Microsoft Windows Server 2003 SP1, you must install additional prerequisite software. Windows Server 2008, Windows Server 2008 R2, and Windows 7 already contain this software. The following list describes software that you must install before installing and using MDT 2010 on Windows Server 2003 SP1 (Windows Server 2003 SP2 requires only Microsoft .NET Framework 2.0):

- **Windows PowerShell** Download Windows PowerShell from the Microsoft Download Center at *http://www.microsoft.com/downloads*.
- **Microsoft .NET Framework 2.0** The Windows AIK distribution media includes the .NET Framework 2.0 installation file. Alternatively, download .NET Framework 2.0 from the following addresses:
  - **x86** *http://www.microsoft.com/downloads/details.aspx?FamilyID=0856eacb-4362-4b0d-8edd-aab15c5e04f5&DisplayLang=en*
  - **x64** *http://www.microsoft.com/downloads/details.aspx?FamilyID=b44a0000-acf8-4fa1-affb-40e78d788b00&DisplayLang=en*
- **Microsoft Management Console (MMC) 3.0** Download MMC 3.0 from the following addresses:
  - **x86** *http://www.microsoft.com/downloads/details.aspx?FamilyID=4c84f80b-908d-4b5d-8aa8-27b962566d9f&DisplayLang=en*
  - **x64** *http://www.microsoft.com/downloads/details.aspx?FamilyID=b65b9b17-5c6d-427c-90aa-7f814e48373b&DisplayLang=en*

> ***NOTE*** **If you choose to install only the MDT 2010 documentation, the only software requirements are .NET Framework 2.0 and MMC 3.0. The remaining software in the previous list is not required to view the documentation.**

To install MDT 2010, perform the following steps:

1. Right-click MicrosoftDeploymentToolkit_*platform*.msi, where *platform* is either x86 or x64, and then click Install.
2. Click Next to skip the Welcome page.
3. On the End-User License Agreement page, review the license agreement, click I Accept The Terms In The License Agreement, and then click Next.
4. On the Custom Setup page, choose the features to install and then click Next. To change a feature's state, click the feature and then choose a state (Will Be Installed On Local Hard Drive and Entire Feature Will Be Unavailable). The following list describes each feature:
   - **Documents** This feature installs the solution's guidance and job aids. By default, this feature is installed in C:\Program Files\Microsoft Deployment Toolkit \Documentation.
   - **Tools and templates** This feature installs the solution's wizards and template deployment files, such as Unattend.xml. By default, this feature is installed in C:\Program Files\Microsoft Deployment Toolkit.
5. Click Install to install the solution.
6. Click Finish to complete the installation and close the installer.

> ***NOTE*** **Versions of MDT earlier than 2008, including Microsoft Solution Accelerator for Business Desktop Deployment 2007, included a feature to create a distribution share. MDT 2010 does not create a distribution share during installation, however. Instead, you create a distribution share or upgrade an existing distribution share by using Deployment Workbench.**

The following list describes the subfolders in the MDT 2010 program folder (C:\Program Files \Microsoft Deployment Toolkit) after installing the solution:

- **Bin** Contains the MMC Deployment Workbench add-in and supporting files
- **Documentation** Contains the MDT 2010 documentation
- **Downloads** Provides storage for components that MDT 2010 downloads
- **ManagementPack** Contains the MDT 2010 management pack files
- **Samples** Contains sample task sequence scripts
- **SCCM** Contains files that support Microsoft System Center Configuration Manager (SCCM) 2007 integration
- **Templates** Contains template files that the Deployment Workbench uses

NOTE The hard drive containing the program folders must have at least 1 gigabyte (GB) of free space available. MDT 2010 downloads components, including the Windows AIK, to the Downloads folder.

Starting Deployment Workbench

Deployment Workbench is the MDT 2010 tool that you use to stock deployment shares, create task sequences, and so on. See Chapter 6 for more information about using Deployment Workbench to stock a distribution share and create custom Windows 7 images. To start Deployment Workbench, click Start, point to All Programs, select Microsoft Deployment Toolkit, and then click Deployment Workbench. The console tree shows the following items:

- **Information Center** This item provides access to the documentation, breaking news about MDT 2010, and the components required for using Deployment Workbench. The Documentation item helps you quickly navigate the solution's guidance. Click a link to open that guide as a compiled help (.chm) file.
- **Deployment Shares** Under Deployment Shares, you see an item for each deployment share that you create. Each deployment share contains applications, operating systems, out-of-box device drivers, packages, and task sequences. Additionally, you can create boot media, link deployment shares, and connect the deployment share to a deployment database.

NOTE For the Deployment Workbench MMC, the default view includes the Action pane. To remove the Action pane, open the management console in author mode. To open the console in author mode, run C:\Program Files\Microsoft Deployment Toolkit\Bin\DeploymentWorkbench.msc /a. Click View, click Customize, clear the Action Pane check box, and then click OK. To save changes, from the File menu, select Save. When prompted to choose whether to display a single window interface, click Yes.

Updating Microsoft Deployment Toolkit Components

After installing MDT 2010 and becoming familiar with Deployment Workbench, download and install the additional components that MDT 2010 requires. The following components are mandatory in MDT 2010:

- **Windows AIK 2.0** You can install Windows AIK 2.0 manually by downloading it from the Microsoft Download Center at *http://www.microsoft.com/downloads* or use Deployment Workbench to download and install it automatically.

- **MSXML Services 6.0** You can preinstall MSXML Services 6.0 or use Deployment Workbench to download and install it. The Windows AIK distribution media includes the MSXML Services 6.0 SP1 installation file. You can also download MSXML Services 6.0 SP1 from *http://www.microsoft.com/downloads/details.aspx?FamilyID=d21c292c-368b-4ce1-9dab-3e9827b70604&displaylang=en*. Download both x86 and x64 versions at this location. Windows Vista with SP1, Windows 7, Windows Server 2008, and Windows Server 2008 R2 already include this feature.

To download components using Deployment Workbench, perform the following steps:

1. In Deployment Workbench, under Information Center, click Components.

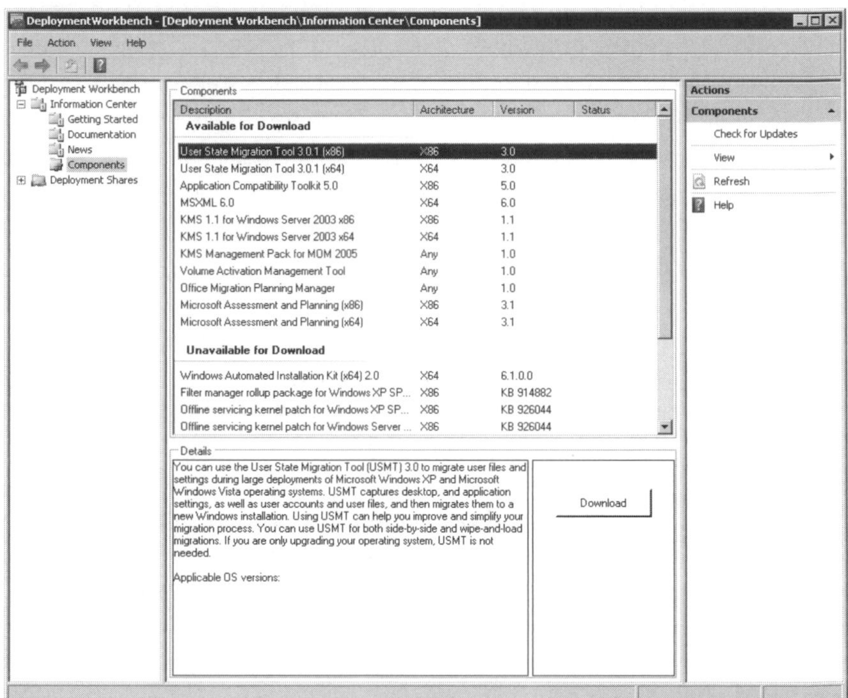

2. In the Available For Download section of the Components list, click a component. In the bottom pane, click Download. Deployment Workbench displays the download status in the Components list. When it finishes downloading the component, it moves the component to the Downloaded section in the right pane.
3. In the Downloaded section of the Components list, click a downloaded component. In the bottom pane, click Install to install the component or Browse to open the folder containing the component in Windows Explorer. MDT 2010 cannot install some components automatically. To install them, click Browse to open the folder containing the component and then manually install the component.

NOTE Check the Internet for updated components frequently. On the Deployment Workbench main menu, from the Action menu, click Check For Updates. On the Check For Updates page of the Check For Updates Wizard, select the Check The Internet check box and then click Check.

Summary

Early planning is important to a successful Windows 7 deployment project. Although MDT 2010 provides the technology framework for deploying Windows 7, MOF 4.0 contains the most comprehensive deployment planning guidance from Microsoft. It includes proven best practices from Microsoft's own experience and that of its partners and its customers.

Planning to deploy Windows 7 is a far larger initiative than just figuring out how to install the operating system. Key planning topics include compatibility testing, application packaging, image engineering, user state migration, security, and deployment. This Resource Kit, MDT 2010, and MOF 4.0 help you plan and develop solutions for each of these topics.

Additional Resources

These resources contain additional information and tools related to this chapter.

- The *Getting Started Guide* in MDT 2010 contains essential information for installing and configuring MDT 2010 as well as preparing your infrastructure for using it.
- Chapter 6, "Developing Disk Images," explains how to plan and engineer Windows 7 disk images by using MDT 2010.
- Chapter 7, "Migrating User State Data," explains how to plan and design a user state migration solution by using USMT.
- Chapter 8, "Deploying Applications," includes more information about packaging and automating application installations. This chapter also discusses application-compatibility remediation.
- Chapter 11, "Using Volume Activation," explains how to account for Windows 7 volume activation in large-scale deployment projects.
- Chapter 12, "Deploying with Microsoft Deployment Toolkit," explains how to use MDT 2010 to deploy Windows 7 by using the LTI process.
- MOF 4.0, at *http://technet.microsoft.com/en-us/library/cc506049.aspx,* provides project management guidance and job aids.

CHAPTER 5

Testing Application Compatibility

Application compatibility is often a deployment-blocking issue. It's also the issue that most deployment projects focus on the least—until things begin to fall apart. By focusing on application compatibility early, you can better ensure a successful deployment project.

Three common reasons that application compatibility blocks operating-system deployment are fear, uncertainty, and doubt. Companies simply don't know what applications are in their environments, whether the applications are compatible with the Windows 7 operating system, and what risks each application poses if it fails after deployment.

To help overcome these issues, this chapter describes the Microsoft tools that are available for discovering the applications in your environment, evaluating their compatibility with Windows 7, and then developing fixes for any issues. The primary tool in Windows 7 is the Microsoft Application Compatibility Toolkit (ACT) 5.5.

Understanding Compatibility

Since the arrival of Microsoft Windows as a ubiquitous application platform, Independent Software Vendors (ISVs) and internal developers have created thousands of applications for it. Many are mission-critical applications—some of which aren't compatible with the latest version of Windows. Types of applications that might not be compatible include the following:

- Line-of-business (LOB) applications, such as enterprise resource-planning suites
- Core applications that are part of standard desktop configurations
- Administrative tools, such as antivirus, compression, and remote-control applications
- Custom tools, such as logon scripts

What Compatibility Means

Applications designed for earlier versions of Windows have been carried forward for a number of reasons. Maybe the application is a necessary tool that is used daily to accomplish some otherwise tedious task. Maybe users have learned the application and are reticent to move to another, similar application. Maybe the application has no replacement because the original creator either is no longer in business or has left the company. All these issues make application compatibility a critical issue that you must consider when deploying a new operating system such as Windows 7. In this chapter, you learn the many issues that affect application compatibility, how to discover the applications on which the organization depends, and what you can do to ensure that mission-critical applications work with Windows 7.

An application is compatible with Windows 7 if it runs as designed in Windows 7—that is, the application should install and uninstall correctly. Users should be able to create, delete, open, and save any data files that are native to the application. Common operations such as printing should work as expected. A compatible application runs on Windows 7 out of the box, without any special assistance. If an application is not compatible, you might find that a newer, compatible version of the application is available or that using one of the tools that Microsoft provides to remediate the compatibility problem is all you need. You might also find that an application will require a combination of fixes to run properly. This chapter discusses all these scenarios.

Why Applications Fail

The following list describes common compatibility issues for Windows 7, particularly when using an application originally designed for Windows XP:

- **User Account Control** In Windows 7, by default, all interactive users, including members of the Administrators group, run as standard users. User Account Control (UAC) is the mechanism through which users can elevate applications to full administrator privileges. Because of UAC, applications that require administrator rights or check for administrator privileges behave differently in Windows 7, even when run by a user as administrator.

- **Windows Resource Protection** Windows Resource Protection (WRP) is designed to protect the system in a read-only state to increase system stability, predictability, and reliability. This will affect specific files, folders, and registry keys. Updates to protected resources are restricted to the operating-system trusted installers (TrustedInstaller group), such as Windows Servicing. This helps to protect features and applications that ship with the operating system from any impact of other applications and administrators. This impact can be an issue for custom installations not detected as set up by Windows 7 when applications try to replace WRP files and registry settings and check for specific versions and values.
- **Internet Explorer Protected Mode** In Windows 7, Windows Internet Explorer 8 processes run in IEPM with greatly restricted privileges to help protect users from attack. Internet Explorer Protected Mode (IEPM) significantly reduces the ability of an attack to write, alter, or destroy data on the user's computer, or to install malicious code. This could affect ActiveX controls and other script code that try to modify higher-integrity-level objects.
- **Operating system and Internet Explorer versioning** Many applications check the version of the operating system and behave differently or fail to run when an unexpected version number is detected. You can resolve this issue by setting appropriate compatibility modes or applying versioning shims (application-compatibility fixes).
- **New folder locations** User folders, My Documents folders, and folders with localization have changed since Windows XP. Applications with hard-coded paths may fail. You can mitigate this by using directory junctions or by replacing hard-coded paths with appropriate API calls to get folder locations.
- **Session 0 isolation** Running services and user applications together in Session 0 poses a security risk because these services run at an elevated privilege level and therefore are targets for malicious agents looking for a means to elevate their own privilege level. In earlier versions of the Windows operating system, services and applications run in the same session as the first user who logs on to the console (Session 0). To help protect against malicious agents in Windows 7, Session 0 has been isolated from other sessions. This could impact services that communicate with applications using window messages.

Choosing the Best Tool

You can use five primary tools to mitigate application-compatibility issues: Program Compatibility Assistant, Program Compatibility Wizard, ACT, Windows XP Mode, and application virtualization. The following sections describe each tool and when it is appropriate to use each tool versus using other tools or technologies.

The first two tools provide approaches for users and one-off support issues but are not for use in a large-scale deployment. The remainder of this chapter focuses on using the ACT to inventory, analyze, and mitigate compatibility issues, because this is the tool that organizations primarily use in large-scale deployment.

> **NOTE** The Microsoft Assessment and Planning (MAP) Toolkit 4.0 is a free tool from Microsoft that you can use to plan your Windows 7 migration project. It can help you assess your environment's readiness for Windows 7. For more information about MAP, see *http://technet.microsoft.com/en-us/solutionaccelerators/dd537566.aspx*.

Program Compatibility Assistant

If you have an individual application that needs Windows 7 compatibility remediation, one mitigation tool that might be effective is the built-in Program Compatibility Assistant. To run the Program Compatibility Assistant, right-click the application's .exe file, click Properties, and then click the Compatibility tab to view the application's compatibility settings, as shown in Figure 5-1. If the program is used by multiple users on the same computer, click Change Settings For All Users to change the settings selected here to affect all users.

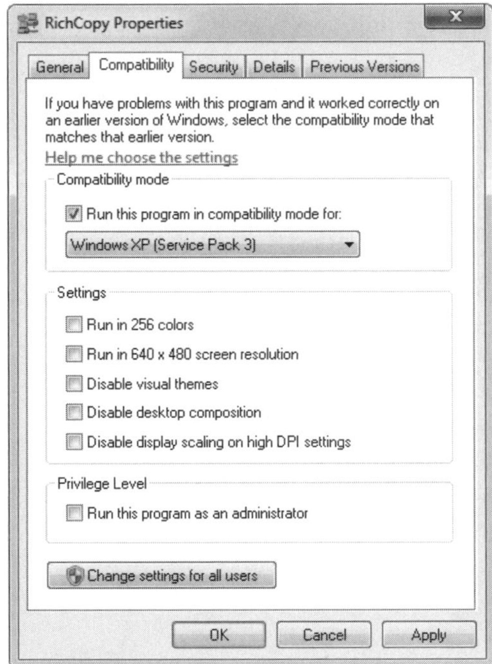

FIGURE 5-1 Compatibility settings

Program Compatibility Troubleshooter

The Program Compatibility troubleshooter can help resolve many application issues. Using the troubleshooter, you can test various compatibility options on various programs to find the setting that allows the programs to run under Windows 7. To start the Program Compatibility troubleshooter, click Start, Control Panel, Programs, and then Run Programs Made For Previous Versions Of Windows. The Program Compatibility troubleshooter starts as shown in Figure 5-2. To begin the application compatibility diagnostic process, click Next.

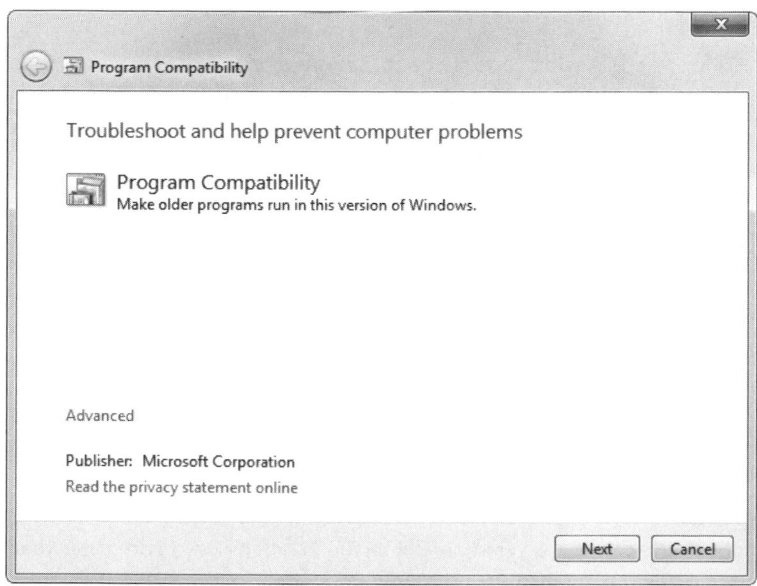

FIGURE 5-2 Program Compatibility troubleshooter

NOTE **To get the most accurate results with this troubleshooter, log on to the computer with a user account that has standard user rights, not administrator rights.**

Application Compatibility Toolkit

You can use the ACT for anything more than a few one-off, simple mitigations. It helps you create an inventory of the applications in your organization. It also helps identify which applications are compatible with Windows 7 and which applications require further testing. The following are some of the major components of the ACT solution:

- **Application Compatibility Manager** A tool that enables you to collect and analyze your data so that you can identify any issues prior to deploying a new operating system or a Windows update in your organization. You use this program heavily during the initial phases of an application migration project. You should consider this tool as the primary user interface for the ACT.
- **Application Compatibility Toolkit Data Collector** The Application Compatibility Toolkit Data Collector is distributed to each computer and scans by using compatibility evaluators. Data is collected and stored in the central compatibility database.

- **Setup Analysis Tool (SAT)** Automates the running of application installations while monitoring the actions taken by each application's installer.
- **Standard User Analyzer (SUA)** Determines the possible issues for applications running as a standard user in Windows 7.

The ACT is indispensable for testing a wide variety of applications across a variety of computers and operating systems within your organization, using solutions based on a common pool of application fixes provided by vendors and users. You can use the ACT tools separately or together, based on your organization's needs. Some tools, such as the SAT and SUA, are intended for developers to enable application remediation and are not necessarily used in the scanning and mitigation process.

Windows XP Mode

In some instances, such as when standard application mitigation strategies fail, virtualization technologies might be appropriate. For example, you can use Windows XP Mode as a safety net for applications that aren't compatible with Windows 7. The Windows XP Mode environment is available for Windows 7 Enterprise, Professional, and Ultimate Edition operating systems.

Using Windows XP Mode, users can run a Windows XP virtual machine on a computer that is running Windows 7. This way, you can proceed with your Windows 7 deployment rather than delay because of application incompatibility. Your organization can take full advantage of the new features and capabilities in Windows 7 and still provide user access to earlier versions of mission-critical applications. In addition, the organization can realize a return on the investment of upgrading to Windows 7 faster than it would by implementing other short-term application compatibility solutions.

Windows XP Mode requires Windows Virtual PC, which is an update that you apply to Windows 7 Enterprise, Professional, and Ultimate Editions. Windows Virtual PC provides a time-saving and cost-saving solution anywhere users must run multiple operating systems (x86 operating systems only) and is an excellent short-term solution for mitigating application compatibility issues; it allows you to continue with Windows 7 deployment. However, you should consider selecting a longer-term solution. Note that Windows Virtual PC requires a CPU with the Intel Virtualization Technology or AMD-V feature turned on. This feature must be enabled in the system BIOS.

Installing Windows XP Mode is easy. You must first install Windows Virtual PC and then install Windows XP Mode. You can perform both tasks from the Windows Virtual PC Web site at *http://www.microsoft.com/windows/virtual-pc/download.aspx*.

> ***MORE INFO*** **For step-by-step instructions on using Windows XP Mode, including installing and using applications, see *http://www.microsoft.com/windows/virtual-pc/support/default.aspx*.**

Application Virtualization

Very often, even if an application does work with Windows 7, it will still create conflicts with other applications running in the same environment because they are competing for system resources. Application virtualization plays a key role in mitigating those concerns.

Microsoft Application Virtualization (App-V) transforms applications into virtualized, network-available services, resulting in dynamic delivery of software that is never installed, never conflicts, and minimizes costly application-to-application regression testing. By using this technology, users and their application environments are no longer computer specific, and the computers themselves are no longer user specific. Although App-V typically provisions applications to run independently of each other in isolated environments, App-V does permit some application interaction. You should carefully examine any dependencies that applications might have on one another and sequence applications together if they rely on interacting with each other.

This allows IT administrators to be flexible and responsive to business needs and significantly reduces the cost of computer management, including enabling application and operating-system migrations, by separating the application deployment from the core operating-system image. App-V is an integral tool in the Microsoft Desktop Optimization Pack for Software Assurance solution, a dynamic desktop solution available to Software Assurance customers that helps reduce application deployment costs, enable delivery of applications as services, and better manage and control enterprise desktop environments. For more information, see *http://www.microsoft.com/windows/enterprise/default.aspx.*

Understanding the ACT

Figure 5-3 illustrates the architecture of the ACT. The following list describes each component of this architecture:

- **Application Compatibility Manager** A tool that enables you to configure, collect, and analyze your data so that you can triage and prioritize any issues prior to deploying a new operating system, updating your version of Internet Explorer, or deploying a Windows update in your organization.
- **Data Collection Package** An .msi file created by the Application Compatibility Manager (ACM) for deploying to each of your client computers. Each Data Collection Package (DCP) can include one or more compatibility evaluators, depending on what you are trying to evaluate.
- **ACT Log Processing Service** A service used to process the ACT log files uploaded from your client computers. It adds the information to your ACT database.
- **ACT Log Processing Share** A file share, accessed by the ACT Log Processing Service, to store the log files that will be processed and added to the ACT database.
- **ACT Database** A Microsoft SQL Server database that stores the collected application, computer, device, and compatibility data. You can view the information stored in the ACT database as reports from the ACM.

- **Microsoft Compatibility Exchange** A Web service that propagates application compatibility issues from the server to the client and enables the client computers to connect to Microsoft via the Internet to check for updated compatibility information. This service does not automatically fix compatibility issues, as it is only an information sharing system.

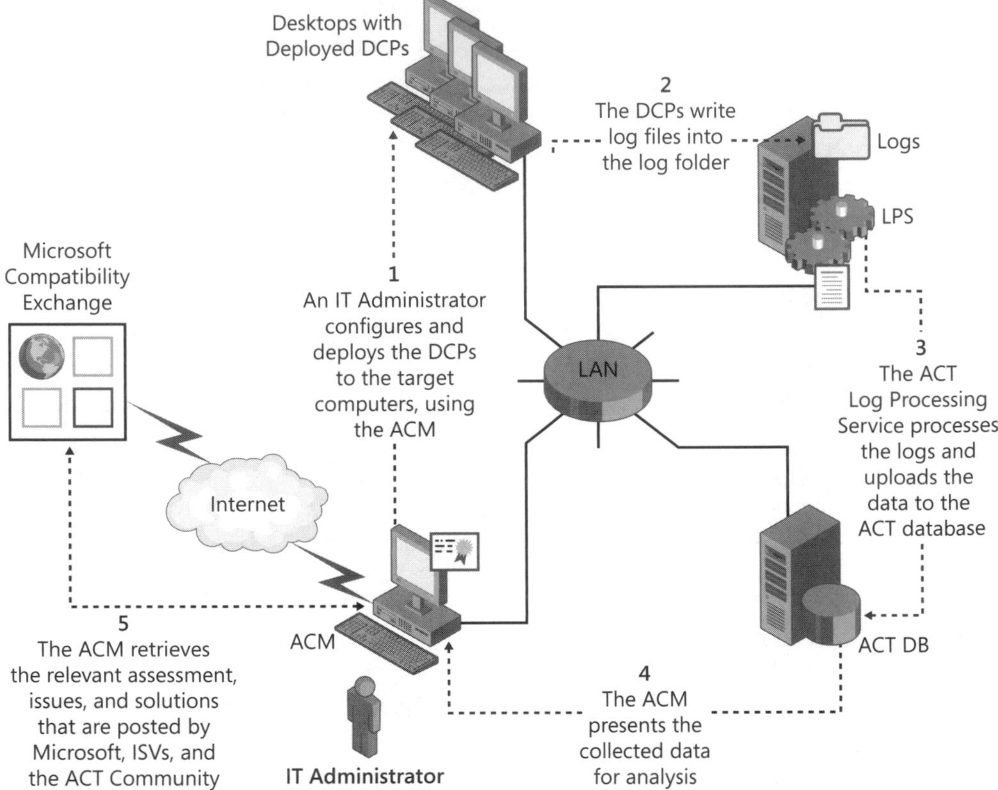

FIGURE 5-3 ACT architecture

Support Topologies

Figure 5-4 shows the topologies that the ACT supports in the order that Microsoft recommends them. For example, Microsoft most highly recommends using the distributed ACT Log Processing Service, ACT Log Processing share, and ACT Database topology, and least recommends using a consolidated server. If you choose to employ a topology based on distributed logging with a rollup to your central share, you must move the files to the ACT Log Processing share before actual processing can occur. You can move the files manually or use a technology such as Distributed File System Replication (DFSR) or any other similar technology already employed in your organization.

Distributed ACT Log Processing Service (LPS), ACT Log Processing Share (LPS Share), and ACT Database

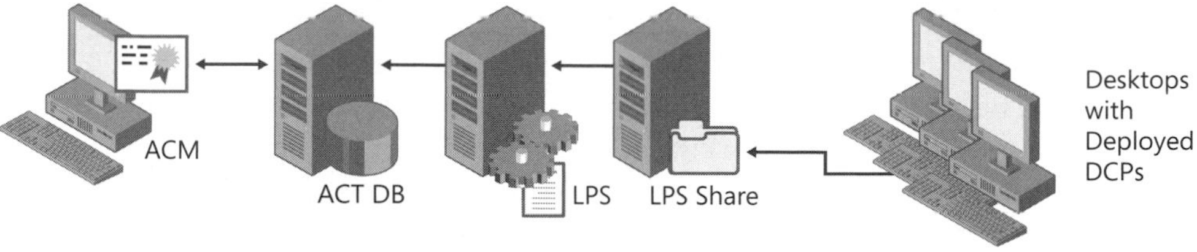

Distributed Logging with Rollup to Central LPS Share

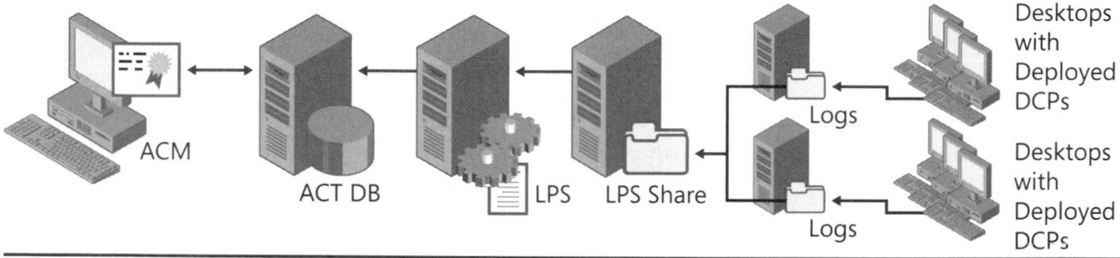

Distributed LPS and ACT Database

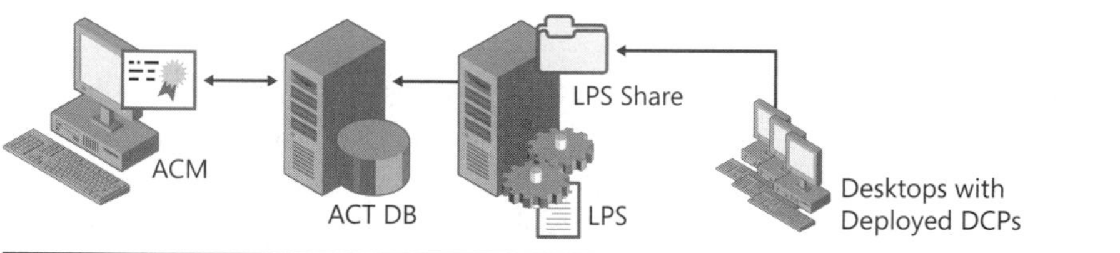

Consolidated Server

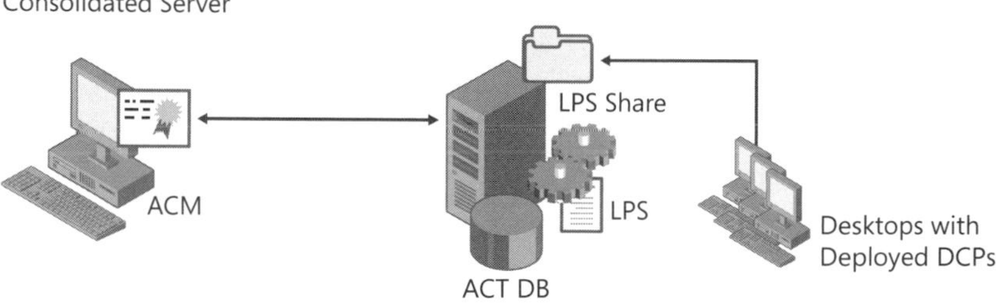

FIGURE 5-4 Supported topologies

Compatibility Evaluators

In addition to collecting application and hardware inventory, the ACT includes compatibility evaluators. Compatibility evaluators are run-time detection tools specifically designed to log behaviors as they occur on the user's computer and locate potential compatibility issues. You should use the compatibility evaluators prior to deploying Windows 7, as they cannot identify problems with an application if the application cannot run. The ACT includes the following compatibility evaluators:

- **Inventory Collector** Examines each of your organization's computers, identifying the installed applications and system information.
- **User Account Control Compatibility Evaluator** Identifies potential compatibility issues because of an application running under a protected administrator (PA) or standard user account on the Windows 7 operating system. When running, the User Account Control Compatibility Evaluator (UACCE) monitors your running applications to verify interactions with the operating system and identify potentially incompatible activities.
- **Update Compatibility Evaluator (UCE)** Identifies the potential impact of a new Windows update. Using the collected update impact data, you can prioritize your testing and reduce the uncertainty in deploying updates.
- **Windows Compatibility Evaluator** Identifies potential compatibility issues resulting from deprecated features in the new operating system, Graphical Identification and Authentication (GINA) dynamic-link libraries (DLLs), and the isolation required by Session 0 applications. Do not run the Windows Compatibility Evaluator (WCE) on Windows 7. If you've already upgraded to Windows 7, you already know about any problems that the WCE has reported.

> ***NOTE*** **Microsoft removed the Internet Explorer Compatibility Evaluator (IECE) from ACT 5.5. You can detect compatibility issues with Internet Explorer 8 by using the Internet Explorer Compatibility Test Tool (IECTT). Microsoft removed the IECE because using the IECTT provides a better experience when testing for Internet Explorer compatibility.**

A DCP can include one or more compatibility evaluators, depending on what you are trying to evaluate. The ACM groups the evaluators based on tasks as described in the following sections.

Planning for the ACT

The ACT provides a way for you to create an inventory for your organization, including your installed applications, computers, and devices. It also enables you to collect compatibility data, to determine the impact of that data in your organization, and, finally, to create mitigation packages to fix the compatibility issues, when possible. The following list describes the three phases for effectively using the ACT in your organization:

- **Collecting data** Before you can analyze your potential compatibility issues, you must first collect your organization's inventory and the associated compatibility issues.
- **Analyzing issues** After collecting your inventory and associated compatibility data, you can organize and analyze your issues. This includes categorizing, prioritizing, setting your deployment status, and setting your application assessment to create customized reports.

- **Testing and mitigating issues** After analyzing your compatibility issue reports, you can test your applications to determine whether the specified compatibility issues are actually problems within your organization. If you determine that the issues are valid, you can create mitigation packages to fix the issues by using the Compatibility Administrator. You can also use the other tools provided with the ACT—including the IECTT, the SAT, and the SUA tool—to determine additional issues and possible mitigation strategies.

Targeting Deployment

For greater control over your collected data, you should deploy DCPs to a small subset of computers based on specific groupings, such as location and department—for example, a DCP for users in the Human Resources department. This enables better categorization and analysis of an application throughout the organization.

If your organization already has a hardware asset inventory list, it is recommended that you sample each unique hardware configuration so that you can synchronize with the Microsoft Compatibility Exchange and obtain the relevant driver compatibility issues. If you do not have a comprehensive inventory, Microsoft recommends that you distribute the DCPs based on the factors described in Table 5-1.

TABLE 5-1 DCP Deployment Considerations

CONSIDERATION	DESCRIPTION
Do you have a managed, unmanaged, or mixed environment?	You categorize your organization as a managed environment, an unmanaged environment, or a mixed management environment through the following criteria: ■ **Managed environment** IT administrators strictly control and manage the application installation and usage based on need and the various divisions in the organization. In this situation, an IT administrator can deploy a DCP on a limited subset of computers for each department, based on known needs and requirements. ■ **Unmanaged environment** Users typically have administrator privileges on their computers and can install applications at their own discretion. Because users in an unmanaged environment can install any software they choose, you need to deploy your DCPs to more computers than you would if you were in a managed environment. ■ **Mixed environment** Your organization uses both managed and unmanaged environments, depending on an individual group's needs and administrative privileges.

CONSIDERATION	DESCRIPTION
How do you use specific applications in your organization?	It is very important that you provide coverage for all applications required by users in your organization, but it's even more important that you provide coverage for your LOB applications. For the most complete coverage of application usage, you must do the following: ■ Consult with your local administrators, support engineers, and department heads to ensure that all applications are in use during the data collection process. ■ Ensure that "seasonal" applications are covered. For example, fiscal year accounting applications might be used only once a year. ■ Attempt to perform the data collection when few employee vacations are scheduled or at the beginning of the week to avoid weekends. Otherwise, you might have limited or incomplete results because of the decreased application usage. In all cases, recruit willing participants that will be responsible for their team and applications and will report everything they find. User acceptance testing is critical.
Do you use role-based applications?	Your organization may use role-based applications, which are applications that relate to job function and the role that a user performs within your organization. A common example is accountants (a financial role) and their finance-related applications. Reviewing application usage in conjunction with job function and roles enables better application coverage in your organization.
How do you distribute your applications in your organization?	You can distribute applications in many ways within an organization—for example, by using Group Policy, IntelliMirror, Microsoft System Center Configuration Manager 2007, or a custom distribution method. Reviewing your software distribution system policies in conjunction with your application inventory enables better application coverage and narrows the deployment of your DCPs.
What is the geographic breakdown of your organization?	You must consider the geographic distribution of your organization when planning for your DCP deployment (for example, if you have branches in North America, Asia, and Europe). You must then consider the application usage patterns across each geographic region. You must account for divisional applications, localized versions of applications, and applications specific to the geographic location and export restrictions. We recommend that you consult with technical and business leaders from each region to understand these differences.

CONSIDERATION	DESCRIPTION
What types of computers do you have in your organization and how are they used?	Computer types and usage patterns can play an important role in your DCP deployment. The following sections describe some of the most common computer types and usage patterns: ▪ **Mobile and laptop computers** Mobile users frequently work offline, occasionally synchronizing with the corporate network through either a LAN or virtual private network (VPN) connection. Because of the high possibility of a user going offline for long periods of time, you must consider the odds of the user being online for the DCP to be downloaded and installed, and then online again for the logged data to be uploaded. ▪ **Multiuser computers** Multiuser computers are typically located in university computer labs, libraries, and organizations that enable job sharing. These computers are highly secure and include a core set of applications that are always available, as well as many applications that can be installed and removed as necessary. Because these computers typically have a basic set of applications assigned to users or computers, you can narrow the application coverage and usage to identify only a subset of client computers to receive the DCP. ▪ **AppStations/TaskStations** AppStations running vertical applications are typically used for marketing, claims and loan processing, and customer service. TaskStations are typically dedicated to running a single application, such as on a manufacturing floor as an entry terminal or in a call center. Because both of these types of computers do not commonly allow users to add or to remove applications and might be designated for specific users and job roles, the application coverage and usage can be narrowed to identify a subset of client computers to receive the DCP. ▪ **Kiosks** Kiosks are generally in public areas. These computers run unattended and are highly secure, generally running a single program by using a single-use account and automatic logon. Because these computers typically run a single application, the application coverage and usage can be narrowed to identify a subset of computers to receive the DCP.

Choosing a Deployment Method

Microsoft recommends that you base your method for deploying the DCP on your existing infrastructure. You can choose one of several ways to distribute a DCP to your identified client computers, including the following (listed in order of preference):

- **System Center Configuration Manager 2007** After performing an inventory of your applications, you can use the software deployment feature in System Center Configuration Manager 2007 to deploy the DCPs to the client computers. Additionally, the inventory information that it contains is a valuable aid.
- **Group Policy Software Installation** Create an .msi package for each DCP, and then use the Group Policy Software Installation feature of Active Directory Domain Services (AD DS) in Windows Server 2008 and Windows Server 2008 R2 for deployment. All client computers to which you will deploy the DCP must be part of the AD DS forest.
- **Logon scripts** While logged on to a domain from the client computers, you can initiate the installation of DCPs using logon scripts in Windows Server 2008 and Windows Server 2008 R2.
- **Non-Microsoft deployment software** If your organization has a non-Microsoft software deployment infrastructure, use that method to deploy the DCPs. For information about the requirements of the non-Microsoft deployment software, consult the software vendor.
- **Manual distribution** For computers that are not connected to the network or that have slow connections, such as small branch offices, manual distribution methods are available. These methods include distributing the collection packages through e-mail or on physical media such as a USB Flash drive (UFD) or CD.

Choosing a Log File Location

When you are creating a DCP in the ACM, you can select an output location for your log files. The following configuration options are available:

- **Select a default ACT Log Processing share location** If you use this option, the DCP automatically writes the log files to the ACT Log Processing share. If the ACT Log Processing share is unavailable when the specified upload time interval is reached, the DCP will make two more attempts. If the problem persists, the DCP will store the log file in the location defined in the next option. All files are then retried during the next upload interval.
- **Select the Local (%ACTAppData%\DataCollector\Output) location** If you use this option, the DCP creates the log files on the local system and the computer Administrator must manually copy the files to the ACT Log Processing share location. This is a good option for mobile users that are not always connected to the network. If you select this option, Microsoft recommends that you either notify your users to copy the collected data to the ACT Log Processing share or employ an alternate method to collect the data from the client computers and copy the information into the ACT Log Processing share.

- **Type an alternate network share location** If you use this option, you must verify that the DCP service can write to the location. This is a good option for companies that are geographically diverse (for example, if you have branches in North America and Europe). An IT administrator can create DCPs and file shares individually for North America and Europe, which further enables administrators at a central location to roll up all the collection log files to a central location. These log files are then mapped to the ACT Log Processing share for final processing and entry into the ACT database.

Preparing for the ACT

Before configuring and running the ACT, you must verify that you are using supported software, that you meet the minimum hardware requirements, and that you have configured the required permissions and infrastructure. Table 5-2 lists the software required by the ACT. Table 5-3 lists the hardware requirements for using the ACT.

You must provide special system requirements before you can successfully use the Update Compatibility Evaluator (UCE), the SAT, or the Compatibility Administrator. For more information, see the ACT 5.5 documentation. The UCE is not compatible with any 64-bit version of Windows.

TABLE 5-2 Software Requirements for the ACT

SOFTWARE	SUPPORTED VERSIONS
Operating systems	■ Windows 7 ■ Windows Vista ■ Windows Vista SP1 ■ Windows Vista SP2 ■ Windows XP SP2 ■ Windows XP SP3 ■ Windows Server 2008 R2 ■ Windows Server 2008 ■ Windows Server 2003 SP2
Proxy server	The ACT supports only the Microsoft Internet Security and Acceleration (ISA) Server proxy server.
Database	After the ACT is installed, it requires one of the following database components: SQL Server 2005, SQL Server 2005 Express, SQL Server 2008, or SQL Server 2008 Express. *Note:* The ACT does not support the Microsoft Database Engine (MSDE) or Microsoft SQL Server 2000.
.NET Framework	The ACT requires Microsoft .NET Framework 2.0 or later.

TABLE 5-3 Hardware Requirements for the ACT

ACT COMPONENT	MINIMUM REQUIREMENT	RECOMMENDED REQUIREMENT
ACM client and ACT Log Processing Service servers	550-megahertz (MHz) processor with 256 megabytes (MB) of RAM	2.8-gigahertz (GHz) processor with 2 gigabytes (GB) of RAM
ACT client databases	1-GHz processor with 512 MB of RAM	2.8-GHz processor with 2 GB of RAM

Sharing the Log Processing Folder

If your DCPs write to a network ACT Log Processing share, you must verify that you have the correct permissions at both the share and the folder levels, as follows:

- **Share-Level Permissions** Verify that the Everyone group has Change and Read permissions for the ACT Log Processing share folder.
- **Folder-Level Permissions (NTFS Only)** Verify that the Everyone group has Write access and that the ACT Log Processing Service account has List Folder Contents, Read, and Write permissions. If the ACT Log Processing Service is running as Local System, this must be the *domain\computer*$ account. If the ACT Log Processing Service is running with a user account, this is the user account information.

Preparing for Microsoft Compatibility Exchange

Configure your organization's infrastructure to support the Microsoft Compatibility Exchange while also protecting your intranet security and stability. The recommended method of configuration requires you to allow the appropriate users, on designated computers, to access the Microsoft Compatibility Exchange through your security and network infrastructure. To configure the infrastructure to support the Microsoft Compatibility Exchange, follow these steps:

1. Configure your firewalls and Uniform Resource Locator (URL) scanners to allow access to the Microsoft Compatibility Exchange by setting the following conditions:
   - Allow outbound access for the standard Secure Sockets Layer (SSL) TCP port 443 on any computer running the ACM.
   - Restrict outbound access to the Microsoft Compatibility Exchange, allowing access only from designated computers and designated users within your organizations.
   - Enable access to the Microsoft Compatibility Exchange (*https://appinfo.microsoft.com/AppProfile50/ActWebService.asmx*), which is necessary only if passing through a firewall.
2. Grant the *db_datareader*, *db_datawriter*, and *db_owner* database roles to any user account that will log on to the computer running the ACT Log Processing Service.
3. Grant the *db_datareader* and *db_datawriter* database roles to any user account that will log on to the computer running the ACM.

Installing the ACT 5.5

You can download the ACT 5.5 from the Microsoft Download Center at *http://www.microsoft.com/downloads*. Before you install the ACT, ensure that the computer on which you're installing it meets the requirements described in the section titled "Preparing for the ACT" earlier in this chapter.

To install the ACT, perform the following steps:

1. Right-click Application Compatibility Toolkit.msi and then click Install.
2. Click Next.
3. On the License Agreement page, click I Accept The Terms In The License Agreement and then click Next.
4. If you want to install the ACT 5.5 in a different location than the default folder, on the Installation Folder page, click Change to change the installation folder and then click Next.
5. Click Install.
6. Click Finish.

Configuring the ACM

Before you can use the ACM to collect and analyze your compatibility data, you must configure the tool. This includes configuring the following: your SQL Server instance and database, your ACT Log Processing Service account, and your ACT Log Processing share.

The ACT Configuration Wizard enables you to configure the ACT database, the ACT Log Processing share, and the ACT Log Processing Service account. Before running the wizard, you must verify the following:

- You are an administrator on the computer, and you have Read and Write permissions to the database.
- Your domain computer has Write permissions to the ACT Log Processing Service share.
- The ACT Log Processing Service account has Read and Write permissions to the ACT database for the *domain\computer*$ account.
- The ACT client is installed on any computer that acts as an ACT Log Processing Server.

To configure the ACM, perform the following steps:

1. Click Start, point to All Programs, Microsoft Application Compatibility Toolkit 5.5, and then select Application Compatibility Manager to start the ACT Configuration Wizard.
2. Review the information on the page and then click Next.
3. On the Select The Configuration Option page, click Enterprise Configuration and then click Next.
4. On the Configure Your ACT Database Settings page, type the name of the SQL Server instance that will contain the ACT database in the SQL Server box and then click Connect.

In the Database box, type a unique name for your new database, such as **ACT_Database**, and then click Create. Click Next.

5. On the Configure Your Log File Location page, type the path of the folder in which to store the ACT log files in the Path box or click Browse to choose an existing folder or create a new folder. In the ShareAs box, type a name for the share and then click Next.
6. On the Configure Your ACT Log Processing Service Account page, click Local System to use your local system account credentials to start the ACT Log Processing Service and then click Next. You also have the option to click User Account. If you choose this option, the ACT will use the local computer user account to start the ACT Log Processing Service. Additionally, for this option, you must enter your user name, password, and domain, and provide Log On As A Service user rights.
7. Click Finish.

You have the option to change any of your ACT configuration settings after completing the configuration wizard. On the Tools menu, select Settings and then make your changes in the Settings dialog box (Figure 5-5).

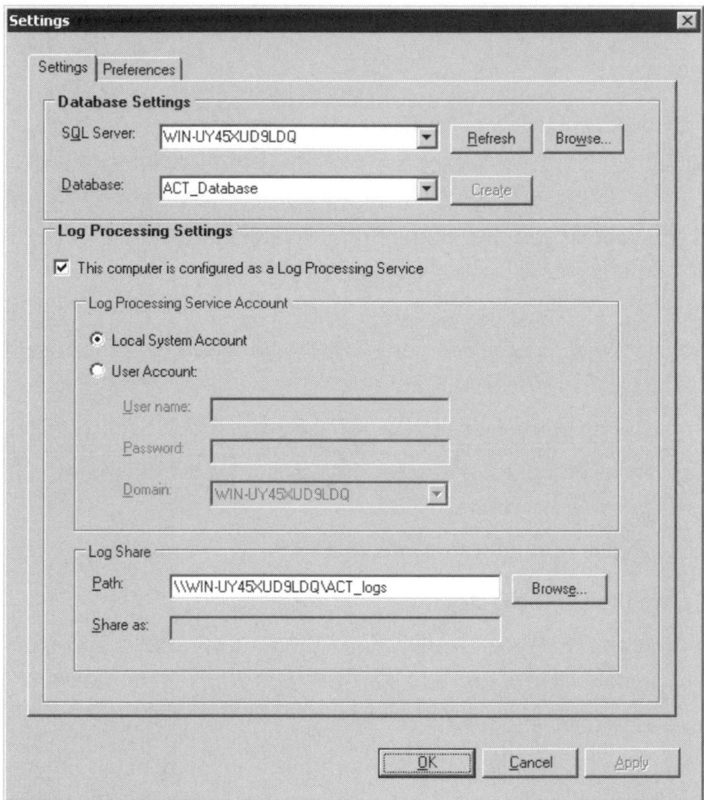

FIGURE 5-5 ACT settings

Collecting Compatibility Data

The ACT enables you to collect an inventory of all installed software, hardware, and devices within your organization. Additionally, the ACT provides compatibility evaluators, which you will use in your DCPs for deployment to your client computers. Compatibility evaluators are run-time detection tools designed to log behaviors as they occur on the user's computer and locate potential compatibility issues.

The ACT collects data according to the following workflow:

1. You create a new DCP by using the ACM. Each DCP can contain one or more compatibility evaluators, including the Inventory Collector.
2. You deploy the DCPs to your identified subset of client computers using System Center Configuration Manager 2007, Group Policy, or any other software distribution technology. The evaluators run for the length of time that you specified when creating the DCP and then the data (.cab) file is uploaded to your ACT Log Processing share.
3. The ACT Log Processing Service, running on a server, accesses the data from the ACT Log Processing share, processes the data, and then uploads the information to your ACT database.
4. The ACM reads the data from your ACT database to determine how many computers have uploaded data and the status of the collection process. The ACM also uses the data from the ACT database to enable reporting and viewing of the collected data.

By using the ACM, you can create DCPs to gather your installed software, hardware, and device information, in addition to determining any associated compatibility issues based on applications, Web sites, or Windows updates for your selected client computers. The ACT includes the compatibility evaluators described in the section titled "Compatibility Evaluators" earlier in this chapter.

After creating a DCP, deploy it using the method chosen from the list in the section titled "Choosing a Deployment Method" earlier in this chapter. Because a DCP is an .msi file that installs silently, deploying it is just like deploying any other application. For more information about deploying applications, see Chapter 8, "Deploying Applications."

To create a DCP for deploying Windows 7, perform the following steps:

1. In the ACM, click File and then click New.
2. The New_Package dialog box appears. In the Package Name box, type a unique name for your DCP, such as **Windows_Deployment**.
3. In the Evaluate Compatibility When area, click Deploying A New Operating System Or Service Pack. This evaluator option includes the Inventory Collector, the UACCE, and the WCE by default. If you want, you can click Advanced to choose the specific evaluators to include in the package.
4. In the When To Monitor Application Usage area, configure the starting time, duration, and upload interval.

5. In the Output Location box, shown here, keep your default value, previously specified in the Configuration Wizard.

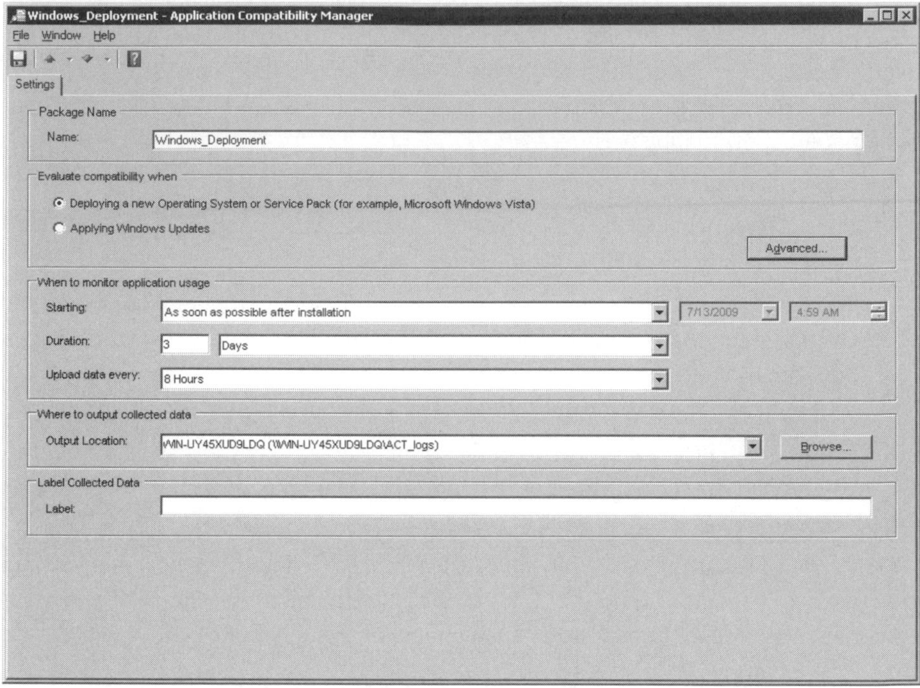

6. On the File menu, click Save And Create Package, saving the compiled DCP as an .msi file in an accessible location, such as a network share.

To view the status of a DCP, perform the following steps:

1. In the left pane of the ACM, click Collect.
2. Click By Status in the Current View section of the Collect screen. The Collect screen changes to show you the deployed DCPs and their status, including whether they are in progress or complete.

Analyzing Compatibility Data

The ACT enables you to organize and to analyze your data by using categorization, prioritization, organizational assessments, issue and solution management, report management, and filtering. You can access and view all your compatibility data by using the Quick Reports area of the ACM, shown in Figure 5-6.

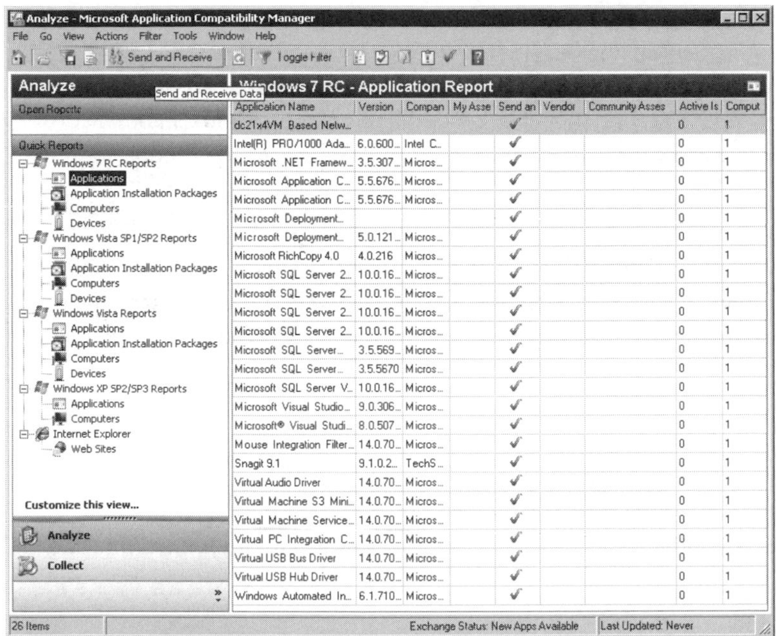

FIGURE 5-6 Quick Reports in the ACM

Creating and Assigning Categories

You can create, modify, and assign categories to all your applications, computers, devices, Web sites, and updates for a more customized ACT compatibility report and for filtering purposes. After assigning the priority categories, the second most commonly used analysis tool is assigning arbitrary categories to each piece of software:

- Software Vendor can be a useful category because you might have varying relationships with each of your vendors. Generating reports and groupings by software vendor can be useful when you have discussions with that vendor and evaluate the vendor's performance with regard to your compatibility needs.
- Test Complexity can be useful for planning and assigning resources. Applications with higher complexity might require additional resources or help to make support decisions. For example, you might assign additional resources to a Business Critical application with an elevated test complexity but remove a Nice To Have application with an elevated test complexity from the supported software list.
- Unit of Deployment is another commonly used set of categories, such as Division and Region. Your organization might choose a different naming convention for this information, but typically, this category enables you to track the software needs of one unit of deployment so that as the necessary software is tested and approved, that deployment unit can proceed.

Because the category option is a completely extensible multiple-selection string value, you can potentially use it for just about anything. Some creative uses include creating a category for signoff from multiple owners so that the software can be authorized only when all categories have been selected (indicating that each group has signed off). You can brainstorm other ideas about how to use categories and how your group perceives the organization of its software ecosystem.

> ***NOTE*** **By default, the Master Category List dialog box has two categories: Software Vendor and Test Complexity. These are the only default subcategories. For more information about creating and assigning categories and subcategories, see "Categorizing Your Data" in the ACT documentation.**

To create new categories and subcategories, perform the following steps:

1. In the ACM, click Analyze.
2. In the Analyze screen, in the Quick Reports pane, click Applications in the Windows 7 Reports section.
3. On the Actions menu, click Assign Categories.
4. In the Assign Categories dialog box, click Category List.
5. In the Categories area of the Category List dialog box, click Add, type the name of the new category, and then press Enter.
6. In the Subcategories area of the Category List dialog box, shown here, click Add, type the name of a new subcategory, and then press Enter. Repeat this step for each subcategory that you want to add to the category.

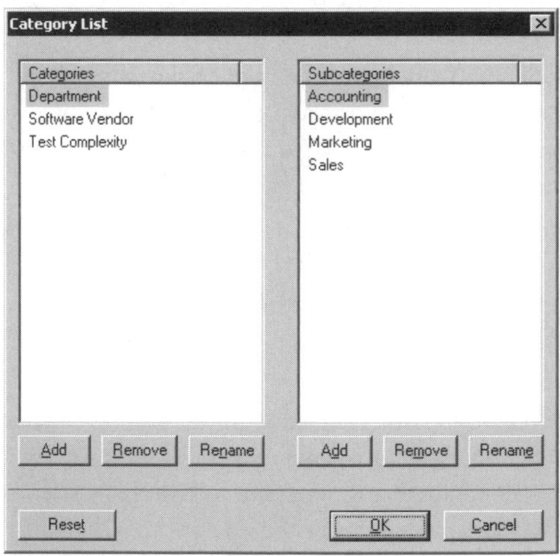

7. Click OK to close the Category List dialog box.

8. Click OK to close the Assign Categories dialog box.

To assign a category or subcategory, perform the following steps:

1. In the ACM, click Analyze.
2. In the Analyze screen, in the Quick Reports pane, click Applications in the Windows 7 Reports section.
3. In the Windows 7 - Application Report, right-click an application and then click Assign Categories.
4. In the Assign Categories dialog box, shown here, select the check box next to each category and subcategory to which you want to assign the application.

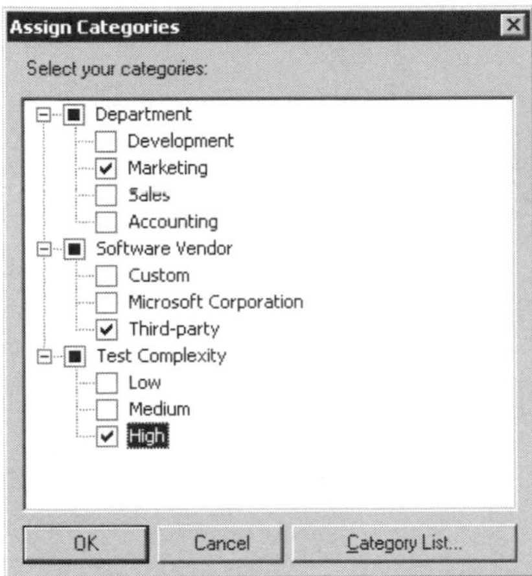

5. Click OK to close the Assign Categories dialog box.

Prioritizing Compatibility Data

You can prioritize any of your collected compatibility data, except for your setup installation packages, based on your organization's requirements. Prioritizing your data enables you to organize your data better, for both a more customized ACT compatibility report and filtering purposes. The following priority levels are available:

- **Priority 1 – Business Critical** Includes any item that is so important to your organization that, unless you can certify it, you will not continue with your deployment.
- **Priority 2 – Important** Includes any item that your organization regularly uses but can continue to function without. It is your choice whether to continue your deployment without certification.
- **Priority 3 – Nice To Have** Includes any item that does not fall into the previous two categories, but that should appear in your ACT compatibility reports. These items will not prevent you from continuing with your deployment.

- **Priority 4 – Unimportant** Includes any item that is irrelevant to your organization's daily operations. You can use this priority level to filter the unimportant items from your reports.
- **Unspecified** The default priority level, which is automatically assigned to any item. Your organization can use this priority level to denote applications that have not yet been reviewed.

To prioritize your compatibility data, perform the following steps:

1. In the left pane of the ACM, click Analyze.
2. In the Quick Reports pane, click Applications in the Windows 7 Reports section.
3. Right-click an application in the Windows 7 - Application Report and then click Set Priority.
4. In the Set Priority dialog box, shown here, click a priority and then click OK.

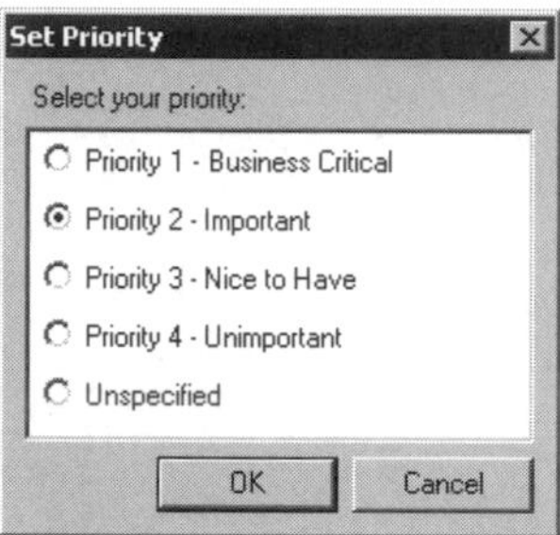

Assessing Application Compatibility

You can set your organization's assessment rating for each application, application installation report, and Web site. Setting your assessment rating enables you to specify which applications might be problematic while going through your organization's testing process. Additionally, setting your assessment enables you to organize your data better, for both a more customized ACT compatibility report and for filtering purposes.

> ***NOTE*** **Microsoft, the application vendor, and the ACT Community also can add assessment ratings. You can view high-level assessment summaries and specific application assessment details in the applicable report screen or report detail screen. For more information about how to view the assessment details, see the ACT documentation.**

Your assessment choices include the following:

- **Works** Indicates that during your organization's testing process, you did not experience any issues.

- **Works With Minor Issues Or Has Solutions** Indicates that during your organization's testing process, you experienced minor issues (severity 3), such as showing a typographical error, or an issue that already had a known solution.
- **Does Not Work** Indicates that during your organization's testing process, you experienced a severity 1 or severity 2 issue.
- **No Data** Neither your organization, Microsoft Corporation, the vendor of the application or Web site, nor the ACT Community has provided any data.

To assess your compatibility data, perform the following steps:

1. In the left pane of the ACM, click Analyze.
2. In the Quick Reports pane, click Applications in the Windows 7 Reports section.
3. Right-click an application in the Windows 7 - Application Report and then click Set Assessment.
4. In the Set Assessment dialog box, shown here, click an assessment and then click OK.

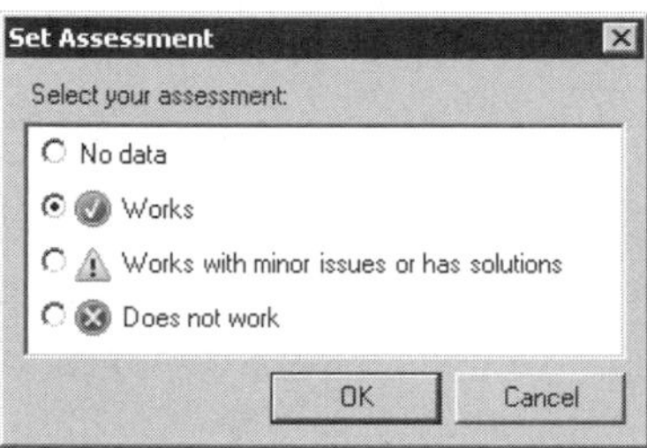

Setting the Deployment Status

You can set your organization's deployment status for each application, application installation report, Web site, and Windows update. Setting your deployment status enables you to determine where each item is in your testing process. Additionally, setting your deployment status enables you to organize your data better, for both a more customized ACT compatibility report and for filtering purposes. Your deployment status choices include the following:

- **Not Reviewed** Your organization has not yet reviewed this item to determine its impact, testing requirements, or deployment options.
- **Testing** Your organization is in the process of locating compatibility issues.
- **Mitigating** Your organization is in the process of creating and applying solutions for your compatibility issues.
- **Ready To Deploy** Your organization has completed its testing and mitigation processes and has determined that you can deploy the item in your organization.
- **Will Not Deploy** Your organization has decided that you will not deploy the item in your organization.

To assess your deployment status, perform the following steps:

1. In the left pane of the ACM, click Analyze.
2. In the Quick Reports pane, click Applications in the Windows 7 Reports section.
3. Right-click an application in the Windows 7 - Application Report and then click Set Deployment Status.
4. In the Set Deployment Status dialog box, shown here, click a deployment status and then click OK.

Managing Compatibility Issues

Although the compatibility evaluators, the Microsoft Compatibility Exchange, and the ACT Community all provide information about application compatibility issues, you might still uncover an undocumented issue. After adding your compatibility issue, you can use the Microsoft Compatibility Exchange to upload and to share your issue information with both Microsoft and the ACT Community, if you are a member. You can also add compatibility solutions to any compatibility issue in your ACT database, regardless of whether you entered the issue.

You also can resolve any active compatibility issue in your ACT database, regardless of whether you entered the issue. Resolving an issue means that you are satisfied with the state of the issue and are closing it from further edits. However, you can still add solutions or reactivate the issue if you discover that you resolved it in error. Marking an issue as resolved also changes the issue status from a red X to a green check mark in your compatibility reports, report detail screens, and for the overall group score in the ACT Community data.

To add a compatibility issue, perform the following steps:

1. In the left pane of the ACM, click Analyze.
2. In the Quick Reports pane, click Applications in the Windows 7 Reports section.
3. In the Windows 7 - Application Report, right-click an application and then click Open.
4. On the Actions menu, click Add Issue to open the New Issue dialog box.
5. In the Title box, type a title for the issue.
6. In the Priority list, click a priority.
7. In the Severity list, click a severity level.

8. In the Symptom list, click a symptom.
9. In the Cause list, click a cause for the issue.
10. In the Affected Operating Systems dialog box, shown here, select the check boxes next to each operating system on which this issue appears.

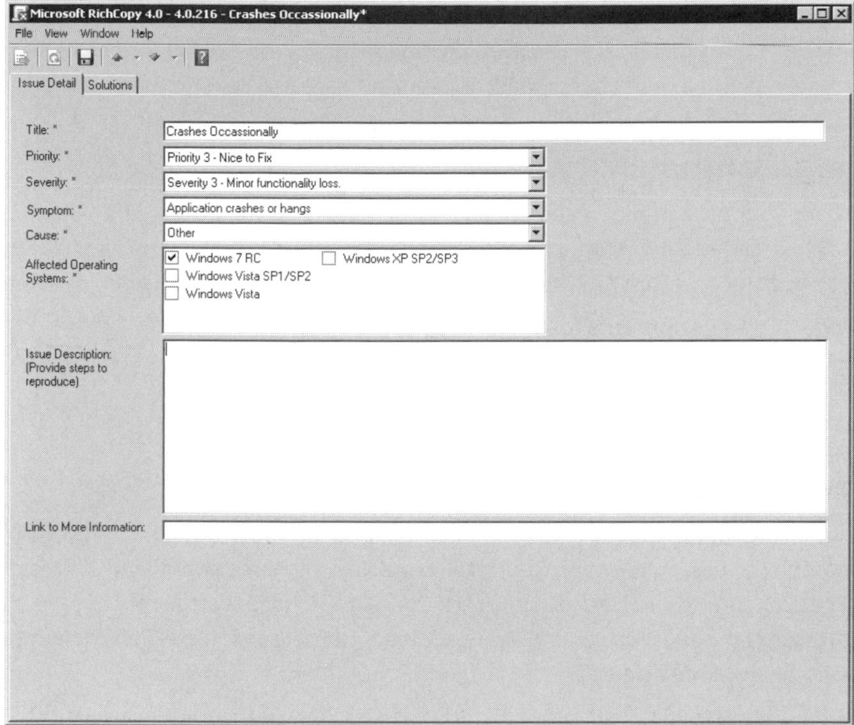

11. In the Issue Description box, type a description of the issue.
12. On the File menu, click Save.

To add a compatibility solution, perform the following steps:

1. In the left pane of the ACM, click Analyze.
2. In the Quick Reports pane, click Applications in the Windows 7 Reports section.
3. In the Windows 7 - Application Report, right-click an application and then click Open.
4. On the Issues tab, double-click the issue for which you want to add a solution.
5. Click the issue's Solutions tab.
6. On the Actions menu, click Add Solution.
7. In the Title box, type a title for the solution.
8. In the Solution Type box, click a solution type.
9. In the Solution Details box, type a description of the solution.
10. Click Save.

To resolve a compatibility issue, perform the following steps:

1. In the left pane of the ACM, click Analyze.
2. In the Quick Reports pane, click Applications in the Windows 7 Reports section.
3. In the Windows 7 - Application Report, right-click an application and then click Open.
4. On the Issues tab, double-click the issue that you want to resolve.
5. On the Actions menu, click Resolve. A note appears in the Issues tab that says the issue is resolved and a green check mark appears in the Status column of the Issues tab.

Filtering Compatibility Data

You can filter your organization's compatibility issue data by selecting specific restriction criteria in context, based on the report that you are viewing. For example, you can filter your applications by category, your Web sites by priority, or a Windows update by deployment status.

To create a filter, perform the following steps:

1. In the ACM, click Analyze.
2. In the Analyze screen, in the Quick Reports pane, click Applications in the Windows 7 Reports section.
3. On the Filter menu, select Toggle Filter to turn on the filter.
4. In the Filter pane, choose a field, an operator, and a value on which to filter. For example, to display only applications with a company name containing *Microsoft*, click Company in the Field column, click Contains in the Operator column, and type **Microsoft** in the Value column. After adding a clause (row), the ACM automatically adds a new, empty clause.
5. Add additional clauses as necessary. You can specify whether all clauses must be true or whether any one of the clauses must be true by choosing And or Or in the And/Or column for each individual clause.
6. Select Refresh from the View menu to display the compatibility database based on your filter.

You can further edit your filter by clicking the Filter menu and then selecting Cut, Copy, Paste, Insert Clause, Delete Clause, or Clear.

To save a filter, perform the following steps:

1. On the File menu, select Save As.
2. In the Save As dialog box, type the path and file name of the ACM Report File (.adq) to save and then click Save.

To export a report, perform the following steps:

1. On the File menu, select Export Report.
2. In the Export Report Data dialog box, choose from one of the following report types in the Save As Type list:

- Microsoft Excel Files (*.xls)
- SV (Comma Delimited) (*.csv)
- XML Document (*.xml)

3. In the File Name box, type the path and file name of the report and then click Save.

Synchronizing with the Compatibility Exchange Service

The ACT enables you to synchronize your ACT database with Microsoft and the ACT Community through the Microsoft Compatibility Exchange Web service. This Web service downloads new information from authoritative sources, such as Microsoft and ISVs, and it uploads your compatibility issues to Microsoft. The ACT only displays applications that your environment has in common with the service.

To synchronize with the Microsoft Compatibility Exchange, perform the following steps:

1. In the ACM, click Actions and then click Send And Receive.
2. If you want, in the Send And Receive Data dialog box, click Review The Data Before Sending to view a list of the applications for which you are sending your compatibility data. You can choose the applications that you will share. You can also click Review All Data to save a list of the data that you're sending in an audit log, as shown here.

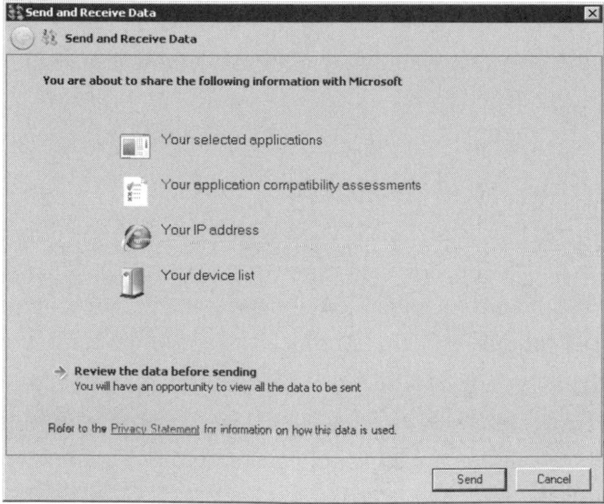

3. Click Send.
4. Review the updated issue data for your applications in the ACM.

Rationalizing an Application Inventory

After you have finished organizing and analyzing your data, Microsoft recommends that you create an application portfolio for your organization. The application portfolio is a list of all the applications in your organization, including their specific details and compatibility status.

To create an application portfolio, perform the following steps:

1. Collect your application inventory and compatibility data by using the ACT.
2. Organize your data based on your organization's requirements and then analyze the information.
3. Identify any applications that are missing from the inventory.
4. Select specific versions of your inventoried applications to be included in your deployment.

Identifying the Missing Applications

You must identify any applications that were not located during the automated inventory collection process. These applications might be located on portable computers or high-security systems that cannot be accessed for inventory. In these situations, you must document the application manually.

To identify missing applications, perform the following steps:

1. Distribute the application portfolio in your organization; specifically, distribute it to those who have knowledge of the required applications currently in use.
2. Request that the group specified in step 1 review the portfolio for errors.
3. Review the feedback provided from step 2 to analyze the errors in the existing portfolio.
4. Make the appropriate changes to the portfolio based on the review.
5. Publish the revised application portfolio and obtain stakeholder approval of the list and application compatibility status.

Selecting Specific Application Versions

To help reduce the long-term total cost of ownership (TCO), you must reduce the number of supported applications in your organization. For each supported application, you must allocate time, training, tools, and resources to plan, deploy, and support the application. Standardizing your list of supported applications can help to reduce the amount of effort required to support your deployed computer configurations.

If you determine that multiple applications are performing the same task in your organization, Microsoft recommends that you select a single application and include it in your standard portfolio, with an emphasis on the following criteria:

- The application is part of a suite of applications. Applications that are part of a suite (for example, Microsoft Office Word 2007) are more difficult to eliminate from your portfolio because you typically must eliminate the entire suite.
- The vendor supports the application on the new operating system. Identifying support options early can reduce your costs later.
- The application adheres to the Designed for Windows logo program. Applications that display the current compatibility logo have met stringent guidelines for compatibility with the current version of Windows.

- The application provides an .msi package for deployment. If the application provides an .msi package, you will spend less time preparing the application for deployment.
- The application is AD DS–aware. You can manage AD DS–aware applications through Group Policy.
- The application is the latest version available in your inventory. Deploying a later version helps ensure the long-term support of the application because of obsolescence policies.
- The application provides multilingual support. Multilingual support within the application, when coupled with multilingual support in the operating system (such as the multilingual support in Windows 7), enables your organization to eliminate localized versions of the application.
- The application provides a greater number of features. Applications that support a greater number of features are more likely to address the business needs of a larger number of your users.

To select the appropriate version of an application, perform the following steps:

1. Identify the latest version of the application currently installed in your organization.
2. Determine whether a later version of the application is currently available. If so, Microsoft recommends that you include the later version of the application in your analysis.
3. Verify that you have vendor support for each version of the application.
4. Identify the license availability and cost for each application and version.
5. From all the versions available, select one version that is supported on all your client computers.
6. Validate the selected version in your test environment, verifying that it is compatible with your new operating system, Windows update, or Internet Explorer version.

Testing and Mitigating Issues

After you analyze your issues in the ACM, you can continue to explore your compatibility issues by using several development tools provided with the ACT. The development tools enable you to test for a variety of compatibility issues, including Web site and Web application issues, issues related to running as a standard user in Windows 7, and issues that might arise because of actions taken by an application's installer program. Additionally, the ACT provides a tool that can help you resolve many of your compatibility issues: the Compatibility Administrator. To resolve your compatibility problems, you must follow these steps:

1. Identify your most critical applications. Create an inventory of your organization's applications and then verify certification status of the included applications to see whether they require testing.
2. Identify any application compatibility problems. Test each application, determining any compatibility issues if necessary.

3. Resolve any application compatibility issues. Identify and create application compatibility solutions by using the ACT tools, which include the IECTT, either the stand-alone version or the virtual version of the SAT, the SUA, and the Compatibility Administrator.
4. Deploy or distribute your test and certified applications and solutions. Use a deployment and distribution tool, such as System Center Configuration Manager 2007, to deploy your certified applications and compatibility issue solution packages to your client desktops.

When testing an application in a new operating system, Microsoft recommends that you retain the default security feature selections. Microsoft also recommends that you thoroughly test the applications, replicating as many of the usage scenarios from within your organization as possible. Finally, Microsoft recommends that you enter your issues and solutions into the ACM so that you can track the data from a central location.

When testing a Web site or a Web application, Microsoft recommends that you include both intranet and extranet sites, prioritizing the list based on how critical the site or the application is to your organization. Microsoft also recommends that you thoroughly test the Web sites and Web applications, replicating as many of the usage scenarios from within your organization as possible. Finally, Microsoft recommends that you enter your issues into the ACM so that you can share that data with both Microsoft and the ACT Community to receive potential solutions for your issues.

Building a Test Lab

Your test environment should be a long-term investment in the overall deployment process. Retain the test environment after the deployment to assist in future deployment projects. To create the test environment, you must determine how to model the production environment in the test environment and configure the test environment to support automated testing of the mitigation strategies.

Microsoft recommends that you establish a dedicated and isolated lab environment for use in developing and testing the application compatibility mitigation. The lab should mirror your production environment as closely as possible. In some cases, you might find that it is better to open up the test network to existing production services, instead of replicating your production environment in detail. For example, you might want to permit your Dynamic Host Configuration Protocol (DHCP) packets to pass through routers into the test network. Some operations can be safely conducted in the production environment, such as the application inventory collection process. At a minimum, your lab environment should include:

- DHCP services
- Domain Name System (DNS) services
- SQL Server 2005 or SQL Server 2005 Express
- Lab test user accounts, with both normal user and administrative privileges
- Network hardware to provide Internet access (for downloading updates, files, and so on)

- Test computers that accurately reflect production computers in both software and hardware configuration
- A software library representing all the applications to be tested
- Windows Server 2008 R2 with Hyper-V
- Windows Internet Naming Service (WINS) services (optional)

In most instances, you must test the mitigation strategies more than once and must be able to revert reliably to a previous test state. Automating your testing process enables you to ensure reproducibility and consistency in your testing process. Using test automation tools enables you to run your test cases in a standardized, reproducible manner. Using disk-imaging software for physical images of the servers and using software virtualization features for reversing changes to virtualized hard disks enables you to restore your test environment back to a previous state.

Modeling the Production Environment

The goal of the test environment is to model your production environment. The more accurate the production environment, the greater the validity of the testing performed in that test environment. Microsoft recommends the following best practices in creating your test environment:

- Use virtual or physical images of production computers to create their test environment counterparts. Virtual or physical images can help ensure that the test environment configuration accurately reflects the production environment. In addition, the images contain live information (such as users, user profiles, and file permissions) to use in testing.
- Separate your test environment physically from your production environment. A physically separate test environment enables you to use an identical IP configuration and helps ensure that tests conducted in the test environment do not affect the production environment. Using the identical IP address, subnets, and other network configuration information helps to ensure the fidelity of the test environment. However, duplicating IP addresses might not always be the best option when applications do not rely on a hard-coded IP address. You might also pass some network traffic through the router from the production environment to reduce the need for replicating network services. For example, opening the ports for DHCP to pass through eliminates the need for a separate DHCP server in the test lab.
- Ensure that your test environment is at the same service pack and update level as your production environment. Before performing application mitigation testing, update your lab environment by applying service packs and updates or by refreshing the virtual or physical images of your production counterparts. Consider adding the test environment to the change-management process to simplify tracking the updates.
- Ensure that you perform all your application mitigation tests by using accounts that have similar permissions as the accounts in your production environment. For example,

if your organization does not allow users to run as administrators on their local computers, ensure that similar permissions are granted to users in the test environment. This process ensures that you can determine potential security issues.

Using the Standard User Analyzer

The SUA tool enables you to test your applications and monitor API calls to detect potential compatibility issues resulting from the User Account Control (UAC) feature in Windows 7. UAC requires that all users (including members of the Administrator group) run as standard users until the application is deliberately elevated. However, not all applications can run properly as a standard user because of access violations. For more information about SUA, see the Standard User Analyzer Usage document (SUAnalyzer.rtf) in the \Microsoft Application Compatibility Toolkit 5\Standard User Analyzer folder, where Microsoft Application Compatibility Toolkit 5 is the folder in which you installed the toolkit.

To test an application using SUA, perform the following steps:

1. Click Start, point to All Programs, select Microsoft Application Compatibility Toolkit 5.5, choose Developer And Tester Tools, and then click Standard User Analyzer.
2. In the Target Application box, type the path and file name of the application that you want to test by using the SUA.
3. In the Parameters box, type any command-line options for the application.
4. Click Launch. Exercise each of the application's features and then close the application.
5. Click through each of the SUA tabs, reviewing the detected issues, as shown here.

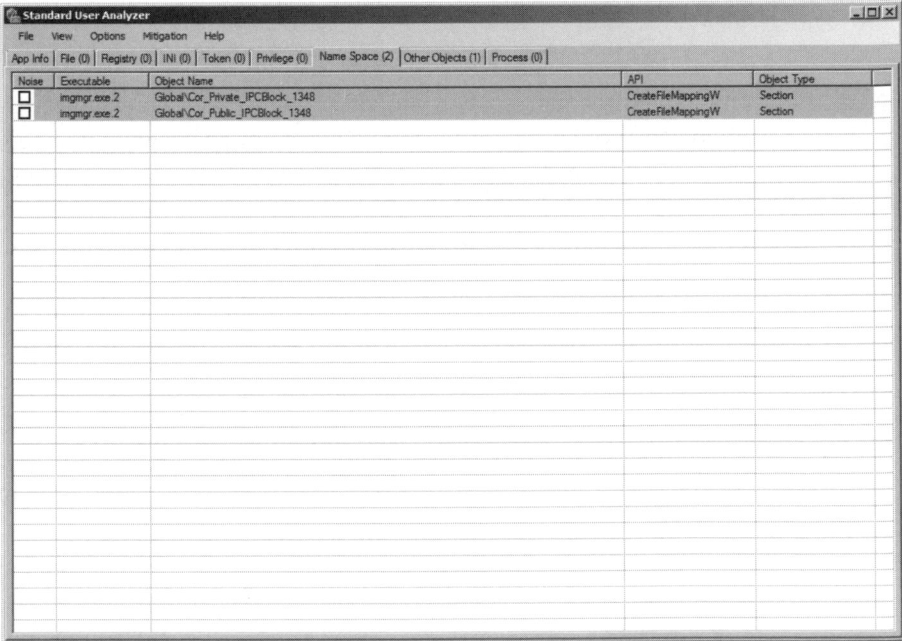

Using the Compatibility Administrator

The Compatibility Administrator tool can help you to resolve many of your compatibility issues by enabling the creation and the installation of application mitigation packages (shims), which can include individual compatibility fixes, compatibility modes, and AppHelp messages. The flowchart in Figure 5-7 illustrates the steps required while using the Compatibility Administrator to create your compatibility fixes, compatibility modes, and AppHelp messages.

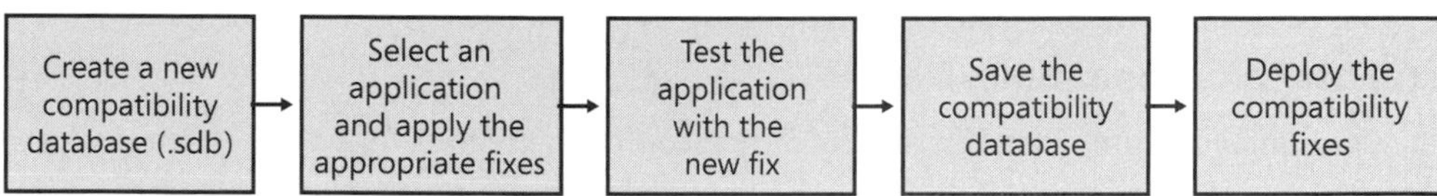

FIGURE 5-7 Using the Compatibility Administrator

The following terminology is used throughout the Compatibility Administrator:

- **Application fix** A small piece of code that intercepts API calls from applications, transforming them so that Windows 7 will provide the same product support for the application as previous versions of the operating system. This can mean anything from disabling a new feature in Windows 7 to emulating a particular behavior of a previous version of the Win32 API set.
- **Compatibility mode** A group of compatibility fixes that work together and are saved and deployed as a single unit.
- **AppHelp message** A blocking or non-blocking message that appears when a user starts an application that you know has major functionality issues with Windows 7.
- **Application mitigation package** The custom database (.sdb) file, which includes any compatibility fixes, compatibility modes, and AppHelp messages that you plan on deploying together as a group.

The Compatibility Administrator is the primary tool that most IT professionals will use when testing and with mitigation application compatibility issues. To start the Compatibility Administrator, click Start, point to All Programs, select Microsoft Application Compatibility Toolkit 5.5, and then choose Compatibility Administrator.

Creating a Custom Compatibility Database

You must apply compatibility fixes, compatibility modes, and AppHelp messages to an application and then store them in a custom database. After creating and applying the fixes, you can deploy the custom databases to your local computers to fix the known issues.

To create a custom database, perform the following steps:

1. On the Compatibility Administrator toolbar, click New.
2. The New Database(*n*) [Untitled_*n*] entry appears under the Custom Databases item in the left pane.

To save a custom database, perform the following steps:

1. On the Compatibility Administrator toolbar, select Save from the File menu.
2. In the Database Name dialog box, type a name for the compatibility database and then click OK.
3. In the Save Database dialog box, type the path and file name of the new compatibility database and then click Save.

Creating a Compatibility Fix

The Compatibility Administrator provides several compatibility fixes found to resolve many common application compatibility issues. You might find that a compatibility fix is not properly associated with an application because it was not found during previous testing by Microsoft or the ISV. If this is the case, you can use the Compatibility Administrator to associate the compatibility fix with the application. Compatibility fixes apply to a single application only. Therefore, you must create multiple fixes if you need to fix the same issue in multiple applications.

To create a new compatibility fix, perform the following steps:

1. In the left pane of the Compatibility Administrator, click the custom database to which you will apply the compatibility fix.
2. From the Database menu, select Create New and then select Application Fix.
3. Type the name of the application to which this compatibility fix applies, type the name of the application vendor, browse to the location of the application file (.exe) on your computer, as shown here, and then click Next.

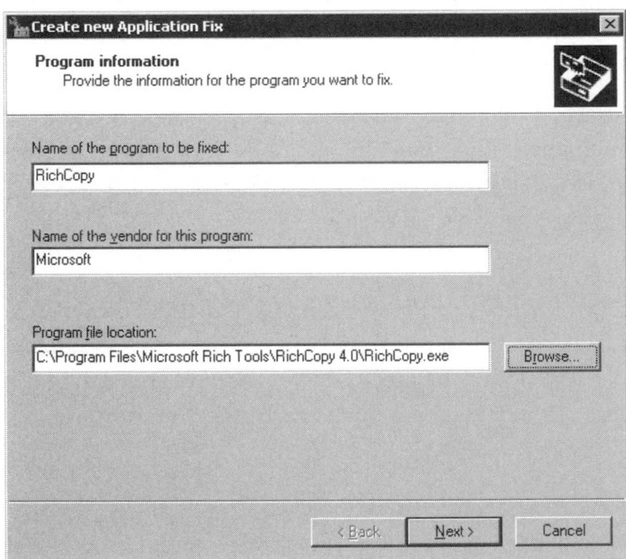

4. Select an operating system to emulate, click any applicable compatibility modes to apply to your compatibility fix, and then click Next. If you know that an application worked properly with a previous operating system version, such as Window XP, you can apply the existing compatibility mode and then test the application to ensure that it works on Windows 7, as shown here.

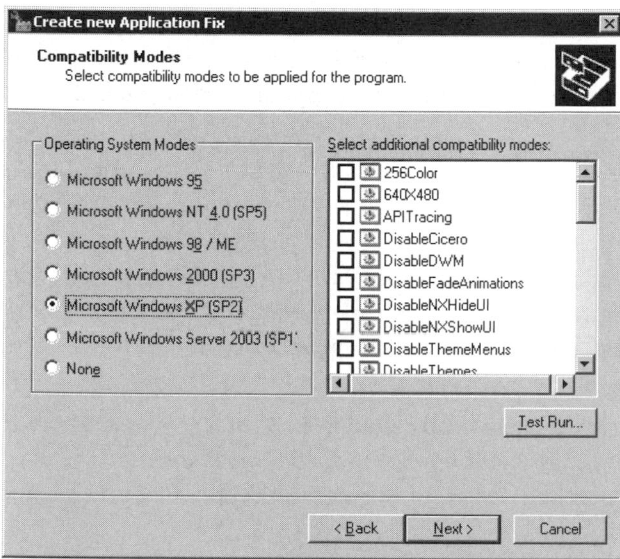

5. Select any additional compatibility fixes to apply to your compatibility fix. Click Test Run to verify that your choices enable the application to work properly. When you are satisfied that the application works, click Next.
6. Click Auto-Generate to automatically select the files that the Compatibility Administrator recommends to represent your application and then click Finish. The Compatibility Administrator adds your compatibility modes, fixes, and matching information to your custom database, and the information appears in the right pane.

Creating a Compatibility Mode

The Compatibility Administrator provides several compatibility modes, which are groups of compatibility fixes found to resolve many common application compatibility issues. You can create custom compatibility modes that contain multiple fixes and then apply these compatibility modes to applications.

To create a compatibility mode, perform the following steps:

1. In the left pane of the Compatibility Administrator, click the custom database to which you will apply the compatibility mode.
2. From the Database menu, select Create New and then select Compatibility Mode.
3. Type the name of your custom compatibility mode in the Name Of The Compatibility Mode text box.

4. Select each of the available compatibility fixes to include in your custom compatibility mode and then click >. If you are unsure which compatibility modes to add, you can click Copy Mode to copy an existing compatibility mode.
5. Click OK after adding all of the applicable compatibility modes.

Creating AppHelp Messages

The Compatibility Administrator enables you to create the following blocking or non-blocking AppHelp messages, which appear when a user starts an application that you know has functionality issues with Windows 7:

- **Blocking AppHelp message (also called a HARDBLOCK)** Prevents the application from starting. Instead, it provides an error message dialog box that explains why the application did not start. In this situation, you can also define a specific URL where the user can download an updated driver or other fix to resolve the issue. When using a blocking AppHelp message, you must also define the file-matching information to identify the problematic version of the application and allow the corrected version to continue.
- **Non-blocking AppHelp message (also called a NOBLOCK)** Allows the application to start but also provides an error message dialog box to the user. The dialog box includes information about security issues, updates to the application, or changes to the location of network resources.

To create an AppHelp message, perform the following steps:

1. In the left pane of the Compatibility Administrator, click the custom database to which you will apply the AppHelp message.
2. On the Database menu, click Create New and then click AppHelp Message.
3. Type the name of the application to which this AppHelp message applies, type the name of the application vendor, browse to the location of the application file (.exe) on your computer, and then click Next.
4. Click Auto-Generate to automatically select the files the Compatibility Administrator recommends to represent your application and then click Next.
5. Select one of the following options for your AppHelp message:
   - Non-blocking Display a message and allow this program to run.
   - Blocking Display a message and do not allow this program to run.
6. Click Next. Type the URL and message text to appear when the user starts the application and then click Finish.

Deploying Application Mitigation Packages

Distribution of the custom compatibility databases (.sdb files) can be facilitated using a variety of methods such as logon scripts, System Center Configuration Manager 2007, injection into disk images, and so on. After the file is on the target system, the actual installation of the custom databases is done using a tool that ships with the operating system called Sdbinst.exe. After the file exists on the target computer, the custom database file must be installed (registered) before the operating system will identify the fixes present when starting the affected applications. (For example, the command line might be *sdbinst* C:\Windows\AppPatch\Myapp.sdb.) After the database file is registered on a computer, the compatibility information will be used any time the application is started. Table 5-4 describes the command-line options for Sdbinst.exe, which has the following syntax:

```
sdbinst [-?] [-q] filename.sdb [-u] [-g {guid}] [-n name]
```

TABLE 5-4 Sdbinst.exe Command-Line Options

OPTION	DESCRIPTION
-?	Displays Help text
-q	Runs quietly with no message boxes
filename.sdb	Specifies the file name of the database to install
-u	Uninstalls the database
-g {guid}	Specifies the globally unique identifier (GUID) of the database to uninstall
-n name	Specifies the name of the database to uninstall

The Sdbinst.exe command can be written into a machine logon script to automatically install the custom database from a share network location when the users log on to their computers. This process could even be accomplished as part of a custom job to be pushed out to the desktops via System Center Configuration Manager 2007 or another third-party management application. One of the best methods of distribution of these custom databases is to include them in your disk image. Installing them as part of the original image before adding the application that needs the fixes ensures that the application will run the first time the user needs it.

Summary

For many companies, issues with application compatibility prevent them from fully taking advantage of the technology that they are already paying for, such as Windows 7. Many of the issues are related to fear, uncertainty, and doubt as to whether the applications in their environment are compatible with Windows 7. You can help overcome these concerns by creating an application inventory and then rationalizing it. In the case of application compatibility, knowledge helps companies overcome challenges.

This chapter described the primary tool that Microsoft provides for gaining this understanding and then putting it to use by creating a rationalized application portfolio as well as testing and mitigating compatibility issues. That tool is the ACT, and it is available as a free download from the Microsoft Download Center.

Additional Resources

These resources contain additional information and tools related to this chapter.

- Chapter 7, "Migrating User State Data," describes how to migrate users' documents and settings as part of a Windows 7 deployment.
- Chapter 8, "Deploying Applications," describes how to deploy applications as part of a Windows 7 deployment.
- "Application Compatibility" in the Windows Client TechCenter on Microsoft TechNet at *http://technet.microsoft.com/en-us/windows/aa905066.aspx.*
- "Microsoft Assessment and Planning (MAP) Toolkit 4.0" at *http://technet.microsoft.com/en-us/solutionaccelerators/dd537566.aspx.*
- "Microsoft Application Compatibility Toolkit (ACT) Version 5.5" at *http://technet.microsoft.com/en-us/library/cc722055.aspx* describes the ACT.
- "Microsoft Application Compatibility Toolkit 5.5" at *http://www.microsoft.com/downloads/details.aspx?FamilyId=24DA89E9-B581-47B0-B45E-492DD6DA2971&displaylang=en* contains the ACT download.
- Chris Jackson's blog at *http://blogs.msdn.com/cjacks/default.aspx.*
- Aaron Margosis's blog at *http://blogs.msdn.com/aaron_margosis/default.aspx.*

CHAPTER 6

Developing Disk Images

Beginning with Windows Vista and continuing with the Windows 7 operating system, the Windows operating system natively supports image-based deployment. In fact, with Windows Vista and later versions, only image-based deployment is supported—even when performing an unattended installation.

Image-based deployment is the most efficient method in high-volume deployment projects. Two factors make image-based deployment superior to other methods: time and cost. Creating a single image that you deploy to each computer is significantly faster than installing the operating system on each computer manually or using unattended installation. Image-based deployment significantly reduces costs by allowing you to better manage the computing environment: You're starting each computer with a known, standardized configuration. It also reduces deployment errors and support costs by using a standardized, stable, and repeatable process to develop and deploy operating systems.

Although the process of building and deploying images is not new, features first introduced with Windows Vista specifically address the challenges of the process. First, servicing images (adding device drivers, security updates, and so on) is easier because you don't have to rebuild and recapture an image every time you need to service it. Second, you can build hardware- and language-independent images that are not dependent on the Hardware Abstraction Layer (HAL), which means you can build and maintain fewer images (and ideally, only one).

The Windows Automated Installation Kit (Windows AIK) 2.0 provides essential tools for building, servicing, and deploying Windows images. These tools include the Windows System Image Manager (Windows SIM) for creating Extensible Markup Language (XML) answer files for unattended installation; the Windows Preinstallation Environment (Windows PE) 3.0 for starting bare-metal destination computers; the new Deployment Image Servicing and Management (DISM) command-line tool for servicing images by adding drivers and packages; and the ImageX command-line tool for capturing images. The Windows AIK also includes extensive documentation about using these tools. You can download the Windows AIK 2.0, including the *Windows Automated Installation Kit User's Guide* and other documentation, from *http://www.microsoft.com/downloads*.

Although the Windows AIK 2.0 provides essential imaging tools, the Microsoft Deployment Toolkit (MDT) 2010 is a complete deployment framework that provides end-to-end guidance for planning, building, and deploying Windows 7 images. MDT 2010 takes full advantage of the Windows AIK 2.0 as well as other tools, such as the User State Migration Tool (USMT) 4.0 (which is now included in the Windows AIK 2.0), the Application Compatibility Toolkit (ACT) 5.5, Microsoft System Center Configuration Manager 2007 Service Pack 2 (SP2), and so on. Microsoft recommends that you use MDT 2010 to develop and deploy Windows 7 images, so this chapter focuses primarily on MDT 2010. For readers who prefer to use the Windows AIK directly, the *Windows Automated Installation Kit User's Guide* provides complete information about using the Windows AIK tools.

Getting Started

A typical difficulty with deployment efforts is the number of images that you must manage. In heterogeneous environments with diverse requirements, many organizations build numerous images. Adding new hardware, language packs, security updates, and drivers usually requires re-creating each disk image. Updating multiple images with a critical security update and testing each of them requires a lot of effort from you. Therefore, a major Microsoft design goal, beginning with Windows Vista and continuing in Windows 7, is to significantly reduce the number of images you must maintain and help you maintain those images more easily.

A key way that Windows 7 helps you reduce the number of images that you must build and maintain is by reducing dependencies on features that typically differ from one image to the next. These include languages, HALs, and device drivers. For example, unlike Windows XP and earlier versions of Windows, Windows Vista and later images are no longer tied to a HAL type. (Windows Vista and later versions support only Advanced Configuration and Power Interface (ACPI)–based computers.) The operating system can redetect the HAL when you apply it to each destination computer. Windows Vista and later versions are also language neutral, which means that all languages are operating system features, and adding or removing language packages is very easy. In addition to reducing dependencies, Microsoft modularized

Windows Vista and later versions to make customization and deployment easier, based the installation of Windows Vista and later versions on the file-based disk imaging format called Windows Imaging (WIM), and made other significant deployment features to the core operating system. (For more information, see Chapter 3, "Deployment Platform.")

MDT 2010 is a framework for these tools and features. Rather than using each tool and feature individually and using scripts to cobble them together, this chapter recommends that you develop and deploy Windows 7 images by using MDT 2010. To learn how to install MDT 2010, see Chapter 4, "Planning Deployment."

Prerequisite Skills

To build Windows 7 images—with or without MDT 2010—you should be familiar with the following tools and concepts:

- Unattended setup answer files (Unattend.xml)
- Windows AIK 2.0, including the following tools:
  - Windows SIM
  - DISM
  - ImageX
- Hardware device drivers and hardware-specific applications
- Microsoft Visual Basic Scripting Edition (VBScript)
- Disk imaging technologies and concepts, including Sysprep
- Windows PE 3.0

Lab Requirements

While developing and testing Windows 7 images, you will copy large volumes of files between the build server and destination computers. Because of these high-volume data transfers, you should establish a lab that is physically separate from the production network. Configure the development lab to represent the production environment as much as possible.

Lab Hardware

Ensure that the following hardware is available in the lab environment:

- **Network switches and cabling** 100 megabits per second (Mbps) or faster is recommended to accommodate the high volumes of data.
- **Keyboard Video Mouse (KVM) switches** It's useful to have the client computers connected to a KVM switch to minimize the floor space required to host the computers.
- **CD and DVD burner** A system should be available in the lab for creating CD-ROMs or DVD-ROMs.

- **Client computers** In the lab, duplicate any unique type of computer configuration found in the production environment to allow for testing each hardware configuration.
- **Build server** This computer (running Windows XP SP2, Windows Server 2003 SP1, or a newer version of Windows) can be a client- or server-class computer. The computer should have at least 50 gigabytes (GB) of disk space and backup equipment, such as a tape drive or a storage area network (SAN). Using Windows Server 2008 R2 is recommended because it already includes the MDT 2010 prerequisites.

Network Services

Make sure that the following network services are available in the lab environment:

- **A Windows domain for the computers to join and to host user accounts** This domain could be a Microsoft Windows 2000, Windows Server 2003, or Windows Server 2008 domain.
- **Dynamic Host Configuration Protocol (DHCP) services** DHCP provides Transmission Control Protocol/Internet Protocol (TCP/IP) addresses to client computers.
- **Domain Name System (DNS) services** DNS provides TCP/IP host name resolution to client and server computers.
- **Windows Internet Naming Service (WINS)** WINS provides NetBIOS name resolution to client and server computers. This service is optional but recommended.
- **Windows Deployment Services** Windows Deployment Services delivers Windows PE to computers that do not yet have an operating system. Windows Deployment Services servers require a Windows Server 2003 or later domain. For more information about Windows Deployment Services, see Chapter 10, "Configuring Windows Deployment Services."
- **Internet access** The lab (or a portion of the lab) should have access to the Internet for downloading software updates.

> ***IMPORTANT*** **Windows protects users against malicious programs by warning them when they try to run a program that they have downloaded from the Internet. Users must acknowledge the warning to continue. This warning, however, prevents MDT 2010 from installing applications automatically during the build process. After verifying that the file is safe, disable the warning by right-clicking the file, clicking Properties, and then clicking Unblock. Windows does not display this warning when files are downloaded from sites listed in the Trusted Sites security zone, and Windows Server 2003 SP1 or later versions do not allow program downloads from untrusted sites.**

Installation Media

The installation media required for your environment include the following:

- Windows media (x86 and x64 editions) and product keys. Windows Vista is available on the volume-licensed media. MDT 2010 also supports retail media.

> **NOTE** Earlier versions of Windows, such as Windows XP, supported slipstreaming. This process allowed you to integrate a service pack into the operating system source files. For example, you can integrate SP1 with the original release of Windows XP to create Windows XP SP1 media. Microsoft does not support slipstreaming service packs into Windows Vista or later versions. Instead, you can download fully integrated media from the volume licensing Web site, TechNet, or MSDN.

- Any additional application media you plan to include in the images, such as the 2007 Microsoft Office system. The 2007 Office system is available on volume-licensed media; MDT 2010 also supports retail media.
- Any hardware-specific software, such as device drivers, CD-ROM burner software, and DVD-viewing software. Downloading all the known device drivers and hardware-specific applications early in the process saves time when developing and building Windows images.

Capturing Images Using Microsoft Deployment Toolkit

Capturing images using MDT 2010 is essentially a Lite Touch Installation (LTI) process, which ends by capturing a customized image of a master or *reference computer* that contains applications, language packs, and various other customizations needed. The following list of steps outlines the overall process for using MDT 2010 to create and capture operating system images as illustrated in Figure 6-1:

- **Create and configure a deployment share** Create a deployment share and then configure the share by adding operating system source files, applications, out-of-box device drivers, and packages to it as needed. The section titled "Creating and Configuring a Deployment Share" later in this chapter describes this step in detail.
- **Create and configure a task sequence** Create a task sequence that associates an operating system with an unattended setup answer file (Unattend.xml) to define a sequence of tasks to run during installation. The section titled "Creating Task Sequences" later in this chapter describes this step in detail.
- **Configure and update the deployment share** Configure and update the deployment share to update the MDT 2010 configuration files and generate a customized version of Windows PE you can use to boot your reference computer. The section titled "Updating the Deployment Share" later in this chapter describes this step in detail.

- **Run the Windows Deployment Wizard on the reference computer** Start your reference computer using the Windows PE image generated when you update your deployment share. Then run the Windows Deployment Wizard on the reference computer to install Windows from your deployment share. During the phase when gathering information, the Windows Deployment Wizard will prompt you to specify whether you want to capture a custom image of the reference computer that you can later deploy to target computers. The section titled "Capturing a Disk Image for LTI" later in this chapter describes this step in detail.
- **Add the custom image as an operating system source** After capturing the custom image of your reference computer, you add it to the deployment share as an operating system source. You can then deploy your custom image by using LTI as described in Chapter 12, "Deploying with Microsoft Deployment Toolkit."

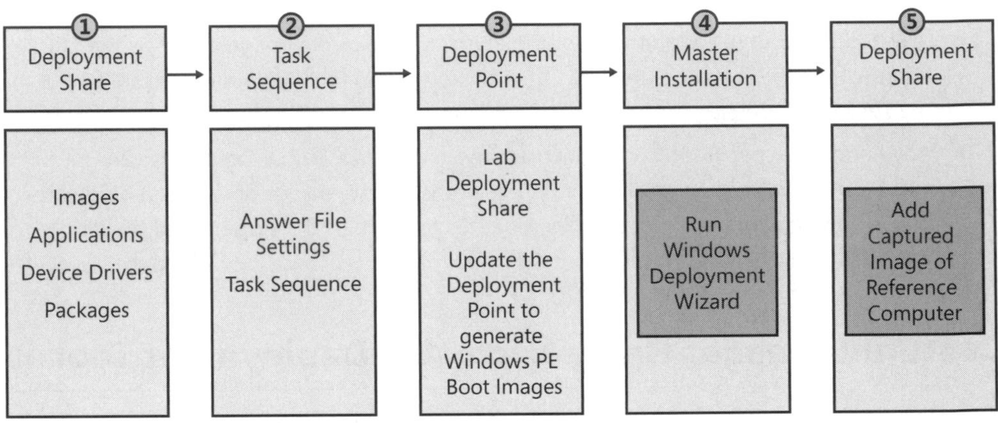

FIGURE 6-1 Image engineering with MDT

Creating and Configuring a Deployment Share

Before you can use MDT 2010 to deploy Windows 7, you must create a deployment share. A *deployment share* is a repository for the operating system images, language packs, applications, device drivers, and other software that will be deployed to your target computers. Deployment shares are new in MDT 2010 and consolidate two separate features found in MDT 2008:

- **Distribution share** Contains operating system source files, application source files, packages, and out-of-box drivers.
- **Deployment point** Contains files needed to connect to the distribution share and install a build from it.

By consolidating these two separate features into a single feature (the deployment share), MDT 2010 simplifies the deployment process. In addition, a deployment share does not have to be located on a specific computer—it can be stored on a local disk volume, a shared folder on the network, or anywhere in a stand-alone Distributed File System (DFS) namespace. (Windows PE cannot access domain-based DFS namespaces.)

> ***NOTE*** **See the Microsoft Deployment Toolkit 2010 Documentation Library for information on how to upgrade to MDT 2010 from previous versions of MDT or Business Desktop Deployment (BDD). After you upgrade to MDT 2010, you must also upgrade any deployment points created using the previous version of MDT or BDD.**

To create a new deployment share, perform the following steps:

1. In the Deployment Workbench console tree, right-click Deployment Shares and then click New Deployment Share.
2. On the Path page, specify the path to the folder for your deployment share. The default path is *<drive>\DeploymentShare,* where *<drive>* is the volume with the most available space. For best performance, you should specify a path to a separate physical disk that has sufficient free space to hold the operating system source files, application source files, packages, and out-of-box drivers you use for your deployments.
3. On the Share page, specify the share name for the deployment share. By default, this will be a hidden share named DeploymentShare$.
4. On the Descriptive Name page, specify a descriptive name for the deployment share. By default, this will be MDT Deployment Share.
5. On the Allow Image Capture page, leave the Ask If An Image Should Be Captured option selected so you will be able to capture an image of your reference computer.
6. On the Allow Admin Password page, choose whether the user will be prompted to set the local Administrator password during installation.
7. On the Allow Product Key page, choose whether the user will be prompted to enter a product key during installation.
8. Finish the remaining steps of the wizard.

Once your deployment share has been created, you can view the hierarchy of folders under it in the Deployment Workbench (Figure 6-2).

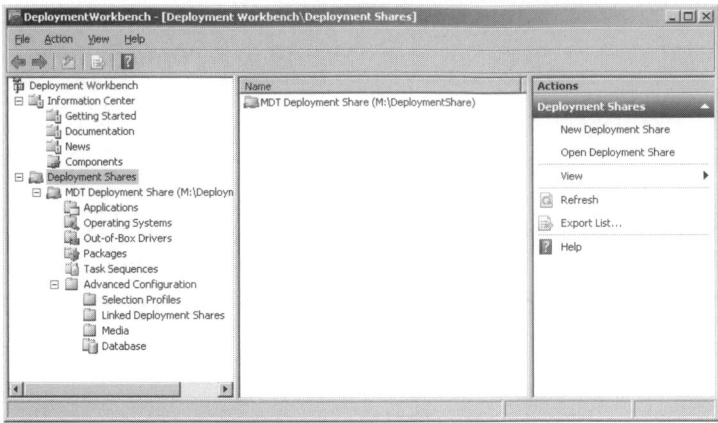

FIGURE 6-2 The folder structure of a deployment share in the Deployment Workbench

> ***NOTE*** **The default view in Deployment Workbench includes the action pane. The action pane often gets in the way of viewing the entire details pane. You can remove the action pane by authoring the management console. To author the console, run C:\Program Files \Microsoft Deployment Toolkit\Bin\DeploymentWorkbench.msc /a. Click View, click Customize, clear the Action Pane check box, and then click OK. Save your changes by clicking File and then clicking Save on the main menu. When prompted whether you want to display a single window interface, click Yes.**

After creating a deployment share, you can configure it in the following ways (at minimum, you must add the Windows 7 source files to deploy Windows 7):

- Add, remove, and configure operating systems.
- Add, remove, and configure applications.
- Add, remove, and configure operating system packages, including updates and language packs.
- Add, remove, and configure out-of-box device drivers.

When you add operating systems, applications, operating system packages, and out-of-box device drivers to a deployment share, Deployment Workbench stores the source files in the deployment share folder specified when you create the deployment share (see Figure 6-3). You will associate these source files and other files with task sequences later in the development process.

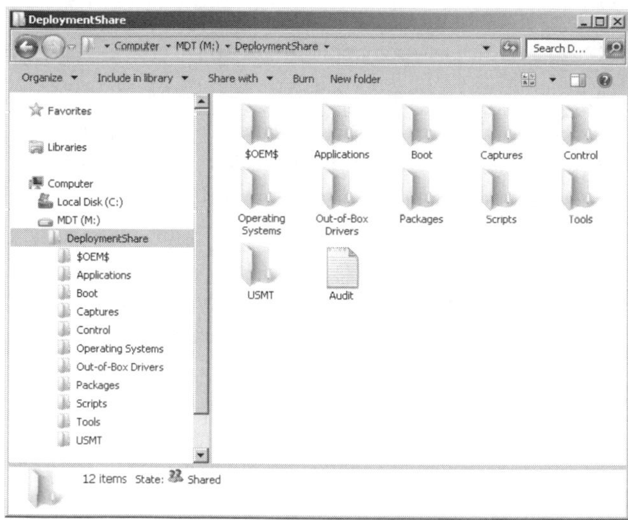

FIGURE 6-3 The folder structure of a deployment share in the file system

In the distribution share's Control folder, Deployment Workbench stores metadata about operating systems, applications, operating system packages, and out-of-box device drivers in the following files:

- **Applications.xml** Contains metadata about applications in the distribution share
- **Drivers.xml** Contains metadata about device drivers in the distribution share
- **OperatingSystems.xml** Contains metadata about operating systems in the distribution share
- **Packages.xml** Contains metadata about operating system packages in the distribution share

Adding Operating Systems

Windows 7 editions are in a single image file, Install.wim, which is in the \Sources folder on the distribution media. For more information about the Windows 7 distribution media and Install.wim, see the Windows AIK 2.0 documentation. To build images based on Windows 7, you must add the Windows 7 media to the MDT 2010 deployment share. Deployment shares must contain at a minimum the Windows 7 source files.

As well as adding Windows 7 media to the deployment share, you can add Windows 7 images that already exist in Windows Deployment Services. MDT 2010 will not copy these files to the deployment share. Instead, MDT 2010 uses the files from their original location during deployment. There is a requirement for doing this.

To add Windows 7 to a deployment share, perform the following steps:

1. In the Deployment Workbench console tree, right-click the Operating Systems folder (or a subfolder you created under this folder) in your deployment share and select Import Operating System to start the Import Operating System Wizard.
2. On the OS Type page, shown here, select Full Set Of Source Files. This option copies the entire set of operating system source files from the distribution media or folder containing the distribution media. Optionally, you can add operating system images from a specific Windows Deployment Services server by selecting Windows Deployment Services Images. You can also click Custom Image File to add a custom image, created by using the Windows Deployment Wizard. For more information about creating a custom image, see the section titled "Capturing a Disk Image for LTI" later in this chapter.

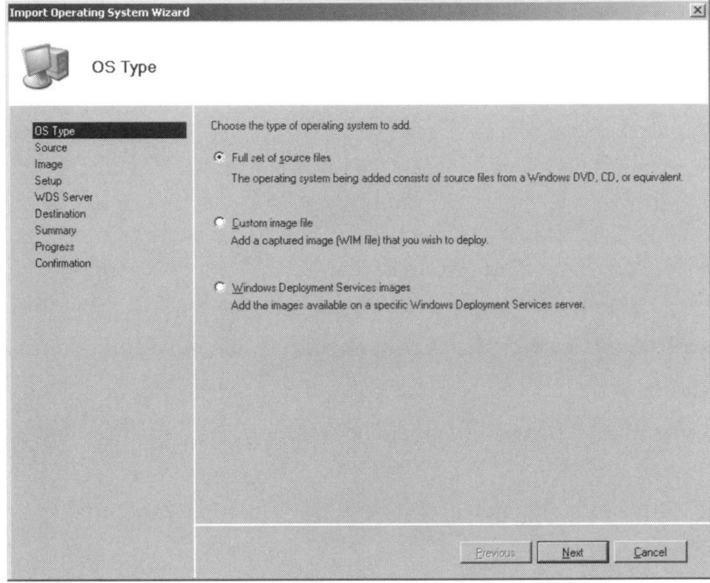

3. On the Source page, type the path containing the operating system source files you're adding to the deployment share, or click Browse to select the path. If you stage (pre-copy the source files to the local computer) the operating system files on the same partition as the deployment share, you can select Move The Files To The Deployment Share Instead Of Copying Them to speed the process.
4. On the Destination page, type the name of the operating system folder to create in the deployment share. You can accept the default name, which Deployment Workbench derives from the source files, or use a name that describes the operating system version and edition. For example, you can use Windows 7 Enterprise and Windows 7 Professional to distinguish between the different operating system editions of Windows 7. Deployment Workbench uses the default name to create a folder for the operating system in the deployment share's Operating Systems folder.
5. Finish the wizard.

The copy process can take several minutes to complete; the move process is much faster. After you add an operating system to the deployment share, it appears in the details pane when Operating Systems is selected in the console tree. Also, the operating system appears in the deployment share in Operating Systems*subfolder[\subfolder]* (shown in Figure 6-4), where *subfolder[\subfolder]* is the destination specified when adding the operating system.

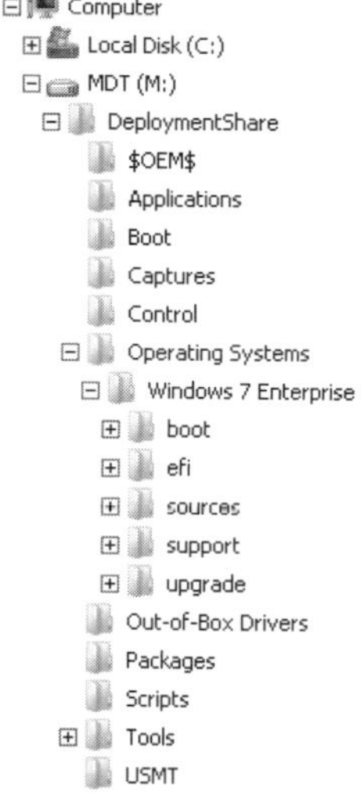

FIGURE 6-4 Operating Systems in the deployment share

To remove Windows 7 from the deployment share, perform the following steps:

1. In the Deployment Workbench console tree, click Operating Systems.
2. In the details pane, right-click the operating system you want to remove and then click Delete.

> ***NOTE*** **When an operating system is deleted from Deployment Workbench, Deployment Workbench also removes it from the Operating Systems folder in the deployment share. In other words, removing an operating system from Deployment Workbench also removes it from the file system.**

Adding Applications

You must add each application to the deployment share that you intend to deploy by using MDT 2010. Deployment Workbench gives you the option to copy the application source files directly into the deployment share or to just add a reference to the application source files to the deployment share and leave them in their original location. Generally, if the network location containing the application source files will not be available during deployment, you should copy the application source files to the deployment share.

In addition to specifying how to add application source files to the deployment share, you can specify the command line for installing the application, dependencies between applications, and other settings for each application. After adding an application to the deployment share, you can install it at one of two points in the process:

- **During the Windows Deployment Wizard** During the interview, the Windows Deployment Wizard prompts the user with a list of applications that are available for installation. The user can then choose which applications to install. You can configure the applications that the Windows Deployment Wizard installs by using the MDT 2010 database and then skip the application installation pages of the wizard—automating application installation without requiring user intervention. For more information about using the MDT 2010 database, see Chapter 12.
- **During the task sequence** Application installations added to the task sequence—the sequence of tasks that occur during installation to prepare, install, and configure the build on the destination computer—occur when the Windows Deployment Wizard executes the task sequence on the destination computer. This is fully automated.

Chapter 8, "Deploying Applications," describes how to plan for and develop automated application installation. Chapter 8 describes differences between core applications, which are common to every desktop in the organization, and supplemental applications, which are not. You deploy each type of application differently depending on the strategy you choose for application deployment. The strategies are as follows:

- **Thick image** You install applications to the build that you're using to create disk images. You can install applications by using the Windows Deployment Wizard or by adding applications to the task sequence.
- **Thin image** Application deployment usually occurs outside of operating system deployment, typically using a systems management infrastructure such as System Center Configuration Manager 2007 SP2.
- **Hybrid image** You install applications to the build you're deploying to destination computers (most likely a custom image) and possibly install additional applications using a systems management infrastructure. You can install the applications by using the Windows Deployment Wizard or by adding them to the task sequence.

WARNING **Do not allow an application to restart the computer. The Windows Deployment Wizard must control reboots or the task sequence will fail. See the section titled "Installation Reboots" later in this chapter for more information about configuring reboots.**

To add an application to the deployment share, perform the following steps:

1. In the Deployment Workbench console tree, right-click the Applications folder (or a subfolder you created under this folder) in your deployment share and select New Application to start the New Application Wizard.

2. On the Application Type page, do one of the following:
   - Select Application With Source Files to copy the application source files to the deployment share. During deployment, the Windows Deployment Wizard installs the application from the deployment share.
   - Select Application Without Source Files Or Elsewhere On The Network. Choosing this option does not copy the application source files to the deployment share. During deployment, the Windows Deployment Wizard installs the application from another location on the network. You also choose this option to run a command that requires no application source files.
   - Select Application Bundle. Choosing this option does not add an application to the deployment share. Instead, it creates a placeholder to which you can associate dependencies. Then, by installing the placeholder application (the bundle), you also install its dependencies.
3. On the Details page, shown here, provide the information described in Table 6-1.

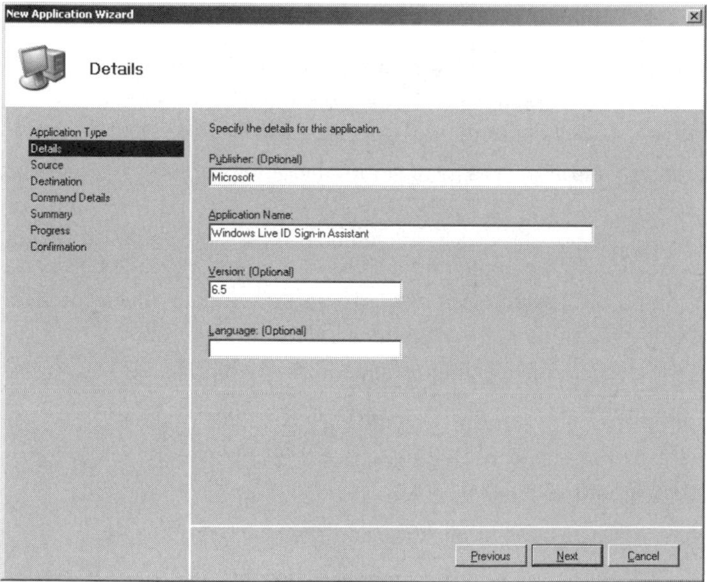

TABLE 6-1 The Specify The Details For This Application Page

IN THIS LOCATION	PROVIDE THIS INFORMATION
Publisher box	Name of the application's publisher
Application Name box	Name of the application
Version box	Version label for the application
Languages box	Languages that the application supports

4. On the Source page, type the path of the folder containing the application to be added or click Browse to open it. If you choose to copy the application source files to the deployment share, Deployment Workbench copies everything in this folder to the deployment share; otherwise, it adds this path to the application's metadata as the application's installation path. If the application source files are staged on the local hard disk, you can select Move The Files To The Distribution Share Instead Of Copying Them to move them quickly to the deployment share instead of copying them.
5. On the Destination page, type the name of the folder to create for the application within the deployment share's Applications folder. The default value is the publisher, application name, and version label concatenated.

> ***WARNING*** **Make sure that the destination specified on the Specify The Destination page is unique. Otherwise, during an LTI deployment, the Windows Deployment Wizard will display multiple applications having the same name but installing different applications. If necessary, change the name on the Destination page to ensure that it is unique.**

6. On the Command Details page, type the command to use to install the application silently. For example, type **msiexec /qb /i *app_name*.msi**. The command is relative to the working directory specified in the Working Directory box. For help finding the appropriate command to automate the installation of various applications, see Chapter 8.
7. Finish the wizard.

After you add an application to the deployment share, it appears in the details pane when the Applications folder (or in a subfolder of this folder) is selected in the console tree. It also appears in the deployment share in Applications*subfolder[\subfolder]*, where *subfolder[\subfolder]* is the destination specified when adding the application.

To edit an application in the deployment share, perform the following steps:

1. In the Deployment Workbench console tree, select the Applications folder (or a subfolder) in deployment share.
2. In the details pane, right-click the application and then click Properties.
3. On the General and Details tabs, edit the application information.

To provide an uninstall registry key name, perform the following steps:

1. In the Deployment Workbench console tree, select the Applications folder (or a subfolder) in your deployment share.
2. In the details pane, right-click the application and then click Properties.
3. On the Details tab, type the uninstall registry key name in the Uninstall Registry Key Name box.

The Windows Deployment Wizard uses the uninstall registry key name to determine whether an application is already installed on the destination computer. This is a subkey of

HKLM\Software\Microsoft\Windows\CurrentVersion\Uninstall. If the Windows Deployment Wizard detects the presence of this key, it assumes that the application is already installed and skips the installation of that application and any dependencies. In the Uninstall Registry Key Name box, type the name of the subkey—not the entire path.

To disable an application, perform the following steps:

1. In the Deployment Workbench console tree, select the Applications folder (or a subfolder) in your deployment share.
2. In the details pane, right-click the application you want to disable and then click Properties.
3. Click the General tab and clear the Enable This Application check box.

If you add an application that you intend to install during the task sequence, disable the application by clearing the Enable This Application check box. The application will still install during the task sequence, but the user will not see it in the applications list.

To remove an application from the deployment share, perform the following steps:

1. In the Deployment Workbench console tree, select the Applications folder (or a subfolder) in your deployment share.
2. In the details pane, right-click the application you want to remove and then click Delete.

When you delete an application from Deployment Workbench, it is also removed from the Applications folder in the deployment share. In other words, removing an application from Deployment Workbench also removes it from the file system.

Specifying Application Dependencies

Using Deployment Workbench, you can specify dependencies between applications. For example, if application A is dependent on application B, Deployment Workbench will ensure that application B is installed before installing application A.

To create a dependency between two applications, perform the following steps:

1. In the Deployment Workbench console tree, select the Applications folder (or a subfolder) in your deployment share.
2. In the details pane, right-click the application that has a dependency and then click Properties.
3. Click the Dependencies tab, as shown here, perform any of the following actions, and then click OK:
   - To add an application to the dependencies list, click Add, and then select an application. Deployment Workbench displays only those applications that have already been added to the deployment share.
   - To remove an application from the dependencies list, select an application from the list, and then click Remove.

- To reorder the applications in the dependencies list, select an application in the list and then click Up or Down. The Windows Deployment Wizard installs the dependent applications in the order specified in the dependencies list.

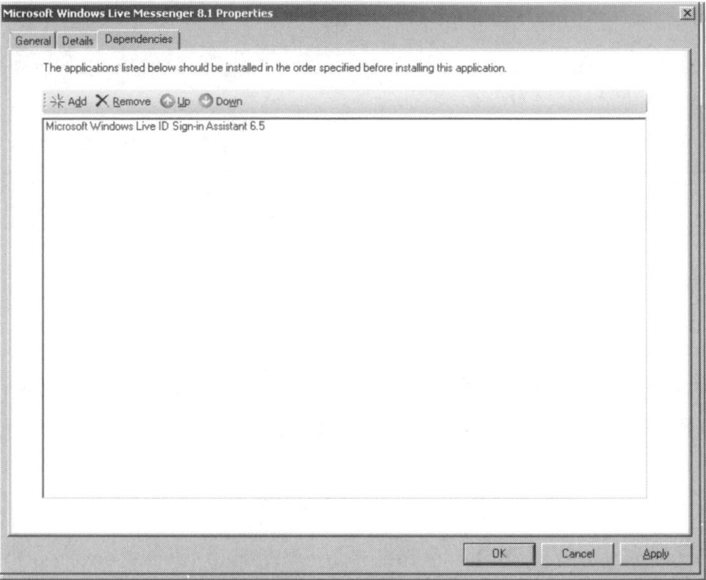

Installation Reboots

Do not allow an application to restart the computer. The Windows Deployment Wizard must control reboots, or the task sequence will fail. For example, you can use REBOOT=REALLYSUPPRESS to prevent some Windows Installer–based applications from restarting. You can cause the Windows Deployment Wizard to restart the computer after installing an application by selecting the Reboot The Computer After Installing This Application check box on the Details tab of the *app_name* Properties, where *app_name* is the name of the application.

To restart the computer after installing an application, perform the following steps:

1. In the Deployment Workbench console tree, select the Applications folder (or a subfolder) in your deployment share.
2. In the details pane, right-click the application for which the Windows Deployment Wizard must restart the computer after installation and then click Properties.
3. Click the Details tab and select the Reboot The Computer After Installing This Application check box. Selecting this check box causes the Windows Deployment Wizard to restart the computer after installing the application and then continue with the next step in the task sequence.

DIRECT FROM THE SOURCE

Reboots in MDT 2010

Michael Niehaus, Lead Developer for Microsoft Deployment Toolkit
Solution Accelerator Team

When a user first logs on to the computer, he can run commands in different ways. One way is to add *RunSynchronous* to the <Microsoft-Windows-Setup> child element *FirstLogonCommands* during the oobeSystem pass.

MDT 2010 doesn't use *RunSynchronous* because it needs to support more complex installation scenarios. For example, an MDT 2010 installation needs to support reboots between application installations, and *RunSynchronous* doesn't support reboot-and-pick-up-where-it-left-off. Instead, MDT 2010 adds a command to *RunSynchronous* to initially start the task sequence. Then, if the task sequence needs to restart the computer, it adds a shortcut to the StartUp group, which continues the task sequence after the computer restarts.

Adding Packages

Packages include operating system updates and language packs. The Windows Deployment Wizard can automatically install operating system updates during deployment. Users can also choose which language packs to install during LTI deployment. The following sections include more information about updates and languages.

To add a package to the deployment share, perform the following steps:

1. In Deployment Workbench, right-click the Packages folder (or a subfolder you created under this folder) in your deployment share and select Import OS Packages to start the Import Package Wizard.
2. On the Specify Directory page, type the path containing the package files you want to add to the deployment share, or click Browse to open it, and then click Finish. Deployment Workbench adds all the packages it finds in the folder and all its subfolders.
3. Finish the wizard. Deployment Workbench adds all the packages it finds in the folder and its subfolders.

After you add a package to the deployment share, it appears in the details pane when the Packages folder (or a subfolder of this folder) is selected in the console tree. It also appears in the deployment share in Packages*subfolder[\subfolder]*, where *subfolder[\subfolder]* is the destination specified when adding the package.

To disable a package and prevent its installation, perform the following steps:

1. In the Deployment Workbench console tree, select the Packages folder (or a subfolder) in your deployment share.
2. In the details pane, right-click the package you want to disable and then click Properties.
3. Click the General tab and clear the Enable (Approve) This Package check box to disable the package.

To remove a package from the deployment share, perform the following steps:

1. In the Deployment Workbench console tree, select the Packages folder (or a subfolder) in your deployment share.
2. In the details pane, right-click the package you want to remove and then click Delete.

When a package is deleted from Deployment Workbench, it is also removed from the Packages folder in the deployment share. In other words, removing a package from Deployment Workbench also removes it from the file system.

Adding Updates

Operating system updates are distributed as Microsoft Standalone Update (.msu) files. For more information about .msu files, see Chapter 23, "Managing Software Updates."

When you are developing an image, take care to ensure that all critical security updates are included in the image so that computers deployed with the image are as up to date as possible. Table 6-2 describes different approaches to performing these updates. (When you use MDT 2010, the first method is recommended.)

TABLE 6-2 Updating Windows 7 Images

METHOD	BENEFITS	DRAWBACKS
Download the security updates from the Microsoft Web site and then install them as part of the image build process. You can search for updates in the Knowledge Base and on the Download Center.	The process is very easy to perform; you can install updates simply by adding them to the deployment share.	The process can be time consuming.
Use Windows Server Update Services (WSUS) or System Center Configuration Manager 2007 SP2 to install the security update post-deployment.	The process is easy to perform and picks up new updates as soon as they are approved.	The image is vulnerable before the updates are installed and the computer is restarted, providing an opportunity for exploitation; the application process can also be time consuming.

METHOD	BENEFITS	DRAWBACKS
		Depending on the System Center Configuration Manager 2007 SP2 server configuration, it may take an hour or more before all updates are applied; having the System Center Configuration Manager 2007 SP2 client included in the image and communicating with a specific site may result in all computers built from the image communicating with only that site.
Download the security updates from the Microsoft Web site and then integrate them into the Windows installation source before beginning the unattended build process.	The image is protected at all times from known security exploits, and the image build process completes faster because all security updates are installed before building the image.	Integrating the security updates takes some effort. It may not be obvious which updates you can integrate; you will need to install some as part of the unattended build process.

NOTE **Download the required Windows security updates from the Microsoft Knowledge Base or Download Center. You can also download updates from the Microsoft Update Catalog at** ***http://catalog.update.microsoft.com/v7/site/*****.**

Adding Language Packs

Language packs make possible a multilingual Windows environment. Windows 7 is language neutral; all language and locale resources are added to Windows 7 through language packs (Lp.cab files). By adding one or more language packs to Windows 7, you can enable those languages when installing the operating system. As a result, you can deploy the same Windows 7 image to regions with different language and locale settings, reducing development and deployment time.

The following resources provide additional information about language packs in Windows Vista:

- Chapter 12 includes instructions on installing language packs during deployment.

- The *Microsoft Deployment Toolkit Reference* in the MDT 2010 documentation lists the properties that you can configure to install language packs automatically.
- The topic, "Understanding Multilingual Deployments," in the *Windows Automated Installation Kit User's Guide for Windows 7* includes more information about Windows Vista language packs.

Adding Out-of-Box Drivers

Depending on the type of computer in the environment and the hardware it contains, you require software from the hardware vendors to make computers in the production environment fully functional. Some of this software may be provided on a CD-ROM or DVD-ROM by the hardware manufacturer; other software must be downloaded from the vendor's Web site.

Deployment Workbench makes adding device drivers to the deployment share an easy process. You simply specify a folder containing one or more device drivers, and Deployment Workbench copies them to the deployment share and organizes them into folders as appropriate. However, you must make sure that you've extracted device drivers from any compressed files containing them. In other words, Deployment Workbench looks for each device driver's .inf file and any related files.

In MDT 2008 you could create driver groups to group together device drivers. You could then associate a driver group with a task sequence. In MDT 2010, you can no longer create driver groups. Instead, you can now create subfolders under the Out-Of-Box Drivers folder in your distribution share. You can import different drivers into different subfolders and then associate each subfolder with a task sequence.

NOTE Windows Deployment Services in Windows Server 2008 R2 also includes new features that make it simpler to ensure that the appropriate drivers are available during a deployment. You can add driver packages to a Windows Deployment Services server and deploy these driver packages to different client computers based on filtering criteria. You can also add boot-critical driver packages to boot images (supported for Windows 7 and Windows Server 2008 R2 images only). For more information on this topic, see Chapter 10.

To add device drivers to the deployment share, perform the following steps:

1. In Deployment Workbench, right-click the Out-Of-Box Drivers folder (or a subfolder you created under this folder) in your deployment share and select Import Drivers to start the Import Driver Wizard.
2. On the Specify Directory page, type the path containing the device drivers you want to add to the deployment share or click Browse to open it.
3. If you want, select the Import Drivers Even If They Are Duplicates Of An Existing Driver check box. Choosing this option allows Deployment Workbench to import duplicate drivers, if they exist, but Microsoft recommends against this.

4. Finish the wizard. Deployment Workbench adds all the device drivers it finds in the folder and its subfolders.

After you add a device driver to the deployment share, it appears in the details pane when the Out-Of-Box Drivers folder (or a subfolder of this folder) is selected in the console tree. It also appears in the deployment share in Out-Of-Box Drivers*subfolder[\subfolder]*, where *subfolder[\subfolder]* is the destination specified when adding the driver.

To disable a device driver, perform the following steps:

1. In the Deployment Workbench console tree, click Out-Of-Box Drivers (or a subfolder) in your deployment share.
2. In the details pane, right-click the device driver you want to disable and then click Properties.
3. Click the General tab, clear the Enable This Driver check box, and then click OK.

To remove a device driver from the deployment share, perform the following steps:

1. In the Deployment Workbench console tree, click Out-Of-Box Drivers (or a subfolder) in your deployment share.
2. In the details pane, right-click the device driver you want to remove and then click Delete.

When a device driver is deleted from Deployment Workbench, it is also removed from the Out-Of-Box Drivers folder in the deployment share. In other words, removing a device driver from Deployment Workbench also removes it from the file system.

Creating Task Sequences

A task sequence binds operating system source files with the steps necessary to install them. A task sequence is associated with the following:

- **Operating system** Choose an operating system image to use for the build.
- **Unattended setup answer file (Unattend.xml)** Create an answer file that describes how to install and configure the operating system on the destination computer. For example, the answer file can contain a product key, organization name, and information necessary to join the computer to a domain. Generally, allow MDT 2010 to control the settings in Unattend.xml and use the MDT 2010 database to configure destination computers.

> ***NOTE*** **This chapter assumes that you are configuring task sequences and deployment points for the purpose of capturing custom images. The settings you configure by using the instructions in this chapter are different than the settings you will configure when deploying images to production computers. For more information about those settings, see Chapter 12.**

To create a task sequence for image capture, perform the following steps:

1. In the Deployment Workbench console tree, right-click the Task Sequences folder (or a subfolder you created under this folder) in your deployment share and select New Task Sequence to start the New Task Sequence Wizard.
2. On the General Settings page, provide the information described in Table 6-3.

TABLE 6-3 The General Settings Page

IN THIS LOCATION	PROVIDE THIS INFORMATION
Task Sequence ID box	Unique ID for the task sequence. You cannot change this ID later, so decide on a naming scheme for task sequence IDs in advance.
Task Sequence Name box	Descriptive name for the task sequence. Users see this name during LTI.
Task Sequence Comments box	Additional information about the task sequence. Users see this description during LTI. Describe the build and what it installs in the image.

3. On the Select Template page, choose a template task sequence to use as a starting point. You can customize the template later. For the purpose of building images, choose the Standard Client Task Sequence template.
4. On the Select OS page, choose an operating system image to install with this task sequence. Only the operating system images previously added to your deployment point are visible.
5. On the Specify Product Key page, select one of the following:
   - Do Not Specify A Product Key At This Time.
   - Specify A Multiple Activation Key (MAK Key) For Activating This Operating System, and then type the product key in the Product Key box.
   - Specify The Product Key For This Operating System, and then type the product key in the Product Key box.

   For more information about volume activation and product keys in MDT 2010, see Chapter 11, "Using Volume Activation." Chapter 11 describes when a product key is necessary. Generally, customers deploying volume-licensed Windows 7 media to 25 or more computers should select the Do Not Use A Product Key When Installing option. Customers deploying volume-licensed Windows 7 media using Windows 7 Multiple Activation Keys (MAKs) should select the Specify A Multiple Activation Key (MAK Key) For Activating This Operating System option and then type a product key in the Product Key box. Customers deploying retail Windows 7 media should select the Specify The Product Key For This Operating System option and then type a product key in the Product Key box.

6. On the OS Settings page, provide the information described in Table 6-4 and then click OK. The values you provide on this page are irrelevant because you are creating a build for image capture, and you will change these values during production deployment.

TABLE 6-4 The OS Settings Page

IN THIS LOCATION	PROVIDE THIS INFORMATION
Full Name box	Owner name
Organization box	Name of the organization
Internet Explorer Home Page box	Uniform Resource Locator (URL) of the default Windows Internet Explorer home page, such as the URL of the organization's intranet home page

7. On the Admin Password page, select Do Not Specify An Administrator Password At This Time. Do not specify a local Administrator password for image task sequences so that you can specialize the password during deployment.
8. Finish the wizard.

After you create a task sequence in your deployment share, it appears in the details pane when the Task Sequences folder (or a subfolder of this folder) is selected in the console tree. It also appears in the deployment share in Task Sequences*subfolder[\subfolder]*, where *subfolder[\subfolder]* is the destination selected when creating the task sequence. Deployment Workbench stores metadata about each build in TaskSequences.xml, which is located in the deployment share's Control folder.

To disable a task sequence, perform the following steps:

1. In the Deployment Workbench console tree, click Task Sequences (or a subfolder) in your deployment share.
2. In the details pane, right-click the task sequence you want to disable and then click Properties.
3. On the General tab, clear the Enable This Task Sequence check box and then click OK. Alternatively, you can hide the task sequence by selecting the Hide This Task Sequence In The Deployment Wizard check box.

NOTE **Disabling a build prevents the Windows Deployment Wizard from displaying it in the list of builds from which a user can choose during an LTI deployment.**

To remove a task sequence, perform the following steps:

1. In the Deployment Workbench console tree, click Task Sequences (or a subfolder) in your deployment share.

2. In the details pane, right-click the task sequence you want to remove and then click Delete.

To edit the task sequence's answer file (Unattend.xml), perform the following steps:

1. In the Deployment Workbench console tree, click Task Sequences (or a subfolder) in your deployment share.
2. In the details pane, right-click the task sequence containing the answer file you want to edit, and then click Properties.
3. On the OS Info tab, click Edit Unattend.xml to open the build's answer file in Windows SIM.

For more information about using Windows SIM to edit Unattend.xml, see the topic "Windows System Image Manager Technical Reference" in the Windows AIK.

DIRECT FROM THE SOURCE

Reducing Image Count

Doug Davis, Lead Architect
Management Operations & Deployment, Microsoft Consulting Services

We put the 2007 Office system and a virus scanner on every image. That way, the customer can be productive regardless of the method we use to deploy other applications. Also, a lot of things just make sense to put in the image so that the user doesn't have to download them later. I can't think of a single customer who doesn't have Adobe Acrobat Reader.

The virtual private network (VPN) and dialer installation programs are in the image, but we don't install them. When we deploy the image, the task sequence checks Windows Management Instrumentation (WMI) to see whether it's a mobile device. If it's a mobile device, we then install the VPN and dialer software; otherwise, we delete the installation programs.

We also never use a product key. Instead, we use the Key Management Service to simplify our images and reduce key loss. Chapter 11 describes the Key Management Service.

Having a single image to deploy is very handy and works well. We encourage people to change an image only when they need new software. Whenever a new update or device driver is required, we just replicate that information and then inject it into the image rather than making a new image every month and replicating the image. If this is the approach you plan to take, image versioning is very important to track.

Editing a Task Sequence

In MDT 2010, the task sequence is a list of tasks to run during deployment. However, it's not a linear list of tasks like a batch script. The task sequence is organized into groups and specifies conditions, or filters, that can prevent tasks and entire groups from running in certain situations.

MDT 2010 uses a *Task Sequencer* to run the task sequence. The Task Sequencer runs the task sequence from top to bottom in the order specified. Each task in the sequence is a step, and steps can be organized into groups and subgroups. When you create a task sequence in Deployment Workbench, you can choose a task sequence template. A key feature of the task sequence is that it stores state data, or variables, on the destination computer. These variables persist, even across reboots. The Task Sequencer can then use these variables to test conditions and possibly filter tasks or groups. The Task Sequencer also can restart the computer and gracefully continue the task sequence where it left off. These are important characteristics when driving a deployment process from beginning to end.

Task sequences contain the following types of items:

- **Steps** Steps are commands that the Task Sequencer runs during the sequence, such as partitioning the disk, capturing user state, and installing the operating system. Within a task sequence, steps do the actual work. In the task sequence templates provided by MDT 2010, most steps are commands that run scripts.
- **Groups** The task sequence steps can be organized into groups, which are folders that can contain subgroups and steps. Groups can be nested as necessary. For example, the default task sequence puts steps in groups by phase and deployment type.

You can filter both steps and groups, including the groups and steps that they contain, based on conditions that you specify. Groups are especially useful for filtering because you can run an entire collection of steps based on a condition, such as the deployment phase or type of deployment.

To edit a task sequence, perform the following steps:

1. In the Deployment Workbench console tree, click Task Sequences (or a subfolder) in your deployment share.
2. In the details pane, right-click the task sequence you want to edit and then click Properties.
3. Click the Task Sequence tab, as shown here, edit the task sequence as described in Table 6-5, and then click OK. For more information about settings on the Properties and Options tabs, see the sections titled "Configuring Group and Task Properties" and "Configuring the Options Tab" later in this chapter.

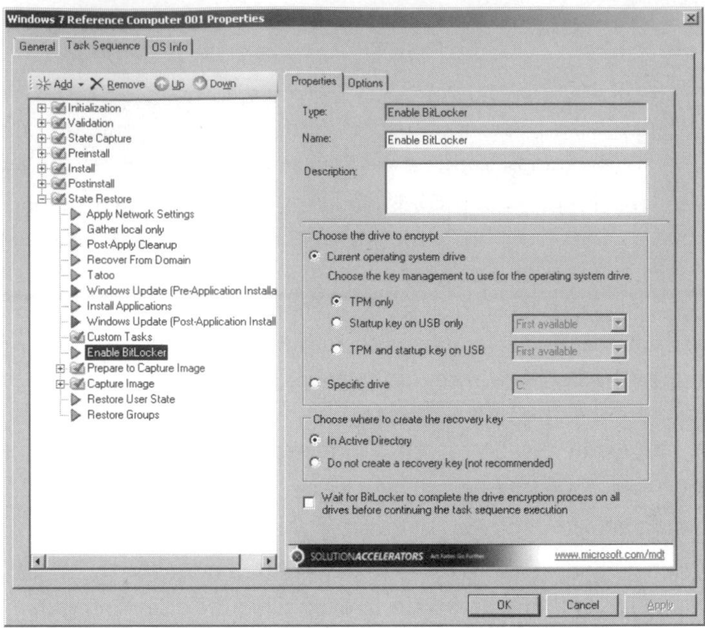

TABLE 6-5 Editing a Task Sequence

TO	USE THESE STEPS
Add a group	In the task sequence, select the item beneath which you want to create a new group, click Add, and then click New Group. Deployment Workbench creates and selects a new group called New Group.
Add a step	In the task sequence, select the item beneath which you want to create a new step and click Add. Then choose the type of step that you want to create by clicking General and then choosing one of the following (MDT 2010 supports more steps than those listed here, but they are already in the task sequence or are primarily for server deployment): ■ Run Command Line ■ Set Task Sequence Variable ■ Run Command Line As Deployment Workbench creates and selects a new step with a name relating to the type of step you're creating.
Add a reboot	In the task sequence, select the item beneath which you want to add a reboot, click Add, click General, and then click Restart Computer. Deployment Workbench creates and selects a new task that restarts the destination computer.

TO	USE THESE STEPS
Add an application	In the task sequence, select the item beneath which you want to add an application installation, click Add, click General, and then click Install Application. Then select the Install Application step you just added, and on the Properties tab, click Install A Single Application. Choose the application you want to install from the Application To Install list.

IMPORTANT **If you install antivirus software as part of the task sequence, be sure to carefully test how the antivirus software interacts with the deployment process before moving to a production environment. Antivirus software can prevent MDT 2010 from successfully deploying Windows 7 and applications. If necessary, you can always disable the antivirus software and then re-enable it at the end of the task sequence.**

To edit an item in a task sequence, select the item you want to work with and then edit the settings in the right pane.

NOTE **MDT 2010 includes a variety of special steps, such as the Enable BitLocker task or Install Operating System step, that you can configure. You change settings for these steps by selecting the step in the left pane and then configuring the step on the Properties tab. In general, the most interesting steps to configure are Validate (under Validation and under Preinstall\New Computer Only), Format and Partition Disk (under Preinstall\New Computer Only), Install Operating System (under Install), Apply Network Settings (under State Restore), and Enable BitLocker (under State Restore).**

To remove an item in a task sequence, select the item you want to work with and then click Remove. If a group is removed, Deployment Workbench removes the group and everything it contains, including subgroups and tasks.

To reorder an item in a task sequence, select the item you want to work with and then click Up or Down to change its position within the task sequence. During deployment, the Windows Deployment Wizard runs the tasks from top to bottom in the order specified.

Configuring Group and Task Properties

In the task sequence, every group and step has a Properties tab. Each group and step has a name and description that you can edit on the Properties tab. The Run Command Line and Run Command Line As steps also have a command line and a starting folder location that you can edit. Other steps have additional properties depending on the type of step. The following list describes what you see on the Properties tab:

- **Type** The Type box indicates the type of step. You cannot change the type.

- **Name** In the Name box, type a short, descriptive name for the group or step. During deployment, this name appears in the status window of the Task Sequencer.
- **Description** In the Description box, type a description of the group or step.
- **Command Line (Run Command Line and Run Command Line As tasks only)** In the Command Line box, type the command to run at this step in the task sequence. Include any command-line arguments. Environment variables are also permitted in command lines.
- **Start In (steps only)** In the Start In box, type the path in which to start the command. This path specifies the current working directory for the command. If you do not provide a path in this box, the paths in the Command Line box must be fully qualified or the command must be in the path.

Configuring the Options Tab

Groups and tasks have the following settings on the Options tab (shown in Figure 6-5):

- **Disable This Step** Select the Disable This Step check box to disable the step or group, including all groups and steps that it contains.
- **Success Codes (steps only)** List the return codes that indicate successful completion. The Windows Deployment Wizard determines whether a step completed successfully by comparing its return code to each code in the Success Codes box. If it finds a match, the step completed successfully. A success code of 0 usually represents successful completion. A success code of 3010 usually represents a successful completion with a reboot required. Thus, most of the steps in the templates that MDT 2010 provides list the success codes as 0 3010.
- **Continue On Error** If an error occurs in the current step, select the Continue On Error check box to continue with the next step in the task sequence. If you clear this check box, the Windows Deployment Wizard stops processing and displays an error message if the step or group does not complete successfully.

Additionally, on the Options tab, you can filter the group or steps based on conditions specified in the Conditions list. If the condition evaluates to true, the group or step runs. If the condition evaluates to false, the group (and all of the groups and steps that group contains) or step does not run. See the following sections for more information about conditions you can add to the Conditions list.

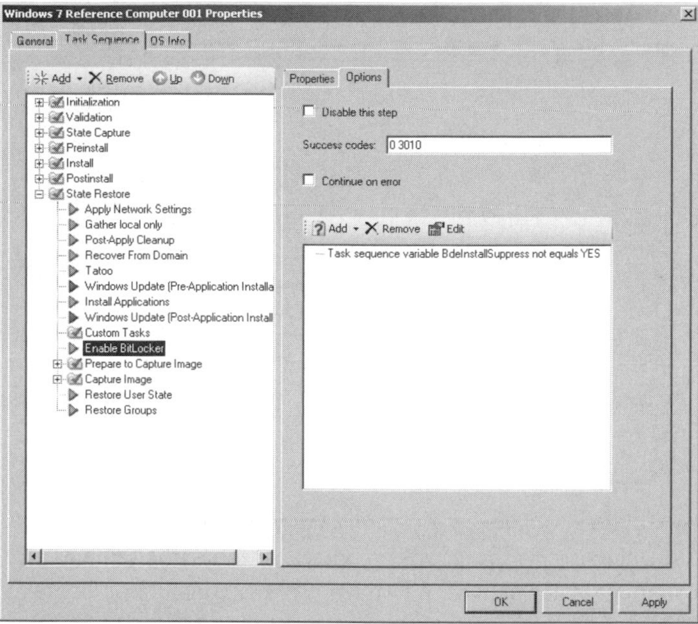

FIGURE 6-5 The Options tab

Task Sequence Variables

Task sequence variables allow you to compare a variable to a static value using a variety of conditions, such as equal, greater than, and less than. The Task Sequencer maintains numerous variables that you can use in these tests. For example, the Task Sequencer defines a variable called *DeploymentMethod* that indicates the method of deployment. One possible value of *DeploymentMethod* is *UNC*. For a complete list of variables that the Task Sequencer maintains, see the *Microsoft Deployment Toolkit Reference* in the MDT 2010 documentation.

To add a variable to an item's Conditions list, perform the following steps:

1. On the Options tab, click Add and then click Task Sequence Variable to display the Task Sequence Variable Condition dialog box, shown here.

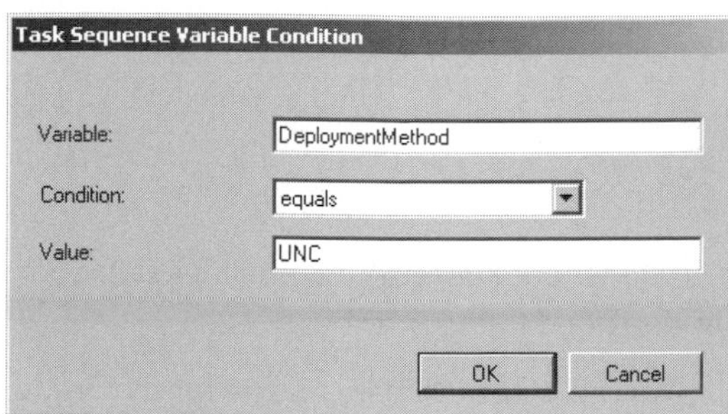

2. In the Variable box, type the name of the variable you want to test.

3. From the Conditions list, choose one of the following conditions:
   - Exists
   - Equals
   - Not equals
   - Greater than
   - Greater than or equals
   - Less than
   - Less than or equals
4. In the Value box, type the static value you want to compare to the variable using the condition specified in the previous step.

if Statements

Use *if* statements to combine variables into bigger expressions. For example, create an *if* statement that evaluates to true only if all the conditions it contains are true (the same as a logical *AND*), or create an *if* statement that evaluates to true if any of the conditions it contains are true (the same as a logical *OR*).

To add an *if* statement to an item's Conditions list, perform the following steps:

1. On the Options tab, click Add and then click If Statement to display the If Statement Properties dialog box, shown here.

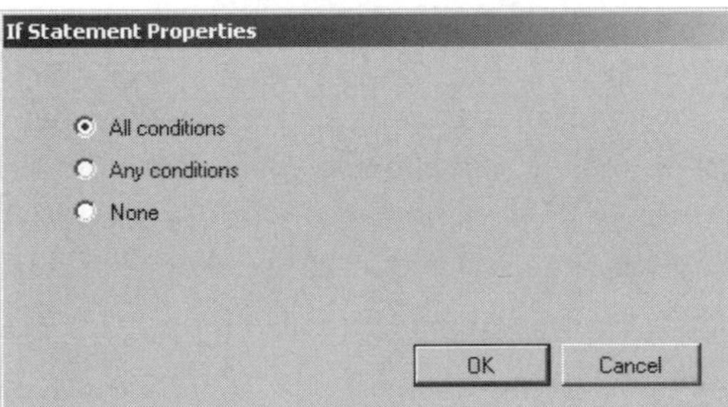

2. In the If Statement Properties dialog box, choose one of the following options and then click OK:
   - All conditions (*AND*)
   - Any conditions (*OR*)
   - None
3. From the Conditions list, select the *if* statement added in the previous step and then add task sequence variables to it as described in the previous section.

If you choose All Conditions, all variables added must evaluate to true for the group or step to run. If you choose Any Conditions, the group or task will run if any one of the variables added evaluates to true.

> **NOTE** You can nest *if* statements to create complex logic. If you are familiar with Boolean logic, represent Boolean expressions as *if* statements in the Conditions list.

Operating System Versions

The Task Sequencer allows you to filter steps and groups based on the computer's current operating system. For example, you can choose to run a preinstallation step only if the destination computer is currently running Windows Vista SP1.

To add an operating system filter to an item's Conditions list, perform the following steps:

1. On the Options tab, click Add, and then click Operating System Version to display the Task Sequence OS Condition dialog box.
2. From the Architecture list, click either X86 or X64.
3. From the Operating System list, choose an operating system version and a service pack level.
4. From the Conditions list, choose one of the following conditions:
   - Equals
   - Not equals
   - Greater than
   - Greater than or equals
   - Less than
   - Less than or equals

WMI Queries

The Task Sequencer allows you to filter steps and groups based on WMI queries. The WMI query must return a collection. If the collection is empty, the result evaluates to false. If the collection is not empty, the result evaluates to true. The following are some sample WMI queries you could use to filter steps in the task sequence:

- SELECT * FROM Win32_ComputerSystem WHERE Manufacturer = 'Dell Computer Corporation'. This is true only if WMI reports the computer's manufacturer as *Dell Computer Corporation*.
- SELECT * FROM Win32_OperatingSystem WHERE OSLanguage = '1033'. This is true only if WMI reports the operating system language as 1033.
- SELECT * FROM Win32_Service WHERE Name = 'WinMgmt'. This is true only if the WinMgmt service is available.
- SELECT * FROM Win32_Processor WHERE DeviceID = 'CPU0' AND Architecture = '0'. This is true only if the processor architecture is x86.
- SELECT * FROM Win32_Directory WHERE Name = 'D:\Somefolder'. This is true only if D:\Somefolder exists on the computer.

To add a WMI query to an item's Conditions list, perform the following steps:

1. On the Options tab, click Add and then click Query WMI to display the Task Sequence WMI Condition dialog box.
2. In the WMI Namespace box, type the WMI namespace in which to run the query, as shown here. The default namespace is *root\cimv2*.

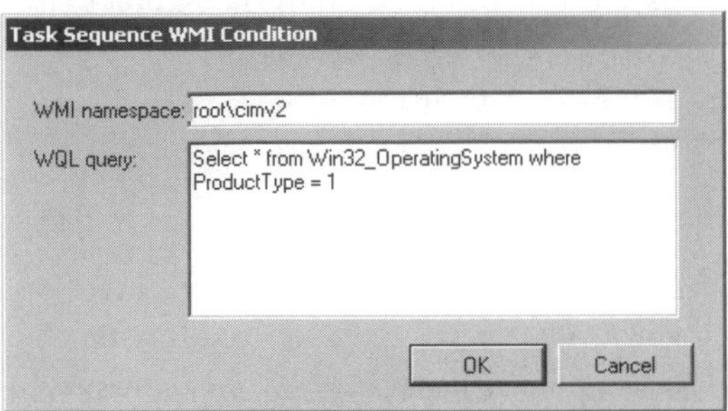

3. In the WQL Query box, type the WMI query.

Updating the Deployment Share

The Windows AIK 2.0 comes with Windows PE 3.0, so no additional files are necessary to create Windows PE boot images for MDT 2010. When you update your deployment share in the Deployment Workbench, MDT 2010 automatically generates the following custom Windows PE images (here *platform* is x86 or x64):

- Lite Touch Windows PE (*platform*) .wim file
- LiteTouchPE_*platform*.iso

If you want, you can configure the deployment share to also generate the following Windows PE images:

- Generic Windows PE (*platform*)
- Generic_*platform*.iso

You don't need to manually customize Windows PE to add network interface card (NIC) device drivers to it. Deployment Workbench automatically adds the NIC device drivers that you add to the deployment share to the Windows PE boot images. You have the additional option of automatically adding video and system device drivers from the deployment share to the Windows PE boot images. You can also perform additional customizations of your Windows PE images. For example, you can customize the background bitmap, add additional directories, and increase the scratch space size from its default value of 32 megabytes (MB) up to a maximum of 512 MB if needed. To learn more about customizing Windows PE, see the *Windows Preinstallation Environment User's Guide for Windows 7* in the Windows AIK.

Updating a deployment share causes Deployment Workbench to update its configuration files, source files, and Windows PE images. Deployment Workbench updates the deployment share's files and generates the Windows PE boot images when you update the deployment share, not when you create it. Deployment Workbench stores these boot images in the deployment share's \Boot folder. After you have updated the deployment share and generated Windows PE images, you can add the .wim image file to Windows Deployment Services. If you want, you can burn the Windows PE .iso images to CD or DVD media by using third-party CD/DVD-burning software. Windows Deployment Services is the best way to start the Windows PE boot images on lab computers. Updating the boot images is faster than burning media, and booting destination computers is quicker. For more information, see Chapter 10.

> ***NOTE*** **You must use the same platform edition of Windows PE to start computers for installing each platform edition of Windows. In other words, you must start destination computers using a x86 edition of Windows PE to install a x86 edition of Windows 7. Likewise, you must use a x64 edition of Windows PE to install a x64 edition of Windows 7. If you use mismatched editions, you might see errors indicating that the image is for a different type of computer. Deployment Workbench automatically chooses the correct platform edition of Windows PE to match the operating system you're deploying.**

To configure a deployment share for imaging in the lab, perform the following steps:

1. In the Deployment Workbench console tree, click Deployment Shares.
2. In the details pane, right-click the deployment share you want to configure and then click Properties.
3. Click the General tab and then choose the platforms that the deployment share supports. To indicate that the deployment share supports the x86 platform, select the x86 check box. To indicate that the deployment share supports the x64 platform, select the x64 check box. This option determines the platforms for which Deployment Workbench generates Windows PE boot images.
4. Click the Rules tab and then edit the deployment share's settings. These settings are located in CustomSettings.ini, which is located in the deployment share's Control folder. For more information about the settings that you can configure on this tab, see the *Microsoft Deployment Toolkit Reference* in MDT 2010.
5. Click the Windows PE Settings (*platform*) tab for each platform and edit the settings described in Table 6-6, as shown on the following page. Then, click OK.

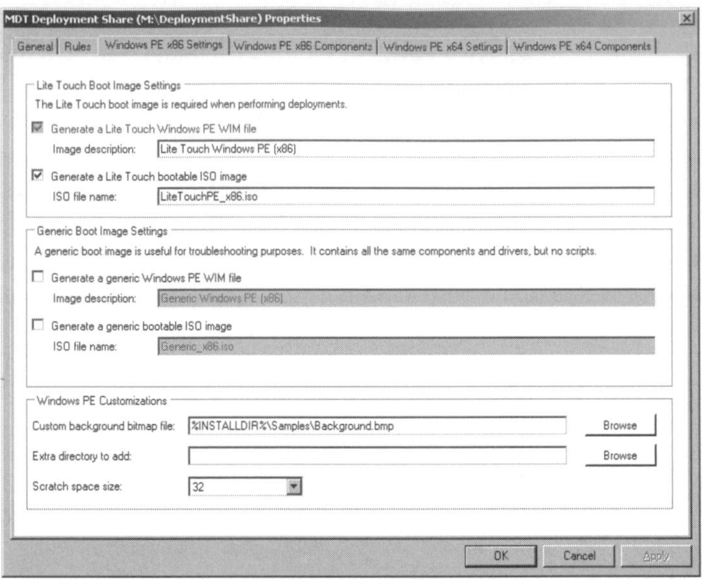

TABLE 6-6 Windows PE Settings Tab

AREA	SETTINGS
Images to Generate	**Generate A Lite Touch Windows PE WIM file** Select this option to generate a customized WIM file that you can use to perform LTI using Windows Deployment Services (this option is selected by default and cannot be cleared). **Generate A Lite Touch Bootable ISO Image** Select this option to generate a bootable customized Windows PE ISO image that you can use to perform LTI by starting your destination computers manually (this option is selected by default). **Generate A Generic Windows PE WIM file** Select this option to generate a generic WIM file that you can use to perform LTI using Windows Deployment Services. **Generate A Generic Bootable ISO Image** Select this option to generate a bootable generic Windows PE ISO image that you can use to perform LTI by starting your destination computers manually.
Windows PE Customizations	**Custom Background Bitmap File** Type the path and file name of a bitmap file to use as the Windows PE background. **Extra Directory To Add** Type the path of a folder containing extra files and subfolders to add to the Windows PE bootable images. **Scratch Space Size** Select the size of the scratch space for your Windows PE image. The available values are 32, 64, 128, 256, and 512 MB, with 32 being the default.

6. Click the Windows PE Components (*platform*) tab for each platform and edit the settings described in Table 6-7, as shown here, and then click OK.

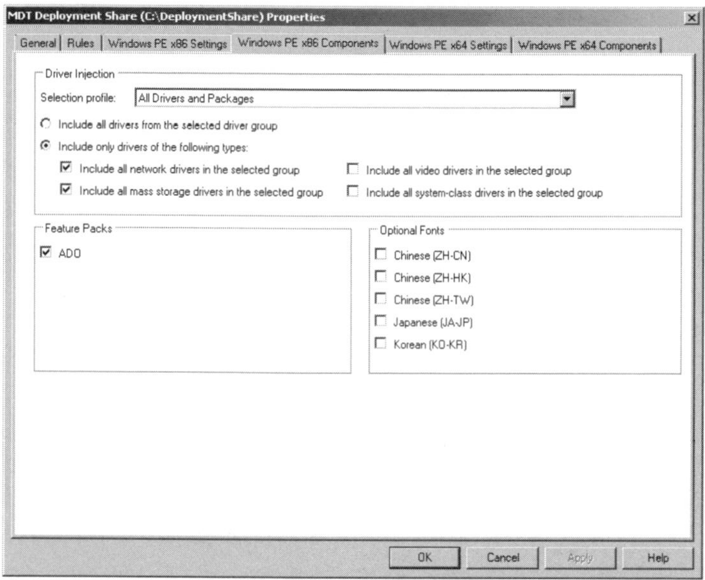

TABLE 6-7 Windows PE Components Tab

AREA	SETTINGS
Feature Packs	**ADO** Select this option to add the Microsoft ActiveX Data Objects (ADO) optional feature to the Windows PE bootable images.
Optional Fonts	Select the font support to add to the Windows PE boot images that Deployment Workbench generates. You must add these fonts when performing an LTI deployment of Windows Vista images when the setup files are Japanese, Korean, or Chinese. The Optional Fonts area provides the following options: ■ Chinese (ZH-CN) ■ Chinese (ZH-HK) ■ Chinese (ZH-TW) ■ Japanese (JA-JP) ■ Korean (KO-KR) Adding additional fonts to Windows PE boot images increases the size of the images. Add additional fonts only if necessary.

AREA	SETTINGS
Driver Injection	**Selection Profile** Use this list box to choose one of the following selection profiles to include the appropriate device drivers in your Windows PE images: ■ **Everything** Includes all folders from all nodes in Deployment Workbench. This selection profile includes all applications, operating systems, device drivers, operating system packages, and task sequences. ■ **All Drivers** Includes all folders from the Out-Of-Box Drivers node in Deployment Workbench. This selection profile includes all device drivers. ■ **All Drivers And Packages** Includes all folders from the Applications and Out-Of-Box Drivers nodes in Deployment Workbench. This selection profile includes all applications and device drivers. ■ **Nothing** Includes no folders in Deployment Workbench. This selection profile includes no items. ■ **Sample** A sample selection profile that illustrates how to select a subset of the items and include all folders from the Packages and Task Sequences nodes in Deployment Workbench. This selection profile includes all operating system packages and task sequences. ***NOTE*** **If you have created any custom selection profiles, these will also be available for selection here.** Selection profiles are new in MDT 2010 and allow you to select one or more folders in Deployment Workbench that contain one or more items in Deployment Workbench, including applications, device drivers, operating systems, operating system packages, and task sequences. For more information concerning selection profiles, see the topic "Managing Selection Profiles" in the MDT 2010 documentation. **Include All Drivers From The Selected Driver Group** Select this option if you want to include all the device drivers in the selection profile you specified in the Selection Profile list box. **Include Only Drivers Of The Following Types** Select this option to include only specific types of device drivers in the selection profile you specified in the Selection Profile list box. If you select this option, you can select one or more of the following:

AREA	SETTINGS
	■ **Include All Network Drivers In The Selected Group** Select this option to inject all the device drivers in the selection profile specified in the Selection profile list box. ■ **Include All Mass Storage Drivers In The Selected Group** Select this option to inject all mass storage drivers found in the deployment share into the Windows PE boot images. ■ **Include All Video Drivers In The Selected Group** Select this option to inject all video drivers found in the deployment share into the Windows PE boot images. ■ **Include All System-Class Drivers In The Selected Group** Select this option to inject all system drivers (such as motherboard drivers) in the deployment share into the Windows PE boot images.

After creating and configuring a deployment share in Deployment Workbench, you must update it to update the deployment share's configuration files and generate Windows PE boot images in the deployment share's \Boot folder. Deployment Workbench always generates .wim image files, which you can use to start destination computers using Windows Deployment Services. Choose to generate only the Windows PE bootable ISO images that are actually required. If you limit the number of images generated, the updating process is faster.

To update a deployment share, perform the following steps:

1. In the Deployment Workbench console tree, click Deployment Shares.
2. In the details pane, right-click the deployment share you want to configure and then click Update.
3. On the Options page of the Update Deployment Share Wizard, shown on the following page, select one of the following options:
   - **Optimize The Boot Image Updating Process** Select this option to update existing versions of the image files in the deployment share. Choosing this option reduces the amount of time required to update the boot images. If you select this option, you can also select Compress The Boot Image Contents To Recover Space Used By Removed Or Modified Content if desired. Selecting this suboption reduces the size of the boot images but may increase the time needed to generate the images.
   - **Completely Regenerate The Boot Images** Select this option to create a new version of all the image files in the deployment share. You can choose this option when you want to force the creation of new images. Note that this can take some time to complete.

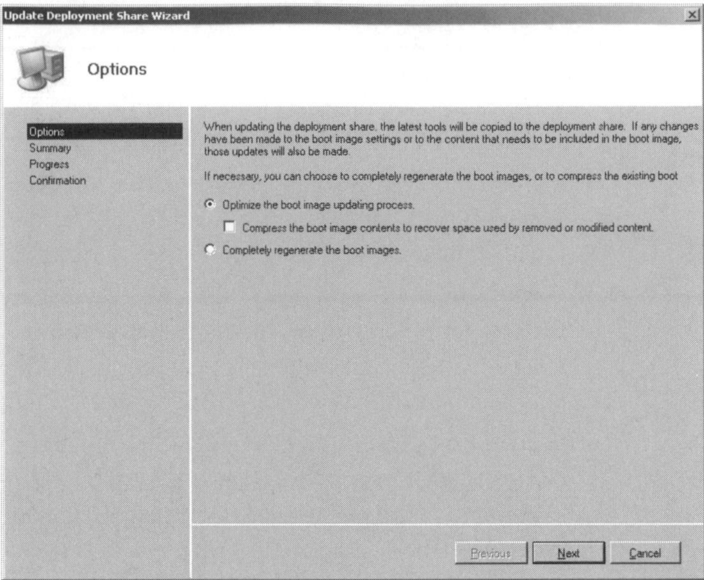

4. Finish the wizard. Depending on how your deployment share is configured and the options you selected in the Update Deployment Share Wizard, generating Windows PE boot images may take some time to complete.

After the deployment share has been updated, Windows PE boot images and other files will be present in the \Boot folder of the deployment share (see Figure 6-6).

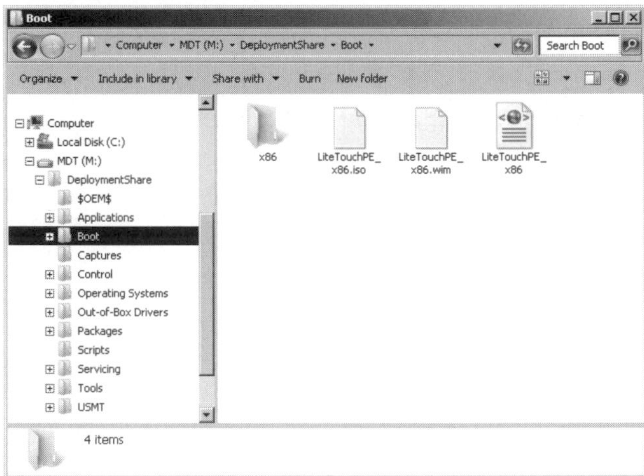

FIGURE 6-6 \Boot folder of updated deployment share showing Windows PE boot images that were generated

IMPORTANT You *must* update your deployment share if you make changes to any the settings on the properties sheet of your deployment share. The Windows PE boot images will not contain your updated settings until you update your deployment share.

Capturing a Disk Image for LTI

In MDT 2010, installing a build and capturing an image is essentially an LTI deployment that ends with the Windows Deployment Wizard capturing an image of the destination computer. When you create a deployment share, Deployment Workbench provides the option of prompting to capture an image (the Ask If An Image Should Be Captured check box). You must enable this option, as described in the section titled "Creating and Configuring a Deployment Share" earlier in this chapter.

Then, when you install the build on the destination lab computer, the Windows Deployment Wizard asks whether you want to capture an image after installation is complete. The wizard also allows you to specify a destination for the image. The default destination is the \Captures folder in the deployment share, and the default file name is task sequence.wim, where *task sequence* is the ID of the task sequence you installed.

To capture an image, start a lab computer using the Windows PE boot image generated by updating the deployment share. Start the Windows PE boot image in either of two ways. One way is to burn the .iso images to a DVD. This process is slow and tedious. These ISO image files reside in the \Boot folder of the deployment share. The other way is to add the LiteTouchPE_x86.wim or LiteTouchPE_x64.wim image files to the Boot Images item of a Windows Deployment Services server. The .wim image files are in the \Boot folder of the deployment share. For more information about installing and configuring Windows Deployment Services, see Chapter 10.

To capture an image using the Windows Deployment Wizard, perform the following steps:

1. Start the lab computer using the Windows PE boot image that you created in the section titled "Updating the Deployment Share" earlier in this chapter. You can start this boot image by burning the .iso file to CD or DVD media or by adding the .wim file to Windows Deployment Services. For more information about Windows Deployment Services, see Chapter 10.
2. In the Welcome Windows Deployment dialog box, click Run The Deployment Wizard To Install A New Operating System.
3. In the User Credentials dialog box, type the credentials necessary to connect to the deployment share (user name, domain, and password) and then click OK. The Windows Deployment Wizard starts automatically. To capture an image using the Windows Deployment Wizard, you must use an account that has Read and Write access to the deployment share, such as an account that is a member of the local Administrators group on the computer that contains the deployment share.

4. On the Select A Task Sequence To Execute On This Computer page, choose a task sequence to run from the list of available task sequences and then click Next.
5. On the Configure The Computer Name page, type a computer name or accept the default and then click Next. The default, randomly generated computer name is reasonable because the computer name will change during deployment to the production environment.
6. On the Join The Computer To A Domain Or Workgroup page, click Join A Workgroup. In the Workgroup box, type a workgroup name or accept the default and then click Next. If you join the computer to a domain, the Windows Deployment Wizard does not prompt you to capture an image.
7. On the Specify Whether To Restore User Data page, select Do Not Restore User Data And Settings and then click Next.
8. On the Packages page (if displayed), choose the packages, such as software updates and language packs, that you want to install on the image and then click Next.
9. On the Locale Selection page, choose your locale and keyboard layout and then click Next. Your choice here is irrelevant, because the Windows Deployment Wizard will configure the locale and keyboard layouts during deployment to the production environment.
10. On the Select The Time Zone page, select a time zone and then click Next. Your choice here is irrelevant, because the Windows Deployment Wizard will configure the time zone during deployment to the production environment.
11. On the Select One Or More Applications To Install page (if displayed), select the check box next to each application that you want to install on the image and then click Next.
12. In the Specify Whether To Capture An Image page, select Capture An Image Of This Reference Computer. In the Location box, type the Universal Naming Convention (UNC) path of the folder in which to store the image or accept the default capture location. In the File Name box, type the file name of the image or accept the default file name for the captured image. The default UNC path is the \Captures folder of the deployment share; the default image file name is the ID of the task sequence being installed. Click Next.
12. Click Next, then on the Ready To Begin page, click Begin.

After you click Begin, the Task Sequencer begins running the build's task sequence. By default, it begins by partitioning and formatting the hard disk. Then it installs and configures the operating system, runs Sysprep to prepare the computer for imaging, and restarts the computer in Windows PE to capture the image. The Windows Deployment Wizard stores the captured image in the folder specified on the Specify Whether To Capture An Image page, which is the deployment share's \Captures folder by default. After capturing the image, you can add it to the deployment share as a custom image by using the steps described in the section titled "Creating and Configuring a Deployment Share" earlier in this chapter. For more information about deploying your custom Windows 7 image, see Chapter 12.

Preparing Images Manually

The deployment share tells Windows Setup how to install and configure Windows 7 on the destination computers. It includes the settings (answer file) as well as device drivers and packages that you want to add to the operating system. It might also contain applications that you want to install.

A common way to deliver operating systems to users is to create an image of the desired configuration. This is particularly true when the deployment share includes other files, such as applications. Creating an image that you install on each destination computer is quicker and more efficient than installing the uncustomized Windows 7 image and then installing applications on each destination computer.

Sysprep prepares a Windows 7 installation for imaging or delivery to end users. Sysprep removes all user-specific information from a system and resets any system-specific security identifiers (SIDs) to allow the system to be duplicated. Once duplicated, systems using the duplicated image will register their own SIDs with the domain in which they are deployed. Sysprep has several command-line options to control its behavior, listed in Table 6-8.

TABLE 6-8 Sysprep Command-Line Options

OPTION	DESCRIPTION
/audit	Restarts the computer into audit mode. In audit mode, you can add additional drivers or applications to Windows Vista. You can also test an installation of Windows Vista before it is sent to an end user. If you specify an unattended Windows Vista setup file, the audit mode of Windows Setup runs the auditSystem and auditUser configuration passes.
/generalize	Prepares the Windows installation to be imaged. If you specify this option, all unique system information is removed from the Windows installation. The system's SID is reset, any System Restore points are cleared, and event logs are deleted. The next time the computer starts, the specialize configuration pass runs. A new SID is created, and the clock for Windows activation resets (if the clock has not already been reset three times).
/oobe	Restarts the computer into Windows Welcome mode. Windows Welcome allows end users to customize the Windows operating system, create user accounts, name the computer, and complete other tasks. Any settings in the oobeSystem configuration pass in an answer file are processed immediately before Windows Welcome starts.
/reboot	Restarts the computer. Use this option to audit the computer and to verify that the first-run experience operates correctly.
/shutdown	Shuts down the computer after Sysprep completes.

OPTION	DESCRIPTION
/quiet	Runs Sysprep without displaying on-screen confirmation messages. Use this option if you automate Sysprep.
/quit	Closes Sysprep after running the specified commands.
/unattend: *answerfile*	Applies settings in an answer file to Windows during unattended installation. You can create this answer file in Windows SIM.
answerfile	Specifies the path and file name of the answer file to use.

When you create a Windows 7 installation that you plan to image, you then use Sysprep to generalize the system. The following command generalizes the system and prepares it to run the Windows Welcome Wizard on the next restart.

```
sysprep /oobe /generalize
```

Most organizations use this command. If you are a system builder or an Original Equipment Manufacturer (OEM), however, you can also use Sysprep to create build-to-order systems. The following command lets you place a system into audit mode on the next restart, wherein you can install additional applications and modify configurations.

```
sysprep /audit /generalize /reboot
```

The following command then completes the customization by preparing the system to run the Windows Welcome on the next boot, which is a typical requirement in a retail environment.

```
sysprep /oobe
```

When all system preparations have been made, the system is ready for imaging. You can use the ImageX command with the */FLAGS* parameter to capture an image of the system. You can then burn the image onto a DVD, import it into a deployment share, or leave it on the system for use on the next system start.

Customizing Microsoft Deployment Toolkit

You can brand some features in MDT 2010. You can customize Deployment Workbench and the Windows Deployment Wizard. For example, you can customize Workbench.xml in C:\Program Files\Microsoft Deployment\Bin to change the text displayed in the Deployment Workbench title bar and for each item in the console tree. Although it's generally safe to customize the <*Name*> tag in Workbench.xml, you should avoid changing other tags.

The LTI process is driven by .xml files called *definition files*. You can brand the entire LTI process by customizing the following files, which are found in the \Scripts folder in your deployment share:

- **BDD_Welcome_ENU.xml** Customize this file to change the text displayed on the Windows Deployment Wizard's Welcome page.

- **Credentials_ENU.xml** Customize this file to change the text displayed in the User Credentials dialog box.
- **DeployWiz_Definition_ENU.xml** Customize this file to change the text for each page displayed by the Windows Deployment Wizard.
- **Summary_Definition_ENU.xml** Customize this file to change the text in the Deployment Summary dialog box, which displays at the end of the LTI process.

Summary

The new installation architecture first introduced in Windows Vista and deployment tools included in the Windows AIK make deploying Windows 7 in your organization easier than deploying earlier versions of Windows. The new .wim file format makes it possible to deploy highly compressed image files. Windows 7 helps reduce image count by removing hardware and other dependencies from the image. Modularization in Windows 7 makes servicing images easier than with legacy methods, so you no longer have to apply, customize, and recapture an image to update it. The new answer file format, Unattend.xml, provides a more flexible and consistent configuration. Finally, deployment tools in the Windows AIK 2.0 provide a robust way to create, customize, and manage Windows 7 images.

Although the Windows AIK 2.0 provides the basic tools for customizing and deploying Windows 7, MDT 2010 provides a more flexible framework for deploying Windows 7 in businesses. MDT 2010 enables you to create and customize multiple image builds. The framework includes automation common to most businesses and is highly extensible to suit any requirements. For example, by using MDT 2010 to deploy Windows 7, you can include custom actions such as installing applications, packages, and drivers that are performed during installation.

Additional Resources

These resources contain additional information and tools related to this chapter.

- Chapter 3, "Deployment Platform," includes information about the Windows 7 installation architecture, its key features and technologies, and how the various features interact.
- Chapter 4, "Planning Deployment," includes information about installing and preparing MDT 2010 for use. This chapter also describes how to use the MDT 2010 documentation.
- Chapter 10, "Configuring Windows Deployment Services," explains how to install and configure Windows Deployment Services and how to add images to and deploy images from Windows Deployment Services.
- Chapter 11, "Using Volume Activation," includes more information about Windows 7 product keys and volume activation.

- Chapter 12, "Deploying with Microsoft Deployment Toolkit," includes more information about using MDT 2010 to deploy Windows 7 images in the production environment.
- *Microsoft Deployment Toolkit Reference* in MDT 2010 lists the properties you can configure in a deployment share.
- *Windows Automated Installation Kit User's Guide for Windows 7* contains detailed information about the tools and technologies included in the Windows AIK 2.0. This guide is in the file Waik.chm in the Windows AIK 2.0.

CHAPTER 7

Migrating User State Data

Operating system deployment always involves user state migration—the process of migrating users' documents and settings from one operating system to another. Even when you don't migrate user state during deployment, users will spend countless hours trying to restore their preferences (such as desktop backgrounds, screensavers, and themes). Because this manual process reduces user productivity and usually increases support calls, organizations often choose to migrate some portion of user state to new operating systems as they are deployed.

User satisfaction is another reason to elevate the importance of user state migration in your project. Users are simply more satisfied and feel less overwhelmed when they sit down in front of a new operating system and they don't have to recover their preferences. The fact is that unsatisfied users can lead to poor post-implementation reviews and can have negative consequences for future deployment projects. For example, user dissatisfaction with previous projects can stall a deployment project that you know will benefit the company in the long term. Keep the users happy.

This chapter helps you decide which user state migration tools best suit your environment. It then explores the User State Migration Tool (USMT) 4.0, including customizing and automating the user state migration process. You'll learn how to identify user state data, how to plan the user state migration project, and how to execute the user state migration using tools such as Windows scripting and Microsoft Deployment Toolkit 2010 (MDT 2010).

Evaluating Migration Technologies

Whether you decide to migrate user state individually, as part of a high-volume deployment project, or not at all, you should evaluate the available options to ensure that you make the best choices for your environment. The size and scope of the migration project factor into your choice, as will the type and amount of user state data you choose to migrate.

The following sections describe the different options that Microsoft provides. Several third-party products are also available for migrating user state. If you're using MDT 2010 as your deployment framework, Microsoft recommends that you use USMT to migrate user state to Windows 7. USMT handles most common scenarios out of the box, and exceptional cases are easy to configure. Additionally, MDT 2010 already includes the pre-deployment and post-deployment logic for saving and restoring user state.

Windows Easy Transfer

Windows Easy Transfer is the Windows 7 equivalent of the Windows XP Files And Settings Transfer Wizard. This tool leads the user through a series of pages to determine how much data to migrate and which migration method to use (removable media, universal serial bus (USB) cable connection, or network). Using Windows Easy Transfer is not appropriate in high-volume deployment projects because it is a completely manual process. However, in bench deployments, Windows Easy Transfer can be a viable tool for migrating user state on individual computers.

> ***NOTE*** **Windows Easy Transfer can transfer user state data using a special USB cable available from most cable vendors. The Easy Transfer Cable includes circuitry that links two computers using their USB ports and can transfer data at approximately 20 gigabytes (GB) per hour.**

User State Migration Tool

Use USMT to migrate user state in high-volume deployment projects. It can execute complex, repeatable migrations of user state data between operating systems. You can script USMT; you can execute it as part of an MDT 2010 Lite Touch Installation (LTI) or Zero Touch Installation (ZTI); or you can execute it directly at the command prompt.

In addition to document and settings migration, USMT can migrate application preferences for Microsoft Office applications between versions of Office. For example, USMT can migrate Office XP settings to the Microsoft 2007 Office system.

Version 4.0 is the new version of USMT supporting Windows 7 migrations. It includes numerous changes from USMT 3.0, but the most notable are:

- **Hard-link migration store** For use in Refresh Computer scenarios only, hard-link migration stores are stored locally on the computer that you're refreshing and can migrate user accounts, files, and settings in less time using far less disk space.
- **Support for offline Windows operating systems** You can gather data from an offline Windows operating system using the ScanState command in Windows Preinstallation Environment (Windows PE). In addition, USMT now supports migrations from previous installations of Windows contained in Windows.old directories.
- **Volume Shadow Copy support** With the */vsc* command-line option, the ScanState command can now use the Volume Shadow Copy service to capture files that are locked for editing by other applications.

This chapter mostly describes USMT because of its power and flexibility in large-scale migrations. Later in this chapter, you will learn how to plan, develop, and deploy a custom migration project by using USMT.

Microsoft IntelliMirror

Microsoft introduced IntelliMirror with Microsoft Windows 2000 so that users' data and settings could follow them from computer to computer on the network. For more information about IntelliMirror, see Chapter 15, "Managing Users and User Data." The following two IntelliMirror features in particular minimize the need to migrate user state when deploying Windows 7 because these features store user state on the network.

- **Roaming user profiles** Roaming user profiles ensure that users' data and settings follow them on the network. This feature copies users' data and settings to a network server when they log off their computers and then restores their data and settings when they log on to another computer anywhere on the network. This feature provides a transparent way to back up users' data and settings to a network server.
- **Folder redirection** Folder redirection allows IT professionals to redirect certain folders (My Documents, Application Data, and so on) from the user's computer to a server. This feature protects user data by storing it on a network server, thereby providing centralized storage and administrator-managed backups. When used with roaming user profiles, folder redirection speeds the logon process by removing documents and other large files from the user profile.

NOTE **Windows 7 and Windows Vista store user profiles using a different folder hierarchy than Windows XP. Therefore, carefully review Chapter 15 before you rely on IntelliMirror in any Windows XP migration project.**

Using Windows Easy Transfer

Although USMT will generally be used in most enterprise environments, some businesses may find Windows Easy Transfer a simple and useful alternative to using USMT. This section briefly describes the basic functionality of Windows Easy Transfer, which can be particularly useful in bench deployments. Before you use Windows Easy Transfer, check for the following prerequisites:

- The destination computer must be running Windows 7. Windows 7 can create a Windows Easy Transfer data collection disk to execute the data collection portion of the migration on previous versions of Windows, but the destination computer must be running Windows 7.
- The source computer can be running any of the following operating systems:
  - Windows XP Service Pack 2 (SP2)
  - Windows Vista
  - Windows 7
- You must decide which user state data to migrate. Windows Easy Transfer does not offer the same degree of control as USMT, but you can choose which user accounts to migrate and the types of files and settings to migrate from each.

Windows Easy Transfer, shown in Figure 7-1, steps the user through a series of pages to define and execute the user state migration. Whether you are refreshing computers or replacing computers, Windows Easy Transfer can move user accounts, files and folders, program settings, Internet settings and favorites, and e-mail settings from a computer running earlier versions of Windows to Windows 7.

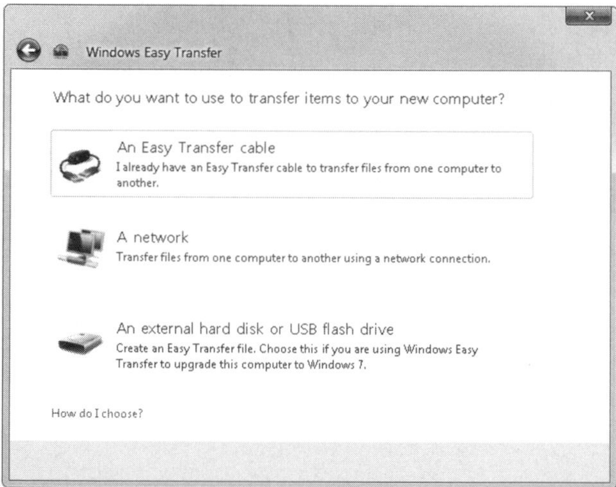

FIGURE 7-1 Windows Easy Transfer

Before using Windows Easy Transfer, though, you must prepare it for use by copying it to media that you can use to run it on earlier versions of Windows. To do this, follow these steps:

1. Close all running programs.
2. Start Windows Easy Transfer by clicking Start, pointing to All Programs, selecting Accessories, selecting System Tools, and then selecting Windows Easy Transfer.
3. On the Welcome To Windows Easy Transfer screen, click Next to continue.
4. Select the method you want to use for transferring files from your old computer from the following options:
   - A Windows Easy Transfer cable
   - A network
   - An external hard disk or USB flash drive
5. Click This Is My New Computer.
6. Click I Need To Install It Now.
7. Choose the destination for the Windows Easy Transfer files. If you want to use a USB Flash Drive (UFD) or portable USB hard drive, make sure it's plugged into the computer. If you want to put the files on a network share, make sure the computer is on the network. In any case, any computer on which you want to run Windows Easy Transfer using these files must also have access to the same hard disk or network share.
8. Choose the path of the folder in which to put the Windows Easy Transfer files and then click OK.

After preparing the Windows Easy Transfer files, you will have a removable drive or network share that contains program files that you run on the source computer—the computer from which you are moving the user's documents and settings. Use the instructions in the following sections, depending on the scenario: Refresh Computer or Replace Computer.

Refresh Computer

This section describes how to use Windows Easy Transfer in the Refresh Computer scenario. Recall that in this scenario, you are not replacing the computer. Instead, you are formatting the hard drive and then installing Windows 7 on it. As a result, you must save user documents and settings in a temporary location. To do this, follow these steps:

1. On the user's computer, run Windows Easy Transfer. To start Windows Easy Transfer, open the path that contains the Windows Easy Transfer files (on a UFD, removable USB drive, or network share) and then double-click the Windows Easy Transfer shortcut.
2. On the Welcome To Windows Easy Transfer screen, click Next.
3. Connect the portable USB drive or network share to the computer and then click An External Hard Disk Or USB Flash Drive.
4. Click This Is My Old Computer.

5. On the Choose What To Transfer From This Computer screen, choose each user account that you want to transfer to Windows 7. Selecting Shared Items, shown in Figure 7-2, migrates public documents, music, pictures, and settings. You can customize what to transfer from each folder by clicking Customize under each one.

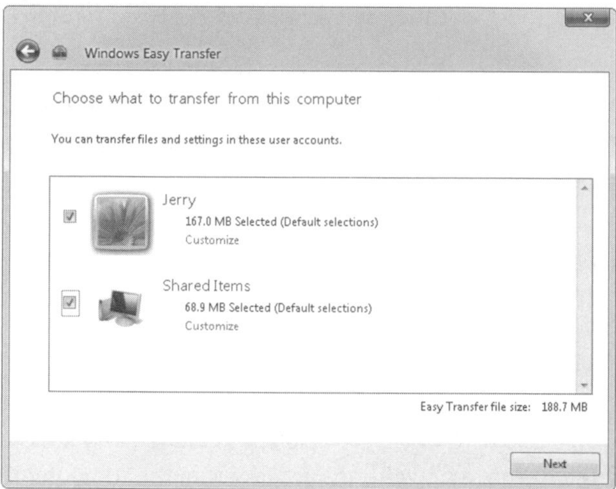

FIGURE 7-2 The Choose What To Transfer From This Computer screen

6. On the Save Your Files And Settings For Transfer screen, type and confirm a password with which you want to protect the migration data and then click Save. Microsoft recommends that you create a password to protect the information, but if you want, you also can click Save without typing and confirming a password.
7. In the Save Your Easy Transfer File dialog box, type the path of the file in which you want to store the migration data. This is not a folder path; it's the path and name of the file you want Windows Easy Transfer to create. The location can be on a network share or it can be on a portable drive. Click Save.
8. After Windows Easy Transfer finishes saving your migration data, click Next.
9. Confirm the location where Windows Easy Transfer saved your migration data and then click Next.
10. Click Close.
11. With the computer's user documents and settings safely in temporary storage, you can now install Windows 7 on the computer. Continue with the remainder of these steps after successfully installing Windows 7.
12. After installing Windows 7, connect the computer to the portable drive or network share on which you stored the migration data. In Windows Explorer, open the folder containing the migration data and then double-click the migration (.mig) file that you created before installing Windows 7. This starts Windows Easy Transfer.

13. On the Choose What To Transfer To This Computer screen, choose the accounts that you want to transfer to Windows 7 and then click Next. You can select which types of files and settings to transfer by clicking Customize. Additionally, you can map account names from the old computer to account names in Windows 7 by clicking Advanced Options.
14. Click Transfer to begin transferring the documents and settings from the migration file to the computer.
15. On the Your Transfer Is Complete screen, do either of the following and then click Close:
    - Click See What Was Transferred to see a detailed list of the accounts, documents, and settings transferred from the previous operating system to Windows 7.
    - Click See A List Of Programs You Might Want To Install On Your New Computer to see a list of applications installed on the previous operating system that you might want to reinstall in Windows 7. Install these applications after you finish migrating your documents and settings to Windows 7.
16. Click Restart Now to restart the computer. You must restart the computer for the changes to take effect.

Replace Computer

This section describes how to use Windows Easy Transfer in the Replace Computer scenario. In this scenario, you are replacing a computer running an earlier version of Windows with a new computer running Windows 7. In this case, you can certainly use the steps described in the previous section to transfer documents and settings from the old computer to temporary storage, replace the computer, and then restore documents and settings to the new computer. However, transferring documents and settings from the old computer to the new computer through the network is a simpler solution, which you can implement by following these steps:

1. Make sure both the old computer and the new computer are on the network.
2. On the new computer, complete the following steps:
    a. Close all running programs.
    b. Start Windows Easy Transfer by clicking Start, pointing to All Programs, selecting Accessories, selecting System Tools, and then selecting Windows Easy Transfer.
    c. On the Welcome To Windows Easy Transfer screen, click Next to continue.
    d. Run Windows Easy Transfer. To start Windows Easy Transfer, open the path that contains the Windows Easy Transfer files (on a UFD, removable USB drive, or network share) and then double-click Migwiz.exe. Do not open the file from the Start menu.
    e. Click A Network.
    f. Click This Is My New Computer.
    g. Click I Already Installed It On My Old Computer.

3. On the old computer, complete the following steps:
   a. Run Windows Easy Transfer. To start Windows Easy Transfer, open the path that contains the Windows Easy Transfer files (on a UFD, removable USB drive, or network share) that you created earlier and then double-click the Windows Easy Transfer shortcut.
   b. On the Welcome To Windows Easy Transfer screen, click Next.
   c. Click A Network.
   d. Click This Is My Old Computer.
   e. Record the Windows Easy Transfer key.
4. On the new computer, complete the following steps:
   a. In Windows Easy Transfer, click Next.
   b. On the Enter Your Windows Easy Transfer Key screen, type the Windows Easy Transfer key that you noted previously for the old computer and then click Next.
   c. On the Choose What To Transfer To This Computer screen, choose the accounts that you want to transfer to Windows 7 and then click Next. You can select which types of files and settings to transfer by clicking Customize. Additionally, you can map account names from the old computer to account names in Windows 7 by clicking Advanced Options.
   d. Click Transfer to begin transferring the documents and settings from the migration file to the computer.
   e. On the Your Transfer Is Complete screen, click See What Was Transferred to see a detailed list of the accounts, documents, and settings transferred from the previous operating system to Windows 7, or click See A List Of Programs You Might Want To Install On Your New Computer to see a list of applications installed on the previous operating system that you might want to reinstall in Windows 7. After reviewing the migration reports, click Close.
   f. Click Restart Now to restart the computer. You must restart the computer for the changes to take effect.

Planning User State Migration Using USMT

Thoughtful planning is a critical factor in the success of any user state migration project. By identifying the scope of the migration, you can plan storage space requirements, labor, and development time required to successfully implement the migration solution. This section describes user state migration planning topics such as using subject matter experts (SMEs), identifying and prioritizing user state data, storing user state data, and testing the effort.

NOTE The team responsible for planning and developing user state migration must work hand-in-hand with the team responsible for application deployment. Both teams will share a lab environment, application portfolio, SMEs, and so on. For more information, see Chapter 8, "Deploying Applications." In some cases, the same IT professionals responsible for application deployment are also responsible for user state migration.

DIRECT FROM THE SOURCE

Planning

Doug Davis, Lead Architect
Management Operations & Deployment, Microsoft Consulting Services

The main thing I have found about user state migration is that very few companies actually know which files they need to migrate. Even fewer have an idea about settings. The largest concern is, of course, lost data—the settings matter less.

Customers who use IntelliMirror features such as folder redirection and offline folders are the easiest to deal with; however, these customers are the minority. There are really only two ways to get user data and files. Asking the client which files they use never works and just drags out the process. You're left with another way that drives user feedback: to do full backups on your proof-of-concept and pilot groups and run standard USMT without any custom settings. When users ask for files to be recovered from the backup, you add them to the custom settings to be retained.

The second way takes a little bit longer and is what I call intern-ware: If you have an intern, you can give him or her this busy work. Figure out which applications are critical to you, search the registry for "open with," and cross-reference the file extensions to the program.

Choosing Subject Matter Experts

Although IT professionals in small organizations probably know each application and the settings used in the computing environment, this is highly unlikely to be the case in large organizations that potentially have thousands of applications. In large organizations, you should use SMEs to help in the planning, development, and stabilizing processes. SMEs, though not necessarily experts, are the users who are most familiar with the applications and data to migrate, and they're usually stakeholders in seeing that the process is properly performed.

Use SMEs to assist with several key tasks:

- Locating application source media, such as CDs or DVDs

- Identifying document storage locations for each application
- Identifying application configuration data and settings to migrate
- Selecting the operating system preferences to migrate
- Consulting on file relocations that will be performed as part of the migration

Identifying User State Data

User state data can consist of many elements: settings that customize the user experience, application data created by the user, e-mail and messaging settings and data, and even personal data. The following sections describe examples of user state data.

Operating System Settings

The following list describes many of the operating system files and settings that you will want to migrate. (USMT migrates most of these by default.)

- **Appearance settings** Examples include desktop background, colors, sounds, and screensaver settings.
- **User interface settings** Examples include mouse pointers, whether double-clicking a folder opens it in a new window or in the same window, and whether users must click or double-click an item to open it.
- **Windows Internet Explorer settings** Examples include home pages, favorites, cookies, security settings, and proxy settings.
- **Mail settings** Examples include mail server settings, signature files, and contact lists.

Application Data and Settings

You will find application data in a number of locations. As you inventory the applications in your environment, consider the following potential locations for application settings and data storage:

- **The Program Files folder** Many applications still store settings and data directly in the Applications folder within Program Files. As you plan the migration, consider whether or not you can safely redirect the application data to a different location. This will assist with future attempts to allow use of the application by standard (non-administrator) users.
- **A specific folder on the local disk** Many applications define a data storage location on the local disk for storage of application settings and data. This location is often the root of the system drive.
- **The user's profile folder** Many applications store data in user profile folders. Search the Documents And Settings folder (in Windows XP) or the Users folder (in Windows Vista and Windows 7) for application settings and data files.

Users' Documents

Users will store data in a variety of locations. The following strategies will help you locate users' documents:

- **Search user profile folders** The Desktop and My Documents folders are only two of many locations where you will find user data in the user profile folders. Ideally, however, these two folders are the primary location of users' documents.
- **Interview users and SMEs** Survey users and interview SMEs to determine common storage locations for documents. An intranet Web site, possibly based on Windows SharePoint Services, is an ideal data-collection tool.
- **Scan a sample of disks** Search the local disks for common document file extensions such as .doc and .xls. Although you can't scan every disk in the organization, you can scan a representative sample to give you an idea of where you'll find documents.
- **Search Recent Documents** Scan the Recent folder in users' profiles to determine the locations most frequently used to store data. This can expose some of the less intuitive storage locations. Search a representative sample of users in the organization.

DIRECT FROM THE SOURCE

USMT and ACT

Doug Davis, Lead Architect
Management Operations & Deployment, Microsoft Consulting Services

Application Compatibility Toolkit 4.0 (ACT 4.0) always grabbed the registered file extensions in the log files but never posted them to the database. In my review of the functional specification of ACT 5.0, I asked to have that log data posted to the database even if it wasn't exposed in the graphical user interface (GUI).

With a little work using SQL Server, you should be able to use ACT to find out which applications you are migrating and then sort the file extensions you need for USMT in a more logical fashion. For example, you can extract the file extensions that are a high priority from the ACT database for applications in the portfolio and then focus on migrating those applications first.

Prioritizing Migration Tasks

As you compile your user state migration requirements, prioritize them according to their impact on the organization. It's important to the success of this project to concentrate first on mission-critical data and later on preferences such as desktop wallpaper or screensaver settings. Prioritizing requirements helps the development personnel to prioritize their work. SMEs are a valuable source of input when prioritizing the migration requirements.

Choosing a Data Store Location

USMT stores user state in a data store. USMT can create the data store in a variety of locations and media during migration. By default, USMT creates a store file that contains compressed user data. It can also encrypt the data store to protect the data during the transition to the new operating system. As you prepare for user state migration, you must determine the best location for the USMT data store.

Consider the following when locating the USMT data store:

- **Hard-link migration reduces storage requirements** During a hard-link migration, USMT maps how a collection of bits on the hard disk is wired into the file system. It allows you to remove the old operating system and install Windows 7 without requiring you to create copies of the original files. After installing Windows 7, USMT restores the original file links. Hard-link migration uses significantly less disk space and takes considerably less time, but you can perform a hard-link migration only in the Refresh Computer scenario.
- **USMT cannot store multiple operations in the same file** USMT operations can collect data from more than one user but cannot store more than one operation in a single store file. In a high-volume migration, you can either locate the data store locally (which is only possible because the Windows 7 imaging process is nondestructive) or locate each data store on the network (possibly organized by computer name). Note that MDT 2010 handles the data store location automatically and provides choices for customizing it.
- **User state data can use significant space** When creating your migration plan, you can run the ScanState component of USMT with the */p:<path to a file>* command-line option to create a size estimate. If you're locating the data store on a server, rather than locally, run this command on a representative sample of computers in the environment to calculate the storage required.
- **The USMT data store must be accessible to both the source and target systems** When writing to or reading from the data store, USMT must have access to that data store. Locate the file somewhere that will be available to both computers. MDT 2010 handles this issue somewhat transparently. If you're locating the data store locally, access is not an issue.

Local Data Stores

You can locate the USMT data store on the local disk in the Refresh Computer scenario. (See Chapter 4, "Planning Deployment," for a description of deployment scenarios.) ImageX and Windows Setup are *nondestructive*, which means that they can install the operating system without destroying the data on the disk. This optimizes the speed of the migration process because network speeds and removable media speeds are factored out of the process. MDT 2010 provides the option to use local data stores.

A better option is using a hard-link migration store, which enables you to perform an in-place migration in which USMT maintains all user state on the local computer while you remove the old operating system and install the new operating system. Therefore, hard-link migration is suitable only for the Refresh Computer scenario. Using a hard-link migration store drastically improves migration performance and significantly reduces hard-disk utilization, reduces deployment costs, and enables entirely new migration scenarios.

Remote Data Stores

In the Replace Computer (side-by-side) and New Computer scenarios, you can put the USMT data store on a network server. In these scenarios, putting the data store on the network is necessary because the local data store will not be available in the postinstallation phase.

Removable Storage

You can also put USMT store files on removable media during the migration process. You can use flash disks and portable hard disks to simplify this process. Because this step adds interaction to the process, it is recommended only in bench deployments or in scenarios in which you've already factored interaction into the deployment process.

Automating USMT

The full power of the USMT is realized when you automate migration. Through the use of scripting techniques—or tools such as MDT 2010 and Microsoft System Center Configuration Manager 2007—you can automate the migration of large numbers of systems. The following list describes each option:

- **Scripting** You can execute USMT with a variety of scripting tools, including Windows PowerShell, VBScript, and batch script files. By including the appropriate command-line options, you can automate the migration process to collect and restore user state data. End users can then execute these scripts to migrate their own data.
- **Microsoft Deployment Toolkit** MDT 2010 fully enables user state migration as part of the LTI and ZTI deployment processes. You can customize the location of the data stores and customize the migration .xml files to include or exclude user state as defined by your requirements (although this is often not necessary with USMT 4.0). Using the default migration .xml files with MDT 2010 is an extremely simple, straightforward process. Thus, the only real effort is in creating custom migration .xml files for USMT, if necessary.
- **Configuration Manager** Configuration Manager can be used as is or with MDT 2010 to automate user state migration as part of operating system deployment. For more information about using USMT with Configuration Manager alone, see the System Center Configuration Manager 2007 documentation.

Testing User State Migration

After you set up the USMT migration .xml files and infrastructure, you should conduct a test pass to ensure that the solution works as planned. Test modularly: start with migration files first, followed by command-line options and automation. As you create the project plan, define testable criteria. With a test plan already established, you will be prepared to begin testing as soon as the development is complete.

Creating a Lab Environment

Establish a test lab with equipment and settings similar to systems in production in your organization. The goal is to test each scenario you will see in the production environment. Duplicate your production environment in as much detail as possible. Set up migration servers and data stores, configure source and target client systems, and prepare and place control files in the appropriate locations. Finally, execute the test and measure the results. The team responsible for user state migration should share a lab environment with the team responsible for application deployment. (For more information, see Chapter 8.)

Choosing Sample Data

If possible, conduct the migration tests on actual production data. You can copy this data from production systems as you prepare for the testing. For example, you can create images of SME computers for testing purposes. Testing on production data helps ensure that you expose the migration infrastructure to all scenarios that will be seen in the production environment.

Be sure to choose the following types of production data:

- **Operating system settings** You should test desktop and appearance settings. Users can nominate elements for testing, or you can select a sample based on the results of user surveys. Test user profile settings and user preference settings to ensure that they are properly migrated. Identify a set of user settings that you can test.
- **Application data and settings** Include application data such as configuration files and data files in your test plan. Test application registry settings and initialization files to ensure that they are properly migrated. Work with developers and SMEs to identify a representative sample of these configuration settings to test.
- **Users' documents** Choose a representative sample of user data. Include sources such as My Documents and any custom data folders found in your environment.

Running the Test

Run the USMT test using the migration .xml files and procedures that you have developed for the production environment. The goal is to simulate the production migration with as much detail as possible. Be sure to use any scripts and processes designed to automate the USMT process.

Validating the Test Results

Following the migration test, verify all user state elements that have been defined for testing. View each setting and test each migrated application. Open the e-mail client and operate applications to ensure that user customizations still exist in the new system. Identify any errors and list any items that failed to migrate. Investigate these elements to ensure that you properly configured the control files for the migration. If necessary, retest to verify that problems have been resolved.

Installing USMT

USMT 4.0 is included in the Windows Automated Installation Kit 2.0 (Windows AIK 2.0). You can download the Windows AIK from the Microsoft Download Center at *http://www.microsoft.com/downloads*. After downloading and installing the Windows AIK, the USMT source files are in C:\Program Files\Windows AIK\Tools\USMT*Platform*, where *Platform* is either amd64 or x86.

You can stage USMT directly on each client computer or on a network share. If you're using MDT 2010, it can install USMT in deployment shares automatically. MDT 2010 already contains logic for using USMT to save and restore user state data on each computer.

You use USMT in a number of ways: on a network share, on Windows PE media, on an MDT 2010 deployment share, or with Configuration Manager. The last two options enable migration during LTI and ZTI deployment projects. The following sections describe each option.

Network Share

After installing the Windows AIK on a local computer, you can copy the contents of the C:\Program Files\Windows AIK\Tools\USMT\ to a network share. Then you can run ScanState and LoadState remotely on each computer.

Windows PE Media

USMT 4.0 supports offline migration. That is, you can run USMT from a Windows PE session to save user state data without actually starting the old operating system. To support this scenario, you must copy the USMT binary files to your Windows PE media. For more information about creating Windows PE media, see Chapter 9, "Preparing Windows PE."

Microsoft Deployment Toolkit

Unlike earlier versions of MDT, MDT 2010 automatically adds USMT to deployment shares when you update them. It copies the files from the Windows AIK to the USMT folder in the deployment share. You do not have to do anything additional to install USMT in a deployment share.

Configuration Manager

You can use USMT with Configuration Manager to manage user state migrations during operating system deployment. For more information, see the System Center Configuration Manager 2007 documentation.

Understanding USMT Components

After downloading and installing the Windows AIK, the USMT source files are in C:\Program Files\Windows AIK\Tools\USMT*Platform*, where *Platform* is either amd64 or x86. The installer copies many files into this folder, including .dll files, feature manifests, and other application initialization files. (See Figure 7-3.) Most of the files support the two main executables: Scanstate.exe and Loadstate.exe.

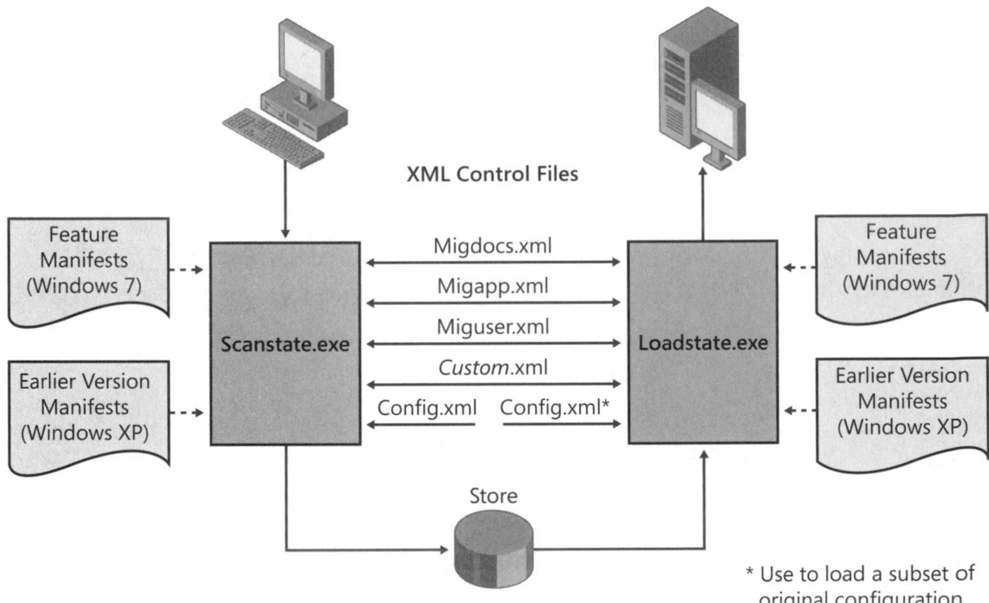

FIGURE 7-3 USMT components

In addition to ScanState and LoadState, USMT uses three XML migration files—MigApp.xml, MigDocs.xml, and MigUser.xml—to perform basic file and settings migrations based on default criteria. You can customize these files, along with custom .xml files, to migrate additional files and settings or to exclude some of the default files and settings. For more information about migration .xml files, see the section titled "Developing Migration Files" later in this chapter.

ScanState and LoadState save and restore user state data, respectively. You can run them directly from a command prompt. They provide several command-line options that control their behavior. USMT 4.0 includes an additional utility called UsmtUtils.exe. This utility helps you to determine cryptographic options for your migration. It also helps remove hard-link stores that you cannot delete otherwise due to a sharing lock.

Scanstate.exe

You use ScanState to save user state data. By default, this program places user state data into the data store location as defined by the three migration .xml files. The following describes an abbreviated syntax of ScanState, and Table 7-1 describes each command-line option.

```
Scanstate.exe [Store][/i:[path\]filename] [/config:[path\]file] [/hardlink /nocompress]
[/o] [/p[:file]] [/vsc]
```

TABLE 7-1 Scanstate.exe Command-Line Options

OPTION	DESCRIPTION
Store	Specifies a path to the data store.
/config:[path\]file	Specifies a Config.xml file. (See the section titled "Developing Migration Files" later in this chapter for more information.)
/hardlink	Enables the creation of a hard-link migration store at the location specified by *Store*. You must specify the */nocompress* option when using this option.
/i:[path\]filename	Identifies a migration .xml file to use when saving state data. You can use this option multiple times.
/nocompress	Disables data compression. Use this option only with the */hardlink* option or when testing in a lab environment.
/o	Overwrites existing data in the data store.
/p[:file]	Creates a size estimate in the path specified. When used without a path, it creates a size estimate file called USMTsize.txt in the location specified by *Store*.
/vsc	Enables use of the Volume Shadow Copy service to migrate files that are locked or in use during migration.

> ***NOTE*** **ScanState supports many other command-line options. For a complete list of these options, see the USMT.chm help file in the Windows AIK.**

Loadstate.exe

You use LoadState to restore user state from the data store. By default, this program restores user state to the location from which ScanState originally saved it—unless one of the migration .xml files redirects it. You must specify the same migration .xml files to LoadState that you did to ScanState. The following describes an abbreviated syntax of LoadState, and Table 7-2 describes each command-line option.

```
Loadstate.exe [Store][/i:[path\]filename] [/hardlink /nocompress]
```

TABLE 7-2 Loadstate.exe Command-Line Options

OPTION	DESCRIPTION
Store	Specifies a path to the data store.
/i:[path\]filename	Identifies a migration .xml file to use when restoring user state data. You can use this option multiple times.
/config:[path\]file	Specifies a Config.xml file. (See the section titled "Developing Migration Files" later in this chapter for more information.)
/hardlink	Enables the creation of a hard-link migration store at the location specified by *Store*. You must specify the */nocompress* option when using this option.
/nocompress	Disables data compression. Use this option only with the */hardlink* option or when testing in a lab environment.

NOTE LoadState supports many other command-line options. For a complete list of these options, see the USMT.chm help file in the Windows AIK.

Migration Files

Both ScanState and LoadState use three migration .xml files to control migrations. In addition to these three files, you can specify one or more custom .xml files to migrate custom applications or customize the standard migrations. The following section, "Developing Migration Files," describes the .xml files that come with USMT and how to build custom migration files.

Developing Migration Files

USMT ships with three standard migration .xml files. You can customize these files to control the behavior of USMT during migration. In addition to the three standard files, you can develop custom .xml files to migrate special application settings and files. The three migration .xml files included with USMT are:

- **MigApp.xml** Contains rules to migrate application settings.
- **MigDocs.xml** Contains rules that can find user documents on a computer automatically without creating extensive custom migration .xml files. Use this migration file if the data set is unknown. Don't use this migration file and MigUser.xml together.
- **MigUser.xml** Contains results to migrate user profiles and user data. Don't use this migration file and MigDocs.xml together.

Customizing USMT

You manage USMT through command-line options and the migration .xml files. You could modify the default files to control some aspects of the migration, but this is not recommended. The better option is to create custom .xml files to migrate specific application settings and data. The following list describes customization points for USMT:

- **Command-Line Control** You can use command-line options, such as */ui* and */ue*, to include and exclude specific users during the migration process. You can also specify custom .xml files and manage encryption and compression options.
- **Customizing the Migration XML Files** You can modify the migration .xml files to exclude portions of a standard migration or to redirect data and settings during the migration process. This capability is helpful for scenarios in which you want to consolidate migrated data, but a better alternative to customizing the existing migration files is creating custom migration files.
- **Generating Config.xml** You can generate a Config.xml file to exclude an entire feature from the migration. For example, you can exclude the entire Documents folder or exclude all of the settings for a specific application. Using this file to exclude features is easier than modifying the migration .xml files because you don't have to understand the migration rules or syntax. Using this file is also the only way to exclude operating system settings when migrating to Windows 7. For more information about Config.xml, see the USMT.chm help file in the Windows AIK.

NOTE You can use migration .xml files that you created for USMT 3.0 with USMT 4.0. To use new USMT features, you must refresh your migration files to use new XML elements and command-line options.

Control File Syntax

The default migration .xml files use XML elements to control migration behavior. These files cover the most common applications, documents, and settings. If you want to migrate settings and application data that the default migration .xml files don't cover, you should create a custom .xml file. The full XML reference for USMT is in the USMT.chm help file in the Windows AIK. Additionally, the XML reference in USMT.chm contains good examples that you can use as your starting point for creating custom migration .xml files.

NOTE The best practice is to create custom migration .xml files instead of adding application data and settings to the default migration .xml files. Doing so makes maintaining those settings easier over time and prevents confusion.

Deploying Migration Files

The following list describes how to deploy custom migration .xml files for stand-alone use, with MDT 2010, and with Configuration Manager:

- **Stand-alone use** You can store the migration .xml files in the USMT program folder or place them in a central location. You must specify the full path to each migration .xml file (Scanstate *server**share**computer* /l:*server**share**migration*.xml).
- **Microsoft Deployment Toolkit** MDT 2010 has a specific organization for deployment shares. You must store custom migration .xml files in the USMT*platform* folder of the deployment share, where *platform* is either x86 or x64.
- **Configuration Manager** Configuration Manager uses USMT to migrate user state data during operating system deployments. You can specify the location of migration .xml files and data stores during the configuration of Configuration Manager. See the System Center Configuration Manager 2007 documentation for more information.

Using USMT in Microsoft Deployment Toolkit

User state migrations can be started and controlled in a number of ways. Among these are direct command-line execution, scripting, MDT 2010, and Configuration Manager. The section titled "Understanding USMT Components" earlier in this chapter describes the command-line options for running USMT directly or driving it by using scripts. This section describes how to enable USMT in MDT 2010, as well as how to add custom migration .xml files to MDT 2010.

HOW IT WORKS

State Migration in MDT 2010

Chapter 6, "Developing Disk Images," describes the task sequence and Task Sequencer that MDT 2010 uses for deploying Windows 7. The default task sequence separates the process into two phases. One of the preinstallation phases is State Capture; one of the postinstallation phases is State Restore. The entire state migration work is tucked into these two phases.

In the State Capture phase, the Capture User State step runs ZTIUserState.wsf /Capture to capture user state. It uses settings from the deployment share's CustomSettings.ini file or the MDT 2010 database. In the State Restore phase, the Restore User State step runs ZTIUserState.wsf /Restore to restore the state data captured in the Capture User Step.

For the */capture* command-line option, ZTIUserState.wsf reads its settings (UDDShare, UDDir, and so on) from the environment and then chooses the best place to create the data store based upon UserDataLocation. In the final step, the script executes ScanState with the command-line arguments that it assembled from the data in the environment, adding the command-line options for hard-link migration. For the */restore* command-line option, ZTIUserState.wsf retrieves information about the data store it created from the environment and then runs LoadState using the command line that it assembled from that information, also adding command-line options for hard-link migration.

Specifying the Data Store Location

Performing hard-link migrations is the recommended action in Refresh Computer scenarios, and this is the default behavior of MDT 2010. For other scenarios, you can create the data stores within the MDT 2010 deployment share. However, creating a share for the data stores on a separate server is better than putting the data stores in the deployment share because it spreads the load and allows you to dedicate resources to user state migration more easily.

After creating the share for the data stores, you configure the data store location by customizing properties in each deployment share's CustomSettings.ini file, as shown in Figure 7-4. To configure CustomSettings.ini, right-click a deployment share in Deployment Workbench and click Properties; then configure CustomSettings.ini on the Rules tab. You can also customize these properties in the MDT 2010 database. Table 7-3 describes these properties. For more information about CustomSettings.ini and the MDT 2010 database, see Chapter 12, "Deploying with Microsoft Deployment Toolkit."

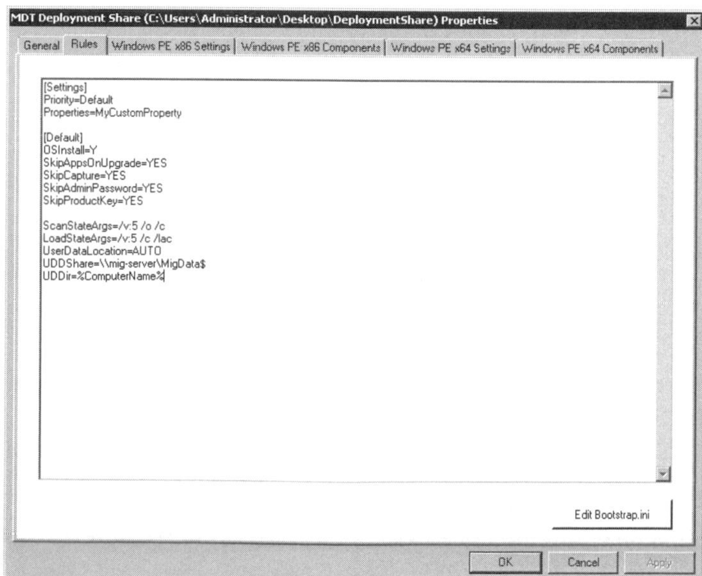

FIGURE 7-4 Configuring USMT settings in CustomSettings.ini

TABLE 7-3 USMT Properties in MDT 2010

PROPERTY	CONTROLS
LoadStateArgs=*arguments*	The arguments passed to LoadState. MDT 2010 inserts the appropriate logging, progress, and data store parameters. If this value is not included in the settings file, ZTIUserState.wsf uses LoadStateArgs=*/v:5 /c /lac*.
ScanStateArgs=*arguments*	The arguments passed to ScanState. MDT 2010 inserts the appropriate logging, progress, and data store parameters. If this value is not included in the settings file, ZTIUserState.wsf uses ScanStateArgs=*/v:5 /o /c*. Use the property *USMTMigFiles* to specify the .xml files to be used by Scanstate.exe instead of using the */i* parameter in the *ScanStateArgs* property. This prevents the ZTIUserState script from potentially duplicating the same list of .xml files.
UDDShare=*Path*	The network share in which to create data stores, such as *UDDShare=\\server\MigData$*. This value is ignored when performing hard-link migrations.
UDDir=*Folder*	The folder where the user state migration data is stored. This folder exists beneath the network shared folder specified in UDDShare. For example, UDDir=%ComputerName%. This value is ignored when performing hard-link migrations.
UserDataLocation=[*blank* | AUTO | NETWORK | NONE]	The location in which user state migration data is stored: ■ *BLANK* For LTI, the Windows Deployment Wizard prompts for the storage location. For ZTI, this is the same as setting the property to NONE. ■ *AUTO* MDT 2010 performs a hard-link migration. ■ *NETWORK* MDT 2010 creates the data store in the location designated by the UDDShare and UDDir properties.
UDProfiles=*Profile1*, *Profile2*, *ProfileN*	A list of user profiles to save during the MDT 2010 State Capture phase by Scanstate.exe, such as UDProfiles=Administrator, Patrice, Dave.

NOTE You can also use removable media and local data stores during a user state migration by not setting the UserDataLocation value. The Windows Deployment Wizard will prompt you for the user data location. See the Toolkit Reference in MDT 2010 for more details about these properties.

Adding Custom Migration Files

MDT 2010 will use only the MigApp.xml and MigDocs.xml files unless you indicate the path to your custom .xml files. As with other properties in MDT 2010, you can configure them in each deployment point's CustomSettings.ini file or add them to the MDT 2010 database.

Set the property USMTMigFiles to the name of each custom migration .xml file. If you don't configure this property, MDT 2010 uses the default migration files: MigApp.xml and MigDocs.xml. If you do configure this option, MDT 2010 uses only the files specified in the property. Therefore, if you configure this property, it must also include the default migration .xml files. For example, the following line in CustomSettings.ini adds Custom.xml to the default .xml files.

```
USMTMigFiles1=MigApp.xml
USMTMigFiles2=MigDocs.xml
USMTMigFiles4=Custom.xml
```

> ***NOTE*** **Do not try to customize the script that drives the USMT process (ZTIUserState.wsf) to add migration .xml files by adding the */i* command-line option. This can potentially cause the script to work improperly and may make upgrading to future versions of MDT problematic. Add custom migration .xml files only by customizing the *USMTMigFiles* property.**

Summary

Migrating user state is an important aspect of desktop deployment because it minimizes lost productivity and increases user satisfaction. User state migration requires thorough planning and a good understanding of user, application, and system settings, as well as knowledge of the location of data files in your environment. SMEs can assist with the identification of files and settings for migration, and you should test all migration projects extensively to ensure that they will function properly in your production environment.

USMT offers the most powerful migration options for high-volume deployment projects. As a user state migration engine, USMT has support built in to MDT 2010. In fact, you can provide support for migrating most common data and settings with not much more effort than customizing each deployment share's CustomSettings.ini. By creating custom migration .xml files, you can add support for corner cases and custom applications that your organization uses.

Additional Resources

These resources contain additional information and tools related to this chapter.

- Chapter 12, "Deploying with Microsoft Deployment Toolkit," includes more information on using MDT 2010 to migrate users.
- Chapter 15, "Managing Users and User Data," includes details on roaming user profiles and Folder Redirection.
- USMT.chm in the Windows AIK includes detailed information about ScanState and LoadState command-line options, creating XML migration files, and other more advanced scenarios like offline migration.
- User State Migration Tool 4.0 documentation on Microsoft TechNet at *http://technet.microsoft.com/en-us/library/dd560801.aspx.*

CHAPTER 8

Deploying Applications

Deploying applications is an important aspect of desktop deployment. Choosing the applications you want to deploy, and deciding how to deploy them, affects the choices that you make when deploying the operating system. For example, will you include applications in the operating system image or deploy them later? Including applications in the operating system image provides good performance but low flexibility; deploying them later provides poorer performance but higher flexibility and lower maintenance costs.

During the planning stages of your deployment project, you must identify each application used in the environment. Then you must prioritize the application inventory so that you can focus on the most important applications first and possibly eliminate applications that are duplicates, no longer in use, or unsupported by the Windows 7 operating system.

After creating a prioritized application inventory, you must find and mitigate compatibility issues (a process described in Chapter 5, "Testing Application Compatibility"). Then you determine how to deploy the applications. This chapter helps you make these decisions and use the tools that Microsoft provides for deploying applications, including Microsoft Deployment Toolkit 2010 (MDT 2010). See Chapter 5 to learn how to create an application inventory, test applications for compatibility with Windows 7, and resolve the compatibility issues that you find.

Preparing the Lab

Planning application deployment requires a lab environment for application repackaging. Within an organization, different teams that work on deployment (image engineering, application packaging, and so on) can and often should share a single lab environment. Sharing a lab enables teams to share deliverables and integration-test their work with other components more easily. In a shared lab environment, however, each team must have its own workspace on the file server and dedicated computers on which to work.

Although the lab must have access to the Internet, it should be insulated from the production network. However, if you don't install any server features like Dynamic Host Configuration Protocol (DHCP), separating the lab from the production network is not a rigid requirement. Application repackaging does not require that the lab mirror the production network. The lab must provide storage space for application source files and repackaged applications.

The following list describes the recommended requirements for a lab used to repackage applications:

- A lab server configured as follows:
  - Windows Server 2008 or Windows Server 2008 R2
  - An Active Directory Domain Services domain
  - DHCP services
  - Domain Name System (DNS) services
  - Windows Internet Naming Service (WINS) services (optional)
  - Microsoft SQL Server 2005 or SQL Server 2008
  - Microsoft Virtual Server 2005, Microsoft Virtual PC 2007, Microsoft Windows Virtual PC, or Microsoft Hyper-V
- Lab test accounts (for standard users and an administrator)
- Network hardware to provide connectivity (consider the routing and bandwidth so that moving large files doesn't impact users on the production network)
- Internet access (for downloading updates, files, and so on)
- Test computers that accurately reflect production computers
- Source files for all applications to be tested and repackaged
- Software repackaging tools

> **_NOTE_** **MDT 2010 provides prescriptive guidance for building and using a deployment lab. For more information, see the "Getting Started Guide" in MDT 2010.**

Planning Deployment

Creating an application inventory is the main task you must complete when planning application deployment. You use the inventory to prioritize applications—determining which are not compatible with Windows 7, which you must repackage for automatic installation, and so on. The Application Compatibility Toolkit (ACT) provides tools for collecting an application inventory based on the production network. For more information about using ACT to inventory applications, see Chapter 5.

After creating an application inventory, you must take the following planning steps for each application in the list:

- **Priorities** Prioritize the application inventory so that you can focus on the most important applications first. Focus on the applications that help your organization provide products and services to customers. While you are prioritizing the inventory, you might discover duplicate applications (different versions of the same application or different applications fulfilling the same purpose) that you can eliminate. You may also discover many applications that were used for a short-term project and are no longer required.
- **Categories** Categorize each application in the inventory as a core application or a supplemental application. A core application is common to most computers (virus scanners, management agents, and so on), whereas a supplemental application is not. Chapter 5 recommends additional ways in which you can categorize applications, such as by department, geography, cost center, worker type, and so on.
- **Installation method** Determine how to install the application automatically. Whether the application is a core or supplemental application, you achieve the best results by completely automating the installation. You cannot automate the installation of some legacy applications; you must repackage them. If so, the best time to choose a repackaging technology is while planning deployment. For more information about repackaging technologies, see the section titled "Repackaging Legacy Applications" later in this chapter.
- **Determine responsibility** Determine who owns and is responsible for the installation and support of each application. Does IT own the application or does the user's organization own it?
- **Subject matter experts** You will not have the in-depth understanding of all applications in the organization that you will need to repackage them all. Therefore, for each application, identify a subject matter expert (SME) who can help you make important decisions. A good SME is not necessarily a highly technical person. A good SME is the person most familiar with an application, its history in the organization, how the organization uses it, where to find the media, and so on.

- **Configuration** Based on feedback from each application's SME, document the desired configuration of each application. You can capture the desired configuration in transforms that you create for Windows Installer–based applications or within packages that you create when repackaging older applications. Configuring older applications is usually as easy as importing Registration Entries (.reg) files on the destination computer after deployment.

ACT 5.5 provides data organization features that supersede the application inventory templates in earlier versions of MDT. With ACT 5.5, you can categorize applications a number of ways: by priority, risk, department, type, vendor, complexity, and so on. You can also create your own categories for organizing the application inventory. For more information, see Chapter 5.

Priorities

After creating an application inventory, the next step is to prioritize the list. Prioritizing the application inventory is not a task that you perform unilaterally. Instead, you will want to involve other team members, management, and user representatives in the review of priorities.

The priority levels you choose to use might include the following:

- **High** High-priority applications are most likely mission-critical or core applications. These are applications that are pervasive in the organization or are complex and must be addressed first. Examples of high-priority applications include virus scanners, management agents, Microsoft Office, and so on.
- **Medium** Medium-priority applications are nice to have but not essential. These are applications that are not as pervasive or complex as high-priority applications. For example, a custom mailing-list program might be a medium-priority application, because you can replicate the functionality in another application. To test whether an application is indeed a medium priority, answer this question: What's the worst that would happen if all the high-priority applications are deployed, but not this application? If you foresee no major consequences, the application is a medium priority.
- **Low** Low-priority applications are applications that deserve no attention in the process. Examples of low-priority applications are duplicate applications, applications that users have brought from home and installed themselves, and applications that are no longer in use. When prioritizing an application as low, record the reason for that status in case you must defend the decision later.

Prioritizing the application list helps you focus on the applications in an orderly fashion. Within each priority, you can also rank applications by order of importance. Ranking applications in an organization using thousands of applications is a foreboding task, however. Instead, you might want to rank only the high-priority applications or repeat the prioritization process with only the high-priority applications.

Categories

After prioritizing the application list, you must categorize each high- and medium-priority application. You can drop the low-priority applications from the list, as you have no intention of addressing them. The following categories help you determine the best way to deploy an application:

- **Core applications** Core applications are applications common to most of the computers in the organization (typically 80 percent or more) or applications that must be available the first time you start a computer after installing the operating system. For example, virus scanners and security software are usually core applications because they must run the first time you start the computer. Mail clients are core applications because they are common to all users and computers. The following list contains specific examples of what most organizations might consider core applications:
  - Adobe Acrobat Reader
  - Corporate screen savers
  - Database drivers and connectivity software
  - Macromedia Flash Player
  - Macromedia Shockwave
  - Microsoft Office
  - Network and client management software, such as OpenManage clients
  - Terminal emulation applications, such as TN3270
  - Various antivirus packages
  - Various Windows Internet Explorer plug-ins
  - Various Microsoft Office Outlook plug-ins
- **Supplemental applications** Supplemental applications are applications that aren't core applications. These are applications that are not common to most computers in the organization (department-specific applications) and aren't required when you first start the computer after installing a new operating system image. Examples of supplemental applications include applications that are department specific, such as accounting software, or role specific, such as dictation software. The following list contains examples of what most organizations consider supplemental applications:
  - Microsoft Data Analyzer 3.5
  - SQL Server 2005 Client Tools
  - Microsoft Visual Studio 2005 and Visual Studio 2008
  - Various Computer-Aided Design (CAD) applications
  - Various Enterprise Resource Planning (ERP) systems

Installation Methods

For each high- and medium-priority application, you must determine the best way to install it. For each, consider the following:

- **Automatic installation** Most applications provide a way to install automatically. For example, if the application is a Windows Installer package file (with the .msi file extension), you can install the application automatically. The section titled "Automating Installation" later in this chapter describes how to install applications packaged with common technologies automatically. In this case, you don't need to repackage the application unless you want to deploy a configuration that isn't possible otherwise.
- **Repackaged application** If an application does not provide a way to install automatically, you can repackage it to automate and customize installation by using one of the packaging technologies described in the section titled "Repackaging Legacy Applications" later in this chapter. Repackaging applications is a complex process and is quite often the most costly and tedious part of any deployment project. Make the decision to repackage applications only after exhausting other possibilities. Doing so requires technical experience with repackaging applications or using third-party companies to repackage the application for you.
- **Screen scraping** You can automate most applications with interactive installers by using a tool that simulates keystrokes, such as Windows Script Host. (See the section titled "Windows Script Host" later in this chapter for more information.) Understand that this method is more of a hack than a polished solution, but sometimes you're left with no other choice. Occasionally, the installation procedure may require the user to use the mouse or otherwise perform some complex task that cannot be automated easily. In these circumstances, automating the installation process may not be feasible.

For each application, record the installation method. Does the application already support automated installation? If so, record the command required to install the application. Are you required to repackage the application? If so, record the packaging technology you'll use and the command required to install the application. If you will use screen scraping to install the application, indicate that decision in the application inventory.

Subject Matter Experts

In a small organization with a few applications, you might know them all very well. In a large organization with thousands of applications, you will know very few of them well enough to make good decisions about repackaging applications. Therefore, for each application you must identify a SME. This SME should be an expert with the application, having the most experience with it. In other words, each application's SME will have insight into how the organization installs, configures, and uses that application. The SME will know the application's history and where to find the application's source media. Record the name and e-mail alias of each application's SME in the application inventory.

Configurations

During planning, with the SME's help, you should review each application and record the following:

- The location of the installation media. Often, the SME is the best source of information about the location of the source media, such as CDs, disks, and so on.
- Settings that differ from the application's default settings that are required to deploy the application in a desired configuration.
- External connections. For example, does the application require a connection to a database, mainframe, Web site, or other application server?
- Constraints associated with the application.
- Deployment compatibility. Is the application compatible with disk imaging and Sysprep? Is the application compatible with 32-bit systems? 64-bit systems?
- Application dependencies. Does the application depend on any patches or other applications?

Choosing a Deployment Strategy

Most companies share a common goal: create a corporate-standard desktop configuration based on a common image for each operating system version. They want to apply a common image to any desktop in any region at any time and then customize that image quickly to provide services to users.

In reality, most organizations build and maintain many images—sometimes even hundreds of images. By making technical and support compromises and disciplined hardware purchases, and by using advanced scripting techniques, some organizations have reduced the number of images they maintain to between one and three. These organizations tend to have the sophisticated software distribution infrastructures necessary to deploy applications—often before first use—and keep them updated.

Business requirements usually drive the need to reduce the number of images that an organization maintains. Of course, the primary business requirement is to reduce ownership costs. The following list describes costs associated with building, maintaining, and deploying disk images:

- **Development costs** Development costs include creating a well-engineered image to lower future support costs and improve security and reliability. They also include creating a predictable work environment for maximum productivity balanced with flexibility. Higher levels of automation lower development costs.
- **Test costs** Test costs include testing time and labor costs for the standard image, the applications that might reside inside it, and those applications applied after deployment. Test costs also include the development time required to stabilize disk images.

- **Storage costs** Storage costs include storage of the deployment shares, disk images, migration data, and backup images. Storage costs can be significant, depending on the number of disk images, number of computers in each deployment run, and so on.
- **Network costs** Network costs include moving disk images to deployment shares and to desktops.

As the size of image files increases, costs increase. Large images have more updating, testing, distribution, network, and storage costs associated with them. Even though you update only a small portion of the image, you must distribute the entire file.

Thick Images

Thick images are monolithic images that contain core applications and other files. Part of the image-development process is installing core applications prior to capturing the disk image, as shown in Figure 8-1. To date, most organizations that use disk imaging to deploy operating systems are building thick images.

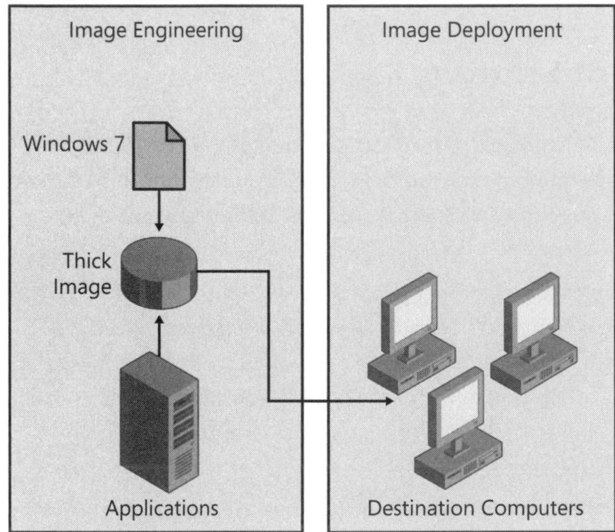

FIGURE 8-1 The thick image process

The advantage of thick images is deployment speed and simplicity. You create a disk image that contains core applications and thus have only a single step to deploy the disk image and core applications to the destination computer. Thick images also can be less costly to develop, as advanced scripting techniques are not often required to build them. In fact, you can build thick images by using MDT 2010 with little or no scripting work. Finally, in thick images, core applications are available on first start.

The disadvantages of thick images are maintenance, storage, and network costs, which rise with thick images. For example, updating a thick image with a new version of an application requires you to rebuild, retest, and redistribute the image. Thick images require more storage and use more network resources in a short span of time to transfer.

If you choose to build thick images that include applications, you will want to install the applications during the disk-imaging process. In this case, see the following sections later in this chapter:

- See "Automating Installation" to learn how to install applications silently.
- See "Injecting in a Disk Image" to learn how to add applications to the deployment shares you create by using MDT 2010 and capturing them in a disk image.

Thin Images

The key to reducing image count, size, and cost is compromise. The more you put in an image, the less common and bigger it becomes. Big images are less attractive to deploy over a network, more difficult to update regularly, more difficult to test, and more expensive to store. By compromising on what you include in images, you reduce the number you maintain and you reduce their size. Ideally, you build and maintain a single, worldwide image that you customize post-deployment. A key compromise is when you choose to build *thin images*.

Thin images contain few if any core applications. You install applications separately from the disk image, as shown in Figure 8-2. Installing the applications separately from the image usually takes more time at the desktop and possibly more total bytes transferred over the network, but spread out over a longer period of time than a single large image transfer. You can mitigate the network transfer by using trickle-down technology that many software distribution infrastructures provide, such as Background Intelligent Transfer Service (BITS).

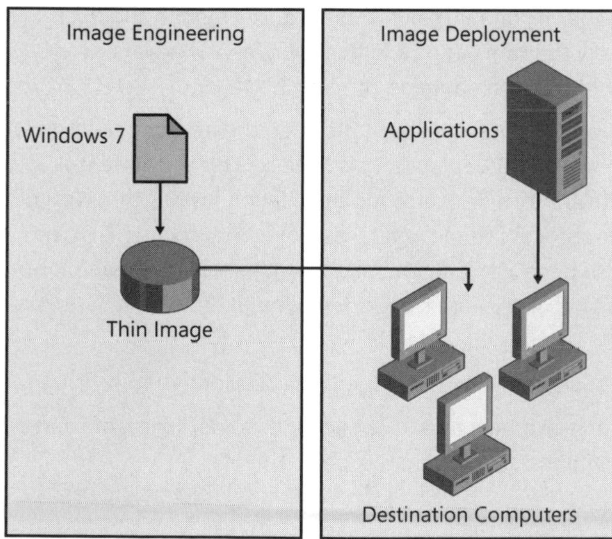

FIGURE 8-2 The thin image process

Thin images have many advantages. First, they cost less to build, maintain, and test. Second, network and storage costs associated with the disk image are lower because the image file is physically smaller. The primary disadvantage of thin images is that postinstallation configuration can be more complex to develop initially, but this is offset by the reduction in costs to build successive images. Deploying applications outside the disk image often requires scripting and usually requires a software distribution infrastructure. Another disadvantage of thin images is that core applications aren't available on first start, which might be necessary in high-security scenarios.

If you choose to build thin images that do not include applications, you should have a systems-management infrastructure, such as Microsoft System Center Configuration Manager 2007, in place to deploy applications. To use a thin image strategy, you will use this infrastructure to deploy applications after installing the thin image. You can also use this infrastructure for other postinstallation configuration tasks, such as customizing operating system settings.

Hybrid Images

Hybrid images mix thin- and thick-image strategies. In a hybrid image, you configure the disk image to install applications on first run, giving the illusion of a thick image but installing the applications from a network source. Hybrid images have most of the advantages of thin images. However, they aren't as complex to develop and do not require a software distribution infrastructure. They do require longer installation times, however, which can raise initial deployment costs.

An alternative is to build one-off thick images from a thin image. In this case, you build a reference thin image. After the thin image is complete, you add core applications and then capture, test, and distribute a thick image. Testing is minimized because creating the thick images from the thin image is essentially the same as a regular deployment. Be wary of applications that are not compatible with the disk-imaging process, however.

If you choose to build hybrid images, you will store applications on the network but include the commands to install them when you deploy the disk image. This is different than installing the applications in the disk image. You are deferring application installs that would normally occur during the disk-imaging process to the image-deployment process. They become a postinstallation task. Also, if you have a systems-management infrastructure in place, you will likely use it to install supplemental applications post-deployment. In this scenario, see the following sections of this chapter:

- See "Automating Installation" to learn how to install applications silently.
- See "Injecting in a Disk Image" to learn how to add applications to deployment shares you create by using MDT 2010 and install them during deployment.

Automating Installation

To achieve a fully automated deployment process, the packages you install must support unattended installation. Many setup programs support */s* or */q* command-line options for silent or quiet installations; others don't.

Often you can find out if the package supports unattended installation by typing ***setup /?*** at the command prompt, where *setup* is the file name of the setup program. If the setup program doesn't provide clues, you need to know which vendor's product was used to create the package. You can usually tell by running the setup program and looking for logos, for example, or checking the file properties. Armed with that information, read the following sections to learn how to install packages created by different packaging software automatically. Table 8-1 summarizes the necessary commands.

TABLE 8-1 Unattended Package Installation

PACKAGE TYPE	COMMAND FOR UNATTENDED INSTALLATION
Windows Installer	**msiexec.exe /i package.msi /qn ALLUSERS=2**
InstallShield Windows Installer	**setup.exe /s /v"/qn"** Optionally, you can extract the Windows Installer database from the compressed file and use the command **msiexec.exe /i setup.msi ISSETUPDRIVEN=1 /qn** to install it.
Legacy InstallShield	**setup.exe /s /sms** To create the Setup.iss file necessary to run setup silently, type **setup.exe /r** to create a Setup.iss from your responses to the setup program's dialog boxes and then copy Setup.iss from %SystemRoot% to the folder containing the package.
Legacy InstallShield PackageForTheWeb	**setup.exe /a /s /sms** To create the Setup.iss file necessary to run setup silently, type **setup.exe /a /r** to create the Setup.iss based on your responses and then copy Setup.iss from %SystemRoot% to the folder containing the package.
Legacy Wise Installation System	**setup.exe /s**

Useful Deployment Web Sites

The following Web sites are outstanding resources for automating the installation of applications, as well as other deployment topics:

- AppDeploy.com at *http://www.appdeploy.com*

  This Web site provides comprehensive information about deploying applications that are packaged using a variety of technologies.

- SourceForge at *http://unattended.sourceforge.net*

  This visually nondescript Web site contains a wealth of information, including information about automating the installation of many legacy installers.

- Real Men Don't Click at *http://isg.ee.ethz.ch/tools/realmen*

  Don't let the name or odd URL detract from this Web site's usefulness. It describes how to automate a variety of processes, including software installation.

- Acresso Software at *http://www.acresso.com/services/education/publications_3812.htm*

  This Web page contains the e-book *The Administrator Shortcut Guide to Software Packaging for Desktop Migrations*. This guide is an excellent resource for learning about packaging applications for deployment.

Windows Installer

Windows Installer is an installation and configuration service that helps reduce ownership costs by providing a component-based application installation architecture. Installation is consistent across all applications packaged for Windows Installer. Packages are easily customizable, installations are protected from errors, and a rollback mechanism provides for recovery in case of failure. Windows Installer supports application and feature advertising. Windows Installer provides many other benefits, and most Independent Software Vendors (ISVs) are now using it to package their applications. Windows 7 includes Windows Installer 5.0. For more information about its new features, see *http://msdn.microsoft.com/en-us/library/aa372796.aspx*.

Windows Installer 5.0 is compatible with User Account Control (UAC) in Windows 7. By using elevated installation, an administrator can authorize Windows Installer to install applications or security updates on behalf of users who aren't members of the Administrators group. For more information about UAC, see Chapter 24, "Managing Client Protection."

Windows Installer packages provide the following to enable flexible application deployment:

- **Command-line options** You use command-line options to specify options, file names, and path names, as well as control the action of the installation at run time.

- **Properties (variables) on the command line** Properties are variables that Windows Installer uses during an installation. You can set a subset of these, called public properties, on the command line.
- **Transforms** A transform is a collection of changes you can apply to a base Windows Installer package (.msi) file. You can customize applications by using Windows Installer transform (.mst) files. You configure transforms to modify a Windows Installer package to dynamically affect installation behavior according to your requirements. You associate transforms with a Windows Installer package at deployment time. Transforms for Windows Installer package files are similar to answer files that you might have used to automate the installation of an operating system such as Windows Vista.

The number of applications packaged as Windows Installer databases is multiplying rapidly. Nearly all software vendors are packaging their applications using this technology. And what often looks like a self-contained, self-extracting setup program with a file name such as Setup.exe is often a file that decompresses to a Windows Installer database. You can usually extract the database by using a tool such as WinZip (from WinZip Computing at *http://www.winzip.com*) or by running the setup program and looking in %UserProfile%\Local Settings\Temp for the package file. Windows Installer databases have the .msi file extension.

To install Windows Installer databases unattended using Msiexec.exe, use the */qb* command-line option for a basic user interface or the */qn* command-line option for no user interface. Also, to ensure that the package installs for all users, add the *ALLUSERS=2* property. For example, the command

```
msiexec.exe /i program.msi /qn ALLUSERS=2
```

installs the package file *Program*.msi with no user interaction and for use by all users who share the computer.

> **NOTE** You can learn more about Windows Installer at ***http://msdn2.microsoft.com/en-us/library/aa372866.aspx***. For a list of command-line options, see ***http://technet2.microsoft.com/WindowsServer/en/library/9361d377-9011-4e21-8011-db371fa220ba1033.mspx?mfr=true***.

InstallShield

Some Windows Installer databases that Macrovision InstallShield (*http://www.acresso.com/products/is/installshield-overview.htm*) creates require that you install them by running Setup.exe. Trying to install the .msi file using Msiexec.exe results in a message that you must run Setup.exe to start the installation. When the developer uses InstallShield Script, this requirement is enforced to ensure that the needed version of the InstallShield Script Engine (ISScript.msi) is installed on the computer before proceeding. If it is not detected, the required version of InstallShield

Script Engine is installed automatically before starting Windows Installer. You can automate this installation a couple of ways:

- Use InstallShield's command-line support that Setup.exe offers. Not only does Setup.exe provide command-line option support, but you may also pass options to the Windows Installer setup database by using the */v* command-line option. Following */v*, you may specify any options you want to pass to the Windows Installer setup database within double quotation marks. For example, the following command installs the application silently and passes the */qn* option.

  ```
  setup.exe /s /v"/qn"
  ```

- Deploy the InstallShield Script Engine separately as part of your core applications before any setup files that require it. You may then safely bypass running Setup.exe by installing the Windows Installer setup database with Msiexec.exe and including the *ISSETUPDRIVEN* public property. You can extract the embedded Windows Installer setup database by looking in the %Temp% folder after the welcome message for the installation wizard is displayed. Then, use the following command to install it.

  ```
  msiexec.exe /i setup.msi ISSETUPDRIVEN=1 /qn
  ```

Legacy InstallShield

Packages created using legacy InstallShield technologies usually have the file name Setup.exe. To create an unattended installation for a legacy InstallShield package, you need to create an InstallShield script, which has the .iss file extension. Many applications come with such a file, but they are also easy to create.

To create an InstallShield response file, perform the following steps:

1. Run the setup program using the */r* command-line option. This creates a Setup.iss file based on how you configure the installation as you step through the setup program. The result is the file Setup.iss in %SystemRoot%.
2. Copy Setup.iss from %SystemRoot% to the folder containing the package.
3. Run the setup program using the */s* command-line option. The setup program runs silently using the responses provided by the Setup.iss file.

> ***IMPORTANT*** **Packages created by InstallShield will spawn a separate process and then return immediately to the calling program. This means that the setup program runs asynchronously, even if you start the setup program using *start /wait*. You can add the */sms* command-line option to force the setup program to pause until installation is finished, however, making the process synchronous.**

Legacy InstallShield PackageForTheWeb

PackageForTheWeb is an InstallShield-packaged application contained in a self-contained, self-extracting file. You create a Setup.iss file and use it in almost the same way as described in the previous section. The difference is that you must use the */a* command-line option to pass the command-line options to the setup program after the file extracts its contents. For example, a file that you downloaded called Prog.exe will expand its contents into the temporary folder and then run Setup.exe when finished. To pass command-line options to Setup.exe, you must use the */a* command-line option. The following procedure demonstrates how this extra option changes the steps.

To create an InstallShield PackageForTheWeb response file, perform the following steps:

1. Run the setup program using the */a /r* command-line options: Type **setup.exe /a /r**. This creates a Setup.iss file based on the way you configure the installation as you step through the setup program. The Setup.iss file is in %SystemRoot%.
2. Copy Setup.iss from %SystemRoot% to the folder containing the package.
3. Run the setup program using the */a /s* command-line options: Type **setup.exe /a /s**. The setup program runs silently using the responses in the Setup.iss file.

Legacy Wise Installation System

Packages created using the legacy Wise Installation System recognize the */s* command-line option for unattended installation. No tool is available to script the installation, however.

Windows Script Host

Some applications cannot be automated with command-line options. These applications might provide a wizard-based setup routine but require the user to click buttons or press keys on the keyboard to install the application. If a user can complete the installation by using only the keyboard, you can automate the installation by creating a script (a series of text commands) that simulates keystrokes. This technique is called *screen scraping*.

You can screen scrape by using Windows Script Host. Specifically, you use the *SendKeys()* method to send keystrokes to an application. For more information about the *SendKeys()* method and an example that you can use to quickly create your own screen-scraping scripts, see *http://windowssdk.msdn.microsoft.com/en-us/library/8c6yea83.aspx*.

ON THE COMPANION MEDIA **The companion media contains the sample script Sendkeys.vbs, which provides a shell for using the *SendKeys()* method without having to write your own script. It accepts two command-line options: sendkeys.vbs *program textfile*, where *program* is the path and file name of the program you want to drive, and *textfile* is the path and file name of the text file containing the keystrokes, one keystroke per line, to send to the program. See *http://windowssdk.msdn.microsoft.com/en-us/library/8c6yea83.aspx* for a list of key codes. If you need to pause before sending more keystrokes, add a line to the file that contains *sleep*. Each line that contains *sleep* will pause for 1 second. The file Sendkeys.txt is a sample *textfile* you can use with Sendkeys.vbs; for example, type sendkeys.vbs notepad.exe sendkeys.txt and watch what happens.**

Repackaging Legacy Applications

Some legacy installers don't support silent installations, and some that do support silent installations don't provide a way to script settings. No legacy installers provide the management capabilities that Windows Installer provides.

If you have an application that is not designed for Windows Installer and does not support another automated installation technique, you can repackage it into the Windows Installer setup database so that you can use the features of Windows Installer to distribute and manage the application. A repackaged application combines the entire feature set of the application into a single feature. After repackaging an application, you use Windows Installer to install it. However, repackaged applications lack the flexibility to customize the application installation efficiently.

WARNING **Do not repackage Microsoft Office. The Office package files include logic that customizes the installation for the destination computer and user. Repackaging the package file loses this logic, potentially preventing the package from installing correctly in some configurations.**

The Repackaging Process

Windows Installer provides no functionality for repackaging applications. However, numerous vendors sell repackaging products for Windows Installer. See the next section, "Repackaging Tools," for a list of vendors.

Repackaging is not new. Organizations have historically repackaged applications to customize their installation and configuration. However, Windows Installer transforms eliminate the need to repackage Windows Installer–based applications just to customize them. In fact, repackaging applications that already install from a Windows Installer setup database is bad practice and is not supported.

Repackaging an application is a process that compares snapshots to determine the contents of the new package. The following steps provide an overview of the repackaging process:

1. Take a snapshot of the computer's current configuration.
2. Install the application.
3. Take a second snapshot of the computer's new configuration.
4. Create a package that contains the differences between the two snapshots. The repackaging tool detects all of the differences between the two snapshots, including all changes to the registry and file system. Because numerous processes are running in Windows 7 at any time, the package file will likely contain settings and files related to processes outside of the application.
5. Clean the package to remove noise (unnecessary files and settings).

> ***WARNING*** **Don't let the simplicity of these five steps trick you into believing that repackaging is easy. Application repackaging is very often the most expensive part of any deployment project. When you undertake the repackaging of an organization's applications, you can count on a labor- and resource-intensive effort, particularly in organizations with thousands of applications, many of which the organization must repackage. Budget, plan, and schedule accordingly.**

Repackaging Tools

You must use tools that are not included with Windows Installer to create Windows Installer packages. The following list includes some of the variety of tools available:

- **AdminStudio** Available in multiple versions, including a free download, AdminStudio is a powerful and flexible repackaging tool. The following versions are available:
  - **AdminStudio Configuration Manager Edition** This free download from Microsoft integrates with System Center Configuration Manager 2007 to simplify repackaging. AdminStudio Configuration Manager Edition prepares legacy Setup.exe packages for deployment by converting them to Windows Installer .msi packages. To download AdminStudio Configuration Manager Edition, see *http://technet.microsoft.com/en-us/configmgr/bb932316.aspx*.
  - **AdminStudio Professional Edition** This full version of AdminStudio is a complete solution for packaging, customizing, testing, and distributing applications. The full version includes all the features included with AdminStudio Configuration Manager Edition, plus additional features. To download a trial version of AdminStudio, see the AdminStudio software overview page at *http://www.acresso.com/products/as/adminstudio-overview.htm*.

- **Wise Package Studio** Wise offers products for repackaging, testing, and configuring the deployment of applications. See *http://www.symantec.com/business/package-studio* for more information.

Injecting in a Disk Image

This section describes how to add applications to deployment shares you build with MDT 2010, and then inject those applications into disk images or install them when deploying the disk image. If you're not using MDT 2010 to build and deploy Windows 7, see Chapter 4, "Planning Deployment," to learn why using MDT 2010 is a better way to deploy Windows 7 than using the Windows Automated Installation Kit (Windows AIK) alone.

When planning application deployment, you choose between three deployment strategies: thick image, thin image, and hybrid image, as we described earlier in this chapter. If you're using a thin-image strategy, you won't be injecting applications into disk images. Instead, you'll use a systems-management infrastructure such as System Center Configuration Manager 2007 to deploy applications after installing the thin disk image. If you're using a thick-image strategy, you will install applications when you create the disk image. In other words, you will add the application installations to the MDT 2010 task sequence that you use to create the disk image. This method should be a last resort, as it's more difficult to maintain and slower to deploy. If you're using a hybrid image strategy, you will install applications during deployment. In this case, you will add the application installations to the MDT 2010 task sequence that you're deploying to destination computers, or you will add application installations to the MDT 2010 database.

NOTE **This chapter does not describe how to start or use Deployment Workbench. For more information about using Deployment Workbench, see Chapter 6, "Developing Disk Images."**

DIRECT FROM THE SOURCE

Infrastructure

Doug Davis, Lead Architect
Management Operations & Deployment, Microsoft Consulting Services

One question I hear repeatedly regarding deployment space concerns the amount of infrastructure required. Even with a moderately large (thick) image, customers still need to deploy additional applications. I typically suggest dynamic application distribution—applications that the user had before are dynamically reinstalled on the new configuration before the user logs on to the computer.

However, this requires a stable infrastructure. On average, three applications will need to be added for each computer—three applications not already included in the thick image. On average, 4,805 files per computer will be migrated by using the User State Migration Tool (USMT), and 900 megabytes (MB) will be transferred per computer. Therefore, a 1,000-computer deployment would require the following infrastructure:

- **Computers: 1,000**
- **Applications: 2,952**
- **Files: 4,805,594**
- **Gigabytes: 977.60**

Adding Applications

When you add an application to a deployment share, you're simply describing for MDT 2010 how to install the application by using the command line and optionally copying the application source files to the deployment share. If you don't copy the application source files to the deployment share, MDT 2010 installs the application from the source location you specify, such as a network share.

To add an application to a deployment share, perform the following steps:

1. In the Deployment Workbench console tree, right-click Applications and then select New Application to begin the New Application Wizard. The Applications option is under Deployment Share. In MDT 2010, you must create a deployment share before adding applications to it. For more information about creating deployment shares, see Chapter 6.
2. On the Application Type page, do one of the following and then click Next:
   - Click the Application With Source Files option. Choosing this option copies the application source files to the deployment share. During deployment, MDT 2010 installs the application from source files it copied to the deployment share.
   - Click the Application Without Source Files Or Elsewhere On The Network option. Choosing this option does not copy the application source files to the deployment share. During deployment, MDT 2010 installs the application from another location on the network. You also choose this option to run a command that requires no application source files.
   - Click the Application Bundle option. This option creates essentially a dummy application with which you can associate other applications (dependencies). If you select the Application Bundle option during deployment, MDT 2010 will install all of its dependencies. For more information about dependencies, see the section titled "Creating Dependencies" later in this chapter.

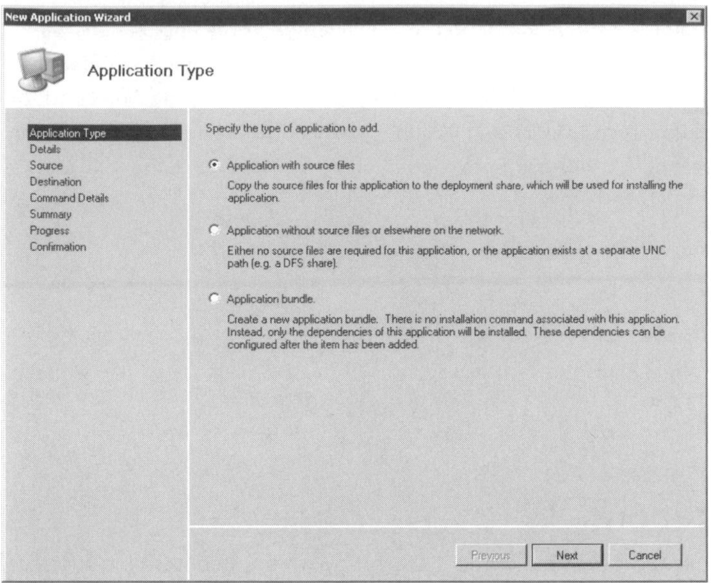

3. On the Details page, provide the following information about the application and then click Next:
    a. In the Publisher box, type the name of the application's publisher (optional).
    b. In the Application Name box, type the name of the application.
    c. In the Version box, type a version label for the application (optional).
    d. In the Languages box, type the languages supported by the application (optional).
4. On the Source page, type the path of the folder containing the application you want to add and then click Next. If you've chosen to copy the application source files to the deployment share, Deployment Workbench copies everything in this folder to the deployment share; otherwise, it adds this path to the application's metadata as the application's installation path.

> ***NOTE*** **If you select the Move The Files To The Deployment Share Instead Of Copying Them check box, the New Application Wizard will move the source files instead of copying them. Use this option if you want to stage applications on the local hard disk before moving them into the deployment share.**

5. On the Destination page, type the name of the folder to create for the application within the deployment share and then click Next. The default value is the publisher, application name, and version label concatenated.
6. On the Command Details page, type the command to use to install the application silently, and then click Next. For example, type **msiexec /qb /i *program*.msi**. The command is relative to the working directory specified in the Working Directory box.

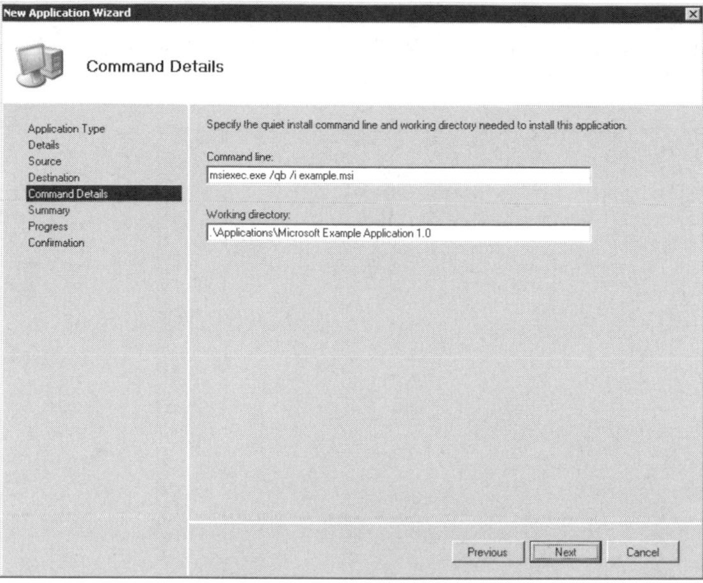

7. On the Summary page, review the application details and then click Next.
8. On the Confirmation page, click Finish.

After adding an application to the deployment share, you see it in the Applications details pane. You also see it in the deployment share in Applications*subfolder*, where *subfolder* is the destination you specified when adding the application.

Creating Dependencies

Often, an application has dependencies. For example, application A is dependent on application B if you must install application B before installing application A. MDT 2010 allows you to specify application dependencies for each application you add to the deployment share. You can make an application dependent only on other applications that you've added to the deployment share.

To add dependencies to an application, perform the following steps:

1. In the Deployment Workbench console tree, click Applications.
2. In the details pane, right-click the application that has a dependency on another application and then click Properties.
3. On the Dependencies tab, shown on the following page, do the following:
   - To add an application to the dependencies list, click Add, select an application, and then click OK. Deployment Workbench only displays applications in this list that you've already added to the deployment share.
   - To remove an application from the dependencies list, select an application in the dependencies list and then click Remove.

- To reorder the applications in the dependencies list, select an application in the dependencies list and then click Up or click Down. MDT 2010 installs the dependent applications in the order specified by the dependencies list.

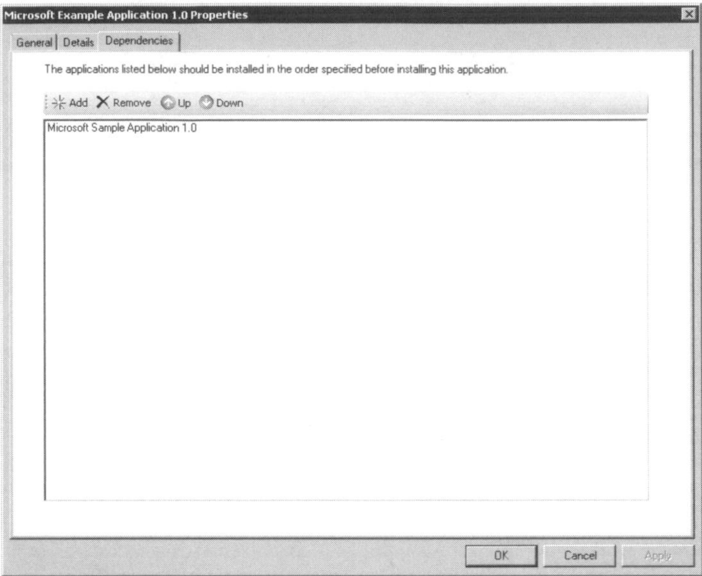

Installing Applications

In MDT 2010, the task sequence specifies the tasks that run during deployment and their order. You can install applications during the imaging process by adding a step to the task sequence that installs the application at the appropriate time. For more information about customizing the task sequence, see Chapter 6. Although this approach is useful for injecting applications into a disk image, using the MDT 2010 database or CustomSettings.ini is more appropriate during deployment in production. For more information, see Chapter 12, "Deploying with Microsoft Deployment Toolkit."

Without creating additional groups in the task sequence, the best place to add application installs is to the Custom Tasks group, which MDT 2010 creates in each task sequence's default task sequence. The instructions in this section show you how to install an application as a step under this group.

> ***NOTE*** **If you add an application to the deployment share without installing it via the task sequence, the Windows Deployment Wizard will allow the user to install the application optionally during deployment. Also, you can choose applications to install automatically during a Zero Touch Installation by configuring the deployment share to install the application automatically.**

To add an application installation to a task sequence, perform the following steps:

1. In the Deployment Workbench console tree, click Task Sequences, which is located under Deployment Share. In MDT 2010, you must create a deployment share before adding applications to it. For more information about creating deployment shares, see Chapter 6.
2. In the details pane, right-click the task sequence in which you want to install an application and then click Properties.
3. On the Task Sequence tab, shown here, click Custom Tasks in the task sequence and then click Add, click General, and then click Install Application.

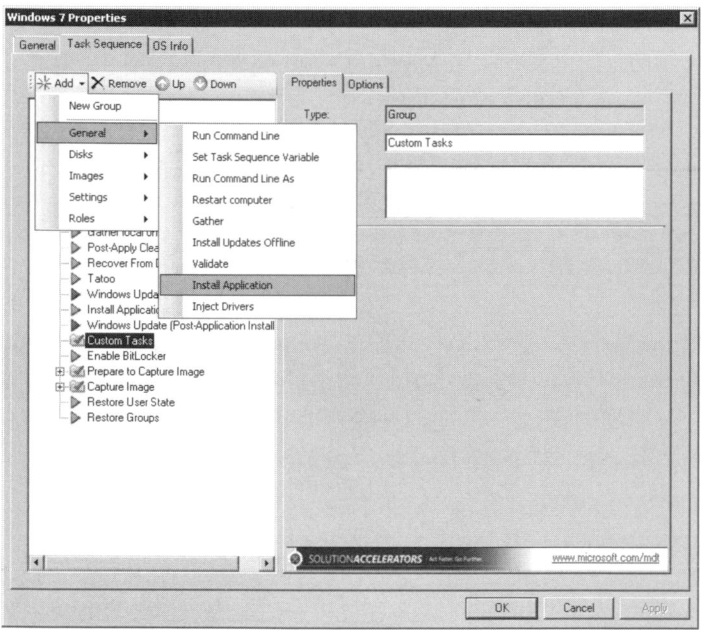

4. Click the Install Application task that you just added to the task sequence, select the Install A Single Application option, click Browse, choose an application, and then click OK, as shown here.

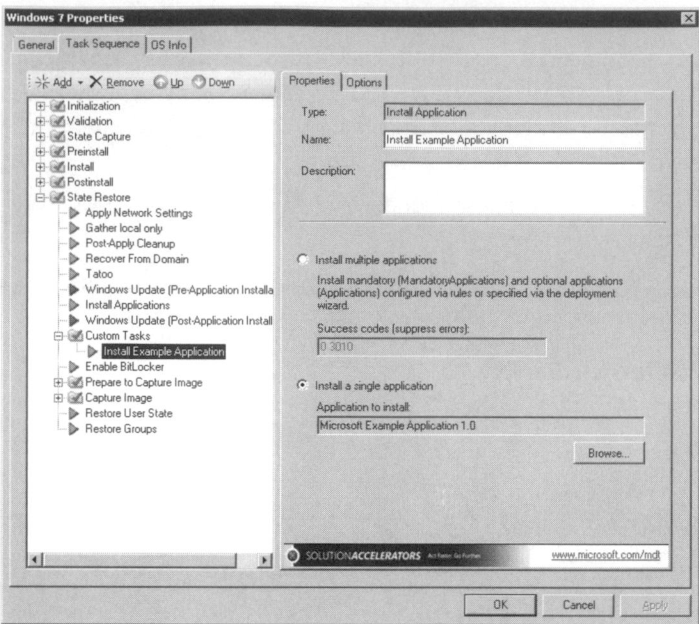

NOTE In MDT 2010, the task sequence is very flexible. For example, you can install applications at almost any point during the State Restore phase. You can filter application installation tasks on a variety of variables. For more information about editing task sequences in MDT 2010, see Chapter 6.

Summary

Careful planning is the most important task you must undertake when deploying applications with Windows 7. The first step is building an application inventory. Then you must prioritize, categorize, and document the installation of each application. MDT 2010 and ACT provide tools that help with this step.

Another key planning step is determining the right type of deployment strategy for your organization. Thick images are monolithic images that contain core applications and other files. They are large and costly to maintain and deploy. Thin images are bare images. You install applications post-deployment using a systems-management infrastructure, such as System Center Configuration Manager 2007. Hybrid images use a combination of both strategies. The deployment strategy you choose determines how you build images.

After careful planning, you repackage the applications that don't provide an automated installation and document the installation commands for those that do. Then add applications to your MDT 2010 deployment share and add steps to the task sequence that installs the application when you build the disk image (thick image) or when you deploy the disk image (hybrid image).

> ***NOTE*** **If you're not using MDT 2010 to deploy Windows 7, see Chapter 4 to learn why using MDT 2010 is a better way to deploy Windows 7 than using the Windows AIK alone. If you're not using MDT 2010, see *Windows Automated Installation Kit User's Guide* to learn how to install applications by using an answer file.**

Additional Resources

These resources contain additional information and tools related to this chapter.

Related Information

- Chapter 2, "Security in Windows 7," includes more information about how Windows 7 security features affect applications.
- Chapter 5, "Testing Application Compatibility," describes how to use ACT 5.5 to create an application inventory, analyze it, and then mitigate compatibility issues.
- Chapter 6, "Developing Disk Images," includes more information about building custom Windows 7 disk images that include applications.
- Chapter 7, "Migrating User State Data," includes more information about migrating application settings from earlier versions of Windows to Windows 7.
- The "2007 Office Resource Kit," found at *http://technet.microsoft.com/en-us/library/cc303401.aspx*, includes more information about customizing and deploying the 2007 Microsoft Office system.
- "SendKeys Method," found at *http://windowssdk.msdn.microsoft.com/en-us/library/8c6yea83.aspx*, includes more information about using Windows Script Host as a screen-scraping tool to automate application installations.
- "Application Compatibility," found at *http://technet.microsoft.com/en-us/windows/aa905066.aspx*, includes more information about downloading and using ACT to resolve compatibility issues.

On the Companion Media

- Sendkeys.vbs
- Sendkeys.txt

CHAPTER 9

Preparing Windows PE

Half the job of installing the Windows 7 operating system or building disk images is starting the computer and preparing for installation. You use Windows Preinstallation Environment (Windows PE) 3.0 to start computers, which is similar to using MS-DOS in the old days. Windows PE allows you to fully automate the preparation and installation process. This chapter describes how to use, customize, and automate Windows PE for the purpose of installing Windows 7 in business environments.

Earlier versions of Windows PE, including Windows PE 2004 and Windows PE 2005, were available only to Software Assurance (SA) customers. Windows 7 installation is entirely based on Windows PE and imaging by using ImageX; therefore, Windows PE 3.0 is freely available as part of the Windows Automated Installation Kit (Windows AIK) 2.0. Windows PE is highly customizable. You can use the *Windows PE User's Guide*, included in the Windows AIK, to accomplish most tasks. This chapter describes the most common ways to customize Windows PE, as well as how to start it in various scenarios.

In most circumstances, you should use Microsoft Deployment Toolkit 2010 (MDT 2010) to deploy Windows 7. In this case, you can use Deployment Workbench to customize Windows 7 and automatically generate images that you can use to start Windows PE with a variety of media. Although the information in this chapter does describe how to customize Windows PE manually, Microsoft recommends that you use MDT 2010 to generate Windows PE images in most cases.

Exploring Windows PE

Windows PE, which is supplied with Windows 7 and in the Windows AIK, is the installation engine for Windows 7. It is directly bootable from CD, DVD, and universal serial bus (USB) flash drives (UFDs). You can also start Windows PE by using Windows Deployment Services and the Pre-Boot Execution Environment (PXE) extensions to Dynamic Host Configuration Protocol (DHCP) (if supported by the network adapters of your computers).

Windows PE is a minimal Windows operating system that provides limited services based on the Windows 7 kernel. It also provides the minimal set of features required to run Windows 7 Setup, install Windows 7 from networks, script basic repetitive tasks, and validate hardware. For example, with Windows PE, you can use powerful batch scripts, Windows Script Host (WSH) scripts, and HTML Applications (HTAs) to fully automate computer preparation and Windows 7 installation, rather than the limited batch commands in MS-DOS. Examples of what you can do with Windows PE include:

- Create and format disk partitions, including NTFS file system (NTFS) partitions, without rebooting the computer before installing Windows 7 on them. Formatting disks with NTFS by using an MS-DOS–bootable disk required third-party utilities. Windows PE replaces the MS-DOS–bootable disk in this scenario, allowing you to format disks with NTFS without using third-party utilities. Also, the file system utilities that Windows PE provides are scriptable, so you can completely automate the setup preparation process.
- Access network shares to run preparation tools or install Windows 7. Windows PE provides network access comparable to Windows 7. In fact, Windows PE provides the same network drivers that come with Windows 7, allowing you to access the network quickly and easily. Customizing MS-DOS–bootable disks to access network shares was time consuming and tedious.
- Use all the mass-storage devices that rely on Windows 7 device drivers. Windows PE includes the same mass-storage device drivers that Windows 7 provides, so you no longer have to customize MS-DOS–bootable disks for use with specialized mass-storage devices. Once again, Windows PE allows you to focus on important jobs rather than on maintaining MS-DOS–bootable disks.
- Customize Windows PE by using techniques and technologies that are already familiar to you. Windows PE is based on Windows 7, so you are already familiar with the techniques and tools used to customize Windows PE. You can customize it in a variety of scenarios:
  - Addition of hardware-specific device drivers
  - Automation through use of Unattend.xml answer files
  - Execution of scripts (batch, WSH, and HTA) to perform specific actions

The following sections provide more detail about the features and limitations of Windows PE. They focus specifically on using Windows PE in high-volume deployment scenarios, rather than in manufacturing environments.

DIRECT FROM THE SOURCE

Windows PE 3.0

Michael Niehaus, Lead Developer for Microsoft Deployment Toolkit
Management and Infrastructure Solutions

Windows PE 3.0, the new version that will be released with Windows 7, is an important part of the deployment process. Even the standard DVD-based installation of Windows 7 uses Windows PE 3.0, and most organizations will be using it (often customized for the organization's specific needs) as part of their deployment processes.

Compared to MS-DOS–based deployment, Windows PE 3.0 brings numerous benefits, including less time spent trying to find 16-bit real-mode drivers. (It's not even possible to find these any more for some newer network cards and mass storage adapters.) Better performance from 32-bit and 64-bit networking stacks and tools, as well as large memory support, are also advantages. And don't forget support for tools such as WSH, VBScript, and hypertext applications.

Windows PE has been available for a few years (the latest version, Windows PE 2.1, was released at the same time as Windows Vista and Windows Server 2008). Previous versions required you to have SA on your Windows desktop operating system licenses. With Windows PE 3.0, that's not the case. All organizations will be able to download Windows PE 3.0 from *http://www.microsoft.com* and use it freely for the purposes of deploying licensed copies of Windows 7.

Like Windows 7 itself, Windows PE 3.0 is provided as an image that is modular and can be serviced both online and offline. As with Windows PE 2.1, several optional features can be added. New tools like Deployment Image Servicing and Management (DISM) are provided for servicing Windows PE 3.0. You can use DISM to add packages and drivers, including mass storage devices, which no longer require any special handling.

Capabilities

Windows PE is a bootable image that you can start by using removable media (CD, DVD, or UFD). You can also use Windows Deployment Services to start Windows PE. Because the Windows 7 deployment tools do not work in 16-bit environments, Windows PE replaces the MS-DOS–bootable disk in *all* deployment scenarios. It's a lightweight 32-bit or 64-bit environment that supports the same set of networking and mass-storage device drivers that Windows 7 supports, and it provides access to similar features, including NTFS and stand-alone Distributed File System (DFS). Windows PE includes the following features:

- **Hardware independence** Windows PE is a hardware-independent Windows environment for both x86 and x64 architectures. You can use the same preinstallation environment on all desktop computers and servers without creating and maintaining different bootable disks for different hardware configurations.
- **APIs and scripting capabilities** Windows PE contains a subset of the Win32 application programming interfaces (APIs); a command interpreter capable of running batch scripts; and support for adding WSH, HTA, and Microsoft ActiveX Data Objects to create custom tools or scripts. The scripting capabilities in Windows PE far exceed the capabilities of MS-DOS–bootable disks. For example, the command interpreter in Windows PE supports a more robust batch-scripting language than does MS-DOS, allowing you to use more advanced scripts.
- **Network access** Windows PE uses Transmission Control Protocol/Internet Protocol (TCP/IP) to provide network access and supports standard network drivers for running Windows 7 Setup and installing images from the network to the computer. You can easily add or remove network drivers from a customized version of Windows PE. In contrast, customizing MS-DOS–bootable disks to access network shares is frustrating, mostly because you need to build and maintain numerous disks. Windows PE alleviates this frustration by supporting the network drivers that Windows 7 supports, and Windows PE is easier to customize with additional network drivers.
- **Mass-storage devices** Windows PE includes support for all mass-storage devices that Windows 7 supports. As new devices become available, you can easily add or remove drivers into a customized version of Windows PE. Customizing an MS-DOS–bootable disk to access atypical mass-storage devices requires tracking down and installing the 16-bit device drivers. However, Windows PE supports many of these mass-storage devices out of the box. And customizing Windows PE to support additional mass-storage devices is easier because it uses standard, readily available Windows device drivers.
- **Disk management** Windows PE includes native support for creating, deleting, formatting, and managing NTFS partitions. Also, Windows PE provides full, unrestricted access to NTFS file systems. With Windows PE, you don't have to restart the computer after formatting a disk.
- **Support for the PXE protocol** If the computer supports PXE, you can start it automatically from a Windows PE image located on a Windows Deployment Services server—and Windows Deployment Services doesn't install the Windows PE image on the computer's hard disk. Starting Windows PE from the network makes it a convenient tool to use in all deployment scenarios. Also, you can customize a Windows PE image for recovery and troubleshooting purposes, and adding it to Windows Deployment Services makes it a convenient tool to use in production.

> ***NOTE*** **You must build a custom Windows PE image from the Windows PE source files, as described in the section titled "Customizing Windows PE" later in this chapter.**

You manage and deploy Windows PE by using the tools included in Windows 7 and the Windows AIK. This toolkit includes the *Windows PE User's Guide* and tools such as:

- **BCDboot.exe** Provides initialization of the boot configuration data (BCD) store, and it enables you to copy boot environment files to the system partition during image deployment.
- **Bootsect.exe** Updates the master boot code for hard disk partitions to alternate between BOOTMGR and NTLDR. This enables you to preinstall Windows 7 from Windows XP.
- **DiskPart.exe** A text-mode command interpreter in Windows 7 that enables you to manage disks, partitions, or volumes by using scripts or direct input at a command prompt.
- **Drvload.exe** A command-line tool for adding out-of-the-box drivers to a booted Windows PE image. It takes one or more driver .inf files as inputs.
- **Oscdimg.exe** A command-line tool for creating an image (.iso) file of a customized 32-bit or 64-bit version of Windows PE. You can then burn the .iso file to a CD-ROM.
- **Dism.exe** A command-line tool that can create and modify a Windows PE 3.0 or Windows 7 image.
- **ImageX.exe** A command-line tool that enables you to capture, modify, and apply file-based disk images for rapid deployment. It can also work with other technologies that use .wim files, such as Setup for Windows 7 and Windows Deployment Services.
- **Winpeshl.ini** The default interface for Windows PE is a command prompt. You can customize Winpeshl.ini to run your own shell application.
- **Wpeinit.exe** A command-line tool that initializes Windows PE every time it boots. Wpeinit replaced the initialization function previously supported by the *Factory.exe -winpe* command in earlier versions of Windows PE.
- **Wpeutil.exe** A command-line tool that enables you to run various commands in a Windows PE session.

NOTE The *Windows PE User's Guide* (Winpe.chm) provides complete, portable documentation of the command-line options for all of the tools discussed in this chapter. This Help file is located in the Windows AIK 2.0, which you can download from the Microsoft Download Center at *http://www.microsoft.com/downloads*.

Limitations

Windows PE has the following limitations:

- To reduce its size, Windows PE includes only a subset of the available Win32 APIs: I/O (disk and network) and core Win32 APIs.

- Windows PE doesn't fit on floppy disks, but you can write a custom Windows PE image to a bootable CD or DVD.
- Windows PE supports TCP/IP and NetBIOS over TCP/IP for network connectivity, but it doesn't support other protocols, such as Internetwork Packet Exchange/Sequenced Packet Exchange (IPX/SPX).
- The Windows on Windows 32 (WOW32) subsystem allows 16-bit applications to run on the 32-bit Windows platform. The WOW32 subsystem isn't available in Windows PE, so 16-bit applications won't run in 32-bit versions of Windows PE. Similarly, in the x64 version of Windows PE, the Windows on Windows 64 (WOW64) subsystem is not available, so applications must be fully 64-bit compliant.
- To install 64-bit Windows 7, you must use 64-bit Windows PE. Likewise, installing 32-bit Windows 7 requires 32-bit Windows PE.
- Drive letter assignments aren't persistent between sessions. After you restart Windows PE, the drive letter assignments will be in the default order.
- Changes to the registry aren't persistent between sessions. To make permanent changes to the registry, you must edit the registry offline by mounting the image with ImageX and then loading hive files into Registry Editor.
- Windows PE supports DFS name resolution to stand-alone DFS roots only.
- You can't access files or folders on a computer running Windows PE from another computer. Likewise, Windows PE can't act as a terminal server, so you can't connect to it by using Remote Desktop.
- Windows PE requires a VESA (Video Electronics Standards Association)-compatible display device and will use the highest screen resolution that it can determine is supported. If the operating system can't detect video settings, it uses a resolution of 640 by 480 pixels.
- Windows PE doesn't support the Microsoft .NET Framework or the Common Language Runtime (CLR).
- Windows PE does not support the installation of Windows Installer package (.msi) files.
- Windows PE does not support 802.1x.
- To prevent its use as a pirated operating system, Windows PE automatically reboots after 72 hours.

New Features of Windows PE 3.0

The following features are changes to Windows PE 3.0 since Windows PE 2.1, the version that shipped with Windows Vista:

- **Deployment Image Servicing and Management (DISM)** DISM is a new command-line tool that you can use to customize a Windows PE 3.0 image offline. DISM replaces Pkgmgr.exe, Intlcfg.exe, and PEImg.exe.

- **Smaller default size** Windows PE version 2.1 contains staged optional features that add additional size and required additional effort to remove. The Windows PE 3.0 default image contains only the minimum resources to support most deployment scenarios. You can add optional features by using DISM.
- **Serviceable** In Windows Vista, you cannot modify a Windows PE image after running *peimg /prep* against it. Windows PE 3.0 images can be serviced at any time by using DISM. The PEImg.exe tool is not supported in Windows PE 3.0.
- **Image optimization** Previous versions of Windows PE provide limited support for optimizing (reducing) the size of an image. Using the new DISM */apply-profiles* command, you can reduce the contents of a Windows PE 3.0 image to only those files necessary to support a given set of applications.
- **System drive letter** You can assign any letter to the system drive using the new DISM */Set-TargetPath* command.
- **Mounted images** Windows PE 3.0 supports mounting a Windows Imaging (WIM) file.
- **Hyper-V support** Windows PE 3.0 includes all Hyper-V drivers except display drivers. This enables Windows PE to run in Hyper-V. Supported features include mass storage, mouse integration, and network adapters.
- **Customizable scratch space** You can now customize the RAM scratch space as 32, 64, 128, 256, or 512 megabytes (MB).

Setting Up the Environment

You will need to build an environment for customizing Windows PE images before deployment. Having everything in the appropriate location will simplify the task of creating builds and will help you establish repeatable methods for creating and updating builds.

Create this environment on a technician or lab computer. If you're using MDT 2010 to deploy Windows 7, configure the Windows PE customization environment on the build server. In fact, installing and configuring MDT 2010 installs all of the requirements for building custom Windows PE images.

Installing the Windows AIK 2.0

Windows PE 3.0 ships with the Windows AIK 2.0, which is available from the Microsoft Download Center at *http://www.microsoft.com/downloads*. Install the Windows AIK on your Windows PE build system from the installation DVD. (Microsoft provides the Windows AIK as a downloadable .iso image.) Installing the Windows AIK 2.0 is a requirement for installing and using MDT 2010. Therefore, a build server containing MDT 2010 already has the files necessary to build and customize Windows PE images. For more information about installing MDT 2010 and the Windows AIK, see Chapter 4, "Planning Deployment." Windows 7 and Windows Server 2008 R2 already contain all of the software prerequisites for the Windows AIK 2.0.

To install the Windows AIK, perform the following steps:

1. From the Windows AIK media or a folder containing the Windows AIK, run **waik*platform*.msi,** where *platform* is either x86 or amd64.
2. Accept the end-user license agreement (EULA) and choose the default location for the installation files. You must use the default installation location if you're using MDT 2010. The examples in this chapter are based on a default Windows AIK installation.
3. Complete the installation wizard to install Windows AIK.

> ***NOTE*** **The Windows Installer file Waik*platform*.msi includes the Windows AIK tools. The file Winpe.cab actually includes the Windows PE source files. To install Windows PE, Winpe.cab must be in the same folder as the .msi file.**

Configuring the Build Environment

The Windows AIK will install the Windows PE build and imaging tools to the following folders:

- **C:\Program Files\Windows AIK\Tools** Contains Windows AIK program files
- **C:\Program Files\Windows AIK\Tools*platform*** Contains ImageX program files for different processor architectures
- **C:\Program Files\Windows AIK\Tools\PETools** Contains Window PE source files
- **C:\Program Files\Windows AIK\Tools\Servicing** Contains servicing files

The Windows AIK also provides a Deployment Tools command prompt that opens on the Windows AIK tools folders (shown in Figure 9-1). You can use commands within this command prompt interface to create your Windows PE build environment. The build environment is a copy of the build scripts and Windows PE source files that you customize and then use to create a new Windows PE image file. The Copype.cmd script is designed to create the build environment. Use the following syntax to create the Windows PE environment, where *platform* is either x86 or amd64 and *destination* is the folder to which you want to copy the files.

```
copype.cmd platform destination
```

> ***NOTE*** **To follow the examples in this chapter, run the command *copype x86 c:\winpe_x86*. You can use an alternative location for your build environment, but you will need to make the appropriate modifications to the examples provided with this chapter. Additionally, you can replace x86 with x64 if you want to build a 64-bit version of Windows PE, which is necessary when you are installing the 64-bit version of Windows 7.**

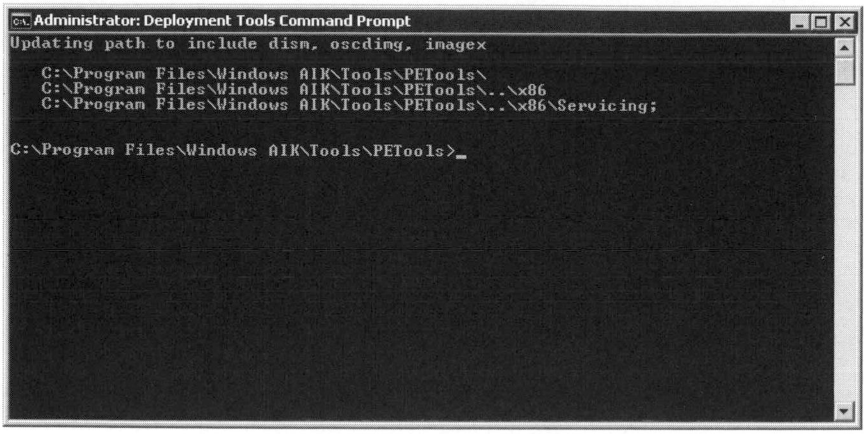

```
Administrator: Deployment Tools Command Prompt
Updating path to include dism, oscdimg, imagex

   C:\Program Files\Windows AIK\Tools\PETools\
   C:\Program Files\Windows AIK\Tools\PETools\..\x86
   C:\Program Files\Windows AIK\Tools\PETools\..\x86\Servicing;

C:\Program Files\Windows AIK\Tools\PETools>_
```

FIGURE 9-1 Use the Windows PE Tools command prompt to work with Windows PE.

Removing the Build Environment

When DISM installs features, it can modify the access control lists (ACLs) of the Windows PE build files and folders, making it difficult to remove them in the future. You can work around this by using the Windows Server 2008 tool Takeown.exe to take ownership of the affected resources.

To remove the Windows PE build environment, perform the following steps:

1. Take ownership of the folder structure using the *Takeown* command.

   ```
   takeown /F c:\winpe_x86\* /R
   ```

2. Use the *Change ACLs* (cacls) command to give yourself permission to remove the folders (*user* is your user account).

   ```
   cacls c:\winpe_x86\* /T /G user:F
   ```

3. Remove the folder.

   ```
   rd /s /q c:\winpe_x86\
   ```

Working with Windows PE

Most Windows PE tasks have just a few basic steps. Applications and customizations might vary the process somewhat, but the basic process is the same. This section gives you an overview of the Windows PE build process. In later sections, you learn how to customize Windows PE in greater depth.

Mounting Windows PE

After you create the Windows PE build environment, the first step in customizing the Windows PE–based image is to mount it so that you can service it by using DISM. An example of the command to mount the base image is shown here (where 1 is the image number within Winpe.wim to be mounted and *C:\Winpe_x86\Mount* is the path on which to mount it):

```
Dism /Mount-Wim /WimFile:C:\Winpe_x86\Winpe.wim /Index:1 /MountDir:C:\Winpe_x86\Mount
```

> ***NOTE*** **With previous versions of Windows PE, you couldn't service the image after you ran *peimg /prep*. This is no longer true with Windows PE 3.0. You can now mount and service Windows PE images as required.**

Adding Packages

The next step is to add the packages that you require. You add packages by using the DISM */Add-Package* option. Additionally, for every feature you want to add to Windows PE, you must add a language-neutral package and a language-specific package. In a default installation of the Windows AIK, you find the language-neutral packages in the folder C:\Program Files\Windows AIK\Tools\PETools\x86\WinPE_FPs and the language-specific packages in C:\Program Files\Windows AIK\Tools\PETools\x86\WinPE_FPs*language*, where *language* is the language identifier (such as *en-US* for U.S. English).

To add a package to the Windows PE image, perform the following steps:

1. Look up in Table 9-1 the names of the packages that you want to install.
2. Add the language-neutral package to the Windows PE image by running the following command at the Deployment Tools command prompt.

   ```
   dism /image:C:\winpe_x86\mount /Add-Package /PackagePath:"C:\Program Files\Windows
   AIK\Tools\PETools\x86\WinPE_FPs\package.cab"
   ```

3. Add the language-specific package to the Windows PE image (look up the actual file name in C:\Program Files\Windows AIK\Tools\PETools\x86\WinPE_FPs\en-us).

   ```
   dism /image:C:\winpe_x86\mount /Add-Package /PackagePath:"C:\Program Files\Windows
   AIK\Tools\PETools\x86\WinPE_FPs\language\package_language.cab"
   ```

For example, the following two commands install the WinPE-Scripting language-neutral and language-specific packages into a Windows PE image mounted at C:\Winpe_x86\Mount.

```
dism /image:C:\winpe_x86\mount /Add-Package /PackagePath:"C:\Program Files\Windows AIK
\Tools\PETools\x86\WinPE_FPs\winpe-scripting.cab"

dism /image:C:\winpe_x86\mount /Add-Package /PackagePath:"C:\Program Files\Windows AIK
\Tools\PETools\x86\WinPE_FPs\en-us\winpe-scripting_en-us.cab"
```

After adding packages to the Windows PE image, you can verify them by listing the image's packages. To list the packages in a Windows PE image mounted to C:\Winpe_x86\Mount, run the following command at the Deployment Tools command prompt.

```
dism /image:c:\winpe_x86\mount /Get-Packages
```

TABLE 9-1 Windows PE Packages

PACKAGE	DESCRIPTION
WinPE-FONTSupport-<language>	Provides additional font support for the following languages: ja-JP, ko-KR, zh-CN, zh-HK, and zh-TW.
WinPE-HTA	Provides HTA support. Enables the creation of graphical user interface (GUI) applications using the Windows Internet Explorer script engine and HTML services.
Winpe-LegacySetup	Contains the Media Setup package. All Setup files from the \Sources folder on the Windows media. Add this package when servicing Setup or the \Sources folder on the Windows media. Must be added with the Setup package. To add a new Boot.wim to the media, add either child package in addition to the Setup and Media packages.
WinPE-MDAC	Provides Microsoft Data Access Component support. Enables queries to SQL servers with Active Directory Objects. For example, you can build a dynamic Unattend.xml file from unique system information.
WinPE-PPPoE	Enables Point-to-Point Protocol over Ethernet (PPPoE) support. Create, connect, disconnect, and delete PPPoE connections from Windows PE.
WinPE-Scripting	Provides WSH support. Enables batch file processing using WSH script objects.
WinPE-Setup	Contains the Setup package. All Setup files from the \Sources folder common to the client and server. This package is the parent package of *winpe-setup-client* and *winpe-setup-server*. You must install *winpe-setup* before you install the child packages.
WinPE-Setup-Client	Contains the Client Setup package. The client branding files for Setup. Must be added after the WinPE-Setup package.
WinPE-Setup-Server	Contains the Server Setup package. The server branding files for Setup. Must be added after the WinPE-Setup package.
WinPE-SRT	Contains the Windows Recovery Environment (Windows RE) package. Provides a recovery platform for automatic system diagnosis and repair and the creation of custom recovery solutions.

PACKAGE	DESCRIPTION
WinPE-WMI	Provides Windows Management Instrumentation (WMI) support. A subset of the WMI providers that enables minimal system diagnostics.
WinPE-WDS-Tools	Contains the Windows Deployment Services tools package. Includes APIs to enable a multicast scenario with a custom Windows Deployment Services client and Image Capture utility.

NOTE **Previous versions of Windows PE included pre-staged optional packages that you had to remove if you didn't want to include them in the image. These included the WinPE-HTA-Package, WinPE-Scripting-Package, and WinPE-MDAC-Package packages. Windows PE 3.0 does not include pre-staged optional features, helping reduce the footprint of Windows PE. You must add all of the packages that you require.**

Copying Applications

You can also copy applications into the Windows PE image so that you can use them during the Windows 7 implementation process. To copy an application into a Windows PE image, use operating system copy commands to copy the application to the appropriate location.

```
xcopy /chery myapp.exe "c:\winpe_x86\mount\program files\myapp\myapp.exe"
```

Adding Device Drivers

Windows PE can use Windows 7 device drivers to provide hardware support for Windows 7 installation processes. Use the DISM */Add-Drive* option to add device drivers to the Windows PE image (*inf_file* is the path and file name of the device driver's .inf file).

```
Dism /image:c:\winpe_x86\mount /Add-Driver /Driver:inf_file
```

Windows PE can also add device drivers dynamically when running. Use the Drvload.exe command to load device drivers while operating.

```
drvload.exe path[,path]
```

Installing Updates

You install updates to Windows PE using the same process by which you add features: You use the DISM */Add-Package* option. Run the following command at the Deployment Tools command prompt, where *update_file* is the path and file name of the update.

```
dism /image:C:\winpe_x86\mount /Add-Package /PackagePath:update_file
```

Committing the Changes

After customizing the mounted Windows PE image, you must dismount the image and commit your changes. This saves your changes into the Winpe.wim file that you mounted. Before dismounting the image, make sure you close any open files and Windows Explorer windows that might prevent you from successfully committing your changes.

To capture the Windows PE image, use the following command.

```
dism /unmount-Wim /MountDir:C:\winpe_x86\mount /Commit
```

Creating Bootable Media

Many Windows maintenance and troubleshooting utilities can make use of Windows PE, including utilities created for managing disks and recovering systems. Windows RE is one example of a recovery tool that uses Windows PE. Many other utilities created by third-party manufacturers also use Windows PE.

This section covers the creation of bootable Windows PE media based on CDs, DVDs, UFDs, and hard disks. You can use all of these technologies for Windows 7 deployment, creating an array of possible solutions for corporate deployments.

Staging a Boot Image

The Windows PE boot image needs supporting files to be made bootable. If you copy your Winpe.wim file to the ISO\Sources folder of the build directory and rename it to Boot.wim, you can create your bootable Windows PE by using the entire ISO folder hierarchy. A completed ISO folder hierarchy looks similar to Figure 9-2.

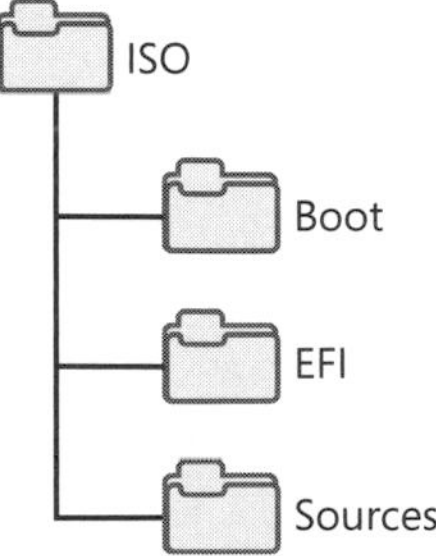

FIGURE 9-2 Windows PE ISO folder hierarchy

To stage a captured Windows PE boot image, copy Winpe.wim from c:\winpe_x86 to the c:\winpe_x86\ISO\Sources folder of the Windows PE build directory.

```
xcopy /chery c:\winpe_x86\Winpe.wim c:\winpe_x86\ISO\Sources\boot.wim
```

Creating Bootable CD/DVD Media

After the boot image is properly staged, you can create a bootable CD or DVD that uses your Windows PE image.

To create a bootable Windows PE CD or DVD, perform the following steps:

1. Use the Oscdimg.exe command to create an .iso image that can be burned onto a CD or DVD.

   ```
   oscdimg -n -bc:\winpe_x86\etfsboot.com c:\winpe_x86\ISO c:\winpe_x86\winpe_x86.iso
   ```

2. Using a CD/DVD burning application, burn the .iso image to a CD or DVD.

Creating Bootable UFD Media

UFDs are available that have the capacity to hold an entire custom Windows 7 deployment. The first step, however, is to make your bootable Windows PE media. After you've accomplished this, you can copy any custom images and Unattend.xml files you have made to the UFD for deployment.

To create bootable Windows PE UFD media, perform the following steps:

1. Insert your bootable UFD device into an available USB port on your system.
2. Use the DiskPart utility to prepare the device for loading Windows PE. To run DiskPart, type **diskpart** at the command prompt and then press Enter.
3. Run the commands shown in Table 9-2 to prepare the UFD.

TABLE 9-2 Preparing a UFD for Windows PE

COMMAND	DESCRIPTION
list disk	Lists available disks.
select disk n	*n* is the UFD you are preparing. Be sure to select the correct disk when using DiskPart. DiskPart will clean your primary hard disk as easily as it will clean your UFD device.
clean	Removes the current partition structures.
create partition primary size=size	*size* is the size of the disk as shown in the list. If you omit *size*, DiskPart will use all of the available space for the partition.
select partition 1	Selects the partition you created in the previous command.
active	Marks the new partition as active.
format fs=FAT32	Formats the UFD partition with the FAT32 file system.
assign	Assigns the next available drive letter to your UFD.
exit	Quits DiskPart.

4. Copy the contents of the ISO folder to your UFD, where e:\ is the drive letter assigned to the UFD device.

```
xcopy /chery c:\winpe_x86\ISO\*.* e:\
```

5. Safely remove your UFD.

NOTE Some UFD devices do not support this preparation process. If necessary, use the UFD device manufacturer's processes and utilities to make the disk bootable.

Making Your UFD Bootable

Creating a bootable UFD requires careful work. First, the computer's BIOS must support booting from a UFD. Second, many UFDs are not bootable and need to be converted before use. They are shipped with a flag value set to cause Windows to detect them as removable media devices rather than USB disk devices.

To make your UFD bootable, consult with the device manufacturer to obtain directions or utilities that will convert the device. Many manufacturers make these instructions available through their product support systems. Ask specifically how to switch the removable media flag. This action will cause Windows to detect the device as a USB hard disk drive and will allow you to proceed with the preparations for creating a bootable UFD.

Booting from a Hard Disk Drive

Although it might seem strange to be booting Windows PE from a hard disk drive, you can do this to perform refresh installations of Windows 7. By loading Windows PE onto the hard disk and booting it to RAM, you can repartition your systems disks and install the new Windows 7 image.

To boot Windows PE from a hard disk drive, perform the following steps:

1. Boot your computer from prepared Windows PE media.
2. Using DiskPart, prepare the computer's hard disk for installation of Windows PE. Use the DiskPart commands shown in Table 9-3.

TABLE 9-3 Preparing a Hard Drive for Windows PE

COMMAND	DESCRIPTION
select disk 0	0 is the primary hard disk drive.
clean	Removes the current partition structures.

COMMAND	DESCRIPTION
create partition primary size=size	*size* is a partition size large enough to hold the Windows PE source files.
select partition 1	Selects the partition created by the previous command.
active	Marks the new partition as active.
format	Formats the new partition.
exit	Quits DiskPart.

3. Copy the Windows PE files from your Windows PE media to your hard disk.

```
xcopy /chery x:\*.* c:\
```

Customizing Windows PE

Most Windows PE customization tasks will involve the processes described in the previous section. First, you will mount the image by using DISM. Then, you will add packages, applications, and updates. Last, you will dismount the image and commit your changes.

Other tasks you might see when customizing your Windows PE implementation include adding hardware-specific device drivers and customizing the actual settings used by Windows PE when it runs. This section covers the installation of device drivers and details changes that you can make to base Windows PE configuration settings. Additional information on automating Windows PE is covered in the section titled "Automating Windows PE" later in this chapter.

Windows PE supports four configuration files to control startup and operation. These files can be configured to launch custom shell environments or execute specified actions:

- **BCD** The BCD file stores the boot settings for Windows PE. This file is edited with the Windows 7 command-line tool, BCDEdit.
- **Winpeshl.ini** During startup, you can start custom shell environments using the Winpeshl.ini file. This file is located in the %SystemRoot%\System32 folder of the Windows PE image. You can configure this file with the path and the executable name of the custom shell application.
- **Startnet.cmd** Windows PE uses the Startnet.cmd file to configure network startup activities. By default, the Wpeinit command is called to initialize Plug and Play devices and start the network connection. You can also add other commands to this script to customize activities during startup.
- **Unattend.xml** Windows PE operates in the windowsPE setup configuration pass of a Windows 7 installation. In this pass, Windows PE uses the appropriate sections of the Unattend.xml file to control its actions. Windows PE looks in the root of the boot device for this file. You can also specify its location by using the Startnet.cmd script or by using Wpeutil.exe with the appropriate command-line options.

Your final environment can run custom application shells (see Figure 9-3).

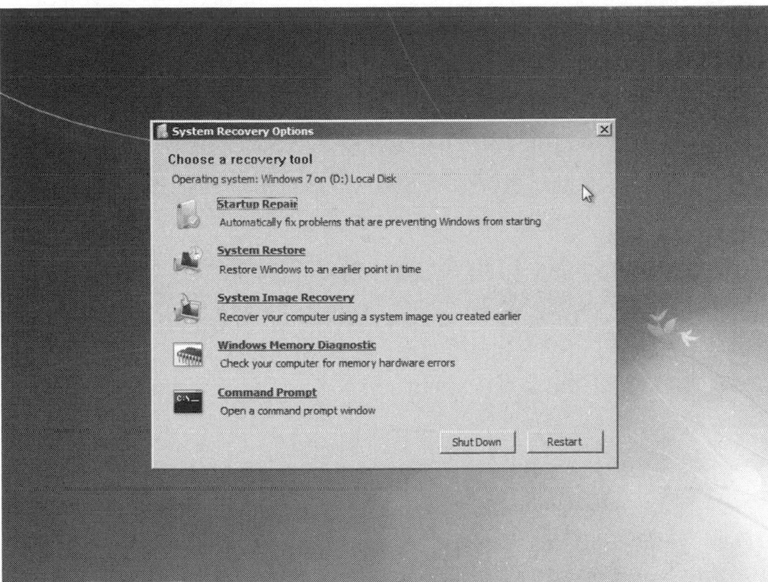

FIGURE 9-3 Windows RE running on Windows PE

Automating Windows PE

Most Windows PE automation is done by customizing Unattend.xml, the Windows 7 unattended answer file. Use the Windows System Image Manager (Windows SIM) to create and edit this file. Unattend.xml allows you to control automation tasks in all the major installation passes. You can put it in the root of your Windows PE media to automate the installation process.

Automating with Unattend.xml

Windows SIM is the primary tool for creating and modifying Unattend.xml. It is designed to validate each automation step against the actual files in an image to ensure that you use proper syntax to build the automation. This provides an extra measure of assurance that unattended installations will work as planned.

When beginning the process of creating an answer file, be sure to create a catalog file if necessary to allow Windows SIM to validate your choices against the image file. Add answer file options to the answer file by right-clicking a feature and choosing Add Setting To Pass 1 WindowsPE. The setting will then appear in the answer file pane, where you can configure it. When you complete answer file customization, you can validate the answer file by clicking Tools and then choosing Validate Answer File. Any settings that are not configured or that use invalid configuration settings will be listed in the Messages pane. When you are satisfied with the answer file, save it to the root folder of your Windows PE media. When you boot a system using this media, the answer file is automatically detected and will control the operation of Windows PE.

> **NOTE** For more detailed information on using Windows SIM to create automation files, see the *Windows Automated Installation Kit User's Guide.*

Adding Images to Windows Deployment Services

When you have completed building a Windows PE image, you can use Windows Deployment Services to deploy it to clients. This allows you to use the PXE boot automation services of Windows Deployment Services to replace portable media as the primary method of initiating Windows 7 installations.

To add a Windows PE boot image to Windows Deployment Services, perform the following steps:

1. In the Windows Deployment Services administration console, shown here, expand your Windows Deployment Services server and right-click Boot Images.

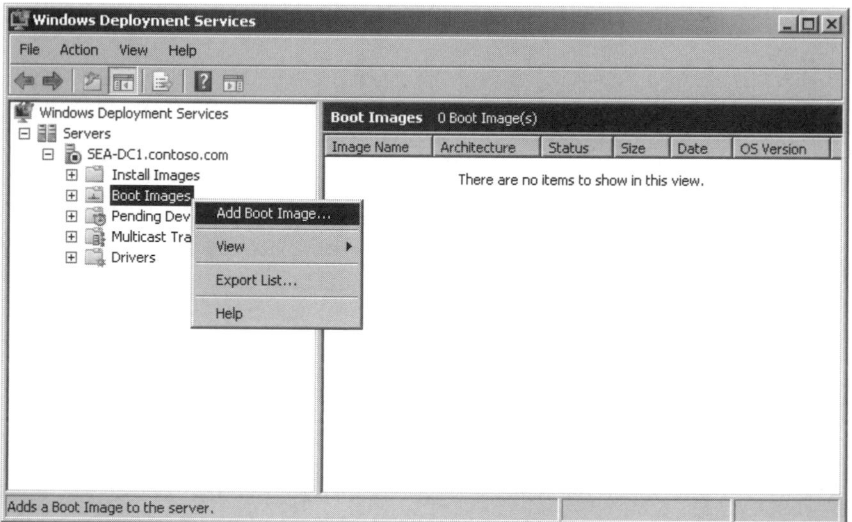

2. Click Add Boot Image to start the Add Image Wizard.
3. Follow the instructions in the wizard to select and import your custom Windows PE image.

> **NOTE** For more information on the configuration and operation of Windows Deployment Services, see Chapter 10, "Configuring Windows Deployment Services."

Using Windows PE with Microsoft Deployment Toolkit

MDT 2010 provides an infrastructure solution for automating the deployment of Windows 7. Part of the infrastructure is the support for automatically customizing and building Windows PE images. You manage the actual process of building the Windows PE image files by using wizards and scripting, greatly simplifying the process of adding device drivers and packages, automating settings, and prepping and capturing the deployment image.

You use Deployment Workbench to manage most operations regarding the creation and deployment of Windows 7 images and applications. This scripted environment is able to dynamically update Windows PE as updates are made to the Windows 7 distribution.

Chapter 6, "Developing Disk Images," describes how to use Deployment Workbench to create deployment shares. Deployment shares automatically generate Windows PE images when you update them. You can customize a deployment share's Windows PE image and choose which types of Windows PE images the deployment share generates when you update it. For more information on the Windows PE customization options available in MDT 2010, see the section titled "Updating the Deployment Share" in Chapter 6.

Summary

Windows PE 3.0 is the only preinstallation platform for installing Windows 7. Windows PE is publicly available in the Windows AIK.

You can approach using Windows PE in two ways. You can customize it through MDT 2010, which is the most appropriate approach if you're using MDT 2010 to deploy Windows 7. Alternatively, you can customize Windows PE manually by using the tools available in the Windows AIK. You can customize Windows PE to fit almost any deployment scenario by adding device drivers and packages, scripts and HTAs, and so on.

You can also start Windows PE in multiple ways. First, you can burn your custom Windows PE image to a CD or DVD and then start the computer using the disk. Second, you can put the Windows PE image on a bootable UFD and then use the UFD to start the computer. Last (and the most convenient option), you can add the custom Windows PE boot image to a Windows Deployment Services server and then start computers remotely.

Additional Resources

These resources contain additional information and tools related to this chapter.

- *Windows Automated Installation Kit User's Guide* (WAIK.chm)
- *Windows PE User's Guide* (WinPE.chm)
- Chapter 6, "Developing Disk Images"
- Chapter 10, "Configuring Windows Deployment Services"

CHAPTER 10

Configuring Windows Deployment Services

Windows Deployment Services in Windows Server 2008 and Windows Server 2008 R2 is the updated and redesigned version of Remote Installation Services (RIS), which was first introduced in Microsoft Windows 2000 Server. You can use Windows Deployment Services to rapidly deploy the Windows 7 operating system by using Pre-Boot Execution Environment (PXE). Using Windows Deployment Services, you can deploy Windows 7 over a network. You can also use Windows Deployment Services to start remote computers using Windows Preinstallation Environment (Windows PE) boot images and then install Windows 7 using customized, scripted deployment solutions, such as Microsoft Deployment Toolkit 2010 (MDT 2010).

Windows Deployment Services delivers a better in-box deployment solution than RIS. It provides platform features that allow for custom solutions, including remote boot capabilities; a plug-in model for PXE server extensibility; and a client-server communication protocol for diagnostics, logging, and image enumeration. Also, Windows Deployment Services uses the Windows Imaging (.wim) file format and provides a greatly improved management experience through the Microsoft Management Console (MMC) and scriptable command-line tools. For organizations that already have a RIS implementation deployed, Windows Deployment Services maintains parity with RIS by providing both coexistence and migration paths for RIS. First, Windows Deployment Services continues to support RIS images in legacy or mixed mode. Second, Windows Deployment Services provides tools to migrate RIS images to the .wim file format.

This chapter describes the architecture of Windows Deployment Services and the requirements for using it. It also describes the key features of Windows Deployment Services and how to use them in specific scenarios, including how MDT 2010 uses Windows Deployment Services to start destination computers and install operating systems. Finally, the chapter describes the improvements to Windows Deployment Services introduced in Windows Server 2008 R2.

Introducing Windows Deployment Services

Windows Deployment Services supports remote, on-demand deployment of Windows 7 and Windows PE images located in a central image store. It is available as an add-on to Windows Server 2003 systems running RIS and is the native remote installation technology provided with Windows Server 2008 and Windows Server 2008 R2.

Windows Deployment Services images are collected from client master systems and stored using the single instancing provided by the .wim imaging format. Clients can be booted from PXE-compliant network adapters or by using remote client boot disks. The Windows Deployment Services client boots into a customized Windows PE image, and the user can select the installation image from a list of images stored on the server. Windows Deployment Services installations can also be scripted for unattended installation support and to support Lite Touch Installation (LTI) and Zero Touch Installation (ZTI) scenarios.

Service Architecture

The Windows Deployment Services architecture has three major categories of features:

- **Management features** Management features are a set of tools that you use to manage the server, operating system images, and client computer accounts. The Windows Deployment Services MMC snap-in is a management feature, and the command-line interface is another.

- **Server features** Server features include a PXE server for network booting a client to load and install an operating system. Server features also include a shared folder and image repository that contains boot images, installation images, a Trivial File Transfer Protocol (TFTP) server, a multicast server, a driver provisioning server, and files that you need specifically for network boot.
- **Client features** Client features include a graphical user interface (GUI) that runs within Windows PE and communicates with the server features to select and install an operating system image.

Figure 10-1 illustrates the various features of Windows Deployment Services. The following sections describe the image store, PXE server, management, and client features in more detail.

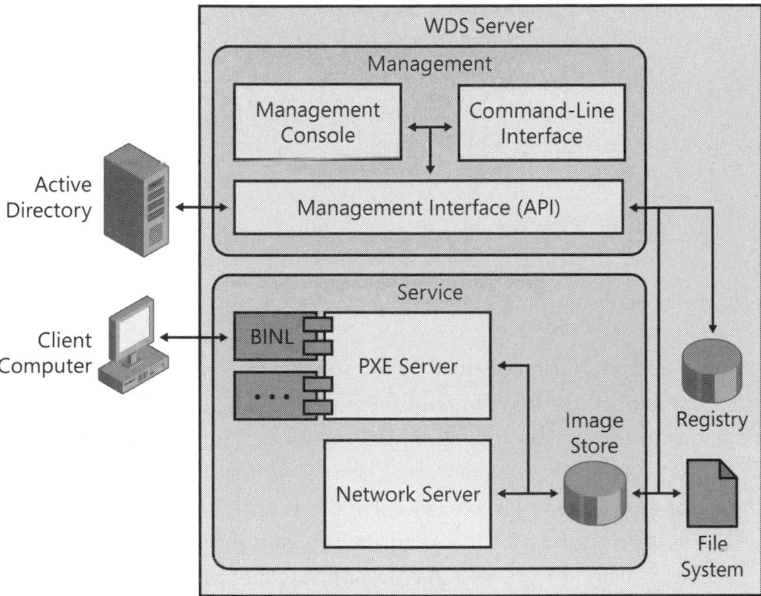

FIGURE 10-1 Windows Deployment Services architecture

Image Store

Figure 10-2 describes how Windows Deployment Services organizes the image store.

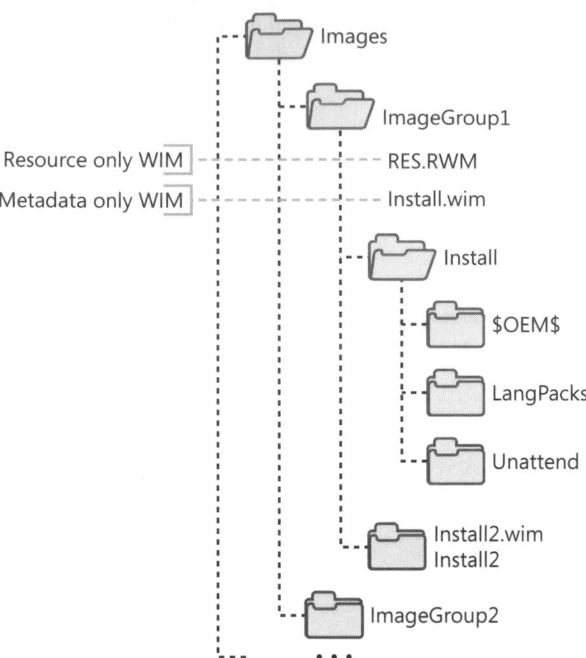

FIGURE 10-2 Windows Deployment Services image store organization

Organizing images into groups, as shown in Figure 10-2, provides two benefits. First, image groups allow you to better manage and organize images. For example, you can manage the security of an entire image group rather than managing the security of individual images. Second, image groups provide units of single instancing. This means that all the images within an image group use Single Instance Storage (SIS) to significantly compress their contents. The file Res.rwm contains all of the file resources for the image group, and this file uses SIS. Each image file (Install.wim and Install2.wim in Figure 10-2) contains only metadata that describes the image file contents based on the contents of Res.rwm.

Windows Deployment Services references images by their group name and image file name. For example, the image ImageGroup1\Install2.wim refers to the image file Install2.wim in the group ImageGroup1.

PXE Services

The Windows Deployment Services PXE server is built on a unified and scalable architecture. As shown in Figure 10-3, it uses plug-ins to provide access to the data store. The PXE server supports one or more plug-ins, and each plug-in can use any data store. Windows Deployment Services provides a default BINL plug-in, as shown earlier in Figure 10-1.

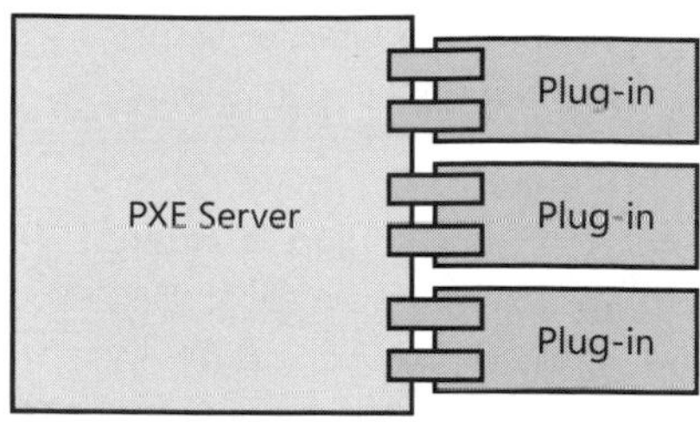

FIGURE 10-3 Windows Deployment Services PXE server

> ***NOTE*** **Windows Deployment Services in Windows Server 2008 R2 also adds a provider called WDSSIPR (SImple PRovider), which is installed with the Transport Server role service and uses an .ini file as a data store.**

Developers can use published application programming interfaces (APIs) to create PXE server plug-ins. You can find these APIs in the Windows Vista Software Development Kit (SDK). The SDK also includes samples that developers can use to create their own plug-ins. For example, a developer can create a PXE server plug-in that works without requiring Active Directory Domain Services (AD DS) and reads settings from a Microsoft SQL Server database.

Management

Windows Deployment Services provides two management tools that significantly simplify management tasks. The first tool is an MMC console that provides a GUI for common management tasks. After installing Windows Deployment Services, you start this console by clicking Windows Deployment Services in the Administrative Tools folder of the Start menu. Examples of common tasks that you can perform using this console include adding images and configuring server settings. The second management tool provided by Windows Deployment Services is the Wdsutil command-line tool. Wdsutil provides all the management functionality that the console provides and more. You can use Wdsutil to perform individual management tasks; you can also use it to automate management tasks by scripting Wdsutil commands. Both tools use the management API that Windows Deployment Services provides, and both tools enable remote administration of Windows Deployment Services servers.

Other management utilities for Windows Deployment Services include:

- **Capture utility** The Windows Deployment Services capture utility captures images to the .wim file format. It includes a light version of the ImageX */capture* functionality and provides a GUI for it. You can use this to add the resulting .wim file to the image store.
- **Active Directory Users And Computers MMC snap-in** You can use this snap-in to administer legacy RIS functionality and configure settings on the Remote Install tab of computer accounts.

- **Risetup and Riprep** Windows Deployment Services provides updated versions of Risetup and Riprep for upgrade scenarios (available in Windows Server 2003 only).

The Windows Deployment Services management console (Figure 10-4) provides significant administrative control. You can add and remove servers. You can configure a variety of options, including computer-naming rules, Dynamic Host Configuration Protocol (DHCP) settings, PXE response settings, and so on. You can add and remove installation and boot images. You can also organize images into image groups. The Windows Deployment Services management console gives you full control over your image groups and the images you add to them. You can configure permissions for each image group and for individual images, too. You can also associate an answer file with each individual image. The Windows Deployment Services management console helps you better manage images for different platforms. For example, you can associate different boot programs and boot images with the x86, x64, and ia64 platforms. You can also associate a global answer file with each platform.

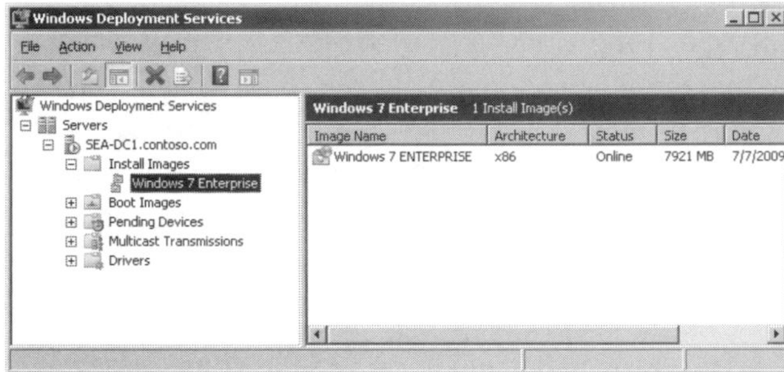

FIGURE 10-4 Windows Deployment Services management console

> ***NOTE*** **Windows Deployment Services in Windows Server 2008 R2 also allows the administrator to choose the preferred boot behavior, such as whether to require an F12 keypress to boot or not.**

Client

The Windows Deployment Services client is a special version of Windows Setup that runs only within Windows PE. In other words, when you deploy Windows 7 to the destination computer using Windows Deployment Services, the Windows Deployment Services client runs within Windows PE on the client computer. This approach allows deployment of Windows 7 as well as images of previous versions of Windows. Note, however, that the version of Windows PE you use has to be at least as recent as the operating system you are deploying. For example, Windows PE 3.0 will deploy Windows 7, Windows Vista, and Windows XP, but Windows PE 2.1 will deploy only Windows Vista and Windows XP.

The Windows Deployment Services client drives the setup experience as follows:

- **Language selection** For Windows 7, the client prompts the user to choose a language. This choice applies to the setup user interface and the operating system installation. The user can also install additional language packs (Windows 7 Enterprise and Windows 7 Ultimate Edition operating systems only).
- **Credentials gathering** The client prompts the user for required credentials to connect to the image store on the Windows Deployment Services server.
- **Image selection** The client displays a list of images available to the user and allows the user to choose an image to install on the destination computer.
- **Disk configuration** The client allows the user to partition and format the destination computer's hard disks. The client provides the same options as Windows Setup.

However, you can automate all of the settings that the client prompts for. To automate these settings, you use Windows System Image Manager (Windows SIM) to create an Unattend.xml file. For more information about creating answer files, see the *Windows Automated Installation Kit User's Guide*, which is installed as part of the Windows Automated Installation Kit (Windows AIK) 2.0.

Operating Modes

To provide a clear path between legacy RIS functionality and Windows Deployment Services functionality, Windows Deployment Services supports three modes (legacy and mixed modes are available only in Windows Server 2003):

- **Legacy mode** This mode uses the Client Installation Wizard (OSChooser) and Riprep (sector-based) images. This mode is compatible with RIS. Moving from RIS-only functionality to legacy mode happens when you install the Windows Deployment Services update on a server running RIS.
- **Mixed mode** This mode supports both OSChooser and Windows PE for boot environments and Riprep and ImageX imaging. Moving from legacy mode to mixed mode happens when you configure Windows Deployment Services and add .wim image files to it.
- **Native mode** This mode supports only the Windows PE boot environment and .wim image files. The final move to native mode occurs after you have converted all legacy images to the .wim image file format and have disabled the OSChooser functionality.

Your choice of operating mode will depend on which client operating systems you are deploying and your investment into legacy Riprep images. You don't need to abandon your current deployment images; operating in mixed mode allows you to continue to deploy legacy RIS images from OSChooser. It also allows you to deploy new .wim images of Windows 7 using Windows PE.

The mode used by Windows Deployment Services is not a simple selection in a dialog box. Each mode is activated in a specific way. The following sections describe each mode in more detail and how to configure each mode.

Legacy Mode

In Windows Deployment Services, legacy mode is functionally equivalent to that of RIS (Windows Deployment Services binaries with RIS functionality). In legacy mode, only OSChooser will be present as the boot operating system. Therefore, only Risetup and Riprep images are supported. You will not be using the Windows Deployment Services management tools; rather, legacy RIS utilities will be the only way to manage the server. Legacy mode is available only on Windows Server 2003.

You configure legacy mode by first installing RIS on Windows Server 2003 and optionally adding legacy images to it. Then, you install the Windows Deployment Services update, as described in the section titled "Installing Windows Deployment Services" later in this chapter. You do not configure Windows Deployment Services by using Wdsutil or the Windows Deployment Services management console.

To configure Windows Deployment Services in legacy mode in Windows Server 2003, perform the following steps:

1. Install the RIS optional feature on Windows Server 2003 Service Pack 1 (SP1) or later and then configure it by running Risetup. Optionally, you can add images to it.
2. If needed, install the Windows Deployment Services update. (Windows Server 2003 SP2 and later installs this update by default.) The Windows AIK 1.1 includes the Windows Deployment Services update for Windows Server 2003 SP1.

Mixed Mode

Mixed mode describes a server state in which both OSChooser and Windows PE boot images are available. In mixed mode, access to the old Risetup and Riprep images is possible through OSChooser. Additionally, you can access the .wim image files via a Windows PE boot image. A boot menu allows users to choose RIS or Windows PE. You will use legacy management tools to manage Risetup and Riprep images and the Windows Deployment Services management tools to manage all facets of the server, including the .wim image files. Windows Deployment Services mixed mode is available only on Windows Server 2003.

You configure mixed mode by first installing RIS on Windows Server 2003 and adding legacy images to it. Then, you install the Windows Deployment Services update, as described in the section titled "Installing Windows Deployment Services" later in this chapter. Last, you run Wdsutil or use the Windows Deployment Services management console to configure Windows Deployment Services and then optionally add .wim images to the image store.

To configure Windows Deployment Services in mixed mode in Windows Server 2003, perform the following steps:

1. Install the RIS optional feature on Windows Server 2003 SP1 or later and then configure it by running Risetup. Optionally, you can add images to it.
2. If needed, install the Windows Deployment Services update. (Windows Server 2003 SP2 and later installs this update by default.)

3. Run **wdsutil /initialize-server** or configure the server in the Windows Deployment Services management console.

Native Mode

Native mode describes a Windows Deployment Services server with only Windows PE boot images. In this mode, OSChooser is not available, and Windows Deployment Services deploys only .wim image files to client computers. You use the Windows Deployment Services management console or Wdsutil to manage Windows Deployment Services in native mode. Native mode is available on Windows Server 2003, Windows Server 2008, and Windows Server 2008 R2. Native mode is the only mode supported on Windows Server 2008 and Windows Server 2008 R2.

To configure Windows Deployment Services in native mode in Windows Server 2003, perform the following steps:

1. Install the RIS optional feature on Windows Server 2003 SP1. Do not configure the RIS service or add images to it.
2. If needed, install the Windows Deployment Services update. (Windows Server 2003 SP2 and later installs this update by default.)
3. Run **wdsutil /initialize-server** or configure the server in the Windows Deployment Services management console.

> ***NOTE*** **The Windows Deployment Services server may be forced to enter native mode from any other mode. This is a one-way operation and is accomplished by using the Wdsutil management utility. The command** `wdsutil /Set-Server /ForceNative` **changes the Windows Deployment Services server to native mode.**

Planning for Windows Deployment Services

Windows Deployment Services doesn't have significant requirements for the system on which you install it, but you need to put some thought into which services and applications must exist in your environment to support Windows Deployment Services, including the actual server requirements, client computer requirements, and network requirements.

Windows Deployment Services supports booting computers directly from a boot image over the network. This image boots using the PXE boot specification and needs to be able to receive broadcast messages from PXE clients. This will require some planning to make sure clients will be able to find and communicate with the Windows Deployment Services server. As a result, you must consider the Windows Deployment Services requirements for DHCP and routing. This section discusses requirements you need to consider for Windows Deployment Services.

Choosing a Version of Windows Deployment Services

Windows Deployment Services is included as an installable server role in Windows Server 2008 and Windows Server 2008 R2. Windows Deployment Services is also available as a separate update for Windows Server 2003 SP1. (This update is included in Windows Server 2003 SP2.) The version of Windows Deployment Services that you use in your environment will depend upon your business needs, budget, and existing network infrastructure.

Supported Operating Systems

The Windows operating systems that can be deployed vary with the version of Windows Deployment Services used. The Windows Deployment Services role in Windows Server 2008 R2 can be used to deploy the following operating systems:

- Windows XP
- Windows Server 2003
- Windows Vista SP1
- Windows Server 2008
- Windows 7
- Windows Server 2008 R2

The Windows Deployment Services role in Windows Server 2008 can deploy all the operating systems listed previously, as well as Windows 2000.

The operating systems that you can deploy using the Windows Deployment Services update for Windows Server 2003 SP1 and later depend upon whether Windows Deployment Services is running in legacy, mixed, or native mode. Specifically:

- **Legacy mode** Supports installing Windows 2000, Windows XP, and Windows Server 2003
- **Mixed mode** Supports installing Windows 2000, Windows XP, Windows Server 2003, Windows Vista, and Windows Server 2008 (You can also deploy Windows 7 and Windows Server 2008 R2 in this mode, as long as you have a Windows PE 3.0 boot image.)
- **Native mode** Supports installing Windows 2000 Professional Edition, Windows XP, Windows Server 2003, Windows Vista, Windows Server 2008, Windows 7, and Windows Server 2008 R2

Supported Image Types

The types of Windows images that can be deployed also vary with the version of Windows Deployment Services used. The Windows Deployment Services role in Windows Server 2008 R2 can deploy the following types of images:

- Windows Imaging (WIM) file format images
- Virtual hard disk (VHD) images

The Windows Deployment Services role in Windows Server 2008 can deploy only WIM images for a new installation of Windows Server 2008. If you upgrade to Windows Server 2008 from Windows Server 2003, you can also convert RIPREP images to WIM images. RISETUP images are not supported, however.

The types of Windows images you can deploy using the Windows Deployment Services update for Windows Server 2003 SP1 and later depend on the mode in which Windows Deployment Services is running, specifically:

- **Legacy mode** RISETUP and RIPREP images
- **Mixed mode** RISETUP, RIPREP, and WIM images
- **Native mode** WIM images only

Boot Environment

The boot environment used for deployment varies with the version of Windows Deployment Services used. The Windows Deployment Services role in Windows Server 2008 R2 uses Windows PE 3.0 as its boot environment. The Windows Deployment Services role in Windows Server 2008 uses Windows PE 2.1. The boot environment used by the Windows Deployment Services update for Windows Server 2003 SP1 and later depends on the mode in which Windows Deployment Services is running, specifically:

- **Legacy mode** OSChooser
- **Mixed mode** OSChooser and Windows PE 2.0, 2.1, or 3.0
- **Native mode** Windows PE 2.0, 2.1, or 3.0

New Features of Windows Deployment Services in Windows Server 2008 R2

The Windows Deployment Services role in Windows Server 2008 R2 has been improved with the following new features:

- **Dynamic driver provisioning** You can now use Windows Deployment Services to add driver packages to boot images so you can deploy these packages to client computers during deployment. For more information on dynamic driver provisioning, see the section titled "Managing and Deploying Driver Packages" later in this chapter.
- **Improved multicasting** Windows Deployment Services can now automatically disconnect slow clients and divide transmissions into multiple streams based on client speeds. Windows Deployment Services also now includes support for IPv6 multicasting. For more information, see the section titled "Creating Multicast Transmissions" later in this chapter.
- **Native booting to VHD images** In Windows 7 and Windows Server 2008 R2, you can now use a VHD as a running operating system without any other parent operating system, virtual machine, or hypervisor. For example, you can deploy a Windows 7 .wim file to a VHD and then copy the .vhd file to client computers. After you do this,

the Windows 7 boot manager must be configured to boot directly into the VHD. Note, however, that if you simply deploy Windows 7 into a VHD, you'll go through the Sysprep specialize pass, which prevents you from using the VHD on physical machines. The workaround for this is to first use the Wim2vhd tool available from *http://code.msdn.microsoft.com/wim2vhd*, create a VHD, and then use ImageX to apply the contents of the WIM into the VHD.

VHD images are not intended to replace WIM images for general deployment purposes. Furthermore, beginning with Windows Server 2008 R2, Windows Deployment Services now supports deploying VHD images in addition to deploying WIM images. Specifically, when you deploy a VHD through Windows Deployment Services, the Bootmgr entries are automatically fixed, so there is no extra step. For example, you can use Windows Deployment Services to deploy VHD images during an unattended installation. For more information on native booting to VHD images, see "Understanding Virtual Hard Disks with Native Boot" in the Windows Client TechCenter on Microsoft TechNet at *http://technet.microsoft.com/en-us/library/dd799282.aspx*. For more information on deploying VHD images using Windows Deployment Services, see "Deploying Virtual Hard Disk Images" in the Windows Server TechCenter on Microsoft TechNet at *http://technet.microsoft.com/en-us/library/dd363560.aspx*.

- **PXE provider for Transport Server** Windows Deployment Services now includes a PXE provider for the Transport Server role service. This lets you use a stand-alone Transport Server to boot from the network or to multicast data without the need of AD DS or Domain Name System (DNS).
- **Additional EFI support** Windows Deployment Services now supports network booting of x64-based computers that use EFI.

> ***MORE INFO*** **For additional information concerning these new features, see *http://technet.microsoft.com/en-us/library/dd735188.aspx*.**

Server Requirements

The hardware requirements for running Windows Server 2003 or Windows Server 2008 are sufficient to support most Windows Deployment Services installations. If you are supporting a large number of images or if you are expecting greater-than-normal client load, investigate adding additional memory for performance and additional hard drive space for image storage. Adding more network adapters can also help with the TFTP download phase if you have a large client load.

The following list describes the software and service requirements for installing and using Windows Deployment Services:

- **AD DS** A Windows Deployment Services server must be either a member of an AD DS domain or a domain controller for a domain. AD DS is used by Windows Deployment

Services to track Windows Deployment Services clients and Windows Deployment Services servers. In addition, systems can be preconfigured in AD DS, instructing Windows Deployment Services on how to image them. Note that AD DS is required only for Deployment Server, not Transport Server.

- **DHCP** You must have a working DHCP server with an active scope on the network because Windows Deployment Services uses PXE, which in turn uses DHCP. The DHCP server does not have to be on the Windows Deployment Services server. The type of DHCP server is not critical for Windows Deployment Services to function properly. To operate Windows Deployment Services and DCHP on the same server, see the section titled "DHCP Requirements" later in this chapter. Note that if you are using Transport Server for multicast only (no PXE), then you don't need DHCP.
- **DNS** A working DNS server on the network is required to run Windows Deployment Services. The DNS server does not have to be running on the Windows Deployment Services server. DNS is used to locate AD DS domain controllers and Windows Deployment Services servers.
- **Installation media** Windows 7 media or a network location that contains the contents of the media are required to install Windows 7 using Windows Deployment Services.
- **An NTFS partition on the Windows Deployment Services server** The server running Windows Deployment Services requires an NTFS File System (NTFS) partition for the image store. You should not create the image store on the partition containing the operating system files, so an additional partition is necessary.
- **SP1 or later version and RIS installed (Windows Server 2003 only)** If you're installing Windows Deployment Services on a server running Windows Server 2003, you must install RIS for the Windows Deployment Services update package to be run. Windows Deployment Services also requires at least SP1.

NOTE Installing and administering Windows Deployment Services requires the administrator to be a member of the local Administrators group on the Windows Deployment Services server. In addition, most administrative tasks for Windows Deployment Services require Domain Admins credentials.

Client Computer Requirements

The client computer requirements to support installation using Windows Deployment Services will vary based on how you intend to use Windows Deployment Services. The following list outlines the requirements for PXE booting to Windows Deployment Services and installing images:

- **Hardware requirements** The client must meet the minimum hardware requirements of the operating system you're installing. The client must also have enough memory to run Windows PE (384 megabytes [MB] required, 512 MB recommended), because Windows Deployment Services uses Windows PE to start the client computer.

- **PXE DHCP-based boot ROM version .99 or later network adapter** To boot directly from the Windows Deployment Services server, the client's network adapter must contain a PXE boot ROM. If this is not the case, the client can be booted using a DVD boot disk, a Windows PE boot image copied to the computer's hard disk, or a USB flash drive (UFD). See the section titled "Preparing Discover Images" later in this chapter.

  All computers meeting the NetPC or PC98 specifications should have the ability to boot from the network adapter. Investigate the basic input/output system (BIOS) settings of the client to determine whether you can enable a Boot From Network option. When the option is enabled, the client should briefly display an option to press F12 to boot from the network during each startup.

- **Network access to the Windows Deployment Services server** The client must have broadcast access to the Windows Deployment Services server to enable PXE booting. Windows PE boot disks can allow you to boot to Windows PE using Windows Deployment Services as an image store without broadcast access.

> ***NOTE*** **The account performing the installation must be a member of the Domain Users AD DS security group. Domain Users have permission to join computers to the domain.**

DHCP Requirements

Windows Deployment Services will configure accessible DHCP servers during installation, adding required scope options to the DHCP scopes. It may be necessary under some circumstances to modify DHCP servers manually to support advanced Windows Deployment Services scenarios. The following list describes how to manage DHCP scope modifications:

- **Microsoft DHCP and Windows Deployment Services on the same server** When Windows Deployment Services is installed on the same physical server as the DHCP service, the Windows Deployment Services PXE server and the DHCP server will both attempt to listen on port 67 for DHCP requests. To prevent this, the Windows Deployment Services PXE server must be configured not to listen on this port. (See Figure 10-5.) This allows booting PXE clients to learn about the presence of the Windows Deployment Services PXE server from the DHCP response generated by the DHCP server.
- **Microsoft DHCP and Windows Deployment Services on separate servers with the clients on the same subnet as the Windows Deployment Services server** When Windows Deployment Services and Microsoft DHCP exist on different servers, no additional settings are required. Both servers respond to DHCP requests. The DHCP server responds with an IP address offer; the Windows Deployment Services PXE server responds with the PXE boot information.

- **Microsoft DHCP and Windows Deployment Services on separate servers with the clients on a different subnet from the Windows Deployment Services server** The recommended approach in this scenario is to use IP Helper tables on the router or switch to forward PXE requests to the Windows Deployment Services server (as well as the DHCP server). An alternative approach is to configure DHCP options 66 and 67 on all scopes to specify the Windows Deployment Services server and the path to the boot program.
- **Third-party DHCP and Windows Deployment Services on separate servers** No additional action should be required for Windows Deployment Services to coexist with third-party DHCP servers. The Windows Deployment Services PXE server will respond with boot file location information only, allowing DHCP to service the IP address request.

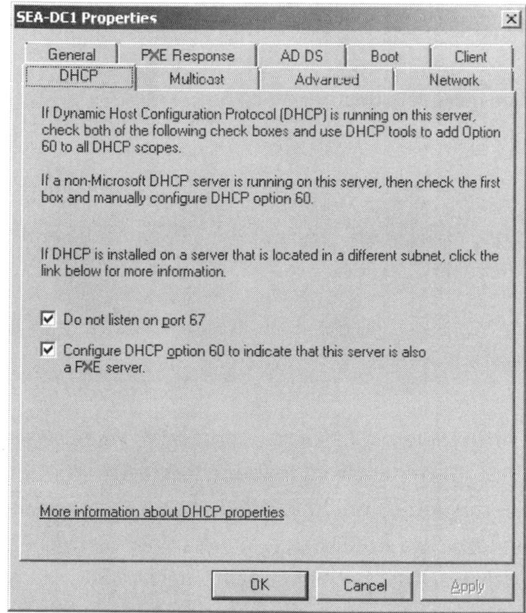

FIGURE 10-5 Configuring DHCP options in Windows Deployment Services

NOTE **RIS requires the RIS server to be authorized as a DHCP server in AD DS. This is not required to operate Windows Deployment Services.**

Routing Requirements

When DHCP and Windows Deployment Services are located on different subnets or if clients are located on a different subnet than the Windows Deployment Services server, IP Helpers must be configured on network routers to enable forwarding of DHCP and PXE boot requests to the appropriate servers. (See Figure 10-6.)

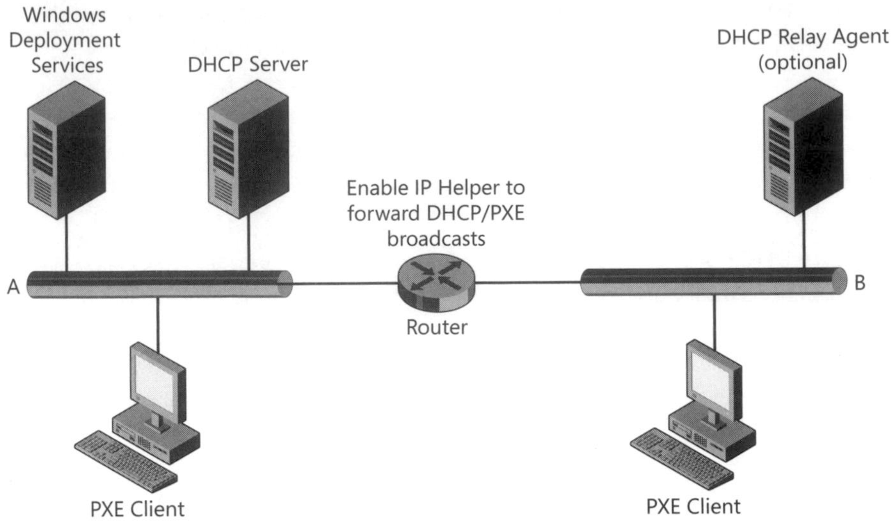

FIGURE 10-6 Windows Deployment Services on multiple subnets

> ***NOTE*** **An alternative to enabling IP Helpers on your routers is to install a DHCP relay agent on the remote network, configuring appropriate scope options to allow the remote clients to locate the Windows Deployment Services server.**

Capacity Requirements

Windows Deployment Services servers can generate a lot of network traffic when servicing multiple, simultaneous client requests. Plan for this network load by designing your deployment network for sufficient capacity. You can deploy multiple Windows Deployment Services servers or use multicasting (requires Windows Server 2008 or later versions) in environments that experience significant installation activity. Note that beyond about 25 to 50 simultaneous clients, the bottleneck becomes TFTP, which is unicast and is required to download Windows PE. (Windows Deployment Services supports multicast download of Windows PE only for x64 Unified Extensible Firmware Interface [UEFI] machines). You can allocate access to Windows Deployment Services by using DHCP scopes and IP subnetting. You can also configure IP Helper tables to direct clients to one or another Windows Deployment Services server based on client network ID.

Installing Windows Deployment Services

Windows Deployment Services is installed as an update to Windows Server 2003 or added as a server role in Windows Server 2008 R2. The following procedures outline the basic installation steps for Windows Deployment Services. Refer to the appropriate guidance (listed in the section titled "Additional Resources" at the end of this chapter) for complete instructions and planning advice.

Windows Server 2003

To completely install Windows Deployment Services on a computer running Windows Server 2003, you must first install RIS. After RIS is installed, you install the Windows Deployment Services update or Windows Server 2003 SP2 (which contains the update). The Windows AIK also includes the Windows Deployment Services update, which you can install on any server after extracting the file from the Windows AIK media.

To install RIS on Windows Server 2003, perform the following steps:

1. In the Add Or Remove Programs utility in Control Panel, click Add/Remove Windows Components.
2. Select the check box next to Remote Installation Services, as shown here, and then click Next.

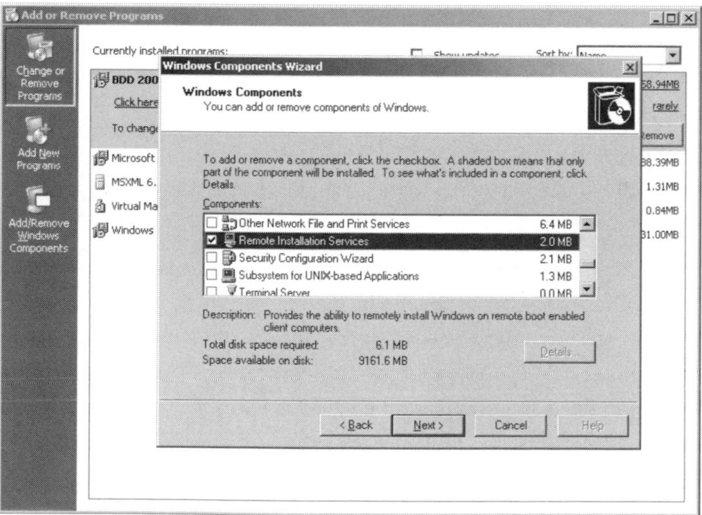

> **NOTE** **In Windows Server 2003 SP2, the Remote Installation Services feature is named Windows Deployment Services.**

To install the Windows Deployment Services update, perform the following steps:

1. Run the Windows Deployment Services update from the Windows AIK. The file is windows-deployment-service-update-*platform*.exe, where *platform* is either x86 or x64, and is found in the WDS folder on the Windows AIK DVD. (If you have already installed SP2 for Windows Server 2003, you do not need to perform this task.)

2. On the Windows Deployment Services Setup Wizard Welcome page, shown here, click Next.

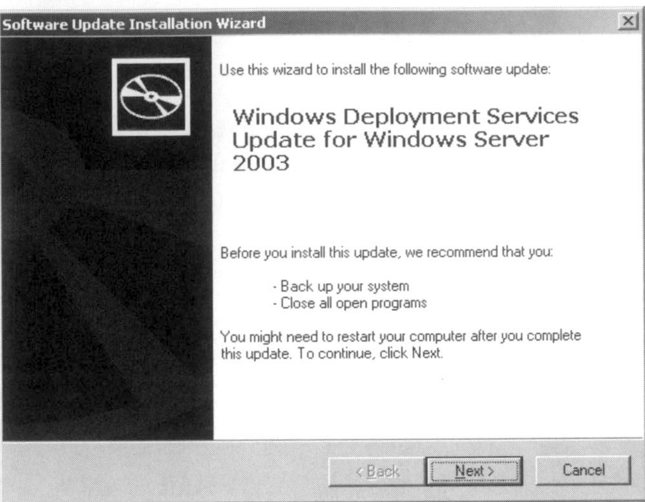

3. On the Microsoft Software License Terms page, click I Accept The Terms In The License Agreement. Click Next.
4. The Updating Your System page displays installation progress.
5. On the Completion page, click Finish to restart the computer.

> ***NOTE*** **Unless you plan to use Riprep legacy images, you can proceed with the configuration of Windows Deployment Services at this point. To enable Windows Deployment Services mixed mode, ensure that you do not install this update until at least one Riprep image is installed on the RIS server. For more information on the installation and configuration of RIS, see "Designing RIS Installations" in the *Windows Server 2003 Resource Kit*.**

Windows Server 2008 R2

You can install Windows Deployment Services by using the Add Roles Wizard, located in Server Manager.

To add the Windows Deployment Services server role, perform the following steps:

1. Start the Add Roles Wizard from Server Manager.
2. Click Next to skip the Before You Begin screen.
3. Select the Windows Deployment Services role, as shown here, and click Next.

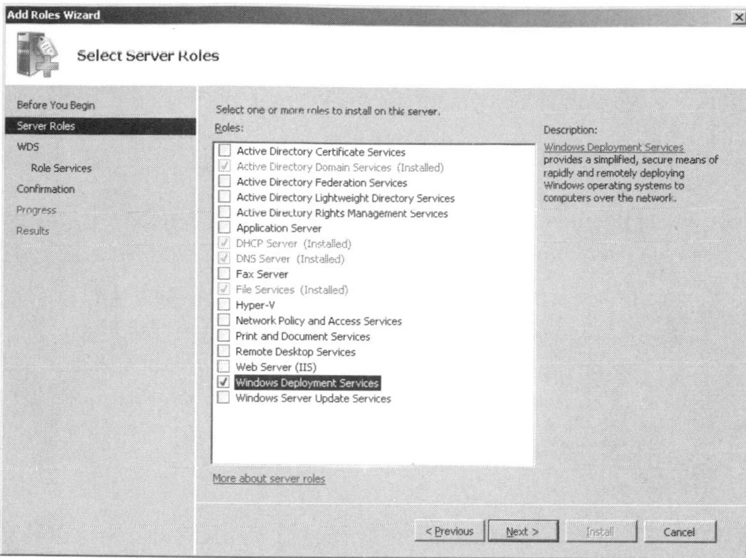

4. Additional information on installing and using Windows Deployment Services is displayed.
5. Click Next when you are ready to proceed.
6. On the Select Role Services page, click Next to install both the Deployment Server and the Transport Server role services. The Deployment Server role service contains all of the core Windows Deployment Services functionality. The Transport Server role service contains the core networking features.
7. On the Confirm Installation Selections page, click Install.
8. Windows Deployment Services is installed.
9. Click Close to complete the Add Roles Wizard.

Configuring Windows Deployment Services

After Windows Deployment Services is installed, you will need to add the server to the management console and then configure it. Windows Deployment Services automatically adds the local computer to the console. If you want to add a remote server, you must add it.

To add a server to Windows Deployment Services, perform the following steps:

1. Open the Windows Deployment Services management console by selecting Windows Deployment Services from Administrative Tools. You can also use the Windows Deployment Services node under Roles in Server Manager.
2. Right-click Servers in the Windows Deployment Services console tree and then click Add Server.

3. In the Add Server dialog box, choose a computer to add to the console. The server will be added and will now need to be configured.

To initially prepare the Windows Deployment Services server, perform the following steps:

1. In the Windows Deployment Services console tree, right-click the server and click Configure Server.
2. On the Windows Deployment Services Configuration Wizard Welcome page, make sure that your environment meets the requirements and then click Next.
3. Enter a path for the image store, as shown here, and then click Next. The folder should be on a partition other than the partition containing the system files. If you choose to create the image store on the system drive, a warning message will appear. Click Yes to continue or click No to choose a new installation location (recommended).

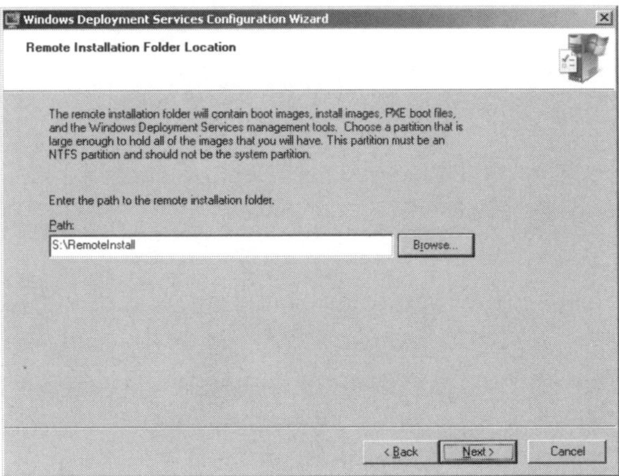

4. Configure DHCP Option 60 settings, as shown here, and then click Next. (Depending upon your configuration, this screen may or may not be displayed.) See the section titled "DHCP Requirements" earlier in this chapter for information on how to properly configure these settings.

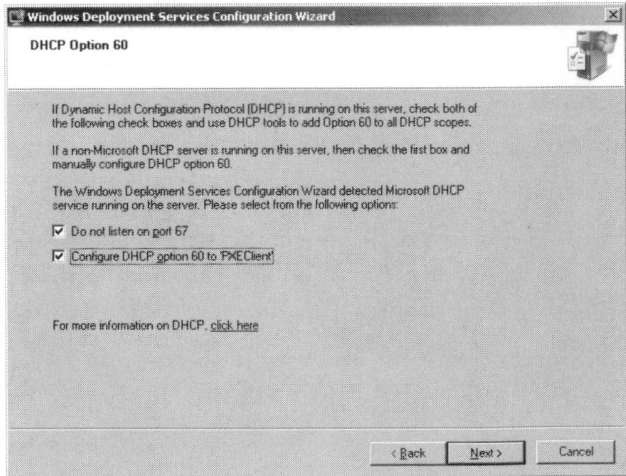

5. Set a PXE Server Initial Settings policy, as shown here, and then click Next.

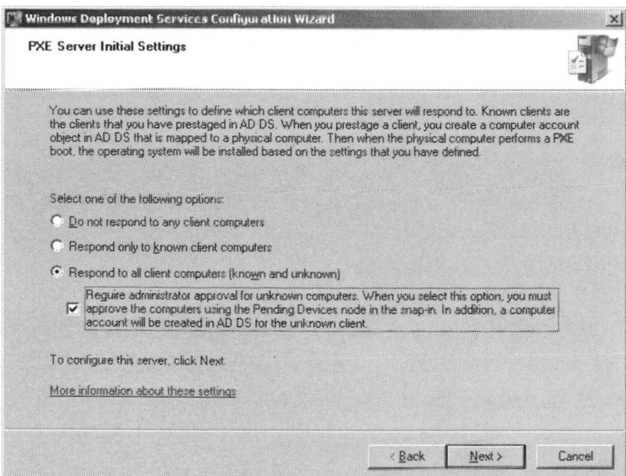

6. On the Configuration Complete page, you can add images to the server (default) or clear the Add Images To The Windows Deployment Services Server Now check box if you want to add images at another time. To add images to your server, see the section titled "Importing Images" later in this chapter.

Preparing Discover Images

For client computers that do not support PXE booting, you can create boot disks using a CD or DVD, a hard disk, or a UFD. You can create these disks by using the Windows Deployment Services administration tools or the Windows PE administration tools from the Windows AIK. The process begins by creating a Windows PE boot image using the Windows Deployment Services console or Wdsutil. After this image is created, a bootable disk is made using the *Oscdimg* command from the Windows AIK.

To create a discover image using the management console, perform the following steps:

1. In the Windows Deployment Services management console, click Boot Images. Boot Images is under Servers, *server_name*, where *server_name* is the name of the Windows Deployment Services server.
2. Right-click a boot image that you previously added to Windows Deployment Services to use as a discover image and then click Create Discover Boot Image.
3. On the Metadata And Location page, type a name and description for the discover image, as shown on the following page. Then choose the location in which to create the image and the Windows Deployment Services server to respond to it. Click Next.

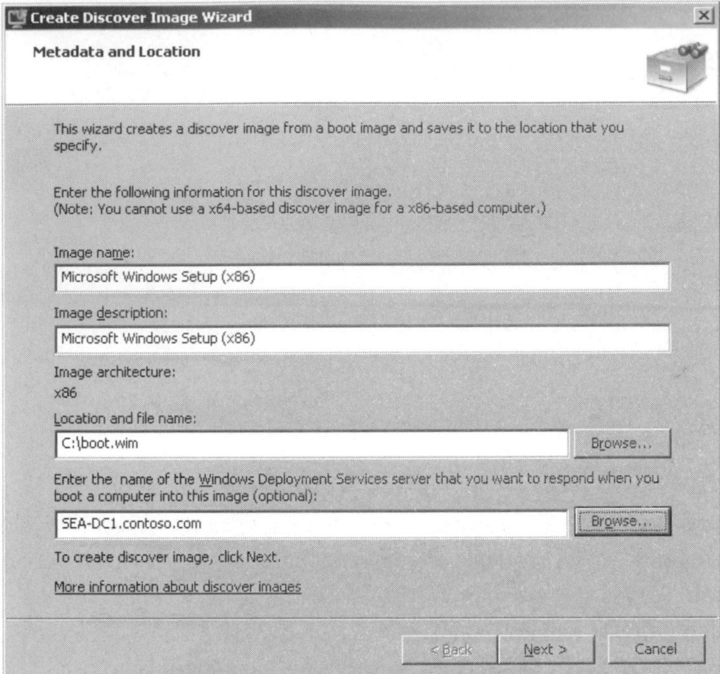

4. Click Finish.

To create a discover image using Wdsutil, perform the following steps:

1. Run the following command using elevated credentials.

   Wdsutil /new-discoverimage /image:*boot_image*/architecture:*architecture* /destinationimage /filepath:*discover_image*

   Boot_image is the name of the boot image you want to use to create the discover image (not the file name), and *discover_image* is the file path and file name of the new Windows PE boot image. *Architecture* is either x86 or x64.

To create a bootable DVD using the discover image, perform the following steps:

1. To create a Windows PE build environment, open a command prompt and run the following commands.

   ```
   Md c:\Winpe\Boot
   Md c:\Winpe\Sources
   ```

2. Copy the discover image created in the previous procedures to the \Sources folder of the build environment with the following command.

   ```
   Copy d:\sources\boot.wim c:\Winpe\Sources
   ```

3. Copy boot files from the Windows AIK with the following command, where *architecture* is the processor architecture for the computer being used (either x86 or x64).

```
Xcopy c:\Program Files\Windows AIK\tools\architecture\boot c:\WinPE\boot
```

4. Run the following command in the folder C:\Program files\Windows AIK\tools*architecture*, where *architecture* is x86 or x64.

```
Oscdimg -n -bc:\winpe\boot\etfsboot.com c:\winpe c:\winpe.iso
```

5. Burn the .iso file Winpe.iso to a DVD by using a third-party DVD mastering program.

> **NOTE** For more information on creating bootable media, see Chapter 9, "Preparing Windows PE."

Importing Images

After you have installed and configured the Windows Deployment Services service, you can add more Windows PE boot images (Boot.wim) and Windows 7 install images (Install.wim). This process is straightforward: The files Boot.wim and Install.wim from the \Sources folder on Windows 7 media are used for this purpose. For example, you can add the boot image that MDT 2010 creates to Windows Deployment Services, allowing you to connect to deployment points and run MDT 2010 task sequences across the network.

> **NOTE** For more information on creating custom boot and install images that you can use with Windows Deployment Services, see Chapter 9 and Chapter 6, "Developing Disk Images."

Importing Boot Images

To prepare to service client computers, you must import a Windows PE boot image. Although Windows Deployment Services in Windows Server 2008 and later versions includes the boot loader code, it does not include the actual Windows PE boot image. You can import boot images directly from the Windows 7 or Windows Server 2008 R2 source files. You can also customize boot images with hooks into services, such as MDT 2010. For example, MDT 2010 builds custom Windows PE boot images that connect to MDT 2010 deployment points to install operating system builds. You can add these custom Windows PE boot images to Windows Deployment Services to streamline the LTI deployment process.

To import a Windows 7 boot image, perform the following steps:

1. Insert a Windows 7 DVD into the server's DVD-ROM drive or make an installation source available to the server over the network.

2. Right-click the Boot Images folder and then click Add Boot Image. Boot Images is located under Servers, *server_name*, where *server_name* is the name of the Windows Deployment Services server to which you're adding the boot image.
3. On the Image File page, click Browse to select the boot image and then click Open. For example, you can select the default boot image \Sources\Boot.wim on the Windows 7 media.
4. On the Image File page, click Next.
5. On the Image Metadata page, type a name and description of the image and then click Next. The default name and description is derived from the contents of the boot image file.
6. On the Summary page, click Next to add the image to Windows Deployment Services.
7. When the import task is completed, click Finish.

Importing Install Images

Windows 7 includes an installation image on the media. The installation image (Install.wim) can include multiple editions of Windows 7. You can import one or more of these editions into Windows Deployment Services for deployment over the network.

ON THE COMPANION MEDIA **This book's companion media includes a sample script, VRKAddInstallImage.vbs, that demonstrates how to script the addition of installation images to Windows Deployment Services. A similar script, VRKListImages.vbs, demonstrates how to write a script that iterates install images. These scripts are samples only and should be customized to meet the specific needs of your deployment environment.**

To import a Windows 7 install image, perform the following steps:

1. Insert a Windows 7 DVD into the server's DVD-ROM drive or make an installation source available to the server over the network.
2. Right-click the Install Images folder in the Windows Deployment Services management console and then click Add Image Group. Install Images is under Servers, *server_name*, where *server_name* is the name of the Windows Deployment Services server to which you're adding the installation image.
3. Name the Image Group and then click OK. This creates a folder for image import. It also allows you to group similar images together for optimal use of disk space and security.
4. Right-click Install Images and then click Add Install Image.
5. Choose the Image Group you created in the previous steps and then click Next.

6. In the Image File page, click Browse, choose the Install.wim file you're adding to the server, and then click Open. This file is located in the \Sources folder of the Windows 7 DVD. Click Next to continue.
7. Choose the image(s) you want to import from the selections presented on the List Of Available Images page. (Be sure to select only images for which you have licenses.) Click Next.
8. Click Next on the Summary page to begin the import process. The process can take several minutes to finish.
9. When the import task is completed, click Finish.

> ***NOTE*** **Copying the source files to the local hard drive first and then importing the image into Windows from the local source files is faster than importing the image directly from the DVD.**

Managing and Deploying Driver Packages

A new feature of Windows Deployment Services in Windows Server 2008 R2 is the ability to manage and deploy driver packages when performing deployment. Specifically, you can:

- Add driver packages to a Window Deployment Services server and deploy these driver packages to different client computers based on filtering criteria.
- Add boot-critical driver packages to boot images (supported for Windows 7 and Windows Server 2008 R2 images only).

These new features make it simpler to ensure that the appropriate drivers are available during a deployment.

Deploying Driver Packages to Clients

You can use Windows Deployment Services in Windows Server 2008 R2 to deploy driver packages to client computers using the following methods:

- **Method 1** Make all driver packages available to all clients. This is the simplest approach, and each type of client will use Plug and Play to install the driver package it needs. This method assumes that the devices that need the driver packages are connected to or attached to the clients before you deploy Windows to them. However, this method can cause problems if two or more incompatible drivers are installed on the same client. If this happens, try method 2.
- **Method 2** Create a different driver group for each type of client and add different driver packages to each driver group as needed. A *driver group* is a collection of driver packages on a Windows Deployment Services server. They use filters to define which type of client has access to the driver group based on the client's hardware and the

operating system being installed. You should use this method if you need to install specific driver packages on specific computers or if your hardware environment is too complex for method 1 above to work properly.

- **Method 3** Create a different driver group for each type of client and add different driver packages to each driver group as needed. Then create an additional driver group and deploy all the driver packages in it to all computers. This method is useful if you have external hardware that is not connected to clients during the installation process. Once the installation is complete, you can connect the hardware and the driver package will install.

The sections that follow describe each method in more detail.

Deploying Driver Packages to Clients Using Method 1

To make all driver packages available to all clients during deployment, do the following:

1. In the Windows Deployment Services console, under the *server_name* node, right-click the Drivers node and select Add Driver Package.
2. Either browse to select a folder containing the driver packages you want to deploy, or browse to select the .inf file of a single driver package you want to deploy, as shown here.

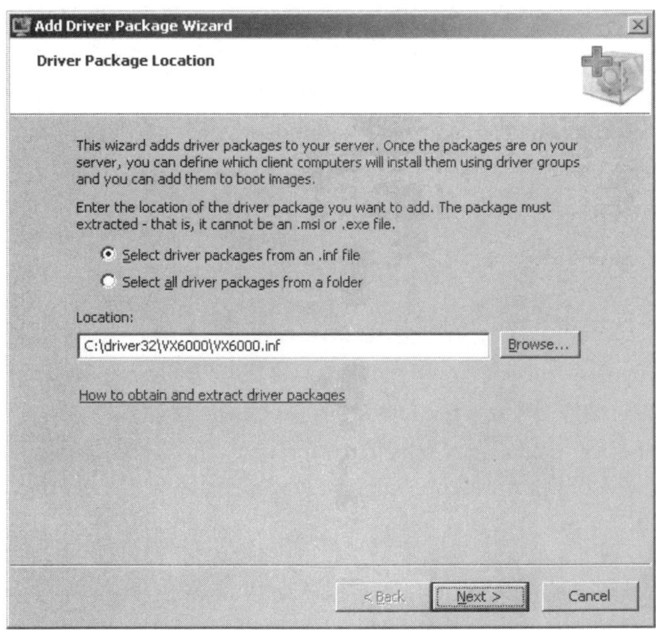

Note that you cannot deploy driver packages that are in the form of .msi or .exe files. You must extract the driver files from these packages to add them to your Windows Deployment Services server.

3. Click Next and select the driver package(s) you want to add to the Windows Deployment Services server.
4. Click Next to add the driver package to the Windows Deployment Services server.
5. Click Next and select the Select An Existing Driver Group option. Then select DriverGroup1 as the driver group to which the driver package will be added. DriverGroup1 is the default driver group and has no filters configured for it. This means that all client computers will have access to the driver packages in this driver group. Plug and Play will ensure that only those driver packages that match the client's hardware will be installed.
6. Finish the Add Driver Packages Wizard. The added driver package will be displayed in the Windows Deployment Services console under DriverGroup1, as shown here.

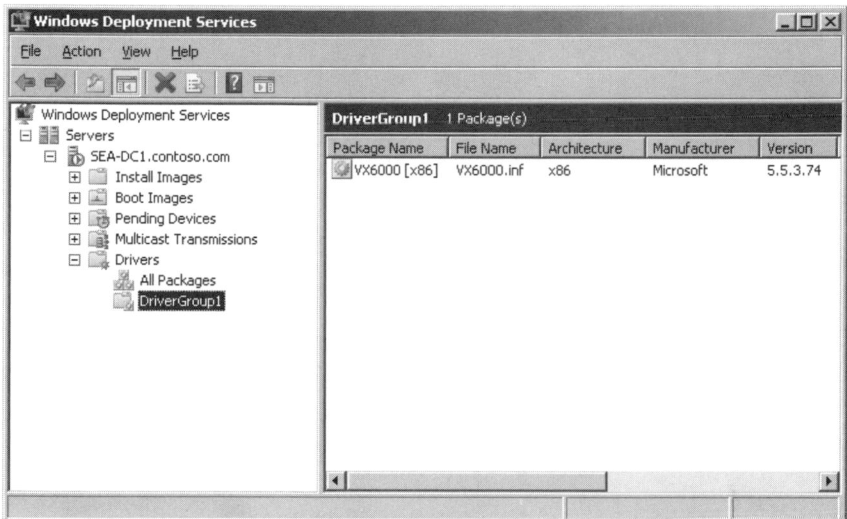

You can test this approach as follows:

1. Make sure that the device for which the driver package is intended is connected to or attached to a client computer.
2. Use Windows Deployment Services to deploy Windows 7 to the client computer.
3. When the install is finished, log on as an administrator and open Device Manager. Verify that the device drivers needed by the device have been installed and that the device is working properly.

Deploying Driver Packages to Clients Using Method 2

To deploy driver packages to different types of clients using driver groups that have been configured with hardware and/or install image filters, do the following:

1. In the Windows Deployment Services console, under the *server_name* node under the Drivers node, right-click on DriverGroup1 and select Disable. You must disable

DriverGroup1 when performing this method because DriverGroup1 does not have any filters configured on it, which means that all driver packages in DriverGroup1 will be deployed to all clients unless DriverGroup1 is disabled.

2. Right-click on the Drivers node and select Add Driver Group. Type a descriptive name for the driver group.
3. Click Next to display the Client Hardware Filters page of the Add Driver Group Wizard.
4. Click Add to open the Add Filter dialog box.
5. Select a filter type. The available filter types are:
   - Manufacturer
   - BIOS Vendor
   - BIOS Version
   - Chassis Type
   - UUID

   Manufacturer is the most common type of filter used, followed by Chassis Type. The others are typically used for troubleshooting.
6. Select either Equal To or Not Equal To as the operator for the filter.
7. Type a value for the filter and click Add. You can add multiple values to a filter if needed—for example, if the name of the manufacturer has multiple possible spellings.
8. Repeat steps 5 through 7 to add additional filters as needed.
9. Click OK when finished. The added filters are displayed, as shown here.

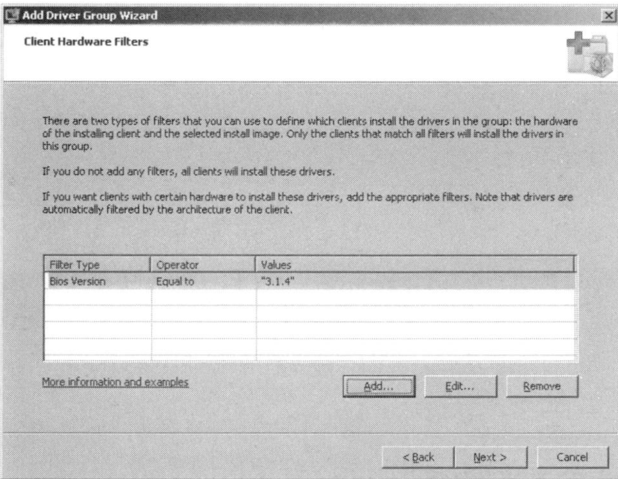

10. Click Next to display the Install Image Filters page.
11. Click Add to open the Add Filter dialog box.
12. Select a filter type. The available filter types are:
    - OS Version

- OS Edition
- OS Language

13. Select either Equal To or Not Equal To as the operator for the filter.
14. Type a value for the filter and click Add.
15. Repeat steps 12 through 14 to add additional filters as needed.
16. Click OK when finished, and then click Next to display the Packages To Install page.
17. On the Packages To Install page, leave Install Only The Driver Packages That Match A Client's Hardware selected. Click Next and then Finish to complete the Add Driver Group Wizard.
18. Now add the driver packages needed to your new driver group. You can do this in two ways:
    - For driver packages not yet added to the Windows Deployment Services server, right-click the Drivers node and select Add Driver Group. Use the Add Driver Packages Wizard to add driver packages, first to the server and then to the driver group.
    - For driver packages already added to the Windows Deployment Services server but in the wrong driver groups, right-click the driver group you just created and select Add Driver Packages To This Group. Use the Add Driver Packages To *driver_group* Wizard to add the driver packages to the driver group.

WARNING **Be sure to test this approach carefully before using it in a production environment. In particular, be careful to specify the values of filters exactly as needed—omitting a period or other character can invalidate a filter.**

Deploying Driver Packages to Clients Using Method 3

To deploy driver packages to different types of clients by skipping the running of Plug and Play enumeration, do the following:

1. Complete steps 1 through 16 of method 2, as outlined in the previous section.
2. On the Packages To Install page, select Install All Driver Packages In This Group.
3. Click Next and then Finish to complete the Add Driver Group Wizard. Then add the driver packages needed to the new driver group as described in step 18 of Method 2.

Alternatively, if you already used method 2 to create driver groups with filters and add driver packages to them, you can right-click a driver group, select Properties, and then select All Driver Packages In The Group, as shown on the following page.

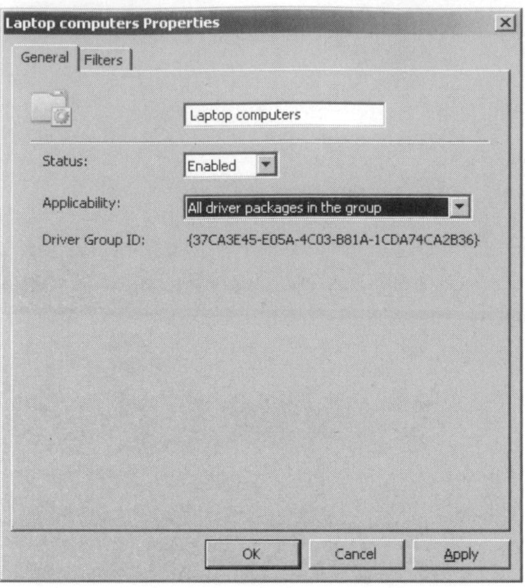

WARNING If incompatible driver packages are deployed using this method, the result can be client computers that fail to boot properly.

Managing Driver Groups and Driver Packages

You can use Windows Deployment Services in Windows Server 2008 R2 to manage driver groups. For example, you can:

- Enable or disable a driver group.
- Duplicate a driver group. (This creates a new group with the same driver packages and filters. It doesn't make any copies of the files, but just references them again.)
- Modify the filters for a driver group.
- Configure the applicability of a driver group.

You can also use Windows Deployment Services in Windows Server 2008 R2 to manage driver packages. For example, you can:

- View the properties of a driver package, including its drivers and files.
- Configure the driver groups to which the driver package belongs.
- Enable or disable the driver package.

Adding Driver Packages to Boot Images

You can also use Windows Deployment Services in Windows Server 2008 R2 to add driver packages for boot-critical drivers to boot images. To add a driver package to a boot image, perform the following steps:

1. In the Windows Deployment Services console, under the *server_name* node under the Boot Images node, right-click a boot image and select Export Image to back up your boot image before proceeding further. This is recommended because adding an incompatible or corrupt boot-critical driver to a boot image can render the boot image unbootable and unrepairable.
2. Right-click the boot image again and select Add Driver Packages To Image to start the Add Driver Packages To *driver_group* Wizard.
3. Click Next to display the Select Driver Packages page, as shown here.

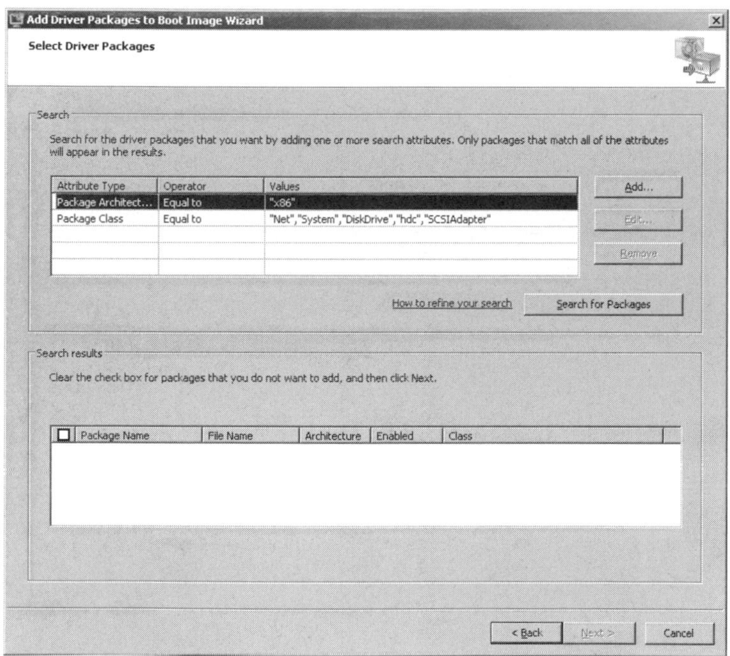

4. Click Add or Remove to add or remove filter criteria for finding driver packages that were previously added to your Windows Deployment Services server. Then click Search For Packages to display all driver packages on the server that match your filter criteria.
5. Select the driver packages you want to add to the boot image from your search results. Then, finish the wizard.

Managing Image Security

It is important to properly secure boot and installation images to prevent their unauthorized use. A fully configured image might include corporate applications and data, proprietary configurations, and even codes and keys required to activate line of business (LOB) applications.

One way to prevent unauthorized installations is by controlling the clients that are allowed to receive images. You can accomplish this through pre-staging, in which clients are registered with AD DS through the use of a globally unique identifier (GUID). Another method is to enable administrative approval for client installations. Finally, you can restrict images by user as shown in the following procedure.

To configure an image file's access control list (ACL), perform the following steps:

1. Right-click the image and then click Properties.
2. On the User Permissions tab, configure the ACL and then click OK. The image's ACL must give a user Read and Execute permissions for the user to be able to install the image. In the following screenshot, members of the Installations group can install the image secured by this ACL.

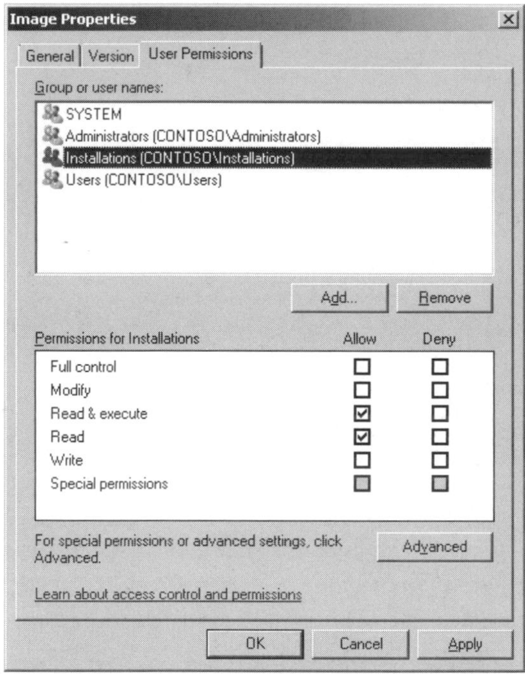

> **NOTE** In addition to securing individual images, you can secure image groups. Right-click an image group, click Security, and then configure the group's ACL on the Security tab. By default, images in an image group inherit the group's permissions.

Pre-staging Client Computers

Pre-staging client computer accounts allows you to restrict Windows Deployment Services to respond only to known clients. You can also cause specific Windows Deployment Services servers to respond to the pre-staged client, assign specific install images, and control client provisioning automatically. You configured these settings earlier by setting the PXE Server Initial Settings policy when you installed Windows Deployment Services, as described in the section titled "Installing Windows Deployment Services" earlier in this chapter.

To pre-stage a client computer's account, you will need to know the computer's GUID. You can find this value in the system's BIOS, in the documentation delivered with the system, or on a tag affixed to the computer's case. This value is entered into the AD DS computer account details for the computer to pre-assign its membership in the AD DS infrastructure.

To pre-stage a client computer, perform the following steps:

1. In Active Directory Users And Computers, find the organizational unit (OU) where the computer will be staged.
2. Right-click the OU, click New, and then click Computer.
3. Type a name for the computer and then click Next. If you want, click Change to choose the user or group with permission to join this computer to the domain.
4. On the Managed page, select the check box next to This Is A Managed Computer. Type the computer's GUID, as shown here, and then click Next.

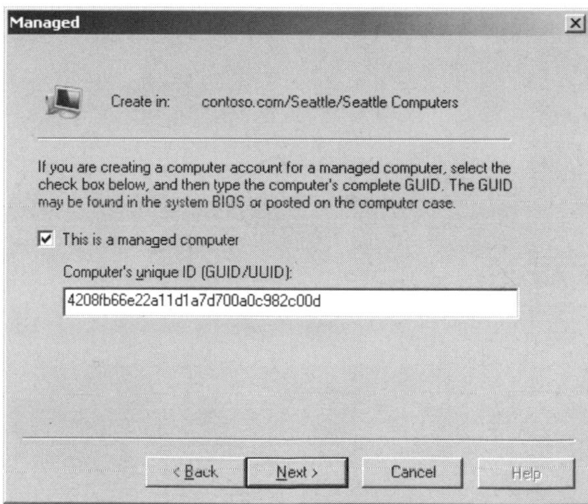

5. On the Host Server page, choose Any Available Remote Installation Server or select the Windows Deployment Services server that will serve this client. Click Next.
6. Click Finish to complete the wizard.

NOTE You can also pre-stage client computer accounts using the ***WDSUTIL /Add-Device*** **command.**

Configuring Administrator Approval

An alternative to pre-staging computers or allowing unrestricted access to Windows Deployment Services images is to require administrator approval before allowing installation. You accomplish this on the PXE Response tab of each server. You can also configure this by setting the PXE Server Initial policy when you install Windows Deployment Services, as described in the section titled "Installing Windows Deployment Services" earlier in this chapter.

To require administrative approval for unknown computers, begin by granting Domain Admin permissions to the computer account of the Windows Deployment Services server. Instructions on how to do this can be found at *http://technet.microsoft.com/en-us/library/cc754005.aspx* under the heading "Approve a Pending Computer." Then perform the following steps:

1. In the Windows Deployment Services management console, right-click the server and then click Properties.
2. On the PXE Response tab, click Respond To All Client Computers (Known And Unknown) and then select the Require Administrator Approval For Unknown Computers check box, as shown here.

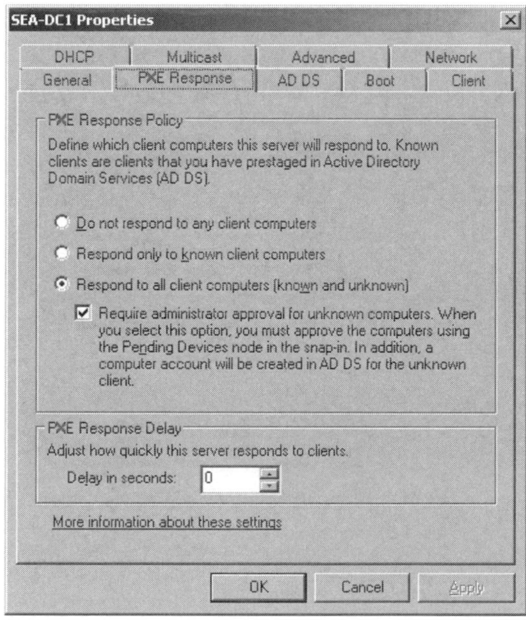

Systems booted to Windows PE will enter a pending state until an administrator approves their installation. You can view systems in this state in the Pending Devices item of the Windows Deployment Services management console.

Installing Windows 7

For ease of installing Windows 7, client computers must support booting from the network. Windows Deployment Services uses PXE technology to boot from the network and start the Windows Deployment Services client. You must also ensure that the computer's BIOS is configured to boot from the network.

To install Windows 7 from Windows Deployment Services, perform the following steps:

1. Start or reboot the client computer.
2. When the client computer starts and the Windows Deployment Services boot loader prompts you to press F12, press F12 to download and start the Windows Deployment Services client. Make sure you enable network boot in the computer's BIOS.
3. On the Windows Deployment Services page, choose a locale and keyboard layout and then click Next.
4. When prompted to connect to the Windows Deployment Services server, type the user account and password to use for the connection and then click OK.
5. On the Select The Operating System You Want To Install page, choose an operating system image and then click Next.
6. On the Where Do You Want To Install Windows? page, choose a partition on which to install Windows 7 and then click Next. To repartition the disk using advanced options, click Drive Options (Advanced).
7. Windows Setup will install Windows 7, prompting for required settings that are not specified in an unattended-setup answer file.

Capturing Custom Images

Windows Deployment Services can deploy more than just default images from the Windows 7 media. You can also create custom boot images and install images and then import them into Windows Deployment Services for automated distribution. Chapter 9 describes how to create custom Windows PE boot images. After creating a custom image, you can import it using the instructions in the section titled "Importing Images" earlier in this chapter.

To create a custom installation image for Windows Deployment Services, you must install an existing image on a reference computer, customize the reference computer as desired by adding drivers and applications, and then capture an image of the reference computer. Image capture is a two-step process. First, you must create a Windows PE capture image to support the image-capture process. Then you capture an image from a reference computer that was prepared for imaging using the Sysprep utility.

To create an image-capture image, perform the following steps:

1. Click the Boot Images item in the Windows Deployment Services console tree.

2. Right-click the image to use as a capture image and then click Create Capture Boot Image.
3. On the Metadata And Location page, type a name and description for the capture image and then specify the location and file name of the image file to create, as shown here. Click Next to create the capture image.

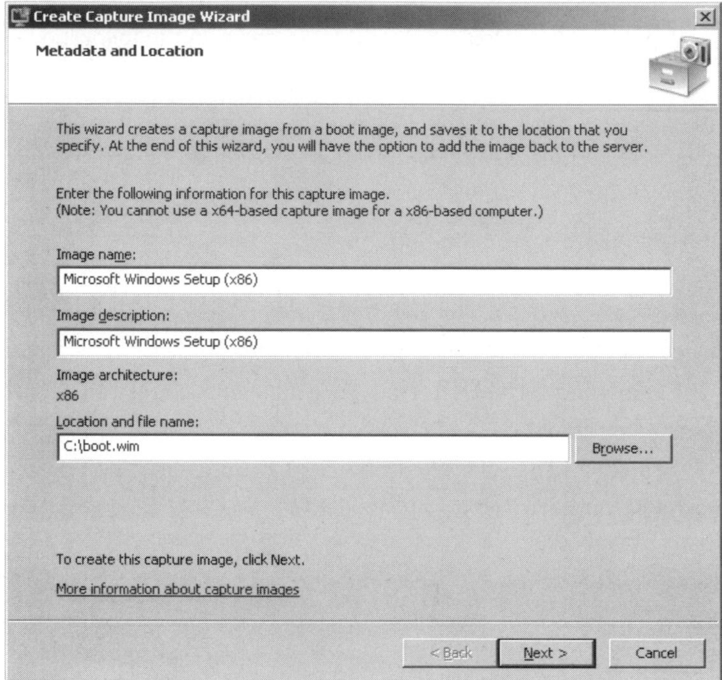

4. Click Finish.
5. Import the custom capture boot image by using the instructions in the section titled "Importing Images" earlier in this chapter. Note that Windows Deployment Services in Windows Server 2008 R2 includes a check box on the last page of this wizard that you can select to automatically re-import the image.

To create a custom Windows 7 install image, perform the following steps:

1. Create a master installation by installing a Windows 7 image on a reference computer and then customizing the installation to meet your requirements. You can install Windows 7 on your reference computer either from media or using Windows Deployment Services. To learn how to install Windows 7 using Windows Deployment Services, see the section titled "Installing Windows 7" earlier in this chapter.
2. From a command prompt on the master computer, change directories to \Windows\System32\Sysprep and run the following command.

```
Sysprep /oobe /generalize /reboot
```

3. When the reference computer reboots and the Windows Deployment Services boot loader prompts you to press F12, press F12 to download and start the Windows Deployment Services client. Make sure you enable network boot in the computer's BIOS.
4. In Windows Boot Manager, select the capture boot image.
5. On the Windows Deployment Wizard Image Capture Wizard, click Next.
6. On the Image Capture Source page, choose the volume to capture from the Volume To Capture list and then provide a name and description for the image. Click Next to continue. (Note that if you have omitted step 2, you won't see any volumes available at this point. This has been a major area of customer confusion.)
7. On the Image Capture Destination page, click Browse to choose the location where you want to store the captured image. In the File Name text box, type a name for the image using the .wim extension and then click Save. Click Upload Image To WDS Server, type the name of the Windows Deployment Services server, and click Connect. If prompted for credentials, provide a user name and password for an account with sufficient privileges to connect to the Windows Deployment Services server. Choose the image group in which to store the image from the Image Group list.
8. Click Finish.

> ***NOTE*** **The reason for saving a local copy in step 7 rather than just uploading it to the server immediately is to minimize the chances of corruption occurring over the network.**

Creating Multicast Transmissions

Multicasting enables you to deploy an image to numerous client computers at the same time without overburdening the network. By using multicast, you transmit image data only once, drastically reducing the amount of network bandwidth that is used to deploy images from Windows Deployment Services.

Consider implementing multicasting if your organization:

- Has network routers that support multicasting.
- Is a large company that requires many concurrent client installations. If your organization deploys images to only a small number of computers at the same time, multicasting might not be the right choice.
- Wants to use network bandwidth efficiently. With this feature, images are sent over the network only once, and you can specify limitations (for example, to only use 10 percent of your bandwidth). If your organization does not have bandwidth overload issues, multicasting might not be worth the effort.

- Has enough disk space on client computers for the image to be downloaded. When multicasting, Windows Deployment Services downloads the image to the client computer instead of installing it from the server.
- Meets the requirements listed in the following section.

Multicast Prerequisites

To use multicast in your organization, it must meet all the following requirements:

- Routers that support multicasting. In particular, your network infrastructure needs to support the Internet Group Management Protocol (IGMP) to properly forward multicast traffic. Without the IGMP, multicast packets are treated as broadcast packets, which can lead to network flooding.
- At least one install image that you want to transmit on the server.
- The Boot.wim file located in the \Sources folder on Windows 7 or Windows Server 2008 R2 media.
- IGMP snooping should be enabled on all devices. This will cause your network hardware to forward multicast packets only to those devices that are requesting data. If IGMP snooping is turned off, multicast packets are treated as broadcast packets and will be sent to every device in the subnet.

Transmission Types

There are two types of multicast transmissions:

- **Auto-Cast** This option indicates that as soon as an applicable client requests an install image, a multicast transmission of the selected image begins. Then, as other clients request the same image, they are also joined to the transmission that is already started.
- **Scheduled-Cast** This option sets the start criteria for the transmission based on the number of clients that are requesting an image, a specific day and time, or both. If you do not select either of the check boxes in Scheduled-Cast, the transmission will not start until you manually start it. Note that in addition to these criteria, you can start a transmission manually at any time by right-clicking it and then clicking Start.

Performing Multicast Deployment

Multicast deployment requires using the Windows Deployment Services server role in Windows Server 2008 or Windows Server 2008 R2. The Windows Deployment Services update for Windows Server 2003 SP1 and later versions does not support multicast deployment.

Multicast deployment is supported for install images only. The Boot.wim file used for multicast deployment must be imported from Windows Server 2008, Windows Vista SP1 or later versions, Windows 7, or Windows Server 2008 R2 media.

New features of multicast deployment for the Windows Deployment Services server role in Windows Server 2008 R2 include the following:

- Enables Windows Deployment Services to automatically disconnect slow clients and to divide transmissions into multiple streams based on client speeds. Note that while multicast deployment requires Windows 3.0, auto-disconnect will work with Windows PE 2.1 or 3.0.
- Supports multicast deployment in IPv6 environments. This feature requires that the boot image comes from Windows Vista SP1 or later versions, Windows Server 2008, Windows 7, or Windows Server 2008 R2.
- Supports boot images for computers that use x64 EFI. This feature can be managed using the Wdsutil command only.

> ***MORE INFO*** **For more information on performing multicast deployment using Windows Deployment Services, see "Performing Multicast Deployments" at** ***http://technet.microsoft.com/en-us/library/dd637994.aspx*****.**

Using Windows Deployment Services with Microsoft Deployment Toolkit

For LTI, MDT 2010 generates Windows PE boot images that connect to the deployment point and starts the Windows Deployment Wizard. The Windows Deployment Wizard allows the user to select an operating build to configure, applications to install, and so on.

MDT 2010 generates boot images when you update deployment points. MDT 2010 generates .iso image files that you can burn to DVD. You find these boot images in the \DeploymentShare$\Boot folder on your MDT 2010 technician computer. The file name is LiteTouchPE_*platform*.iso, where *platform* is x86 or x64. After you burn the .iso image to DVD and then use this DVD to start destination computers.

MDT 2010 also generates Windows PE .wim boot images that you can add to Windows Deployment Services. Starting the MDT 2010 Windows PE boot images by using Windows Deployment Services is more convenient and quicker than using DVDs. You find these boot images in the \DeploymentShare$\Boot folder on your MDT 2010 technician computer. The file name is LiteTouchPE_*platform*.wim, where *platform* is x86 or x64. You can import this boot image into Windows Deployment Services using the instructions in the section titled "Importing Images" earlier in this chapter.

> ***ON THE COMPANION MEDIA*** **This book's companion CD includes a sample script, VRKAddBootImage.vbs, that adds boot images to Windows Deployment Services. You can use this script to quickly add MDT 2008 boot images. These scripts are samples only and should be customized to meet the specific needs of your deployment environment.**

MDT 2010 can also use Windows 7 installation images from Windows Deployment Services. By doing so, you can use installation sources that already exist in a Windows Deployment Services server without duplicating the files in an MDT 2010 deployment share. This requires that you copy Wdsclientapi.dll, Wdscsl.dll, and Wdsimage.dll from the \Sources folder of the Windows 7 media to the C:\Program Files\Microsoft Deployment Toolkit\Bin folder. It also requires that at least one Windows 7 source must exist within the deployment share and that you must create and update a deployment share. MDT 2010 uses the setup program files from the deployment share to install the Windows 7 image from the Windows Deployment Services server.

To add images from Windows Deployment Services to an MDT 2010 deployment share, perform the following steps:

1. Add a full set of Windows 7 source files to an MDT 2010 deployment share. See Chapter 6 for more information on this topic.
2. Copy the following files from the \Sources folder of the Windows 7 media to the C:\Program Files\Microsoft Deployment Toolkit\Bin folder:
   - Wdsclientapi.dll
   - Wdscsl.dll
   - Wdsimage.dll
3. In the MDT 2010 Deployment Workbench console tree, right-click Operating Systems under your deployment share and click Import Operating System to start the New Operating System Wizard.
4. On the OS Type page, select Windows Deployment Services Images and then click Next to add an image from a Windows Deployment Services server to the distribution share.
5. On the WDS Server page, type the name of the Windows Deployment Services server from which to add the operating system images and then click Finish.
6. Deployment Workbench adds all the installation images it finds in Windows Deployment Services to the Operating Systems folder.

Summary

Windows Deployment Services provides a solution for the network-based installation of Windows 7. It's built on standard Windows 7 setup technologies, including Windows PE, .wim image files, and image-based setup. Using Windows Deployment Services can help reduce the cost and complexity of Windows 7 deployments.

In Windows Server 2008 R2, Windows Deployment Services replaces RIS. Windows Deployment Services is also available as an update for Windows Server 2003, and it provides a clear migration path from RIS for customers using legacy RIS images.

Although Windows Deployment Services provides the technology necessary to capture and remotely deploy custom operating system images, it does not provide end-to-end technology or guidance for high-volume deployment projects. It also does not provide tools or guidance for customizing the custom images you deploy with settings, applications, device drivers, and so on. MDT 2010 builds on Windows Deployment Services by adding both end-to-end guidance and tools for building and customizing images and then deploying them by using Windows Deployment Services.

Additional Resources

These resources contain additional information and tools related to this chapter.

Related Information

- The "Windows Deployment Services" section of the Windows Server TechCenter on Microsoft TechNet at *http://technet.microsoft.com/en-us/library/cc772106.aspx* for more information concerning Windows Deployment Services.
- *Infrastructure Planning and Design Guide for Windows Deployment Services* at *http://technet.microsoft.com/en-us/library/cc265612.aspx.*
- *Windows Deployment Services Getting Started Guide* at *http://go.microsoft.com/fwlink/?LinkId=84628* for step-by-step instructions on using Windows Deployment Services.
- The "Setup Deployment" forum on Microsoft TechNet at *http://go.microsoft.com/fwlink/?LinkId=87628.*
- Chapter 6, "Developing Disk Images," includes more information about building custom Windows Vista images that you can deploy using Windows Deployment Services.
- Chapter 9, "Preparing Windows PE," includes more information about creating custom Windows PE images that you can use with Windows Deployment Services.
- Chapter 12, "Deploying with Microsoft Deployment Toolkit," includes more information about using Windows Deployment Services to deploy Windows Vista with MDT 2008 and Windows Deployment Services.

On the Companion Media

- VRKAddBootImage.vbs
- VRKAddInstallImage.vbs
- VRKListImages.vbs

CHAPTER 11

Using Volume Activation

Volume Activation is a configurable solution that helps IT professionals automate and manage the product activation process on computers running the Windows Vista, Windows 7, Windows Server 2008, and Windows Server 2008 R2 operating systems licensed under a Microsoft Volume Licensing program and other programs that provide Volume License editions of Microsoft Windows. This chapter describes Volume Activation for Windows 7.

Introduction

Product activation is the process of validating software with the manufacturer. Activation confirms the genuine status of a product and that the product key is not compromised. It is analogous to the activation of credit cards or new mobile phones. Activation establishes a relationship between the software's product key and a particular installation of that software on a device.

All methods of activation used by Microsoft are designed to help protect user privacy. Data that is sent during activation is not traceable to the computer or user. The data that is gathered is used to confirm a legally licensed copy of the software. It is then aggregated for statistical analysis. Microsoft does not use this information to identify or contact the user or organization. For example, during online activations, information such as the software version, language, and product key are sent, as well as the IP address and information about the hardware of the device. The IP address is used only to verify the location of the request, as some editions of Windows—such as Windows 7 Starter—can be activated only within certain target market geographies.

ON THE COMPANION MEDIA The complete set of Volume Activation guides is included on the companion media. The *Volume Activation Planning Guide* provides guidance for deployment planning. The *Volume Activation Deployment Guide* includes detailed guidance for deploying Volume Activation in enterprise environments. Also, the *Volume Activation Operations Guide* describes how to support Volume Activation in enterprise environments. The *Volume Activation Technical Reference Guide* is a useful reference for Volume Activation.

Activation Options

Licenses for Windows 7 can be obtained through one of three basic channels: retail, Original Equipment Manufacturer (OEM), or Volume Licensing. Each channel has its own unique methods of activation. Because organizations can obtain their operating systems through any of the three available channels, they can choose a combination of activation methods.

Retail

Windows 7 products acquired through a retail store are licensed individually and are activated in the same way as retail versions of Windows Vista. Each purchased copy comes with one unique product key, found on the product packaging, which is typed in during the installation of the product. The computer uses this product key to complete the activation after the installation of the operating system is complete. This activation can be accomplished either online or by telephone.

Original Equipment Manufacturer

Most OEMs sell systems that include a standard build of Windows 7. Hardware vendors perform OEM activation by associating Windows with the firmware (basic input/output system, or BIOS) of the physical computer. This process occurs before the computers are sent to the customer so that no additional actions are required of the user. This method of activation is known as OEM Activation.

OEM Activation is valid as long as the customer uses the OEM-provided image on a system. To create a customized image, customers can use the image provided by the OEM as the basis for creating the custom image. Otherwise, a different activation method must be used.

> **NOTE** Some editions of Windows 7, such as Windows 7 Enterprise, are available only through the Volume Licensing channel. OEM Activation is applicable to computers purchased through OEM channels with Windows installed.

Volume Licensing

Volume Licensing offers customized programs tailored to the size and purchasing preference of the organization. These programs provide simple, flexible, and affordable solutions that enable organizations to manage their licenses. To become a Volume Licensing customer, an organization needs to set up a Volume License agreement with Microsoft.

There are only two legal ways to acquire a full Windows desktop license for a new computer system. The first and most economical way is preinstalled through the computer hardware manufacturer. The other option is with a full, packaged retail product. Volume Licensing programs such as Open License, Select License, and Enterprise agreements cover Windows upgrades only and do not provide a full Windows desktop license. After the computers have a full Windows desktop license, a Windows Volume Licensing agreement can be acquired and used to provide version upgrade rights. For more information on Volume Licensing, go to *http://go.microsoft.com/fwlink/?LinkId=73076*.

Volume Activation is designed to allow Volume License customers to automate the activation process in a way that is transparent to users. Volume Activation applies to computers that are covered under a Volume Licensing program. It is used strictly as a tool for activation and is in no way tied to license invoicing or billing. Volume Activation provides two different models for completing volume activations: Key Management Service (KMS) and Multiple Activation Key (MAK). KMS allows organizations to activate systems within their own network, whereas MAK activates systems on a one-time basis using Microsoft's hosted activation services.

Customers can use either or both key types to activate systems in their environment. The model chosen depends on the size, network infrastructure, connectivity, and security requirements of the organization. IT professionals can choose to use just one or a combination of these activation models. For more information about choosing an activation model, see the section titled "Volume Activation Scenarios," later in this chapter.

DIRECT FROM THE SOURCE

Choosing the Activation Method

Kim Griffiths, Product Manager
Genuine Windows

Aaron Smith, Program Manager
Windows Genuine Platform Team

Which method to use? That is one of the most common questions that we hear from our customers about Volume Activation. It is a decision that you need to make before any systems are deployed. When we were designing Volume Activation, it was clear that there were a wide variety of customer deployment models and use cases that needed to be considered. For example, a well-connected, global corporate intranet would have very different requirements from a disconnected development and test lab. Accordingly, two methods were developed to give the level of flexibility that our customers needed: KMS and MAK. Customers can use one or both methods, depending on how they deploy and use their machines.

KMS is the recommended solution for most customer use cases, for a variety of reasons. First, it is automated and simple for the administrator to configure. The KMS clients detect and use the service for activation on their own, without any configuration changes to the image or end-user involvement. Second, activation happens within the customer environment. After the service is activated, all communication stays inside the organization. None of the KMS clients will ever connect to Microsoft to activate.

MAK is best suited to a smaller set of systems, individual stand-alone machines, or those that are disconnected from the corporate network. It is very similar to retail activation and can be configured as part of system provisioning, making it transparent to the end user as well.

Key Management Service

KMS activates computers on a local network, eliminating the need for individual computers to connect to Microsoft. To do this, KMS uses a client–server topology. KMS clients can locate KMS hosts by using Domain Name System (DNS) or a static configuration. KMS clients contact the KMS host by using Remote Procedure Call (RPC). KMS can be hosted on computers running the Windows 7, Windows Vista, Windows Server 2008 R2, Windows Server 2008, or Windows Server 2003 operating systems.

Minimum Computer Requirements

If you are planning to use KMS activation, the network must meet or exceed the activation threshold (the minimum number of qualifying computers that KMS requires). IT professionals must also understand how the KMS host tracks the number of computers on the network.

KMS Activation Thresholds

KMS can activate both physical computers and virtual machines (VMs). To qualify for KMS activation, a network must have a minimum number of qualifying computers, called the *activation threshold.* KMS hosts activate clients only after meeting this threshold. To ensure that the activation threshold is met, a KMS host counts the number of computers requesting activation on the network.

The Windows Server operating systems (starting with Windows Server 2008) and Windows client operating systems (starting with Windows Vista) are activated after meeting different thresholds. The Windows Server activation threshold is 5 computers, and the Windows client activation threshold is 25 computers. The threshold includes Windows client and server operating systems running on physical computers or VMs.

A KMS host responds to each valid activation request from a KMS client with the count of how many computers have contacted the KMS host for activation. Clients that receive a count below their activation threshold are not activated. For example, if the first two computers that contact the KMS host are running Windows 7, the first receives an activation count of 1, and the second receives an activation count of 2. If the next computer is a Windows 7 VM, it receives an activation count of 3, and so on. None of these computers is activated because computers running Windows 7 must receive an activation count greater than or equal to 25 to be activated. KMS clients in the grace state that are not activated because the activation count is too low will connect to the KMS host every two hours to get the current activation count and will be activated when the threshold is met.

If the next computer that contacts the KMS host is running Windows Server 2008 R2, it receives an activation count of 4, because activation counts are a combination of computers running Windows Server 2008 R2 and Windows 7. If a computer running Windows Server 2008 or Windows Server 2008 R2 receives an activation count that is greater than or equal to 5, it is activated. If a computer running Windows 7 receives an activation count greater than or equal to 25, it is activated.

Activation Count Cache

To track the activation threshold, the KMS host keeps a record of the KMS clients that request activation. The KMS host gives each KMS client a client machine identification (CMID) designation, and the KMS host saves each CMID in a table. Each activation request remains in the table for 30 days. When a client renews its activation, the cached CMID is removed from the table, a new record is created, and the 30-day period begins again. If a KMS client does not renew its activation within 30 days, the KMS host removes the corresponding CMID from the table and reduces the activation count by 1.

The KMS host caches twice the number of CMIDs that KMS clients require to help ensure that the CMID count does not drop below the activation threshold. For example, on a network with clients running Windows 7, the KMS activation threshold is 25. The KMS host caches the CMIDs of the most recent 50 activations. The KMS activation threshold for Windows Server 2008 R2 is 5. A KMS host that is contacted only by clients running Windows Server 2008 R2 KMS would cache the 10 most recent CMIDs. If a client running Windows 7 later contacts that KMS host, KMS increases the cache size to 50 to accommodate the higher threshold. KMS never reduces the cache size.

How KMS Works

KMS activation requires Transmission Control Protocol/Internet Protocol (TCP/IP) connectivity. By default, KMS hosts and clients use DNS to publish and find the KMS. The default settings can be used, which require little to no administrative action, or KMS hosts and clients can be configured manually based on network configuration and security requirements.

KMS Activation Renewal

KMS activations are valid for 180 days. This is called the *activation validity interval.* To remain activated, KMS clients must renew their activation by connecting to the KMS host at least once every 180 days. By default, KMS client computers attempt to renew their activation every seven days. If KMS activation fails, the client will reattempt every two hours. After a client's activation is renewed, the activation validity interval begins again.

Publication of the KMS

The KMS uses service (SRV) resource records (RRs) in DNS to store and communicate the locations of KMS hosts. KMS hosts use Dynamic DNS (DDNS), if available, to publish the KMS SRV RRs. If DDNS is not available, or the KMS host does not have rights to publish the RRs, the DNS records must be published manually or IT professionals must configure client computers to connect to specific KMS hosts. The *Volume Activation Deployment Guide* at *http://go.microsoft.com/fwlink/?LinkId=150083* describes the steps necessary to publish the KMS in DNS.

> ***NOTE*** **DNS changes may take time to propagate to all DNS hosts, depending on the complexity and topology of the network.**

Client Discovery of the KMS

By default, KMS clients query DNS for KMS information. The first time a KMS client queries DNS for KMS information, it randomly chooses a KMS host from the list of SRV RRs that DNS returns.

The address of a DNS server containing the SRV RRs can be listed as a suffixed entry on KMS clients, which allows advertisement of SRV RRs for KMS in one DNS server and allows KMS clients with other primary DNS servers to find KMS.

Also, priority and weight parameters can be added to the DnsDomainPublishList registry value for KMS. Doing so allows IT professionals to establish KMS host priority groupings and weighting within each group, which specify the KMS host to try first, to balance traffic among multiple KMS hosts. Only Windows 7 and Windows Server 2008 R2 use the priority and weight parameters.

If the KMS host that a client selects does not respond, the KMS client removes that KMS host from its list of SRV RRs and randomly selects another KMS host from the list. After a KMS host responds, the KMS client caches the name of the KMS host and uses it for subsequent activation and renewal attempts. If the cached KMS host does not respond on a subsequent renewal, the KMS client discovers a new KMS host by querying DNS for KMS SRV RRs.

By default, client computers connect to the KMS host for activation by using anonymous RPCs through TCP port 1688. (IT professionals can change the default port.) After establishing a TCP session with the KMS host, the client sends a single request packet. The KMS host responds with the activation count. If the count meets or exceeds the activation threshold for that operating system, the client is activated and the session is closed. The KMS client uses this same process for renewal requests. The communication each way is 250 bytes.

Planning a KMS Deployment

The KMS does not require a dedicated server. The KMS can be co-hosted with other services, such as Active Directory Domain Services (AD DS) domain controllers and read-only domain controllers (RODCs). KMS hosts can also run on physical computers or VMs running any supported Windows operating system, including Windows Server 2003. Although a KMS host running on Windows Server 2008 R2 can activate any Windows operating system that supports Volume Activation, a KMS host running on Windows 7 can activate only Windows client operating systems. A single KMS host can support unlimited numbers of KMS clients; however, Microsoft recommends deploying a minimum of two KMS hosts for failover. Most organizations can use as few as two KMS hosts for their entire infrastructure.

NOTE KMS is not included automatically in Windows Server 2003. To host KMS on machines running Windows Server 2003, download and install KMS for Windows Server 2003 SP1 and later from *http://go.microsoft.com/fwlink/?LinkID=82964*. KMS is available in several languages. The 64-bit version is available at *http://go.microsoft.com/fwlink/?Linkld=83041*.

Planning DNS Server Configuration

The default KMS auto-publishing feature requires SRV RR and DDNS support. Microsoft DNS or any other DNS server that supports SRV RRs (per Internet Engineering Task Force [IETF] RFC 2782) and dynamic updates (per RFC 2136) can support KMS client default behavior and KMS SRV RR publishing. Berkeley Internet Domain Name (BIND) versions 8.*x* and 9.*x* support both SRV records and DDNS, for example.

The KMS host must be configured so that it has the credentials needed to create and update SRV, A (IP version 4, or IPv4), and AAAA (IP version 6, or IPv6) RRs on the DDNS servers, or the records need to be created manually. The recommended solution for giving the KMS host the needed credentials is to create a security group in AD DS and add all KMS hosts to that group. In the Microsoft DNS server, ensure that this security group is given full control over the _VLMCS._TCP record on each DNS domain that will contain the KMS SRV RRs.

Activating the First KMS Host

KMS hosts on the network need to install a KMS key and then be activated with Microsoft. Installation of a KMS key enables the KMS on the KMS host. After installing the KMS key, complete the activation of the KMS host by telephone or online. Beyond this initial activation, a KMS host does not communicate any information to Microsoft.

KMS keys are installed only on KMS hosts, never on individual KMS clients. Windows 7 and Windows Server 2008 R2 have safeguards to help prevent inadvertently installing KMS keys on KMS client computers. Any time users try to install a KMS key, they see a warning, but they can continue to install the KMS key.

Activating Subsequent KMS Hosts

Each KMS key can be installed on up to six KMS hosts, which can be physical computers or VMs. After activating a KMS host, the same host can be reactivated up to nine more times with the same key.

If the organization needs more than six KMS hosts, IT professionals can request additional activations for the organization's KMS key. An example of this would be if 10 separate physical locations were under one Volume Licensing agreement, and IT wanted each location to have a local KMS host. To request this exception, call the Activation Call Center. For more information, see the Volume Licensing Web site at *http://go.microsoft.com/fwlink/?LinkID=73076*.

Upgrading Existing KMS Hosts

KMS hosts operating on Windows Server 2003, Windows Vista, or Windows Server 2008 can be configured to support KMS clients running Windows 7 and Windows Server 2008 R2. For Windows Vista and Windows Server 2008, it will be necessary to update the KMS host with a package containing the files supporting the expanded KMS client support. This package is available through the Microsoft Download Center at *http://www.microsoft.com/downloads* or through Windows Update and Windows Server Update Services (WSUS). Once the KMS host is updated, a KMS key that is designed to support Windows 7 and Windows Server 2008 R2 can be applied as described earlier in this chapter. Note that a KMS key supporting these new versions of Windows provides backward support for all previous versions of Volume License editions of Windows acting as KMS clients.

In the case of updating a Windows Server 2003 KMS host, all necessary files are contained within the KMS 1.2 downloadable package, which is available through the Microsoft Download Center at *http://www.microsoft.com/downloads*. Once the KMS host is updated, a KMS key designed to support Windows 7 and Windows Server 2008 R2 can be applied as described earlier in this chapter. A KMS key supporting these new versions of Windows provides backward support for all previous versions of Volume License editions of Windows acting as KMS clients.

Planning KMS Clients

By default, computers running Volume Licensing editions of Windows Vista, Windows 7, Windows Server 2008, and Windows Server 2008 R2 are KMS clients, and no additional configuration is needed. KMS clients can locate a KMS host automatically by querying DNS for SRV RRs that publish the KMS. If the network environment does not use SRV RRs, a KMS client can be configured manually to use a specific KMS host. The steps needed to configure KMS clients manually are described in the *Volume Activation Deployment Guide* at *http://go.microsoft.com/fwlink/?LinkId=150083.*

Activating as a Standard User

Windows 7 does not require administrator privileges for activation. However, this change does not allow standard user accounts to remove Windows 7 from the activated state. An administrator account is required for other activation- or license-related tasks, such as rearming.

Multiple Activation Key

A MAK is used for one-time activation with Microsoft's hosted activation services. Each MAK has a predetermined number of allowed activations; this number is based on Volume Licensing agreements and does not match the organization's exact license count. Each activation using a MAK with Microsoft's hosted activation service counts toward the activation limit.

There are two ways to activate computers using a MAK:

- **MAK Independent activation** MAK Independent activation requires that each computer independently connect and be activated with Microsoft, either over the Internet or by telephone. MAK Independent activation is best suited for computers within an organization that do not maintain a connection to the corporate network.
- **MAK Proxy activation** MAK Proxy activation enables a centralized activation request on behalf of multiple computers with one connection to Microsoft. MAK Proxy activation is configured using the Volume Activation Management Tool (VAMT).

MAK Proxy activation is appropriate for environments in which security concerns may restrict direct access to the Internet or the corporate network. It is also suited for development and test labs that lack this connectivity.

MAK is recommended for computers that rarely or never connect to the corporate network and for environments in which the number of computers needing activation does not meet the KMS activation threshold. MAK can be used for individual computers or with an image that can be bulk-duplicated or installed using Microsoft deployment solutions. MAK can also be used on a computer that was configured originally to use KMS activation—useful for moving a computer off the core network to a disconnected environment.

Volume Activation Management Tool

Included in the Windows Automated Installation Kit (Windows AIK), VAMT is a stand-alone application that collects activation requests from several computers and then sends them to Microsoft in bulk. VAMT allows IT professionals to specify a group of computers to activate using AD DS, workgroup names, IP addresses, or computer names. After receiving the activation confirmation IDs, VAMT distributes them to the computers that requested activation. Because VAMT also stores these confirmation IDs locally, it can reactivate a previously activated computer after it is reimaged without recontacting Microsoft. The communication between VAMT and client computers is via Windows Management Instrumentation (WMI), so Windows Firewall on client computers must be configured to allow WMI traffic. Additionally, VAMT can be used to transition computers easily between MAK and KMS activation methods. Download Windows AIK, which includes VAMT, at *http://go.microsoft.com/fwlink/?LinkId=136976*.

MAK Architecture

MAK Independent activation installs a MAK product key on a client computer and instructs that computer to activate itself against Microsoft servers over the Internet. In MAK Proxy activation, VAMT installs a MAK product key on a client computer, obtains the Installation Identifier (IID) from the target computer, sends the IID to Microsoft on behalf of the client, and obtains a Confirmation Identifier (CID). The tool then activates the client by installing the CID.

Volume Activation Scenarios

Each Volume Activation method is best suited to a particular network configuration. To select the best activation method or methods for the organization, assess the network environment to identify how different groups of computers connect to the network. Connectivity to the corporate network, Internet access, and the number of computers that regularly connect to the corporate network are some of the important characteristics to identify. Most medium-sized to large organizations use a combination of activation methods because of the varied ways their client computers connect to their networks.

KMS is the recommended activation method for computers that are well connected to the organization's core network or that have periodic connectivity, such as computers that are offsite. MAK activation is the recommended activation method for computers that are offsite with limited connectivity or that cannot connect to the core network because of security restrictions. These include computers in lab and development environments that are isolated from the core network.

Table 11-1 lists common network configurations and the best practice recommendations for each type. Each solution factors in the number of computers and network connectivity of the activation clients.

TABLE 11-1 Volume Activation Recommendations by Scenario

NETWORK INFRASTRUCTURE	RECOMMENDATIONS	CONSIDERATIONS
Core network Well-connected LAN Most common scenario	If total computers > KMS activation threshold: ■ Small (< 100 machines): KMS host = 1 ■ Medium (> 100 machines): KMS host ≥ 1 ■ Enterprise: KMS host > 1 If total computers ≤ KMS activation threshold: ■ MAK (by telephone or Internet) ■ MAK Proxy	Minimize the number of KMS hosts Each KMS host must consistently maintain a count of total machines > KMS activation threshold KMS hosts are autonomous KMS host is activated by telephone or Internet
Isolated network Branch office, high-security network segments, perimeter networks Well-connected zoned LAN	If ports on firewalls can be opened between KMS clients and hosts: ■ Use KMS hosts in core network If policy prevents firewall modification: ■ Use local KMS hosts in an isolated network ■ MAK (by telephone or Internet) ■ MAK Proxy	Firewall configuration ■ RPC over TCP (TCP port 1688) ■ Initiated by the client Change management on firewall rule sets

NETWORK INFRASTRUCTURE	RECOMMENDATIONS	CONSIDERATIONS
Test or development lab Isolated network	If total computers > KMS activation threshold: ■ KMS host = 1 (per isolated network) If total computers ≤ KMS activation threshold: ■ No activation (reset grace period) ■ MAK (by telephone) ■ MAK Proxy performed manually	Variable configuration Limited number of computers KMS host and MAK activation through telephone; MAK Proxy performed manually
Individual disconnected computer No connectivity to the Internet or core network Roaming computers that periodically connect to the core network or connect through a virtual private network (VPN) Roaming computers with Internet access but no connection to the core network	For clients that connect periodically to the core network: ■ Use the KMS hosts in the core network For clients that never connect to the core network or have no Internet access: ■ MAK (by telephone) For networks that cannot connect to the core network: ■ If total computers > KMS activation threshold: • Small: KMS host = 1 • Medium: KMS host ≥ 1 • Enterprise: KMS host > 1 ■ If total computers ≤ KMS activation threshold, MAK Independent or MAK Proxy performed manually For clients that never connect to the core network but have Internet access: ■ MAK (by Internet)	Restricted environments or networks that cannot connect to other networks KMS host can be activated and then moved to disconnected network KMS host and MAK activation by telephone; MAK Proxy performed manually

The following sections describe examples of Volume Activation solutions in heterogeneous corporate environments that require more than one activation method. Each scenario has a recommended activation solution, but some environments may have infrastructure or policy requirements that are best suited to a different solution.

Core Network

A centralized KMS solution is recommended for computers on the core network. This solution is for networks that have well-connected computers on multiple network segments that also have a connection to the Internet. Figure 11-1 shows a core network with a KMS host. The KMS host publishes the KMS using DDNS. KMS clients query DNS for KMS SRV RRs and activate themselves after contacting the KMS host. The KMS host is activated directly through the Internet.

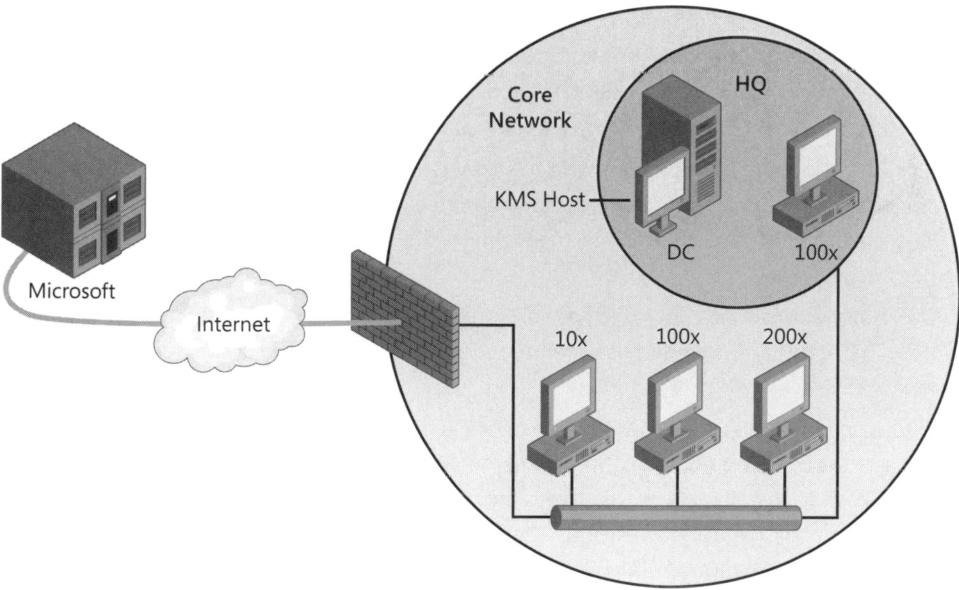

FIGURE 11-1 Core network scenario

> ***NOTE*** **A KMS host can be installed on a VM, but select a VM that is unlikely to be moved to a different host computer. If the virtual KMS host is moved to a different host computer, the operating system detects the change in the underlying hardware and the KMS host must reactivate with Microsoft. KMS hosts can activate with Microsoft up to nine times.**

Isolated Networks

Many organizations have networks that are separated into multiple security zones. Some networks have a high-security zone that is isolated because it has sensitive information, whereas other networks are separated from the core network because they are in a different physical location (branch office locations).

High-Security Zone

High-security zones are network segments separated by a firewall that limits communication to and from other network segments. If the computers in a high-security zone are allowed access to the core network by allowing TCP port 1688 outbound from the high-security zone and an RPC reply inbound, activate computers in the high-security zone by using KMS hosts located in the core network. This way, the number of client computers in the high-security network does not have to meet any KMS activation threshold.

If these firewall exceptions are not authorized and the number of total computers in the high-security zone is sufficient to meet KMS activation thresholds, add a local KMS host to the high-security zone. Then, activate the KMS host in the high-security zone by telephone.

Figure 11-2 shows an environment with a corporate security policy that does not allow traffic between computers in the high-security zone and the core network. Because the high-security zone has enough computers to meet the KMS activation threshold, the high-security zone has its own local KMS host. The KMS host itself is activated by telephone.

If KMS is not appropriate because there are only a few computers in the high-security zone, MAK Independent activation is recommended. Each computer can be activated independently with Microsoft by telephone.

MAK Proxy activation using VAMT is also possible in this scenario. VAMT can discover client computers by using AD DS, computer name, IP address, or membership in a workgroup. VAMT uses WMI to install MAK product keys and CIDs and to retrieve status on MAK clients. Because this traffic is not allowed through the firewall, there must be a local VAMT host in the high-security zone and another VAMT host in another zone that has Internet access.

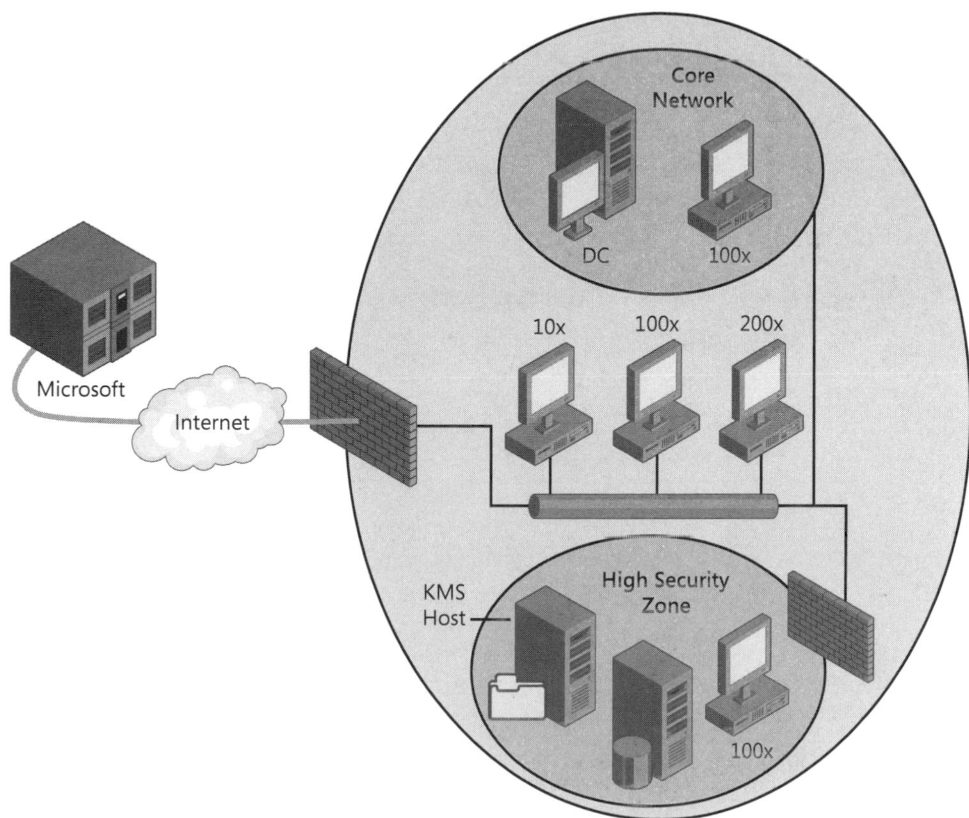

FIGURE 11-2 High-security network scenario

Branch Office Locations

Figure 11-3 shows an enterprise network that supports client computers in three branch offices. Site A uses a local KMS host because it has more than 25 client computers, and it does not have secure TCP/IP connectivity to the core network. Site B uses MAK activation because KMS does not support sites with fewer than 25 KMS client computers, and the site is not connected by a secure link to the core network. Site C uses KMS because it is connected to the core network by a secure connection over a private wide area network (WAN), and activation thresholds are met using core network KMS clients.

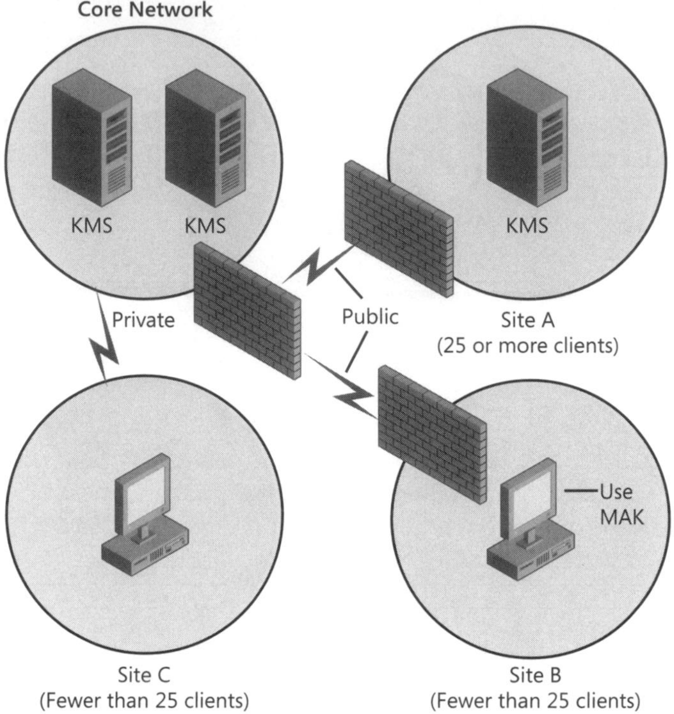

FIGURE 11-3 Branch office scenario

Individual Disconnected Computers

Some users in an organization may be in remote locations or may travel to many locations. This scenario is common for roaming clients, such as the computers of salespeople or other users who are offsite but not at branch locations. This scenario can also apply to remote branch office locations that have no connection or an intermittent connection to the core network.

Disconnected computers can use KMS or MAK, depending on how often the computers connect to the core network. Use KMS activation for computers that connect to the core network—either directly or through a VPN—at least once every 180 days and when the core network is using KMS activation. Use MAK Independent activation—by telephone or the Internet—for computers that rarely or never connect to the core network. Figure 11-4 shows disconnected clients using MAK Independent activation through the Internet and also through the telephone.

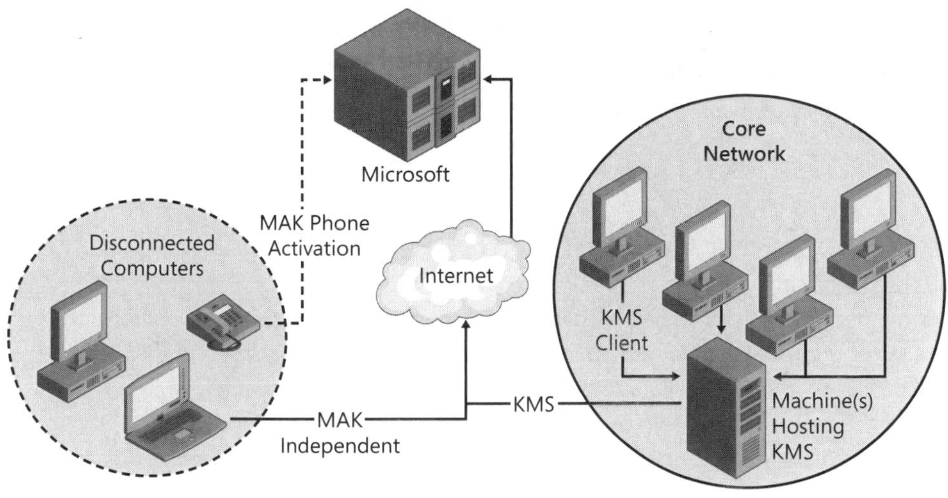

FIGURE 11-4 Disconnected computer scenario

Test/Development Labs

Lab environments usually have large numbers of VMs, and computers in labs are reconfigured frequently. First, determine whether the computers in test and development labs need activation. The initial 30-day grace period of a computer running Windows 7 or Windows Server 2008 R2 can be reset three times without activating it. Therefore, if you are rebuilding lab computers within 120 days, these computers need not be activated.

If lab computers do require activation, use KMS or MAK activation. Use KMS activation if the computers have connectivity to a core network that is using KMS. If the number of computers in the lab meets the KMS activation threshold, deploy a local KMS host.

In labs that have a high turnover of computers as well as a small number of KMS clients, it is important to monitor the KMS activation count to maintain a sufficient number of cached CMIDs on the KMS host. A KMS host caches activation requests from computers for 30 days. (See the section titled "Minimum Computer Requirements" earlier in this chapter for more information about how CMIDs affect activations.) If the lab environment needs activation but does not qualify for KMS activation, use MAK activation. MAK clients are activated by telephone or over the Internet, whichever is available to the lab.

MAK Proxy activation with VAMT can also be used in this scenario. Install VAMT in the isolated lab network and also in a network that has access to the Internet. In the isolated lab, VAMT performs discovery, obtains status, installs a MAK product key, and obtains the IID of each computer in the lab. This information can then be exported from VAMT, saved to removable media, and then the file can be imported to a computer running VAMT that has access to the Internet. VAMT sends the IIDs to Microsoft and obtains the corresponding CIDs needed to complete activation. After exporting this data to removable media, take it to the isolated lab to import the CIDs so that VAMT can complete the activations.

NOTE In High Security mode, VAMT removes all personally identifiable information (PII) from the file that it exports. This file is a readable Extensible Markup Language (XML) file that can be reviewed in any XML or text editor.

What If Systems Are Not Activated?

Activation is designed to provide a transparent activation experience for users. If activation does not occur immediately after the operating system is installed, Windows 7 and Windows Server 2008 R2 still provide the full functionality of the operating system for a limited amount of time (a grace period). The length of the grace period is 30 days for Windows 7 and Windows Server 2008 R2. After the grace period expires, both operating systems remind the user through notifications to activate the computer.

Grace Period

During the initial grace period, there are periodic notifications that the computer requires activation. Computers in this grace period have a set period of time to activate the operating system. Once per day, during the logon process, a notification bubble reminds the user to activate the operating system. This behavior continues until there are three days left in the grace period. For the first two of the final three days of the grace period, the notification bubble appears every four hours. During the final day of the grace period, the notification bubble appears every hour on the hour.

Grace Period Expiration

After the initial grace period expires or activation fails, Windows 7 continues to notify users that the operating system requires activation. Until the operating system is activated, reminders that the computer must be activated appear in several places throughout the product:

- Notification dialog boxes appear during logon after users enter their credentials.
- Notifications appear at the bottom of the screen above the notification area.
- A persistent desktop notification will be shown on a black desktop background.
- A reminder might appear when users open certain Windows applications.

Product Keys

Volume Activation does not change how Volume Licensing customers obtain their product keys. They can obtain MAK and KMS keys at the Volume Licensing Service Center (VLSC) Web page at *http://go.microsoft.com/fwlink/?LinkId=107544* or by calling an Activation Call Center. Service Provider License Agreement (SPLA) partners can obtain keys only by calling an Activation Call Center. Customers in the United States can call 888-352-7140. International customers should contact their local Support Center. For the telephone numbers of Activation Call Centers worldwide, go to *http://go.microsoft.com/fwlink/?LinkId=107418*. When calling a Support Center, customers must have the Volume License agreement.

Volume Licensing customers can log on to the VLSC Web page at any time to view their KMS key information. The VLSC Web site also contains information on how to request and use MAKs. For more information about MAK and KMS keys, including information about increasing the number of allowed activations, go to the Existing Customers page at *http://go.microsoft.com/fwlink/?LinkId=74008*.

Summary

Volume Activation helps IT professionals automate and manage the product activation process on computers running Windows 7 editions that are licensed under a Volume Licensing program or other programs that provide Volume License editions of Windows. Two options are available for Volume Activation: KMS and MAK. KMS activation provides a solution that is easy to deploy and manage, requiring little interaction. Environments that don't meet the minimum requirements for KMS can use MAK activation to activate systems with the Microsoft-hosted activation service.

Additional Resources

These resources contain additional information and tools related to this chapter.

Related Information

- Genuine Microsoft Software at *http://go.microsoft.com/fwlink/?LinkId=151993*.
- Genuine Microsoft Software validation page at *http://go.microsoft.com/fwlink/?LinkId=64187*.
- "Key Management Service 1.1 (x64) for Windows Server 2003 SP1 and Later" at *http://go.microsoft.com/fwlink/?LinkId=83041*.
- "Microsoft Activation Centers Worldwide Telephone Numbers" at *http://go.microsoft.com/fwlink/?LinkId=107418*.
- Microsoft Volume Licensing at *http://go.microsoft.com/fwlink/?LinkId=73076*.
- Microsoft Volume Licensing Service Center at *http://go.microsoft.com/fwlink/?LinkId=107544*.
- "Product Activation and Key Information" at *http://go.microsoft.com/fwlink/?LinkId=74008*.
- "System Center Pack Catalog" at *http://go.microsoft.com/fwlink/?LinkID=110332*.
- "Volume Activation 2.0 Technical Guidance" at *http://go.microsoft.com/fwlink/?LinkID=75674*.
- *Volume Activation Deployment Guide* at *http://go.microsoft.com/fwlink/?LinkId=150083*.

- Volume Activation on TechNet at *http://technet.microsoft.com/en-us/windows/dd197314.aspx.*
- *Volume Activation Operations Guide* at *http://go.microsoft.com/fwlink/?LinkId=150084.*
- *Volume Activation Planning Guide* at *http://go.microsoft.com/fwlink/?LinkID=149823.*
- *Volume Activation Technical Reference Guide* at *http://go.microsoft.com/fwlink/?LinkId=152550.*
- "Windows Vista Privacy Notice Highlights" at *http://go.microsoft.com/fwlink/?LinkID=52526.*
- "Windows Automated Installation Kit (Windows AIK) for Windows 7 RC" at *http://go.microsoft.com/fwlink/?LinkId=136976.*

On the Companion Media

- *Volume Activation Planning Guide*
- *Volume Activation Deployment Guide*
- *Volume Activation Operations Guide*
- *Volume Activation Technical Reference Guide*

CHAPTER 12

Deploying with Microsoft Deployment Toolkit

The Windows 7 operating system and the Windows Automated Installation Kit (Windows AIK) include the low-level tools necessary to deploy the operating system. However, they don't provide a framework for managing and automating high-volume Windows 7 deployments or business logic for managing complex projects. Microsoft Deployment Toolkit 2010 (MDT 2010) provides this framework and business logic, making it Microsoft's primary tool for deploying Windows 7.

This chapter describes how to use MDT 2010 to deploy Windows 7. It assumes that you've already created a deployment share in a lab and populated it with applications, device drivers, and packages. It also assumes that you've already designed and built custom Windows 7 disk images, as described in Chapter 6, "Developing Disk Images." This chapter helps you configure and customize MDT 2010 for Lite Touch Installation (LTI). For more information about Zero Touch Installation (ZTI) by using MDT 2010 with Microsoft System Center Configuration Manager 2007, see the MDT 2010 documentation.

Introducing MDT 2010

The following sections introduce key concepts for using MDT 2010 to deploy Windows 7. Specifically, the section titled "Deployment Scenarios" describes the scenarios that MDT 2010 supports. For LTI, MDT 2010 relies entirely on MDT 2010, the Windows AIK, and potentially Windows Deployment Services.

Deployment Scenarios

The following list describes the scenarios supported by MDT 2010:

- **New Computer** A new installation of Windows is deployed to a new computer. This scenario assumes that there is no user data or profile to preserve.
- **Upgrade Computer** The current Windows operating system on the target computer is upgraded to the target operating system. The existing user state data and applications are retained (as supported by the target operating system).
- **Refresh Computer** A computer currently running a supported Windows operating system is refreshed. This scenario includes computers that must be reimaged for image standardization or to address a problem. This scenario assumes that you're preserving the existing user state data on the computer. Applications are not preserved in this scenario.
- **Replace Computer** A computer currently running a supported Windows operating system is replaced with another computer. The existing user state migration data is saved from the original computer. Then, a new installation of Windows is deployed to a new computer. Finally, the user state data is restored to the new computer.

Based on your existing environment, you can select any combination of these scenarios in the deployment. For example, if you are upgrading only existing computers, only the Refresh Computer scenario or the Upgrade Computer scenario is necessary. If you're deploying new computers for some users and upgrading the remaining computers, use the Upgrade Computer, Replace Computer, and Refresh Computer scenarios as appropriate.

Resource Access

Before starting the deployment, create additional shared folders in which to store the user state migration data and the deployment logs. You can create these shared folders on any server that is accessible to destination computers. Refer to your deployment plan to guide you on server placement. The following list describes the shared folders you should create:

- **MigData** Stores the user state migration data during the deployment process
- **Logs** Stores the deployment logs during the deployment process

> ***NOTE*** **MigData and Logs are recommended shared folder names. You can use any name for these shared folders; however, the remainder of this chapter refers to these shared folders by these names.**

During deployment to destination computers, the MDT 2010 deployment scripts connect to the deployment shares and shared folders. Create accounts for use by these scripts when accessing these resources.

After creating the additional shared folders, configure the appropriate shared folder permissions. Ensure that unauthorized users are unable to access user state migration information and the deployment logs. Only the destination computer creating the user state migration information and the deployment logs should have access to these folders.

For each shared folder, disable inheritance and remove existing permissions. Then give the domain Computers group the Create Folder/Append Data permission for each folder only, and do the same for the domain Users group. Also, add the Creator Owner group to each shared folder, giving it the Full Control permission for subfolders and files only. Also, give each group that will have administrator access to migration data and log files the same permissions.

The permissions that you set in these steps allow a target computer to connect to the appropriate share and create a new folder in which to store user state information or logs. The folder permissions prevent other users or computers from accessing the data stored in the folder.

Using LTI with MDT 2010

Prior to deploying Windows 7 by using LTI with MDT 2010, be sure to perform the following steps, as described in Chapter 6:

- Create a deployment share, possibly in a lab environment, and add the appropriate resources to it. To add applications to the deployment share, see Chapter 8, "Deploying Applications."
- In the deployment share, create and customize task sequences that install Windows 7 as required.
- Build any custom Windows 7 images required for deployment.
- Test your deployment share and custom disk images in the lab.

Chapter 6 describes how to fully stock the deployment share with applications, device drivers, packages, and operating system source files. It also describes how to create task sequences and build custom Windows 7 disk images. In this chapter, you learn how to replicate your deployment share onto the production network and how to perform an LTI deployment by using it.

Replicating a Deployment Share

For LTI, you need to replicate the deployment share in the production environment or copy it to removable media. This process enables you to develop in a controlled environment and then easily move the deployment share into the production environment when you're ready to deploy Windows 7. MDT 2010 provides both capabilities.

When you replicate a deployment share, you can replicate everything or you can choose which folders in the deployment share to replicate. You choose folders to replicate by creating selection profiles. A selection profile simply selects folders across applications, operating systems, out-of-box drivers, packages, and task sequences. You create a selection profile in advance, and then you choose that selection profile when you set up replication.

During replication, Deployment Workbench updates the boot media. The updated boot media contains an updated Bootstrap.ini file that is configured to connect to the replicated deployment share. In other words, each deployment share has its own boot media associated with it, and that boot media is configured to connect a specific share.

To create a selection profile, perform the following steps:

1. In the Deployment Workbench console tree under the Advanced Configuration folder of your deployment share, right-click Selection Profiles and click New Selection Profile.
2. In the Selection Profile Name box, type a descriptive name for the selection profile and then click Next. For example, a selection profile that selects files for deployment in a particular department might use the department name for its title.
3. On the Folder page, select the folders that you want to include in the selection profile and then click Next.
4. On the Summary page, review the details and click Next.
5. Click Finish to close the New Selection Profile Wizard.

To link deployment shares for replication, perform the following steps:

1. In the production environment, create a share in which to replicate the deployment share. Make sure that your account has full control of the product sharing.
2. In the Deployment Workbench console tree under the Advanced Configuration folder of your deployment share, right-click Linked Deployment Shares and then click New Linked Deployment Share.
3. On the General Settings page, shown on the following page, do the following and then click Next:
    a. In the Linked Deployment Share UNC Path box, type the Universal Naming Convention (UNC) path of the deployment share in the production environment.
    b. From the Selection Profile list, click the profile that contains the folders that you want to replicate to the production environment.
    c. Click the Merge The Selected Contents Into The Target Deployment Share option to merge this deployment share with the production share; alternatively, click the Replace The Contents Of The Target Deployment Share Folder With Those Selected option to replace the contents of the production share with this share.

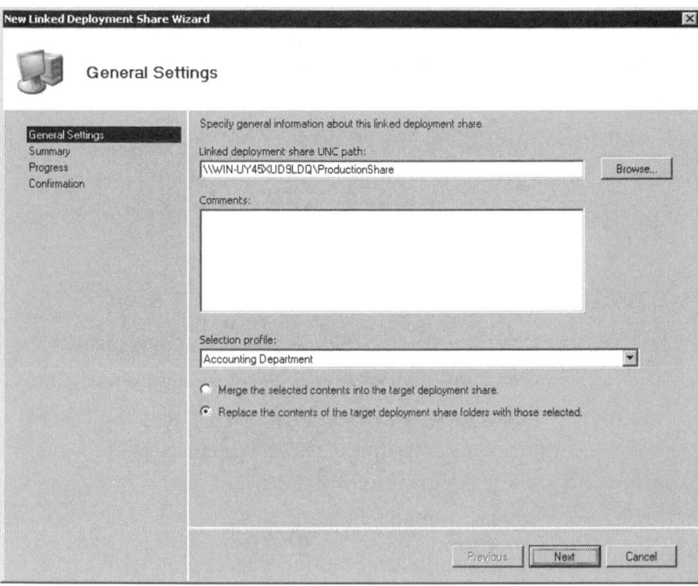

4. On the Summary page, review the details and then click Next.
5. On the Confirmation page, click Finish to close the New Linked Deployment Share Wizard.

To replicate the lab deployment share to production, perform the following steps:

1. In the Deployment Workbench console tree under the Advanced Configuration folder of your deployment share, click Linked Deployment Shares.
2. In the Details pane, right-click the replication partnership you created previously and then click Replicate Content.
3. On the Confirmation page, click Finish to close the Replicate To Linked Deployment Share dialog box.

To link removable media to the deployment share, perform the following steps:

1. In the Deployment Workbench console tree under the Advanced Configuration folder of your deployment share, right-click Media and click New Media.
2. On the General Settings page, do the following and then click Next:
   a. In the Media Path box, type the path of the removable media to which you want to copy the deployment share.
   b. From the Selection Profile list, click the profile that contains the folders you want to replicate to the production environment.
3. On the Summary page, review the details and click Next.
4. On the Confirmation page, click Finish to close the New Media Wizard.

To replicate the lab deployment share to removable media, perform the following steps:

1. In the Deployment Workbench console tree under the Advanced Configuration folder of your deployment share, click Media.
2. In the details pane, right-click the media link you created previously and then click Update Media Content.
3. On the Confirmation page, click Finish to close the Updated Media Content dialog box.

Preparing Windows Deployment Services

In the deployment process, Windows Deployment Services servers are responsible for starting Windows Preinstallation Environment (Windows PE) on destination computers to prepare the computers for image installation. After you install and initially configure Windows Deployment Services, ensure that Windows PE images created by updating deployment shares in Deployment Workbench have the appropriate flat-file image structures and add them to the Windows Deployment Services server.

Windows Deployment Services is responsible for initiating the deployment process for Pre-Boot Execution Environment (PXE) boot-enabled destination computers. For more information about setting up and configuring the Windows Deployment Services server, see Chapter 10, "Configuring Windows Deployment Services."

Configuring Resources

In addition to the shared folders described in the section titled "Resource Access" earlier in this chapter, the MDT 2010 scripts may require access to other resources, including application or database servers, such as Microsoft SQL Server 2008. The resources that the installation requires access to depend on the applications you've added to the distribution and the customizations you've made to MDT 2010 and the task sequence.

For LTI, you need to grant access to the deployment share to the credentials specified in one the following ways:

- UserID, UserPassword, and UserDomain properties in the CustomSettings.ini file. MDT 2010 uses these credentials to connect to the deployment share and other network resources. Make sure the credentials used in these properties have Read and Execute permissions on the deployment share. By providing these credentials in CustomSettings.ini, you can fully automate the LTI installation process.
- If you don't provide the credentials in CustomSettings.ini, you provide the credentials necessary to connect to the deployment share when you start the Windows Deployment Wizard on the destination computer. Make sure that the credentials used to start the Windows Deployment Wizard have at least Read and Execute permissions on the deployment share.

Make sure that the credentials used for LTI (defined in CustomSettings.ini or used to start the Windows Deployment Wizard) have Read and Execute permissions to access the following resources:

- **Deployment share** Configure access to the deployment share created in Deployment Workbench.
- **Any resources on application or database servers** Configure access to applications or databases that are accessed through the SQLServer, SQLShare, and Database properties.

> ***NOTE*** **Other connections to the same servers, such as Named Pipes and Remote Procedure Call (RPC), use the same credentials listed here. Use the ZTIConnect.wsf script to establish these connections. For more information about the ZTIConnect.wsf script, see the MDT 2010 documentation.**

Configuring CustomSettings.ini

CustomSettings.ini is the primary customization file for MDT 2010. The customizations you perform are specific to your organization. The names of the servers, default gateways for each subnet, media access control (MAC) addresses, and other details are unique to your organization, of course. The customization that you perform configures the deployment processes to run properly in your network environment. The examples in this section are provided as guides to help you in your customization. For more information on other configuration scenarios, see the MDT 2010 documentation.

The following listing shows a customized version of the CustomSettings.ini file after completing the New Deployment Share Wizard in Deployment Workbench. The initial contents of CustomSettings.ini depend on the answers given to the New Deployment Share Wizard, of course. The section titled "Customizing CustomSettings.ini" later in this chapter describes in more detail how to customize these settings for different computers.

CustomSettings.ini Modified by Deployment Workbench

```
[Settings]
Priority=Default
Properties=MyCustomProperty

[Default]
OSInstall=Y
SkipAppsOnUpgrade=YES
SkipCapture=NO
SkipAdminPassword=YES
SkipProductKey=YES
```

The CustomSettings.ini file in the listing contains the property values for all the target computers to be deployed using this version of the file. This version of the file contains no values that are unique to a specific target computer, because all of the settings are defined in the [Default] section. In this case, the target computer–specific configuration values are provided manually during the installation process by using the Windows Deployment Wizard. Table 12-1 explains the properties and corresponding values used in the listing.

NOTE In MDT 2010, the document *Microsoft Deployment Toolkit Reference* defines these and dozens of other settings that you can define in CustomSettings.ini. Of all the guides in MDT 2010, the *Microsoft Deployment Toolkit Reference* is the most useful, particularly for IT professionals already familiar with the MDT 2010 basic concepts.

TABLE 12-1 Explanation of CustomSettings.ini Properties for LTI

LINE IN CUSTOMSETTINGS.INI	PURPOSE
[Settings]	Indicates the start of the *[Settings]* section.
Priority=Default	Establishes the sequence in which the process parses subsections to locate values for the variables. In this example, the *[Default]* section is the only subsection that is parsed for variables.
Properties=MyCustomProperty	Indicates any additional properties to locate. The properties listed here are in addition to the properties listed in ZTIGather.xml. ZTIGather.wsf parses ZTIGather.xml to obtain a list of the properties. The property names defined here are added to them.
[Default]	Indicates the start of the *[Default]* section. The settings defined in this section apply to all computers.
OSInstall=Y	Indicates that the computer is supposed to perform an operating system deployment.
SkipAppsOnUpgrade=YES	Indicates whether the Windows Deployment Wizard prompts the user to install applications during an upgrade. If the property is set to *YES*, the wizard page is not displayed.
SkipCapture=NO	Indicates whether the Windows Deployment Wizard prompts to capture an image. If the property is set to *YES*, the wizard page is not displayed.
SkipAdminPassword=YES	Indicates whether the Windows Deployment Wizard prompts to set the local Administrator password. If the property is set to *YES*, the wizard page is skipped and not displayed.
SkipProductKey=YES	Indicates whether the Windows Deployment Wizard prompts for a product key. If the property is set to *YES*, the wizard page is skipped and not displayed.

Automating the LTI Process

You can use LTI to automate much of the deployment process. ZTI provides full deployment automation using the MDT 2010 scripts, System Center Configuration Manager 2007, and Windows Deployment Services. However, LTI is designed to work with fewer infrastructure requirements.

You can reduce (or eliminate) the wizard pages that are displayed in the Windows Deployment Wizard during the LTI deployment process. You can also skip the entire Windows Deployment Wizard by specifying the SkipWizard property in CustomSettings.ini. To skip individual wizard pages, use the following properties (see the *Microsoft Deployment Toolkit Reference* in MDT 2010 for a description of each property):

- SkipAdminPassword
- SkipApplications
- SkipAppsOnUpgrade
- SkipBDDWelcome
- SkipBitLocker
- SkipBitLockerDetails
- SkipTaskSequence
- SkipCapture
- SkipComputerBackup
- SkipComputerName
- SkipDeploymentType
- SkipDomainMembership
- SkipFinalSummary
- SkipLocaleSelection
- SkipPackageDisplay
- SkipProductKey
- SkipSummary
- SkipTimeZone
- SkipUserData

> ***NOTE*** **Automating LTI by using CustomSettings.ini alone is not realistic. Defining custom settings for each computer by using CustomSettings.ini is difficult. The ideal tool to use for fully automating LTI is the MDT 2010 database, which enables you to easily associate settings with individual computers and define settings that apply to groups of computers. For more information about using the MDT 2010 database, see the section titled "Using the MDT 2010 Database" later in the chapter.**

For each wizard page that you skip, provide the values for the corresponding properties that normally are collected through the wizard page in the CustomSettings.ini and BootStrap.ini files (or by using the MDT 2010 database). For more information on the properties that you need to configure in the CustomSettings.ini and BootStrap.ini files, see the MDT 2010 documentation.

The following listing illustrates a CustomSettings.ini file used for a Refresh Computer scenario to skip all Windows Deployment Wizard pages. In this sample, the properties to provide when skipping the wizard page are immediately beneath the property that skips the wizard page.

CustomSettings.ini File for a Refresh Computer Scenario

```
[Settings]
Priority=Default
Properties=MyCustomProperty

[Default]
OSInstall=Y
ScanStateArgs=/v:5 /o /c
LoadStateArgs=/v:5 /c /lac /lae
SkipAppsOnUpgrade=Yes
SkipCapture=Yes
SkipAdminPassword=YES
SkipProductKey=YES

SkipDeploymentType=Yes
DeploymentType=REFRESH

SkipDomainMembership=Yes
JoinDomain=Americas
DomainAdmin=Administrator
DomainAdminDomain=Americas
DomainAdminPassword=

SkipUserData=yes
UserDataLocation=AUTO
UDShare=\\nyc-am-dep-01\Dellimage\OSDUsmt
UDDir=%ComputerName%

SkipComputerBackup=yes
ComputerBackuplocation=AUTO
BackupShare=\\nyc-am-dep-01\Dellimage\OSDBackup
BackupDir=%ComputerName%

SkipTaskSequence=Yes
TaskSequenceID=Enterprise

SkipComputerName=Yes
```

```
ComputerName=%ComputerName%

SkipPackageDisplay=Yes
LanguagePacks1={3af4e3ce-8122-41a2-9cf9-892145521660}
LanguagePacks2={84fc70d4-db4b-40dc-a660-d546a50bf226}

SkipLocaleSelection=Yes
UILanguage=en-US
UserLocale=en-CA
KeyboardLocale=0409:00000409

SkipTimeZone=Yes
TimeZoneName=China Standard Time

SkipApplications=Yes
Applications1={a26c6358-8db9-4615-90ff-d4511dc2feff}
Applications2={7e9d10a0-42ef-4a0a-9ee2-90eb2f4e4b98}
UserID=Administrator
UserDomain=Americas
UserPassword=P@ssw0rd

SkipBitLocker=Yes
SkipSummary=Yes
Powerusers1=Americas\JoinRis
```

Performing LTI Deployments

To deploy a computer using LTI, start the destination computer by running LiteTouch.vbs from the deployment share or by using the Windows PE boot image generated by updating the deployment share. Start the Windows PE boot image in any of three ways:

- Burn the .iso images to a DVD. This process is slow and tedious. These ISO image files reside in the \Boot folder of the deployment share.
- Copy the contents of the Windows PE boot image to a bootable USB Flash drive (UFD). This is far more convenient than DVDs, and most modern computers support booting from UFDs. For more information about creating bootable UFDs, see Chapter 9, "Preparing Windows PE."
- Add the LiteTouchPE_x86.wim or LiteTouchPE_x64.wim image files to the Boot Images item of a Windows Deployment Services server. The .wim image files are in the \Boot folder of the deployment share. For more information about installing and configuring Windows Deployment Services, see Chapter 10.

Before beginning installation, verify that the folders in the following list no longer exist on any drive on the target computer (MDT 2010 creates them on the drive with the most free space):

- **MININT** This folder is preserved through the deployment process and contains deployment state information (such as user state migration information and log files).
- **SMSTaskSequence** This folder contains state information specific to Task Sequencer.

The Windows Deployment Wizard creates and uses these folders (on the drive where the operating system is installed) during the deployment process. If a previous deployment terminates abnormally, these folders may still exist on the target computer, and if you don't remove them manually, the process will continue from the point where the process abnormally terminated instead of starting from the beginning. Be sure to remove these folders, if they exist, before initiating deployment.

To start an LTI deployment using Windows Deployment Wizard, perform the following steps:

1. Start the Windows Deployment Wizard using one of the following methods:
   - Start the wizard manually from an existing Windows installation by connecting to the appropriate deployment share (for example, *servername*\DeploymentShare$ \Scripts) and typing **cscript litetouch.vbs**.
   - Start the Lite Touch Windows PE image by using a bootable DVD, bootable UFD, or Windows Deployment Services. Any images created by Deployment Workbench automatically start the Windows Deployment Wizard. See Chapter 10 to learn how to add these boot images to Windows Deployment Services.
2. If prompted by the Welcome To Windows Deployment dialog box, click Run The Deployment Wizard To Install A New Operating System and then click Next.
3. If prompted by the User Credentials dialog box, type the credentials necessary to connect to the deployment share (user name, domain, and password) and then click OK. The Windows Deployment Wizard starts automatically. You must use an account that has Read and Write access to the deployment share.
4. Follow the Windows Deployment Wizard instructions to choose a task sequence, answer prompts not skipped by CustomSettings.ini or the MDT 2010 database, and begin installation. The actual experience is based entirely on the customizations you made to CustomSettings.ini and the MDT 2010 database.

NOTE Windows 7 can use the new Offline Domain Join feature to join a domain without a connection to it. This process requires Windows 7 and Windows Server 2008 R2. First, you provision the computer account on the domain controller, which creates a metadata file containing the information required to join the domain. Then, you transfer the metadata to the joining computer. The computer performs the domain join without having connectivity to the domain controller. For more information, type **djoin.exe /?** on a domain controller running Windows Server 2008 R2.

Customizing MDT 2010

MDT 2010 customization provides the necessary configuration settings for the destination computers. The configuration settings include the values that you would normally provide if you were deploying the operating system manually. You accomplish this customization by using one or more of these options:

- Configure the CustomSettings.ini file.
- Configure the BootStrap.ini file.
- Retrieve information from the MDT 2010 database.

For LTI-based deployments, any configuration settings that you don't specify in the CustomSettings.ini file, the BootStrap.ini file, or the database must be provided when running the Windows Deployment Wizard. This gives you the flexibility to automate the LTI process fully or have the majority of configuration settings provided when running the Windows Deployment Wizard.

MORE INFO **For more information, see the following resources:**

- **For the syntax and structure of the CustomSettings.ini file, see the MDT 2010 documentation.**
- **For the syntax and structure of the BootStrap.ini file, see the MDT 2010 documentation.**

Configuring Multiple Computers

Whenever possible, apply configuration settings to multiple computers. You can define groups of computers and then apply configuration settings to the groups you define. Group-based configuration settings allow you to apply the same settings to a group of client computers. After you apply group-based settings, you can apply computer-specific configuration settings through computer-based settings.

Selecting a Grouping Method

You can use different methods to group client computers. After you determine how you want to group computers, select the appropriate properties.

Using the processing rules in MDT 2010, you can group computers based on any property that might be applied to a group of computers (such as Make, Model, DefaultGateway, and so on). Table 12-2 lists methods of grouping computers, descriptions of the methods, and the properties that you can use to group the computers.

TABLE 12-2 Grouping Methods

GROUPING METHOD	DESCRIPTION	PROPERTIES
Geographically	Group configuration settings based on resources located within a geographic region (such as a shared folder on a computer within a geographic region).	DefaultGateway
Target computer hardware attributes	Group configuration settings based on hardware attributes (such as the make of the computer or processor architecture of the target computer).	Architecture CapableArchitecture Make Model HALName
Target computer software attributes	Group configuration settings based on software attributes (such as the operating system version of the target computer).	OSVersion
Default attributes	Apply configuration settings to all target computers when the properties are not located in other sections.	Default

In most instances, you can nest computer groupings. For example, you can use the DefaultGateway property to designate the IP subnets on which a computer resides within a geographic location. You can define locations by using the user-defined properties in the *[DefaultGateway]* section, as shown in the following listing. When grouping computers by hardware configuration, you can use a variety of methods, and the script searches for the substituted value. For instance, if you specify *Priority=Make*, the script substitutes the value for *Make* that it determines through a Windows Management Instrumentation (WMI) call and looks for the corresponding section, such as *[Dell Computer Corporation]*.

Grouping with [DefaultGateway]

```
[DefaultGateway]
172.16.0.3=NYC
172.16.1.3=NYC
172.16.2.3=NYC
172.16.111.3=DALLAS
172.16.112.3=DALLAS
172.16.116.3=WASHINGTON
172.16.117.3=WASHINGTON

[NYC]
UDShare=\\NYC-AM-FIL-01\MigData
SLShare=\\NYC-AM-FIL-01\Logs
Packages1=NYC00010-Install
Packages2=NYC00011-Install
```

```
Administrator1=WOODGROVEBANK\NYC Help Desk Staff

[DALLAS]
UDShare=\\DAL-AM-FIL-01\MigData
SLShare=\\DAL-AM-FIL-01\Logs
Administrator1=WOODGROVEBANK\DAL Help Desk Staff
```

> ***MORE INFO*** **You can find the complete source of the CustomSettings.ini file used in these examples in the MDT 2010 documentation.**

Applying the Properties to the Groups

After you identify the ways you want to group configuration settings, determine which properties and corresponding configuration settings you will apply to each group. Properties that you can group are properties that you can apply to multiple computers. Properties that you can apply to groups of computers include:

- BackupDir
- BackupShare
- CaptureGroups
- ComputerBackupLocation
- Packagesx
- SLShare
- UDDir
- UDShare
- UDProfiles

You should not apply properties that are specific to individual computers to groups of computers. These properties include:

- AssetTag
- HostName
- IPAddress
- OSDNewMachineName
- SerialNumber

> ***NOTE*** **MDT 2010 supports dozens of properties in CustomSettings.ini. The *Microsoft Deployment Toolkit Reference* in MDT 2010 contains a complete reference of all the settings it supports.**

Configuring Individual Computers

For LTI, configuration settings that you apply to a group of computers may be sufficient. You can supply the remainder of the computer-specific settings interactively in the Windows Deployment Wizard.

If you want to automate your LTI-based deployment fully, you need to provide computer-specific configuration settings in addition to the settings that apply to groups of computers. You can use the configuration settings for individual computers to override or augment settings for groups of computers based on the priority. For more information about determining the priority of processing rules, see the MDT 2010 documentation.

Selecting an Identification Method

More than one method is available for identifying individual computers (just as when identifying groups of computers). After you select the method for identifying an individual target computer, you can select the appropriate properties.

The processing rules in MDT 2010 allow you to identify individual computers based on any property that might be applied to only one computer (such as AssetTag, MACAddress, UUID, and so on). Table 12-3 lists the methods of identifying individual computers, descriptions of the methods, and properties that you can use to identify the individual computers.

TABLE 12-3 Identifying Individual Computers

IDENTIFICATION METHOD	DESCRIPTION	PROPERTIES
Target computer hardware attributes	Identify the target computer by using the hardware configuration.	MACAddress
Target computer software attributes	Identify the target computer by using the software or firmware configuration.	Product (in conjunction with Make and Model) UUID
Target computer user-defined attributes	Identify the target computer by using attributes that are assigned to the computer but are not a part of the hardware or software configuration.	AssetTag SerialNumber

Applying the Properties to Individual Computers

After you select the methods for identifying individual computers, determine which properties and corresponding configuration settings you will apply to each destination computer. These configuration settings typically apply to only one computer because the configuration settings are unique to that computer. In instances in which a configuration setting is being applied to several computers, use group-based processing rules.

Properties that are typically applied to individual computers include:

- AssetTag
- HostName
- IPAddress
- OSDNewMachineName
- SerialNumber

If a group-based setting has a higher priority and the configuration setting is found in that group, the same configuration setting for an individual computer is ignored. For more information about deployment processing rule priority, see the MDT 2010 documentation.

Customizing CustomSettings.ini

The CustomSettings.ini file is the primary configuration file for MDT 2010. All configuration settings are specified either directly or indirectly:

- Directly, in the CustomSettings.ini file
- Indirectly, in the MDT 2010 database that is referenced in the CustomSettings.ini file

The CustomSettings.ini file syntax is very similar to many .ini files. The CustomSettings.ini file in the following listing illustrates a CustomSettings.ini file customized for a LTI-based deployment. For further explanation of the CustomSettings.ini file in the listing, see the MDT 2010 documentation.

CustomSettings.ini for LTI

```
[Settings]
Priority=Default, MACAddress
Properties=CustomProperty

[Default]
OSInstall=Y
ScanStateArgs=/v:5 /o /c
LoadStateArgs=/v:5 /c /lac
UserDataLocation=NONE
CustomProperty=TRUE

[00:0F:20:35:DE:AC]
ComputerName=HPD530-1

[00:03:FF:FE:FF:FF]
ComputerName=BVMXP
```

A CustomSettings.ini file includes:

- **Sections** Sections are identified by brackets that surround the section name (for example, *[Settings]*). In the previous listing, the sections include *[Settings]*, *[Default]*, *[00:0F:20:35:DE:AC]*, and *[00:03:FF:FE:FF:FF]*. CustomSettings.ini has the following types of sections:
  - **Required sections** Only the *[Settings]* section is required. All other sections are optional. The MDT 2010 scripts require the *[Settings]* section in CustomSettings.ini to locate the reserved properties (Priority and Properties).
  - **Optional sections** The optional sections in the CustomSettings.ini file are used to assign a group of configuration settings to groups of computers or to individual computers. In the previous listing, the configuration settings in the *[Default]* section are applied to more than one computer, and the configuration settings in the *[00:0F:20:35:DE:AC]* and *[00:03:FF:FE:FF:FF]* sections are applied to the corresponding computers.
- **Properties** Properties are variables that need to have values assigned. Properties are followed by an equals sign (=). The scripts scan the CustomSettings.ini file to locate the properties.
- **Values** Values are the configuration settings assigned to the properties. Values are preceded by an equals sign. The scripts scan the CustomSettings.ini file to locate the values. In the previous listing, the value assigned to the *LoadStateArgs* property is */v:5 /c /lac*.

> ***MORE INFO*** **For more information on the syntax of the CustomSettings.ini file, see the MDT 2010 documentation.**

Customizing BootStrap.ini

Configure the BootStrap.ini file to specify property settings prior to accessing the CustomSettings.ini file. In other words, the BootStrap.ini file describes how to connect to the deployment share, which contains the CustomSettings.ini file. Configure the BootStrap.ini file to help the MDT 2010 scripts locate the appropriate MDT 2010 deployment share.

The syntax of the BootStrap.ini file is identical to the CustomSettings.ini file. The BootStrap.ini file contains a subset of the properties that are used in the CustomSettings.ini file. The following lists the common properties that are configured in BootStrap.ini:

- DeployRoot
- SkipBDDWelcome
- UserDomain
- UserID
- UserPassword
- KeyboardLocale

MORE INFO Deployment Workbench creates the BootStrap.ini file when a deployment share is created. After the initial creation, make all further customizations manually. For more information on configuring the BootStrap.ini file syntax, see the MDT 2010 documentation.

Using the MDT 2010 Database

You can configure the rules for LTI deployment in the MDT 2010 database by using Deployment Workbench. The benefits of using the database include:

- **A more generic version of CustomSettings.ini** Storing the configuration settings in the MDT 2010 database removes most of the detail from CustomSettings.ini. This change helps make the CustomSettings.ini file more generic so that you can use the same file in multiple deployment shares.
- **A centralized repository for all property configuration settings** Centralizing the configuration for all property settings ensures consistency across all deployment shares.

To configure the rules in the configuration database, perform the following steps:

1. Create the database by using Deployment Workbench. The following section, "Creating the MDT 2010 Database," describes this step.
2. Configure the property values in the MDT 2010 database by using the Database item in Deployment Workbench. The section titled "Configuring the MDT 2010 Database" later in this chapter describes this step in more detail.
3. Configure CustomSettings.ini to include the appropriate database queries for returning the property values stored in the MDT 2010 database. The section titled "Configuring the Database Access" later in this chapter describes this step in more detail.

Creating the MDT 2010 Database

Before configuring the database, you must create it in SQL Server. Deployment Workbench creates this database automatically by using the New DB Wizard. Of course, this section assumes that SQL Server is already installed and configured locally or remotely in your environment and that you have permission to create databases.

To create the MDT 2010 database in SQL Server, perform the following steps:

1. In Deployment Workbench, right-click Database and then click New Database. Database is located under Advanced Configuration in the deployment share.
2. On the SQL Server Details page, in the SQL Server Name box, type the name of the server hosting SQL Server and click Next. If you want, provide an instance and port and specify the network library to use for the connection.

3. On the Database page, shown here, choose Create A New Database, type the name of the database in the Database text box, and then click Next. You can also choose to repair or connect to an existing database.

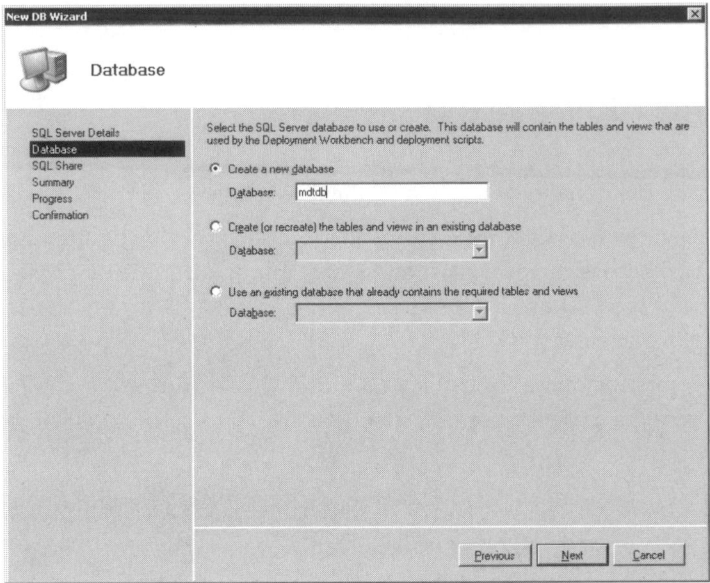

4. If you want, on the SQL Share page, type the name of any share on the server running SQL Server and then click Finish. MDT 2010 uses this share only if necessary to create a secure connection to the computer running SQL Server when using integrated security. Specify this share only if the Windows Deployment Wizard is not able to connect to SQL Server during deployment. The wizard will attempt to connect to this share using the connection credentials specified as described in the section titled "Configuring Resources" earlier in this chapter.

Configuring the MDT 2010 Database

MDT 2010 organizes the property values in the database by the method for applying them to destination computers. An item beneath the Database item in Deployment Workbench represents each method, as shown in Figure 12-1 and as listed in Table 12-4.

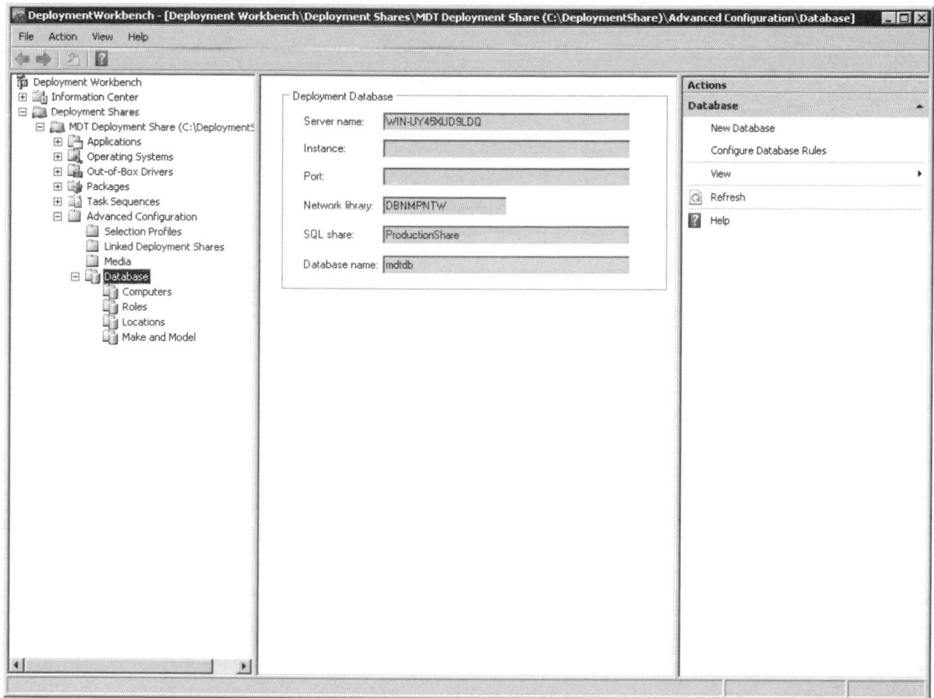

FIGURE 12-1 Database organization in Deployment Workbench

TABLE 12-4 Database Items in Deployment Workbench

NODE	ITEMS DEFINED BY THIS NODE
Computers	Specific target computers based on the AssetTag, UUID, SerialNumber, and MACAddress properties. You can associate property settings, applications, packages, roles, and administrative-level accounts with a computer. For more information on configuring this node, see the MDT 2010 documentation.
Roles	A group of computers based on the tasks performed by the users of the target computers (by using the Role property). You can associate property settings, applications, packages, and administrative-level accounts with a role. For more information on configuring this node, see the MDT 2010 documentation.
Locations	A group of computers using the DefaultGateway property of the target computers to identify a geographic location. You can associate property settings, applications, packages, roles, and administrative-level accounts with a location. For more information on configuring this node, see the MDT 2010 documentation.

NODE	ITEMS DEFINED BY THIS NODE
Make And Model	A group of computers using the Make And Model properties of the target computers. You can associate property settings, applications, packages, roles, and administrative-level accounts with target computers that are of the same make and model. For more information on configuring this node, see the MDT 2010 documentation.

NOTE Create the items in the Roles node before you create the other items beneath other nodes (Computers, Locations, and Make And Model), because the other nodes can be associated with roles.

Configuring the Database Access

After you have configured the property values in the MDT 2010 database, you need to configure CustomSettings.ini to perform the appropriate database queries. You can do this easily by using the Configure DB Wizard in Deployment Workbench. Run the Configure DB Wizard for each deployment share defined in Deployment Workbench with which you want to use the database.

To configure CustomSettings.ini for database queries, perform the following steps:

1. In the Deployment Workbench console tree, right-click Database and then click Configure Database Rules. Database is under Advanced Configuration in the deployment share.
2. On the Computer Options page, shown on the following page, choose from the following options and then click Next:
   - **Query For Computer-Specific Settings** Queries the settings configured on the Details tab of the Properties dialog box of the computer item.
   - **Query For Roles Assigned To This Computer** Queries the roles associated with the computer on the Roles tab of the Properties dialog box of the computer item.
   - **Query For Applications To Be Installed On This Computer** Queries the applications to be installed on the computer, as configured on the Applications tab of the Properties dialog box of the computer item.
   - **Query For Administrators To Be Assigned To This Computer** Queries the accounts that will be made members of the local Administrators group on the target computer, as configured on the Administrators tab of the Properties dialog box of the computer item.

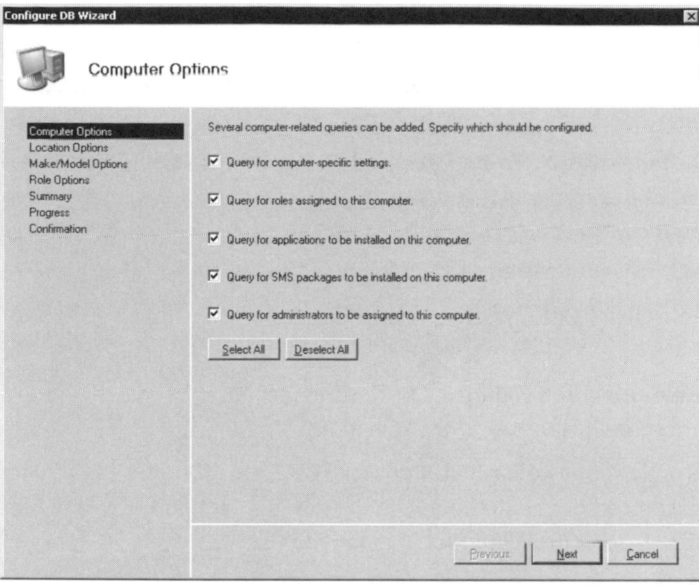

3. On the Location Options page, choose from the following options and then click Next:
   - **Query For Location Names Based On Default Gateways** Queries for location names based on the IP addresses of the default gateways configured on the Identity tab of the Properties dialog box of the location item.
   - **Query For Location-Specific Settings** Queries the settings configured on the Details tab of the Properties dialog box of the location item.
   - **Query For Roles Assigned For This Location** Queries the roles associated with the location on the Roles tab of the Properties dialog box of the location item.
   - **Query For Applications To Be Installed For This Location** Queries the applications to be installed on the target computers within the location configured on the Applications tab of the Properties dialog box of the location item.
   - **Query For Administrators To Be Assigned For This Location** Queries the accounts that will be made members of the local Administrators group on the target computers within the location configured on the Administrators tab of the Properties dialog box of the location item.
4. On the Select Make And Model Query Options page, choose from the following options and then click Next:
   - **Query For Model-Specific Settings** Queries the settings configured on the Details tab of the Properties dialog box of the make and model item.
   - **Query For Roles Assigned To Computers With This Make And Model** Queries the roles associated with the make and model on the Roles tab of the Properties dialog box of the make and model item.

- **Query For Applications To Be Installed On Computers With This Make And Model** Queries the applications to be installed on the target computers with the make and model configured on the Applications tab of the Properties dialog box of the make and model item.
- **Query For Administrators To Be Assigned To Machines With This Make And Model** Queries the accounts that will be made members of the local Administrators group on the target computer with the make and model configured on the Administrators tab of the Properties dialog box of the make and model item.

5. On the Select Role Query Options page, choose from the following options and then click Finish:
   - **Query For Role-Specific Settings** Queries the settings configured on the Details tab of the Properties dialog box of the role item.
   - **Query For Applications To Be Installed For This Role** Queries the applications to be installed on computers that perform this role, as configured on the Applications tab of the Properties dialog box of the role item.
   - **Query For Administrators To Be Assigned For This Role** Queries the accounts that will be made members of the local Administrators group on computers that perform this role, as configured on the Administrators tab of the Properties dialog box of the role item.

> ***MORE INFO*** After you complete the Configure DB Wizard, the CustomSettings.ini file is configured to perform the selected queries. For more information, see the MDT 2010 documentation. See the corresponding section for each table and view in the configuration database under "Tables and Views in the MDT DB" in *Microsoft Deployment Toolkit Reference*.

Summary

This chapter provided step-by-step instructions for configuring MDT 2010 to deploy Windows 7 using LTI. LTI is a simple way to deploy Windows 7 in small and medium-sized businesses. It requires no infrastructure and is very easy to set up and customize.

Additional Resources

These resources contain additional information and tools related to this chapter.

- Chapter 3, "Deployment Platform," includes information about the Windows 7 installation architecture and its main components and technologies. This chapter describes how the various components interact.

- Chapter 4, "Planning Deployment," includes information about installing and preparing MDT 2010 for use. This chapter also describes how to use the MDT 2010 guidance.
- Chapter 6, "Developing Disk Images," explains how to design and develop custom Windows 7 disk images for use with MDT 2010 LTI.
- Chapter 10, "Configuring Windows Deployment Services," explains how to install and configure Windows Deployment Services and how to use it with MDT 2010.
- Chapter 11, "Using Volume Activation," includes more information about Windows 7 product keys and volume activation.
- *Microsoft Deployment Toolkit Reference* in MDT 2010 lists the properties you can configure in a deployment share.
- *Windows Automated Installation Kit User's Guide* includes detailed information about the tools and technologies included in the Windows AIK 2.0. This guide is in the file Waik.chm in the Windows AIK.

PART III

Desktop Management

CHAPTER 13

Overview of Management Tools

As an administrator, you will need tools for managing computers running the Windows 7 operating system. The tools you will use, however, will depend on many factors, such as the number of computers you need to manage, the experience level of your IT staff, and the size of your organization's budget. Windows 7 and the Windows Server 2008 R2 operating system include numerous tools and technologies for managing Windows 7 client computers. There are also select tools available only to volume-licensed customers and free tools that anyone can download from the Microsoft Download Center. Large enterprises and mid-sized businesses may also consider investing in a comprehensive suite of management tools like the Microsoft System Center family of products.

This chapter provides you with a brief overview of the different kinds of tools available for managing Windows 7 computers and points you to where you can learn more about these tools, either within this book or elsewhere online. The chapter also provides you with a comprehensive introduction on how to use Windows PowerShell 2.0, which is included in Windows 7 and provides a powerful language for scripting the remote administration of Windows 7 clients.

Included Tools

Windows 7 and Windows Server 2008 R2 include a number of tools and technologies that you can use to manage computers running Windows 7 in your organization. The sections that follow describe some of the key tools with which you should be familiar and where you can find out more about how to use them. Note that this is only a brief overview; it is not intended as a comprehensive list of included tools available on these platforms.

Group Policy

Group Policy works with Active Directory Domain Services (AD DS) to allow administrators to deliver and apply configurations or policy settings remotely to a set of targeted users or computers across an enterprise. Group Policy provides an infrastructure that allows centralized configuration management of the Windows 7 operating system and supported applications such as the Microsoft Office 2007 system without the need to physically visit each computer on the network.

Group Policy can be managed by using the Group Policy Management Console (GPMC), which provides a Microsoft Management Console (MMC) snap-in and a set of scriptable interfaces that let you deploy, manage, and troubleshoot Group Policy. The GPMC is available as a feature you can install on Windows Server 2008 R2. The GPMC can also be used on administrative workstations running the Windows 7 Professional, Enterprise, or Ultimate Edition operating systems. To use the GPMC on a computer running Windows 7, first install the Remote Server Administration Tools (RSAT) for Windows 7 on the computer and then enable the Group Policy Management Tools feature by selecting Remote Server from Control Panel and then selecting Administration Tools, Feature Administration Tools, Turn Windows Features On Or Off.

New in Windows 7 and Windows Server 2008 R2 is the ability to use Windows PowerShell to automate common Group Policy tasks such as creating, configuring, linking, backing up Group Policy objects (GPOs), and direct editing of registry-based policy settings. Windows 7 and Windows Server 2008 R2 also include other enhancements to Group Policy including additional policy settings, additional types of preference items, improvements to Starter GPOs, and an improved user interface for configuring Administrative Template policy settings. For more information about using Group Policy to manage Windows 7 computers, see Chapter 14, "Managing the Desktop Environment."

Windows Management Instrumentation

Windows Management Instrumentation (WMI) is Microsoft's implementation of Web-Based Enterprise Management (WBEM), an industry initiative for developing a standard technology for accessing management information across an enterprise. WMI uses the Common Information Model (CIM) industry standard in order to represent systems, networks, devices, applications, and other managed features. WMI can be used to obtain management data from both local and remote Windows-based computers. WMI can also be used to automate the configuration of some aspects of Windows-based computers. Remote WMI connections can be made either through the Distributed Component Object Model (DCOM) or by using Windows Remote Management.

WMI can be used to manage Windows 7 computers in several ways:

- Interactively, by using the Windows Management Instrumentation Command-line (WMIC)
- In batch mode, by using WMI scripts written in Microsoft VBScript
- Either interactively or in batch mode by using Windows PowerShell

> ***MORE INFO*** **For information on how to use WMI to manage Windows 7 computers, see the various resources available on the Script Center on Microsoft TechNet at *http://www.microsoft.com/technet/scriptcenter/default.mspx*. A collection of sample administration scripts can also be found on the Script Center Script Repository at *http://www.microsoft.com/technet/scriptcenter/scripts/default.mspx?mfr=true*.**

Windows PowerShell

Windows PowerShell is a command-line shell and scripting language designed for system administration of Windows-based computers. Windows PowerShell helps administrators control and automate the administration of Windows operating systems and applications. Windows PowerShell is built on the Microsoft .NET Framework and uses standardized command-line tools called cmdlets to manage Windows-based computers locally and remotely across an enterprise. Windows PowerShell is also extensible, allowing application developers to create their own cmdlets, providers, and functions and package them in modules that they can share with others.

Windows PowerShell 2.0, which is included in both Windows 7 and Windows Server 2008 R2 and will be available as a download for some earlier versions of Windows, provides new features such as additional cmdlets, enhanced remote administration capabilities, an Integrated Scripting Environment (ISE), and more. Learning how to use Windows PowerShell can provide administrators with powerful new capabilities for automating many common Windows system administration tasks. For a comprehensive introduction to using Windows PowerShell, see the section titled "Introduction to Windows PowerShell" later in this chapter.

> ***MORE INFO*** **For more information about Windows PowerShell, see the "Scripting with Windows PowerShell" section of the Script Center at *http://www.microsoft.com/technet/scriptcenter/hubs/msh.mspx*. For information about what's new in Windows PowerShell 2.0, see *http://technet.microsoft.com/en-us/library/dd367858.aspx*. For the latest news about Windows PowerShell and tips on using it, see the Windows PowerShell blog at *http://blogs.msdn.com/PowerShell/*.**

Windows Remote Management

The Windows Remote Management (WinRM) service implements the WS-Management protocol for remote management on Windows 7 and Windows Server 2008 R2. WS-Management is a standard Web services protocol based on the Simple Object Access Protocol (SOAP) that is used for remote hardware and software management. When it is enabled and configured on the computer, the WinRM service listens on the network for WS-Management requests and processes them. Administrators can use the Windows Remote Shell (WinRS), a command-line tool (Winrs.exe) that enables administrators to execute commands remotely using the WS-Management protocol.

Before you can manage a remote computer using WinRS, the WinRM service on the remote computer needs to be enabled and configured with a listener, a management service that implements WS-Management protocol to send and receive messages. A listener is defined by a transport (HTTP or HTTPS) and an IPv4 or IPv6 address. For Windows 7 and Windows Server 2008 R2, enabling the WinRM service and configuring a listener can be done either by using the Winrm.cmd command-line tool or by using the Group Policy settings found under Computer Configuration\Policies\Administrative Templates\Windows Components\Windows Remote Management (WinRM). Additional Group Policy settings for configuring WinRS can be found under Computer Configuration\Policies\Administrative Templates\Windows Components\Windows Remote Shell.

MORE INFO For more information about WinRM and WinRS, see Windows Remote Management on MSDN at *http://msdn.microsoft.com/en-us/library/aa384426.aspx.*

Command-Line Tools

Windows 7 includes more than two hundred built-in command-line tools. Administrators can use these tools to perform various tasks ranging from configuring networking settings to performing backups. Examples of using some of these commands are found in various places throughout this resource kit:

- Chapter 16, "Managing Disks and File Systems," contains examples of using the Wbadmin.exe command-line tool to create and manage backups on Windows 7 computers.
- Chapter 17, "Managing Devices and Services," contains examples of using the Powercfg.exe command-line tool to configure and manage power management policy on Windows 7 computers.
- Chapter 21, "Maintaining Desktop Health," contains examples of using the Schtasks.exe command-line tool to create and manage scheduled tasks on Windows 7 computers.
- Chapter 23, "Managing Software Updates," contains examples of using the Bitsadmin.exe command-line tool to manage Background Intelligent Transfer Service (BITS) jobs running on Windows 7 computers.

- Chapter 26, "Configuring Windows Firewall and IPsec," contains examples of using the Netsh.exe command-line tool to manage various aspects of Windows Firewall on Windows 7 computers.

> ***MORE INFO*** **For a list of available commands and their detailed syntax, see the "Command Reference" section of "Commands, References, and Tools for Windows Server 2008 R2," which can be found in the Windows Server TechCenter on Microsoft TechNet at** ***http://technet.microsoft.com/en-us/library/dd695747.aspx.***

Remote Desktop

The Remote Desktop feature of Windows 7 allows users with appropriate permissions to access the entire desktop of a Windows 7 computer from another Windows-based computer. After a Remote Desktop connection has been established, the user of the remote computer can run applications and perform other tasks on the local computer as if he or she were sitting at the local computer's console and interactively logged on. If the remote user also has administrative credentials on the local computer, he or she can perform any administrative task on the computer that a locally logged-on administrator could perform. This enables administrators to connect to and remotely manage a Windows 7 computer on their network when the need arises. For more information about Remote Desktop in Windows 7, see Chapter 27, "Connecting Remote Users and Networks."

By using Remote Desktop Connection (Mstsc.exe) on an administrative workstation, an administrator can connect remotely to any Windows 7 computer on the network that has Remote Desktop enabled when needed to perform maintenance or troubleshooting tasks on the computer. After a Remote Desktop session has been established with a remote computer, the administrator can collect information concerning the computer, modify configuration settings on the computer, and manage the computer by running any built-in applications locally on the computer, including:

- **Task Manager** Lets you view the programs, processes, and services running on the computer, terminate a program that is not responding, and monitor the computer's performance. For more information about using Task Manager, see Chapter 21.
- **Resource Monitor** Lets you view detailed resource utilization information for the CPU, memory, disk, and network on a process-by-process basis. For more information about using Resource Monitor, see Chapter 30, "Troubleshooting Hardware, Driver, and Disk Issues."
- **Event Viewer** Lets you browse and manage event logs to monitor the health of the computer and troubleshooting issues that arise. For more information about using Event Viewer, see Chapter 21.
- **Services console** Lets you view and modify settings for services running on the computer. For more information about managing services, see Chapter 17.

- **Action Center** Lets you scan the computer for spyware, configure security settings, view the computer's reliability history, run troubleshooters, perform system recovery actions, and perform other maintenance tasks. For more information about using the Action Center, see Chapter 1, "Overview of Windows 7 Improvements."

Other useful tools for administrators to use during a Remote Desktop session are the Windows command prompt (Cmd.exe) and the Windows PowerShell command prompt (PowerShell.exe). Alternatively, you can run Windows commands remotely on the computer using WinRM/WinRS or use the new remoting capabilities found in Windows PowerShell 2.0.

Downloadable Tools

At the time of writing, the Microsoft Download Center (*http://www.microsoft.com/downloads/*) has several free tools that you can download and use to manage computers running Windows 7 in your organization. Additional tools for managing Windows 7 will likely become available during the product life cycle. The sections that follow describe a few useful tools administrators will likely want to download and add to their toolbox.

Microsoft Network Monitor

Microsoft Network Monitor is a network protocol analyzer that lets you capture network traffic, view it, and analyze it. Version 3.3 of Network Monitor is available in 32- and 64-bit versions and can be downloaded from *http://www.microsoft.com/downloads/details.aspx?displaylang=en&FamilyID=983b941d-06cb-4658-b7f6-3088333d062f*. A good source of information on how to use this tool is the Network Monitor blog at *http://blogs.technet.com/netmon/*.

Microsoft Baseline Security Analyzer

The Microsoft Baseline Security Analyzer (MBSA) is an easy-to-use tool designed to help administrators of small and medium-sized businesses ensure that their Windows-based computers are secure. You can use MBSA to determine the security state of your computers in accordance with Microsoft security recommendations. MBSA also offers specific remediation guidance for security problems it detects, such as misconfigurations and missing security updates.

The current version (2.1) of MBSA is available in 32- and 64-bit versions for several languages but will not install on Windows 7. A new version of MBSA will be released sometime in the future that will support running on Windows 7, and information concerning the new version will be made available at *http://www.microsoft.com/mbsa/*.

Microsoft IPsec Diagnostic Tool

The Microsoft IPsec Diagnostic Tool helps network administrators troubleshoot network-related failures, focusing primarily on Internet Protocol security (IPsec). The tool checks for common network problems on the host machine and, if it finds any problems, it suggests repair commands that you can use. The tool also collects IPsec policy information on the system and parses the IPsec logs to try to determine why the failure might have happened. The tool also provides trace collection for virtual private network (VPN) connections, the Network Access Protection (NAP) client, Windows Firewall, Group Policy updates, and wireless and system events. The diagnostic report generated by the tool is derived from the system logs collected by the tool during its analysis phase.

The Microsoft IPsec Diagnostic Tool can be installed on both 32- and 64-bit versions of Windows and can be downloaded from *http://www.microsoft.com/downloads/details.aspx?displaylang=en&FamilyID=1d4c292c-7998-42e4-8786-789c7b457881*.

Windows NT Backup-Restore Utility

Windows Vista introduced a new Backup utility that is not backward compatible with the file format used by the old NTBackup.exe utility on earlier versions of Windows. For this reason, Microsoft has a new Windows NT Backup-Restore Utility available for download which can be used to restore backups on Windows XP and Windows Server 2003 to computers running Windows Vista and later versions. The tool requires that the Removable Storage Management feature be enabled on the computer. The tool is available in both 32- and 64-bit versions. The tool can be found at *http://www.microsoft.com/downloads/details.aspx?displaylang=en&FamilyID=7da725e2-8b69-4c65-afa3-2a53107d54a7*.

Windows Sysinternals Suite

The Windows Sysinternals Suite is a set of advanced tools for troubleshooting issues with Windows-based computers. These tools were originally developed by Winternals Software LP, a company that Microsoft acquired in 2006. Winternals was established in 1996 by Mark Russinovich and Bryce Cogswell, recognized industry leaders in operating system design and architecture. Examples of some useful tools in this suite include the following:

- **Autoruns** This tool lets you see what programs are configured to start up automatically when your system boots. It also displays the full list of registry and file locations where applications can configure autostart settings.
- **BgInfo** This tool automatically generates desktop backgrounds that include important information about the system, including IP addresses, computer name, network adapters, and more.
- **Process Explorer** This tool lets you find out what files, registry keys, and other objects that your processes have open, which dynamic-link libraries (DLLs) they have loaded, and who owns each process.

- **Process Monitor** This tool lets you monitor the file system, registry, process, thread, and DLL activity on your computer in real time.
- **PsTools** This set of command-line tools can be used for listing the processes running on local or remote computers, running processes remotely, rebooting computers, dumping event logs, and performing other tasks.
- **RootkitRevealer** This tool lets you scan your system for rootkit-based malware.
- **ShellRunas** This tool allows you to launch programs as a different user using a shell context-menu entry.
- **TCPView** This tool lets you view active sockets on the computer in real time.

The entire Sysinternals Suite can be downloaded as a compressed archive file from *http://download.sysinternals.com/Files/SysinternalsSuite.zip*. For more information about any of these tools, click the link for the tool on the Sysinternals Utility Index at *http://technet.microsoft.com/en-us/sysinternals/bb545027.aspx*. For news concerning the release of new and updated tools, see the Sysinternals site blog at *http://blogs.technet.com/Sysinternals/*. For helpful examples on how to use these tools, see Mark Russinovich's blog at *http://blogs.technet.com/markrussinovich/default.aspx*. An index of Mark's blog posts can also be found at *http://technet.microsoft.com/en-us/sysinternals/bb963890.aspx*.

Windows 7 Enterprise and the Microsoft Desktop Optimization Pack

Windows 7 Enterprise is a special edition of Windows 7 that is only available to customers through the Microsoft Software Assurance for Volume Licensing program. Software Assurance is a comprehensive maintenance offering that helps customers maximize the business value of their technology investments by providing new version rights, packaged services, round-the-clock Problem Resolution Support, and other benefits depending on the Volume Licensing program to which the customer subscribes. For more information about the Microsoft Software Assurance for Volume Licensing program, see *http://www.microsoft.com/licensing/software-assurance/default.aspx*.

Windows 7 Enterprise includes the following features not available in Windows 7 Professional:

- **AppLocker** Allows administrators to use Group Policy to control what software can run on users' computers. For more information about AppLocker, see Chapter 2, "Security in Windows 7."
- **BitLocker and BitLocker To Go** Helps safeguard data on laptops and removable drives should they be lost or stolen. For more information about BitLocker and BitLocker To Go, see Chapter 16.
- **BranchCache** Allows organizations to decrease the time branch office users spend waiting to download files across a slow wide area network (WAN) link. For more information about BranchCache, see Chapter 27.

- **DirectAccess** Provides mobile users with seamless access to corporate networks without needing to use a VPN. For more information about DirectAccess, see Chapter 27.
- **Enterprise Search scopes** Enables users to find information on network locations, such as Windows SharePoint sites, using a simple user interface. For more information about this feature, see Chapter 19, "Managing Search."
- **Multi-lingual User Interface (MUI) Packs** Enables administrators to create a single operating system image for worldwide deployment. For more information, see Part II, "Deployment."
- **Virtual Desktop Infrastructure (VDI) Optimizations** Provides an improved user experience for Microsoft VDI implementations that includes multimon and microphone support and also enables the reuse of virtual machine images to boot a physical computer. For more information about emerging VDI solutions, see *http://www.microsoft.com/windows/enterprise/products/virtual-desktop.aspx.*

MORE INFO For more information about Windows 7 Enterprise Edition, see *http://www.microsoft.com/windows/enterprise/products/windows-7-enterprise.aspx.*

The Microsoft Desktop Optimization Pack (MDOP) is a suite of six products that are available only to customers who subscribe to the Software Assurance program. MDOP 2009, the newest release of this suite of products, employs innovative technologies that can help businesses reduce the Total Cost of Ownership (TCO) of deploying, maintaining, and troubleshooting the Windows desktop. The sections that follow briefly describe the six Microsoft technologies that make up MDOP 2009.

MORE INFO For more information about MDOP, see *http://www.microsoft.com/windows/enterprise/technologies/mdop.aspx.* For the latest news about MDOP products and tips on how to use them, see the Official MDOP blog at *http://blogs.technet.com/mdop/default.aspx.* If you are a Software Assurance customer, you can download MDOP 2009 from the Microsoft Volume Licensing Services (MVLS) site at *https://licensing.microsoft.com/eLicense/L1033/Default.asp.*

Microsoft Application Virtualization

Microsoft Application Virtualization (App-V) helps organizations deploy software applications that follow users anywhere on demand but are never installed and never need regression testing. App-V works by transforming applications into virtualized, network-available services that are delivered automatically as users need them and do not need to be installed on users' computers.

MORE INFO For more information about App-V 4.5, the latest version of this product, see *http://www.microsoft.com/windows/enterprise/products/app-virtualization.aspx*.

Microsoft Advanced Group Policy Management

Microsoft Advanced Group Policy Management (AGPM) helps administrators take control of the Windows desktop through effective change management, versioning, and resets. AGPM is an extension to Group Policy that enables more flexible administration by allowing administrators to develop, review, and modify GPOs without affecting users and computers targeted by those GPOs. AGPM also lets administrators configure, test, and approve changes before they go live in the production environment and to quickly roll back changes if this is needed.

MORE INFO For more information about AGPM, see *http://www.microsoft.com/windows/enterprise/products/advanced-group-policy-management.aspx*.

Microsoft Asset Inventory Service

Microsoft Asset Inventory Service (AIS) helps administrators make better asset-management decisions by enabling them to inventory their networks by scanning desktop computers for installed software. AIS also helps you ensure that your organization is in compliance with licenses you have purchased by facilitating the tracking of Microsoft Volume Licenses across an enterprise.

MORE INFO For more information about AIS 1.5, the latest version of this product, see *http://www.microsoft.com/windows/enterprise/products/ais.aspx*.

Microsoft Diagnostics and Recovery Toolset

Microsoft Diagnostics and Recovery Toolset (DaRT) is a suite of special troubleshooting tools that administrators can use to boot into a Windows Recovery Environment to repair unbootable or locked-out computers. Using these tools, you can perform recovery tasks such as restoring lost data, removing malware from infected systems, and diagnosing various kinds of problems.

MORE INFO For more information about DaRT, see *http://www.microsoft.com/windows/enterprise/products/dart.aspx*.

Microsoft Enterprise Desktop Virtualization

Microsoft Enterprise Desktop Virtualization (MED-V) version 1 is new in MDOP 2009 and enables the deployment and management of Microsoft Virtual PC images on a desktop running the Windows operating system while enabling a seamless user experience independent of the local desktop configuration and operating system. MED-V 1.0 can help businesses resolve difficult application compatibility problems by allowing them to deploy legacy applications on top of a single virtualized Windows image.

> ***MORE INFO*** **For more information about MED-V 1.0, see *http://www.microsoft.com/windows/enterprise/products/med-v.aspx*.**

Microsoft System Center Desktop Error Monitoring

Microsoft System Center Desktop Error Monitoring (DEM) can provide administrators with insight into the reasons behind application and operating system failures that cause desktop computers to stop operating. DEM can help make desktop computers more stable by enabling administrators to manage failures by implementing a low-cost, scalable error-filtering and error-alerting solution.

> ***MORE INFO*** **For more information about DEM, see *http://www.microsoft.com/windows/enterprise/products/dem.aspx*.**

Microsoft System Center

Microsoft System Center is a comprehensive set of products and solutions for IT management. System Center products provide technologies and solutions for capacity planning, operating system and application deployment and inventory, performance and availability monitoring, software update and data storage and recovery management, operations management, and reporting. Organizations that have hundreds or even thousands of desktop computers running Windows 7 can benefit from integrating System Center products into their IT management infrastructure. The sections that follow briefly describe the five core System Center products.

System Center Configuration Manager

System Center Configuration Manager allows organizations to assess, deploy, and update servers, client computers, and devices comprehensively across physical, virtual, distributed, and mobile networking environments. System Center Configuration Manager is extensible and is fully optimized for Windows. System Center Configuration Manager 2007 R2, the latest version of the platform, includes the following new features:

- Support for App-V management
- Microsoft Forefront Client Security integration
- Microsoft SQL Server Reporting Services reporting
- Client status reporting
- Operating system deployment enhancements for multicast deployment and unknown computer support

MORE INFO For more information about System Center Configuration Manager 2007 R2, see *http://www.microsoft.com/systemcenter/configurationmanager/en/us/default.aspx*. For the latest news about System Center Configuration Manager and tips on using the platform, see the System Center Configuration Manager Team blog at *http://blogs.technet.com/configmgrteam/default.aspx*. For information on resolving issues with System Center Configuration Manager, see the Configuration Manager Support Team blog at *http://blogs.technet.com/configurationmgr/default.aspx*.

System Center Operations Manager

System Center Operations Manager provides end-to-end monitoring for enterprise IT environments. By using System Center Operations Manager, you can monitor thousands of servers, applications, and clients across an enterprise and obtain comprehensive information concerning the health of these systems and applications. System Center Operations Manager 2007 R2, the latest version of the platform, includes the following new features:

- Import Management Packs Wizard
- Process Monitoring Management Pack Template
- Microsoft Exchange Server 2007 Client Access Server Monitoring Management Pack Template
- Exchange Server 2007 Intra-organizational Mail Flow Monitoring Management Pack Template
- Support for custom queries in OLE DB Data Source Management Pack Template
- Support for discovery and monitoring of UNIX- and LINUX-based computers
- Service Level Tracking
- Health Explorer
- Updated Microsoft Visio export functionality
- Improvements to setup and recovery, reporting, Management Pack authoring, and the user interface experience

MORE INFO For more information about System Center Operations Manager 2007 R2, see *http://www.microsoft.com/systemcenter/operationsmanager/en/us/default.aspx*. For the latest news about System Center Operations Manager and tips on using the platform, see the System Center Operations Manager Team blog at *http://blogs.technet.com/momteam/default.aspx*. For information on resolving issues with System Center Operations Manager, see the Operations Manager Support Team blog at *http://blogs.technet.com/operationsmgr*.

System Center Data Protection Manager

System Center Data Protection Manager provides enterprise-level solutions for Windows backup and recovery that enable delivery of continuous data protection for Microsoft application and file servers using integrated disk and tape media. System Center Data Protection Manager 2007 Service Pack 1 (SP1), the latest version of the platform, adds support for the following:

- Windows SharePoint Services (WSS) and Microsoft Office SharePoint Server (MOSS), including significant performance improvements when protecting WSS farms and support for search index backups for both WSS and MOSS
- Exchange Server Standby Continuous Replication (SCR)
- Mirrored SQL Server databases and mirrored clusters
- Hyper-V guest-based and host-based protection

For more information about System Center Data Protection Manager 2007 SP1, see *http://www.microsoft.com/systemcenter/dataprotectionmanager/en/us/default.aspx*. For the latest news about System Center Data Protection Manager and tips on using the platform, see the System Center Data Protection Manager blog called "Rescue Data Like A Hero" at *http://blogs.technet.com/dpm/*.

System Center Virtual Machine Manager

System Center Virtual Machine Manager provides centralized administration for an organization's virtual machine infrastructure. By using System Center Virtual Machine Manager, you can configure and deploy new virtual machines and centrally manage your physical and virtual infrastructure from a single administrative console. System Center Virtual Machine Manager 2008 R2, the latest version of the platform, adds support for the following:

- Live migration, including queuing support
- Rapid provisioning of virtual machines
- Multiple virtual machines per logical unit number (LUN) and other storage area network (SAN)–related enhancements
- Storage migration
- Host compatibility checks

- Third-party clustered file system support
- Veritas Volume Manager support

For more information about System Center Virtual Machine Manager 2008 R2, see *http://www.microsoft.com/systemcenter/virtualmachinemanager/en/us/default.aspx*. For the latest news about System Center Virtual Machine Manager and tips on using the platform, see the System Center Virtual Machine Manager Product and Support Team blog at *http://blogs.technet.com/scvmm/*.

System Center Essentials

System Center Essentials is a unified management product that provides end-to-end monitoring along with software and update deployment for midmarket businesses that have up to 500 client computers and 30 servers. By using System Center Essentials, you can monitor servers, applications, clients, and network devices and obtain views of their health states. System Center Essentials 2007 SP1, the latest version of the product, includes the following:

- Improvements in performance, usability, and supportability
- Improved backup and disaster recovery guidance
- Improvements in Management Pack quality
- Support for managing workgroup-joined computers
- Support for monitoring SNMPv1 (Simple Network Management Protocol) network devices
- Support for using multiple auto-approval rules in update management
- Support for using a remote SQL Server 2005 instance running on a computer with a different architecture than the management server
- Support for running the management server, console, and agent on computers running Windows Server 2008

For more information about System Center Essentials 2007 SP1, see *http://www.microsoft.com/systemcenter/sce/default.mspx*. For the latest news about System Center Essentials and tips on using the platform, see the System Center Essentials Team blog at *http://blogs.technet.com/systemcenteressentials/*.

Introduction to Windows PowerShell Scripting

System and network administrators and other IT professionals can simplify and automate the administration of Windows 7 across their organizations by learning how to use Windows PowerShell as a management tool. The rest of this chapter provides a basic tutorial on using Windows PowerShell for performing and scripting administrative tasks. Some of the new features of Windows PowerShell 2.0 are also demonstrated. Familiarity with VBScript scripting is assumed throughout, and familiarity with Windows PowerShell 1.0 can also be helpful when reading this tutorial.

DIRECT FROM THE SOURCE

Understanding Cmdlets

James O'Neill, Evangelist
Developer and Platform Group

Windows PowerShell can run several different kinds of commands including scripts, external programs, and user-defined functions. It also has compiled cmdlets (pronounced command-lets), which are loaded into the Windows PowerShell environment from .NET DLL files. Windows PowerShell loads a default set of these DLLs when it starts; without them, it would have just the basic grammar of a scripting language without any vocabulary. These DLLs, which can be registered and loaded as snap-ins or included as part of a Windows PowerShell module, can also contain the providers that Windows PowerShell uses to create drives: PowerShell has drives for the Windows Registry and for variables as well as for file systems. Developers can provide DLLs to add extra cmdlets and providers. For example, in Windows Server 2008 R2, the Active Directory team provides a module whose DLL implements a rich set of commands and a provider so Active Directory can be treated as a drive. System administrators can write their own commands, known as functions, in Windows PowerShell.

Cmdlets have a standardized naming convention that takes the form verb-noun, which makes them easy to discover. However, to save typing and to allow old familiar names to be used, Windows PowerShell also has one other type of command—the alias, which replaces one command name with another. When we talk about a command in Windows PowerShell, we may be referring to cmdlets, functions, alias scripts, external programs, or any combination of these linked together in a pipeline (in which the output of one command becomes the input of the next).

Working with Windows PowerShell Cmdlets

For people who come from a Windows background, Windows PowerShell will take some getting used to, because it provides a new kind of capability to the environment. On the one hand, the Windows PowerShell console enables you to type commands in an interactive manner. On the other hand, Windows PowerShell is a language that lets you write scripts. It is similar to taking the command prompt and putting VBScript inside it. In other words, you get two tools in one.

The heart of Windows PowerShell is the cmdlets that are included with the product. These cmdlets are built into Windows PowerShell, but they can also be written by other people to provide additional capability. You can open Windows PowerShell and obtain information about all the processes running on your computer. The Get-Process cmdlet returns information about the process ID, how much CPU time is being consumed, and the level of memory consumption. The command is Get-Process, and the results are seen in Figure 13-1.

```
Windows PowerShell
Windows PowerShell
Copyright (C) 2006 Microsoft Corporation. All rights reserved.

PS C:\> Get-Process

Handles  NPM(K)    PM(K)      WS(K) VM(M)   CPU(s)     Id ProcessName
-------  ------    -----      ----- -----   ------     -- -----------
    104       5     1144       3532    32     0.03    328 alg
     99       3     1960       3304    24     0.19   1084 ati2evxx
    115       3     2152       3740    29     1.45   1688 ati2evxx
    499       7     1904       5576    38    34.72    816 csrss
    187       7     1056       4268    37     2.27   2384 ctfmon
    481      15    21984      14368   109    19.66   2220 explorer
      0       0        0         16     0              0 Idle
    137      10     4508       6740    54     0.34    420 InoRpc
    136       5    29344      32784    84    30.39    560 InoRT
    174       7    29984      34680    91     1.36    592 InoTask
    405       9     4052       2676    42     8.67    900 lsass
     85       3      852       3036    31     0.05    552 OfficeLiveSignIn
    242       5    29324      25584   127     0.70   2328 powershell
    320      10     4924       8832    51     0.66   1140 SeaPort
    304       7     1756       3484    35     4.22    888 services
     19       1      168        400     4     0.03    760 smss
    278      16    10524       4716   107     3.61   1836 SnagIt32
    278      24    15696      30072   118    11.53   2416 SnagItEditor
     42       2      588       2404    20     0.05   2160 SnagPriv
    171       6     3904       7288    52     0.89   1756 spoolsv
    110       3     1260       3708    35     0.05    360 svchost
    203       5     3016       4876    60     0.45   1100 svchost
    322      14     2020       4688    39     4.45   1212 svchost
   1817      72    18700      29048   151    13.98   1336 svchost
    107       3     2308       3320    31     0.06   1376 svchost
     91       4     1664       3892    31     0.42   1432 svchost
    172       5     1544       3968    35     0.11   1576 svchost
    300       0        0        220     2    33.45      4 System
     40       2      632       2456    26     0.03    508 TscHelp
    622      42     8480       6248    65     2.02    844 winlogon
   1427      34    67064       4324   404   621.50   2812 WINWORD
     35       2      536       2092    26     0.02   1716 wscntfy
     90       4     2908       3420    22     0.02   1852 ZuneBusEnum

PS C:\>
```

FIGURE 13-1 The Get-Process cmdlet provides detailed process information.

If you are interested in services, the Windows PowerShell cmdlet is Get-Service. When you run this command, you obtain information about the service name, status, and even the display name. The results are shown in Figure 13-2.

If you want to obtain the date, the command is Get-Date, and if you want to find the culture settings on the computer, you use Get-Culture. But you are not limited to just using Windows PowerShell cmdlets within the PowerShell console. You can also use external commands such as Getmac.exe, as shown in Figure 13-3.

```
PS C:\> Get-Service

Status   Name               DisplayName
------   ----               -----------
Stopped  AdobeActiveFile... Adobe Active File Monitor V6
Stopped  Alerter            Alerter
Running  ALG                Application Layer Gateway Service
Stopped  AppMgmt            Application Management
Stopped  aspnet_state       ASP.NET State Service
Running  Ati HotKey Poller  Ati HotKey Poller
Running  AudioSrv           Windows Audio
Running  BITS               Background Intelligent Transfer Ser...
Running  Browser            Computer Browser
Stopped  cisvc              Indexing Service
Stopped  ClipSrv            ClipBook
Stopped  clr_optimizatio... .NET Runtime Optimization Service v...
Stopped  COMSysApp          COM+ System Application
Running  CryptSvc           Cryptographic Services
Running  DcomLaunch         DCOM Server Process Launcher
Running  Dhcp               DHCP Client
Stopped  dmadmin            Logical Disk Manager Administrative...
Running  dmserver           Logical Disk Manager
Running  Dnscache           DNS Client
Stopped  Dot3svc            Wired AutoConfig
Stopped  EapHost            Extensible Authentication Protocol ...
Running  ERSvc              Error Reporting Service
Running  Eventlog           Event Log
Running  EventSystem        COM+ Event System
Running  FastUserSwitchi... Fast User Switching Compatibility
Stopped  FLEXnet Licensi... FLEXnet Licensing Service
Stopped  FontCache3.0.0.0   Windows Presentation Foundation Fon...
Stopped  fsssvc             Windows Live Family Safety
Running  helpsvc            Help and Support
Running  HidServ            HID Input Service
Stopped  hkmsvc             Health Key and Certificate Manageme...
Stopped  HTTPFilter         HTTP SSL
Stopped  idsvc              Windows CardSpace
Stopped  ImapiService       IMAPI CD-Burning COM Service
Running  InoRPC             eTrust Antivirus RPC Server
Running  InoRT              eTrust Antivirus Realtime Server
Running  InoTask            eTrust Antivirus Job Server
Running  lanmanserver       Server
Running  lanmanworkstation  Workstation
Running  LmHosts            TCP/IP NetBIOS Helper
Stopped  Messenger          Messenger
```

FIGURE 13-2 The Get-Service cmdlet provides service information.

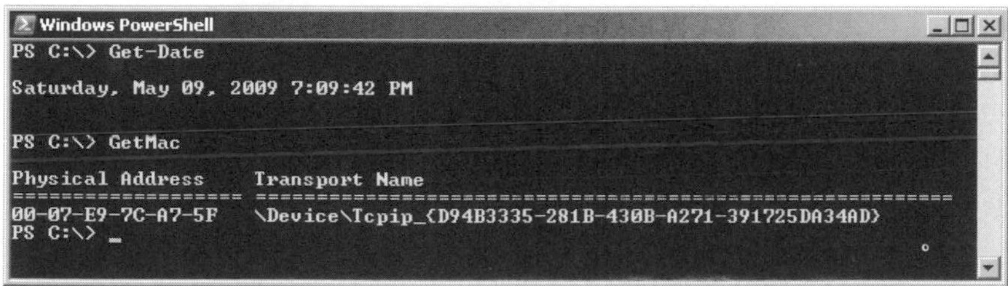
Windows PowerShell
PS C:\> Get-Date
Saturday, May 09, 2009 7:09:42 PM
PS C:\> GetMac
Physical Address   Transport Name
00-07-E9-7C-A7-5F   \Device\Tcpip_{D94B3335-281B-430B-A271-391725DA34AD}
PS C:\>

FIGURE 13-3 Both Windows PowerShell cmdlets and external commands can be combined in the same PowerShell session.

Up to this point in the discussion, all commands have begun with the word *Get* and were followed by some other word. All Windows PowerShell cmdlets have two-part names. The first part of the cmdlet name is called a *verb,* and the second part is called a *noun*. These do not correspond exactly to the grammatical terms, but the idea can be summarized as follows: "What do you want to do, and what do you want to do it to?" A standard set of verbs makes it easy to remember cmdlet names. For example, a common task IT professionals must perform is to stop a process. Many different utilities require you to remember to stop, unload, delete, kill, terminate, or some other command to stop a process. In Windows PowerShell, it is easy—

the verb is always *stop*. If you want to start something, you use the *start* verb. A listing of common verbs is seen in Table 13-1.

TABLE 13-1 Common Windows PowerShell Verbs and Grouping

VERB	GROUP
Add	Common
Clear	Common
Copy	Common
Enter	Common
Exit	Common
Format	Common
Get	Common
Hide	Common
Join	Common
Lock	Common
Move	Common
New	Common
Pop	Common
Push	Common
Redo	Common
Remove	Common
Rename	Common
Search	Common
Select	Common
Set	Common
Show	Common
Split	Common
Undo	Common
Use	Common
Unlock	Common
Backup	Data
Checkpoint	Data
Compare	Data

VERB	GROUP
Compress	Data
Convert	Data
ConvertFrom	Data
ConvertTo	Data
Dismount	Data
Expand	Data
Export	Data
Import	Data
Initialize	Data
Limit	Data
Merge	Data
Mount	Data
Out	Data
Publish	Data
Redo	Repeats the last action on a resource. Pairs with Undo.
Restore	Data
Save	Data
Undo	Returns a resource to its previous state. Pairs with Redo.
Unpublish	Data
Update	Data
Complete	Lifecycle
Disable	Lifecycle
Enable	Lifecycle
Install	Lifecycle
Register	Lifecycle
Restart	Lifecycle
Resume	Lifecycle
Start	Lifecycle
Stop	Lifecycle
Suspend	Lifecycle
Uninstall	Lifecycle

VERB	GROUP
Unregister	Lifecycle
Wait	Lifecycle
Debug	Diagnostic
Measure	Diagnostic
Ping	Diagnostic
Repair	Diagnostic
Resolve	Diagnostic
Test	Diagnostic
Trace	Diagnostic
Connect	Communications
Disconnect	Communications
Read	Communications
Receive	Communications
Send	Communications
Write	Communications
Block	Security
Grant	Security
Revoke	Security
Unblock	Security
Use	Other

In addition to employing the new Windows PowerShell cmdlets, you can use Windows PowerShell in ways that may already be familiar to you. For example, if you want to obtain a directory listing, you can type **dir**, and sample results of this command are shown in Figure 13-4. Keep in mind that some of the advanced features of the old *dir* command do not behave in exactly the same way that the Windows PowerShell *dir* command does. But the similarity is strong enough to facilitate learning the Windows PowerShell syntax.

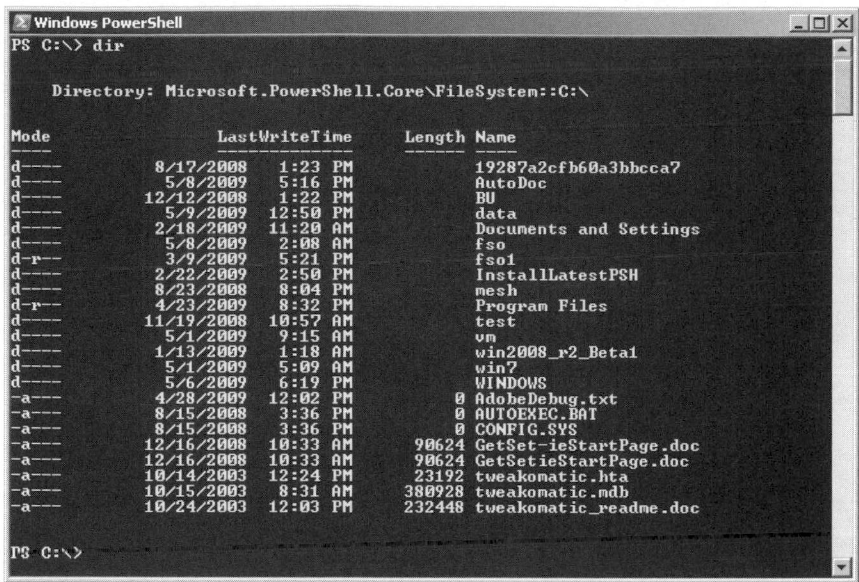

FIGURE 13-4 The *dir* command produces a directory listing of files and folders.

To create a directory, you can use the *md* command and supply the name of the directory you need to create. As soon as a directory is created, you can create a text file by using the redirection arrows to capture the results of a command, such as the *dir* command that was used earlier. These results are shown in Figure 13-5.

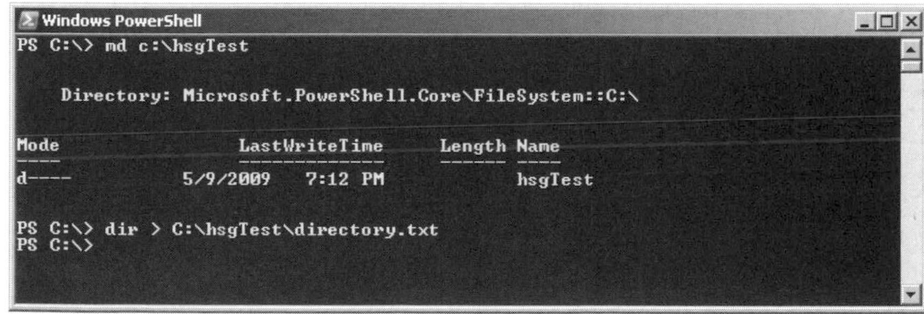

FIGURE 13-5 To create a new directory, use the *md* command.

No feedback is displayed in Windows PowerShell when creating a file by redirection. The text file that was created in the previous command is shown in Figure 13-6.

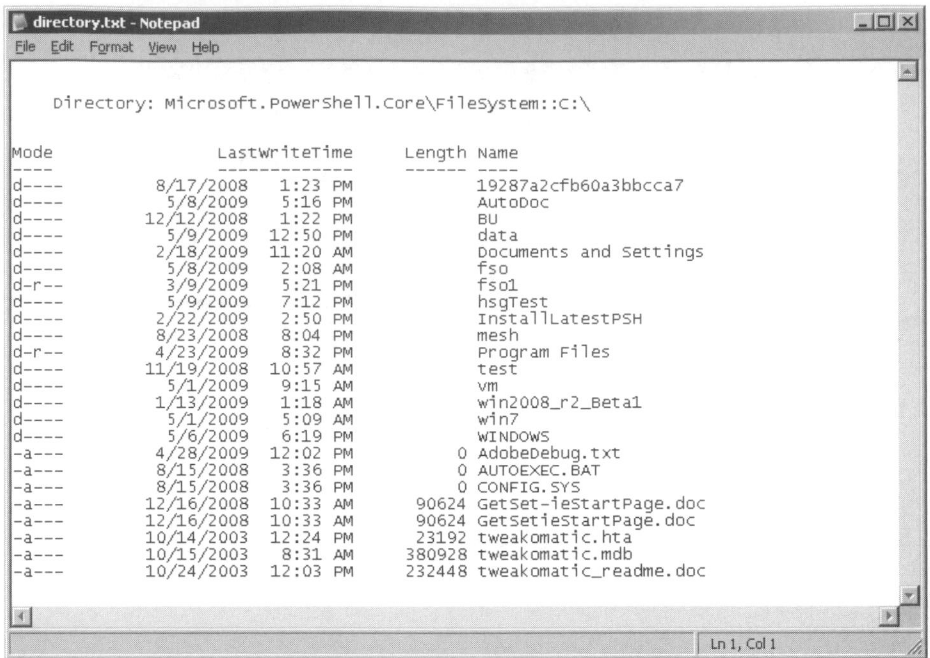

FIGURE 13-6 The text file of a directory listing created by using the redirection operator

The last thing that might have to be done is to delete a text file and a folder. To do this, you use the *del* command (the Windows PowerShell alias for the Remove-Item cmdlet) to delete both the file and the folder. The first thing that you might need to do is to change your working directory to the C:\HsgTest folder that was created earlier in this chapter via the *md* command (see Figure 13-5). To do this, you use the *cd* command. After you are in the directory, you can obtain another directory listing by using the *dir* command. Next, you use the *del* command to delete the Directory.txt file. As shown in Figure 13-7, the file name is preceded by the ".\" characters. This means that you are interested in the file in the current directory. When you type the first few letters of the file name and press the Tab key, ".\" is added to the file name automatically as the complete file name is expanded. This enables you to avoid typing the complete file name. The feature, known as a *tab expansion,* is a great time saver.

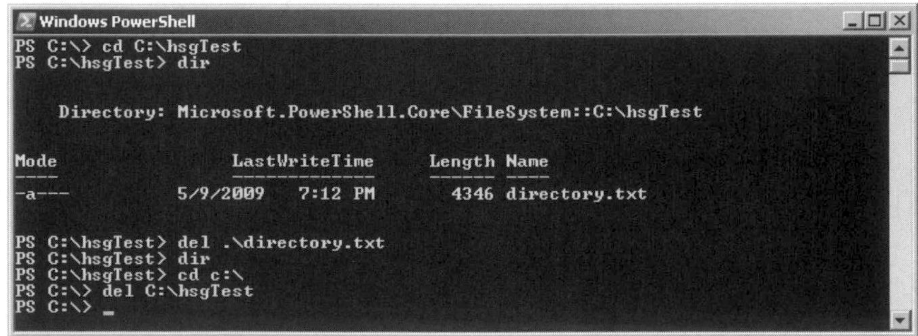

FIGURE 13-7 Use the *del* command to delete a file or a folder.

Using the Pipeline to Read Text Files

A common scripting task faced by IT professionals is reading text files. This usually involves using a script similar to the SearchTextFileForSpecificWord.vbs script. In the SearchTextFileForSpecificWord.vbs script, you create an instance of the *Scripting.FileSystemObject*, open the file, and store the resulting *TextStream* object in the file variable. You then use the *Do...Until...Loop* statement to work your way through the text stream. Inside the loop, you read one line at a time from the text stream. As soon as you find a specific line, you use the *InStr* statement to see whether you can find a specific word. If it does, you display the sentence to the screen. The SearchTextFileForSpecificWord.vbs script is shown here.

SearchTextFileForSpecificWord.vbs

```
filepath = "C:\fso\testFile.txt"
word = "text"
set fso = CreateObject("Scripting.FileSystemObject")
Set file = fso.OpenTextFile(filepath)

Do Until file.AtEndOfStream
 line = file.ReadLine
 If InStr(line, word) Then
  WScript.Echo line
 End If
Loop
```

The technique of using the *ReadLine* method is very efficient, and it is the recommended way to work with large files from within VBScript. The other way of reading content from a text file in VBScript is the *ReadAll* method. The problem with using the *ReadAll* method is that it stores the contents of a text file in memory. This is not a problem if the file is small, but for a large file, it consumes a large amount of memory. In addition to the memory consumption issue, if you plan on working with the file one line at a time, which is one of the main reasons for reading a text file, you now have to figure out artificial methods to work your way through the file. With the *ReadLine* method and the *TextStream* object, you stream the file and it never is stored in memory. The *TextStream* object from VBScript is similar to pipelining in Windows PowerShell.

With Windows PowerShell, you do not have to write a script to do the same thing that the SearchTextFileForSpecificWord.vbs script does. You can, in fact, perform the operation in just three lines of code, as shown here.

```
PS C:\> $filepath = "C:\fso\TestFile.txt"
PS C:\> $word = "test"
PS C:\> Get-Content -Path $filepath | ForEach-Object {if($_ -match $word){$_}}
```

When you run these commands, you will see the output shown in Figure 13-8.

```
PS C:\> $filepath = "C:\fso\TestFile.txt"
PS C:\> $word = "test"
PS C:\> Get-Content -Path $filepath | ForEach-Object {if($_ -match $word){$_}}
This is a test file.
PS C:\>
```

FIGURE 13-8 Script-like commands can be typed directly into the Windows PowerShell console.

Before you go any further, examine TestFile.txt in Figure 13-9. This will give you a better idea of what you are working with.

FIGURE 13-9 TestFile.txt contains several lines of text.

The first two lines that were typed into the Windows PowerShell console assign string values to variables. This serves the same purpose as the first two lines of the SearchTextFileForSpecificWord.vbs script. The last line typed in the Windows PowerShell console is actually two separate commands. The first one reads the contents of the text file. This is the same as creating an instance of the *Scripting.FileSystemObject*, opening the text file by using the *Do...While...Loop* construction, and calling the *ReadLine* method. Here is the Get-Content command.

```
Get-Content -Path $filepath
```

The results of the Get-Content cmdlet are pipelined to the ForEach-Object cmdlet. The ForEach-Object cmdlet enables you to work inside the pipeline to examine individual lines as they come across the pipe. The variable *$_* is an automatic variable that is created when you are working with a pipeline. It is used to enable you to work with a specific item when it is located on the pipeline. In VBScript, you used the *If...Then...End If* construction. In Windows PowerShell, you use an *If(...){...}* construction. The two serve the same purpose, however—decision making. In VBScript, the condition that is evaluated goes between the *If* and the *Then* statement. In Windows PowerShell, the condition that is evaluated goes between parentheses. In VBScript, the action that is taken when a condition is matched goes between the *Then* and the *End If* statements. In Windows PowerShell, the action that is matched goes between a pair of braces.

In VBScipt, you used the *Instr* function to look inside the sentence to see whether a match could be found. In Windows PowerShell, you use the *–match* operator. In VBScript, you use the *Wscript.Echo* command to display the matching sentence to the screen, and in Windows PowerShell, you only need to call the *$_* variable and it is displayed automatically.

Of course, you do not have to use the Get-Content cmdlet if you do not want to, because Windows PowerShell has a cmdlet called Select-String, which will look inside a text file and retrieve the matching lines of text. The three lines of code seen earlier can therefore be shortened to this one-line command.

```
PS C:\> Select-String -Path C:\fso\TestFile.txt -Pattern "text"
```

The results of this command are shown in Figure 13-10.

```
PS C:\> Select-String -Path C:\fso\TestFile.txt -Pattern "text"

fso\TestFile.txt:2:It contains text that we can use.
fso\TestFile.txt:3:It does not have a lot of text in it.

PS C:\> _
```

FIGURE 13-10 The Select-String cmdlet reads a file and searches content at the same time.

DIRECT FROM THE SOURCE

Command Output

James O'Neill, Evangelist
Developer and Platform Group

Something that takes some getting used to in Windows PowerShell is that anything that PowerShell generates is treated as output (and the possible input to a later command in a pipeline) unless you explicitly say you want to do something else with it. Thus, you never need to use an echo, print, or write command. Windows PowerShell does have commands to do these things, although many of them are redundant. Write-Host is useful to force something to go to the console without being redirected. In other words, an external command like TaskList.exe generates text and sends it to standard output as part of the command. A cmdlet like Get-Process returns .NET process objects. Windows PowerShell loads formatting information from PS1XML files, and when it has no other instructions, it checks to see whether there is known formatting to apply to the object and uses that to send output to standard output. Sometimes that standard formatting won't work, and you want to apply your own formatting. Windows PowerShell can output objects to comma-separated variable (CSV) files or convert them to HTML tables, which can save a lot of programming effort, but the most commonly used commands are Format-List and Format-Table.

One of the things that you will really like to do with Windows PowerShell is to use the formatting cmdlets. There are three formatting cmdlets that are especially helpful. They are listed here, in the reverse order in which you will use them:

- Format-Wide
- Format-Table
- Format-List

Consider the Format-Wide cmdlet. Format-Wide is useful when you want to display a single property across multiple columns. This might happen because you want to have a list of all process names that are currently running on the workstation. Such a command would resemble the following.

```
PS C:\> Get-Process | Format-Wide -Property name -AutoSize
```

The first thing you do is use the Get-Process cmdlet to return all the processes that are running on the computer. You next pipe the process objects to the Format-Wide cmdlet. You use the *–property* parameter to select the name of each process, and you use the *–autosize* parameter to tell Format-Wide to use as many columns as possible in the Windows PowerShell console without truncating any of the process names. You can see the results of this command in Figure 13-11.

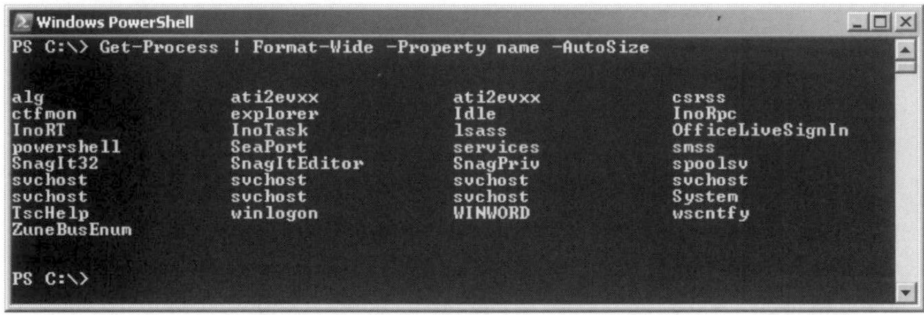

FIGURE 13-11 The Format-Wide cmdlet displays a single property.

If you are interested in displaying between two and four properties from the processes, you can use the Format-Table cmdlet. The command might resemble the following.

```
PS C:\> Get-Process | Format-Table -Property Name, Path, Id -AutoSize
```

You first use the Get-Process cmdlet and then you pipeline the process objects to the Format-Table cmdlet. You select three properties from the process objects: *name, path,* and *Id.* The Format-Table cmdlet also has an *–autosize* parameter exactly as the Format-Wide cmdlet does. This helps to arrange the columns in such a way that you do not waste space inside the console. As shown in Figure 13-12, because of the length of some paths to process executables, the *–autosize* parameter had no effect in this example, and the ID column was removed. As a best practice, you always should include the parameter when you are unsure what the output will actually resemble.

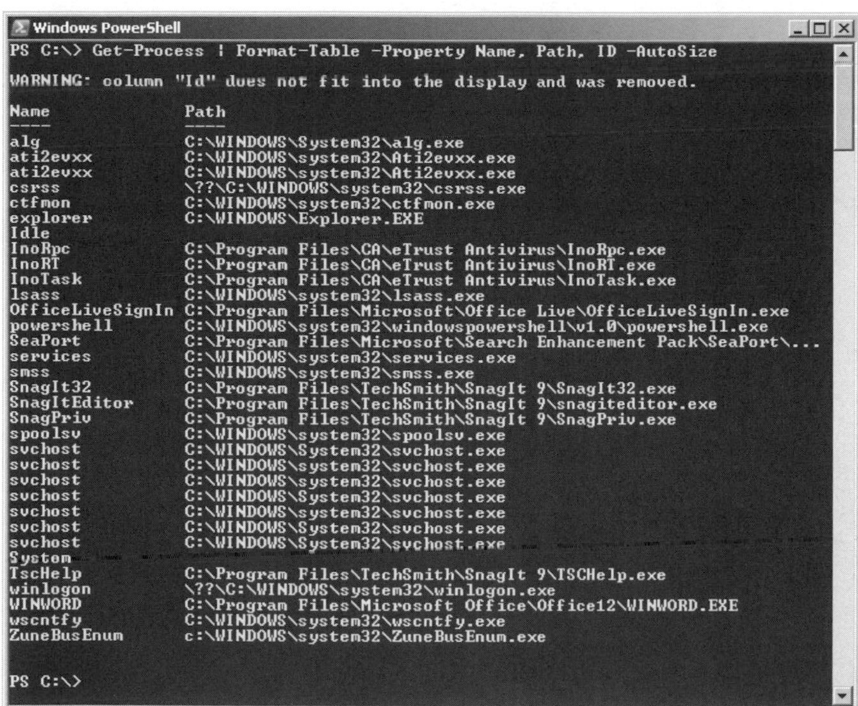

Windows PowerShell
PS C:\> Get-Process | Format-Table -Property Name, Path, ID -AutoSize
WARNING: column "Id" does not fit into the display and was removed.
Name Path
---- ----
alg C:\WINDOWS\System32\alg.exe
ati2evxx C:\WINDOWS\system32\Ati2evxx.exe
ati2evxx C:\WINDOWS\system32\Ati2evxx.exe
csrss \??\C:\WINDOWS\system32\csrss.exe
ctfmon C:\WINDOWS\system32\ctfmon.exe
explorer C:\WINDOWS\Explorer.EXE
Idle
InoRpc C:\Program Files\CA\eTrust Antivirus\InoRpc.exe
InoRT C:\Program Files\CA\eTrust Antivirus\InoRT.exe
InoTask C:\Program Files\CA\eTrust Antivirus\InoTask.exe
lsass C:\WINDOWS\system32\lsass.exe
OfficeLiveSignIn C:\Program Files\Microsoft\Office Live\OfficeLiveSignIn.exe
powershell C:\WINDOWS\system32\windowspowershell\v1.0\powershell.exe
SeaPort C:\Program Files\Microsoft\Search Enhancement Pack\SeaPort\...
services C:\WINDOWS\system32\services.exe
smss C:\WINDOWS\system32\smss.exe
SnagIt32 C:\Program Files\TechSmith\SnagIt 9\SnagIt32.exe
SnagItEditor C:\Program Files\TechSmith\SnagIt 9\snagiteditor.exe
SnagPriv C:\Program Files\TechSmith\SnagIt 9\SnagPriv.exe
spoolsv C:\WINDOWS\system32\spoolsv.exe
svchost C:\WINDOWS\System32\svchost.exe
svchost C:\WINDOWS\system32\svchost.exe
svchost C:\WINDOWS\system32\svchost.exe
svchost C:\WINDOWS\System32\svchost.exe
svchost C:\WINDOWS\system32\svchost.exe
svchost C:\WINDOWS\System32\svchost.exe
svchost C:\WINDOWS\System32\svchost.exe
System
TscHelp C:\Program Files\TechSmith\SnagIt 9\TSCHelp.exe
winlogon \??\C:\WINDOWS\system32\winlogon.exe
WINWORD C:\Program Files\Microsoft Office\Office12\WINWORD.EXE
wscntfy C:\WINDOWS\system32\wscntfy.exe
ZuneBusEnum c:\WINDOWS\system32\ZuneBusEnum.exe
PS C:\>

FIGURE 13-12 The Format-Table cmdlet makes it easy to create tables.

The format cmdlet that you will use the most is Format-List, because it is the best way to display lots of information. It is also a good way to see what kind of data might be returned by a particular command. Armed with this information, you then determine whether you want to focus on a more select group of properties and perhaps output the data as a table or just leave it in a list. When you use the Format-List cmdlet, you will usually use the wildcard * to select all the properties from the objects. Here is an example of obtaining all the property information from all your processes.

```
PS C:\> Get-Process | Format-List -Property *
```

This command displays information that scrolls off the display. A small sampling of the information is shown in Figure 13-13.

```
PS C:\> Get-Process | Format-List -Property *

__NounName                 : Process
Name                       : alg
Handles                    : 104
VM                         : 33849344
WS                         : 3616768
PM                         : 1171456
NPM                        : 5328
Path                       : C:\WINDOWS\System32\alg.exe
Company                    : Microsoft Corporation
CPU                        : 0.03125
FileVersion                : 5.1.2600.5512 (xpsp.080413-0852)
ProductVersion             : 5.1.2600.5512
Description                : Application Layer Gateway Service
Product                    : Microsoftr Windowsr Operating System
Id                         : 328
PriorityClass              : Normal
HandleCount                : 104
WorkingSet                 : 3616768
PagedMemorySize            : 1171456
PrivateMemorySize          : 1171456
VirtualMemorySize          : 33849344
TotalProcessorTime         : 00:00:00.0312500
BasePriority               : 8
ExitCode                   :
HasExited                  : False
ExitTime                   :
Handle                     : 660
MachineName                : .
MainWindowHandle           : 0
MainWindowTitle            :
MainModule                 : System.Diagnostics.ProcessModule (alg.exe)
MaxWorkingSet              : 1413120
MinWorkingSet              : 204800
Modules                    : {alg.exe, ntdll.dll, kernel32.dll, msvcrt.dll...}
NonpagedSystemMemorySize   : 5328
NonpagedSystemMemorySize64 : 5328
PagedMemorySize64          : 1171456
PagedSystemMemorySize      : 36148
PagedSystemMemorySize64    : 36148
PeakPagedMemorySize        : 1196032
PeakPagedMemorySize64      : 1196032
```

FIGURE 13-13 The Get-Process cmdlet displays process information.

There is so much information that all the properties and their values for a single process will not fit on a single screen. When you work with the Format-List cmdlet, if you want to look through all the data, you can pipeline the information to the *more* function. This works in the same manner as the *more* command does in the command shell. If you use shortcut names, or aliases, you have a very compact command at your disposal. As shown here, *gps* is an alias for the Get-Process cmdlet. The *fl* command is an alias for Format-List. Because the first parameter of the Format-List cmdlet is the *–property* parameter, you can leave it out of the command. You then pipeline the results to *more,* which will cause the information to be displayed one page at a time. This command is shown here.

```
PS C:\> gps | fl * | more
```

Additional Pipeline Techniques

The use of the pipeline is a fundamental Windows PowerShell technique. It is, therefore, important to examine different ways to use the pipeline. In this section, you will examine the use of the pipeline to avoid positional errors. You will also see how to use the pipeline to filter result sets and make decisions on the data that crosses the pipeline.

Use the Pipeline to Avoid Positional Errors

If you want to obtain information about the Notepad process (assuming that Notepad is actually running), you use the Get-Process cmdlet, as seen here.

```
Get-Process Notepad
```

You do not have to specify the *name* parameter if you do not want to because the *name* parameter is the default with Get-Process. You can, of course, type the *name* parameter and obtain information about the Notepad process as shown here.

```
PS C:\> Get-Process -name notepad

Handles  NPM(K)    PM(K)      WS(K) VM(M)   CPU(s)     Id ProcessName
-------  ------    -----      ----- -----   ------     -- -----------
     47       2      976       3512    59     0.10   3960 notepad
```

To stop the Notepad process, you use the Stop-Process cmdlet. If, however, you are not used to using the *name* parameter with the Get-Process cmdlet, you will receive a surprise when you try the same syntax with Stop-Process. The result of this is seen here.

```
PS C:\> Stop-Process notepad
Stop-Process : Cannot bind parameter 'Id'. Cannot convert value "notepad" to type
"System.Int32". Error: "Input string was not in a correct format."
At line:1 char:13
+ Stop-Process <<<<  notepad
    + CategoryInfo          : InvalidArgument: (:) [Stop-Process],
ParameterBindingException
    + FullyQualifiedErrorId : CannotConvertArgumentNoMessage,Microsoft.PowerShell.
Commands.StopProcessCommand
```

The reason for the error is that the *name* parameter occupies the first position for the Get-Process cmdlet and the *id* parameter is the first-position parameter for the Stop-Process cmdlet. When you did not use any named parameters, the Stop-Process cmdlet looked for a process with the process ID of *notepad*, which is not an integer, and this caused the error. The *name* parameter is a named parameter in the Stop-Process cmdlet. This means if you want to use the name of a process to stop, you must specify the *name* parameter, as seen here.

```
Stop-Process -name notepad
```

To avoid these kinds of errors, you can always use the parameters (which is a best practice when you write scripts), or you can use the pipeline. The advantage of using the pipeline is that you do not have to worry about all the parameters. You can use Windows PowerShell to find the process that you are interested in and pipeline the results of the first command to the second command that will stop the process, as seen here.

```
Get-Process notepad | Stop-Process
```

A session that starts an instance of Notepad and identifies the Notepad process is seen in Figure 13-14.

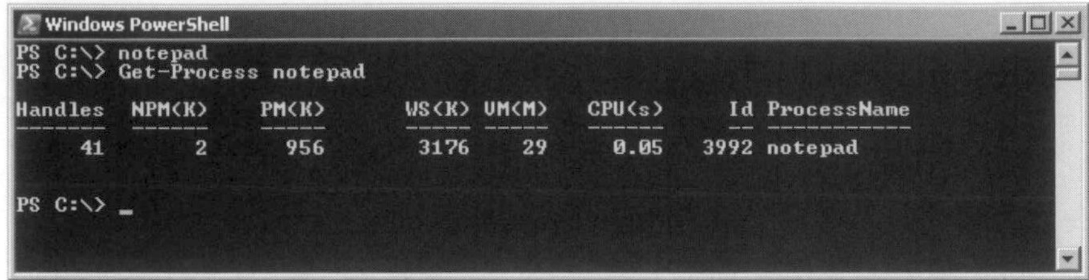

FIGURE 13-14 Using the pipeline simplifies parameter complications.

You can use wildcard characters to identify processes. This technique can be both dangerous and useful. Here is an example of using wildcard characters to simplify finding all the Notepad processes.

```
PS C:\> Get-Process note*

Handles  NPM(K)    PM(K)      WS(K) VM(M)   CPU(s)     Id ProcessName
-------  ------    -----      ----- -----   ------     -- -----------
     47       2      976       3464    59     0.05   2056 notepad
     47       2      976       3488    59     0.09   3292 notepad
```

You can then pipeline the result to the Stop-Process cmdlet and stop all the instances of the Notepad process that are running on the computer, as seen here.

```
Get-Process note* | Stop-Process
```

An example of working with processes by using wildcard characters is seen in Figure 13-15.

```
Windows PowerShell
PS C:\> notepad
PS C:\> notepad
PS C:\> Get-Process note*

Handles  NPM(K)    PM(K)      WS(K) VM(M)   CPU(s)     Id ProcessName
-------  ------    -----      ----- -----   ------     -- -----------
     41       2      956       3164    29     0.05   2412 notepad
     41       2      956       3176    29     0.03   2996 notepad

PS C:\>
```

FIGURE 13-15 By using wildcard characters, it is easy to identify processes.

Using the wildcard characters can be dangerous if you are not careful, however. An example of such a dangerous command is seen in the following code, which would obtain a list of all the processes that are running on the computer and pipeline them to the Stop-Process cmdlet. This will stop every process that is running on the computer, which for most operating systems will cause the computer to shut down (on Windows Vista and later versions, this command must be run by someone with administrative rights).

```
Get-Process * | Stop-Process
```

Of course, if you want to shut down the operating system, it is best to use the shutdown method from the Win32_OperatingSystem WMI class.

Use the Pipeline to Filter Results

Suppose you have several instances of Notepad that are running. One instance has been running for a while and has consumed more CPU time than the other processes. You can obtain this information as seen here.

```
PS C:\> Get-Process notepad

Handles  NPM(K)    PM(K)      WS(K) VM(M)   CPU(s)     Id ProcessName
-------  ------    -----      ----- -----   ------     -- -----------
     47       2      976       3452    59     0.10   2688 notepad
     49       2     1160       3936    60     1.13   3984 notepad
```

Whereas you could definitely use the process ID, 3984 in this example, to stop the process that is using the most CPU time, you may not want to type two separate commands (or perhaps you want to stop a process automatically if it is using too much CPU time). Instead, you can pipeline the results of the first query to the Where-Object cmdlet. You can use *Where*, the alias for Where-Object, to reduce some typing that is required for this command without sacrificing any readability. If you were not worried about readability, you could use *gps* as an alias for the Get-Process cmdlet, and you could use *?* as the alias for the Where-Object.

As you become more proficient with Windows PowerShell, you might decide you like using the aliases for the different cmdlet names. If you are curious about which cmdlets have aliases defined for them, you can use the Get-Alias cmdlet to find aliases. You will need to specify the *–definition* parameter when you use the command. The command to discover aliases for the Get-Process cmdlet is seen here.

```
PS C:\> Get-Alias -Definition Get-Process

CommandType     Name                                                  Definition
-----------     ----                                                  ----------
Alias           gps                                                   Get-Process
Alias           ps                                                    Get-Process
```

The short command is shown here.

```
PS C:\> gps notepad | ? { $_.cpu -gt 1 }

Handles  NPM(K)    PM(K)      WS(K) VM(M)   CPU(s)     Id ProcessName
-------  ------    -----      ----- -----   ------     -- -----------
     47       2     1316       4080    60     1.38   2420 notepad
```

The way you generally type the command is to spell out Get-Process. (You use Tab completion to spell it out. Therefore, you only have to type **Get-P** and then press the Tab key.) The Where-Object cmdlet is used to filter the process objects as they come across the pipeline. Each instance of a process with the name of Notepad is returned by the Get-Process cmdlet. As the process comes across the pipeline, the *$_* automatic variable represents the current process object on the pipeline. This enables you to examine the properties of the process object. Inspect the amount of CPU time that is being used by the process to see whether it exceeds 1. If it does, the filter will enable the process object to continue. The example here displays basic information about the process on the console.

```
PS C:\> Get-Process notepad | Where { $_.cpu -gt 1 }

Handles  NPM(K)    PM(K)      WS(K) VM(M)   CPU(s)     Id ProcessName
-------  ------    -----      ----- -----   ------     -- -----------
     49       2     1160       3936    60     1.13   3984 notepad
```

If you are not sure which properties are available for you to use in the Where-Object filter, you can use the Get-Member cmdlet. If you select the properties, you will eliminate the methods. This command is seen here.

```
PS C:\> Get-Process | Get-Member -MemberType property
```

However, you will also miss the *ScriptProperty* and the *AliasProperty* properties. To make sure that you can find the other properties that were added by the Windows PowerShell team, use a wildcard in front of the *MemberType* property. The *CPU* property is one that was added by the Windows PowerShell team. It is a *ScriptProperty* property, and the code is seen here.

```
PS C:\> Get-Process | Get-Member -MemberType *property

   TypeName: System.Diagnostics.Process

Name                           MemberType     Definition
----                           ----------     ----------
Handles                        AliasProperty  Handles = Handlecount
Name                           AliasProperty  Name = ProcessName
NPM                            AliasProperty  NPM = NonpagedSystemMemorySize
PM                             AliasProperty  PM = PagedMemorySize
VM                             AliasProperty  VM = VirtualMemorySize
WS                             AliasProperty  WS = WorkingSet
__NounName                     NoteProperty   System.String __NounName=Process
BasePriority                   Property       System.Int32 BasePriority {get;}
Container                      Property       System.ComponentModel.IContainer C...
EnableRaisingEvents            Property       System.Boolean EnableRaisingEvents...
ExitCode                       Property       System.Int32 ExitCode {get;}
ExitTime                       Property       System.DateTime ExitTime {get;}
Handle                         Property       System.IntPtr Handle {get;}
HandleCount                    Property       System.Int32 HandleCount {get;}
HasExited                      Property       System.Boolean HasExited {get;}
Id                             Property       System.Int32 Id {get;}
MachineName                    Property       System.String MachineName {get;}
MainModule                     Property       System.Diagnostics.ProcessModule M...
MainWindowHandle               Property       System.IntPtr MainWindowHandle {get;}
MainWindowTitle                Property       System.String MainWindowTitle {get;}
```

```
MaxWorkingSet              Property       System.IntPtr MaxWorkingSet {get;s...
MinWorkingSet              Property       System.IntPtr MinWorkingSet {get;s...
Modules                    Property       System.Diagnostics.ProcessModuleCo...
NonpagedSystemMemorySize   Property       System.Int32 NonpagedSystemMemoryS...
NonpagedSystemMemorySize64 Property       System.Int64 NonpagedSystemMemoryS...
PagedMemorySize            Property       System.Int32 PagedMemorySize {get;}
PagedMemorySize64          Property       System.Int64 PagedMemorySize64 {get;}
PagedSystemMemorySize      Property       System.Int32 PagedSystemMemorySize...
PagedSystemMemorySize64    Property       System.Int64 PagedSystemMemorySize...
PeakPagedMemorySize        Property       System.Int32 PeakPagedMemorySize {...
PeakPagedMemorySize64      Property       System.Int64 PeakPagedMemorySize64...
PeakVirtualMemorySize      Property       System.Int32 PeakVirtualMemorySize...
PeakVirtualMemorySize64    Property       System.Int64 PeakVirtualMemorySize...
PeakWorkingSet             Property       System.Int32 PeakWorkingSet {get;}
PeakWorkingSet64           Property       System.Int64 PeakWorkingSet64 {get;}
PriorityBoostEnabled       Property       System.Boolean PriorityBoostEnable...
PriorityClass              Property       System.Diagnostics.ProcessPriority...
PrivateMemorySize          Property       System.Int32 PrivateMemorySize {get;}
PrivateMemorySize64        Property       System.Int64 PrivateMemorySize64 {...
PrivilegedProcessorTime    Property       System.TimeSpan PrivilegedProcesso...
ProcessName                Property       System.String ProcessName {get;}
ProcessorAffinity          Property       System.IntPtr ProcessorAffinity {g...
Responding                 Property       System.Boolean Responding {get;}
SessionId                  Property       System.Int32 SessionId {get;}
Site                       Property       System.ComponentModel.ISite Site {...
StandardError              Property       System.IO.StreamReader StandardErr...
StandardInput              Property       System.IO.StreamWriter StandardInp...
StandardOutput             Property       System.IO.StreamReader StandardOut...
StartInfo                  Property       System.Diagnostics.ProcessStartInf...
StartTime                  Property       System.DateTime StartTime {get;}
SynchronizingObject        Property       System.ComponentModel.ISynchronize...
Threads                    Property       System.Diagnostics.ProcessThreadCo...
TotalProcessorTime         Property       System.TimeSpan TotalProcessorTime...
UserProcessorTime          Property       System.TimeSpan UserProcessorTime ...
VirtualMemorySize          Property       System.Int32 VirtualMemorySize {get;}
VirtualMemorySize64        Property       System.Int64 VirtualMemorySize64 {...
WorkingSet                 Property       System.Int32 WorkingSet {get;}
WorkingSet64               Property       System.Int64 WorkingSet64 {get;}
Company                    ScriptProperty System.Object Company {get=$this.M...
CPU                        ScriptProperty System.Object CPU {get=$this.Total...
Description                ScriptProperty System.Object Description {get=$th...
FileVersion                ScriptProperty System.Object FileVersion {get=$th...
Path                       ScriptProperty System.Object Path {get=$this.Main...
Product                    ScriptProperty System.Object Product {get=$this.M...
ProductVersion             ScriptProperty System.Object ProductVersion {get=...
```

Use the Pipeline to Take Action

As soon as you have the filter working correctly and see that it is returning the results you are interested in obtaining, you can just pipeline the resulting process object to the Stop-Process cmdlet. This action is shown here.

```
PS C:\> Get-Process notepad | Where { $_.cpu -gt 1 } | Stop-Process
```

The ability to add pipelines together by feeding the results of one pipeline into another pipeline, as shown earlier, is how you harness the real power of Windows PowerShell. This is a new concept for people who have a background working with graphical user interface (GUI) tools, but it is something that people have done for years at the command line. The big difference for them is that Windows PowerShell passes objects through the pipeline, not merely text.

Working with Cmdlets

One of the exciting benefits of using Windows PowerShell and learning how to use the built-in cmdlets is that it frees you from worrying about all the details. You may know that Windows PowerShell is built on the Microsoft .NET Framework, but you do not have to worry about .NET Framework programming. If you are interested in working with files and folders, you can use cmdlets to provide this functionality. You therefore avoid writing .NET Framework code.

Filtering Cmdlet Output

If you want to produce a listing of all the folders and the date when each folder was modified, you could use the *FileSystemObject* and write a VBScript that is similar to the ListFoldersAndModifiedDates.vbs script. You will notice that you first create an instance of the *FileSystemObject* and store it in the *objFSO* variable. You then return a folder object by using the *GetFolder* method to connect to the root of the C drive. Next, you return a folder collection by calling the *SubFolders* method. You then walk through the collection by using the *For...Each ...Next* statement and display both the name of the folder and the date the folder was changed. The ListFoldersAndModifiedDates.vbs script is seen here.

ListFoldersAndModifiedDates.vbs

```
Set objFSO = CreateObject("Scripting.FileSystemObject")
Set objFolder = objFSO.GetFolder("C:\")
Set colFOlders = objFolder.SubFolders
For Each subFolder In colFOlders
  WScript.Echo subFolder.Name, subFolder.DateLastModified
Next
```

In Windows PowerShell, you can obtain a collection of files and folders by using the Get-ChildItem cmdlet. When you use the Get-ChildItem cmdlet without supplying any values for the parameters, it returns a list of all the files and folders in the root directory. This is seen in Figure 13-16.

```
Windows PowerShell
PS C:\> Get-ChildItem

    Directory: Microsoft.PowerShell.Core\FileSystem::C:\

Mode                LastWriteTime     Length Name
----                -------------     ------ ----
d----         8/17/2008   1:23 PM            19287a2cfb60a3bbcca7
d----          5/8/2009   5:16 PM            AutoDoc
d----        12/12/2008   1:22 PM            BU
d----          5/9/2009  12:50 PM            data
d----         2/18/2009  11:20 AM            Documents and Settings
d----          5/8/2009   2:08 AM            fso
d-r--          3/9/2009   5:21 PM            fso1
d----         2/22/2009   2:50 PM            InstallLatestPSH
d----         8/23/2008   8:04 PM            mesh
d-r--         4/23/2009   8:32 PM            Program Files
d----        11/19/2008  10:57 AM            test
d----          5/1/2009   9:15 AM            vm
d----         1/13/2009   1:18 AM            win2008_r2_Beta1
d----          5/1/2009   5:09 AM            win7
d----          5/6/2009   6:19 PM            WINDOWS
-a---         4/28/2009  12:02 PM          0 AdobeDebug.txt
-a---         8/15/2008   3:36 PM          0 AUTOEXEC.BAT
-a---         8/15/2008   3:36 PM          0 CONFIG.SYS
-a---        12/16/2008  10:33 AM      90624 GetSet-ieStartPage.doc
-a---        12/16/2008  10:33 AM      90624 GetSetieStartPage.doc
-a---        10/14/2003  12:24 PM      23192 tweakomatic.hta
-a---        10/15/2003   8:31 AM     380928 tweakomatic.mdb
-a---        10/24/2003  12:03 PM     232448 tweakomatic_readme.doc

PS C:\>
```

FIGURE 13-16 The Get-ChildItem cmdlet returns a directory listing of the root drive when you use it without parameters.

To return a listing of only directories, you have to determine a way to separate the directories from the files that are returned by the default use of the Get-ChildItem cmdlet. There are actually several ways to do this, but they all involve pipelining the results of the Get-ChildItem cmdlet to the Where-Object cmdlet. Most of the time, you can examine the column headings in the display results to find a property that you can use with the Where-Object cmdlet to create a filter for your command. The default column headings used with the Get-ChildItem cmdlet are Mode, LastWriteTime, Length, and Name. Of the four, the Mode column will be of the most use, because it has a *d* in the first position if the item is a directory. You use the Get-ChildItem cmdlet to retrieve the file and folder objects from the root drive. Then you pipeline the objects to the Where-Object cmdlet. Inside the script block (which is delineated by a pair of braces) for the Where-Object cmdlet, you use the *$_* automatic variable to examine each object as it comes across the pipeline. The property that you are interested in is the *mode* property. You use the *–like* operator to perform a wildcard match of any value that begins with the letter *d* and is followed by any other value. The command to list directories on the root drive is seen here.

```
PS C:\> Get-ChildItem | Where-Object { $_.mode -like 'd*' }
```

The results of the list directory command are seen in Figure 13-17.

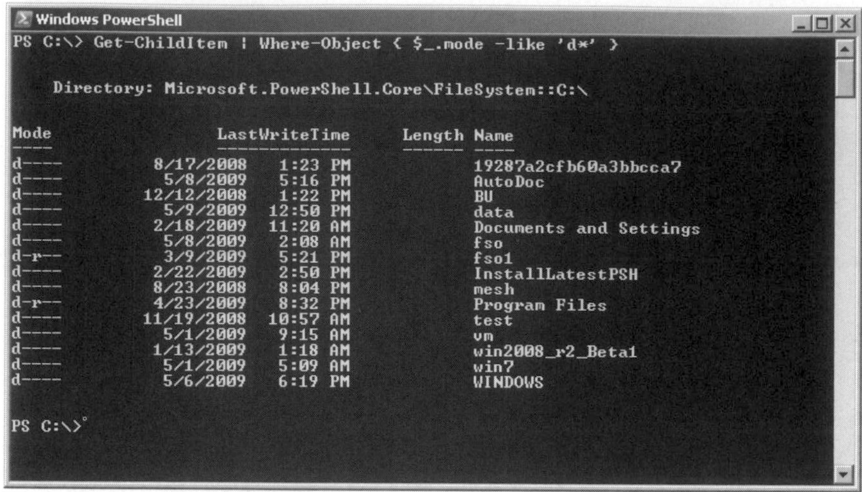

FIGURE 13-17 By using wildcard characters, you can separate directories from files.

If you want to replicate the output from the ListFoldersAndModifiedDates.vbs script exactly, you have to pass the results further down the pipeline so that you can reduce the information that is returned. You can use the Select-Object cmdlet to choose only the *name* and the *LastWriteTime* properties. When you use the Select-Object cmdlet to select certain properties, the object that is returned is a custom object that contains only the properties that you select and the methods that are common to all Windows PowerShell objects. By piping the output of Select-Object into the Get-Member cmdlet, the members of the newly created custom object are shown here.

```
   TypeName: System.Management.Automation.PSCustomObject

Name         MemberType   Definition
----         ----------   ----------
Equals       Method       System.Boolean Equals(Object obj)
GetHashCode  Method       System.Int32 GetHashCode()
GetType      Method       System.Type GetType()
ToString     Method       System.String ToString()
LastWriteTime NoteProperty System.DateTime LastWriteTime=8/17/2008 1:23:10 PM
Name         NoteProperty System.String Name=19287a2cfb60a3bbcca7
```

Understanding Cmdlet Output Objects

It is important to understand the object that is returned by a cmdlet so that you can perform additional processing on the object if you want to do so. The Get-ChildItem command, which lists the name and last write time of all the directories on the root drive, is shown here. This code is a single command that is broken at the pipeline character for readability.

```
PS C:\> Get-ChildItem | Where-Object { $_.mode -like 'd*' } |
Select-Object -Property Name, LastWriteTime
```

The results of the Get-ChildItem command are shown in Figure 13-18.

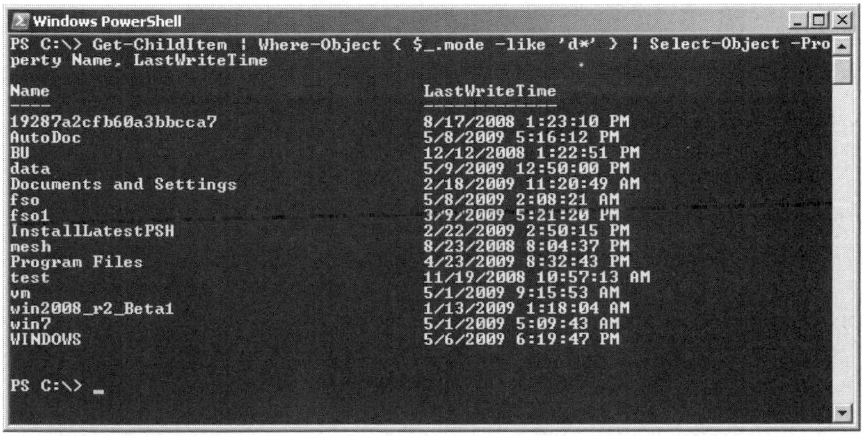

```
Windows PowerShell
PS C:\> Get-ChildItem | Where-Object { $_.mode -like 'd*' } | Select-Object -Pro
perty Name, LastWriteTime

Name                                    LastWriteTime
----                                    -------------
19287a2cfb60a3bbcca7                    8/17/2008 1:23:10 PM
AutoDoc                                 5/8/2009 5:16:12 PM
BU                                      12/12/2008 1:22:51 PM
data                                    5/9/2009 12:50:00 PM
Documents and Settings                  2/18/2009 11:20:49 AM
fso                                     5/8/2009 2:08:21 AM
fso1                                    3/9/2009 5:21:20 PM
InstallLatestPSH                        2/22/2009 2:50:15 PM
mesh                                    8/23/2008 8:04:37 PM
Program Files                           4/23/2009 8:32:43 PM
test                                    11/19/2008 10:57:13 AM
vm                                      5/1/2009 9:15:53 AM
win2008_r2_Beta1                        1/13/2009 1:18:04 AM
win7                                    5/1/2009 5:09:43 AM
WINDOWS                                 5/6/2009 6:19:47 PM

PS C:\> _
```

FIGURE 13-18 You can reduce the information returned from a command by using the Select-Object cmdlet.

You can reduce the typing without sacrificing any of the readability of the command by using *dir* as the alias for Get-ChildItem, *Where* as the alias for Where-Object, and *Select* as the alias for Select-Object. You can also omit the *–property* parameter, because it is the default parameter for the Select-Object cmdlet. The revised command is shown here.

```
PS C:\> dir | where { $_.mode -like 'd*'} | select name, lastwritetime
```

Another way to produce a listing of the name and the last write time of each directory in the root directory is to send the output to the Format-Table cmdlet, as illustrated here.

```
PS C:\> Get-ChildItem | Where-Object { $_.mode -like 'd*' } |

Format-Table -Property Name, LastWriteTime
```

The output produced by using the Format-Table cmdlet is almost the same as the output produced by using the Select-Object cmdlet. This is seen in Figure 13-19.

```
PS C:\> Get-ChildItem | Where-Object { $_.mode -like 'd*' } | Format-table -Prop
erty Name, LastWriteTime

Name                                        LastWriteTime
----                                        -------------
19287a2cfb60a3bbcca7                        8/17/2008 1:23:10 PM
AutoDoc                                     5/8/2009 5:16:12 PM
BU                                          12/12/2008 1:22:51 PM
data                                        5/9/2009 12:50:00 PM
Documents and Settings                      2/18/2009 11:20:49 AM
fso                                         5/8/2009 2:08:21 AM
fso1                                        3/9/2009 5:21:20 PM
InstallLatestPSH                            2/22/2009 2:50:15 PM
mesh                                        8/23/2008 8:04:37 PM
Program Files                               4/23/2009 8:32:43 PM
test                                        11/19/2008 10:57:13 AM
vm                                          5/1/2009 9:15:53 AM
win2008_r2_Beta1                            1/13/2009 1:18:04 AM
win7                                        5/1/2009 5:09:43 AM
WINDOWS                                     5/6/2009 6:19:47 PM

PS C:\> _
```

FIGURE 13-19 By using the Format-Table cmdlet, you can create almost the same results as the output produced by the Select-Object cmdlet.

The problem with using Format-Table to format your output is that if you have to do anything else to the data, you are left with a series of five different format objects that are basically useless for additional data manipulation. Depending on what you are trying to achieve, even the custom Windows PowerShell object that is created by the Select-Object cmdlet will cause you problems. As a best practice, you should always perform all data manipulation before sending your object to an output cmdlet.

At this point, you have one last thing that you can do easily in your pipeline—send the output to a text file. The easiest way to do this is to use the >> redirection operator as shown here (once again, the single command is broken at the pipeline character for readability).

```
PS C:\> Get-ChildItem | Where-Object { $_.mode -like 'd*' } |
Format-Table -Property Name, LastWriteTime >> c:\fso\directoryFile.txt
```

The text file that is produced by the redirection operator maintains the format that is displayed on the console. This is seen in Figure 13-20.

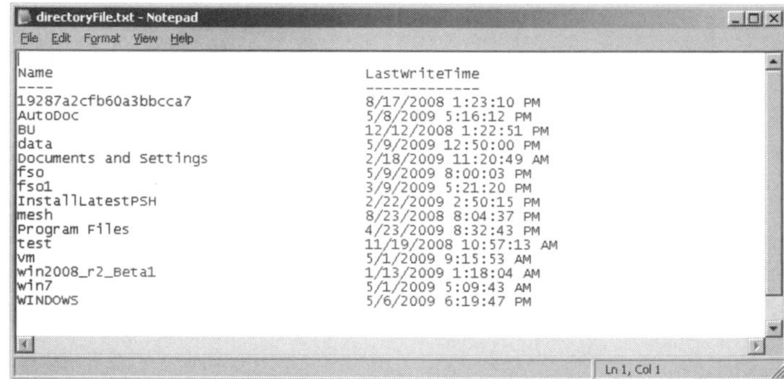

```
Name                                        LastWriteTime
----                                        -------------
19287a2cfb60a3bbcca7                        8/17/2008 1:23:10 PM
AutoDoc                                     5/8/2009 5:16:12 PM
BU                                          12/12/2008 1:22:51 PM
data                                        5/9/2009 12:50:00 PM
Documents and Settings                      2/18/2009 11:20:49 AM
fso                                         5/9/2009 8:00:03 PM
fso1                                        3/9/2009 5:21:20 PM
InstallLatestPSH                            2/22/2009 2:50:15 PM
mesh                                        8/23/2008 8:04:37 PM
Program Files                               4/23/2009 8:32:43 PM
test                                        11/19/2008 10:57:13 AM
vm                                          5/1/2009 9:15:53 AM
win2008_r2_Beta1                            1/13/2009 1:18:04 AM
win7                                        5/1/2009 5:09:43 AM
WINDOWS                                     5/6/2009 6:19:47 PM
```

FIGURE 13-20 The redirection operator maintains formatting seen on the Windows PowerShell console.

This concludes our overview of using Windows PowerShell to simplify working with directories and files.

Scripting Fundamentals

In its most basic form, a Windows PowerShell script is a collection of Windows PowerShell commands, such as the following.

```
Get-Process notepad | Stop-Process
```

You can put that command into a Windows PowerShell script and run it directly as it is written. The StopNotepad.ps1 script is shown in Figure 13-21.

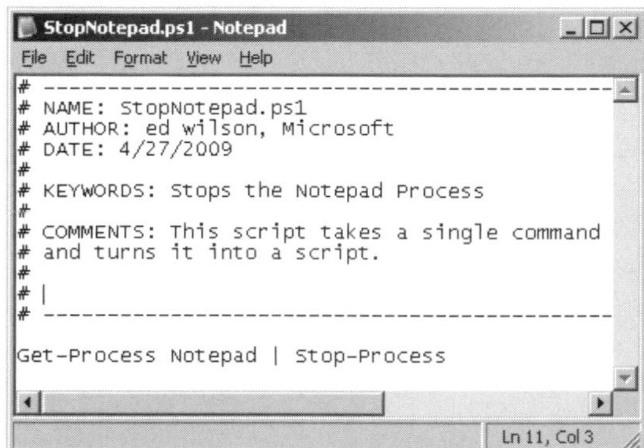

FIGURE 13-21 StopNotepad.ps1 script seen in Notepad

To create a Windows PowerShell script, you only have to copy the command in a text file and save the file by using a .ps1 extension. If you double-click the file, it will open with the graphical version of Windows PowerShell. The graphical version of Windows PowerShell is called Windows PowerShell ISE.

Running Windows PowerShell Scripts

To run the script, if you are running Windows XP or Windows Server 2003, you can open the Windows PowerShell console and drag the file to the console. In Windows Vista, the capability of dragging to a command line was removed due to potential security implications. To replace it, Windows Vista introduced a very helpful command that you can use instead: the Copy As Path command. You hold down the Shift key, right-click the PS1 file, and select Copy As Path from the action menu shown in Figure 13-22.

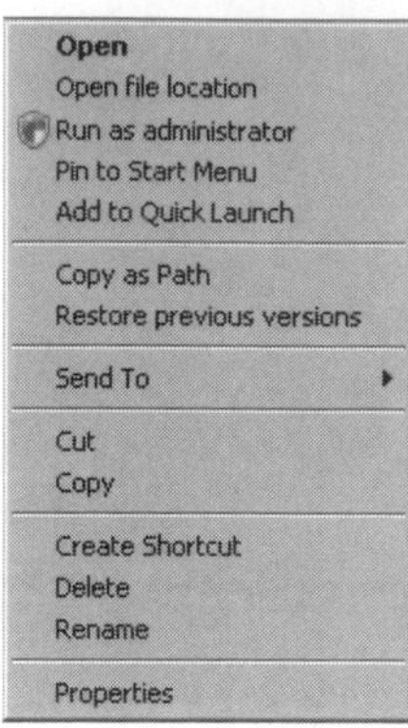

FIGURE 13-22 Windows Vista introduced the Copy As Path command to simplify working with long paths inside the Windows PowerShell console.

Windows 7 has fixed dragging and dropping to the console, and it keeps the Copy As Path action as well, giving you the best of both worlds. Now you are ready to run your first script. To do this, copy the path of the script, right-click inside the Windows PowerShell console to paste the path of your script there, and press Enter. You just printed out a string that represents the path of the script as seen here.

```
PS C:\> "C:\BestPracticesBook\StopNotepad.ps1"
C:\BestPracticesBook\StopNotepad.ps1
```

DIRECT FROM THE SOURCE

Expressions and Paths

James O'Neill, Evangelist
Developer and Platform Group

Windows PowerShell can execute commands and evaluate "expressions." For example, 2 + 2 is an expression, and so is *$Host* (the value of the variable named host). "Hello world" is a common example of an expression, and 1..100 (numbers from 1 to 100) is also an expression. If you enter an expression in Windows PowerShell, PowerShell will work out its value and pass it on—so an expression on its own just generates output to the console, but it can be piped into a command. This poses a problem when you try to execute something like "C:\Program Files (x86)\Internet Explorer\iexplore.exe". Without the quotation marks, Windows PowerShell uses the spaces to break up the path and understand it; with the quotation marks, PowerShell thinks it is a string constant. To tell Windows PowerShell to execute a string as a command, prefix it with an ampersand (&).

In Windows PowerShell, when you want to print a string in the console, you put it in quotation marks. You do not have to use Wscript.Echo or similar commands, as you had to do in VBScript. It is easier and simpler to print a string in Windows PowerShell, but it can be difficult to become accustomed to doing so. If you display a string, remove the quotation marks and press Enter. This time, you receive a real error message. "What now?" you may ask. The error message, seen in Figure 13-23, is related to the script execution policy that disallows the running of scripts.

```
Administrator: Windows PowerShell
PS C:\> "C:\BestPracticesBook\StopNotepad.ps1"
C:\BestPracticesBook\StopNotepad.ps1
PS C:\> C:\BestPracticesBook\StopNotepad.ps1
File C:\BestPracticesBook\StopNotepad.ps1 cannot be loaded because the executio
n of scripts is disabled on this system. Please see "get-help about_signing" fo
r more details.
At line:1 char:37
+ C:\BestPracticesBook\StopNotepad.ps1 <<<<
    + CategoryInfo          : NotSpecified: (:) [], PSSecurityException
    + FullyQualifiedErrorId : RuntimeException

PS C:\>
```

FIGURE 13-23 By default, an attempt to run a Windows PowerShell script generates an error message.

Enabling Windows PowerShell Scripting Support

By default, support for running Windows PowerShell scripts is disallowed. Script support can be controlled by using Group Policy, but if it is not and if you have administrator rights on your computer, you can use the Set-ExecutionPolicy Windows PowerShell cmdlet to turn on script support. There are four levels that can be enabled by using the Set-ExecutionPolicy cmdlet:

- **Restricted** Does not load configuration files or run scripts. Restricted is the default setting.
- **AllSigned** Requires that all scripts and configuration files be signed by a trusted publisher, including scripts that you write on the local computer.
- **RemoteSigned** Requires that all scripts and configuration files downloaded from the Internet be signed by a trusted publisher.
- **Unrestricted** Loads all configuration files and runs all scripts. If you run an unsigned script that is downloaded from the Internet, you are prompted for permission before it runs.

In Windows PowerShell 2.0, two additional levels are available:

- **Bypass** Nothing is blocked, and there are no warnings or prompts.
- **Undefined** Removes the currently assigned execution policy from the current scope. This parameter will not remove an execution policy that is set in a Group Policy scope.

With so many choices for a script execution policy available to you, you may be wondering which one is appropriate for you. The Windows PowerShell team recommends the RemoteSigned setting, stating that it is "appropriate for most circumstances." Remember that, even though descriptions of the various policy settings use the term *Internet,* this may not always refer to the World Wide Web or even to locations outside your own firewall because Windows PowerShell obtains its script origin information by using the Windows Internet Explorer zone settings. This basically means that anything that comes from a computer other than your own is in the Internet zone. You can change the Internet Explorer zone settings by using Internet Explorer, the registry, or Group Policy.

DIRECT FROM THE SOURCE

Execution Policy

James O'Neill, Evangelist
Developer and Platform Group

The Windows PowerShell execution policy is governed by a registry entry that you set directly, bypassing the command. Whether it is set through Windows PowerShell itself or by going to the registry, changing this entry requires administrator access. Alternatively, there is an Administrative Template (ADM) file available for download that allows you to set the policy centrally using Group Policy instead of on a machine-by-machine basis. Note that unlike batch files, Windows PowerShell scripts are not run automatically by double-clicking them in Windows Explorer, and scripts that you download will be flagged as such unless you remove the flag.

When you use the Set-ExecutionPolicy cmdlet to change the script execution policy in Windows PowerShell 1.0, the change occurs silently and without incident. In Windows PowerShell 2.0, the behavior now requires confirmation of the command. This is seen in Figure 13-24.

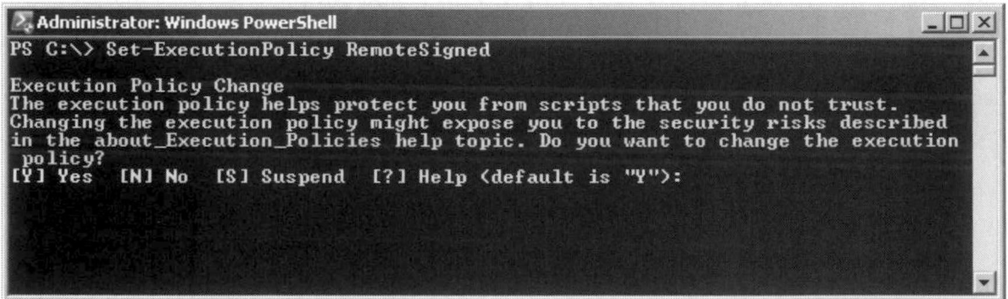

FIGURE 13-24 In Windows PowerShell 2.0, the Set-ExecutionPolicy cmdlet requires confirmation.

If you do not want to see the confirmation message when you change the script execution policy in Windows PowerShell 2.0, use the *–force* parameter to make the behavior the same as it was in Windows PowerShell 1.0. Unfortunately, Windows PowerShell 1.0 does not have a *–force* parameter for the Set-ExecutionPolicy cmdlet, so attempts to use this parameter will fail. A batch file command that will change the script execution policy on Windows PowerShell 2.0 is seen in the following code.

```
ChangeScriptExecutionPolicyPs2.bat
REM ChangeExecutionPolicyPs2.bat
REM Ed Wilson, 4/27/2009
REM Sets the script execution policy to remotesigned. Other values:
REM AllSigned, Restricted, Unrestricted, ByPass
cls
Powershell -noexit -command "& {Set-ExecutionPolicy remotesigned -Force}"
```

To perform the same command in Windows PowerShell 1.0, you remove the *–force* parameter. The rest of the batch file can remain the same, as seen here.

```
ChangeExecutionPolicyPs1.bat
REM ChangeExecutionPolicyPs1.bat
REM Ed Wilson, 4/27/2009
REM Sets the script execution policy to remotesigned. Other values:
REM AllSigned, Restricted, Unrestricted
cls
Powershell -noexit -command "& {Set-ExecutionPolicy remotesigned}"
```

Transitioning from the Command Line to Script

Now that you have everything set up to enable script execution, you can run your StopNotepad.ps1 script. This is seen here.

```
StopNotepad.ps1
Get-Process Notepad | Stop-Process
```

If an instance of the Notepad process is running, everything is successful. If not, the error seen here is generated.

```
Get-Process : Cannot find a process with the name 'Notepad'. Verify the process
 name and call the cmdlet again.
At C:\Documents and Settings\ed\Local Settings\Temp\tmp1DB.tmp.ps1:14 char:12
+ Get-Process  <<<< Notepad | Stop-Process
```

When using Windows PowerShell, you should get in the habit of reading the error messages. The first part of the error message gives a description of the problem. In this example, it could not find a process with the name of Notepad. The second part of the error message shows the position in the code where the error occurred. This is known as the position message. The first line of the position message states the error occurred on line 14. The second portion has a series of arrows that point to the command that failed. The Get-Process cmdlet command is the one that failed, as shown here.

```
At C:\Documents and Settings\ed\Local Settings\Temp\tmp1DB.tmp.ps1:14 char:12
+ Get-Process  <<<< Notepad | Stop-Process
```

The easiest way to eliminate this error message is to use the *–erroraction* parameter and specify the *SilentlyContinue* value. This is basically the same as using the *On Error Resume Next* command in VBScript. The really useful feature of the *–erroraction* parameter is that it can be specified on a cmdlet-by-cmdlet basis. In addition, there are four values that can be used:

- *Continue* (the default value)
- *SilentlyContinue*
- *Inquire*
- *Stop*

In the StopNotepadSilentlyContinue.ps1 script, you add the *–erroraction* parameter to the Get-Process cmdlet to skip any error that may arise if the Notepad process does not exist. To make the script easier to read, break the code at the pipeline character. Windows PowerShell will allow you to split a command over multiple lines if the line appears to be incomplete, including the pipeline character on the first line *ensures* that the line *is* incomplete, but it is not a line continuation character. The backtick (`) character, also known as the grave character, is used when a line of code is too long and must be broken into two physical lines of code, but the position of the break makes the first part a valid command to Windows PowerShell. The main thing to be aware of is that the two physical lines form a single logical line of code. An example of how to use line continuation is seen here.

```
Write-Host -foregroundcolor green "This is a demo " `
         "of the line continuation character"
```

The StopNotepadSilentlyContinue.ps1 script is shown here.

StopNotepadSilentlyContinue.ps1

```
Get-Process -name Notepad -erroraction SilentlyContinue |
Stop-Process
```

Because you are writing a script, you can take advantage of some of the script features. One of the first things you can do is use a variable to hold the name of the process to be stopped. This has the advantage of enabling you to change the script easily to allow for the stopping of processes other than Notepad. All variables begin with the dollar sign (*$*). The line that holds the name of the process in a variable is seen here.

```
$process= "notepad"
```

Another improvement to the script is one that provides information about the process that is stopped. The Stop-Process cmdlet returns no information when it is used. But by using the *–passthru* parameter, the process object is passed along in the pipeline. You use this parameter and pipeline the process object to the ForEach-Object cmdlet. You use the *$_* automatic variable to refer to the current object on the pipeline and select the name and the process ID of the process that is stopped. The concatenation operator in Windows PowerShell is the plus (+) sign, and you use it to display the values of the selected properties in addition to the strings completing your sentence. This line of code is seen here.

```
ForEach-Object { $_.name + ' with process ID: ' +  $_.ID + ' was stopped.'}
```

The complete StopNotepadSilentlyContinuePassThru.ps1 script is seen here.

StopNotepadSilentlyContinuePassThru.ps1

```
$process = "notepad"
Get-Process -name $Process -erroraction SilentlyContinue |
Stop-Process -passthru |
ForEach-Object { $_.name + ' with process ID: ' +  $_.ID + ' was stopped.'}
```

When you run the script with two instances of Notepad running, the following output is seen.

```
notepad with process ID: 2088 was stopped.
notepad with process ID: 2568 was stopped.
```

An additional advantage of the StopNotepadSilentlyContinuePassThru.ps1 script is that you can use it to stop different processes. You can assign multiple process names (an array) to the *$process* variable, and when you run the script, each process will be stopped. In this example, you assign the Notepad and the Calc process to the *$process* variable, as seen here.

```
$process= "notepad", "calc"
```

When you run the script, both processes are stopped, as shown here.

```
calc with process ID: 3428 was stopped.
notepad with process ID: 488 was stopped.
```

You could continue changing your script—you could put the code in a function, write command-line help, and change the script so that it accepts command-line input or even reads a list of processes from a text file. As soon as you move from the command line to a script, such options suddenly become possible.

Using the *while* Statement

In VBScript, you had the *While...Wend* loop. An example of using the *While...Wend* loop is the WhileReadLineWend.vbs script. The first thing you do in the script is create an instance of the *FileSystemObject* and store it in the *objFSO* variable. You then use the *OpenTextFile* method to open a test file and store that object in the *objFile* variable. You then use the *While...Not ...Wend* construction to read one line at a time from the text stream and display it on the screen. You continue to do this until you are at the end of the *TextStream* object. A *While ... Wend* loop continues to operate as long as a condition is evaluated as true. In this example, as long as you are not at the end of the stream, you will continue to read the line from the text file. The WhileReadLineWend.vbs script is shown here.

WhileReadLineWend.vbs

```
Set objFSO = CreateObject("Scripting.FileSystemObject")
Set objFile = objFSO.OpenTextFile("C:\fso\testfile.txt")

While Not objFile.AtEndOfStream
 WScript.Echo objFile.ReadLine
Wend
```

Constructing the *while* Statement

As you probably already guessed, you have the same kind of construction available to you in Windows PowerShell. The *while* statement in Windows PowerShell is used in the same way that the *While...Wend* statement is used in VBScript. In the DemoWhileLessThan.ps1 script, you first initialize the variable *$i* to be equal to 0. You then use the *while* keyword to begin the *while* loop. In Windows PowerShell, you must include the condition that will be evaluated inside a set of parentheses. For this example, you determine the value of the *$i* variable with each pass through the loop. If the value of *$i* is less than 5, you will perform the action that is specified inside the braces (curly brackets) which set off the script block. In VBScript, the condition that is evaluated is positioned on the same line with the *While* statement, but no parentheses are required. Although this is convenient from a typing perspective, it actually makes the code a bit confusing to read. In Windows PowerShell, the statement is outside the parentheses and the condition is clearly delimited by the parentheses. In VBScript, the action that is performed is added between two words: *While* and *Wend*. In Windows PowerShell, there is no *wend* statement, and the action to be performed is positioned inside a pair of braces. Although shocking at first to users coming from a VBScript background, the braces are always used to contain code. This is what is called a *script block,* and they are used everywhere. As soon as you are used to seeing them here, you will find them with other language statements as well. The good thing is that you do not have to look for items such as the keyword *Wend* or the keyword *Loop* (of *Do...Loop* fame).

UNDERSTANDING EXPANDING STRINGS

In Windows PowerShell, there are two kinds of strings: literal strings and expanding strings. In the DemoWhileLessThan.ps1 script, you use the expanding string (signified when you use the double quotation marks; the literal string uses the single quotation mark). You want to display the name of the variable, and you want to display the value that is contained in the variable. In an expanding string, the value that is contained in a variable is displayed to the screen when a line is evaluated. As an example, consider the following code. You assign the value 12 to the variable *$i.* You then put *$i* inside a pair of double quotation marks, making an expanding string. When the line "$i is equal to $i" is evaluated, you obtain "12 is equal to 12," which while true is hardly illuminating. This rather unhelpful code is shown here.

```
PS C:\> $i = 12
PS C:\> "$i is equal to $i"
12 is equal to 12
PS C:\>
```

UNDERSTANDING LITERAL STRINGS

What you probably want to do is display both the name of the variable and the value that is contained inside it. In VBScript you use concatenation. For this example to work, you have to use the literal string, as seen here.

```
PS C:\> $i = 12
PS C:\> '$i is equal to ' + $i
$i is equal to 12
PS C:\>
```

If you want to use the advantage of the expanding string, you have to suppress the expanding nature of the expanding string for the first variable. To do this, you use the escape character, which is the backtick (or grave character), as seen here.

```
PS C:\> $i = 12
PS C:\> "`$i is equal to $i"
$i is equal to 12
PS C:\>
```

In the DemoWhileLessThan.ps1 script, you use the expanding string to print your status message of the value of the *$i* variable during each trip through the *While* loop. You suppress the expanding nature of the expanding string for the first *$i* variable so you can see which variable you are talking about. Then, you increment the value of the *$i* variable by 1. To do this, you use the *$i++* syntax. This is identical to saying the following.

```
$i = $i + 1
```

The advantage is that the *$i++* syntax requires less typing. The DemoWhileLessThan.ps1 script is seen here.

DemoWhileLessThan.ps1

```
$i = 0
While ($i -lt 5)
 {
  "`$i equals $i. This is less than  5"
  $i++
 } #end while $i lt 5
```

When you run the DemoWhileLessThan.ps1 script, you receive the following output.

```
$i equals 0. This is less than  5
$i equals 1. This is less than  5
$i equals 2. This is less than  5
$i equals 3. This is less than  5
$i equals 4. This is less than  5
PS C:\>
```

A Practical Example of Using the *while* Statement

Now that you know how to use the *while* loop, let's examine the WhileReadLine.ps1 script. The first thing you do is initialize the *$i* variable and set it equal to 0. You then use the Get-Content cmdlet to read the contents of the TestFile.txt file and store the contents into the *$fileContents* variable. The TestFile.txt file is shown in Figure 13-25.

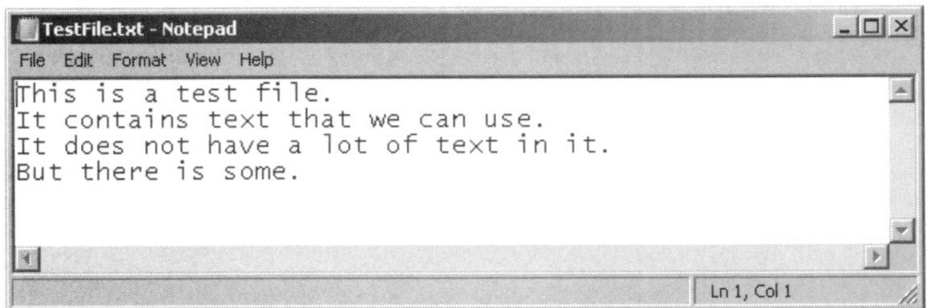

FIGURE 13-25 You can read the contents of the TestFile.Txt file by using the Get-Content cmdlet.

Now you use the *while* statement to loop through the contents of the text file. You do this as long as the value of the *$i* variable is less than or equal to the number of lines in the text file. The number of lines in the text file is represented by the *length* property. Inside the script block, you treat the contents of the *$fileContents* variable as though it is an array (which it is), and you use the *$i* variable to index into the array to print the value of each line in the *$fileContents* variable. You then increment the value of the *$i* variable by 1. The WhileReadLine.ps1 script is shown here.

WhileReadLine.ps1

```
$i = 0
$fileContents = Get-Content -path C:\fso\testfile.txt
While ( $i -le $fileContents.length )
 {
  $fileContents[$i]
  $i++
 }
```

Using the Special Features of Windows PowerShell

If you are thinking the WriteReadLine.ps1 script is a bit difficult, it is really only about as difficult as the VBScript version. The difference is you resorted to using arrays to work with the content you received from the Get-Content cmdlet. The VBScript version uses a *FileSystemObject* and a *TextStreamObject* to work with the data. In reality, you do not need to use a script exactly like the WhileReadLine.ps1 script to read the contents of the text file because the Get-Content cmdlet does this for you automatically. All you really have to do to display the contents of TestFile.txt is use Get-Content. This command is shown here.

```
Get-Content -path c:\fso\TestFile.txt
```

The results of the command are shown in Figure 13-26.

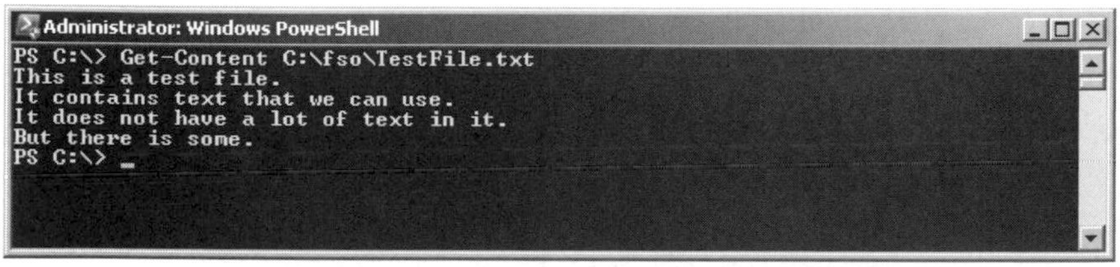

```
Administrator: Windows PowerShell
PS C:\> Get-Content C:\fso\TestFile.txt
This is a test file.
It contains text that we can use.
It does not have a lot of text in it.
But there is some.
PS C:\> _
```

FIGURE 13-26 Get-Content reads and displays content from a text file.

By not storing the results of the command in a variable, the contents are emitted automatically to the screen. The Get-Content command can be shortened further by using the GC alias (shortcut name for Get-Content) and by omitting the name of the *–path* parameter (which is the default parameter). When you do this, you create a command that resembles the following.

```
GC c:\fso\TestFile.txt
```

To find the available aliases for the Get-Content cmdlet, you use the Get-Alias cmdlet with the *–definition* parameter. The Get-Alias cmdlet searches for aliases that have definitions that match Get-Content. Here is the command and the output you receive.

```
PS C:\> Get-Alias -Definition Get-content

CommandType     Name                             Definition
-----------     ----                             ----------
Alias           cat                              Get-Content
Alias           gc                               Get-Content
Alias           type                             Get-Content
```

In this section, you learned that you can use the *while* statement in Windows PowerShell to perform looping. You also learned that activities in VBScript that require looping do not always require you to use the looping behavior in Windows PowerShell, because some cmdlets automatically display information. Finally, you learned how to find aliases for cmdlets you frequently use.

Using the *do...while* Statement

The *Do While...Loop* statement is often used when working with VBScript. This section covers some of the advantages of using the *do...while* statement in Windows PowerShell, too.

The DemoDoWhile.vbs script illustrates using the *Do...While* statement in VBScript. The first thing you do is assign the value of 0 to the variable *i*. You then create an array. To do this, you use the *Array* function and assign the numbers 1 through 5 to the variable *ary*. You then use the *Do...While...Loop* construction to walk through the array of numbers. As long as the value of the variable *i* is less than the number 5, you display the value of the variable *i*. You then increment the value of the variable *i* and loop back around. The DemoDoWhile.vbs script is seen here.

DemoDoWhile.vbs

```
i = 0
ary = Array(1,2,3,4,5)
Do While i < 5
 WScript.Echo ary(i)
 i = i + 1
Loop
```

When you run the DemoDoWhile.vbs script in Cscript at the command prompt, you see the numbers 1 through 5 displayed, as shown in Figure 13-27.

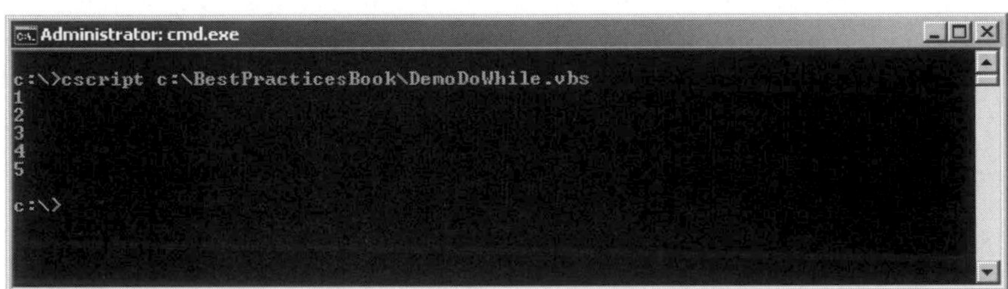

FIGURE 13-27 The numbers 1 through 5 are displayed by the DemoDoWhile.vbs script when it is run in Cscript.

You can do exactly the same thing using Windows PowerShell. The DemoDoWhile.ps1 script and the DemoDoWhile.vbs scripts are essentially the same. The differences between the two scripts are due to syntax differences between Windows PowerShell and VBScript. The first thing you do is assign the value of 1 to the variable *$i*. You then create an array of the numbers 1 through 5 and store that array in the *$ary* variable. You use a shortcut in Windows PowerShell to make this a bit easier. Actually, arrays in Windows PowerShell are fairly easy anyway. If you want to create an array, you just have to assign multiple pieces of data to the variable. To do this, you separate each piece of data by a comma, as seen here.

```
$ary = 1,2,3,4,5
```

Using the *range* Operator

If you needed to create an array with 32,000 numbers in it, it would be impractical to type each number and separate it with a comma. In VBScript, you would have to use a *For...Next... Loop* to add the numbers to the array. In Windows PowerShell, you can use the *range* operator. To do this, you use a variable to hold the array of numbers that is created and type the beginning and the ending number separated with two periods, as seen here.

```
$ary = 1..5
```

Unfortunately, the *range* operator does not work for letters. But there is nothing to prevent you from creating a range of numbers that represent the ASCII value of each letter and then casting it to a string later.

Operating over an Array

You are now ready for the *Do...While...Loop* in Windows PowerShell. You use the *do* statement and open a set of braces (curly brackets). Inside the curly brackets is a script block. The first thing you do is index into the array. After you pass through the array, the value of *$i* is equal to 0. You therefore display the first element in the *$ary* array. You next increment the value of the *$i* variable by 1. You are now done with the script block, so you look at the *while* statement. The condition you are examining is the value of the *$i* variable. As long as it is less than 5, the program will continue to loop around. As soon as the value of *$i* is no longer less than the number 5, the program will stop looping, as seen here.

DemoDoWhile.ps1

```
$i = 0
$ary = 1..5
do
{
 $ary[$i]
 $i++
} while ($i -lt 5)
```

When you run the DemoDoWhile.ps1 script, you receive the results shown in Figure 13-28.

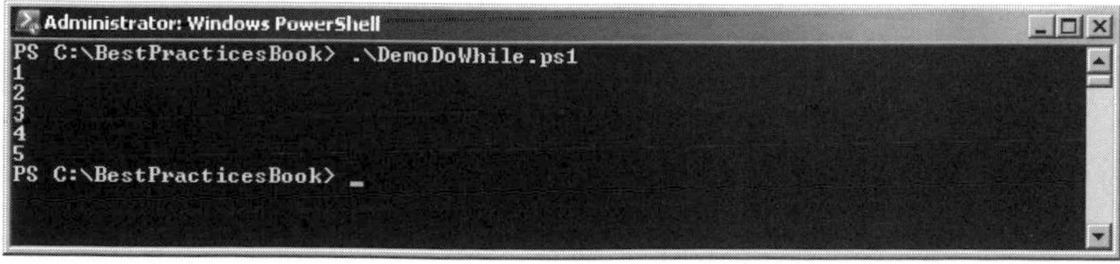

FIGURE 13-28 While the value of *$i* is less than 5, a number is displayed.

Because it can be a bit confusing, be aware that you are evaluating the value of *$i*. You initialize *$i* at 0. The first number in your array is 1. But the first element number in the array is always 0 in Windows PowerShell (unlike VBScript, which can start arrays with 0 or 1). The *while* statement evaluates the value contained in the *$i* variable, not the value that is contained in the array. That is why you see the number 5 displayed.

Casting to ASCII Values

You can change your DemoDoWhile.ps1 script and display the uppercase letters from *A* to *Z*. To do this, you first initialize the *$i* variable and set it to 0. You then create a range of numbers from 65 through 91. These are the ASCII values for the capital letter *A* through the capital letter *Z*. Now you begin the *do* statement and open your script block. To this point, the script is identical to the previous one. To obtain letters from numbers, cast the *integer* data type to a *char* data type. To do this, you use the *char* data type and put it in square brackets. You then use this to convert an *integer* to an uppercase letter. To display the uppercase letter *B* from the ASCII value of 66, the code would resemble the following.

```
PS C:\> [char]66

B
```

Because you know that the *$caps* variable contains an array of numbers ranged from 65 through 91 and that the variable *$i* will hold numbers from 0 through 26, you index into the *$caps* array, cast the integer to a *char* data type, and display the results as shown in the following code.

```
[char]$caps[$i]
```

You then increment the value of *$i* by 1, close the script block, and enter the *while* statement, where you check the value of *$i* to make sure it is less than 26. As long as *$i* is less than 26, the program continues to loop around. The complete DisplayCapitalLetters.ps1 script is seen here.

DisplayCapitalLetters.ps1

```
$i = 0
$caps = 65..91
do
{
 [char]$caps[$i]
 $i++
} while ($i -lt 26)
```

Using the *do...until* Statement

Looping technology is something that is essential to master. It occurs everywhere, and it should be a tool that you can use without thought. When you are confronted with a collection or bundle of items or an array, you have to know how to walk easily through the mess without resorting to research, panic, or hours searching the Internet with Windows Live Search.

This section examines the *Do...Until...Loop* construction. Most of the scripts that do looping at the Microsoft Technet Script Center seem to use *Do...While...Loop*. The scripts that use *Do...Until...Loop* are typically used to read through a text file (until the end of the stream) or to read through a Microsoft ActiveX Data Object (ADO) record set (until the end of the file). As you will see here, these are not required coding conventions and are not meant to be limitations. You can frequently perform the same thing by using any of the different looping constructions.

Comparing the VBScript *Do...Until...Loop* Statement

Before you get too far into this topic, consider the DemoDoUntil.vbs script. In the DemoDoUntil.vbs script, you first assign a value of 0 to the variable *i*. You then create an array with the numbers 1 through 5 contained in it. You use the *Do...Until...Loop* construction to walk through the array until the value of the variable *i* is equal to the number 5. The script will continue to run until the value of the variable *i* is equal to 5. A *Do...Until...Loop* construction runs until a condition is met. The difference between a *Do...Until...Loop* and the *Do...While...Loop* examined in the previous section is that the *Do...While...Loop* runs while a condition is true, and the *Do...Until...Loop* runs until a condition becomes true. In VBScript, this means that a *Do...Until...Loop* will always run at least once, because the condition is evaluated at the bottom of the loop, whereas the *Do...While...Loop* is evaluated at the top of the loop and therefore may never run if the condition is not true. This is not true for Windows PowerShell, however, as will be shown later in this section.

Inside the loop, you first display the value that is contained in the array element 0 on the first pass through the loop, because you first set the value of the variable *i* equal to 0. You next increment the value of the variable *i* by 1 and loop around until the value of *i* is equal to 5. The DemoDoUntil.vbs script is seen here.

DemoDoUntil.vbs

```
i = 0
ary = array(1,2,3,4,5)
Do Until i = 5
 wscript.Echo ary(i)
 i = i+1
Loop
```

Using the Windows PowerShell *do...loop* Statement

You can write the same script by using Windows PowerShell. In the DemoDoUntil.ps1 script, you first set the value of the *$i* variable to 0. You then create an array with the numbers 1 through 5 in it. You store that array in the *$ary* variable. You then arrive at the *do...loop* (*do-until*) construction. After the *do* keyword, you open a set of braces (curly brackets). Inside the curly brackets, you use the *$i* variable to index into the *$ary* array and to retrieve the value that is stored in the first element (element 0) of the array. You then increment the value of the *$i* variable by 1. You continue to loop through the elements in the array until the value of the *$i* variable is equal to 5. At that time, you end the script. This script resembles the DemoDoWhile.ps1 script examined in the previous section.

DemoDoUntil.ps1

```
$i = 0
$ary = 1..5

Do
{
 $ary[$i]
 $i ++
} Until ($i -eq 5)
```

THE *DO...WHILE* AND *DO...UNTIL* STATEMENTS ALWAYS RUN ONCE

In VBScript, if a *Do...While...Loop* condition is never true, the code inside the loop never executes. In Windows PowerShell, the *do...while* and the *do...until* constructions always run at least once. This can be unexpected behavior, and it is something that you should focus on. This is illustrated in the DoWhileAlwaysRuns.ps1 script. The script assigns the value of 1 to the variable *$i*. Inside the script block for the *do...while* loop, you print out a message that states you are inside the *do* loop. The loop condition is *while* the variable *$i* is equal to 5. As you can see, the value of the *$i* variable is 1. Therefore, the value of the *$i* variable will never reach 5 because you are not incrementing it. The DoWhileAlwaysRuns.ps1 script is seen here.

DoWhileAlwaysRuns.ps1

```
$i = 1

Do
{
 "inside the do loop"
} While ($i -eq 5)
```

When you run the script, the text "inside the do loop" is printed out once. This is seen in Figure 13-29.

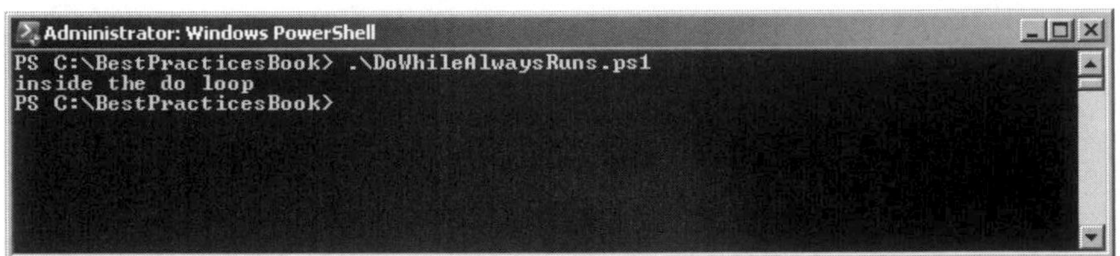

FIGURE 13-29 The script block of a *do-while* statement always runs one time.

What about a similar script that uses the *do...until* construction? The EndlessDoUntil.ps1 script is the same script as the DoWhileAlwaysRuns.ps1 script except for one small detail. Instead of using *do...while*, you are using *do...until*. The rest of the script is the same. The value of the *$i* variable is equal to 1, and in the script block for the *do...until* loop, you print the string "inside the do loop." This line of code should execute once for each *do* loop until the value of *$i* is equal to 5. Because the value of *$i* is never increased to 5, the script will continue to run. The EndlessDoUntil.ps1 script is shown here.

EndlessDoUntil.ps1

```
$i = 1

Do
{
 "inside the do loop"
} Until ($i -eq 5)
```

Before you run the EndlessDoUntil.ps1 script, you should know how to interrupt the running of the script: You hold down the Ctrl key and press C (Ctrl+C). This was the same keystroke sequence that would break a runaway VBScript that was run in Cscript. The results of running the EndlessDoUntil.ps1 script are seen in Figure 13-30.

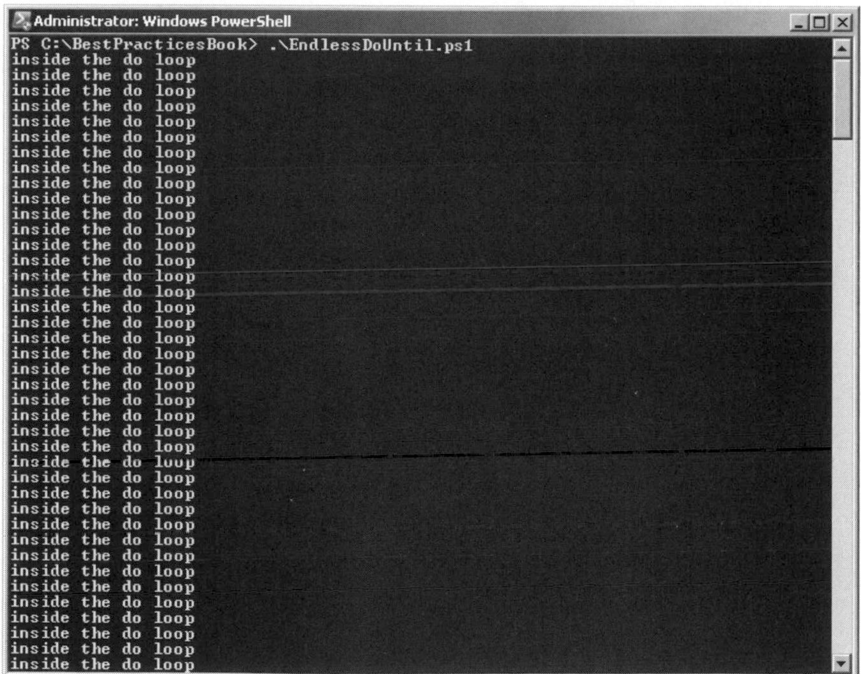

FIGURE 13-30 If the *until* condition is never met, the *do...until* construction will run forever unless interrupted by Ctrl+C.

THE *WHILE* STATEMENT IS USED TO PREVENT UNWANTED EXECUTION

If you have a situation in which the script block must not execute if the condition is not true, you should use the *while* statement. The use of the *while* statement was examined in an earlier section. Again, you have the same kind of script. You assign the value of 0 to the variable *$i*, and instead of using a *do* ... kind of construction, you use the *while* statement. The condition you are looking at is the same condition you used for the other scripts: *while* the value of *$i* is equal to 5. Inside the script block, you display a string that states you are inside the *while* loop. The WhileDoesNotRun.ps1 script is shown here.

WhileDoesNotRun.ps1

```
$i = 0

While ($i -eq 5)
{
 "Inside the While Loop"
}
```

It is perhaps a bit anticlimactic, but go ahead and run the WhileDoesNotRun.ps1 script. When you run the WhileDoesNotRun.ps1 script, you are greeted with the display shown in Figure 13-31. (On your computer, the display will be the color blue.) There should be no output displayed to the console.

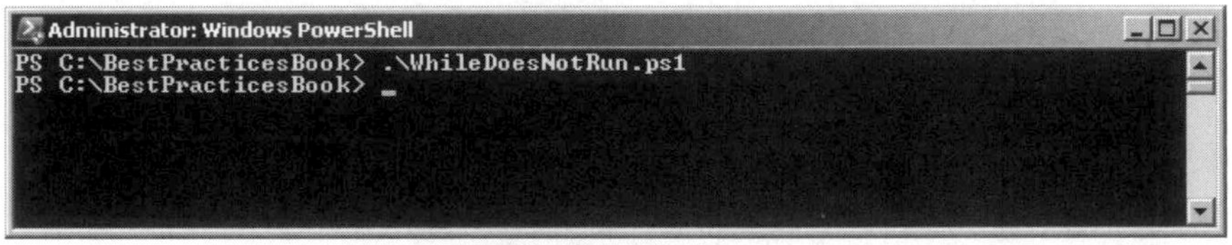

```
Administrator: Windows PowerShell
PS C:\BestPracticesBook> .\WhileDoesNotRun.ps1
PS C:\BestPracticesBook> _
```

FIGURE 13-31 If the *while* condition is not satisfied, the script block does not execute.

The *for* Statement

In VBScript, a *For...Next ...Loop* was easy to create. An example of a simple *For...Next...Loop* is seen in DemoForLoop.vbs. You use the *For* keyword, define a variable to keep track of the count, indicate how far you will go, define your action, and specify the *Next* keyword. That is about all there is to it. It sounds more difficult than it is. The DemoForLoop.vbs script is shown here.

DemoForLoop.vbs

```
For i = 1 To 5
 WScript.Echo i
Next
```

Using the *for* Statement

You can achieve the same thing in Windows PowerShell. The structure of the *for...loop* in Windows PowerShell resembles the structure for VBScript. They both begin with the keyword *for*, they both initialize the variable, and they both specify how far the loop will progress. One thing that is different, however, is that a *For...Loop* in VBScript automatically increments the counter variable. In Windows PowerShell, the variable is not incremented automatically, and you add *$i++* to increment the *$i* variable by 1. Inside the script block (braces, curly brackets), you display the value of the *$i* variable. The DemoForLoop.ps1 script is shown here.

DemoForLoop.ps1

```
For($i = 0; $i -le 5; $i++)
{
 '$i equals ' + $i
}
```

The Windows PowerShell *for* statement is very flexible, and you can leave out one or more elements. In the DemoForWithoutInitOrRepeat.ps1 script, you exclude the first and the last sections of the *for* statement. You set the *$i* variable equal to 0 on the first line of the script. You next come to the *for* statement. In the DemoForLoop.ps1 script, `$i = 0` is moved from inside the *for* statement to the first line of the script. The semicolon is still required because it is used to separate the three sections of the statement. The condition portion, `$i -le 5`, is the same as in the previous script. The repeat section, `$i ++`, is not used either.

In the script section of the *for* statement, you display the value of the *$i* variable, and you also increment the value of *$i* by 1. There are two kinds of Windows PowerShell strings: expanding and literal. These two types of strings were examined earlier in this chapter. In the DemoForLoop.ps1 script, you see an example of a literal string—what is entered is what is displayed, as shown here.

```
'$i equals ' + $i
```

In the DemoForWithoutInitOrRepeat.ps1 script, you see an example of an expanding string. The value of the variable is displayed—not the variable name itself. To suppress the expanding nature of the expanding string, escape the variable by using the backtick character. When you use the expanding string in this manner, it enables you to avoid concatenating the string and the variable as you did in the DemoForLoop.ps1 script, as shown here.

```
"`$i is equal to $i"
```

The value of *$i* must be incremented somewhere. Because it was not incremented in the repeat section of the *for* statement, you have to be able to increment it inside the script block. The DemoForWithoutInitOrRepeat.ps1 script is shown here.

DemoForWithoutInitOrRepeat.ps1

```
$i = 0
For(;$i -le 5; )
{
 "`$i is equal to $i"
 $i++
}
```

When you run the DemoForWithoutInitOrRepeat.ps1 script, the output that is displayed resembles the output produced by the DemoForLoop.ps1 script seen in Figure 13-32. You would never be able to tell it was missing two-thirds of the parameters.

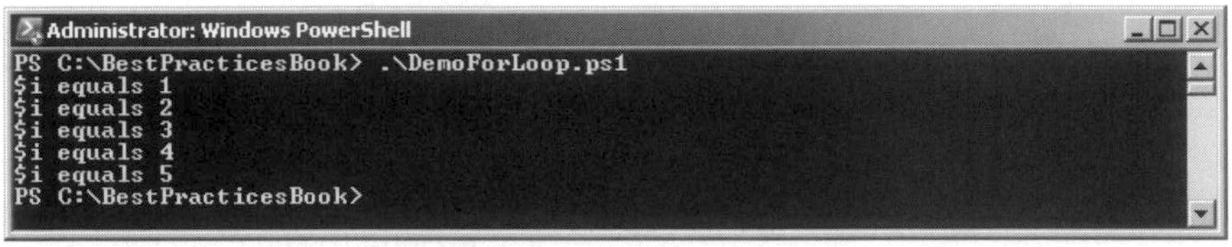

```
PS C:\BestPracticesBook> .\DemoForLoop.ps1
$i equals 1
$i equals 2
$i equals 3
$i equals 4
$i equals 5
PS C:\BestPracticesBook>
```

FIGURE 13-32 The output from DemoForWithoutInitOrRepeat.ps1

You can put your *for* statement into an infinite loop by omitting all three sections of the *for* statement. You must leave the semicolons as position holders. When you omit the three parts of the *for* statement, the *for* statement will resemble the following.

```
for(;;)
```

The ForEndlessLoop.ps1 script will create an endless loop, but you do not have to do this if you do not wish. You could use an *if* statement to evaluate a condition and to take action when the condition was met. You will look at *if* statements in the section titled "The If Statement" later in this chapter. In the ForEndlessLoop.ps1 script, you display the value of the *$i* variable and increment it by 1. The semicolon is used to represent a new line. The *for* statement could therefore be written on three lines if you wanted to do this. This would be useful if you had a very complex *for* statement, because it would make the code easier to read. The script block for the ForEndlessLoop.ps1 script could be written on different lines and exclude the semicolon, as seen here.

```
{

 $i

 $i++

}
```

ForEndlessLoop.ps1

```
for(;;)
{
 $i ; $i++
}
```

When you run the ForEndlessLoop.ps1 script, you are greeted with a long line of numbers. To break out of the endless loop, press Ctrl+C inside the Windows PowerShell prompt. The long line of numbers is shown in Figure 13-33.

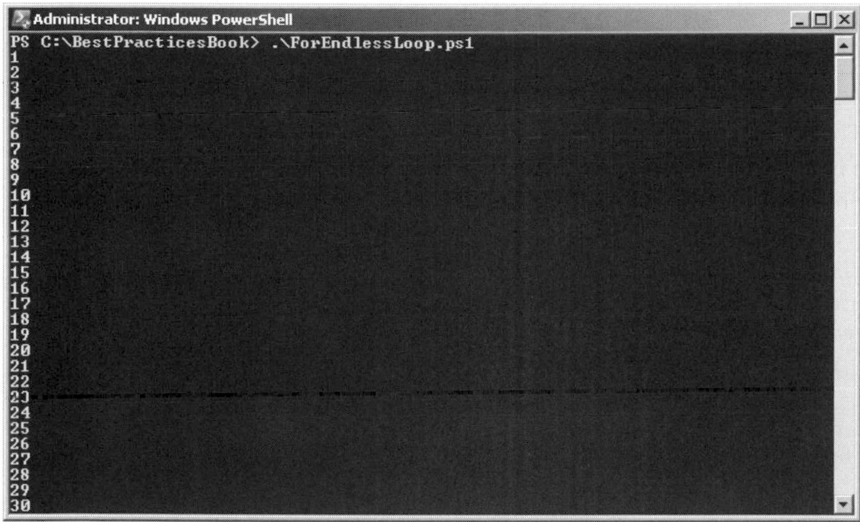

FIGURE 13-33 To break out of this endless loop of numbers, type **Ctrl+C**.

You can see that working with Windows PowerShell is all about choices. You need to decide how you want to work and the things that you want to try to achieve. The *for* statement in Windows PowerShell is very flexible, and maybe one day, you will find just the problem waiting for the solution that you have.

Using the *foreach* Statement

The *foreach* statement resembles the *For...Each...Next* construction from VBScript. In the DemoForEachNext.vbs script, you create an array of five numbers, 1 through 5. You then use the *For...Each...Next* statement to walk your way through the array that is contained in the variable *ary*. The variable *i* is used to iterate through the elements of the array. The *For Each* block is entered so long as there is at least one item in the collection or array. When the loop is entered, all statements inside the loop are executed for the first element. In the DemoForEachNext.vbs script, this means that the following command is executed for each element in the array.

```
Wscript.Echo i
```

As long as there are more elements in the collection or array, the statements inside the loop continue to execute for each element. When there are no more elements in the collection or array, the loop is exited, and execution continues with the statement following the *Next* statement. This is seen in DemoForEachNext.vbs.

```
DemoForEachNext.vbs
ary = Array(1,2,3,4,5)
For Each i In ary
  WScript.Echo i
Next
Wscript.echo "All done"
```

The DemoForEachNext.vbs script works exactly like the DemoForEach.ps1 script. In the DemoForEach.ps1 Windows PowerShell script, you first create an array that contains the numbers 1 through 5 and store that array in the *$ary* variable, as seen here.

```
$ary = 1..5
```

Then you use the *foreach* statement to walk through the array contained in the *$ary* variable. Use the *$i* variable to keep track of your progress through the array. Inside the script block (the curly brackets), you display the value of each variable. The DemoForEach.ps1 script is seen here.

```
DemoForEach.ps1
$ary = 1..5
Foreach ($i in $ary)
{
 $i
}
```

USING THE *FOREACH* STATEMENT FROM THE WINDOWS POWERSHELL CONSOLE

The great thing about Windows PowerShell is that you can also use the *foreach* statement from inside the Windows PowerShell console, as seen here.

```
PS C:\> $ary = 1..5
PS C:\> foreach($i in $ary) { $i }
1
2
3
4
5
```

The ability to use the *foreach* statement from inside the Windows PowerShell console can give you excellent flexibility when you are working interactively. However, much of the work done at the Windows PowerShell console consists of using pipelining. When you are working with the pipeline, you can use the ForEach-Object cmdlet. This cmdlet behaves in a similar manner to the *foreach* statement but is designed to handle pipelined input. The difference is that you do not have to use an intermediate variable to hold the contents of the array. You can create the array and send it across the pipeline. The other difference is that you do not have to create a variable to use for the enumerator. You use the *$_* automatic variable (which represents the current item on the pipeline) instead, as seen here.

```
PS C:\> 1..5 | ForEach-Object { $_ }
1
2
3
4
5
```

Exiting the *foreach* Statement Early

Suppose that you do not want to work with all the numbers in the array. In VBScript terms, leaving a *For...Each...Loop* early is called an *Exit For* statement. You have to use an *If* statement to perform the evaluation of the condition. When the condition is met, you call *Exit For*. In the DemoExitFor.vbs script, you use an inline *If* statement to make this determination. The inline syntax is more efficient for these kinds of things than spreading the statement across three different lines. The main thing to remember about the inline *If* statement is that it does not conclude with the final *End If* statement. The DemoExitFor.vbs script is seen here.

DemoExitFor.vbs

```
ary = Array(1,2,3,4,5)
For Each i In ary
 If i = 3 Then Exit For
 WScript.Echo i
Next
WScript.Echo "Statement following Next"
```

USING THE *BREAK* STATEMENT

In Windows PowerShell terms, you use the *break* statement to leave the loop early. Inside the script block, you use an *if* statement to evaluate the value of the *$i* variable. If it is equal to 3, you call the *break* statement and leave the loop. This line of code is seen here.

```
if($i -eq 3) { break }
```

The complete DemoBreakFor.ps1 script is seen here.

DemoBreakFor.ps1

```
$ary = 1..5
ForEach($i in $ary)
{
 if($i -eq 3) { break }
 $i
}
"Statement following foreach loop"
```

When the DemoBreakFor.ps1 script runs, it displays the numbers 1 and 2. Then it leaves the *foreach* loop and runs the line of code following the *foreach* loop, as seen here.

```
1
2
Statement following foreach loop
```

USING THE *EXIT* STATEMENT

If you did not want to run the line of code after the loop statement, you would use the *exit* statement instead of the *break* statement. This is shown in the DemoExitFor.ps1 script, as shown here.

DemoExitFor.ps1

```
$ary = 1..5
ForEach($i in $ary)
{
 if($i -eq 3) { exit }
 $i
}
"Statement following foreach loop"
```

When the DemoExitFor.ps1 script runs, the line of code following the *foreach* loop never executes, because the *exit* statement ends the script. The results of running the DemoExitFor.ps1 script are shown here.

```
1
2
```

You could achieve the same thing in VBScript by using the *Wscript.Quit* statement instead of *Exit For*. As with the DemoExitFor.ps1 script, the DemoQuitFor.vbs script never comes to the line of code following the *For...Each...Loop*. This is seen in DemoQuitFor.vbs.

DemoQuitFor.vbs

```
ary = Array(1,2,3,4,5)
For Each i In ary
 If i = 3 Then WScript.Quit
 WScript.Echo i
Next
WScript.Echo "Statement following Next"
```

In this section, the use of the *foreach* statement was examined. It is used when you do not know how many items are contained within a collection. It allows you to walk through the collection and to work with items from that collection on an individual basis. In addition, two techniques for exiting a *foreach* statement were examined.

The *if* Statement

In VBScript, the *If...Then...End If* statement was somewhat straightforward. There were several things to understand:

- The *If* and the *Then* statements must be on the same line.
- The *If...Then... End If* statement must conclude with *End If.*
- *End If* is two words, not one word.

The VBScript *If...Then...End If* statement is seen in the DemoIf.vbs script.

DemoIf.vbs

```
a = 5
If a = 5 Then
 WScript.Echo "a equals 5"
End If
```

In the Windows PowerShell version of the *If...Then...End If* statement, there is no *Then* keyword, nor is there an *End If* statement. The Windows PowerShell *if* statement is easier to type, but this simplicity comes with a bit of complexity. The condition that is evaluated in the *if* statement is positioned in a set of parentheses. In the DemoIf.ps1 script, you are checking whether the variable *$a* is equal to 5, as seen here.

```
If ($a -eq 5)
```

The code that is executed when the condition is true is positioned inside a pair of braces (curly brackets). The script block for the DemoIf.ps1 script is seen here.

```
{
   '$a equals 5'
}
```

The Windows PowerShell version of the DemoIf.vbs script is the DemoIf.ps1 script.

DemoIf.ps1

```
$a = 5
If($a -eq 5)
 {
   '$a equals 5'
 }
```

The one thing that is different about the Windows PowerShell *if* statement is the comparison operators. In VBScript, the equals sign (=) is used as an assignment operator. It is also used as an equality operator for comparison. On the first line of code, the variable *a* is assigned the value 5. This uses the equals sign as an assignment. On the next line of code, the *If* statement is used to see whether the value of *a* is equal to the number 5. On this line of code, the equals sign is used as the equality operator, as seen here.

```
a = 5
If a = 5 Then
```

In simple examples such as this, it is fairly easy to tell the difference between an equality operator and an assignment operator. In more complex scripts, however, things could be confusing. Windows PowerShell removes that confusion by having special comparison operators. As mentioned earlier, this clarity can be a bit confusing until you take the time to learn the Windows PowerShell comparison operators. One thing that might help is to realize that main operators are two letters long. (Case-sensitive operators all begin with the letter *c*, such as *ceq* for case-sensitive equals. You can type **Get-Help about_operators** for more information). Comparison operators are seen in Table 13-2.

TABLE 13-2 Comparison Operators

OPERATOR	DESCRIPTION	EXAMPLE	RESULT
–eq	Equals	$a = 5 ; $a –eq 4	False
–ne	Not equal to	$a = 5 ; $a –ne 4	True
–gt	Greater than	$a = 5 ; $a –gt 4	True
–ge	Greater than or equal to	$a = 5 ; $a –ge 5	True
–lt	Less than	$a = 5 ; $a –lt 5	False
–le	Less than or equal to	$a = 5 ; $a –le 5	True
–like	Wildcard comparison	$a = "This is Text" ; $a –like "Text"	False
–notlike	Wildcard not comparison	$a = "This is Text" ; $a –notlike "Text"	True
–match	Regular expression comparison	$a = "Text is Text" ; $a –match "Text"	True
–notmatch	Regular expression not comparison	$a = "This is Text" ; $a –notmatch "Text$"	False

Using Assignment and Comparison Operators

Any value assignment will evaluate to true, and therefore the script block is executed. In this example, you assign the value 1 to the variable *$a*. In the condition for the *if* statement, you assign the value of 12 to the variable *$a*. Any assignment evaluates to true, and the script block executes.

```
PS C:\> $a = 1 ; If ($a = 12) { "its true" }
its true
```

Rarely do you test a condition and perform an outcome. Most of the time, you have to perform one action if the condition is true and another action if the condition is false. In VBScript, you used the *If...Else...End If* construction. You put the *Else* clause immediately after the first outcome to be performed if the condition were true. This is seen in the DemoIfElse.vbs script.

DemoIfElse.vbs

```
a = 4
If a = 5 Then
 WScript.Echo "a equals 5"
Else
 WScript.Echo "a is not equal to 5"
End If
```

In Windows PowerShell, the syntax is not surprising. Following the closing curly brackets from the *if* statement script block, you add the *else* keyword and open a new script block to hold the alternative outcome, as seen here.

demoIfElse.ps1

```
$a = 4
If ($a -eq 5)
{
 '$a equals 5'
}
Else
{
 '$a is not equal to 5'
}
```

Things become confusing with VBScript when you want to evaluate multiple conditions and have multiple outcomes. The *Else If* clause provides for the second outcome. You have to evaluate the second condition. The *Else If* clause receives its own condition, which is followed by the *Then* keyword. Following the *Then* keyword, you list the code that you want to execute. This is followed by the *Else* keyword and a pair of *End If* statements. This is seen in the DemoIfElseIfElse.vbs script.

DemoIfElseIfElse.vbs

```
a = 4
If a = 5 Then
 WScript.Echo "a equals 5"
Else If a = 3 Then
 WScript.Echo "a equals 3"
Else
 WScript.Echo "a does not equal 3 or 5"
End If
End If
```

Evaluating Multiple Conditions

The Windows PowerShell demoIfElseIfElse.ps1 script is a bit easier to understand because it avoids the double *End If* kind of scenario. For each condition that you want to evaluate, you use *elseif*. Be aware that this is a single word. You put the condition inside a pair of smooth parentheses, and open your script block. The demoIfElseIfElse.ps1 script demonstrates this.

demoIfElseIfElse.ps1

```
$a = 4
If ($a -eq 5)
{
 '$a equals 5'
}
ElseIf ($a -eq 3)
{
 '$a is equal to 3'
}
Else
{
 '$a does not equal 3 or 5'
}
```

The *switch* Statement

As a best practice, you generally avoid using the *elseif* type of construction from either VBScript or Windows PowerShell, because there is a better way to write the same code.

In VBScript, you use the *Select Case* statement to evaluate a condition and select one outcome from a group of potential statements. In the DemoSelectCase.VBS script, the value of the variable *a* is assigned the value of 2. The *Select Case* statement is used to evaluate the value of the variable *a*. The syntax is seen here.

```
Select Case testexpression
```

The test expression that is evaluated is the variable *a*. Each of the different cases contains potential values for the test expression. If the value of the variable *a* is equal to 1, the code Wscript.Echo "a = 1" is executed as seen here.

```
Case 1
   WScript.Echo "a = 1"
```

Each of the different cases is evaluated in the same manner. The *Case Else* expression is run if none of the previous expressions evaluate to true. The complete DemoSelectCase.vbs script is seen here.

DemoSelectCase.vbs

```
a = 2
Select Case a
 Case 1
   WScript.Echo "a = 1"
 Case 2
   WScript.Echo "a = 2"
 Case 3
   WScript.Echo "a = 3"
 Case Else
   WScript.Echo "unable to determine value of a"
End Select
WScript.Echo "statement after select case"
```

Using the *switch* Statement

In Windows PowerShell, there is no *Select Case* statement. There is, however, the *switch* statement. The *switch* statement is the most powerful statement in the Windows PowerShell language. The *switch* statement begins with the *switch* keyword, and the condition to be evaluated is inside a pair of smooth parentheses, as seen here:

```
Switch ($a)
```

Next, a pair of braces (curly brackets) is used to mark off the script block for the *switch* statement. Inside the script block, each condition to be evaluated begins with a value followed by the script block to be executed in the event the value matches the condition, as shown here.

```
1 { '$a = 1' }
2 { '$a = 2' }
3 { '$a = 3' }
```

DEFINING THE *DEFAULT* CONDITION

If no match is found and the *default* statement is not used, the *switch* statement exits, and the line of code that follows the *switch* statement is executed. The *default* statement performs a function similar to the one performed by the *Case Else* statement from the *Select Case* statement. The *default* statement is seen here.

```
Default { 'unable to determine value of $a' }
```

The complete DemoSwitchCase.ps1 script is seen here.

```
DemoSwitchCase.ps1
$a = 2
Switch ($a)
{
 1 { '$a = 1' }
 2 { '$a = 2' }
 3 { '$a = 3' }
 Default { 'unable to determine value of $a' }
}
"Statement after switch"
```

UNDERSTANDING MATCHING

With the *Select Case* statement, the first matching case is the one that is executed. As soon as that code executes, the line following the *Select Case* statement is executed. If the condition matches multiple cases in the *Select Case* statement, only the first match in the list is executed. Matches from lower in the list are not executed. Therefore, make sure that the most desirable code to execute is positioned highest in the *Select Case* order.

With the *switch* statement in Windows PowerShell, order is not a major design concern because every match from inside the *switch* statement will be executed. An example of this is seen in the DemoSwitchMultiMatch.ps1 script shown here.

```
DemoSwitchMultiMatch.ps1
$a = 2
Switch ($a)
{
 1 { '$a = 1' }
 2 { '$a = 2' }
 2 { 'Second match of the $a variable' }
 3 { '$a = 3' }
 Default { 'unable to determine value of $a' }
}
"Statement after switch"
```

When the DemoSwitchMultiMatch.ps1 script runs, the second and third conditions will both be matched, and therefore their associated script blocks are executed. The DemoSwitchMultiMatch.ps1 script produces the output seen here.

```
$a = 2
Second match of the $a variable
Statement after switch
```

EVALUATING AN ARRAY

If an array is stored in the variable *a* in the DemoSelectCase.vbs script, a type mismatch error will be produced. This error is seen here.

```
Microsoft VBScript runtime error: Type mismatch
```

The Windows PowerShell *switch* statement can handle an array in the variable *$a* without any modification. The array is seen here.

```
$a = 2,3,5,1,77
```

The complete DemoSwitchArray.ps1 script is seen here.

DemoSwitchArray.ps1

```
$a = 2,3,5,1,77
Switch ($a)
{
 1 { '$a = 1' }
 2 { '$a = 2' }
 3 { '$a = 3' }
 Default { 'unable to determine value of $a' }
}
"Statement after switch"
```

When the DemoSwitchArray.ps1 script is run, the results seen in Figure 13-34 are produced.

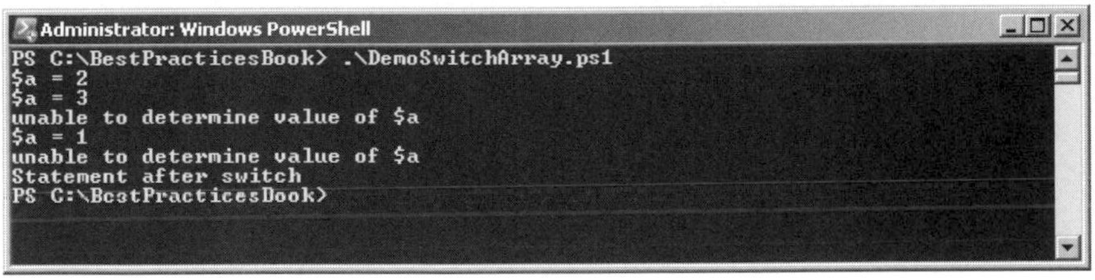

```
Administrator: Windows PowerShell
PS C:\BestPracticesBook> .\DemoSwitchArray.ps1
$a = 2
$a = 3
unable to determine value of $a
$a = 1
unable to determine value of $a
Statement after switch
PS C:\BestPracticesBook>
```

FIGURE 13-34 The *switch* statement produces multiple matches.

Controlling Matching Behavior

If you do not want the multimatch behavior of the *switch* statement, you can use the *break* statement to change the behavior. In the DemoSwitchArrayBreak.ps1 script, the *switch* statement will be exited when the first match occurs because each of the match condition script blocks contains the *break* statement, as seen here.

```
1 { '$a = 1' ; break }
2 { '$a = 2' ; break }
3 { '$a = 3' ; break }
```

You are not required to include the *break* statement with each condition; instead, you could use it to exit the switch only after a particular condition is matched. The complete DemoSwitchArrayBreak.ps1 script is seen here.

DemoSwitchArrayBreak.ps1

```
$a = 2,3,5,1,77
Switch ($a)
{
 1 { '$a = 1' ; break }
 2 { '$a = 2' ; break }
 3 { '$a = 3' ; break }
 Default { 'unable to determine value of $a' }
}
"Statement after switch"
```

When the DemoSwitchArrayBreak.ps1 script runs, the output shown in Figure 13-35 appears.

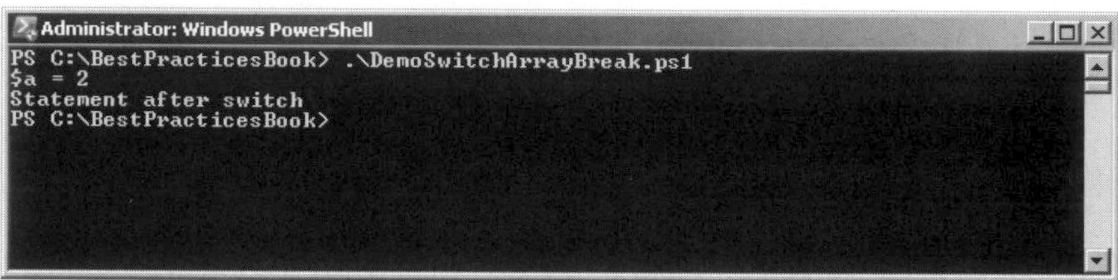

FIGURE 13-35 The first match exits the *switch* statement.

In this section, the use of the Windows PowerShell *switch* statement was examined. The matching behavior of the *switch* statement and the use of *break* were also discussed.

Understanding Modules

Windows PowerShell 2.0 introduces the concept of modules. A module is a package that can contain Windows PowerShell cmdlets, aliases, functions, variables, and even providers. In short, a Windows PowerShell module can contain the kinds of things that you might put into your profile, but it can also contain things that Windows PowerShell 1.0 required a developer to incorporate into a PowerShell snap-in. There are several advantages of modules over snap-ins:

- Anyone who can write a Windows PowerShell script can create a module.
- A module does not have to be written in C++ or C#; it can be a collection of Windows PowerShell scripts of PowerShell functions.
- To install a module, you do not need to write a Windows Installer package.
- To install a module, you do not have to have administrator rights.

These advantages should be of great interest to the IT professional.

Including Functions

In Windows PowerShell 1.0 you could include functions from previously written scripts by dot-sourcing the script, but the use of a module offers greater flexibility because of the ability to create a module manifest that specifies exactly which functions and programming elements will be imported into the current session.

DIRECT FROM THE SOURCE

Scopes and Dot-Sourcing

James O'Neill, Evangelist
Developer and Platform Group

Windows PowerShell has three logical drives that can be thought of as holding the variables ENV: (which holds environment variables), VARIABLE: (which holds Windows PowerShell variables), and FUNCTION: (which holds Windows PowerShell functions). You can refer to the contents of an environment variable as $ENV:name. Windows PowerShell also has the concept of scopes, which can be summarized as "what happens in the script, stays in the script." That is, a variable, alias, or function that is changed in a script won't affect the Windows PowerShell environment after the script terminates. This is usually a good thing. Actions taken at the command prompt affect a global scope, and scripts and functions only affect their local scope. A function that must change something in the global scope can explicitly work on $Global:name. However, this still presents a problem for scripts that set variables we want to use later in the session or that load functions because, as soon the script is completed, the variables and functions are lost. Windows PowerShell allows a command to be prefixed with a dot (.) character. The dot operator says "Run this command in the current scope and not in a scope of its own," a process that is known as "dot-sourcing."

Using Dot-Sourcing

This technique of dot-sourcing still works in Windows PowerShell 2.0, and it offers the advantage of simplicity and familiarity. In the TextFunctions.ps1 script, two functions are created. The first function is called *New-Line*. The second function is called *Get-TextStatus*. The TextFunctions.ps1 script is seen here.

TextFunctions.ps1

```
Function New-Line([string]$stringIn)
{
 "-" * $stringIn.length
} #end New-Line

Function Get-TextStats([string[]]$textIn)
{
 $textIn | Measure-Object -Line -word -char
} #end Get-TextStats
```

The *New-Line* function will create a line that is the length of an input text. This is helpful when you want an underline for text separation purposes that is sized to the text. Traditional VBScript users copy the function they need to use into a separate file and run the newly produced script. An example of using the *New-Line* text function in this manner is seen here.

CallNew-LineTextFunction.ps1

```
Function New-Line([string]$stringIn)
{
 "-" * $stringIn.length
} #end New-Line

Function Get-TextStats([string[]]$textIn)
{
 $textIn | Measure-Object -Line -word -char
} #end Get-TextStats

# *** Entry Point to script ***
"This is a string" | ForEach-Object  {$_ ; New-Line $_}
```

When the script runs, it returns the following output.

```
This is a string

----------------
```

Of course, this is a bit inefficient, and it limits your ability to use the functions. If you have to copy the entire text of a function into each new script you want to produce or edit a script each time you want to use a function in a different manner, you dramatically increase your workload. If the functions were available all the time, you might be inclined to use them more often. To make the text functions available in your current Windows PowerShell console, you need to dot-source the script containing the functions into your console. You will need to use the entire path to the script unless the folder that contains the script is in your search path. The syntax to dot-source a script is so easy, it actually becomes a stumbling block for some people who are expecting some complex formula or cmdlet with obscure parameters. It is none of that—just a period (dot) and the path to the script that contains the function. This is why it is called dot-sourcing: you have a dot and the source (path) to the functions you want to include as seen here.

```
PS C:\> . C:\fso\TextFunctions.ps1
```

When you include the functions into your current console, all the functions in the source script are added to the Function drive. This is seen in Figure 13-36.

```
Administrator: Windows PowerShell
PS C:\> . C:\fso\TextFunctions.ps1
PS C:\> dir function:

CommandType     Name                          Definition
-----------     ----                          ----------
Function        A:                            Set-Location A:
Function        B:                            Set-Location B:
Function        C:                            Set-Location C:
Function        cd..                          Set-Location ..
Function        cd\                           Set-Location \
Function        Clear-Host                    $space = New-Object System.M...
Function        D:                            Set-Location D:
Function        Disable-PSRemoting            ...
Function        E:                            Set-Location E:
Function        F:                            Set-Location F:
Function        G:                            Set-Location G:
Function        Get-TextStats                 param([string[]]$textIn)...
Function        Get-Verb                      ...
Function        H:                            Set-Location H:
Function        help                          ...
Function        I:                            Set-Location I:
Function        ImportSystemModules           ...
Function        J:                            Set-Location J:
Function        K:                            Set-Location K:
Function        L:                            Set-Location L:
Function        M:                            Set-Location M:
Function        mkdir                         ...
Function        more                          param([string[]]$paths)...
Function        N:                            Set-Location N:
Function        New-Line                      param([string]$stringIn)...
Function        O:                            Set-Location O:
Function        P:                            Set-Location P:
Function        prompt                        $(if (test-path variable:/PS...
Function        Q:                            Set-Location Q:
Function        R:                            Set-Location R:
Function        S:                            Set-Location S:
Function        T:                            Set-Location T:
Function        TabExpansion                  ...
Function        U:                            Set-Location U:
Function        V:                            Set-Location V:
Function        W:                            Set-Location W:
Function        X:                            Set-Location X:
Function        Y:                            Set-Location Y:
Function        Z:                            Set-Location Z:
```

FIGURE 13-36 Functions from a dot-sourced script are available via the Function drive.

Using Dot-Sourced Functions

When the functions have been introduced to the current console, you can incorporate them into your normal commands. This flexibility should also influence the way you write the function. If you write the functions so they will accept pipelined input and do not change the system environment (by adding global variables, for example), you will be much more likely to use the functions, and they will be less likely to conflict with either functions or cmdlets that are present in the current console.

As an example of using the *New-Line* function, consider the fact that the Get-WmiObject cmdlet allows the use of an array of computer names for the *–computername* parameter. The problem is that the output is confusing, because you do not know which piece of information is associated with which output. In this example, basic input/output system (BIOS) information is obtained from two separate workstations.

```
PS C:\> Get-WmiObject -Class Win32_bios -ComputerName berlin, vista

SMBIOSBIOSVersion : 080002
Manufacturer      : A. Datum Corporation
Name              : BIOS Date: 02/22/06 20:54:49  Ver: 08.00.02
SerialNumber      : 2096-1160-0447-0846-3027-2471-99
Version           : A D C  - 2000622

SMBIOSBIOSVersion : 080002
Manufacturer      : A. Datum Corporation
Name              : BIOS Date: 02/22/06 20:54:49  Ver: 08.00.02
SerialNumber      : 2716-2298-1514-1558-4398-7113-73
Version           : A D C  - 2000622
```

You can improve the display of the information returned by Get-WmiObject by pipelining the output to the *New-Line* function so that you can underline each computer name as it comes across the pipeline. You do not need to write a script to produce this kind of display. You can type the command directly into the Windows PowerShell console. The first thing you need to do is to dot-source the TextFunctions.ps1 script. This makes the functions directly available in the current Windows PowerShell console session. You then use the same Get-WmiObject query that you used earlier to obtain BIOS information via WMI from two computers. Pipeline the resulting management objects to the ForEach-Object cmdlet. Inside the script block section, you use the $_ automatic variable to reference the current object on the pipeline and retrieve the *System.Management.ManagementPath* object. From the *ManagementPath* object, you can obtain the name of the server that is supplying the information. You send this information to the *New-Line* function so the server name is underlined, and you display the BIOS information that is contained in the *$_* variable.

The command to import the *New-Line* function into the current Windows PowerShell session and use it to underline the server names is shown here.

```
PS C:\> . C:\fso\TextFunctions.ps1
PS C:\> Get-WmiObject -Class win32_Bios -ComputerName vista, berlin |
>> ForEach-Object { $_.Path.Server ; New-Line $_.Path.Server ; $_ }
```

The results of using the *New-Line* function are seen in Figure 13-37.

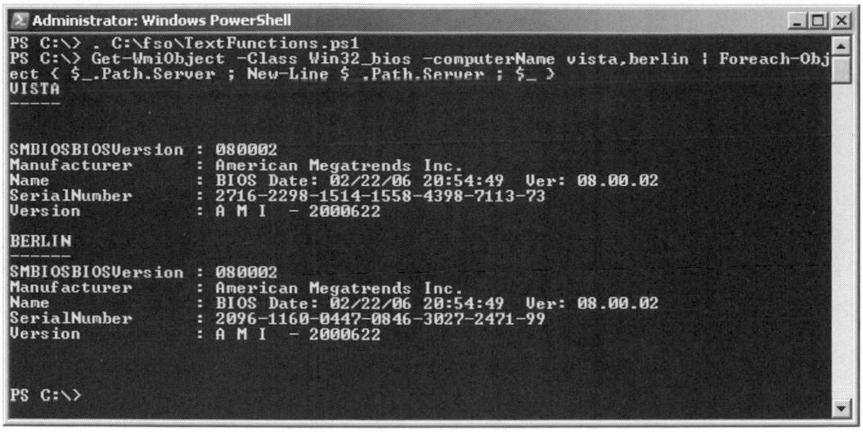

```
PS C:\> . C:\fso\TextFunctions.ps1
PS C:\> Get-WmiObject -Class Win32_bios -computerName vista,berlin | Foreach-Obj
ect { $_.Path.Server ; New-Line $_.Path.Server ; $_ }
VISTA
-----

SMBIOSBIOSVersion : 080002
Manufacturer      : American Megatrends Inc.
Name              : BIOS Date: 02/22/06 20:54:49  Ver: 08.00.02
SerialNumber      : 2716-2298-1514-1558-4398-7113-73
Version           : A M I  - 2000622

BERLIN
------
SMBIOSBIOSVersion : 080002
Manufacturer      : American Megatrends Inc.
Name              : BIOS Date: 02/22/06 20:54:49  Ver: 08.00.02
SerialNumber      : 2096-1160-0447-0846-3027-2471-99
Version           : A M I  - 2000622


PS C:\>
```

FIGURE 13-37 Functions that are written to accept pipelined input will find an immediate use in your daily work routine.

The *Get-TextStats* function from the TextFunctions.ps1 script provides statistics based on an input text file or text string. When the TextFunctions.ps1 script is dot-sourced into the current console, the statistics that it returns when the function is called are word count, number of lines in the file, and number of characters. An example of using this function is seen here.

```
Get-TextStats "This is a string"
```

When the *Get-TextStats* function is used, the following output is produced.

```
                    Lines                    Words              Characters Property
                    -----                    -----              ---------- --------
                        1                        4                      16
```

In this section, the use of functions was discussed. The reuse of functions could be as simple as copying the text of the function from one script into another script. It is easier to dot-source the function. This can be done from within the Windows PowerShell console or from within a script.

Adding Help for Functions

There is one problem that is introduced when dot-sourcing functions into the current Windows PowerShell console. Because you are not required to open the file that contains the function to use it, you may be unaware of everything the file contains within it. In addition to functions, the file could contain variables, aliases, Windows PowerShell drives, or a wide variety of other things. Depending on what you are actually trying to accomplish, this may or may not be an issue. The need arises, however, to have access to help information about the features provided by the Windows PowerShell script.

Using the here-string Technique for Help

In Windows PowerShell 1.0, you could solve this problem by adding a *–help* parameter to the function and storing the help text within a here-string. You can use this approach in Windows PowerShell 2.0 as well, but as discussed in the next section, there is a better approach to providing help for functions. The classic here-string approach for help is seen in the GetWmiClassesFunction.ps1 script. The first step that needs to be done is to define a switched parameter named *$help*. The second step involves creating and displaying the results of a here-string that includes help information. The GetWmiClassesFunction.ps1 script is shown here.

GetWmiClassesFunction.ps1

```
Function Get-WmiClasses(
                 $class=($paramMissing=$true),
                 $ns="root\cimv2",
                 [switch]$help
                )
{
  If($help)
   {
    $helpstring = @"
    NAME
      Get-WmiClasses
    SYNOPSIS
      Displays a list of WMI Classes based upon a search criteria
    SYNTAX
     Get-WmiClasses [[-class] [string]] [[-ns] [string]] [-help]
    EXAMPLE
     Get-WmiClasses -class disk -ns root\cimv2"
     This command finds wmi classes that contain the word disk. The
     classes returned are from the root\cimv2 namespace.
"@
   $helpString
     break #exits the function early
   }
  If($local:paramMissing)
    {
      throw "USAGE: getwmi2 -class <class type> -ns <wmi namespace>"
    } #$local:paramMissing
  "`nClasses in $ns namespace ...."
  Get-WmiObject -namespace $ns -list |
  where-object {
                 $_.name -match $class -and `
                 $_.name -notlike 'cim*'
               }
  # end Get-WmiClasses function} #end get-wmiclasses
```

The here-string technique works fairly well for providing function help. If you follow the cmdlet help pattern, it works well, as seen in Figure 13-38.

```
PS C:\> . C:\fso\GetWmiClassesFunction.ps1
PS C:\> Get-WmiClasses -help
    NAME
      Get-WmiClasses"
    SYNOPSIS
      Displays a list of WMI Classes based upon a search criteria
    SYNTAX
     Get-WmiClasses [[-class] [string]] [[-ns] [string]] [-help]
    EXAMPLE
     Get-WmiClasses -class disk -ns root\cimv2"
     This command finds wmi classes that contain the word disk. The
     classes returned are from the root\cimv2 namespace.
PS C:\>
```

FIGURE 13-38 Manually created help can mimic the look of core cmdlet help.

The drawback to manually creating help for a function is that it is tedious. As a result, only the most important functions receive help information when using this methodology. This is unfortunate, because it then requires the user to memorize the details of the function contract. One way to work around this is to use the Get-Content cmdlet to retrieve the code that was used to create the function. This is much easier to do than searching for the script that was used to create the function and opening it in Notepad. To use the Get-Content cmdlet to display the contents of a function, you type **Get-Content** and supply the path to the function. All functions available to the current Windows PowerShell environment are available via the PowerShell Function drive. You can therefore use the following syntax to obtain the content of a function.

```
PowerShell C:\> Get-Content Function:\Get-WmiClasses
```

The technique of using Get-Content to read the text of the function is seen in Figure 13-39.

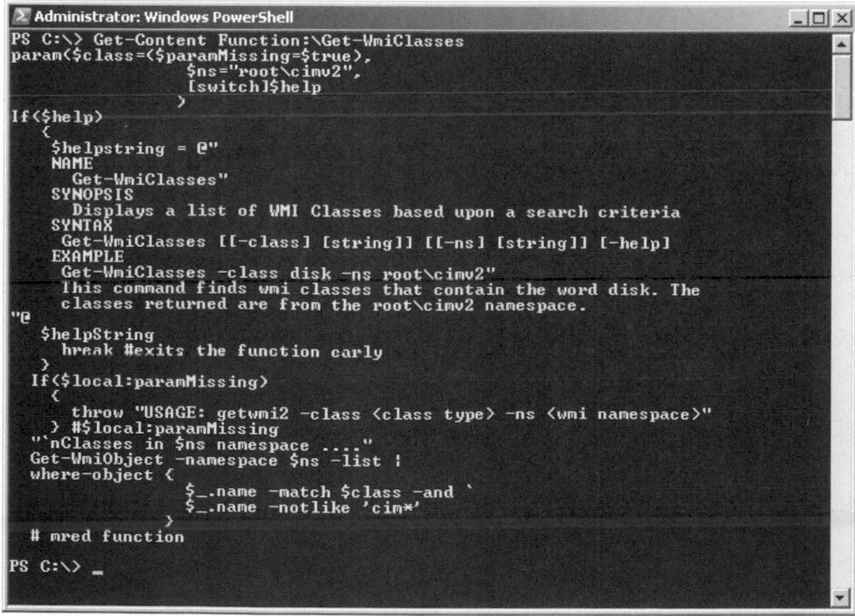

FIGURE 13-39 The Get-Content cmdlet can retrieve the contents of a function.

Using *–help* Function Tags to Produce Help

Much of the intensive work of producing help information for your functions is removed when you use the stylized *–help* function tags that are available in Windows PowerShell 2.0. To use the *help* function tags, you place the tags inside the block comment tags when you are writing your script. When you write help for your function and employ the *–help* tags, the use of the tags allows for complete integration with the Get-Help cmdlet. This provides a seamless user experience for those utilizing your functions. In addition, it promotes the custom user-defined function to the same status within Windows PowerShell as native cmdlets. The experience of using a custom user-defined function is no different than using a cmdlet, and indeed, to the user there is no need to distinguish between a custom function that was dot-sourced or loaded via a module or a native cmdlet. The *–help* function tags and their associated meanings are shown in Table 13-3.

TABLE 13-3 Function *–help* Tags and Meanings

HELP TAG NAME	HELP TAG DESCRIPTION
.Synopsis	A very brief description of the function. It begins with a verb and informs the user as to what the function does. It does not include the function name or how the function works. The function synopsis appears in the *SYNOPSIS* field of all help views.
.Description	Two or three full sentences that briefly list everything that the function can do. It begins with "The *<function name>* function..." If the function can get multiple objects or take multiple inputs, use plural nouns in the description. The description appears in the *DESCRIPTION* field of all help views.
.Parameter	Brief and thorough. Describes what the function does when the parameter is used and the legal values for the parameter. The parameter appears in the *PARAMETERS* field only in Detailed and Full help views.
.Example	Illustrates the use of a function with all its parameters. The first example is simplest with only the required parameters; the last example is most complex and should incorporate pipelining if appropriate. The example appears in the *EXAMPLES* field only in the Example, Detailed, and Full help views.
.Inputs	Lists the .NET Framework classes of objects that the function will accept as input. There is no limit to the number of input classes you may list. The inputs appear in the *INPUTS* field only in the Full help view.
.Outputs	Lists the .NET Framework classes of objects that the function will emit as output. There is no limit to the number of output classes you may list. The outputs appear in the *OUTPUTS* field only in the Full help view.

HELP TAG NAME	HELP TAG DESCRIPTION
.Notes	Provides a place to list information that does not fit easily into the other sections. This can be special requirements required by the function, as well as author, title, version, and other information. The notes appear in the *NOTES* field only in the Full help view.
.Link	Provides links to other Help topics and Internet sites of interest. Because these links appear in a command window, they are not direct links. There is no limit to the number of links you may provide. The links appear in the *RELATED LINKS* field in all help views.

You do not need to supply values for all the *–help* tags. As a best practice, however, you should consider supplying the *.Synopsis* and the *.Example* tags, because these provide the most critical information required to assist a person in learning how to use the function.

An example of using the *–help* tags is shown in the GetWmiClassesFunction1.ps1 script. The help information provided is exactly the same as the information provided by the GetWmiClassesFunction.ps1 script. The difference happens with the use of the *–help* tags. First, you will notice that there is no longer a need for the switched *$help* parameter. The reason for not needing the switched *$help* parameter is the incorporation of the code with the Get-Help cmdlet. When you do not need to use a switched *$help* parameter, you also do not need to test for the existence of the *$help* variable. By avoiding the testing for the *$help* variable, your script can be much simpler. You gain several other bonuses by using the special *–help* tags. These bonus features are listed here:

- The name of the function is displayed automatically and displayed in all help views.
- The syntax of the function is derived from the parameters automatically and displayed in all help views.
- Detailed parameter information is generated automatically when the *–full* parameter of the Get-Help cmdlet is used.
- Common parameters information is displayed automatically when Get-Help is used with the *–detailed* and *–full* parameters.

In the GetWmiClassesFunction.ps1 script, the *Get-WmiClasses* function begins the help section with the Windows PowerShell 2.0 multiline comment block. The multiline comment block special characters begin with the left angle bracket followed with a pound sign (<#) and end with the pound sign followed by the right angle bracket (#>). Everything between the multiline comment characters is considered to be commented out. Two special *–help* tags are included: the *.Synopsis* and the *.Example* tags. The other *–help* tags that are listed in Table 13-3 are not used for this function.

```
<#
  .SYNOPSIS
    Displays a list of WMI Classes based upon a search criteria
  .EXAMPLE
```

```
    Get-WmiClasses -class disk -ns root\cimv2"
    This command finds wmi classes that contain the word disk. The
    classes returned are from the root\cimv2 namespace.
#>
```

When the GetWmiClassesFunction.ps1 script is dot-sourced into the Windows PowerShell console, you can use the Get-Help cmdlet to obtain help information from the *Get-WmiClasses* function. When the Get-Help cmdlet is run with the *–full* parameter, the help display seen in Figure 13-40 appears.

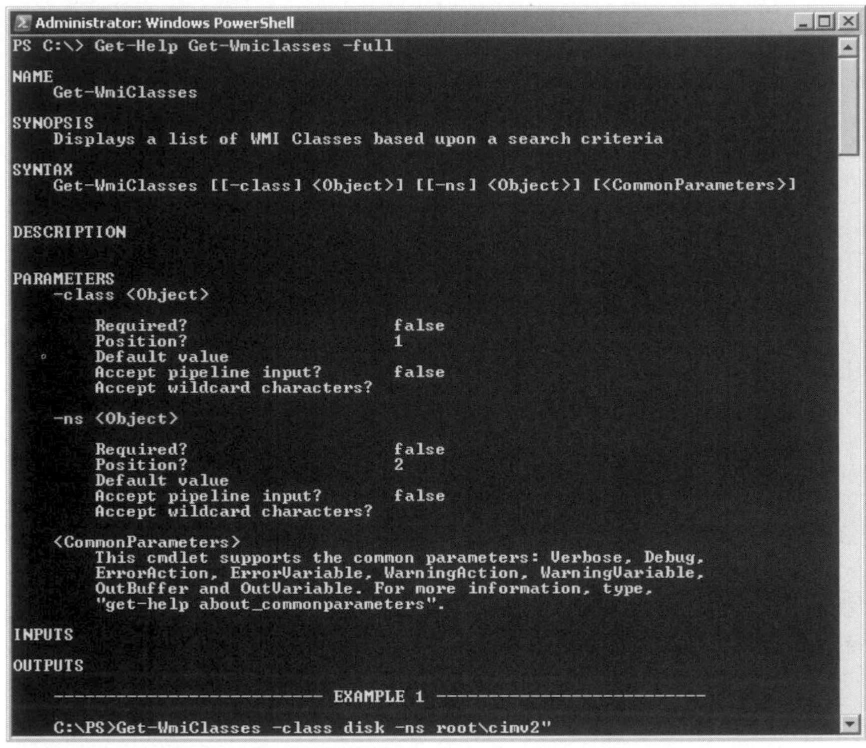

FIGURE 13-40 Full help obtained from the function *Get-WmiClasses*

The complete GetWmiClassesFunction.ps1 script is seen here.

GetWmiClassesFunction1.ps1

```
Function Get-WmiClasses(
                        $class=($paramMissing=$true),
                        $ns="root\cimv2"
                       )
{
<#
    .SYNOPSIS
      Displays a list of WMI Classes based upon a search criteria
    .EXAMPLE
```

```
    Get-WmiClasses -class disk -ns root\cimv2"
    This command finds wmi classes that contain the word disk. The
    classes returned are from the root\cimv2 namespace.
#>
  If($local:paramMissing)
    {
      throw "USAGE: getwmi2 -class <class type> -ns <wmi namespace>"
    } #$local:paramMissing
  "`nClasses in $ns namespace ...."
  Get-WmiObject -namespace $ns -list |
  where-object {
                 $_.name -match $class -and `
                 $_.name -notlike 'cim*'
               }
  #
} #end get-wmiclasses
```

If you intend to use the dot-source method for including functions into your working Windows PowerShell environment, it makes sense to add the directory that contains your scripts to the path. You can add your function Storage directory as a permanent change by using the Windows GUI tools, or you can simply make the addition to your path each time you start Windows PowerShell by making the change via your PowerShell profile. If you decide to add your Function directory by using Windows PowerShell commands, you can use the PowerShell Environmental drive to access the system path variable and make the change. The code seen here first examines the path, and then it appends the C:\Fso folder to the end of the path. Each directory that is added to the search path is separated by a semicolon. When you append a directory to the path, you must include that semicolon as the first item that is added. You can use the += operator to append a directory to the end of the path. The last command checks the path once again to ensure the change took place as intended.

```
PS C:\> $env:path
C:\Windows\system32;C:\Windows;C:\Windows\System32\Wbem;C:\Windows\System32
\Windows System Resource Manager\bin;C:\Windows\idmu\common;C:\Windows\system32
\WindowsPowerShell\v1.0\
PS C:\> $env:path += ";C:\fso"
PS C:\> $env:path
C:\Windows\system32;C:\Windows;C:\Windows\System32\Wbem;C:\Windows\System32
\Windows System Resource Manager\bin;C:\Windows\idmu\common;C:\Windows\system32
\WindowsPowerShell\v1.0\;C:\fso
```

A change made to the path via the Windows PowerShell Environmental drive is temporary; it only lasts for the length of the current PowerShell console session. It will take effect immediately, and therefore it is a convenient method to alter your current Windows PowerShell environment quickly without making permanent changes to your system environmental settings.

A very powerful feature of modifying the path via the Windows PowerShell Environmental drive is that the changes are applied immediately and are at once available to the current PowerShell session. This means you can add a directory to the path, dot-source a script that contains functions, and use the Get-Help cmdlet to display help information without the requirement to close and to open Windows PowerShell. After a directory has been appended to the search path, you can dot-source scripts from that directory without the need to type the entire path to that directory. The technique of modifying the path, dot-sourcing a directory, and using Get-Help is illustrated here.

```
PS C:\> $env:Path += ";C:\fso"
PS C:\> . GetWmiClassesFunction1.ps1
PS C:\> Get-Help Get-WmiClasses
```

Figure 13-41 displays the results of using the technique of adding a directory to the path, dot-sourcing a script that resides in the newly appended folder, and then calling the Get-Help cmdlet to retrieve information from the newly added functions.

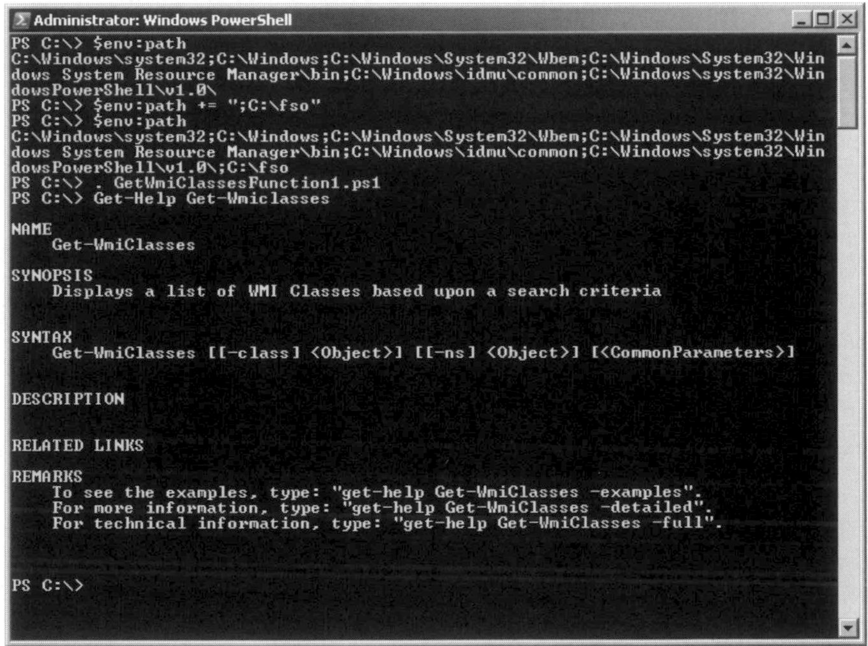

FIGURE 13-41 By appending to the path, functions can be dot-sourced easily into the current Windows PowerShell environment.

DIRECT FROM THE SOURCE

Folders and Locations

James O'Neill, Evangelist
Developer and Platform Group

If you type DIR Variable: you will see the locations Windows PowerShell uses to get its configuration information. *$PSHome* holds the folder where Windows PowerShell is installed, and this contains .PS1XML files, which control the default formatting and type extensions. It also contains language folders that hold the Windows PowerShell online help and a Modules folder. *$Profile* contains the path to the user's profile, which is a script that is run when Windows PowerShell starts. In fact, Windows PowerShell supports four profiles—two that are host specific, and two for all hosts. One of each kind is for the current user, and the other of each kind applies to all users. You can see these as properties of *$Profile* named *.AllUsersAllHosts*, *AllUsersCurrentHost*, *CurrentUserAllHosts*, and *CurrentUserCurrentHost*. Windows PowerShell uses a Windows environment variable, *$env:psModulePath*, to determine where modules should be located. The default is the $PSHome folder and the folder containing the users profile.

Locate and Load Modules

There are two default locations for Windows PowerShell modules. The first location is found in the user's Home directory, and the second is in the Windows PowerShell Home directory. The Modules directory in the Windows PowerShell Home directory always exists. However, the Modules directory in the user's Home directory is not present by default. The Modules directory will exist only in the user's Home directory if it has been created. The creation of the Modules directory in the user's Home directory does not normally happen until someone decides to create and to store modules there. A nice feature of the Modules directory is that when it exists, it is the first place that Windows PowerShell uses when it searches for a module. If the user's Modules directory does not exist, the Modules directory within the Windows PowerShell Home directory is used.

Listing Available Modules

Windows PowerShell modules exist in two states: loaded and unloaded. To display a list of all loaded modules, use the Get-Module cmdlet without any parameters, as shown here.

```
PS C:\> Get-Module

ModuleType Name                    ExportedCommands
---------- ----                    ----------------
Script     helloworld              {Hello-World, Hello-User}
```

If multiple modules are loaded when the Get-Module cmdlet is run, each module will appear along with its accompanying exported commands on their own individual lines, as seen here.

```
PS C:\> Get-Module

ModuleType Name                     ExportedCommands
---------- ----                     ----------------
Script     GetFreeDiskSpace         Get-FreeDiskSpace
Script     HelloWorld               {Hello-World, Hello-User}
Script     TextFunctions            {New-Line, Get-TextStats}
Manifest   BitsTransfer             {Start-BitsTransfer, Remove-BitsTransfe...
Script     PSDiagnostics            {Enable-PSTrace, Enable-WSManTrace, Sta...


PS C:\>
```

If no modules are loaded, nothing will be displayed to the Windows PowerShell console. No errors are displayed, nor is there any confirmation that the command has actually run, as shown here.

```
PS C:\> Get-Module
PS C:\>
```

To obtain a listing of all modules that are available on the system but are not loaded, you use the Get-Module cmdlet with the *–ListAvailable* parameter. The Get-Module cmdlet with the *–ListAvailable* parameter lists all modules that are available whether or not the modules are loaded into the Windows PowerShell console, as seen here.

```
PS C:\> Get-Module -ListAvailable

ModuleType Name                     ExportedCommands
---------- ----                     ----------------
Manifest   GetFreeDiskSpace         Get-FreeDiskSpace
Script     HelloWorld               {}
Script     TextFunctions            {}
Manifest   BitsTransfer             {}
Manifest   PSDiagnostics            {Enable-PSTrace, Enable-WSManTrace, Sta...
```

Loading Modules

After you identify a module you want to load, you use the Import-Module cmdlet to load the module into the current Windows PowerShell session, as shown here.

```
PS C:\> Import-Module -Name GetFreeDiskSpace
PS C:\>
```

If the module exists, the Import-Module cmdlet completes without displaying any information. If the module is already loaded, no error message is displayed. This is seen in the code here, where you use the up arrow to retrieve the previous command and press Enter to execute the command. The Import-Module command is run three times.

```
PS C:\> Import-Module -Name GetFreeDiskSpace
PS C:\> Import-Module -Name GetFreeDiskSpace
PS C:\> Import-Module -Name GetFreeDiskSpace
PS C:\>
```

After you import the module, you may want to use the Get-Module cmdlet to quickly see what functions are exposed by the module, as seen here.

```
PS C:\> Get-Module -Name GetFreeDiskSpace

ModuleType Name                        ExportedCommands
---------- ----                        ----------------
Script     GetFreeDiskSpace            Get-FreeDiskSpace


PS C:\>
```

The GetFreeDiskSpace module exports a single command: the *Get-FreeDiskSpace* function. The one problem with using the Get-Module cmdlet is that it does not include other information that could be exported by the module. It lists only commands.

When working with modules that have long names, you are not limited to typing the entire module name. You are allowed to use wildcards. When using wildcards, it is a best practice to type a significant portion of the module name so that you match only a single module from the list of modules that are available to you, as seen here.

```
PS C:\> Import-Module -Name GetFree*
PS C:\>
```

IMPORTANT **If you use a wildcard pattern that matches more than one module name, the first matched module is loaded, and the remaining matches are discarded. This can lead to inconsistent and unpredictable results. No error message is displayed when more than one module matches a wildcard pattern.**

If you want to load all the modules that are available on your system, you can use the Get-Module cmdlet with the *–ListAvailable* parameter and pipeline the resulting *PSModuleInfo* objects to the Import-Module cmdlet as seen here.

```
PS C:\> Get-Module -ListAvailable | Import-Module
PS C:\>
```

If you have a module that uses a verb that is not on the allowed verb list, a warning message displays when you import the module. The functions in the module still work, and the module will work, but the warning is displayed to remind you to check the authorized verb list, as seen here.

```
PS C:\> Get-Module -ListAvailable | Import-Module
WARNING: Some imported command names include unapproved verbs which might make
them less discoverable.  Use the Verbose parameter for more detail or type
Get-Verb to see the list of approved verbs.
PS C:\>
```

To obtain more information about which unapproved verbs are being used, you use the *–verbose* parameter of Import-Module. This command is seen here.

```
PS C:\> Get-Module -ListAvailable | Import-Module -Verbose
```

The results of the Import-Module *–verbose* command are seen in Figure 13-42.

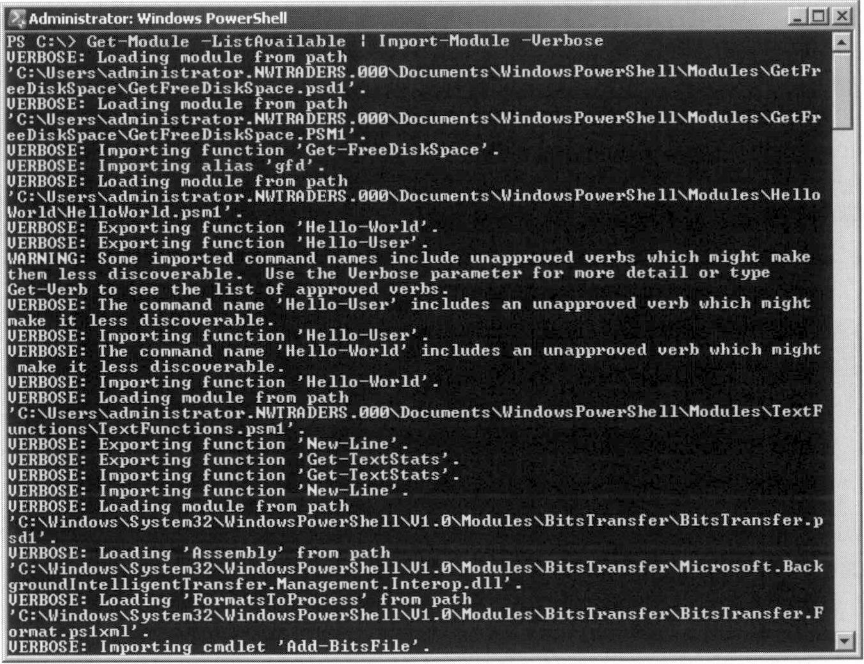

FIGURE 13-42 The *–verbose* parameter of Import-Module displays information about each function, as well as illegal verb names.

Install Modules

One of the features of modules is that they can be installed without elevated rights. Because each user has a Modules folder in the %UserProfile% directory that he or she has the right to use, the installation of a module does not require administrator rights. An additional feature of modules is that they do not require a specialized installer. The files associated with a module can be copied by using the XCopy utility, or they can be copied by using Windows PowerShell cmdlets.

Creating a Modules Folder

The user's Modules folder does not exist by default. To avoid confusion, you may decide to create the Modules directory in the user's profile prior to deploying modules, or you may simply create a module installer script that checks for the existence of the user's Modules folder, creates the folder if it does not exist, and then copies the modules. One thing to remember when directly accessing the user's Modules directory is that it is in a different location depending on the version of the operating system. On Windows XP and Windows Server 2003, the user's Modules folder is in the My Documents folder, whereas on Windows Vista and later versions, the user's Modules folder is in the Documents folder. In the Copy-Modules.ps1 script, you solve the problem of different Modules folder locations by using a function, *Get-OperatingSystemVersion*, that retrieves the major version number of the operating system. The *Get-OperatingSystemVersion* function is seen here.

```
Function Get-OperatingSystemVersion
{
 (Get-WmiObject -Class Win32_OperatingSystem).Version
} #end Get-OperatingSystemVersion
```

The major version number of the operating system is used in the *Test-ModulePath* function. If the major version number of the operating system is greater than or equal to 6, it means the operating system is at least Windows Vista and will therefore use the Documents folder in the path to the modules. If the major version number of the operating system is less than 6, the script will use the My Documents folder for the module location. After you have determined the version of the operating system and have ascertained the path to the module location, it is time to determine whether the Modules folder exists. The best tool to use for checking the existence of folders is the Test-Path cmdlet. The Test-Path cmdlet returns a Boolean value. As you are only interested in the absence of the folder, you can use the *–not* operator, as shown here in the completed *Test-ModulePath* function.

```
Function Test-ModulePath
{
 $VistaPath = "$env:userProfile\documents\WindowsPowerShell\Modules"
 $XPPath =  "$env:Userprofile\my documents\WindowsPowerShell\Modules"
 if ([int](Get-OperatingSystemVersion).substring(0,1) -ge 6)
   {
     if(-not(Test-Path -path $VistaPath))
       {
         New-Item -Path $VistaPath -itemtype directory | Out-Null
       } #end if
   } #end if
 Else
```

```
    {
      if(-not(Test-Path -path $XPPath))
        {
          New-Item -path $XPPath -itemtype directory | Out-Null
        } #end if
    } #end else
} #end Test-ModulePath
```

After the user's Modules folder has been created, it is time to create a child folder to hold the new module. A module is always installed into a folder that has the same name as the module itself. The name of the module is the file name that contains the module without the .psm1 extension. This location is shown in Figure 13-43.

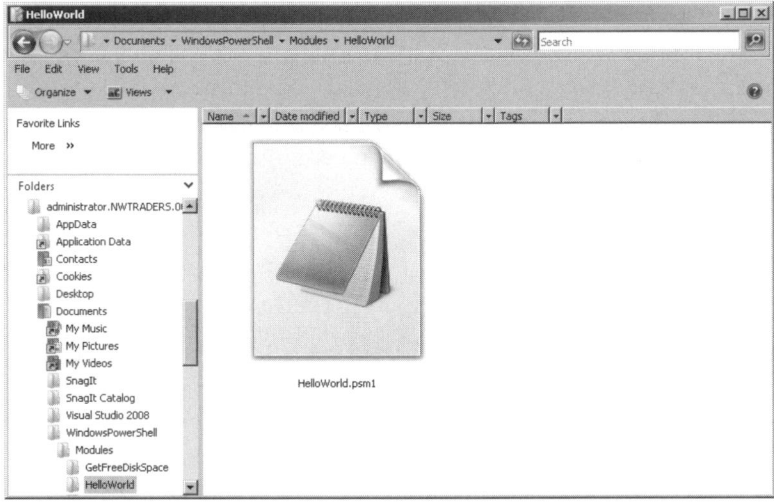

FIGURE 13-43 Modules are placed in the user's Modules directory.

In the *Copy-Module* function from the Copy-Modules.ps1 script, the first action that is taken is to retrieve the value of the *PSModulePath* environment variable. Because there are two locations that modules can be stored, the *PSModulePath* environment variable contains the path to both locations. *PSModulePath* is not stored as an array; it is stored as a string. The value contained in *PSModulePath* is seen here.

```
PS C:\> $env:psmodulePath
C:\Users\administrator.NWTRADERS.000\Documents\WindowsPowerShell\Modules;C:\Windows
\System32\WindowsPowerShell\V1.0\Modules\
```

If you attempt to index into the data stored in the *PSModulePath* environment variable, you will retrieve one letter at a time, as seen here.

```
PS C:\> $env:psmodulePath[0]
C
PS C:\> $env:psmodulePath[1]
:
```

```
PS C:\> $env:psmodulePath[2]
\
PS C:\> $env:psmodulePath[3]
U
```

Attempting to retrieve the path to the user's Modules folder one letter at a time would be difficult at best and error-prone at worst. Because the data is a string, you can use string methods to manipulate the two paths. To break a string into an array that can be utilized easily, you use the *split* method from the *System.String* class. You need only to pass a single value to the *split* method—the character to split upon. Because the value stored in the *PSModulePath* variable is a string, you can access the *split* method directly, as shown here.

```
PS C:\> $env:psmodulePath.split(";")
C:\Users\administrator.NWTRADERS.000\Documents\WindowsPowerShell\Modules
C:\Windows\System32\WindowsPowerShell\V1.0\Modules\
```

You can see from this output that the first string displayed is the path to the user's Modules folder, and the second path is the path to the system Modules folder. Because the *split* method turns a string into an array, it means you can now index into the array and retrieve the path to the user's Modules folder by using the [0] syntax. You do not need to use an intermediate variable to store the returned array of paths if you do not want to do so. You can index into the returned array directly. If you were to use the intermediate variable to hold the returned array and then index into the array, the code would resemble the following.

```
PS C:\> $aryPaths = $env:psmodulePath.split(";")
PS C:\> $aryPaths[0]
C:\Users\administrator.NWTRADERS.000\Documents\WindowsPowerShell\Modules
```

Because the array is immediately available after the *split* method has been called, you directly retrieve the user's Modules folder, as seen here.

```
PS C:\> $env:psmodulePath.split(";")[0]
C:\Users\administrator.NWTRADERS.000\Documents\WindowsPowerShell\Modules
```

Working with the *$modulePath* Variable

The path that will be used to store the module is stored in the *$modulePath* variable. This path includes the path to the user's Modules folder and a child folder that is the same name as the module itself. To create the new path, it is a best practice to use the Join-Path cmdlet instead of doing string concatenation and attempting to build the path to the new folder manually. The Join-Path cmdlet will put together a parent path and a child path to create a new path, as seen here.

```
$ModulePath = Join-Path -path $userPath `
               -childpath (Get-Item -path $name).basename
```

In Windows PowerShell 2.0, the PowerShell team added a script property called *basename* to the *System.Io.FileInfo* class. This makes it easy to retrieve the name of a file without the file extension. Prior to Windows PowerShell 2.0, it was common to use the *split* method or some other string manipulation technique to remote the extension from the file name. Use of the *basename* property is shown here.

```
PS C:\> (Get-Item -Path C:\fso\HelloWorld.psm1).basename
HelloWorld
```

The last step that needs to be accomplished is to create the subdirectory that will hold the module and to copy the module files into the directory. To avoid cluttering the display with the returned information from the New-Item and the Copy-Item cmdlets, the results are pipelined to the Out-Null cmdlet, as seen here.

```
New-Item -path $modulePath -itemtype directory | Out-Null
Copy-item -path $name -destination $ModulePath | Out-Null
```

The entry point to the Copy-Modules.ps1 script calls the *Test-ModulePath* function to determine whether the user's Modules folder exists. It then uses the Get-ChildItem cmdlet to retrieve a listing of all the module files in a particular folder. The *–Recurse* parameter is used to retrieve all the module files in the path. The resulting *FileInfo* objects are pipelined to the ForEach-Object cmdlet. The *fullname* property of each *FileInfo* object is passed to the Copy-Module function, as shown here.

```
Test-ModulePath
Get-ChildItem -Path C:\fso -Include *.psm1,*.psd1 -Recurse |
Foreach-Object { Copy-Module -name $_.fullName }
```

The complete Copy-Modules.ps1 script is seen here.

Copy-Modules.ps1

```
Function Get-OperatingSystemVersion
{
 (Get-WmiObject -Class Win32_OperatingSystem).Version
} #end Get-OperatingSystemVersion

Function Test-ModulePath
{
 $VistaPath = "$env:userProfile\documents\WindowsPowerShell\Modules"
 $XPPath =  "$env:Userprofile\my documents\WindowsPowerShell\Modules"
 if ([int](Get-OperatingSystemVersion).substring(0,1) -ge 6)
   {
     if(-not(Test-Path -path $VistaPath))
       {
         New-Item -Path $VistaPath -itemtype directory | Out-Null
       } #end if
   } #end if
 Else
   {
     if(-not(Test-Path -path $XPPath))
```

```
        {
          New-Item -path $XPPath -itemtype directory | Out-Null
        } #end if
    } #end else
} #end Test-ModulePath

Function Copy-Module([string]$name)
{
 $UserPath = $env:PSModulePath.split(";")[0]
 $ModulePath = Join-Path -path $userPath `
               -childpath (Get-Item -path $name).basename
 New-Item -path $modulePath -itemtype directory | Out-Null
 Copy-item -path $name -destination $ModulePath | Out-Null
}

# *** Entry Point to Script ***
Test-ModulePath
Get-ChildItem -Path C:\fso -Include *.psm1,*.psd1 -Recurse |
Foreach-Object { Copy-Module -name $_.fullName }
```

NOTE Scripting support does not need to be enabled in Windows PowerShell to use modules unless the module contains functions, such as the diagnostic modules. However, to run the Copy-Modules.ps1 script to install modules to the user's profile, you need script support. To enable scripting support in Windows PowerShell, you use the Set-ExecutionPolicy cmdlet. You could also use Xcopy to copy modules to the user's Modules folder.

Creating a Module Drive

An easy way to work with modules is to create a couple of Windows PowerShell drives using the FileSystem provider. Because the modules are in a location to which it is not easy to navigate from the command line and because the *$PSModulePath* returns a string that contains the path to both the user's and the system Modules folders, it makes sense to provide an easier way to work with the modules' location. To create a Windows PowerShell drive for the user's Modules folder location, you use the New-PSDrive cmdlet, specify a name such as **mymods,** use the FileSystem provider, and obtain the root location from the *$PSModulePath* environment variable by using the *split* method from the .NET Framework string class. For the user's Modules folder, you use the first element from the returned array, as shown here.

```
PS C:\> New-PSDrive -Name mymods -PSProvider filesystem -Root `
(($env:PSModulePath).Split(";")[0])

WARNING: column "CurrentLocation" does not fit into the display and was removed
.

Name           Used (GB)     Free (GB) Provider      Root
----           ---------     --------- --------      ----
mymods                           47.62 FileSystem    C:\Users\administrator....
```

The command to create a Windows PowerShell drive for the system module location is exactly the same as the one used to create a Windows PowerShell drive for the user's Modules folder location, with the exception of specifying a different name, such as **sysmods,** and choosing the second element from the array you obtain by using the *split* method on the *$PSModulePath* variable. This command is seen here.

```
PS C:\> New-PSDrive -Name sysmods -PSProvider filesystem -Root `
(($env:PSModulePath).Split(";")[1])

WARNING: column "CurrentLocation" does not fit into the display and was removed
.

Name           Used (GB)     Free (GB) Provider      Root
----           ---------     --------- --------      ----
sysmods                          47.62 FileSystem    C:\Windows\System32\Win...
```

You can also write a script that creates Windows PowerShell drives for each of the two module locations. To do this, you first create an array of names for the Windows PowerShell drives. You then use a *for* statement to walk through the array of Windows PowerShell drive names and call the New-PSDrive cmdlet. Because you are running the commands inside a script, it means the new Windows PowerShell drives would live within the script scope by default. When the script ends, the script scope goes away. This means the Windows PowerShell drives would not be available when the script ended, which would defeat your purposes in creating them in the first place. To solve this scoping problem, you need to create the Windows PowerShell drives within the global scope, which means they will be available in the Windows PowerShell console once the script has completed running. To avoid displaying confirmation messages when creating the Windows PowerShell drives, you pipe the results to the Out-Null cmdlet.

In the New-ModulesDrive.ps1 script, another function is created. This function displays global FileSystem provider Windows PowerShell drives. When the script is run, the *New-ModuleDrives* function is called. It is followed by calling the *Get-FileSystemDrives* function. The complete New-ModulesDrive.ps1 script is shown here.

New-ModulesDrive.ps1

```
Function New-ModuleDrives
{
<#
    .SYNOPSIS
    Creates two PSDrives: myMods and sysMods
    .EXAMPLE
    New-ModuleDrives
    Creates two PSDrives: myMods and sysMods. These correspond
    to the users' modules folder and the system modules folder respectively.
#>
 $driveNames = "myMods","sysMods"

 For($i = 0 ; $i -le 1 ; $i++)
 {
  New-PsDrive -name $driveNames[$i] -PSProvider filesystem `
  -Root ($env:PSModulePath.split(";")[$i]) -scope Global |
  Out-Null
 } #end For
} #end New-ModuleDrives

Function Get-FileSystemDrives
{
<#
    .SYNOPSIS
    Displays global PS Drives that use the Filesystem provider
    .EXAMPLE
    Get-FileSystemDrives
    Displays global PS Drives that use the Filesystem provider
#>
 Get-PSDrive -PSProvider FileSystem -scope Global
} #end Get-FileSystemDrives

# *** EntryPoint to Script ***
New-ModuleDrives
Get-FileSystemDrives
```

Summary

This chapter has provided an overview of tools that you can use for managing a Windows 7 desktop infrastructure. The tools covered included in-box tools, free tools available from the Microsoft Download Center, the Windows Sysinternals Suite of system troubleshooting tools, the six products included in the Microsoft Desktop Optimization Pack for Software Assurance, and the Microsoft System Center family of products. The chapter also includes an extensive tutorial on Windows PowerShell for administrators, including demonstrations of some of the new features in Windows PowerShell 2.0.

Additional Resources

These resources contain additional information and tools related to this chapter.

Related Information

The information below is organized according to topic to make it easier to use.

Related Information on In-box Tools

- For information on how to use WMI to manage Windows 7 computers, see the various resources available on the Script Center on Microsoft TechNet at *http://www.microsoft.com/technet/scriptcenter/default.mspx.*
- For a collection of sample administration scripts, see the Script Center Script Repository at *http://www.microsoft.com/technet/scriptcenter/scripts/default.mspx?mfr=true.*
- For more information about Windows PowerShell, see the "Scripting with Windows PowerShell" section of the Script Center at *http://www.microsoft.com/technet/scriptcenter/hubs/msh.mspx.*
- For information about what's new in Windows PowerShell 2.0, see *http://technet.microsoft.com/en-us/library/dd367858.aspx.*
- For the latest news about Windows PowerShell and tips on using it, see the Windows PowerShell blog at *http://blogs.msdn.com/PowerShell/.*
- For information about WinRM and WinRS, see "Windows Remote Management" on MSDN at *http://msdn.microsoft.com/en-us/library/aa384426.aspx.*
- For a list of Windows commands and their detailed syntax, see the "Command Reference" section of "Commands, References, and Tools for Windows Server 2008 R2" at *http://technet.microsoft.com/en-us/library/dd695747.aspx.*

Related Information on Downloadable Tools

- Search the Microsoft Download Center at *http://www.microsoft.com/downloads/* for free system tools you can use to manage different aspects of Windows 7 in your environment.

Related Information on Windows Sysinternals Tools

- For information concerning each of the tools in the Windows Sysinternals Suite, click on the link for the tool on the Sysinternals Utility Index at *http://technet.microsoft.com/en-us/sysinternals/bb545027.aspx*.
- You can download the entire Sysinternals Suite as a compressed archive file from *http://download.sysinternals.com/Files/SysinternalsSuite.zip*.

Related Information on MDOP for Software Assurance

- For information about the Microsoft Software Assurance for Volume Licensing program, see *http://www.microsoft.com/licensing/software-assurance/default.aspx*.
- For information about Windows 7 Enterprise Edition, see *http://www.microsoft.com/windows/enterprise/products/windows-7-enterprise.aspx*.
- For information about MDOP, see *http://www.microsoft.com/windows/enterprise/technologies/mdop.aspx*.
- For the latest news about MDOP products and tips on how to use them, see the Official MDOP blog at *http://blogs.technet.com/mdop/default.aspx*.
- Software Assurance customers can download MDOP 2009 from the MVLS site at *https://licensing.microsoft.com/eLicense/L1033/Default.asp*.
- For information about App-V 4.5, see *http://www.microsoft.com/windows/enterprise/products/app-virtualization.aspx*.
- For information about AGPM, see *http://www.microsoft.com/windows/enterprise/products/advanced-group-policy-management.aspx*.
- For information about AIS 1.5, see *http://www.microsoft.com/windows/enterprise/products/ais.aspx*.
- For information about DaRT, see *http://www.microsoft.com/windows/enterprise/products/dart.aspx*.
- For information about MED-V 1.0, see *http://www.microsoft.com/windows/enterprise/products/med-v.aspx*.
- For information about DEM, see *http://www.microsoft.com/windows/enterprise/products/dem.aspx*.

Related Information on Microsoft System Center

- For information about System Center Configuration Manager 2007 R2, see *http://www.microsoft.com/systemcenter/configurationmanager/en/us/default.aspx*.
- For the latest news about System Center Configuration Manager and tips on using the platform, see the System Center Configuration Manager Team blog at *http://blogs.technet.com/configmgrteam/default.aspx*.

- For information on resolving issues with System Center Configuration Manager, see the Configuration Manager Support Team blog at *http://blogs.technet.com/configurationmgr/default.aspx*.
- For more information about System Center Operations Manager 2007 R2, see *http://www.microsoft.com/systemcenter/operationsmanager/en/us/default.aspx*.
- For the latest news about System Center Operations Manager and tips on using the platform, see the System Center Operations Manager Team blog at *http://blogs.technet.com/momteam/default.aspx*.
- For information on resolving issues with System Center Operations Manager, see the Operations Manager Support Team blog at *http://blogs.technet.com/operationsmgr*.
- For more information about System Center Data Protection Manager 2007 SP1, see *http://www.microsoft.com/systemcenter/dataprotectionmanager/en/us/default.aspx*.
- For the latest news about System Center Data Protection Manager and tips on using the platform, see the System Center Data Protection Manager blog called "Rescue Data Like a Hero" at *http://blogs.technet.com/dpm/*.
- For more information about System Center Virtual Machine Manager 2008 R2, see *http://www.microsoft.com/systemcenter/virtualmachinemanager/en/us/default.aspx*.
- For the latest news about System Center Virtual Machine Manager and tips on using the platform, see the System Center Virtual Machine Manager Product and Support Team blog at *http://blogs.technet.com/scvmm/*.
- For more information about System Center Essentials 2007 SP1, see *http://www.microsoft.com/systemcenter/sce/default.mspx*.
- For the latest news about System Center Essentials and tips on using the platform, see the System Center Essentials Team blog at *http://blogs.technet.com/systemcenteressentials/*.

Related Information on Learning Windows PowerShell

- Additional resources for learning how to use Windows PowerShell can be found on the "Scripting with Windows PowerShell" section of the Script Center at *http://www.microsoft.com/technet/scriptcenter/hubs/msh.mspx*.

On the Companion Media

Windows PowerShell (.ps1) scripts:

- BlockForStatement.ps1
- CallNew-LineTextFunction.ps1
- Copy-Modules.ps1
- DemoBreakFor.ps1
- DemoDoUntil.ps1

- DemoDoWhile.ps1
- DemoExitFor.ps1
- DemoForEach.ps1
- DemoForEachObject.ps1
- DemoForLoop.ps1
- DemoForWithoutInitOrRepeat.ps1
- DemoIf.ps1
- demoIfElse.ps1
- demoIfElseIfElse.ps1
- DemoLineContinuation.ps1
- DemoSwitchArray.ps1
- DemoSwitchArrayBreak.ps1
- DemoSwitchCase.ps1
- DemoSwitchMultiMatch.ps1
- DisplayCapitalLetters.ps1
- DoLoopForStatement.ps1
- DoUntilBios.ps1
- DoWhileAlwaysRuns.ps1
- EndlessDoUntil.ps1
- Export-XML.ps1
- ForEndlessLoop.ps1
- ForProcesses.ps1
- Get-ISEHost.ps1
- Get-PsCmdlet.ps1
- GetWmiClasses.ps1
- GetWmiClassesFunction.ps1
- GetWmiClassesFunction1.ps1
- MultiCountForLoop.ps1
- New-ModulesDrive.ps1
- ScanForSoftware.ps1
- StopNotepad.ps1
- StopNotepadSilentlyContinue.ps1
- StopNotepadSilentlyContinuePassThru.ps1
- Test-ModulePath.ps1
- TextFunctions.ps1

- TextFunctions1.ps1
- WhileDemo1.ps1
- WhileDoesNotRun.ps1
- WhileReadLine.ps1

VBScript (.vbs) scripts:

- DemoDoUntil.vbs
- DemoDoWhile.vbs
- DemoExitFor.vbs
- DemoForEachNext.vbs
- DemoForLoop.vbs
- DemoIf.vbs
- DemoIfElse.vbs
- DemoIfElseIfElse.vbs
- DemoQuitFor.vbs
- DemoSelectCase.vbs
- ListFoldersAndModifiedDates.vbs
- SearchTextFileForSpecificWord.vbs
- WhileReadLineWend.vbs

CHAPTER 14

Managing the Desktop Environment

Group Policy is a powerful tool for managing the computer and user configuration of client computers in enterprise environments. Using Group Policy, administrators can configure, manage, and lock down different aspects of desktop and mobile PCs and the experience of users on these clients. This chapter describes the new features of Group Policy in the Windows 7 and Windows Server 2008 R2 operating systems and how they build on the earlier Group Policy enhancements introduced in Windows Vista and Windows Server 2008.

Understanding Group Policy in Windows 7

Windows Vista and Windows Server 2008 introduced new and enhanced features in the area of Group Policy management, processing, and settings. These features and enhancements make Group Policy easier to manage, more reliable, better performing, and easier to troubleshoot in enterprise environments where Active Directory Domain Services (AD DS) is deployed. Windows 7 and Windows Server 2008 R2 build on the foundation of Group Policy improvements made in Windows Vista and Windows Server 2008 by adding powerful new features that make enterprise network management easier than ever. For the benefit of administrators who are migrating desktop computers from Windows XP to Windows 7, this section begins by reviewing the Group Policy improvements made previously in Windows Vista and Windows Server 2008 compared with how Group Policy was implemented in earlier versions of Windows.

> **MORE INFO** This chapter deals mainly with the core administrative issues of managing Group Policy in Windows 7 environments. For detailed task-oriented help on managing all aspects of Group Policy, see the *Windows Group Policy Administrator's Pocket Consultant* by William R. Stanek (Microsoft Press, 2009).

Group Policy Before Windows Vista

In earlier versions of Windows such as Microsoft Windows 2000 Server, Windows XP, and Windows Server 2003, Group Policy had a number of limitations due to how it was implemented on these platforms. These limitations included the following:

- Administrative Template (ADM) files used a proprietary syntax that made it complicated for administrators to create their own custom ADM template files to extend Group Policy management functionality by extending or introducing new registry-based policy settings for Windows, other Microsoft software products, third-party applications from Independent Software Vendors (ISVs), and custom internal applications. In addition, the syntax for ADM template files made it difficult for administrators to develop localized versions that they could use to view registry-based ADM policy settings in their own languages. (Using multiple languages with ADM files resulted in a mixture of languages in the user interface—the ADM file with the latest date/timestamp overwrote the other ADM files.) All of these limitations made it difficult for administrators to create their own custom Group Policy solutions for managing registry-based settings, especially in global enterprises with multilingual environments.
- Whenever you used the Group Policy Management Editor on an administrative workstation to create a new domain-based Group Policy object (GPO), the entire set of default ADM template files was automatically copied from the %SystemRoot%\inf folder on the computer where the GPO was being edited to the Group Policy Template (GPT), which is the physical portion of the GPO stored on the domain controllers for your domain. For each GPO that you create, the GPT is created at %SystemRoot%\SYSVOL*domain*\Policies*GPO_GUID* and also appears in the SYSVOL share at *domain_controller_name*\SYSVOL*domain_name*\Policies*GPO_GUID*, where *GPO_GUID* is a folder named after the globally unique identifier (GUID) of the GPO. (The other logical portion of each GPO is stored in the Group Policy Container [GPC], found in the CN=Policies,CN=System container in AD DS.) The File Replication Service (FRS) replicates the contents of each GPT folder within the SYSVOL share to all domain controllers in the domain, and the storage cost of having copies of all of the default ADM template files stored in each GPT is at least 4 megabytes (MB) per GPO. The result of these conditions in large enterprise environments—where dozens or even hundreds of GPOs are deployed—was SYSVOL bloat, a condition that caused excessive replication traffic and consumption of hard drive space whenever a change was made to the settings in a GPO. For domain controllers at different sites linked by slow wide

area network (WAN) links, such excessive replication traffic could at times affect the availability and performance of network applications relying on other forms of traffic. This issue was exacerbated when events occurred that caused all GPOs to change simultaneously, such as when permissions on GPOs were modified when upgrading a domain from Windows 2000 to Windows Server 2003.

- To help reduce Group Policy traffic over slow WAN links, a feature called slow-link detection was used on earlier versions of Windows. Slow-link detection used exchanges of Internet Control Message Protocol (ICMP) packets to detect increased network latency and reduced responsiveness. When a slow link was detected, which by default corresponded to a latency of more than 10 milliseconds, the client pinged the domain controller three times using 2-kilobyte (KB) Echo Request packets and then used the returned Echo Reply packets to determine the effective bandwidth for the network link to the domain controller. If the effective bandwidth was determined to be fewer than 400 kilobits per second (Kbps), the client identified the network link as a slow link and informed the domain controller. If the link was identified as a slow link, Group Policy processed only security and ADM settings during background policy refresh. Because slow-link detection used ICMP for determining effective network bandwidth, problems arose if host or perimeter firewalls blocked ICMP traffic. In addition, being unable to block ICMP traffic increased the attack surface of computers.
- Group Policy processing took place only during startup (processing of machine settings), logon (processing of user settings), and at scheduled background policy refresh intervals, which by default for client computers and member servers was every 90 minutes plus a random offset of up to 30 minutes. For domain controllers, the interval was every 5 minutes. However, Group Policy was implemented on earlier versions of Windows in such a way that Group Policy processing would not take place during the following types of events: when a client computer recovered from hibernation or standby, when a mobile computer was docked with its docking station, when a computer established a virtual private network (VPN) connection with a remote computer or network, and when a client computer successfully exited network quarantine. As a result of these limitations and circumstances, earlier versions of Windows might not have the latest Group Policy settings for the domain applied to them. If updates to the Group Policy settings mitigated security vulnerabilities, this could result in temporary security vulnerabilities until the next round of background policy refresh occurred.
  In addition, if a domain controller temporarily became unavailable when scheduled background policy refresh was to occur, no mechanism was available to alert the client computer that the policy should be refreshed when the domain controller became available again. Instead, the client computer would log an error event in the event log and attempt policy refresh at the next scheduled refresh time.
- Configuring the Local Computer Policy (also called the local Group Policy object [LGPO]) on stand-alone computers resulted in settings that applied to all users (including administrators) on the computer. This limitation made it difficult to lock down and administer shared computers for kiosk use in environments such as libraries and other

public places, as well as for Windows computers used in other non–AD DS environments, because all configured settings applied not just to ordinary users but also to local administrators on the computer.

- Troubleshooting Group Policy currently requires being enabled to log on to the core Group Policy engine Userenv.dll. Log files generated by Userenv.dll are stored in the %WinDir%\Debug\Usermode folder and contain Group Policy function trace statements conflated with roaming profile load and unload function statements, making these log files hard to interpret when trying to diagnose Group Policy failure.
- Although Windows XP Service Pack 2 (SP2) and Windows Server 2003 SP1 and later versions support more than 1,800 different policy settings covering a wide variety of areas, you can't use Group Policy to manage many of these features on earlier versions of Windows. For example, there is no native way to use Group Policy to control power management; to block the installation and use of removable drives, such as universal serial bus (USB) key drives; or to deploy printers to users based on the location of their computers. (Third-party solutions do exist, however, for adding some of these functionalities to Group Policy on these platforms.)

Group Policy in Windows Vista and Windows Server 2008

To address the limitations described previously, Windows Vista and Windows Server 2008 introduced the following new features and enhancements for Group Policy:

- **ADMX templates** Windows Vista uses Extensible Markup Language (XML)–based Administrative Template (ADMX) files that use standard XML syntax instead of the proprietary syntax used in ADM template files in previous versions of Windows. Language-specific resources are stored in separate Architecture Description Markup Language (ADML) files so that administrators can display Group Policy settings in their own localized languages. For more information about this feature, see the section titled "Understanding ADMX Template Files" later in this chapter.
- **Central store** In Windows Vista, ADMX template files can be stored in a central store in the SYSVOL share on domain controllers instead of within each GPT. In addition, when you configure a central store for ADMX files, the Group Policy Management Console (GPMC) included in Remote Server Administration Tools (RSAT) will not copy or read ADMX files in an individual GPO. These enhancements considerably reduce SYSVOL bloat, which reduces replication traffic and makes Group Policy processing more efficient. Placing ADMX template files in a central store also makes them easier to manage and update across a domain. For more information, see the section titled "Configuring the Central Store" later in this chapter.
- **ICMP deprecated** Instead of using ICMP, Windows Vista uses Network Location Awareness version 2.0 (NLA 2.0) to allow Group Policy to detect the current state of network connectivity for the computer. With NLA, computers running Windows Vista can determine when domain controllers become available or unavailable to the client. NLA also allows computers running Windows Vista to refresh Group Policy in the back-

ground after they wake up from Sleep, when they establish a VPN connection, when they dock with a docking station, and when they successfully exit network quarantine. And with NLA, Group Policy can detect slow links without using ICMP and can process Group Policy on the client even when a firewall blocks all ICMP traffic.

- **MLGPOs** Support for multiple local Group Policy objects (MLGPOs) is available in Windows Vista. Using MLGPOs provides increased flexibility for configuring standalone computers for shared use, and you can even configure MLGPOs in domain environments if required. For more information, see the section titled "Understanding Multiple Local Group Policy" later in this chapter.
- **Trace logging** Windows Vista includes a new method to enable trace logging for troubleshooting issues with Group Policy Processing. This method separates Group Policy function trace statements from those created by other operating system activities so that log files are easier to interpret when you are trying to diagnose Group Policy failure.
- **New categories of policy settings** Windows Vista supports more than 2,500 different policy settings compared with the 1,800 settings supported on previous Windows platforms. These settings include new policy categories such as power management, blocking device installation, printer deployment based on location, and more. For a summary of policy setting categories introduced in Windows Vista, see the section titled "Group Policy Policy Settings in Windows 7" later in this chapter. For detailed information concerning the policy settings for a particular feature, see the chapter in this resource kit that deals with that feature. For example, for more information about using Group Policy to assign printers based on location, see Chapter 18, "Managing Printing."
- **RSAT** GPMC is now included as part of the RSAT, which is provided both as a built-in feature of Windows Server 2008 and as a separate download for Windows Vista SP1. (Note that you cannot install the downloadable RSAT on Windows Vista RTM computers; you can install it only on Windows Vista SP1 or later.) RSAT provides tools for managing Windows Server 2008 roles and services, and the downloadable RSAT for Windows Vista SP1 has the same version of GPMC that is included with the built-in RSAT feature of Windows Server 2008 and is available in both 32-bit and 64-bit platforms. The new version of GPMC that is included as part of RSAT provides access to the following features:
  - **Starter GPOs** Starter GPOs provide a foundation for creating GPOs with preconfigured ADM policy settings. A new GPO created from a Starter GPO contains all of the policy settings included in the Starter GPO. Windows Vista SP1 supports two types of Starter GPOs: Custom Starter GPOs, which allow user-created Starter GPOs, and System Starter GPOs, which are read-only Starter GPOs used to distribute predefined configurations. Like GPOs, Starter GPOs can be backed up and restored. Also, you can import and export Starter GPOs from .cab files, which makes them very portable.

- **ADM policy setting filtering** This feature lets you apply inclusive filters against the Administrative Templates All Settings node. This allows you to filter ADM policy settings to include Managed/Unmanaged and Configured/Not Configured policy settings. Also, you can use keywords for searching within the policy title, explain text, or comments of ADM policy settings. Last, you can filter on the application or platform requirements, such as filtering for all policy settings that meet the At Least Windows Server 2008 standard.
- **Comments tab** In Windows Vista, each ADM policy setting and GPO has an additional property tab named Comments. This provides a location that allows administrators to add descriptive comments to the policy setting or GPO. You can also filter on the contents of the comments field.
- **Group Policy Preferences** This feature extends the functionality of existing Group Policy by allowing administrators to perform functions that previously required scripting knowledge. Group Policy preferences allows managing drive mappings, registry settings, Local Users And Groups, files, folders, and shortcuts to client computers. Group Policy preferences can be managed from Windows Vista SP1 with RSAT or Windows Server 2008. Preference client-side extensions (CSEs) are included in Windows Server 2008, whereas downloadable versions of the preference's CSEs are available for Windows Vista RTM or later, Windows XP SP2 or later, and Windows Server 2003 SP1 or later from the Microsoft Download Center.

New Group Policy Features in Windows 7 and Windows Server 2008 R2

Windows 7 and Windows Server 2008 R2 build on the foundation of Group Policy improvements made in Windows Vista and Windows Server 2008. The key improvements to Group Policy in Windows 7 and Windows Server 2008 R2 are as follows:

- **New categories of policy settings** Windows 7 and Windows Server 2008 R2 include new categories of Group Policy policy settings and also some additional policy settings for existing policy categories. For more information on this improvement, see the section titled "Group Policy Policy Settings in Windows 7" later in this chapter.
- **Default Starter GPOs** Windows 7 and Windows Server 2008 R2 now include a number of default Starter GPOs that you can use to help ensure compliance with security best practices for enterprise environments. In Windows Vista and Windows Server 2008, you had to download these Starter GPOs separately before using them. For more information on this improvement, see the section titled "Using Starter GPOs" later in this chapter.
- **Windows PowerShell cmdlets for Group Policy** In Windows 7 and Windows Server 2008 R2, you can now use Windows PowerShell to create, edit, and maintain GPOs using the new Windows PowerShell cmdlets for Group Policy available within the Windows Server 2008 R2 GPMC. This allows administrators to automate many common

Group Policy management tasks and to perform such tasks from the command line. Note that this feature does not work with Local Group Policy. Also, it only works with registry-based settings and not with security policies or other aspects of policy. For more information on this improvement, see the section titled "Creating and Managing GPOs Using Windows PowerShell" later in this chapter.

- **Enhancements to ADM Settings** ADM policy settings (ADMX templates) are enhanced in Windows 7 and Windows Server 2008 R2 with an improved user interface that makes it easier to add comments to policy settings. Support for multi-string and QWORD registry value types is also now supported by ADMX templates for Windows 7. The overall authoring experience is also improved with the new ADMX user interface as the windows are more integrated and dialog boxes are now resizable. For information on configuring policy settings, see the section titled "Configuring Policy Settings" later in this chapter.
- **Enhancements to Group Policy Preferences** Group Policy preferences has been enhanced in Windows 7 and Windows Server 2008 R2 with new capabilities for managing Power Plan settings in Windows Vista and later versions, creating scheduled tasks for Windows Vista and later versions, creating immediate tasks for Windows Vista and later versions that run immediately upon Group Policy refresh, and managing settings for Windows Internet Explorer 8. In addition, a new preference item called Immediate Tasks lets you create tasks. For information on configuring preference items, see the section titled "Configuring Preference Items" later in this chapter.
- **Advanced Audit Policy Configuration** Group Policy in Windows 7 and Windows Server 2008 R2 now includes more than fifty Advanced Audit Policy Configuration settings that can be used to provide detailed control over 10 different areas of audit policies, and they can be used to identify possible attacks on your network or to verify compliance with your organization's security requirements. In Windows Vista and Windows Server 2008, these advanced audit policy categories can be managed from the command line using the Auditpol.exe utility. Starting in Windows 7 and Windows Server 2008, however, these advanced audit policy categories can be managed using Group Policy and are found under Computer Configuration\Policies\Windows Settings \Security Settings\Advanced Audit Policy Configuration. For more information about this feature, see Chapter 2, "Security in Windows 7."
- **Application Control Policies** Group Policy in Windows 7 and Windows Server 2008 R2 now includes Windows AppLocker, which replaces the Software Restriction Policies feature of Windows Vista and Windows Server 2008. AppLocker is found under Computer Configuration\Policies\Windows Settings\Security Settings\Application Control Policies. AppLocker includes new capabilities and extensions that can help reduce administrative overhead and allow administrators to control how users access and use executable files, scripts, Windows Installer files (.msi and .msp files), and dynamic-link libraries (DLLs). For more information on AppLocker, see Chapter 24, "Managing Client Protection."

- **Name Resolution Policy** Group Policy in Windows 7 and Windows Server 2008 R2 has been enhanced with support for Name Resolution Policy, which can be used to store configuration settings for Domain Name System security (DNSsec) and DirectAccess in a Name Resolution Policy Table (NRPT) on client computers. This new policy setting can be found under Computer Configuration\Policies\Windows Settings\Name Resolution Policy.

Group Policy Policy Settings in Windows 7

Windows Vista and Windows Server 2008 introduced many new categories of policy settings and enhanced some existing policy settings. Windows 7 and Windows Server 2008 R2 also present new policy setting categories by which administrators can configure and lock down various aspects of client computers and the experience of those who use them.

Table 14-1 summarizes many of the new and enhanced policy categories on these different platforms and indicates their location within the Group Policy Management Editor. This table also indicates whether you can find additional information on these policy settings within this resource kit. Categories of policy settings that are prefixed with an asterisk (*) are new in Windows 7 and Windows Server 2008 R2, and categories of policy settings prefixed with a double asterisk (**) are enhanced with new policy setting subcategories of policy settings in Windows 7 and Windows Server 2008 R2.

TABLE 14-1 New and Enhanced Group Policy Areas in Windows 7, Windows Server 2008 R2, Windows Vista, and Windows Server 2008

CATEGORY	DESCRIPTION	LOCATION	MORE INFO
Attachment Manager	Configures behavior for evaluating high-risk attachments	User Configuration\Policies \Administrative Templates\Windows Components\Attachment Manager	Not covered
**BitLocker Drive Encryption	Configures behavior of BitLocker Drive Encryption	Computer Configuration\Policies \Administrative Templates\Windows Components\BitLocker Drive Encryption	Chapter 16
*BranchCache	Configures BranchCache caching behavior	Computer Configuration\Policies \Administrative Templates\Network \BranchCache	Chapter 27
Deployed Printers	Deploys a printer connection to a computer	Computer Configuration\Policies \Windows Settings\Deployed Printers User Configuration\Windows Settings\Deployed Printers	Chapter 18

CATEGORY	DESCRIPTION	LOCATION	MORE INFO
Device Installation	Permits or restricts device installation based on device class or ID	Computer Configuration\Policies \Administrative Templates\System \Device Installation	Chapter 17
Disk Diagnostic	Configures level of information displayed by disk-failure diagnostics	Computer Configuration\Policies \Administrative Templates\System \Troubleshooting And Diagnostics \Disk Diagnostic	Chapter 30
Disk NV Cache	Configures hybrid hard disk properties	Computer Configuration\Policies \Administrative Templates\System \Disk NV Cache	Chapter 16
Event Log Service	Configures behavior for event logs	Computer Configuration\Policies \Administrative Templates\Windows Components\Event Log Service	Chapter 21
*Filesystem	Configures compression and other NTFS file system (NTFS) behaviors	Computer Configuration\Policies \Administrative Templates\System \Filesystem	Chapter 16
*HomeGroup	Prevents computers from joining a HomeGroup	Computer Configuration\Policies \Administrative Templates\Windows Components\HomeGroup	Chapter 25
**Internet Explorer	Configures Internet Explorer	Computer Configuration\Policies \Administrative Templates\Windows Components\Internet Explorer User Configuration\Policies \Administrative Templates\Windows Components\Internet Explorer	Chapter 20
*Network Connectivity Status Indicator	Is used by Network Awareness to verify the network environment	Computer Configuration\Policies \Administrative Templates\Network \Network Connectivity Status Indicator	Not covered
Network Sharing	Prevents users from sharing from within their profile paths	User Configuration\Policies \Administrative Templates\Windows Components\Network Sharing	Not covered
Offline Files	Configures slow-link mode for offline files	Computer Configuration\Policies \Windows Settings\Network \Offline Files	Chapter 14

CATEGORY	DESCRIPTION	LOCATION	MORE INFO
Online Assistance	Configures whether users can access untrusted Help content and other Help-related settings	Computer Configuration\Policies \Administrative Templates \Online Assistance User Configuration\Administrative Templates\Online Assistance	Not covered
Performance Control Panel	Disables access to performance tool	Computer Configuration\Policies \Administrative Templates\System \Performance Control Panel User Configuration\Policies \Administrative Templates\System \Performance Control Panel	Chapter 21
Power Management	Configures Power Management options, notifications, behavior of Power button, Sleep behavior, hard disk settings, and video settings	Computer Configuration\Policies \Administrative Templates\System \Power Management	Chapter 17
Regional and Language Options	Restricts access to regional and language options	Computer Configuration\Policies \Administrative Templates\Control Panel\Regional And Language Options User Configuration\Policies \Administrative Templates \Control Panel\Regional And Language Options	Not covered
Remote Assistance	Configures the behavior of remote assistance	Computer Configuration\Policies \Administrative Templates\System \Remote Assistance	Chapter 22
Removable Storage	Controls reading data from and writing data to removable storage devices	Computer Configuration\Policies \Administrative Templates\System \Removable Storage Access User Configuration\Policies \Administrative Templates\System \Removable Storage Access	Chapter 16
Search	Prevents indexing files in offline files cache	Computer Configuration\Policies \Administrative Templates\Windows Components\Search	Chapter 19

CATEGORY	DESCRIPTION	LOCATION	MORE INFO
*TCP/IP Settings	Configures IPv6 transition technologies for DirectAccess	Computer Configuration\Policies \Administrative Templates\Network \TCP/IP Settings	Chapter 27
Terminal Services	Configures Remote Desktop client behavior	Computer Configuration\Policies \Administrative Templates\Windows Components\Terminal Services User Configuration\Policies \Administrative Templates\Windows Components\Terminal Services	Chapter 27
**Troubleshooting and Diagnostics	Controls the behavior of built-in diagnostics	Computer Configuration\Policies \Administrative Templates\System \Troubleshooting And Diagnostics	Chapter 30
User Account Protection	Configures elevation-prompt behavior and related settings	Computer Configuration\Policies \Windows Settings\Security Settings \Local Policies\Security Options	Chapter 24
*Windows Anytime Upgrade	Prevents Windows Anytime Upgrade from running	Computer Configuration\Policies \Administrative Templates\Windows Components\Windows Anytime Upgrade User Configuration\Policies \Administrative Templates \Windows Components \Windows Anytime Upgrade	Not covered
Windows Customer Experience Improvement Program	Configures Customer Experience Improvement Program behavior	Computer Configuration\Policies \Administrative Templates\Windows Components\Windows Customer Experience Improvement Program	Chapter 12
Windows Defender	Configures Windows Defender behavior	Computer Configuration\Policies \Administrative Templates\Windows Components\Windows Defender	Chapter 24

CATEGORY	DESCRIPTION	LOCATION	MORE INFO
Windows Error Reporting	Configures Windows Error Reporting behavior, including advanced settings and consent behavior	Computer Configuration\Policies \Administrative Templates\Windows Components\Windows Error Reporting User Configuration\Policies\Windows Components\Administrative Templates\Windows Error Reporting	Chapter 21
Windows Firewall with Advance Security	Configures Windows Firewall and Internet Protocol security (IPsec) settings	Computer Configuration\Policies \Windows Settings\Security Settings \Windows Firewall With Advance Security	Chapter 26
Windows Logon Options	Displays message when logging on with cached credentials and configures behavior when logon hours expire	Computer Configuration\Policies \Administrative Templates\Windows Components\Windows Logon Options User Configuration\Policies \Administrative Templates\Windows Components\Windows Logon Options	Not covered
*Windows Reliability Analysis	Configures Reliability WMI providers	Computer Configuration\Policies \Administrative Templates\Windows Components\Windows Reliability Analysis	Chapter 21
Windows Update	Enables Windows Update Power Management to wake the system automatically to install scheduled updates	Computer Configuration\Policies \Administrative Templates\Windows Components\Windows Update	Chapter 23

Table 14-2 summarizes some of the new and enhanced policy setting categories that include policy settings for locking down the desktop experience for users in enterprise environments. Categories of policy settings that are prefixed with an asterisk (*) are new in Windows 7 and Windows Server 2008 R2.

TABLE 14-2 Categories of Group Policy Policy Settings for Locking Down User Desktops in Windows 7, Windows Server 2008 R2, Windows Vista, and Windows Server 2008

CATEGORY	DESCRIPTION	LOCATION	MORE INFO
Desktop	Configures desktop wallpaper	User Configuration\Policies \Administrative Templates\Desktop	Not covered
*Desktop Gadgets	Configures desktop gadget behavior	Computer Configuration\Policies \Administrative Templates\Windows Components\Desktop Gadgets User Configuration\Policies \Administrative Templates\Windows Components\Desktop Gadgets	Not covered
Desktop Windows Manager	Configures Desktop Windows Manager (DWM) behavior	User Configuration\Policies \Administrative Templates\Windows Components\Desktop Windows Manager	Not covered
Folder Redirection	Enables localization of redirected subfolders of Start menu and documents	Computer Configuration\Policies \Administrative Templates\System \Folder Redirection User Configuration\Policies \Administrative Templates\System \Folder Redirection	Chapter 15
*Instant Search	Configures custom Instant Search Internet search provider	User Configuration\Policies \Administrative Templates\Windows Components\Instant Search	Chapter 19
Logon	Removes entry point for Fast User Switching	Computer Configuration\Policies \Administrative Templates\System \Logon	Not covered
*Personalization	Configures theme, screen saver, and other desktop settings	User Configuration\Policies \Administrative Templates\Control Panel\Personalization	Not covered
Programs	Hides programs in Control Panel	User Configuration\Policies \Administrative Templates\Control Panel\Programs	Not covered
Start Menu And Taskbar	Locks down behavior of Start menu and taskbar	User Configuration\Policies \Administrative Templates\Start Menu And Taskbar	Not covered

CATEGORY	DESCRIPTION	LOCATION	MORE INFO
User Profiles	Configures behavior of roaming and locally cached profiles	Computer Configuration\Policies \Administrative Templates\System \User Profiles User Configuration\Policies \Administrative Templates\System \User Profiles	Chapter 15
Windows Explorer	Configures behavior of Windows Explorer current and previous versions	User Configuration\Policies \Administrative Templates\Windows Components\Windows Explorer	Not covered

Tables 14-1 and 14-2 are not meant to be an exhaustive list of all new and enhanced categories of policy settings in Windows 7 and Windows Server 2008 R2. For a complete list of all Group Policy settings in Windows 7 and Windows Server 2008 R2, download the Group Policy Settings Reference spreadsheet for these platforms from the Microsoft Download Center at *http://www.microsoft.com/downloads/*.

Understanding ADMX Template Files

In previous versions of Windows, ADM (.adm) files are used to surface the registry-based policy settings found under Computer Configuration\Administrative Templates and User Configuration\Administrative Templates in the Group Policy Management Editor. These ADM template files use a complex, text-based syntax that makes it difficult to provide a localized view of ADM settings. Windows XP and Windows Server 2003 come with five default ADM template files: Conf.adm, Inetres.adm, System.adm, Wmplayer.adm, and Wuau.adm. Most ADM settings are described in Inetres.adm and System.adm. These default ADM template files are located in the %WinDir%\inf folder, and when a GPO is created, the ADM template files on the administrative workstation are copied to the GPO in the SYSVOL share and replicated to other domain controllers in the domain.

Beginning with Windows Vista, however, ADMX template files replace ADM template files. ADMX template files use an XML-based syntax instead of the proprietary syntax used by ADM template files. ADMX template files provide the following benefits over ADM template files:

- SYSVOL bloat is avoided because ADMX template files are not stored within GPO folders on SYSVOL.
- You can now store ADMX template files in a single, central store for the whole domain, making them easier to maintain.
- With ADMX template files, Local Group Policy Editor can display policy settings in the local language for the user without affecting any other user's view of the policy settings.
- ADMX template files support strong versioning, which simplifies their creation and management.

Types of ADMX Template Files

There are two types of ADMX template files:

- **ADMX language-neutral files** These files have the extension .admx and surface the actual registry-based policy settings that you can configure using the Group Policy Management Editor user interface. Windows 7 has more than one hundred different .admx files—generally one for each category of Group Policy settings. For example, the RemovableStorage.admx file contains the registry-based settings that surface in the Local Group Policy Editor under Computer Configuration\Policies\Administrative Templates\System\Removable Storage Access and User Configuration\Policies \Administrative Templates\System\Removable Storage Access.
- **ADML language-specific files** These files have the extension .adml and comply with the ADML syntax. For each .admx file, there can be multiple .adml files, one for each installed language. These .adml files provide the localized display text for ADM settings in the Group Policy Management Editor using the currently installed language of the user.

  For example, consider an administrator of a global enterprise who resides in the United States. This administrator creates a GPO from his administrative workstation running Windows 7 with RSAT that is configured to use U.S. English as its default language. If an administrator in Germany then browses the same domain and uses the GPMC to edit this GPO, the policy settings will be displayed in German in the Group Policy Management Editor because this administrator's workstation is configured to use German as its default language. This multilingual Group Policy behavior will occur as long as .adml files for both English and German are found in the central store so that administrators in different geographical locations can access them.

HOW IT WORKS

"Supported on" and "Requirements" Text

Judith Herman, Group Policy Programming Writer
Windows Enterprise Management Division UA

Group Policy is an enterprise configuration management system. ADMX files are always supersets of previous operating systems' registry-based policy settings. This allows an administrator to support management of multiple operating systems from a single platform. The Group Policy Management Editor registry-based policy settings display values for the "Requirements:" (in extended view) or "Supported on:" (in the Properties page) context of an ADM policy setting to allow an administrator to determine which systems will be affected by different ADMX policy settings. The policy setting will apply to a specific operating system version based on the "Supported on:" text information. Note: If the policy setting is not applicable to a client workstation operating system, it will not have any effect.

Local Storage of ADMX Template Files

ADMX template files are stored locally on Windows 7 computers in the following locations:

- **ADMX language-neutral (.admx) files** Found under the %SystemRoot%\PolicyDefinitions folder.
- **ADML language-specific (.adml) files** Found under the %SystemRoot%\PolicyDefinitions*MUI_culture* folders, where *MUI_culture* is the name of the installed language and culture. For example, .adml files for U.S. English are found under the %SystemRoot%\PolicyDefinitions\en-US folder.

Domain Storage of ADMX Template Files

You can copy ADMX template files to a central store in AD DS environments running Windows Server 2003, Windows Server 2008, or Windows Server 2008 R2. This makes it easier to maintain a single master set of ADMX template files for all computers in the domain running Windows 7, Windows Vista, Windows Server 2008, and Windows Server 2008 R2. In addition, the GPMC in RSAT will automatically look for this central store; when the GPMC finds it, it will use the ADMX template files stored in this location instead of the ADMX template files stored on the local computer. Copying an ADMX template file from a computer running Windows 7 to the central store makes this ADMX template file available to Group Policy administrators anywhere in the domain and makes Group Policy settings display properly regardless of the administrator's locally installed language.

In a domain environment where the central store has been created and configured, ADMX template files are stored in the following locations on your domain controllers:

- **ADMX language-neutral (.admx) files** Found under the %SystemRoot%\sysvol\domain\policies\PolicyDefinitions folder.
- **ADML language-specific (.adml) files** Found under the %SystemRoot%\sysvol\domain\policies\PolicyDefinitions*MUI_culture* folders, where *MUI_culture* is the name of the installed language. For example, .adml files for U.S. English are found under the %SystemRoot%\sysvol\domain\policies\PolicyDefinitions\en-US folder.

> ***NOTE*** **You must create and populate the central store with ADMX template files manually if you want to use this feature. For more information, see the section titled "Configuring the Central Store" later in this chapter.**

HOW IT WORKS

ADMX Central Store on Windows 2000 Server and Windows Server 2003 Domains

Judith Herman, Group Policy Programming Writer
Windows Enterprise Management Division UA

A central store can be created in a Windows 2000 or Windows 2003 server domain. The ADMX central store is simply a set of specifically named folders on the SYSVOL of the domain to contain the ADMX files. The Group Policy Management Editor will be able to access the ADMX central store, no matter which version of domain exists, as long as an administrator is using the Group Policy Management Editor on a Windows Vista or later workstation.

Considerations When Working with ADMX Template Files

The following considerations apply when working with ADMX template files:

- Windows 7 includes only ADMX template files and does not include any of the default ADM template files used in versions of Windows earlier than Windows Vista. The default ADMX template files in Windows 7 supersede the default ADM template files used in earlier platforms.
- If you add the default ADM files to a GPO, the version of Group Policy Management Editor in Windows 7 will not read them. For example, if you have customized the System.adm file from a previous version of Windows and this ADM file is in the GPO, you will not see your customized settings when you open this GPO in the Group Policy Management Editor of a computer running Windows 7.
- If ADMX template files exist on both the local computer running Windows 7 and in a central store on domain controllers, the ADMX template files in the central store are used for surfacing policy settings when the Group Policy Management Editor is used on domain computers.
- Policy settings in ADMX template files containing Supported On text that reads "At least Windows 7" are available only to computers running Windows 7 or Windows Server 2008 R2. These settings are not available to computers running earlier versions of Windows and have no effect on the registry of these computers when they are targeted by the GPO. In addition, domain-based policy settings that exist only in ADMX template files can be managed only from computers running Windows 7 with RSAT or Windows Server 2008 R2 because the policy settings are not exposed in the versions of Group Policy Management Editor available on earlier versions of Windows.

- You can import an ADM template file into the %WinDir%\inf folder on a computer running Windows 7 in the usual way by right-clicking the appropriate (computer or user) Administrative Templates node in the Group Policy Management Editor and selecting Add/Remove Templates. Windows 7 has no interface for importing ADMX template files into %SystemRoot%\PolicyDefinitions, however.
- Administrators who develop custom ADM template files can migrate these files to the new ADMX format by using ADMX Migrator. For more information, see the section titled "Migrating ADM Templates to ADMX Format" later in this chapter.
- The Group Policy Management Editor included with Windows 7 can read and display both ADMX template files and custom-developed ADM files but not the default ADM template files used with earlier versions of Windows. (Note that this does not cause any issues because the ADMX files of Windows 7 and Windows Vista contain a superset of the policy settings found in the ADM files of earlier versions of Windows.) If a computer running Windows 7 includes a custom (non-default) ADM template file stored in the %WinDir%\inf folder on the local computer, the policy settings defined in this file will be displayed in a separate node called Classic Administrative Templates (ADM) found under Computer Configuration\Administrative Templates or User Configuration \Administrative Templates depending on the location to which the ADM template file was imported (see Figure 14-1). If ADM template files are stored in a GPO in SYSVOL, the same behavior occurs when you use the Group Policy Management Editor on a computer running Windows 7 to open the GPO.
- If you use the GPMC to create a new GPO from a Windows 7 or Windows Vista SP1 computer running RSAT and this GPO is never edited using the Group Policy Management Editor in an earlier version of Windows, the GPO folder will not contain either ADM or ADMX template files. This approach helps reduce the size of each GPO folder by about 4 MB over previous platforms and thus helps reduce SYSVOL bloat on your domain controllers. However, if you create a new GPO from a computer running Windows 7 or Windows Vista SP1 by using the GPMC and then edit the GPO using the Group Policy Management Editor from an earlier version of Windows, the ADM template files found in %WinDir%\inf on the earlier version of Windows are automatically copied to the GPO folder and replicated to all domain controllers in the domain.

> ***IMPORTANT*** **It is a best practice that after you edit GPOs using the GPMC included in Windows Server 2008 R2 or the GPMC included with RSAT for Windows 7, you do not use earlier versions of either the GPMC or the Group Policy Management Editor to edit those GPOs.**

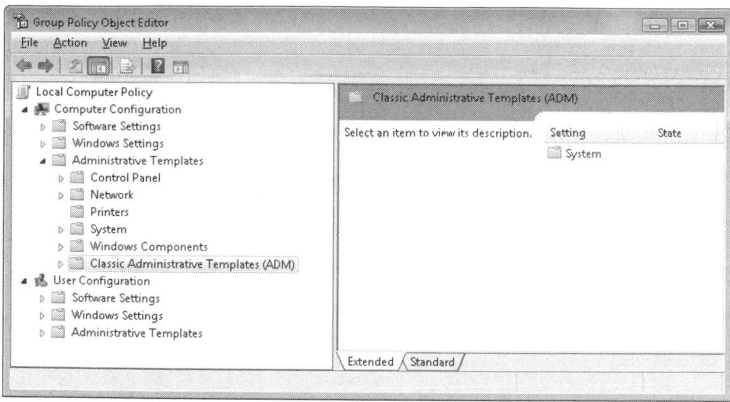

FIGURE 14-1 In the Classic Administrative Templates (ADM) node, policy settings surfaced by ADM template files are displayed in the Group Policy Management Editor.

WARNING Just as with earlier versions of Windows, Microsoft does not recommend that you customize the default ADMX files used in Windows 7. If you customize the default ADMX or ADM files, your customization settings may be lost when Microsoft releases updated versions of these files.

DIRECT FROM THE SOURCE

Fixing the SYSVOL Bloat Issue

Judith Herman, Group Policy Programming Writer
Windows Enterprise Management Division UA

SYSVOL bloat is caused by the operation of the Group Policy Management Editor automatically populating each GPO with the default set of ADM files during the editing session. This causes approximately 4 MB to be copied to SYSVOL for every GPO created and edited. This happens whether or not you are setting registry-based policy settings. A large organization can easily have a thousand or more GPOs. This adds up to quite a large amount of disk space being used for storing ADM files in each GPO.

ADMX files are not copied into individual GPOs when created or edited using a Windows 7 workstation. Using Windows 7 workstations to create and edit GPOs, you can fix the SYSVOL space bloat issue. A word of caution here: You will see a SYSVOL space savings only if all Group Policy administrators are using Windows 7 workstations to create and edit GPOs. The existing GPOs or GPOs edited by previous operating systems might contain ADM files on SYSVOL, even if the GPO was created using a Windows 7 version of Gpedit.msc.

Understanding Multiple Local Group Policy

Another feature of Group Policy that was introduced in Windows Vista is support for MLGPOs. MLGPOs simplify the task of locking down shared-use computers, such as kiosk computers in libraries. Although MLGPOs are primarily intended for use on stand-alone computers, they can also be used on domain-joined computers (although you're better off creating multiple domain GPOs whenever possible).

Types of MLGPOs

Earlier versions of Windows supported only a single LGPO per computer—also known as Local Computer Policy. With these Windows platforms, you could manage stand-alone computers with Group Policy only by configuring their LGPO. You could manage domain-joined computers with Group Policy both by configuring their LGPO and also by using one or more domain-based GPOs to target the AD DS container (domain, organizational unit [OU], or site) to which the computer or user belongs.

Although you cannot manage LGPOs on earlier versions of Windows using GPMC, you can open them in the Group Policy Management Editor and configure them on the local computer. An earlier version of Windows that has been clean-installed has no LGPO until created when an administrator first uses the Local Group Policy Editor. The newly created LGPO is stored in the hidden directory, %WinDir%\System32\GroupPolicy, and has a file structure similar to the GPT for a domain-based GPO. Not all domain-based policy settings are included in the local GPO.

Computers running Windows 7, however, have three levels of LGPO (which is why they are called MLGPOs):

- **Local Computer Policy** This is the default LGPO. It will affect all users on the computer and also contains the only available Local Computer Policy. This level consists of a single MLGPO whose policy settings apply to all users on the computer, including local administrators. Local Group Policy contains both computer and user settings, and its behavior in Windows 7 is the same as in versions of Windows earlier than Windows Vista. Because this is the only MLGPO that contains computer settings, however, you typically use this MLGPO to apply a set of policy settings uniformly to all users of the computer.
- **Administrators and Non-Administrators Local Group Policy** Users on a computer running Windows 7 are either members or not members of this group. Users that are members of Administrators have full administrative privileges on the computer (although elevation may be required to realize these privileges); those who are not members of this group have limited privileges. This level has two MLGPOs: one for users who belong to the Administrators group and one for those who don't. These MLGPOs have user settings only and do not contain any machine settings. You can use these MLGPOs to apply different policy settings to administrators and standard users. These settings apply only to user-based policy and do not affect the computer side.

- **User-Specific Local Group Policy** This level consists of one or more MLGPOs—one per local user account that you create on the computer. These MLGPOs have user settings only, do not contain any machine settings, and allow you to apply a different set of policy settings to each local user on the computer if necessary. These settings apply only to user-based policy and do not affect the computer side.

> **NOTE** Windows 7 does not support using ad hoc local groups to configure Local Group Policy for groups of users on the computer, nor can you use any built-in groups other than Administrators (and Non-Administrators) to configure Local Group Policy for groups of users on the computer. For example, you cannot create an MLGPO for users who belong to the Backup Operators built-in group on the computer.

MLGPOs and Group Policy Processing

In earlier versions of Windows, Group Policy processing is applied in the following order:

1. Local Computer Policy
2. Site GPOs
3. Domain GPOs
4. Organizational unit GPOs

Policy is applied so that the policy setting closest to the user or computer takes precedence unless the ordering is changed using GPMC capabilities (overriding, blocking from above, disabling GPO or computer/user portions of the GPO). For example, if a certain policy is configured as Enabled at the domain level but Disabled at the OU level and if the computer and/or user objects are also contained at this OU level, the last value (Disabled) wins and is the effective value for the policy.

Windows 7 uses the same Group Policy processing order, as well as the "last writer wins" method. However, because Windows 7 includes three levels of local policy, processing this policy requires additional steps:

1. Local Computer Policy
2. Administrators and Non-Administrators Local Group Policy (user-based policy only)
3. User-Specific Local Group Policy (user-based policy only)

For information on how to configure MLGPOs, see the section titled "Understanding Multiple Local Group Policy" earlier in this chapter. For information on how to disable the processing of Multiple Local Group Policy in a domain environment, see the section titled "Configuring Group Policy Processing" later in this chapter.

Managing Group Policy

Managing Group Policy for the Windows 7 platform involves various tasks, including the following:

- Configuring the central store
- Adding ADMX templates to the store
- Creating and managing GPOs
- Editing GPOs
- Managing MLGPOs
- Migrating ADM templates to ADMX format
- Configuring Group Policy processing
- Using Advanced Group Policy Management

The following sections explain how to perform these tasks and more.

Configuring the Central Store

You should create and configure the central store manually for ADMX template files in AD DS domains running Windows Server 2008 R2, Windows Server 2008, and Windows Server 2003. To create and configure the central store, follow these steps:

1. Log on to the domain controller hosting the PDC Emulator flexible single master operations (FSMO) role using a user account that is a member of the Domain Admins built-in group.
2. Open Windows Explorer and select the following folder from the left folder tree: %SystemRoot%\sysvol\domain\policies.
3. Create a subfolder named PolicyDefinitions within this folder.
4. Select the newly created PolicyDefinitions folder from the left folder tree and create a subfolder for each language that your Group Policy administrators will use. You must name these subfolders using the appropriate ISO language identifiers. For example, U.S. administrators should create a subfolder named EN-US under the PolicyDefinitions folder, as shown in Figure 14-2.

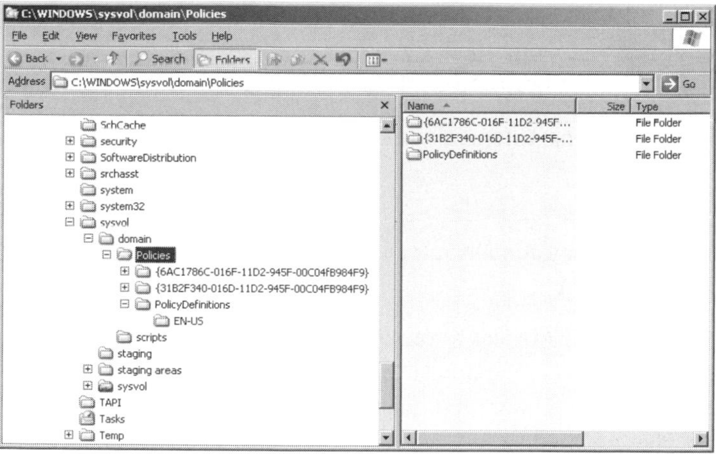

FIGURE 14-2 The folder structure for the central store where ADMX template files are stored for the domain

> ***NOTE*** For a list of ISO language identifiers, see *http://msdn.microsoft.com/en-us/library/dd318691.aspx.*

After you create this folder structure for the central store on the PDC Emulator, the FRS will replicate this structure to all domain controllers in the domain. You choose the PDC Emulator as the domain controller on which to create this folder structure manually because the PDC Emulator is the default choice for the focus of the GPMC.

> ***NOTE*** **Creating a central store is not a requirement for using Group Policy to manage computers running Windows Vista or later. For example, in the absence of a central store, an administrator can use the GPMC on an RSAT administrative workstation running Windows 7 to create GPOs and then use the GPMC to configure these GPOs. The advantage of configuring a central store is that all GPOs created and edited after the store is configured have access to all of the ADMX files within the store, which makes the central store useful for deploying any custom ADMX files that you want to share with other administrators in your domain.**

Adding ADMX Templates to the Store

After you configure the central store, you must populate it using ADMX template files. You can copy these ADMX template files from a computer running Windows 7 by following these steps:

1. Log on to an administrative workstation running Windows 7 using a user account that is a member of the Domain Admins built-in group.
2. Open a command prompt and type the following command.

```
xcopy %SystemRoot%\PolicyDefinitions\* %LogonServer%\sysvol\%UserDNSDomain%\
policies\
PolicyDefinitions /s /y
```

3. Repeat this process from any administrator workstations running Windows 7 that have different languages installed.

After you copy the ADMX template files to the central store, the central store will be replicated to all domain controllers in the domain as the contents of the SYSVOL share are replicated by the FRS. Whenever you want to update the files or copy a custom ADMX file, you must do this manually.

DIRECT FROM THE SOURCE

Create and Populate the ADMX Central Store in a Single Step

Judith Herman, Group Policy Programming Writer
Windows Enterprise Management Division UA

As long as the ADMX central store directory exists, the Group Policy Management Editor will ignore the local versions of the ADMX files. It is recommended that as soon as the central store is created, the ADMX (and associated ADML files) are used to populate the central store. If there is an empty central store directory when the Group Policy Management Editor in Windows 7 is started, the ADM nodes will not display any policy settings because the Group Policy Management Editor reads ADM policy settings display information only from the empty central store.

Creating and Managing GPOs

After your central store is configured and you have copied ADMX template files to it, you are ready to create GPOs for managing your environment. Beginning with Windows 7, you can create and manage GPOs in two ways:

- From the graphical user interface (GUI) by using the GPMC. This is the only method available for managing Group Policy on earlier versions of Windows.
- From the command line or via script automation by using the new Windows PowerShell Group Policy cmdlets. This method for managing Group Policy is new in Windows 7 and Windows Server 2008 R2 and is described in the section titled "Creating and Managing GPOs Using Windows PowerShell" later in this chapter.

Obtaining the GPMC

The GPMC is not included in a default Windows 7 install. Instead, you must download and install the RSAT for Windows 7 to use the GPMC on a Windows 7 computer. To do this, follow these steps:

1. Obtain the appropriate RSAT package (x86 or x64) for your Windows 7 administrative workstation from the Microsoft Download Center at *http://www.microsoft.com/downloads/* and install the RSAT .msu package on your computer.
2. Open Programs And Features from Control Panel and select Turn Windows Features On Or Off.
3. In the Windows Features dialog box, expand Remote Server Administration Tools, followed by Feature Administration Tools.
4. Select the check box next to Group Policy Management Tools and click OK.

Alternatively, instead of managing Group Policy by installing RSAT on a computer running Windows 7, you can manage it directly from a computer running Windows Server 2008 R2 by installing the RSAT feature using the Add Features Wizard in Server Manager.

Using Starter GPOs

Starter GPOs, introduced in the GPMC for Windows Server 2008 and Windows Vista SP1 with RSAT, are read-only collections of configured Administrative Template (.admx) policy settings that you can use to create a live GPO. Starter GPOs provide baselines of Group Policy settings designed for specific scenarios. By using Starter GPOs as templates for creating domain-based GPOs, you can deploy Group Policy quickly in different kinds of environments. Note that Starter GPOs can contain only policy settings (ADM settings); they cannot include preference items, security settings, or other types of Group Policy settings.

In Windows Vista SP1 and Windows Server 2008, you had to download Starter GPOs before using them. Now, however, a default set of Starter GPOs are included in RSAT for Windows 7 and in the GPMC feature of Windows Server 2008 R2.

RSAT for Windows 7 includes two different categories of Starter GPOs:

- **Enterprise Client (EC)** Client computers in this type of environment are members of an AD DS domain and need to communicate only with systems running Windows Server 2003. The client computers in this environment may include a mixture of Windows versions, including Windows 7, Windows Vista, and Windows XP.
- **Specialized Security Limited Functionality (SSLF)** Client computers in this type of environment are members of an AD DS domain and must be running Windows Vista or later. Concern for security in this environment is a higher priority than functionality and manageability, which means that the majority of enterprise organizations do not use this environment. The types of environments that might use SSLF are military and intelligence agency computers.

In addition to these two categories, the default Starter GPOs in RSAT for Windows 7 can also be categorized by whether they do the following:

- Apply only to clients running Windows XP SP2 or later or Windows Vista SP1 or later.
- Apply to users or to computers.

The result of this categorization is the following eight types of Starter GPOs included in RSAT for Windows 7:

- Windows Vista EC Computer
- Windows Vista EC User
- Windows Vista SSLF Computer
- Windows Vista SSLF User
- Windows XP EC Computer
- Windows XP EC User
- Windows XP SSLF Computer
- Windows XP SSLF User

For more information concerning the default configuration of policy settings in Starter GPOs designed for Windows Vista SP1 or later, see the *Windows Vista Security Guide* at *http://go.microsoft.com/?linkID=5744573*. For more information concerning the default configuration of policy settings in Starter GPOs designed for Windows XP SP2 or later, see the Windows XP Security Compliance Management Toolkit at *http://go.microsoft.com/fwlink/?LinkId=14839*. Updated information on Starter GPOs should also be available; search for *Windows 7 Security Guide* on the Microsoft Download Center.

Before you can use Starter GPOs, you must prepare your environment by creating a separate folder for these GPOs in the SYSVOL share on your domain controllers. If your forest has more than one domain, you must create a separate Starter GPOs folder in each domain of your forest. To create the Starter GPOs folder, perform the following steps:

1. Open the GPMC and select the Starter GPOs node in the console tree for the domain.
2. Click the Create Starter GPOs Folder button in the details pane (see Figure 14-3).
3. Repeat for each domain in your forest.

After you create your Starter GPOs folder, you can use the default Starter GPOs as templates when you create new GPOs, as described in the next section. You can also create and manage your own Starter GPOs by right-clicking the Starter GPOs node in the console tree of the GPMC.

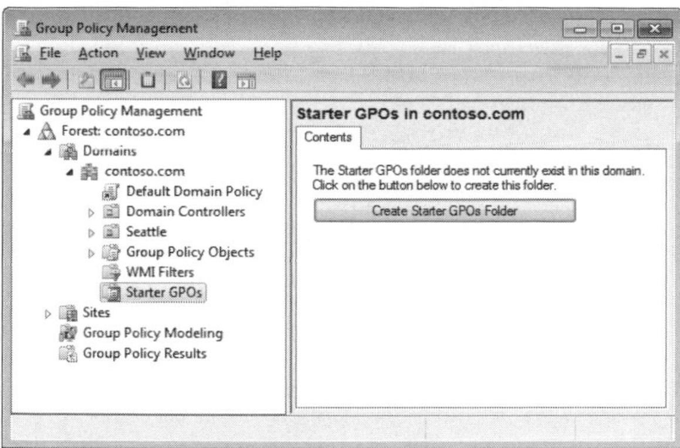

FIGURE 14-3 Creating the Starter GPOs folder in SYSVOL for the domain

Creating and Managing GPOs Using the GPMC

To create and configure a GPO using the GPMC, follow these steps:

1. Log on to an administrative workstation running Windows 7 with RSAT using a user account that is a member of the Domain Admins built-in group.
2. Right-click Start and then click Properties. On the Start Menu tab, click Customize. Then in the Customize Start Menu dialog box, scroll down to System Administrative Tools, select Display On The All Programs Menu And The Start Menu, and click OK.
3. Click Start, then Administrative Tools, and then Group Policy Management. (Alternatively, you can type **gpmc.msc** in the Start Search box and then click gpmc.msc when it appears under Programs in your search results.)
4. Expand the console tree to select the domain or OU to which you will link the new GPO when you create it.
5. Right-click this domain or OU and select Create A GPO In This Domain And Link It Here.
6. Type a descriptive name for your new GPO, such as **Seattle Computers GPO,** and (optionally) select a Starter GPO as a template for it. Then click OK.
7. Expand the domain or OU to display the GPO link for your new GPO beneath it, as shown in the following image.

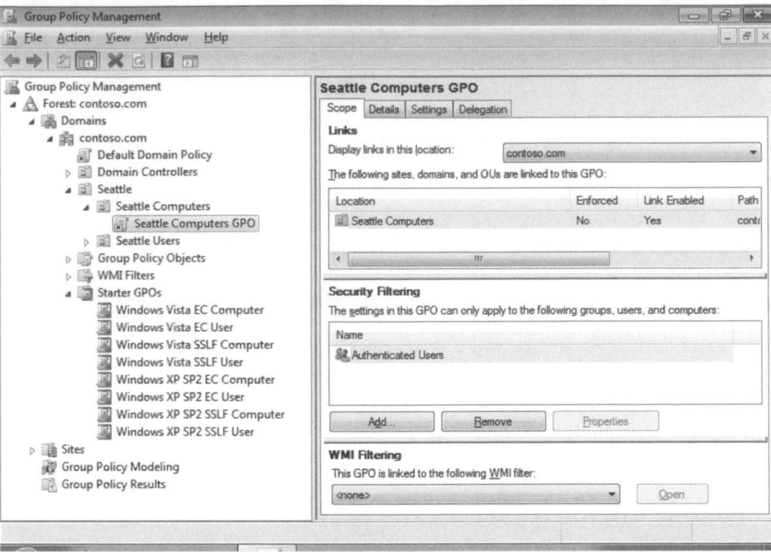

8. Right-click the GPO link and then select Edit to open the GPO.
9. Configure policy settings and preference items in the GPO as desired for the computers and/or users targeted by the GPO.

> **NOTE** If a domain controller is unavailable when a computer running Windows 7 tries to log on to the network, the computer will log on using cached credentials and will use the local copies of the ADMX template files to surface ADM policy settings in the Local Group Policy Editor. Also, if an administrator uses a computer running Windows 7 with RSAT to start GPMC or the Local Group Policy Editor and no central store is found, local copies of the ADMX template files will be used to surface ADM policy settings in the Local Group Policy Editor.

Creating and Managing GPOs Using Windows PowerShell

Beginning with Windows 7 and Windows Server 2008 R2, you can also use 25 new Windows PowerShell cmdlets to create and manage GPOs from the PowerShell command line or by using PowerShell scripts. This new capability builds upon the earlier Component Object Model (COM)–based Group Policy scripting capabilities found in Windows Vista and Windows Server 2008. This feature enables administrators to manage the full life cycle of GPOs, including creating, deleting, copying, configuring, linking, backing up and restoring, generating Resultant Set of Policy (RSoP) reports, configuring permissions, and migrating (importing and exporting) GPOs across domains and forests and from test to production environments.

This new functionality is implemented using the GPMC application programming interfaces (APIs) and is available as a module that you can import from the Windows PowerShell command line. This means that the GPMC must be installed on the computer from which you run your Windows PowerShell commands. These new cmdlets provide functionality both for performing GPMC operations and for reading and writing registry settings to GPOs (including both policy settings and preference items).

You can also use Group Policy to configure policy settings that specify whether Windows PowerShell scripts can run before non-PowerShell scripts during user computer startup and shutdown and during user logon and logoff. By default, Windows PowerShell scripts run after non-PowerShell scripts.

As shown in Table 14-3, the Windows PowerShell cmdlets in Group Policy can be organized into five different categories according to their verb.

TABLE 14-3 Windows PowerShell cmdlets for Group Policy in Windows 7 and Windows Server 2008 R2

VERB	CMDLETS
Get	Get-GPInheritance Get-GPO Get-GPOReport Get-GPPermissions Get-GPPrefRegistryValue Get-GPRegistryValue Get-GPResultantSetofPolicy Get-GPStarterGPO
New	New-GPLink New-GPO New-GPStarterGPO
Set	Set-GPInheritance Set-GPLink Set-GPPermissions Set-GPPrefRegistryValue Set-GPRegistryValue
Remove	Remove-GPLink Remove-GPO Remove-GPPrefRegistryValue Remove-GPRegistryValue
Misc	Backup-GPO Copy-GPO Import-GPO Rename-GPO Restore-GPO

As an example of using these new cmdlets, the procedure described here creates a new Seattle Users GPO and links it to the Seattle Users OU beneath the Seattle OU in the contoso.com domain to complement the Seattle Computers GPO created using the GPMC in the previous section.

1. Log on to your domain controller and click the Administrator: Windows PowerShell icon pinned to the taskbar. This opens the Windows PowerShell command-prompt window.
2. Type **import-module GroupPolicy** to import the Group Policy module into Windows PowerShell. This step is required at the beginning of each Windows PowerShell script or series of PowerShell commands that you execute to manage Group Policy.
3. Type **$gpo = New-GPO "Seattle Users GPO"** to create a new GPO named Seattle Users GPO and assign the GPO to the Windows PowerShell variable named $gpo.
4. Type **Get-GPO $gpo.DisplayName** to retrieve the properties of the newly created GPO and verify its creation, as shown here.

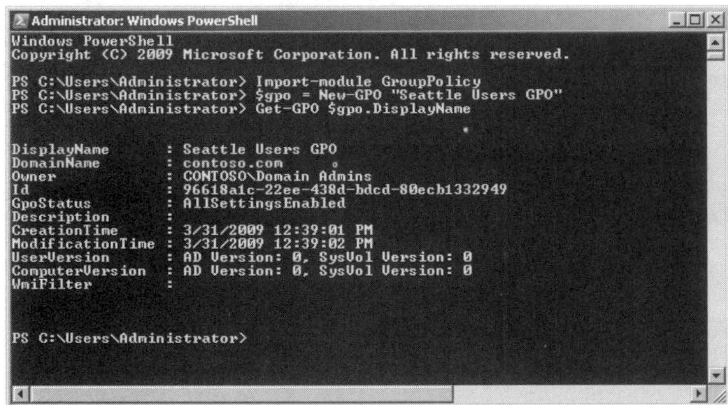

5. Type **New-GPLink $gpo.DisplayName –target "ou=Seattle Users,ou=Seattle,dc= contoso,dc=com" –order 1** to link the new GPO to the Seattle Users OU beneath the Seattle OU in the contoso.com domain and assign the GPO a link order of 1.

If you refresh the GPMC view, you should now see the newly created GPO linked to the OU you specified.

For more examples on how to use these new Group Policy cmdlets to create and manage Group Policy, see the Windows PowerShell section of the Group Policy Team Blog on Microsoft TechNet at *http://blogs.technet.com/grouppolicy/archive/tags/PowerShell/default.aspx.* For a general introduction to the Windows PowerShell capabilities of Windows 7, see Chapter 13, "Overview of Management Tools."

Editing GPOs

After you've created a GPO, you can edit the settings that it contains using one of two methods:

- From the GUI by using the Group Policy Management Editor, which can be started from the GPMC. This is the only method available for editing GPOs in earlier versions of Windows. Using this method, you can modify any GPO setting, including policy settings, preference items, and security settings.
- From the command line or via script automation by using the Set-GPRegistryValue, SetGPPrefRegistryValue, Get-GPRegistryValue, Get-GPPrefRegistryValue, Remove-GPRegistryValue, and Remove-GPPrefRegistryValue cmdlets, which are among the new Windows PowerShell Group Policy cmdlets in Windows 7. Using this method, you can modify either policy settings or Group Policy preferences registry-based preference items (you cannot modify other types of preference items using the cmdlets). You cannot use Windows PowerShell to modify security settings, software installation settings, or any other types of GPO settings.

Configuring Policy Settings

To configure a policy setting in a GPO, follow these steps:

1. Right-click the GPO or its associated GPO link in GPMC and select Edit to open the GPO in the Group Policy Management Editor.
2. Expand the Policies node under either Computer Configuration or User Configuration as desired.
3. Expand the Administrative Templates node under Policy and browse to select the policy you want to configure, as shown here.

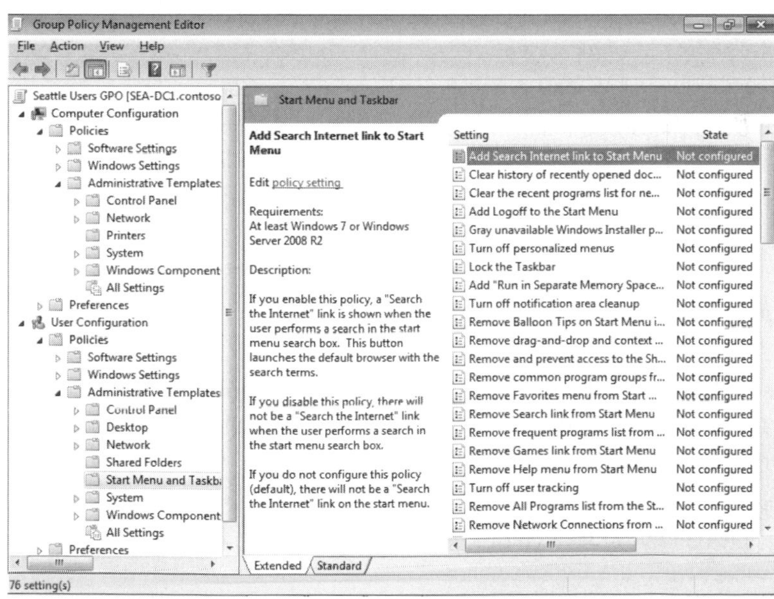

4. Double-click the policy setting to open its properties, then enable or disable the setting as desired, and (optionally) type a comment to document your action, as shown here.

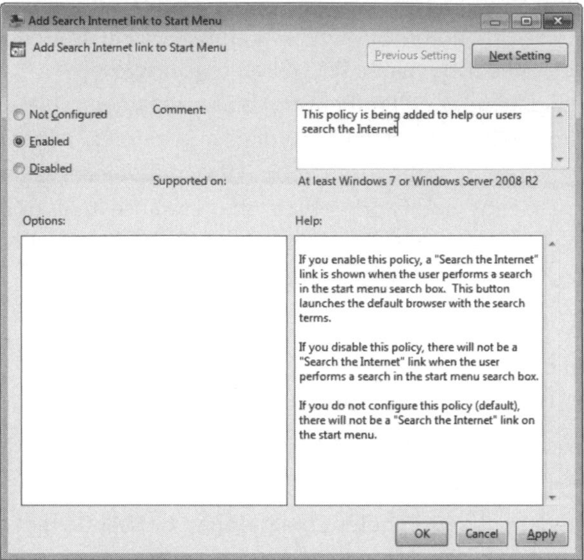

5. Click OK to apply the change to the GPO.

After Group Policy is updated for the users or computers targeted by the GPO, the policy setting will be applied. This policy setting, which applies only to Windows 7 and later versions, displays a Search The Internet link above the Start menu button whenever a user types something into the Search box on the Start menu.

In addition to using the Group Policy Management Editor to configure policy settings, you can use Windows PowerShell to do this if you have the GPMC installed on a computer running Windows 7 or Windows Server 2008 R2. For example, to edit the Seattle Users GPO and enable the Add Search Internet Link To Start Menu policy setting as was done previously, open a Windows PowerShell command-prompt window and follow these steps:

1. Type **Import-module GroupPolicy** to import the GroupPolicy module into Windows PowerShell.
2. Type **$key = "HKCU\Software\Policies\Microsoft\Windows\Explorer"** to assign the registry path for the Add Search Internet Link To Start Menu policy setting to the variable named $key.
3. Use the Set-GPRegistryValue cmdlet, as shown in Figure 14-4, to create a new DWORD registry value named AddSearchInternetLinkinStartMenu under the registry key and assign a value of 1 to this registry value.

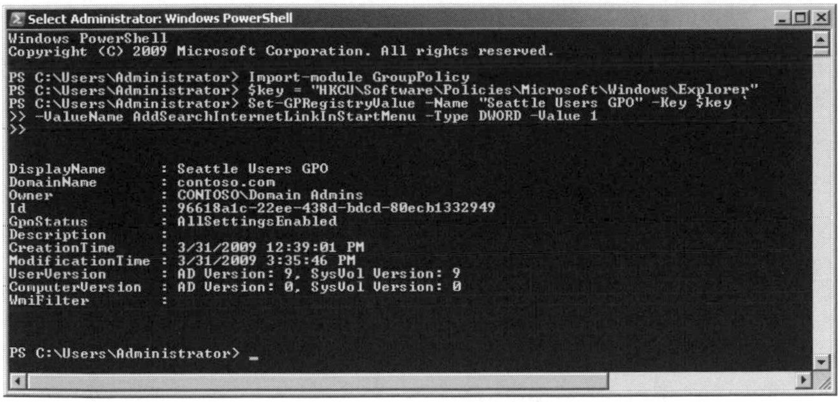

```
Select Administrator: Windows PowerShell
Windows PowerShell
Copyright (C) 2009 Microsoft Corporation. All rights reserved.

PS C:\Users\Administrator> Import-module GroupPolicy
PS C:\Users\Administrator> $key = "HKCU\Software\Policies\Microsoft\Windows\Explorer"
PS C:\Users\Administrator> Set-GPRegistryValue -Name "Seattle Users GPO" -Key $key `
>> -ValueName AddSearchInternetLinkInStartMenu -Type DWORD -Value 1
>>

DisplayName      : Seattle Users GPO
DomainName       : contoso.com
Owner            : CONTOSO\Domain Admins
Id               : 96618a1c-22ee-438d-bdcd-80ecb1332949
GpoStatus        : AllSettingsEnabled
Description      :
CreationTime     : 3/31/2009 12:39:01 PM
ModificationTime : 3/31/2009 3:35:46 PM
UserVersion      : AD Version: 9, SysVol Version: 9
ComputerVersion  : AD Version: 0, SysVol Version: 0
WmiFilter        :

PS C:\Users\Administrator> _
```

FIGURE 14-4 Configuring a policy setting in a GPO using Windows PowerShell

To verify that the policy setting has been modified as desired in the GPO, open the GPO in the Group Policy Management Editor and double-click the policy setting to display its properties. You can also select the GPO under the Group Policy Objects node in the GPMC and then select the Settings tab in the details pane to view details concerning all configured policy settings within the GPO.

NOTE **To modify a policy setting using the Set-GPRegistryValue cmdlet, you need to know the registry setting associated with the policy setting. A simple way to obtain this information is to download the Group Policy Settings Reference spreadsheet for Windows Server 2008 R2 and Windows 7 from the Microsoft Download Center, open it in Microsoft Office Excel, select the Administrative Templates worksheet, find the row that has the name of the policy setting under the Policy Setting Name column, and then find the registry key and value name for the policy under the Registry Information column for the selected row. Note that this spreadsheet doesn't state the value type or range of possible values of the registry value—to determine this (if it's not obvious), you can enable, disable, or otherwise configure the policy setting on a test computer and then open the registry value for the policy using Registry Editor to view the results.**

Configuring Preference Items

To configure a preference item in a GPO, follow these steps:

1. Right-click the GPO or its associated GPO link in GPMC and select Edit to open the GPO in the Group Policy Management Editor.
2. Expand the Preferences node under either Computer Configuration or User Configuration as desired.

3. Right-click a preference setting node and select the appropriate menu option to create, replace, update, or remove a preference setting, as shown here.

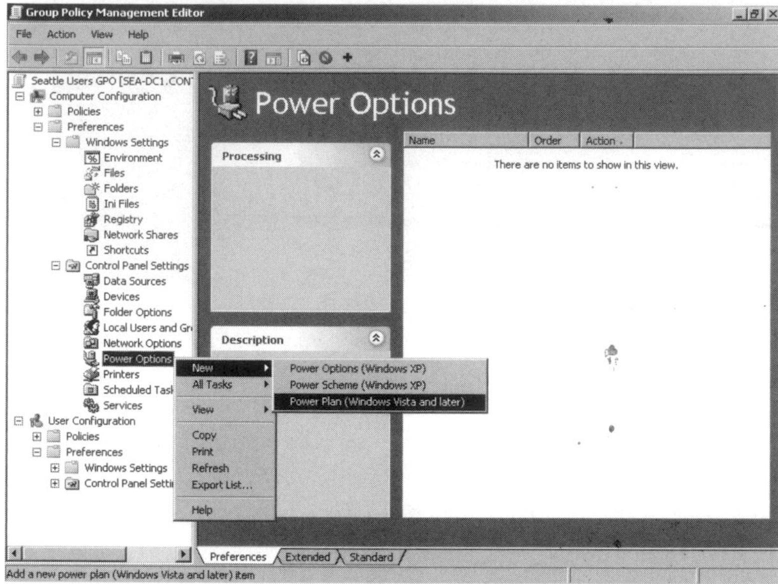

You can also use the Get-GPPrefRegistrySetting cmdlet to configure preference items using Windows PowerShell. For more examples on how to use the Group Policy cmdlets, see the Windows PowerShell section of the Group Policy Team Blog on Microsoft TechNet at *http://blogs.technet.com/grouppolicy/archive/tags/PowerShell/default.aspx.*

DIRECT FROM THE SOURCE

Group Policy Settings vs. Group Policy Preferences*

William R. Stanek
Author

One way to think of Group Policy is as a set of rules that you can apply throughout the enterprise. Although you can use Group Policy to manage servers and workstations running Windows 2000 or later, Group Policy has changed since it was first implemented with Windows 2000. For Windows Vista with SP1 or later and Windows Server 2008, Group Policy includes both managed settings, referred to as policy settings, and unmanaged settings, referred to as policy preferences. When you deploy the Group Policy CSEs to Windows XP with SP2 or later, Windows Vista, or Windows Server 2003 with SP1 or later, these older operating systems can use Group Policy preferences as well.

- Group Policy settings enable you to control the configuration of the operating system and its features. You can also use policy settings to configure computer and user scripts, folder redirection, computer security, software installation, and more.
- Group Policy preferences enable you to configure, deploy, and manage operating system and application settings that you were not able to manage using earlier implementations of Group Policy, including data sources, mapped drives, environment variables, network shares, folder options, shortcuts, and more. In many cases, you'll find that using Group Policy preferences is a better approach than configuring these settings in Windows images or using logon scripts.
- The key difference between preferences and policy settings is enforcement. Group Policy strictly enforces policy settings. You use policy settings to control the configuration of the operating system and its features. You also use policy settings to disable the user interface for settings that Group Policy is managing, which prevents users from changing those settings. Most policy settings are stored in policy-related branches of the registry. The operating system and compliant applications check the policy-related branches of the registry to determine whether and how various aspects of the operating system are controlled. Group Policy refreshes policy settings at a regular interval, which is every 90 to 120 minutes by default.
- In contrast, Group Policy does not strictly enforce policy preferences. Group Policy does not store preferences in the policy-related branches of the registry. Instead, it writes preferences to the same locations in the registry that an application or operating system feature uses to store the setting. This allows Group Policy preferences to support applications and operating system features that aren't Group Policy–aware and also does not disable application or operating system features in the user interface to prevent their use. Because of this behavior, users can change settings that were configured using policy preferences. Finally, although Group Policy by default refreshes preferences using the same interval as Group Policy settings, you can prevent Group Policy from refreshing individual preferences by choosing to apply them only once.

When working with policy settings, keep the following in mind:

- Most policy settings are stored in policy-based areas of the registry.
- Settings are enforced.
- User interface options might be disabled.
- Settings are refreshed automatically.
- Settings require Group Policy–aware applications.
- Original settings are not changed.
- Removing the policy setting restores the original settings.

When working with policy preferences, keep the following in mind:

- **Preferences are stored in the same registry locations as those used by the operating system and applications.**
- **Preferences are not enforced.**
- **User interface options are not disabled.**
- **Settings can be refreshed automatically or applied once.**
- **Preferences support non-Group Policy–aware applications.**
- **Original settings are overwritten.**
- **Removing the preference item does not restore the original setting.**

In the real world, the way you use policy settings or policy preferences depends on whether you want to enforce the item. To configure an item without enforcing it, use policy preferences and then disable automatic refresh. To configure an item and enforce the specified configuration, use policy settings or configure preferences and then enable automatic refresh.

*Excerpted with permission from the *Windows Group Policy Administrator's Pocket Consultant* (Microsoft Press, 2009).

Managing MLGPOs

To edit different MLGPOs on a computer running Windows 7, follow these steps:

1. Log on to an administrative workstation running Windows 7 using a user account that is a member of the local Administrators built-in group.
2. Type **mmc** in the Start menu and then click mmc.exe when it appears under Programs in your search results.
3. Select File and then select Add/Remove Snap-in.
4. Select Group Policy Management Editor from the list of available snap-ins and then click Add.
5. Do one of the following:
   - To create a custom Microsoft Management Console (MMC) for editing the Local Computer Policy, click Finish.
   - To create a custom MMC for editing the Administrators Local Group Policy, click Browse, click the Users tab, select Administrators, click OK, and then click Finish.
   - To create a custom MMC for editing the Non-Administrators Local Group Policy, click Browse, click the Users tab, select Non-Administrators, click OK, and then click Finish.
   - To create a custom MMC for editing the Local Group Policy for a specific local user account, click Browse, click the Users tab, select that user account, click OK, and then click Finish.

6. Alternatively, instead of creating multiple different custom MMCs, you can add multiple instances of the Group Policy Management Editor snap-in to a single custom MMC console with each snap-in having a different MLGPO as its focus, as shown in Figure 14-5.

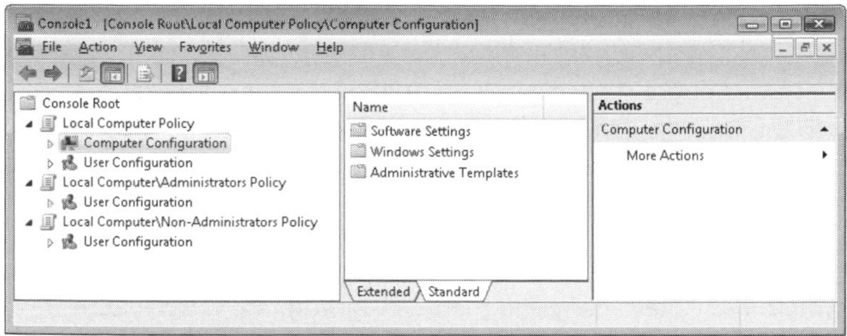

FIGURE 14-5 Editing Local Computer Policy, Administrators Local Group Policy, and Non-Administrators Local Group Policy, all from a single MMC console

MLGPOs do not exist until you actually configure their settings using the Local Group Policy Editor. You can delete MLGPOs that you no longer need by following these steps:

1. Log on to an administrative workstation running Windows 7 using a user account that is a member of the local Administrators built-in group.
2. Click the Start button, type **mmc** in the Start menu Search box, and then click mmc.exe when it appears under Programs in your search results.
3. Respond to the User Account Control (UAC) prompt by clicking Continue.
4. Select File and then select Add/Remove Snap-in.
5. Select Group Policy Management Editor from the list of available snap-ins and then click Add.
6. Click Browse and then click the Users tab, as shown here.

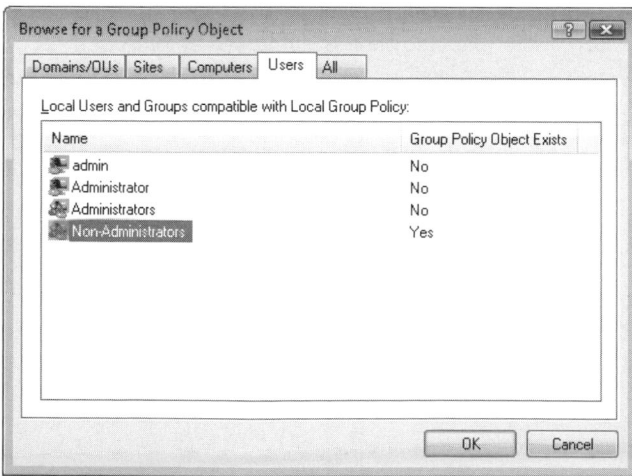

7. Right-click the user or group (Administrators or Non-Administrators) for which you want to delete the associated MLGPO, select Remove Group Policy Object, click Yes, and then click OK.

NOTE You can also disable an MLGPO temporarily by right-clicking its associated user or group, selecting Properties, and then selecting the check boxes to disable the user and machine (if available) portions of the MLGPO.

You can also choose to edit only the Local Computer Policy on a computer running Windows 7 (similar to the way it is done in earlier versions of Windows) by following these steps:

1. Log on to an administrative workstation running Windows 7 using a user account that is a member of the Administrators built-in group.
2. Type **gpedit.msc** in the Start menu and then click gpedit.msc when it appears under Programs in your search results.
3. Respond to the UAC prompt by clicking Continue.
4. Configure policy settings as desired.

Migrating ADM Templates to ADMX Format

ADMX Migrator is an MMC snap-in developed and supported by FullArmor Corporation (*http://www.fullarmor.com*) that simplifies the task of converting existing Group Policy ADM template files to ADMX template files so that your enterprise can take advantage of the additional capabilities of this new format. ADMX Migrator is available from the Microsoft Download Center at *http://go.microsoft.com/fwlink/?LinkId=103774* and can be installed on Windows 7, Windows Server 2008 R2, Windows Vista, Windows Server 2008, Windows Server 2003 SP1 or later, and Windows XP SP2 or later, provided that MMC 3.0 and the Microsoft .NET Framework 2.0 are installed.

IMPORTANT ADMX Migrator was developed by and is supported by FullArmor Corporation. For support issues involving ADMX Migrator, go to *http://www.fullarmor.com/admx-migrator-issue-report.htm*.

With ADMX Migrator, administrators can do any of the following:

- Use a GUI called ADMX Editor to convert ADM files to ADMX format and to create and edit custom ADMX template files.
- Use a command-line tool called ADMX Migrator Command Window to control template migration settings granularly.
- Choose multiple ADM template files for conversion to ADMX format.
- Detect collisions resulting from duplicate names.

During the conversion process, any items that cannot be validated against the ADMX schema are preserved in an Unsupported section instead of being deleted.

NOTE Annotations within ADM template files are removed during the conversion process.

Converting ADM Template Files to ADMX Format

To convert a custom ADM file into ADMX format, install ADMX Migrator and then follow these steps:

1. Click Start, click All Programs, click FullArmor, expand FullArmor ADMX Migrator, and then click ADMX Editor.
2. Respond to the UAC prompt as required to open ADMX Migrator.
3. Right-click the root node in the console tree and then select Generate ADMX From ADM.
4. Browse to locate and select your custom ADM file and then click Open.
5. Click Yes when the message appears stating that the ADM file was successfully converted to ADMX format. This will load the new ADMX file into the ADMX Migrator, as shown here.

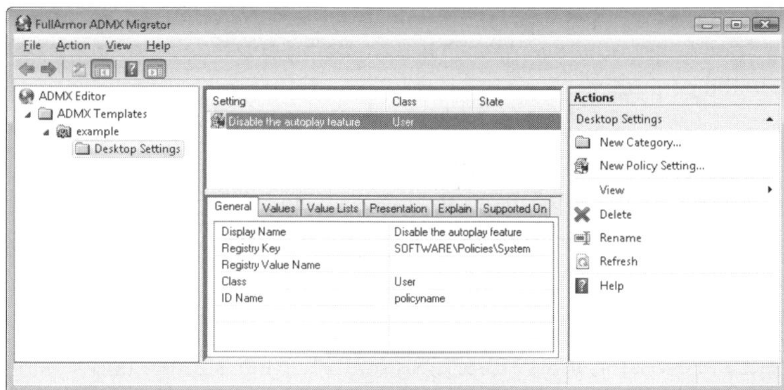

The converted ADMX template file is saved in the %UserProfile%\AppData\Local\Temp folder using the same name as the .adm file but with the .admx extension. Copy this .admx file to the central store for your domain and you'll be able to configure the policy settings defined by it when you create and edit domain-based GPOs.

Creating and Editing Custom ADMX Template Files

You can create new ADMX template files and modify existing ones by using ADMX Migrator. Follow these steps:

1. Click Start, click All Programs, click FullArmor, expand FullArmor ADMX Migrator, and then click ADMX Editor.
2. Respond to the UAC prompt as required to open ADMX Migrator.
3. Right-click the ADMX Templates node under the root node and select one of the following:

- Select New Template to create a new ADMX template file. After you create this file, you can right-click this template and select New Category to add categories of policy settings. After you add categories, you can right-click these categories and select New Policy Setting to define new registry-based policy settings. Type a descriptive name, a full path to the registry key, and a default value (optional) for the key.
- Select Load Template to open an existing ADMX template file for editing. After you open the file, you can add or delete categories and policy settings as desired.

> ***WARNING*** **Do not modify the default ADMX template files included with Windows 7.**

Configuring Group Policy Processing

Beginning with Windows Vista, there are two policy settings you can configure that affect how Group Policy processing is performed:

- **Turn Off Local Group Policy Objects Processing** This policy setting is found under Computer Configuration\Policies\Administrative Templates\System\Group Policy. Enabling this policy setting prevents LGPOs from being applied when Group Policy is processed on the computer.

> ***WARNING*** **Do not enable this policy setting within LGPOs on a stand-alone computer; the Group Policy service does not honor this policy setting from an LGPO when in a workgroup. Enable this policy only on domain-based GPOs if you want to disable application of LGPOs completely during Group Policy processing.**

- **Startup Policy Processing Wait Time** This policy setting is found under Computer Configuration\Policies\Administrative Templates\System\Group Policy. Enabling and configuring this policy setting determines how long Group Policy must wait for network availability notifications during startup policy processing. The default value for this policy setting when it is enabled is 120 seconds, and configuring this policy setting overrides any system-determined wait times. (The default wait time for computers running Windows 7 is 30 seconds.) If you are using synchronous startup policy processing, the computer is blocked until the network becomes available or the configured wait time is reached. If you are using asynchronous startup policy processing, the computer is not blocked and policy processing takes place in the background. In either case, configuring this policy setting overrides any system-computed wait times.

Using Advanced Group Policy Management

Microsoft Advanced Group Policy Management (AGPM) 4.0, which supports Windows 7 and Windows Server 2008 R2, will be part of the R2 release of the Microsoft Desktop Optimization Pack (MDOP) 2009, a dynamic desktop solution available to Software Assurance (SA) customers that helps application deployment costs, supports delivery of applications as services, and allows for easier management and control of enterprise desktop environments. AGPM was originally based on GPOVault Enterprise Edition, a software solution developed by Desktop-Standard and acquired by Microsoft. AGPM integrates seamlessly with the GPMC and provides the following benefits relating to Group Policy management in enterprise environments:

- More granular administrative control through role-based administration, a robust delegation model, and change-request approval
- Reduced risk of Group Policy failures by supporting offline editing of GPOs, recovery of deleted GPOs, repair of live GPOs, difference reporting, and audit logging
- More effective Group Policy change management through the creation of GPO template libraries, version tracking, history capture, quick rollback of deployed changes, and subscription to policy change e-mail notifications

> ***MORE INFO*** **For more information about AGPM and other MDOP technologies, see *http://www.microsoft.com/windows/enterprise/default.aspx*. For detailed task-oriented help on using AGPM to manage Group Policy in enterprise environments, see the *Windows Group Policy Administrator's Pocket Consultant* by William R. Stanek (Microsoft Press, 2009).**

Troubleshooting Group Policy

Beginning with Windows Vista SP1, the Group Policy engine no longer records information in the Userenv.log. Instead, you can find detailed logging of information concerning Group Policy issues by using the following methods:

- Use Event Viewer to view events in the Group Policy operational log for resolving issues relating to Group Policy processing on the computer.
- Enable debug logging for the Group Policy Management Editor to generate a GpEdit.log for resolving issues relating to malformed ADMX files.

> ***MORE INFO*** **For additional information on how to troubleshoot Group Policy application issues for Windows 7 and Windows Vista SP1, see "Troubleshooting Group Policy Using Event Logs" at *http://technet2.microsoft.com/WindowsVista/en/library/7e940882-33b7-43db-b097-f3752c84f67f1033.mspx?mfr=true*.**

DIRECT FROM THE SOURCE

An Ordered Approach to Troubleshooting Group Policy

Mark Lawrence, Senior Program Manager*
Windows Enterprise Management Division (WEMD)

To successfully troubleshoot Group Policy issues on Windows Vista and later versions, we recommend performing the following sequence of steps:

1. **Start with Administrative Events under Custom Views in Event Viewer. Identify any policy failures that occurred and then examine their descriptions, the Details tab, and the More Information link for these events.**
2. **Open the Group Policy Operational log and obtain the activity ID from a failure event. Then use GPLogView.exe with the –a option to filter events for this activity ID and export the results as either HTML or XML for analysis and archiving.**
3. **Analyze the GPLogView.exe output to review step-by-step policy-processing scenario events to identify any failure point and error codes for possible future troubleshooting.**

*With the help of information provided by Dilip Radhakrishnan of the Group Policy Program Managers Team.

Using Event Viewer

The operational log for Group Policy processing on the computer can be found in Event Viewer under Applications And Service Logs\Microsoft\Windows\Group Policy\Operational, as shown in Figure 14-6.

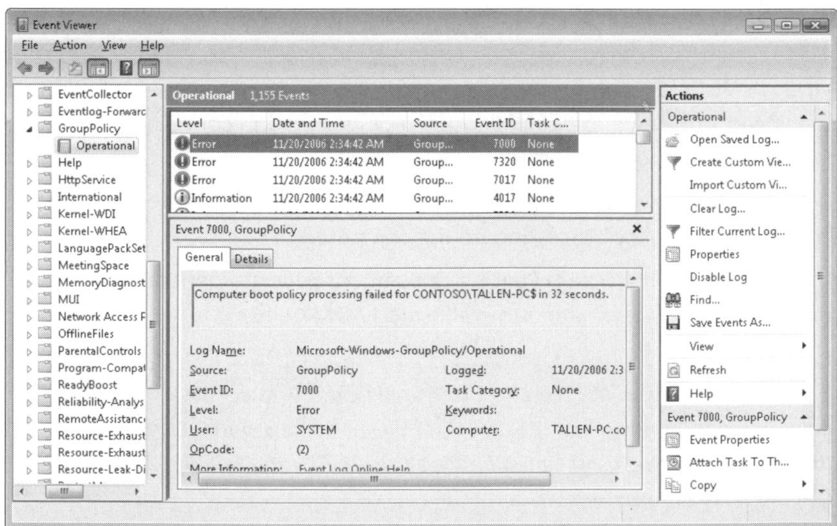

FIGURE 14-6 Operational log for Group Policy in Event Viewer

MORE INFO For more information on using Event Viewer in Windows 7, see Chapter 21, "Maintaining Desktop Health."

This Group Policy Application channel within Event Viewer records each of the step-by-step policy-processing events that occurs as Group Policy is applied on the client. This logging channel is an administrator-friendly replacement for the Userenv.log used on previous versions of Windows for troubleshooting Group Policy processing. (The Userenv.log was challenging to parse on those platforms for Group Policy events because several other types of events could be recorded in the same log.) These Group Policy operational events can provide valuable troubleshooting information such as user name, GPO list, and policy-processing metrics, such as total processing time and individual extension processing time. In addition, a unique activity ID allows for the grouping of events that occur during each Group Policy processing cycle.

NOTE Only the Group Policy engine logs events in the System Event Log. Group Policy extension DLLs do not log events in this channel—they log their events in the Group Policy Operational Event Log.

Table 14-4 summarizes the different ranges of event IDs in the Group Policy Application channel and their meaning.

TABLE 14-4 Event ID Ranges for the Group Policy Operational Log

RANGE	MEANING
4000–4299	Scenario Start Events
5000–5299	Corresponding success scenario End Events (Scenario Start Event + 1000)
5300–5999	Informational Events
6000–6299	Corresponding warning scenario End Events (Scenario Start Event + 2000)
6300–6999	Warning Events (Corresponding Informational Event +1000)
7000–7299	Corresponding error scenario End Events (Scenario Start Event + 3000)
7300–7999	Error Events (Corresponding Informational Event +2000)
8000–8999	Policy scenario Success Events

NOTE Administrative events relating to Group Policy are still logged in the System Event Log as on older Windows platforms, except that the event source for these events is now Group Policy instead of USERENV. Another advantage beginning with Windows Vista is that Group Policy script-processing errors (the scripts deployed through the Group Policy script extension) are now logged through the same mechanism as the rest of the Group Policy errors.

MORE INFO For another way of categorizing these events, see the posting named Group Policy Troubleshooting – Helpful Event Log Categories on the Group Policy Team Blog at *http://blogs.technet.com/grouppolicy/archive/2009/03/04/group-policy-troubleshooting-helpful-event-log-categories.aspx.*

Enabling Debug Logging

There are optional debug logging for the Group Policy Editor that provide much more detailed logging than is available from within Event Viewer. You can enable debug logging by creating and configuring the following REG_DWORD registry value.

HKLM\Software\Microsoft\Windows NT\CurrentVersion\Winlogon\GPEditDebugLevel

The value normally used for troubleshooting purposes is 0x10002. Configuring this registry value will create a GpEdit.log in the %SystemRoot%\debug\usermode folder. The following sample output for this log file indicates malformed ADMX files named test.admx and test.adml.

```
GPEDIT(b6c.10c8) 12:10:03:713 PDX parser: Parsing file 'C:\Windows\PolicyDefinitions
    \FolderRedirection.admx'.
GPEDIT(b6c.10c8) 12:10:03:716 PDX parser: Obtained appropriate PDX resource file
    'C:\Windows\PolicyDefinitions\en-US\FolderRedirection.adml' for language 'en-US'.
GPEDIT(b6c.10c8) 12:10:03:717 PDX parser: Parsing resource file
    'C:\Windows\PolicyDefinitions\en-US\FolderRedirection.adml'.
GPEDIT(b6c.10c8) 12:10:03:719 PDX parser: Parsing resource file completed successfully.
GPEDIT(b6c.10c8) 12:10:03:720 PDX parser: Successfully parsed file.
GPEDIT(b6c.10c8) 12:10:03:720 PDX parser: Parsing file 'C:\Windows\PolicyDefinitions
    \test.admx'.
GPEDIT(b6c.10c8) 12:10:03:721 CSAXErrorHandlerImpl::fatalError: Parsing error, hr =
    0xc00cee2d, message = 'Incorrect document syntax.
GPEDIT(b6c.10c8) 12:10:11:223 CSAXParser::ParseURL: parseURL for C:\Windows
    \PolicyDefinitions\test.admx failed with 0xc00cee2d.
GPEDIT(b6c.10c8) 12:10:11:223 PDX parser: Failed to parse C:\Windows\PolicyDefinitions
    \test.admx with 0xc00cee2d.
```

Using Group Policy Log View

GPLogView.exe is a command-line troubleshooting tool that you can use to export Group Policy–related events logged in the System Event Log channel and the Group Policy Operational Event Log channel into a text, HTML or XML file. GPLogView.exe works only on Windows Vista and later; it is not included with Windows 7 or Windows Server 2008 R2, but it is available as a separate download from *http://go.microsoft.com/fwlink/?LinkId=75004*. The command-line options for this tool are the following:

- **–?** Shows this usage message.

- **–o *output_filename*** Output filename required for text, XML, or HTML; not valid if *–m* is specified.
- **–n** Do not output the activity ID.
- **–p** Dump the process ID and thread ID associated with each event.
- **–a *activity_ID_GUID*** Shows only events matching the given activity ID.
- **–m** Runs the tool in monitor mode displaying events in real time.
- **–x** Dumps the event in XML; the only other options allowed with this option are *–m* and *–a,* but not both together.
- **–h** Dumps the events in HTML format; the *–m* or *–x* option is not allowed, and *–a* and *–n* are allowed, but not both together. Also must specify the *–o* option.
- **–q *query_filename*** Uses the query specified by the query file.
- **–l *publisher_name*** If *–q* is specified, the publisher name must be specified.

The following examples illustrate the use of this tool:

- GPLogView.exe -o GPEvents.txt
- GPLogView.exe -n -o GPEvents.txt
- GPLogView.exe -a ea276341-d646-43e0-866c-e7cc35aecc0a -o GPEvents.txt
- GPLogView.exe -p -o GPEvents.txt
- GPLogView.exe -x -o GPEvents.xml
- GPLogView.exe -x -m
- GPLogView.exe -x -a ea276341-d646-43e0-866c-e7cc35aecc0a -o GPEvents.xml
- GPLogView.exe -h -o GPEvents.html
- GPLogView.exe -h -a ea276341-d646-43e0-866c-e7cc35aecc0a -o GPEvents.html
- GPLogView.exe -h -q somequeryFile.txt -l Microsoft-Windows-GroupPolicy -oGPEvents.html

Using GPResult

GPResult.exe is a command-line tool built into Windows 7, Windows Server 2008 R2, Windows Vista, and Windows Server 2008 that can be used for displaying Group Policy settings and RSoP for a specified user or a computer. Two new command-line switches were added to GPResult.exe beginning with Windows Vista SP1 and Windows Server 2008:

- **/x *filename*** Saves the report in XML format at the location and with the filename specified by the filename parameter
- **/h *filename*** Saves the report in HTML format at the location and with the filename specified by the filename parameter

In addition, GPResult now requires command-line parameters when it is run. For more information concerning GPResult.exe syntax and usage, see *http://technet2.microsoft.com/windowsserver2008/en/library/dfaa3adf-2c83-486c-86d6-23f93c5c883c1033.mspx?mfr=true.* For additional information, see this posting on the Ask The Directory Services Team Blog: *http://blogs.technet.com/askds/archive/2007/12/04/an-old-new-way-to-get-group-policy-results.aspx.*

DIRECT FROM THE SOURCE

Prerequisites for Using Preferences on Previous Versions of Windows

The Group Policy Team at Microsoft

It's important to know the CSE and XMLLite install requirements for Group Policy preferences because this is the number one Group Policy issue for Microsoft Product Support Services (PSS). To ensure that the preference items are applied to clients, complete the following prerequisite tasks:

1. Install the Group Policy CSEs on any clients in which you plan to deploy preference items if the CSEs are not already installed by default. These are required for clients to process Group Policy preferences.
2. Install XMLLite on the same clients if it is not already installed by default (see *http://msdn.microsoft.com/en-us/library/ms752838.aspx* for more information).

One option for installing the CSEs and XMLLite is to use a script (see *http://heidelbergit.blogspot.com/2008/03/how-to-install-gpp-cses-using-startup.html* for an example). Alternatively, you can obtain the CSEs through Windows Update or Windows Server Update Services (WSUS) or from the Microsoft Download Center. Then, you can obtain XMLLite from the Download Center.

The following information will help you determine whether the CSEs and XMLLite need to be installed and whether you can obtain them from the Microsoft Download Center or from Windows Update.

Requirements for CSEs

The following are the requirements for installing CSEs on earlier versions of Windows:

- **Windows Server 2008** CSEs are already included and therefore do not need to be installed.
- **Windows Vista and Windows Vista with SP1** Download and install the 32-bit edition of CSEs from *http://go.microsoft.com/fwlink/?LinkId=111859* and the 64-bit edition from *http://go.microsoft.com/fwlink/?LinkID=111857.*

- **Windows XP with SP2 or later** Download and install the 32-bit edition of CSEs from *http://go.microsoft.com/fwlink/?LinkId=111851* and the 64-bit edition from *http://go.microsoft.com/fwlink/?LinkId=111862*.
- **Windows Server 2003 with SP1 or later** Download and install the 32-bit edition of CSEs from *http://go.microsoft.com/fwlink/?LinkId=111852* and the 64-bit edition from *http://go.microsoft.com/fwlink/?LinkId=111863*.

Requirements for XMLLite

Note that XMLLite is not needed if:

- Your clients run Windows Server 2008 or Windows Vista.
- Your Windows XP and Windows Server 2003 clients run Internet Explorer 7 and/or the latest service packs.

For clients that run Windows Server 2003 and Windows XP operating system versions that support the CSEs, the following list indicates the requirements and where to obtain XMLLite from the Download Center:

- **Windows XP SP3** XMLLite is already included and does not need to be installed.
- **Windows XP SP2** Unless Internet Explorer 7 is installed (in which case XMLLite is included), you must download and install XMLLite from *http://go.microsoft.com/fwlink/?LinkId=111843*.
- **Windows Server 2003 SP2** XMLLite is already included and does not need to be installed.
- **Windows Server 2003 SP1** Unless Internet Explorer 7 is installed (in which case XMLLite is included), you must download and install XMLLite from *http://go.microsoft.com/fwlink/?LinkId=111843*.

Summary

Best practices for using Group Policy to manage Windows 7 computers include the following:

- Install RSAT on your Windows 7 administrative workstations so you can use them to manage Group Policy.
- After you edit GPOs using the GPMC included in Windows Server 2008 R2 or the GPMC included with RSAT for Windows 7, do not use earlier versions of either the GPMC or the Group Policy Management Editor to edit those GPOs any further.
- Create a central store on domain controllers running Windows Server 2008 R2, Windows Server 2008, or Windows Server 2003 and copy the ADMX files from your computers running Windows 7 to this store.

- Migrate your custom ADM files to ADMX format using ADMX Migrator. Do not migrate the default ADM files found on previous versions of Windows; Windows 7 does not need them.
- If you are an SA customer, obtain the MDOP so that you can use the enhanced functionality provided by AGPM.

Additional Resources

These resources contain additional information and tools related to this chapter.

Related Information

- The Windows Server Group Policy TechCenter at *http://technet.microsoft.com/en-us/windowsserver/grouppolicy/default.aspx*.
- "What's New in Group Policy" in Windows Server 2008 R2 and Windows 7 at *http://technet.microsoft.com/en-us/library/dd367853.aspx*.
- "Group Policy Frequently Asked Questions (FAQ)" at *http://technet.microsoft.com/en-us/windowsserver/grouppolicy/cc817587.aspx*.
- "Group Policy Preferences Frequently Asked Questions (FAQ)" at *http://technet.microsoft.com/en-us/windowsserver/grouppolicy/cc817590.aspx*.
- The white paper, "Group Policy Preferences Overview," available at *http://www.microsoft.com/downloads/details.aspx?FamilyID=42e30e3f-6f01-4610-9d6e-f6e0fb7a0790&DisplayLang=en*.
- The white paper, "Planning and Deploying Group Policy," available at *http://www.microsoft.com/downloads/details.aspx?FamilyID=73d96068-0aea-450a-861b-e2c5413b0485&DisplayLang=en*.
- The white paper, "Advanced Group Policy Management Overview," available at *http://www.microsoft.com/downloads/details.aspx?FamilyID=993a34d0-c274-4b46-b9fc-568426b81c5e&DisplayLang=en*.
- ADMX Migrator available at *http://www.microsoft.com/downloads/details.aspx?FamilyID=0f1eec3d-10c4-4b5f-9625-97c2f731090c&DisplayLang=en*.
- Group Policy Log View (GPLogView) available at *http://www.microsoft.com/downloads/details.aspx?FamilyID=bcfb1955-ca1d-4f00-9cff-6f541bad4563&DisplayLang=en*.
- "Group Policy Settings Reference for Windows 7 and Windows Server 2008 R2" available from the Microsoft Download Center.
- "Overview Series: Advanced Group Policy Management" at *http://technet.microsoft.com/en-us/library/cc749396.aspx*.
- "Step-by-Step Guide to Managing Multiple Local Group Policy Objects" at *http://technet.microsoft.com/en-us/library/cc766291.aspx*.

- *Managing Group Policy ADMX Files Step-by-Step Guide* at *http://technet.microsoft.com/en-us/library/cc709647.aspx.*
- *Deploying Group Policy Using Windows Vista* at *http://technet.microsoft.com/en-us/library/cc766208.aspx.*
- "Troubleshooting Group Policy Using Event Logs" at *http://technet.microsoft.com/en-us/library/cc749336.aspx.*
- *Windows Group Policy Resource Kit: Windows Server 2008 and Windows Vista* (Microsoft Press, 2008).
- *Windows Group Policy Administrator's Pocket Consultant* by William R. Stanek (Microsoft Press, 2009).
- "ADMX Schema" on MSDN at *http://msdn2.microsoft.com/en-us/library/aa373476.aspx.*
- Group Policy Team Blog at *http://blogs.technet.com/grouppolicy/.*
- "Automating Group Policy Management with Windows PowerShell" in TechNet Magazine at *http://technet.microsoft.com/en-us/magazine/dd797571.aspx.*
- Knowledge Base article 929841, "How to Create a Central Store for Group Policy Administrative Templates in Windows Vista," at *http://support.microsoft.com/kb/929841.*

On the Companion Media

- Get-ComputerRsop.ps1
- Get-ComputerIEEE80211GroupPolicySetting.ps1
- Get-IPSECPolicySetting.ps1
- Get-RegistryPolicySetting.ps1
- Get-RSOPRestrictedGroup.ps1
- Get-ComputerRsop.ps1
- Get-ComputerRsopGPLink.ps1
- Get-ComputerRsopSOM.ps1
- Get-OptionalFeatures.ps1
- ListCodec.ps1
- Get-Games.ps1
- TroubleshootPerformance.ps1

CHAPTER 15

Managing Users and User Data

Large enterprises need secure, reliable, and highly available methods of managing user data and settings. These methods must also work in a variety of networking scenarios ranging from mobile users to shared computer environments to connections over slow and unreliable wide area network (WAN) links. Beginning with Windows Vista, enhancements were made to three corporate roaming technologies available on earlier versions of Microsoft Windows: Roaming User Profiles (RUP), Folder Redirection, and Offline Files. Further enhancements to these technologies have now been introduced in the Windows 7 operating system, which make managing user data and settings for Windows 7 computers easier and provide users with a more consistent and reliable experience as they share computers, work from remote sites, or travel.

Understanding User Profiles in Windows 7

Beginning with Windows Vista, the way user profiles are implemented significantly changed compared with how they were implemented in earlier versions of Windows. One example of this change is the default storage location for local user profiles, which changed from C:\Documents And Settings in Windows XP to C:\Users in Windows Vista. Another example is the default location where documents are saved, which changed from the My Documents known folder in Windows XP to the Documents known folder in Windows Vista.

Windows 7 does not introduce any significant changes to the underlying structure of user profiles or where they are stored. However, Windows 7 does change the user experience of accessing user profile folders by introducing a new feature called Libraries. The following sections describe in detail the underlying structure of user profiles in Windows 7 and how the new Libraries feature helps users keep their documents and other files organized.

It's important for administrators to understand how user profiles work and how they are implemented. For example, because of user profile differences, a roaming user profile cannot be shared between a computer running Windows 7 (or Windows Vista) and one running Windows XP. Understanding how user profiles are implemented can also help administrators troubleshoot issues with users who cannot access their desktop or documents. Finally, an understanding of how user profiles work can provide guidance for training users on how they store and organize their documents.

Types of User Profiles

A user profile is a collection of folders and registry data that describes a user's environment when the user logs on to a client computer. Specifically, user profiles contain:

- A folder hierarchy that stores desktop icons, shortcut links, startup applications, and other data and settings. The structure of this folder hierarchy is discussed further in the section titled "User Profile Namespace in Windows Vista and Windows 7" later in this chapter.
- A registry hive that stores user-defined desktop settings, application settings, persistent network connections, printer connections, and so on. The registry hive for a user profile, which is the Ntuser.dat file in the root of the user's profile folder, is mapped to the HKEY_CURRENT_USER portion of the registry when the user logs on. Ntuser.dat (a system file located in the root of the user's profile folder) maintains the user environment preferences when the user is logged on to the computer.

Windows clients support two kinds of user profiles:

- **Local user profiles** Local user profiles are stored on the client computer. When a user logs on to a Windows computer for the first time, a local user profile is created for the user and stored by default on %SystemDrive% inside the \Users*user_name* folder on Windows Vista and later versions and in the \Documents And Settings*user_name* folder on previous versions of Windows. Whenever the user logs on to the computer, the user's local user profile is loaded and the user's desktop environment is configured according to the data and settings stored in this profile. When the user logs off the computer, any configuration changes made to the user's desktop environment are saved in the user's profile when the profile unloads.

  All Windows computers support local user profiles by default, and the advantage of local user profiles is that they maintain the unique desktop environment of each user who logs on to the computer. Local user profiles thus enable several users to share the same computer while keeping their own user settings and data. The disadvantage of local user profiles is that they are local to the computer. This means that when the user logs on to a different computer, the user's data and settings do not follow her. This makes it difficult for users to roam, or use any available computer, in an enterprise environment.

- **Roaming user profiles** Roaming user profiles are stored in a central location on the network, which is generally a shared folder on a file server. When the user logs on to a client computer, the roaming user profile is downloaded from the network location and loaded onto the client computer to configure the user's desktop environment. When the user logs off the computer, any configuration changes made to the user's desktop are saved to the network share. In addition to maintaining a copy of the roaming profile on the network share, Windows also keeps a locally cached copy of the roaming profile on each computer to which the user logs on.

  Roaming user profiles are supported only in Active Directory Domain Services (AD DS) environments and must be deployed and configured appropriately. An advantage of roaming user profiles is that they allow a user to log on to any available computer on the network, download her profile, load the profile, and experience her unique desktop environment. Another advantage of roaming profiles is that they can be assigned to individual users or to groups of users, which provides flexibility in how desktop environments are deployed. The Windows XP implementation of RUP has several disadvantages that have been improved, first in Windows Vista and later with additional improvements in Windows 7. The section titled "Understanding Roaming User Profiles and Folder Redirection" later in this chapter discusses these disadvantages and enhancements.

  Mandatory user profiles and *super-mandatory* user profiles are two variations of roaming user profiles. Mandatory user profiles are read-only versions of roaming user profiles that have been preconfigured to provide a consistent desktop environment that the user cannot modify. When a user account is configured to use a mandatory user profile, the user downloads the profile from the network share during logon. When the user logs off, any changes made to the user's desktop environment are not uploaded to the profile stored on a network location, and the changes made are overwritten during the next logon when the roaming profile is downloaded from the server. Super-mandatory user profiles have these same characteristics of mandatory user profiles: They are read-only and are not copied back to the network during logoff. What makes them different, however, is that super-mandatory profiles are required for the user to log on. Any condition that prevents the super-mandatory user profile from loading also prevents the user from logging on to the computer. Therefore, super-mandatory user profiles should be used only in environments in which the network infrastructure is very reliable and the presence of the user profile is critical.

User Profiles for Service Accounts

In Windows Vista and later versions, special identities that are used for service accounts—such as Local System, Local Service, and Network Service—also have user profiles. The profiles for these accounts are located as follows:

- **LocalSystem** %WinDir%\System32\config\systemprofile
- **LocalService** %WinDir%\ServiceProfiles\LocalService
- **NetworkService** %WinDir%\ServiceProfiles\NetworkService

User Profile Namespace

The hierarchy of folders within a user's profile folder is called the *user profile namespace*. In Windows Vista and later versions of Windows, this namespace is organized in a significantly different manner than in earlier versions of Windows, including Windows XP and Microsoft Windows 2000. Understanding these differences is essential for understanding how RUP works in mixed environments, such as a network that has computers running Windows 7 and computers running Windows XP. Such an environment is a common scenario during a gradual desktop migration in a large enterprise.

User Profile Namespace in Windows XP

In Windows XP and Windows 2000, the user profile namespace is characterized as follows:

- Local user profiles are stored within the root folder %SystemDrive%\Documents And Settings.
- Each user who has logged on at least once to the computer has a user profile folder named after his user account. For example, user Michael Allen (mallen@contoso.com) has the user profile folder %SystemDrive%\Documents And Settings\mallen; the local Administrator account has the user profile folder %SystemDrive%\Documents And Settings\Administrator; and so on.
- A special profile folder, %SystemDrive%\Documents And Settings\All Users, contains common program items, such as Start Menu shortcuts and desktop items that are accessible to all users who log on to the computer. By customizing the contents of the All Users profile, you can provide all users who log on to the computer with access to programs and shortcuts that they need, in addition to those items within their own personal Start Menu and Desktop folders. The All Users profile does not contain a registry hive because Windows does not load this profile. Instead, Windows writes all shared settings to the HKEY_LOCAL_MACHINE hive of the registry on the computer.
- A special hidden profile folder, %SystemDrive%\Documents And Settings\Default User, is used as a template for all new local user profiles created on the computer. When a user logs on to the computer for the first time and no Default Domain User profile

is stored in the NETLOGON share on domain controllers (and no roaming profile is already stored in a network location for users with a roaming user profile configured), the Default User profile is loaded and copied to %SystemDrive%\Documents And Settings*user_name* as the user's local profile. If a Default User profile is stored in the NETLOGON share, this profile (instead of SystemDrive%\Documents And Settings \Default User) is copied to %SystemDrive%\Documents And Settings*user_name* as the user's local profile.

- %SystemDrive%\Documents And Settings\LocalService and %SystemDrive%\Documents And Settings\NetworkService are two special, super-hidden profile folders automatically created for the LocalService and NetworkService built-in accounts used by the Service Control Manager to host services that don't need to run as LocalSystem. Windows requires these special profiles; you should not modify them.

The hierarchy of folders (the namespace) within a user folder on Windows XP consists of a mix of application settings folders and user data folders, many of which are hidden. Some of the important folders in this namespace include:

- **Application Data** Contains application-specific data, such as custom dictionaries or vendor-specific data. The directories inside Application Data are roamed between computers.
- **Cookies** Contains Windows Internet Explorer cookies.
- **Desktop** Contains desktop items, including files and shortcuts.
- **Favorites** Contains Internet Explorer favorites.
- **Local Settings** Contains application settings and data that are either computer specific or are too large to roam effectively with the profile. (The directories inside Local Settings are not roamed between computers.) Subfolders of this folder include Application Data, History, Temp, and Temporary Internet Files.
- **My Documents** This folder is the default location for any documents the user creates. Subfolders of this folder include My Pictures, My Music, and other application-specific folders.
- **NetHood** Contains shortcuts to My Network Places items.
- **PrintHood** Contains shortcuts to printer folder items.
- **Recent** Contains shortcuts to files, programs, and settings used recently.
- **SendTo** Contains shortcuts to document storage locations and applications.
- **Start Menu** Contains shortcuts to program items.
- **Templates** Contains shortcuts to template items.

In Windows XP, user profile folders such as My Documents and Favorites are known as *special folders*. These special folders are identified to the operating system using constant special item ID list (CSIDL) values, which provide a unique, system-independent method for identifying folders that are used frequently by applications but which may not have the same name or location on any given system because of the installation method or Folder Redirection.

The implementation of the user profile namespace in Windows XP has several disadvantages:

- A user profile consists of a mixture of application and user data folders stored at the root of the profile. This means that the user profile provides no clean separation of user data from application data. For example, the %SystemDrive%\Documents And Settings *user_name*\Local Settings\Application Data folder contains either computer-specific data and settings that cannot (or should not) roam with the user's profile, or it contains data and settings that are too large to roam effectively. (They would delay the logon experience if they were roamed.) On the other hand, the %SystemDrive% \Documents And Settings*user_name*\Application Data folder contains data and settings that should roam when RUP is implemented. This confusion of having roaming and non-roaming data and settings stored in two similarly named folders sometimes leads to third-party vendors creating applications that store their data and settings in the wrong folder, affecting the ability of these applications to roam along with the user who uses them.
- My Pictures, My Music, and My Videos are subfolders of My Documents even though they are designed to contain media files rather than conventional documents. This makes configuring Folder Redirection unnecessarily complex and sometimes leads to nondocument, user-managed data being unnecessarily redirected.
- No guidelines or restrictions exist for how third-party applications should store their per-user settings and data within the user's profile. For example, third-party applications might create new subfolders of the user profile root folder for storing per-user information instead of storing it within existing folders in the namespace. Third-party applications also sometimes combine computer-specific and per-user settings within the Application Data folder, which can make it difficult for certain applications to roam when RUP is configured.
- Users have no simple and intuitive way of securely sharing portions of their user profiles and the data they contain with other users to access over the network. This makes it difficult, for example, for inexperienced users to share specific documents within their My Documents folders.
- The system of using CSIDL values to identify special folders has several disadvantages. For example, CSIDL values could not be extended, which means that application vendors could not add their own special folders to user profiles easily. In addition, no application programming interface (API) was available on Windows XP for enumerating all CSIDL values available on the system. Finally, under the CSIDL system, only the My Documents folder could be redirected to a different location.

User Profile Namespace in Windows Vista and Windows 7

To address concerns with using the user profile namespace in earlier versions of Windows, the following changes have been implemented for user profiles starting with Windows Vista:

- The root of the user profile namespace has been moved from %SystemDrive% \Documents And Settings to %SystemDrive%\Users. This means, for example, that the user profile folder for user Michael Allen (mallen@contoso.com) is now found at %SystemDrive%\Users\mallen instead of %SystemDrive%\Documents And Settings \mallen.

- The "My" prefix has been dropped from folders storing user-managed data files to simplify their appearance. For example, documents are now stored in a folder named Documents instead of in a folder named My Documents. Note that in Windows Vista, these folders are displayed in the same way (that is, without the "My" prefix) in both the Windows Explorer shell and at the command prompt. Beginning with Windows 7, however, these folders display a "My" prefix when viewed within Windows Explorer but not when viewed at the command prompt. In other words, the Windows Explorer shell in Windows 7 adds a "My" prefix to the displayed representation of these folders, but the actual folders in the underlying file system do not include this prefix in their names.
- The Windows Vista and later versions of My Music, My Pictures, and My Videos are no longer subfolders of My Documents. Instead, these and similar user-managed data folders are now stored under the root profile folder and are peers of the My Documents folder. The user profile namespace has been flattened in this way to help provide better separation between user-managed data and application settings and to simplify how Folder Redirection works.
- New subfolders have been added under the root profile folder to help to better organize user-managed data and settings and to help prevent "profile pollution," when users or applications save data files in the root profile folder or in subfolders not intended for that particular purpose. Specifically, the following new profile subfolders have been added beginning with Windows Vista:
  - **Contacts** The default location for storing the user's contacts
  - **Downloads** The default location for saving all downloaded content
  - **Searches** The default location for storing saved searches
  - **Links** The default location for storing Windows Explorer favorites
  - **Saved Games** The default location for storing saved games
- The system of using CSIDL values used in Windows XP to identify special folders, such as My Documents, used by applications has been replaced. These special folders are now referred to as *known folders,* and they are identified to the operating system by a set of globally unique identifier (GUID) values called Known Folder IDs. The Known Folder system provides a number of advantages over the older CSIDL system. For example, Independent Software Vendors (ISVs) can extend the set of Known Folder IDs to define additional application-specific known folders, assign IDs to them, and register them with the system. In contrast, the system of CSIDL values cannot be extended. A known folder added by an ISV can also add custom properties that allow the folder to expose its purpose and intended use to the user. All the known folders on a system can also be enumerated using the *GetFolderIds* method of the *IKnownFolderManager* interface. Finally, 13 known folders can be redirected to new locations by using Folder

Redirection. By comparison, under the CSIDL system, only the My Documents folder could be redirected. A new, hidden folder named AppData located under the profile root is used as a central location for storing all per-user application settings and binaries. In addition, the following three subfolders under AppData are better at separating state information and helping applications roam:

- **Local** This folder stores computer-specific application data and settings that cannot (or should not) roam, as well as user-managed data or settings too large to support roaming effectively. The AppData\Local folder within a Windows Vista or later user profile is essentially the same as the Local Settings\Application Data folder under the root folder of a Windows XP user profile.
- **Roaming** This folder stores user-specific application data and settings that should (or must) roam along with the user when RUP is implemented. The AppData \Roaming folder within a Windows Vista or later user profile is essentially the same as the Application Data folder under the root folder of a Windows XP user profile.
- **LocalLow** This folder allows low-integrity processes to have Write access to it. Low-integrity processes perform tasks that could compromise the operating system. For example, applications started by the Protected Mode of Internet Explorer must use this profile folder for storing application data and settings. The LocalLow profile folder has no counterpart in Windows XP.

- The All Users profile has been renamed Public to better describe its purpose. (Anything stored in this folder is publicly available to all users on the computer.) The contents of certain subfolders within this profile, such as Desktop, merge with the user's own profile when the user logs on to the computer, just as the All Users profile does in Windows XP. As with All Users in Windows XP, the Public profile in Windows Vista and later versions has no per-user registry hive because the operating system never loads the profile. In addition, application data stored in the All Users profile in Windows XP is now stored in the hidden %SystemDrive%\ProgramData folder in Windows Vista.
- Users now can share individual files easily and securely from within their user profile folders and subfolders.
- The Default User profile has been renamed Default. As with Default User in Windows XP, the Default profile in Windows Vista and later versions is never loaded and is copied only when creating new profiles. The Default profile thus acts as a template for creating each user's profile when he logs on for the first time.

NOTE **Only the local default user folder has changed from Default User to Default. The default roaming user profile located on the NETLOGON share on domain controllers is now called Default User.v2.**

Table 15-1 compares the user profile namespace for Windows Vista and later versions with that of Windows XP. The folders in the first column are subfolders (or special files) of the root profile folder %SystemDrive%\Users*user_name*; the folders in the second column are rooted at %SystemDrive%\Documents And Settings*user_name*. Many of these folders are hidden.

TABLE 15-1 The User Profile Namespace in Windows Vista and Later Versions Compared with Windows XP

WINDOWS VISTA AND LATER VERSIONS	WINDOWS XP
N/A	Local Settings
AppData	N/A
AppData\Local	Local Settings\Application Data
AppData\Local\Microsoft\Windows\History	Local Settings\History
AppData\Local\Temp	Local Settings\Temp
AppData\Local\Microsoft\Windows\Temporary Internet Files	Local Settings\Temporary Internet Files
AppData\LocalLow	N/A
AppData\Roaming	Application Data
AppData\Roaming\Microsoft \Windows\Cookies	Cookies
AppData\Roaming\Microsoft\Windows\Network Shortcuts	NetHood
AppData\Roaming\Microsoft\Windows\Printer Shortcuts	PrintHood
AppData\Roaming\Microsoft\Windows\Recent	Recent
AppData\Roaming\Microsoft\Windows\Send To	SendTo
AppData\Roaming\Microsoft\Windows\Start Menu	Start Menu
AppData\Roaming\Microsoft\Windows\Templates	Templates
Contacts	N/A
Desktop	Desktop
Documents	My Documents
Downloads	N/A
Favorites	Favorites
Links	N/A
Music	My Documents\My Music
Pictures	My Documents\My Pictures
Searches	N/A
Saved Games	N/A
Videos	My Documents\My Videos

NOTE Windows Vista and later versions allow users to use the Encrypting File System (EFS) to encrypt all files and folders within their user profiles except for Ntuser.dat and the AppData\Roaming\Microsoft\Credentials subfolder, which is essentially the same behavior as user profile encryption in Windows XP. To encrypt files that EFS cannot encrypt, use Windows BitLocker. For more information, read Chapter 16, "Managing Disks and File Systems."

Application Compatibility Issues

Because of the significant changes to the user profile namespace beginning with Windows Vista, particularly the new root profile folder %SystemDrive%\Users and the flattening of the profile folder hierarchy, some application compatibility issues may arise with older, third-party, and in-house developed applications. For example, if an older application developed for Windows XP has %SystemDrive%\Documents And Settings*user_name*\My Documents hard-coded as the location for storing user data files created with the application, the application might fail because this path does not exist in Windows Vista and later.

To resolve these compatibility issues, a number of directory junction (DJ) points have been created within user profile folders beginning with Windows Vista. These junction points automatically cause applications trying to access older profile paths to traverse the junction and be redirected to the new profile paths used in Windows Vista and later versions. For example, a junction under %SystemDrive% named Documents And Settings points to %SystemDrive%\Users so that any older application that tries to access the nonexistent %SystemDrive%\Documents And Settings folder in Windows Vista and later versions is redirected automatically to %SystemDrive%\Users.

Junction points are super-hidden (the *system* and *hidden* attributes are set) and can be displayed by using the *dir /AL* command at the command prompt, where the *L* option displays all reparse points (junction points or symbolic links) within the current directory. For example, running this command from within the root profile folder for user Michael Allen displays 10 junction points.

```
C:\Users\mallen>dir /AL
 Volume in drive C has no label.
 Volume Serial Number is 70E7-7600

 Directory of C:\Users\mallen

11/17/2006  10:36 AM    <JUNCTION>     Application Data [C:\Users\mallen\AppData\
Roaming]
11/17/2006  10:36 AM    <JUNCTION>     Cookies [C:\Users\mallen\AppData\Roaming\
Microsoft\
Windows\Cookies]
11/17/2006  10:36 AM    <JUNCTION>     Local Settings [C:\Users\mallen\AppData\Local]
```

```
11/17/2006  10:36 AM    <JUNCTION>     My Documents [C:\Users\mallen\Documents]
11/17/2006  10:36 AM    <JUNCTION>     NetHood [C:\Users\mallen\AppData\Roaming\
Microsoft\Windows
\Network Shortcuts]
11/17/2006  10:36 AM    <JUNCTION>     PrintHood [C:\Users\mallen\AppData\Roaming\
Microsoft
\Windows\Printer Shortcuts]
11/17/2006  10:36 AM    <JUNCTION>     Recent [C:\Users\mallen\AppData\Roaming\
Microsoft\Windows
\Recent]
11/17/2006  10:36 AM    <JUNCTION>     SendTo [C:\Users\mallen\AppData\Roaming\
Microsoft\Windows
\SendTo]
11/17/2006  10:36 AM    <JUNCTION>     Start Menu [C:\Users\mallen\AppData\Roaming\
Microsoft
\Windows\Start Menu]
11/17/2006  10:36 AM    <JUNCTION>     Templates [C:\Users\mallen\AppData\Roaming\
Microsoft
\Windows\Templates]
               0 File(s)              0 bytes
              10 Dir(s)  35,494,162,432 bytes free
```

DIRECT FROM THE SOURCE

Working with Directory Junction Points

Ming Zhu, Software Design Engineer
Microsoft Windows Shell Team

It's important to mention that directory junction (DJ) points are not designed for enumeration. This means you can't use the command **dir <DJ>** to list the contents under the folder to which the junction points because this results in an infinite loop. For example, %UserProfile%\AppData\Local\Application Data actually points to %UserProfile%\AppData\Local itself. To prevent this from happening, there is a Deny Read access control entry (ACE) on these DJs. Instead of enumeration, applications can access only files directly using a path that contains the DJ. For example, you can't use the command dir %UserName%\My Documents, but if you have a Example.txt file in your Documents directory, you can use Notepad %UserProfile%\My Documents\Example.txt to open the file directly.

One impact of this change is that you cannot use the traditional XCopy command to copy user profiles anymore because it doesn't handle DJs correctly. Instead, you should use the new Robocopy command (which is included in Windows Vista and later versions) because it has an */XJD* option to ignore all DJs during the copy.

Windows Vista and later versions actually use two types of junction points:

- **Per-user junctions** Per-user junctions are created inside user profiles to provide compatibility for older applications. The junction from %SystemDrive%\Users *user_name*\My Documents to C:\Users*user_name*\Documents is an example of a per-user junction created by the Profile service when the user profile is created.
- **System junctions** System junctions include any other junctions created on the system that are not located within the user profile namespace for a user that has logged on to the system. The junction from %SystemDrive%\Documents And Settings to %SystemDrive%\Users is an example of a system junction created when Windows Vista and later versions are installed on the system. In addition, any junctions found in the All Users, Public, and Default User profiles are also system junctions because these profiles are never loaded.

Tables 15-2 through 15-5 show the various junction points implemented in Windows Vista and later versions to provide compatibility with legacy applications developed for Windows XP or Windows 2000.

TABLE 15-2 Junctions Within User Profiles on Windows Vista and Later Versions

JUNCTION CREATION LOCATION	JUNCTION DESTINATION
JUNCTION FOR PARENT FOLDER	
Documents And Settings	Users
JUNCTIONS FOR USER DATA LEGACY FOLDERS	
Documents And Settings*user_name*\My Documents	Users*user_name*\Documents
Documents And Settings*user_name*\My Documents\My Music	Users*user_name*\Music
Documents And Settings*user_name*\My Documents\My Pictures	Users*user_name*\Pictures
Documents And Settings*user_name*\My Documents\My Videos	Users*user_name*\Videos
JUNCTIONS FOR PER-USER APPLICATION DATA LEGACY FOLDERS	
Documents And Settings*user_name*\Local Settings	Users*user_name*\AppData\Local
Documents And Settings*user_name*\Local Settings\Application Data	Users*user_name*\AppData\Local

JUNCTION CREATION LOCATION	JUNCTION DESTINATION
Documents And Settings*user_name*\Local Settings\Temporary Internet Files	Users*user_name*\AppData\Local\Microsoft\Windows\Temporary Internet Files
Documents And Settings*user_name*\Local Settings\History	Users*user_name*\AppData\Local\Microsoft\Windows\History
Documents And Settings*user_name*\Application Data	Users*user_name*\AppData\Roaming
JUNCTIONS FOR PER-USER OPERATING SYSTEM SETTINGS LEGACY FOLDERS	
Documents And Settings*user_name*\Cookies	Users*user_name*\AppData\Roaming\Microsoft\Windows\Cookies
Documents And Settings*user_name*\Recent	Users*user_name*\AppData\Roaming\Microsoft\Windows\Recent Items
Documents And Settings*user_name*\NetHood	Users*user_name*\AppData\Roaming\Microsoft\Windows\Network Shortcuts
Documents And Settings*user_name*\PrintHood	Users*user_name*\AppData\Roaming\Microsoft\Windows\Printer Shortcuts
Documents And Settings*user_name*\SendTo	Users*user_name*\AppData\Roaming\Microsoft\Windows\Send To
Documents And Settings*user_name*\StartMenu	Users*user_name*\AppData\Roaming\Microsoft\Windows\Start Menu
Documents And Settings*user_name*\Templates	Users*user_name*\AppData\Roaming\Microsoft\Windows\Templates

TABLE 15-3 Junctions for Older Default User Profiles on Windows Vista and Later Versions

JUNCTION CREATION LOCATION	JUNCTION DESTINATION
Documents And Settings\Default User	Users\Default
Documents And Settings\Default User\Desktop	Users\Default\Desktop
Documents And Settings\Default User\My Documents	Users\Default\Documents
Documents And Settings\Default User\Favorites	Users\Default\Favorites
Documents And Settings\Default User\My Documents\My Music	Users\Default\Music

JUNCTION CREATION LOCATION	JUNCTION DESTINATION
Documents And Settings\Default User\My Documents\My Pictures	Users\Default\Pictures
Documents And Settings\Default User\My Documents\My Videos	Users\Default\Videos
Documents And Settings\Default User\Application Data	Users\Default\AppData\Roaming
Documents And Settings\Default User\Start Menu	Users\Default\AppData\Roaming\Microsoft\Windows\Start Menu
Documents And Settings\Default User\Templates	Users\Default\AppData\Roaming\Microsoft\Windows\Templates
Program Files (Localized Name)	Program Files
Program Files\Common Files (Localized Name)	Program Files\Local Files

TABLE 15-4 Junctions for Older All Users Folders on Windows Vista and Later Versions

JUNCTION CREATION LOCATION	JUNCTION DESTINATION
Users\All Users	ProgramData
ProgramData\Public Desktop	Users\Public\Public Desktop
ProgramData\Public Documents	Users\Public\Public Documents
ProgramData\Favorites	Users\Public\Favorites
Users\Public\Public Documents\Public Music	Users\Public\Public Music
Users\Public\Public Documents\Public Pictures	Users\Public\Public Pictures
Users\Public\Public Documents\Public Videos	Users\Public\Public Videos
ProgramData\Application Data	ProgramData
ProgramData\Start Menu	ProgramData\Microsoft\Windows\Start Menu
ProgramData\Templates	ProgramData\Microsoft\Windows\Templates

TABLE 15-5 Older Profile Folders in Which Junctions Are Not Required on Windows Vista and Later Versions

PREVIOUS LOCATION	REASON
Documents And Settings\ *user_name*\Desktop	Handled by the junction at Documents And Settings
Documents And Settings\ *user_name*\Favorites	Handled by the junction at Documents And Settings
Documents And Settings\ *user_name*\Local Settings\Temp	Handled by the junction at Local Settings

> ***NOTE*** **The junction from Users\All Users to ProgramData shown in Table 15-4 is actually a symbolic link and not a junction point. Symbolic links (symlinks) were introduced in Windows Vista and are not supported on previous versions of Windows. You can create symlinks, junction points, and hard links using the *mklink* command. For more information on new NTFS features in Windows Vista and later versions, see Chapter 16.**

Disabling Known Folders

Administrators who want to minimize user confusion around known folders being recreated by applications can disable specific known folders in Windows 7 by enabling and configuring the following Group Policy setting:

User Configuration\Administrative Templates\Windows Components\Windows Explorer \Disable Known Folders

For example, the Sample Videos known folder has the Known Folder ID of {440fcffd-a92b-4739-ae1a-d4a54907c53f} and the Canonical ID name of SampleVideos. By enabling this policy setting and specifying either the Known Folder ID or Canonical ID of this folder, you can prevent the folder from being created using the known folder API. If the folder already exists before the policy setting is applied, the folder must be deleted manually (the policy only blocks the creation of the folder).

> ***WARNING*** **Disabling a known folder can introduce application compatibility issues for applications that depend on the folder.**

HOW IT WORKS

Moving User Profiles

In previous versions of Windows, the Moveuser utility (part of the Windows Server 2003 Resource Kit Tools) can be used to map an existing local user account profile to a new domain account profile when a computer in a workgroup is being joined to a domain. The Moveuser utility can also be used to map an existing domain account profile to a new domain account profile. In Windows Vista and later versions, however, Moveuser will not work and has been replaced by a downloadable User Profile Windows Management Instrumentation (WMI) provider. For more information on obtaining this WMI provider, see Microsoft Knowledge Base article 930955, "Moveuser.exe Is Incompatible with Windows Vista and Is Replaced by the New Win32_UserProfile WMI Functionality," at *http://support.microsoft.com/kb/930955*.

Understanding Libraries

Libraries are a new feature in Windows 7 that makes it easier for users to organize, find, and use their documents, pictures, and other data files. By using libraries, users can access files that are stored in different locations as a single collection. For example, documents that are stored in the My Documents folder, the Public documents folder, an external hard drive, and a network share can be accessed as a single set of files in the Documents library—as if they were all stored in the same place. Libraries are also integrated with the Windows Search service to enable users to find the files they need on their computers or on network file servers quickly. Libraries were introduced in Windows 7 to address the problem of the tendency of users to store their files in multiple locations on their computers, which can make it difficult for them to find the files when they need them.

To point a library to different locations, you must include a folder in the library. When you include a folder, it is associated with the library so that the contents of the folder—or library location—are displayed within the library and are searchable from the library. Library locations can be folders on the local system or shared folders on the network.

As Figure 15-1 shows, when Windows 7 is installed on a system, four default libraries are created:

- Documents
- Pictures
- Music
- Videos

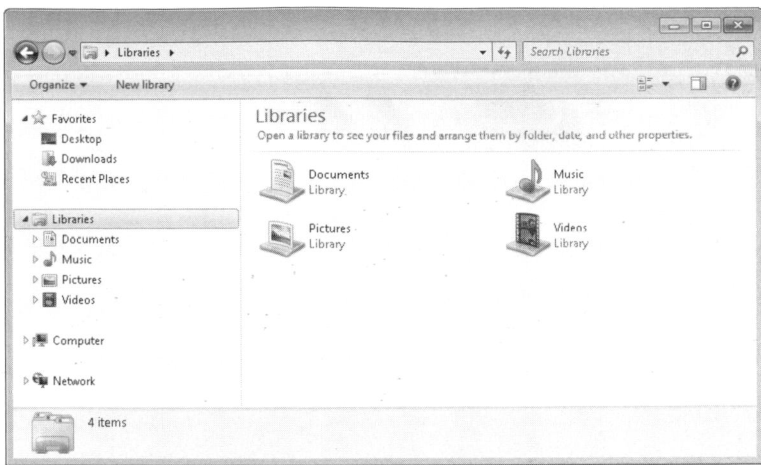

FIGURE 15-1 The four default libraries created by Windows 7

Each of these default libraries has two locations configured. For example, the Documents library has the following two locations configured by default:

- **My Documents** The C:\Users*user_name*\Documents folder within the user's profile
- **Public Documents** The C:\Users\Public\Documents folder that can be accessed by any user who is logged on to the computer interactively

Only one library location can be configured as the default save location for a library. The *default save location* is the folder to which files that are moved, copied, or saved to the library are stored. The default save location for the four default libraries are the known folders within the user's profile. For example, the default save location for the Documents library is the My Documents folder. As Figure 15-2 shows, the default save location for a library can be viewed or modified by opening the properties sheet for the library. If the location representing the default save location is removed from the library, the next available location in the Library Locations list will become the new default save location.

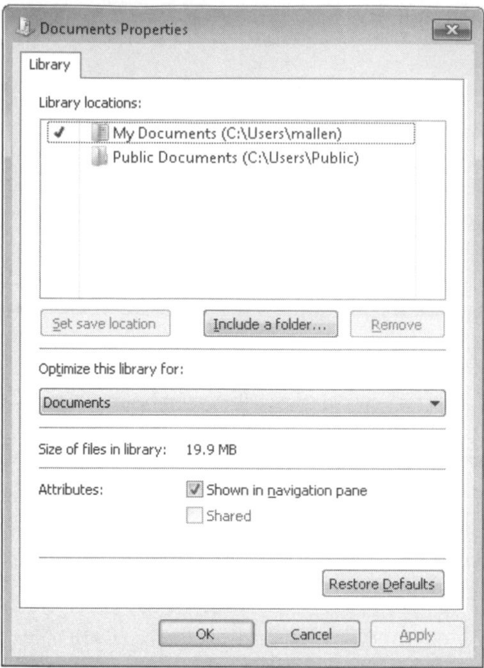

FIGURE 15-2 Use the properties sheet of a library to modify the default save location for the library.

Libraries support two levels of functionality:

- **Full functionality** If all library locations included in a library are indexed using the Windows Search service, the full Windows 7 library experience is available for users, including:
  - **Rich metadata views** Allows you to arrange files by properties such as date, type, author, and tags
  - **Fast, full-content searching** Searching library contents provides customized filter search suggestions based on the types of files included in the library
- **Basic functionality** If one or more nonindexed locations are included in a library, some library functionality will not be available, including:
  - You cannot search the library from the Start menu.
  - You cannot perform a full-text search (grep search is used instead).
  - You cannot access search filter suggestions other than Date Modified and Size.
  - There are no file snippets in the search results.
  - You cannot use metadata browsing using Arrange By views.

For more information on the levels of library functionality, see the section titled "Managing Libraries" later in this chapter.

NOTE The Windows Explorer user interface will not allow you to add a nonindexed remote location to a library.

Working with Libraries

Users can include additional folders or remove existing ones from each of the default libraries. These new library locations can either be local folders on the computer or shared folders on other computers on the network.

For a folder to be included in a library, it must already be indexed or be available for indexing by the Windows Search service. If a folder on the local system is not yet indexed, including the folder in the library automatically causes the folder to be indexed.

Locations can be indexed in two ways:

- **By indexing the location using the Windows Search service on the local system** Automatically including a local folder in a library causes the folder to be added to the local indexer scope. If a folder is stored remotely and is not indexed on the remote system, making the folder available for offline use adds the location to the local indexer scope. For more information, see the section titled "Adding Nonindexed Remote Locations to a Library" later in this chapter.
- **By federating from the local indexer to files indexed on a remote system** The remote system must have the Windows Search service installed and running on it and must be one of the following platforms:
  - Windows 7, with additional features installed
  - Windows Vista Service Pack 1 (SP1) or later, with no additional features installed
  - Windows Server 2008 R2, with the File Services role and the File Server and Windows Search Service role services added
  - Windows Server 2008, with the File Services role and the File Server and Windows Search Service role services added
  - Windows XP SP2 or later, with Windows Search 4.0 installed
  - Windows Server 2003 SP2 or later, with Windows Search 4.0 installed

Table 15-6 summarizes the types of locations that are supported and not supported for inclusion in libraries in which full library functionality is enabled.

TABLE 15-6 Supported and Unsupported Library Locations

SUPPORTED LOCATIONS	UNSUPPORTED LOCATIONS
Fixed local volumes (NTFS or FAT)	Removable drives and media such as DVDs
Remote shared folders that are indexed or that are available for offline use either manually or through Folder Redirection	Remote network shares that are not indexed and that are not available for offline use
	Other data sources such as Windows SharePoint sites, Microsoft Exchange Server, Windows Live SkyDrive, and so on

Including Indexed Folders in a Library

Users can include indexed folders in a library, such as the Documents library, by performing the following steps:

1. Right-click the Documents library and select Properties to open the properties sheet for the library.
2. Click Include A Folder to open the Include Folder In Documents dialog box.
3. Browse to the local folder or network share that you want to include and select Include Folder.

Figure 15-3 shows the Documents library with five library locations:

- The My Documents folder in the user's profile
- The Public Documents folder on the user's computer
- A folder in the root of the user's C drive.
- A folder on a different local drive
- A shared folder on a network file server running Windows Server 2008 R2

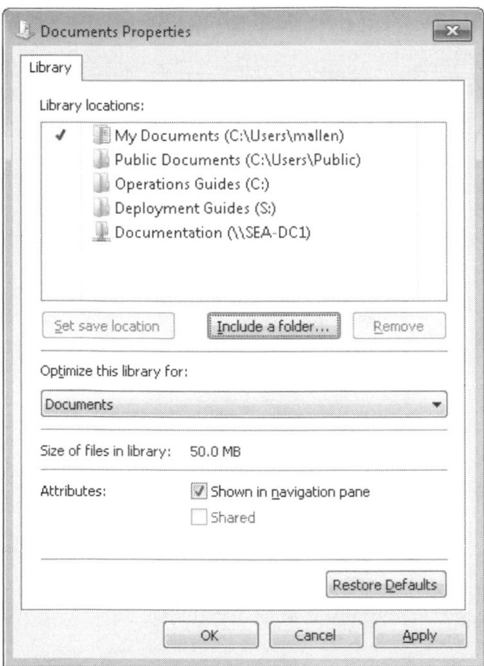

FIGURE 15-3 The Documents library with five locations configured

Users can also include an indexed folder in a library by right-clicking the folder or network share in Windows Explorer and selecting the Include In Library option from the context menu.

Adding Nonindexed Remote Locations to a Library

Users can also add nonindexed remote locations, such as shared folders, on file servers running older versions of Windows. To do this, you must make the shared folder available for offline use. This adds the contents of the folder to the Offline Files cache on the local system so that it can be indexed by the local indexer. Windows then automatically keeps the local and remote copies of the folder in sync.

To add a nonindexed shared folder on a remote computer to the Documents library on your system, follow these steps:

1. On the Start menu, in the Search box, type ***computername*** and press Enter, where *computername* is the name of the remote computer. This will open Windows Explorer and display any shared folders on the remote computer.
2. Right-click the shared folder you want to add to your library and select Always Available Offline. A green sync icon will be added to the shared folder icon when synchronization is complete between the shared folder on the remote system and the Offline Files cache on the local system.

3. Follow the steps in the previous section to add the remote location to your library. When you are done, the remote location should appear in the list of library locations on the library's properties sheet, as shown in Figure 15-4.

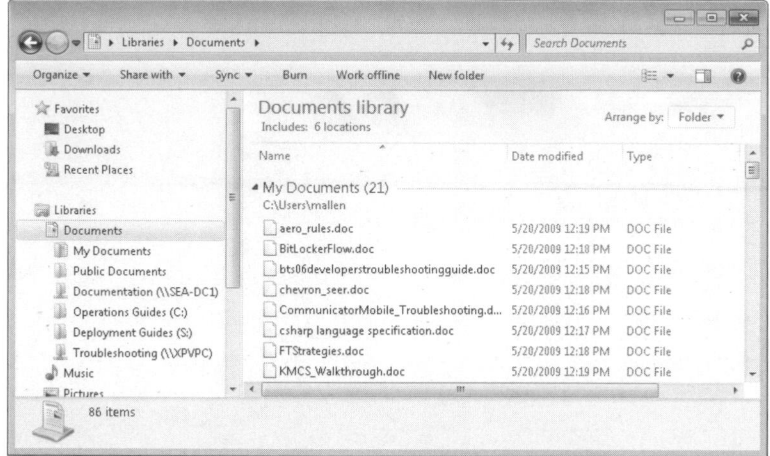

FIGURE 15-4 A nonindexed shared folder on a remote computer is added to the Documents library after making it available for offline use.

Creating Additional Libraries

Users can create additional libraries to organize their work better. To create a new library, follow these steps:

1. Click the New Library button on the toolbar, as shown in Figure 15-1, and type a name for your new library. This will create a new library that has no library locations and is configured for general content (mixed file types).
2. Right-click the new library you created and select Properties to open the properties sheet for the new library.
3. Include one or more folders in your new library as needed using the procedure outlined in the section titled "Adding Nonindexed Remote Locations to a Library" earlier in this chapter.
4. Select the Optimize This Library For option and select the type of file content that you plan on storing in your library.

Users can also create a new library and include an indexed folder in the library in a single step by right-clicking the folder or network share in Windows Explorer, selecting Include In Library, and then selecting Create New Library.

Customizing Libraries

By opening the properties sheet for a library, the following library attributes can be modified:

- Library name
- Library locations
- Default save location
- Type of file content for which the library is optimized
- Visibility of the library in navigation pane
- Whether the library is shared (only in HomeGroup scenarios)

Libraries can be customized further by editing their Library Description files, which are Extensible Markup Language (XML) files with the file extension .library-ms that are stored in the %Appdata%\Microsoft\Windows\Libraries folder.

> ***MORE INFO*** **For more information on editing Library Description files, see the post titled "Understanding Windows 7 Libraries" on the Windows blog at *http://windowsteamblog.com/blogs/developers/archive/2009/04/06/understanding-windows-7-libraries.aspx.***

Viewing Libraries

When a library is displayed in the navigation pane of Windows Explorer, selecting the library node will display all of the files in all configured locations (as shown in Figure 15-5). This allows users to view the contents of both local folders and remote shares from a single place, making it easier for them to browse for specific files they want.

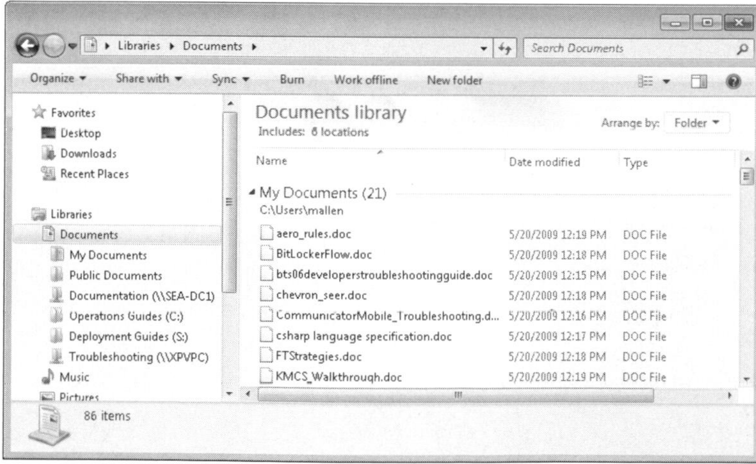

FIGURE 15-5 All files from all configured locations are displayed when you select a library in the navigation pane of Windows Explorer.

Users can include more folders in a library or remove existing ones by clicking Locations (next to Includes) beneath the library name, as shown in Figure 15-5. Doing this opens a dialog box displaying a list of configured locations, as shown in Figure 15-6.

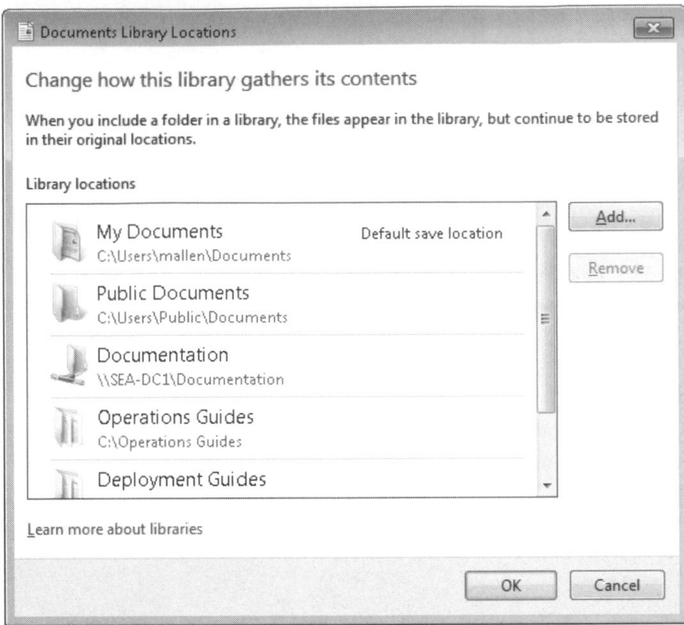

FIGURE 15-6 Users can quickly include folders in a library or remove existing folders.

As shown in Figure 15-7, typing text in the Search box when a library is selected in Windows Explorer will result in searching the entire library and all its locations for the specified text.

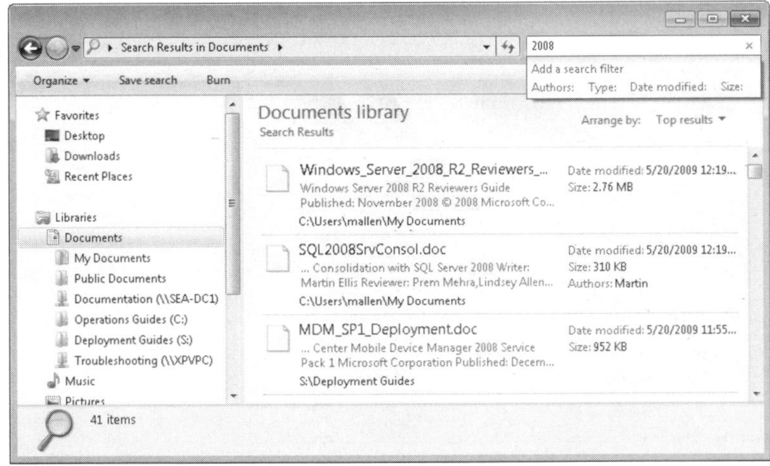

FIGURE 15-7 Searching a library searches all configured locations for that library.

For more information on the search functionality included in Windows 7, see Chapter 19, "Managing Search."

Managing Libraries

Administrators can control which default libraries are available directly on a user's Start menu by configuring the following Group Policy settings found under User Configuration\Policies \Administrative Templates\Start Menu And Taskbar:

- Remove Documents Icon From Start Menu
- Remove Pictures Icon From Start Menu
- Remove Music Icon From Start Menu
- Remove Videos Link From Start Menu

These policy settings will be applied to the targeted users after their next logon.

Administrators can also hide selected default libraries such as Music and Videos in business environments where such libraries are not appropriate. However, hiding a library from view only removes the library from the navigation pane of Windows Explorer. To hide a default library such as the Music library, use Group Policy to run the following script the next time the targeted users log on.

```
@echo off
%SystemDrive%
cd\
cd %appdata%\Microsoft\Windows\Libraries
attrib +h Music.library-ms
```

> ***NOTE*** **If you hide a library using this script, you should also remove it from the users' Start menus.**

Administrators can deploy additional custom libraries to users by manually creating Library Description files for them and then deploying them to users by using either logon scripts or Group Policy preferences to copy the Library Description files to the %UserProfile%\Appdata \Roaming\Microsoft\Windows\Libraries folder on the targeted computers.

Administrators that have environments in which known folders are redirected to server shares that are not indexed remotely and cannot be made available for offline use can configure libraries to use basic-level functionality by enabling the following Group Policy setting:

User Configuration\Administrative Templates\Windows Components\Windows Explorer \Turn off Windows Libraries Features That Rely On Indexed File Data

Note that library functionality is severely degraded if this policy setting is enabled, even for libraries that contain only indexed files. However, if your environment does not support local indexing, enabling this Group Policy may help minimize user feedback, indicating that an unsupported location is included in a library, and can help reduce network impact from grep searches of remote nonindexed locations.

Enabling this policy disables the following library functionality:

- Searching libraries in the Start menu
- Applying Arrange By views other than By Folder and Clear Changes
- Using Library Search Filter suggestions other than Date Modified and Size
- Using the Unsupported tag in the Library Management dialog box
- Applying rich functionality to user-created libraries
- Viewing file content snippets in the Content View mode
- Notifying users that unsupported locations are included in libraries

Implementing Corporate Roaming

RUP and Folder Redirection are two technologies that provide enterprises with the ability for users to roam between computers and access their unique, personal, desktop environments with their personal data and settings. Corporate roaming also provides enterprises with flexibility in seating arrangements: Users are not (or need not be) guaranteed the same computer each time they work, such as in a call center where users have no assigned desk or seating and must therefore share computers with other users at different times or on different days. Corporate roaming has the additional benefit of simplifying per-user backup by providing administrators with a centralized location for storing all user data and settings, namely the file server where roaming user profiles are stored.

Understanding Roaming User Profiles and Folder Redirection

RUP is a technology that has been available on Windows platforms since Microsoft Windows NT 4.0. Roaming profiles work by storing user profiles in a centralized location, typically within a shared folder on a network file server called the *profile server*. Because roaming profiles store the entire profile for a user (except for the Local Settings profile subfolder), all of a user's data and application settings can roam. When roaming profiles are enabled, a user can log on to any computer on the corporate network and access his desktop, applications, and data in exactly the same way as on any other computer.

Understanding Roaming User Profiles in Earlier Versions of Windows

Because of how it was implemented in Windows NT 4.0, Windows 2000, and Windows XP, RUP originally had the following drawbacks as a corporate roaming technology:

- **User profiles can grow very large over time** For example, the Documents folder for a user might contain numerous spreadsheets, Microsoft Office Word documents, and other user-managed data files. Because the entire profile for the user is downloaded from the profile server during logon and uploaded again during logoff, the logon/

logoff experience for the user can become very slow during profile synchronization, particularly over slow WAN links or over dial-up connections for mobile users.

- **Roaming profiles are saved only at logoff.** This means that although administrators can easily back up profiles stored on the central profile server, the contents of these profiles (including user data within them) may not be up to date. Roaming profiles therefore present challenges in terms of providing real-time access to user-managed data and ensuring the integrity of this data.
- **Roaming profiles cause all settings for a user to be roamed, even for applications that do not have roaming capabilities and even for data and settings that have not changed.** If a user has a shortcut on his desktop to an application installed on one computer and then roams to a second computer where that application has not been installed, the shortcut will roam, but it will not work on the second computer, which can cause frustration for users.
- **Roaming profiles do not support multiple simultaneous logons by a user across several computers.** For example, if a user is logged on to two computers simultaneously and modifies the desktop background differently on each computer, the conflict will be resolved on a last-writer-wins basis.
- **Roaming profiles take some effort to configure and manage on the part of administrators.** Specifically, a profile file server must be deployed, roaming profiles must be created and stored on the server, and user accounts must be configured to use these roaming profiles. You can also use Group Policy to manage different aspects of roaming profiles.

HOW IT WORKS

Roaming User Profiles and Terminal Services

There are four different ways to configure roaming profiles for users. Windows 7 reads these roaming profile configuration settings in the following order and uses the first configured setting that it finds:

1. The Remote Desktop Services roaming profile path as specified by Remote Desktop Services policy setting
2. The Remote Desktop Services roaming profile path as specified on the Remote Desktop Services Profile tab of the properties sheet for the user account in Active Directory Users And Computers
3. The per-computer roaming profile path as specified using the policy setting Computer Configuration\Policies\Administrative Templates\System\User Profiles \Set Roaming Profile Path For All Users Logging Onto This Computer

4. The per-user roaming profile path as specified on the Profile tab of the properties sheet for the user account in Active Directory Users And Computers

Note that Remote Desktop connections to a Windows 7 computer do not support the Remote Desktop Server Profile path or Group Policy settings regarding Remote Desktop Services. Even though both use the Remote Desktop Protocol (RDP), Remote Desktop Services policies do not apply to Windows 7 Remote Desktop.

Understanding Folder Redirection in Earlier Versions of Windows

Because of the limitations of roaming profiles, a second corporate roaming technology called Folder Redirection was first introduced in Windows 2000 and was basically unchanged in Windows XP. Folder Redirection works by providing the ability to change the target location of special folders within a user's profile from a default location within the user's local profile to a different location either on the local computer or on a network share. For example, an administrator can use Group Policy to change the target location of a user's My Documents folder from the user's local profile to a network share on a file server. Folder Redirection thus allows users to work with data files on a network server as if the files were stored locally on their computers.

Folder Redirection provides several advantages as a corporate roaming technology:

- You can implement Folder Redirection with RUP to reduce the size of roaming user profiles. This means that not all the data in a user's profile needs to be transferred every time the user logs on or off of the network—a portion of the user's data and settings is transferred instead using Folder Redirection. This can considerably speed up logon and logoff times for users compared with using RUP alone.
- You can also implement Folder Redirection without RUP to provide users with access to their data regardless of which computer they use to log on to the network. Folder Redirection thus provides full corporate roaming capabilities for any folders that are redirected. On Windows XP, these include the My Documents (which can optionally include My Pictures), Application Data, Desktop, and Start Menu folders within a user's profile.

Folder Redirection as implemented on earlier versions of Windows has some drawbacks, however:

- Folder Redirection is hard-coded to redirect only a limited number of user profile folders. Some key folders, such as Favorites and Cookies, are not redirected, which limits the usefulness of this technology for corporate roaming purposes unless combined with RUP.

- Folder Redirection by itself does not roam an application's registry settings, limiting its usefulness as a corporate roaming technology. For an optimum roaming experience, implement Folder Redirection with RUP.

NOTE **RUP is the only way of roaming user settings (the HKCU registry hive); Folder Redirection is the primary way of roaming user data.**

Enhancements to Roaming User Profiles and Folder Redirection Previously Introduced in Windows Vista

Because of the limitations of the way that RUP and Folder Redirection were implemented in earlier versions of Windows, these two corporate roaming technologies were enhanced in Windows Vista in several ways:

- The changes made to the user profile namespace (described in the section titled "User Profile Namespace In Windows Vista and Windows 7" earlier in this chapter) separate user data from application data, making it easier to roam some data and settings using roaming profiles and to roam others using Folder Redirection.
- The number of folders that can be redirected using Group Policy is considerably increased, providing greater flexibility for administrators in choosing which user data and settings to redirect. The list of folders that can be redirected in Windows Vista and later versions now includes AppData, Desktop, Start Menu, Documents, Pictures, Music, Videos, Favorites, Contacts, Downloads, Links, Searches, and Saved Games.
- When you implement RUP with Folder Redirection, Windows Vista and later versions copy the user's profile and redirect folders to their respective network locations. The net result is an enhanced logon experience that brings up the user's desktop much faster than when you implement these two technologies on earlier versions of Windows. Specifically, when all user data folders are redirected and RUP is deployed, the only thing slowing logon is the time it takes to download Ntuser.dat (usually a relatively small file) from the profile server. (A small part of the AppData\Roaming\Microsoft directory is also roamed, even when the AppData\Roaming folder has been redirected. This folder contains some encryption certificates.)
- Offline Files, which can be used in conjunction with Folder Redirection, is enhanced in a number of ways in Windows Vista (and even more so in Windows 7). For more information concerning this, see the section titled "Working with Offline Files" later in this chapter.

Additional Enhancements to Roaming User Profiles and Folder Redirection Introduced in Windows 7

Additional enhancements to support corporate roaming have now been introduced in Windows 7, especially concerning RUP. These enhancements, described in the next section, make using RUP together with Folder Redirection a more robust and reliable corporate roaming technology.

BACKGROUND REGISTRY ROAMING

Beginning in Windows 7, users with roaming user profiles will have their current user settings in HKCU (in other words, the entire NTuser.dat from their profile) periodically synchronized back to the server while they are logged on to their computers. This is a change from RUP in Windows Vista and earlier versions, in which roaming user profiles were synchronized back to the server only on logoff.

This change will especially benefit enterprises that have a remote workforce with mobile computers because laptop users typically hibernate or sleep their computers instead of logging off. In previous versions of Windows, this meant that changes to user profiles might never get pushed up to the server, thus putting corporate data at risk. The change will also benefit enterprises that have mobile users who use virtual private network (VPN) connections to connect to their corporate network. VPN connections are typically initiated after the user logs on and before the user logs off, which again can prevent profiles from being properly synchronized to the server.

Note that background synchronization of roaming user profiles takes place in only one direction: from the client to the server. As in previous versions of Windows, synchronization of roaming user profiles from the server to the client still occurs only at logon. Also as in previous versions of Windows, any conflicts that arise roaming user settings are resolved based on timestamp at the file level. For example, when a user logs on using a roaming user profile, Windows checks whether the timestamp of the local version of NTuser.dat is newer than the server copy of NTuser.dat. If this is true, Windows loads the existing local version of NTuser.dat for the user and presents the user with her desktop. If this is false, Windows roams the newer version of NTuser.dat from the server to the local client, loads the new roamed version of NTuser.dat for the user, completes the rest of the load profile operation, and presents the user with her desktop. A similar process occurs during logoff.

Background registry roaming is disabled by default in Windows 7 and can be enabled on targeted computers by using Group Policy. The following Group Policy setting can be used to control this behavior:

Computer Configuration\Policies\Administrative Templates\System\User Profiles
\Background Upload Of A Roaming User Profile's Registry File While User Is Logged On

When you enable this policy setting, you can configure background registry roaming to synchronize on either of the following schedules:

- At a set time interval (the default is 12 hours and can range from 1 to 720 hours)

- At a specified time of day (the default is 3 A.M.)

A random offset of up to a one-hour delay is added to both of these scheduling options to avoid overloading the server with simultaneous uploads.

For monitoring and troubleshooting background registry roaming, Windows 7 logs additional events in the following event log:

Applications And Services Logs\Microsoft\Windows\User Profile Service\Operational

The additional events logged include:

- Background upload started
- Background upload finished successfully
- Hive not roamed due to a slow link
- Hive not roamed due to the storage server being unavailable

In addition, Windows will log the failure event "Background RUP upload failed, with error details" in the Windows Logs\Application event log.

IMPROVED FIRST LOGON PERFORMANCE WITH FOLDER REDIRECTION

Folder Redirection in Windows Vista and earlier versions has one large drawback: the potentially poor logon performance when a user logs on to her computer for the first time after it has been enabled. This occurs because, in Windows Vista and earlier versions, the user is blocked from logging on until all of her redirected data is migrated to the server. For a user with large amounts of data, this can result in long wait times during which she is prevented from doing useful work on her computer. The problem can be especially frustrating for a user who is logging on over a slow connection. In circumstances in which the user has large amounts of data that needs to be redirected, it can take an hour or longer for the user's desktop to appear when she logs on for the first time after Folder Redirection has been enabled.

Beginning in Windows 7, however, if Offline Files is enabled on the user's computer, first logon performance with Folder Redirection can be significantly improved, particularly for organizations with slower networks. This happens because instead of copying the user's redirected data to the server during the logon process and forcing the user to wait for this operation to finish, the user's redirected data is instead copied into the local Offline Files cache on the user's computer, which is a much faster operation. The user's desktop then appears and the Offline Files cache uploads the user's redirected data to the server using Offline Files synchronization and continues copying the user's data to the server until all of the data is been copied.

Additional enhancements in Windows 7 for improving first logon performance with Folder Redirection include the following:

- Before Windows attempts to copy the user's redirected data to the local Offline Files cache, it now checks to make sure there is enough room in the cache to hold the data. If the data won't fit in the cache, the data will be uploaded to the server during logon, resulting in behavior similar to what happens in Windows Vista and a possibly lengthy delay before the user's desktop appears.

- If the local Offline Files cache has been disabled on the user's computer, Windows now checks whether the server has room for the user's data before attempting to upload the data to the server. If there is not enough room on the server, no data is uploaded, resulting in the user's desktop quickly becoming available. An event is logged in the event log to indicate that the logon occurred without redirecting any data.

Because Offline Files is enabled by default on Windows 7 computers, this improved first logon performance with Folder Redirection also occurs by default.

> ***NOTE*** **A new feature of Offline Files in Windows 7 called background sync also enhances how Folder Redirection works. For more information on this feature, see the section titled "Additional Enhancements to Offline Files Introduced in Windows 7" later in this chapter.**

Implementing Folder Redirection

You can use Group Policy to implement Folder Redirection in enterprise environments. The policy settings for configuring Folder Redirection of known folders is found under User Configuration\Policies\Windows Settings\Folder Redirection (shown in Figure 15-8).

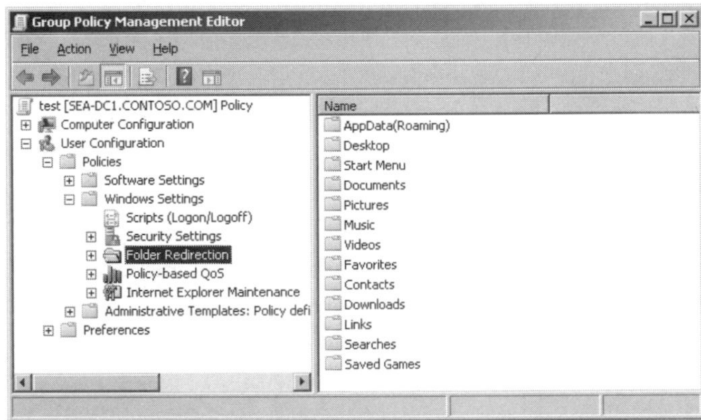

FIGURE 15-8 Folder Redirection policies in Group Policy

To implement Folder Redirection in an AD DS environment, follow these steps:

1. Create a share on the file server where you will be storing redirected folders and assign suitable permissions to this share. (See the sidebar titled "Direct from the Source: Securing Redirected Folders" later in this chapter for information on the permissions needed for this share.)
2. Create a Folder Redirection Group Policy object (GPO) or use an existing GPO and link it to the organizational unit (OU) that contains the users whose folders you want to redirect.

3. Open the Folder Redirection GPO in the Group Policy Object Editor and navigate to User Configuration\Policies\Windows Settings\Folder Redirection. Configure each Folder Redirection policy as desired.

NOTE Group Policy may take up to two processing cycles to apply GPOs that contain Folder Redirection settings successfully. This occurs because Windows XP and later versions have Fast Logon Optimization, which basically applies Group Policy in the background asynchronously. Some parts of Group Policy, such as Software Installation and Folder Redirection, require Group Policy to apply synchronously, however. This means that on first policy application, Folder Redirection policy is recognized, but because it is applied asynchronously, it cannot be processed immediately. Therefore, Group Policy flags synchronous application to occur on the next logon.

DIRECT FROM THE SOURCE

Securing Redirected Folders

Mike Stephens, Technical Writer
Group Policy

The following recommendations for secure Folder Redirection permissions are based on Microsoft Knowledge Base article 274443.

When using Basic Redirection, follow these steps to make sure that only the user and the domain administrators have permissions to open a particular redirected folder:

1. Select a central location in your environment where you want to store Folder Redirection and then share this folder. This example uses FLDREDIR.
2. Set Share Permissions for the Authenticated Users group to Full Control.
3. Use the following settings for NTFS Permissions:
   - CREATOR OWNER – Full Control (Apply to: Subfolders And Files Only)
   - System – Full Control (Apply to: This Folder, Subfolders, And Files)
   - Domain Admins – Full Control (Apply to: This Folder, Subfolders, And Files) (This is optional and is needed only if you require that administrators have full control.)
   - Authenticated Users – Create Folder/Append Data (Apply to: This Folder Only)
   - Authenticated Users – List Folder/Read Data (Apply to: This Folder Only)
   - Authenticated Users – Read Attributes (Apply to: This Folder Only)
   - Authenticated Users – Traverse Folder/Execute File (Apply to: This Folder Only)

4. Use the option Create A Folder For Each User under the redirection path or the option Redirect To The Following Location and use a path similar to \\Server\FLDREDIR\%Username% to create a folder under the shared folder, FLDREDIR.

When using Advanced Redirection, follow these steps:

1. Select a central location in your environment where you want to store Folder Redirection and then share this folder. This example uses FLDREDIR.
2. Set Share Permissions for the Authenticated Users group to Full Control.
3. Use the following settings for NTFS Permissions:
   - CREATOR OWNER – Full Control (Apply to: Subfolders And Files Only)
   - System – Full Control (Apply to: This Folder, Subfolders, And Files)
   - Domain Admins – Full Control (Apply to: This Folder, Subfolders, And Files) (This option is required only if you want administrators to have full control.)
   - <each group listed in policy> – Create Folder/Append Data (Apply to: This Folder Only)
   - <each group listed in policy> – List Folder/Read Data (Apply to: This Folder Only)
   - <each group listed in policy> – Read Attributes (Apply to: This Folder Only)
   - <each group listed in policy> – Traverse Folder/Execute File (Apply to: This Folder Only)
4. Use the option Create A Folder For Each User under the redirection path or use the option Redirect To The Following Location and use a path similar to \\Server\FLDREDIR\%Username% to create a folder under the shared folder, FLDREDIR.

When using advanced Folder Redirection policies, you must complete the last four steps in the preceding list for each group listed in the policy. Most likely, the user will belong to only one of these groups, but for the user folder to create properly, the access control lists (ACLs) on the resource must account for all the groups listed in the Folder Redirection settings. Additionally, one hopes that the administrator will use Group Policy filtering to ensure that only the users listed in the Folder Redirection policy settings actually apply the policy. Otherwise, it's just a waste of time because the user will try to apply the policy, but Folder Redirection will fail because the user is not a member of any of the groups within the policy. This creates a false error condition in the event log, but it's actually a configuration issue.

Configuring the Redirection Method

You can configure the redirection method for redirecting folders on the Target tab of the properties sheet for each policy setting. Three redirection methods are possible, plus a fourth option for certain folders:

- **Not Configured** Choosing this option returns the Folder Redirection policy to its default state. This means that previously redirected folders stay redirected and folders that are local to the computer remain so. To return a redirected folder to its original target location, see the section titled "Configuring Policy Removal Options" later in this chapter.
- **Basic Redirection** Administrators should choose this option if they plan to store redirected folders for all of their users targeted by the GPO on the same network share (see Figure 15-9).

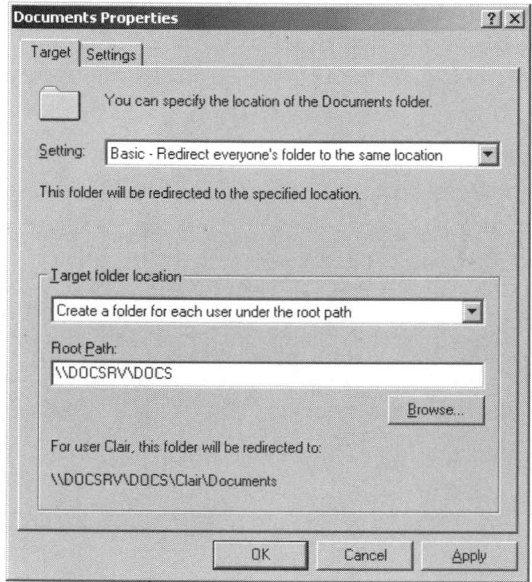

FIGURE 15-9 Choosing a redirection method and target folder location on the Target tab of a Folder Redirection policy

- **Advanced Redirection** Administrators should choose this option if they want to store redirected folders for different groups of users on different network shares. For example, the Documents folders for users in the Human Resources group could be redirected to \\DOCSRV\HRDOCS, the Documents folders for users in the Managers group could be redirected to \\DOCSRV\MGMTDOCS, and so on.

  If a user belongs to more than one security group listed for a redirected folder, the first security group listed that matches the group membership of the user will be used to determine the target location for the user's redirected folder.
- **Follow The Documents Folder** This option is available only for the Music, Pictures, and Videos folders. Choosing this option redirects these folders as subfolders of the redirected Documents folder and causes these subfolders to inherit their remaining Folder Redirection settings from the Folder Redirection settings for the Documents folder.

Configuring Target Folder Location

If you select either the Basic Redirection or Advanced Redirection option on the Target tab, you have three possible target folder locations from which to choose, plus a fourth location for the Documents folder:

- **Create A Folder For Each User Under The Root Path** This is the default setting for the target folder location option. Choosing this option lets you specify a root path for redirecting the selected folder for all users targeted by the GPO. You must specify this path as a Universal Naming Convention (UNC) path. For example, if you select this option for the Documents policy setting and the root path \\DOCSRV\DOCS is specified, any users targeted by this GPO will have a folder named \\DOCSRV\DOCS*user_name* \Documents created on the file server the next time they start their computers, where *user_name* is a folder named after the user name of each user targeted by the GPO.
- **Redirect To The Following Location** Choose this option if you want to redirect several users to the same redirected folder using the specified UNC path. For example, if you redirect the Desktop folder to \\DOCSRV\DESKTOP and select this option, all users targeted by the GPO will load the same desktop environment when they log on to their computers.

  Another use for this option is to redirect the Start Menu folder to ensure that all targeted users have the same Start menu. If you do this, be sure to configure suitable permissions on the redirected folder to allow all users to access it.
- **Redirect To The Local UserProfile Location** Choose this option if you want to redirect a previously redirected folder back to its local user profile location. For example, selecting this option for the Documents policy setting redirects the Documents folder back to %SystemDrive%\Users*user_name*\Documents.
- **Redirect To The User's Home Directory** This option is available only for the Documents folder. Choosing this option redirects the Documents folder to the user's home folder. (The user's home folder is configured on the Profile tab of the properties sheet for the user's account in Active Directory Users And Computers.) If you also want the Pictures, Music, and Videos folders to follow the Documents folder to the user's home folder, select the Also Apply Redirection Policy To Windows 2000, Windows 2000 Server, Windows XP And Windows Server 2003 Operating Systems option on the Settings tab of the policy setting.

NOTE **You can specify only a UNC path for the root path when redirecting folders to a network share. You cannot specify a mapped drive for this path because network drives are mapped only after all Group Policy extensions have been processed on the client computer.**

NOTE You can use any of the following environment variables within the UNC path you specify for a target folder location in a Folder Redirection policy: %USERNAME%, %USERPROFILE%, %HOMESHARE%, and %HOMEPATH%. You cannot use any other environment variables for UNC paths specified in Folder Redirection policies because other environment variables are not defined when the Group Policy service loads the Folder Redirection extension (Fdeploy.dll) during the logon process.

Configuring Redirection Options

You can configure three redirection options for each Folder Redirection policy (but only two for certain policy settings). These redirection options are specified on the Settings tab of the policy setting (as shown in Figure 15-10).

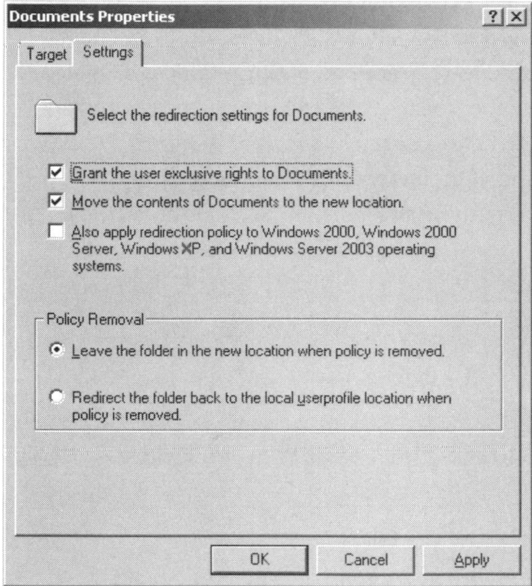

FIGURE 15-10 Choosing additional redirection options and policy removal options on the Settings tab of a Folder Redirection policy

The three redirection options available on the Settings tab are:

- **Grant The User Exclusive Rights To *folder_name*** This option is selected by default and provides Full Control NTFS permissions on the redirected folder to the user to whom the policy is applied. For example, user Michael Allen (mallen@contoso.com) would have Full Control permissions on the folder \\DOCSRV\DOCS\mallen\Documents. In addition, the LocalSystem account has Full Control so that Windows can sync the contents of the local cache with the target folder. Changing this option after the policy has been applied to some users will only affect any new users who receive the policy, and the option will only apply to newly created folders. (If the folder already exists, ownership is the only item checked.)

Clear this option if you want Folder Redirection to check the ownership of the folder. Also clear this option if you want to allow members of the Administrators group access to each user's redirected folder. (This requires that administrators have appropriate NTFS permissions assigned to the root folder.)

- **Move The Contents Of *folder_name* To The New Location** This option is selected by default and causes any files the user has in the local folder to move to the target folder on the network share. Clear this option if you only want to use the Folder Redirection policy to create the target folders on the file server for users targeted by the GPO but want to leave users' documents on their local computers.
- **Also Apply Redirection Policy To Windows 2000, Windows 2000 Server, Windows XP And Windows Server 2003 Operating Systems** This option is not selected by default and is available only for known folders that could be redirected on earlier versions of Windows, which include Documents, Pictures, Desktop, Start Menu, and Application Data. If you choose to redirect one of these folders by leaving this option cleared and then try to apply the policy, a dialog box will appear indicating that Windows wants to write this redirection policy in a format that only Windows Vista and later computers can understand. If you select this option and apply the policy setting, the policy will be written in a format that these earlier versions of Windows can understand.

Configuring Policy Removal Options

In the following scenarios, a Folder Redirection policy can move out of scope for a specific user:

- The Folder Redirection GPO becomes unlinked from the OU to which it was previously linked.
- The Folder Redirection GPO is deleted.
- The user's account is moved to a different OU and the Folder Redirection GPO is not linked to that OU.
- The user becomes a member of a security group to which security filtering has been applied to prevent the Folder Redirection GPO from applying to the group.

In any of these scenarios, the configured policy removal option determines the behavior of the Folder Redirection policy. The two policy removal options for Folder Redirection policies are as follows:

- **Leave The Folder In New Location When Policy Is Removed** This is the default option and leaves the redirected folder in its present state when the policy goes out of scope. For example, if a GPO redirects the Documents folder to \\DOCSRV\DOCS*user_name*\Documents and this GPO goes out of scope for the users to which it applies, the users' Documents folders will remain on the file server and will not be returned to the users' local profiles on their computers.

- **Redirect The Folder Back To The Local UserProfile Location When Policy Is Removed** Choosing this option causes the redirected folder to be returned to the user's local profile when the GPO goes out of scope.

Folder Redirection and Sync Center

When Folder Redirection policy is first processed by a Windows Vista or later computer, a message appears above the notification area indicating that a sync partnership is being established to keep the local and network copies of the redirected folders synchronized. Clicking this notification opens Sync Center, where the user can view additional details. For more information about Sync Center, see the section titled "Managing Offline Files Using Sync Center" later in this chapter.

DIRECT FROM THE SOURCE

Folder Redirection Server Path and Folder Name Concerns

Ming Zhu, Software Design Engineer
Microsoft Windows Shell Team

When specifying a path for a user's redirected folder, the recommended technique is to put the folder under the user's name so as to have a similar folder hierarchy as the local profile. For example, put the Documents folder under \\Server\Share*user_name*\Documents and the Pictures folder under \\Server\Share*user_name*\Pictures.

Sometimes administrators may want to redirect different folders into different shares. In this case, you can use %UserName% as the target folder, such as by redirecting the Documents folder to \\Server\Docs*user_name* and the Pictures folder to \\Server\Pics*user_name*. This is not recommended, however, and here's why: In Windows Vista and later versions, names of special folders such as Documents and Pictures are enabled for Multi-lingual User Interface (MUI), which means that all the localized names of the folder are actually stored in a file named Desktop.ini. The Desktop.ini file has an entry like this: LocalizedResourceName=@%SystemRoot%\system32\shell32.dll,-21770. This means that when displaying the folder in Windows Explorer, it actually goes into Shell32.dll, fetches the resource ID 21770, and then uses that resource to display the folder's name. The result is called the display name of the folder. Different users can choose different user interface languages—the resources of these different languages will be different, so the same folder will show different names for different users.

The result is that each folder under a user's profile has a display name, and this display name will not change as long as the same Desktop ini file is there, even if the underlying file system folder name is changed. So if you redirect the Documents folder to \\Server\Docs*user_name*, the display name will still be Documents. Similarly, if you redirect the Pictures folder to \\Server\Pics*user_name*, the folder will still show Pictures as the display name. The user won't see any difference on his Windows Vista and later client computer. So far, so good—at least as far as the user is concerned. The bad news, however, is for the administrator: If the administrator examines the \\Server\Docs folder, she will see a huge number of Documents folders and not the *user_name* folder as expected.

Therefore, you should specify the redirected folder path to match the local folder if possible. If you have to choose the %UserName% pattern, one solution to this problem is to select the Give Exclusive Access option for the redirected folder so that administrators won't be able to access the Desktop.ini file. Windows Explorer will then fall back to showing the real file system folder name. If that is not an option, you'll need to use a script to modify each of the permissions of each user's Desktop.ini file to remove Allow Read access for administrators. This might be your only choice if you select the Redirect To Home Directory option for the Documents folder because a Home directory usually uses the user name as the folder name, and Give Exclusive Access does not work with Home directories, either.

Considerations for Mixed Environments

The following considerations apply when you implement Folder Redirection in mixed environments that consist of a combination of computers running Windows 7 or Windows Vista and computers running Windows XP or Windows 2000:

- If you configure a Folder Redirection policy on a computer running an earlier version of Windows and apply it to Windows Vista and later computers, the Windows Vista and later computers will apply this policy as if they are running the earlier version of Windows. For example, suppose that you create a Folder Redirection policy on Windows Server 2003 that redirects the My Documents folder belonging to users targeted by this GPO to \\DOCSRV\DOCS*user_name*\My Documents. When you apply this policy to Windows Vista and later computers, it will redirect users' Documents folders to \\DOCSRV\DOCS*user_name*\My Documents and not to \\DOCSRV\DOCS*user_name*\Documents. The policy will also automatically cause Music, Videos, and Pictures to follow Documents. (Pictures will follow only if the policy for the Pictures folder hasn't been configured separately, however.)
- If you configure a Folder Redirection policy on a Windows 7, Windows Vista, or Windows Server 2008 computer and apply it to both Windows Vista and later computers and computers running an earlier version of Windows, the best practice is to configure the policy only for known folders that can be redirected on computers

running earlier versions of Windows. (You can also use Folder Redirection policies configured from Windows 7, Windows Vista, or Windows Server 2008 computers to manage Folder Redirection for earlier versions of Windows, but only for shell folders that can be redirected on those earlier versions of Windows.) For example, you can configure redirection of the Documents folder, which will redirect both the Documents folder on Windows Vista and later computers and the My Documents folder on Windows XP or Windows 2000 computers. If you configure redirection of the Favorites folder, however, this policy will redirect the Favorites folder on Windows Vista and later computers, but the policy will be ignored by earlier versions of Windows targeted by this policy. In environments in which users are undergoing gradual or staged transition from versions earlier than Windows Vista, following this approach will minimize confusion for users. In a pure Windows Vista and later environment, however, you can redirect any of the known folders supported by Folder Redirection policy on Windows 7, Windows Vista, or Windows Server 2008.

- When you create a Folder Redirection policy from a computer running an earlier version of Windows, the policy settings for Folder Redirection are stored in a hidden configuration file named Fdeploy.ini, which is stored in SYSVOL in the Group Policy Template (GPT) under *GPO_GUID*\Users\Documents And Settings\Fdeploy.ini. This file contains a FolderStatus section that lists the different folders that are being redirected by this policy, a flag for each folder indicating its redirection settings, and a list of UNC paths to which the folder should be redirected for users belonging to different security groups represented by the security identifiers (SIDs) of these groups. If the Folder Redirection policy is then modified from a Windows 7, Windows Vista, or Windows Server 2008 computer, a second file named Fdeploy1.ini is created in the same location as Fdeploy.ini, and only Windows Vista and later computers can recognize and apply the Folder Redirection policy settings contained in this file. The presence or absence of these two files and their configuration indicates to Windows Vista and later computers targeted by this GPO whether they are in pure Windows Vista and later environments or mixed environments containing earlier versions of Windows. Thus, if you configure a Folder Redirection policy on a Windows 7, Windows Vista, or Windows Server 2008 computer and select the Also Apply Redirection Policy To Windows 2000, Windows 2000 Server, Windows XP And Windows Server 2003 Operating Systems option described previously, no Fdeploy1.ini file is created in the GPO. (If such a file is already present, it is deleted.) Instead, when the policy is applied, the Fdeploy.ini file is configured so that the policy can also be applied to earlier versions of Windows.
- Adding a known folder from Windows Vista and later versions to an existing Folder Redirection policy previously created from an earlier version of Windows will remove the ability to save Folder Redirection settings from an earlier version of Windows. This is due to the way that the Folder Redirection snap-in works in Windows Vista and later versions. Specifically, if you add a known folder from Windows Vista and later versions to an existing policy setting that is compatible with earlier versions of Windows, the Windows Vista and later version of the Folder Redirection snap-in writes both files

(Fdeploy.ini and Fdeploy1.ini). However, the snap-in marks the Fdeploy.ini file as read-only. This prevents earlier versions of the Folder Redirection snap-in from changing the Folder Redirection settings. The administrator then gets an Access Denied error message because the Folder Redirection settings must now be managed from Windows Vista and later versions. (Windows Vista and later versions keep both policy files synchronized.)

- In mixed environments in which a Folder Redirection policy is configured on a Windows 7, Windows Vista, or Windows Server 2008 computer and applied to both Windows Vista and later computers and computers running an earlier version of Windows, be sure to choose Follow The Documents Folder as the redirection method for the Music and Videos folders. If you try to redirect the Music and Videos folders to a location other than under the Documents folder, compatibility with earlier versions of Windows will be broken. You can, however, redirect the Pictures folder to a location other than under Documents. (This option is available in earlier versions of Windows.)
- In mixed environments, administrators can even configure folders such as Favorites—which cannot be roamed on earlier versions of Windows—so that they roam between Windows Vista and later computers and computers running an earlier version of Windows. To do this, simply redirect the %SystemDrive%\Users*user_name*\Favorites folder in Windows Vista and later versions to \\Profile_server\Profiles*user_name*\Favorites within the roaming profile of the earlier version of Windows. Unfortunately, this method adds data to the user profile to enable having user data in both versions of Windows. This additional data can slow down logons and logoffs when logging on clients running previous versions of Windows.

HOW IT WORKS

Folder Redirection and/or Roaming User Profiles in Mixed Environments

Mike Stephens, Technical Writer
Group Policy

One of the major benefits of Folder Redirection is to expedite logons by removing information from the profile. However, Folder Redirection in mixed environments works only with RUP, which involves adding data back into the Windows XP profile. The net result is the following in different mixed-environment scenarios:

- **Mixed environment with Folder Redirection only** This can't be done—to redirect folders such as Favorites, you have to implement RUP. Adding RUP in this scenario has the potential to cause slow logons because users are required to wait for the profile to download. Is implementing RUP so that you can roam user data worth the tradeoff here?

- **Mixed environment with RUP only** You can do this by implementing Folder Redirection for Windows Vista and later clients but not for Windows XP clients. Windows Vista and later Folder Redirection redirects special folders, such as Favorites, back into the Windows XP user profile. The Good: Windows Vista and later version user data is copied to the server using Folder Redirection. The Bad: Windows XP profiles can become larger and subsequently cause longer logons and logoffs. Additionally, user data is available immediately on Windows Vista and later versions; user data is only as current as the last logon on Windows XP.
- **Mixed with both Folder Redirection and RUP** Current Folder Redirection policy should redirect the five folders (the ones prior to Windows Vista) outside the user profile. The Good: This choice speeds up logons and logoffs (especially for My Documents). The Bad: New Folder Redirection policy for Windows Vista and later clients is required to redirect special folders, such as Favorites, back into the user profile, and this adds more data back into the Windows XP user profiles, which can again slow down logons and logoffs. But when users no longer use Windows XP, you can change the Folder Redirection policy to redirect all of the known folder data out of the user profile, thereby speeding up logons.

Additional Group Policy Settings for Folder Redirection

You can configure additional behavior for Folder Redirection by using the following Group Policy settings:

- **Use Localized Subfolder Names When Redirecting Start And My Documents** You can find this setting under Computer Configuration\Policies\Administrative Templates \System\Folder Redirection and User Configuration\Policies\Administrative Templates \System\Folder Redirection; it applies only to computers running Windows Vista or later versions. Administrators can use this setting to specify whether Folder Redirection should use localized names for the All Programs, Startup, My Music, My Pictures, and My Videos subfolders when redirecting the parent Start menu and legacy My Documents folder, respectively. Enabling this policy setting causes Windows Vista and later versions to use localized folder names for these subfolders in the file system when redirecting the Start menu or legacy My Documents folder. Disabling this policy setting or leaving it Not Configured causes Windows Vista and later versions to use the standard English names for these subfolders when redirecting the Start menu or legacy My Documents folder. (This policy is valid only when Windows Vista and later versions computers process an older redirection policy already deployed for these folders in an existing localized environment.)
- **Do Not Automatically Make Redirected Folders Available Offline** You can find this user setting under User Configuration\Policies\Administrative Templates\System

\Folder Redirection; it applies to computers running Windows XP or later versions. By default, all redirected shell folders are available for offline use. This setting lets you change this behavior so that redirected shell folders are not automatically available for offline use. (Users can still choose to make files and folders available offline, however.) Enabling this setting forces users to select the files manually if they want to make them available offline. Disabling this setting or leaving it Not Configured automatically makes redirected folders available offline (including subfolders within these redirected folders). Enabling this setting, however, does not prevent files from being automatically cached if the network share is configured for Automatic Caching, nor does it affect the availability of the Make Available Offline menu option in the user interface. (Do not enable this setting unless you are sure that users will not need access to their redirected files if the network share becomes unavailable.)

NOTE **Some policy settings for managing Offline Files can also affect Folder Redirection behavior because Folder Redirection subscribes to Offline Files. You can find these policy settings under Computer Configuration\Policies\Administrative Templates\Network\Offline Files and User Configuration\Policies\Administrative Templates\Network\Offline Files. Before you configure any of these Offline Files policy settings, be sure to investigate what impact (if any) they may have on Folder Redirection if you have implemented it in your environment. For more information concerning Group Policy settings for Offline Files, see the section titled "Managing Offline Files Using Group Policy" later in this chapter.**

Troubleshooting Folder Redirection

A common issue with Folder Redirection occurs when administrators precreate target folders instead of allowing Folder Redirection policies to create these folders automatically. Typically, the problems that arise result from one of three causes:

- The target folder does not exist.
- The target folder has incorrect NTFS permissions.
- The user is not the owner of the target folder.

The Folder Redirection extension (Fdeploy.dll) logs events in the Application log, so be sure to check this log if you experience problems with Folder Redirection. In addition, you can enable diagnostic logging of the Folder Redirection extension by configuring the *FdeployDebugLevel* registry value found under the following registry key:

HKLM\Software\Microsoft\Windows NT\CurrentVersion\Diagnostics Set

FdeployDebugLevel is a DWORD value that you should set to 0x0F to enable Folder Redirection debugging. In earlier versions of Windows, the resulting log file is saved under %WinDir%\Debug\UserMode\Fdeploy.log. In Windows Vista and later versions, however, adding this registry key simply means that more detailed information on Folder Redirection activity is logged in the event logs.

NOTE The failure of Folder Redirection policies affects the Folder Redirection extension (Fdeploy.dll) only on a per-folder basis.

Implementing Roaming User Profiles

To implement RUP for users of Windows Vista and later computers in an AD DS environment, follow these steps:

1. Prepare the file server where you want to store roaming user profiles for users by creating a shared folder on the server. (This server is sometimes called the profile server; a typical share name for this shared folder is Profiles.)
2. Assign the permissions shown in Tables 15-7 and 15-8 to the underlying folder being shared and to the share itself. Also, confirm that the permissions in Table 15-9 are automatically applied to each roaming user profile folder.
3. Create a default network profile for users and copy it to the NETLOGON share on a domain controller. Let it replicate to other domain controllers in the domain. (This step is optional and is typically necessary only if you want to preconfigure a roaming user profile for your users so that they will all have the same desktop experience when they first log on. If you do not create a default network profile, Windows Vista and later versions will use the local %SystemRoot%\Users\Default profile instead.)
4. Open Active Directory Users And Computers and configure the profile path on the Profile tab for each user who will roam.

Additional optional steps include configuring roaming profiles as mandatory profiles or as super-mandatory profiles if desired.

TABLE 15-7 NTFS Permissions for the Roaming Profile Parent Folder

USER ACCOUNT	MINIMUM PERMISSIONS REQUIRED
Creator/Owner	Full Control – Subfolders And Files Only
Administrator	None
Security group of users needing to put data on the share	List Folder/Read Data, Create Folders/Append Data – This Folder Only
Everyone	No Permissions
LocalSystem	Full Control – This Folder, Subfolders, And Files

TABLE 15-8 Share-Level Server Message Block Permissions for the Roaming Profile Share

USER ACCOUNT	DEFAULT PERMISSIONS	MINIMUM PERMISSIONS REQUIRED
Everyone	Full Control	No Permissions
The security group of the users needing to put data on the share	N/A	Full Control

TABLE 15-9 NTFS Permissions for Each User's Roaming Profile Folder

USER ACCOUNT	DEFAULT PERMISSIONS	MINIMUM PERMISSIONS REQUIRED
%UserName%	Full Control, Owner Of Folder	Full Control, Owner Of Folder
LocalSystem	Full Control	Full Control
Administrators	No Permissions*	No Permissions
Everyone	No Permissions	No Permissions

**This is true unless you set the Add The Administrator Security Group To The Roaming User Profile Share policy, in which case the Administrators group has Full Control (requires Windows 2000 SP2 or later versions).*

Creating a Default Network Profile

As explained earlier in this chapter, when a user logs on to a Windows Vista or later computer for the first time, Windows tries to find a profile named Default User.v2 in the NETLOGON share on the domain controller authenticating the user. If Windows finds a profile named Default User.v2 in the NETLOGON share, this profile is copied to the user's computer to form the user's local profile on the computer. If Windows does not find a profile named Default User.v2 in NETLOGON, the Default profile under %SystemDrive%\Users on the user's computer is copied instead as the user's local profile.

To create a default network profile, follow these steps:

1. Log on to any computer running Windows Vista and later versions using the Administrator account or any account that has administrative credentials.
2. Configure the desktop settings, Start menu, and other aspects of your computer's environment as you want users who log on to Windows for the first time to experience them.
3. Create an Unattend.xml file that contains the Microsoft-Windows-Shell-Setup\CopyProfile *parameter* and set this parameter to True in the specialized configuration pass.
4. At a command prompt, type the **sysprep.exe /generalize /unattend:unattend.xml** command. Running this command will copy any customizations you made to the default user profile and will delete the Administrator account.

5. Restart the computer and log on using the Administrator account. Click Start, right-click Computer, select Properties, select Advanced System Settings, and then click Settings under User Profiles. The User Profiles dialog box opens.
6. Select Default Profile from the list of profiles stored on the computer and click Copy To. The Copy To dialog box opens.
7. Type ***domain_controller*\NETLOGON\Default User.v2** in the Copy To dialog box.
8. Click Change, type **Everyone**, and then click OK twice to copy the local user profile you previously configured to the NETLOGON share as the default network profile Default User v.2.
9. Type ***domain_controller*\NETLOGON** in the Quick Search box and press Enter to open the NETLOGON share on your domain controller in a Windows Explorer window. Verify that the profile has been copied.

NOTE You may already have a Default User profile in NETLOGON that you created previously as a default network profile for users of computers running Windows XP or earlier versions. This network profile is not compatible with Windows Vista and later versions. See the section titled "Considerations for Mixed Environments" earlier in this chapter for more information.

Configuring a User Account to Use a Roaming Profile

After you have created a PROFILES share and configured it with suitable permissions on a file server, you can configure new user accounts to use roaming user profiles. To do this, follow these steps:

1. Log on to a domain controller as a member of the Domain Admins group (or any administrator workstation running an earlier version of Windows on which adminpak.msi has been installed).
2. Open Active Directory Users And Computers and select the OU containing the new user accounts for which you want to enable roaming.
3. Select each user account in the OU that you want to configure. For each account, right-click it and select Properties.
4. Click the Profile tab, select the check box labeled Profile Path, type ***profile_server* \Profiles\%username%** in the Profile Path text box, and then click OK.

The selected new user accounts are now ready to use roaming profiles. To complete this procedure, have each user log on to a Windows Vista and later computer using her user credentials. When the user logs on to Windows Vista and later versions for the first time, the Default User.v2 profile is copied from NETLOGON to the user's local profile and then copied as *user_name*.v2 to the PROFILES share on the profile server. For example, a user named Jacky Chen (jchen@contoso.com) who logs on to a Windows Vista and later computer for the first time will receive the roaming user profile *profile_server*\Profiles\jchen.v2. The .v2 suffix identifies this profile as compatible only with Windows Vista or later versions.

Implementing Mandatory Profiles

The procedure for implementing mandatory user profiles is similar to the procedure for implementing RUP described earlier in the chapter, with the following differences:

- Instead of assigning the Authenticated Users built-in group Full Control permission of the Profiles folder on the profile server, assign this group Read permission and the Administrators group Full Control instead.
- Follow the steps in the section titled "Creating a Default Network Profile" earlier in this chapter, but instead of copying the domain user profile that you configured to *domain_controller*\NETLOGON\Default User.v2, copy the profile to *profile_server*\Profiles\Mandatory.v2.
- Browse to locate the super-hidden *profile_server*\Profiles\Mandatory.v2\Ntuser.dat file and change its name to Ntuser.man. (Super-hidden files have the *hidden* and *system* attributes set.)
- Follow the steps in the section titled "Configuring a User Account to Use a Roaming Profile" earlier in this chapter, but instead of typing ***profile_server*\Profiles\%username%** in the Profile Path text box, type ***profile_server*\Profiles\Mandatory**.

Any user who now logs on with this mandatory user profile will be able to configure the desktop environment while logged on to the network, but when the user logs off, any changes made to the environment will not be saved.

> **WARNING** Do not add .v2 to the profile path of the user object in Active Directory Users And Computers. Doing so may prevent Windows Vista and later versions from locating the roaming or mandatory profile. You should apply the .v2 suffix only to the name of the user folder on the central file server.

> **WARNING** It is acceptable to use the existing server and file share where you store your current roaming user profiles. If you do so, however, each user will have two roaming profile folders: one for Windows Vista and later versions and one for Windows XP. The added folder also means additional storage requirements for the server. Ensure that the server hosting the share has adequate free disk space, and adjust any disk-quota policies accordingly.

Implementing Super-Mandatory Profiles

The procedure for implementing super-mandatory profiles is similar to the procedure for implementing mandatory user profiles described earlier, with the following differences:

- Instead of copying the domain user profile you configured to *domain_controller*\NETLOGON\Default User.v2, copy the profile to *profile_server*\Profiles\Mandatory.man.v2.
- Instead of typing ***profile_server*\Profiles\%*username*%** in the Profile Path text box, type ***profile_server*\Profiles\Mandatory.man.**

After you have implemented these profiles, users will be able to configure their desktop environments while logged on to the network, but when they log off, any changes they made to their environments will not be saved. In addition, if the profile server is unavailable when the user tries to log on to the network (or if the super-mandatory profile does not load for any other reason), Windows Vista and later versions will not allow the user to log on to the computer.

Using Roaming User Profiles with Folder Redirection

If you implement both Folder Redirection and RUP, do not store redirected folders within the user's roaming profiles. Instead, store them on the network share where Folder Redirection is targeted. This reduces the size of a user's roaming profile, speeds up its download time, and improves the user's logon experience.

In general, the best practice is to configure Folder Redirection first, make sure it applies successfully, and then deploy roaming user profiles. Also, users should log off all computers and follow these steps on one computer first (with all of their main data).

Considerations for Mixed Environments

The following considerations apply when implementing RUP in mixed environments that consist of a combination of computers running Windows Vista and later versions and computers running Windows XP or Windows 2000:

- Default network profiles created for computers running an earlier version of Windows are not compatible with default network profiles created for Windows Vista and later computers because the profile namespace of Windows Vista and later versions is incompatible with the profile namespace of Windows XP. Because of this incompatibility, users who log on to a computer running an earlier version of Windows cannot roam their profiles to Windows Vista and later computers and vice versa. If users must use Windows Vista and later computers as well as computers running earlier versions of Windows, they will need separate roaming profiles for each computer and must manage the profiles separately. If Folder Redirection is implemented, however, part of the user profiles (the redirected folders) can be shared between the two desktop environments.
- If users need to roam across both Windows Vista and later computers and computers running earlier versions of Windows, you will need twice the usual space to store their roaming profiles. For example, if user Jacky Chen roams across both Windows Vista

and later versions and computers running an earlier version of Windows, he will have two roaming profiles on the profile server:

- *Profile_server*\Profiles\jchen, which is his roaming profile on earlier versions of Windows
- *Profile_server*\Profiles\jchen.v2, which is his roaming profile on Windows Vista and later computers

  These two user profiles are incompatible and will not share any data unless you also implement Folder Redirection for the user. Specifically, if you implement all available Folder Redirection policies for this user (including those that apply to earlier versions of Windows), only the HKCU settings will be unavailable between platforms.

In Windows Vista and later versions, disk quotas configured on roaming profiles no longer prevent users from logging off as disk quotas do on earlier versions of Windows. However, disk quotas will prevent roaming profiles from being uploaded to the profile server when the user logs off. No user data is lost because the data still remains in the user's local user profile on the computer, but data could be lost if profiles are set to be deleted after the user logs off—for example, in a Terminal Services scenario. In this case, any changes the user made during his current session would be gone, but the server copy of his profile is still intact.

NOTE **For information about how to migrate user profiles for previous versions of Windows to environments running Windows Vista and later versions and Windows Server 2008, see Knowledge Base article 947025, "Support Guidelines for Migrating Roaming User Profiles Data to Windows Vista or to Windows Server 2008" found at *http://support.microsoft.com/kb/947025*.**

Managing User Profiles Using Group Policy

You can manage the behavior of user profiles (especially roaming user profiles) in AD DS environments by using Group Policy settings found under Computer Configuration\Policies\Administrative Templates\System\User Profiles and User Configuration\Policies\Administrative Templates\System\User Profiles. You do not need to reboot or log off for these settings to take effect after you configure them.

Tables 15-10 and 15-11 describe the per-computer and per-user policy settings for user profiles new to Windows Vista and later versions.

TABLE 15-10 New Per-Computer Group Policy Settings for Managing User Profiles in Windows Vista and Later Versions

POLICY SETTING	NOTES
Background Upload Of A Roaming User Profile's Registry File While User Is Logged On (Applies only to Windows 7 and Windows Server 2008 R2)	Sets the schedule for background uploading of a roaming user profile's registry file (Ntuser.dat). This setting will upload only the user profile's registry file (other user data will not be uploaded) and will upload it only if the user is logged on. Only the registry file of a roaming user profile will be uploaded—regular profiles will not be affected. This policy does not stop the roaming user profile's registry file from being uploaded when the user logs off. If this setting is disabled or not configured, the registry file for a roaming user profile will not be uploaded in the background while the user is logged on. To use this setting, first choose which scheduling method to use: ■ If Run At Set Interval is chosen, an interval must be set with a value ranging from 1 to 720 hours. Once set, the profile's registry file will be uploaded at the specified interval after the user logs on. For example, if the value is 6 hours and a user logs on at 6:00 A.M. and is still logged on at 12:00 P.M., her registry file will be uploaded at that time. Further, if she is still logged on at 6 P.M., it will upload then as well and then again every 6 hours until logoff. The next time the user logs on, the timer will start again, so the registry file will upload 6 hours later (in this example). ■ If Run At Specified Time Of Day is chosen, then a time of day must be specified. Once set, the registry hive will be uploaded at that same time every day, assuming the user is logged on at that time.
Delete User Profiles Older Than A Specified Number Of Days On System Restart (Applies to Windows Vista or later versions)	Allows administrators to delete user profiles automatically on system restart if the profiles have not been used within a specified number of days. Enabling this policy setting causes the User Profile Service to delete all user profiles on the computer automatically upon reboot that have not been used within the specified number of days on the next system restart.

POLICY SETTING	NOTES
Do Not Forcefully Unload The Users Registry At User Logoff (Applies to Windows Vista or later versions)	Allows administrators to prevent Windows Vista from forcefully unloading the user's registry at user logoff. (By default, Windows Vista will always unload the user's registry even if there are open handles to per-user registry keys during user logoff.) Enabling this policy setting causes Windows Vista not to forcefully unload the user's registry during logoff, but instead to unload the registry when all open handles to per-user registry keys have been closed. Disabling this policy setting or leaving it Not Configured causes Windows Vista to always unload the user's registry at logoff even if there are open handles to per-user registry keys during user logoff. Do not enable this policy by default because it may prevent users from getting updated versions of their roaming user profiles. Instead, only enable this policy when you are experiencing application compatibility issues related to unloading the user's registry.
Set Maximum Wait Time For The Network If A User Has A Roaming User Profile Or Remote Home Directory (Applies to Windows Vista or later versions)	Allows administrators to specify how long Windows Vista should wait for the network to become available if the user has a roaming user profile or remote Home directory and the network is currently unavailable. (By default, when the user has a roaming user profile or a remote Home directory, Windows Vista waits 30 seconds for the network to become available when the user logs on to the computer.) If the network is still unavailable after the maximum wait time expires, Windows Vista continues the logon for the user without a network connection, but the user's roaming profile will not synchronize with the server, nor will the remote Home directory be used for the logon session. However, if the network does become available before the maximum wait time expires, Windows Vista proceeds immediately with the user logon. (Windows Vista will not wait if the physical network connection is unavailable on the computer—for example, if the media is disconnected.) Enabling this policy setting causes Windows Vista to wait for the network to become available up to the maximum wait time specified in this policy setting. (Specifying a value to zero will cause Windows Vista to proceed without waiting for the network.) Disabling this policy setting or leaving it Not Configured causes Windows Vista to wait for the network for a maximum of 30 seconds.

POLICY SETTING	NOTES
	You should enable this policy setting in scenarios in which the network takes longer to initialize than is typical—for example, when using a wireless network.
Set Roaming Profile Path For All Users Logging Onto This Computer (Applies to Windows Vista or later versions)	Allows administrators to specify whether Windows Vista should use the specified network path (usually *Computername**Sharename*\%UserName%) as the roaming user profile path for all users logging on to the computer. (If %UserName% is not specified, all users logging on to the computer will use the same roaming profile folder specified in the policy.) Enabling this policy setting causes all users logging on to the computer to use the specified roaming profile path. Disabling this policy setting or leaving it Not Configured causes users logging on to the computer to use their local profile or standard roaming user profile.

TABLE 15-11 New Per-User Group Policy Setting for Managing User Profiles in Windows Vista and Later Versions

POLICY SETTING	NOTES
Network Directories To Sync At Logon/Logoff Time Only (Applies to Windows Vista or later versions)	Allows administrators to specify which network directories should be synchronized only at logon and logoff using Offline Files. Use this policy setting in conjunction with Folder Redirection to help resolve issues with applications that do not function well with Offline Files while the user is online. (See the section titled "Implementing Folder Redirection" earlier in this chapter for more information.) Enabling this policy setting causes the network paths specified in this policy setting to be synchronized only by Offline Files during user logon and logoff and to be taken offline while the user is logged on. Disabling this policy setting or leaving it Not Configured causes the network paths specified in this policy setting to behave like any other cached data using Offline Files and to continue to remain online while the user is logged on (provided that the network paths are accessible). Do not use this policy setting to suspend root redirected folders such as AppData\Roaming, Start Menu, or Documents. You should suspend only subfolders of these parent folders.

The following user profile policy settings are no longer supported in Windows Vista and later versions:

- Connect Home Directory To Root Of The Share
- Maximum Retries To Unload And Update The User Profile
- Timeout For Dialog Boxes

In addition, the behavior of two user profile policy settings has changed in Windows Vista and later versions:

- **Limit Profile Size** Instead of preventing the user from logging off, the roaming user profile will not be copied to the server on logoff. Disabling this setting or leaving it Not Configured means that the system does not limit the size of user profiles. When you enable this setting, you can:
  - Set a maximum permitted user profile size.
  - Determine whether the registry files are included in the calculation of the profile size.
  - Determine whether users are notified when the profile exceeds the permitted maximum size.
  - Specify a customized message notifying users of the oversized profile.
  - Determine how often the customized message is displayed.

  This setting affects both local and roaming profiles.
- **Prompt User When A Slow Network Connection Is Detected** Provides users with the ability to download their roaming profiles even when a slow network connection with the profile server is detected. Enabling this policy setting allows users to specify whether they want their roaming profiles to be downloaded when a slow link with the profile server is detected. In earlier versions of Windows, a dialog box is displayed to the user during logon if a slow network connection is detected. The user can then choose whether to download the remote copy of the user profile. In Windows Vista and later versions, a check box appears on the logon screen instead and the user must choose whether to download the remote user profile before Windows detects the network connection speed.

  Disabling this policy setting or leaving it Not Configured means that the system uses the local copy of the user profile and does not consult the user. If you have also enabled the Wait For Remote User Profile policy setting, the system downloads the remote copy of the user profile without consulting the user. In Windows Vista and later versions, the system will ignore the user choice made on the logon screen.

  If you enable the Do Not Detect Slow Network Connections policy setting, this policy setting is ignored. If you enable the Delete Cached Copies Of Roaming Profiles policy setting, no local copy of the roaming profile is available to load when the system detects a slow connection.

NOTE For additional information on policy settings for user profiles, see "Group Policy Settings Reference for Windows Server 2008 R2 and Windows 7" available from the Microsoft Download Center.

Working with Offline Files

Offline Files is a feature of Windows 7 Professional, Enterprise, and Ultimate Edition operating systems that allows users to access files stored in shared folders on network file servers even when those shared folders are unavailable, such as when a network problem occurs or when a file server is offline. The Offline Files feature has been around since Windows 2000 and provides several advantages for corporate networks:

- Users can continue working with files stored on network shares even when those file servers become unavailable because of network interruption or some other problem.
- Users in branch offices can continue working with files stored on file servers at corporate headquarters when the WAN link between the branch office and headquarters fails, becomes unreliable, or becomes congested.
- Mobile users can continue working with files stored on network shares when they are traveling and unable to connect to the remote corporate network.

Some common deployment scenarios for Offline Files include the following:

- **Using Folder Redirection** Implementing Offline Files with Folder Redirection provides a robust solution for ensuring that users can access their files when disconnected from the corporate network. This scenario also enables administrators to ensure that users' data files are backed up centrally from network servers.
- **Working on cached drives** By using logon scripts to map network drives to server message block (SMB) shares on network file servers and then making these network drives available for offline use, users can open and work on files in the network drive even when their computers are disconnected from the corporate network.
- **Pinning remote shares or specific files** By making an individual network share or a file within a share available for offline use, users can open and work on that file or the files in that share when their computers are disconnected from the corporate network.

Windows Vista included numerous enhancements to Offline Files, and Windows 7 builds on these earlier enhancements by providing additional Offline Files functionality. The sections that follow summarize the improvements made to Offline Files, first in Windows Vista and later in Windows 7.

Enhancements to Offline Files Introduced Previously in Windows Vista

Offline Files functionality was completely redesigned for Windows Vista to improve performance, reliability, flexibility, manageability, and ease of use. The following list summarizes the enhancements and changes to Offline Files in Windows Vista compared with Windows XP:

- The user experience with Offline Files in Windows Vista is more seamless and less disruptive when a transition occurs between online and offline mode. Synchronization occurs automatically when configured, and users are notified concerning sync conflicts by the appearance of the Sync icon in the notification area of the taskbar. By clicking or right-clicking this icon, users can choose from various options provided to resolve conflicts, including opening the new Sync Center utility in Control Panel, which is described later in this chapter in the section titled "Managing Offline Files Using Sync Center." Synchronization of other files in which no conflict occurs then continues in the background while the user decides how to resolve each conflict.
- The user also has a more consistent user interface experience in Windows Vista (compared with Windows XP) when files have been transitioned to offline mode. For example, if a network folder on Windows XP contains a number of files and two of them are made available for offline use, only those two files will be visible when the user has the folder open in Windows Explorer when the server is unavailable. In the same scenario in Windows Vista, however, all of the files will be visible in Windows Explorer, and the unavailable files will be displayed with ghosted placeholders (see Figure 15-11). This change causes less confusion for users by providing a consistent view of the namespace on the file server regardless of whether any files are available offline. In addition, if you configure caching on the network folder so that all files that users open from the share will automatically be made available offline, Offline Files will create placeholders for all the files within the folder automatically.

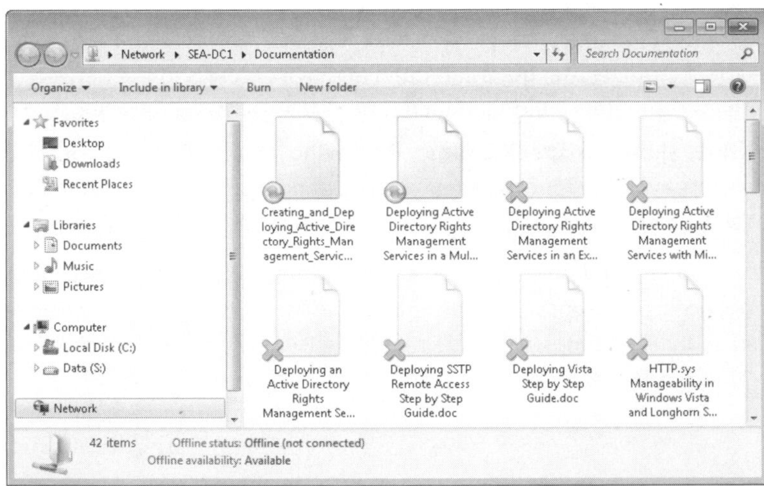

FIGURE 15-11 Working offline with a network folder that contains a number of files, two of which have been made available for offline use

- The synchronization process for Offline Files in Windows Vista has been streamlined and made more efficient by the use of a new sync algorithm known as Bitmap Differential Transfer (BDT). BDT keeps track of which blocks of a file in the local cache (also called client-side cache, or CSC) are being modified when you are working offline. Then, when a sync action occurs, BDT sends only those blocks that have changed to the server. This provides a definite performance improvement over Windows XP, in which the entire file is copied from the local cache to the server even if only a small portion of the file has been modified. In addition, because of the performance improvement brought about by BDT, any file type can now be marked for offline use in Windows Vista. This is another improvement over Windows XP, in which certain file types, such as .pst and .mdb files, are excluded by default from being made available offline, either because of their large size or because of the frequency of modification. Note that BDT is used only when syncing from the client to the server, not the other way around. Also, it works only for files that are modified in place and hence does not work for certain applications like Microsoft Office PowerPoint, Office Word, and so on.
- Mobile users and users at branch offices where network latency is high benefit from an improved slow-link mode of operation in Windows Vista. When Windows Vista determines that the network throughput between the local computer and the remote server has dropped below a specified level, Offline Files automatically transitions to the new slow-link mode of operation. When Offline Files is running in slow-link mode, all read and write requests are satisfied from the local cache, and any sync operations must be initiated manually by the user. Offline Files will continue running in slow-link mode until the user attempts to transition back to online mode by clicking Work Online on the command bar of Windows Explorer. When online mode is operational again, Windows Vista will test network throughput and packet latency every two minutes by default to determine whether to remain online or transition back to slow-link mode again.
- Offline Files in Windows Vista lets you configure a limit for the total amount of disk space used for your local cache, which includes both automatically and manually cached files. In addition, you can also configure a second limit within this total local cache size limit to specify the total disk space that can be used for automatically cached files. By contrast, in Windows XP, you can specify a limit only for the total amount of disk space to be used for automatically cached files; you have no way to limit the amount of disk space used in Windows XP for manually cached files.
- Limits for total cached files and automatically cached files can be configured using Group Policy. Note that when the limit for automatically cached files is reached, the files that have been least-used recently drop out of the cache to make room for newer ones. By contrast, manually cached files are never removed from the cache unless you specifically delete them.
- Offline Files modes of operation apply to both individual SMB shared folders and DFS scopes. By contrast, Offline Files modes in Windows XP apply only to an entire network file server or domain-based DFS namespace. This means, for example, that when a network error is detected when trying to connect to a file or folder within a DFS

namespace in Windows Vista, only the DFS link that includes that file or folder will be transitioned from online mode to offline. When the same scenario occurs with Windows XP, the entire DFS namespace is taken offline.

- Offline Files in Windows Vista allows each file within the local cache to be encrypted using the EFS certificate of the user doing the encryption. By contrast, in Windows XP you can encrypt the entire local cache only by using the LocalSystem account. This change improves privacy of information by preventing access to cached files by other users of the computer. When the local cache is encrypted, the first user who makes a particular file available offline will be the only user who will be able to access that file when working offline; other users will be able to access that file only when working online. Encryption of the Offline Files cache can be configured using Group Policy; see the section titled "Understanding Offline File Sync" later in this chapter for more information. Note that you cannot encrypt files that are currently in use. Also, when an encrypted file is made available offline, the file is automatically encrypted in the client-side cache.
- Offline Files in Windows Vista can also be programmatically managed using either the WMI provider or Win32/COM interfaces. For more information, see *http://msdn2.microsoft.com/en-us/library/cc296092.aspx.*

> ***NOTE*** **All changes to Offline Files in Windows Vista, including BDT, are compatible with any Windows Server operating system that fully supports the SMB protocol, including Windows Server 2000, Windows Server 2003, Windows Server 2003 R2, and Windows Server 2008.**

Additional Enhancements to Offline Files Introduced in Windows 7

To improve Offline Files performance and overall user experience, the following additional enhancements have been made to Offline Files in Windows 7:

- **Slow-link mode enabled** Slow-link mode is on by default for Offline Files in Windows 7. The default slow-link threshold in Windows 7 is now an 80-millisecond round-trip latency to ensure an optimal user experience when accessing files made available for offline use over a slow WAN link.
- **Background sync** Beginning with Windows 7, Offline Files synchronization between the client and the server can now occur automatically in the background without the user needing to choose between online and offline modes. This means that synchronization is now completely transparent to users and they no longer need to worry about manually synchronizing their data over slow networks (provided that the server is available, either over a LAN connection, WAN link, or VPN connection). Administrators

also benefit by knowing that users' files are synchronized automatically with the server, making it easier to ensure that users' files are always backed up.

The new background sync feature of Offline Files in Windows 7 also makes Folder Redirection more powerful and more transparent to users. For example, if you use Folder Redirection to redirect the Documents folder to a network share and have Offline Files enabled, background sync will ensure that users' local copies of documents will be synchronized automatically with copies on the network share.

Full two-way background sync occurs whenever Windows determines that Offline Files is operating in slow-link mode. By default, network folders in slow-link mode are synchronized every 6 hours with the server plus an offset of up to 1 hour. Background sync is fully configurable by using Group Policy. For information on how to configure background sync, see the section titled "Additional Offline Files Policy Settings for Windows 7" later in this chapter.

- **Transparent caching** In Windows Vista and earlier versions, when client computers had to open a file across a slow network, the client had to retrieve the file from the server even if the client had retrieved the file recently. Beginning with Windows 7, client computers can now cache remote files to reduce the number of times the file needs to be retrieved from the remote server.

  The first time that the user opens a file in an SMB share on a network server, the file is read from the server and is cached locally on the client in the Offline Files cache. On subsequent occasions that the user needs to read the same file, the client contacts the server to determine whether the locally cached version of the file is still up to date. If the local copy is still up to date, the client reads the file from its local cache. If the file is no longer up to date, the client retrieves a new copy of the file from the server. If the server becomes unavailable, the user cannot access the file—the locally cached copy of the file is not available to the user when the user is offline.

  The locally cached copy is not kept in sync automatically with the copy on the server and does not show up in Sync Center. The server must still be available for the client to access the file, either from its local cache or over the network. If the client makes any modifications to a file and then saves it, the modifications are made on the server to ensure that the server always has an up-to-date copy of the file. If the server is not available when the client tries to save the modified file, the save operation will fail with an error.

  Transparent caching can be configured using Group Policy and takes place whenever a specified network latency value is exceeded. Transparent caching is not enabled by default on fast networks (for example, those with LAN connections). For information on how to configure transparent caching, see the section titled "Additional Offline Files Policy Settings for Windows 7" later in this chapter.

  Transparent caching can benefit users at branch offices by enabling them to access files quickly over slow WAN links by retrieving them from the client's local cache when they are available. Transparent caching also benefits administrators by reducing bandwidth utilization on slow WAN links. Administrators can further reduce unwanted WAN traffic and improve end-user experience for file access by implementing BranchCache, a feature of Windows Server 2008 R2 and Windows 7 that enables content from file and Web servers on a WAN to be cached on computers at a local branch office. For more information about BranchCache, see Chapter 27, "Connecting Remote Users and Networks."

- **Offline Files exclusion list** Administrators can now specify file types that should be blocked from being available for offline use. This exclusion list is configured using Group Policy by specifying the file extensions of the files that should not be made available for offline use. For information on how to configure an exclusion list, see the section titled "Additional Offline Files Policy Settings for Windows 7" later in this chapter.

  The Offline Files exclusion list benefits administrators by allowing them to enforce organizational security policies by preventing users from storing restricted types of content, such as music or video files, on network servers. The exclusion list also enables administrators to save disk space on both clients and servers and also save bandwidth by reducing the amount of sync traffic occurring.

Understanding Offline File Sync

When a user chooses to make a particular file available for offline use, Windows automatically creates a copy of that file within the local cache on the user's local computer. When the network becomes unavailable (for example, when a mobile user disconnects from the network), the user can then work with the local copy of the file by opening it and editing it using the appropriate application. Later, when the network becomes available again (for example, when the mobile user reconnects to the network), Windows will synchronize (sync) the local and remote copies of the file. In addition, users can also manually sync their locally cached versions of files with the remote copies whenever they choose.

When a file that has been made available for offline use is modified, the local and remote copies become different. What happens now when a sync operation occurs depends on which copy of the file has been modified:

- If the local copy of the file stored in the local cache on the user's computer has been modified but the remote copy is unchanged, the sync operation typically will overwrite the remote copy with the local version because the local copy is the more recent version of the file.
- If the local copy is unchanged but the remote copy has been modified, the sync operation typically will overwrite the local copy with the remote version because the remote copy is the more recent version of the file.
- If both the local and remote copies of the file have been modified, a sync conflict will occur and Windows will prompt the user to resolve the conflict in one of three ways:
  - By deciding which copy (local or remote) of the file should be considered the master copy and which copy should be updated

- By deciding to keep both copies of the file as is, in which case one copy of the file is renamed and both versions are then copied and stored in both locations (local and remote)
- By ignoring the conflict, in which case the conflict will usually occur again the next time you try to sync the file

Sync operations also have an effect when offline files are added or deleted. For example, when the local copy of a file is deleted, the remote copy will also be deleted during the next sync operation. And when a file is added to one location (local or remote) but not the other, it will be copied to the other location when sync next occurs.

Modes of Operation in Offline Files

Offline Files in Windows Vista and later versions has four modes of operation:

- **Online mode** This is the default mode of operation and provides the user with normal access to files and folders stored on network shares and DFS scopes. In online mode, any changes made to files or folders are applied first to the network server and then to the local cache. Reads, however, are satisfied from the cache, thus improving the user experience.
- **Auto offline mode** If Offline Files detects a network error during a file operation with an SMB shared folder or a DFS scope, Offline Files automatically transitions the network share to auto offline mode. In this mode, file operations are performed against the local cache. Certain file operations cannot be performed in auto offline mode, however, such as accessing previous versions of files. When Offline Files is in auto offline mode, by default it automatically tries to reconnect to the network share every two minutes. If the reconnection is successful, Offline Files transitions back to online mode. Note that users also cannot initiate a manual sync when in auto offline mode.
- **Manual offline mode** When a user has a particular network share open in Windows Explorer, the user can force a transition from online mode to manual offline mode for that share by clicking Work Offline on the command bar of Windows Explorer. Available file operations in manual offline mode are the same as when in auto offline mode. Manual offline mode persists across restarting the computer, and the user has the options of manually syncing an offline item by clicking Sync on the command bar of Windows Explorer and of forcing a transition to online mode by clicking Work Online on the command bar of Windows Explorer. If the user forces synchronization of an offline item, the item remains offline.
- **Slow-link mode** If the Configure Slow-Link Mode policy setting has been enabled and applied to the user's computer using Group Policy, a network share will transition automatically to slow-link mode when Offline Files is in online mode but network performance degrades below the specified threshold. For more information, see the section titled "Managing Offline Files Using Group Policy" later in this chapter.

NOTE Beginning with Windows Vista SP1, you can now rename and delete offline files when in offline mode. However, this feature must first be enabled in the registry. See *http://support.microsoft.com/kb/942845* for more information.

Figure 15-12 summarizes the conditions under which transitions occur between different modes.

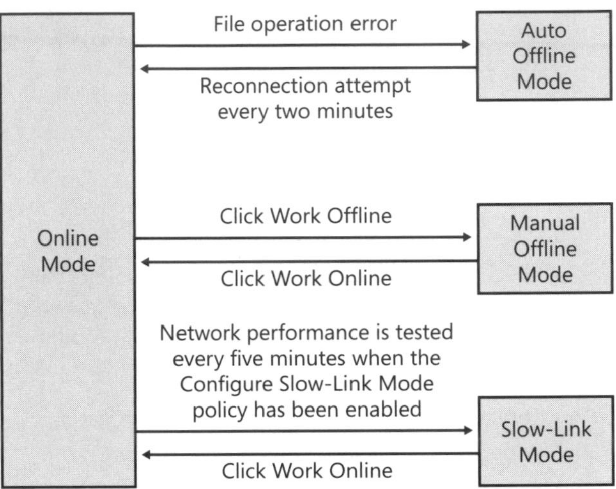

FIGURE 15-12 How transitions occur between different modes

Table 15-12 summarizes where various file operations are satisfied (on the local cache or network server) for each mode.

TABLE 15-12 Where File Operations Are Satisfied for Each Mode

MODE	OPEN/CREATE FILE	READ FROM FILE	WRITE TO FILE	BROWSE FOLDER
Online	Server	Cache (if in sync with server)	Server then cache	Server
Auto offline	Cache	Cache	Cache	Cache
Manual offline	Cache	Cache	Cache	Cache
Slow-link	Cache	Cache	Cache	Cache

Table 15-13 summarizes the availability of synchronization (manual or automatic) for each mode.

TABLE 15-13 Availability of Synchronization for Each Mode

MODE	AUTOMATIC SYNCHRONIZATION	MANUAL SYNCHRONIZATION
Online	Available	Available
Auto offline	Not available	Not available
Manual offline	Not available	Available
Slow-link	Not available	Available

Managing Offline Files

Windows 7 and Windows Server 2008 R2 provide several tools for managing Offline Files:

- Windows Explorer
- Offline Files in Control Panel
- Sync Center in Control Panel
- Offline Settings on the server
- Group Policy

> **NOTE** The Client-Side Caching Command-Line Options (CSCCMD) command-line tool (Csccmd.exe) used for managing Offline Files in Windows XP is no longer supported in Windows Vista and later versions.

Managing Offline Files Using Windows Explorer

As shown previously in Figure 15-11, items (files or folders) that are available offline are displayed in Windows Explorer with a Sync icon overlay, whereas items that are unavailable offline are displayed in ghosted form as placeholders with an X icon overlay. To make an item in a network share available offline, right-click the file and then select Always Available Offline (you must be online to perform this action). You can also make an item available offline using the Offline Files tab of the item's properties sheet (see Figure 15-13).

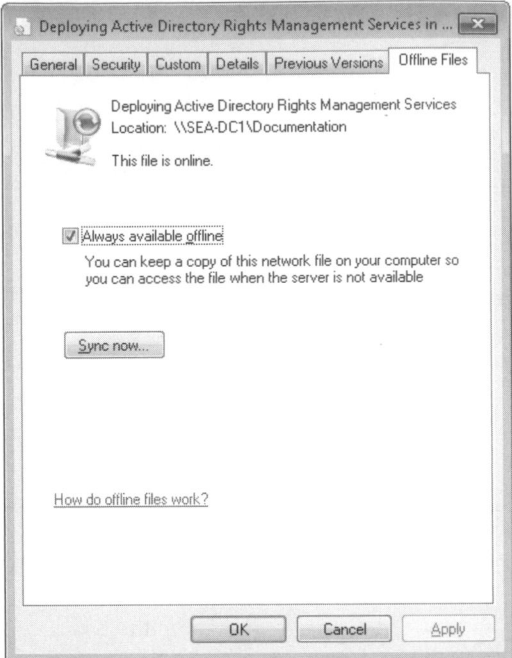

FIGURE 15-13 The Offline tab on a file's properties sheet

You can also configure the Details view of Windows Explorer to show the offline status and availability of items in network shares (see Figure 15-14). The offline availability of an item can be either of the following:

- **Available** The item has been made available for offline use.
- **Not available** The item has not been made available for offline use.

The offline status of an item can be:

- **Online** Offline Files is in online mode so that both the network version and the locally cached version of the item are available. (Reads are satisfied from cache; writes, opens, and creates go to the server.)
- **Offline (not connected)** Offline Files is in auto offline mode, so only the locally cached version of the item is available.
- **Offline (working offline)** Offline Files is in manual offline mode, so only the locally cached version of the item is available.
- **Offline (slow connection)** Same behavior as Offline (not connected).
- **Offline** Neither version of the item is available because the item has not been made available for offline use.

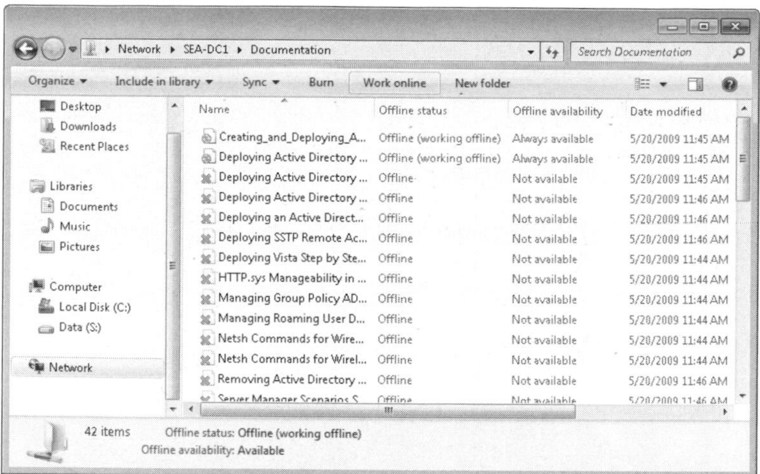

FIGURE 15-14 Two additional columns are available for Offline Files in the Details view of Windows Explorer.

To synchronize a particular offline item in Windows Explorer, right-click the file and select Sync. To synchronize all offline items in a network share manually, click Sync on the command bar. If an offline item is online, you can also synchronize it by clicking Sync Now on the Offline Files tab of the item's properties sheet. Other ways of synchronizing offline items are described in the section titled "Managing Offline Files Using Sync Center" later in this chapter.

Managing Offline Files Using the Offline Files Control Panel

Users of unmanaged computers can configure their Offline Files settings using the Offline Files Control Panel tool (see Figure 15-15). On managed networks where Group Policy is used to manage Offline Files settings for users' computers, configuration settings in the Offline Files Control Panel on users' computers will appear dimmed (unavailable). For more information on Group Policy settings for managing Offline Files, see the section titled "Managing Offline Files Using Group Policy" later in this chapter.

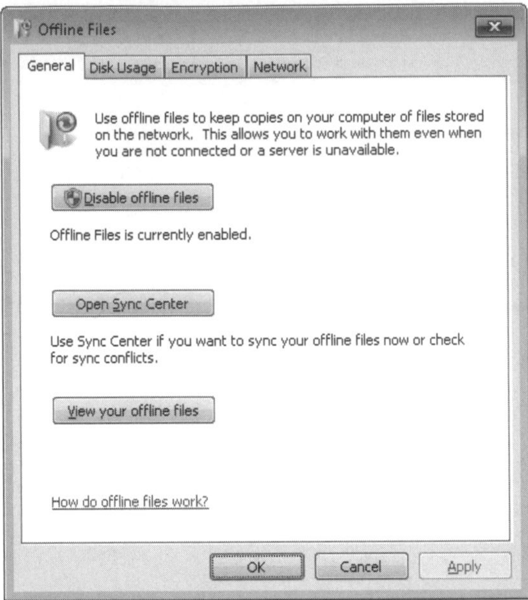

FIGURE 15-15 The General tab of the Offline Files Control Panel tool

The Offline Files Control Panel tool includes the following four tabs:

- **General** Lets you enable or disable Offline Files on the computer, open Sync Center, and view all offline files on your computer, including files in SMB shared folders, DFS scopes, and mapped network drives. Note that Offline Files is enabled by default on Windows Vista and later versions.
- **Disk Usage** Lets you view and configure the total disk space used by Offline Files on your computer and the space available for temporary offline files. You also can use this tab to delete all temporary offline files on your computer. Note that All Offline Files refers to both automatically cached and manually cached offline files, whereas Temporary Offline Files refers only to automatically cached files.
- **Encryption** Lets you encrypt or unencrypt the local cache on your computer using EFS. Note that you can encrypt only the locally cached versions of these files, not their network versions.
- **Network** Lets you see whether Offline Files slow-link mode has been enabled for your computer and how often your computer checks the connection speed after you manually transition to online mode. Note that the user cannot configure the settings on this tab directly; slow-link settings can be configured only by using Group Policy.

> ***NOTE*** **Windows Vista and later versions index offline files by default. Indexing of offline files can be toggled on and off by using the Indexing Options Control Panel. For more information, see Chapter 19.**

Managing Offline Files Using Sync Center

Sync Center, introduced in Windows Vista, lets you synchronize versions of offline files between the client computer and a network server. You can also use Sync Center to synchronize content between a client computer and mobile devices, such as portable music players, digital cameras, and mobile phones, either by plugging these devices into your computer using a universal serial bus (USB) connection or over a wireless networking connection. You can use Sync Center for the following tasks:

- Set up sync partnerships between your computer and the remote server or mobile device.
- Initiate or stop synchronization between members of a sync partnership.
- Schedule synchronization to occur for a partnership at a scheduled time or when an action or event occurs.
- Resolve sync conflicts when the same file is modified in different locations.
- View the status of sync partnerships and identify sync errors and warnings (as shown in Figure 15-16).

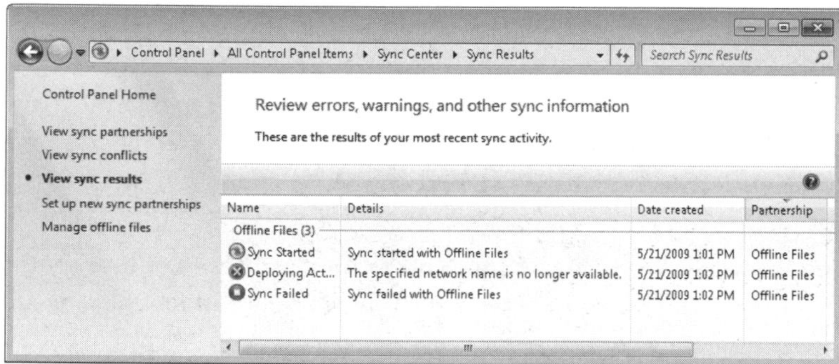

FIGURE 15-16 Using Sync Center to identify sync errors

You can also open Sync Center by clicking the Sync icon in the notification area of the taskbar. You can also right-click this icon and initiate or terminate synchronization, view sync conflicts, or view synchronization results.

Configuring Offline Files on the Server

When you create a shared folder on a Windows Server 2008 R2 file server, you also have the option of configuring Offline Files settings for items located within that folder. To do this, open the properties sheet for the shared folder and select the Sharing tab. Click Advanced Settings to open the Advanced Settings dialog box. Then click Caching to display the Offline Settings dialog box shown in Figure 15-17.

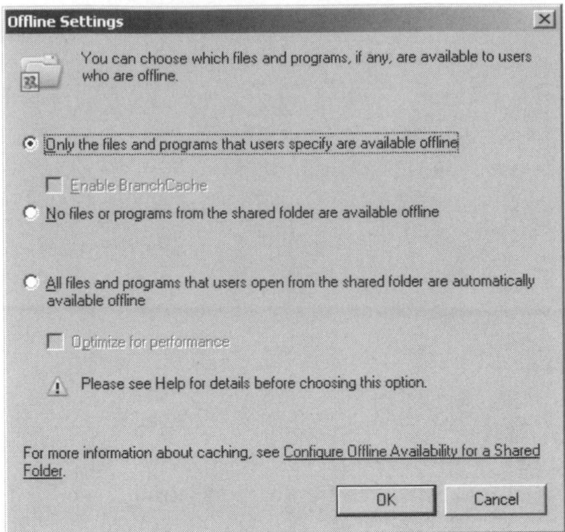

FIGURE 15-17 Offline Files settings for a shared folder on a network server

Three caching options are available for shared folders:

- **Only The Files And Programs That Users Specify Are Available Offline** This is the default setting and is used to configure manual caching of items in the folder. This means that if the user wants an item to be available offline, the user must manually select it to be made available offline by using one of the methods described earlier in this chapter.
- **No Files Or Programs From The Shared Folder Are Available Offline** With this setting, no caching is performed. (Items in the shared folder cannot be made available offline.)
- **All Files And Programs That Users Open From The Shared Folder Are Automatically Available Offline** This setting is used to configure automatic caching of items, which means that every time a user accesses an item in the shared folder, the item will be made temporarily available offline on his computer. If you also select the Optimized For Performance option, all programs are cached automatically so that they can run locally. (This option is particularly useful for file servers that host applications because it reduces network traffic and improves server scalability.)

NOTE **You can also select specific files to be cached automatically using Group Policy by enabling and configuring the Administratively Assigned Offline Files policy setting. For more information, see the next section of this chapter titled "Managing Offline Files Using Group Policy."**

DIRECT FROM THE SOURCE

CSC Server Settings for Roaming User Profiles/Folder Redirection

Ming Zhu, Software Design Engineer
Microsoft Windows Shell Team

When setting up an RUP or Folder Redirection server, one thing to consider is how to set the CSC settings on the share. RUP and Folder Redirection behave quite differently when used with CSC: RUP uses its own synchronization algorithm to keep the local copy in sync with the server, so it does not rely on CSC. As a best practice, Microsoft always recommends that you configure the RUP server to disable CSC (with the setting Files Or Programs From This Share Will Not Be Available Offline). Folder Redirection, on the other hand, depends heavily on CSC to provide synchronization between the client cache and the server. So the typical setting on a Folder Redirection share is manual caching (Only The Files Or Programs That Users Specify Are Available Offline). You don't need to set it to auto caching (All Files And Programs That Users Open From The Shared Folder Are Automatically Available Offline) because the Folder Redirection client side will pin the folder automatically so that it will always be available offline.

However, the preceding recommendation has an exception. Because Windows Vista and later versions and Windows XP have separate profiles in the server (the Windows Vista and later profile has a .v2 suffix), if you have both Windows XP and Windows Vista and later clients in your organization and have RUP deployed on both platforms, you can't share data between them. To share a specific folder between them, you can deploy a special folder redirection policy for Windows Vista and later client computers to redirect only a certain folder (such as Favorites) to the Windows XP RUP share. In this configuration, you cannot disable CSC entirely on the RUP share. Instead, you need to set up manual caching to let CSC work against this share for Windows Vista and later versions. Don't worry about RUP in Windows XP, though—RUP tries to keep the CSC out of the picture by bypassing CSC to talk directly to the server.

Managing Offline Files Using Group Policy

A number of aspects of Offline Files can be configured using Group Policy, These policy settings are found in the following locations:

- Computer Configuration\Policies\Administrative Templates\Network\Offline Files
- User Configuration\Policies\Administrative Templates\Network\Offline Files

Some policy settings for Offline Files can apply to both computers and users; other settings apply only to computers. See Table 15-14 for more information about which policy settings are per user and which are per machine.

Windows Vista introduced several new policy settings for managing Offline Files. These policy settings are described in the section titled "Offline Files Policy Settings Introduced in Windows Vista" later in this chapter. Windows 7 also introduces additional new policy settings for managing Offline Files. These additional policy settings are described in the section titled "Additional Offline Files Policy Settings for Windows 7" later in this chapter.

Note that some policy settings for Offline Files used by earlier versions of Windows, such as Windows XP and Windows Server 2003, no longer apply to Windows Vista and later. Table 15-14 summarizes which Offline Files policy settings apply to Windows Vista and to Windows 7.

TABLE 15-14 Offline Files Policy Settings for Windows Vista and Windows 7

NAME OF POLICY SETTING	PER MACHINE	PER USER	APPLIES TO WINDOWS VISTA	APPLIES TO WINDOWS 7
Action On Server Disconnect	✓	✓		
Administratively Assigned Offline Files	✓	✓	✓	✓
Allow Or Disallow Use Of The Offline Files Feature	✓		✓	✓
At Logoff, Delete Local Copy Of User's Offline Files	✓			
Configure Background Sync	✓			✓
Configure Slow-Link Speed	✓			
Configure Slow-Link Mode	✓		✓ (replaces Configure Slow-Link Speed policy)	✓
Default Cache Size	✓			
Enable Transparent Caching	✓			✓
Encrypt The Offline Files Cache	✓		✓	✓
Event Logging Level	✓	✓		
Exclude Files From Being Cached	✓			✓
Files Not Cached	✓			

NAME OF POLICY SETTING	PER MACHINE	PER USER	APPLIES TO WINDOWS VISTA	APPLIES TO WINDOWS 7
Initial Reminder Balloon Lifetime	✓	✓		
Limit Disk Space Used By Offline Files	✓		✓ (replaces Default Cache Size policy)	✓
Non-Default Server Disconnect Actions	✓	✓		
Prevent Use Of Offline Files Folder	✓	✓		
Prohibit 'Make Available Offline' For These Files And Folders	✓	✓		
Prohibit User Configuration Of Offline Files	✓	✓		
Reminder Balloon Frequency	✓	✓		
Reminder Balloon Lifetime	✓	✓		
Remove 'Make Available Offline'	✓	✓	✓	✓
Subfolders Always Available Offline	✓			
Synchronize All Offline Files Before Logging Off	✓	✓		
Synchronize All Offline Files When Logging On	✓	✓		
Synchronize Offline Files Before Suspend	✓	✓		
Turn Off Reminder Balloons	✓	✓		
Turn On Economical Application Of Administratively Assigned Offline Files	✓		✓	✓

OFFLINE FILES POLICY SETTINGS INTRODUCED IN WINDOWS VISTA

The following Group Policy settings for managing Offline Files were introduced with Windows Vista and still apply in Windows 7:

- **Configure Slow-Link Mode** This policy setting allows you to enable and configure the slow-link mode of Offline Files. When Offline Files is operating in slow-link mode, all file requests are satisfied from the Offline Files cache, just as when the user is working offline. However, the user can initiate synchronization manually on demand. When the synchronization completes, the system continues to operate in the slow-link mode until the user transitions the share to online mode.

  If you enable this policy setting, Offline Files will operate in slow-link mode if the end-to-end network throughput between the client and the server is below the throughput threshold parameter or if the network latency is above the latency threshold parameter.

  You can configure slow-link mode by specifying thresholds for throughput (bits per second) and latency (in milliseconds) for specific UNC paths. You can specify one or both threshold parameters.

  When a share is transitioned to slow-link mode, the user can force the share to transition to online mode. However, the system periodically checks to see whether a connection to a server is slow. If the connection is slow, the share will again be transitioned to slow-link mode.

  > ***NOTE*** **You can use wildcards (*) for specifying UNC paths.**

  If you disable or do not configure this policy setting, Offline Files will not transition to slow-link mode.

  > ***NOTE*** **The Configure Slow-Link Mode policy setting replaces the Configure Slow Link Speed policy setting used by earlier versions of Windows.**

- **Limit Disk Space Used By Offline Files** This policy limits the amount of the computer's disk space that can be used to store offline files. Using this setting, you can configure how much total disk space (in megabytes) is used for storing offline files. This includes the space used by automatically cached files and files that are specifically made available offline. Files can be cached automatically if the user accesses a file on an automatic caching network share. This setting also disables the ability to adjust the disk space limits on the Offline Files cache using the Offline Files Control Panel tool. This prevents users from trying to change the option while a policy setting controls it.

  If you enable this policy setting, you can specify the disk space limit for offline files and also specify how much of that disk space can be used by automatically cached files.

  If you disable this policy setting, the system limits the space that offline files occupy to 25 percent of the total space on the drive where the Offline Files cache is located. The limit for automatically cached files is 100 percent of the total disk space limit.

If you do not configure this policy setting, the system limits the space that offline files occupy to 25 percent of the total space on the drive where the Offline Files cache is located. The limit for automatically cached files is 100 percent of the total disk space limit. However, the users can change these values using the Offline Files Control Panel tool.

If you enable this setting and specify a total size limit greater than the size of the drive hosting the Offline Files cache and that drive is the system drive, the total size limit is automatically adjusted downward to 75 percent of the size of the drive. If the cache is located on a drive other than the system drive, the limit is automatically adjusted downward to 100 percent of the size of the drive.

If you enable this setting and specify a total size limit less than the amount of space currently used by the Offline Files cache, the total size limit is automatically adjusted upward to the amount of space currently used by offline files. The cache is then considered full.

If you enable this setting and specify an auto-cached space limit greater than the total size limit, the auto-cached limit is automatically adjusted downward to equal the total size limit.

> ***NOTE*** **The Limit Disk Space Used By Offline Files policy setting replaces the Default Cache Size policy setting used by earlier versions of Windows.**

- **Turn On Economical Application Of Administratively Assigned Offline Files** This policy setting allows you to turn on economical application of administratively assigned Offline Files.

  If you enable this policy setting, only new files and folders in administratively assigned folders are synchronized at logon. Files and folders that are already available offline are skipped and are synchronized later.

  If you disable or do not configure this policy setting, all administratively assigned folders are synchronized at logon.

ADDITIONAL OFFLINE FILES POLICY SETTINGS FOR WINDOWS 7

The following Group Policy settings for managing Offline Files are new in Windows 7:

- **Configure Background Sync** This policy setting applies to any user who logs on to the specified machine while this policy is in effect. This policy is in effect when a network folder is determined by the Configure Slow-Link Mode policy to be in slow-link mode.

  For network folders in slow-link mode, a sync will be initiated in the background on a regular basis, according to these settings, to synchronize the files in those shares/folders between the client and server. By default, network folders in slow-link mode will be synchronized with the server every 360 minutes, with the start of the sync varying between 0 and 60 additional minutes (as shown in Figure 15-18).

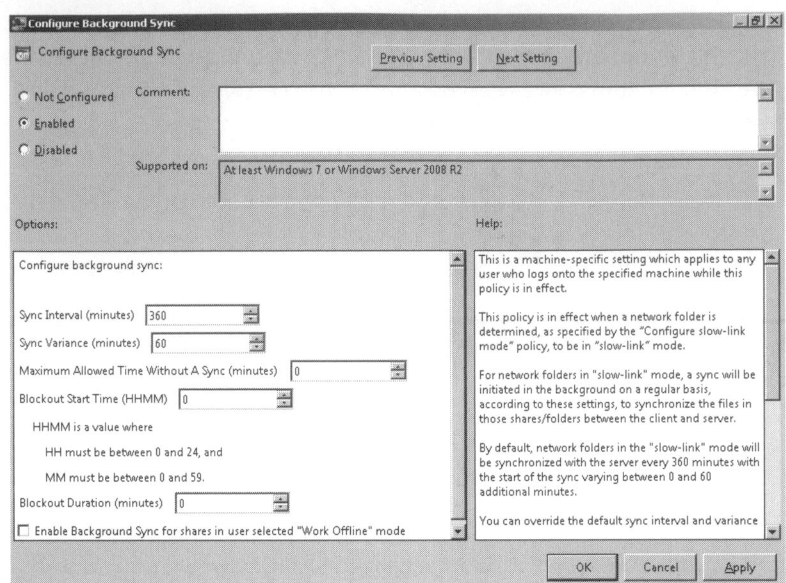

FIGURE 15-18 The new Configure Background Sync policy setting in Windows 7

You can override the default sync interval and variance by setting Sync Interval and Sync Variance values. You can also set a period of time in which background sync is disabled by setting *Blockout Start Time and Blockout Duration values*. To ensure that all the network folders on the machine are synchronized with the server on a regular basis, you may also set the *Maximum Allowed Time Without A Sync value*.

You may also configure Background Sync for network shares that are in user-selected Work Offline mode. This mode is in effect when a user selects the Work Offline option for a specific share. When selected, all configured settings will apply to shares in user-selected Work Offline mode as well.

- **Enable Transparent Caching** Enabling this policy optimizes subsequent reads to network files by a user or an application. This is done by caching reads to remote files over a slow network in the Offline Files cache. Subsequent reads to the same file are then satisfied from the client after verifying the integrity of the cached copy. This policy not only improves user response times but also decreases bandwidth consumption over the WAN links to the server. The cached files are temporary and are not available to the user when offline. The cached files are not kept in sync with the version on the server, and the most current version from the server is always available for subsequent reads.

  This policy is triggered by the configured round-trip network latency value (shown in Figure 15-19). We recommend using this policy when the network connection to the server is slow. For example, you can configure a value of 60 milliseconds as the round-trip latency of the network above which files should be transparently cached in the Offline Files cache. If the round-trip latency of the network is less than 60 milliseconds, reads to remote files will not be cached. If you do not configure this setting, remote files will not be transparently cached on user clients.

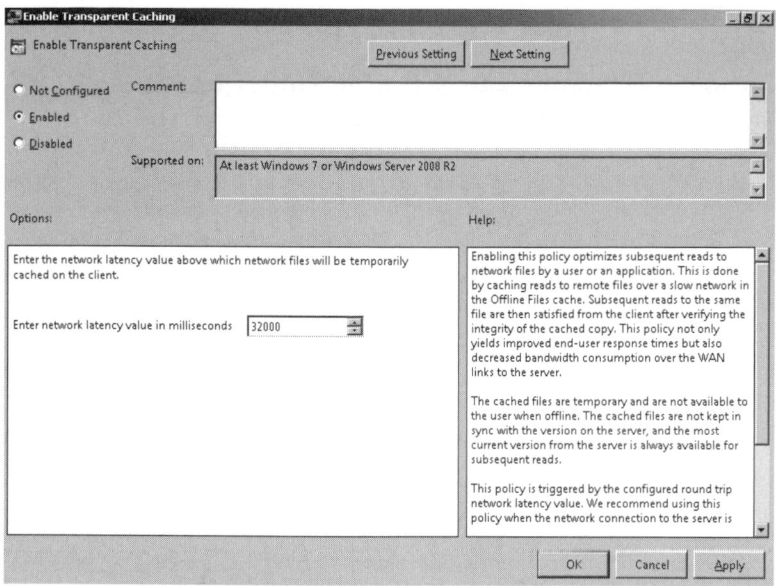

FIGURE 15-19 The new Enable Transparent Caching policy setting in Windows 7

- **Exclude Files From Being Cached** This policy enables administrators to exclude certain file types from being made available offline. You need to specify the file extensions of the file types that should be excluded (shown in Figure 15-20). A user then will be unable to create a file of this type in the folders that are available offline.

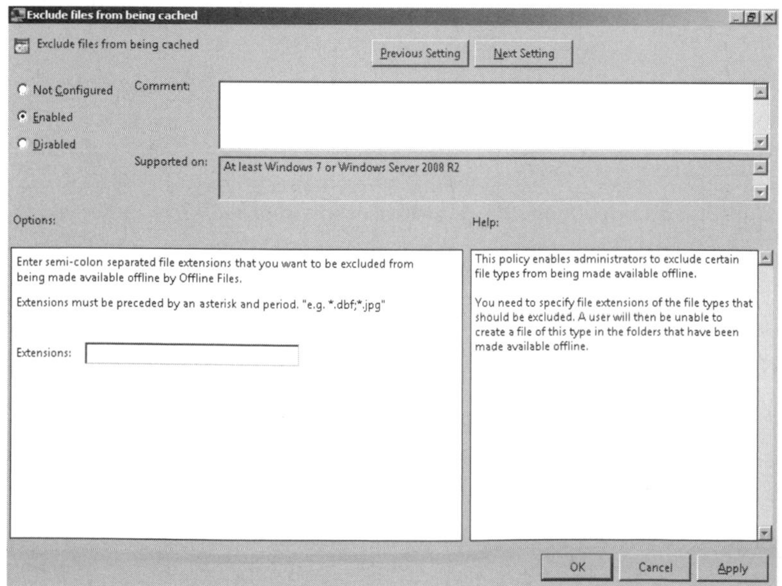

FIGURE 15-20 The new Exclude Files From Being Cached policy setting in Windows 7

DIRECT FROM THE SOURCE

Troubleshooting Roaming User Profile Folder Redirection, and Client-Side Caching Issues in Windows Vista and Later Versions

Paul D. LeBlanc, Manager
Supportability Program

The following lists describe some common support issues with Folder Redirection, RUP, and CSC in Windows Vista and later versions.

Roaming User Profile Issue Troubleshooting

Symptom: Loading temporary profile error during user logon: "Windows cannot find the local profile and is logging you on with a temporary profile. Changes you make to this profile will be lost when you log off."

- Possible cause #1: SID in ProfileList structure deleted

  Explanation: Microsoft does not recommend that you delete user profiles using anything other than the Control Panel item (Computer Properties \Advanced System Settings\User Profiles\Settings). When the folder structure for a user profile is deleted using Windows Explorer or the command prompt, the corresponding registry entries under the ProfileList registry key are left behind.

  Resolution: Remove the corresponding SID entry under the ProfileList registry key:

  HKEY_LOCAL_MACHINE\Software\Microsoft\Windows NT\CurrentVersion \ProfileList.

- Possible cause #2: User in Guests group

  Explanation: During logon, the interactive user is checked for membership in the local Guests group and the domain Guest group (if the user is the member of a domain).

  Resolution: If appropriate, remove the affected user from the local Guests /Domain Guest membership (see *http://support.microsoft.com/kb/940453*).

- Possible cause #3: Insufficient permissions (roaming profile)

  Explanation: If permissions have been altered on a working roaming profile, the user may encounter this error.

  Resolution: Correct the permissions so that the user has Full Control over her Roaming User Profile folders. If a locked-down user profile is required, use a mandatory user profile.

Folder Redirection Troubleshooting

Symptom: Duplicate folders in user profile

- Possible cause #1: Partial sync

  Explanation: Users of Windows Vista and later versions can select various folders within their user profiles to redirect to a local or remote drive. If only some of the contents of a folder are moved, the user may see multiple folders under a user profile, such as two folders named Documents or Music.

  Resolution: Allow the session to complete data transfer before logoff.

- Possible cause #2: Local and remote copies of files kept

  Explanation: When a user's folder is being redirected, the user will be asked whether she wants to move all current content. If the user chooses not to move the contents but only to copy them, duplicate folders will appear under the user profile—one local, one remote.

  Resolution: This is by design.

- Possible cause #3: Program creating folder locally (application compatibility)

  Explanation: After a user redirects a user profile folder or folders successfully, on running an application, a local instance of the user profile folder(s) may be created. This behavior is due to the application using only local resources or having a fixed path for resources and not using the environment variables. This is an application-specific issue.

  Resolution: Update the application or do not redirect the affected user profile folder(s).

Client-Side Caching Troubleshooting

Symptom: Files/folders not seen while offline

- Possible cause #1: Sync has not completed (because it occurs during background)

  Explanation: This is a fundamental change from Windows XP. In Windows Vista and later versions, Offline Files will synchronize in the background as user activity allows. This means that users will not have to wait for files to synchronize before completing a logoff. However, this also means that, depending on the volume and type of data that is to be synchronized, synchronization may need further logon sessions to complete.

  Resolution: Allow longer logon sessions for larger amounts of data to be synchronized.

- Possible cause #2: Sync has not completed

  Explanation: Another possible root cause of incomplete synchronization is the same as in Windows XP—namely, if a file is in use, open file handles will prevent the file from synchronizing.

  Resolution: This is an unchanged behavior and is by design.

- Possible cause #3: Offline files respond slowly over a VPN connection

  Explanation: On computers running Windows Vista and later versions, you experience slow performance after you establish a VPN connection. Additionally, it may take several minutes to open a redirected shell folder. This problem occurs if the following conditions are true:

  - Offline files are enabled on the computer.
  - Some offline files are cached on the local computer.
  - You logged on to the computer when you were offline.
  - The VPN connection is based on a slow connection.

  This problem usually lasts several minutes and then disappears.

  Resolution: See *http://support.microsoft.com/kb/934202*. (This issue has been fixed in SP1.)

- Possible cause #4: Changes to an offline file are not saved to the server when files are synchronized

  Explanation: When you modify an offline file in Windows Vista and later versions, the changes are not saved to the server when files are synchronized. When this problem occurs, you receive the following error message: "Access Denied." Additionally, a .tmp file that corresponds to the file appears on the server. You may experience this symptom even when you have Change permissions to the shared resource.

  Resolution: See *http://support.microsoft.com/kb/935663*. (This issue has been fixed in SP1.)

Summary

Folder Redirection, Offline Files, and Roaming User Profiles have been enhanced in Windows 7 to provide better support for corporate roaming scenarios and high availability for file server scenarios. You can implement these features using the procedures outlined in this chapter; you can manage various aspects of their behavior using Group Policy and from the user interface.

Additional Resources

These resources contain additional information and tools related to this chapter.

Related Information

- "Folder Redirection Overview" found at *http://technet.microsoft.com/en-us/library/cc732275.aspx*.
- "File Sharing and Offline Files Enhancements" found at *http://technet.microsoft.com/en-us/library/dd637828.aspx*.
- "Windows Browse and Organize Features" found at *http://technet.microsoft.com/en-us/library/dd744693.aspx*.
- *Managing Roaming User Data Deployment Guide* found at *http://technet.microsoft.com/en-us/library/cc766489.aspx*. Note that this information is for Windows Vista, so check first to see whether this topic has been updated for Windows 7 either here or elsewhere on TechNet.

On the Companion Media

- AddLocalUserToLocalGroup.ps1
- Change-LocalUserPassword.ps1
- CreateLocalGroup.ps1
- CreateLocalUser.ps1
- Remove-LocalUserFromLocalGroup.ps1
- Get-LocalGroupMembers.ps1
- LocateDisabledUsers.ps1
- Get-LocalGroups.ps1
- Get-LocalUsers.ps1
- LocateLockedOutLocalUsers.ps1
- ListUserLastLogon.ps1
- FindAdmin.ps1
- EnableDisableUser.ps1
- BackupFolderToServer.ps1
- GetSystemRestoreSettings.ps1

CHAPTER 16

Managing Disks and File Systems

The most important aspect of a computer is the user data. Businesses depend on the privacy of their intellectual property to stay competitive, and government organizations depend on confidentiality for national security. Thus, it's critical that Windows protects the availability, integrity, and privacy of the user data on client computers. The Windows 7 operating system provides several important improvements to disk and file management.

Windows 7 includes several improvements that both users and administrators will appreciate. By default, backups automatically create a System Image backup of the entire system drive. Additionally, you can store System Image backups to shared folders. System Image backups greatly reduce the time required to restore a computer after a hard disk failure or system corruption.

To improve data security, you can use Windows BitLocker Drive Encryption to encrypt an entire volume, protecting the data on the disk even if the disk is physically removed from the computer. BitLocker works alongside Encrypting File System (EFS): BitLocker can encrypt system files and the page file along with any other files on the volume, whereas EFS is intended primarily to encrypt user files. Windows 7 supports BitLocker To Go, enabling removable flash drives to be encrypted with BitLocker. The BitLocker To Go Reader enables earlier versions of Windows to read encrypted files from the removable flash drive if the user has the required password.

This chapter describes these features, as well as features introduced in Windows Vista, in more detail.

Overview of Partitioning Disks

Before you can format disks into volumes that applications can access, you must partition them. Windows 7 provides flexible partitioning that you can change even after you have formatted a volume. However, it's still important to plan ahead when creating partitions for features such as BitLocker Drive Encryption, which has very specific partitioning requirements.

> ***NOTE*** **If Windows discovers a problem with a volume, it might schedule ChkDsk to run the next time the computer starts. Large volumes, especially volumes bigger than a terabyte, can take a very long time to check—more than an hour. During this time, the computer will be offline. Therefore, when you plan the size of your partitions, consider the time required for Windows to perform a ChkDsk operation at startup.**

The sections that follow describe how to partition disks in Windows 7.

How to Choose Between MBR or GPT

Master Boot Record (MBR) and Globally Unique Identifier Partition Table (GPT) are two different disk-partitioning systems. MBR is the most common system and is supported by every version of Windows, including Windows Vista and Windows 7. GPT is an updated and improved partitioning system and is supported on Windows Vista, Windows 7, Windows Server 2008, and 64-bit versions of Windows XP and Windows Server 2003 operating systems.

GPT offers several advantages over MBR:

- In Windows, GPT can support up to 128 partitions. MBR supports only four partitions.
- GPT accurately describes physical disk geometry, allowing Windows to create partitions and logical drives on cylinder boundaries. Although Windows attempts to do this for MBR, the geometry that MBR reports has no relationship to a modern drive's physical geometry because it has been altered to enable larger capacities. Different disk vendors have created vendor-specific workarounds for this problem that are difficult to manage. Therefore, partitioning is more reliable when using GPT.

- GPT can support larger partition sizes. In theory, a GPT disk can be up to 18 exabytes in size (about 18,000,000 terabytes).
- GPT uses primary and backup partition tables for redundancy and CRC32 fields for improved partition data structure integrity. MBR does not have redundant partition tables.

NOTE All GPT disks start with a protective MBR partition to prevent previously released MBR disk tools, such as Microsoft MS-DOS FDISK or Microsoft Windows NT Disk Administrator, from damaging the GPT partition because they don't recognize the partition type. If you mount an MBR disk in a 32-bit version of Windows XP, it will see only the protective MBR partition.

To boot from a GPT disk, the computer must support the Extensible Firmware Interface (EFI). Basic input/output system (BIOS)–based systems must boot from an MBR disk, although they can use a second GPT disk as a data disk. All removable media must use MBR.

MORE INFO For more information about GPT, read the "Windows and GPT FAQ" at *http://www.microsoft.com/whdc/device/storage/GPT_FAQ.mspx.*

Converting from MBR to GPT Disks

You can convert disks only from MBR to GPT, or vice versa, if the disk does not contain partitions or volumes. You can convert a disk in two ways:

- In the Disk Management snap-in, right-click the MBR drive you want to convert to GPT and then click Convert To GPT Disk. If the drive is not empty or contains partitions, this option is unavailable.
- In the DiskPart command-line tool, select the drive you want to convert and run the command *convert gpt*. Similarly, to convert from GPT to MBR, run the command *convert mbr*.

NOTE When a dynamic disk is converted between MBR and GPT types, it must first be converted to a basic disk, then converted to MBR or GPT as appropriate, and then converted back to a dynamic disk. When you use the Disk Management snap-in, the conversion to a basic disk and then back to a dynamic disk happens automatically in the background. If you're using the command-line DiskPart tool, you must explicitly make the conversions.

GPT Partitions

For EFI computers that boot from a GPT disk, the boot disk must contain at least the following partitions:

- **EFI System Partition** On EFI computers, the EFI System Partition (ESP) is about 100 megabytes (MB) and contains the Windows Boot Manager files. For more information about startup files, read Chapter 29, "Configuring Startup and Troubleshooting Startup Issues." The ESP has the following partition globally unique identifier (GUID):

```
DEFINE_GUID (PARTITION_SYSTEM_GUID, 0xC12A7328L, 0xF81F, 0x11D2, 0xBA, 0x4B, 0x00,
0xA0, 0xC9, 0x3E, 0xC9, 0x3B)
```

- **Microsoft Reserved Partition** The Microsoft Reserved Partition (MSR) reserves space on each disk drive for subsequent use by operating system software. On drives smaller than 16 gigabytes (GB), the MSR is 32 MB. On drives 16 GB or larger, the MSR is 128 MB. GPT disks do not allow hidden sectors. Software features that formerly used hidden sectors now allocate portions of the MSR for feature-specific partitions. For example, converting a basic disk to a dynamic disk causes the MSR on that disk to be reduced in size, and a newly created partition holds the dynamic disk database. The MSR has the following partition GUID:

```
DEFINE_GUID (PARTITION_MSFT_RESERVED_GUID, 0xE3C9E316L, 0x0B5C, 0x4DB8, 0x81,
0x7D,
0xF9, 0x2D, 0xF0, 0x02, 0x15, 0xAE)
```

- **Data partition** This partition stores Windows 7 system files and user files. The data partition has the following partition GUID:

```
DEFINE_GUID (PARTITION_BASIC_DATA_GUID, 0xEBD0A0A2L, 0xB9E5, 0x4433, 0x87, 0xC0,
0x68, 0xB6, 0xB7, 0x26, 0x99, 0xC7);
```

Additionally, dynamic disks can use two different GPT partitions:

- A data container partition corresponding to the MBR partition 0x42, with the following GUID:

```
DEFINE_GUID (PARTITION_LDM_DATA_GUID, 0xAF9B60A0L, 0x1431, 0x4F62, 0xBC, 0x68,
0x33, 0x11, 0x71, 0x4A, 0x69, 0xAD);
```

- A partition to contain the dynamic configuration database with the following GUID:

```
DEFINE_GUID(PARTITION_LDM_METADATA_GUID, 0x5808C8AAL, 0x7E8F, 0x42E0, 0x85, 0xD2,
0xE1, 0xE9, 0x04, 0x34, 0xCF, 0xB3);
```

Data disks (non-boot disks) must have an MSR and a data partition. Standard users will typically see only the data partitions; however, the other partitions will be visible to administrators using the Disk Management snap-in or the DiskPart tool.

Choosing Basic or Dynamic Disks

Traditional hard disks are called basic disks in Windows Vista and Windows 7, and they have the same functionality that basic disks have always had, plus a few extras. You can create new partitions (called *simple volumes* in Windows Vista and Windows 7), delete partitions, and extend or shrink the existing partitions. The ability to extend or shrink an existing partition is an important new feature in Windows Vista and continues to be supported in Windows 7.

Dynamic disks, first introduced in Microsoft Windows 2000, provide all of the functionality of the basic disk, plus the ability to span a volume across multiple dynamic disks or stripe multiple dynamic disks to create a larger (and faster) volume. Dynamic disks present difficulties, however, because they are not accessible from operating systems other than the operating system instance that converted the disk to dynamic. This makes dynamic disks inaccessible in multiboot environments and makes recovering data more difficult in the event of partial hard disk failure. You should always use basic disks unless you have a specific requirement that can be met only by dynamic disks.

Working with Volumes

In earlier versions of Windows, your choices for resizing volumes and partitions after they have been created are limited. If you need to add space to a volume, your only choice is to make the disk a dynamic disk and then create a spanned volume. If you want to expand or contract a partition, your only choice is to use third-party tools. In Windows Vista and Windows 7, however, you can now expand and contract volumes without data loss and without requiring a reboot.

How to Create a Simple Volume

In Windows Vista and Windows 7, the term *simple volume* has been expanded to include both partitions on basic disks and simple volumes on dynamic disks. If your only need is a simple volume, your best choice is a basic disk because a simple volume doesn't use the advanced features of a dynamic disk.

To create a simple volume, open the Disk Management snap-in and follow these steps:

1. Right-click an unallocated space on one of the disks and then click New Simple Volume. The New Simple Volume Wizard appears.
2. Click Next. On the Specify Volume Size page, enter the size of volume you want to create in megabytes. The default is the maximum space available on the disk. Click Next.
3. On the Assign Drive Letter Or Path page, assign a drive letter or mount point. Click Next.
4. On the Format Partition page, choose the formatting options for the volume and then click Next.
5. Click Finish on the summary page of the wizard and the volume will be created and formatted according to your selections.

NOTE The Disk Management snap-in always creates simple volumes on dynamic disks or primary partitions on basic GPT disks. For basic MBR disks, the first three volumes created will be primary partitions. The fourth simple volume on a basic MBR disk is created as an extended partition and a logical drive. Further simple volumes on the basic MBR disk are logical drives.

Creating simple volumes using the command line or a script requires that you know whether the disk you're creating the volume on is a dynamic or basic disk. The DiskPart tool is not as flexible as the Disk Management snap-in, which automatically adjusts to create either a volume or a partition depending on the disk type. With DiskPart, you must create a partition on a basic disk and a volume on a dynamic disk.

How to Create a Spanned Volume

A spanned volume uses the free space on more than one physical hard disk to create a bigger volume. The portions of disk used to create the volume do not need to be the same size and can actually include more than one free space on a disk. A spanned volume provides no additional speed benefits and increases the risk of catastrophic failure leading to data loss. The failure of any disk involved in the spanned volume will make the entire volume unavailable.

NOTE To achieve a speed benefit with multiple disks, you must use striping, such as that provided by RAID 1 or RAID 5. With striping, every file on a volume is evenly distributed between multiple physical disks. With striping, files can be read from or written to multiple disks simultaneously, increasing throughput. Spanning simply appends one disk to the next, so any given file is probably stored only on a single disk. The best way to add striping is to use a computer or add-on card that supports hardware RAID.

If you still want to create a spanned volume, follow these steps:

1. Open the Disk Management snap-in.
2. Right-click a free-space segment that you want to include in the spanned volume and then select New Spanned Volume from the shortcut menu. The New Spanned Volume Wizard appears.
3. Click Next. On the Select Disks page, select from the available disks and then click Add to add the disks to the spanned volume. Select each disk in the Selected column and set the amount of space to use on that disk for the spanned volume. Click Next.
4. On the Assign Drive Letter Or Path page, the default is to assign the next available drive letter to the new volume. You can also mount the volume on an empty NTFS folder on an existing volume. Click Next.

5. On the Format Volume page, choose the formatting options for the new volume. Windows Vista and Windows 7 support only NTFS formatting from the Disk Management snap-in. To format with FAT or FAT32, you need to use the command line. Click Next.
6. Click Finish on the summary page to create the volume.

Creating a spanned volume using DiskPart is a somewhat more complicated process than creating a simple volume. You can't just create the spanned volume in one step; you need to first make sure that the disks to be used are converted to dynamic. Then you create a simple volume on the first disk of the spanned volume, extend the volume to the second disk, and then add any additional disks involved in the span. Finally, you must assign the volume to a drive letter or mount point.

How to Create a Striped Volume

A striped volume uses the free space on more than one physical hard disk to create a bigger volume. Unlike a spanned volume, however, a striped volume writes across all volumes in the stripe in small blocks, distributing the load across the disks in the volume. The portions of disk used to create the volume need to be the same size; the size of the smallest free space included in the striped volume will be the determinant.

A striped volume is faster than a simple volume because reads and writes happen across multiple disks at the same time. However, this additional speed comes with an increased risk of catastrophic failure leading to data loss when compared to a volume residing on a single physical disk because the failure of any disk involved in the spanned volume will make the entire volume unavailable. Therefore, it is critical to regularly back up striped volumes.

To create a striped volume, follow these steps:

1. Open the Disk Management snap-in.
2. Right-click a free-space segment that you want to include in the striped volume and then click New Striped Volume. The New Striped Volume Wizard appears.
3. Click Next. On the Select Disks page, select from the available disks and then click Add to add the disks to the striped volume. Set the amount of space to use on the disks for the striped volume. Click Next.
4. On the Assign Drive Letter Or Path page, the default is to assign the next available drive letter to the new volume. You can also mount the volume on an empty NTFS folder on an existing volume. Click Next.
5. On the Format Volume page of the New Striped Volume Wizard, choose the formatting options for the new volume. Windows Vista and Windows 7 support only NTFS formatting from the Disk Management snap-in. To format with FAT or FAT32, you need to use the command line. Click Next.
6. Click Finish on the summary page to create the volume. If the disks are basic disks, you'll be warned that this operation will convert them to dynamic disks. Click Yes to convert the disks and create the striped volume.

How to Resize a Volume

New in Windows Vista, and also included in Windows 7, is the ability to expand and contract simple volumes without a third-party tool. You can also expand and contract spanned volumes, but striped volumes are fixed in size. To change the size of a striped volume, you need to delete and re-create it.

> **NOTE** **Third-party products offer additional flexibility in resizing partitions, allowing the resizing of partitions with no available unallocated space immediately adjacent to the partition that you want to extend and also allowing you to control the placement of the unallocated space after shrinking the partition.**

To shrink a volume, follow these steps:

1. Open the Disk Management snap-in.
2. Right-click the volume you want to shrink and then click Shrink Volume.
3. The Shrink dialog box opens and shows the maximum amount by which you can shrink the volume in megabytes. If desired, decrease the amount to shrink the volume and then click Shrink. The shrink process will proceed without further prompting.

You can also use DiskPart interactively from an elevated command line, using exactly the same steps as you would use with a script. The following interactive steps show how to shrink a volume as much as possible.

```
DiskPart
```

```
Microsoft DiskPart version 6.1.7100
Copyright (C) 1999-2008 Microsoft Corporation.
On computer: WIN7
```

```
DISKPART> list volume
```

```
  Volume ###  Ltr  Label        Fs     Type        Size     Status     Info
  ----------  ---  -----------  -----  ----------  -------  ---------  --------
  Volume 0     F   New Volume   NTFS   Simple        20 GB  Healthy
  Volume 1     E   New Volume   NTFS   Simple        40 GB  Healthy
  Volume 2     R                       DVD-ROM        0 B   No Media
  Volume 3     C                NTFS   Partition     75 GB  Healthy    System
  Volume 4     D   New Volume   NTFS   Partition     52 GB  Healthy
```

```
DISKPART> select volume 4
```

```
Volume 4 is the selected volume.
```

```
DISKPART> shrink querymax

The maximum number of reclaimable bytes is:   26 GB

DISKPART> shrink

DiskPart successfully shrunk the volume by:   26 GB
```

> **NOTE** In the code list, the command *shrink querymax* queries the volume to determine the maximum amount of shrinkage that the volume will support. The actual number will depend on the amount of free space on the volume, the fragmentation level, and where critical files are located on the volume.

To extend a volume, the steps are similar:

1. Open the Disk Management snap-in.
2. Right-click the volume you want to extend and then click Extend Volume. The Extend Volume Wizard appears.
3. Click Next. The Select Disks page appears.
4. Select the disks and set the amount of space from each disk to include in the extended volume. If you are extending a volume on a basic disk and you choose noncontiguous unallocated space or space on a second disk, the extension will also convert any disks involved to dynamic disks as part of the extension. Click Next.
5. On the Completing The Extend Volume Wizard page, click Finish. If the extension requires conversion to a dynamic disk, you'll see a warning.

How to Delete a Volume

You can delete a volume from either the Disk Management snap-in or the command line. Deleting a volume permanently erases the data stored on the volume.

From the Disk Management snap-in, simply right-click the volume and then click Delete Volume. From the DiskPart command-line tool at an elevated command prompt, select the volume and then use the *delete volume* command, as the following code demonstrates.

```
DiskPart

Microsoft DiskPart version 6.1.7100
Copyright (C) 1999-2008 Microsoft Corporation.
On computer: WIN7

DISKPART> list volume
```

```
Volume ###  Ltr  Label        Fs     Type        Size     Status     Info
----------  ---  -----------  -----  ----------  -------  ---------  --------
Volume 0     F   New Volume   NTFS   Simple        20 GB  Healthy
Volume 1     E   New Volume   NTFS   Simple        40 GB  Healthy
Volume 2     R                       DVD-ROM        0 B   No Media
Volume 3     C                NTFS   Partition     75 GB  Healthy    System
Volume 4     D   New Volume   NTFS   Partition     52 GB  Healthy
```

```
DISKPART> select volume 0
```

```
Volume 0 is the selected volume.
```

```
DISKPART> delete volume
```

```
DiskPart successfully deleted the volume.
```

How to Create and Use a Virtual Hard Disk

Virtual hard disks (VHDs) are a file type that acts like a hard disk. In previous versions of Windows, VHDs were used by virtual machines, such as those created by Microsoft Virtual Server 2005 or Microsoft Virtual PC. Additionally, Complete PC Backup in Windows Vista created a copy of the computer's hard disk as a VHD disk image.

Beginning with Windows 7, you can now mount VHDs exactly like a physical disk. By mounting a VHD, you can easily copy files to and from the virtual disk. Additionally, Windows 7 can be configured to boot from a VHD, as described in Chapter 29.

You can create a VHD from either the Disk Management snap-in or the command line. After you create the VHD, you must attach it and then format it before you can use it, just like a physical partition.

From the Disk Management console, following these steps:

1. Right-click Disk Management and then click Create VHD. Follow the prompts that appear.
2. Right-click the new disk and then click Initialize Disk. Click OK.
3. Right-click the new disk and then click New Simple Volume (or select a different volume type, if available). Follow the prompts that appear.

The new virtual disk is ready to be used, just like any other disk.

From the DiskPart command-line tool at an elevated command prompt, run the *create vdisk* command and specify the *file* (to name the file) and *maximum* (to set the maximum size in megabytes) parameters. The following code demonstrates how to create a VHD file at C:\vdisks\disk1.vdh with a maximum file size of 16 GB (or 16,000 MB).

```
DiskPart
```

```
Microsoft DiskPart version 6.1.7100
Copyright (C) 1999-2008 Microsoft Corporation.
On computer: WIN7
```

```
DISKPART> create vdisk file="C:\vdisks\disk1.vhd" maximum=16000
```

```
  Volume ###  Ltr  Label        Fs     Type        Size     Status     Info
  ----------  ---  -----------  -----  ----------  -------  ---------  --------
  Volume 0     F   New Volume   NTFS   Simple        20 GB  Healthy
  Volume 1     E   New Volume   NTFS   Simple        40 GB  Healthy
  Volume 2     R                       DVD-ROM        0 B   No Media
  Volume 3     C                NTFS   Partition     75 GB  Healthy    System
  Volume 4     D   New Volume   NTFS   Partition     52 GB  Healthy
```

```
DISKPART> select volume 0
```

```
Volume 0 is the selected volume.
```

```
DISKPART> delete volume
```

```
DiskPart successfully deleted the volume.
```

For additional options, run the command *help create vdisk* at the DiskPart command prompt.

After you create a VHD, you must attach it, create a partition, assign it a drive letter, and format it before it can be used. The following script (which must be run within a DiskPart session) demonstrates how to do this.

```
create vdisk file="C:\vdisks\disk1.vhd" maximum=16000
attach vdisk
create partition primary
assign letter=g
format
```

File System Fragmentation

As files are created, deleted, and modified over time, their size and physical location on the hard disk will change. If a file size needs to increase and the hard disk doesn't have room directly adjacent to the existing file, the file system automatically places the new portion of the file where it can find the room and then marks the necessary structures so that the file system can find the entire file when an application needs it. The file is now in two (or more) fragments.

Fragmentation is normal behavior and is completely transparent to both applications and users. The problem is that over time, more and more files become fragmented and even highly fragmented, increasing the amount of time that it takes for the hard disk controller to locate all of the fragments. Not only does this slow down file access, but it also places additional stress on the hard disk itself.

By default, Windows Vista and Windows 7 will defragment the hard drive at 1:00 A.M. every Wednesday. If the computer is off at this time, defragmentation will start shortly after the computer boots next. Ideally, defragmentation will run when the computer is not in use, minimizing the performance impact. However, the user impact is minimal because the defragmenter uses both low CPU priority and low-priority input/output (I/O).

Unlike earlier versions of Windows, Windows 7 recognizes solid-state drives (SSDs) and disables automatic defragmentation. Defragmentation does not improve the performance of SSDs and can decrease the lifetime of the SSD by unnecessarily reading and writing data.

HOW IT WORKS

Defragmentation Algorithm Improvements

Many systems administrators have been captivated by the graphical defragmentation displays in previous versions of Windows. You'll notice the graphics are gone in Windows Vista and Windows 7. Unfortunately, displaying the layout of files and highlighting files that had even one fragmentation made many performance-focused administrators obsessed with eliminating every single fragmented file.

Fragmentation does reduce disk performance, but having a few fragments in a large file doesn't make a difference—even years of reading and writing a large file with a single fragment would never add up to a significant amount of time. For this reason, Microsoft tweaked the defragmentation algorithm so that it does not defragment a file if a segment is longer than 64 MB. In those circumstances, the relatively significant effort required to rearrange files just to combine two 64-MB fragments isn't worth the effort, so Windows doesn't bother.

If you run a different defragmentation tool (including the defragmenter in Windows XP), those fragments will show up, and they'll probably look significant because the fragmented file is so large. (Typically, the entire file appears red if it has even a single fragment.) Trust the algorithm, though—a few fragments don't matter.

To defragment a file system or configure the automatic disk defragmentation schedule manually, follow these steps:

1. Click Start and then click Computer.
2. Right-click the drive and then click Properties.
3. Click the Tools tab and then click Defragment Now. The Disk Defragmenter appears, as shown in Figure 16-1.

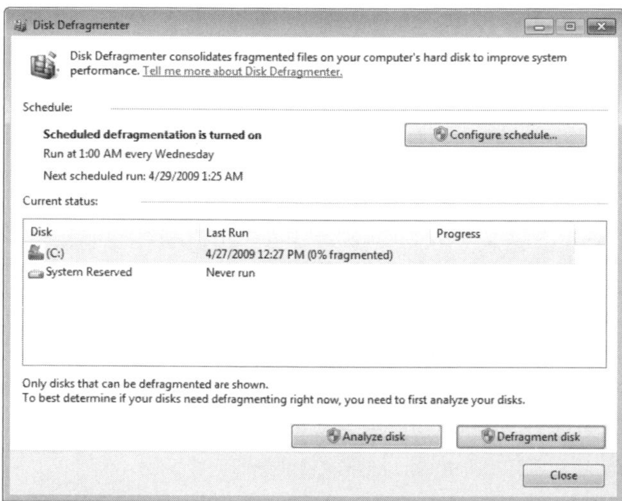

FIGURE 16-1 The Windows 7 Disk Defragmenter interface

4. In the Disk Defragmenter dialog box, click Defragment Disk to begin defragmentation.

You can continue to use the computer while defragmentation takes place, but it might be a little slower. You can also adjust the defragmentation schedule for a single computer from this interface.

For more complete control of defragmentation, you can use the command-line defragmentation tool, Defrag.exe, from an elevated command prompt. Defrag.exe has the following syntax, which has changed since Windows Vista.

```
Defrag <volume> | /C | /E <volumes> [/A | /X | /T] [/H] [/M] [/U] [/V]
```

The options for Defrag.exe are:

- ***<volume>*** The drive letter or mount point of the volume to defragment.
- ***/C*** Defragment all local volumes on the computer.
- ***/E*** Defragment all local volumes on the computer except those specified.
- ***/A*** Display a fragmentation analysis report for the specified volume without defragmenting it. Analysis reports resemble the following.

```
Post Defragmentation Report:

        Volume Information:
                Volume size                             = 68.56 GB
                Free space                              = 58.78 GB
                Total fragmented space                  = 0%
                Largest free space extent               = 31.64 GB

You do not need to defragment this volume
```

- ***/X*** Perform free-space consolidation. Free-space consolidation is useful if you need to shrink a volume, and it can reduce fragmentation of future files.
- ***/T*** Track an operation already in progress on the specified volume.
- ***/H*** Run the operation at normal priority instead of the default low priority. Specify this option if a computer is not otherwise in use.
- ***/M*** Defragment multiple volumes simultaneously, in parallel. This is primarily useful for computers that can access multiple disks simultaneously, such as those using SCSI- or SATA-based disks rather than disks with an IDE interface.
- ***/U*** Print the progress of the operation on the screen.
- ***/V*** Verbose mode. Provides additional detail and statistics.

Backup And Restore

Windows 7 includes the Backup And Restore Control Panel tool, as shown in Figure 16-2, which is an updated version of the Backup And Restore Center. The Backup And Restore Center uses Shadow Copy to take a snapshot of your files, even allowing the backup to back up open files completely without problems.

The Backup And Restore Center supports two kinds of backup:

- **System Image** Previously known as Complete PC Backup in Windows Vista, the System Image backup backs up an entire volume to a virtual hard disk (.vhd) disk-image file (compacted to remove empty space), allowing you to quickly restore a computer and all running applications. However, backups take up much more space and are more time consuming. System Image backups typically need to be done only once after a computer is initially configured. Complete PC Backup in Windows Vista could be stored only on local media, such as a DVD or a removable hard disk, but System Image backups in Windows 7 can also be saved to shared folders.
- **Files and folders** Stores user files and documents to compressed (.zip) files. File backups are incremental by default and thus are very quick. Additionally, file backups do not back up system files, program files, EFS-encrypted files, temporary files, files in the Recycle Bin, or user profile settings. File backups can back up to either local media or a shared folder on the network.

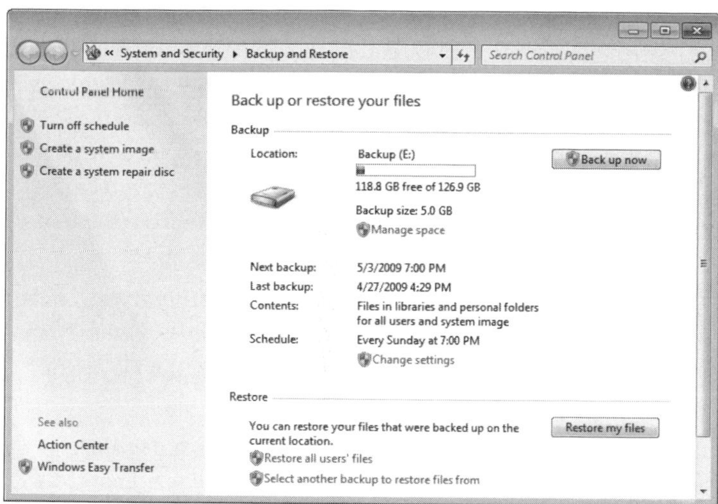

FIGURE 16-2 The Backup And Restore Control Panel tool

> ***NOTE*** **File backups are faster because they don't back up system or application files. However, System Image backups are surprisingly fast. Because System Image backups read the disk block by block, the read performance is faster than reading the disk file by file, which requires the disk to jump between different files.**

Backup And Restore supports backing up data files to CD, DVD, hard disk (fixed or removable), or a network share. The default settings for the first backup and for scheduled backups perform both a System Image backup and a files and folders backup on a weekly basis.

> ***NOTE*** **You cannot save backups to a universal serial bus (USB) flash drive, but you can use an external USB hard drive or CF or SD memory cards.**

How File Backups Work

Backup And Restore provides graphical tools for manually initiating backup and restore sessions and for scheduling automatic backups. All client computers that store important data should have automatic backup scheduled. For more information, read the section titled "Best Practices for Computer Backups" later in this chapter.

After you first configure automatic file backup using Backup And Restore, Windows 7 will regularly back up all files. The first time a backup is performed, a full backup is done, including all important user documents. Subsequent backups are incremental, backing up only changed files. Older backups are discarded when the disk begins to run out of space.

For example, if you configure a nightly scheduled backup and change a file every day, a copy of that file will be stored in each day's Backup Files folder (described in "File and Folder Backup Structure" later in this chapter). By storing multiple versions of a single file, Windows 7 gives users the opportunity to choose from several older copies of a file when using the Previous Versions tool (also described later in this chapter). When you restore files, you only need to restore from a single backup because Windows 7 automatically locates the most recent version of each file. In previous versions of Windows, you need to first restore from the last full backup and then restore any updates from incremental or differential backups.

Windows 7 uses Shadow Copy to back up the last saved version of a file. Therefore, if a file is open during the backup (such as the storage file for local e-mail or an open document), the file will be backed up. However, any changes the user makes since last saving the file are not backed up.

Only administrators can configure scheduled backups or manually initiate a backup. However, once configured, scheduled backups do not require a user to provide administrative credentials. Restoring files does not require administrative privileges unless a user attempts to restore another user's file.

If you perform a file backup to a shared folder, the credentials used to run the backup must have Full Control share and NTFS permissions for the destination folder (known as Co-owner permissions in the Windows 7 Setup Wizard). To reduce security risks, set up a user account to be used only by the backup application, and configure share and NTFS permissions to grant access only to the backup user. The backup account requires administrative privileges to the computer being backed up, but it needs permissions only to the share and folder on the target computer.

File and Folder Backup Structure

The Backup tool in Windows XP creates a single file with a .bkf extension when you perform a backup. Backups in Windows Vista and Windows 7 provide a more flexible and reliable file structure.

When a user chooses to perform a backup to an external hard disk, Windows 7 automatically creates a folder in the root of the hard disk using the computer name. Within that folder, backups are saved in this format: "Backup Set *<year-month-day>* *<time>*". For example, if your computer name is Computer, your backup location is E, and you backed up on January 22, 2007, at 16:32:00, that backup would be located in "E:\Computer\Backup Set 2007-01-22 163200".

The folder structure is created when the user first performs a backup. Automatic incremental backups that occur afterward store additional copies of changed files within subfolders. However, the name of the Backup Set folder is never updated, so the date indicated by the folder name will be older than the dates of the files contained within the folder. A new Backup Set folder is created only when the user performs a full backup.

Within each Backup Set folder, Backup creates a series of Backup Files folders that are named using the date on which the incremental backup was performed. Additionally, Backup creates a Catalogs folder within the root Backup Set folder. Figure 16-3 shows a backup folder structure for a computer named WIN7 that is configured to save backups to the E drive. The File And Folder backup is stored in the WIN7 folder, whereas the System Image backup is stored in the WIndowsImageBackup folder. File permissions on all folders and files are restricted to administrators, who have full control, and to the user who configured the backup, who has read-only permissions by default.

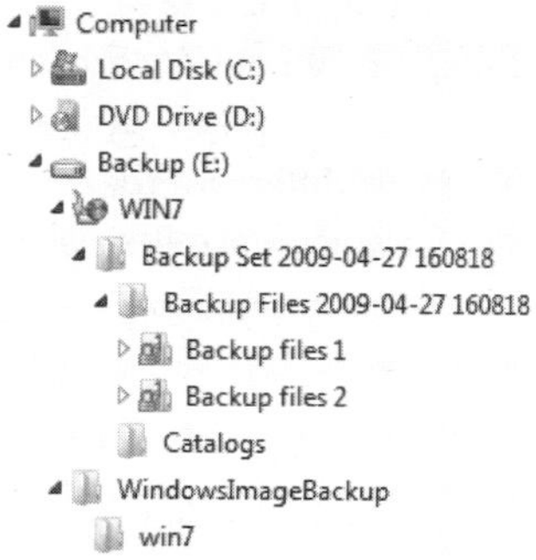

- Computer
  - Local Disk (C:)
  - DVD Drive (D:)
  - Backup (E:)
    - WIN7
      - Backup Set 2009-04-27 160818
        - Backup Files 2009-04-27 160818
          - Backup files 1
          - Backup files 2
        - Catalogs
    - WindowsImageBackup
      - win7

FIGURE 16-3 The backup folder structure includes separate folders for each computer, backup set, backup session, and catalog.

> ***NOTE*** **When restoring files, Windows 7 looks for a folder with the current computer's name in the root of the backup media. If you need to restore files created on a different Windows 7 computer, you can either rename the folder to the current computer's name or perform an Advanced Restore and select the Files From A Backup Made On A Different Computer option on the What Do You Want To Restore page of the Restore Files (Advanced) Wizard.**

Within each of the backup folders is a series of compressed (.zip) files named "Backup files *xxx*.zip", where *xxx* is an incremental number to make each filename unique. For example, a backup folder might contain the following files:

- Backup files 1.zip
- Backup files 2.zip
- Backup files 138.zip

> ***NOTE*** **Because the .zip files used for backups are compressed and stored in fewer files, they take up less space on the backup media. Overall, backups take about half the space of the original files. Compression levels vary widely, though. Text and Extensible Markup Language (XML) files are typically compressed to less than one-tenth the original space. Backups of video, music, and picture files take up the same space as the original files because the files are already compressed.**

These are standard ZIP files that you can open by using the ZIP decompression capabilities in Windows or by using other ZIP file tools. Because Windows can search .zip files, you can quickly find a backup of a specific file by searching the backup folders and then extracting that file from the compressed folder without directly accessing the Backup And Restore tool. This makes restoring files possible even if you need to use a different operating system.

The Catalogs folder contains a file named GlobalCatalog.wbcat. This file uses a proprietary format and contains an index of the individual files that have been backed up and the ZIP file within which the backup is contained, which Windows 7 uses to locate a file quickly for restoration. The Catalogs folder also contains a list of file permissions for each backed-up file. Therefore, permissions will be intact if you restore files using the Backup And Restore tool. However, if you restore a file from the compressed folder directly, the file will inherit the permissions of the parent folder rather than keeping the file permissions of the original file.

How System Image Backups Work

System Image backups make a block-by-block backup of your system volume to a .vhd file, which must be stored on local storage, such as a second hard disk. Like file backups, subsequent backups to the same media automatically perform only an incremental backup. In other words, only the portions of the hard disk that have changed are copied to the existing System Image backup. Unlike file backups, only a single version of the System Image backup is kept—multiple versions are not stored.

The Backup And Restore tool does not provide a graphical tool for scheduling automatic System Image backups. Instead, you should rely on automatic file backups and manually create a System Image backup only after you have made significant changes to a computer's configuration. Alternatively, you can use the WBAdmin command-line tool to schedule a System Image backup, as described in the next section.

How to Start a System Image Backup from the Command Line

The simplest way to initiate a System Image backup is to follow the prompts in the Backup And Restore Center. If you want to automate or schedule System Image backups, however, you can use the WBAdmin.exe command-line tool.

For example, to initiate a System Image backup of the C drive to the L drive, you can run the following command line from an elevated command prompt.

```
Wbadmin start backup -backupTarget:L: -include:C: -quiet
```

```
wbadmin 1.0 - Backup command-line tool
(C) Copyright 2004 Microsoft Corp.

Retrieving volume information...
```

```
This will back up volume Local Disk(C:) to L:.

The backup operation to L: is starting.

Creating a shadow copy of the volumes specified for backup...
Creating a backup of volume Local Disk(C:), copied (0%).
Creating a backup of volume Local Disk(C:), copied (18%).
Creating a backup of volume Local Disk(C:), copied (40%).
Creating a backup of volume Local Disk(C:), copied (77%).
Creating a backup of volume Local Disk(C:), copied (98%).
The backup of volume Local Disk(C:) successfully completed.
The backup operating successfully completed.

Summary of the backup operation:
------------------

Backup of volume Local Disk(C:) completed successfully.
```

The behavior is identical to the System Image backups initiated from the graphical Backup And Restore tool. The first time you initiate a System Image backup, it backs up every block on the system volume. Each subsequent time, it simply updates the previous backup.

You can use the same command to schedule a task from the command line. If you use Task Scheduler, you must configure the task to run with administrative privileges. You can do this by providing an administrative user account and selecting the Run With Highest Privileges check box on the General tab of the task's Properties dialog box.

How to Restore a System Image Backup

Because System Image backups must rewrite the entire contents of the disk, you can restore System Image backups only by booting from the Windows 7 DVD and loading System Recovery tools. Restoring a System Image backup from System Recovery tools allows you to quickly get a computer running after replacing a failed hard disk or when the previous operating system installation has been corrupted (for example, by an irreparable malware installation).

To restore a System Image backup, follow these steps:

1. Connect the backup media to your computer. For example, if the System Image backup was performed to an external USB hard drive, connect that drive to your computer.
2. Insert the Windows 7 DVD in your computer. Ensure that the computer is configured to boot from the DVD.
3. Restart your computer. When prompted to boot from the DVD, press a key. If you are not prompted to boot from the DVD, you might have to configure your computer's startup sequence.

4. Windows 7 Setup loads. When prompted, select your regional preferences and then click Next.
5. Click Repair Your Computer to launch RecEnv.exe.
6. In the System Recovery Options dialog box, click Restore Your Computer Using A System Image That Was Created Earlier, as shown in Figure 16-4. If the backup was saved to a DVD, insert the DVD now. Click Next. The Windows System Image Restore Wizard appears.

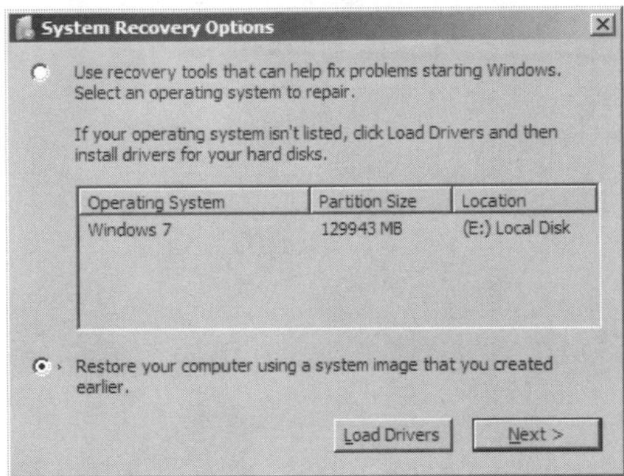

FIGURE 16-4 You can restore a System Image backup from System Recovery.

On the Select A System Image Backup page, the most recent backup will be automatically selected. If this is the correct backup to restore, click Next, as shown in Figure 16-5. Otherwise, click Select A System Image, click Next, and then select the correct backup.

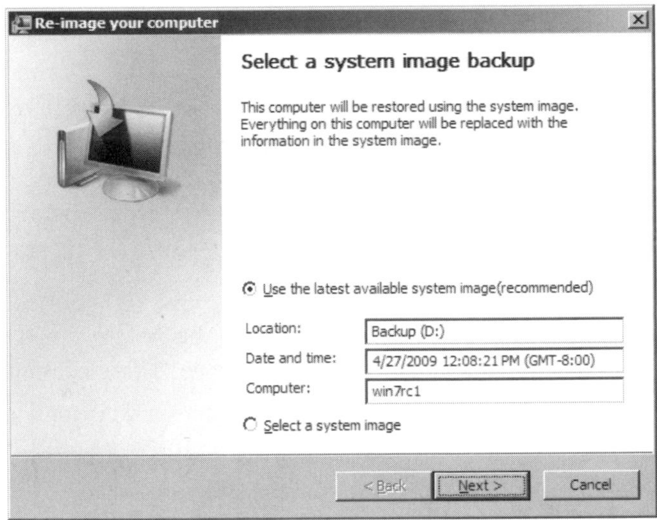

FIGURE 16-5 Select the correct System Image backup to restore.

7. On the next page, select the Format And Repartition Disks check box only if the disk is not formatted. Be sure that you are prepared to overwrite all of the data on your current disk and then click Next, as shown in Figure 16-6.

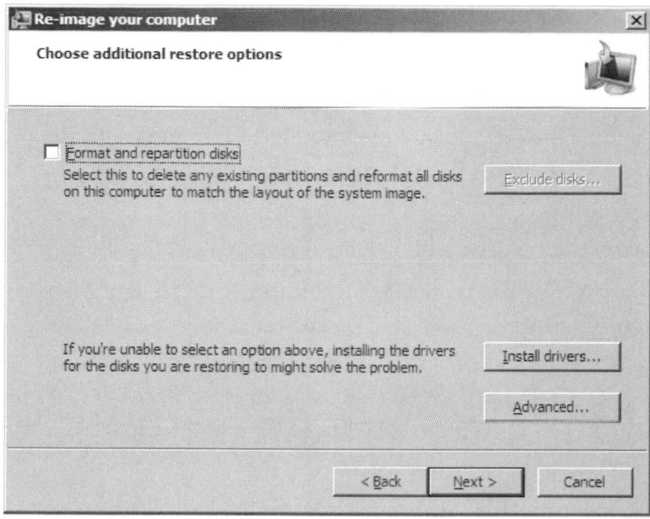

FIGURE 16-6 The System Image Restore Wizard writes an entire disk image, including system files and user documents.

8. On the final page, click Finish. When prompted, click Yes.

Windows System Image Restore reads the data from the backup and overwrites existing files. Typically, the restore will take 30 to 60 seconds per gigabyte. You can restore to a different-sized hard disk as long as the hard disk is large enough to store the backup. After the restore is complete, the computer will restart using the restored files.

System Image Backup Structure

System Image backups use a similar folder structure to file backups. When you create a System Image backup, Windows creates a WindowsImageBackup folder in the root of the backup media. Within that folder, it creates a folder with the current computer's name. It then creates a Catalog folder containing the GlobalCatalog and BackupGlobalCatalog files and a "Backup *<year>-<month>-<date> <time>*" folder containing the disk image file.

To back up an entire volume, System Image creates a .vhd disk image file, which is the same file format used by Virtual PC and Virtual Server. In fact, you can mount the .vhd files as secondary disks in either Virtual PC or Virtual Server, granting you quick access to individual files contained within the backup from a virtual computer. You cannot easily boot from a System Image .vhd file, however.

System Image backups also create several other files:

- A MediaId file in the *<ComputerName>* folder to identify the disk image

- GlobalCatalog and BackupGlobalCatalog files in the Catalog folder to track the System Image backup image versions
- Numerous XML files in the Backup folder, which contain configuration settings for the backup file

Best Practices for Computer Backups

The backup and restore tools built into Windows 7 are intended for home users and small businesses. Typically, enterprises will need a third-party backup-management tool to manage the large number of client computers.

However, Windows 7 backup can be very useful in many common scenarios:

- **Mobile users** Mobile users often travel with their computers, preventing network backups from succeeding. For these users, you should provide external storage that they can use to back up their computers while they are away from the office. Typically, this would be an external USB hard drive. Mobile users can also back up to writable DVDs (if the computer is equipped with a DVD burner) or a large-capacity portable audio player that can act as an external hard disk.
- **Users who work from home** Users who work from home may not have sufficient bandwidth to participate in network backups. Additionally, their connectivity may not always be stable enough to allow them to store important files on your internal servers. To reduce the risk of these workers losing important data, equip users with external storage and configure automatic backups.
- **Small or branch offices** To back up computers in small or branch offices with a 100-Mbps or faster LAN, configure a server with sufficient disk storage for backups from each computer. Then schedule automatic backups to store files to a shared folder on the server. Alternatively, you can use network attached storage (NAS).

Keeping an external hard disk attached to a computer with automatic updates enabled is the most convenient and reliable way to back up a computer. However, because the backup media is physically close to the computer, this configuration does not protect against common data recovery scenarios such as theft, fire, or electrical surges. To protect against these threats, users should perform weekly full backups to a second external storage device and then store that storage device securely at a different location. For the best protection, users should have two off-site storage devices and alternate between them so that one device is always off-site, even when a backup is being performed.

How to Manage Backup Using Group Policy Settings

You can use Group Policy to manage Windows Backup options in an enterprise environment. The policy settings for Windows Backup are both user and computer settings. The user-specific settings are client-only settings and are found in the following location:

User Configuration\Policies\Administrative Templates\Windows Components\Backup\Client

The computer settings are for both the client and the server and are found in the following locations:

Computer Configuration\Policies\Administrative Templates\Windows Components\Backup\Client

Computer Configuration\Policies\Administrative Templates\Windows Components\Backup\Server

Table 16-1 lists the available policy settings for Windows Backup. Client settings are available for both User and Computer scopes, but Server settings are available only in the Computer scope. These settings are written to the registry on targeted computers under the following registry key:

HKLM\Software\Policies\Microsoft\Windows\Backup

TABLE 16-1 Group Policy Settings for Windows Backup

POLICY	CLIENT OR SERVER	DESCRIPTION
Prevent The User From Running The Backup Status And Configuration Program	Client	Enabling this policy prevents the user from running the Backup Status And Configuration program. The user will be unable to configure, initiate, or restore a backup.
Prevent Backing Up To Local Disks	Client	Enabling this policy prevents the user from choosing a local disk (internal or external) as a backup target.
Prevent Backing Up To Network Location	Client	Enabling this policy prevents the user from choosing a network share as a backup target.
Prevent Backing Up To Optical Media (CD/DVD)	Client	Enabling this policy prevents the user from choosing a CD or DVD as a backup target.
Turn Off The Ability To Back Up Data Files	Client	Enabling this policy prevents the user from running the file backup application. The restore functionality is still available, as is Windows System Image Backup.
Turn Off Restore Functionality	Client	Enabling this policy prevents the user from using restore. File backups and Windows System Image Backup are still available.
Turn Off The Ability To Create A System Image	Client	Enabling this policy prevents the user from using Windows System Image Backup. File backups and restores are still available.
Allow Only System Backup	Server	Enabling this policy prevents the user from backing up non-system volumes.
Disallow Locally Attached Storage As Backup Target	Server	Enabling this policy prevents the user from backing up to locally attached storage devices.

POLICY	CLIENT OR SERVER	DESCRIPTION
Disallow Network As Backup Target	Server	Enabling this policy prevents the user from backing up to a network share.
Disallow Optical Media As Backup Target	Server	Enabling this policy prevents the user from backing up to CD or DVD drives.
Disallow Run-Once Backups	Server	Enabling this policy prevents the user from running on-demand backups.

Previous Versions and Shadow Copies

Windows 7 can also restore earlier versions of files so that users can quickly recover a file that has been accidentally modified, corrupted, or deleted. Depending on the type of file or folder, users can open, save to a different location, or restore a previous version. The sections that follow describe the Volume Shadow Copy technology and the Previous Versions user interface.

How Volume Shadow Copy Works

To provide backups for files that are in use, Windows 7 uses the Volume Shadow Copy service, which was first introduced with Windows XP. Volume Shadow Copy mitigates file access between applications and the backup process. In other words, if a backup tool needs to access a file currently in use, Volume Shadow Copy creates a shadow copy of that file and then provides the backup process access to the shadow copy. Figure 16-7 illustrates the relationship between Volume Shadow Copy features.

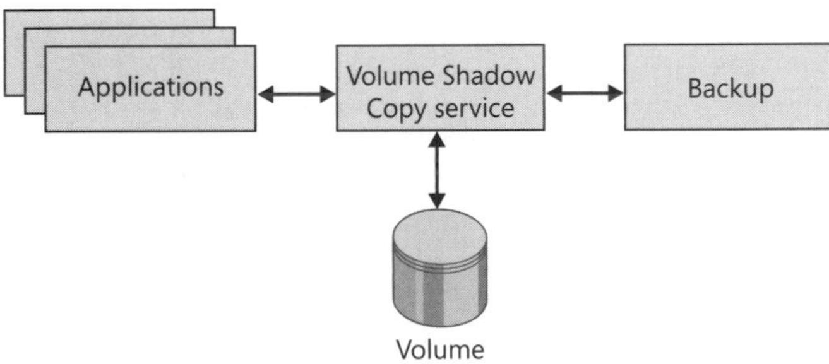

FIGURE 16-7 Volume Shadow Copy allows you to back up open files.

Volume Shadow Copy works with any application. Some applications, however, can communicate directly with the Volume Shadow Copy service to ensure that backed-up files are consistent. If an application keeps several files in use at the same time, they might become inconsistent if two files must be synchronized and one of those files is updated after another is backed up in an earlier state.

NOTE Application developers can build Volume Shadow Copy integration into their applications using the Volume Shadow Copy Service software development kit (SDK). For more information, go to *http://www.microsoft.com/downloads/details.aspx?FamilyID=0b4f56e4-0ccc-4626-826a-ed2c4c95c871*.

To provide backup access to a file that is open and being updated, Volume Shadow Copy needs to be able to make two versions of the file accessible: one that is currently in use by the application and a second that is a snapshot of the file when backup first requested access to a volume shadow copy. Volume Shadow Copy handles this transparently by storing copies of changed files in Volume Shadow Copy storage. Volume Shadow Copy stores a copy of the original state of any modified portion of a file, which allows the original file to be updated without interrupting the backup process. In other words, if a user modifies a file after the backup starts, the file will be in the state it was in when the backup began.

How to Manage Shadow Copies

You can manage the Volume Shadow Copy service using the Vssadmin command-line tool from an elevated command prompt. You can use this tool to run the following commands:

- **Vssadmin List Providers** Lists registered Volume Shadow Copy providers. Windows 7 includes Microsoft Software Shadow Copy Provider 1.0.
- **Vssadmin List Shadows** Lists existing volume shadow copies, the time the shadow copy was created, and its location. The following sample output shows two shadow copies.

```
vssadmin 1.1 - Volume Shadow Copy Service administrative command-line tool
(C) Copyright 2001-2005 Microsoft Corp.

Contents of shadow copy set ID: {79f6e5e8-0211-43bf-9480-c65e51b4b40d}
   Contained 1 shadow copies at creation time: 12/20/2006 1:05:08 PM
      Shadow Copy ID: {26fc6f1c-9610-4c0c-b10b-7e9f6fab042c}
         Original Volume: (C:)\\?\Volume{3e59796e-cf1b-11da-af4b-806d6172696f}\
         Shadow Copy Volume: \\?\GLOBALROOT\Device\HarddiskVolumeShadowCopy1
         Originating Machine: WIN7
         Service Machine: WIN7
         Provider: 'Microsoft Software Shadow Copy provider 1.0'
         Type: DataVolumeRollback
         Attributes: Persistent, No auto release, No writers, Differential

Contents of shadow copy set ID: {d14c728d-ff85-4be1-b048-24f3aced48a9}
   Contained 1 shadow copies at creation time: 12/20/2006 4:42:12 PM
      Shadow Copy ID: {271752a4-e886-4c92-9671-10624ca36cd4}
         Original Volume: (C:)\\?\Volume{3e59796e-cf1b-11da-af4b-806d6172696f}\
         Shadow Copy Volume: \\?\GLOBALROOT\Device\HarddiskVolumeShadowCopy2
```

```
Originating Machine: WIN7
Service Machine: WIN7
Provider: 'Microsoft Software Shadow Copy provider 1.0'
Type: DataVolumeRollback
Attributes: Persistent, No auto release, No Writers, Differential
```

- **Vssadmin List ShadowStorage** Lists the volume shadow storage space currently in use, the space that is reserved for future use (labeled as allocated), and the maximum space that might be dedicated. This space is used to store changes while a shadow copy is active. The following sample output was generated using a computer that currently has about 3 GB of files stored in a shadow copy, but that might allocate as much as 6.4 GB.

```
Vssadmin 1.1 - Volume Shadow Copy Service administrative command-line tool
(C) Copyright 2001-2005 Microsoft Corp.

Shadow Copy Storage association
   For volume: (C:)\\?\Volume{3e59796e-cf1b-11da-af4b-806d6172696f}\
   Shadow Copy Storage volume: (C:)\\?\Volume{3e59796e-cf1b-11da-af4b-
806d6172696f}\
   Used Shadow Copy Storage space: 32.703 MB (0%)
   Allocated Shadow Copy Storage space: 1.904 GB (1%)
   Maximum Shadow Copy Storage space: 38.061 GB (30%)
```

- **Vssadmin List Volumes** Lists volumes that are eligible for shadow copies.
- **Vssadmin List Writers** Lists shadow copy writers, which support communicating with the Volume Shadow Copy service to ensure that files are captured in a consistent state. By default, subscribed writers include an operating system writer, a registry writer, a Windows Management Instrumentation (WMI) writer, and a search service writer, among others. SQL Server also provides a Volume Shadow Copy writer.
- **Vssadmin Resize ShadowStorage** Resizes Volume Shadow Copy storage. You can use this command to increase the maximum space that might be used by Volume Shadow Copy. Typically, this is unnecessary. However, if you discover that backups are failing on a computer because of an extremely high volume of changes during a backup and if Vssadmin List ShadowStorage reveals that the used Shadow Copy Storage space is at the maximum, you might be able to resolve the problem by manually increasing the maximum size.

NOTE **Vssadmin in Windows 7 does not provide all of the commands that Windows Server 2008 provides because the ability to manually create and manage shadow copies typically is unnecessary on client computers.**

How to Restore a File with Previous Versions

With Previous Versions, users can quickly restore a file to an earlier state that was established either when a shadow copy or a file backup was made. Previous Versions cannot restore a file from a System Image backup, even though you might be able to extract the file manually from the System Image disk image. However, System Image backups do initiate a Volume Shadow Copy, and a version of a file might be available from the shadow copy.

To restore an earlier version of a file, follow these steps:

1. Right-click the file and then click Restore Previous Versions. The Previous Versions tab appears, as shown in Figure 16-8.

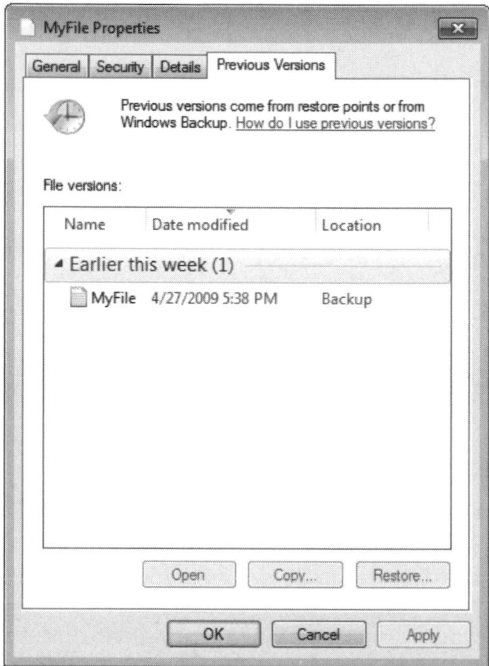

FIGURE 16-8 Previous Versions allows users to restore an earlier version of the file without calling the Support Center.

> ***NOTE*** **If you delete a file but remember the filename, create a file with the exact same filename in the same folder, and follow the steps in this section using the new file. The file can be empty; as long as the filename matches, you'll be able to restore an earlier version. Otherwise, you can view the Previous Versions tab in the Properties dialog box for the parent folder and restore only the file you need. You can also browse for the file manually using the Backup And Restore Center.**

2. If an earlier version of the file is available, click it and then click Restore if the button is available. For system files, you can click Open or Copy. The Copy File dialog box appears, as shown in Figure 16-9.

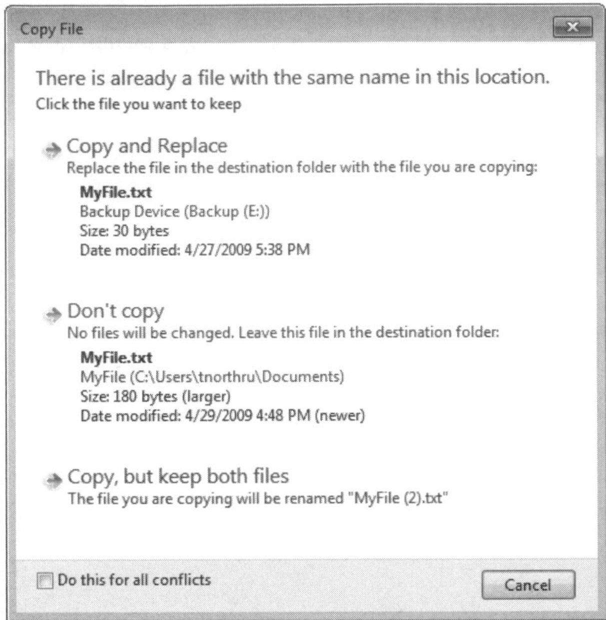

FIGURE 16-9 When restoring a file, you can overwrite the existing file or save it with a different name.

3. You can choose to overwrite the existing file or save the recovered file with a different name.
4. Click Finish.

To allow users to take advantage of previous versions, provide them with an online backup solution using the Backup And Restore Center. Most often, backups for computers connected to your internal network are saved to a shared folder on a server. For mobile users, backups can be saved to external hard disks.

How to Configure Previous Versions with Group Policy Settings

You can configure Previous Versions with six Group Policy settings, located in Policies\Administrative Templates\Windows Components\Windows Explorer\Previous Versions (under both Computer Configuration and User Configuration):

- **Prevent Restoring Previous Versions From Backups** When you enable this setting, the Restore button is disabled on the Previous Versions tab. Users will still be able to see whether previous versions are available (unless you enable the following setting), but the versions will be inaccessible. This setting is disabled by default.

- **Prevent Restoring Local Previous Versions** When you enable this setting, the Restore button on the Previous Versions tab is disabled when the file to be restored is a local file. This setting is disabled by default.
- **Prevent Restoring Remote Previous Versions** When you enable this setting, the Restore button on the Previous Versions tab is disabled when the file to be restored is on a remote computer. This setting is disabled by default.
- **Hide Previous Versions List For Local Files** When you enable this setting, the Previous Versions tab is removed from the file Properties dialog box, and the Restore Previous Versions menu item is removed from the file shortcut menu. This setting is disabled by default.
- **Hide Previous Versions List For Remote Files** When you enable this setting, the behavior is the same as with the previous setting, but it affects files on remote computers instead of local files. This setting is disabled by default.
- **Hide Previous Versions Of Files On Backup Location** When you enable this setting, previous versions that were created with a backup are hidden. Previous versions created by shadow copies will still be available. This setting is disabled by default.

Windows ReadyBoost

Windows 7 supports Windows ReadyBoost, originally introduced with Windows Vista. ReadyBoost uses external USB flash drives as a hard disk cache, thus improving disk read performance in some circumstances. Supported external storage types include USB thumb drives as shown in Figure 16-10, SD cards, and CF cards.

FIGURE 16-10 ReadyBoost uses flash storage to improve disk read performance.

Unlike Windows Vista, Windows 7 recognizes that ReadyBoost will not provide a performance gain when the primary disk is an SSD. Windows 7 disables ReadyBoost when reading from an SSD drive.

External storage must meet the following requirements:

- Capacity of at least 256 MB, with at least 64 kilobytes (KB) of free space. The 4-GB limit of Windows Vista has been removed.
- At least a 2.5 MB/sec throughput for 4-KB random reads
- At least a 1.75 MB/sec throughput for 1-MB random writes

Unfortunately, most flash storage provides only raw throughput performance statistics measured under ideal conditions, not the very specific 4-KB random reads required by

ReadyBoost. Therefore, the most effective way to determine whether a specific flash drive meets ReadyBoost requirements is simply to test it. Windows Vista and Windows 7 automatically test removable storage when attached. If a storage device fails the test, Windows will automatically retest the storage on a regular basis.

Some devices will show the phrase "Enhanced for Windows ReadyBoost" on the packaging, which means that Microsoft has tested the device specifically for this feature. If you connect a flash drive that meets these requirements, AutoPlay will provide ReadyBoost as an option, as shown in Figure 16-11.

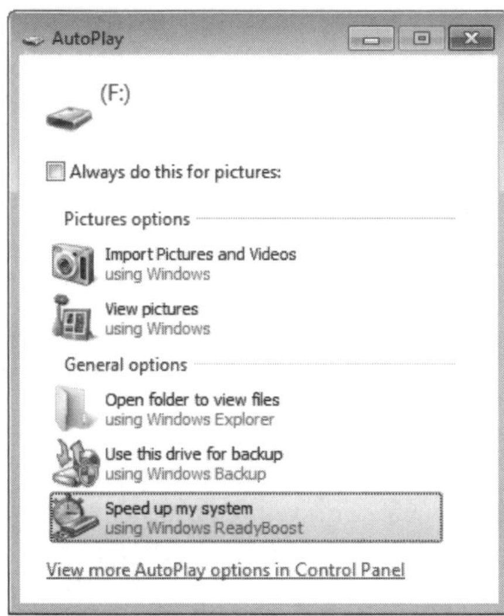

FIGURE 16-11 AutoPlay will prompt the user to use a compatible device with ReadyBoost.

Alternatively, you can configure ReadyBoost by right-clicking the device in Windows Explorer, clicking Properties, and then clicking the ReadyBoost tab. The only configuration option is to configure the space reserved for the cache. You must reserve at least 256 MB. Larger caches can improve performance, but the ReadyBoost cache cannot be greater than 4 GB on a FAT32 file system or greater than 32 GB on an NTFS file system.

Windows Vista and Windows 7 use the Windows SuperFetch algorithm (the successor to Windows Prefetcher) to determine which files should be stored in the cache. SuperFetch monitors files that users access (including system files, application files, and documents) and preloads those files into the ReadyBoost cache. All files in the cache are encrypted using 128-bit AES if the flash storage device is removable, but hardware manufacturers can choose to disable encryption on internal, nonremovable ReadyBoost devices. Because the ReadyBoost cache stores a copy of the files, the flash drive can be removed at any point without affecting the computer—Windows will simply read the original files from the disk.

ReadyBoost provides the most significant performance improvement under the following circumstances:

- The computer has a slow hard disk drive. Computers with a primary hard disk Windows Experience Index (WEI) subscore lower than 4.0 will see the most significant improvements.
- The flash storage provides fast, random, nonsequential reads. Sequential read speed is less important.
- The flash storage is connected by a fast bus. Typically, USB memory card readers are not sufficiently fast. However, connecting flash memory to an internal memory card reader might provide sufficient performance.

Computers with fast hard disks (such as 7,200- or 10,000-RPM disks) might realize minimal performance gains because of the already high disk I/O. ReadyBoost will read files from the cache only when doing so will improve performance. Hard disks outperform flash drives during sequential reads, but flash drives are faster during nonsequential reads (because of the latency caused when the drive head must move to a different disk sector). Therefore, ReadyBoost reads from the cache only for nonsequential reads.

NOTE **In the author's informal experiments, enabling ReadyBoost on a 1-GB flash drive on a laptop computer with a WEI disk rating of 3.7 decreased Windows startup times by more than 30 percent. Gains on computers with a WEI disk rating of more than 5 were minimal.**

ReadyBoost creates a disk cache file named ReadyBoost.sfcache in the root of the flash drive. The file is immediately created for the full size of the specified cache; however, Windows will gradually fill the space with cached content.

To monitor ReadyBoost performance, use the System Tools\Performance\Monitoring Tools\Performance Monitor tool in the Computer Management console and add the ReadyBoost Cache counters. These counters enable you to monitor how much of the cache is currently being used and when the cache is read from or written to. It does not tell you exactly what performance benefit you are achieving by using ReadyBoost, however.

BitLocker Drive Encryption

BitLocker Drive Encryption is a new Windows Vista and Windows 7 feature that improves data integrity and confidentiality by encrypting entire volumes. Windows Vista must have Service Pack 1 (SP1) installed to encrypted non-system volumes. BitLocker can use Trusted Platform Module (TPM) security hardware to wrap and seal the keys used to encrypt the system volume, helping to protect the volumes from offline attacks. Alternatively, BitLocker can use a USB flash drive to store the startup key used to encrypt the volumes. BitLocker is available in the Enterprise and Ultimate Editions of Windows 7.

BitLocker should be used with a TPM when used to encrypt the system volume. A TPM is a hardware module embedded in the motherboards of many new laptops and some desktops. TPM modules must be version 1.2 for use with BitLocker.

If a TPM 1.2 module is not available, computers can still take advantage of BitLocker encryption technology on system volumes as long as the computer's BIOS supports reading from a USB flash device before the operating system is loaded. However, you cannot use BitLocker's integrity verification capabilities without a TPM 1.2 module.

Unlike EFS, BitLocker can encrypt entire volumes, including the page file, hibernation file, registry, and temporary files, which might hold confidential information. EFS can encrypt only user files. Additionally, when used with TPM hardware, BitLocker can help protect your system integrity by ensuring that critical Windows startup files have not been modified (which might occur if a rootkit or other malware was installed). Also, if the hard disk is moved to a different computer (a common method for extracting data from a stolen hard disk), the user will be forced to enter a recovery password before gaining access to the protected volumes.

How BitLocker Encrypts Data

BitLocker encrypts entire volumes. The contents of the volumes can be decrypted only by someone with access to the decryption key, known as the Full Volume Encryption Key (FVEK). Windows 7 actually stores the FVEK in the volume metadata; this is not a problem because the FVEK itself is encrypted using the Volume Master Key (VMK).

Both the FVEK and the VMK are 256 bits. The FVEK always uses AES encryption to protect the volume. By editing the Computer Configuration\Administrative Templates\Windows Components\BitLocker Drive Encryption\Choose Drive Encryption Method And Cipher Strength Group Policy setting, you can set the specific AES encryption strength to one of four values:

- AES 128 bit with Diffuser (this is the default setting)
- AES 256 bit with Diffuser (this is the strongest setting, but using it might negatively affect performance)
- AES 128 bit
- AES 256 bit

MORE INFO **For more information about the encryption algorithms used and the use of diffusers, read "AES-CBC + Elephant Diffuser: A Disk Encryption Algorithm for Windows Vista," at** ***http://download.microsoft.com/download/0/2/3/0238acaf-d3bf-4a6d-b3d6-0a0be4bbb36e/BitLockerCipher200608.pdf.***

Windows Vista and Windows 7 encrypt and decrypt disk sectors on the fly as data is read and written (as long as it has access to the FVEK) using the FVE Filter Driver (Fvevol.sys). As shown in Figure 16-12, the FVE Filter Driver, like all filter drivers, resides between the file system (which expects to receive the unencrypted contents of files) and the volume manager (which provides access to the volume). Therefore, applications and users are not aware of encryption when everything is functioning normally.

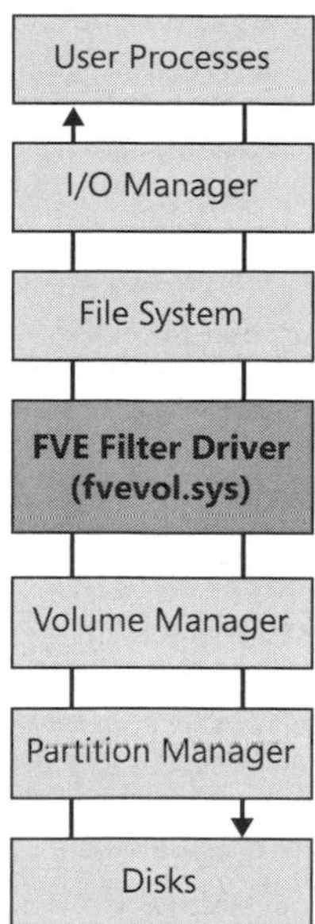

FIGURE 16-12 The FVE Filter Driver transparently encrypts and decrypts disk contents.

Encrypting and decrypting data do affect performance. While reading from and writing to a BitLocker-encrypted volume, some processor time will be consumed by the cryptographic operations performed by BitLocker. The actual impact depends on several factors, including caching mechanisms, hard drive speed, and processor performance. However, Microsoft has put great effort into implementing an efficient AES engine so that the performance impact on modern computers is minimal.

How BitLocker Protects Data

Before BitLocker grants access to the FVEK and the encrypted volume, it needs to obtain a key from the authorized user and/or the computer. If the computer has a TPM chip, authentication can happen in several different ways. If the computer doesn't have a TPM chip, you can use only a USB key. The sections that follow describe the different authentication techniques.

TPM (Use BitLocker Without Additional Keys)

BitLocker uses the TPM to unlock the VMK. The Windows startup process uses the TPM to verify that the hard disk is attached to the correct computer (and thus, the hard disk has not been removed) and that important system files are intact (preventing access to the hard drive if malware or a rootkit has compromised system integrity). When the computer is validated, TPM unlocks the VMK, and Windows 7 can start without prompting the user, as illustrated in

Figure 16-13. This validation technique provides some level of protection without affecting the user at all.

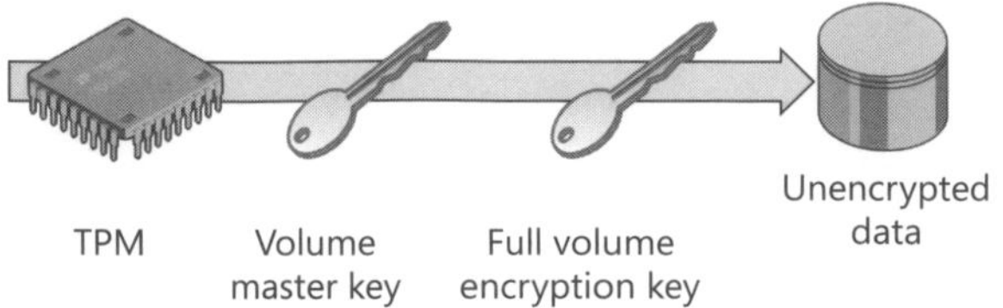

FIGURE 16-13 TPM-only authentication validates computer integrity without prompting the user.

TPM with External Key (Require Startup USB Key At Every Startup)

In addition to the protection described in the previous paragraph, the TPM requires an external key provided by the user (see Figure 16-14). This requires the user to insert a USB flash drive (or any other BIOS-enumerable storage device) containing the key, effectively authenticating both the user and the integrity of the computer. This can protect the data in the event the computer is stolen while the computer is shut down or in hibernation; resuming from standby does not require BitLocker protection. For this authentication technique to be effective, the user must store the external key separately from the computer to reduce the risk that they will be stolen simultaneously.

> ***NOTE*** **An excellent way to prevent yourself from losing your startup key and to avoid leaving it connected to your computer is to connect your USB startup key to your key ring. If you leave the USB key connected, it is more likely to be stolen with the computer, and malicious software might be able to copy the key.**

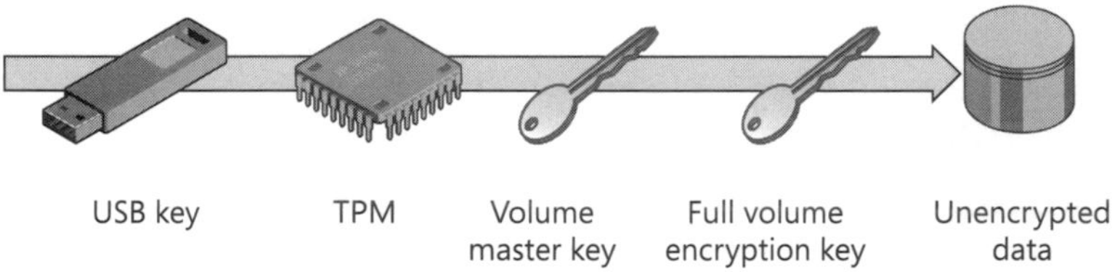

FIGURE 16-14 For better security, require users to insert a USB flash drive to authenticate them to TPM.

TPM with PIN (Require PIN At Every Startup)

This requirement prevents the computer from starting until the user types a personal identification number (PIN), as illustrated in Figure 16-15. This helps to protect the data in the event the computer is stolen while shut down. You should never use PINs to protect computers that need to start automatically without a human present, such as computers that are configured to start up for maintenance or backup purposes or computers that act as servers.

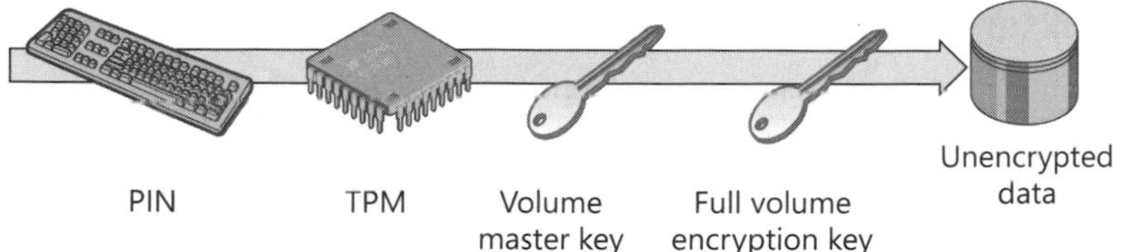

FIGURE 16-15 For better security, require users to type a PIN to authenticate them to TPM.

NOTE Be sure to change your PIN frequently. Although Trusted Computing Group (TCG)–compliant TPMs offer protection from password-guessing attacks by forcing the user to wait between attempts, laptop keys show wear. This is especially true if you enter the PIN using your rarely used function keys (on most keyboards, you can use the standard number keys as well). If you use the same PIN for years, the keys in your PIN may show more wear than other keys, allowing a sophisticated attacker to guess the characters in your PIN, thus reducing the number of keys the attacker needs to guess. To minimize this risk further, use a long PIN and use the same key multiple times in your PIN.

When requiring a PIN, the computer's TPM hardware forces a non-resettable delay between PIN entry attempts (the exact delay varies between TPM vendors). Because of this delay, a four-digit PIN might take an entire year to crack. Without this delay, a random four-digit PIN could be cracked in less than a day. Because of this password-guessing weakness when a delay is not enforced by TPM, BitLocker does not allow PIN authentication on computers that do not have TPM hardware.

HOW IT WORKS

PIN Authentication

In this authentication scenario, the administrator sets up a PIN when BitLocker is turned on. BitLocker hashes the PIN using SHA-256. The resulting nonreversible hash is used as authorization data sent to the TPM to seal the VMK. The VMK is now protected by both the TPM and the PIN. To unseal the VMK, the user enters the PIN when the computer starts, the PIN is hashed, and the result is submitted to the TPM. If the submitted hash and other platform configuration registers (PCRs) are correct (proving that the user entered the same PIN), the TPM unseals the VMK.

The following authentication techniques are available regardless of whether the computer has a TPM.

TPM with PIN and External Key

In Windows 7 and Windows Vista SP1, you have an additional option for BitLocker security on computers with a TPM: requiring the user to type a PIN and insert a USB key. This provides the highest level of BitLocker protection by requiring something the user knows (the PIN) and something the user has (the external key). For an attacker to successfully access data on a BitLocker-protected partition, the attacker needs to acquire the computer with the hard disk, have the USB key, and work with the computer's owner to acquire the PIN.

You must use the Manage-bde.exe BitLocker command-line tool to configure this authentication option. Manage-bde.exe is discussed later in this section.

External Key (Require Startup USB Key At Every Startup)

The user provides the VMK on a USB flash drive or similar external storage so that BitLocker can decrypt the FVEK and the volume without requiring TPM hardware. The external key can be either the standard key or a recovery key created to replace a lost external key.

Using a startup key without TPM does allow you to encrypt a volume without upgrading your hardware. However, it does not provide boot integrity, and it will not detect whether the hard disk has been moved to a different computer.

Recovery Password

The user enters a 48-character recovery password, which decrypts the VMK, granting access to the FVEK and the volume. The recovery password is designed with checksums so that IT support can read the password to a user over the phone and easily detect whether a user has mistyped a character. For more information, read the section titled "How to Recover Data Protected by BitLocker" later in this chapter.

Clear Key

No authentication occurs. BitLocker does not check the integrity of the computer or operating system, and the VMK is freely accessible, encrypted with a symmetric key stored in the clear on the hard disk. However, the volume remains, in fact, encrypted. This is used only when BitLocker is disabled (to upgrade the computer's BIOS, for example). When BitLocker is re-enabled, the clear key is removed and the VMK is rekeyed and re-encrypted. For more information, read the section titled "How to Disable or Remove BitLocker Drive Encryption" later in this chapter.

BitLocker To Go

BitLocker To Go enables users to encrypt removable drives using a password or a smart card. When a BitLocker To Go–protected drive is connected, Windows 7 prompts the user to enter the password. When the correct password is entered, the contents of the drive are available from Windows Explorer, and accessing the drive is completely transparent to the user.

When a BitLocker To Go–protected drive is connected to an earlier version of Windows, the user can run the BitLocker To Go Reader application, as shown in Figure 16-16. If the user chooses to run the tool, it prompts the user for a password. The BitLocker To Go Reader application can only be used with drives formatted in the FAT file system and those drives that have been configured to be unlocked with a password.

FIGURE 16-16 The BitLocker To Go Reader enables earlier versions of Windows to access BitLocker To Go–protected drives.

When the correct password is entered, the contents of the drive are available from the BitLocker To Go Reader, as shown in Figure 16-17. Users can drag files from the BitLocker To Go Reader to any Windows Explorer window, where they can access the files normally. Note that versions of Windows prior to Windows 7 cannot transparently access a BitLocker To Go–protected drive; instead, they must used the BitLocker To Go Reader.

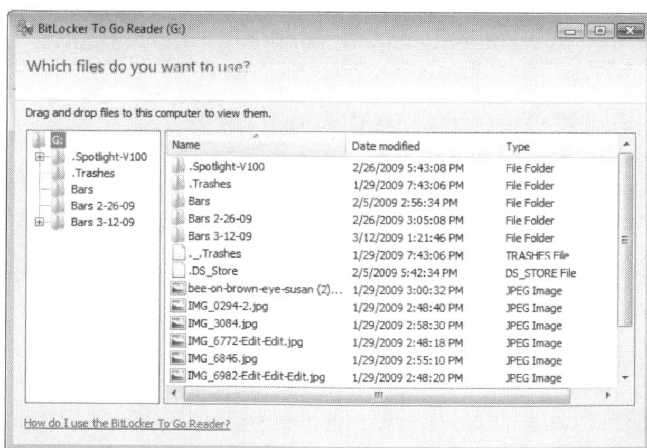

FIGURE 16-17 Users can drag files from the BitLocker To Go Reader to a Windows Explorer window.

You can use Group Policy settings to configure BitLocker To Go. Within the Computer Configuration\Policies\Administrative Templates\Windows Components\BitLocker Drive Encryption\Removable Data Drives node, you can define the following policies:

- **Control Use Of Bitlocker On Removable Drives** Allows you to prevent users from using BitLocker To Go and block users from suspending encryption or decrypting BitLocker To Go–protected drives.
- **Configure Use Of Smart Cards On Removable Data Drives** Allows you to require the use of a smart card to protect a drive with BitLocker To Go or prevent users from using smart cards.
- **Deny Write Access To Removable Drives Not Protected By BitLocker** Enables you to require BitLocker To Go before allowing users to save files to a removable drive.
- **Allow Access To Bitlocker-Protected Removable Data Drives From Earlier Versions Of Windows** Controls whether the BitLocker To Go Reader is installed on BitLocker To Go–protected drives.
- **Configure Use Of Passwords For Removable Data Drives** Enables you to require passwords for BitLocker To Go–protected drives and to enforce password complexity requirements.
- **Choose How Bitlocker-Protected Removable Drives Can Be Recovered** Allows recovery agents and determines whether recovery agents, 48-digit recovery passwords, or 256-bit recovery keys can be used to recover a BitLocker-protected drive. You can also use this policy setting to save BitLocker To Go recovery information to Active Directory Domain Services (AD DS).

BitLocker Phases

The stages of BitLocker startup are as follows:

- **System integrity verification (if a TPM is present)** Features of the computer and the Windows Boot Manager write values to the PCRs of the TPM as the boot process proceeds, including a measurement of the MBR executable code.
- **User authentication (optional)** If user authentication is configured, the Windows Boot Manager collects a key from USB storage or a PIN from the user.
- **VMK retrieval** The Windows Boot Manager requests that the TPM decrypt the VMK. If the hashes of the measurements written to the PCR match those taken when BitLocker was set up, the TPM will supply the VMK. If any measurement does not match the recorded value, the TPM does not supply the decryption key, and BitLocker gives the user the option to enter the recovery key.
- **Operating system startup** At this point, the Windows Boot Manager has validated the system integrity and now has access to the VMK. The VMK must be passed to the operating system loader; however, the Windows Boot Manager must avoid passing it to a potentially malicious operating system loader and thus compromising the security of the VMK. To ensure that the operating system loader is valid, the Windows Boot Manager verifies that operating system loader executables match a set of requirements. The Windows Boot Manager also verifies that the boot configuration data (BCD) settings have not been modified. It does so by comparing them to a previously generated digital signature known as a message authenticity check (MAC). The BCD MAC is generated using the VMK, ensuring that it cannot be easily rewritten.

After the operating system loader is started, Windows can use the VMK to decrypt the FVEK and then use the FVEK to decrypt the BitLocker-encrypted volume. With access to the unencrypted data on the volume, Windows loads normally.

DIRECT FROM THE SOURCE

BitLocker Volumes

Jamie Hunter, Lead Software Development Engineer
Many-Core Strategies and Incubation

Prior to transitioning to the operating system, the OS Loader ensures that it will hand off at most one key (VMK) to the operating system. Prior to handing off the key to the operating system, the following conditions must apply:

- All features, up to and including BOOTMGR, must be correct. If they are not correct, the VMK will not be available.
- The VMK must be correct to validate the MAC of the metadata. BOOTMGR verifies this MAC.
- OS Loader must be the loader approved by metadata associated with the VMK. Verified by BOOTMGR.
- BCD settings must be the settings approved by metadata associated with the VMK. Verified by BOOTMGR.
- The VMK must correctly decrypt the FVEK stored in the validated metadata. Verified by BOOTMGR.
- The FVEK must successfully decrypt data stored on the volume. An incorrect FVEK will result in invalid executable code or invalid data. In some cases, this is caught by code integrity.
  - The Master File Table (MFT) must be encrypted by the correct FVEK to access all files.
  - Phase 0 drivers, including Fvevol.sys, must be encrypted by the correct FVEK.
  - Registry must be encrypted by the correct FVEK.
  - Kernel and Hardware Abstraction Layer (HAL) must be encrypted by the correct FVEK.
  - Phase 1 features must be encrypted by the FVEK because Fvevol.sys (encrypted by the FVEK) will only decrypt using the same FVEK.
  - Phase 2 features must also be encrypted by the FVEK as stated in the previous entry.

The last point is particularly important, and it is true only if the data on the volume is entirely encrypted. In other words, a volume in which encryption is paused halfway through is not secure.

Requirements for Protecting the System Volume with BitLocker

To enable BitLocker to protect the system volume on a Windows 7 computer, the computer must meet the following requirements:

- Unless you plan to rely solely on a USB startup key, the computer must have a TPM 1.2 module (revision 85 or later), and it must be enabled. (TPM chips can be disabled by default and can be turned on using the computer's BIOS.) The TPM provides boot-process integrity measurement and reporting.
- The computer must have a version 1.21 (revision 0.24 or later), TCG-compliant BIOS with support for TCG specified Static Root Trust Measurement (SRTM) to establish a chain of trust prior to starting Windows.
- If you plan to use a USB startup key, the BIOS must support the USB Mass Storage Device Class2, including both reading and writing small files on a USB flash drive in the preoperating system environment.
- The computer must have at least two volumes to operate. Windows 7 setup automatically configures volumes to meet these requirements. On computers running Windows Vista, you can use the BitLocker Drive Preparation Tool, available at *http://www.microsoft.com/downloads*, to modify existing partitions to meet these requirements:
  - The boot volume is the volume that contains the Windows operating system and its support files; it must be formatted with NTFS. Data on this volume is protected by BitLocker.
  - The system volume is the volume that contains the hardware-specific files needed to load Windows 7 computers after the BIOS has booted the platform. For BitLocker to work, the system volume must not be encrypted, must differ from the operating system volume, and must be formatted with NTFS. Your system volume should be at least 100 MB. Data written to this volume—including additional user data—is not protected by BitLocker.

You can have multiple instances of Windows Vista or Windows 7 installed on a computer with a BitLocker-encrypted volume, and they will all be able to access the volume if you enter the respective recovery password every time you need to access the volume from a different partition. You can also install earlier versions of Windows on volumes not encrypted with BitLocker. However, earlier versions of Windows will not be able to access the BitLocker-encrypted volume.

How to Enable the Use of BitLocker on the System Volume on Computers Without TPM

BitLocker can store decryption keys on a USB flash drive instead of using a built-in TPM module. This allows you to use BitLocker on computers that do not have the TPM hardware. Using BitLocker in this configuration can be risky, however, because if the user loses the USB flash drive, the encrypted volume will no longer be accessible and the computer will not be able to start without the recovery key. Windows 7 does not make this option available by default.

To use BitLocker encryption on a computer without a compatible TPM, you will need to change a computer Group Policy setting by following these steps:

1. Open the Group Policy Editor by clicking Start, typing **gpedit.msc**, and then pressing Enter.
2. Navigate to Computer Configuration\Policies\Administrative Templates\Windows Components\BitLocker Drive Encryption\Operating System Drives\Require Additional Authentication At Startup. For computers running Windows Vista and Windows Server 2008 (prior to Windows Server 2008 R2), select the Require Additional Authentication At Startup (Windows Server 2008 And Windows Vista) policy.
3. Enable the setting and then select the Allow BitLocker Without A Compatible TPM check box.

How to Enable BitLocker Encryption on System Volumes

To enable BitLocker on a system volume, follow these steps:

1. Perform a full backup of the computer. Then, run a check of the integrity of the BitLocker partition using ChkDsk. For more information about using ChkDsk, read Chapter 30, "Troubleshooting Hardware, Driver, and Disk Issues."
2. Open Control Panel. Click System And Security. Under BitLocker Drive Encryption, click Protect Your Computer By Encrypting Data On Your Disk.
3. On the BitLocker Drive Encryption page, click Turn On BitLocker (see Figure 16-18).

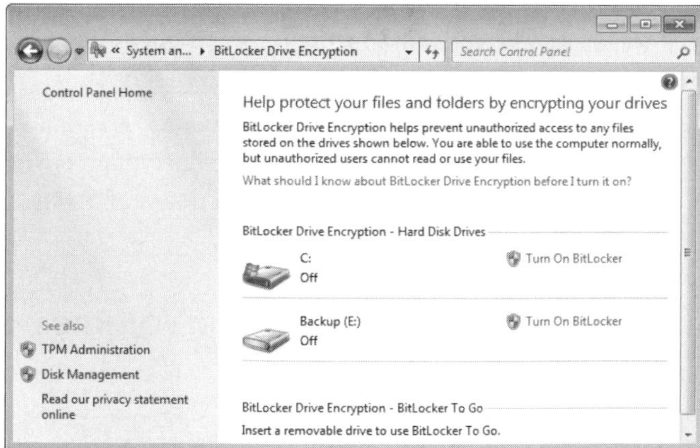

FIGURE 16-18 If your partitions are properly configured and your computer has a TPM (or the TPM requirement has been disabled), you can enable BitLocker.

4. If available (the choice can be blocked by a Group Policy setting), in the Set BitLocker Startup Preferences dialog box, select your authentication choice.

5. If you choose to use a USB key, the Save Your Startup Key dialog box appears. Select the startup key and then click Save.
6. Choose the destination to save your recovery password. The recovery password is a small text file containing brief instructions, a drive label and password ID, and the 48-digit recovery password. The choices are to store it on a USB drive, save it to a local or remote folder, or print the password. Be sure to save the password and the recovery key on separate devices. You can repeat this step to save the password to multiple locations. Keep the recovery passwords safe—anyone with access to the recovery password can bypass BitLocker security. Click Next.

> ***NOTE*** **It is strongly recommended that you save your recovery password to more than one location or device to ensure that you can recover it in the event that the BitLocker drive becomes locked. Keep the recovery keys safe and separate from the protected computer. Additionally, ensure that BitLocker-protected volumes are regularly backed up.**

7. Select the Run BitLocker System Check check box and click Continue if you are ready to begin encryption. Click Restart Now. Upon rebooting, BitLocker will ensure that the computer is fully compatible and ready to be encrypted. BitLocker displays a special screen confirming that the key material was loaded. Now that this is confirmed, BitLocker will begin encrypting the drive after Windows starts, and BitLocker will be enabled. If you do not select the Run BitLocker System Check check box, click Start Encrypting.

Encryption occurs in the background; the user can work on the computer (although free disk space and processor time will be partially consumed by BitLocker). If BitLocker encounters a disk-related problem, it will pause encryption and schedule a ChkDsk to run the next time you restart your computer. After the problem is fixed, encryption will continue.

A notification message is displayed in the system tray during encryption. An administrator can click the BitLocker system tray icon and then choose to pause the encryption process if the computer's performance is impacted, although the computer will not be protected until encryption is completed.

How to Enable BitLocker Encryption on Data Volumes

To enable BitLocker on a data volume, follow these steps:

1. Perform a full backup of the computer. Then, run a check of the integrity of the BitLocker partition using ChkDsk. For more information about using ChkDsk, read Chapter 30.
2. In Windows Explorer, right-click the drive you want to protect, and then click Turn On BitLocker.

3. On the Choose How You Want To Unlock This Drive page, select one or more protection methods:
   - Use A Password To Unlock This Drive. Users will be prompted to type a password before they can access the contents of the drive.
   - Use My Smart Card To Unlock The Drive. Users will be prompted to insert a smart card before they can access the contents of the drive. You can use this option with removable drives; however, you will not be able to access the drive using Windows Vista or Windows XP because smart cards cannot be used with the BitLocker To Go Reader.
   - Automatically Unlock This Drive On This Computer. Windows will automatically unlock non-removable data drives without prompting the user. Selecting this option requires that the system volume be protected by BitLocker. If you move the drive to a different computer, you will be prompted for credentials.
4. On the How Do You Want To Store Your Recovery Key page, choose the method to save the recovery key. Click Next.
5. On the Are You Ready To Encrypt This Drive page, click Start Encrypting.

How to Manage BitLocker Keys on a Local Computer

To manage keys on a local computer, follow these steps:

1. Open Control Panel and click System And Security. Under BitLocker Drive Encryption, click Manage BitLocker.
2. In the BitLocker Drive Encryption window, click Manage BitLocker.

Using this tool, you can save the recovery key to a USB flash drive or a file, or you can print the recovery key.

How to Manage BitLocker from the Command Line

To manage BitLocker from an elevated command prompt or from a remote computer, use the Manage-bde.exe tool. The following example demonstrates how to view the status.

```
manage-bde -status
```

```
BitLocker Drive Encryption: Configuration Tool
Copyright (C) Microsoft Corporation. All rights reserved.

Disk volumes that can be protected with
BitLocker Drive Encryption:
Volume C: []
[OS Volume]

    Size:                 74.37 GB
```

```
BitLocker Version:    Windows 7
Conversion Status:    Fully Encrypted
Percentage Encrypted: 100%
Encryption Method:    AES 128 with Diffuser
Protection Status:    Protection On
Lock Status:          Unlocked
Identification Field: None
Key Protectors:
    TPM
    Numerical Password
```

Run the following command to enable BitLocker on the C drive, store the recovery key on the Y drive, and generate a random recovery password.

manage-bde -on C: -RecoveryKey Y: -RecoveryPassword

```
BitLocker Drive Encryption: Configuration Tool version 6.1.7100
Copyright (C) Microsoft Corporation. All rights reserved.

Volume C: []
[OS Volume]
Key Protectors Added:
    Saved to directory Y:\

    External Key:
      ID: {7B7E1BD1-E579-4F6A-8B9C-AEB626FE08CC}
      External Key File Name:
        7B7E1BD1-E579-4F6A-8B9C-AEB626FE08CC.BEK

    Numerical Password:
      ID: {75A76E33-740E-41C4-BD41-48BDB08FE755}
      Password:
        460559-421212-096877-553201-389444-471801-362252-086284

    TPM:
      ID: {E6164F0E-8F85-4649-B6BD-77090D49DE0E}

ACTIONS REQUIRED:

    1. Save this numerical recovery password in a secure location away from
    your computer:

    460559-421212-096877-553201-389444-471801-362252-086284

    To prevent data loss, save this password immediately. This password helps
    ensure that you can unlock the encrypted volume.
```

```
    2. Insert a USB flash drive with an external key file into the computer.

    3. Restart the computer to run a hardware test.
    (Type "shutdown /?" for command line instructions.)

    4. Type "manage-bde -status" to check if the hardware test succeeded.

NOTE: Encryption will begin after the hardware test succeeds.
```

After you run the command, restart the computer with the recovery key connected to complete the hardware test. After the computer restarts, BitLocker will begin encrypting the disk.

Run the following command to disable BitLocker on the C drive.

```
manage-bde -off C:
```

```
BitLocker Drive Encryption: Configuration Tool
Copyright (C) Microsoft Corporation. All rights reserved.

Decryption is now in progress.
```

You can also use the Manage-bde.exe script to specify a startup key and a recovery key, which can allow a single key to be used on multiple computers. This is useful if a single user has multiple computers, such as a user with both a Tablet PC computer and a desktop computer. It can also be useful in lab environments, where several users might share several different computers. Note, however, that a single compromised startup key or recovery key will require all computers with the same key to be rekeyed.

For detailed information about using Manage-bde.exe, run *manage-bde.exe -?* from a command prompt.

How to Recover Data Protected by BitLocker

When you use BitLocker, the encrypted volumes will be locked if the encryption key is not available, causing BitLocker to enter recovery mode. Likely causes for the encryption key's unavailability include:

- Modification of one of the boot files.
- The BIOS is modified and the TPM is disabled.
- The TPM is cleared.
- An attempt is made to boot without the TPM, PIN, or USB key being available.
- The BitLocker-encrypted disk is moved to a new computer.

After the drive is locked, you can boot only to recovery mode, as shown in Figure 16-19. In recovery mode, you enter the recovery password using the function keys on your keyboard (just as you do when entering the PIN), pressing F1 for the digit 1, F2 for the digit 2, and so forth, with F10 being the digit 0. You must use function keys because localized keyboard support is not yet available at this phase of startup.

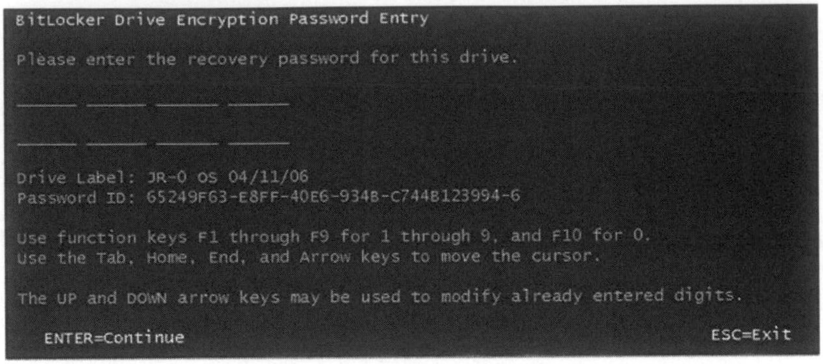

```
BitLocker Drive Encryption Password Entry

Please enter the recovery password for this drive.

______ ______ ______ ______

______ ______ ______ ______

Drive Label: JR-0 OS 04/11/06
Password ID: 65249F63-E8FF-40E6-934B-C744B123994-6

Use function keys F1 through F9 for 1 through 9, and F10 for 0.
Use the Tab, Home, End, and Arrow keys to move the cursor.

The UP and DOWN arrow keys may be used to modify already entered digits.

  ENTER=Continue                                              ESC=Exit
```

FIGURE 16-19 Recovery mode prompts you for a 48-character recovery password.

If you have the recovery key on a USB flash drive, you can insert the recovery key and press Esc to restart the computer. The recovery key will be read automatically during startup.

If you cancel recovery, the Windows Boot Manager will provide instructions for using Startup Repair to fix a startup problem automatically. Do not follow these instructions because Startup Repair cannot access the encrypted volume. Instead, restart the computer and enter the recovery key.

> ***MORE INFO*** **Additionally, you can use the BitLocker Repair Tool, Repair-bde.exe, to help recover data from an encrypted volume. If a BitLocker failure prevents Windows 7 from starting, you can run *repair-bde* from the Windows Recovery Environment (Windows RE) command prompt. For more information about *repair-bde*, run *repair-bde /?* at a command prompt. For more information about troubleshooting startup problems, including using *repair-bde*, refer to Chapter 29.**

How to Disable or Remove BitLocker Drive Encryption

Because BitLocker intercepts the boot process and looks for changes to any of the early boot files, it can cause problems in the following nonattack scenarios:

- Upgrading or replacing the motherboard or TPM
- Installing a new operating system that changes the MBR or the Boot Manager
- Moving a BitLocker-encrypted disk to another TPM-enabled computer
- Repartitioning the hard disk
- Updating the BIOS
- Installing a third-party update outside the operating system (such as hardware firmware updates)

To avoid entering BitLocker recovery mode, you can temporarily disable BitLocker, which allows you to change the TPM and upgrade the operating system. When you re-enable BitLocker, the same keys will be used. You can also choose to decrypt the BitLocker-protected volume, which will completely remove BitLocker protection. You can only re-enable BitLocker by repeating the process to create new keys and re-encrypt the volume. To disable or decrypt BitLocker, follow these steps:

1. Log on to the computer as Administrator.
2. From Control Panel, open BitLocker Drive Encryption.
3. To temporarily disable BitLocker by using a clear key, click Suspend Protection and then click Yes. To disable BitLocker permanently, click Turn Off BitLocker and then click Decrypt Drive.

How to Decommission a BitLocker Drive Permanently

Compromises in confidentiality can occur when computers or hard disks are decommissioned. For example, a computer that reaches the end of its usefulness at an organization might be discarded, sold, or donated to charity. The person who receives the computer might extract confidential files from the computer's hard disk. Even if the disk has been formatted, data can often be extracted.

BitLocker reduces the risks of decommissioning drives. For example, if you use a startup key or startup PIN, the contents of the volume are inaccessible without this additional information or the drive's saved recovery information.

You can decommission a drive more securely by removing all key blobs from the disk. By deleting the BitLocker keys from the volume, an attacker needs to crack the encryption—a task that is extremely unlikely to be accomplished within anyone's lifetime. As a cleanup task, you should also discard all saved recovery information, such as recovery information saved to AD DS.

To remove all key blobs on a secondary drive (data volume), you can format that drive from Windows or the Windows RE. Note that this format operation will not work on a drive that is currently in use. For example, you cannot use it to more securely decommission the drive used to run Windows.

To remove all key blobs on a running drive, you can create a script that performs the following tasks:

1. Calls the *Win32_EncryptableVolume.GetKeyProtectors* method to retrieve all key protectors (*KeyProtectorType 0*).
2. Creates a not-to-be-used recovery password blob (discarding the actual recovery password) by using *Win32_EncryptableVolume.ProtectKeyWithNumericalPassword* and a randomly generated password sequence. This is required because *Win32_EncryptableVolume.DeleteKeyProtector* will not remove all key protectors.
3. Uses *Win32_EncryptableVolume.DeleteKeyProtector* to remove all of the usable key protectors associated with the identifiers mentioned previously.

4. Clears the TPM by calling the *Win32_TPM.Clear* method.

For more information about developing a script or application to perform secure decommissioning on a BitLocker-encrypted drive, refer to the *Win32_EncryptableVolume* WMI provider class documentation at *http://msdn.microsoft.com/en-us/library/aa376483.aspx* and the *Win32_TPM* WMI provider class documentation at *http://msdn.microsoft.com/en-us/library/aa376484.aspx*.

How to Prepare AD DS for BitLocker

BitLocker is also integrated into AD DS. In fact, although you can use BitLocker without AD DS, enterprises really shouldn't—key recovery and data recovery agents are an extremely important part of using BitLocker. AD DS is a reliable and efficient way to store recovery keys so that you can restore encrypted data if a key is lost, and you must use Group Policy settings to configure data recovery agents.

If your AD DS is at the Windows Server 2008 or later functional level, you do not need to prepare the AD DS for BitLocker. If your AD DS is at a functional level of Windows Server 2003 or earlier, however, you will need to update the schema to support BitLocker. For detailed instructions on how to configure AD DS to back up BitLocker and TPM recovery information, read "Configuring Active Directory to Back Up Windows BitLocker Drive Encryption and Trusted Platform Module Recovery Information" at *http://go.microsoft.com/fwlink/?LinkId=78953*. For information about retrieving recovery passwords from AD DS, read "How to Use the BitLocker Recovery Password Viewer For Active Directory Users And Computers Tool to View Recovery Passwords for Windows Vista" at *http://support.microsoft.com/?kbid=928202*.

How to Configure a Data Recovery Agent

Earlier versions of Windows supported storing BitLocker recovery keys in AD DS. This works well, but each BitLocker-protected volume has a unique recovery key. In enterprises, this can consume a large amount of space in AD DS. By using a data recovery agent instead of storing recovery keys in AD DS, you can store a single certificate in AD DS and use it to recover any BitLocker-protected volume.

To configure a data recovery agent, follow these steps:

1. Publish the future data recovery agent's certificate to AD DS. Alternatively, export the certificate to a .cer file and have it available.
2. Open a Group Policy object that targets the Windows 7 computers using the Group Policy object Editor and then select Computer Configuration\Policies\Windows Settings\Security Settings\Public Key Policies.
3. Right-click BitLocker Drive Encryption, click Add Data Recovery Agent to start the Add Recovery Agent Wizard, and then click Next.

4. On the Select Recovery Agents page, click Browse Directory (if the certificate is stored in AD DS) or Browse Folders (if you have saved the .cer file locally). Select a .cer file to use as a data recovery agent. After the file is selected, it will be imported and will appear in the Recovery Agents list in the wizard. You can specify multiple data recovery agents. After you specify all of the data recovery agents that you want to use, click Next.
5. The Completing The Add Recovery Agent page of the wizard displays a list of the data recovery agents that will be added to the Group Policy object. Click Finish to confirm the data recovery agents and close the wizard.

The next time Group Policy is applied to the targeted Windows 7 computers, the data recovery agent certificate will be applied to the drive. At that point, you will be able to recover a BitLocker-protected drive using the certificate configured as the data recovery agent. Because of this, you must carefully protect the data recovery agent certificate.

How to Manage BitLocker with Group Policy

BitLocker has several Group Policy settings located in Computer Configuration\Policies\Administrative Templates\Windows Components\BitLocker Drive Encryption that you can use to manage the available features. Table 16-2 lists these policies, which are written to the registry on targeted computers under the following registry key:

HKLM\Software\Policies\Microsoft\FVE

TABLE 16-2 Group Policy Settings for BitLocker Drive Encryption

POLICY	DESCRIPTION
Store BitLocker Recovery Information In Active Directory Domain Services (Windows Server 2008 And Windows Vista)	Enabling this policy silently backs up BitLocker recovery information to AD DS. For computers running Windows 7 and Windows Server 2008 R2, enable the Fixed Data Drives\Choose How BitLocker-Protected Fixed Drives Can Be Recovered, Operating System Drives\Choose How BitLocker-Protected Operating System Drives Can Be Recovered, or Removable Data Drives\Choose How BitLocker-Protected Removable Drives Can Be Recovered policies.
Choose Default Folder For Recovery Password	Enabling this policy and configuring a default path for it sets the default folder to display when the user is saving recovery information for BitLocker. The user will have the ability to override the default.

POLICY	DESCRIPTION
Choose How Users Can Recover BitLocker-Protected Drives (Windows Server 2008 And Windows Vista)	Enabling this policy allows you to control which recovery mechanisms the user can choose. Disabling the recovery password will disable saving to a folder or printing the key because these actions require the 48-digit recovery password. Disabling the 256-bit recovery key will disable saving to a USB key. If you disable both options, you must enable AD DS backup or a policy error will occur. For computers running Windows 7 and Windows Server 2008 R2, enable the Fixed Data Drives\Choose How BitLocker-Protected Fixed Drives Can Be Recovered, Operating System Drives\Choose How BitLocker-Protected Operating System Drives Can Be Recovered, or Removable Data Drives\Choose How BitLocker-Protected Removable Drives Can Be Recovered policies.
Choose Drive Encryption Method And Cipher Strength	Enabling this policy allows configuration of the encryption method used by BitLocker Drive Encryption. The default if this key is not enabled is 128-bit AES with Diffuser. Other choices that can be configured are 256-bit AES with Diffuser, 128-bit AES, and 256-bit AES.
Prevent Memory Overwrite On Restart	Enabling this policy prevents Windows from overwriting memory on restarts. This potentially exposes BitLocker secrets but can improve restart performance.
Provide The Unique Identifiers For Your Organization	Enable this policy if you want to prevent users from mounting BitLocker-protected drives that might be from outside organizations.
Validate Smart Card Certificate Usage Rule Compliance	Enable this policy only if you want to restrict users to smart cards that have an object identifier (OID) that you specify.
Operating System Drives \Require Additional Authentication At Startup or Operating System Drives \Require Additional Authentication At Startup (Windows Server 2008 And Windows Vista)	Enabling this policy allows configuring additional startup options and allows enabling of BitLocker on a non–TPM-compatible computer. On TPM-compatible computers, a secondary authentication can be required at startup—either a USB key or a startup PIN, but not both.
Allow Enhanced PINs For Startup	Enhanced PINs permit the use of characters including uppercase and lowercase letters, symbols, numbers, and spaces. By default, enhanced PINs are disabled.

POLICY	DESCRIPTION
Operating System Drives\Configure Minimum PIN Length For Startup	Enables you to require a minimum PIN length.
Operating System Drives\Choose How BitLocker-Protected Operating System Drives Can Be Recovered	Enabling this policy allows you to control which recovery mechanisms the user can choose and whether recovery information is stored in the AD DS. Disabling the recovery password will disable saving to a folder or printing the key because these actions require the 48-digit recovery password. Disabling the 256-bit recovery key will disable saving to a USB key.
Operating System Drives\Configure TPM Platform Validation Profile	Enabling this policy allows detailed configuration of the PCR indices. Each index aligns with Windows features that run during startup.
Fixed Data Drives\Configure Use Of Smart Cards On Fixed Data Drives	Enables or requires smart cards for BitLocker to protect non–operating system volumes.
Fixed Data Drives\Deny Writer Access To Fixed Drives Not Protected By BitLocker	Requires drives to be BitLocker-protected before users can save files.
Fixed Data Drives\Allow Access To BitLocker-Protected Fixed Data Drives From Earlier Versions Of Windows	Allows you to prevent the BitLocker To Go Reader from being copied to fixed data drives, preventing users of earlier versions of Windows (including Windows Server 2008, Windows Vista, and Windows XP SP2 or SP3) from entering a password to access the drive.
Fixed Data Drives\Configure Use Of Passwords For Fixed Drives	Requires passwords to access BitLocker-protected fixed drives and configures password complexity.
Fixed Data Drives\Choose How BitLocker-Protected Fixed Drives Can Be Recovered	Enabling this policy allows you to control which recovery mechanisms the user can choose and whether recovery information is stored in the AD DS. Disabling the recovery password will disable saving to a folder or printing the key because these actions require the 48-digit recovery password. Disabling the 256-bit recovery key will disable saving to a USB key.

For information about BitLocker To Go policies (which are configured in the Removable Data Drives node), refer to the section titled "BitLocker To Go" earlier in this chapter.

The Costs of BitLocker

Most security features require a tradeoff. The benefit to any security feature is that it reduces risk and thus reduces the cost associated with a security compromise. Most security features also have a cost—purchase price, increased maintenance, or decreased user productivity.

The benefit of using BitLocker is reduced risk of loss of data confidentiality in the event of a stolen hard disk. Like most security features, BitLocker has costs (aside from any software or hardware costs):

- If a PIN or external key is required, the startup experience is not transparent to the user. If the user loses his PIN or startup key, he will need to wait for a Support Center representative to read him the password so that he can start his computer.
- In the event of hard disk failure or data corruption, recovering data from the disk can be more difficult.

> ***MORE INFO*** **You should implement BitLocker in your organization only if the reduced security risks outweigh these costs. For more information about cost/benefit analysis, read the *Security Risk Management Guide* at *http://technet.microsoft.com/en-us/library/cc163143.aspx*.**

Encrypting File System

BitLocker is not a replacement for the EFS introduced in Windows 2000, but it is a supplement to the EFS that ensures that the operating system itself is protected from attack. Best practices for protecting sensitive computers and data will combine the two features to provide a high level of assurance of the data integrity on the system.

EFS continues to be an important data-integrity tool in Windows 7. EFS allows the encryption of entire volumes or individual folders and files and can support multiple users using the same computer, each with protected data. Additionally, EFS allows multiple users to have secure access to sensitive data while protecting the data against unauthorized viewing or modification. EFS cannot be used to encrypt system files, however, and it should be combined with BitLocker to encrypt the system drive where sensitive data must be protected. EFS is susceptible to offline attack using the SYSKEY, but when you combine EFS with BitLocker to encrypt the system volume, this attack vector is protected.

EFS uses symmetric key encryption along with public key technology to protect files and folders. Each user of EFS is issued a digital certificate with a public and private key pair. EFS uses the keys to encrypt and decrypt the files transparently for the logged-on user. Authorized users work with encrypted files and folders just as they do with unencrypted files and folders. Unauthorized users receive an Access Denied message in response to any attempt to open, copy, move, or rename the encrypted file or folder.

Files are encrypted with a single symmetrical key, and then the symmetrical key is encrypted twice: once with the user's EFS public key to allow transparent decryption and once with the recovery agent's key to allow data recovery.

The sections that follow describe how to manage EFS keys. For general information about EFS, read "Encrypting File System in Windows XP and Windows Server 2003" at *http://technet.microsoft.com/en-us/library/bb457065.aspx*.

How to Export Personal Certificates

To prevent being unable to access an encrypted file, you can export your personal certificate. When you export your certificate, you can then copy or move the encrypted file to another computer and still access it by importing the certificate you exported.

To export your personal certificate, follow these steps:

1. Open Windows Explorer and select a file that you have encrypted.
2. Right-click the file and then select Properties.
3. Click Advanced on the General tab.
4. Click Details on the Advanced Attributes tab to open the User Access dialog box.
5. Select your user name and then click Back Up Keys to open the Certificate Export Wizard.
6. Click Next to select the file format to use.
7. Click Next and enter a password to protect the key. Repeat the entry and then click Next.
8. Enter a path and filename to save the file to, or browse for a path. Click Next.
9. Click Finish to export the certificate and then click OK to confirm that it was saved successfully.

How to Import Personal Certificates

You can share encrypted files with other users if you have the certificate for the other user. To allow another user to use a file that you have encrypted, you need to import her certificate onto your computer and add her user name to the list of users who are permitted access to the file.

To import a user certificate, follow these steps:

1. Click Start, type **mmc**, and then press Enter to open a blank Microsoft Management Console (MMC).
2. Click File and then click Add/Remove Snap-in.
3. Select Certificates and click Add. Select My User Account and click Finish. Click OK to close the Add Or Remove Snap-in dialog box.
4. Click Certificates and then double-click Trusted People.

5. Under Trusted People, right-click Certificates. On the All Tasks menu, click Import to open the Certificate Import Wizard.
6. Click Next and then browse to the location of the certificate you want to import.
7. Select the certificate and then click Next.
8. Type the password for the certificate and then click Next.
9. Click Next to place the certificate in the Trusted People store.
10. Click Finish to complete the import.
11. Click OK to acknowledge the successful import and then exit the MMC.

How to Grant Users Access to an Encrypted File

When you have a user's certificate, you can add that user to the list of users who have access to a file. A user's certificate will be on a computer automatically if the user has logged on to the computer previously.

To add a user whose certificate you have imported to the users who can access a file, follow these steps:

1. Open Windows Explorer and highlight the file you want to receive access.
2. Right-click the file and then select Properties.
3. Click Advanced on the General tab.
4. Click Details on the Advanced Attributes tab to open the User Access dialog box.
5. Click Add to open the Encrypting File System dialog box and then select the user you want to permit to use the encrypted file.
6. Click OK to add the user to the list of users who have access to the file.
7. Click OK until you've exited out of the dialog boxes.

You do not need to grant EFS access to allow users to access files across the network—EFS does not affect shared folders.

Symbolic Links

Windows Vista and Windows 7 include *symbolic links*. Symbolic links act like shortcuts, but they provide a transparent link to the target file at the file-system level rather than within Windows Explorer. Therefore, although a user can double-click a shortcut from Windows Explorer to open the original file, a symbolic link will actually trick applications into thinking they are directly accessing the target file.

As an administrator, you might need to use symbolic links for backward compatibility. For example, if an application expects to find a file in the root of the C drive but you need to move the file to a different location on the local disk, you can create a symbolic link in the root of the C drive to the file's new location, allowing the application to continue to access the file in the root of the C drive. Windows Vista and Windows 7 use symbolic links for backward compatibility with user profiles in earlier versions of Windows. For more information, read Chapter 15, "Managing Users and User Data."

HOW IT WORKS

Symbolic Links, Hard Links, Junction Points, and Shortcuts

Windows Vista and Windows 7 support four different types of links, each providing a slightly different function:

- **Shortcuts** Shortcuts are files with a .lnk extension. If you double-click them within the Windows Explorer shell, Windows will open the target file. However, the file system treats .lnk files just like any other files. For example, opening a .lnk file from a command prompt does not open the target file.
- **Hard links** Hard links create a new directory entry for an existing file, so a single file can appear in multiple folders (or in a single folder using multiple filenames). Hard links must all be on a single volume.
- **Junction points** Also known as soft links, junction points reference a folder using an absolute path. Windows automatically redirects requests for a junction point to the target folder. Junction points do not have to be on the same volume.
- **Symbolic links** A pointer to a file or folder. Like junction points, symbolic links are almost always transparent to users. (Occasionally, a program might use an outdated application programming interface [API] that does not respect a symbolic link.) Symbolic links use relative paths rather than absolute paths.

How to Create Symbolic Links

By default, only administrators can create symbolic links. However, you can grant other users access using the Computer Configuration\Windows Settings\Security Settings\Local Policies\User Rights Assignment\Create Symbolic Links setting.

To create a symbolic link, open a command prompt with administrative privileges and use the *mklink* command. For example, the following command creates a symbolic link from C:\Myapp.exe to Notepad in the system directory.

```
C:\>mklink myapp.exe %windir%\system32\notepad.exe
```

```
Symbolic link created for myapp.exe <<===>> C:\Windows\system32\notepad.exe
```

NOTE Developers can call the *CreateSymbolicLink* function to create symbolic links. For more information, go to *http://msdn.microsoft.com/en-us/library/aa363866.aspx*.

After you create this symbolic link, the Myapp.exe link behaves exactly like a copy of the Notepad.exe file. Windows Explorer displays symbolic links using the standard shortcut symbol. However, shortcuts always have a .lnk extension, whereas symbolic links can have any extension. At a command prompt, the *dir* command uses the <SYMLINK> identifier to distinguish symbolic links and displays the path to the target file.

```
C:\>dir
```

```
 Volume in drive C has no label.
 Volume Serial Number is BC33-D7AC

 Directory of C:\

09/18/2006  04:43 PM                24 AUTOEXEC.BAT
09/18/2006  04:43 PM                10 config.sys
12/27/2006  12:16 PM    <SYMLINK>      myapp.exe [C:\Windows\system32\notepad.exe]
12/23/2006  04:47 PM    <DIR>          Program Files
11/29/2006  03:31 PM    <DIR>          Users
12/27/2006  08:39 AM    <DIR>          Windows
```

Because a symbolic link is only a link, any changes made to the link actually affect the target file and vice versa. If you create a symbolic link and then delete the target file, the symbolic link will remain, but any attempts to access it will return a File Not Found error because Windows will attempt to access the link target automatically. If you delete a target file and later replace it with a file of the same name, that new file will become the link target. Deleting a link does not affect the link target. Attribute changes to the symbolic link, such as marking a file as hidden or as a system file, are applied to both the symbolic link and the target file.

How to Create Relative or Absolute Symbolic Links

Relative symbolic links identify the location of the target based on their own folder. For example, a relative symbolic link to a target file in the same folder will always attempt to access a target with the specified filename in the same folder, even if the symbolic link is moved. You can create relative or absolute symbolic links, but all symbolic links are relative by default. For example, consider the following commands, which attempt to create a symbolic link named Link.txt to a file named Target.txt and then attempt to access the symbolic link before and after moving the target file.

```
C:\>mklink link.txt target.txt
C:\>type link.txt
```

```
Hello, world.
```

```
C:\>REM Move link.txt to a different folder
C:\>move link.txt C:\links
        1 file(s) moved.

C:\>cd links
C:\links>type link.txt
The system cannot find the file specified.

C:\links>move \target.txt C:\links
C:\links>type link.txt
Hello, world.
```

In the previous example, moving the symbolic link to a different folder causes Windows to be unable to locate the target because the symbolic link is a relative link pointing to a file named Target.txt in the same folder. When both the link and the target are moved to the same folder, the symbolic link works again.

Now consider the same example using an absolute symbolic link, created by specifying the full path to the target file:

```
C:\>mklink link.txt C:\target.txt
C:\>type link.txt
Hello, world.

C:\>REM Move link.txt to a different folder
C:\>move link.txt C:\links
        1 file(s) moved.

C:\>cd links
C:\links>type link.txt
Hello, world.

C:\links>move C:\target.txt C:\links\
C:\links>type link.txt
The system cannot find the file specified.
```

In the last example, specifying the full path to the target file creates an absolute symbolic link that references the full path to the target file. Therefore, the symbolic link still works after it is moved to a different folder. However, moving the target file makes it inaccessible.

How to Create Symbolic Links to Shared Folders

You can create symbolic links on the local file system to files stored on other local drives or shared folders. However, when you use the *mklink* command, you must always specify the absolute path to the remote target file because the *mklink* command by default assumes that the location is relative. For example, suppose you want to create a symbolic link named C:\Link.txt that targets a file on a shared folder at Z:\Target.txt. If you run the following commands, you will successfully create a symbolic link at C:\Link.txt.

```
C:\>Z:
Z:\>mklink C:\link.txt target.txt
```

However, that file will link to C:\Target.txt and not the intended Z:\Target.txt. To create a link to the Z:\Target.txt file, you need to run the following command.

```
C:\>mklink C:\link.txt Z:\target.txt
```

The *mklink* command also allows you to create a symbolic link targeting a Universal Naming Convention (UNC) path. For example, if you run the following command, Windows will create a symbolic link file called Link.txt that opens the Target.txt file.

```
Mklink link.txt \\server\folder\target.txt
```

If you enable remote symbolic links (discussed later in this section), they can be used to store symbolic links on shared folders and automatically redirect multiple Windows network clients to a different file on the network.

By default, you can use symbolic links only on local volumes. If you attempt to access a symbolic link located on a shared folder (regardless of the location of the target) or copy a symbolic link to a shared folder, you will receive an error. You can change this behavior by configuring the following Group Policy setting:

Computer Configuration\Administrative Templates\System\NTFS File System\Selectively Allow The Evaluation Of A SymbolicLink

When you enable this policy setting, you can select from four settings:

- **Local Link To Local Target** Enabled by default, this allows local symbolic links to targets on the local file system.
- **Local Link To Remote Target** Enabled by default, this allows local symbolic links to targets on shared folders.
- **Remote Link To Remote Target** Disabled by default, this allows remote symbolic links to remote targets on shared folders.
- **Remote Link To Local Target** Disabled by default, this allows remote symbolic links to remote targets on shared folders.

Enabling remote links can introduce security vulnerabilities. For example, a malicious user can create a symbolic link on a shared folder that references an absolute path on the local computer. When a user attempts to access the symbolic link, he will actually be accessing a different file that might contain confidential information. In this way, a sophisticated attacker might be able to trick a user into compromising the confidentiality of a file on his local computer.

How to Use Hard Links

Hard links create a second directory entry for a single file, whereas symbolic links create a new file that references an existing file. This subtle difference yields significantly different behavior.

You can create hard links by adding the */H* parameter to the *mklink* command. For example, the following command creates a hard link from Link.txt to Target.txt.

```
C:\>mklink /H link.txt target.txt
```

```
Hardlink created for link.txt <<===>> target.txt
```

As with symbolic links, any changes made to the hard link are made automatically to the target (including attribute changes) and vice versa because the file itself is stored only once on the volume. However, hard links have several key differences:

- Hard links must refer to files on the same volume, while symbolic links can refer to files or folders on different volumes or shared folders.
- Hard links can refer only to files, while symbolic links can refer to either files or folders.
- Windows maintains hard links, so the link and the target remain accessible even if you move one of them to a different folder.
- Hard links survive deleting the target file. A target file is deleted only if the target file and all hard links are deleted.
- If you delete a symbolic link target and then create a new file with the same name as the target, the symbolic link will open the new target. Hard links will continue to reference the original target file, even if you replace the target.
- Hard links do not show up as symbolic links in *dir* command-line output, and Windows Explorer does not show a shortcut symbol for them. Hard links are indistinguishable from the original file.
- Changes made to file permissions on a hard link apply to the target file and vice versa. With symbolic links, you can configure separate permissions on the symbolic link, but the permissions are ignored.

Windows XP supports hard links by using the *fsutil hardlink* command. Windows Vista and Windows 7 hard links are compatible with Windows XP hard links, and the *fsutil hardlink* command continues to function in Windows Vista and Windows 7.

Disk Quotas

Administrators can configure disk quotas to control how much of a volume a single user can fill with files. This is most useful when implemented on a server that hosts shared folders. However, you might also need to implement disk quotas on client computers in environments in which multiple users access a single computer because they can help prevent a single user from completely filling a volume and thereby preventing other users from saving files. Disk quotas have not changed significantly since Windows XP.

Before enabling disk quotas, consider whether they are worthwhile. Managing disk quotas requires administrators to monitor disk quota events, such as a user exceeding a disk storage threshold. Administrators must then work with users to either increase the quota or identify files that can be removed. Often, it is less expensive to simply add more disk storage, even if the users do not closely manage their disk usage.

How to Configure Disk Quotas on a Single Computer

To configure disk quotas on a single computer, follow these steps:

1. Click Start and then click Computer.
2. In the right pane, right-click the drive on which you want to configure the quotas and then click Properties.
3. Click the Quota tab and then click Show Quota Settings. The Quota Settings dialog box appears.
4. Select the Enable Quota Management check box, as shown in Figure 16-20.

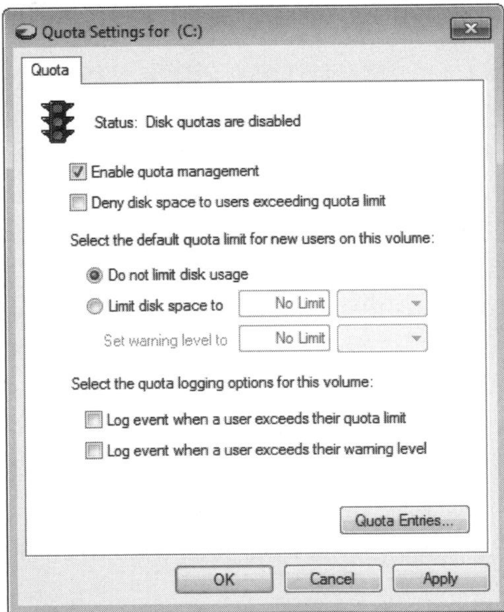

FIGURE 16-20 Disk quotas control how much of a disk users can fill.

From this dialog box, you can configure the following disk quota options:

- **Enable Quota Management** Quota management is disabled by default. Select this check box to enable quota management.
- **Deny Disk Space To Users Exceeding Quota Limit** By default, users are warned only if they exceed their quota limits. Selecting this check box causes Windows to block disk access after the quota is exceeded. Typically, warning users is sufficient, provided that you also log the events and follow up with users who do not clean up their disk space. Denying disk access will cause applications to fail when they attempt to write more data to the disk and can cause users to lose unsaved work.

> ***NOTE*** **To determine quota limitations for users, developers can call the *ManagementObjectSearcher.Get WMI* method to retrieve a *ManagementObjectCollection* object and then access the collection's QuotaVolume item.**

- **Do Not Limit Disk Usage** Does not configure disk quotas for new users by default. You can still use the Quota Entries window to configure disk quotas for users.
- **Limit Disk Space To and Set Warning Level To** Creates a disk quota by default for new users. The value in the Set Warning Level To box should be lower than that in the Limit Disk Space To box so that the user receives a warning before running out of available disk space.
- **Log Event When A User Exceeds Their Quota Limit and Log Event When A User Exceeds Their Warning Level** Configures Windows to add an event when the user exceeds her quota. You should typically select this check box and then monitor the events so that IT support can communicate directly with the user to keep the user within her quotas (or increase the quotas as needed).

Additionally, you can click Quota Entries to configure quota settings for existing users and groups.

How to Configure Disk Quotas from a Command Prompt

To view and manage disk quotas from scripts or from the command line, use the Fsutil administrative command-line utility. Useful Fsutil commands include:

- ***fsutil quota query C:*** Displays quota information about the C volume, as the following example shows.

```
C:\>fsutil quota query C:
```

```
FileSystemControlFlags = 0x00000301
    Quotas are tracked on this volume
    Logging for quota events is not enabled
    The quota values are incomplete
```

```
Default Quota Threshold = 0xffffffffffffffff
Default Quota Limit     = 0xffffffffffffffff

SID Name           = BUILTIN\Administrators (Alias)
Change time        = Tuesday, April 11, 2006   7:54:59 AM
Quota Used         = 0
Quota Threshold = 18446744073709551615
Quota Limit        = 18446744073709551615
```

- ***fsutil quota track C:*** Enables disk quotas on the C volume.
- ***fsutil quota disable C:*** Disables disk quotas on the C volume.
- ***fsutil quota enforce C:*** Enables disk quota enforcement on the C volume, which causes Windows to deny disk access if a quota is exceeded.
- ***fsutil quota modify C: 3000000000 5000000000 Contoso\User*** Creates a disk quota entry for the user Contoso\User. The first number (3,000,000,000 in the preceding example) enables a warning threshold at about 3 GB, and the second number (5,000,000,000 in the preceding example) enables an absolute limit of about 5 GB.

For complete usage information, run *fsutil /?* from a command prompt.

How to Configure Disk Quotas by Using Group Policy Settings

To configure disk quotas in an enterprise, use the AD DS Group Policy settings located at Computer Configuration\Administrative Templates\System\Disk Quotas. The following settings are available:

- Enable Disk Quotas
- Enforce Disk Quota Limit
- Default Quota Limit And Warning Level
- Log Event When Quota Limit Exceeded
- Log Event When Quota Warning Level Exceeded
- Apply Policy To Removable Media

Each of these settings relates directly to a local computer setting described earlier except for Apply Policy To Removable Media. If you enable this setting, quotas also apply to NTFS-formatted removable media. Quotas never apply to fixed or removable media unless they are formatted with NTFS.

Disk Tools

Microsoft provides several free tools that are very useful for managing disks and file systems, as the sections that follow describe. For information about tools used for troubleshooting disk problems, refer to Chapter 30.

Disk Usage

Perhaps the biggest challenge of managing file systems is managing disk usage. Quotas can help, but often you will still need to manually identify folders and files that are consuming large amounts of disk space.

The free Disk Usage (Du) tool, available for download from *http://technet.microsoft.com/en-us/sysinternals/bb896651.aspx*, can identify the mount of disk space a folder and its subfolders consume. Run Du.exe with the folder you want to analyze, as in the following example.

Du C:\users

```
Du v1.33 - report directory disk usage
Copyright (C) 2005-2007 Mark Russinovich
Sysinternals - www.sysinternals.com

Files:        96459
Directories:  19696
Size:         51,641,352,816 bytes
Size on disk: 47,647,077,498 bytes
```

EFSDump

Users can share EFS-encrypted files by adding other user certificates to a file. However, auditing the users who have rights to files would be very time-consuming using the Windows Explorer graphical interface. To list users who have access to encrypted files more easily, use EFSDump, available for download from *http://technet.microsoft.com/en-ca/sysinternals/bb896735.aspx*.

For example, to list the users who have access to files in the encrypted subfolder, run the following command.

Efsdump -s encrypted

```
EFS Information Dumper v1.02
Copyright (C) 1999 Mark Russinovich
Systems Internals - http://www.sysinternals.com

C:\Users\User1\Documents\Encrypted\MyFile.txt:
DDF Entry:
```

```
    COMPUTER\User1:
        User1(User1@COMPUTER)
DDF Entry:
    COMPUTER\User2:
        User2(User2@COMPUTER)
DRF Entry:
```

SDelete

When you delete a file, Windows removes the index for the file and prevents the operating system from accessing the file's contents. However, an attacker with direct access to the disk can still recover the file's contents until it has been overwritten by another file—which might never happen. Similarly, files that have been EFS-encrypted leave behind the unencrypted contents of the file on the disk.

With the SDelete tool, available for download from *http://technet.microsoft.com/en-us/sysinternals/bb897443.aspx*, you can overwrite the contents of free space on your disk to prevent deleted or encrypted files from being recovered.

To use SDelete to overwrite deleted files on the C drive, run the following command.

Sdelete -z C:

```
SDelete - Secure Delete v1.51
Copyright (C) 1999-2005 Mark Russinovich
Sysinternals - www.sysinternals.com

SDelete is set for 1 pass.
Free space cleaned on C:
```

Streams

NTFS files can contain multiple streams of data. Each stream resembles a separate file but is listed within a single filename. Streams are accessed using the syntax *file*:*stream*, and by default, the main stream is unnamed (and hence is accessed when you simply specify the filename).

For example, you can use the *echo* command to create a file or a specific stream. To create a stream named Data for the file named Text.txt, run the following command.

Echo Hello, world > text.txt:data

Directory listings will show that the Text.txt file is zero bytes long, and opening the file in a text editor will show nothing. However, it does contain data in the Data stream, which you can demonstrate by running the following command.

```
More < text.txt:data
```

```
Hello, world
```

Legitimate programs often use streams. However, malicious software also uses streams to hide data. You can use the Streams program, available at *http://technet.microsoft.com/en-ca/sysinternals/bb897440.aspx*, to list streams. For example, to list all files with streams within the Windows directory, run the following command.

```
Streams -s %windir%
```

```
Streams v1.56 - Enumerate alternate NTFS data streams
Copyright (C) 1999-2007 Mark Russinovich
Sysinternals - www.sysinternals.com

C:\Windows\Thumbs.db:
      :encryptable:$DATA 0
C:\Windows\PLA\System\LAN Diagnostics.xml:
   :0v1ieca3Feahez0jAwxjjk5uRh:$DATA   2524
   :{4c8cc155-6c1e-11d1-8e41-00c04fb9386d}:$DATA        0
C:\Windows\PLA\System\System Diagnostics.xml:
   :0v1ieca3Feahez0jAwxjjk5uRh:$DATA   5384
   :{4c8cc155-6c1e-11d1-8e41-00c04fb9386d}:$DATA        0
C:\Windows\PLA\System\System Performance.xml:
   :0v1ieca3Feahez0jAwxjjk5uRh:$DATA   500
   :{4c8cc155-6c1e-11d1-8e41-00c04fb9386d}:$DATA        0
C:\Windows\PLA\System\Wireless Diagnostics.xml:
   :0v1ieca3Feahez0jAwxjjk5uRh:$DATA   3240
   :{4c8cc155-6c1e-11d1-8e41-00c04fb9386d}:$DATA        0
C:\Windows\ShellNew\Thumbs.db:
      :encryptable:$DATA 0
C:\Windows\System32\Thumbs.db:
      :encryptable:$DATA 0
```

As you can see from this output, several files in subdirectories within the C:\Windows\ directory have a stream named $DATA.

Sync

In some cases, Windows might cache data before writing it to the disk. When a computer is shut down normally, all cached data is written to the disk. If you plan to shut down a computer forcibly (by initiating a Stop error or disconnecting the power), you can run the Sync command to flush all file system data to the disk. Sync is also useful to ensure that all data is written to removable disks.

You can download Sync from *http://technet.microsoft.com/en-ca/sysinternals/bb897438.aspx*. The simplest way to use Sync is to run it with no parameters and with administrative privileges, which flushes data for all disks.

sync

```
Sync 2.2: Disk Flusher for Windows 9x/Me/NT/2K/XP
Copyright (C) 1997-2004 Mark Russinovich
Sysinternals - www.sysinternals.com

Flushing: C E F
```

To flush data for the F drive removable disk and then eject it, run the following command.

Sync -r -e F:

```
Sync 2.2: Disk Flusher for Windows 9x/Me/NT/2K/XP
Copyright (C) 1997-2004 Mark Russinovich
Sysinternals - www.sysinternals.com

Flushing: F
```

MoveFile and PendMoves

Files can't be moved when they're in use by the operating system or an application. If a file is constantly in use, you can schedule Windows to move the file during startup using the MoveFile tool, available for download from *http://technet.microsoft.com/en-ca/sysinternals/bb897556.aspx*.

Use MoveFile exactly as you would use the *move* command as in the following example.

Movefile file.txt test\file.txt

```
Movefile v1.0 - copies over an in-use file at boot time
Move successfully scheduled.
```

The file will not be moved immediately. However, the next time the computer is restarted, Windows will move the file. If you want to delete a file that is constantly in use (a common requirement for removing malicious software), provide "" as the destination as in the following example.

Movefile file2.txt ""

```
Movefile v1.0 - copies over an in-use file at boot time
Move successfully scheduled.
```

The same download that includes MoveFile includes the PendMoves tool, which displays moves and deletions that have been scheduled. You can simply run the command without parameters, as the following example demonstrates.

pendmoves

```
PendMove v1.1
Copyright (C) 2004 Mark Russinovich
Sysinternals - wwww.sysinternals.com

Source: C:\Users\User1\Documents\file.txt
Target: C:\Users\User1\Documents\dest\file.txt

Source: C:\Users\User1\Documents\file2.txt
Target: DELETE

Time of last update to pending moves key: 2/27/2008 10:08 AM
```

Summary

Windows 7 uses local storage, which is typically based on hard disks, to store critical operating system files. Users rely on the same storage for confidential files. Because the integrity of the operating system and the security of your organization depend on the disks and file systems stored within each Windows computer, you must carefully consider your client-storage management requirements.

Fortunately, Windows 7 provides simple disk and volume management using either graphical or command-line tools. Windows Vista and Windows 7 improve on Windows XP by allowing partitions to be dynamically resized and thereby allowing administrators to reconfigure partitions without reformatting a disk or using third-party tools.

Windows 7 provides several features for managing disks and file systems. To provide data recovery in the event of a failed hard disk, corrupted files, or accidentally deleted data, Windows 7 provides both manual and scheduled backups. If backups are available online, users can use Previous Versions to recover a file without contacting the Support Center. System Image backup and restore enables you to replace a hard disk and get a computer up and running within minutes without needing to reinstall user applications.

To improve random access disk performance, ReadyBoost can use removable flash storage to cache disk contents. ReadyBoost will prompt the user automatically when compatible media is attached unless an administrator has disabled the feature. ReadyBoost offers the biggest performance gains on computers with slow disk access.

As with earlier versions of Windows, Windows 7 supports EFS to encrypt user files. To encrypt the system volume, including the hibernation and paging file, Windows 7 also supports BitLocker Drive Encryption. BitLocker requires a decryption key before Windows can start. The key can be provided by a hardware TPM chip, a USB key, a combination of the two, or a combination of a TPM chip and a PIN. BitLocker To Go is new in Windows 7 and allows removable drives to be encrypted while providing the BitLocker To Go Reader tool to enable previous versions of Windows to access the contents of the encrypted drive using a password.

Additional Resources

These resources contain additional information and tools related to this chapter.

Related Information

- Chapter 29, "Configuring Startup and Troubleshooting Startup Issues," includes more information about startup files and startup repair.
- Chapter 30, "Troubleshooting Hardware, Driver, and Disk Issues," includes more information about ChkDsk.
- "Windows and GPT FAQ" at *http://www.microsoft.com/whdc/device/storage/GPT_FAQ.mspx* includes detailed information about GPT.
- "BitLocker Drive Encryption: Technical Overview" at *http://technet.microsoft.com/en-us/library/cc732774.aspx* includes detailed information about BitLocker.
- *Security Risk Management Guide* at *http://technet.microsoft.com/en-us/library/cc163143.aspx/guidance/complianceandpolicies/secrisk/default.mspx* includes more information about cost/benefit analysis.
- "BitLocker Drive Encryption Team Blog" at *http://blogs.technet.com/bitlocker/* provides the latest BitLocker news direct from the Microsoft BitLocker team.

On the Companion Media

- Get-DefragAnalysis.ps1
- Get-DiskDriveInventory.ps1
- Get-DiskPerformance.ps1
- Get-LogicalDiskInventory.ps1
- Get-PageFile.ps1
- Get-PercentFreeSpace.ps1
- Set-CheckDisk.ps1
- Get-VolumeDirty.ps1
- Get-VolumeInventory.ps1
- Get-VolumeLabel.ps1
- ListFreeSpace.ps1
- Set-VolumeAutoCheck.ps1
- Set-VolumeLabel.ps1
- Start-Defrag.ps1

CHAPTER 17

Managing Devices and Services

The Windows 7 operating system builds upon the improvements previously made in the Windows Vista operating system in the areas of device installation and management, power management, and service implementation and management. These enhancements not only make it easy for users to connect and use devices and conserve battery life on their mobile computers, but they also enable administrators to manage the device installation process better and ensure energy efficiency across an enterprise. This chapter examines how to manage devices, energy efficiency, and services on desktop and mobile computers and describes the various improvements in these areas in Windows 7.

Understanding Device Installation and Management

Installing and managing devices and device drivers is an important aspect of overall desktop management for enterprises. Windows Vista introduced a number of improvements to the way that you install, configure, and manage devices. Windows 7 adds a number of new important features and enhancements in the way devices are installed, configured, and managed.

Device Enhancements in Windows 7

The device experience in Windows 7 builds upon the many improvements previously made in this area in Windows Vista. The following list summarizes some of the changes to device management implemented in Windows Vista. Many of these changes are significant for IT professionals who manage computers in enterprise environments, and later sections of this chapter explain how many of these enhancements work.

- **Driver store** Provides a central and authoritative point from which device driver files are copied to their final location when devices are installed.
- **Windows Resource Protection** Replaces Windows File Protection (WFP) and protects the integrity of system files and system registry settings, including device drivers and device settings. Drivers are added to the list of Windows Resource Protection (WRP)–protected files on the system only if they have been specifically flagged for protection by WRP when being staged to the driver store.
- **New standards for driver development** The Windows Logo Program Requirements 3.0 details new guidelines for vendors developing drivers to ensure that devices can be installed silently under nonprivileged standard user accounts without the need for reboots or local administrative privileges on the system.
- **Driver staging** Speeds up device installation and provides driver verification to prevent Plug and Play (PnP) detection of devices from causing the computer to stop responding or crash during device installation as a result of poorly written or corrupt drivers.
- **Driver packaging** Keeps all files needed for device installation in a single location during staging.
- **New tools for managing driver packages** Administrators can use PnPutil.exe, Drvload.exe, and other tools to add or remove driver packages from the driver store using either online or offline staging.
- **Mandatory driver signing** Requires all device drivers developed for 64-bit versions of Windows to be digitally signed.
- **Internal and third-party driver signing** Provides enterprises with guidelines and tools for signing in-house and third-party-developed drivers.
- **INF changes** Changes to INF file syntax to verify compatibility and ensure that only verified drivers are added to the store.
- **New driver-ranking algorithm** A new algorithm that Windows uses to determine which version of a driver is the most stable version for a particular device.
- **Recursive searching for driver paths** During driver installation, driver paths—including the specified directory and all its subdirectories—are searched recursively to find suitable drivers with fewer user prompts. In addition, Windows automatically searches multiple paths, including the local driver store, removable media, network shares, and even Windows Update, to locate and install the most suitable driver for a newly detected device.
- **New diagnostic logging** When enabled, driver diagnostic logging now writes information to the event logs instead of to a separate log file.

- **Windows Error Reporting** When a device driver or device install fails for any reason, the user is prompted to send information to Microsoft using Windows Error Reporting (WER). Microsoft and Independent Software Vendors (ISVs) can then analyze the information and provide updated drivers if needed.
- **Windows Update/Microsoft Update** Microsoft and ISVs can provide updated drivers that can be silently and transparently downloaded and installed on users' computers when they become available.
- **Windows Display Driver Model** A new video device driver model called Windows Display Driver Model (WDDM) replaces the XP Device Driver Model (XDDM) and provides enhanced functionality, including full Advanced Configuration and Power Interface (ACPI) support for video output devices, support for Windows Aero Glass, and improved video driver stability.
- **Windows System Assessment** Windows System Assessment (WinSAT) can be used for benchmarking system performance and determining the level of Aero Glass that can be used on the system. You can also use WinSAT to troubleshoot device driver issues during system startup.
- **New Group Policy settings for managing device installation and error reporting** Provide enhanced ways for using WER to control device installation and report driver failures. Blocking installation of devices by device manufacturer, device class, or specific device ID using Group Policy is also supported, and users can receive customized feedback when installation of a device is blocked.
- **New Group Policy settings for blocking installation and use of removable storage devices** Help to protect enterprises against accidental or malicious information leakage using portable storage devices, such as universal serial bus (USB) flash drives and portable media players. Policies can be configured to either block installation of removable media entirely or allow users only to read from such media but not write to them.
- **New Group Policy settings for power management** Provide enterprises with a way of configuring and enforcing power policy across computers in the enterprise.
- **Removal of support for standard Hardware Abstraction Layers** Standard (non-ACPI) Hardware Abstraction Layers (HALs) are no longer supported.
- **Removal of support for IEEE 1394 (FireWire)** Support for IEEE 1394 network has been removed.

The next list summarizes the additional changes to device management that have been introduced in Windows 7.

- **Devices And Printers** A new Start menu and Control Panel item in Windows 7 that provides users with a single location where they can discover, configure, and use devices connected to their computers. For more information about this feature, see the section titled "Using the Devices And Printers Folder" later in this chapter.

- **Device Stage** A new, intuitive visual interface for supported devices that makes it easier for users to configure, use, and manage devices connected to their computers. For more information about this feature, see the section titled "Understanding Device Stage" later in this chapter.
- **Device containers** An enhancement to the Windows PnP infrastructure that allows grouping together the various functions supported by a device. For more information about this feature, see the section titled "Device Containers" later in this chapter.
- **Improved device driver installation experience** The device installation experience has been improved in Windows 7 to make it easier than ever for users to connect devices to their computers, including both wired and wireless devices. For an overview of these improvements, see the section titled "Enhancements to the Device Installation Experience in Windows 7" later in this chapter.
- **New Group Policy settings for device installation** New Group Policy settings have been added to Windows 7 and the Windows Server 2008 R2 operating system for managing new features, such as Device Stage, and to enhance the manageability of the Windows device installation experience. These new policy settings are covered in the appropriate sections later in this chapter.
- **Display enhancements** Windows 7 includes numerous display enhancements that provide improved display performance and reliability. For an overview of some of these enhancements, see the sidebar titled "Display Enhancements in Windows 7" later in this chapter.
- **Other device enhancements** Windows 7 includes numerous other device enhancements, including the following:
    - Windows Biometric Framework (WBF), which provides a technology stack for supporting fingerprint biometric devices by Independent Hardware Vendors (IHVs).
    - Windows Mobile Broadband Driver Model, which defines the standards for driver integration and the use of the native broadband functionality included in Windows 7.
    - Windows Portable Devices (WPD), which provides a new way for computers to communicate with attached media and storage devices. WPD introduces two new features: an object-based Device-Driver Interface (DDI) and the Media Transfer Protocol (MTP). In addition, WPD supersedes the Windows Media Device Manager (WMDM) and Windows Image Acquisition (WIA) features used in earlier versions of Windows.

Display Enhancements in Windows 7

Windows 7 now supports WDDM 1.1, which reduces memory consumption for Windows Aero and provides improved display performance, improved video overlay presentation, a better viewing experience on TVs and widescreen laptops, and improved reliability and ability to diagnose problems. Windows 7 includes improved support for high-dot-per-inch (DPI) monitors, and users can configure DPI settings by using the enhanced Display utility in Control Panel, as shown here.

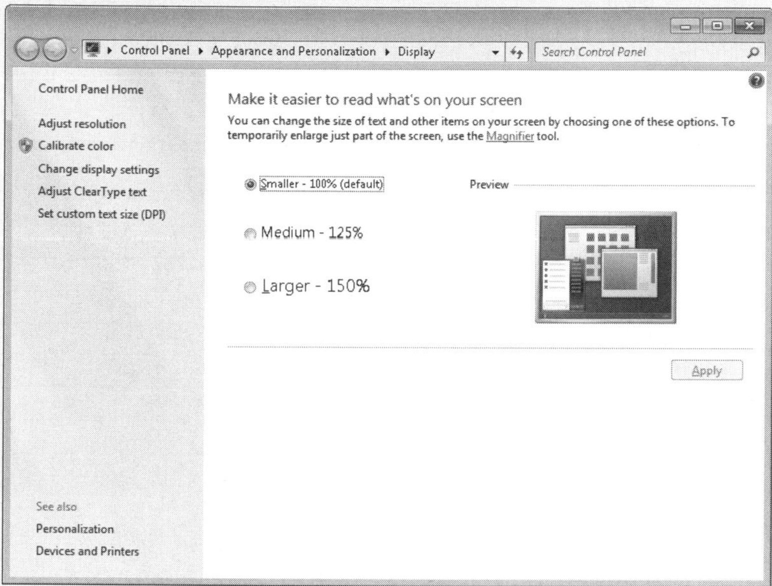

In Windows 7, the Display utility uses scaling percentages instead of the raw DPI values for a more intuitive user experience by allowing users to adjust their text size and other elements to make it easier for them to read their screens. The correlation between the scaling percentages and DPI settings presented by the Display utility are as follows:

- 100% scaling equals 96 DPI
- 125% scaling equals 120 DPI
- 150% scaling equals 144 DPI (this High DPI option is new in Windows 7)

Similar to Windows Vista, advanced users can still access the Custom DPI Setting dialog box in Windows 7 to specify a custom DPI setting for their monitors. To open this dialog box, select the Set Custom Text Size (DPI) setting in the image shown above in this sidebar.

Beginning with Windows 7, however, DPI settings can be configured on a per-user basis instead of on a per-machine basis. In addition, DPI settings can now be changed without the need for rebooting the system, although a logoff/logon is still required for the changes to take effect. Windows Internet Explorer 8 also includes native support for High DPI.

DPI settings can now be configured during deployment by configuring the <DPI> setting under <Display> in the Unattend.xml answer file to a value of 96, 120, or 144. Note that some applications can have rendering issues at nonstandard DPIs. To resolve such issues, Windows 7 (like Windows Vista before it) includes support for automatic scaling (also known as DPI Virtualization) to enable ISV applications that are not yet DPI aware to be displayed properly. Automatic scaling can be disabled on a per-application basis by selecting the Disable Display Scaling On High DPI Settings check box on the Compatibility tab of the application's Properties dialog box.

Other display enhancements found in Windows 7 include support for integrated display brightness control, a new Display Color Calibration (DCC) tool, and an enhanced Windows Touch technology that supports multi-touch. For additional information on display enhancements in Windows 7, see the Hardware Design For Windows 7 page on Windows Hardware Developer Central (WHDC) at *http://www.microsoft.com/whdc/system/hwdesign/HWdesign_Win7.mspx*.

Understanding Device Installation

Deploying, managing, and troubleshooting devices and device drivers in Windows 7 requires knowledge of how device installation works, including the following concepts:

- The driver store
- Driver packaging
- Driver staging vs. installation
- Driver ranking
- Driver signing
- Tools for managing driver packages

NOTE The 64-bit versions of Windows Vista or later versions do not support 32-bit device drivers or 16-bit applications. For more information, see Knowledge Base article 946765, "A Description of the Differences Between 32-Bit Versions of Windows Vista and 64-Bit Versions of Windows Vista," found at *http://support.microsoft.com/kb/946765*.

Driver Store and Driver Packaging

Introduced in Windows Vista, the driver store is a central location where all driver files are stored before they are copied to their final destinations during device installation. The location of the driver store on a Windows Vista or later system is the following:

%SystemRoot%\System32\DriverStore

Driver files are stored in folders called *driver packages,* which are located within the FileRepository subfolder under the preceding path. For example, the driver package developed by Microsoft that contains core mouse support files is contained in the following folder:

%SystemRoot%\System32\DriverStore\FileRepository\msmouse.inf_3dfa3917

Within this folder are the driver (.sys) files, driver setup (.inf) files, Precompiled INF (.pnf) files, and an Extensible Markup Language (XML) manifest (.man) file that contains the manifest of all the files within the driver package. Together, all these files add up to the driver package, which contains all the files needed to install the device. To protect these driver files, the NTFS File System (NTFS) permissions on the driver store and all its subfolders and files is Full Control for the LocalSystem account and Read and Execute for the Everyone built-in identity.

This central store and driver package architecture is different from Windows XP, where driver source files needed for installing devices are typically found in several locations, including the following:

- %SystemRoot%\Driver Cache\I386\Drivers.cab
- %SystemRoot%\Driver Cache\I386\Service_pack.cab (for example, Sp2.cab)
- .inf files under %Windir%\Inf
- .sys files under %SystemRoot%\System32\Drivers
- Support dynamic-link libraries (DLLs) under %SystemRoot%\System32
- Third-party co-installers in various locations

The following benefits result from maintaining a single, central store as an authoritative point from which to install driver files when new PnP devices are detected:

- Allows for potentially faster device installations, more reliable driver rollback, and a single standard for uninstalling drivers
- Allows you to protect drivers by using WRP
- Uses index files to minimize the performance impact on installing devices when the driver store grows in size as a result of the addition of new packages

Driver Staging vs. Installation

When the PnP service detects a new device in Windows XP, the driver files are extracted from .cab files found under %SystemRoot%\Driver Cache\I386, from .cab files on vendor-supplied media, or directly from Windows Update. The files are then copied to different locations as required to install the drivers and enable the device. Installing a device on Windows XP works like this: You connect the device, the PnP service detects it, and then Windows searches the driver search path for a suitable driver and installs the device. In Windows XP, therefore, the device has to be present on (or connected to) the system for device driver installation to occur.

Beginning with Windows Vista, however, device installation takes place in two distinct steps:

1. **Staging** The process of adding driver packages to the driver store
2. **Installation** The process of installing drivers from the driver store when the PnP service detects a device

Driver staging is performed under the LocalSystem security context. Adding driver packages to the driver store requires administrative privileges on the system. During driver staging, driver files are verified, copied to the store, and indexed for quick retrieval, but they are not installed on the system. The staging process verifies the driver packages against the following criteria to ensure that the drivers will not destabilize the system when they are installed later:

- The driver package must be complete and contain all files needed to install the device. This means that the INF file for the device must specify all the files needed during driver installation, and all those files must also be present.
- When drivers are installed, they cannot display any interactive user mode prompts or require any software-first installation facilities because Windows Vista and later versions require all device drivers to be installed under the noninteractive LocalSystem security context.
- PnP device driver files must be able to be installed in their entirety under the noninteractive LocalSystem security context. If the driver installation routine attempts to display any interactive user interface (UI) elements, installation will hang, timing out after five minutes. The user will be prompted to specify the location of new drivers for the device. (You can use Group Policy to modify the default device installation time-out value—see the section titled "Managing Device Installation Behavior" later in this chapter for more information.)
- The INF files and other driver files must not have been tampered with or modified. The integrity of the driver files is verified by the PnP service.
- The driver must not be listed on the known bad drivers list, which is maintained within a DLL on the system and cannot be modified.

If the driver package fails any of these criteria, staging of the package to the driver store will fail (except in the case of the third bullet item in the preceding list). This prevents Windows from being destabilized and possibly crashing when the user attempts to install the device requiring the package. Staging failure, however, has no impact on the system—it simply means that the package is not added to the store.

The device does not need to be present on (or connected to) the system when its driver package is being staged. Driver packages can be staged from media (CD, DVD, and so on) or from network locations. Windows Vista comes with numerous in-box drivers that are staged during Windows Setup so that they can be available for device installs when the user first logs on to the system. Beginning with Windows 7, however, the number of in-box device drivers has been reduced considerably because of the inclusion of Windows Update in the default device path. For more information about this change, see the section titled "Enhancements to the Device Installation Experience in Windows 7" later in this chapter.

Third-party driver packages can be staged in two ways:

- When the device is connected, by using vendor-supplied media and the Add New Hardware Wizard. (The Add New Hardware Wizard is for devices not recognized by PnP.)
- When the device is disconnected, by using staging tools such as PnPutil.exe or DrvLoad.exe. In addition, many device vendors are likely to provide .exe files that will stage drivers to the driver store.

You can also stage driver packages on Windows 7 by using the Microsoft Deployment Toolkit 2010 (MDT 2010). Using MDT 2010, an administrator can stage new drivers with simple drag-and-drop operations. In addition, you can group drivers so that they can be targeted to specific makes and models of computers that require them. For more information on MDT 2010, see Part II, "Deployment."

Finally, you can stage driver packages by using Windows Automated Installation Kit 2.0 (Windows AIK 2.0) to embed them in deployment images. For more information on Windows AIK 2.0, see Part II.

> ***NOTE*** **There is no hard-coded limit on the size to which the driver store can grow as new driver packages are staged. The driver store uses index files that are updated during stages to minimize the performance impact on installation time as the driver store grows in size.**

DRIVER STAGING AND INSTALLATION PROCESS

The driver staging and installation process alternates between user mode and kernel mode as follows:

1. The files in the driver package are copied to a temporary secure location within the user profile as Configuration Management Interface (CMI) objects. The driver store then validates trust for the driver package under the LocalSystem context.
2. If verification succeeds, the driver package is copied from the temporary location to the driver store under the LocalSystem context. After the driver package has been added to the store, its INF file is parsed to determine the names and locations of the required driver files. This information is added to the index files for the store. The driver package in the temporary location is then deleted.

   In addition, during the staging process, a system restore point is created to allow for quick rollback to an earlier state in case installing the driver destabilizes the system.

(You can use Group Policy to disable the creation of automatic restore points when drivers are updated or installed. See the section titled "Managing Device Installation Behavior" later in this chapter for more information.)

3. If the driver package needs updating later (for example, if a new version of the driver is released on Windows Update), this is initiated under the User context but takes place under the System context. (This step is optional.)
4. When the PnP service detects the presence of the device, the driver is installed from the driver store under the LocalSystem context. Installation takes place silently and transparently from the user's perspective because no additional prompts for files are needed.

   Note that a Found New Hardware message balloon may appear above the notification area as the device is being installed, and a second balloon notifies the user after the device is installed. However, you can use Group Policy to disable these notifications. See the section titled "Managing Device Installation Behavior" later in this chapter for more information.
5. If the vendor-supplied driver requires the installation of support software (for example, a control center for a display driver) in addition to the core device driver, a Finish Install page is displayed and runs under the User context (requires local administrative privileges or elevation) to allow the user to install the required support software for the device. (This step is optional.)

For more information about driver staging, see the section titled "Managing Driver Packages" later in this chapter.

DETAILED INSTALLATION PROCESS

The following steps offer a detailed description of the device installation process:

1. Windows detects that a new device is present.
2. The PnP service queries the device for identifiers.
3. Windows checks the three driver store index files—Infpub.dat, Infstore.dat, and Drvindex.dat—found under %SystemRoot%\Inf to determine whether an in-box or previously staged driver package is available for the device. If the driver was previously staged, Windows can install the driver without requiring the user to provide administrative credentials. In other words, standard users can install devices that have drivers staged in the driver store.
4. If no driver package for the device is found within the driver store, Windows recursively searches for a driver package for the device within the configured driver search locations, which in Windows 7 now includes Windows Update by default. If a suitable driver package is found, Windows confirms that the user has the permissions needed to install the device and verifies that the package has a trusted and valid digital signature. If the driver package satisfies these conditions, the package is then copied (staged) to the driver store.

5. The PnP service copies the driver files from the driver store to their final locations on the system.
6. The PnP service configures the registry so that Windows can use the new driver.
7. The PnP service starts the driver and the device becomes functional.

For more information about the device driver installation process in Windows 7, see the section titled "Enhancements to the Device Installation Experience in Windows 7" later in this chapter.

Managing Driver Packages

Managing driver packages involves adding and removing packages from the driver store. Drivers can be staged in two ways:

- **Online staging** This involves adding driver packages to the driver store while Windows is running on the system. You can perform online staging of driver packages by using tools such as PnPutil.exe or the Deployment Image Servicing and Management (DISM) command-line tool. For more information about using PnPutil.exe, see the next section. For information about using the DISM tool, see the section titled "Using DISM.exe" later in this chapter.
- **Offline staging** This involves adding driver packages to images for deploying Windows Vista with prestaged drivers needed by the targeted computer systems. You can perform offline staging of driver packages by using the DISM command-line tool or by using drag-and-drop operations with MDT 2010 to add driver packages to the Out-Of-Box Drivers folder under a deployment share in Deployment Workbench. For more information on how to perform offline staging of driver packages, see Part II.

> ***NOTE*** **You can use the Out-Of-Box Drivers folder under a deployment share in the MDT 2010 Deployment Workbench only to deploy core device drivers. If you also need to deploy a supporting application (Setup.exe file) for a third-party driver, you need to package it and deploy it as an application in MDT 2010. For more information on using MDT 2010 to deploy Windows 7, see Part II.**

USING PNPUTIL.EXE

PnPutil.exe can be used for online staging of driver packages on Windows 7 systems. This procedure is known as online servicing of Windows. PnPutil.exe supersedes the DevCon.exe tool for managing device drivers on earlier versions of Windows. You can run PnPutil.exe to add, remove, and enumerate PnP drivers from a Command Prompt window, or you can script it for batch operations.

The following examples use PnPutil.exe to perform various actions against the driver store. For the full syntax of this command, type **pnputil /?** at an elevated command prompt.

- **pnputil –a a:\usbcam.inf** Adds the package specified by Usbcam.inf into the driver store. This command requires you to run PnPutil.exe with administrator credentials but does not require that the device be connected to the computer.
- **pnputil –a path_to_INF_files*.inf** Stages multiple drivers using a single command or script. You must first place all driver packages into the central directory referenced in the command.
- **pnputil –e** Enumerates all packages that have been published (staged) in the driver store. If no third-party drivers are published, it will return the error "No published driver packages were found on the system."
- **pnputil.exe –d INF_name** Deletes the specified package from the driver store, provided that no currently installed device is using the driver. This command also purges the index of any reference to the driver package being removed. Note that this INF_name is the "published" name of a third-party package in the driver store, as returned by the pnputil –e command. This command requires you to run Pnputil.exe with administrator credentials.
- **pnputil.exe –f –d INF_name** Forcibly deletes the specified driver package. (You can use this if necessary to remove a package associated with a device that is physically installed in the system or when using –d alone returns an error accessing the package. However, this is not recommended because doing this causes problems for the device[s] that are still left referencing the driver package that was forcibly removed.) Note that this INF_name is the "published" name of a third-party package in the driver store, as returned by the pnputil –e command. This command requires you to run Pnputil.exe with administrator credentials.

Sample output from enumerating staged drivers on a Windows 7 computer might look like this.

```
C:\Users\tallen>pnputil -e
Microsoft PnP Utility


Published name :              oem0.inf
Driver package provider :     Microsoft
Class :                       Printers
Driver date and version :     06/21/2006 6.1.7100.0
Signer name :                 Microsoft Windows

Published name :              oem1.inf
Driver package provider :     NVIDIA
Class :                       Network adapters
Driver date and version :     05/03/2007 65.7.4
Signer name :                 Microsoft Windows Hardware Compatibility Publisher
```

Note that when using pnputil –a to stage multiple drivers using a single command or script, the command or script can sometimes halt before finishing. This can occur if either of the following conditions is true:

- The driver package is incomplete or damaged.
- The driver paths in the INF span multiple media.

If this problem occurs, troubleshoot the issue by stepping through the command or script to identify the problem driver and replace it with an updated driver designed for Windows 7.

USING DISM.EXE

The new DISM command-line tool (DISM.exe) is included both in a default install of Windows 7 and in the Windows AIK 2.0. DISM.exe can be used to service both online (running) and offline Windows images by adding or removing device drivers, hotfixes, and operating system packages; configuring international settings; and upgrading a Windows installation to a different edition, such as from Business to Ultimate. DISM.exe can be used to service images in the following versions of Windows:

- Windows Vista Service Pack 1 (SP1) or later versions
- Windows Server 2008
- Windows 7
- Windows Server 2008 R2

To service an offline Windows image using a technician computer on which Windows AIK 2.0 has been installed, you use DISM.exe to do the following:

1. Mount the image.
2. Enumerate, add, or remove drivers.
3. Unmount the image and commit the changes.

Servicing an online Windows image, however, does not require mounting or unmounting the image because the operating system is already running. In addition, any changes made to the driver store (for example, by adding or removing a device driver) are committed immediately when a DISM command is executed to service an online image. To indicate that the current running image is to be serviced, specify the */online* parameter in the DISM command.

For example, the following DISM command enumerates a list of installed out-of-box device drivers on a running Windows 7 system.

```
C:\Windows\system32>dism /online /get-drivers

Deployment Image Servicing and Management tool
Version: 6.1.7100.0

Image Version: 6.1.7100.0

Obtaining list of 3rd party drivers from the driver store...

Driver packages listing:

Published Name : oem0.inf
```

```
Original File Name : prnms001.inf
Inbox : No
Class Name : Printer
Provider Name : Microsoft
Date : 6/21/2006
Version : 6.1.7100.0

Published Name : oem1.inf
Original File Name : nvfd6032.inf
Inbox : No
Class Name : Net
Provider Name : NVIDIA
Date : 5/3/2007
Version : 65.7.4.0

The operation completed successfully.
```

To get more information about the driver named Oem0.inf, use the */get-driverinfo* parameter of DISM, as follows.

```
C:\Windows\system32>dism /online /get-driverinfo /driver:oem0.inf

Deployment Image Servicing and Management tool
Version: 6.1.7100.0

Image Version: 6.1.7100.0

Driver package information:

Published Name : oem0.inf
Driver Store Path : C:\Windows\System32\DriverStore\FileRepository\prnms001.inf_
x86_neutral_d9580ee0743299f4\prnms001.inf
Class Name : Printer
Class Description : Printers
Class GUID : {4D36E979-E325-11CE-BFC1-08002BE10318}
Date : 6/21/2006
Version : 6.1.7100.0
Boot Critical : No

Drivers for architecture : x86

    Manufacturer : Microsoft
    Description : Microsoft XPS Document Writer
    Architecture : x86
    Hardware ID : MicrosoftMicrosoft_X00AC
    Service Name :
    Compatible IDs :
    Exclude IDs :

The operation completed successfully.
```

Out-of-box device drivers can be added to or removed from a running Windows 7 system by using the /add-driver and /remove-driver parameters, respectively. Note that DISM driver servicing commands only support .inf files; you cannot use DISM to add or remove Windows Installer packages (.msi files) or other driver package types (such as .exe files) using DISM.exe. For more information on servicing online images using DISM.exe, see "Driver Servicing Command-Line Options" on Microsoft TechNet at *http://technet.microsoft.com/en-us/library/dd799258.aspx*.

Driver Signing

Using the Windows Driver Kit (WDK), enterprise administrators can sign custom-developed drivers using Authenticode and then stage these drivers to Windows systems or images. Windows 7 provides the ability to digitally sign drivers using an organization's own digital certificate, such as one generated by an enterprise certification authority (CA). An organization can use its digital certificate to sign unsigned drivers or to replace the driver vendor's signature with its own. The administrator can then use Group Policy settings to distribute the digital certificate to client computers and configure them to install only those drivers that the organization has signed. For information on how to do this, see *Device Management and Installation Step-by-Step Guide*: "Signing and Staging Device Drivers in Windows Vista and Windows Server 2008" found at *http://technet.microsoft.com/en-us/library/cc754052.aspx*. For information on the WDK, see *http://www.microsoft.com/whdc/DevTools/WDK/*.

> ***NOTE*** **Although you can use unsigned drivers with 32-bit versions of Windows Vista or later versions, 64-bit versions of Windows Vista or later versions require all device drivers to be digitally signed by the developer. For more information, see Knowledge Base article 946765, "A Description of the Differences Between 32-Bit Versions of Windows Vista and 64-Bit Versions of Windows Vista," found at *http://support.microsoft.com/kb/946765*.**

Driver Ranking

Windows XP uses the following algorithm to arbitrate between several possible drivers when installing a device:

1. In-box drivers are given first preference.
2. Windows Hardware Quality Labs (WHQL)–signed drivers are given next preference, with the most recent driver preferred.
3. Unsigned drivers are given lowest preference, with the most recent driver preferred.

Windows Vista and later versions support the following eight levels of digital signature, listed in order of decreasing preference:

1. Microsoft-signed WHQL-Certified drivers
2. Microsoft-signed in-box drivers (NT Build Lab Certified)
3. Microsoft-signed WinSE-Certified drivers

4. Drivers that have been signed using Authenticode (Enterprise CA)
5. Drivers that have been signed using Authenticode (Class 3 CA Certified)
6. Drivers that have been signed using Authenticode (MAKECERT.EXE Certified)
7. Microsoft-signed WHQL-Certified drivers for a previous version of the Windows operating system
8. Unsigned drivers

> ***NOTE*** **For the purpose of calculating rank, WHQL, DQS, INBOX, STANDARD, and PREMIUM are all equal for both Windows XP and Windows Vista.**

In addition to if (and how) drivers are signed, Windows Vista and later versions use the following criteria to determine which version of a driver should be installed for a particular device:

- The value of the feature score specified in the driver INF file if one is provided
- How closely the Plug and Play ID (PNPID) of the device matches the PNPID of the driver
- How recent is the driver compared to other suitable drivers
- The driver version

> ***NOTE*** **Date and version are considered only if every other aspect of the driver rank is equal—such as signed/unsigned, same hardware ID match, and so on.**

For WDDM display drivers, the driver arbitration algorithm is more complex, including the following:

1. WHQL or in-box driver
2. WHQL-Certified or Authenticode-signed driver for an earlier version of the Windows operating system
3. Unsigned driver
4. WDDM driver preferred over any other technology
5. Device ID
6. Driver date
7. Driver version

> ***NOTE*** **Driver arbitration for audio devices and printers follows a similar algorithm to that used for WDDM display drivers.**

Although the default driver-ranking process favors Microsoft-signed drivers over Authenticode-signed drivers, you can modify this behavior by configuring the following Group Policy setting:

Computer Configuration\Policies\Administrative Templates\System\Device Installation \Treat All Digitally Signed Drivers Equally In The Driver Ranking And Selection Process

For more information, see the section titled "Managing Device Installation Behavior" later in this chapter.

Installing and Using Devices

The device experience has been improved in Windows 7 to make it easier for users to install and use devices with their computers. Some of the key improvements in this area include:

- Enhancements to the device installation experience.
- The new Devices And Printers folder.
- Device Stage and its underlying device architecture changes.

The overall goal of these improvements is to make it simple for users to install device drivers and device-related applications simply by connecting their devices to the computer, either by using a connecting cable for wired devices or by using the Add A Device wizard to discover and connect to wireless and networked devices of all types, including Bluetooth devices, Web Services devices, Universal Plug and Play (UPnP) devices, WiFi devices, network scanners, printers, media players, and so on—even networked devices connected using LAN cabling. The result is that devices "just work" with Windows 7, and the latest driver for a device is automatically installed for optimal experience.

Enhancements to the Device Installation Experience in Windows 7

The device installation experience has been enhanced in Windows 7 in four ways:

- **It is automatic** When a device has been connected, Windows 7 automatically searches all configured device driver locations to find the most recent driver for the device. The device is then installed without any wizard or elevation prompt being displayed. Only a balloon notification (Windows can be configured to hide this) above the animated PnP icon in the system tray is visible to provide an indication that drivers are being installed for the device, and by clicking on this balloon notification (or the animated PnP icon) the user can view extended status information that indicates which device driver location is currently being searched. The device installation process in Windows 7 is thus entirely automatic from the user's perspective and can even happen when no user is logged on to the system.
- **It is easier** In previous versions of Windows, Bluetooth pairing was a complex experience for users. Beginning with Windows 7, however, this is no longer the case. The Add A Device wizard now makes this task extremely easy and intuitive. The Add A Device wizard also supports Vertical Pairing, which means that when you connect a WiFi device to your network, Windows will automatically pair your computer with the device. You no longer have to manually perform multiple steps such as connecting the device to a WiFi network, pairing with the device, and so on.

- **It is accurate** In Windows Vista, when a new device is connected to the computer, Windows checks the driver store for a supported device driver for the device. If a driver is found, the driver is installed, and the driver installation process ends without checking whether Windows Update might have a newer version of the driver. Beginning with Windows 7, however, Windows by default queries Windows Update first when searching for a driver for a device that has just been connected to or discovered by the system. If no driver can be found for the device on Windows Update, then Windows 7 checks its own driver store for a supported driver for the device. This default device path in Windows 7 (namely, using Windows Update first followed by the driver store) is fully configurable using Group Policy for administrators who want to have greater control over device installation. For more information, see the section titled "Managing Device Installation Using Group Policy" later in this chapter.
- **Performance has improved** To make device installation occur more quickly, a system restore point in Windows 7 is no longer captured prior to installing a new device. Users can also cancel lengthy driver downloads if they need to do so, and in special cases, certain devices can be configured not to search Windows Update for supported drivers.

> ***NOTE*** **The Add Hardware Control Panel utility found in Windows Vista has been removed from Control Panel of Windows 7. Users who still need the Add Hardware wizard to install older devices connected to their computers manually can do so by typing hdwwiz in the Search box on the Start menu and pressing Enter.**

To understand how device installation works in Windows 7, it is useful to consider a number of different scenarios, including:

1. A driver is found in the driver store.
2. A driver is found on Windows Update.
3. A driver is found in the driver store, but a better one is found on Windows Update.
4. A driver is found somewhere in the device path on the corporate network as configured using Group Policy.
5. No driver is found for the device in the driver store, on Windows Update, on the corporate network, or on media the user possesses.
6. Media supplied by the device vendor is in the possession of the user. Such media typically contains software that provides additional device functionality beyond what can be provided by the device driver alone.
7. No media has been supplied by the device vendor, but vendor software is needed to achieve device functionality beyond what can be provided by the device driver alone. This additional software is available for download from the vendor.

The sections that follow examine each of these driver installation scenarios by comparing what happened in Windows Vista with how things have changed in Windows 7. These scenarios describe the device installation experience for all PnP devices on Windows 7, including both external and internal devices, single- or multifunction devices, and wireless devices.

By examining these scenarios, you will see that, by default, Windows 7 searches Windows Update for compatible device drivers before checking the driver store on the computer. The main purpose of this change in device driver installation behavior is to ensure that Windows obtains the latest driver for a device. In previous versions of Windows, the driver installation process ended as soon as a compatible driver was found, even if a better-ranked driver was available in another location. In Windows 7, however, if a driver for a device is found in both the driver store and on Windows Update, the better-ranked driver is installed. For more information on configuring this behavior, see the section titled "Managing Device Installation Using Group Policy" later in this chapter.

SCENARIO 1: DRIVER FOUND IN DRIVER STORE

In Windows Vista, the following steps must be performed for this scenario:

1. The user connects the device to the computer.
2. A balloon notification appears, saying "Installing device driver software, click here for status."
3. When the driver found in the driver store has been installed, the balloon notification message changes to "Your devices are ready to use, device driver software installed successfully."
4. The user can now use the connected device to perform its function.

In Windows 7, the steps for this scenario are identical to the steps listed previously for Windows Vista. Although Windows 7 now checks Windows Update before querying the driver store, no driver for the device was found when Windows Update was queried in this case.

SCENARIO 2: DRIVER FOUND ON WINDOWS UPDATE

In Windows Vista, the following steps must be performed for this scenario:

1. The user connects the device to the computer.
2. A balloon notification appears, saying "Installing device driver software, click here for status."
3. A Found New Hardware dialog box is displayed, indicating that Windows Needs To Install Driver Software For Your Unknown Device. The device is labeled Unknown because Windows Vista has not found a driver for the device in the driver store on the computer.
4. The user must now select the Locate And Install Driver Software (Recommended) option from the dialog box to search Windows Update for a suitable driver. Because of the way User Account Control (UAC) is implemented in Windows Vista, selecting the Locate And Install Driver Software (Recommended) option causes an elevation prompt to be displayed.

5. Once the user makes the selection in step 4 and responds to the elevation prompt, Windows Vista queries Windows Update, finds an appropriate driver, and begins downloading the driver.
6. When the driver found in Windows Update has been downloaded and installed, the balloon notification message changes to "Your devices are ready to use, device driver software installed successfully."

In Windows 7, the steps for this same scenario are as follows:

1. The user connects the device to the computer.
2. A balloon notification appears, saying "Installing device driver software, click here for status." If the user clicks the balloon notification, a Driver Software Installation dialog box is displayed indicating that Windows is searching Windows Update for a suitable driver and that this might take a while.

   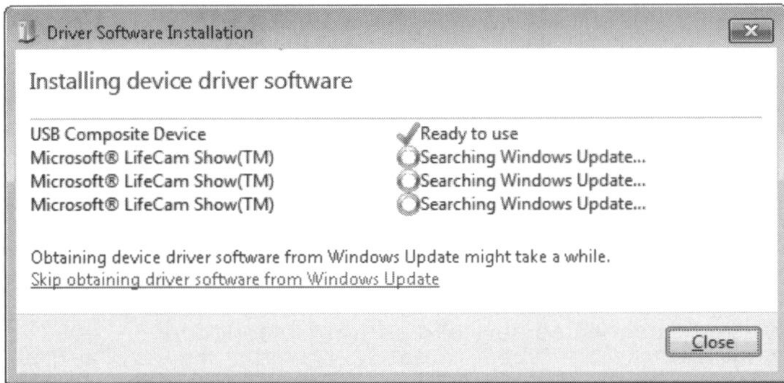

   If the download progress is too slow for the user, the user has the option of clicking Close and canceling downloading the latest available driver for the device from Windows Update.
3. When the driver found in Windows Update has been downloaded and installed, the balloon notification message changes to "Your devices are ready to use, device driver software installed successfully." If the Driver Software Installation dialog box has been opened, it will indicate Ready To Use when the driver has been installed successfully.
4. The user can now use the connected device to perform its function.

Note that in this scenario, the Windows Vista user must make two decisions that can determine whether the driver for the device will be installed successfully: making the correct selection in the Found New Hardware dialog box and responding appropriately to the elevation prompt. The improved device experience in Windows 7 removes the need for these two decisions, making it easier for the user to install the device.

SCENARIO 3: DRIVER IN DRIVER STORE, BUT BETTER DRIVER ON WINDOWS UPDATE

On Windows Vista, the following steps must be performed for this scenario:

1. The user connects the device to the computer.

2. A balloon notification appears, saying "Installing device driver software, click here for status."
3. When the driver found in the driver store has been installed, the balloon notification message changes to "Your devices are ready to use, device driver software installed successfully."
4. The user can now use the connected device, but it may not perform optimally because the latest driver, which is available on Windows Update, has not been downloaded and installed for the device. In other words, in this scenario, you have not obtained the latest driver for the device, so you are being deprived of the best possible functioning.

In Windows 7, the steps for this same scenario are as follows:

1. The user connects the device to the computer.
2. A balloon notification appears, saying "Installing device driver software, click here for status."
3. When the driver found in Windows Update has been downloaded and installed, the balloon notification message changes to "Your devices are ready to use, device driver software installed successfully."
4. The user can now use the connected device, which should function optimally because the latest driver has been installed for the device.

SCENARIO 4: DRIVER IS FOUND SOMEWHERE IN THE CONFIGURED DEVICE PATH

In both Windows Vista and Windows 7, the steps for this scenario are the same as the steps in Scenario 2.

SCENARIO 5: NO DRIVER CAN BE FOUND FOR THE DEVICE

In Windows Vista, the following steps must be performed for this scenario:

1. The user connects the device to the computer.
2. A balloon notification appears, saying "Installing device driver software, click here for status."
3. A Found New Hardware dialog box is displayed, indicating that Windows Needs To Install Driver Software For Your Unknown Device.
4. The user selects the Locate And Install Driver Software (Recommended) option from this dialog box and accepts the elevation prompt to search the driver path for a suitable driver.
5. The Found New Hardware wizard appears with the message "Insert the disk that came with your <*name of device*>.
6. Because the user doesn't have media containing the driver, the user selects Next in the Found New Hardware wizard to continue searching the configured driver path for a suitable driver.

7. After searching the configured driver path, no driver is found for the device, so the Found New Hardware wizard displays the message "Windows was unable to install your unknown device."
8. The user selects Back in the Found New Hardware wizard and selects I Don't Have The Disk, Show Me Other Options.
9. The Found New Hardware wizard displays the message "Windows couldn't find driver software for your device" and provides two options for the user to choose from: Check For A Solution and Browse My Computer For Driver Software (Advanced).
10. The user selects Browse My Computer For Driver Software (Advanced) and then specifies a local folder on the system where additional drivers are located. Unfortunately, the driver needed for the device is not in that folder, so the Found New Hardware wizard again displays the message "Windows was unable to install your unknown device."
11. The user selects Back again and this time selects Check For A Solution.
12. The Found New Hardware wizard again shows the message "Windows was unable to install your unknown device." After making 10 different decisions (which button to click or option to select), the user gives up and the device installation fails.

In Windows 7, the steps for this scenario are as follows:

1. The user connects the device to the computer.
2. A balloon notification appears with the message "Installing device driver software, click here for status."
3. When Windows has searched everywhere in the configured driver path and does not find a compatible driver for the device, another balloon notification message appears, saying "Device driver software was not successfully installed, click here for details." Clicking this link indicates No Driver Found and lets the user choose between always automatically searching Windows Update for the latest drivers (the default) or letting the user choose what to do. For more information on these options, see the section titled "Configuring Device Installation Settings" later in this chapter.

SCENARIO 6: VENDOR-SUPPLIED MEDIA IS AVAILABLE

The steps for this scenario depend upon whether you begin by installing software supplied by the device vendor or by connecting the device to your system. In both Windows Vista and Windows 7, if you begin by inserting the vendor-supplied media for the device into your CD/DVD-ROM drive, you are typically presented with an elevation prompt before the installation can continue. Once your vendor-supplied software has been installed, you connect your device and the steps follow as described in Scenario 1.

In Windows Vista, if you begin by connecting the device to your computer, the following steps must be performed to complete the device installation:

1. The user connects the device to the computer.
2. A balloon notification appears, saying "Installing device driver software, click here for status."

3. A Found New Hardware dialog box is displayed, indicating that Windows Needs To Install Driver Software For Your Unknown Device.
4. The user selects the Locate And Install Driver Software (Recommended) option from this dialog box and accepts the elevation prompt to search the driver path for a suitable driver.
5. The Found New Hardware wizard appears with the message "Insert the disk that came with your *<name of device>*."
6. The user inserts the vendor-supplied media for the device into the CD/DVD-ROM drive.
7. The user selects Next in the Found New Hardware wizard. Windows searches the media for a compatible driver, finds one, installs the driver, and displays the message "The software for this device has been successfully installed." However, because the Setup.exe program on the vendor-supplied media was not run in this scenario, any software provided by the vendor in addition to the device driver will not be installed. This may mean that the full functionality of the device may not be available to the user.

In Windows 7, if you begin by connecting the device to your computer, the following steps must be performed to complete the device installation:

1. The user connects the device to the computer.
2. A balloon notification appears, saying "Installing device driver software, click here for status."
3. The balloon notification message is replaced with another, saying "Your devices are ready to use, device driver software successfully installed."
4. The user inserts the vendor-supplied media for the device into the CD/DVD-ROM drive and responds to the elevation prompt that appears.
5. Once the vendor-supplied software for the device has been installed, the device is ready to use with its full functionality.

SCENARIO 7: ADDITIONAL DEVICE SOFTWARE IS AVAILABLE FOR DOWNLOAD FROM VENDOR

In Windows Vista, the following steps must be performed for this scenario:

1. The user connects the device to the computer.
2. A balloon notification appears, saying "Installing device driver software, click here for status."
3. When the driver found in the driver store has been installed, the balloon notification message changes to "Your devices are ready to use, device driver software installed successfully."
4. The user must open Internet Explorer and visit the vendor's Web site, locate the vendor's support page, and download and install the additional software needed for the device to achieve its full functionality. This may be beyond the ability of some users to perform on their own without expert assistance.

In Windows 7, the steps for this same scenario are as follows:

1. The user connects the device to the computer.
2. A balloon notification appears, saying "Installing device driver software, click here for status."
3. When the appropriate driver has been installed, the balloon notification message changes to "Your devices are ready to use, device driver software installed successfully."
4. A new balloon notification message then appears, saying "*<device name>* software is not installed, download software for *<device name>*."
5. When the user clicks the balloon, a dialog box is displayed, prompting the user to download the additional software needed from the vendor. This dialog box is generated by the Action Center on the user's Windows 7 computer.

CONFIGURING DEVICE INSTALLATION SETTINGS

During the Out-Of-Box Experience (OOBE) stage of a Windows 7 installation, a Set Up Windows dialog box is displayed, offering three choices:

- Use Recommended Settings
- Install Important Updates Only
- Ask Me Later

If the Use Recommended Settings option is selected, either by the user during a manual install or using an answer file during an unattended setup, the Windows 7 device installation experience will be configured automatically to search Windows Update for the latest device drivers before searching the driver store on the computer.

If users later want to change this behavior, they can do so by performing these steps:

1. Click Start, then Device And Printers to open the Devices And Printers folder.
2. Right-click the computer icon and select Device Installation Settings.
3. Select an appropriate option on the Device Installation Settings dialog box:

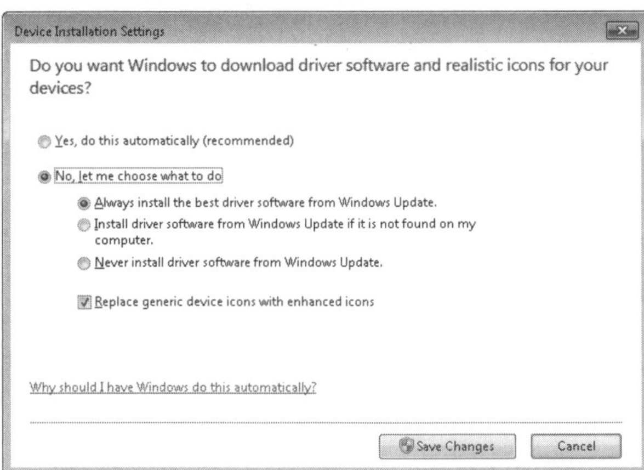

Administrators can prevent users from modifying the Device Installation Settings on their computers by using Group Policy. For more information, see the section titled "Managing Device Installation Using Group Policy" later in this chapter.

Using the Devices And Printers Folder

Devices And Printers is a new Start menu and Control Panel item in Windows 7 that provides users with a single location where they can discover, connect, configure, use, and manage devices connected to their computers. In previous versions of Windows, there was no central location where users could view and manage wired and wireless devices connected to their computers. Beginning with Windows 7, however, users can now use the Devices And Printers folder to view and manage all devices connected to or discovered by their computer, including printers, fax machines, scanners, cameras, removable storage devices, networked devices, paired WiFi and Bluetooth devices, multifunction devices (which appear as a single device), and other machines.

Figure 17-1 shows the Devices And Printers folder on a computer that has a printer, webcam, and music player attached to it.

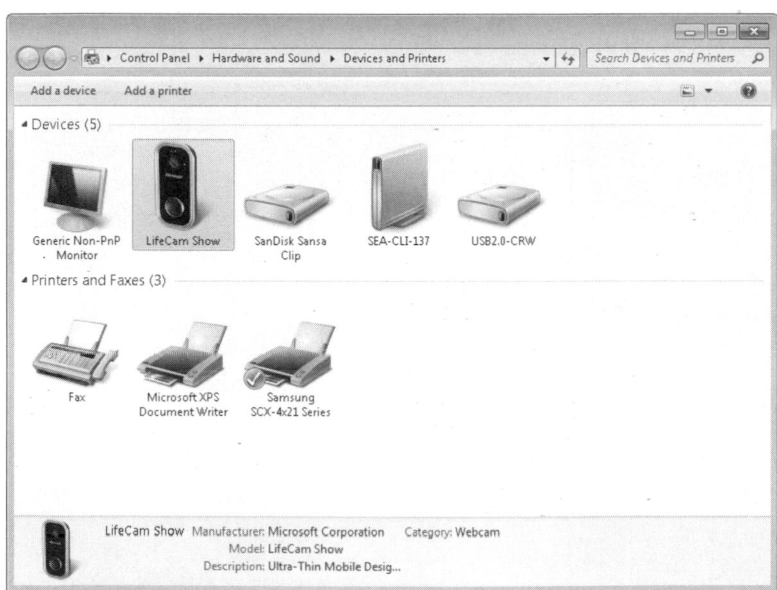

FIGURE 17-1 The new Devices And Printers folder in Windows 7

Features of the Devices And Printers folder include:

- A context-sensitive command bar that varies depending upon the device selected. Regardless of which device is selected, the command bar always displays the Add A Device (which is used for discovering and connecting with wireless devices) and Add A Printer (which launches the Add Printer wizard) options.

- A context-sensitive right-click menu that also varies depending upon the device selected. For example, you can access the properties for a device by right-clicking the device and selecting Properties. These properties pages are extensible by the device manufacturer, who can add additional tabs and register them for device management and configuration purposes. Note that the default double-click action for the right-click menu is also configurable.
- A device metadata system and a set of XML schemas that device vendors can use to customize the way their devices are presented to users in the Devices And Printers folder. For example, Devices And Printers can automatically download additional metadata for a newly connected device to display a photorealistic image of the device and additional manufacturer information that is not available from the hardware or device driver. For more information, see the section titled "Device Metadata System" later in this chapter.
- Integration with the new Device Stage feature of Windows 7, which is discussed in the next section of this chapter.

The Windows 7 computer itself appears as a device within the Devices And Printers folder. As Figure 17-2 illustrates, right-clicking your computer device icon displays a menu of actions that you can perform to configure and manage your computer.

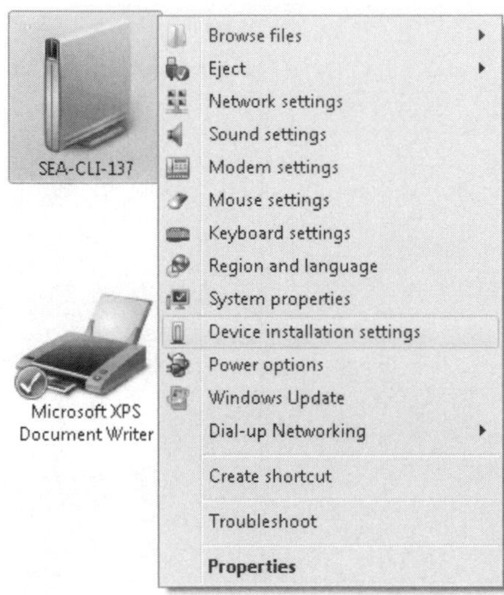

FIGURE 17-2 The context menu for the computer device icon in Devices And Printers

> ***NOTE*** **Advanced users can perform even more device configuration tasks, such as rolling back drivers, by right-clicking the computer device icon in Devices And Printers, selecting System Properties, and selecting Device Manager.**

Understanding Device Stage

Device Stage is a new, intuitive visual interface for supported devices that makes it easier for users to configure, use, and manage devices connected to their computers. Microsoft is working with IHVs to help them support Device Stage for their devices. Currently, Device Stage is supported by only a small selection of multifunction printers, music players, and mobile phones.

Figure 17-3 shows the new UI for a device that supports Device Stage, which shows branding information and various tasks from which the user can choose to use and manage the device. In addition, when the Device Stage UI is open for a device, a photo-realistic shell icon for the device is displayed on the taskbar. Clicking this icon displays a thumbnail preview of the device and of the Device Stage UI for the device.

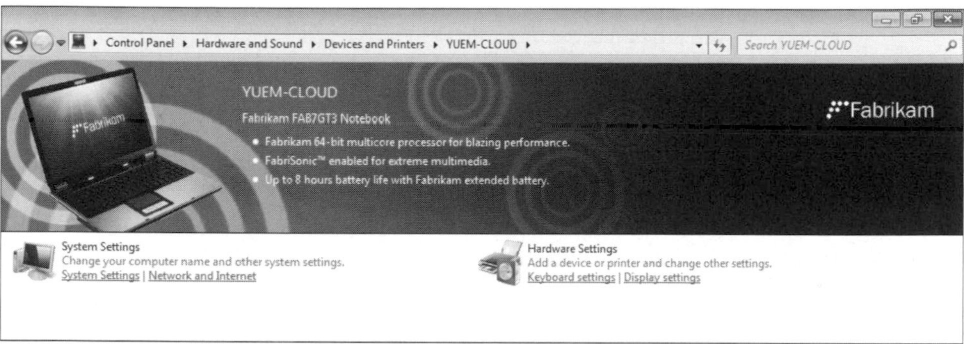

FIGURE 17-3 An example of the Device Stage user interface for a compatible device

Understanding the Device Experience Architecture

Figure 17-4 shows the architecture of the new device experience in Windows 7. New elements of Windows 7 include:

- Two new UIs (the Devices And Printers folder and the Device Stage experience).
- Two underlying features (Device Display Object and Device Metadata System) that make the new UIs possible.

The device manufacturer must supply the following for each device:

- XML metadata for the device, which includes both Device Stage XML and Device Display XML metadata
- Vendor applications for using the device, which may be Web applications and/or Windows applications
- Device drivers for physical layer connectivity with and use of the device

These features of the Windows 7 device experience are described in more detail below.

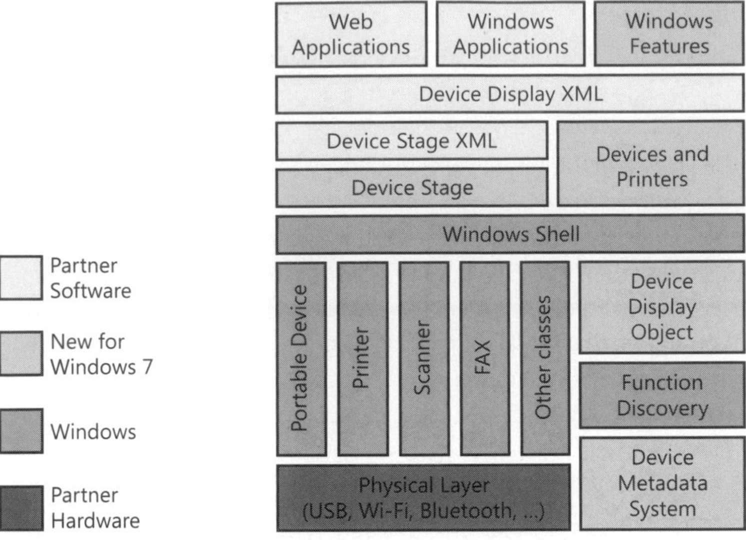

FIGURE 17-4 The architecture of the new device experience in Windows 7

DEVICE CONTAINERS

Because of the growing popularity of multifunction devices, such as printer/copier/fax /scanners, the PnP architecture has been enhanced in Windows 7 to support the detecting and grouping together of the different functions that a device supports. This new feature is called *device container*, a new PnP device property that groups device functions together into a single container representing the physical device. Device containers preserve the existing devnode model of Windows while providing users with a more natural representation of a physical device. (A *devnode* is an internal structure that represents a device on a system. It contains the device stack and information about whether the device has been started and which drivers have registered for notification on the device. Each device on a computer has a devnode, and these devnodes are organized into a hierarchical device tree. The Plug and Play Manager creates a devnode for a device when the device is configured.)

By using device containers, a multifunction device such as a printer/copier/fax/scanner can be presented to the user as a single device icon in the Devices And Printers folder (and also in the Device Stage interface if this is supported by the device). Device containers are identified by a container ID, which is a globally unique identifier (GUID) that is individual to each physical device. The container ID for a device is generated automatically by PnP. All devnodes belonging to the device container on a given bus share the same container ID.

DEVICE DISPLAY OBJECT

The Device Display Object is responsible for acquiring the XML metadata for a device and using it to render that device in the Devices And Printers folder (and in the Device Stage UI if the device supports Device Stage). The Device Display Object includes the Device Metadata

Retrieval Client (DMRC), which matches devices to Device Stage metadata packages. The Device Display Object is an internal feature of Windows 7 and is not configurable.

DEVICE METADATA SYSTEM

The Device Metadata System is new in Windows 7 and provides a process for defining and distributing metadata packages for devices that users connect to their computers. Device metadata is information that enriches the way that devices are displayed by and used with Windows; it consists of two types of metadata:

- **Device Display XML metadata** This type of metadata is conceptually similar to sleeve art for music CDs and allows a photorealistic device icon to be displayed along with additional device information, such as manufacturer, model, and description fields. Figure 17-5 shows an example of how Device Display XML metadata can enhance how the device is displayed in the Devices And Printers folder. (The bottom portion of the Devices And Printers window in the figure has been enlarged by dragging its upper border upward.)
- **Device Experience XML metadata** This type of metadata is conceptually similar to a simple Web page and is used by the Device Stage UI. For example, such metadata can enable branding by allowing background and overlay images to be displayed and can display a large, photorealistic image of the device, provide real-time device status information, display a vendor logo and marketing information, and describe what the user can do with the device. See Figure 17-3 earlier in this chapter for an example of how this metadata can be used to display a device that supports Device Stage.

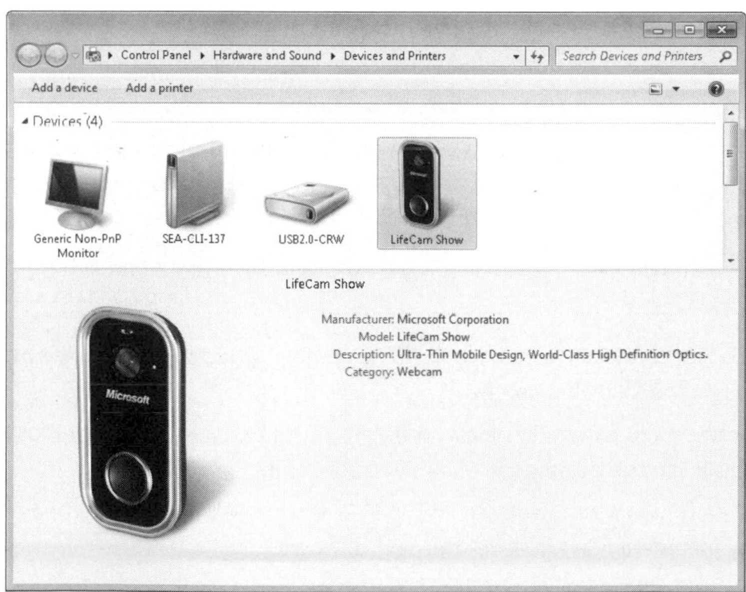

FIGURE 17-5 Device Display XML metadata can enhance how a device is displayed.

The device metadata system for Windows 7 delivers device metadata in the form of a package. This package consists of XML files, graphics files, and icon files and typically contains the following:

- **PackageInfo.xml** Contains the hardware IDs, model ID, timestamp, schemas, and index and locale information for the device
- **DeviceInfo.xml** Contains additional device information with an icon file for the device
- **WindowsInfo.xml** Contains additional information needed by Windows

If the device supports Device Stage, the following additional metadata files are included in the device metadata package:

- **Behavior.xml** Defines the layout of the Device Stage UI with any branding graphics included by the vendor
- **Task.xml** Defines the tasks that the user can perform with the device using the Device Stage interface with associated icons and commands for these tasks
- **Resource.xml** Contains any localized resources needed for the Device Stage interface

> ***NOTE*** **XML metadata can be associated with a device using either the hardware ID or model ID of the device, with model ID being the preferred method.**

IHVs that create metadata packages for their devices must submit this metadata to Windows Quality Online Services (Winqual). This must be done to validate the quality of the metadata and digitally sign the package to guard against tampering. Once the package has been signed by Winqual, it can be distributed to users by the following methods:

- Embedding the metadata in the hardware of the device
- Including the metadata in the vendor's software that is included with the device
- Installing the metadata on user's computers as an Original Equipment Manufacturer (OEM) add-on
- Making the metadata available for download from Windows Metadata and Internet Services (WMIS)

When a device is first connected to a Windows 7 computer, Windows acquires the metadata for the device by using the following process:

1. The DMRC checks the computer's local metadata cache and metadata store for metadata that applies to the device.
2. If no metadata is found for the device, the DMRC visits the WMIS Web site to determine whether any metadata is available for the device.
3. If no metadata is available for the device from WMIS, a standard icon is displayed for the device and descriptive information found in the device's driver is displayed. The

device is then displayed in the Unspecified Device section at the bottom of the Devices And Printers folder.

4. If metadata is found and downloaded for the device from WMIS, the Device Display Object feature parses the metadata and uses it to display the device in the Devices And Printers folder (and in the Device Stage interface if the device supports Device Stage).

Users can opt out of downloading metadata from WMIS by configuring the Device Installation Settings on their computers. For more information, see the section titled "Configuring Device Installation Settings" earlier in this chapter. Administrators can also prevent the downloading of metadata from WMIS by using Group Policy. See the following section titled "Managing Device Installation Using Group Policy" for information.

> **NOTE** Some older systems may display some internal devices, such CD/DVD-ROM drives, USB root hubs, and other devices, as separate devices in the Devices And Printers folder because the system is reporting these devices as removable when they actually are not. Updating the basic input/output (BIOS) on these older systems may resolve this problem.

Managing Device Installation Using Group Policy

Group Policy is the recommended method for managing device installation behavior across an enterprise network where Active Directory Domain Services is deployed. The following sections summarize the various policy settings available for managing the device installation experience on Windows 7.

Managing Device Installation Behavior

Policy settings for controlling device installation behavior in Windows 7 are found under the following node in Group Policy Object Editor:

Computer Configuration\Policies\Administrative Templates\System\Device Installation

Policies controlling device installation behavior, described in Table 17-1, are per-computer policies only. They may apply to Windows Vista and Windows Server 2008 only, to Windows 7 and Windows Server 2008 R2 only, or to all of these platforms—see the first column of the table for more information on which platforms to apply each policy. Policy settings that are new in Windows 7 are prefixed with an asterisk (*). Policy settings that were introduced in Windows Vista but have now been deprecated in Windows 7 are prefixed with two asterisks (**).

Although configured policy settings will be available for use on the computer without a reboot, they will take effect for only device installations initiated after the policy settings have been applied. In other words, the policy settings are not retroactive, and they will not affect the state of any devices that were installed previously.

TABLE 17-1 Policies for Managing Device Installation Behavior

POLICY NAME	DESCRIPTION
Allow Remote Access To The Plug And Play Interface (Applies to Windows Vista or later versions)	Specifies whether remote access to the PnP interface is allowed. If you enable this setting, remote connections to the PnP interface will be allowed. If you disable or do not configure this setting, the PnP interface will not be available remotely. Note that this policy should be enabled only if the administrator of the system requires the ability to retrieve information about devices on this system from another remote computer, such as using Windows Device Manager to connect to this system from a remote computer.
Configure Device Installation Timeout (Applies to Windows Vista or later versions)	Specifies the number of seconds the system will wait for a device installation task to complete. If the task is not completed within the specified number of seconds, the system will terminate the installation. If you disable or do not configure this setting, the system will wait 300 seconds (5 minutes) for any device installation task to complete before terminating installation.
**Do Not Create System Restore Point When New Device Driver Installed (Applies only to Windows Vista and Windows Server 2008)	If you enable this setting, system restore points will not be created when a new device driver is installed or updated. If you disable or do not configure this setting, a system restore point will be created whenever a new driver is installed or an existing device driver is updated.
Do Not Send A Windows Error Report When A Generic Driver Is Installed On A Device (Applies to Windows Vista or later versions)	If you enable this setting, a Windows error report will not be sent when a generic driver is installed. If you disable or do not configure this setting, a Windows error report will be sent when a generic driver is installed.

POLICY NAME	DESCRIPTION
*Prevent Creation Of A System Restore Point During Device Activity That Would Normally Prompt Creation Of A Restore Point (Applies to Windows Vista or later versions)	Lets you prevent Windows from creating a system restore point during device activity that normally prompts Windows to create a system restore point. Windows usually creates restore points for certain driver activity, such as the installation of an unsigned driver. A system restore point enables you to restore your system to its state before the activity more easily. If you disable or do not configure this policy setting, Windows creates a system restore point as it normally does. Note: This policy setting replaces the Do Not Create System Restore Point When New Device Driver Installed policy setting used in Windows Vista.
*Prevent Device Metadata Retrieval From The Internet (Applies only to Windows 7 and Windows Server 2008 R2)	If you enable this policy setting, Windows does not retrieve device metadata for installed devices from the Internet. This policy setting overrides the setting in the Device Installation Settings dialog box on the user's computer. If you disable or do not configure this policy setting, the setting in the Device Installation Settings dialog box controls whether Windows retrieves device metadata from the Internet.
*Prevent Windows From Sending An Error Report When A Device Driver Requests Additional Software During Installation (Applies only to Windows 7 and Windows Server 2008 R2)	If you enable this policy setting, Windows does not send an error report when a device driver that requests additional software is installed. If you disable or do not configure this policy setting, Windows sends an error report when a device driver that requests additional software is installed.

POLICY NAME	DESCRIPTION
Prioritize All Digitally Signed Drivers Equally During The Driver Ranking And Selection Process (Applies to Windows Vista or later versions)	When selecting which driver to install, do not distinguish between drivers signed by a Windows Publisher certificate and drivers signed by others. If you enable this setting, all valid Authenticode signatures are treated equally for the purpose of selecting a device driver to install. Selection is based on other criteria (such as matching hardware or compatible IDs) rather than whether the driver was signed by a Windows Publisher certificate or by another Authenticode certificate. A signed driver is still preferred over an unsigned driver. However, drivers signed by Windows Publisher certificates are not preferred over drivers signed by other Authenticode certificates. If you disable or do not configure this setting, drivers signed by a Windows Publisher certificate are selected for installation over drivers signed by other Authenticode certificates. Note: In Windows Vista, this policy setting was named Treat All Digitally Signed Drivers Equally In The Driver Ranking And Selection Process.
*Specify Search Order For Device Driver Source Locations (Applies only to Windows 7 and Windows Server 2008 R2)	If you enable this policy setting, you can select whether Windows searches Windows Update first, searches Windows Update last, or does not search Windows Update. If you disable or do not configure this policy setting, members of the Administrators group can determine the order in which Windows searches source locations for device drivers.
Turn Off "Found New Hardware" Balloons During Device Installation (Applies to Windows Vista or later versions)	If you enable this setting, "Found New Hardware" balloons will not appear while a device is being installed. If you disable or do not configure this setting, "Found New Hardware" balloons will appear while a device is being installed unless the driver for the device has suppressed the balloons.

Best practices for configuring these policy settings include the following:

- To ensure that users of Windows 7 computers have an optimal device experience, enable the Specify Search Order For Device Driver Source Locations policy setting and configure the setting to Search Windows Update First. This will prevent users from being able to modify their device installation settings, as described in the section titled "Configuring Device Installation Settings" earlier in this chapter.

- If you enable the Configure Device Installation Timeout policy setting, you cannot specify a time shorter than the default value of 300 seconds. Some devices, such as redundant array of independent disks (RAID) controllers and other boot-critical devices, can take a long time to initialize, and the default value for this setting was chosen to accommodate PnP installation of such devices to prevent boot failure. The reason an installation time-out value is specified at all is that improperly written driver installation packages can stop responding during installation, causing the system itself to stop responding. This was a problem in earlier versions of Windows because an improperly written driver could cause an interactive prompt to be displayed in the background where it couldn't be accessed. In Windows Vista, however, device installation has been moved out of Newdev.dll into the PnP service (DrvInst.exe), and the PnP service starts a separate, new process instance for each device installation. These architectural changes to how device installation works in Windows Vista make it much harder for an improperly written driver to make the PnP service stop responding. If the installation process instance does stop responding, however, the time-out value set here kills the process and displays the Add New Hardware wizard, allowing the user to specify a different driver to install. However, the reason for allowing administrators to be able to configure this policy setting is that if the administrator knows that the installation of some driver package(s) on some device(s) will take longer than the default time-out period (but not actually stop responding from the UI), she can allow the system to wait for a longer period of time for the installation to complete.

Managing Driver Installation Behavior

Policy settings for controlling driver installation behavior, including driver signing and driver search, are found under Computer Configuration\Policies\Administrative Templates\System \Driver Installation or User Configuration\Policies\Administrative Templates\System\Driver Installation, or both. However, the only driver installation policy setting that still applies in Windows 7 is the one that can be used to manage the driver installation behavior for standard users, specifically the following machine policy setting:

Computer Configuration\Policies\Administrative Templates\System\Driver Installation \Allow Non-Administrators To Install Drivers For These Device Setup Classes

This policy applies to Windows Vista or later versions and can be used to specify a list of device setup class GUIDs describing device drivers that standard users can install on the system. Enabling this setting allows users to install new drivers for the specified device setup classes. (The drivers must be signed according to Windows Driver Signing Policy or by publishers already in the TrustedPublisher store.) Disabling this policy setting or leaving it Not Configured means that only members of the local Administrators built-in group can install new device drivers on the system.

To configure this policy, follow these steps:

1. Using Group Policy Object Editor on a Windows Vista computer, open the Group Policy object (GPO) linked to the organizational unit (OU) where your target users have their computer accounts.
2. Navigate to the policy setting and double-click it to open it.

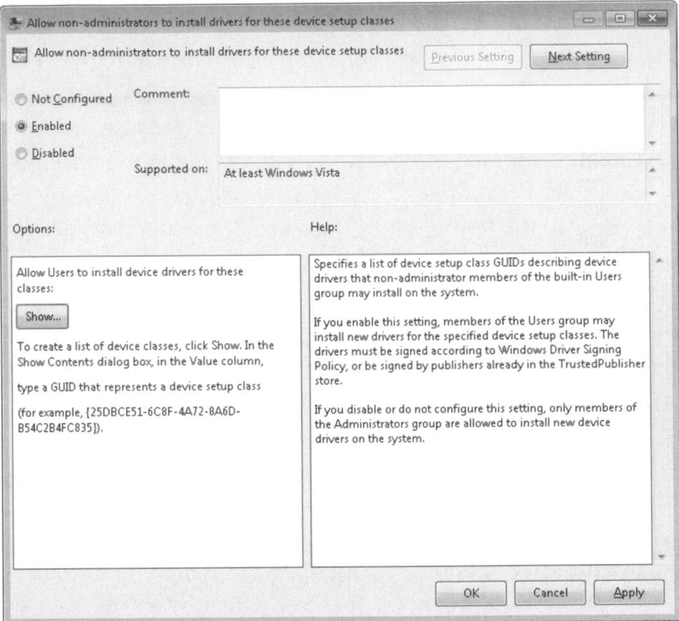

3. Enable the policy. Click Show and then click Add.
4. Type the GUID for the device setup class for the device type that you want to allow standard users to be able to install on computers targeted by the GPO. For example, to allow users to install imaging devices, such as digital cameras and scanners, type **{6bdd1fc6-810f-11d0-bec7-08002be2092f}** in the Add Item text box. Continue by adding other GUIDs as needed.

MORE INFO **For a list of device setup classes and their GUIDs, see** ***http://msdn2.microsoft.com/en-US/library/ms791134.aspx.***

Blocking Installation of Removable Devices

Policy settings for blocking device installation are found under the following node in the Group Policy Object Editor:

Computer Configuration\Policies\Administrative Templates\System\Device Installation \Device Installation Restrictions

Policies for blocking device installation, described in Table 17-2, are per-computer policies only. All but one of these policies apply to Windows Vista or later versions (the policy setting marked with an asterisk applies only to Windows 7 and Windows Server 2008 R2). In addition, two of these policy settings (marked with a double asterisk) have been updated in Windows 7 with new functionality.

Configured policy settings will be applied during the next background refresh of Group Policy. In other words, these policies do not require a reboot or logon/logoff to take effect after you configure them.

TABLE 17-2 Computer Policies for Blocking Device Installation

POLICY NAME	DESCRIPTION
Allow Administrators To Override Device Installation Restriction Policies (Applies to Windows Vista or later versions)	Allows members of the Administrators group to install and update the drivers for any device, regardless of other policy settings. If you enable this setting, administrators can use Add Hardware wizard or Update Driver wizard to install and update the drivers for any device. If you disable or do not configure this setting, administrators are subject to all policies that restrict device installation. If this computer is a Remote Desktop server, enabling this policy also affects redirection of the specified devices from a Remote Desktop client to this computer.
Allow Installation Of Devices That Match Any Of These Device IDs (Applies to Windows Vista or later versions)	Specifies a list of PnP hardware IDs and compatible IDs that describe devices that can be installed. This setting is intended for use only when the Prevent Installation Of Devices Not Described By Other Policy Settings setting is enabled and does not take precedence over any policy setting that would prevent a device from being installed. If you enable this setting, any device with a hardware ID or compatible ID that matches an ID in this list can be installed or updated if that installation has not been prevented specifically by any of the following policy settings: Prevent Installation Of Devices That Match Any Of These Device IDs, Prevent Installation Of Devices For These Device Classes, or Prevent Installation Of Removable Devices. If another policy setting prevents a device from being installed, the device cannot be installed even if it is also described by a value in this policy setting. If you disable or do not configure this setting and no other policy describes the device, the Prevent Installation Of Devices Not Described By Other Policy Settings setting determines whether the device can be installed. If this computer is a Remote Desktop server, enabling this policy also affects redirection of the specified devices from a Remote Desktop client to this computer.

POLICY NAME	DESCRIPTION
Allow Installation Of Devices Using Drivers That Match These Device Setup Classes (Applies to Windows Vista or later versions)	Specifies a list of device setup class GUIDs describing devices that can be installed. This setting is intended for use only when the Prevent Installation Of Devices Not Described By Other Policy Settings setting is enabled and does not have precedence over any setting that would prevent a device from being installed. If you enable this setting, any device with a hardware ID or compatible ID that matches one of the IDs in this list can be installed or updated if that installation has not been specifically prevented by any of the following policy settings: Prevent Installation Of Devices That Match Any Of These Device IDs, Prevent Installation Of Devices For These Device Classes, or Prevent Installation Of Removable Devices. If another policy setting prevents a device from being installed, the device cannot be installed even if it is also described by a value in this setting. If you disable or do not configure this setting and no other policy describes the device, the setting Prevent Installation Of Devices Not Described By Other Policy Settings determines whether the device can be installed. If this computer is a Remote Desktop server, enabling this policy also affects redirection of the specified devices from a Remote Desktop client to this computer.
Display A Custom Message Title When Installation Is Prevented By Policy (Applies to Windows Vista or later versions)	Specifies a customized message that is displayed to the user in the title of the notification balloon when policy prevents the installation of a device. If you enable this setting, this text is displayed as the title text of the message displayed by Windows Vista whenever device installation is prevented by policy. If you disable or do not configure this setting, Windows Vista displays a default title whenever device installation is prevented by policy. Note: In Windows Vista, this policy was named Display A Custom Message When Installation Is Prevented By Policy (Balloon Title).
Display A Custom Message When Installation Is Prevented By Policy (Applies to Windows Vista or later versions)	Specifies a customized message that is displayed to the user in the text of the notification balloon when policy prevents the installation of a device. If you enable this setting, this text is displayed as the main body text of the message displayed by Windows Vista whenever device installation is prevented by policy.

POLICY NAME	DESCRIPTION
	If you disable or do not configure this setting, Windows Vista displays a default message whenever device installation is prevented by policy. Note: In Windows Vista, this policy was named Display A Custom Message When Installation Is Prevented By Policy (Balloon Text).
Prevent Installation Of Devices Not Described By Other Policy Settings (Applies to Windows Vista or later versions)	This setting controls the installation policy for devices that are not specifically described by any other policy. If you enable this setting, any device that is not described by either Allow Installation Of Devices That Match These Device IDs or Allow Installation Of Devices For These Device Classes cannot be installed or have its driver updated. If you disable or do not configure this setting, any device that is not described by the Prevent Installation Of Devices That Match Any Of These Device IDs, Prevent Installation Of Devices For These Device Classes, or Deny Installation Of Removable Devices policies can be installed and have its driver updated. If this computer is a Remote Desktop server, enabling this policy also affects redirection of the specified devices from a Remote Desktop client to this computer.
**Prevent Installation Of Devices That Match Any Of These Device IDs (Applies to Windows Vista or later versions and is updated in Windows 7)	Lets you specify a list of PnP hardware IDs and compatible IDs for devices that Windows is prevented from installing. This policy setting takes precedence over any other policy setting that allows Windows to install a device. If you enable this policy setting, Windows is prevented from installing a device whose hardware ID or compatible ID appears in the list you create. If you enable this policy setting on a remote desktop server, the policy setting affects redirection of the specified devices from a remote desktop client to the remote desktop server. If you disable or do not configure this policy setting, devices can be installed and updated as allowed or prevented by other policy settings. Note: This policy has been updated in Windows 7 to add retroactive uninstall functionality, that is, to enable the removal of devices that were installed before the application of the policy (for example, during an OEM preload of Windows onto a system). To enable retroactive uninstall functionality, enable the policy setting and select the Also Apply To Matching Devices That Are Already Installed check box. Then be sure to enable and configure the Time (In Seconds) To Force Reboot When Required For Policy Changes To Take Effect policy setting because uninstalling previously installed devices will trigger a reboot.

POLICY NAME	DESCRIPTION
**Prevent Installation Of Devices Using Drivers That Match These Device Setup Classes (Applies to Windows Vista or later versions and is updated in Windows 7)	Lets you specify a list of device setup class GUIDs for device drivers that Windows is prevented from installing. This policy setting takes precedence over any other policy setting that allows Windows to install a device. If you enable this policy setting, Windows is prevented from installing or updating device drivers whose device setup class GUIDs appear in the list you create. If you enable this policy setting on a remote desktop server, the policy setting affects redirection of the specified devices from a remote desktop client to the remote desktop server. If you disable or do not configure this policy setting, Windows can install and update devices as allowed or prevented by other policy settings. Note: This policy has been updated in Windows 7 to add retroactive uninstall functionality, that is, to enable the removal of devices that were installed before the application of the policy (for example, during an OEM preload of Windows onto a system). To enable retroactive uninstall functionality, enable the policy setting and select the Also Apply To Matching Devices That Are Already Installed check box. Then be sure to also enable and configure the Time (In Seconds) To Force Reboot When Required For Policy Changes To Take Effect policy setting because uninstalling previously installed devices will trigger a reboot.
Prevent Installation Of Removable Devices (Applies to Windows Vista or later versions)	Prevents removable devices from being installed. If you enable this setting, removable devices may not be installed, and existing removable devices cannot have their drivers updated. If you disable or do not configure this setting, removable devices can be installed and existing removable devices can be updated as permitted by other policy settings for device installation. Note: This policy setting takes precedence over any other policy settings that allow a device to be installed. If this policy setting prevents a device from being installed, the device cannot be installed or updated, even if it matches another policy setting that would allow installation of that device. For this policy, a device is considered removable when the drivers for the device to which it is connected indicate that the device is removable. For example, a USB device is reported to be removable by the drivers for the USB hub to which the device is connected. If this computer is a Remote Desktop server, enabling this policy also affects redirection of the specified devices from a Remote Desktop client to this computer.

POLICY NAME	DESCRIPTION
*Time (In Seconds) To Force Reboot When Required For Policy Changes To Take Effect (Applies only to Windows 7 and Windows Server 2008 R2)	If you enable this setting, set the number of seconds that you want the system to wait until a reboot to enforce a change in device installation restriction policies. (The default is 120 seconds.) If you disable or do not configure this setting, the system will not force a reboot. Note: If no reboot is forced, the device installation restriction right will not take effect until the system is restarted.

MORE INFO **For information on how to identify device IDs for PnP devices, see** ***http://msdn2.microsoft.com/en-us/library/ms791083.aspx.***

Managing Device Redirection Behavior

A new addition to Windows 7 is a number of policy settings that you can use to control the redirection of USB devices on your system. These policy settings are supported only on Windows 7 and Windows Server 2008 R2 and are machine policies that are found in the following location:

Computer Configuration\Policies\Administrative Templates\System\Device Redirection \Device Redirection Restrictions

The two policies available for configuration are as follows:

- **Prevent Redirection Of USB Devices** Prevents redirection of USB devices.
  - If you enable this setting, an alternate driver for USB devices cannot be loaded.
  - If you disable or do not configure this setting, an alternate driver for USB devices can be loaded.
- **Prevent Redirection Of Devices That Match Any Of These Device IDs** Prevents redirection of specific USB devices (see Figure 17-6).
  - If you enable this setting, an alternate driver for the USB device cannot be loaded.
  - If you disable or do not configure this setting, an alternate driver for the USB device can be loaded.

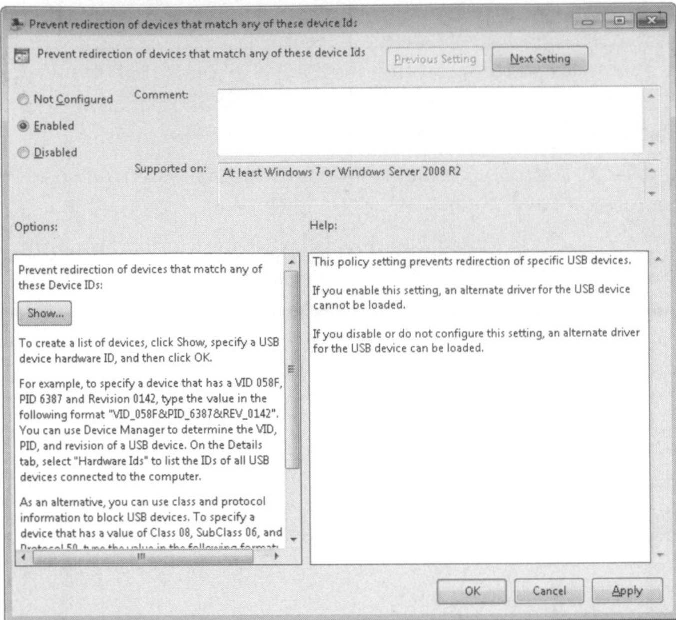

FIGURE 17-6 Details of the new Prevent Redirection Of Devices That Match Any Of These Device IDs policy setting

Troubleshooting Device Installation

The following sections outline specific troubleshooting steps with regard to device installation. For general guidance on troubleshooting hardware problems in Windows 7, see Chapter 30, "Troubleshooting Hardware, Driver, and Disk Issues."

Using Event Logs

Windows event logs can be useful for troubleshooting device installation problems and driver issues. In addition to checking the System Event Log, you should check the Operational Event Logs under Applications And Services Logs\Microsoft\Windows\DriverFrameworks-UserMode when experiencing problems installing devices and device drivers. For more information on using Event Viewer, see Chapter 21, "Maintaining Desktop Health."

Using WinSAT

WinSAT is a tool included in Windows 7 that provides a benchmark of system performance based on ratings of the following hardware:

- Processor
- Physical memory (RAM)
- Hard disk (%SystemDrive% only)

- Graphics and gaming graphics

WinSAT results are saved in both the registry and in an XML file saved in the %SystemRoot%\Performance\WinSAT\Datastore directory. You can also run WinSAT on demand by opening Performance Information And Tools in Control Panel and clicking Re-run The Assessment. WinSAT stores a history of up to one hundred system assessments and discards the oldest assessment when the limit is reached. WinSAT never deletes the initial assessment produced during the Machine Out-Of-Box Experience (MOOBE).

WinSAT can also be useful to determine which drivers are slowing down the boot process or blocking a system from Sleep mode. Problem drivers will be flagged under Performance Issues with messages such as "Drivers are causing Windows to start slowly" or "Drivers are interfering with Windows entering sleep mode." The solution to these situations is usually to update the problem drivers. However, these messages might also be reported as a result of configuration issues with devices.

Using Windows Error Reporting

When a device driver or device install fails for any reason, the user is prompted to send information to Microsoft using WER, where Microsoft, ISVs, and IHVs can analyze the information and provide updated drivers if needed. When a user makes a report, an entry is created on the WER site, logging the problem. Data is collected for the following types of device installation failures:

- **Device errors** Errors with distinct Device Manager codes.
- **Import errors** Problems staging device drivers.
- **Install errors** Reported when a driver has successfully staged but fails to install when the device is connected to the system.
- **Driver not found** Reported when a matching driver package cannot be located.
- **Driver protection errors** WRP processing errors: driver is flagged as protected but fails to meet criteria.
- **Generic driver found** Reported when a specific driver for a device is not available and Windows Vista installs a generic driver.
- **Windows Update errors** When a user encounters one of these errors and elects to report it, additional data is collected. The data gathered depends on the nature of the problem.

In each case, WER tracks the following information:

- Number of users (hits) who have seen the same problem in the last 30 days
- Number of hits per locale (English, German, French, and so on)
- Number of hits by operating system version
- Total number of hits
- Bugs filed on this problem

Developers use the information gathered to track high-profile driver requests and petition manufacturers to provide drivers through either Windows Update or the WER interface itself. Both internal Microsoft employees and manufacturers have access to WER data and the Winqual site found at *https://winqual.microsoft.com*. If a driver becomes available, it can be added to the response portion of the WER interface. After users elect to report the data, they are prompted to fill out a survey. (Note that if the IHV or ISV creates a response for the given error, the user can see the response without filling out a survey.) This response may be edited to provide a link to the driver on the third-party Web site, which should decrease the number of support calls requesting drivers for devices.

NOTE **By default, Windows 7 sends a Windows error report when a generic driver is installed on a device. You can use Group Policy to modify this behavior. See the section titled "Managing Device Installation Behavior" earlier in this chapter for more information.**

Using the SetupAPI Log File

In Windows XP, the SetupAPI.log found under %Windir% is a plain text log file that you can use to troubleshoot issues with installing devices. Beginning with Windows Vista, this log is moved to %Windir%\Inf and consists of two separate log files: SetupAPI.app.log and SetupAPI.dev.log. Each log file is made up of distinct sections, with each section representing one device install.

```
<Log Header>
>>>  Section header
     Device Driver install section 1
<<<  End Section
>>>  Section header
     Device Driver install section 2
<<<  End Section
>>>  Section header
     Device Driver install section 3
<<<  End Section
...
```

The INF file for the device driver controls device installation, and the SetupAPI logs record a series of entries corresponding to each instruction in the INF file, along with whether the action succeeded or failed. When parsing these logs to troubleshoot device installation issues, a good place to start is looking for problem descriptions such as "device did not install" or "wrong driver installed" or a message saying "Exit status: FAILURE".

The following example illustrates a device installation problem reported in the SetupAPI logs.

```
>>>  [Device Install (Hardware initiated) - USB\VID_045E&PID_00BD\{0D51C6EB-7E08-D342-
9E60-177B6A619B96}]
>>>  Section start 2006/08/17 13:40:16.348
     ump: Creating Install Process: DrvInst.exe 13:40:16.348
     ndv: Retrieving device info...
     ndv: Setting device parameters...
     ndv: Building driver list...
     dvi: {Build Driver List} 13:40:16.645
     dvi:      Searching for hardware ID(s):
     dvi:           usb\vid_045e&pid_00bd&rev_0100
     dvi:           usb\vid_045e&pid_00bd
     dvi:      Searching for compatible ID(s):
     dvi:           usb\class_ff&subclass_ff&prot_ff
     dvi:           usb\class_ff&subclass_ff
     dvi:           usb\class_ff
     dvi:      Enumerating INFs from path list 'C:\Windows\INF'
     inf:      Searched 0 potential matches in published INF directory
     inf:      Searched 34 INFs in directory: 'C:\Windows\INF'
     dvi: {Build Driver List - exit(0x00000000)} 13:40:16.818
     ndv: Selecting best match...
     dvi: {DIF_SELECTBESTCOMPATDRV} 13:40:16.819
     dvi:      No class installer for 'Microsoft® Fingerprint Reader'
     dvi:      No CoInstallers found
     dvi:      Default installer: Enter 13:40:16.821
     dvi:           {Select Best Driver}
!!!  dvi:                Selecting driver failed(0xe0000228)
     dvi:           {Select Best Driver - exit(0xe0000228)}
!!!  dvi:      Default installer: failed!
!!!  dvi:      Error 0xe0000228: There are no compatible drivers for this device.
     dvi: {DIF_SELECTBESTCOMPATDRV - exit(0xe0000228)} 13:40:16.824
     ndv: {Core Device Install}
     ndv:      Device install status=0xe0000203
     ndv:      Performing device install final cleanup...
     ndv:      Queueing up error report since device installation failed...
     ndv: {Core Device Install - exit(0xe0000203)}
     ump: Server install process exited with code 0xe0000203 13:40:16.832
<<<  Section end 2006/08/17 13:40:16.837
<<<  [Exit status: FAILURE(0xe0000203)]
```

The problem reported is failure to install the Microsoft Fingerprint Reader, and the cause of the problem is reported in the error message "There are no compatible drivers for this device."

By default, Windows Vista and later versions log device behavior in the SetupAPI logs at a more verbose level than in previous versions of Windows. You can use the following DWORD registry value to configure the verbosity level for these logs:

HKLM\Software\Microsoft\Windows\CurrentVersion\Setup\LogLevel

The default setting for this value is 0x2000ffff. For information on how to configure logging levels for the SetupAPI logs, see the white paper, "Debugging Device Installation in Windows Vista," found at *http://www.microsoft.com/whdc/driver/install/diagnose.mspx*.

Using Driver INF Files

WRP protects the integrity of system files and system registry settings, including device drivers and device settings. Drivers are added to the list of WRP-protected files on the system only if they have been specifically flagged for protection by WRP when being staged to the driver store.

When a driver package has been specifically flagged for WRP protection and that driver package is staged to the driver store, an event is logged to the event logs to indicate this. To verify that a third-party driver you plan to install will be protected using WRP, open the INF file for the driver and look for Pnplockdown=1 in the [Version] section. Microsoft recommends that ISVs who develop third-party drivers for Windows 7 include this setting (called the *lockdown flag*) in their INF files, which causes WRP to prevent users with administrative privileges from deleting or modifying the driver files referenced in the INF file. However, this is only a recommendation; ISVs are not required to include this setting in case compatibility issues should arise.

Using Device Manager Error Codes

Device Manager error codes are the codes that accompany icons displayed with exclamation points (also known as *bangs*) in the Device Manager console (Devmgmt.msc). To view these error codes, open the properties of the problem device in Device Manager and look under Device Status on the General tab. You can view the hardware ID of the problem device by selecting Hardware Ids from the Property list box on the Details tab. When you parse SetupAPI logs, this ID can be useful for gaining further understanding of why the device did not install or is not working properly.

Windows 7 reports the same Device Manager error codes as previous versions of Windows. Knowledge Base article 245386, found at *http://support.microsoft.com/kb/245386*, documents these codes, explaining the meaning of each and the kinds of scenarios that can cause them to be reported.

> ***NOTE*** **During a device installation, if a user is prompted to install the device in the future and responds by choosing No, a driver must still be installed. Otherwise, the PnP service will continue to redetect the driver and prompt for installation. In this scenario, the Null driver (which actually means that the device is configured not to use a driver) is installed and Device Manager displays error code 28. If the user later wants to install the device, the user must select the Update Driver option in Device Manager because the device previously was assigned an error code because it could not be installed with any driver.**

Device Manager error codes are reported only during device installation; they are never reported during driver staging. This means that if a Device Manager error code is reported, the problem occurred during device installation and not driver staging. A good place to start troubleshooting is looking at how physical installation of the device occurred and whether it was done properly. Device Manager error codes are also reported in the SetupAPI.dev.log file. See the section titled "Using the SetupAPI Log File" earlier in this chapter for more information.

Using Driver Verifier

Another device driver troubleshooting tool is Driver Verifier, which can monitor kernel-mode drivers and graphics drivers and detect illegal function calls or other actions that could corrupt the system. Driver Verifier can subject drivers to a variety of stresses to uncover improper driver behavior. The Driver Verifier Manager tool (Verifier.exe) is located in %WinDir%\System32 and can be run either graphically (press Windows Logo Key+R, type **verifier**, and press Enter) or from an elevated command prompt using various parameters (type **verifier /?** to learn more about these parameters).

> ***MORE INFO*** **For more information about using Driver Verifier, see** ***http://msdn2.microsoft.com/en-us/library/ms792872.aspx.***

Repairing Driver Store Corruption

If the driver store becomes corrupt, new drivers cannot be added to it and Windows may not be able to copy driver files from it. The inability to add new drivers or install new devices could therefore indicate problems with the driver store. Possible causes of driver store corruption can include:

- Interrupted write operations from sudden power loss.
- Damaged clusters on %SystemDrive% (use ChkDsk.exe to resolve).
- Bad memory being accessed during memory-mapped input/output (I/O).
- Malware or possibly even misbehaving anti-malware software.

If you suspect that driver store corruption is the problem, contact Microsoft Product Support Services (PSS) for troubleshooting.

Repairing Index File Corruption

If the files used to index the driver store are missing or corrupt, new drivers cannot be added to the driver store. The inability to add new drivers or install new devices could therefore indicate problems with these index files. Possible causes of index file corruption are similar to causes of driver store corruption.

If index files become corrupt, restore them from your most recent system backup. The three index files for the driver store are Infpub.dat, Infstore.dat, and Drvindex.dat, and they are found under %SystemRoot%\Inf. You can also use System Restore to restore index files because these files are added to protection points, but this approach is generally not recommended because reverting to a previous restore point can affect other aspects of the system and its installed software. Restoring from backup is therefore preferred.

DIRECT FROM THE SOURCE

Troubleshooting Driver Signing Issues

Sampath Somasundaram, SDET
DMI Team, Windows

If you see a Windows Security dialog box with a check box that says Windows Can't Verify The Publisher Of This Driver Software, you should verify the validity of the driver signature by checking the following:

1. See whether the INF file contains the CatalogFile=FileName entry and whether the FileName matches the CAT file in the same directory.
2. If the preceding step is successful, double-click the catalog file, view the signature, view the certificate, and check the Certification Path tab. Verify that the entire chain of certificates is trusted. If not, add them all to the trusted root CA store on the local computer. The last one should be added to the TrustedPublisher store.

If you see a Windows Security dialog box with a check box that says Always Trust Software From Some_name, install the certificate in the TrustedPublisher store on the local computer. Alternatively, you can select the check box and click Install, and the system will add the certificate automatically to the TrustedPublisher store. Note that you must use Mmc.exe to install the certificate, not the Certmgr.exe UI, because Certmgr.exe installs the certificate in the current user's store only.

If the package is signed but an unsigned dialog box still shows, determine whether any older unsigned versions of the driver are in the driver store. Open a command prompt and type pnputil.exe –e. To remove a driver from the driver store, type pnptuil –d OEMfilename.inf, where OEMFilename.inf is the OEM file name listed by pnputil –e for the driver package.

To check whether the catalog file actually contains the driver files, use the Signtool.exe utility from the WDK/Platform Software Development Kit (SDK) and type **signtool verify /c catalogfilename filename**.

Finally, to determine why your new latest freshly signed driver is losing to in-box drivers, do the following:

- Select the option to treat all signing as equal.
- Compare the date of your driver with that of the in-box driver.
- Check the version to see whether the dates are equal.

Understanding Power Management

The goal of power management in Windows is to maximize energy efficiency. This is accomplished by minimizing the amount of power used while automatically providing required performance on demand. Power management is an increasingly important issue for businesses as a result of rising energy costs and energy consumption by today's desktop and mobile computers. In the United States, the Environmental Protection Agency has estimated that PCs at home and in the workplace use about 2 percent of all electrical energy consumed. Leaving a PC on at home can add up to 8 percent to the total household power usage for the average home.

By contrast, putting a PC into Sleep mode for 14 hours a day can save between 600 and 760 kWh per year of electricity consumption. In 2009, this means savings of approximately $63,000 per year per 1,000 PCs for which this is done. The business and environmental importance of improving the power efficiency of PCs is compelling, and Microsoft has made numerous enhancements in this area in Windows 7.

Power Management Enhancements in Windows 7

Windows XP delivered improvements in the area of power management, such as support for hibernation and standby and the ability of Windows to automatically power down monitors and hard drives to reduce energy consumption. Windows Vista built upon these advances with a number of improved power management capabilities, including:

- Improved support for ACPI 2.0. In addition, Windows Vista also provides support for selected features of ACPI 3.0.
- Standard (non-ACPI) HALs are no longer supported in Windows Vista; only the ACPI Programmable Interrupt Controller (PIC) HAL and ACPI Advanced Programmable Interrupt Controller (APIC) HAL are supported in Windows Vista.
- Simplified power plan model, including three default power plans:
  - **Balanced** Automatically balances system performance with energy consumption—for example, by speeding up the processor when performing CPU-intensive activities, such as playing a 3D game, and slowing down the processor when performing activities that require little CPU, such as editing a document in Microsoft Office Word. Balanced is the default power plan in Windows Vista.
  - **Power Saver** Saves power at the expense of maximum performance. On mobile systems, this helps to maximize battery life. On desktop and server platforms, it works to reduce energy consumption.
  - **High Performance** Maximizes system performance at the expense of power savings.
- Mobile users can easily switch between power plans using the enhanced battery meter in the notification area or the battery tile in Windows Mobility Center. Desktop and server users can switch power plans in Power Options in Control Panel.

- OEMs can customize the default power plans or create their own and install them as the system default. In addition, users can easily create their own custom power plans and manage them.
- A new Sleep mode called Hybrid Sleep is available. It combines the benefits of standby and hibernation. When the system transitions to Hybrid Sleep, a hibernation file is generated, and the system transitions to sleep (ACPI S3 state). Sleep and resume time are improved because in most cases, the system is resuming from memory (ACPI S3). In the event of a power failure, system state is still preserved and the computer will resume from the hibernation file.
- Sleep reliability improvements. Windows Vista does not query applications or services before transitioning to any of the Sleep states. This is a departure from how Windows XP behaves. Applications may no longer prevent the system from going to sleep when a user clicks the sleep button or closes the lid on a mobile PC. This helps prevent the system from accidentally remaining powered on when in a laptop bag or other closed environment.
- Resume performance improvements. Waking from Sleep mode is much faster, and improved power transition diagnostics help ensure consistent and predictable power transitions.
- Support for managing power settings using Group Policy. This allows businesses to easily configure the policies for powering off monitors and computers after a period of inactivity, saving money in utility expenses.
- Extensible power settings. Third-party drivers and applications can add new power settings to the system, and custom power settings can be managed in the same manner as system power settings.

Windows 7 builds upon the foundation of Windows Vista with additional improvements in this area. For instance, numerous changes were made in Windows 7 to reduce power usage while the system is idle, which is the key issue for ensuring maximum battery life for mobile computers because periodic background activity can significantly increase the power consumption of a system. Very frequent events can greatly affect processor and chipset power usage, and long-running infrequent events can prevent the system from idling to sleep to conserve battery power. The changes made in Windows 7 to reduce idle activity and extend idle periods include:

- Windows 7 is now more aggressive about placing the system in Sleep mode when idle by responding to user input and application availability requests only.
- You can now configure how much idle time must elapse before Windows automatically transitions the computer to sleep. This energy efficiency feature is also configurable by Group Policy; see the section titled "Configuring Power Management Settings Using Group Policy" later in this chapter for more information.
- You can now configure Windows so that only user input and not application and driver activity can prevent Windows from automatically transitioning to Sleep mode. This

energy efficiency feature is also configurable by Group Policy; see the section titled "Configuring Power Management Settings Using Group Policy" later in this chapter for more information.

- A new /requests option for the Powercfg.exe command now lets you enumerate application and driver requests that prevent the computer from automatically turning off the display or entering Sleep mode.
- A new /requestsoverride option for the Powercfg.exe command now lets you override either individual availability requests or all availability requests.
- A new feature called Intelligent Timer Tick Distribution (ITTD) enables timer interrupts to be handled by a single processor on a multiprocessor system so that cores and processors can stay in Sleep states longer.
- A new feature called Timer Coalescing expires multiple distinct software timers at the same time to increase the average processor idle period.
- Open files in the client-side cache (offline files) will no longer prevent the system from sleeping. This energy efficiency feature is also configurable by Group Policy; see the section titled "Configuring Power Management Settings Using Group Policy" later in this chapter for more information.
- The Transmission Control Protocol (TCP) Distributed Program Call (DPC) timer is eliminated on every system timer interrupt.
- The frequency of USB driver maintenance timers is reduced.

Windows 7 also includes a number of new power policies that administrators can use to manage power on client computers. The policies for the Default (Balanced) power plan are summarized in Table 17-3.

TABLE 17-3 New Power Policies in Windows 7 for the Default (Balanced) Power Plan

NAME	GUID	DESCRIPTION	DEFAULT (BALANCED)	
			AC	DC
Unattended sleep time-out	7bc4a2f9-d8fc-4469-b07b-33eb785aaca0	Determines the amount of inactivity time before the system automatically sleeps if the computer resumed without a user present	2 minutes	2 minutes

NAME	GUID	DESCRIPTION	DEFAULT (BALANCED)	
			AC	DC
System cooling policy	94d3a615-a899-4ac5-ae2b-e4d-8f634367f	Determines whether active or passive cooling should be favored for thermal zones	Active	Active
Reserve battery level	f3c5027d-cd16-4930-aa6b-90db844a8f00	Configures the percentage of battery capacity remaining before displaying the reserve battery warning	N/A	7%
Advanced Host Controller Interface (AHCI) link power mode	0b2d69d7-a2a1-449c-9680-f91c70521c60	Configures AHCI link power modes (HIPM, DIPM) and link power states (Partial, Slumber, Active)	HIPM, Partial	HIPM, Slumber
Allow System Required Policy	a4b195f5-8225-47d8-8012-9d41369786e2	Enable applications to prevent the system from idling to sleep	Enabled	Enabled
Dim Display After	17aaa29b-8b43-4b94-aafe-35f64daaf1ee	Determines the amount of inactivity time before the system automatically reduces the brightness of the display on a mobile PC	5 minutes	2 minutes

Another new feature of Windows 7 that improves energy efficiency is a unified architecture that drives the scheduling of both services and scheduled tasks and enables trigger-starting of services. For more information on this new unified architecture and on Trigger Start services, see the section titled "Understanding Services" later in this chapter.

Windows 7 also allows you to run power efficiency diagnostics using the new /energy option of the Powercfg.exe command on a system to detect common energy efficiency problems. This command can detect power efficiency issues such as inefficient power policy settings, platform firmware problems, battery capacity issues, USB device selective suspend, and other problems. Enterprise system builders and OEMs can use this command option to validate the energy efficiency of Windows 7 computers prior to imaging them for deployment rollout. The command is also executed automatically when a Windows 7 system is idle and the data collected is uploaded to the Customer Experience Improvement Program (CEIP) at Microsoft. For information on how to use this new command option, see the section titled "Configuring Power Management Settings Using the PowerCfg Utility" later in this chapter.

Other new energy efficiency features in Windows 7 include:

- Wake timers are now disabled by default on Windows 7 mobile computers to prevent spurious wake events, such as a system waking up in a laptop bag due to an application request. Wake timers will continue to be enabled by default, however, on desktop systems.
- You can now configure the percentage of battery capacity remaining that triggers the reserve power mode. This energy efficiency feature is also configurable by Group Policy; see the section titled "Configuring Power Management Settings Using Group Policy" later in this chapter for more information.
- Adaptive Display Brightness can dim the display on a mobile computer automatically after a period of user inactivity. Adaptive Display Brightness is an intelligent policy whose time-out value automatically adjusts with user input and does not interfere with presentations, such as full-screen media playback. This energy efficiency feature is also configurable by Group Policy; see the section titled "Configuring Power Management Settings Using Group Policy" later in this chapter for more information.
- Wired LAN run-time idle detection, whereby network interface cards can enter low-power D3 (device sleep) state automatically when media is disconnected and return to D0 (working) state when it is reconnected.
- Wake on LAN (WoL), which is turned off by default in Windows Vista, is turned on by default in Windows 7. This feature uses a revised set of wake patterns to prevent spurious transitions from sleep.
- Support for the latest Intel HD Audio low-power specifications.
- Support for USB audio class selective suspend.
- Bluetooth radio now enters selective suspend when connections are in sniff mode.
- Updates to the core performance state algorithm.
- Core parking on supported hardware.
- Refined optical drive spin-down mechanism.

DIRECT FROM THE SOURCE

ACPI Sleep States

Pat Stemen, Senior Program Manager
Windows Kernel Team

The ACPI defines system power states using the Sx abbreviation (where x is the state number). For example, the S3 state refers to Sleep in Windows, when the system is in a low-power mode and the memory contents are preserved. The following table describes the other ACPI Sx states.

ACPI STATE NAME	WINDOWS STATE NAME	DESCRIPTION
S0	[On]	In the S0 state, the computer is on and running applications. The processor is executing instructions and the user can interact with the system.
S1	[Sleep]	The S1 state is also referred to as Sleep in Windows, but it is rarely used on modern computers. The S1 state leaves all system devices on, but the processor is halted, and the processor is not executing instructions.
S2	[Sleep]	S2 is a lower-power version of S1. Very few systems support the S2 state.
S3	Sleep	S3 is the common Windows Sleep state. In the S3 state, the processor and most system devices are turned off. Main memory (that is, RAM) is powered on to preserve the user's open applications and documents. Only devices needed to wake the system from sleep (such as LAN adapters and USB mice/keyboards) remain powered on.
S4	Hibernate	S4 is the Windows Hibernate state. In Hibernate, memory contents are written to a file on the disk. This file is called the hibernation file. All devices are powered off, and the processor is powered off as well. No instructions are executed on the processor.
S5	Shutdown	In Shutdown, no memory contents are preserved, and all system devices are powered off.

Configuring Power Management Settings

Beginning with Windows Vista, administrators could use Group Policy to configure power management settings on client computers in enterprise environments. In addition, the Power Options Control Panel item was enhanced to expose more advanced settings, and the Powercfg.exe command provided full support for managing all power configuration options from the command line. Windows 7 builds upon these Windows Vista features by refining the UI for power management, adding new Group Policy policy settings for configuring power management, and adding new command-line options for the Powercfg.exe command. You can also now script the configuration of power management settings by using Windows Management Instrumentation (WMI).

Configuring Power Management Settings Using the Power Options Utility in Control Panel

The Power Options utility in Control Panel provides a central location where users can configure how their computer balances power consumption against performance, create and manage power plans, configure the behavior of the power buttons on the computer, and configure other advanced settings. In Windows 7, this utility has been enhanced by hiding the High Performance plan by default under the Show Additional Plans option (see Figure 17-7). This was done to encourage users to conserve energy by not making the High Performance plan as visible as the Balanced and Power Saver plans.

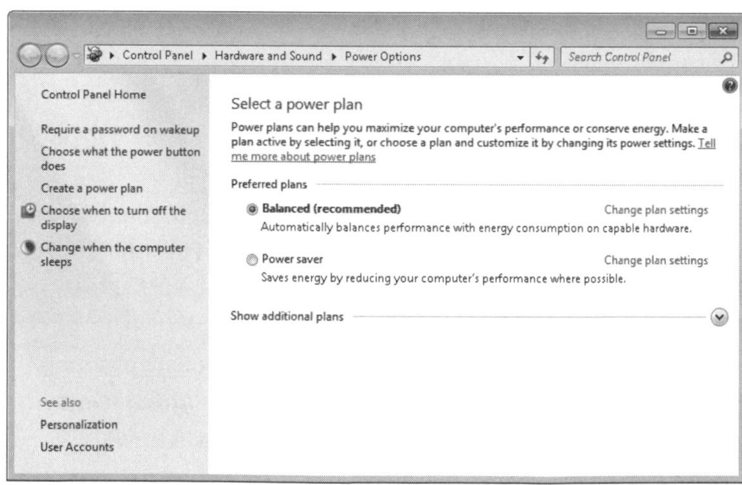

FIGURE 17-7 The Power Options Control Panel

Selecting either of the top two links on the left opens a screen where the user can configure the behavior of the power button on the computer and require that a password be specified when returning from Sleep mode (see Figure 17-8).

FIGURE 17-8 Configuring resume password and power button behavior

Beginning with Windows Vista, standard (non-Administrator) users can manage most power management settings on their computers. In earlier versions of Windows, users had to be local administrators to manage power settings on their computers. In addition, in Windows Vista and later versions, there is a single set of power plans for the computer. All users have access to the same power settings across the computer, helping to avoid situations in which power policy changes based on which user, if any, is currently logged on. This is a departure from Windows XP, where one portion of the power policy was specified on a per-user basis and the remainder on a per-computer basis.

To manage advanced power options, select either of the lower two links on the upper left of the main Power Options screen and then select Change Advanced Power Settings to open the Advanced Settings tab for Power Options (see Figure 17-9).

Advanced power settings provide more detailed control over power consumption and the ability to change some settings not displayed elsewhere in Power Options. Additional settings include the power-saving mode for wireless adapters, USB selective suspend, PCI Express Active-State Power Management, and Search and Indexing activity on the system.

Note that some systems (particularly mobile computers) may have additional power settings in advanced power settings. For example, third-party drivers and applications may add new power settings. Common third-party settings include power management options for video adapters.

> ***NOTE*** **When you select Change Settings That Are Currently Unavailable and respond to the UAC prompt, no new items will appear in the list, which can seem confusing. However, some options that could not be edited before can now be edited.**

FIGURE 17-9 Configuring advanced power settings

HOW IT WORKS

Power-Saving Modes for Wireless Network Adapters

On the Advanced Settings tab for Power Options, four different power-saving modes are displayed under Wireless Network Adapter (the On Battery settings are relevant only on mobile systems and computers with batteries):

- Maximum Performance
- Low Power Saving
- Medium Power Saving
- Maximum Power Saving

If Maximum Performance is chosen, the wireless adapter will not use any power management features but will communicate with the wireless access point at the maximum speed. However, if Maximum Power Saving is chosen, the wireless adapter will conserve energy by communicating with the wireless access point at a lower speed. This reduces wireless performance but conserves power and helps extend battery life on mobile PCs. The Low Power Saving and Medium Power Saving settings balance power savings and performance.

NOTE You can configure additional advanced power settings by using the Powercfg.exe command. See the section titled "Configuring Power Management Settings Using the Powercfg Utility" later in the chapter for more information.

Configuring Power Management Settings Using Group Policy

Power Management policy settings in Windows Vista or later versions are per-computer settings that apply only to computers running Windows Vista or later versions. Each Power Management policy setting may be configured independently for when the computer is plugged in or running on battery power.

Group Policy settings for Power Management are found in the following location:

Computer Management/Policies/Administrative Templates/System/Power Management

The subnodes beneath this location are as follows:

- **Button Settings** Used to configure the behavior of pressing the power and sleep buttons and the Start menu power button, and the lid switch on laptops.
- **Hard Disk Settings** Used to specify the period of inactivity after which the hard drive will turn off.
- **Notification Settings** Used to specify low and critical battery levels and behaviors.
- **Sleep Settings** Used to specify sleep and hibernation time-outs and behaviors.
- **Video and Display Settings** Used to configure the display time-out. The display time-out controls the length of the period of inactivity before the display automatically turns off.

Table 17-4 lists all Power Management policy settings for Windows 7, showing only the "On Battery" setting whenever a corresponding "Plugged In" setting also exists. The table also indicates the policy settings that are new in Windows 7 by prefixing them with an asterisk (*).

TABLE 17-4 Selected Power Management Policy Settings for Windows Vista

POLICY NAME	DESCRIPTION
	FOUND UNDER /SYSTEM/POWER MANAGEMENT
Select An Active Power Plan (Applies to Windows Vista or later versions)	If you enable this setting, you can specify the active power plan from a list of default Windows Vista power plans. To specify a custom power plan, use the Custom Active Power Plan setting. If you disable this policy or do not configure it, users can see and change this setting.

POLICY NAME	DESCRIPTION
Specify A Custom Active Power Plan (Applies to Windows Vista or later versions)	If you use this policy, you can specify a custom active power plan when you enter a power plan's GUID. Retrieve the custom power plan GUID by using Powercfg, the power configuration command-line tool. Enter the GUID using the following format: *XXXXXXXX-XXXX-XXXX-XXXX-XXXXXXXXXXXX* (For example, enter **103eea6e-9fcd-4544-a713-c282d8e50083**.) If you disable this policy or do not configure it, users can see and change this setting. Note that this is a general setting that is not specific to mobile computers. Also, a plan corresponding to the GUID-specified power plan must exist on the target computer.
	FOUND UNDER /SYSTEM/POWER MANAGEMENT/BUTTON SETTINGS
Select The Lid Switch Action (On Battery) (Applies to Windows Vista or later versions)	If you enable this policy, you can specify the action that Windows Vista takes when a user closes the lid on a mobile PC. Possible actions include: ■ Take No Action ■ Sleep ■ Hibernate ■ Shut Down If you disable this policy setting or do not configure it, users can see and change this setting.
Select The Power Button Action (On Battery) (Applies to Windows Vista or later versions)	If you enable this policy setting, you can specify the action that Windows Vista takes when a user presses the power button. Possible actions include: ■ Take No Action ■ Sleep ■ Hibernate ■ Shut Down If you disable this policy setting or do not configure it, users can see and change this setting.
Select The Sleep Button Action (On Battery) (Applies to Windows Vista or later versions)	If you enable this policy setting, you can specify the action that Windows Vista takes when a user presses the sleep button. Possible actions include: ■ Take No Action ■ Sleep ■ Hibernate ■ Shut Down If you disable this policy setting or do not configure it, users can see and change this setting.

POLICY NAME	DESCRIPTION
Select The Start Menu Power Button Action (On Battery) (Applies only to Windows Vista)	If you enable this policy setting, you can specify the action that Windows takes when a user presses the UI sleep button. Possible actions include: ■ Take No Action ■ Sleep ■ Hibernate ■ Shut Down If you disable this policy setting or do not configure it, users can see and change this setting.
	FOUND UNDER /SYSTEM/POWER MANAGEMENT/HARD DISK SETTINGS
Turn Off The Hard Disk (On Battery) (Applies to Windows Vista or later versions)	If you enable this policy, you can specify, in seconds, how much idle time should elapse before Windows Vista turns off the hard disk. If you disable this policy or do not configure it, users can see and change this setting. Note that this is a general setting that is not specific to mobile computers.
	FOUND UNDER /SYSTEM/POWER MANAGEMENT/NOTIFICATION SETTINGS
Critical Battery Notification Action (Applies to Windows Vista or later versions)	If you enable this policy setting, you can specify the action that Windows takes when battery capacity reaches the critical-battery notification level. Possible actions include: ■ Take No Action ■ Sleep ■ Hibernate ■ Shut Down If you disable this policy setting or do not configure it, users can see and change this setting.
Critical Battery Notification Level (Applies to Windows Vista or later versions)	Specifies the percentage of battery capacity remaining that triggers the critical-battery notification action. If you enable this policy, you must enter a numeric value (as a percentage) to set the battery level that triggers the critical-battery notification. To set the action that is triggered, see the Critical Battery Notification Action policy setting. If you disable this policy setting or do not configure it, users can see and change this setting.

POLICY NAME	DESCRIPTION
Low Battery Notification Action (Applies to Windows Vista or later versions)	If you enable this policy setting, you can specify the action that Windows takes when battery capacity reaches the low-battery notification level. Possible actions include: ■ Take No Action ■ Sleep ■ Hibernate ■ Shut Down If you disable this policy setting or do not configure it, users can see and change this setting.
Low Battery Notification Level (Applies to Windows Vista or later versions)	Specifies the percentage of battery capacity remaining that triggers the low-battery notification action. If you enable this policy, you must enter a numeric value (as a percentage) that triggers the low-battery notification. To set the action that is triggered, see the Low Battery Notification Action policy setting. If you disable this policy setting or do not configure it, users can see and change this setting.
*Reserve Battery Notification Level (Applies only to Windows 7 or Windows Server 2008 R2)	Specifies the percentage of battery capacity remaining that triggers the reserve power mode. If you enable this policy setting, you must enter a numeric value (as a percentage) to set the battery level that triggers the reserve power notification. If you disable this policy setting or do not configure it, users can see and change this setting.
Turn Off Low Battery User Notification (Applies to Windows Vista or later versions)	Disables a user notification when the battery capacity remaining equals the low-battery notification level. If you enable this policy, Windows will not show a notification when the battery capacity remaining equals the low-battery notification level. To configure the low-battery notification level, see the Low Battery Notification Level policy setting. The notification will be shown only if you configure the Low Battery Notification Action policy setting to No Action. If you do not configure this policy setting, users can see and change this setting.

POLICY NAME	DESCRIPTION
	FOUND UNDER /SYSTEM/SLEEP SETTINGS
*Allow Applications To Prevent Automatic Sleep (On Battery) (Applies only to Windows 7 or Windows Server 2008 R2)	Allows applications and services to prevent Windows from automatically transitioning to sleep after a period of user inactivity. If you disable this policy setting, applications, services, or drivers may not prevent Windows from automatically transitioning to sleep. Only user input will be used to determine whether Windows should sleep automatically.
*Allow Automatic Sleep With Open Network Files (On Battery) (Applies only to Windows 7 or Windows Server 2008 R2)	If you enable this policy setting, the computer will sleep automatically when network files are open. If you disable this policy setting, the computer will not automatically sleep when network files are open.
Allow Standby States (S1-S3) When Sleeping (On Battery) (Applies to Windows Vista or later versions)	When this policy is enabled, Windows may use Stand By states to sleep the computer. If this policy is disabled, the only Sleep state a computer may enter is Hibernate.
Require A Password When A Computer Wakes (On Battery) (Applies to Windows Vista or later versions)	If you enable this policy or if this policy is not configured, the user is prompted for a password when the system resumes from sleep. If you disable this policy, the user is not prompted for a password when the system resumes from sleep.
Specify The System Hibernate Timeout (On Battery) (Applies to Windows Vista or later versions)	If you enable this policy setting, you must provide a value, in seconds, indicating how much idle time should elapse before Windows transitions to Hibernate. If you disable this policy setting or do not configure it, users can see and change this setting.

POLICY NAME	DESCRIPTION
Specify The System Sleep Timeout (On Battery) (Applies to Windows Vista or later versions)	If you enable this policy setting, you must provide a value, in seconds, indicating how much idle time should elapse before Windows transitions to sleep. If you disable this policy setting or do not configure it, users can see and change this setting.
*Specify The Unattended Sleep Timeout (On Battery) (Applies only to Windows 7 or Windows Server 2008 R2)	If you enable this policy setting, you must provide a value, in seconds, indicating how much idle time should elapse before Windows automatically transitions to sleep when the user leaves the computer unattended. If you specify 0 seconds, Windows will not transition to sleep automatically. If you disable this policy setting or do not configure it, users can see and change this setting.
Turn Off Hybrid Sleep (On Battery) (Applies to Windows Vista or later versions)	Disables Hybrid Sleep, which refers to the use of hibernation during sleep to store the contents of the computer's memory. If you enable this policy setting, a hibernation file (Hiberfile.sys) is not generated when the system transitions to sleep (Stand By). If you do not configure this policy setting, users can see and change this setting.
Turn Off The Ability For Applications To Prevent Sleep Transitions (On Battery) (Applies to Windows Vista or later versions)	If you enable this policy setting, an application or service may prevent the system from sleeping (using the Hybrid Sleep, Stand By, or Hibernate setting). If you disable this policy setting or do not configure it, users can see and change this setting.
	FOUND UNDER /SYSTEM/VIDEO AND DISPLAY SETTINGS
*Reduce Display Brightness (On Battery) (Applies only to Windows 7 or Windows Server 2008 R2)	If you enable this policy setting, you must provide a value, in seconds, indicating how much idle time should elapse before Windows automatically reduces the brightness of the display. Windows will reduce the brightness of only the primary display integrated into the computer. If you disable this policy setting or do not configure it, users can see and change this setting.

POLICY NAME	DESCRIPTION
*Specify The Display Dim Brightness (On Battery) (Applies only to Windows 7 or Windows Server 2008 R2)	If you enable this policy setting, you must provide a value, as a percentage, indicating the level at which Windows automatically reduces the brightness of the display. If you disable this policy setting or do not configure it, users can see and change this setting.
Turn Off Adaptive Display Timeout (On Battery) (Applies to Windows Vista or later versions)	Manages how Windows controls the setting that specifies how long a computer must be inactive before Windows Vista turns off the computer's display. If you enable this policy, Windows automatically adjusts the setting based on what the user does with the keyboard or mouse to keep the display turned on. If you disable this policy, Windows uses the same setting regardless of the user's keyboard or mouse behavior. If you don't configure this setting, users can see and change this setting.
Turn Off The Display (On Battery) (Applies to Windows Vista or later versions)	If you enable this policy, you must provide a value, in seconds, indicating how much idle time should elapse before Windows turns off the display. If you disable this policy or do not configure it, users can see and change this setting.
*Turn Off Desktop Background Slideshow (On Battery) (Applies only to Windows 7 or Windows Server 2008 R2)	If you enable this policy setting, the desktop background slideshow is enabled. If you disable this policy setting, the desktop background slideshow is disabled. if you do not configure this setting, users can see and change this setting.

DIRECT FROM THE SOURCE

Problems with Automatic Sleep

Nick Judge, Senior Development Lead
Windows Kernel Development

Although a manually requested sleep (initiated, for example, by closing your laptop's lid or pushing the power button) cannot be prevented by software in Windows Vista, you can still prevent automatic sleep (idling-to-sleep) in several ways:

- **API calls** Applications, services, or drivers may call an application programming interface (API) (SetThreadExecutionState, PoRegisterSystemState) to prevent automatic sleep because they are performing an important task that should not be interrupted. Common examples include burning a DVD, copying a large network file, and performing a system scan.
- **Consistent processor (CPU) utilization greater than 20%** The power manager checks processor utilization in an attempt to prevent automatic sleep when an application may be busy. Windows Vista has a power setting that adjusts the amount of processor activity that prevents automatic sleep.
- **Network file sharing** If, for example, a computer has shared files or printers that are currently opened by a remote computer, automatic sleep will be prevented on both computers.
- **Media sharing** Media sharing prevents automatic sleep because not all remote computers or media devices are capable of waking the computer from sleep over the network. This behavior may be configured in Advanced Settings in Power Options. The When Sharing Media setting under Multimedia settings configures this behavior.

Configuring Power Management Settings Using the Powercfg Utility

Powercfg is a command-line utility for configuring Windows 7 power management policy. Powercfg.exe exposes all power management settings, including those that are not available in the UI or from Group Policy.

Power management settings are represented by GUIDs, so using Powercfg.exe generally requires that you know the GUIDs for the settings you want to modify. However, Powercfg.exe also supports aliases for most common GUIDs, and you can type **powercfg –aliases** to display a list of supported aliases as shown here (the output has been truncated).

```
C:\Windows\system32\>powercfg -aliases

a1841308-3541-4fab-bc81-f71556f20b4a  SCHEME_MAX
8c5e7fda-e8bf-4a96-9a85-a6e23a8c635c  SCHEME_MIN
381b4222-f694-41f0-9685-ff5bb260df2e  SCHEME_BALANCED
fea3413e-7e05-4911-9a71-700331f1c294  SUB_NONE
238c9fa8-0aad-41ed-83f4-97be242c8f20  SUB_SLEEP
29f6c1db-86da-48c5-9fdb-f2b67b1f44da  STANDBYIDLE
9d7815a6-7ee4-497e-8888-515a05f02364  HIBERNATEIDLE
94ac6d29-73ce-41a6-809f-6363ba21b47e  HYBRIDSLEEP
d4c1d4c8-d5cc-43d3-b83e-fc51215cb04d  REMOTEFILESLEEP
7516b95f-f776-4464-8c53-06167f40cc99  SUB_VIDEO
...
```

For example, this means you can type **powercfg -setactive SCHEME_BALANCED** instead of having to specify the GUID for the Balanced power plan.

The examples that follow illustrate the use of Powercfg.exe on Windows Vista and later systems. You can run most of these commands while logged on as a standard user, but a few, such as –export (for exporting power plans) and –h (for enabling or disabling hibernation support), must be run from an administrator-level (elevated) command prompt.

> ***NOTE*** **To display detailed help for Powercfg.exe, type powercfg /? at a command prompt.**

To list the available power plans (called *power schemes*) in Powercfg.exe:

```
C:\Windows\system32\>powercfg -L

Existing Power Schemes (* Active)
-----------------------------------
Power Scheme GUID: 381b4222-f694-41f0-9685-ff5bb260df2e  (Balanced)
Power Scheme GUID: 8c5e7fda-e8bf-4a96-9a85-a6e23a8c635c  (High performance) *
Power Scheme GUID: a1841308-3541-4fab-bc81-f71556f20b4a  (Power saver)
```

Listing power schemes lets you determine the GUID for each scheme. The asterisk beside the High Performance scheme indicates that it is the active power plan. You can also determine the active power scheme quickly as follows.

```
C:\Windows\system32\>powercfg -getactivescheme
Power Scheme GUID: 8c5e7fda-e8bf-4a96-9a85-a6e23a8c635c  (High performance)
```

To display detailed information concerning the High Performance power scheme in the preceding example, see the code here (the output has been truncated).

```
C:\Windows\system32\>powercfg -q 8c5e7fda-e8bf-4a96-9a85-a6e23a8c635c


Power Scheme GUID: 8c5e7fda-e8bf-4a96-9a85-a6e23a8c635c  (High performance)
  Subgroup GUID: fea3413e-7e05-4911-9a71-700331f1c294  (Settings belonging to no
subgroup)
    Power Setting GUID: 0e796bdb-100d-47d6-a2d5-f7d2daa51f51  (Require a password on
wakeup)
      Possible Setting Index: 000
      Possible Setting Friendly Name: No
      Possible Setting Index: 001
      Possible Setting Friendly Name: Yes
    Current AC Power Setting Index: 0x00000001
    Current DC Power Setting Index: 0x00000001

  Subgroup GUID: 0012ee47-9041-4b5d-9b77-535fba8b1442  (Hard disk)
    Power Setting GUID: 6738e2c4-e8a5-4a42-b16a-e040e769756e  (Turn off hard disk after)
      Minimum Possible Setting: 0x00000000
      Maximum Possible Setting: 0xffffffff
      Possible Settings increment: 0x00000001
      Possible Settings units: Seconds
    Current AC Power Setting Index: 0x000004b0
    Current DC Power Setting Index: 0x000004b0

  Subgroup GUID: 0d7dbae2-4294-402a-ba8e-26777e8488cd  (Desktop background settings)
    Power Setting GUID: 309dce9b-bef4-4119-9921-a851fb12f0f4  (Slide show)
      Possible Setting Index: 000
      Possible Setting Friendly Name: Available
      Possible Setting Index: 001
      Possible Setting Friendly Name: Paused
    Current AC Power Setting Index: 0x00000000
    Current DC Power Setting Index: 0x00000000

  Subgroup GUID: 19cbb8fa-5279-450e-9fac-8a3d5fedd0c1  (Wireless Adapter Settings)
    Power Setting GUID: 12bbebe6-58d6-4636-95bb-3217ef867c1a  (Power Saving Mode)
      Possible Setting Index: 000
      Possible Setting Friendly Name: Maximum Performance
      Possible Setting Index: 001
      Possible Setting Friendly Name: Low Power Saving
      Possible Setting Index: 002
      Possible Setting Friendly Name: Medium Power Saving
      Possible Setting Index: 003
      Possible Setting Friendly Name: Maximum Power Saving
    Current AC Power Setting Index: 0x00000000
    Current DC Power Setting Index: 0x00000000...
```

The following code changes the active power scheme to Balanced in the preceding example.

```
C:\Windows\system32\>powercfg -setactive SCHEME_BALANCED
```

Verify the result as follows.

```
C:\Windows\system32\>powercfg -L

Existing Power Schemes (* Active)
-----------------------------------
Power Scheme GUID: 381b4222-f694-41f0-9685-ff5bb260df2e  (Balanced) *
Power Scheme GUID: 8c5e7fda-e8bf-4a96-9a85-a6e23a8c635c  (High performance)
Power Scheme GUID: a1841308-3541-4fab-bc81-f71556f20b4a  (Power saver)
```

The following code determines the available Sleep states supported by the system.

```
C:\Windows\system32\>powercfg -a
The following sleep states are available on this system: Standby ( S1 S3 ) Hibernate
Hybrid Sleep
The following sleep states are not available on this system:
Standby (S2)
        The system firmware does not support this standby state.
```

> ***MORE INFO*** **For information concerning the differences between these different Sleep states, see *http://msdn2.microsoft.com/en-gb/library/ms798270.aspx*.**

The following code displays the source that has awakened the system from sleep.

```
C:\Windows\system32\>powercfg -lastwake
Wake History Count - 1
Wake History [0]
  Wake Source Count - 1
  Wake Source [0]
    Type: Device
    Instance Path: ACPI\PNP0C0C\2&daba3ff&1
    Friendly Name:
    Description: ACPI Power Button
    Manufacturer: (Standard system devices)
```

The following code changes the monitor time-out when running on AC power for the active power scheme to 30 minutes.

```
C:\Windows\system32\>powercfg -setacvalueindex SCHEME_CURRENT SUB_VIDEO VIDEOIDLE 1800
C:\Windows\system32\>powercfg -setactive SCHEME_CURRENT
```

The following code exports a power scheme to a .pow file (proprietary binary format).

```
C:\Windows\system32\>powercfg -export C:\newscheme.pow 8c5e7fda-e8bf-4a96-9a85-
a6e23a8c635c
```

Use the *–import* switch to import a .pow file.

The following code disables hibernation on the computer.

```
C:\Windows\system32\>powercfg -h off
```

To evaluate the energy efficiency of the computer, first close all applications and documents, let the system remain idle for 10 minutes, and then run the following command.

```
C:\Windows\system32>powercfg -energy
Enabling tracing for 60 seconds...
Observing system behavior...
Analyzing trace data...
Analysis complete.

Energy efficiency problems were found.

7 Errors
1 Warnings
11 Informational

See C:\Windows\system32\energy-report.html for more details.
```

Opening the Hypertext Markup Language (HTML) file generated by the command displays a Power Efficiency Diagnostic Report with errors, warnings, and informational issues. Figure 17-10 shows the error section of a report run on an older system that is not configured for optimal energy efficiency.

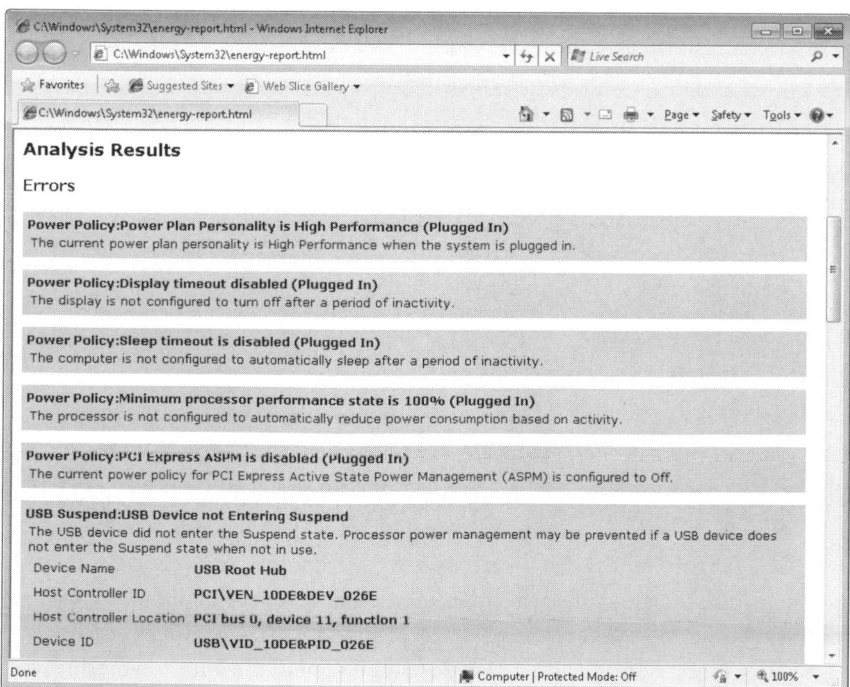

FIGURE 17-10 Part of a Power Efficiency Diagnostic Report generated using *powercfg –energy*

Configuring Power Management Settings Using the Power WMI Provider

Windows 7 now includes a WMI provider that lets you configure power policy through the standard WMI interface. Using this provider, you can script actions such as:

- Changing power setting values by using the Win32_PowerSetting class.
- Activating a specific power plan by using the *Win32_Plan.Activate()* method.

> ***MORE INFO*** See MSDN for more information on using WMI to manage power settings in Windows 7.

Understanding Services

Services are long-running applications that run in the background, typically start up on boot, and run independently of users who log on. Services handle low-level tasks such as managing authentication and networking and other tasks that need little or no user interaction to function. Third-party services, such as firewalls and antivirus software, can also run on Windows.

Services are implemented using the Services API and are managed by the Service Control Manager (SCM). SCM maintains a database of information concerning the services installed on the system and exposes these services to management using both UI and command-line tools. Using these tools, administrators can:

- Configure a service to start automatically on system startup, to start the service manually on demand, or to disable the service.
- Start, stop, pause, and resume a service (depending on whether it is currently running).
- Specify a security context under which the service runs—typically one of the following: LocalSystem; a lower-privileged identity such as LocalService or NetworkService; or a custom user account created specifically for the service.
- Specify recovery actions to be taken when the service fails.
- View the dependencies of a service on other services.

Service Enhancements in Windows 7

The implementation of services in Windows 7 builds on improvements previously made in this area in Windows Vista. The following list summarizes some of the changes to services that were implemented in Windows Vista to enhance the security, reliability, and performance of services as they run on the system.

- **Running with least privileges** Enhances security by removing unnecessary privileges from the process token under which the service runs. For stand-alone services, SCM does this by checking the list of required privileges against the process token and removing any unnecessary privileges. A service can be configured with required privileges; this is typically a service designer action as opposed to an administrator action because the list of required privileges is tied to the service design. SCM strips unnecessary privileges present in the service's account before starting the service process. If the service process hosts multiple services, SCM computes the union of the required privileges of all hosted services and strips unnecessary privileges. By default, no privilege stripping is performed, thus pre–Windows Vista services running on Windows Vista are not affected by this feature.

- **Service isolation** Uses restricted security identifiers (SIDs) to enhance security by allowing services to run with fewer privileges while still maintaining access to objects, such as registry keys, that are configured to allow access only to administrators. In earlier versions of Windows, many services are configured to run under the powerful LocalSystem account because the resources that they need to access are secured using ACLs for LocalSystem access (because it is worrisome to allow access to any less-privileged process). Running under the LocalSystem account causes security vulnerabilities in the service code to have a huge impact, however. In Windows Vista (similar to earlier versions of Windows), services can be configured to run under less-privileged accounts. However, only in Windows Vista can the service designer configure the service to have a unique SID added to the process token (called the *service SID*) and use ACLs to secure the resources used by the service (registry keys, for example) to allow full access by the service SID alone. This keeps the service account at a lower privilege level yet allows only the service process access to the resources, as opposed to any process running the service account accessing the resources.
- **Restricted service SID** If the service designer chooses this option, the service SID is added to the process token at service process startup as in the service SID case. (In the case of a shared process, the SID is in a disabled state until the service starts.) In addition, the process token is marked Write Restricted, meaning that the service process code can write only to those resources explicitly secured with ACLs for the service SID. For example, consider a registry key that allows full access to the LocalService account. A restricted service process would not get Write access to that key even if it were running under the LocalService account. The restricted service would get access only if the key were secured with ACLs to allow the service SID to be written to. This feature is intended to mitigate the damage that a service can do to the system if it is exploited. Typically, these features are implemented by the service designer, not the administrator.
- **Restricted network access** Uses Windows Service Hardening (WSH) and per-service SIDs to enhance security by restricting access by a service to network resources, such as ports and protocols.
- **Session 0 isolation** Enhances security by isolating services from user applications by running all services in Session 0 while user applications are required to run in Session 1 or higher. This means that a service that is marked as Interactive in earlier versions of Windows and can show a UI will no longer be able to show a UI in Windows Vista. Note that such services are already broken in previous versions of Windows with the introduction of Fast User Switching (FUS). Such services are expected to run a UI

process in the user's session, which can throw the UI and communicate with the service using COM or Remote Procedure Call (RPC).

- **Delayed Start** A new service startup type that enhances performance immediately after startup by allowing startup of less-critical services to be delayed until approximately 2 minutes after Windows has started. This feature enables Windows and applications to be usable sooner after startup. An example of a service that is configured for Delayed Start is the Windows Update service.
- **Service state change notifications** Enhances performance by enabling SCM to detect when a service has been created or deleted or has changed its status without having to poll the status of the service. SCM can then notify the client of the change of status of the service. This feature works for local as well as remote clients.
- **Preshutdown notifications** Enhances reliability by allowing SCM to notify services in advance of shutdown so that they have more time to clean up and shut down gracefully. In earlier versions of Windows and in Windows Vista as well, the computer shutdown has a fixed time limit by default. Although most services are unaffected by this, some services can have a dirty shutdown, which can cause long delays in starting up during the next boot (for example, a database recovery after a dirty shutdown might be quite time consuming). In Windows Vista, such services can subscribe to preshutdown notifications. The system will send this notification after all users are logged off and before the computer shutdown is initiated. The services can take up as much time as they want before they stop. However, this can affect shutdown time negatively and has to be considered by the service designer. Again, this is a feature for the service designer to implement—it cannot be configured by the administrator.
- **Shutdown ordering** Enhances reliability by allowing service owners to specify dependencies between services in a global dependency list to control the shutdown order for services. This is applicable only for services that subscribe to preshutdown notifications. In this case, such services can experience either an ordered or unordered shutdown. If the services add themselves to the ordered list in the registry, SCM will wait for the service to stop before proceeding to shut down the next service in the list. After ordered preshutdown is complete, unordered preshutdown begins. Note that the computer shutdown ordering of services is arbitrary, as described previously.
- **Detection of and recovery from nonfatal errors** Enhances reliability by allowing SCM to detect nonfatal errors with services, such as memory leaks, and initiate specified recovery actions. In earlier versions of Windows, only allowed services could be configured with recovery actions (restart, run a script, and so on) when the process crashed. In Windows Vista, in addition, services can be configured to have recovery actions initiated if they stop with an error as opposed to crashing. Therefore, services can recover from memory leaks and other issues by using this feature.
- **Stop reason** An administrator that stops a service can now specify the reason for stopping the service. This allows postmortem reliability analysis to find out why a service is failing. If the administrator specifies the stop reason using the Sc.exe stop

option, SCM logs an event with the stop reason to the event log. A new API called ControlServiceEx has also been added to accept the stop reason.

- **Localization** A service designer now can configure a service property, such as a display name or description, as a localizable string and have SCM load the specified resource from a resource DLL when a user queries the service property. The name is in the form *@resource_dll,-resource_ID*.

Windows 7 introduces additional enhancements to how services are implemented to increase the security, performance, and energy efficiency of Windows computers. These enhancements include the following:

- **New unified architecture** Windows 7 has a new unified architecture that drives the scheduling of background processes (services and scheduled tasks) on Windows. This is transparent to users, IT professionals, and existing APIs, and it enables trigger-starting services as described next.
- **Trigger Start** Windows 7 now allows the starting or stopping (but not pausing or resuming) of a service when a specific event, known as a *trigger*, occurs. Examples of triggers that can be used to start or stop a service can include the following:
  - First IP address arrival
  - Last IP address departure
  - Connecting or disconnecting a hardware device
  - Joining or leaving a domain
  - Group Policy change
  - Custom triggers raised from either kernel or user mode

  For example, connecting a scanner to a Windows 7 computer can trigger the start of the imaging service used by the device. Disconnecting the scanner can also trigger the stopping of the service. Trigger Start improves the performance of Windows by reducing the number of running services on the computer. It also enhances security because having fewer running services means there is less attack surface. Finally, Trigger Start can improve boot performance by reducing the number of services that need to be started when Windows is started. For a complete list of triggers, see *http://msdn.microsoft.com/en-us/library/dd405512.aspx*.
- **New Sc.exe command options** The Sc.exe command-line tool for managing services has been enhanced in Windows 7 with new command options for managing service triggers, including the following:
  - **qtriggerinfo** Queries the trigger parameters of a service
  - **triggerinfo** Configures the trigger parameters of a service
- **Managed service accounts** Managed service accounts in Windows Server 2008 R2 and Windows 7 are managed domain accounts that provide the following features to simplify service administration:
  - Automatic password management

- Simplified service principal name (SPN) management, including delegation of management to other administrators

- **Virtual accounts** Virtual accounts in Windows Server 2008 R2 and Windows 7 are "managed local accounts" that provide the following features to simplify service administration:
  - No password management is required
  - The ability to access the network with a computer identity in a domain environment

DIRECT FROM THE SOURCE

Troubleshooting Service Issues

Chittur Subbaraman, Software Design Engineer
Windows Kernel Development

Here are a few points about troubleshooting for IT administrators and service developers:

- **Performance issues** Sluggish service performance is one of the primary culprits for lengthier logon times and being unable to elevate programs after logon. If you experience these symptoms, use Event Viewer to check the System Log for warning or error messages from SCM. In addition, you can use the Sc.exe in-box tool to run commands, such as sc.exe queryex, that will allow you to see which services are blocked in the START_PENDING state. You can also use the Services Microsoft Management Console (MMC) snap-in to check the status of services. Such blocked services are likely causes of sluggish system performance.
- **Services tab in Task Manager** In Windows Vista, the Task Manager has a new Services tab that can display various service-related information. This can be particularly useful for identifying services that use up significant amounts of CPU or other resources. You could then choose to right-click the culprit services and stop them to solve the problem for the moment before contacting the service vendor for support.
- **General tip** If some scenario is not working, it is useful to check the state of any services that might implement parts of the feature. For instance, if antivirus real-time monitoring is not working, perhaps the real-time monitoring service has failed to start up. Check the System Log in Event Viewer for warning or error messages from SCM related to the service. In addition, you can use the Sc.exe in-box tool to run commands, such as sc.exe queryex service_short_name, and see details of the service status. The Services MMC snap-in can also help.

Managing Services

Windows provides four main tools for managing services:

- The Services snap-in (Services.msc)
- Task Manager
- Group Policy
- The Sc.exe command

Managing Services Using the Services Snap-in

The Services snap-in in Windows 7 is the same as in Windows Vista. Compared to this snap-in in Windows XP, the main difference is that the Startup value for a service can be configured as Automatic (Delayed Start) on the General tab of the properties sheet for the service (see Figure 17-11).

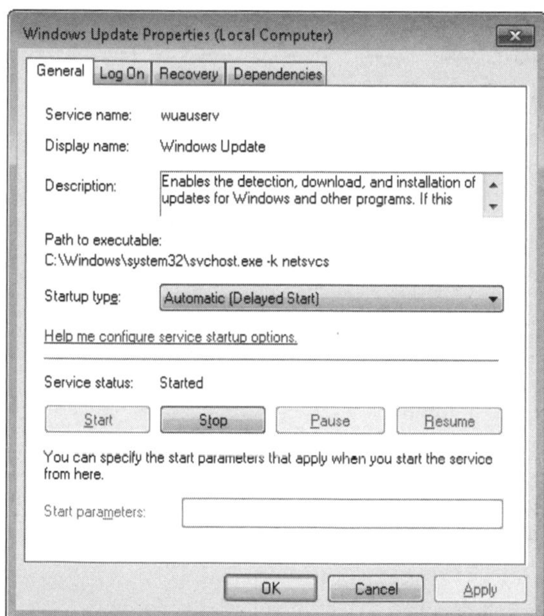

FIGURE 17-11 Configuring a service for Delayed Start

> ***IMPORTANT*** **Before configuring a service for Delayed Start, be sure that you understand the possible ramifications. Delayed Start does not provide any time guarantee for when a delayed service will start after the boot process finishes, and if a client application attempts to use the service before it starts, the client application may fail. This means that client applications should be designed to start up the service on demand if they need the service before the Delayed Start sequence starts it. In addition, if a particular service is configured for Delayed Start and SCM detects other services that depend on this service, SCM will ignore the Delayed Start setting on the service and will start it during the boot process.**

The only other change from Windows XP is the option of enabling actions for stops with errors. This option can be configured on the Recovery tab, and configuring it enables detection of and recovery from nonfatal errors.

Managing Services Using Task Manager

A Services tab was added to Task Manager in Windows Vista and is still available in Windows 7 (see Figure 17-12). This tab allows you to:

- View the name, Process Identifier (PID), description (which is actually the service's friendly name), status (running or stopped), and service group for all services running on the system.
- Stop or start a service by right-clicking it and then selecting the appropriate option.
- View the process within which a service is running by right-clicking the service and then selecting Go To Process.

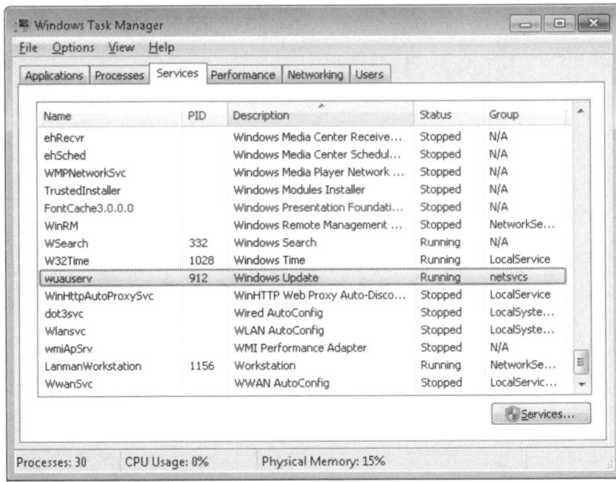

FIGURE 17-12 The Services tab in Task Manager

> ***NOTE*** **To view the process associated with a service, you should first click the Show Processes From All Users button on the Processes tab. This is a necessary step because many services run within an SvcHost.exe process to reduce the memory footprint that would result if each service ran separately. After processes for all users are displayed on the Processes tab, right-click a service that has a PID number on the Services tab and then select Go To Process. The focus will switch to the Processes tab and highlight the SvcHost.exe process used to host that particular service.**

Managing Services Using Group Policy

You can use Group Policy to configure the startup state (Automatic, Manual, or Disabled) and ACLs for services in the same way that you do this on previous versions of Windows. A policy setting for each system service on a computer can be found under the following node:

Computer Configuration\Policies\Windows Settings\Security Settings\System Services

Managing Services Using the Sc.exe Command

You can use the Sc.exe command to start, stop, configure, and manage various aspects of services in the same way that you can on earlier versions of Windows. The Sc.exe command provides administrators with far more flexibility in configuring services than the Services snap-in or Group Policy.

The Sc.exe command was previously enhanced in Windows Vista with additional command-line switches, including the following:

- New switches for specifying required privileges for a service, including:
  - **privs** Sets the required privileges for a service
  - **qprivs** Queries for the required privileges of a service
- New switches that support per-service SIDs, including:
  - **sidtype** Changes a service's SID
  - **qsidtype** Retrieves the setting for a service's SID
- New switches to enable configuration of the FailureActionsOnNonCrashFailures setting, including:
  - **failureflag** Changes the setting of the *FailureActionsOnNonCrashFailures* flag
  - **qfailureflag** Retrieves the setting for the *FailureActionsOnNonCrashFailures* flag
  - **showsid** Displays the service SID string corresponding to an arbitrary name
  - **stop** This is an old setting that was enhanced in Windows Vista to specify the stop reason. This setting enables postmortem reliability analysis to find an administrator's reasons (by examining the event logged by SCM with the stop reason) for stopping a service.

New in Windows 7 are command options for Sc.exe that allow configuring and querying a service for supported triggers. For information about how to use these new command options, see the sidebar titled "Direct from the Source: Sc.exe Command Support for Service Triggers" later in this chapter.

For more information about the command-line switches for Sc.exe, type **sc /?** at a command prompt.

DIRECT FROM THE SOURCE

Sc.exe Command Support for Service Triggers

CSS Global Technical Readiness (GTR) Team

The Sc.exe command-line tool has been updated for Windows 7 and Windows Server 2008 R2 to include the triggerinfo command option for configuring a service for supported triggers and the qtriggerinfo command option for querying the trigger information for a service.

The syntax for the triggerinfo option is as follows.

```
sc <server> triggerinfo [service name] <parameter1> <parameter2>...
```

Possible parameters for the -triggerinfo command option are as follows:

- **start/device/UUID/HwId1/...** Starts the service on arrival of the specified device interface class UUID string with one or more hardware ID strings and/or compatible ID strings.
- **start/custom/UUID/data0/...** Starts the service on arrival of an event from the specified custom ETW provider UUID string with one or more binary data items in hexadecimal string format, such as ABCDABCD to set 4-byte data.
- **stop/custom/UUID/data0/...** Stops the service on arrival of an event from the specified custom ETW provider UUID string with one or more binary data items in hexadecimal string format, such as ABCDABCD to set 4-byte data.
- **start/strcustom/UUID/data0/...** Starts the service on arrival of an event from the specified custom ETW provider UUID string with one or more optional string data items.
- **stop/strcustom/UUID/data0/...** Stops the service on arrival of an event from the specified custom ETW provider UUID string with one or more optional string data items.
- **start/networkon** Starts the service on first IP address.
- **stop/networkoff** Stops the service on zero IP addresses.
- **start/domainjoin** Starts the service if a domain member.
- **stop/domainleave** Stops the service if not a domain member.
- **start/portopen/parameter** Starts the service on the opening of a network port. The parameter is of the semicolon-delimited form portnumber;protocol name;imagepath;servicename.
- **stop/portclose/parameter** Stops the service on the closing of a network port. The parameter is of the semicolon-delimited form portnumber;protocol name;imagepath;servicename.

- **start/machinepolicy** Starts the service when machine group policy changes or is present at boot.
- **start/userpolicy** Starts the service when user group policy changes or is present at boot.
- **delete** Deletes the existing trigger parameters.

Using the sc -qtriggerinfo command and the Windows Time (W32Time) service as an example, you can see that this service is configured to start when the system is joined to a domain and stop when the system is not joined to a domain.

```
C:\Windows\system32>sc qtriggerinfo w32time
[SC] QueryServiceConfig2 SUCCESS

SERVICE_NAME: w32time

START SERVICE
  DOMAIN JOINED STATUS: 1ce20aba-9851-4421-9430-1ddeb766e809 [DOMAIN
JOINED]

STOP SERVICE
  DOMAIN JOINED STATUS: ddaf516e-58c2-4866-9574-c3b615d42ea1 [NOT DOMAIN
JOINED]
```

For all services that specify trigger actions, a TriggerInfo subkey is created in the registry in the service configuration key, which is located at:

HKEY_LOCAL_MACHINE\SYSTEM\CurrentControlSet\Services\<Service Name>

The TriggerInfo registry key for the Windows Time service is shown here.

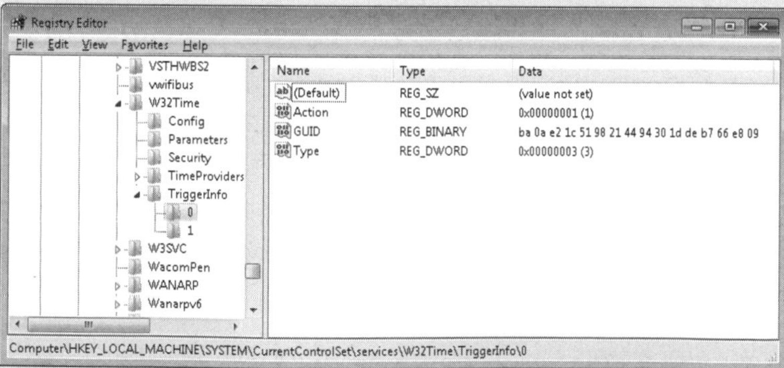

The first trigger is assigned a subkey of 0, selected in the image above. The 0 subkey for the Windows Time service indicates the Start trigger action. The second trigger action is assigned a subkey of 1. For the Windows Time service, the second trigger is used for the Stop trigger action.

The following values are contained within the TriggerInfo subkey(s):

- Value Name: Action

  Value Type: REG_DWORD

  Description: Specifies the action to take when triggered:

  - 0x00000001 = Service Start
  - 0x00000002 = Service Stop

- Value Name: GUID

  Value Type: REG_BINARY!

  Description: A GUID may be specified if it applies to the trigger type. For a device arrival trigger, the interface class GUID would be specified. For an ETW event trigger, the ETW provider GUID would be specified.

- Value Name: Type

  Value Type: REG_DWORD

  Description: Specifies the type of trigger:

  - 0x00000001 = Device arrival trigger
  - 0x00000002 = IP address trigger
  - 0x00000003 = Domain join trigger
  - 0x00000020 = Custom trigger

Note that for Trigger Start services, the Start value should be 0x00000003 to specify the Demand-Start Startup Type. Also, the Startup Type for Demand-Start services is listed as Manual in the Services MMC console.

Summary

Windows 7 provides an improved device installation experience for users that always searches Windows Update for the latest compatible drivers when a device is connected to the computer. The new Devices And Printers folder and Device Stage make it easier than ever for users to install, configure, and use both wired and wireless devices. Windows 7 also includes significant improvements in energy efficiency that increase battery life for mobile computers and can help businesses reduce their electric bills. Finally, Windows 7 includes support for Trigger Start of services to reduce the memory footprint, reduce the attack surface, and increase the boot- and run-time performance of Windows computers.

Additional Resources

These resources contain additional information and tools related to this chapter.

Related Information

- "Device Management and Installation" found at *http://technet.microsoft.com/en-us/library/cc766437.aspx*.
- "Power Management in Windows 7 Overview" found at *http://technet.microsoft.com/en-us/library/dd744300.aspx*.
- "What's New in Service Accounts" found at *http://technet.microsoft.com/en-us/library/dd367859.aspx*.
- "What's New in Services" found at *http://msdn.microsoft.com/en-us/library/dd405528.aspx*.
- "Service Accounts Step-by-Step Guide" found at *http://technet.microsoft.com/en-us/library/dd548356.aspx*.
- "Windows Logo'd Products List updated for Windows 7" found at *http://winqual.microsoft.com/HCL/Default.aspx*.
- "Windows Logo Program" found at *http://www.microsoft.com/whdc/winlogo/default.mspx*.
- "Microsoft Hardware Support for Windows 7" found at *http://www.microsoft.com/hardware/windows7/support.mspx*.
- *Device Management and Installation Step-by-Step Guide*: "Controlling Device Driver Installation and Usage with Group Policy" found at *http://technet.microsoft.com/en-us/library/cc731387.aspx*.
- *Device Management and Installation Step-by-Step Guide*: "Signing and Staging Device Drivers in Windows Vista and Windows Server 2008" found at *http://technet.microsoft.com/en-us/library/cc754052.aspx*.
- *Device Management and Installation Operations Guide* found at *http://technet.microsoft.com/en-us/library/cc753759.aspx*.
- "Overview of Device and Driver Installation" (from the Windows Driver Kit) found at *http://msdn.microsoft.com/en-us/library/ms791091.aspx*.
- "Device and Driver Technologies" (from the Windows Driver Kit) found at *http://msdn.microsoft.com/en-us/library/aa972913.aspx*.
- "Device Identification Strings" (from the Windows Driver Kit) found at *http://msdn.microsoft.com/en-us/library/ms791083.aspx*.
- "How Setup Ranks Drivers (Windows Vista and Later)" found at *http://msdn.microsoft.com/en-us/library/aa477022.aspx*.

On the Companion Media

- AcceptPause.ps1
- AutoServicesNotRunning.ps1
- ChangMmodeThenStart.ps1
- ChangeServiceAccountLogon.ps1
- CheckServiceThenStart.ps1
- CheckServiceAThenStop.ps1
- CountRunningServices.ps1
- EvaluateServices.ps1
- FindPortableDeviceEvents.ps1
- GetMultipleServices.ps1
- GetServiceStatus.ps1
- MonitorService.ps1
- ServiceDependencies.ps1
- StartMultipleServices.ps1
- StopMultipleServices.ps1

CHAPTER 18

Managing Printing

Previous to the introduction of the Windows 7 operating system, the Windows Vista operating system included enhanced capabilities for printing to provide high-fidelity print output, better print performance, improved manageability of printers and print servers, integrated support for XML Paper Specification (XPS), and the Windows Color System (WCS), which provides a richer color-printing experience. The Windows 7 operating system builds on these earlier printing improvements by adding Location-Aware Printing, printer driver isolation, configurable default spooler security settings, and an improved Point and Print experience for users. This chapter describes the printing capabilities of Windows 7 and how to manage printers in enterprise environments.

Enhancements to Printing in Windows 7

The printing subsystem in Windows 7 and Windows Server 2008 R2 builds on the printing improvements made previously in Windows Vista and Windows Server 2008, so we will discuss the improvements that were introduced in the earlier versions of the operating systems in the next section, followed by a section that describes the new printing features that have now been added in Windows 7.

Printing Enhancements Previously Introduced in Windows Vista

A number of print subsystem, print management, and printing experience improvements were first introduced in Windows Vista, and these continue to be included in Windows 7. The new features and enhancements to printing in Windows Vista were as follows:

- **Integrated support for XPS** Windows Vista includes support for XPS, which is a set of conventions for using Extensible Markup Language (XML) to describe the content and appearance of paginated documents.
- **XPS print path** In addition to supporting the Graphics Device Interface (GDI) print path used by earlier versions of Windows, the printing architecture of Windows Vista includes a print path that uses XPS as a document format, a Windows spool file format, and a page description language (PDL) for printers.
- **XPS document graphics fidelity and performance** The XPS document printing capability in Windows Vista supports vector-based graphics that can be scaled to a high degree without creating jagged or pixilated text, producing high-fidelity print output for graphics-rich documents. An XPS document is created by default when you print from any application running on Windows Vista, and you can print this document without rendering it again to an XPS-capable printer. Therefore, you can reduce print processing time by as much as 90 percent compared with printing in previous versions of Windows, depending on the richness of the content being printed and the capabilities of the printer.
- **Microsoft XPS Document Writer** Windows Vista includes the Microsoft XPS Document Writer, which you can use through any Windows application to print graphics-rich application output as XPS documents. You can then view these documents in Windows Internet Explorer by using the Microsoft XPS Viewer or by printing them directly to an XPS-capable printer without rendering them again.
- **Client-Side Rendering (CSR)** By default, Windows Vista renders print jobs on the client instead of the print server. This can significantly reduce print processing times when printing to XPS-capable printers. CSR works on non-XPS printers as well and is useful for reducing CPU and memory load on the server (servers can host more queues); it also reduces network traffic for some drivers.
- **Resource Reuse** XPS documents include the capability of rendering an image once and reusing the rendered image when it appears on multiple pages of a print job. This can reduce the print processing time for documents that have graphics-rich corporate logos and reduces the amount of data sent over the network to remote printers.
- **Windows Color System** Windows Color System (WCS) works with the Windows Vista print subsystem to provide a richer color-printing experience that supports wide-gamut printers (inkjet printers that use more than four ink colors) for lifelike printing of color photos and graphics-rich documents.

- **Print Management** Print Management, a Microsoft Management Console (MMC) snap-in that was first included in Windows Server 2003 R2, is installed by default on Windows Vista, allowing administrators to manage printers, print servers, and print jobs easily across an enterprise. Print Management in Windows Vista has also been enhanced with new capabilities.
- **Network Printer Installation Wizard** Windows Vista replaces the Add Printer Wizard, which was used in previous versions of Windows, with the Network Printer Installation Wizard, which is easier to use and has new capabilities. This new wizard makes it easier for users to connect to remote printers and to local printers that are not Plug and Play.
- **Non-admin printer installation** Standard users (that is, users who are not local administrators on their computers) can install printers without requiring administrative privileges or elevation at a User Account Control (UAC) prompt.
- **Deploying and managing printers using Group Policy** Using Group Policy to deploy printer connections—first introduced in Windows Server 2003 R2—was enhanced in Windows Vista by eliminating the requirement to prepare client computers first using a startup script that installs PushPrinterConnections.exe client software on them. New policy settings have also been added in Windows Vista to enhance the capability of managing printers and printing using Group Policy. You can also use the Group Policy Results Wizard in the Group Policy Management Console (GPMC) to display Resultant Set of Policy (RSoP) for deployed printers.
- **Assigning printers based on location** In Windows Vista, you can assign printers based on location by deploying printers using Group Policy and linking Group Policy objects (GPOs) to sites in Active Directory Domain Services (AD DS). When mobile users move to a different site, Group Policy updates their printer connections for the new location; when the users return to their primary site, their original default printers are restored.
- **Easier printer migration** You can use a new Printer Migration Wizard (including a command-line version called PrintBRM) to back up printer configurations on print servers, move printers between print servers, and consolidate multiple print servers onto a single server.

Additional Printing Enhancements in Windows 7

In addition to the previously listed printing improvements first introduced in Windows Vista, printing in Windows 7 and Windows Server 2008 R2 has now been enhanced in the following ways:

- **XPS printing system** The XPS printing system has been enhanced in Windows 7 and Windows Server 2008 R2 by the inclusion of a new rendering service for XPS printer drivers, new application programming interfaces (APIs), XPS Viewer enhancements, and miscellaneous performance enhancements. For information concerning one of these enhancements, see the sidebar titled "Direct from the Source: New Rasterization Service for Print Drivers" later in this chapter.

- **Devices And Printers** Windows 7 and Windows Server 2008 R2 include a new item on the Start menu and Control Panel called Devices And Printers, which provides a single, central location where users can interact with all of the devices connected to their computer. Devices And Printers can display different types of devices, including universal serial bus (USB), WiFi, and Bluetooth devices. Devices And Printers also integrates with Device Stage, a new feature of Windows 7 that makes it easier for users to connect, recognize, and use their devices. For more information about Devices And Printers, see the section titled "Using Devices and Printers" later in this chapter. For more information about Device Stage, see Chapter 17, "Managing Devices and Services."
- **Installing printer drivers using Windows Update** The Add Printer Driver Wizard has been enhanced in Windows 7 and Windows Server 2008 R2 to enable downloading of additional printer drivers directly from the Windows Update Web site. This change also means that fewer in-box printer drivers need to be included in Windows. It also makes the Point and Print experience for users easier because if a compatible in-box driver is not found when installing a printer, Windows Update is silently queried for a compatible driver to complete the installation. For more information about this feature, see the sections titled "Managing Printer Drivers" and "Extending Point and Print Using Windows Update" later in this chapter.
- **Cross-platform Point and Print** Improvements to the Point and Print experience now make it easy for users having Windows 7 computers running different processor architectures (x86 or x64) to share their printers. For more information about this feature, see the section titled "Extending Point and Print Using Windows Update" later in this chapter.
- **Location-Aware Printing** This feature allows mobile users running Windows 7 on their laptop computers to set a different default printer for each configured network location. For more information about this feature, see the section titled "Using Location-Aware Printing" later in this chapter.
- **Printer driver isolation** This enhancement to the printing subsystem in Windows Server 2008 R2 can increase the stability of print servers by allowing administrators to isolate unstable printer drivers in a separate process instead of within the spooler process. When this is done and an unstable printer driver crashes, the crash doesn't halt the spooler, which will stop all other printers from functioning on the server. For more information about this feature, see the sections titled "Understanding Printer Driver Isolation" and "Configuring Printer Driver Isolation Mode" later in this chapter.
- **Custom default security settings for print servers** Administrators can now define custom default security settings on Windows Server 2008 R2 print servers that apply to all printers installed on the print server. For more information about this feature, see the section titled "Configuring Default Security for Print Servers" later in this chapter.
- **Print Management enhancements** The Print Management MMC snap-in has been enhanced in Windows 7 and Windows Server 2008 with new functionality that allows administrators to configure default security settings for print servers and printer driver

isolation settings. The filtering capabilities of custom filters have also been enhanced with additional filter criteria to make filtering more powerful. For more information concerning these enhancements, see the section titled "Enhancements to the Print Management Console in Windows 7" later in this chapter.

- **PrintBRM** The PrintBRM command-line tool has been enhanced in Windows 7 and Windows Server 2008 R2 to provide more flexibility and improved instrumentation for the administrator. For more information concerning these improvements, see the sidebar titled "Direct from the Source: Enhancements to PrintBRM in Windows 7 and Windows Server 2008 R2" later in this chapter.

How Printing Works in Windows 7

Understanding how printing works in Windows 7 is important for administrators who need to know how to configure, manage, and troubleshoot printers and printing on this platform. The key topics to understand are:

- XPS
- The Windows printing subsystem

Understanding XPS

XPS is a platform-independent, royalty-free, open-standard document format developed by Microsoft that uses XML, Open Packaging Conventions (OPC), and other industry standards to create cross-platform documents. XPS was designed to simplify the process for creating, sharing, viewing, printing, and archiving digital documents that are accurate representations of application output. Using APIs provided by the Windows SDK and the Microsoft .NET Framework 3.0, developers can create Windows Presentation Foundation (WPF) applications that take advantage of XPS technologies.

XPS support, which is native to Windows Vista and later versions, allows users to open XPS documents in Internet Explorer 7.0 or higher and to generate XPS documents from any Windows application using the Microsoft XPS Document Writer. When you install additional features, some earlier versions of Windows can also use some of the capabilities of XPS:

- By installing the .NET Framework 3.0 redistributable on Windows XP Service Pack 2 (SP2) or Windows Server 2003, users of these platforms can open XPS documents using Internet Explorer 6.0 or later versions.
- By installing Microsoft Core XML Services 6.0 on Windows XP SP2 or later versions, users can generate XPS documents from any Windows application using the Microsoft XPS Document Writer.
- By installing the Microsoft XPS Essentials Pack and Microsoft Core XML Services 6.0 on Microsoft Windows 2000, Windows XP, or Windows Server 2003, users can open XPS documents in a stand-alone XPS Viewer application.

NOTE You can download these additional features from the Microsoft Download Center at *http://www.microsoft.com/downloads.*

You can find detailed information on XPS in the version 1.0 document for this specification at *http://www.microsoft.com/whdc/xps/downloads.mspx* on Microsoft Windows Hardware Developer Central (WHDC). You can find additional news concerning this specification on the XPS Team Blog at *http://blogs.msdn.com/xps/.*

Understanding the Windows Printing Subsystem

The print subsystem on versions of Windows earlier than Windows Vista used the GDI print path. The GDI print path processes print jobs as follows:

- **Client processes** When a user on a client computer sends a print job from an application, the application calls the GDI, which then calls the printer driver for information about how to render the print job in a format that the printer can understand. The printer driver resides on the user's computer and is specific to the type of printer being used. After the GDI renders the print job, it sends the job to the spooler. By default on Windows 2000 and later versions, the GDI renders print jobs using the Enhanced Metafile (EMF) format, a standard print job format that is highly portable but needs to be further rendered by the spooler before being sent to the printer. When an EMF print job is sent to the spooler, control returns to the user and the spooler then completes rendering the job for printing. (Because the EMF job is quickly handed off to the spooler, the time during which the user's computer is busy is minimized.)
- **Spooler processes** The print spooler is a collection of features that resides on both the client computer that sends the print job and a network print server that receives the job for printing. The spooler takes the job as rendered by the GDI and, if necessary, renders it further to ensure that it prints correctly. The spooler then hands the job off to the printer.
- **Printer processes** The printer receives the print job from the spooler, translates it into a bitmap, and prints the document.

Beginning with Windows Vista, the printing subsystem still includes a GDI print path (for Type 3 – User Mode) to support printing to existing printers. Kernel-mode GDI (Type 2 – Kernel Mode) drivers, however, are no longer supported.

NOTE Type 3 (User Mode) means that the driver is compatible with Windows 2000, Windows XP, Windows Server 2003, Windows Server 2003 R2, Windows Vista, Windows Server 2008, Windows 7, and Windows Server 2008 R2.

Beginning with Windows Vista, the printing subsystem also includes a second print path that is based on XPS. This additional print path, called the XPS print path, is built on the XPS printer driver model (XPSDrv) and provides the following benefits over the GDI model:

- Maintains the XPS document format from the point when an application sends a print job to the final processing by the print driver or device. By comparison, the GDI print path first renders the job into EMF, and then the print driver or device renders the job a second time into the language the printer can understand.
- The XPS print path can be more efficient and can provide support for advanced color profiles, which include 32 bits per channel (bpc), CMYK, named colors, n-inks, and native support of transparency and gradients when XPS-capable printers are being used.
- Provides "what you see is what you get" (WYSIWYG) printing.

Applications can print documents in Windows Vista and later versions by using either the GDI or XPS print path. For example, if a Win32 application sends the print job to a print queue that uses a GDI-based print driver, the print job is processed using the same GDI print path used in previous versions of Windows. However, if a WPF application sends the job to a print queue that uses a new XPSDrv print driver, the job is spooled using the XPS Spool File format and is processed using the XPS print path. The print path taken by the print job is therefore determined by the type of printer driver (GDI-based or XPSDrv) installed on the target print queue.

Figure 18-1 illustrates the two print paths (GDI and XPS) available in Windows Vista and later versions. Although not shown in the diagram, both of these paths use the same Print Spooler service (%SystemRoot%\System32\spoolsv.exe).

Depending on the presentation system of the application from which the document is being printed, the print job might need to be converted before being spooled in the target print path. For example, when you print from a Win32 application to an XPS-capable printer, GDI spooling functions must perform GDI-to-XPS conversion, which simulates a WPF application and spools the job in XPS Spool File format. Similarly, when you print from a WPF application to a legacy GDI-based printer, the WPF Print Support functions must perform XPS-to-GDI conversion, which simulates GDI calls by a Win32 application and spools the job in EMF format. These two conversion technologies are built into Windows Vista and later versions for maximum application compatibility when printing from different kinds of applications to either legacy or XPS-capable printers.

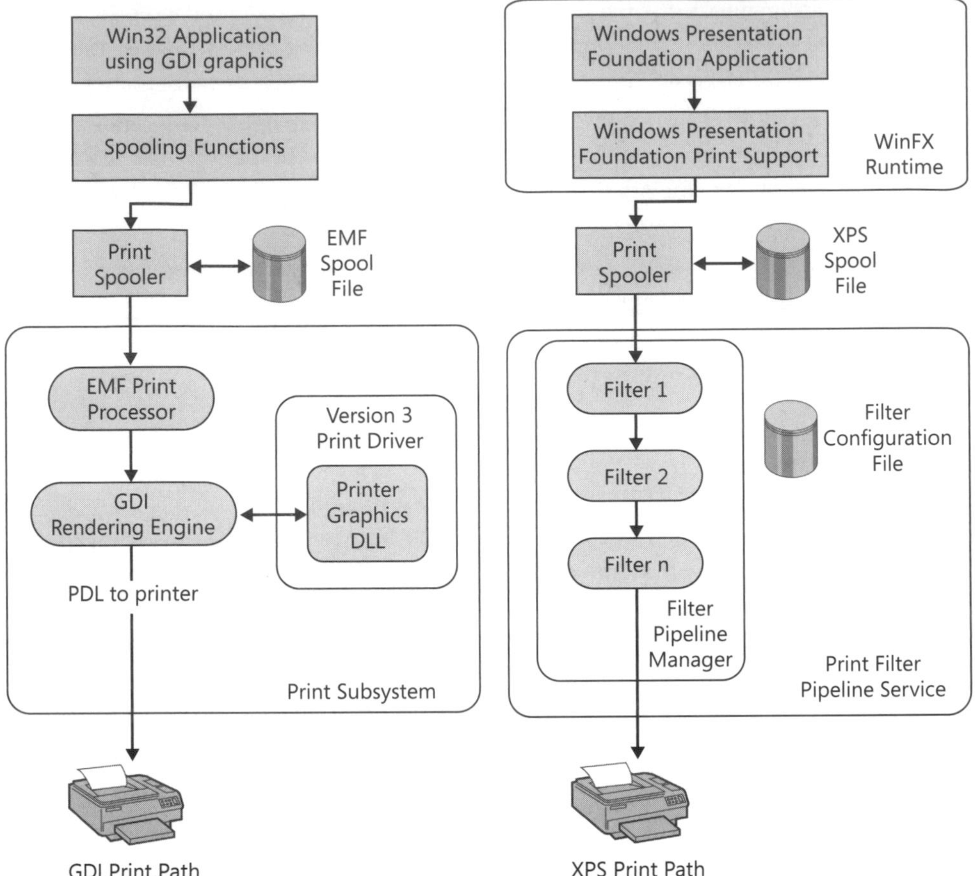

FIGURE 18-1 GDI and XPS print paths in Windows Vista and later versions

For more information on the XPS print path and XPSDrv print drivers, see the white paper titled "The XPSDrv Filter Pipeline" on WHDC at *http://www.microsoft.com/whdc/device/print/XPSDrv_FilterPipe.mspx.*

DIRECT FROM THE SOURCE

New Rasterization Service for Print Drivers

CSS Global Technical Readiness (GTR) Team

The XPS print path, introduced in Windows Vista and Windows Server 2008, did not provide any rendering services and therefore placed a higher burden on vendors developing drivers with support for the XPS print path. Rendering services provide the ability within the printing subsystem to convert a print job into a format that can be sent to the printer. In the GDI print path, the operating system provides

rendering services that support conversion to raster, printer control language (PCL), PostScript, and HP-GL for output.

A rasterization service enables printer drivers to render a print job and send it to the printer in PDL format. In Windows 7 and Windows Server 2008 R2, the XPS Rasterization service (XPSRas) provides print driver developers with the capability to rasterize XPS content in the Windows print path. This service enables printer driver developers to provide better support for printers and other document peripherals on the Windows platform and provides an XPS service that is better than the rasterization capability provided in previous versions of Windows.

Understanding Printer Driver Isolation

Printer driver isolation is a new feature of the printing subsystem in both Windows 7 and Windows Server 2008 R2 that can increase the stability of print servers by allowing administrators to isolate unstable printer drivers within a separate PrintIsolationHost.exe process instead of within the spooler process. The advantage of doing this is that when an unstable printer driver crashes, the crash doesn't halt the spooler, which would stop all other printers from functioning on the print server.

When the Print Server role service of the Print and Document Services server role is installed on Windows Server 2008 R2, each printer driver on the print server can run in one of three possible driver Isolation modes:

- **None** In this mode, the printer driver will run in the spooler process and not in a separate process. If a driver crashes, the spooler will crash, and administrators must restart the Print Spooler service. All print queues on the server will be offline while the spooler is offline. This mode is the only option on Windows 2000, Windows 2003, and Windows 2008 print servers.
- **Shared** The printer driver will run in a separate process with all of the other drivers that are also configured in Shared mode. If the driver crashes, the spooler will not crash, but all print queues with drivers in the shared process will be offline (print queues with drivers in isolated processes or within the spooler process will remain online). The shared process will be recycled, the drivers in it will be restarted, and the queues associated with these drivers will return to the online state.
- **Isolated** In this mode, the printer driver will run by itself in a separate process isolated from all other drivers. If the driver crashes, only the print queue associated with this driver will be offline. The isolated process will be recycled, the print queue will be restarted, and the queue associated with the driver will return to the online state. No other print queues or drivers on the server will be affected by this crash/restart.

Therefore, a Windows Server 2008 R2 print server can have the following:

- Legacy mode (always present)
- Shared process (always present)
- One or more isolated processes (optional)

> ***NOTE*** **The default driver Isolation mode for in-box printer drivers in Windows 7 and Windows Server 2008 R2 is Shared, whereas the default driver Isolation mode for virtual printer drivers (such as the Microsoft XPS Document Writer), fax, and print-to-file drivers (such as Print To OneNote) is None. Group Policy and .inf settings can override these System Default driver isolation settings. For more information, see the section titled "Configuring Printer Driver Isolation Mode" later in this chapter.**

Printer vendors can indicate whether a particular printer driver that they provide has been tested and verified to support running in a shared or isolated process. They can do this by adding a DriverIsolation entry in the Version section of the .inf file for the driver. For example, the following .inf file entry indicates that the driver does not support running in a separate (shared or isolated) process.

```
[Version]
...
DriverIsolation=0
```

The following .inf entry indicates that the driver can be run in a separate process.

```
[Version]
...
DriverIsolation=2
```

> ***NOTE*** **The values 1 and 3 for DriverIsolation are reserved for future use. Any value other than DriverIsolation=2 assumes DriverIsolation=0.**

Regardless of whether this .inf file entry is present or what its value is, administrators can override this setting and configure driver Isolation mode for any print driver by using the Print Management console. Administrators can also configure global driver isolation settings by using Group Policy. For information on how to configure driver isolation using Print Management and Group Policy, see the section titled "Configuring Printer Driver Isolation Mode" later in this chapter.

NOTE Print servers might experience a small degradation of performance when driver isolation is implemented due to the increased number of processes running on the system and the additional interprocess communication overhead incurred when the driver calls spooler functions, and vice versa. Additional temporary performance degradation might also be incurred when a new process is created or needs to be recycled. This performance degradation is much more evident when there are many drivers running in Isolated mode than when using Shared mode.

DIRECT FROM THE SOURCE

Printer Driver Isolation

CSS Global Technical Readiness (GTR) Team

The Printer Driver isolation feature of Windows 7 and Windows Server 2008 R2 allows some print driver functionality to be executed in a process, or processes, separate from the print spooler. By invoking print drivers in a separate process, problems associated with faulty print drivers are isolated from the Print Spooler service and will not cause it to fail. In addition, the ability to isolate print drivers from each other further increases the reliability of the printing system.

Prior to Windows 7 and Windows Server 2008 R2, the failure of third-party drivers was a leading print server support issue at Microsoft. The crash of a driver loaded into the print spooler process would crash the process, leading to an outage of the entire printing system. The impact of a spooler crash on a print server is particularly significant because of the number of users and printers that are typically affected.

In addition to the benefit of improving overall printing system stability, this new feature provides a means to:

- Isolate new drivers for testing and debugging without affecting the spooler.
- Identify which drivers have been causing spooler crashes.

The Printer Driver isolation feature is not intended to isolate print driver functionality from applications other than the print spooler. If an application loads a print driver into its own process space and the driver crashes, then the application might crash as well. For example, if an application directly calls into a printer's configuration module to set or get print capabilities, a failure in the configuration module will crash the application itself. In this scenario, the application is directly loading the printer driver into its process space. If the print driver's rendering module is loaded in the process space of the application, a failure in the driver will again cause a crash of the application itself.

Understanding the Print Management Console

Print Management is a snap-in for the MMC that administrators can use to manage multiple printers and print servers on a network. Using the Print Management console, an administrator can manage hundreds of print servers and thousands of print queues on Microsoft Windows 2000 Server, Windows Server 2003, and Windows Server 2008.

NOTE The Print Management console is designed as a general systems-management tool for administering print servers and print queues. For Help desk scenarios or printer-specific troubleshooting, however, enterprises might need to use vendor-supplied tools from printer manufacturers.

Enhancements to the Print Management Console in Windows 7

The Print Management console was introduced in Windows Server 2003 R2 and was enhanced in a number of ways in Windows Vista:

- **Network Printer Installation Wizard** The Add Printer Wizard used in earlier versions of Windows has been replaced by the Network Printer Installation Wizard, which can automatically search the network for TCP/IP printers and Web Services for Devices (WSD) printers and add them to the print server. You can also use the wizard to manually add TCP/IP and WSD printers, add printers to an existing port, or add a new port and a new printer.
- **All Drivers filter** The new All Drivers filter displays details concerning all installed printer drivers for all print servers managed by Print Management. The All Drivers filter shows the version of printer drivers on multiple servers, which allows administrators to quickly and easily see which print servers must receive updated drivers (when they are updating printer drivers in their organization). The All Drivers filter also allows administrators to easily remove printer driver packages from the driver store when they are no longer needed.
- **Export/import print queues and printer drivers** You can now use Print Management to export the configuration of all print queues and printer drivers on a print server to a Printer Migration (*.printerExport) file, which you can then import on either the same print server or a different one. This is useful for administrators who want to back up printer configurations or migrate printers to a different print server.
- **Comma-separated list in Add/Remove Servers** Administrators can now quickly add multiple print servers to Print Management by specifying a comma-separated list of print servers in the Add/Remove Servers dialog box. Administrators can also copy and paste a list of servers (one per line) to the text box in the dialog box. In addition, the print servers being specified in this dialog box no longer need to be online when added to Print Management.

- **More filter conditions** When creating a new custom filter, administrators now have the option of specifying up to six filter conditions instead of only three as supported previously.
- **Less detailed logging by default** By default, only Error and Warning Events are now logged in the event logs for the Print Spooler service. If desired, however, administrators can still enable logging of Informational Events for detailed logging purposes, such as auditing print queue activity.
- **Migrate Printers option** By right-clicking the root node in Print Management, administrators now have the option of using the Printer Migration Wizard to export or import print queues and printer drivers to move printers to a different print server, such as for consolidation purposes.

In addition to the enhancements to the Print Management console found in Windows Vista and Windows Server 2008 that were described earlier in this chapter, several new enhancements can be found in the Print Management console in Windows 7 and Windows Server 2008 R2. These new enhancements include the following:

- **Security tab added for print servers** When you open the properties of a print server found under the Print Servers node in Print Management, a Security tab is now displayed. Using this tab, you can configure default print permissions for all new printers installed on the server. For information on how to do this, see the section titled "Configuring Default Security for Print Servers" later in this chapter.
- **New custom printer filter criteria** The New Printer Filter Wizard has been enhanced with additional criteria for creating custom printer filters. For more information on this enhancement, see the section titled "Creating and Using Printer Filters" later in this chapter.
- **Custom driver filters** A New Driver Filter Wizard is included that can be used to filter printer drivers according to a wide range of criteria. For more information on this enhancement, see the section titled "Creating and Using Driver Filters" later in this chapter.
- **Configure Driver Isolation mode** You can now configure the Driver Isolation mode as None, Shared, or Isolated using the context menu that appears when you right-click a printer driver found under the Drivers node in Print Management. For information on how to do this, see the section titled "Configuring Printer Driver Isolation Mode" later in this chapter.
- **Installing printer drivers using Windows Update** The Add Printer Driver Wizard has been enhanced to enable downloading of additional printer drivers directly from the Windows Update Web site. This change also means that fewer in-box printer drivers need to be included in Windows. The Network Printer Installation Wizard has also been enhanced to provide this functionality. For more information about this feature, see the section titled "Managing Printer Drivers" later in this chapter.

To use the Print Management console directly on a remote computer (for example, on a remote print server), connect to the computer using Remote Desktop. The remote computer must be running Windows Server 2003 R2 or later, and the Print Management console must be installed on the computer. You might need to use this approach if the computer on which you are running Print Management does not have all of the printer drivers needed to manage the printers because Print Management pulls its printer drivers from the computer on which Print Management is running.

To take advantage of the new Print Management console features in Windows 7 and Windows Server 2008 R2, your computer should be running one of these versions of Windows. On Windows Server 2008 R2, the Print Management console is available from Administrative Tools when you install the Print and Document Services server role. On Windows 7, the Print Management console is available from Administrative Tools, which is found under System And Security in Control Panel.

The Print Management Console

As shown in Figure 18-2, Print Management displays a root node and three main subnodes. You expose the functionality of these different nodes in the Action pane (or by right-clicking a node). They can be summarized as follows:

- **Print Management (root) node** Adds or removes print servers to/from the console and launches the Printer Migration Wizard to export or import printer configurations.
- **Custom Filters node** Displays all custom filters, including four default filters:
  - **All Printers** Displays all printers on all print servers and allows administrators to open the printer queue for a selected printer, pause or resume printing, print a test page from a printer, configure printer properties, and deploy a printer connection using Group Policy.
  - **All Drivers** Displays all printer drivers for all printers and allows administrators to view driver properties and remove driver packages from the driver store.
  - **Printers Not Ready** Displays all print queues that are in a Not Ready state for any reason.
  - **Printers With Jobs** Displays all print queues that currently have jobs pending in them.

  When you create a new custom filter using the New Printer Filter Wizard, you can configure an e-mail notification for troubleshooting purposes to alert administrators when a printer matches the filter conditions. You can also configure a script action so that a specified script can be run when a printer matches the condition—for example, a script to restart the Print Spooler service on a print server.

  In addition, the Show Extended View option (available by right-clicking a custom filter) displays jobs pending on the print queue and—if supported by the print device—the Web page from which the printer can be managed.

- **Print Servers node** Displays all print servers being managed by Print Management, together with a manageable view of their drivers, forms, ports, and print queues. You can also use this node to export/import print queues and printer drivers, configure e-mail notifications or script actions during times when the spooler or server is down, and launch the Network Printer Installation Wizard to add new printers manually or automatically search for TCP/IP and WSD printers and add them to the list of printers being managed by Print Management.
- **Deployed Printers node** Displays printer connections that have been deployed using Group Policy. For more information, see the section titled "Deploying Printers Using Group Policy" later in this chapter.

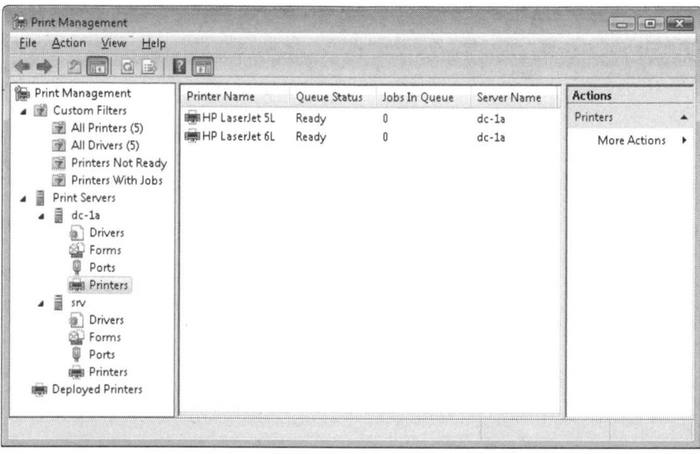

FIGURE 18-2 Overview of Print Management

> ***NOTE*** **Print Management also lets you view print queues on both a UNIX or Linux server running Samba and on Apple Macintosh computers. You can view these queues and also monitor these print servers by receiving notifications when they go down, but you cannot use Print Management to add or remove printers to such servers. To view print queues on UNIX or Linux servers, you must authenticate to *server_name*\ipc$ before you can add the server to the list of print servers you want to monitor.**

Adding and Removing Print Servers

To add or remove print servers so that Print Management can manage them, follow these steps:

1. Click Start, point to All Programs, select Administrative Tools, and then select Print Management.
2. Respond to the UAC prompt either by clicking Continue or by supplying administrator credentials as required.

3. Right-click either the root node or the Print Servers node, select Add/Remove Servers to open the Add/Remove Servers dialog box, and then do one of the following:
   - Click Add The Local Server to add the local computer to the list of managed print servers.
   - Click Browse to open Network Explorer and browse to select print servers on the network.
   - Type a comma-separated list of print servers and click Add To List.

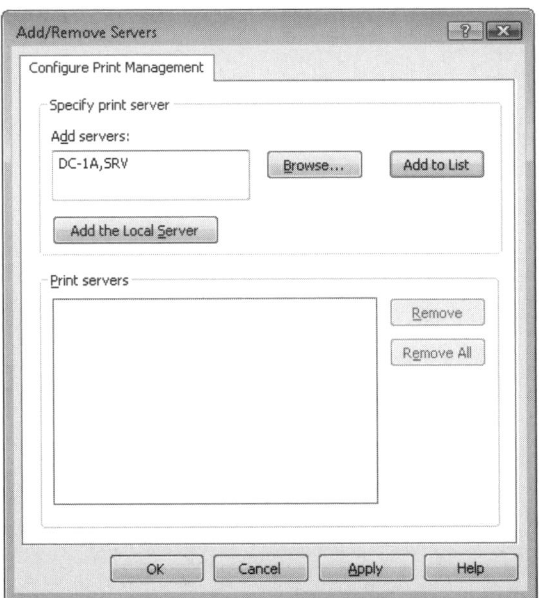

To remove a print server from the list of managed print servers, open the Add/Remove Services dialog box, select the print server, and then click Remove. You can also remove all print servers by clicking Remove All.

Configuring Default Security for Print Servers

In Windows Server 2008 and earlier versions, the following permissions are assigned by default when a new printer is added to the Print Management console:

- Administrator has Print, Manage Printers, and Manage Documents permissions.
- Creator Owner has Manage Documents permission.
- Everyone has Print permission.

If an administrator wants to modify these permissions for all printers on a print server running on one of these platforms, he needs to open the properties for each printer individually and make the necessary changes on the Security tab of each printer's properties sheet. This can be inconvenient if the administrator needs to modify printer permissions to comply with corporate security policy.

New in Windows Server 2008 R2 is the capability of modifying the default security settings for all printers installed on a print server. This can be configured by using the new Security tab on the properties sheet for a print server (as shown in Figure 18-3). Any changes made to these default security settings will then be inherited automatically by any new printers added to the print server. Changes to these default security settings do not modify the permissions for any existing printers on the print server.

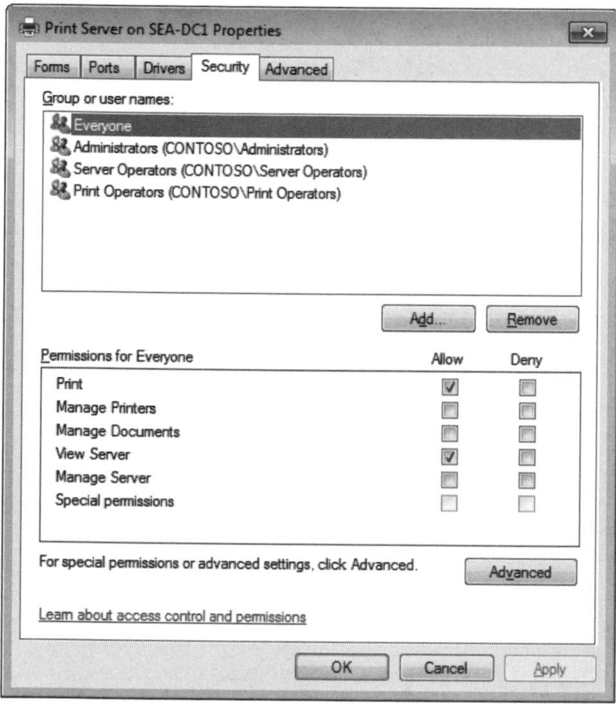

FIGURE 18-3 Configuring default security settings for new printers created on a print server

You can modify a print server's default security settings by using Print Management running on Windows 7 or Windows Server 2008 R2. You can also take or assign ownership of a print server by clicking Advanced and selecting the Owner tab of the Advanced Security Settings dialog box.

> ***NOTE*** **A user must have View Server permission to view printer settings on a print server. A user must have Manage Server permission to add or delete printers, drivers, ports, and forms on printers or to modify settings on a print server.**

Adding Printers Using the Network Printer Installation Wizard

To add printers using the Network Printer Installation Wizard, follow these steps:

1. Add at least one print server to the list of managed print servers.
2. Right-click a print server and select Add Printer to start the Network Printer Installation Wizard.

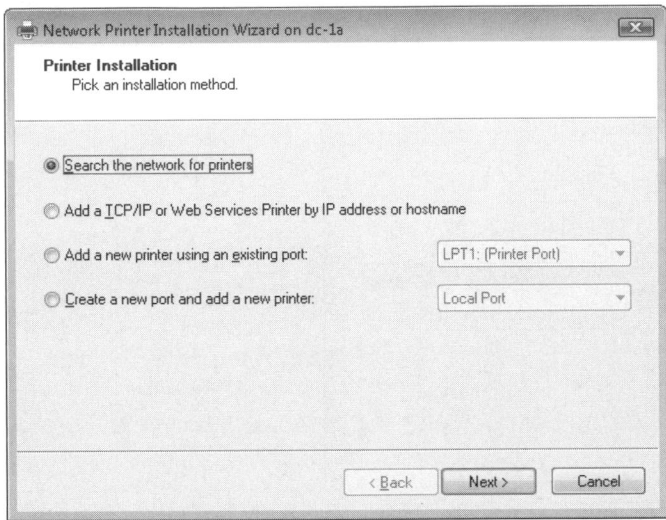

3. Do one of the following:
   - To scan the local subnet for TCP/IP or WSD network printers automatically, select Search The Network For Printers and then click Next. As the scan progresses, Windows will display a list of available network printers and will install them automatically on the selected print server. (You might be required to specify a driver for a printer manually if Windows cannot find one automatically.)
   - To add a specific TCP/IP or WSD network printer to the list of printers managed by the print server manually, select Add A TCP/IP Or Web Services Printer By IP Address Or Hostname, specify the name or IP address of the printer, and then click Next.
   - To add a new printer using an existing port, which can be either a local port (LTP or COM) or a previously added TCP/IP port, select Add A New Printer Using An Existing Port, click Next, and either install the printer driver automatically selected by the wizard, select an existing driver, or install a new driver either from the CD media included with the driver or by using Windows Update.
   - To create a new local port and install a printer on it, select Create A New Port And Add A New Printer, click Next, specify a name for the new port, and then either install the printer driver automatically selected by the wizard, select an existing driver, or install a new driver.

NOTE The option for automatically detecting printers on the local subnet using Search The Network For Printers cannot work across a firewall. If you want to use this feature to detect printers for another location, such as a remote subnet at a branch office location that is located behind a firewall, use Remote Desktop to connect to a Windows Server 2003 R2 or later computer at the remote location, start Print Management, and then select Search The Network For Printers as described previously.

In addition to the new Network Printer Installation Wizard, the end-user Add Printer Wizard is still present in Windows 7 and has been enhanced to allow users to add local, network, wireless, and Bluetooth printers and also to search Windows Update for printer drivers when needed. For more information on this topic, see the section titled "Client-Side Management of Printers" later in this chapter.

HOW IT WORKS

WSD Printers

WSD is a new type of network connectivity supported by Windows Vista and later versions. With WSD, users can have a Plug and Play experience similar to that with universal serial bus (USB) devices over the network rather than only with locally connected devices.

In Windows Vista and later versions, WSD printer ports are serviced by the WSD Port Monitor (WSDMon) instead of the Standard Port Monitor (TCPMon) used to service TCP/IP ports. WSDMon is used by default if a printer supports it; otherwise, it defaults to TCPMon.

For more information about the various Web Services specifications and their support on Windows platforms, see *http://msdn.microsoft.com/en-us/library/ms951274.aspx* on MSDN. You can find additional information on WSD printer support in Windows Vista and later versions on WHDC at *http://www.microsoft.com/whdc/device/print/default.mspx*.

Creating and Using Printer Filters

You can use Print Management to create custom printer filters to simplify the task of managing hundreds of print servers and thousands of printers. To create a custom printer filter, follow these steps:

1. Right-click the Custom Filters node in Print Management and select Add New Printer Filter.
2. Type a name and description for the new filter. For example, type **All HP Printers** for a filter that displays printers whose driver names begin with HP, indicating Hewlett-

Packard printers. If desired, select the check box labeled Display The Total Number Of Printers Next To The Name Of The Printer Filter and then click Next.

3. Specify up to six filter criteria for your new filter. For example, to filter for printers whose driver names begin with HP, select the Driver Name field and the Begins With condition and type **HP** as the value.

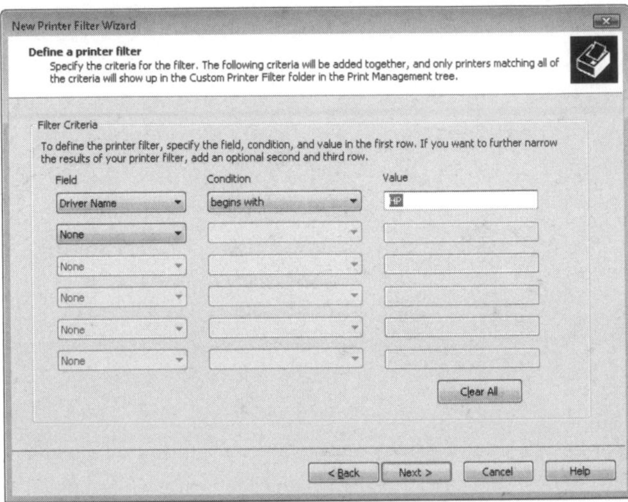

4. Click Next and configure an e-mail notification or script action that occurs when a printer matches the filter criteria specified by the filter. Configuration notification is optional and is described further in the section titled "Monitoring and Troubleshooting Printers" later in this chapter.

5. Click Finish to create the new filter. Select the new filter to activate it and display printers that meet the criteria specified by the filter.

Table 18-1 lists the filter criteria fields, conditions, and possible values that you can specify when you create a custom printer filter. Filter criteria fields marked with an asterisk (*) are new to Print Management in Windows 7 and Windows Server 2008 R2.

TABLE 18-1 Fields, Conditions, and Possible Values for Printer Filter Criteria

FIELD	CONDITIONS	VALUE
Printer Name Server Name Comments Driver Name Location Shared Name Driver Version* Provider*	Is exactly, is not exactly, begins with, not begin with, ends with, not end with, contains, not contains	(type a value to specify)

FIELD	CONDITIONS	VALUE
Queue Status	Is exactly, is not exactly	Ready, paused, error, deleting, paper jam, out of paper, manual feed required, paper problem, offline, IO active, busy, printing, output bin full, not available, waiting, processing, initializing, warming up, toner/ink low, no toner/ink, page punt, user intervention required, out of memory, door open
Jobs in Queue	Is exactly, is not exactly, is less than, is less than or equal to, is greater than, is greater than or equal to	(type a value to specify)
Is Shared	Is exactly, is not exactly	False, true

NOTE **To modify a printer filter after you create it, right-click the filter and then select Properties.**

Creating and Using Driver Filters

A new feature of Print Management in Windows 7 and Windows Server 2008 R2 is the ability to create custom driver filters to simplify the task of managing all of your printer drivers on your print servers. To create a custom driver filter, follow these steps:

1. Right-click the Custom Filters node in Print Management and select Add New Driver Filter.
2. Type a name and description for the new filter. For example, type **Legacy Drivers** for a filter that displays printer drivers that don't support driver isolation.
3. Click Next and specify up to six filter criteria for your new filter. For example, to filter for printer drivers that don't support driver isolation, select the Driver Isolation field and the Is Exactly condition, and type **None** for the value.
4. Click Next and continue configuring the filter as described in the previous section.

Table 18-2 lists the filter criteria fields, conditions, and possible values that you can specify when you create a custom driver filter.

TABLE 18-2 Fields, Conditions, and Possible Values for Driver Filter Criteria

FIELD	CONDITIONS	VALUE
Driver Name Driver Version Provider Environment Driver File Path Config File Path Data File Path Default Datatype Hardware ID Help File Path Language Monitor Manufacturer OEM URL Inf Path Print Processor Driver Data Type Driver Isolation Server Name	Is exactly, is not exactly, begins with, not begin with, ends with, not end with, contains, not contains	(type a value to specify)
Packaged	Is exactly, is not exactly	False, true

Managing Printers Using Print Management

After you add print servers to Print Management and create printer filters to display and easily select different types of printers, you can begin managing these printers and print servers. Printer management tasks that you can perform using Print Management include:

- Configuring properties of printers.
- Publishing printers in AD DS so that users can find them easily.
- Adding, removing, and managing printer drivers.
- Exporting and importing printer configurations.
- Performing bulk actions, such as pausing all print queues on a print server.

Configuring Properties of Printers

You can use Print Management to configure the properties of printers on your network. To do this, you might be required to install additional printer drivers locally on the Windows 7 computer from which you are running Print Management because some printer properties might not be configurable unless the printer's driver is installed on the local computer, Therefore, if the in-box (default) printer drivers included with Windows 7 do not include a driver for a network printer you want to manage, you must first download and install a driver for the printer from the print server before you can configure the printer's properties using Print Management.

To configure the properties of a printer, follow these steps using Print Management:

1. Right-click the printer you want to configure and then select Properties.
2. Respond to one of the following messages if they appear:
   - A message might appear saying, "To use the shared printer *server_name**printer_sharename*, you need to install the printer driver on your computer. If you do not recognize or trust the location or name of the printer, do not install the driver." If this message appears and you want to manage the printer, click Install Driver to automatically download and install the printer's driver from the print server.
   - A message might appear saying, "The *printer_sharename* driver is not installed on this computer. Some printer properties will not be accessible unless you install the printer driver. Do you want to install the printer driver now?" If this message appears and you want to manage the printer, click Yes to open the Add Printer Wizard. Follow the steps of the wizard to manually install the printer driver for the printer by supplying the necessary driver media.
   - If no message appears and the printer's Properties dialog box appears, the printer driver is either already installed on the local computer or is included as an in-box driver in Windows 7.
3. Configure the settings on the various tabs of the printer's Properties dialog box as desired. See Help And Support for addition information about configuring printer properties in Windows 7.

Publishing Printers in AD DS

By default, when printers are installed on Windows Server 2003 or later print servers and are shared over the network, they are also automatically listed in AD DS. However, other network printers—such as stand-alone TCP/IP or WSD network printers—might not be listed in AD DS. You will need to add them manually to the directory so that users can search for them in the directory.

To add a network printer to AD DS manually, do one of the following using Print Management:

- Right-click the printer and select List In Directory.
- Open the printer's Properties dialog box, click the Sharing tab, and then select the List In The Directory check box.

You can also remove printers from AD DS either by clearing the List In The Directory check box or by right-clicking the printer and selecting Remove From Directory. You can remove printers from AD DS to prevent users from installing them manually by using the Add Printer Wizard from the Printers Control Panel item.

After a printer is published in AD DS, users can search AD DS using the Add Printer Wizard and manually install a printer connection on their computers. This allows users to print to a network printer. For more information, see the section titled "Searching for Printers" later in this chapter.

Managing Printer Drivers

If client computers need additional printer drivers, you can use Print Management to add them to print servers, and you can also remove print drivers from print servers when clients no longer need them. For example, you can add additional printer drivers for network printers to support 64-bit Windows client computers by following these steps:

1. Open Print Management and expand the console tree to select the Drivers node beneath the print server to which you want to add additional drivers.
2. Right-click the Drivers node, select Add Driver to open the Add Printer Driver Wizard, and then click Next.
3. Select the types of system architectures for which you need to install additional drivers.

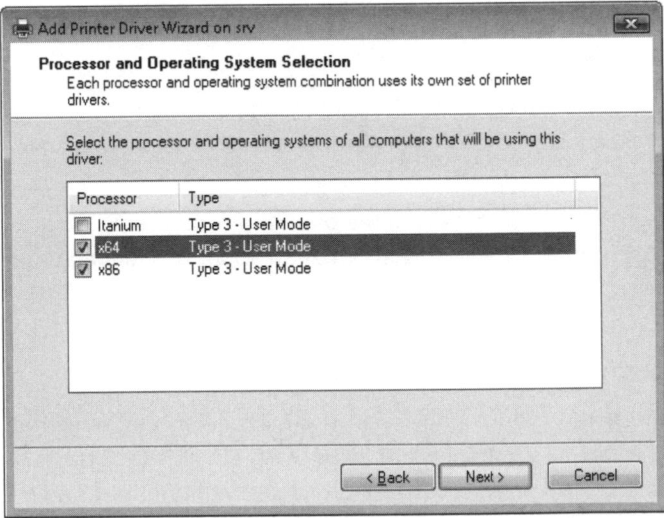

4. Click Next. If the drivers you need to install are not already staged within the driver store on the local computer, you will need to do one of the following:
   - Click Have Disk and provide driver media or specify a network location where the driver packages are available.

- Click Windows Update if this is available to display a list of printer drivers available on Windows Update. Note that it can take several minutes for the list of printer drivers to be downloaded from Windows Update the first time that this is done.

Continue stepping through the wizard to add the drivers to the print server and make them available for clients that need them.

The following considerations apply when adding additional drivers using Print Management:

- Using the Add Printer Drivers Wizard from Print Management running on Windows Server 2003 R2 or later lets you add additional x86, x64, and Itanium drivers for versions of Windows prior to Windows Vista.
- Using the Add Printer Drivers Wizard from Print Management running on Windows Vista or later lets you add Type 3 (User Mode) printer drivers only for x86, x64, and Itanium systems running Windows Vista, Windows 7, Windows Server 2008, or Windows Server 2008 R2. To add additional drivers for earlier versions of Windows, use Print Management on Windows Server 2003 R2 or later versions instead of Windows 7.

> ***NOTE*** **There are no differences in the installation method for adding 32-bit and 64-bit drivers.**

You can also remove printer drivers from print servers when client computers no longer need these drivers. To remove a printer driver from a print server, follow these steps:

1. Open Print Management and expand the console tree to select the Drivers node beneath the print server from which you want to remove drivers.
2. Right-click a driver under the Drivers node and select Delete.
3. Click Yes to confirm your action.

> ***NOTE*** **When you use the preceding steps to remove a printer driver from the local print server (when using a Windows Vista, Windows 7, Windows Server 2008, or Windows Server 2008 R2 computer as a print server), the driver package is uninstalled but remains staged in the driver store. Windows will pick and install the driver again when a compatible TCP/IP or Plug and Play printer is added to the system. If you selected Remove Driver Package instead of Delete, however, Windows will remove the package and not use the driver again.**

You can display detailed information for all printer drivers installed on a print server by following these steps:

1. Open Print Management and expand the console tree to select the Drivers node beneath a print server.
2. From the View menu, select Add/Remove Columns.
3. Add additional columns from the list of available columns to display more detail concerning each driver installed on the server.

To save detailed information concerning each driver installed on a print server and import it into Microsoft Office Excel for reporting purposes, follow the preceding procedure to add the columns desired and then right-click the Drivers node and select Export List. Save the detailed driver as a comma-separated (*.csv) file and import it into Office Excel. The Export List command is available for any node in an MMC snap-in.

DIRECT FROM THE FIELD

Is Your Printer Compatible with Windows 7?

Mitch Tulloch, MVP
http://www.mtit.com

Let's say your company is thinking of upgrading your Windows XP clients to Windows 7. Question: Will the printers you currently have installed on your Windows Server 2003 R2 print server work for users when their computers are upgraded?

Here's a quick way to determine the answer: Use Print Management to examine the version of each printer driver on your print server. If a driver says Windows XP or Windows Server 2003 (that is, Type 3 drivers), the associated printer will be compatible with Windows 7 and Windows Vista. If the driver says Windows NT 4.0 (Type 2), however, the printer uses a Kernel Mode driver and you will need an update for the driver before Windows 7 clients can use that printer.

Configuring Printer Driver Isolation Mode

Administrators can use Print Management to configure the Driver Isolation mode for each printer driver installed on a print server. There are several scenarios in which doing this might be useful to increase print server reliability. For example, if a print queue associated with a particular driver keeps crashing, the administrator can change the Driver Isolation mode for the driver to Isolated so that the driver runs within its own separate process. That way, other print queues on the server won't be affected when the driver crashes. The administrator can then contact the vendor to request an updated driver for the printer.

Another example might be when a vendor supplies the administrator with a printer driver whose quality is unknown. In this case, the best practice is to assign the driver to an isolated process and then collect and analyze crash statistics for the print queue associated with the driver over a period of time. Once the driver is determined to be sufficiently stable, the administrator can move the driver to the shared process.

Configuring Printer Driver Isolation Mode Using the Print Management Console

You can configure the Printer Driver Isolation mode for a printer driver from under the All Drivers node, a custom driver filter node, or the Drivers node for a print server. To configure the Driver Isolation mode for a printer driver, right-click the driver and select Set Driver Isolation from the context menu (see Figure 18-4). Doing this displays four choices:

- **None** Runs the driver within the spooler process (legacy Isolation mode).
- **Shared** Runs the driver within the shared process.
- **Isolated** Creates a new isolated process for this driver only.
- **System Default** This menu option displays (None) if the DriverIsolation entry in the driver's .inf file is missing or has a value of 0, or it displays (Shared) if the DriverIsolation entry in the driver's .inf file has a value of 2. In other words, None indicates that the driver is not designed to support driver isolation, and Shared indicates that it is designed to support driver isolation.

Note also the new Driver Isolation column in the details pane when drivers are being displayed in Print Management, which is new in Windows 7 and Windows Server 2008 R2.

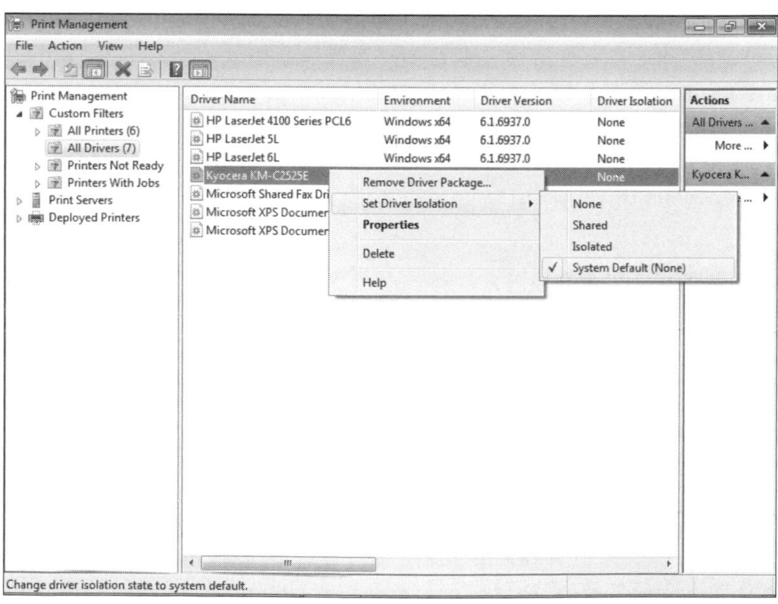

FIGURE 18-4 Configuring the Printer Driver Isolation mode for a printer driver

> ***NOTE*** **If you are using the Print Management console on a computer running Windows 7 or Windows Server 2008 R2 and connect to a print server running a previous version of Windows, the Print Management console will indicate that driver isolation is not supported on that server, and you will not have the option to change modes.**

Configuring Printer Driver Isolation Mode Using Group Policy

You can configure certain aspects of printer driver isolation globally on a Windows Server 2008 R2 print server by using the following two Group Policy settings, which are new in Windows 7 and Windows Server 2008 R2 and apply only to those platforms:

- Computer Configuration\Policies\Administrative Templates\Printers\Execute Print Drivers In Isolated Processes

  This policy setting determines whether the print spooler will execute printer drivers in an isolated or separate process. If you enable or do not configure this policy setting, the print spooler will attempt to execute printer drivers in an isolated process. If you disable this policy setting, no driver isolation is attempted, and the print spooler will execute printer drivers in the print spooler process. In other words, adjusting this policy setting to Disable lets you completely disable driver isolation and force everything to run in legacy mode (mode = None). Any other setting allows driver isolation to work as specified by a driver's .inf file and Print Management console settings.

- Computer Configuration\Policies\Administrative Templates\Printers\Override Print Driver Compatibility Execution Setting Reported By Print Driver

  This policy setting determines whether the print spooler will override the driver isolation compatibility reported by the printer driver via the DriverIsolation entry in its .inf file. Doing this enables you to execute printer drivers in an isolated process even if the driver does not report compatibility. If you enable this policy setting, the print spooler will attempt to execute the driver in Isolation mode regardless of the DriverIsolation entry in the driver's .inf file. If you disable or do not configure this policy setting, the print spooler will honor the DriverIsolation entry in the driver's .inf file.

> ***NOTE*** **Both of these policy settings apply only to printer drivers loaded by the print spooler; print drivers loaded by applications are not affected. After changing these policy settings, use *gpupdate /force* and then restart the Print Spooler service to ensure that the new policies take effect.**

Troubleshooting Driver Isolation

Administrators can troubleshoot driver isolation issues using the event logs. By default, Admin logging for the PrintService is enabled in Windows 7 and Windows Server 2008 R2, and you should monitor the Application and System Event Logs for events coming from the print spooler.

To see additional events related to driver isolation activities, you can enable Operational logging as follows:

1. Open Event Viewer and expand the following:

   Application and Services\Logs\Microsoft\Windows\PrintService.

2. Right-click Operational and select Enable Log.

After you enable Operational logging, look for Informational Events with an Event ID of 842 and with a Source that is PrintService. This event indicates the Isolation mode that was used to print a particular print job and provides information such as the following.

```
The print job <x> was sent through the print processor <print processor name> on printer
<printer name>, driver <print driver name>, in the isolation mode <x> (0 - loaded in the
spooler, 1 - loaded in shared sandbox, 2 - loaded in isolated sandbox). Win32 error code
returned by the print processor: 0x0.
```

Exporting and Importing Print Server Configurations

You can export the configuration of all print queues and printer drivers on a print server to a Printer Migration file (*.printerExport), which you then import on either the same print server or a different one. This is useful for administrators who want to back up printer configurations or migrate printers to a different print server. Exporting print queue configuration settings and printer drivers is also a useful method for backing up the configuration of a print server as part of your organization's Business Continuity Plan (BCP).

To export all printer drivers and the configuration of all print queues for a print server, right-click the print server's node in Print Management and select Export Printers To A File. This opens the Printer Migration Wizard, which displays a list of print queues and printer drivers that will be exported. Save the resulting *.printerExport file on a network share so that you can import it again during a disaster recovery scenario or when consolidating print servers.

You can import previously exported print server configurations by using either of the following methods:

- Right-click the print server's node in Print Management, select Import Printers From A File, and then browse to select a *.printerExport file and import it.
- Double-click a *.printerExport file while logged on to the print server into which you want to import the configuration information to start the Printer Migration Wizard and import the configuration.

For more information on using the Printer Migration Wizard, see the section titled "Migrating Print Servers" later in this chapter.

> ***NOTE*** **The PrintBRM command-line tool can also be used in Task Scheduler to perform nightly backups of your print server configurations.**

HOW IT WORKS

Printer Export Files

The printer export file has a .printerExport file extension and is essentially a compressed cabinet (.cab) file that contains XML definition files for the drivers, ports, forms, and printers on a computer. It also contains all of the driver files for each printer.

The following files are part of the printer export file:

- **BrmDrivers.xml** Printer driver description file. This file contains a list of every driver installed on the computer and the driver files for each driver.
- **BrmForms.xml** Forms description file. This file contains a list of all of the installed forms.
- **BrmLMons.xml** Port monitor definition file. This file usually contains either Windows NT x86 or Windows x64 as the architecture and a list of port monitors and port monitor files installed on the computer.
- **BrmPorts.xml** Printer ports definition file. This file contains a list of all printer ports that have been installed on the computer. This list does not include printer connections.
- **BrmPrinters.xml** Printer definition file. This file contains a list of all printers that have been installed on the computer. This list does not include printer connections.
- **BrmSpoolerAttrib.xml** Spooler attributes definition file. This file contains information about the spooler directory path and a value that determines whether the source computer was a cluster server.

Performing Bulk Actions Using Print Management

You can also use Print Management to perform bulk actions for printers and printer drivers on a print server.

- You can perform the following bulk actions on printers by selecting several (or all) printers on a print server or as displayed within a printer filter:
  - Pause Printing
  - Resume Printing
  - Cancel All Jobs
  - List In Directory
  - Remove From Directory
  - Delete

- You can perform the following bulk actions for printer drivers by selecting several (or all) printer drivers for a printer or as displayed within a printer filter, such as the All Drivers default filter:
  - Remove Driver Package
  - Delete

DIRECT FROM THE SOURCE

Managing Print Queues and Servers with the Print Management Console

Frank Olivier, User Experience Program Manager
Windows Client

With Windows 7 client computers and the Windows 7 Print Management console, printer administrators can easily provide users with high printer availability. This can be achieved by moving users from the print queues on one server to identical print queues (for the same physical printers) on another server when the first server is unavailable.

First, use the Print Management console to deploy printers to a number of users using a GPO (such as \\ServerA\ColorPrinter with GPO1), and link GPO1 to an organizational unit (OU) with a number of users or computers.

Then, using the Print Server import/export tool, do a backup of a print server. In the Print Management console, right-click a print server and select Export Printers To A File. All the print queues and printer drivers will be exported to a .printerExport file. Alternatively, you can use the command-line PrintBRM tool (in %WinDir%\System32\spool\tools), either from the command line or from Task Scheduler, to do periodic backups of the print server.

When a print server goes down because of a hardware failure, the administrator can easily move users to a new server. On the new server (Server2), use the Print Management console to import the .printerExport file. New print queues will now be created (such as \\Server2\ColorPrinter if the old server had \\Server1\ColorPrinter).

Using the deploy printers functionality in the Print Management console, deploy the printers using GPO2. With the Group Policy Management tool, disable the link to GPO1. The print queues from Server1 will be undeployed, and the print queues from GPO2 (Server2) will be installed.

When the old print server is online again, the link to GPO2 can be disabled, and the link to GPO1 can be enabled.

Client-Side Management of Printers

Depending on Group Policy settings, end users of Windows 7 computers in managed environments might be able to find and install their own printers when needed. See the section titled "Managing Client-Side Printer Experience Using Group Policy" later in this chapter for more information on the policy settings that apply.

Installing Printers Using the Add Printers Wizard

In addition to the new Network Printer Installation Wizard used in Print Management, the end-user Add Printer Wizard is still available in Windows 7, and it has been enhanced to allow users to easily add local, network, wireless, and Bluetooth printers. This wizard is not needed when installing USB printers, however, because the user can simply attach the printer to a USB port on the computer and the printer is automatically installed.

> **NOTE** In Windows 7, standard users can install network printers without administrator credentials provided the driver is safe (i.e., signed and packaged). If you see an elevation prompt that says, "Do you trust this printer?" when you try to install a printer, it is because the printer driver is not trustable. Only local administrators can install an untrusted driver.

To start the Add Printer Wizard in Windows 7, follow these steps:

1. Click Start and select Devices And Printers.
2. Click Add Printer on the toolbar to start the Add Printer Wizard.

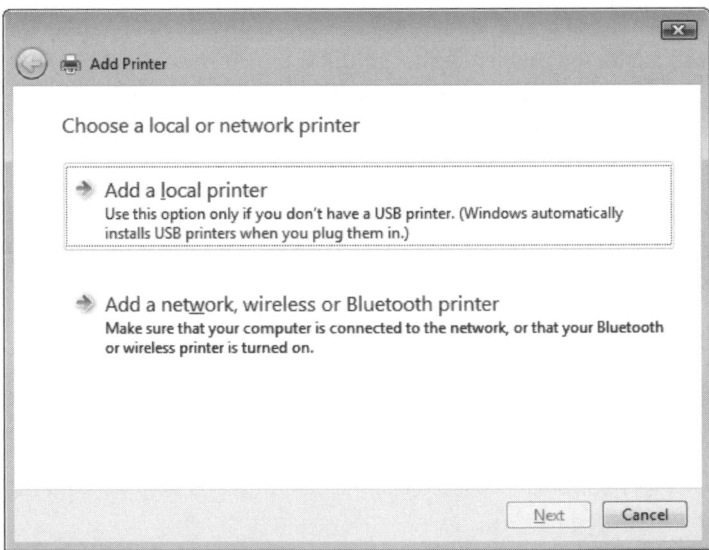

3. Do one of the following:

   - To install a local (non USB) printer, click Add A Local Printer and specify the port, printer driver, and other information required by the wizard. Installing a local printer manually like this is needed only for non–Plug and Play printers. USB printers are detected and installed automatically when they are connected to a USB port on the computer.
   - To install a network, wireless, or Bluetooth printer, click Add A Network, Wireless Or Bluetooth Printer, select the printer you want to install from the list of found printers, and then click Next to install the printer.

On a managed network where AD DS is deployed, the Add A Network, Wireless Or Bluetooth Printer option in the Add Printer Wizard finds network printers published in AD DS as well as available wireless Bluetooth printers. On an unmanaged network without AD DS, selecting this option causes the Add Printer Wizard to scan the local subnet for TCP/IP, WSD, wireless, and Bluetooth printers.

> ***NOTE*** **Network administrators can also set the number and type of printers to find using Group Policy settings found under Computer Configuration\Policies\Administrative Templates\Printers. If you do not want a printer to show up, set the number of printers of each type to 0 in either Add Printer Wizard – Network Scan Page (Managed Network) or Add Printer Wizard – Network Scan Page (Unmanaged Network).**

Searching for Printers

After a printer is published in AD DS, users can use the Add Printer Wizard to search for network printers in AD DS and manually install a printer connection on their computers so that they can print to the printer. To search for a published printer to install, the user can follow these steps using Printers in Control Panel:

1. Click Add A Printer on the toolbar of the Devices And Printers Control Panel item.
2. In the Add Printer Wizard on the Choose A Local Or Network Printer page, click Add A Network, Wireless Or Bluetooth Printer to display a list of printers published in AD DS.

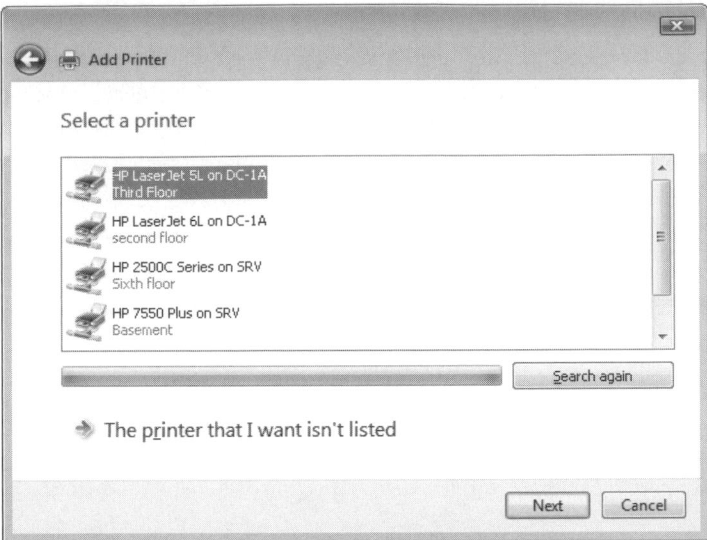

3. Select the published printer for which you want to install a connection and click Next to continue stepping through the wizard and install the printer connection on the local computer.
4. If the printer you want to install is not listed in the directory or if the number of published printers displayed is very large and the user wants to search for a specific type of printer in AD DS, click The Printer That I Want Isn't Listed to open the Find A Printer By Name Or TCP/IP Address page of the Add Printer Wizard.

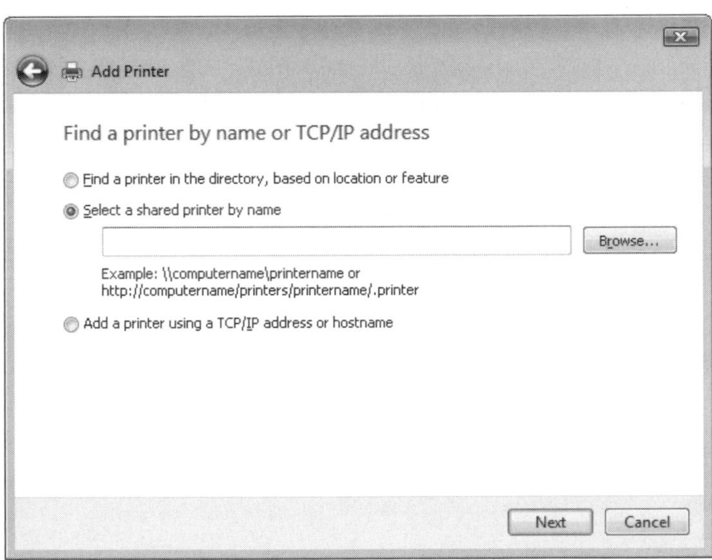

5. Select one of the following options:
   - To browse for a shared printer using Network Explorer, select the Select A Shared Printer By Name check box and then click Browse. You can also type the Universal Naming Convention (UNC) path to the shared printer if you know the path.
   - To install a printer connection to a stand-alone TCP/IP or WSD network printer, select the Add A Printer Using A TCP/IP Address Or Hostname check box and then click Next. Type the IP address or host name of the printer, select Autodetect to automatically detect whether the printer is TCP/IP or WSD type, select Query The Printer And Automatically Select The Driver To Use, and then click Next to install a printer connection to the network printer.
   - To search AD DS for a printer that meets specified criteria, select the Find A Printer In The Directory Based On Location Or Feature check box and click Next to open the Find Printers dialog box. Specify the criteria for the type of printer you want to search for and then click Find Now to query AD DS. Double-click the desired printer to install a printer connection for it.

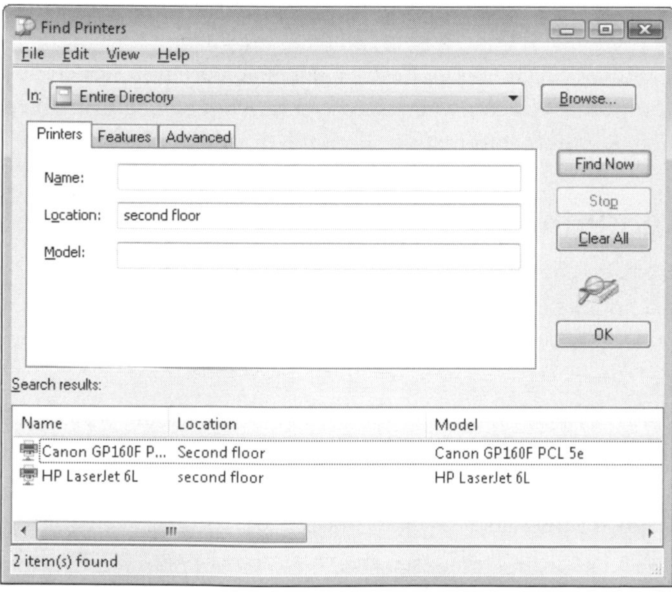

You can control the maximum number of printers of each type that the Add Printer Wizard will display on a computer on a managed network by using the following Group Policy setting:

Computer Configuration\Policies\Administrative Templates\Printers\Add Printer wizard - Network Scan Page (Managed Network)

For more information on this policy setting, see the section titled "Managing Client-Side Printer Experience Using Group Policy" later in this chapter.

> **NOTE** Advanced users can also search for printers to install by opening a command prompt, typing **rundll32 dsquery.dll,OpenQueryWindow**, selecting Printers from the Find list box, and continuing as described in the preceding steps.

Installing Printers Using Point and Print

End users can also use Point and Print to install printers over a network. When using Point and Print, the print server sends the client computer the following information concerning the printer being installed:

- The name of the server on which printer driver files are stored
- Printer model information that specifies which printer driver to install
- The actual printer driver files needed by the client

End users can install printer connections using Point and Print by browsing Network Explorer to find a print server, double-clicking the print server to display its shared printers, right-clicking a shared printer, and then clicking Connect. If a driver for the printer is not found in the driver store on the local computer, the user will need administrator credentials to respond to the UAC prompt that appears when the driver is being copied from the print server to the local computer. For more information about the driver store, see Chapter 17.

Using Devices And Printers

Once a printer is installed, you can begin configuring and using it with the Devices And Printers user interface. Devices And Printers is a new feature in Windows 7 that provides users with a single, central location where they can install and manage all of the devices connected to their computer.

Selecting a printer in Devices And Printers causes additional toolbar buttons to appear on the Devices And Printers toolbar (shown in Figure 18-5). These toolbars, along with the context menu that appears when you right-click the printer, let you perform a number of client-side management tasks for the selected printer, including:

- **See What's Printing** Opens the print queue for the selected printer and displays documents currently being printed and pending print jobs.
- **Print Server Properties** Lets you configure settings on the print server if you have permissions to do so.
- **Set As Default Printer** Sets the printer as the default printer for the user's computer. (Note that some client applications can maintain their own default printer setting that overrides the one set here.)

- **Printing Preferences** Allows the user to select page layout and paper/quality options for the printer.
- **Printer Properties** Lets the user configure different properties of the printer.
- **Troubleshoot** Lets the user start the Printer Troubleshooter to identify and resolve any issues when printing to the printer.
- **Remove Device** Removes the printer from the user's computer.

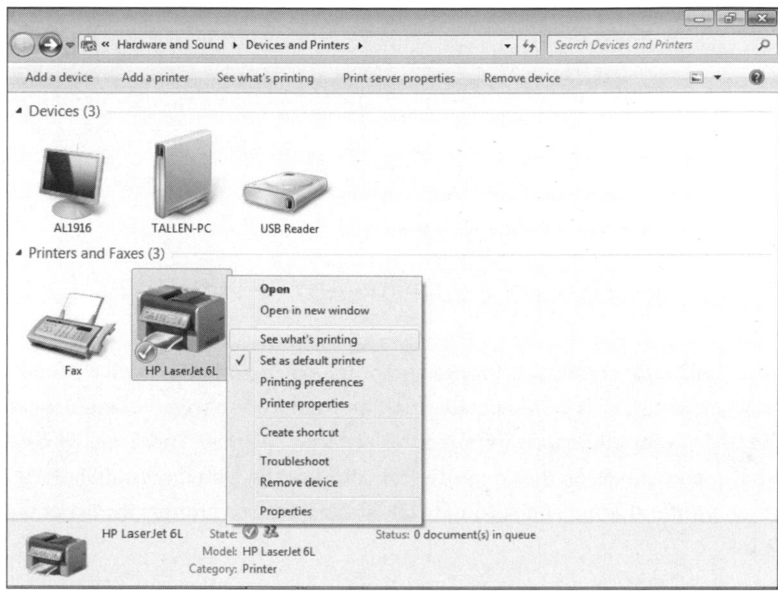

FIGURE 18-5 The new Devices And Printers user interface in Windows 7

Additional toolbar buttons or context menu options might be available depending on the type of printer installed. In addition, if the computer running Windows 7 is a laptop computer and connects to more than one network, the user can use the new Location-Aware Printing feature of Windows 7 to assign a different default printer to each connected network. For more information about this new feature, see the next section titled "Using Location-Aware Printing." Devices And Printers also integrates with Device Stage, a new feature of Windows 7 that makes it easier for users to connect, recognize, and use their devices. When a printer supports Device Stage, you can simply double-click the printer's icon in Devices And Printers to display the Device Stage user interface for the printer, which is designed to make the printer easier to manage and use (see Figure 18-6).

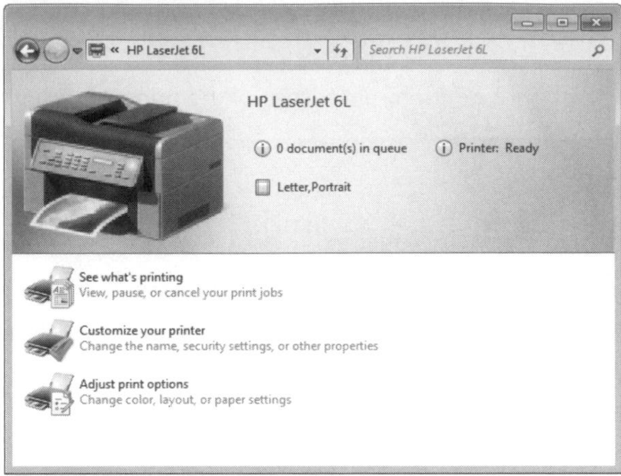

FIGURE 18-6 A basic Device Stage user interface for a printer

For more information about Device Stage, see Chapter 17.

NOTE Local administrator credentials for the computer are required to share a printer displayed in Devices And Printers. These credentials are required so that the end user can respond to the UAC prompt that appears when this action is selected. End users who have local administrator credentials on the computer can also use the Network And Sharing Center to turn on printer sharing and automatically share installed printers for other network users to use.

Using Location-Aware Printing

Location-Aware Printing is a new feature of Windows 7 that lets a user assign a different default printer to each network to which the user's computer connects. Location-Aware Printing is supported only on mobile computers running Windows 7 and is different from assigning printers based on location, a feature that was introduced in Windows Vista to allow administrators to deploy different printers using Group Policy based on the AD DS site in which the target computers reside. For information about assigning printers based on location, see the section titled "Assigning Printers Based on Location" later in this chapter.

Location-Aware Printing is introduced in Windows 7 because of the increasing importance of mobile computers to enterprises. A typical scenario in which this feature is useful might be the following:

1. Karen is supplied with a new laptop computer from her company, Contoso Ltd. While at work, she adds a printer connection to a work printer via the Add Printer Wizard. The printer is set automatically as the default for her work network.
2. Later in the day, she adds a USB printer at home. That printer is set automatically as the default for her home printer.

3. When she comes back to work the next day, she sees that the printer connection to the work printer is set as the default for her.
4. When she returns home again, her home printer is once again the default.

The result of implementing this feature is that whenever Karen is at work, her work printer is her default printer, and whenever she is at home, her home printer becomes the default. In other words, Karen doesn't have to switch her default printer every time she switches networks, as she did in previous versions of Windows. Instead, she can simply start printing to the most appropriate printer without needing to set up or configure anything as she moves from network to network.

When Location-Aware Printing is available on a computer running Windows 7, an additional button named Manage Default Printers will be displayed on the toolbar of Devices And Printers. By clicking this button, the user can configure default printers for each connected network. There is also a new link on the final window of the Add Printer Wizard that will take you to Manage Default Printers.

For more information on how Location-Aware Printing works, see the following sidebar titled "Direct from the Source: Location-Aware Printing and Network Location Awareness."

DIRECT FROM THE SOURCE

Location-Aware Printing and Network Location Awareness

CSS Global Technical Readiness (GTR) Team

Location-Aware Printing depends on the Network Location Awareness service and the Network List Service to determine the network, or networks, to which the laptop is currently connected.

Using the Network List Manager APIs, you can enumerate either networks or network connections. For this feature, networks are enumerated, so if a user is connected to a managed corporate network, whether via a wired or wireless connection, the same corporate domain network is detected regardless of the specific network connection used.

However, if a user is connected to different wired and wireless networks, the conflict is resolved using the following order of precedence for choosing one of multiple networks as an active one:

1. **A wired network connection to a managed network. (Wired networks are always saved by default.)**
2. **All WLAN networks that the user has saved or unsaved. (Wireless networks are not saved by default. Saved networks show up in Control Panel\Network and Internet\Manage Wireless Networks.)**
3. **A wired network connection to any unmanaged network.**
4. **No network.**

Using the Color Management CPL

Windows XP includes support for Image Color Management (ICM) 2.0 to ensure that colors printed from a color printer are accurately reproduced. Beginning with Windows Vista, ICM functions have been enhanced to use WCS, which provides applications with the ability to perform wide-gamut, high-dynamic-range color processing of spool file data in a way that exceeds the possibilities of ICM in previous versions of Windows.

Windows Vista and later versions also include a Color Management CPL that end users can use to manage the following aspects of color printing:

- Add or remove color profiles and specify a default color profile for each printer and display device used by the local computer
- Configure advanced color management settings to ensure accurate display or printing of color information

For more information on using the Color Management CPL, open Color Management in Control Panel and click Understanding Color Management Settings on the Devices tab to access Help And Support information on this topic.

Managing Client-Side Printer Experience Using Group Policy

In managed environments where AD DS is deployed, administrators can use Group Policy to manage different aspects of the end user's experience of installing, configuring, and using printer connections.

You can find Group Policy settings for managing the client-side printer experience in the following two locations in Group Policy Object Editor:

- Computer Configuration\Policies\Administrative Templates\Printers
- User Configuration\Policies\Administrative Templates\Control Panel\Printers

The following sections describe printer policy settings that are new to Windows 7 and Windows Vista. For general information concerning printer policy settings introduced in earlier versions of Windows that still apply to Windows 7, see the "Group Policy Settings Reference for Windows Server 2008 R2 and Windows 7," which can be obtained from the Microsoft Download Center (*http://www.microsoft.com/downloads/*).

You can also use Group Policy Preferences in Windows 7 and Windows Server 2008 R2 to configure local printers and to map network and TCP/IP printers. Group Policy Preferences provide an alternative to Group Policy Policies. The main difference between them is enforcement: policy settings are always enforced, whereas preferences can be overridden by end users. For more information about Group Policy Preferences, see Chapter 14, "Managing the Desktop Environment."

Configuring the Add Printer Wizard

You can find the following two policies that control how the Add Printer Wizard works on client computers under Computer Configuration\Policies\Administrative Templates\Printers:

- **Add Printer Wizard – Network Scan Page (Managed Network)** This policy sets the maximum number of printers (of each type) that the Add Printer Wizard will display on a computer on a managed network (when the computer is able to reach a domain controller, such as a domain-joined laptop on a corporate network).

  If this setting is disabled, the network scan page is not displayed. If this setting is not configured, the Add Printer Wizard displays the default number of printers of each type:

  - Directory printers: 20
  - TCP/IP printers: 0
  - Web Services printers: 0
  - Bluetooth printers: 10
  - Shared printers: 0

  If you don't want to display printers of a certain type, enable this policy and set the number of printers to display to 0. You can control the number of printers of each type that are displayed by configuring the settings contained in this policy, as shown in Figure 18-7.

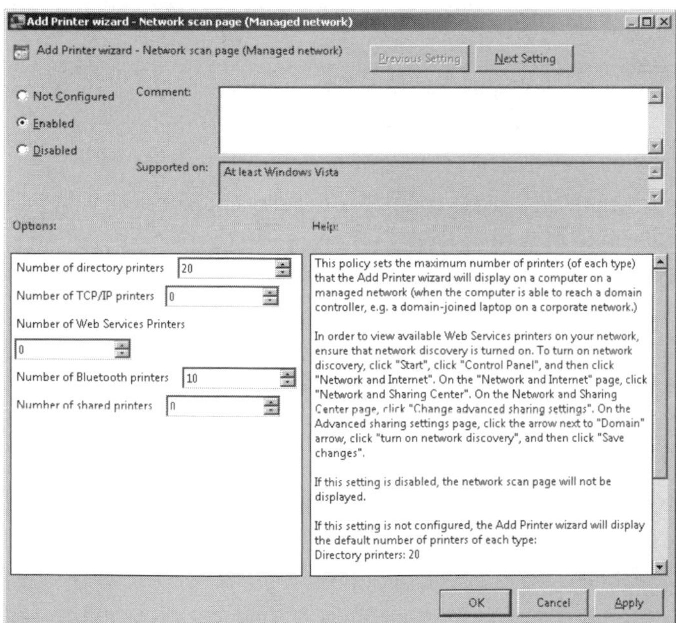

FIGURE 18-7 Configuring the Add Printer Wizard Network Scan Page (Managed Network) policy setting

- **Add Printer Wizard – Network Scan Page (Unmanaged Network)** This policy sets the maximum number of printers (of each type) that the Add Printer Wizard will display on a computer on an unmanaged network (when the computer is not able to reach a domain controller, such as a domain-joined laptop on a home network).

  If this setting is disabled, the network scan page is not displayed. If this setting is not configured, the Add Printer Wizard displays the default number of printers of each type:

  - TCP/IP printers: 50
  - Web Services printers: 50
  - Bluetooth printers: 10

  Again, if you don't want to display printers of a certain type, enable this policy and set the number of printers to display to 0.

Disable Client-Side Printer Rendering

Administrators can also use Group Policy to prevent printer rendering from occurring on client computers. By default, when an application running on a Windows 7 or Windows Vista computer sends a job to a printer hosted on a print server, the job is rendered on the client computer before it is sent to the print server. The following policy setting controls print job rendering behavior on Windows 7 and Windows Vista computers:

Computer Configuration\Policies\Administrative Templates\Printers\Always Render Print Jobs On The Server

When printing through to printers hosted on a print server, this policy determines whether the print spooler on the client will process print jobs itself or will pass them on to the server to do the work. This policy setting only affects printing to a Windows print server.

If you enable this policy setting on a client computer, the client spooler will not process print jobs before sending them to the print server. This decreases the workload on the client at the expense of increasing the load on the server.

If you disable this policy setting on a client computer, the client itself will process print jobs into printer device commands. These commands will then be sent to the print server, and the server will simply pass the commands to the printer. This increases the workload of the client while decreasing the load on the server. If you do not enable this policy setting, the behavior is the same as disabling it.

Keep the following considerations in mind when using this policy:

- This policy does not determine whether offline printing will be available to the client. The client print spooler can always queue print jobs when not connected to the print server. On reconnecting to the server, the client will submit any pending print jobs.
- Some printer drivers require a custom print processor. In some cases, the custom print processor might not be installed on the client computer, such as when the print server does not support transferring print processors during Point and Print. In the case of a

print processor mismatch, the client spooler will always send jobs to the print server for rendering. Disabling the preceding policy setting does not override this behavior.

- In cases in which the client print driver does not match the server print driver (mismatched connection), the client will always process the print job regardless of the setting of this policy.

Configuring Package Point and Print Restrictions

Windows XP SP1 and Windows Server 2003 introduced the following Group Policy setting:

User Configuration\Policies\Administrative Templates\Control Panel\Printers\Point And Print Restrictions

This policy setting controls the servers to which a client computer can connect for Point and Print. A new feature of this policy setting for Windows 7 and Windows Vista is the ability to control the behavior of UAC prompts when installing printer drivers on Windows Vista computers using Point and Print (see Figure 18-8). This policy setting applies only to non–Print Administrators clients and only to computers that are members of a domain.

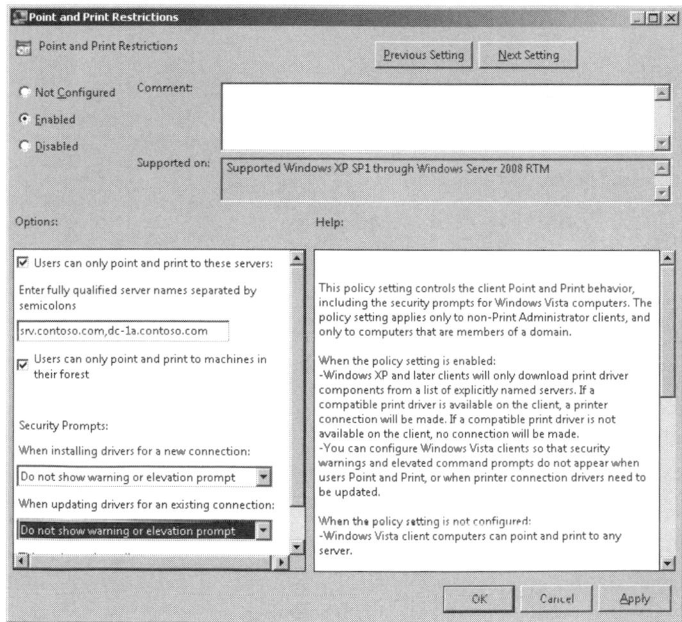

FIGURE 18-8 Controlling the behavior of security prompts using the Point And Print Restrictions policy setting when installing printers using Point and Print

When you enable the policy setting, the client is restricted to only Point and Print to a list of explicitly named servers. You can configure Windows 7 and Windows Vista clients to not show security warnings or elevation prompts when users Point and Print or when drivers for printer connections need to be updated.

If you do not configure the policy setting:

- Windows XP and Windows Server 2003 client computers can point and print to any server in their forest.
- Windows Vista and later client computers can point and print to any server.
- Windows Vista and later computers will show a warning and an elevation prompt when users point and print to any server.
- Windows Vista and later computers will show a warning and an elevation prompt when a driver for an existing printer connection needs to be updated.

If you disable the policy setting:

- Windows XP and Windows Server 2003 client computers can point and print to any server.
- Windows Vista and later client computers can point and print to any server.
- Windows Vista and later computers will not show a warning or an elevation prompt when users point and print to any server.
- Windows Vista and later computers will not show a warning or an elevation prompt when a driver for an existing printer connection needs to be updated.

Note that the Users Can Only Point And Print To Machines In Their Forest setting applies only to Windows XP SP1 (and later service packs) and Windows Server 2003.

In addition to this updated Point And Print Restrictions policy setting, Windows 7 and Windows Vista include two new policy settings related to Point and Print:

- **Only Use Package Point And Print** This policy restricts clients' computers to use Package Point and Print only. If you enable this setting, users will only be able to point and print to printers that use package-aware drivers. When using Package Point and Print, client computers will check the driver signature of all drivers that are downloaded from print servers. If you disable or don't configure this setting, users will not be restricted to Package Point and Print only.
- **Package Point And Print – Approved Servers** Restricts Package Point and Print to approved servers. If you enable this setting, users will only be able to use Package Point and Print on print servers approved by the network administrator. When using Package Point and Print, client computers will check the driver signature of all drivers that are downloaded from print servers. If you disable or don't configure this setting, Package Point and Print will not be restricted to specific print servers.

In Package Point and Print, the complete driver package is put in the driver store on the Windows 7 or Windows Vista client computer. All files in the printer driver are installed on the client, and the installation process ensures that the package is digitally signed properly before adding it to the store. This result is a more secure form of Point and Print than found on previous versions of Windows.

NOTE Printing from Windows Vista and later versions to print servers running earlier versions of Windows uses legacy Point and Print.

Extending Point and Print Using Windows Update

By default, Windows Update is checked for a compatible driver whenever a user uses the Add Printer Wizard to install a new printer. When a compatible in-box driver cannot be found when Group Policy is used to deploy a printer to a client computer, Windows Update is again checked for a compatible driver. This failover behavior can be turned off in enterprise environments using the following Group Policy setting, which is new in Windows 7 and Windows Server 2008 R2:

Computer Configuration\Policies\Administrative Templates\Printers\Extend Point And Print Connection To Use Windows Update And Use An Alternate Connection If Needed

If you enable or do not configure this policy setting, the client computer will continue to search for compatible Point and Print drivers from Windows Update after it fails to find the compatible driver from the local driver store and the server driver cache. If the client computer is unable to find a compatible Point and Print driver, it will attempt to create a CSR mismatch connection using any available driver that supports the hardware. If you disable this policy setting, the client computer will search only the local driver store and server driver cache for compatible Point and Print drivers. If it is unable to find a compatible driver, then the Point and Print connection will fail.

If this policy is enabled, the new cross-platform Point and Print feature of Windows 7 is also enabled. Cross-platform Point and Print is designed to allow users who have computers running different processor architectures (x86 or x64, for example) to share their printers easily. Cross-platform Point and Print is designed to enable the following types of scenarios:

- Karen brings home a new Windows 7 laptop for her son to use in school. She decides to upgrade her old Windows XP desktop to Windows 7 at the same time. She enrolls both PCs to her new HomeGroup during the setup process. She takes her existing inkjet printer and plugs it into her desktop system through the USB port. A short while later, she notices that her son's laptop already has a print queue for her office printer so he can print reports and other documents. She is unaware of the fact that the desktop is running an x86 version of Windows and the laptop is running an x64 version of Windows. This setup works because, in Windows 7, a user can add a printer locally to one system in a HomeGroup, and every other PC in the HomeGroup will search their local driver store, the print server, and Windows Update to find a suitable driver to make a print connection.

- Tony brings home a new Windows 7 laptop for working on personal projects. He already has a home network set up, including an older Windows XP file and print server in his office. After the new laptop is set up, Tony uses the Add Printer Wizard to create a new connection to his office printer. The new laptop is running an x64 edition of the Windows 7 Business operating system. The printer is older, and there are no in-box drivers. Without any prompts or elevations, the system searches Windows Update to find a suitable driver, installs it, and creates the connection to the printer. Tony then brings his laptop to work because he wants to use it for a presentation. After the meeting, he is asked to print out a copy of the slides for his manager. He navigates to the print server at work through Windows Explorer and opens the printer. After a few minutes, it is available to print, and he makes a copy of the slides even though Windows Update is blocked by his company's IT department.

In business environments, you might want to disable the automatic querying Windows Update for compatible printer drivers, especially when Group Policy is used to deploy printers as described in the next section. An example of a scenario in which you disable this Group Policy setting might be the following:

- Tony is setting up a small business computer environment for a startup. He is using Windows 7 for all of the systems. He writes some scripts to set up the servers, including a connection to a shared printer for printing out logs and other reports periodically. He also uses the Print Management console to set up the print server and push printer connections out to all of the clients. On the first client box he tests, he notices that it is going to Windows Update to find a print driver for the push printer connection. This is not the behavior he wants, so he investigates and finds out that a new feature in Windows 7 allows clients to search Windows Update for drivers when they aren't available on the server. He also discovers that Group Policy can be configured to disable this failover case. He disables this policy setting and adds the driver found on Windows Update to the print server so that the remaining clients can use standard Point and Print.

Deploying Printers Using Group Policy

The ability to deploy printer connections to Windows-based client computers using Group Policy was first introduced in Windows Server 2003 R2. You can use Group Policy to deploy printer connections in two ways:

- As per-computer printer connections available for all users who log on to the client computer. You can deploy per-computer printer connections to computers running Windows XP or later versions.
- As per-user printer connections available to the user on any client computer to which the user logs on. You can deploy per-user printer connections to users of computers running Windows 2000 or later versions.

Deploying printers using Group Policy is useful in scenarios in which every user or computer in a room or office needs access to the same printer. Deploying printers using Group Policy can also be useful in large enterprises where users and computers are differentiated by function, workgroup, or department.

DIRECT FROM THE FIELD

Configuring Printer Connections Using Group Policy Preferences

Jerry Honeycutt
Deployment Forum

Group Policy preferences, a new feature of Windows Server 2008, provides administrators with another means of deploying, configuring, and managing printer connections on Windows 7 computers. Configuring printer connections is a common task that administrators typically perform by writing logon scripts. The Printers preference extension, however, enables you to easily create, update, replace, or delete shared printers, TCP/IP printers, and local printers to multiple, targeted users or computers. Using preference targeting, you can deploy printer connections based on location, department, computer type, and so on.

Windows 7 Group Policy provides native support for deploying printers. However, it supports only shared printers and requires AD DS schema extensions. In contrast, the Printers extension supports shared, local, and TCP/IP printers on Windows XP SP2, Windows Vista, and Windows 7. It also allows you to set the default printer and map shared printers to local ports.

NOTE **For more information about Group Policy Preferences, see Chapter 14.**

Preparing to Deploy Printers

Deploying printers using Group Policy requires you to perform the following preparatory steps:

- If you are not using Windows Server 2008 domain controllers, your AD DS schema must first be upgraded to Windows Server 2003 R2 or later. This means the schema revision number must be 9 (for Windows Server 2003) and the schema version number must be 31 (for the R2 schema update). You can use ADSI Edit to determine your current schema version number by looking under the Schema node, right-clicking the object named *CN=Schema,CN=Configuration,DC=forest_root_domain*, selecting Properties, and then examining the value of the *objectVersion* attribute. The R2 schema update is required so that Print Management can create the following two objects in AD DS:

- *CN=Schema,CN=Policies,CN=GPO_GUID,CN=Machine,CN=PushPrinterConnections*
- *CN=Schema,CN=Policies,CN=GPO_GUID,CN=User,CN=PushPrinterConnections*

- If your client computers are running an earlier version of Windows, you must deploy the PushPrinterConnections.exe utility to these clients prior to using Group Policy to deploy printer connections to these computers. The PushPrinterConnections.exe utility reads the GPOs that are used to deploy printer connections and adds or removes these connections on the client as needed. The easiest way to deploy PushPrinterConnections.exe is to use a GPO as follows:
  - As a user logon script for deploying per-user printer connections
  - As a computer startup script for deploying per-computer printer connections

  The simplest approach is to use the same GPO to deploy both PushPrinterConnections.exe to targeted users and/or computers using startup/logon scripts and the actual printer connections themselves to those users and/or computers. Beginning with Windows Vista, however, you do not need to first deploy PushPrinterConnections.exe to client computers because Windows Vista and later versions include this capability in the operating system.

Deploying a Printer Connection

After you complete the preceding preparatory steps, you can deploy a printer connection by following these steps:

1. Create a new GPO for deploying the connections, or use an existing GPO linked to the OU, domain, or site where the users or computers being targeted reside.
2. Open Print Management, right-click the printer you want to deploy, and select Deploy With Group Policy.
3. In the Deploy With Group Policy dialog box, click Browse, find and select the GPO you will use to deploy the printer, and then click OK.
4. Choose whether to deploy the printer as a per-computer connection, a per-user connection, or both.

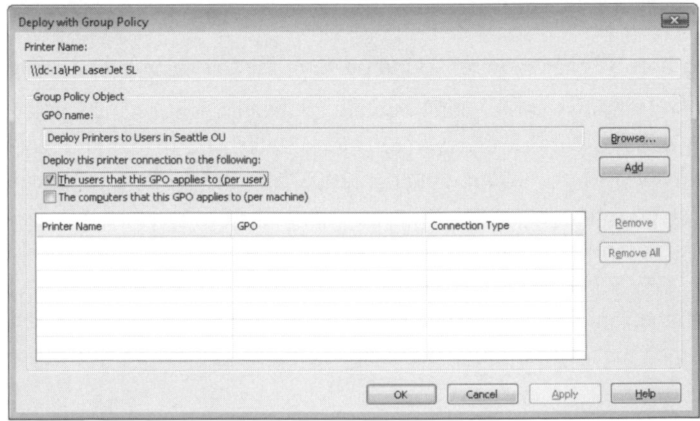

5. Click Add to add the printer connection settings to the GPO.
6. If needed, repeat steps 3 through 5 to deploy the same printer to additional GPOs.
7. Click OK when finished. The printer connection to be deployed using Group Policy will be displayed under the Deployed Printers node in Print Management.

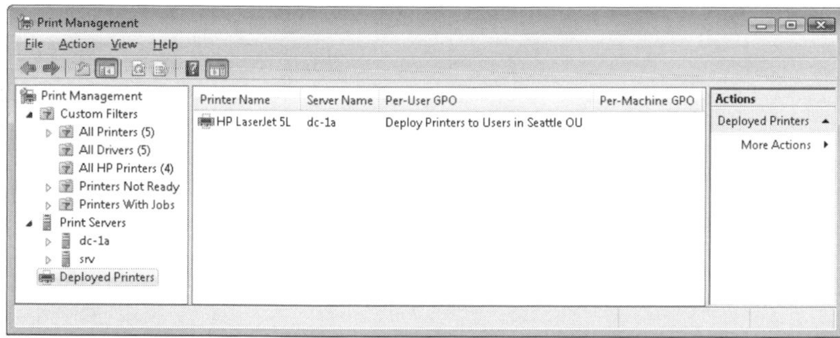

Per-user printer connections can be deployed immediately using Group Policy if the user next logs off and then logs on again to a targeted client computer. Per-computer printer connections can also be deployed immediately if the user's computer is restarted. Neither type of connection will be deployed on earlier versions of Windows during normal background refresh of Group Policy. On Windows Vista and later clients, however, background policy refresh can also deploy both per-user and per-computer printer connections.

NOTE **On Windows Vista and later versions, users can also force printer connections to be deployed immediately by typing gpupdate /force at an elevated command prompt.**

The deployed printer connection is also displayed in the GPO used to deploy the connection. To view this, open the Group Policy Management Console (GPMC), right-click the GPO you used to deploy the connection, and then click Edit to open the GPO using the Group Policy Object Editor (see Figure 18-9). To remove the deployed printer connection from the targeted users or computers during the next background refresh of Group Policy, right-click the connection and then click Remove. Unlinking the GPO from the OU, domain, or site where the targeted users or computers reside also removes the deployed connections.

NOTE **You can also use the Group Policy Results Wizard in the GPMC to collect RSoP information to verify the success or failure of deploying printers using Group Policy. For more information on using Group Policy with Windows 7, see Chapter 14.**

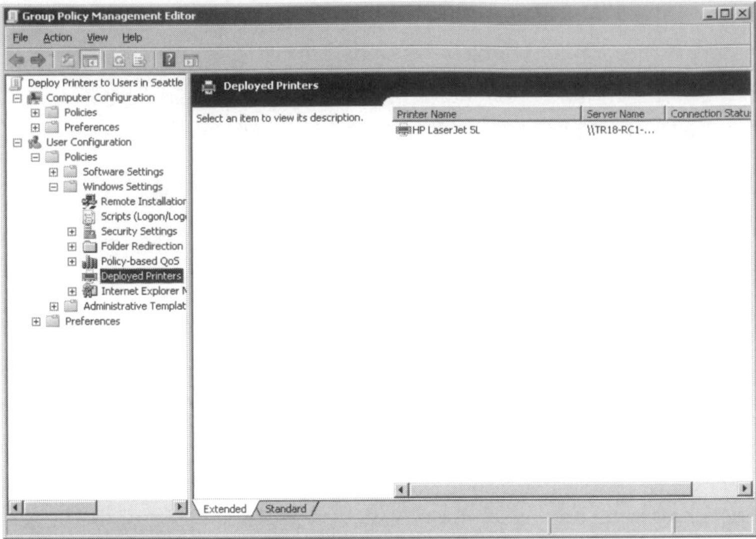

FIGURE 18-9 Viewing a deployed printer connection in a GPO

Limitations of Deploying Printers Using Group Policy

The following limitations apply when deploying printer connections to Windows 7 clients using Group Policy:

- You cannot configure the default printer on the targeted client using Group Policy.
- Loopback mode is not supported.

Assigning Printers Based on Location

Windows Vista introduced a feature with the ability to assign printers based on location. This can be useful in large enterprises that span more than one geographical location, allowing mobile users to update their printers as they move to new locations. When mobile users return to their primary locations, their original default printers are restored.

To assign printers based on location, deploy printers using GPOs linked to AD DS sites. When a mobile computer moves to a new site, the printer connections for the computer are updated using normal Group Policy processing.

DIRECT FROM THE SOURCE

Managing Deployed Printer Connections

Alan Morris, Software Design Engineer
Test, Windows Printing

There are two ways of managing deployed printer connections in Windows 7:

- Using the Print Management console
- Using the Group Policy Management Editor

The following sections of this sidebar describe the differences between these two approaches.

Managing Deployed Printer Connections Using the Print Management Console

Deployed printer connections will be displayed in Print Management's Deployed Printers node for the connections hosted by the current list of monitored servers when the Print Management operator has Read access to the domain policies in which printer connections are deployed.

To deploy connections to a Group Policy using the Print Management console, you must have Write access to the domain policy, and the server that shares the printer must be added to the list of servers that Print Management is monitoring. The operator in charge of printer deployment does not need to have administrative rights on the print server.

The deployed printer connections feature is not used to create local printers, but anyone with administrative rights can add printer connections to the local policy of a computer. Local Policy-deployed printer connections are useful when AD DS is not fully implemented or when setting up systems in a workgroup environment. Some form of peer-to-peer authentication is required when the workgroup computers or users cannot authenticate to a domain controller.

Deployed printer connections do not need to be published to the AD DS.

Deployed printers do not require any driver download prompts during installation. The user does not have access to delete deployed printer connections. The printer needs to be removed from the policy or the user must be unlinked from the policy for the printer removal to occur.

Managing Deployed Printer Connections Using the Group Policy Management Editor

This tool has a few advantages over the Print Management snap-in. You don't need to monitor the server sharing the deployed printers. You can deploy printer shares that have yet to be created. The user interface works directly within the selected GPO. The user does not need to be logged on to the same domain as the GPO.

The big disadvantage when using this tool rather than the Print Management snap-in is the lack of any print share validation. If valid server and share information is improperly entered, the connection will fail. When no share validation is performed, the advantage is that this method allows for deployment of connections prior to creating the share. After the share is created, the connections will be added for the user during the next policy refresh on Windows 7 clients and the next time PushPrinterConnections.exe is run on previous-version clients.

Printers hosted on a server in one domain can easily be deployed to clients in another trusted domain.

Another important use of the Group Policy Management Editor is in the removal of deployed printers after a print server is retired. The Group Policy Management Editor will display the printers deployed to a policy and allow the operator to remove them after the server is no longer available on the network.

Migrating Print Servers

You can use either the Printer Migration Wizard or the PrintBRM command-line tool to export print queues, printer settings, printer ports, and language monitors and then import them on another print server running Windows. This is an efficient way to consolidate multiple print servers onto a single computer or to replace an older print server with a newer system. The Printer Migration Wizard and the PrintBRM command-line tool were introduced in Windows Vista to replace the earlier Print Migrator 3.1 tool available from the Microsoft Download Center.

NOTE **The Printer Migration Wizard can also be useful for backing up print server configurations for disaster recovery purposes. For more information on this topic, see the section titled "Exporting and Importing Print Server Configurations" earlier in this chapter.**

Migrate Print Servers Using Print Management

To migrate print servers using Print Management, follow these steps:

1. Open Print Management, right-click the printer server that contains the print queues and printer drivers that you want to export, and then click Export Printers To A File. This launches the Printer Migration Wizard.

2. Review the list of items to be exported and then click Next.
3. Click Browse to specify the location where you want to save your printer export file (*.printerExport), type a name for this file, and then click Open.
4. Click Next to export the print server's print queues and printer drivers as a compressed cabinet (CAB) file with the .printerExport extension.
5. If errors are reported during the export process, click Open Event Viewer to view the related events.
6. Click Finish to complete the export process.
7. Right-click the destination print server to which you want to import the previously exported print queues and printer drivers and then click Import Printers From A File.
8. Click Browse, find the previously saved printer export file, and double-click it.
9. Click Next, review the items to be imported, and then click Next again.
10. Choose the options you want to select on the Select Import Options page of the wizard (these options are described following this procedure).

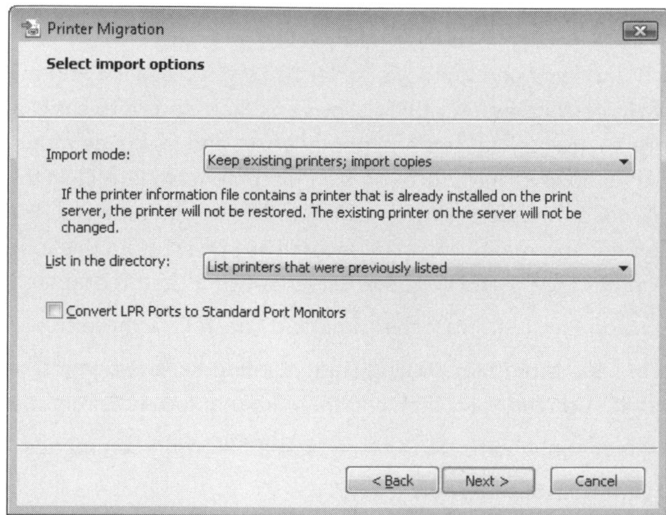

11. Click Next. If errors are reported during the import process, click Open Event Viewer to view the related events.
12. Click Finish to complete the export process.

> ***NOTE*** **If the printers being migrated were deployed using Group Policy, you can use Group Policy to remove the deployed printer connections from users' computers before migrating your print server. When the migration is complete, you can use Group Policy to redeploy the migrated printers.**

The available options on the Select Import Options page are:

- **Import Mode** Specifies what to do if a specific print queue already exists on the destination print server. The possible choices are:
  - Keep Existing Printers; Import Copies (the default)
  - Overwrite Existing Printers
- **List In The Directory** Specifies whether to publish the imported print queues in AD DS. The possible choices are:
  - List Printers That Were Previously Listed (the default)
  - List All Printers
  - Don't List Any Printers
- **Convert LPR Ports To Standard Port Monitors** Specifies whether to convert Line Printer Remote (LPR) printer ports in the printer settings file to the faster Standard Port Monitor when importing printers.

Migrating Print Servers Using PrintBRM

PrintBRM was introduced in Windows 7 and Windows Server 2008 to replace the Printmig.exe utility used in previous versions of Windows. PrintBRM allows an administrator to easily back up, restore, and migrate print queues, printer settings, printer ports, and language monitors. Windows 7 and Windows Server 2008 R2 introduce some enhancements to PrintBRM that are designed to provide more flexibility and better instrumentation for the administrator. For more information concerning these enhancements, see the sidebar titled "Direct from the Source: Enhancements to PrintBRM in Windows 7 and Windows Server 2008 R2" in this chapter.

To migrate print servers using PrintBRM from the command line, follow these steps:

1. Open an elevated command prompt by clicking Start, pointing to All Programs, selecting Accessories, right-clicking Command Prompt, and then clicking Run As Administrator.
2. To export the print server configuration to a file, type the following commands:

   cd %WinDir%\System32\Spool\Tools

   Printbrm -s \\print_server_name -b -f file_name.printerExport
3. To import the previously saved print server configuration file, type the following command:

   Printbrm -s \\print_server_name -r -f file_name.printerExport

DIRECT FROM THE SOURCE

Enhancements to PrintBRM in Windows 7 and Windows Server 2008 R2

CSS Global Technical Readiness (GTR) Team

PrintBRM has been enhanced in Windows 7 and Windows Server 2008 R2 in the following ways:

- Better error handling and reporting
- The ability to perform a partial restore of print objects from a backup
- The option to not restore security settings for print queues during a restore
- Driver isolation settings are migrated

The sections that follow describe these improvements.

Better Error Handling and Reporting

Many general improvements have been made to the reporting and handling of error conditions during the backup and restore processes. Any problems encountered during an export or import should be reported to the administrator either in the export/import dialog box or in the event logs.

Refer to the following Event Viewer logs for messages from the tool:

- Custom Views\Administrative Events
- Custom Views\Printer Migration Events
- Windows Logs\Application
- Windows Logs\System
- Applications and Services Logs\Microsoft\Windows\PrintService\Admin
- Applications and Services Logs\Microsoft\Windows\PrintService\Operational

Selective Restore

Administrators have a means of performing a selective restore of printers and related objects using the command-line tool, PrintBRM.exe. This option is not available using PrintBRMUI.exe.

Option to Not Restore Print Queue ACLs

There might be situations in which it is not desirable to restore security settings for print queues. For example, if printers are being migrated to another domain or if print queues with permissions for local users and groups are being migrated, you likely will not want the access control lists (ACLs) to be migrated.

The PrintBRM.exe command-line tool allows the administrator to prevent the restoration of print queue ACLs.

Driver Isolation Settings Are Migrated

The print driver isolation settings are exported along with other spooler settings in BRMSpoolerAttrib.xml. The following line is added to the XML file with the current driver isolation settings.

```
<DriverIsolation value="<PrintDriverIsolationGroups>"/>
```

The value for <PrintDriverIsolationGroups> comes from the registry key value:

HKLM\System\CurrentControlSet\Control\Print\PrintDriverIsolationGroups

The string value can be manipulated in the XML file before an import/restore operation if desired.

Monitoring and Troubleshooting Printers

Printer troubleshooting can involve numerous considerations, including device problems such as paper jams, incompatible printer drivers, misconfigured printer settings, problems with the Print Spooler service on the client or the print server, and more. Detailed procedures for troubleshooting printer problems are beyond the scope of this chapter and are not presented here. Instead, following are some general considerations and recommendations regarding monitoring printers so that support personnel can quickly identify and respond to problems.

The new Windows Troubleshooting Platform in Windows 7 includes a Printer Troubleshooter that end users can use to identify and resolve printer problems themselves without calling the Help desk. For information on how to start this troubleshooter, see the section titled "Using Devices And Printers" earlier in this chapter.

NOTE For general guidance on how to troubleshoot hardware issues, see Chapter 30, "Troubleshooting Hardware, Driver, and Disk Issues." For additional information about how device drivers are implemented and managed on Windows 7, see Chapter 16, "Managing Disks and File Systems."

Configuring E-Mail Notifications

When you create a custom printer filter, you have the option of sending an automatic e-mail notification to someone when the conditions of the filter are met. This can be useful for resolving printer problems, particularly in an organization with multiple buildings and administrators. For example, you can set up a view of all printers managed by a particular print server where the status does not equal Ready. Then, if a printer changes from the Ready status to another status, the administrator can receive a notification e-mail from Print Management. (You can also configure e-mail notifications for existing printer filters, including the Printers Not Ready and Printers With Jobs default filters.) To send e-mail notifications, you must specify a Simple Mail Transfer Protocol (SMTP) server that can forward these e-mail messages.

To configure e-mail notifications, follow these steps:

1. To set a notification on an existing printer filter, open Print Management, right-click a printer filter, click Properties, and then click the Notification tab.
2. Select the Send E-mail Notification check box.
3. Specify the following information:
   - In the Recipient E-mail Address(es) text box, type the e-mail address(es) of the recipient(s) using the format *account@domain*. (Use semicolons to separate multiple accounts.)
   - In the Sender E-mail Address text box, type the e-mail address of the sender using the format *account@domain*.
   - In the SMTP Server text box, type the fully qualified host name or IP address of the SMTP server that will forward the e-mail notifications.
   - In the Message text box, type a text message describing the conditions of the printer problem.
4. Click Test to verify your SMTP configuration for sending e-mail notifications and then click OK if the test is successful.

Configuring Print Server Notifications

In addition to setting notifications on a custom set of printers by using a printer filter, you can also set notifications for print servers. For example, if the print server is offline or the spooler goes down, an e-mail notification can be sent.

To configure print server notifications, right-click a print server in Print Management, select Set Notifications, and then follow the steps described previously to configure e-mail message parameters.

Configuring Script Actions

When you create a custom printer filter for specific printer criteria, you have the option of running a script when the conditions of the filter are met. Script notifications are also defined in the previously described Notifications tab of the printer filter's Properties dialog box.

Setting script notifications can be useful for resolving printer problems and troubleshooting. For example, you can automatically run a script to restart the Print Spooler service on a print server when its printers go offline. You can also automatically run a script that prints a test page or that notifies your internal monitoring system of a potential problem. Scripts can be written in VBScript or any scripting language available on the computer. The script must be on the computer that is running Print Management, and the script should be running with suitable credentials and have the permissions needed to accomplish what you want the script to do.

An example of a command that you might use in a script to start the Print Spooler service is the *net start spooler* command. For sample scripts that you can use and customize to manage print queues, see the list in the section titled "On the Companion Media" at the end of this chapter. You can also find additional scripts on Microsoft TechNet at *http://www.microsoft.com/technet/scriptcenter/scripts/printing/default.mspx*.

Configuring Detailed Event Logging

To save a record of print jobs and their details, you can enable detailed Information event logging as follows:

1. Right-click a print server in Print Management and then select Properties.
2. Click the Advanced tab.
3. Select the Log Spooler Information Events check box.

You can use Event Viewer to view the resulting Informational Events and then use them either for troubleshooting or auditing purposes. For example, if a bad printer driver is causing reams of paper to be printed with random data on them, you can use these events to identify the user name, print queue, document title, size in pages, and other useful information to determine the possible cause of the problem.

> ***NOTE*** **For troubleshooting information about event log events related to printing issues, see** ***http://technet.microsoft.com/en-us/library/cc771594.aspx*****.**

Summary

Windows 7 and Windows Vista include numerous enhancements in printing technologies and new tools for managing print queues and migrating print servers. Using these new features and tools can provide a more satisfying printing experience for end users and make the job of managing printers within an enterprise easier.

Additional Resources

These resources contain additional information and tools related to this chapter.

Related Information

- "What's New in Print Management for Windows 7" at *http://technet.microsoft.com/en-us/library/dd878494.aspx.*
- "What's New In Print and Document Services for Windows Server 2008 R2" at *http://technet.microsoft.com/en-ca/library/dd878502(WS.10).aspx.*
- The Windows Server 2008 Print Services section of the Windows Server TechCenter at *http://technet.microsoft.com/en-ca/windowsserver/2008/dd448602.aspx.*
- *Windows TIFF IFilter Installation and Operations Guide* at *http://technet.microsoft.com/en-ca/library/dd755985(WS.10).aspx.*
- "Script Repository: Printing (Windows PowerShell Scripts)" at *http://www.microsoft.com/technet/scriptcenter/scripts/msh/printing/default.mspx?mfr=true.*
- TechNet Forum for Print/Fax discussions at *http://social.technet.microsoft.com/Forums/en-US/winserverprint/threads.*
- "Printing – Architecture and Driver Support" at *http://www.microsoft.com/whdc/device/print/default.mspx.*
- XPS Team Blog at *http://blogs.msdn.com/xps/.*
- PrintVerifier Team Blog at *http://blogs.msdn.com/printverifier/default.aspx.*
- "Printing and Print System Management" at *http://msdn.microsoft.com/en-us/library/aa970449.aspx.*

On the Companion Media

- FindPrinterDrivers.ps1
- FindPrinterPorts.ps1
- Get-PrinterPorts.ps1
- Get-PrintQueueStatistics.ps1
- Get-SharedPrinter.ps1
- InstallPrinterDriver.ps1
- InstallPrinterDriverFull.ps1
- ListPrinterDrivers.ps1
- listPrinters.ps1
- ListSharedPrintersAddPrintConnection.ps1
- notepad
- TroubleshootPrinter.ps1
- WorkWithPrinters.ps1

CHAPTER 19

Managing Search

Beginning with Windows Vista, the Search feature has been enhanced and extended in many ways compared to previous Windows platforms. A new search-engine architecture provides improved performance and better query capabilities for faster and more focused information retrieval. Integration of Search throughout the user interface (UI) makes it easier to look for files, e-mail, and other information from within the currently open window. Search produces nearly instantaneous search results as users type their queries, so that they can better focus their queries and narrow search results on the fly as they type. Also, users now have a simple way of saving the results of their queries so that they can quickly access frequently needed data, which reduces the need for users to manually organize how they store information on their computers. This chapter explains how search and indexing work in Windows 7 and how to use Group Policy to manage these capabilities from within the UI.

Search and Indexing Enhancements

Rapidly growing storage capabilities in business environments mean that the ability to quickly and efficiently find information is essential for knowledge workers. To meet these growing requirements, search and indexing capabilities were significantly enhanced in Windows Vista. These capabilities have now been improved further in Windows 7 to provide users with an even better search experience.

Search in Windows XP

Search in Windows XP suffered from the following issues and limitations:

- Using the Search Companion to search for files was often a slow process. As a result, users often had to spend much of their time organizing their data into hierarchical sets of folders to make information easier to find through folder-specific searches.
- Searching for text within files required enabling the Indexing Service (Cisvc.exe) on the computer, and by default this service is stopped and set for manual startup.
- The Indexing Service, when enabled, tended to be intrusive in its operation by being CPU and input/output (I/O) intensive, which sometimes interfered with other user activity on the system.
- E-mail search capabilities in applications such as Microsoft Office Outlook were not integrated with how search and indexing worked in Windows.
- The search query syntax was limited in scope and capabilities. Specifically, there was no support for keywords, such as From:, and the Indexing Service was restricted to file content.

Search in Windows Vista

Search was significantly improved in Windows Vista to make it more powerful and easier to use. The following new features and enhancements in search and indexing functionality were added in Windows Vista:

- Windows Vista introduced a completely new search engine architecture called the Windows Search service, which was based on the earlier Windows Desktop Search (WDS) add-on for Windows XP and Windows Server 2003. The Windows Search service supersedes the earlier Indexing Service and provides better performance and improved query capabilities. For information about this new search engine architecture and how it works, see the section titled "How Windows Search Works" later in this chapter. For information concerning the different versions of Windows Search, see the section titled "Understanding the Windows Search Versions" later in this chapter.
- In Windows XP, indexing of content had to be enabled before it could be used. Beginning with Windows Vista, indexing of content is enabled by default and supports querying both the metadata (properties) of any file type and the full text of many common document formats. The extensibility of Windows Search also allows Independent Software Vendors (ISVs) to provide plug-ins that allows users to search third-party document formats, such as Adobe Portable Document Format (PDF). Beginning with Windows Vista, users can also search for e-mail messages in Office Outlook 2007 and for content stored in Microsoft Office OneNote 2007 notebooks. Users can also use Advanced Query Syntax (AQS) to create complex queries that return highly focused results and then save these queries for future use.

- In Windows XP, the Indexing service did not try to avoid indexing content when the system was under heavy use. Beginning with Windows Vista, however, the Windows Search service includes algorithms that prevent the indexing of content when the system is too busy. This improvement makes Windows Search less intrusive than the previous Indexing service. A new feature of Windows Search is word-wheeled search (or search-as-you-type) functionality, whereby users can watch the results of their queries narrow as they type the characters of the file name or word they are looking for. This makes the search experience for the user much more responsive than in earlier platforms, where users had to type their entire search string and click Search each time they wanted to run a query.
- Beginning with Windows Vista, search capability is integrated into the shell in more places, making searching easy to perform because of the ubiquitous presence of the Search box within the Start menu, Control Panel, any Windows Explorer window, and other Windows Vista experiences. In addition, each instance of the Search box is tuned to provide results appropriate for the types of queries that users might perform from within that instance.
- Windows Vista introduced new searching and organizing capabilities that make it much easier for users to find files on their computers without having to spend a lot of time organizing them into hierarchical sets of folders. These capabilities include enhanced column headers; the ability to sort, group, and stack files and folders; and the ability to tag files and folders with descriptive keywords.
- Beginning with Windows Vista, client-side caching (CSC) is enabled by default so that redirected folders are accessible to users when their computers are not connected to the network. These redirected folders are indexed locally so that users can search their contents even when their computers are not on the network or when the server to which their user profile folders have been redirected is down. The cached versions of offline folders are also indexed locally so that network shares marked offline can even be searched when the user's computer is not connected to the network.
- Beginning with Windows Vista, users can search for information stored in shared folders on other computers running Windows Vista and later versions. The results of such searches are security trimmed so that search results display only those files and documents that the user has permission to access.

Search in Windows 7

Windows 7 builds upon the foundation of Windows Vista by adding the following new features and enhancements in search and indexing functionality:

- Start Menu Search has been significantly enhanced to make it a universal entry point for starting programs, finding Control Panel settings, and searching for almost anything on the local computer, the corporate network, or the Internet. For more information about these improvements, see the section titled "Using Start Menu Search" later in this chapter.

- The Advanced Search option in Windows Vista, which became available only after searching, has been replaced with a new Advanced Search pane that helps users create complex queries while learning AQS. For more information on this improvement, see the section titled "Searching Libraries" and the How It Works sidebar titled "Advanced Query Syntax" later in this chapter.
- Beginning with Windows 7, when the indexer is up to date on the system, all items in the indexed location that would be returned by a grep search are now also returned by the indexer, with the exception of reparse points such as junction points and hard links. This is a change from Windows Vista, where certain types of files were always excluded from being indexed by default. For more information on this change, see the section titled "Understanding the Indexing Process" later in this chapter.
- A new feature of Windows 7 called Libraries now makes it easier for users to organize and search for documents and other types of files. For more information about libraries, see Chapter 15, "Managing Users and User Data." For information about searching libraries, see the section titled "Searching Libraries" later in this chapter.
- Indexing prioritization has been implemented to ensure that particular scopes are given higher priority during indexing. Windows Explorer uses this feature to ensure that index-backed views are always given priority to improve the speed and relevance of searches issued against libraries. For example, if a user has the Music library open and is viewing it via an index-backed view (for example, by artist), Windows Explorer requests that the index scopes associated with that view are given priority. The result is that if indexing hasn't yet finished for those scopes, indexing for this location takes priority over the indexing of other content on the system.
- Indexing performance has been improved by significantly reducing resource requirements for the indexer. New functionality has also been added to the indexer to facilitate troubleshooting, reporting, and feedback concerning indexing issues. For more information, see the section titled "Troubleshooting Search and Indexing Using the Built-in Troubleshooter" later in this chapter.
- In Windows Vista, a user needed to be a local administrator on the computer to add new locations to the indexer using Indexing Options in Control Panel. Beginning with Windows 7, this restriction has been removed, and standard users can now add to or remove locations from the indexer.
- Beginning with Windows 7, Windows Search is also now an optional feature that can be enabled or disabled using the Turn Windows Features On Or Off task option in Control Panel. Note that the Windows Search feature is enabled by default, and significant loss of functionality will occur for users who disable Search in this way.
- Files encrypted using the Encrypting File System (EFS) and locally stored on the user's computer can now be indexed and searched as easily as unencrypted files. For more information concerning this feature, see the section titled "Configuring Indexing of Encrypted Files Using Group Policy" later in this chapter.

- Windows 7 now enables users to search for Tagged Image File Format (TIFF) images based on textual content, such as text contained in images of faxed documents. For more information on this new feature, see the section titled "Configuring Indexing of Text in TIFF Image Documents" later in this chapter.
- Windows 7 minimizes the impact of indexing e-mail stored on Microsoft Exchange Server. Support for indexing digitally signed e-mail is also new in Windows 7.
- Windows 7 allows searching the content of network file shares on computers running Windows 7, Windows Server 2008 R2, Windows Vista, Windows Server 2008, Windows XP, or Windows Server 2003. Some of these operating systems require the installation of an additional feature to support remote queries from computers running Windows 7. For more information, see the section titled "Understanding Remote Search" later in this chapter.
- Federated Search is a new feature of Windows 7 that enables users to search remote data sources from within Windows Explorer. Federated Search uses search connectors to enable users to work with files stored in repositories, such as Windows SharePoint sites, as easily as if they were browsing the local file system on their computers. For more information about Federated Search, see the section titled "Using Federated Search" later in this chapter.

Understanding the Windows Search Versions

Organizations that are in the process of performing a large-scale desktop migration may find that they have several different versions of Windows Search on their computers. This can have implications for administrators who need to manage search and indexing functionality across an enterprise. It is therefore important to understand the different versions of Windows Search that are available for or included in various version of Windows.

Windows Search is provided in several different forms:

- As a built-in service called Windows Search in Windows 7 and Windows Vista
- As a role service called Windows Search Service, which you can install from within the File Services role in Windows Server 2008 and Windows Server 2008 R2
- As a downloadable add-on from the Microsoft Download Center for Windows XP, Microsoft Windows 2000 Server, and Windows Server 2003

Search Versions Included in Windows 7 and Windows Vista

Table 19-1 lists the different versions of Windows Search included in Windows 7 and Windows Vista.

TABLE 19-1 Versions of Windows Search in Windows 7 and Windows Vista

WINDOWS VERSION	WINDOWS SEARCH VERSION
Windows 7	4.00.6001.16503
Windows Vista Service Pack 2 (SP2)	4.00.6001.16503
Windows Vista SP1	3.00.6001.18000
Windows Vista RTM	3.00.6000.16386

In addition, Windows Search 4.0 (version 4.00.6001.16503) is available for Windows Vista SP1 as a downloadable add-on from the Microsoft Download Center.

Search Versions Included in Windows Server 2008

Table 19-2 lists the different versions of the Windows Search service included in Windows Server 2008.

TABLE 19-2 Versions of the Windows Search Service in Windows Server 2008

WINDOWS VERSION	WINDOWS SEARCH VERSION
Windows Server 2008 R2	4.00.6001.16503
Windows Server 2008 SP2	4.00.6001.16503
Windows Server 2008 RTM	3.00.6001.18000

In addition, Windows Search 4.0 (version 4.00.6001.16503) is available for Windows Server 2008 as a downloadable add-on from the Microsoft Download Center.

Search Versions Available for Earlier Versions of Windows

Windows Search, which was previously known as Windows Desktop Search (WDS), is currently available from the Microsoft Download Center in the following versions:

- Windows Search 4.0
- WDS 3.01
- WDS 2.6.6

Windows Search 4.0 (version 4.00.6001.16503) can be installed on the following platforms:

- Windows Vista SP1
- Windows XP SP2 or later versions
- Windows Server 2003 R2
- Windows Server 2003 SP2 or later versions
- Windows Search

WDS 3.01 (version 3.01.6000.72) could be installed on the following platforms:

- Windows XP SP2 or later versions
- Windows Server 2003 SP1 or later versions

WDS 2.6.6 (version 2.06.6000.5414) could be installed on the following platforms:

- Windows XP SP2
- Windows Server 2003 SP1
- Windows 2000 SP4

> **NOTE** You can use the *GetIndexerVersionStr* method of the ISearchManager interface to retrieve the current version number of Windows Search on a system. For more information, see *http://msdn.microsoft.com/en-us/library/bb231477.aspx.*

How Windows Search Works

The underlying architecture and operation of indexing has changed considerably in Windows 7 and Windows Vista compared with search capabilities built into earlier versions of Windows. Understanding how search and indexing works can be helpful for configuring, maintaining, and troubleshooting search and indexing.

Understanding Search Engine Terminology

The following terminology describes search and indexing as it has been implemented in Windows 7 and Windows Vista:

- **Catalog** The index with the property cache.
- **Crawl scopes (inclusions and exclusions)** Included and excluded paths within a search root. For example, if a user wants to index the D drive but exclude D:\Temp, he would add a crawl scope (inclusion) for "D:*" and a crawl scope (Exclusion) for "D:\Temp*". The Crawl Scope Manager would also add a start address for "D:\".
- **Gathering** The process of discovering and accessing items from a data store using protocol handlers and IFilters.
- **IFilter** A feature of the Windows Search engine that is used to extract text from documents so that it can be added to the index. (IFilters can also be used to extract format-specific properties, such as Subject or Author; however, in Windows Vista and Windows 7, property handlers are the preferred mechanism for extracting these properties.) Microsoft provides IFilters for many common document formats by default, while third-party vendors such as Adobe provide their own IFilters for indexing other types of content.

- **Property handler** A feature of Windows that is used to extract format-dependent properties. This feature is used both by the Windows Search engine to read and index property values and also by Windows Explorer to read and write property values directly in the file. Microsoft provides property handlers for many common formats by default.
- **Indexing** The process of building the system index and property cache, which together form the catalog.
- **Master index** A single index formed by combining shadow indexes together using a process called the master merge. This is a content index and conceptually maps words to documents or other items.
- **Master merge** The process of combining index fragments (shadow indexes) together into a single content index called the master index.
- **Property cache** The persistent cache of properties (metadata) for indexed items. Basic file properties (such as the file size or last date modified) are added to the property cache for each indexed item; additional properties are added for items with format-specific properties collected by a property handler or IFilter. Indexing item properties allows users to search quickly through this information and create rich pivoted views based on available metadata.
- **Property store** Another name for the property cache.
- **Protocol handler** A feature of the Windows Search engine that is used to communicate with and enumerate the contents of stores such as the file system, Messaging Application Program Interface (MAPI) e-mail database, and the CSC or offline files database. Like IFilters, protocol handlers are also extensible.
- **Start address** A Uniform Resource Locator (URL) that points to the starting location for indexed content. When indexing is performed, each configured starting address is enumerated by a protocol handler to find the content to be indexed.
- **Search root** The base namespace of a given protocol handler.
- **Search defaults** The default crawl scope(s) for a given search root.
- **Shadow indexes** Temporary indexes that are created during the indexing process and then combined into a single index called the master index.
- **Shadow merge** The process of combining index fragments (shadow indexes) together into the next level of index. The resulting index file will still be a shadow index, but merging indexes into bigger entities improves query performance.
- **System index** The entire index on the system, including the master index, shadow indexes, and various configuration files, log files, and temporary files.

> ***NOTE*** **Existing IFilters, such as the Plain Text filter, can also be used to index unregistered file types or file types that are not content indexed by default. For example, you can register the Plain Text filter for use with .cpp files.**

DIRECT FROM THE SOURCE

The Evolution of Windows Desktop Search

Joe Sherman, Principal Program Manager
Windows Experience Find & Organize Team

Content indexing was first introduced by Index Server in the NT4 Option Pack and then was included in every version of Windows beginning with Windows 2000. The Index Server name was later changed to Indexing Service. This feature includes a file indexer but no gathering or crawling functionality and was not extensible to non-file system content. Site Server introduced the first Microsoft gatherer (or crawler) and reused the content index technology from Index Server. At the same time, content indexing was also added to Microsoft SQL Server 7 and has been enhanced in later versions of SQL Server (as well as Exchange Server). The indexing pipeline was rewritten for SQL Server 2005 to provide enormous increases in indexing throughput and scale for large databases.

Microsoft SharePoint Portal Server 2001 and later versions built on the gathering and content indexing features from SQL Server 2000 and Exchange 2000 Server to provide aggregated gathering for portal and non-portal content. Eventually, this code base was retuned for the client desktop by the MSN team that produced WDS. WDS 3.0 was then integrated into Windows Vista as a system service and platform for use by applications (including the 2007 Microsoft Office system). Now WDS 4.0 is included as part of Windows Vista SP2 and Windows Server 2008 SP2 and is integrated into Windows 7 and Windows Server 2008 R2.

Note for trivia buffs: Microsoft Office XP shipped a version of the indexing engine for use on Microsoft Windows NT 4 and Microsoft Windows 98 (but would use the Indexing Service on Windows 2000).

Windows Search Engine Processes

The new Windows Search engine in Windows 7 and Windows Vista is based on the MSSearch indexing and search engine developed previously for SQL Server, SharePoint Portal Server, Microsoft Office SharePoint Server, and other Microsoft products. The new Windows Search engine replaces the Indexing Service (Cisvc.exe) used in earlier Windows platforms, including Windows XP and Windows Server 2003.

The Windows Search engine logically consists of the following four processes:

- **Indexer process** The indexer process (SearchIndexer.exe) is the main feature of the Windows Search engine and is responsible for core indexing and querying activity on the system. This process is implemented as a Windows service named Windows Search service (WSearch) and is exposed for management in the shell through the Service Control Manager (Services.msc). This service runs in the context of the LocalSystem account but has all privileges removed except for the following two privileges:

- **SE_BACKUP_PRIVILEGE** This privilege allows the service to read every file on the system so that it can be indexed.
- **SE_MANAGE_VOLUME_PRIVILEGE** This privilege allows the service to interact with the NTFS change journal.

- **System-wide Protocol Host** The system-wide Protocol Host (SearchProtocolHost.exe) is a separate process that hosts protocol handlers to isolate them from the main indexer process. Protocol handlers are plug-ins assessing different stores, retrieving documents, and pushing the information to the SearchFilterHost process for filtering. The system-wide Protocol Host runs within the same LocalSystem context as the main indexer process. This security context is needed because the Protocol Host requires access to all files on the system. The system-wide Protocol Host also supports cross-user notifications and enumeration of per-computer data stores such as the local file system.
- **Per-user Protocol Host** The per-user Protocol Host (also SearchProtocolHost.exe) is another separate process that hosts protocol handlers to isolate them from the main indexer process. The difference between this process and the system-wide Protocol Host is that this process runs within the security context of the logged-on user. (If two users are logged on to the computer using Fast User Switching, it is likely that two per-user Protocol Hosts will be running.) A per-user Protocol Host is necessary because some data stores must be accessed using the credentials of the logged-on user to be indexed. Examples of such stores include Outlook e-mail (using MAPI), the CSC, and remote file shares.
- **Search Filter Host process** This process (which runs as SearchFilterHost.exe) hosts IFilters, which are used to extract text from files and other items. IFilters are hosted within a separate process instead of within the main indexer process to protect the Windows Search service from possible crashes and ensure the stability and security of the indexing engine. This process is needed because, although many IFilters are written by Microsoft, other IFilters may be written by third-party vendors and are therefore considered to be untrusted code. Hosting IFilters within a separate process (such as a filtering host) that has very restricted permissions (such as a restricted token) provides a level of isolation that protects the main indexer process if an IFilter crashes. The indexer process runs a single instance of SearchFilterProcess.exe, and this process holds all IFilter parsing documents that come from the system-wide and per-user SearchProtocolHost processes. This Search Filter Host process only reads streams of content, runs IFilters, and returns text to the indexer process.

In normal operation, each of these processes starts immediately after Windows boots and the desktop appears. The main indexer process (SearchIndexer.exe) is the only one that always continues to run, however—the other processes may or may not be running, depending on the immediate needs of the Windows Search engine. The main indexer process uses the standard service control mechanism (Service Control Manager) to detect when the service is not running and restart itself. The conditions for restarting the service can be found on the Recovery tab of the Windows Search Service Properties dialog box, which can be viewed using the Services console. These restart conditions are as follows:

- Restart the service immediately after the first failure occurs.
- Restart the service immediately after the second failure occurs.
- Take no action after subsequent failures occur.
- Reset the failure count after 1 day.

Additional applications can also attempt to restart the indexer if it stops. For example, Windows Explorer does this whenever you attempt to execute a search from either the Start menu or Search Explorer. You can see this by stopping the Windows Search service and then typing in the Start menu or the Explorer search box. To prevent Windows Explorer or any other application from restarting the Windows Search service, you must disable the service, not just stop it.

Enabling the Indexing Service

The Indexing Service (Cisvc.exe) used in previous Windows platforms is still available in Windows 7 and Windows Vista as an optional feature that administrators can turn on if needed by following these steps:

1. Select Programs from Control Panel.
2. Under Programs And Features, click Turn Windows Features On Or Off and respond to the User Account Control (UAC) prompt that appears.
3. In the Turn Windows Features On Or Off dialog box, select the Indexing Service check box and then click OK.

The main reason enterprises might need to enable the previous Indexing Service would be for application compatibility reasons. For example, if enterprises develop applications that depend on Cisvc.exe, they can enable this service to support those applications. The Microsoft Office Visio shape-finding process also uses Cisvc.exe to index shapes. Therefore, if you need to search for shapes quickly in Office or Office Visio on some computers, you can enable Cisvc.exe on those computers.

> ***NOTE*** **Microsoft does not recommend running the older Indexing Service on computers running Windows 7 unless you have a compelling need to do so. The Indexing Service will likely be removed in a future version of Windows.**

Windows Search Engine Architecture

The architecture of the Windows Search engine in Windows 7, shown in Figure 19-1, illustrates the interaction between the four search engine processes described previously, the user's desktop session and client applications, user data (including local and network file stores, MAPI stores, and the CSC), and persistent index data stored in the catalog. The sections that follow outline in detail how Windows Search works and how the catalog is created and configured.

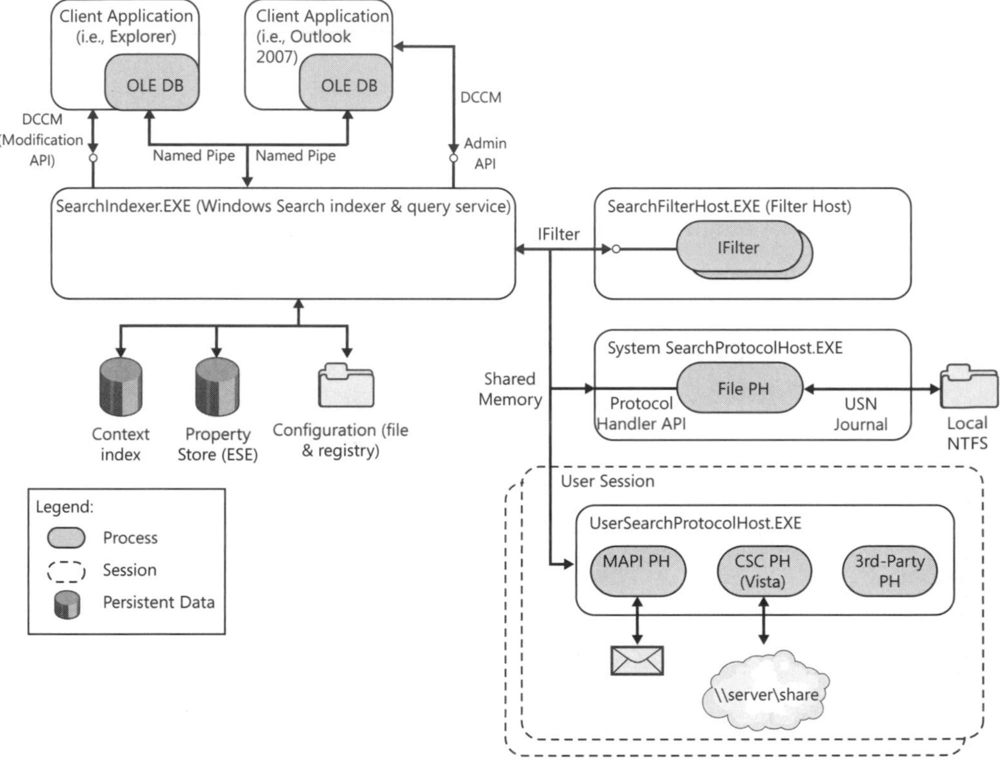

FIGURE 19-1 Architecture of the Windows Search engine in Windows 7

Understanding the Catalog

The catalog contains the results of the indexing process running on the local computer. Each Windows 7 computer has a single catalog that is located by default in the Search subfolder under the %SystemDrive%\ProgramData\Microsoft folder. (You must make hidden files visible to view the ProgramData folder and its contents.) The catalog contains three main types of information:

- The full-text index of all content that has been crawled by the indexer.

- The property store, which is a Jet database that contains the properties of files that have been indexed. (The Windows 7 property schema is used to decide which properties are cached.)
- Configuration files that control how the indexer works. (Additional configuration settings are stored in the registry.)

Although the catalog indexes items for all users who use the computer, the property store contains security descriptors for each item. Thus the indexer can security-trim the results of queries against the index so that the results returned include only items that the user who is performing the query can access.

NOTE **The location of the catalog can be changed using either Indexing Options in Control Panel or Group Policy. For more information, see the section titled "Configuring the Index" later in this chapter.**

DIRECT FROM THE SOURCE

Windows Search Service Files and Subfolders Structure

Denny Gursky, Software Development Engineer
Windows Experience Find & Organize Team

The configuration and data files of the Windows Search service are stored by default under %ProgramData%\Microsoft\Search. There are two folders under Search: Config and Data.

%ProgramData%\Microsoft\Search\Config

The only file kept in the Config folder is Msscolmn.txt. This is a configuration file describing human-readable names for the properties associated with documents and corresponding full property specifications and property types.

%ProgramData%\\Microsoft\Search\Data

There are two subfolders under the Data folder: Temp and Applications.

%ProgramData%\\Microsoft\Search\Data\Temp

The Temp subfolder is used by Windows Search for creating temporary files.

%ProgramData%\\Microsoft\Search\Data\Applications

The Applications subfolder contains more subfolders corresponding to the applications in the Windows Search service. In this context, "Applications" is not equivalent to "program"; rather, it is a logical entity bound to a specific property store. The only application supported in Windows 7 and Windows Vista is "Windows," so the only subfolder under Applications is Windows.

%ProgramData%\\Microsoft\Search\Data\Applications\Windows

The Windows subfolder contains the subfolders Config, GatherLogs, and Projects, along with a number of *.edb and MSS*.* files. These are Jet database data files and logs that contain the property store.

%ProgramData%\\Microsoft\Search\Data\Applications\Windows\Config

The Config subfolder is always empty in Windows Search 4.0 and later.

%ProgramData%\\Microsoft\Search\Data\Applications\Windows\GatherLog

The GatherLog subfolder contains the single subfolder SystemIndex, which corresponds to the only catalog supported by the Windows Search service. (See the following Projects folder description for details.)

%ProgramData%\\Microsoft\Search\Data\Applications\Windows\GatherLog \SystemIndex

The SystemIndex subfolder contains a number of SystemIndex.*.Crwl and SystemIndex.*.gthr files. The .Crwl files are log files tracking crawl transaction processing results. The .gthr files contain processing results for the notification transactions.

%ProgramData%\\Microsoft\Search\Data\Applications\Windows\Projects

The Projects subfolder contains subfolders corresponding to the different catalogs (projects). Catalogs are the way to partition the index. The only catalog supported by the Windows Search service is SystemIndex, so this SystemIndex folder is the only subfolder under Projects.

%ProgramData%\\Microsoft\Search\Data\Applications\Windows\Projects \SystemIndex

The SystemIndex subfolder contains the subfolders Indexer, PropMap, and SecStore.

%ProgramData%\\Microsoft\Search\Data\Applications\Windows\Projects \SystemIndex\PropMap

The PropMap subfolder contains data files of the proprietary database used for mapping full property specifications to internal property identificators.

%ProgramData%\\Microsoft\Search\Data\Applications\Windows\Projects \SystemIndex\SecStore

The SecStore subfolder contains data files of the proprietary database used for keeping access permissions in the form of security IDs (SIDs) for all indexed documents.

%ProgramData%\\Microsoft\Search\Data\Applications\Windows\Projects \SystemIndex\Indexer

The Indexer subfolder contains only one subfolder: CiFiles.

%ProgramData%\\Microsoft\Search\Data\Applications\Windows\Projects \SystemIndex\Indexer\CiFiles

The CiFiles subfolder contains the full text index files themselves, including shadow indexes and the master index. These index files include:

- The SETTINGS.DIA file, which contains diacritic settings.
- The *.ci files, which are index files containing indexed words, occurrence information, and references to the documents containing these words.
- The *.dir files, which are index directory files containing lookup tables for the *.ci files' content to enable fast positioning inside the index without scanning the index file from the very beginning.
- The *.wid and *.wsb files, which are the fresh test, meaning a table of the documents specifying which information is up to date in the corresponding *.ci file. The trick is to write every *.ci file only once when it is created and never modify it later. If the information in the *.ci file concerning some document is no longer valid, the indexer just marks the document as invalid for this particular *.ci file.
- The files INDEX.000, INDEX.001, INDEX.002, which implement transactional persistent storage for the index table, which is keeping records concerning all index files in use.
- The CiMG*.* files, which are merge progress logs that enable the index merge process to continue when interrupted by service shutdown (or even a crash) without having to restart indexing from the very beginning.
- The CiAD*.* and CiAB*.* files, which are average document length logs that are used for relevance metric calculations.

Default System Exclusion Rules

System exclusion rules define which files will be excluded from being indexed. By default, the following folders and files are excluded in Windows 7:

- %SystemDrive%\ProgramData* (with some exceptions, such as %SystemDrive% \ProgramData\Windows\StartMenu)
- %SystemDrive%\Windows\CSC* (excludes the CSC for Offline Files)
- %SystemDrive%\Windows.** (excludes any old Windows installation directories)
- %SystemDrive%\Windows* (excludes the Windows directory)
- *\System volume information*
- *\$Recycle.bin*
- %SystemDrive%\Windows*\Temp*

- C:\Users*username*\AppData* (with an exclusion for the AppData directory under each user profile being added when the user's profile is created, with one explicit exclusion being created for each user on the computer)
- %SystemDrive%\Users*\AppData\Local\Microsoft\Windows\Temporary Internet Files* (excludes Windows Internet Explorer temporary files, but note that this exclusion is not updated if you move the location of these files)
- *\Windows.**
- *\Dfsrprivate*

The location of the indexer files is also excluded. This location is %SystemDrive%\ProgramData\Microsoft\Search\Data* by default, but it is configurable and the exclusion will be updated if the user changes the location.

In addition, beginning with Windows 7, super-hidden files (protected operating system files that have both the *hidden* and *system* attributes set on them) and files that have their *FILE_ATTRIBUTE_NOT_CONTENT_INDEXED* attribute (FANCI bit) set are indexed. However, only basic properties for these types of files, such as file name, size, and date modified, are indexed—IFilter property handlers are not used when indexing these types of files. Note also that because hidden files are marked as hidden in the index, they are displayed in search results only if the user's folder settings are set to Show Hidden Files/Folders.

HOW IT WORKS

Understanding the FANCI Attribute

When the FILE_ATTRIBUTE_NOT_CONTENT_INDEXED attribute (also known as the FANCI bit) is set on a file, only basic properties of the file will be indexed—the file's contents will not be indexed, even if the location is an indexed location. Removing this attribute (by selecting the check box) allows the file to be indexed if it is in an indexed location, but it does not automatically make that location an indexed location. The attribute never indicates whether a file is indexed, only whether it should be indexed if it is in an indexed location. The order of operation at indexing time is to look in the set of indexed locations and then to index only items that do not have the FANCI attribute set. If the attribute is set (or removed) on an item outside of an indexed location, it has no effect.

Just to be clear: to set the FANCI bit on a file (or folder or volume), right-click the item, select Properties, click Advanced, and clear the check box labeled Index This File [or Folder or Volume] For Faster Searching. To clear the FANCI bit on the item, right-click and select Properties, and select the check box. You can also toggle the FANCI bit using the *attrib +i* command from the command prompt.

If the FANCI bit is set as an attribute on a folder (or drive), you will be given the option to either set only the attribute on the root location or to also cascade the change down to all subfolders and files. In addition, any new files created within the directory will inherit the folder FANCI bit. Existing files that are copied into the directory, however, will retain the current state of their FANCI bit (set or cleared). You can also set the attribute on a directory and, when applying the change, have it propagate recursively to all descendent files and folders.

Note that selecting the Index This Drive [or Folder] For Faster Searching check box for a volume or directory only enables the Windows Search service to index the volume or directory; it doesn't actually cause the contents of the volume or directory to be indexed. To do that, you need to add the volume or directory to the list of indexed locations using Indexing Options in Control Panel. For example, if you want to index the contents of a volume or directory, open Indexing Options in Control Panel, click Modify, and examine the check box under Change Selected Locations for the volume or directory. If the check box is selected, the volume or directory is already being indexed. If the check box is cleared but available, the volume or directory is not yet being indexed. To index the volume or directory, select the check box and then click OK. If the check box is cleared and the volume or directory name appears dimmed (unavailable), this is because either Group Policy is preventing indexing of the location or the FANCI bit is set for the location. The location will appear dimmed regardless of the check box being checked or cleared, but this doesn't mean it is unavailable for indexing. To determine whether this is due to the FANCI bit being set, place your mouse over the volume or directory name to reveal text that calls out whether the FANCI bit is preventing indexing of the contents of this location.

To index the volume or directory, right-click the dimmed volume or directory name and select Properties, then click Advanced and select the Index This Drive [or Folder] For Faster Searching check box. Close all properties pages by clicking OK several times, then reopen the Indexed Locations dialog box from Indexing Options and select the check box for the volume or directory.

Be cautious about changing the FANCI attribute for locations that by default have the FANCI bit set, because this can have a negative impact on the indexer. Some locations (such as the location for indexer data files, \ProgramData\Microsoft\Search) should never have the FANCI bit removed. Other locations, such as the ProgramData directory, may contain files that get updated on a very frequent basis. Having these files within the indexing scope will cause the indexer to index them each time they are updated, and this could adversely impact system performance.

A quick way to see all files that have the FANCI bit set for a drive is to use the *dir* command. For example, to find all FANCI files under the C:\Test directory and all subdirectories, you can run dir C:\Test /AI /S from an elevated command prompt. If you have a large number of files or a big directory structure that you want to parse across, you can output the results to a file such as C:\Fanci.txt by running dir C:\Test /AI /S >C:\fanci.txt from an elevated command prompt.

Default Indexing Scopes

Indexing scopes (also called *crawl scopes* and *start addresses*) are URLs that point to the starting locations for indexed content. When indexing is performed, each configured start address is enumerated by the appropriate protocol handler so that the indexing engine can find the content that needs to be indexed. By default, the following locations are indexed for the local volume:

- The Start menu (file:///%SystemDrive%\ProgramData\Microsoft\Windows\Start Menu).
- The Users folder ((file:///%SystemDrive%\Users) and all user profile folders within it except for the Default user profile folder. (The AppData subfolder is excluded, however, for each user profile.)
- The Offline Files cache (Csc://{user's SID}) for all users who use the computer. (This indexing scope is used only if CSC is enabled on the computer.)

By default, all files and folders within these locations are indexed unless they are specifically excluded by a system exclusion rule as described previously.

> ***NOTE*** **You can add additional indexing scopes by using Indexing Options in Control Panel. See the section "Configuring the Index" later in this chapter for more information. If Outlook 2007 is installed on the computer, this also appears as a default indexed location.**

Initial Configuration

When Windows 7 is installed on a computer, the Windows Search engine configuration code performs the following steps:

1. The Windows Search service is started.
2. The system catalog is created (the first time).
3. The file, MAPI, and CSC protocol handlers are registered.
4. Predefined system exclusion and inclusion rules are added (the first time).
5. Predefined start addresses are added (the first time).

HOW IT WORKS

Internationalization

Microsoft Global Technical Readiness Platforms Team

Search in Windows 7 and Windows Vista is language agnostic, but the accuracy of searches across languages may vary because of the tokenization of text performed by features called wordbreakers. Wordbreakers implement the variable tokenization rules for languages. Wordbreakers will break down both the language of the indexed text and the query string; a mismatch between query and indexed language can cause unpredictable results.

Windows ships with a well-defined set of wordbreakers and includes new tokenization code based on the Lexical Service Platform (LSP) for some languages. For others, LSP will delegate to the class wordbreakers. If no wordbreaker is installed for a language, a neutral white-space breaker will be used. (Windows provides wordbreakers for 43 different languages.)

At index time, the IFilter should determine the language of a property or chunk. If a file format does not encode language information, the language auto-detect logic is used to determine the language. At query time, the calling application (the shell, for example) designates the locale of the query.

Understanding the Indexing Process

Understanding how the indexing process works is helpful for troubleshooting issues regarding searching and indexing. The sections that follow outline different aspects of this process.

Types of Files Indexed

IFilters, property handlers, and the Windows property system are used to extract text from documents so that they can be indexed. Microsoft provides IFilters and property handlers for many common document formats by default, while installing other Microsoft applications may also install additional IFilters and property handlers to allow indexing of additional properties and content for documents created by these applications. In addition, third-party vendors may provide their own IFilters and property handlers for indexing proprietary document formats.

IFilters and property handlers are selected on the basis of the file's extension. IFilters understand file formats, whereas property handlers typically just understand file properties. For example, files having the extension .txt are scanned using the Plain Text filter, while files having the .doc extension are scanned using the Office filter and files having the .mp3 extension are scanned using the Audio property handler. All of these extensions are additionally scanned with the Windows property system to extract basic properties, such as file name and size. The Plain Text filter emits full-text content only because text files do not have extended properties (metadata). The Office filter, however, emits both full-text content and metadata because .doc files and other Office files can have extended properties such as Title, Subject, Authors, Date Last Saved, and so on.

Table 19-3 lists common document formats, their associated file extensions, and the IFilter dynamic-link library (DLL) included in Windows 7 that is used to scan each type of document. (Table 19-4 then provides similar information for property handlers.) Note that the indexer scans files based on their file extension, not the type of content within the file. For example, a text file named Test.txt will have its contents scanned and indexed by the Plain Text filter, but a text file named Test.doc will not—the Office filter will be used to scan the file and will expect the file to be a .doc file and not a text file.

NOTE **In Windows Vista, just over one hundred different file extensions were excluded by default from being indexed, including .bin, .chk, .log, .manifest, .tmp, and so on. Beginning with Windows 7, however, the indexer no longer excludes any file extensions by default. This change was made because many of these exclusions were no longer needed, while others had a good probability of reducing the relevance of search results. Some of these exclusions had also been in place to deal with performance issues that could arise if files were indexed. For instance, .log files can be updated very frequently, which in Windows Vista would have caused the indexer to index them repeatedly. Support for smart retry indexing, however, which was added in Windows 7, mitigate the impact of this type of issue. For more information concerning smart retry indexing, see the sidebar titled "Direct from the Source: Indexing and Libraries—Hard Disk Drives vs. Removable Storage" later in this chapter**

DIRECT FROM THE SOURCE

How Retry Logic Works

Michael Novak, Principal Software Development Engineer
Windows Experience Find & Organize Team

Indexing of a document can sometimes fail due to reasons that can be handled at a later point. Examples of this include server availability and sharing violations. When indexing of a document fails, the indexer attempts to index the document again in the future. The time between indexing attempts starts at 1 second, and if the document continues to fail, they expand logarithmically out to 24 hours. If the type of failure is not known to the indexer, the retry attempts may begin at 1 hour rather than 1 second. After a fixed number of attempts, the item falls into permanent failure and ceases to be attempted until the indexer is notified that it has changed again.

TABLE 19-3 IFilters Included in Windows 7 by Document Format and File Extension

DOCUMENT FORMAT	FILE EXTENSIONS	IFILTER DLL
Plain Text	.a, .ans, .asc, .asm, .asx, .bas, .bat, .bcp, .c, .cc, .cls, .cmd, .cpp, .cs, .csa, .csv, .cxx, .dbs, .def, .dic, .dos, .dsp, .dsw, .ext, .faq, .fky, .h, .hpp, .hxx, .i, .ibq, .ics, .idl, .idq, .inc, .inf, .ini, .inl, .inx, .jav, .java, .js, .kci, .lgn, .lst, .m3u, .mak, .mk, .odh, .odl, .pl, .prc, .rc, .rc2, .rct, .reg, .rgs, .rul, .s, .scc, .sol, .sql, .tab, .tdl, .tlh, .tli, .trg, .txt, .udf, .udt, .usr, .vbs, .viw, .vspscc, .vsscc, .vssscc, .wri, .wtx	Query.dll
Rich Text Format (RTF)	.rtf	RTFfilt.dll
Microsoft Office Document	.doc, .dot, .pot, .pps, .ppt, .xlb, .xlc, .xls, .xlt	Offfilt.dll
WordPad	.docx, .otd	WordpadFilter.dll
Multipurpose Internet Mail Extensions (MIME)	.dll	Mimefilt.dll
Hypertext Markup Language (HTML)	.ascx, .asp, .aspx, .css, .hhc, .hta, .htm, .html, .htt, .htw, .htx, .odc, .shtm, .shtml, .sor, .srf, .stm, .wdp, .vcproj	Nlhtml.dll
MIME HTML	.mht, .mhtml	Mimefilt.dll
Extensible Markup Language (XML)	.csproj, .user, .vbproj, .vcproj, .xml, .xsd, .xsl, .xslt	Xmlfilt.dll
Favorites	.url	ieframe.dll
Journal	.jnt	Jntfiltr.dll
XML Paper Specification (XPS)	.dwfx, .easmx, .edrwx, .eprtx, .jtx, .xps	Mscoree.dll

TABLE 19-4 Property Handlers Included in Windows 7 by Document Format and File Extensions

DOCUMENT FORMAT	FILE EXTENSIONS	PROPERTY HANDLER DLL
Contacts	.contact	Wab32.dll
System	.cpl, .dll, .exe, .ocx, .rll, .sys	Shell32.dll
Fonts	.fon, .otf, .ttc, .ttf	Shell32.dll
.Group Shell Extension	.group	Wab32.dll
Application Reference	.appref-ms	Dfshim.dll

DOCUMENT FORMAT	FILE EXTENSIONS	PROPERTY HANDLER DLL
Audio/Video Media	.3gp, .3gp2, .3gpp, .aac, .adts, .asf, .avi, .dvr-ms, .m1v, .m2t, .m2ts, .m2v, .m4a, .m4b, .m4p, .m4v, .mod, .mov, .mp2, .mp2v, .mp3, .mp4, .mp4v, .mpe, .mpeg, .mpg, .mpv2, .mts, .ts, .tts, .vob, .wav, .wma, .wmv	Mf.dll
Internet Shortcut	.url	Leframe.dll
Images	.bmp, .dib, .gif, .ico, .jfif, .jpe, .jpeg, .jpg, .png, .rle, .tif, .tiff, .wdp	PhotoMetadataHandler.dll
Installer	msi, .msm, .msp, .mst, .pcp	Propsys.dll
Library Folder	.library-ms	Shell32.dll
Microsoft XPS	.xps, .dwfx, .easmx, .eadrwx, .eprtx, .jtx	Xpsshhdr.dll
Microsoft Office Document	.doc, .dot, .pot, .ppt, .xls, .xlt, .msg	Propsys.dll
Property Labels	.label	Shdocvw.dll
Search Connector	.searchConnector-ms	Shell32.dll
Search Folder	.search-ms	Shdocvw.dll
Shell Messages	.eml, .nws	Inetcomm.dll
Shortcut	.lnk	Shell32.dll
Media Center Recorded TV	.wtv	Sbe.dll

In Windows 7, all of the file types (extensions) listed in Table 19-4 are enabled for indexing by default. Note, however, that the Plain Text filter will scan files having the extension .txt but not files having the extension .log, even though the filter supports scanning of .log files. To configure the indexer to scan such files using the default filter, see the section "Modifying IFilter Behavior" later in this chapter.

Two additional (implicit) IFilters and their extensions are not shown in Table 19-4:

- **File Properties filter** This filter is used to index the file system properties only of files for which there is no registered IFilter or for which there is a registered IFilter but the user has explicitly gone into Control Panel and selected the Index Properties Only option for the extension. File extensions that use this filter include .cat, .evt, .mig, .msi, .pif, and about 300 other types of files. Note that the File Properties filter isn't really a filter per se, but instead represents the absence of a registered filter for these extensions. In other words, it relies on the File System Protocol Handler to provide the file properties.

- **Null filter** This filter extracts the same properties as a File Properties filter and is used to deal with backward compatibility issues with older methods for registering IFilters. Again, this is not really a filter per se and relies upon the File System Protocol Handler to provide the file properties. The file extensions that use the Null filter are .386, .aif, .aifc, .aiff, .aps, .art, .asf, .au, .avi, .bin, .bkf, .bmp, .bsc, .cab, .cda, .cgm, .cod, .com, .cpl, .cur, .dbg, .dct, .desklink, .dib, .dl_, .dll, .drv, .emf, .eps, .etp, .ex_, .exe, .exp, .eyb, .fnd, .fnt, .fon, .ghi, .gif, .gz, .hqx, .icm, .ico, .ilk, .imc, .in_, .inv, .jbf, .jfif, .jpe, .jpeg, .jpg, .latex, .lib, .m14, .m1v, .mapimail, .mid, .midi, .mmf, .mov, .movie, .mp2, .mp2v, .mp3, .mpa, .mpe, .mpeg, .mpg, .mpv2, .mv, .mydocs, .ncb, .obj, .oc_, .ocx, .pch, .pdb, .pds, .pic, .pma, .pmc, .pml, .pmr, .png, .psd, .res, .rle, .rmi, .rpc, .rsp, .sbr, .sc2, .scd, .sch, .sit, .snd, .sr_, .sy_, .sym, .sys, .tar, .tgz, .tlb, .tsp, .ttc, .ttf, .url, .vbx, .vxd, .wav, .wax, .wll, .wlt, .wm, .wma, .wmf, .wmp, .wmv, .wmx, .wmz, .wsz, .wvx, .xix, .z, .z96, .zfsendtotarget, and .zip.

NOTE **Beginning with Windows 7, you won't see the name Null Filter in the Indexing Options Control Panel any longer. Instead, extensions that use this IFilter will just be associated with the File Properties Filter. You are able to tell that the Null IFilter is being used for a file extension only if you looked up the appropriate entry in the registry. This change was made in Windows 7 because the name "Null Filter" was confusing to some users.**

HOW IT WORKS

Get the Microsoft Filter Pack

The Windows Search service can be enhanced by installing the Microsoft Filter Pack, which provides additional IFilters to support critical search scenarios across multiple Microsoft Search products. The Filter Pack includes the following IFilters:

- **Metro (.docx, .docm, .pptx, .pptm, .xlsx, .xlsm, .xlsb)**
- **Visio (.vdx, .vsd, .vss, .vst, .vdx, .vsx, .vtx)**
- **OneNote (.one)**
- **Zip (.zip)**

These IFilters are designed to provide enhanced search functionality for the following products: SPS2003, MOSS2007, Search Server 2008, Search Server 2008 Express, WSSv3, Exchange Server 2007, SQL Server 2005, SQL Server 2008, and WDS 3.01.

When you install the Filter Pack, the IFilters in the preceding list are installed and registered with the Windows Search service. Note that the Filter Pack does not

need to be installed if Office 2007 is installed. The Filter Pack is available from *http://www.microsoft.com/downloads/details.aspx?FamilyId=60C92A37-719C-4077-B5C6-CAC34F4227CC&displaylang=en* for both x86 and x64 versions of Windows 7, Windows Vista, Windows Server 2008 R2, Windows Server 2008, Windows XP, and Windows Server 2003.

Modifying IFilter Behavior

When the indexer is crawling the file system, each IFilter has three options from which to choose for a file that has one of the file extensions associated with the IFilter:

- Index both the contents of the file and the file's properties
- Index only the properties of the file
- Do not index files of this type

NOTE The indexer will always try to index properties from a property handler (IPropertyStore) shell implementation. IFilter properties are overridden if there is a property handler. IFilter properties will override property handler properties for the property store. However, the system index will contain properties from both the property handlers and the IFilters.

To modify how a particular file type (extension) is handled during indexing by its associated IFilter, follow these steps:

1. Open Indexing Options in Control Panel.
2. Click Advanced and respond to the UAC prompt to open the Advanced Options properties dialog box.
3. Click the File Types tab and select or clear the check box for the file extension depending on whether you want to modify that particular file type. (See Figure 19-2.)

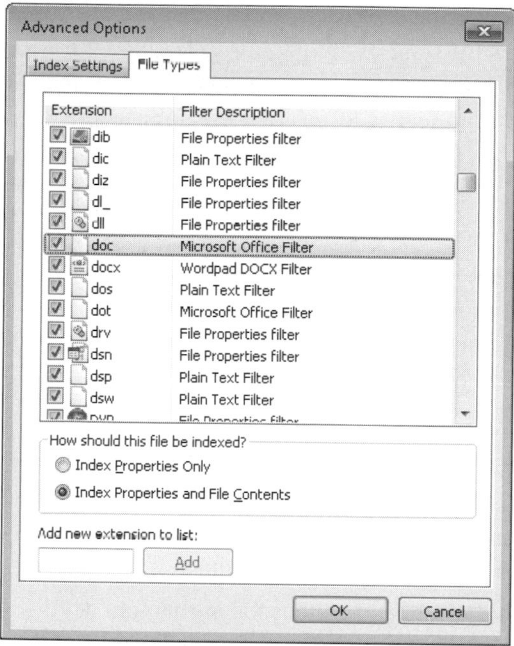

FIGURE 19-2 Configuring how file extensions are handled by their associated IFilters

Note that by default, files that have no file extension have only their properties indexed, not their contents. Beginning with Windows 7, however, you can change this behavior by performing the following steps:

1. In Control Panel, open Indexing Options and click Advanced.
2. Select the File Types tab, type a period (.) in the Add New Extension To List text box, and click Add to associate files that have no extension with the File Properties filter.
3. Select Index Properties And File Contents to associate files with no extension with the Plain Text filter.

> ***IMPORTANT*** **Because the Plain Text filter does not differentiate between binary and plain text files, you must be aware of the impact of making the changes described previously. Specifically, making this change may result in binary files being indexed, which will send useless information to the indexer.**

How Indexing Works

To illustrate the indexing process, consider what happens when a new document is added to an indexed location (a location that is configured for being indexed) on an NTFS volume. The following high-level description explains the steps that take place during the indexing of new file system content:

1. The NTFS change journal detects a change to the file system and notifies the main indexer process (SearchIndexer.exe). To view the state of this flag for a file, open the file's properties in Windows Explorer and click Advanced. A file change notification is then recorded in the USN journal, and the indexing service listens to these notifications.
2. The indexer process starts the Search Filter Host process (SearchFilterHost.exe) if it isn't currently running, and the system protocol handler loads the file protocol handler and Protocol Host.
3. The file's URL is sent to the gatherer's queue. When the indexer retrieves the URL from the queue, it picks the file protocol handler to access the item (based on the file: scheme in the URL). The file protocol handler accesses the system properties (for example, name and size), calls the property handler if one is available, and then reads the content stream from the file system and sends it to the Search Filter Host.
4. In the Search Filter Host, the appropriate IFilter is loaded and the filter returns text and property chunks to the indexer.
5. Back in the indexer process, the chunks are tokenized using the appropriate language wordbreaker (each chunk has a locale ID), and the text is sent into the indexing pipeline.
6. In the pipeline, the indexing plug-in sees the data and creates the in-memory word lists (word to item ID/occurrence counts index). Occasionally, these are written to shadow indexes and then to the master index via master merge.
7. Another plug-in reads the property values and stores them in the property cache.
8. If you have a Tablet PC, you may have activated another plug-in that looks for text you write and uses it to help augment handwriting recognition.

> ***NOTE*** **In Windows 7, both NTFS and FAT32 volumes support notification-based indexing (crawling or pull-type indexing). For NTFS volumes, the NTFS change journal enables notification-based indexing. For FAT volumes, an initial crawl is performed when the location is added and then recrawl is done whenever the location is disconnected (for example, when using an external universal serial bus (USB) drive formatted with FAT) or when the system is rebooted. Once the crawl is complete, however, the ReadDirectoryChangesW application programming interface (API) can be used to listen for any updates.**

REBUILDING THE INDEX

Rebuilding the index can also be forced on demand, but doing so can take a long time. To force a catalog rebuild, follow these steps:

1. Open Indexing Options in Control Panel.
2. Click Advanced and then respond to the UAC prompt to open the Advanced Options properties dialog box.
3. Click Rebuild and then click OK.

NOTE **You should rebuild the index only if your searches are producing inconsistent results or your search results are often out of date. Rebuilding the index can take a long time on a computer that has a large corpus (collection of files to be indexed).**

VIEWING INDEXING PROGRESS

You can view the progress of the indexing from the status message displayed in Indexing Options in Control Panel (shown in Figure 19-3). When user activity is present on the system, the search engine throttles back so as not to interfere with what the user is doing (that is, indexing still goes on but at a slower pace). When this happens, the message "Indexing speed is reduced due to user activity" is displayed. When all indexed locations have been indexed and no more items remain in the gather queue, the message "Indexing complete" is displayed.

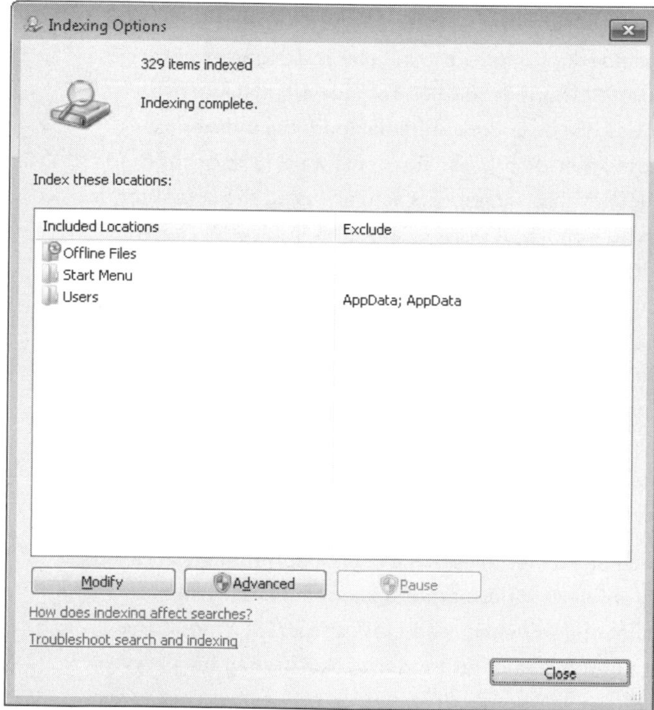

FIGURE 19-3 Using Indexing Options in Control Panel to view indexing progress

NOTE **Clicking Pause causes the Windows Search service to stop indexing new content for 15 minutes.**

You can also view indexing progress by using the Reliability and Performance Monitor. For example, the Search Indexer\Documents Filtered counter displays the number of documents that have been scanned for indexing, while the Search Indexer\Master Merge Progress counter indicates progress made during a master merge on a scale of 0 to 100 percent completed. Performance objects for monitoring the indexer include Search Indexer, Search Gatherer, and Search Gatherer Projects. For more information on using the Reliability and Performance Monitor, see Chapter 21, "Maintaining Desktop Health."

DIRECT FROM THE SOURCE

Windows Search Backoff Logic

Darren Baker, Program Manager, and Max Georgiev, Software Development Engineer
Windows Experience Find & Organize Team

Backoff logic was implemented in the Windows Search service to reduce the impact of the indexing process on user activities and other applications running on the same computer. To provide users with an optimal searching and browsing experience while keeping the index up to date, the indexer is designed to process incoming document change notifications as soon as possible after they arrive. When the computer is otherwise idle or under a minimal load, the indexer uses the available system resources to quickly process any items waiting to be indexed. However, when the indexer detects that someone is actively using the computer or that other applications are using significant system resources, it throttles back its indexing speed to minimize its impact on system performance. In most common user scenarios (for example, when a person is performing lightweight user UI-based activities like browsing the Web, reading e-mail, or composing a document), the indexer simply slows down to free up system resources. This allows users to still search their most recently updated content without experiencing any noticeable negative impact on UI responsiveness. In more extreme cases in which the system is heavily loaded by other processes, the indexer may suspend its processing entirely until resources become available.

To detect the presence of other agents (either users or processes) that are accessing system resources, the Windows Search service monitors a number of system parameters, such as the amount of free memory and disk space. Each monitored parameter has an associated threshold value to trigger backoff; when the parameter reaches or exceeds this threshold, the Windows Search service switches to the backoff state. Backoff thresholds are initialized from the registry on service startup. (Administrators can update or disable some of these backoff thresholds using Group Policy.)

When a backoff condition is detected, the backoff controller (a section of code that implements the backoff logic) pauses the Windows Search indexing thread, and all threads that are processing merge. As described previously, pausing these threads causes indexing to slow down in cases in which backoff is caused by user activity, and it causes it to stop entirely in other cases.

Overview of Supported Backoff Types

This section lists all default backoff conditions with their descriptions.

- **User activity** Indexing will be paused if user activity is detected. Any key press or mouse movement made by the user who is logged in from either the console or a Remote Desktop session is recognized as a user activity event. During this event, indexing will be reduced to consume not more than 30 percent of CPU. One minute after the last user activity event is detected, the maximum CPU consumption will be increased to 60 percent; after 30 more seconds, indexing will resume at full speed. The 30 percent and 60 percent CPU consumption limits can be configured using the registry values BackOffOnUserActivityInterval1 and BackOffOnUserActivityInterval2 correspondingly. This backoff on user activity feature is enabled by default and can be disabled using the Disable Indexer Backoff policy setting.
- **Low memory** Indexing is paused when the system is low on memory. The backoff controller monitors available space for the system page file (this can be examined using the Systeminfo.exe command-line utility) and pauses indexing when available space becomes less than the threshold configured. The default threshold value for this settings is 65,536 kilobytes (KB). This feature doesn't have a corresponding disable flag.
- **Low disk space** Low free disk space on the partition where the index resides (the system partition in the default configuration) can block the indexing process, and the Windows Search service pauses if the index home partition is short on space. The default threshold value for this setting is 600 megabytes (MB). This setting can be adjusted by the Stop Indexing On Limited Hard Drive Space policy setting. This feature doesn't have a disable flag, so the only way to disable it is to set the threshold value to 0.

Understanding Remote Search

In addition to being able to search content stored on the local computer, users of Windows 7 can also search content stored in shared folders on the network. To do this, the following prerequisites are required:

- The remote computer must be running Windows 7, Windows Vista, Windows Server 2008, Windows Server 2008 R2, or Windows XP or have Windows Server 2003 with WDS 4.0 installed.
- The Windows Search (WSearch) service must be running on the remote computer (on Windows Server 2008, you can enable the search service by installing the File Services role and then enabling the Windows Search role service within that role).
- The shared directory on the remote computer must be included in the indexed scope on the remote computer.

NOTE To provide an optimal experience for remote search, Microsoft recommends that computers running older installed versions of Windows with WDS 2.6.6 or WDS 3.01 be upgraded to WDS 4.0. For more information concerning support for WDS, see the section titled "Understanding the Windows Search Versions" earlier in this chapter.

Remote search performed from the local computer uses the Windows Search service on the remote computer to perform the query against the index on the remote computer. Results of the user's search are security trimmed based on the permissions assigned to the files in the shared folder. For example, if a document in the share contains the text "Microsoft" but the document's permissions do not allow the user to read the document, the document will not be returned as part of the search results when the user searches the share for documents containing the text "Microsoft."

NOTE Windows Search 4.0 automatically indexes all share folder locations. WDS 3.01 and the Windows 7 (and Windows Server 2008 R2) Search feature do not index shared folders automatically. To disable automatic indexing of shared folder locations, enable the Prevent Automatically Adding Shared Folders To The Index setting in Group Policy.

The following example illustrates how you can use a computer running Windows 7 to search for text within documents stored in a shared folder on a file server running Windows Server 2008:

1. Install the File Services role on the computer running Windows Server 2008, being sure to add the Windows Search Service role service.
2. Add some documents to a folder named Data that is in the indexing scope for the computer running Windows Server 2008. These should include a text file named Findme.txt that contains the text "Hello world".
3. Share the Data folder as DATA, granting Read permissions to Domain Users.
4. Log on to a computer running Windows 7 using a domain user account and press the Windows Logo key+R.
5. Type the Universal Naming Convention (UNC) path to the remote share (***SERVERNAME*\DATA**) and press Enter.
6. In the Windows Explorer window that opens, type **Hello** in the Search box. You should immediately see Findme.txt in the results set for your search.

NOTE If a yellow information bar appears saying "Network locations and connected devices are searched more slowly than indexed locations," the remote location is not being indexed and the slower grep method is being used to search the remote directory.

Managing Indexing

You can configure and manage the Windows Search engine in two ways:

- Locally, using Indexing Options in Control Panel
- Remotely, using Group Policy by configuring policy settings in Group Policy objects (GPOs) linked to organizational units (OUs) where targeted computers running Windows 7 reside

The sections that follow describe many of the search and indexing settings that you can configure in Windows 7, both from Control Panel and using Group Policy.

> **NOTE** All the Group Policy settings for configuring search and indexing in Windows Vista are computer settings and also apply to earlier Windows platforms that have previous versions of WDS installed on them, with the exception of the policy for preventing indexing of the Offline Files cache. (This policy applies only to Windows Vista or later versions.)

Configuring the Index

Administrative tasks for configuring the index include:

- Moving the index to a new location.
- Changing the locations indexed (modifying indexing scopes and exclusion rules for indexing).
- Rebuilding the index.
- Changing how file types are indexed.

> **NOTE** For information on how to rebuild the index, see the section titled "How Indexing Works" earlier in this chapter. For information on changing the way that file types are indexed, see the section titled "Types of Files Indexed" earlier in this chapter.

Configuring the Index Location Using Control Panel

You may need to change the location of the index if the system drive is running low on free space. To change the location of the index using the Indexing Options item in Control Panel, follow these steps:

1. Click Advanced to open the Advanced Options properties dialog box.
2. Click Select New and choose a new volume or folder for storing the index on the system.
3. Restart the Windows Search service on the computer.

NOTE The index can be located only on a fixed disk. You cannot move the index to a removable or network-attached disk. In addition, any volume or folder to which the index is moved should be set to read-only for non-administrators. Specifically, be sure to verify that \Search\Data\Applications\Windows only provides access to BUILTIN\Administrators and NT Authority\System. Access for any other users, such as Users or Authenticated Users, should be removed.

Configuring the Index Location Using Group Policy

To change the location of the index using Group Policy, configure the following policy setting for targeted computers:

> Computer Configuration\Policies\Administrative Templates\Windows Components\Search \Indexer Data Location

Enable the policy and type a path for the new location of the catalog using up to a maximum of 128 characters.

Configuring Indexing Scopes Using Control Panel

To specify the locations that are indexed manually (that is, to add or remove indexing scopes), perform the following steps:

1. Open Indexing Options in Control Panel and click Modify.
2. Expand the folder tree and select the volumes and directories that you want to have indexed on the computer (see Figure 19-4).

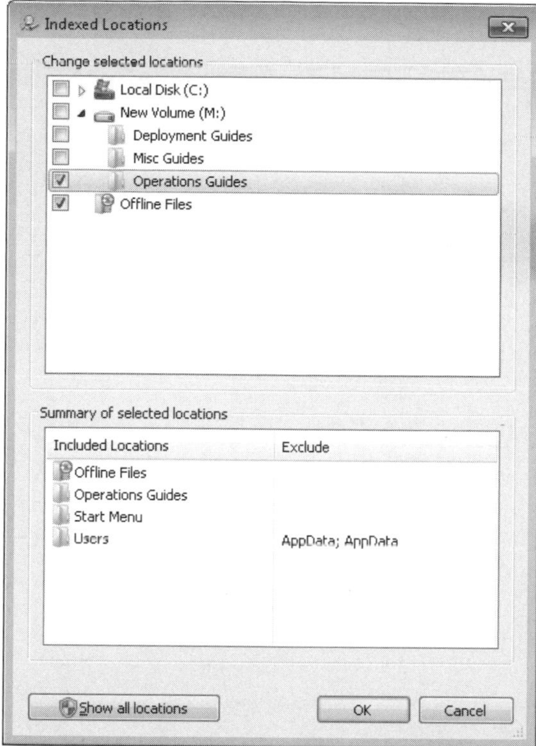

FIGURE 19-4 Modifying the locations that are indexed

For example, to index the entire system volume, select the check box for this volume (usually C). This adds the system drive to the list of start addresses for the indexer, with the following default exclusions: ProgramData, Data, AppData, Windows, and CSC.

You can override these exclusions by making hidden and system files visible in Windows Explorer and then clicking Show All Locations (as shown in Figure 19-4), expanding the system volume in the folder tree, and selecting each excluded folder. This is not recommended, however, because adding program and operating system files to the index can slow search queries and degrade the search experience for users. In addition, if the FANCI bit is set on a directory, the directory will appear dimmed, and when you point to it, additional info will be displayed on how to index the contents of that directory (see Figure 19-5).

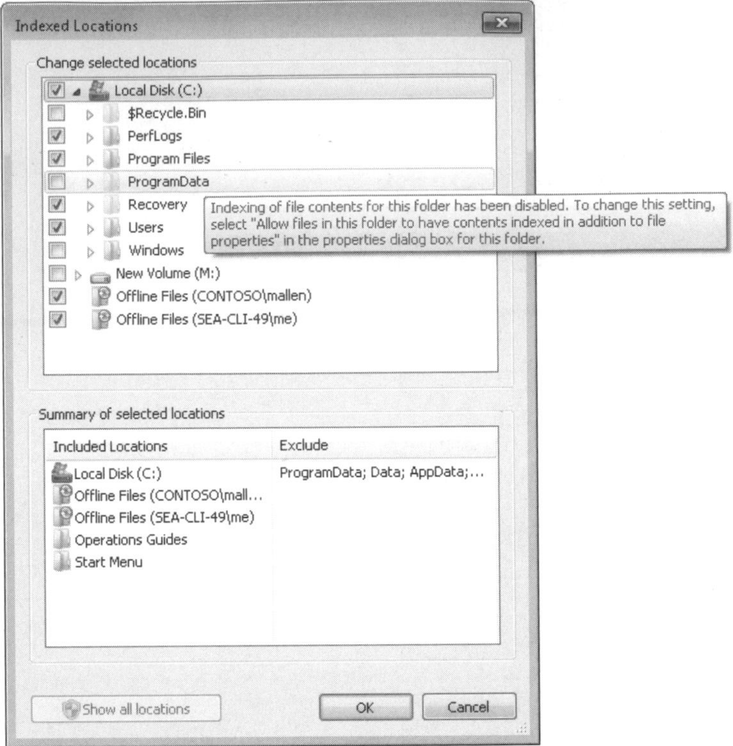

FIGURE 19-5 Indexing a hidden system folder

Configuring Indexing Scopes and Exclusions Using Group Policy

To specify locations to be indexed by using Group Policy, enable the following policy setting for targeted computers:

> Computer Configuration\Policies\Administrative Templates\Windows Components\Search \Default Indexed Paths

Then configure this policy by specifying the local file system paths for the volumes and directories that you want to include as indexed scopes on the targeted computers.

To specify locations to be excluded from indexing by using Group Policy, enable the following policy setting for targeted computers:

> Computer Configuration\Policies\Administrative Templates\Windows Components\Search \Default Excluded Paths

Then configure this policy by specifying the local file system paths for the volumes and directories that you want to exclude from being indexed on the targeted computers.

NOTE Users whose computers are targeted by these two policy settings can override them manually using Indexing Options in Control Panel. For example, a location that is indexed because of the first Group Policy setting can be excluded manually from being indexed by the user. Similarly, a location that is excluded from being indexed because of the second Group Policy setting can be included for indexing manually by the user.

Configuring Offline Files Indexing

Indexing of offline content in the CSC store is enabled by default, but you can disable it by using Indexing Options in Control Panel or by using Group Policy. Only the entire per-user offline cache can be indexed—individual files within the cache cannot be included or excluded from being indexed.

Configuring Offline Files Indexing Using Control Panel

To disable indexing of the Offline Files cache using Indexing Options in Control Panel, follow these steps:

1. Click Modify to open the Indexed Locations dialog box.
2. Clear the check box labeled Offline Files.

The preceding procedure disables indexing of offline files for the current user. To disable indexing of offline files for a different user of the computer using Indexing Options in Control Panel, follow these steps:

1. Click Modify to open the Indexed Locations dialog box.
2. Click Show All Locations and respond to the UAC prompt.
3. Clear the check box for the particular user's Offline Files cache.

NOTE To disable offline files indexing for all users of a computer, you must disable it using Group Policy, as explained in the next section.

Configuring Offline Files Indexing Using Group Policy

Using Group Policy, you can disable indexing of offline files only for all users of the computer, not for a particular user. To disable indexing of offline files for all users, enable the following policy setting for targeted computers:

Computer Configuration\Policies\Administrative Templates\Windows Components\Search \Prevent Indexing Files In Offline Files Cache

Configuring Indexing of Encrypted Files

Indexing files encrypted using EFS are disabled by default in Windows 7, but you can enable them by using Indexing Options in Control Panel or by using Group Policy. Beginning with Windows 7, indexing the contents of encrypted files is supported, which makes searching encrypted content as easy as searching unencrypted content. (In Windows 7, the non-encrypted properties of a file are always indexed, regardless of whether the file itself is encrypted.) The only limitation is that users can search only encrypted content stored on the local file systems of their computers, not encrypted content stored on network shares. Prior to Windows Vista SP2, only encrypted files that were made available for offline use could be indexed.

> ***IMPORTANT*** **If you decide to enable indexing of encrypted content on a computer running Windows 7, Microsoft recommends that you use Windows BitLocker Drive Encryption to encrypt the disk volume on which the index resides on your computer. Microsoft does not recommend using EFS to encrypt the index.**

Configuring Indexing of Encrypted Files Using Control Panel

To enable indexing of encrypted files using Indexing Options in Control Panel, follow these steps:

1. Click Advanced to open the Advanced Options properties dialog box.
2. Select the Index Encrypted Files check box.
3. If the disk volume where the index resides is not yet protected by Windows BitLocker, the following warning dialog box is displayed:

4. Click Continue to enable the indexing of encrypted content on your computer.
5. If you use a smart card to access encrypted files, a balloon notification appears above the notification area, indicating that EFS needs your smart card personal identification number (PIN). Clicking this notification opens a Windows Security dialog box in which you can type the PIN for your smart card.

> **IMPORTANT** Selecting or clearing the Index Encrypted Files check box rebuilds the index immediately. Depending on how many files you have, this can take up to several hours to complete, and searches might be incomplete while the index is being rebuilt.

Configuring Indexing of Encrypted Files Using Group Policy

To enable indexing of encrypted files using Group Policy, enable the following policy setting for targeted computers:

Computer Configuration\Policies\Administrative Templates\Windows Components\Search \Allow Indexing Of Encrypted Files

If you enable this policy setting, indexing disregards encryption flags (although access restrictions still apply) and attempts to decrypt and index the content. If you disable this setting, the Windows Search service (including third-party features) should not index encrypted items, such as files or e-mails, to avoid indexing encrypted stores.

Configuring Indexing of Similar Words

By default, words that differ only in diacritics (accents) are considered the same word by the indexer (at least for English and some other languages). If you want such words to be treated as different words by the indexer, you can use Indexing Options in Control Panel or you can use Group Policy. Note that changing this policy results in a full rebuild of the index because it changes the internal structure of the content index.

> **NOTE** The default setting for how diacritics are handled varies by language. For example, the default is Off in English, but it is On in several other languages.

Configuring Indexing of Similar Words Using Control Panel

To cause words that differ only in diacritics to be indexed as different words using Indexing Options in Control Panel, follow these steps:

1. Click Advanced and respond to the UAC prompt to open the Advanced Options properties dialog box.
2. Select the Treat Similar Words With Diacritics As Different Words check box.

Configuring Indexing of Similar Words Using Group Policy

To cause words that differ only in diacritics to be indexed as different words using Group Policy, enable the following policy setting for targeted computers:

Computer Configuration\Policies\Administrative Templates\Windows Components\Search \Allow Using Diacritics

Configuring Indexing of Text in TIFF Image Documents

New in Windows 7 is the ability for users to search for text within TIFF image documents that are compliant with the TIFF 6.0 specification. This capability uses Optical Character Recognition (OCR) processing and is not enabled by default.

> ***IMPORTANT*** **Enabling the indexing of text in TIFF image documents can result in significant processing overhead.**

Configuring Indexing of Text in TIFF Image Documents Using Control Panel

To enable the indexing of text in TIFF image documents manually on a computer running Windows 7, perform the following steps:

1. Open Control Panel, click Programs, and then click Turn Windows Features On Or Off.
2. Select the Windows TIFF IFilter check box and click OK.
3. Rebuild the index if you have existing TIFF image documents in the indexing scope on your computer.

> ***NOTE*** **If your TIFF image documents are stored on a computer running Windows Server 2008 R2, you can use the Add Features Wizard to add the Windows TIFF IFilter feature so you can enable the indexing of text in TIFF image documents stored on the server.**

Configuring Indexing of Text in TIFF Image Documents Using Group Policy

You can use Group Policy to configure how indexing text in TIFF image documents takes place. The applicable policy settings are found under:

Computer Configuration\Policies\Administrative Templates\Windows Components\Search\OCR\

The policy settings for configuring the indexing of text in TIFF image documents are as follows:

- **Force TIFF IFilter To Perform OCR For Every Page In A TIFF Document** Lets users turn off the performance optimization so that the TIFF IFilter performs OCR for every page in a TIFF document, which allows indexing of all recognized text. By default, the TIFF IFilter optimizes its performance by skipping OCR for document pages that have non-text content (such as photos). In some cases, pages that contain text can be misclassified as non-text pages. If this is the case, the text in these pages will not be indexed.

If you enable this setting, TIFF IFilter will perform OCR for every page in a TIFF document to index all recognized text. Therefore, the OCR process will be slower. This decrease in performance can be significant if there are a great deal of non-text pages in TIFF documents on the system.

If you disable or do not configure this setting, TIFF IFilter optimizes its performance by skipping non-text content during the OCR process.

- **Select OCR Languages From A Code Page** This policy setting allows the selection of OCR languages that belong to one of the supported code pages. If you enable this policy setting, the selected OCR languages are used in OCR processing during the indexing of TIFF files. The default system language is ignored unless it is among the selected OCR languages. If you disable or do not configure this policy setting, only the default system language is used.

  All selected OCR languages must belong to the same code page. If you select languages from more than one code page, the entire OCR language selection is ignored and only the default system language is used.

  Re-indexing is not initiated when you enable this policy and select OCR languages. This policy setting applies only to the indexing of new files unless re-indexing is initiated manually.

Other Index Policy Settings

Table 19-5 lists some additional policy settings for configuring indexing in Windows 7. All the policy settings listed in this table are found in the following location:

Computer Configuration\Policies\Administrative Templates\Windows Components\Search

For detailed information concerning all policy settings for indexing, see the *Windows Server 2008 R2 and Windows 7 Group Policy Settings Reference*, which can be obtained from the Microsoft Download Center at *http://www.microsoft.com/downloads/*.

Policy settings for configuring the user search experience for Windows Explorer in Windows 7 are described in the section titled "Using Search" later in this chapter.

TABLE 19-5 Additional Group Policy Settings for Windows Search

POLICY	DESCRIPTION
Prevent Indexing E-mail Attachments	Enabling this policy setting prevents the indexing of the content of e-mail attachments.
Prevent Indexing Microsoft Office Outlook	Enabling this policy setting prevents the indexing of all Outlook items, including messages, contacts, calendar items, notes, and so on.

POLICY	DESCRIPTION
Prevent Indexing Public Folders	Enabling this policy setting prevents the indexing of Exchange Server public folders in Outlook 2003 or later versions when the user is running in cached mode and the Download Public Folder Favorites option is turned on. When this policy setting is set to Disabled or Not Configured, Outlook users have the option of indexing cached public folders.
Prevent Displaying Advanced Indexing Options In The Control Panel	Enabling this policy setting will prevent users of targeted computers from being able to open Indexing Options in Control Panel to locally configure search and indexing settings on their computers.

DIRECT FROM THE SOURCE

Indexing and Libraries—Hard Disk Drives vs. Removable Storage

Anton Kucer, Senior Program Manager
Windows Experience Find & Organize Team

In Windows 7, hard disk drives appear in the Hard Disk Drives location in Windows Explorer. Typical devices in this category include internal and external hard drives. Examples of external hard drives are drives connected via a USB, FireWire, or ESATA cable to an external port on a PC. All drives that appear under Hard Disk Drives and are formatted as NTFS, FAT, FAT32, or exFAT can be included in a library and added to the indexer.

By contrast, devices with removable storage appear in the Devices With Removable Storage category in Windows Explorer. Typical storage devices in this category include DVD drives, CD drives, flash card readers, and USB flash drives. This category is intended to represent devices that have media that can be removed. However, not all devices accurately report supporting removable media. As a result, it is common to see devices in this category that do not have removable media, such as USB flash drives or portable media players such as a Zune or an iPod. Drives or media that appear under Devices With Removable Storage cannot be added to a library or added to the indexer.

Understanding Drive Letter Assignment Rules

To simplify the description of how drive letter assignment rules work, only the following devices are considered: devices that can be externally connected to a PC, require only one drive letter, and are not floppy disk, CD, or DVD drives. For a complete description of drive letter assignments, see the following: *http://support.microsoft.com/kb/234048*.

When a device that will be assigned a drive letter is attached to Windows for the first time, it is assigned the next available letter (that is, one that is not currently being used for an attached device or resource) starting with C. If the drive is removed and then reattached, Windows assigns the same drive letter unless that drive letter has been recycled for use with a different device or resource. If the drive letter has been recycled, the device once again is assigned the next available drive letter starting with C.

For example, let's say that before any external devices are attached, the computer has two hard disk drives (C and D) and a DVD/CD-RW drive (G). When an external drive is plugged in for the first time, the lowest available drive letter (E) is assigned to External Drive 1. If External Drive 1 is unplugged and External Drive 2 is plugged in, drive letter E is recycled and assigned to External Drive 2. If External drive 1 is then plugged back in again, it is assigned a new drive letter, F.

As long as drive letters are not recycled (for example, due to a new device being plugged in while one of the other devices is unplugged), both external drives can be removed and added in any order and they maintain their current drive letters. For example, if both external drives are removed and then External Drive 1 is plugged back in, it is still assigned the drive letter F.

Drive Letter Assignment and Its Impact on Indexing

The indexer does not support tracking indexed locations via a unique ID. Indexed locations are just tracked via their Uniform Resource Identifier (for example, file:///F:\Music). The indexer has the following limitations when it is indexing a location on a drive and the drive letter changes:

- When a drive letter changes, the indexer does not have the ability to dynamically update the path information for indexed items. For example, if the location E:\Music from External Drive 1 is added to the indexer and External Drive 1 is later assigned the drive letter F, the indexer does not recognize F:\Music as a location that should be indexed. Instead, it maintains the old index scope, E:\Music.
- When the drive letter is assigned to a new drive, the indexer is able to detect that content has changed. If the new drive is supported, it removes all indexed content from the old drive and attempts to index the new drive.

Drive Letter Assignment and Its Impact on Libraries

Libraries also do not support tracking locations that have been added to them via a unique ID. However, they do store additional information about locations, such as creation time, and they have link tracking functionality that can use this information to resolve locations in many cases when drive letters have changed, as follows:

- Link tracking can resolve locations in cases in which folders are added to a library and drive letters have changed as a result. When this occurs, the library is updated to point to the new location (for example, E:\Music gets updated to F:\Music). Additionally, the library notifies the indexer to remove the old location (in this case, E:\Music) and add the new location (F:\Music).
- Libraries do not resolve locations when drive letters change after the root of a drive has been added to a library.

Behavior When a Drive Is Not Available

When an external drive is no longer available (for example, it is unplugged from the computer) after a location from the drive has been added to a library and the indexer and the drive letter have not been recycled, the indexer trims any results from that location for any queries that are sent to it. The indexing control panel shows the location as being indexed but identifies it as unavailable.

Best Practices for Using External Hard Drives with Libraries

Best practices when using external hard drives with libraries include:

- Attaching all drives that you will use with the computer at the same time prevents the recycling of drive letters.
- Do not add a device that is assigned A or B drive letters to a library. The indexing of these drive letters is not supported and prevents the addition of these locations to a library. Note that Windows 7 will never automatically assign drive letter A or B to an external drive. You would need to have manually forced assignment of these drive letters (for example, via the Disk Management console).

Mitigating Drive Letter Recycling

The resolutions given previously, in which you need to manually remove a location and then add a location back to resolve issues caused by drive letter recycling, need to be done only once in most cases. However, after the root of a drive is added to a library, there can be situations in which its drive letter is continually recycled.

For example, suppose that a user has two external hard drives that are never attached to the computer at the same time. One hard drive (External Drive 1) is attached to the laptop only when the user is at work, and the other hard drive (External Drive 2) is attached to the laptop only when the user goes home. When External Drive 1 is plugged in, it is assigned drive letter E; and whenever External Drive 2 is plugged in, it is also assigned drive letter E. So if E\ from External Drive 1 is added to a library, every time External Drive 2 is plugged in, it shows up in the library instead. Each time this occurs, the indexer ends up re-indexing the entire drive.

One solution for this problem is to plug both drives into the system at the same time. If this isn't possible, the other solution is to manually assign a higher drive letter to one or both of the drives. For example, using the Disk Management console, you could assign the drive letter S to External Drive 2. Picking a high drive letter significantly reduces the possibility that the drive letter will be recycled. Picking a letter in the middle of the alphabet is best because Windows assigns drive letters from the end of the alphabet for mapped drives by default.

Using Search

Managing the search experience for users mainly requires educating them about the powerful new search capabilities built into Windows 7. The sections that follow provide an overview of these search capabilities and how to configure the search experience for users using Group Policy.

Configuring Search Using Folder Options

With the new Search tab found in Folder Options in Control Panel (see Figure 19-6), users can configure different aspects of the Windows Search experience to meet their needs, including what to search, how to search, and what should happen when searching nonindexed locations within Windows Explorer.

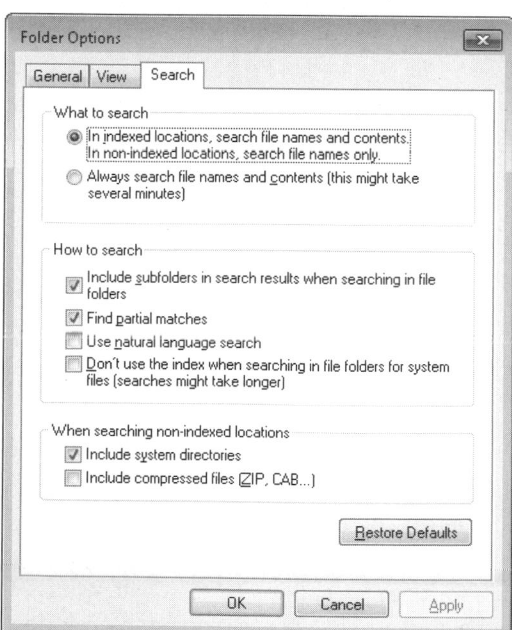

FIGURE 19-6 Configuring your search experience using the Search tab found in Folder Options in Control Panel

Configuring What to Search

By default, Windows 7 Search is configured to search for both file names and the contents of files when searching indexed locations. When searching nonindexed locations, only file names are searched. For example, searching the %Windir% folder for *log* will return all files and subfolders under %Windir% that satisfy any of these conditions:

- The files are named "log" or "Log" (the function is case insensitive).
- The file names use *log* as a prefix. This means, for example, that searching for *log* might return *logger, logarithm,* or even *fire-log* (the hyphen acts as a word separator), but it won't return *blog* or *firelog* because these file names do not have *log* as a prefix.
- The files have the .log file extension.

To perform such a search, open Windows Explorer, select the C:\Windows directory in the navigation pane, and type **log** in the Search box at the upper-right part of the window (see Figure 19-7). Note that the %Windir% folder is not indexed by default, so searching this folder is slow because it uses the grep method instead of the Windows Search service. (This method was used by the Search Assistant in Windows XP.) On the other hand, searching the user's Documents library returns results almost instantaneously because the user's Documents library is indexed by default and the Windows Search service simply has to query the catalog to obtain the results.

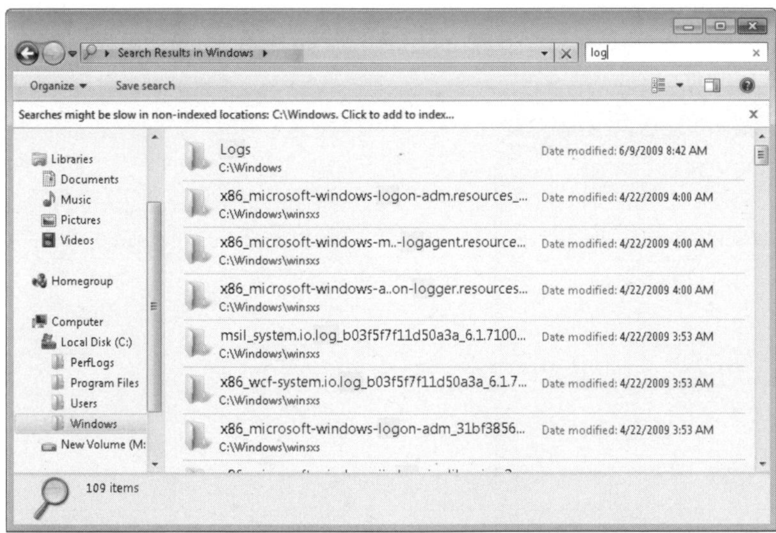

FIGURE 19-7 Results of searching the nonindexed %Windir% directory for the search string *log*

By selecting Always Search File Names And Contents (This Might Take Several Minutes) under What To Search on the Search tab of the Folder Options window, users can modify this default search behavior so that Windows searches for both file names and the contents of files, even when searching locations that are not being indexed. Note that doing this can slow down the search process considerably for such locations. A better approach is to mark these locations for indexing. As shown in Figure 19-7, searching a nonindexed folder using Windows Explorer causes a yellow notification bar to be displayed that says "Searching might be slow for nonindexed locations: *foldername*. Click to add to index." By clicking this notification bar and selecting Add To Index, users can cause the selected folder to be added to the indexing scope on their computer.

Configuring How To Search

The following options configure how searching is performed:

- **Include Subfolders In Search Results When Searching In File Folders** This option is enabled by default and causes Windows to search within subfolders when you search from any Windows Explorer window. Clearing this option will cause Windows to search only within the selected folder.
- **Find Partial Matches** This option is enabled by default and causes Windows to display results as you type your search. For example, if you type **fi** in the Search box on the Start menu, one of the results returned will be "Windows Firewall" because the second word in this program name begins with *fi*. If you disable this option, however, you will need to type the entire word **Firewall** before it will be displayed in your search results.
- **Use Natural Language Search** Selecting this option causes Windows to interpret the search string as natural language. For example, searching for "e-mail from Karen" would return all mail messages received from users named Karen.
- **Don't Use The Index When Searching In File Folders For System Files (Searches Might Take Longer)** Selecting this option causes Windows to always use the slower grep method for searching file names. The contents of files are not searched when this is selected and the setting Always Search File Names And Contents (Might Be Slow) is also selected.

Configuring What Happens When Searching Nonindexed Locations

Users can enable the following search behaviors when they search nonindexed locations:

- **Include System Directories** Selecting this option causes system directories to be included when searching a volume or folder using the grep method of searching. Note that beginning with Windows 7, this option is selected by default.
- **Included Compressed Files (ZIP, CAB...)** Selecting this option causes compressed files to have their contents searched both for matching file names and matching content within these files.

Using Start Menu Search

Start Menu Search has been enhanced significantly in Windows 7 compared with how it was implemented in Windows Vista. These numerous enhancements now make Start Menu Search a universal entry point that users can use to find programs, settings, and files quickly and easily.

For example, in Windows Vista, the results from Start Menu Search were hard-coded into four groups: Programs, Favorites And History, Communications, and Files. Beginning with Windows 7, however, these groups have changed to include Control Panel, Libraries, and all indexed locations, with Programs and Control Panel having the highest priority and with Favorites And History and Communications removed altogether. For example, Figure 19-8 shows a Start Menu Search for the string *remote* that returns two programs, several Control Panel items, and a number of documents and other types of files.

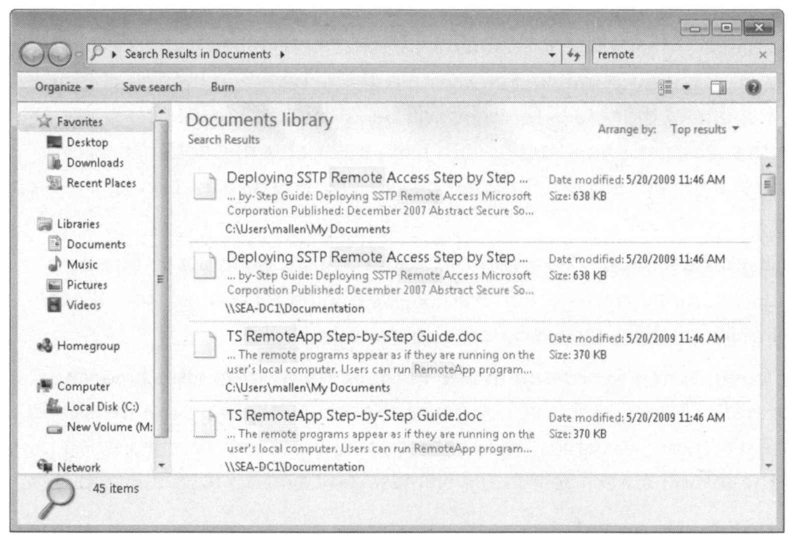

FIGURE 19-8 Start Menu Search now returns Programs, Control Panel items, and other types of files.

Clicking a group heading now returns all search results for that group. For example, Figure 19-9 shows that clicking the Documents heading opens Windows Explorer and displays the search results returned from the Documents library for this search string.

Using the Start menu is now the best way to find a particular Control Panel setting quickly. For example, if you want to change the display settings on your computer, simply type **display** in the Start Menu Search box, and the setting you are looking for is usually one of the results listed. Figure 19-10 illustrates that items listed in the Control Panel group of Start Menu Search results include not only Control Panel utilities, such as the Display applet, but also Control Panel actions, such as Change Display Settings. This enhancement makes using Start Menu Search a much faster way to find configuration settings for your computer than browsing Control Panel.

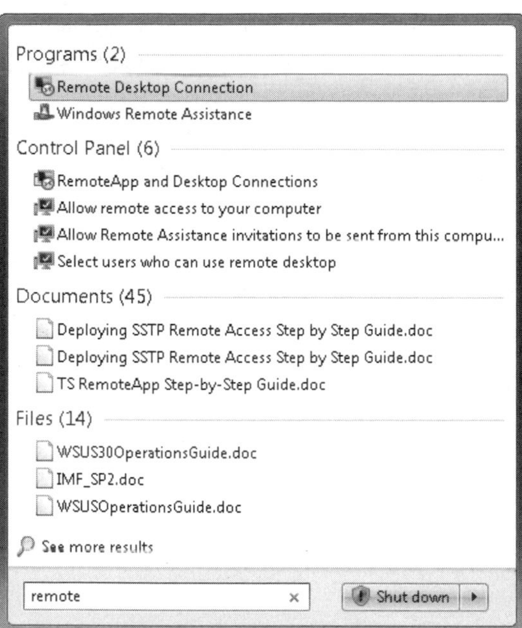

FIGURE 19-9 Clicking the Documents heading returns all documents that contain the string *remote* in the file name or document contents.

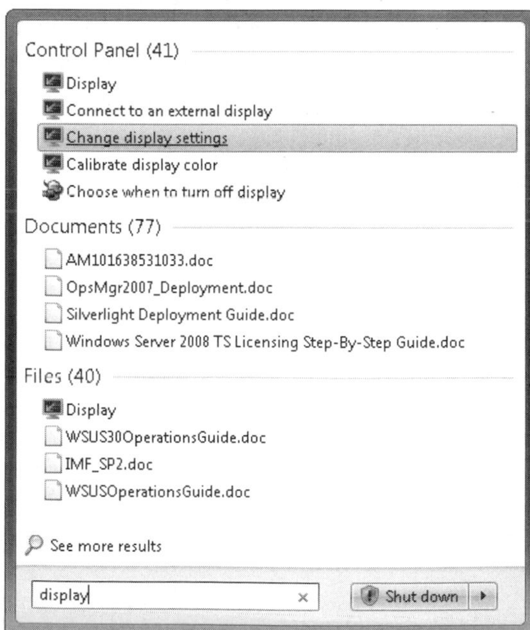

FIGURE 19-10 Searching how to change display settings using Start Menu Search

Re-scope links can be displayed at the bottom of the Start Menu Search results to allow users to re-scope their search to other locations quickly. In Figure 19-10, the re-scope link See More Results is pinned by default, and clicking this link opens Windows Explorer and reruns the query against all indexed locations. Up to three additional re-scope links can be pinned to the Start menu using Group Policy. You can pin the following types of re-scope links:

- **Search The Internet** Reruns the query using the default Web browser and the default search engine
- **Custom Library link** Reruns the query against the specified library using Windows Explorer
- **Search connector link** Reruns the query against the specified federated location via a search connector using Windows Explorer
- **Custom Internet search site link** Reruns the query against a specified Internet or intranet site that supports the OpenSearch standard using the default Web browser

The following Group Policy settings are new in Windows 7 and are used to pin or unpin re-scope links to the Start menu:

- **Add Search Internet Link To Start Menu** Allows users to re-scope searches to their default Internet search engine when searching from the Start menu. This policy setting is found in the following location:

  User Configuration\Policies\Administrative Templates\Start Menu And Taskbar
- **Pin Internet Search Sites To The "Search Again" Links And The Start Menu** Allows users to resend searches to customized Internet or intranet sites from Windows Explorer and the Start menu. This policy setting is found in the following location:

  User Configuration\Policies\Administrative Templates\Windows Components\Windows Explorer
- **Pin Library And Search Connectors To The "Search Again" Links And The Start Menu** Allows users to re-scope searches to customized Library or Search Connector locations from Windows Explorer and the Start menu. This policy setting is found in the following location:

  User Configuration\Policies\Administrative Templates\Windows Components\Windows Explorer
- **Remove See More Results/Search Everywhere Link** Hides the See More Results/ Search Everywhere link on the Start menu. This policy setting is found in the following location:

  User Configuration\Policies\Administrative Templates\Start Menu And Taskbar

> ***MORE INFO*** **For additional information on how Start Menu Search works in Windows 7 and the groups of results that can be displayed, see the *Windows Search, Browse, and Organize Administrator's Guide* found on Microsoft TechNet at *http://technet.microsoft.com/en-us/library/dd744681.aspx.***

Searching Libraries

Libraries are a new feature of Windows 7 that makes it easier for users to organize and search for documents and other types of files. Libraries allow files from multiple storage locations to be browsed and searched as if they were stored in a single location. For example, the Documents Library on a user's computer could contain:

- The user's own My Documents folder (included by default).
- The Public Documents folder on the user's computer (included by default).
- Additional volumes or folders on the user's computer.
- Shared folders on the network.

Libraries are integrated fully in Windows 7 with fast, full-content search and provide customized filter search suggestions based on the types of files the library contains. Figure 19-11 shows the Documents library on a user's computer where one of the library locations is the network share \\SEA-DC1\Documentation.

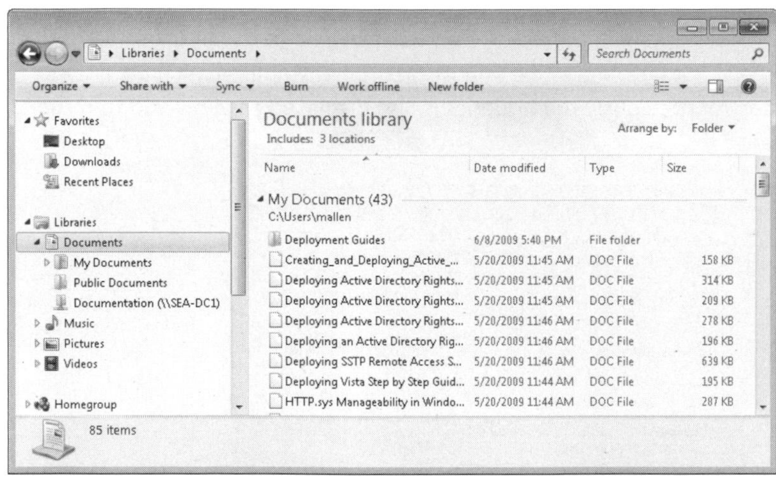

FIGURE 19-11 This Documents library includes files located on a network share.

Typing a search string into the search box in the upper right section of Windows Explorer searches the Documents library for the text specified. As Figure 19-12 shows, the results returned include highlighting of file names that contain the search string and snippets of text from documents that contain the search string.

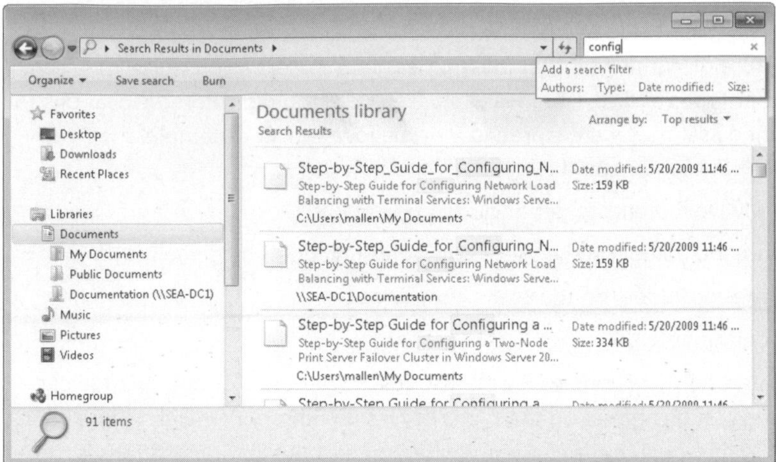

FIGURE 19-12 Results returned when searching the Documents library

As Figure 19-12 shows, clicking within the Search box allows you to use filters to narrow your search for documents that have a specific Author, Size, Date Modified, or Type. Figure 19-13 shows that a history of previously tried queries is also displayed to allow you to rerun a query quickly if you want.

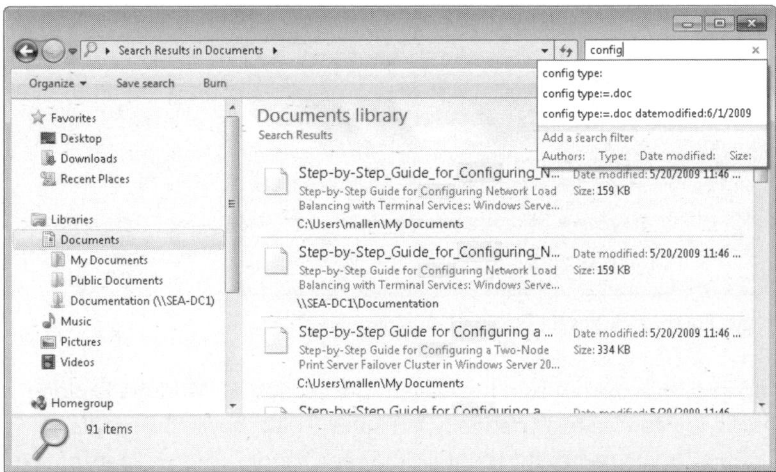

FIGURE 19-13 Narrow your search using search filters or rerun a previous query.

The search filters displayed vary depending upon the type of library being searched. For example, searching the Music library provides search filters for searching by Album, Artist, Genre, or Length. Search filters are a new feature in Windows 7 that make it easier for users to construct queries using AQS, which could only be entered manually when creating search strings in Windows Vista. For more information on AQS, see the sidebar "How It Works: Advanced Query Syntax" later in this chapter.

Once you perform a search, you can save it so you can run it again in the future. To save your search, click the Save Search button on the toolbar. Windows automatically suggests a name for your saved search based on your search string and any filters you selected. Figure 19-14 shows a saved search named *config type=.doc sizelarge.search-ms*, whose name was constructed as follows:

- Search string: "config"
- Type: .doc file (Microsoft Office Word document)
- Size: large (1–16 MB)

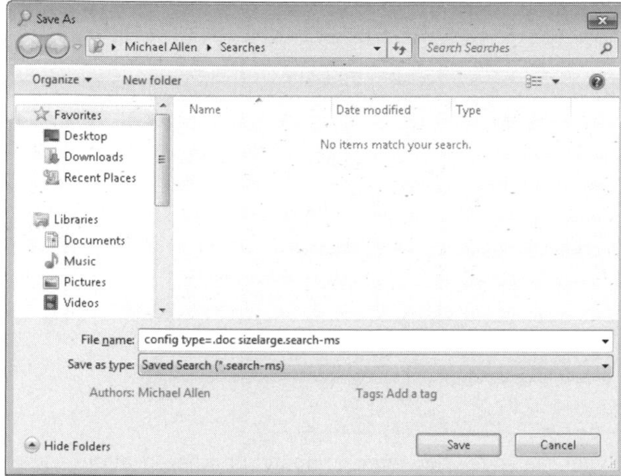

FIGURE 19-14 Saving a search as a *.search-ms file

Saved searches are saved by default in the Searches subfolder of your user profile and have *.search-ms* as their file extension. Saved searches are displayed under Favorites in the navigation pane of Windows Explorer. To rerun a saved search, simply select it in Windows Explorer (as shown in Figure 19-15).

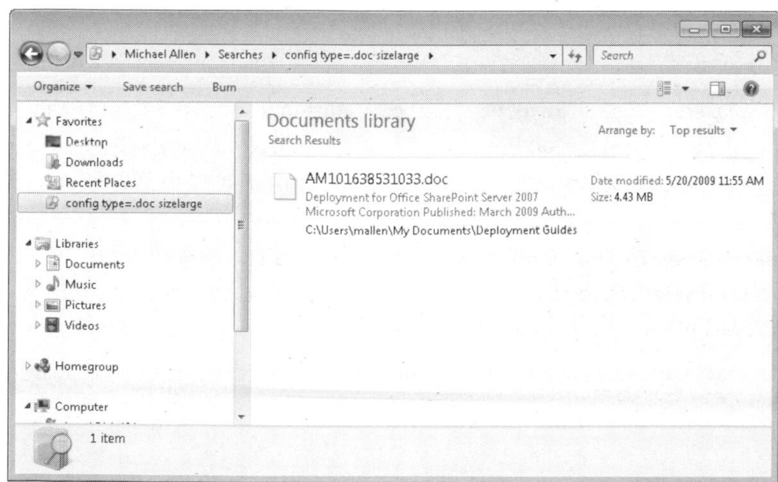

FIGURE 19-15 Rerunning a saved search by selecting it in the navigation pane of Windows Explorer

If searching the Documents library doesn't return the result you are looking for, you can broaden your search focus to other libraries, the entire computer, or even the Internet by selecting one of the re-scope links shown at the bottom of your search results. For example, by clicking the Computer link, you can re-scope your search to files stored in any location on your computer (as shown in Figure 19-16). You can even define a custom scope for this search only by clicking the Custom link and specifying the locations, both local and network, that you want to search.

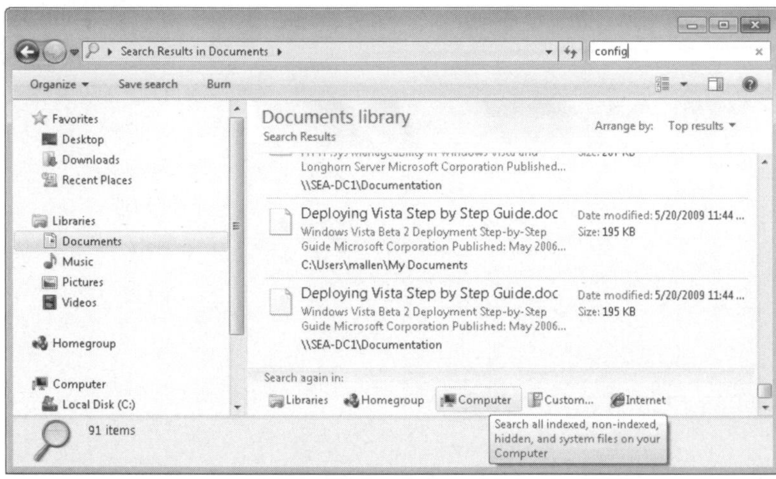

FIGURE 19-16 You can broaden the focus of your search to your entire computer or other locations using re-scope links.

> ***NOTE*** **To quickly search all indexed locations on a computer running Windows 7, press the Windows Logo key+F and type your search string. Other methods for doing this include pressing Ctrl+F from any Windows Explorer window and clicking Start, followed by pressing F3.**

The re-scope links displayed at the bottom of the search results in Windows Explorer can be customized by administrators using Group Policy. The following Group Policy settings are new in Windows 7 and are used to customize the re-scope links displayed in Windows Explorer:

- **Pin Internet Search Sites To The "Search Again" Links And The Start Menu** Allows users to resend searches to customized Internet or intranet sites from Windows Explorer and the Start menu. This policy setting is found in the following location:

  User Configuration\Policies\Administrative Templates\Windows Components\Windows Explorer

- **Pin Library And Search Connectors To The "Search Again" Links And The Start Menu** Allows users to re-scope searches to customized library or Search Connector locations from Windows Explorer and the Start menu. This policy setting is found in the following location:

  User Configuration\Policies\Administrative Templates\Windows Components\Windows Explorer

- **Remove The Search The Internet "Search Again" Button** Blocks access to Internet search from Windows Explorer. This policy setting is found in the following location:

  User Configuration\Policies\Administrative Templates\Windows Components\Windows Explorer

Also new in Windows 7 are the following Group Policy settings, which can be used to configure further how search results are displayed:

- **Turn Off The Display Of Snippets In Content View** Disables the showing of snippets of file contents when search results are returned. This policy setting is found in the following location:

  User Configuration\Policies\Administrative Templates\Windows Components\Windows Explorer

- **Turn Off Display Of Recent Search Entries In The Windows Explorer Search Box** Prevents the display of recent searches and prevents search strings from persisting in the user portion of the registry. This policy setting is found in the following location:

  User Configuration\Policies\Administrative Templates\Windows Components\Windows Explorer

- **Turn Off Numerical Sorting In Windows Explorer** Causes Windows Explorer to use logical file name sorting, as in previous versions of Windows. This policy setting is found in the following location:

  User Configuration\Policies\Administrative Templates\Windows Components\Windows Explorer

> ***MORE INFO*** **For more information concerning libraries and how to manage and work with them, see Chapter 15. For additional information on using Group Policy to manage searching in Windows 7, see the *Windows Search, Browse, and Organize Administrator's Guide* found on TechNet at *http://technet.microsoft.com/en-us/library/dd744681.aspx*.**

HOW IT WORKS

Advanced Query Syntax

AQS is a syntax used for creating complex search queries using the Search feature of Windows 7. AQS is not case sensitive (except for the Boolean operators AND, OR, and NOT) and uses the implicit AND when multiple search terms are specified. Supported syntax includes the following:

- Logical operators. AND (or + prefixed to term), OR, and NOT (or <;$MI> prefixed to term) plus parentheses for grouping. (No assumption should be made about the relative precedence between **AND**, **OR,** and **NOT**, so parentheses should always be used to make queries unambiguous.)
- Individual words. By default partial matches are accepted, so a query **sea** will return items with "sea", "seal", "Seattle", etc. Partial matches will always be accepted, even when the Find partial matches setting is off, if a word ends with a wildcard character (*). Thus a query **sea*** will always return items containing any word beginning with "sea". Multiple words separated by punctuation but no white space will implicitly be treated like a phrase, so a query **love/hate** will search for the word "love" immediately followed by the word "hate". The search is done across all (string) properties.
- Exact phrases enclosed in double quotes. For example, a query **"Majestik Møøse"** will return items containing those two words in sequence. (There is an indexing option controlling whether diacritics such as that in "ø" need to be matched exactly.) If a wildcard character (*) follows immediately after the closing double quote, partial matches will be accepted for each word in the phrase, so a query **"my dog"*** will return items containing the phrase "mystic dogfood". The double quotes also make sure that the enclosed words are interpreted literally, rather than as AQS keywords. The search is done across all (string) properties.
- Property searches on the form **Property: Operation Value**, where **Operation** is optional and one of those described below. **Property** is any term identifying a property of an item; in particular, the label of a property is a valid AQS keyword. For string-valued properties, **Value** is any word or phrase as described above, while for properties with other types of values (such as integer, date/time, or Boolean), values are recognized according to the user locale. An item is returned if **Value** is found in **Property** in the way specified by **Operation** (see below). If **Operation** is omitted, word search is used for string-valued properties and = is used for other properties. For example, a query **tags:John** returns documents where the *Tags* property contains (a word beginning with) "John", while a query **taken:>2007** returns taken in the year 2007 or later.

- Comparison operations include >, >=, <, <=, =, and <>, with the obvious meanings, and can be applied to numeric properties as well as string and date/time properties.
- Character-based operations include ~< (value starts with), ~> (value ends with), and ~~ (value contains). For example, a query **author:~>ing** returns items for which the *Author* property ends with the characters "ing", while a query **title:~~"ill a mock"** returns items containing the character sequence "ill a mock" anywhere in the *Title* property (when used with these operations, the double quotes allow white space in the search string). The character operations are generally much slower than the word-based operations. The character operations can only be applied to specific properties; there is no syntax for searching for an arbitrary character sequence across all properties.
- The fourth character-based operation is ~, which interprets the wildcard character (*) and the single wildcard character (?) like the file system does: matching zero or more arbitrary characters and matching one arbitrary character, respectively. For example, a query **author:~?oe** will return items in which the *Author* property is "joe" or "moe". (Note that the match will be against the whole value, so a more realistic query may be **author:~"?oe *"**, which will return items where the second, third and fourth characters are "o", "e" and a space, respectively, with anything in the other characters.)
- Word search and word prefix search can be specified explicitly using the operations **$$** and **$<**, respectively (but because they are the default operations for string-valued properties, this is rarely necessary).
- The special value **[]** represents "no value" or "null value." So the query **tag:=[]** returns all items that have no value for the *Tags* property, while the query **tag:<>[]** (or **–tag:=[]**, or **tag:-[]**) returns all items that have a value for the *Tags* property.
- For any property that has "symbolic" values, these strings can be used as values in AQS. For example, **importance:normal** returns all items where the *Importance* property is between 2 and 4, **size:small** returns all items with a Size between 10241 and 102400, **kind:docs** returns all items where Kind contains "document", and **flashmode:flashredeye** returns all images where the *Flash mode* property is 65.
- There are also symbolic values for some relative date values: **today**, **yesterday**, **tomorrow**, **this week**, **last week**, **next week**, **this month**, **last month**, **next month**, **this year**, **last year**, and **next year**. These all denote the current, previous, or next complete calendar day/week/month/year. One can also specify **the last day**, **the next day**, **the last week**, **the next week**, **the last month**, **the next month**, **the last year**, and **the next year**. These denote a time period of the specified length beginning or ending at the current time. For example, **modified:last month** (or **modified:lastmonth**;

the space is optional here) returns items where the *Date Modified* property has a value in the previous calendar month, while **taken:the last week** (or **taken:thelastweek**) returns pictures with Date taken in the previous 24 × 7 hours. As mentioned above, one can also use absolute date/time values expressed according to the user's locale; so if the user locale is Thai with the Thai solar calendar, a query **created:19/6/2552** or **created:19 มิถุนายน 2552** will return items created on the day that is June 19, 2009 in the Gregorian calendar.

- A range of values can be specified as **FirstValue .. LastValue**. For example, **taken:March 2007 .. June 2008** will return pictures taken between March 1, 2007 and June 30, 2008 (assuming a user locale that uses the Gregorian calendar).
- Integer suffixes for kilobytes, Megabytes, etc., are recognized, so a query **size:<=1MB** will return items with a size that is at most 1,048,576 bytes.
- There are some "virtual" properties for special purposes available only through AQS: **before:DateTime** and **after:DateTime** return items where the primary *Date* property is less than or greater than the specified date/time. **from:** searches over both sender name and address of messages; similarly, so does **to:**, **cc:**, **bcc:**, **organizer:**, **required:**, **optional:** and **resources:**. Likewise, **file:** will interpret its value as some combination of a path, a file name, and a file extension, and **?** and ***** will be interpreted as wildcards. So the query **file:report*.doc** will return all documents having a name beginning with "report" and a "doc" extension; a query **file:report?.doc** will return all documents with a name consisting of "report" plus one character and a "doc" extension; a query **file:\\lab\files*** will return all files with a path rooted in "\\lab\files"; while a query **file:"C:\Program Files\SomeCompany**.log"** will return all files with extension "log" under the folder "C:\Program Files \SomeCompany".
- One can delimit the scope of a search by placing restrictions on properties such as *Folder*, *Folder path*, *File path*, and *File name*. For example, **folder:"My Stuff"** returns items from any folder having the phrase "My Stuff" in the name, and **folderpath:~<"C:\Budgets\2006\"** returns items from "C:\Budgets\2006" and its subfolders.
- What goes after Property: may actually be multiple values combined using **AND**, **OR**, and **NOT**, each with an optional operation; so a query **kind:(communication –email)** will return items that have *Kind* "communication" but not "email" (note that *Kind* is a multivalued property), and **taken:(> last month < next month)** would be a somewhat convoluted way of expressing the same query as **taken:this month**.
- Property names and symbolic values must all be expressed in the user's default UI language to be recognized as such. In this way, users can express

queries in a language consistent with the rest of their UI. This means that a query **title:zoo** will return items with "zoo" in the title for a user with English UI but not for one with Swedish UI. In order to make it possible to write queries (for programmatic use) that work regardless of the user's UI language, the synonyms for each property include the "canonical name" of that property. For example, the canonical form of the previous query is **System.Title:zoo** (or even **System.Title:$<zoo** to make sure that partial matching will be used).

- A more relaxed form of AQS in which colons are not required after property names is activated by using the Use Natural Language Search option, which allows users to create queries that resemble natural language. When this option is turned on, a query **music by REM** will return items with *Kind* music created by REM (**by** is a synonym for the *Creators* property). This is a somewhat experiemental feature as it increases ambiguity (a word to be searched for may be misinterpreted as a property name, for example) and should be used with caution.

For more information on AQS, see *http://msdn.microsoft.com/en-us/library/bb266512.aspx* on MSDN and *http://www.microsoft.com/windows/products/winfamily/desktopsearch/technicalresources/advquery.mspx*. To build complex search queries without using AQS, use the Advanced Search pane described previously in this chapter.

Using Federated Search

Federated Search enables users to use the familiar Windows Explorer interface to search content located on repositories such as Windows SharePoint sites, intranet sites, and other types of remote data sources, including sites on the Internet. The goal of Federated Search is to allow users to work with files stored on these repositories as easily as they can work with files on their local computers' file systems.

NOTE Federated Search in Windows 7 does not interleave results from multiple sources. You must search each source separately.

How Federated Search Works

Federated Search uses search connectors, which are XML files that store information on how to connect to a remote data source. Search connectors are installed using OpenSearch Description (OSDX) files, which are XML files that have the .osdx file extension. When opened, these files create a .searchConnector-ms file in the %UserProfile%\Searches folder on the computer and a shortcut to this file in the Favorites area of the navigation pane of Windows Explorer. For example, the XML for a search connector named MSDN.OSDX that enables searching of content on *http://social.msdn.microsoft.com* looks like this.

```
<?xml version="1.0" encoding="UTF-8"?>
<OpenSearchDescription xmlns="http://a9.com/-/spec/opensearch/1.1/">
  <ShortName>MSDN</ShortName>
  <Description>Search MSDN. Powered by live.com</Description>
  <Language></Language>
  <Url type="text/html" template="http://social.msdn.microsoft.com/Search
/en-US/?Query={searchTerms}"/>
  <Url type="application/rss+xml" template="http://social.msdn.microsoft.com/Search
/Feed.aspx?locale=en-US&amp;Query={searchTerms}&amp;format=RSS&amp;StartIndex=
{startIndex}"/>
</OpenSearchDescription>
```

Double-clicking this search connector to open it displays the dialog box shown in Figure 19-17.

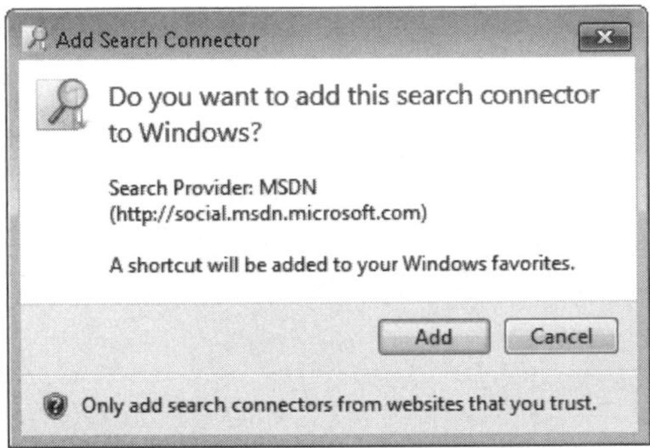

FIGURE 19-17 Adding a search connector for searching MSDN

Clicking Add in this dialog box installs the MSDN search connector (MSDN.searchConnector-ms) in the Favorites area of the navigation pane of Windows Explorer to allow the easy searching of content on MSDN (see Figure 19-18).

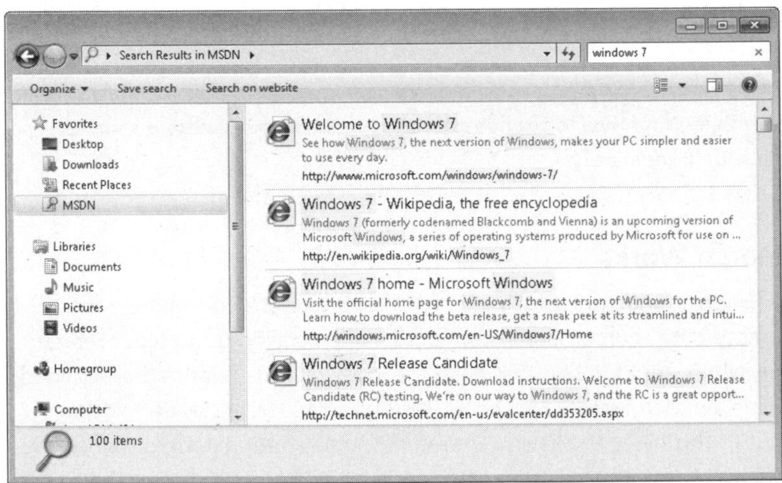

FIGURE 19-18 Searching MSDN for information about Windows 7

Deploying Search Connectors

Search connectors must be installed on computers running Windows 7 before they can be used. To install a search connector, you need the .osdx file that creates that connector. There are three ways of deploying .osdx files:

- **Pull Method** The administrator either sends the OSDX file to the user by using a method such as e-mailing it as an attachment or directs the user to a location (such as a Web page or a network share) from which the user can obtain and install the .osdx file. The user is then responsible for installing the search connector by opening the OSDX file, by clicking a link on a Web page, or by some other method.
- **Push Method** The administrator uses either Group Policy preferences (the preferred method) or a logon script to perform the following actions on the user's computer automatically:
  - Copies the *.searchConnector-ms file to the %UserProfile%\Searches folder on the user's computer to install the search connector on the computer
  - Creates a shortcut (.lnk file) to the %UserProfile%\Links folder on the user's computer to expose the search connector in the Favorites area of the navigation pane of Windows Explorer

  In addition, the administrator can use the following Group Policy setting to pin a re-scope link for the search connector to the Start menu and the Search Again area of Windows Explorer:

  User Configuration\Policies\Administrative Templates\Windows Components\Windows Explorer\Pin Libraries Or Search Connectors To The "Search Again" Links And The Start Menu
- **Imaging Method** Before deploying desktop computers to users, the administrator modifies a master installation of Windows 7 by performing the following actions:
  - Copies the *.searchConnector-ms file to the C:Users\Default\Searches folder on the master computer to install the search connector on the computer
  - Creates a shortcut (.lnk file) to the % C:Users\Default \Links folder on the master computer to expose the search connector in the Favorites area of the navigation pane of Windows Explorer

  The administrator then syspreps the master computer, uses the Windows Automated Installation Kit (Windows AIK) to capture an image of the master computer, and then deploys this image onto destination computers using WDS or some other deployment method. When the user logs on to her computer for the first time, the user's profile is created from the default profile that the administrator has configured.

> ***MORE INFO*** **For additional information on how Federated Search works and how to implement it, see the *Windows 7 Federated Search Provider Implementer's Guide*, which can be downloaded from *http://www.microsoft.com/downloads/details.aspx?FamilyID=c709a596-a9e9-49e7-bcd4-319664929317&DisplayLang=en*.**

Troubleshooting Search and Indexing Using the Built-in Troubleshooter

New in Windows 7 is the Windows Troubleshooting Platform (WTP), which can help organizations reduce Help desk calls by enabling users to fix common issues themselves using built-in troubleshooters. One of these troubleshooters can be used for diagnosing and resolving issues with search and indexing on the computer. The quickest way for a user to start this troubleshooter is to type **fix search** in the Start Menu Search box (as shown in Figure 19-19).

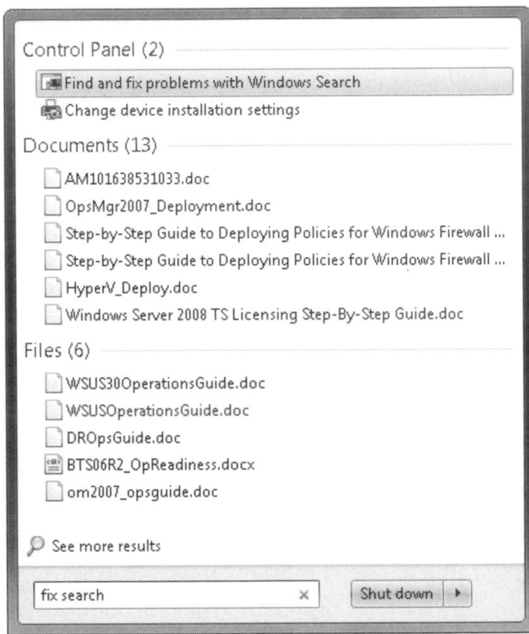

FIGURE 19-19 Starting the Search And Indexing troubleshooter

In the Control Panel group of the Start Menu Search results is Find And Fix Problems With Windows Search. Clicking this item or pressing Enter opens the first page of the Search And Indexing troubleshooter (see Figure 19-20).

> ***NOTE*** **The troubleshooter can also be invoked using the links at the bottom of the Indexing Options Control Panel dialog box or on the Troubleshooting Control Panel page. It may be necessary to click View All to find the Search And Indexing troubleshooter if it is not displayed on the front page of the Troubleshooting Control Panel.**

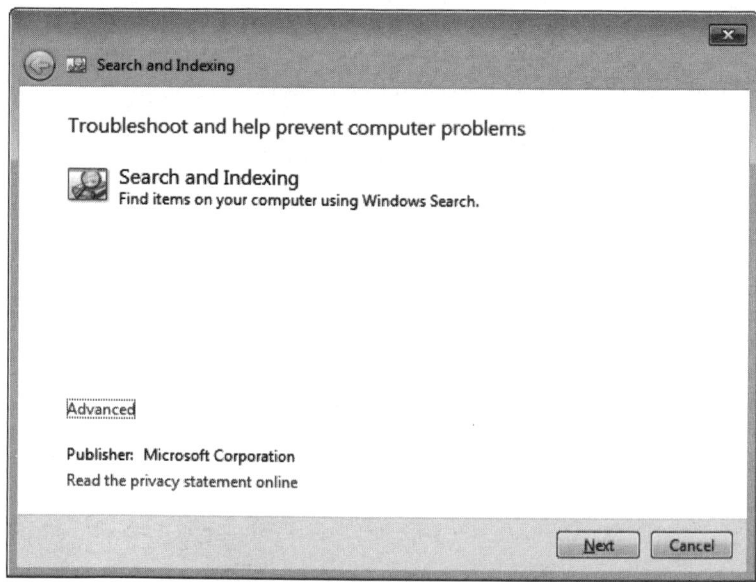

FIGURE 19-20 The opening page of the Search And Indexing troubleshooter

When the troubleshooter opens, clicking Next displays a page on which the user can choose from a list of common search problems to indicate the symptoms of her problem (see Figure 19-21).

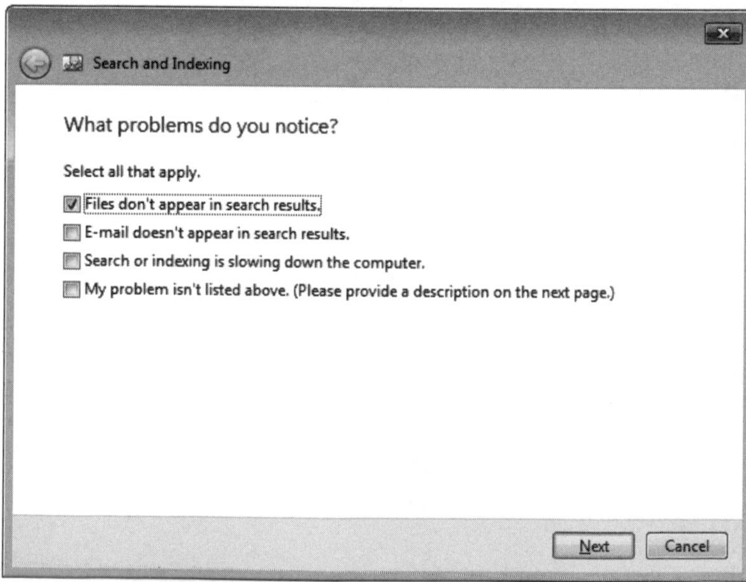

FIGURE 19-21 Choosing the issues a user is experiencing with Search

Once the user has selected the types of problems that she is experiencing, clicking Next either identifies and provides information on how to resolve the problem or directs the user to sources where additional help can be found or solicited (see Figure 19-22).

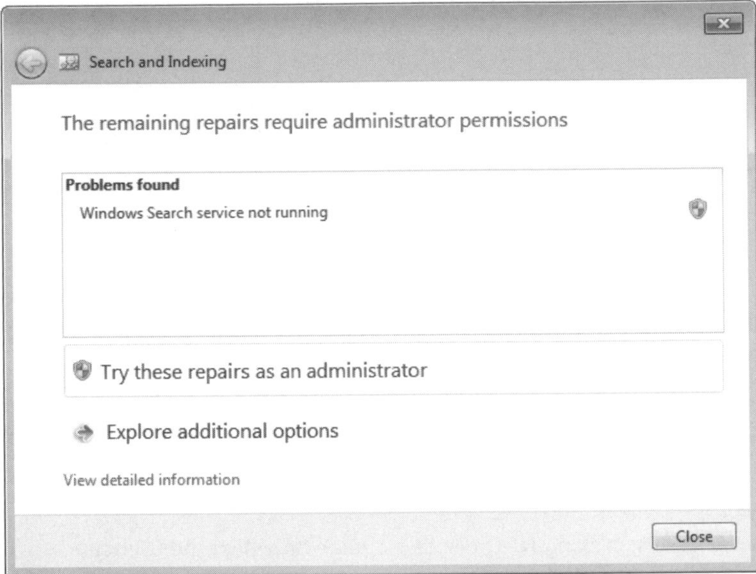

FIGURE 19-22 The troubleshooter identifying the problem

Summary

Search and indexing has been enhanced in Windows 7 in numerous ways, making it much easier for users to manage large amounts of information stored on their computers. Administrators can use Group Policy to manage the functionality of search and indexing, and users who are computer administrators can use Indexing Options and Folder Options in Control Panel to fine-tune the operation of search and indexing on their systems.

Additional Resources

These resources contain additional information and tools related to this chapter.

Related Information

- "What's New in Windows Search, Browse, and Organization" found at *http://technet.microsoft.com/en-us/library/dd349340.aspx*.
- *Windows Search, Browse, and Organize Administrator's Guide* found at *http://technet.microsoft.com/en-us/library/dd744681.aspx*.

On the Companion Media

- Get-SearchService.ps1
- Set-SearchService.ps1
- Stop-SearchService.ps1
- TroubleshootSearch.ps1

CHAPTER 20

Managing Windows Internet Explorer

For many users, accessing Web sites is a critical part of their jobs. The Web browser—specifically, Windows Internet Explorer—provides the graphical user interface for many vital intranet and Internet Web applications. Additionally, many users must access Web sites for research and communications purposes.

Microsoft offers Internet Explorer 8 with the Windows 7 operating system to make accessing the Web as productive as possible. With new features—especially Accelerators, Web slices, and Tab Isolation—users can work more efficiently. The security features of Internet Explorer, including InPrivate Browsing, Domain Highlighting, and SmartScreen, help to significantly reduce security threats posed by potentially malicious Web sites, which might attempt to install malware on your organization's computers. For administrators, Internet Explorer 8 is more manageable than earlier versions because almost any aspect of Internet Explorer can now be configured by using Group Policy settings.

Internet Explorer 8 Improvements

Internet Explorer 8 provides improvements to the user interface, browsing capabilities, security, and manageability. The sections that follow provide only a high-level overview of the Internet Explorer 8 features that affect users and IT professionals. The remainder of the chapter provides information relevant to managing Internet Explorer in enterprise environments.

InPrivate Browsing

When users browse the Web, they leave a record of their visits on the local computer. The browser records the visits directly in the history. Pictures are stored on the local disk as part of the browser cache. Words the user types might be recorded so AutoComplete can fill them in later.

Although these records improve performance and make it easier for users to find sites later, users occasionally want to browse without leaving a record of the Web sites they visit. InPrivate Browsing provides that capability by opening a new browser window that is specially configured to not leave traces of the Web sites they visit.

To open an InPrivate browsing window:

1. Create a new tab by clicking a blank tab or pressing Ctrl+T.
2. Click Open An InPrivate Browsing Window.

Alternatively, users can click the Safety button on the toolbar and then click InPrivate Browsing. Finally, users can press Ctrl+Shift+P. A new window appears, as shown in Figure 20-1, showing InPrivate in the title and address bars.

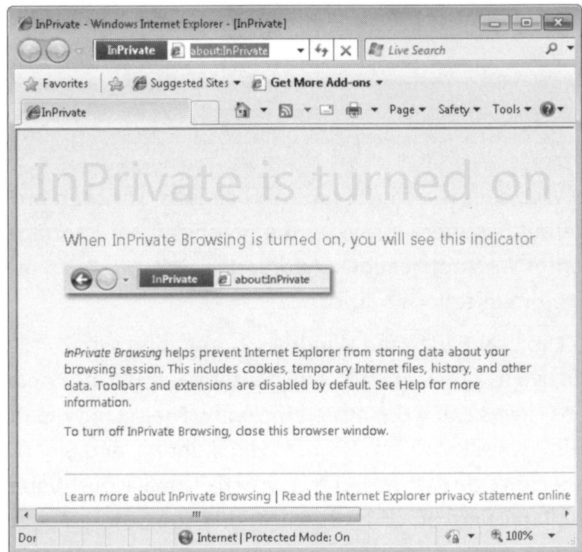

FIGURE 20-1 InPrivate prevents sites from being stored in the history or files from being saved in the cache.

To erase any records of the Web sites visited while InPrivate is enabled, simply close the browser.

NOTE InPrivate Browsing does not protect against many types of monitoring, including firewalls, routers, or proxy servers that might record Web sites visited, keyboard monitors that might record Uniform Resource Locators (URLs) typed, and monitoring software that might record screenshots. Nonetheless, it does improve a user's privacy.

IT professionals might not want users to make use of InPrivate. To disable InPrivate, enable the Administrative Templates\Windows Components\Internet Explorer\InPrivate\Turn Off InPrivate Browsing Group Policy setting, as described in the section titled "New Group Policy Settings for Internet Explorer 8" later in this chapter.

InPrivate Filtering

InPrivate Browsing's primary benefit is eliminating any local history of the Web sites visited by a user, whereas InPrivate Filtering attempts to improve privacy by blocking ads, images, analytics, and other tracking content that might allow Web sites to track a visitor across multiple Web sites. To the user, it's typically not obvious that the tracking content is coming from an outside Web site because the tracking content might be an image or video integrated into the Web page, or it could be completely hidden within the Web page.

For example, if Blue Yonder Airlines advertises on both Contoso.com and Fabrikam.com, Blue Yonder Airlines might be able to determine when the same user visited Contoso.com and Fabrikam.com and use that information to develop a profile about the user. In the future, that profile can be used to generate advertisements targeted toward the user's specific habits. However, users might not want Blue Yonder Airlines to know that much about their browsing habits. InPrivate Filtering attempts to block such cross-site tracking.

InPrivate Filtering is turned off by default and must be enabled on a per-session basis. To use this feature, select InPrivate Filtering from the Safety menu or press Ctrl+Shift+F. InPrivate Filtering can be enabled in a standard browsing session or an InPrivate Browsing session.

By default, InPrivate Filtering blocks content that is shared across 10 different sites or more. You can reduce the number of sites by using the InPrivate Filtering Settings dialog box, as shown in Figure 20-2, or by configuring the Administrative Templates\Windows Components\Internet Explorer\InPrivate\InPrivate Filtering Threshold Group Policy setting.

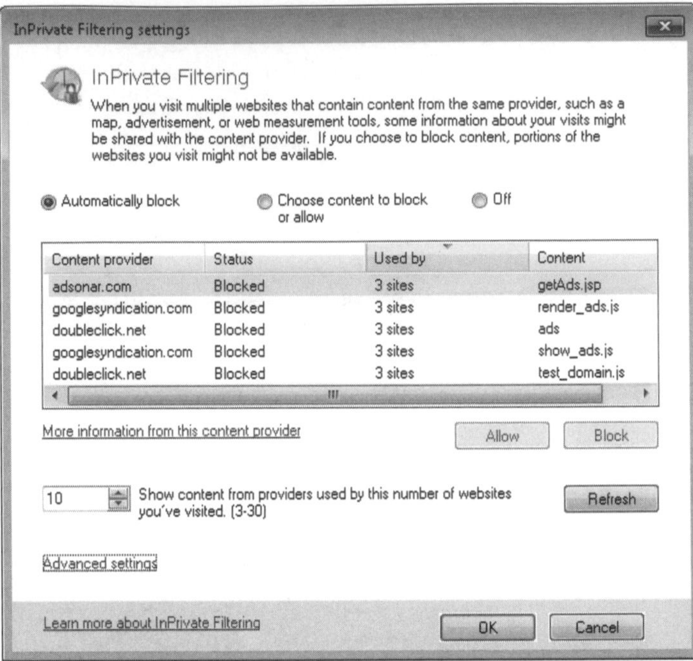

FIGURE 20-2 InPrivate Filtering blocks content that might track users across multiple Web sites.

InPrivate Filtering determines how many Web sites a content provider might track a user across by logging data. To disable this logging, enable the Administrative Templates\Windows Components\Internet Explorer\InPrivate\Do Not Collect InPrivate Filtering Data Group Policy setting.

To disable InPrivate Filtering, enable the Administrative Templates\Windows Components \Internet Explorer\InPrivate\Turn Off InPrivate Filtering Group Policy setting.

Compatibility View

Internet Explorer 8 includes a rendering engine that is more standards compliant. The new rendering engine displays most Web pages exactly as the Web designer intended. However, some Web designers might need to update the style sheets and HTML used to render their page so that the page appears correctly in Internet Explorer 8.

If you discover a page that does not display correctly in Internet Explorer 8, you can enable Compatibility View to render the page similar to the way it is rendered in Internet Explorer 7. To display the current page using Compatibility View, click Page and then click Compatibility View. Internet Explorer will re-render the current page and display it similar to the way it appears if you open it in Internet Explorer 7.

To configure Internet Explorer to always use Compatibility View for specific pages, click Page and then click Compatibility View Settings. Use the Compatibility View Settings dialog box to create a list of Web sites. Additionally, you can select the Include Updated Websites

Lists From Microsoft, Display Intranet Sites In Compatibility View, and Display All Websites In Compatibility View check boxes to control the rendering for different sites.

In Group Policy, you can modify these settings for all computers in your domain. Typically, you should do this only if testing shows that Internet Explorer 8 cannot correctly render an important Web site (such as an internal Web site) without using Compatibility View. Even then, a better approach is to update the Web site so that it renders correctly. If that is not immediately possible, use the Administrative Templates\Windows Components\Internet Explorer\Compatibility View\Use Policy List Of Internet Explorer 7 Sites Group Policy setting to add the URL to the list of URLs that use Compatibility View.

Web site authors can force Internet Explorer 8 to use Compatibility View for a Web page by adding the following metatag.

```
<meta http-equiv="X-UA-Compatible" content="IE=EmulateIE7" />
```

SmartScreen

Many Web sites attempt to trick users into providing credit card numbers, typing user names and passwords, or installing malicious software. Some Web sites are so effective at this that they can successfully deceive even IT professionals and security experts.

Internet Explorer 8 includes SmartScreen, which communicates with a Microsoft Web service to check the integrity of sites before users visit them. If a site is listed as potentially malicious, Internet Explorer 8 warns users before allowing them to connect to the site, as shown in Figure 20-3.

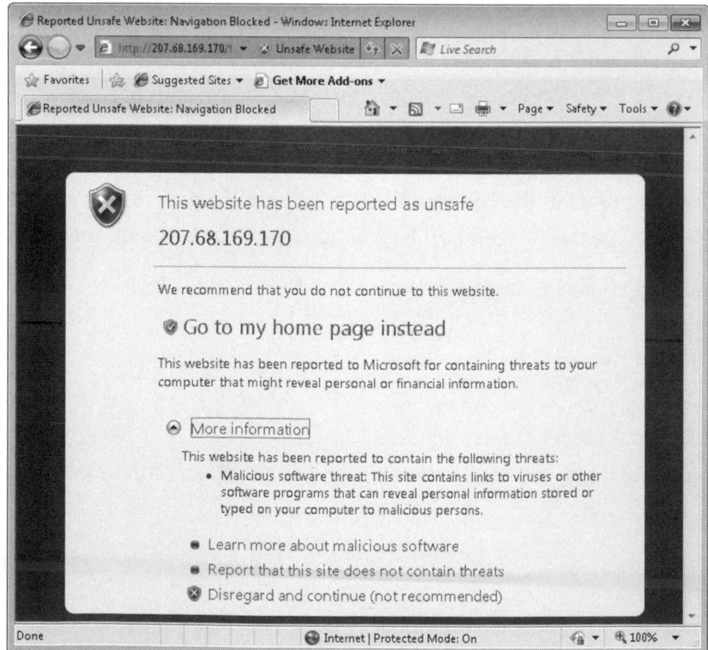

FIGURE 20-3 SmartScreen warns users if a Web site might be malicious.

You can enable or disable the SmartScreen filter using the Administrative Templates \Windows Components\Internet Explorer\Compatibility View\Turn Off Managing SmartScreen Filter Group Policy setting. If you enable this policy and set Select SmartScreen Filter Mode to On, Internet Explorer will send all Web sites not already contained in the filter's allow list to Microsoft and then warn users if a site might be dangerous. If you set the filter mode to Off or don't enable this policy setting, Internet Explorer 8 prompts the user to decide whether to use SmartScreen the first time the user runs Internet Explorer 8.

One way to improve the security of SmartScreen is to enable the Administrative Templates \Windows Components\Internet Explorer\Compatibility View\Prevent Bypassing SmartScreen Filter Warnings Group Policy setting. When enabled, Internet Explorer 8 will prevent users from visiting any site that SmartScreen lists as potentially malicious. Users still might find a way around this by using a different Web browser or a mobile device without SmartScreen protection, but enabling the policy does reduce security risks.

Domain Highlighting

Part of the way a user assesses the trustworthiness of a site is by checking the URL. For example, many users trust the Microsoft.com URL, and they might be willing to enter a user name and password into Microsoft.com if prompted.

Attackers can abuse the trust of URLs by using carefully structured URLs to trick users into thinking they are visiting a legitimate Web site, however. For example, a Web site owner might use the host name *www.microsoft.com.contoso.com* to make a user think they are visiting the *www.microsoft.com* site—even though *contoso.com* controls the address of the Web site.

Domain Highlighting helps users more easily interpret URLs to avoid deceptive Web sites that attempt to trick users with misleading addresses. It does this by highlighting the domain name in the address bar in black, as shown in Figure 20-4, with the remainder of the URL string appearing in gray, making for easier identification of the site's true identity. In this example, if there are distracting elements in the URL (such as an outside domain name), they appear in the lighter shade of gray. The user's attention is instead drawn to the black text.

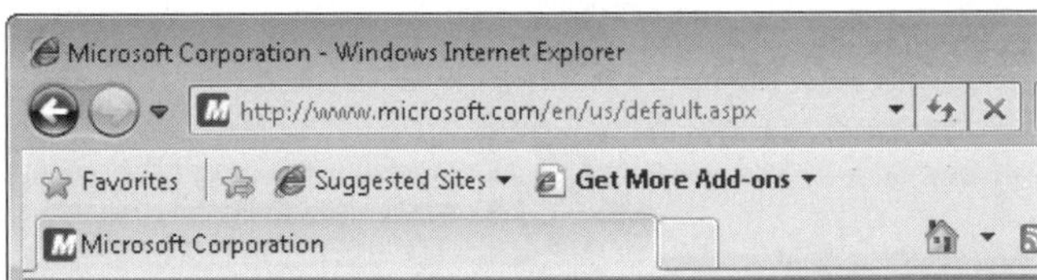

FIGURE 20-4 Domain Highlighting makes it easier to identify the domain name within a URL.

Domain Highlighting cannot completely eliminate the risk of attackers using malicious URLs to trick users. However, it does help to reduce the risk.

Tab Isolation

To improve reliability, Internet Explorer 8 features a new process known as Loosely Coupled Internet Explorer (LCIE). This process model also requires a new session model. Each tab is a separate process, and if a single Web page crashes, Windows will close only the one tab. Figure 20-5 shows an instance of Internet Explorer 8 with four processes: one for the frame and one for each of the three tabs. Each portion of the window that is represented by a separate process is boxed. Unlike Internet Explorer 7, Internet Explorer 8 can host tabs when Protected Mode is both enabled and disabled within a single browser window.

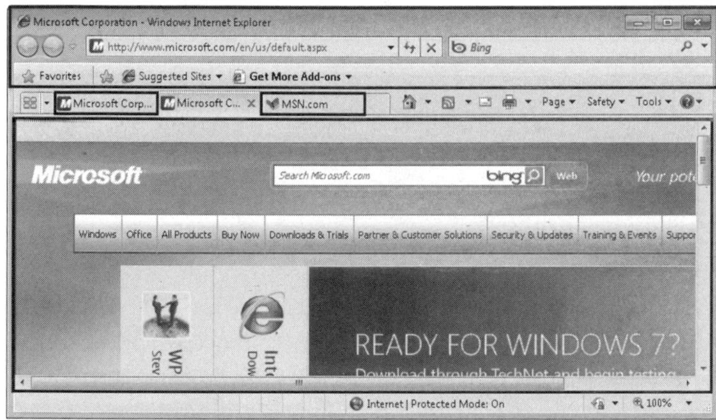

FIGURE 20-5 Tab Isolation separates tabs into different processes.

All tabs and browser instances share a single session, however. This means that different tabs and different browser windows will, by default, use the same set of cookies.

Internet Explorer 7 uses different sessions for different browser windows. Therefore, a user can log on to a Web site as User1 in a browser window, open a second browser window, and log on to the same Web site as User2. In Internet Explorer 8, the user is automatically logged on as User1 in the second browser window. If the user logs out and then logs back on as User2 in the second browser window, they are also be logged on as User1 in the first browser window.

To work around this, the user can start a new session in a new browser window by clicking the File menu and then clicking New Session. Alternatively, you can start Internet Explorer 8 by using the *–nomerge* command-line parameter. For example, you can replace the standard Internet Explorer 8 shortcut with a shortcut to Iexplore.exe–nomerge.

DIRECT FROM THE SOURCE

Understanding Iexplore.exe Processes

Brent Goodpaster, Principal Escalation Engineer
Developer Support/Internet

Due to the changes in LCIE for Internet Explorer 8, it can be very challenging to determine which Internet Explorer tabs belong to which Iexplore.exe process. To help with this confusion, add the Command Line and PID (Process Identifier) columns to the Processes tab in Task Manager.

From within Task Manager, you can see two Iexplore.exe processes after starting Internet Explorer. The lower Iexplore.exe process is the first process (initial frame process) that loads when the Internet Explorer icon is clicked on the desktop. Next, the top Iexplore.exe process (tab process) loads the Web site that you have set up as your home page. Now, open a second tab, and a third Iexplore.exe process appears.

In Task Manager, examine the Command Line column. The initial frame process is simply Iexplore.exe. All tab processes show the SCODEF parameter. The SCODEF number is the PID of the initial frame process.

You can use Process Explorer, available from *http://live.sysinternals.com/procexp.exe*, to determine which tab is associated with each process. First, select the tab in Internet Explorer. Then, from the Find window in Process Explorer, drag the Process toolbar button to the Web page. Process Explorer highlights the Iexplore.exe process associated with that tab. Don't drag the Process toolbar button to the tab itself, or you'll identify the Iexplore.exe process associated with the frame.

When using Internet Explorer 8 in Windows 7, Windows 7 uses a timer to detect tabs that might be nonresponsive. If a tab doesn't respond within a given interval of time, Internet Explorer 8 allows the user to choose to cover the tab, close the page, or wait for the tab to respond.

Accelerators

Accelerators improve productivity by allowing users to select text, click the Accelerator icon, and process the selection by using a Web service. For example, Internet Explorer 8 includes Accelerators that allow users to blog about a Web page, e-mail selected text, and display an address on a map. Figure 20-6 shows the default Accelerators being used to display a map of a selected address.

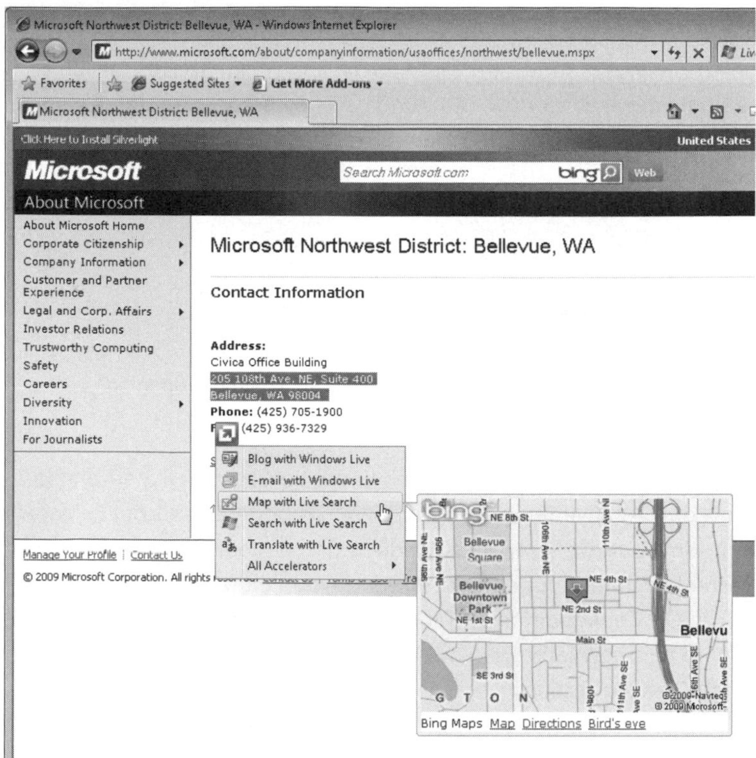

FIGURE 20-6 Accelerators give quick access to Web tools.

You can use the Group Policy settings in Administrative Templates\Windows Components\Internet Explorer\Accelerators to deploy new Accelerators, limit Accelerators to those you deploy, or disable Accelerators entirely.

Improvements Previously Introduced in Internet Explorer 7

Internet Explorer 8 includes all of the improvements found in Internet Explorer 7. The sections that follow describe the improvements previously introduced in Internet Explorer 7 to assist those readers currently using Internet Explorer 6. Where Internet Explorer 8 has improved features introduced in Internet Explorer 7 (such as upgrading the Phishing Filter with SmartScreen), those improvements are noted.

User Interface Changes

The Internet Explorer user interface has been redesigned to minimize the space required for menus, toolbars, the status bar, and display of Favorites, Feeds, and History. This design allows more screen space for the Web page itself.

Tabbed Browsing

The introduction of tabbed browsing, as shown in Figure 20-7, allows users to keep several Web pages open within a single browser window. Although users could open multiple windows to view different pages simultaneously in previous versions of Internet Explorer, tabbed browsing reduces taskbar clutter.

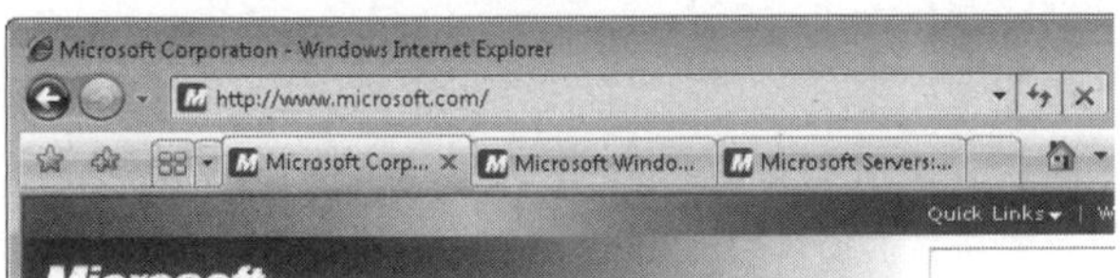

FIGURE 20-7 With tabbed browsing, users can keep multiple Web pages open without opening multiple browsers.

To turn off tabbed browsing, enable the Turn Off Tabbed Browsing Group Policy setting located in User Configuration\Administrative Templates\Windows Components\Internet Explorer\ or Computer Configuration\Administrative Templates\Windows Components\Internet Explorer\. You can also configure Internet Explorer to open pop-up windows in either new windows or new tabs by defining the Turn Off Configuration Of Tabbed Browsing Pop-Up Behavior setting. Finally, you can configure how new tabs open by defining the Turn Off Configuration Of Default Behavior Of New Tab Creation setting.

Search Bar

Beginning with Internet Explorer 7, a Search bar has been added to the toolbar. The Search bar allows users to perform Internet searches from their current windows using a variety of predefined search engines. By default, Internet Explorer 8 is configured to use the Bing search engine. You can also add search engines—including almost any public search engine or even a search engine on your intranet—to the Search bar selection menu.

You can configure other search providers on individual computers by visiting *http://www.microsoft.com/windows/ie/searchguide/*. The sections that follow describe different techniques for configuring computers within your organization.

How to Create a Web Link to Add a Custom Search Provider

You can publish a link on a Web page to allow users to add a custom search engine. First, create an OpenSearch 1.1 Extensible Markup Language (XML) file that describes your search engine. For example, the following XML file describes a search engine that can be used to search the Microsoft.com Web site.

```
<?xml version="1.0" encoding="UTF-8" ?>
<OpenSearchDescription xmlns="http://a9.com/-/spec/opensearch/1.1/">
    <ShortName>Microsoft.com</ShortName>
    <Description>Microsoft.com provider</Description>
    <InputEncoding>UTF-8</InputEncoding>
```

```
    <Url type="text/html"
    template="http://search.microsoft.com/results.aspx?q={searchTerms}" />
</OpenSearchDescription>
```

To create your own OpenSearch XML document, simply replace the *template* attribute in the *<URL>* element with the URL of your search engine, inserting *{searchTerms}* at the location in the URL where search terms appear.

> **NOTE** For detailed information about OpenSearch documents, visit *http://www.opensearch.org/home.*

After you create an OpenSearch XML document, you can allow users to add it from a Web page by using a window.external.AddSearchProvider("*<URL>*") call within a link. When users click the link, they will be prompted to add the search engine. The following example demonstrates the required HTML. (You must replace "*<URL>*" with the location of your OpenSearch XML document.)

```
<a Href="#"
    onClick="window.external.AddSearchProvider(&quot;<URL>&quot;);">Add Search Engine
</a>
```

How to Configure Custom Search Providers Using the Registry

Search providers are stored in the registry in either the HKEY_CURRENT_USER or HKEY_LOCAL_MACHINE hives at Software\Microsoft\Internet Explorer\SearchScopes. To automate the process of adding search providers to computers, use a test computer to configure the search engines manually, including specifying the default search engine. Then, create a .reg file based on this registry key and its subkeys and distribute it to your client computers.

To create a .reg file, follow these steps:

1. To start the Registry Editor, click Start, type **Regedit**, and then press Enter.
2. To configure search engines for individual users, select HKEY_CURRENT_USER \Software\Microsoft\Internet Explorer\SearchScopes. To configure search engines for all users on a computer, select HKEY_LOCAL_MACHINE\Software\Microsoft\Internet Explorer\SearchScopes.
3. Select Export from the File menu. Save the .reg file.

You can now distribute the .reg file to computers in your organization. To configure the search engines, double-click the .reg file to open the Registry Editor and apply the settings. Unfortunately, this requires administrative credentials. If you need to distribute the updated settings without explicitly providing administrative credentials, have a developer create a Windows Installer package that creates the registry values and distribute the Windows Installer package by using Group Policy software distribution.

How to Configure Custom Search Providers Using Group Policy

You can provide a search provider list by using Group Policy settings. However, by default, this policy setting is not available. To include it, you must create administrative template files that update the proper registry keys on client computers. For detailed instructions, read Microsoft Knowledge Base article 918238 at *http://support.microsoft.com/kb/918238*.

If you do not want the Search bar to appear, disable the Prevent The Internet Explorer Search Box From Displaying Group Policy setting in User Configuration\Administrative Templates\Windows Components\Internet Explorer\ or Computer Configuration \Administrative Templates\Windows Components\Internet Explorer\.

How to Use the Internet Explorer Administration Kit to Configure Custom Search Providers

If you plan to use the Internet Explorer Administration Kit (IEAK), you can use that tool to configure search providers. First, configure the computer you are using with the desired search providers. Then, when you reach the Search Providers page, click Import to copy the configured search providers. For more information, see the section titled "Using the Internet Explorer Administration Kit" later in this chapter.

RSS Feeds

Today, Really Simple Syndication (RSS) is used to distribute updates from news sites, blogs, and other regularly updated sources. Internet Explorer 7 and later versions include a new Feed Discovery feature that integrates feed display into the Web browser. With RSS, users can easily keep track of updates to many different Web sites, including intranet sites.

If you have internal blogs or news sites that publish an RSS feed, you can add them to Internet Explorer on the computers in your organization. The easiest way to configure custom feeds is to use the Favorites, Favorites Bar And Feeds page of the IEAK, as shown in Figure 20-8.

Feeds are stored in the %LocalAppData%\Microsoft\Feeds folder. For example, the feeds for a user named Jane using the default file locations is C:\Users\Jane\AppData\Local \Microsoft\Feeds. The FeedsStore.feedsdb-ms file is a set of Object Linking and Embedding (OLE) documents that stores the settings for each feed and the last time each feed was synchronized. The *.feed-ms files are used to cache content downloaded from each feed. To copy a feed to other computers, simply copy the *.feed-ms file.

> ***NOTE*** **Developers: If you want to create a program that views or modifies feeds to Internet Explorer by editing the FeedsStore.feedsdb-ms file, examine the sample program at *http://www.codeproject.com/KB/XML/rssstoreviewer.aspx*.**

You can configure several aspects of RSS feed behavior using Group Policy. Feed-related Group Policy settings are located within both Computer Configuration and User Configuration under Administrative Templates\Windows Components\RSS Feeds.

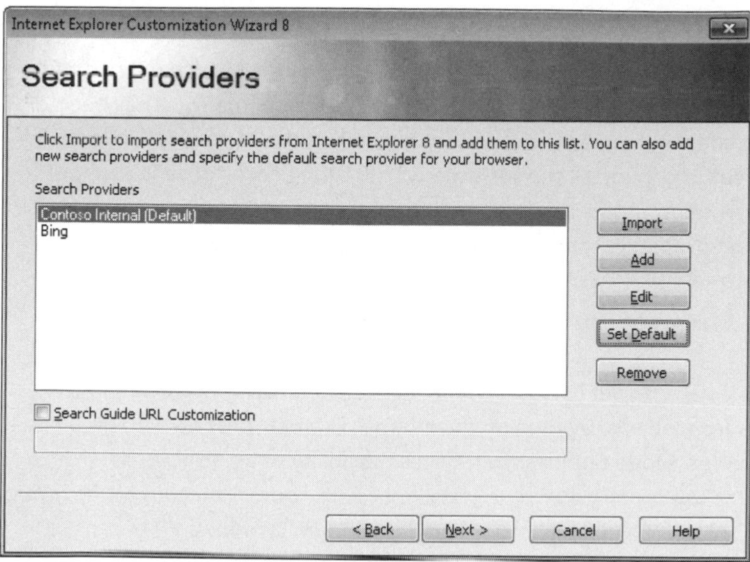

FIGURE 20-8 Use the IEAK to add custom RSS feeds.

Improved Standards Support

Web developers have expressed some frustration with certain peculiarities in the behavior of Internet Explorer 6, especially in the areas of standards support. Beginning with Internet Explorer 7, the browser architecture has been re-engineered to address standards compatibility problems and will offer additional support for popular standards.

- **CSS improvements** CSS is a widely used standard for creating Web pages. Internet Explorer 7 and later versions are prioritizing compliance to CSS standards by first implementing the features that developers have said are most important to them. Microsoft has fixed some positioning and layout issues related to the way in which Internet Explorer 6 handles *<div>* tags.
- **Transparent PNG support** Internet Explorer 7 and later versions support rendering of Portable Network Graphics (PNG) format images, including the optional alpha channel transparency. PNG files use a typographical file format that can include an indication of the exact degree of transparency a picture should have through a measurement called the alpha channel. With an *alpha channel*, designers can use special effects that were not previously supported, such as creating Web page images that have shadows but do not obscure the background image behind them.

Expanded Group Policy Settings

Internet Explorer 7 and later versions include more than 1,200 Group Policy settings, enabling administrators to manage even the smallest aspects of Internet Explorer behavior. For detailed information about Internet Explorer Group Policy settings, read the section titled "Managing Internet Explorer Using Group Policy" later in this chapter.

Defending Against Malware

Malware, a term used to describe malicious software such as spyware and adware, has had a significant negative impact on IT departments in recent years. Often, malware has been distributed through Web sites that either trick users into installing the software or bypass the Web browser's security features to install the software without the user's consent. Internet Explorer 7 has been hardened to reduce the potential for malicious Web sites to compromise a user's browser or the rest of the operating system. The sections that follow describe other improvements that reduce security risks when users browse the Web.

Protected Mode

Beginning with Windows Vista, Internet Explorer 7 and later versions run in Protected Mode, which helps protect users from attacks by running the Internet Explorer process with greatly restricted privileges. Protected Mode significantly reduces the ability of an attacker to write, alter, or destroy data on the user's computer or to install malicious code. Protected Mode is not available when Internet Explorer 7 and later versions are installed on Windows XP because it requires several security features unique to Windows Vista and later operating systems.

HOW PROTECTED MODE IMPROVES SECURITY

When Internet Explorer runs in Protected Mode, Mandatory Integrity Control (MIC), a Windows Vista and later operating systems feature, forces Internet Explorer to be a low-integrity process. MIC does not allow low-integrity processes to gain write access to high-integrity–level objects, such as files and registry keys, in a user's profile or system locations. Low-integrity processes can write only to folders, files, and registry keys that have been assigned a low-integrity MIC access control entry (ACE) known as a *mandatory label.* Table 20-1 describes the different integrity levels.

TABLE 20-1 Mandatory Integrity Control Levels

INTEGRITY ACCESS LEVEL	SYSTEM PRIVILEGES
High	Administrative. Processes can install files to the Program Files folder and write to sensitive registry areas, such as HKEY_LOCAL_MACHINE.
Medium	User. Processes can create and modify files in the user's Documents folder and write to user-specific areas of the registry, such as HKEY_CURRENT_USER. Most files and folders on a computer have a medium-integrity level because any object without a mandatory label has an implied default integrity level of Medium.
Low	Untrusted. Processes can write only to low-integrity locations, such as the Temporary Internet Files\Low folder or the HKEY_CURRENT_USER \Software\Microsoft\Internet Explorer\LowRegistry key.

As a result of being a low-integrity process, Internet Explorer and its extensions run in Protected Mode, which can write only to low-integrity locations, such as the new low-integrity temporary Internet files folder, the History folder, the Cookies folder, the Favorites folder, and the Windows temporary file folders. By preventing unauthorized access to sensitive areas of a user's system, Protected Mode limits the amount of damage that a compromised Internet Explorer process can cause. An attacker cannot, for example, silently install a keystroke logger to the user's startup folder.

Furthermore, the Protected Mode process runs with a low desktop integrity level. Because of User Interface Privilege Isolation (UIPI), a compromised process cannot manipulate applications on the desktop through window messages, thus helping to reduce the risk of *shatter attacks*. Shatter attacks compromise processes with elevated privileges by using window messages.

If a Web page or add-on does require more privileges than provided by Protected Mode or the compatibility layer, it will prompt the user to grant those privileges using User Account Control (UAC). This can occur, for example, if the user needs to install an add-on that requires elevated rights, as shown in Figure 20-9. Most add-ons can run within Protected Mode, however, and loading them will not prompt the user.

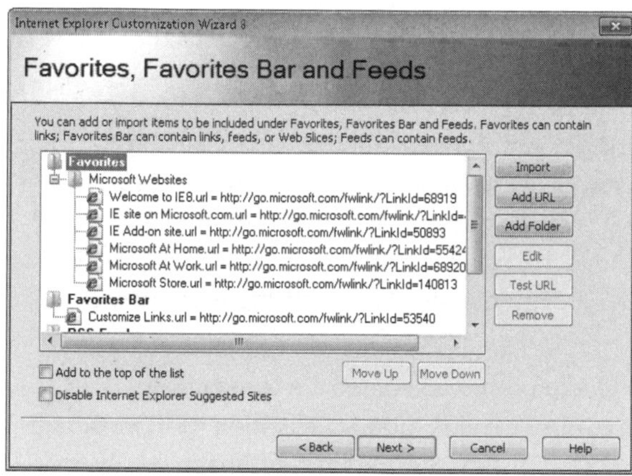

FIGURE 20-9 Internet Explorer protects elevated privileges.

Because Protected Mode also protects extensions, vulnerabilities in extensions, such as buffer overflows, cannot be exploited to access any part of the file system or other operating system object to which Protected Mode does not normally have access. Therefore, the damage that a successful exploit can cause is very limited.

Defense-in-Depth

Protected Mode is not the first line of defense against malware; it's a form of defense-in-depth. Protected Mode offers protection in the event that a malicious Web page successfully bypasses the other security measures of Internet Explorer. In the case of a successful exploit, Protected Mode restricts the processes' privileges to limit the damage that malware can do. In other words, even if your browser gets hacked, Protected Mode might still keep your computer safe.

HOW THE PROTECTED MODE COMPATIBILITY LAYER WORKS

To minimize the impact of the strict security restrictions, Protected Mode provides a compatibility architecture that redirects some requests to protected resources and prompts the user to approve other requests. Figure 20-10 illustrates this behavior.

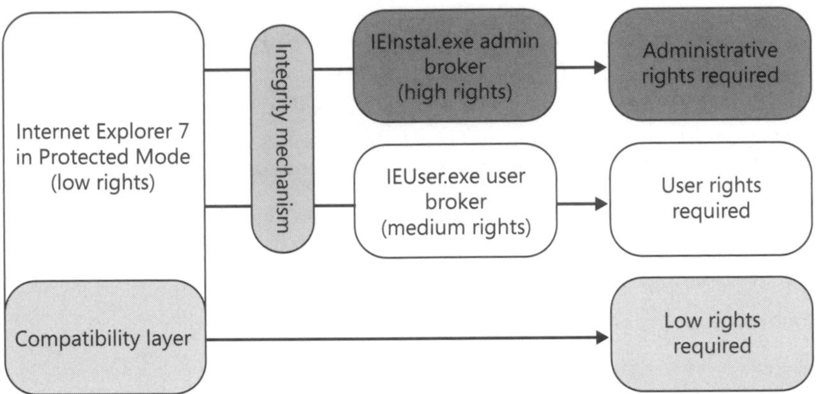

FIGURE 20-10 Internet Explorer Protected Mode provides both security and compatibility.

The *compatibility layer* handles the needs of extensions written for earlier versions of Windows that require access to protected resources by redirecting the requests to safer locations. Specifically, the Documents folder is redirected to \%UserProfile%\AppData\Local\Microsoft\Windows\Temporary Internet Files\Virtualized, and the HKEY_CURRENT_USER registry hive is redirected to HKEY_CURRENT_USER\Software\Microsoft\InternetExplorer\InternetRegistry.

The first time an add-on attempts to write to a protected object, the compatibility layer copies the object and then modifies the copy. After the first modification is made, the compatibility layer forces add-ons to read from the copy. The Internet Explorer compatibility layer virtualization is used instead of the Windows Vista and later operating systems UAC virtualization.

> ***NOTE*** **Add-ons developed for Windows Vista and later operating systems can bypass the compatibility layer to save a file by calling the SaveAs application programming interface (API), so no functionality is lost. To allow the user to select a location to save a file, call *IEShowSaveFileDialog* to prompt the user for a folder and then call *IESaveFile* to write the file. Use *IEGetWriteableFolderPath* and *IEGetWriteableHKCU* to find low-integrity locations to which your add-on can write. To determine whether Protected Mode is active, call the *IEIsProtectedModeProcess* method. For more information, visit *http://msdn.microsoft.com/en-us/library/ms537319.aspx*.**

Two higher-privilege *broker* processes allow Internet Explorer and extensions to perform elevated operations given user consent:

- The User Broker (IEUser.exe) process provides a set of functions that lets the user save files to areas outside of low-integrity areas.
- The Admin Broker (IEInstal.exe) process allows Internet Explorer to install ActiveX controls.

HOW TO SOLVE PROTECTED MODE INCOMPATIBILITIES

Some applications that were designed to work with Internet Explorer 6 might not work with Internet Explorer 7 or later versions on Windows Vista and later operating systems because of restrictions imposed by Protected Mode. Applications that are failing because of Protected Mode have the following characteristics:

- Applications that use Iexplore.exe cannot write directly to disk while in the Internet zone.
- Applications might not know how to handle new Internet Explorer 7 or later versions or Windows Vista or later operating system prompts.

Before upgrading users to Internet Explorer 7 or later versions , whether upgrading the browser on Windows XP or upgrading users to Windows Vista or later operating systems, you need to ensure that critical Web applications still work correctly. Because Internet Explorer has a different rendering engine and higher security, some applications might not work correctly using the standard settings.

If you do identify a compatibility problem, you should enable Compatibility Logging to help you isolate the exact cause of the problem. To enable Compatibility Logging using a Group Policy setting, enable the Turn On Compatibility Logging setting under Computer Configuration\Administrative Templates\Windows Components\Internet Explorer or User Configuration\Administrative Templates\Windows Components\Internet Explorer.

For more information about Compatibility Logging, read "Finding Security Compatibility Issues in Internet Explorer 7" at *http://msdn.microsoft.com/en-us/library/bb250493.aspx*.

After using logging to identify the problem, you might be able to resolve Protected Mode incompatibilities using the following techniques:

- **Add the site in question to the Trusted Sites zone** Sites in the Trusted Sites zone have more privileges than sites in other zones. For more information, read the section titled "Security Zones" later in this chapter.
- **Change the application to handle Protected Mode, including responding to any related prompts that might be displayed** Most applications can run successfully in Protected Mode if they are written to follow Microsoft best practices and use minimal privileges. However, many existing applications might not have been created to follow these guidelines. Work with your developers to design applications for Protected Mode. For more information, read "Understanding and Working in Protected Mode Internet Explorer" at *http://msdn.microsoft.com/en-us/library/bb250462.aspx*.

- **Disable Protected Mode (not recommended)** Protected Mode is an important security feature that can reduce the damage caused by malicious sites and malware. If Protected Mode is causing problems that cost you more than the security improvements benefit you, you can disable Protected Mode for individual security zones. To disable Protected Mode, open the Internet Options dialog box, click the Security tab, select the zone, and clear the Enable Protected Mode check box. Then restart Internet Explorer. Protected Mode is disabled by default for the Trusted Sites zone. You can also disable Protected Mode using the Group Policy setting named Turn On Protected Mode. For more information, read the section titled "Security Zones" later in this chapter.

NOTE **If you disable Protected Mode, Internet Explorer runs at the medium-integrity level.**

To confirm compatibility with key Web applications, use the Microsoft Application Compatibility Toolkit (ACT). For more information about the ACT, visit *http://technet.microsoft.com/en-us/windows/aa905066.aspx*. In addition to the ACT, the Internet Explorer 8 Readiness Toolkit has detailed information and tools to identify and resolve compatibility issues. To download the Internet Explorer 8 Readiness Toolkit, visit *http://www.microsoft.com/windows/internet-explorer/readiness/developers.aspx*. For more information about Web page problems caused by security settings, read "Finding Security Compatibility Issues in Internet Explorer 7" at *http://msdn.microsoft.com/en-us/library/bb250493.aspx*.

Windows Defender

Extending the protections against malware at the browser level, Windows Defender helps prevent malware from entering the computer via a "piggyback" download, a common mechanism by which spyware is distributed and installed silently along with other applications. Although the improvements in Internet Explorer 7 cannot stop non-browser–based spyware from infecting the computer, using it with Windows Defender will provide a solid defense on several levels. For more information about Windows Defender, read Chapter 24, "Managing Client Protection."

URL-Handling Protection

Historically, many browser-based attacks used intentionally malformed URLs to perform a buffer overflow attack and execute malicious code. Internet Explorer 7 benefits from these experiences and the analysis of attack signatures. Microsoft drastically reduced the internal attack surface of Internet Explorer 7 by rewriting certain sections of the code and by defining a single function to process URL data. This new data handler ensures higher reliability and provides better features and flexibility to address the changing nature of the Internet, URL formats, domain names, and international character sets.

HOW IT WORKS

Buffer Overflow Attacks

A buffer overflow (also known as a buffer overrun) occurs when an application attempts to store too much data in a buffer, and memory not allocated to the buffer is overwritten. A particularly crafty attacker can even provide data that instructs the operating system to run the attacker's malicious code with the application's privileges.

One of the most common types of buffer overflows is the stack overflow. To understand how this attack is used, you must first understand how applications normally store variables and other information on the stack. Figure 20-11 shows a simplified example of how a C console application might store the contents of a variable on the stack. In this example, the string "Hello" is passed to the application and is stored in the variable *argv[1]*. In the context of a Web browser, the input would be a URL instead of the word "Hello."

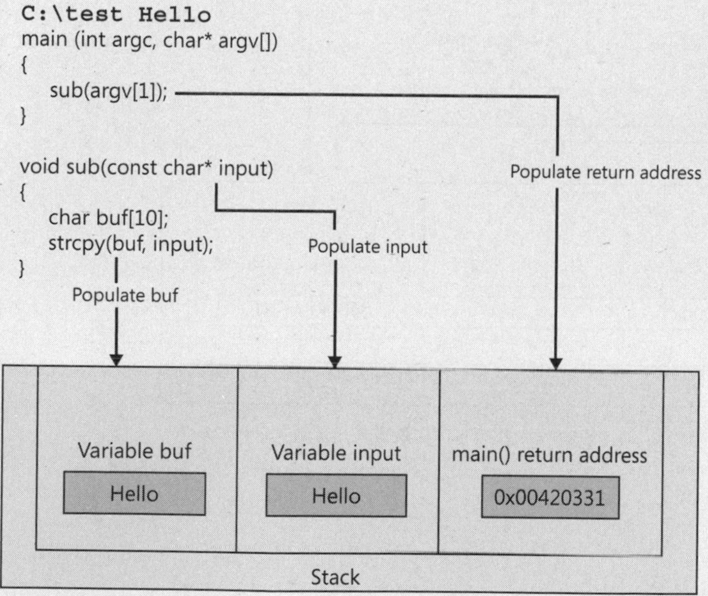

FIGURE 20-11 A simple illustration of normal stack operations

Notice that the first command-line parameter passed to the application is ultimately copied into a 10-character array named *buf*. While the program runs, it stores information temporarily on the stack, including the return address where processing should continue after the subroutine has completed and the variable is passed to the subroutine. The application works fine when fewer than 10 characters are passed to it. However, passing more than 10 characters will result in a buffer overflow.

Figure 20-12 shows that same application being deliberately attacked by providing input longer than 10 characters. When the line strcpy(buf, input); is run, the application attempts to store the string "hello-aaaaaaaa0066ACB1" into the 10-character array named *buf*. Because the input is too long, the input overwrites the contents of other information on the stack, including the stored address that the program will use to return control to main(). After the subroutine finishes running, the processor returns to the address stored in the stack. Because it has been modified, execution begins at memory address 0x0066ACB1, where the attacker has presumably stored malicious code. This code will run with the same privilege as the original application. After all, the operating system thinks the application called the code.

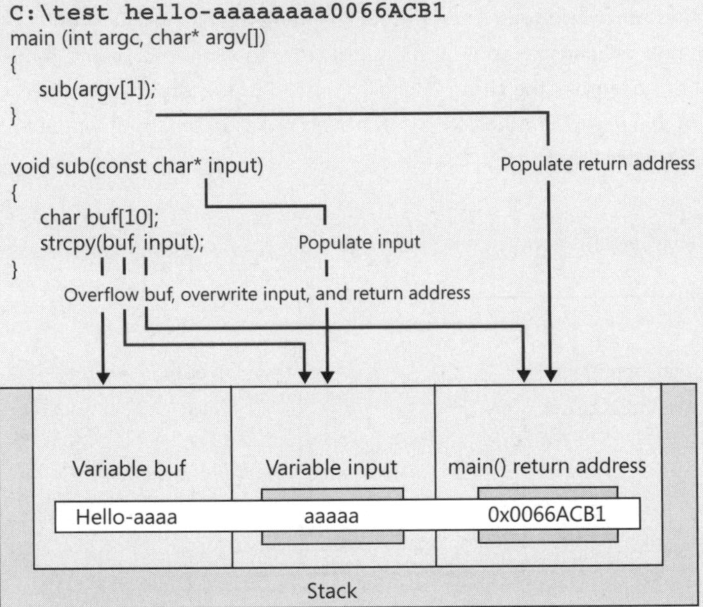

FIGURE 20-12 A simplified buffer overflow attack that redirects execution

Address Bar Visibility

Attackers commonly rely on misleading users into thinking they are looking at information from a known and trusted source. One way attackers have done this in the past is to hide the true URL information and domain name from users by providing specially crafted URLs that appear to be from different Web sites.

To help limit this type of attack, all Internet Explorer 7 and later browser windows now require an address bar. Attackers often have abused valid pop-up window actions to display windows with misleading graphics and data as a way to convince users to download or install their malware. Requiring an address bar in each window ensures that users always know more about the true source of the information they are seeing.

Cross-Domain Scripting Attack Protection

Cross-domain scripting attacks involve a script from one Internet domain manipulating content from another domain. For example, a user might visit a malicious page that opens a new window containing a legitimate page (such as a banking Web site) and prompts the user to enter account information, which is then extracted by the attacker.

Internet Explorer 7 helps to deter this malicious behavior by appending the domain name from which each script originates and by limiting that script's ability to interact only with windows and content from that same domain. These cross-domain scripting barriers help ensure that user information remains in the hands of only those to whom the user intentionally provides it. This new control will further protect against malware by limiting the potential for a malicious Web site to manipulate flaws in other Web sites and initiate the download of some undesired content to a user's computer.

Controlling Browser Add-ons

Browser add-ons can add important capabilities to Web browsers. Unreliable add-ons can also reduce browser stability, however. Even worse, malicious add-ons can compromise private information. Internet Explorer 7 provides several enhancements to give you control over the add-ons run by your users. The sections that follow describe these enhancements.

INTERNET EXPLORER ADD-ONS DISABLED MODE

Internet Explorer 7 includes the No Add-ons mode, which allows Internet Explorer to run temporarily without any toolbars, ActiveX controls, or other add-ons. Functionality in this mode reproduces that of manually disabling all add-ons in the Add-on Manager, and it is very useful if you are troubleshooting a problem that might be related to an add-on.

To disable add-ons using the Add-ons Disabled mode, follow these steps:

1. Open the Start menu and point to All Programs.
2. Point to Accessories, click System Tools, and then click Internet Explorer (No Add-ons).
3. Note the Information bar display in your browser indicating that add-ons are disabled, as shown in Figure 20-13.

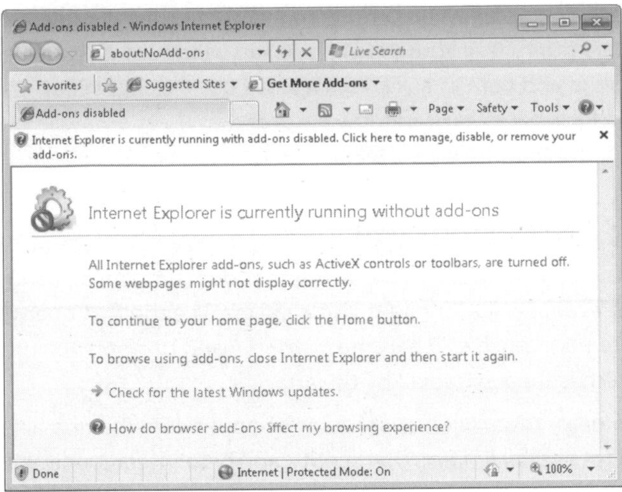

FIGURE 20-13 You can disable add-ons to troubleshoot Internet Explorer problems.

Running Internet Explorer from the standard Start menu shortcut will return the functionality to its prior state.

ADD-ON MANAGER IMPROVEMENTS

The Add-on Manager provides a simple interface that lists installed add-ons, add-ons that are loaded when Internet Explorer starts, and all add-ons that Internet Explorer has ever used. By reviewing these lists, you can determine which add-ons are enabled or disabled and disable or enable each item by simply clicking the corresponding item.

To disable specific add-ons, follow these steps:

1. In your browser, open the Tools menu, select Manage Add-ons, and then click Enable Or Disable Add-ons.
2. Click the Show list and select the set of add-ons that you want to manage.
3. Select the add-on that you want to disable, as shown in Figure 20-14, and then click Disable.
4. Click OK to close the Manage Add-ons dialog box.

In troubleshooting scenarios, disable add-ons one by one until the problem stops occurring.

CONTROLLING ADD-ONS USING GROUP POLICY

As with earlier versions of Internet Explorer, you can use the Group Policy settings in User Configuration\Administrative Templates\Windows Components\Internet Explorer \Security Features\Add-on Management to enable or disable specific add-ons throughout your organization.

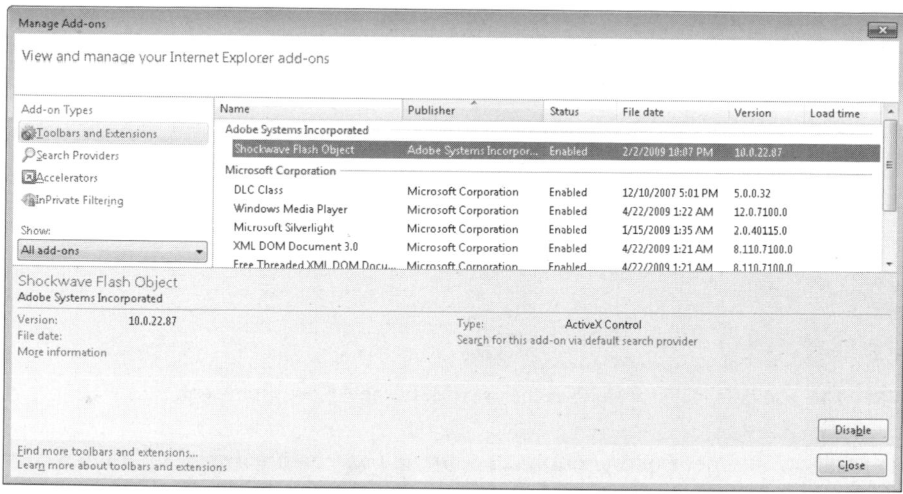

FIGURE 20-14 The Manage Add-ons dialog box makes it easy to disable problematic add-ons.

Protecting Against Data Theft

Most users are unaware of how much personal, traceable data is available with every click of the mouse while they browse the Web. The extent of this information continues to grow as browser developers and Web site operators evolve their technologies to enable more powerful and convenient user features. Similarly, most online users are likely to have trouble discerning a valid Web site from a fake or malicious copy. As described in the following sections, Internet Explorer provides several features to help give users the information they need to determine whether a site is legitimate.

Security Status Bar

Although many users have become quite familiar with Secure Sockets Layer (SSL) and its associated security benefits, a large proportion of Internet users remain overly trusting that any Web site asking for their confidential information is protected. Internet Explorer 7 addresses this issue by providing clear and prominent visual cues to the safety and trustworthiness of a Web site.

Previous versions of Internet Explorer place a gold padlock icon in the lower-right corner of the browser window to designate the trust and security level of the connected Web site. Given the importance and inherent trust value associated with the gold padlock, Internet Explorer 7 and later versions display a Security Status bar at the top of the browser window to highlight such warnings. By clicking this lock, users can quickly view the Web site identification information, as shown in Figure 20-15.

FIGURE 20-15 The gold lock that signifies the use of SSL is now more prominent.

In addition, Internet Explorer displays a warning page before displaying a site with an invalid certificate, as shown in Figure 20-16.

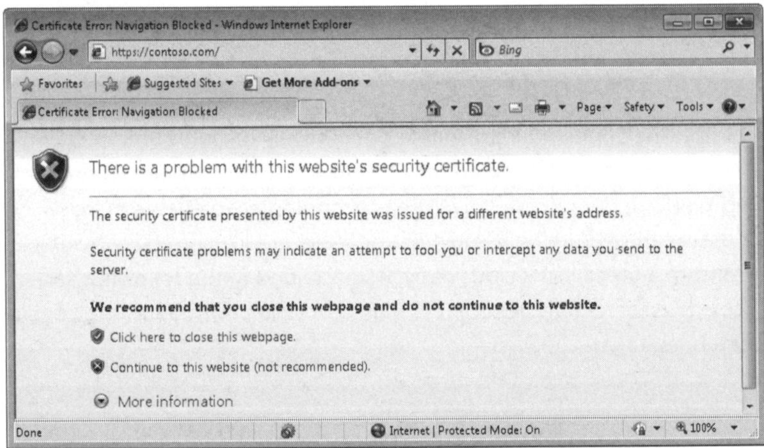

FIGURE 20-16 Internet Explorer warns users about invalid certificates.

Finally, if a user continues on to visit a site with an invalid certificate, the address bar, shown in Figure 20-17, now appears on a red background.

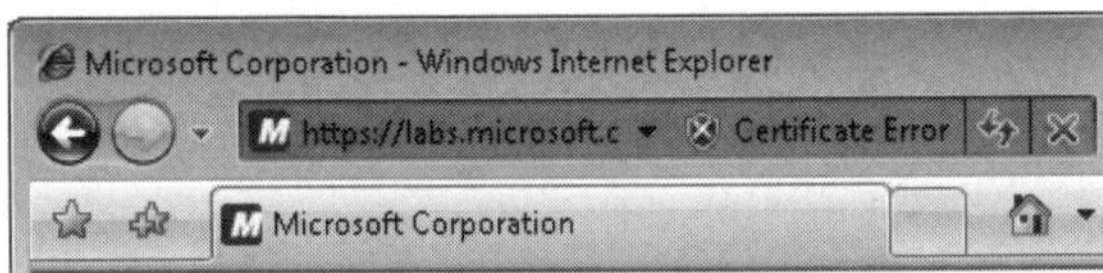

FIGURE 20-17 The red background leaves no doubt that the site's SSL certificate has a problem.

Phishing

Phishing—a technique used by many malicious Web site operators to gather personal information—is the practice of masquerading online as a legitimate business to acquire private information, such as social security numbers or credit card numbers. These fake Web sites, designed to look like the legitimate sites, are referred to as *spoofed* Web sites. The number of phishing Web sites is constantly growing, and the Anti-Phishing Working Group received reports of more than 10,000 different phishing sites in August 2006 that were attempting to hijack 148 different Web sites.

> ***NOTE*** **For more information about the Anti-Phishing Working Group, visit *http://www.antiphishing.org/*.**

Unlike direct attacks, in which attackers break into a system to obtain account information, a phishing attack does not require technical sophistication but instead relies on users willingly divulging information, such as financial account passwords or social security numbers. These socially engineered attacks are among the most difficult to defend against because they require user education and understanding rather than merely issuing an update for an application. Even experienced professionals can be fooled by the quality and details of some phishing Web sites as attackers become more experienced and learn to react more quickly to avoid detection.

HOW THE SMARTSCREEN FILTER WORKS

Phishing and other malicious activities thrive on lack of communication and limited sharing of information. To effectively provide anti-phishing warning systems and protection, the new SmartScreen filter in Internet Explorer 8 consolidates the latest industry information about the ever-growing number of fraudulent Web sites spawned every day in an online service that is updated several times an hour. SmartScreen feeds this information back to warn and help protect Internet Explorer 8 customers proactively.

SmartScreen is designed around the principle that an effective early-warning system must ensure that information is derived dynamically and updated frequently. This system combines client-side scanning for suspicious Web site characteristics with an opt-in Phishing Filter that uses three checks to help protect users from phishing:

- Compares addresses of Web sites a user attempts to visit with a list of reported legitimate sites stored on the user's computer
- Analyzes sites that users want to visit by checking those sites for characteristics common to phishing sites
- Sends Web site addresses to a Microsoft online service for comparison to a frequently updated list of reported phishing sites

The service checks a requested URL against a list of known, trusted Web sites. If a Web site is a suspected phishing site, Internet Explorer 8 displays a yellow button labeled Suspicious Website in the address bar. The user can then click the button to view a more detailed warning.

If a Web site is a known phishing site, Internet Explorer 8 displays a warning with a red status bar. If the user chooses to ignore the warnings and continue to the Web site, the status bar remains red and prominently displays the Phishing Website message in the address bar, as shown in Figure 20-18.

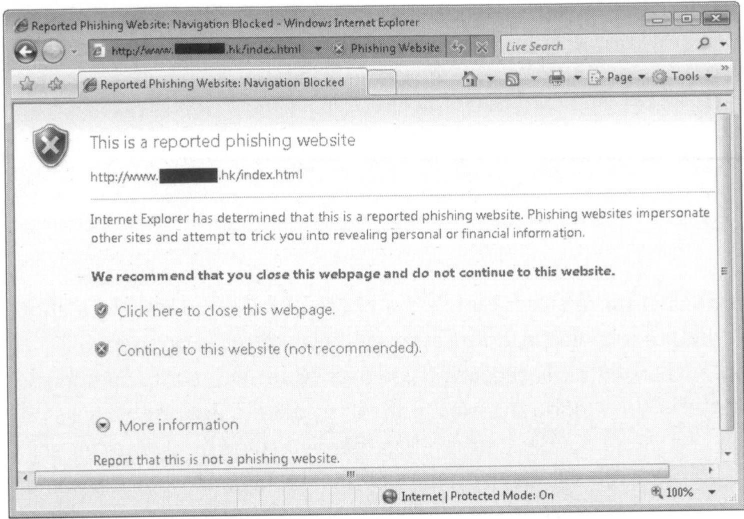

FIGURE 20-18 Internet Explorer can detect phishing Web sites and warn users before they visit them.

Internet Explorer first checks a Web site against a *legitimate list* (also known as an *allow list*) of sites stored on your local computer. This legitimate list is generated by Microsoft based on Web sites that have been reported as legitimate. If the Web site is on the legitimate list, the Web site is considered safe, and no further checking is done. If the site is not on the legitimate list or if the site appears suspicious based on heuristics, Internet Explorer can use two techniques to determine whether a Web site might be a phishing Web site:

- **Local analysis** Internet Explorer examines the Web page for patterns and phrases that indicate it might be a malicious site. Local analysis provides some level of protection against new phishing sites that are not yet listed in the online list. Additionally, local analysis can help protect users who have disabled online lookup.
- **Online lookup** Internet Explorer sends the URL to Microsoft, where it is checked against a list of known phishing sites. This list is updated regularly.

When you use SmartScreen to check Web sites automatically or manually (by selecting SmartScreen Filter from the Tools menu and then clicking Check This Website), the address of the Web site you are visiting is sent to Microsoft (specifically, to *https://urs.microsoft.com*, using TCP port 443), together with some standard information from your computer such as IP address, browser type, and SmartScreen version number. To help protect your privacy, the information sent to Microsoft is encrypted using SSL and is limited to the domain and path of the Web site. Other information that might be associated with the address, such as search terms, data you enter in forms, or cookies, will not be sent.

NOTE Looking up a Web site in the online Phishing Filter can require transferring 8 KB of data or more. Most of the 8 KB is required to set up the encrypted HTTPS connection. The Phishing Filter will send a request only once for each domain you visit within a specific period of time. However, a single Web page can have objects stored in multiple servers, resulting in multiple requests. Requests for different Web pages require separate HTTPS sessions.

For example, if you visit the Bing search Web site at *http://www.bing.com* and enter **MySecret** as the search term, instead of sending the full address *http://www.bing.com/search?q=MySecret&FORM=QBLH*, SmartScreen removes the search term and only sends *http://www.bing.com/search*. Address strings might unintentionally contain personal information, but this information is not used to identify you or contact you. If users are concerned that an address string might contain personal or confidential information, users should not report the site. For more information, read the Internet Explorer 8 privacy statement at *http://www.microsoft.com/windows/internet-explorer/privacy.aspx*.

DIRECT FROM THE SOURCE

Real-Time Checking for Phishing Sites

Rob Franco, Lead Program Manager
Federated Identity Group

Readers asked why we decided to use real-time lookups against the anti-phishing server as opposed to an intermittent download list of sites in the way that an antispyware product might. We included real-time checking for phishing sites because it offers better protection than using only static lists and avoids overloading networks.

SmartScreen does have an intermittently downloaded list of "known-safe" sites, but we know phishing attacks can strike quickly and move to new addresses, often within a 24- to 48-hour time period, which is faster than we can practically push out updates to a list of "known-phishing" sites. Even if SmartScreen downloaded a list of phishing sites 24 times a day, you might not be protected against a confirmed, known phishing site for an hour at a time, at any time of day.

Because SmartScreen checks unknown sites in real time, you always have the latest intelligence. Requiring users to constantly download a local list can also cause network scale problems. We think the number of computers that can be used to launch phishing attacks is much higher than the number of spyware signatures that users deal with today. In a scenario in which phishing threats move rapidly, downloading a list of newly reported phishing sites every hour could significantly clog Internet traffic.

Anonymous statistics about your usage will also be sent to Microsoft, such as the time and total number of Web sites browsed since an address was sent to Microsoft for analysis. This information, along with the information described earlier, will be used to analyze the performance and improve the quality of the SmartScreen service. Microsoft will not use the information it receives to personally identify you. Some URLs that are sent may be saved to be included in the legitimate list and then provided as client updates. When saving this information, additional information—including the SmartScreen and operating system version and your browser language—will be saved.

Although the online list of phishing sites is regularly updated, users might find a phishing site that is not yet on the list. Users can help Microsoft identify a potentially malicious site by reporting it. Within Internet Explorer 8, select SmartScreen Filter from the Tools menu and then click Report Unsafe Website. Users are then taken to a simple form they can submit to inform Microsoft of the site.

HOW TO CONFIGURE SMARTSCREEN OPTIONS

To enable or disable SmartScreen, follow these steps:

1. In your browser, open the Tools menu and select Internet Options.
2. In the Internet Options dialog box, click the Advanced tab, scroll down to the Security group in the Settings list, and then select or clear the Enable SmartScreen Filter check box.

You can use the following Group Policy settings to configure whether users need to configure the SmartScreen filter:

- Computer Configuration\Administrative Templates\Windows Components\Internet Explorer\Turn Off Managing SmartScreen Filter
- User Configuration\Administrative Templates\Windows Components\Internet Explorer \Turn Off Managing SmartScreen Filter

If you enable the setting, you can choose to enable or disable SmartScreen. Additionally, in the same group, you can enable the Prevent Bypassing SmartScreen Filter Warnings policy.

DIRECT FROM THE SOURCE

Anti-Phishing Accuracy Study

Tony Chor, Group Program Manager
Internet Explorer Product Team

As we worked on the new Phishing Filter in Internet Explorer 7, we knew the key measure would be how effective it is in protecting customers. In addition to our internal tests, we wanted to find some external measure of our progress to date as well as point to ways we could improve. We didn't know of a publicly available study covering the area, only some internal and media product reviews.

To help us answer this question, we asked 3Sharp LLC to conduct a study of the Phishing Filter in Internet Explorer 7 along with seven other products designed to protect against phishing threats. 3Sharp LLC tested these eight browser-based products to evaluate their overall accuracy in catching 100 live, confirmed phishing Web sites over a six-week period (May through July 2006) and also to understand the false-positive error rate on 500 good sites. We were pleased to see that the Phishing Filter in Internet Explorer 7 finished at the top of 3Sharp's list as the most accurate anti-phishing technology, catching nearly 9 of 10 phishing sites while generating no warning or block errors on the 500 legitimate Web sites tested.

It's great to see so many companies looking for different ways to address the significant problem of phishing. We think that the results reported by 3Sharp validate the unique approach we've taken of combining a service-backed block list with client-side heuristics. That said, we understand that the threat posed by phishing is constantly evolving, as are the tools designed to protect users. This set of results represents only the relative performance during that period. We know we need to keep working to keep up with the changes in the attacks, and we are already using the results of this test to further improve the efficacy of the Phishing Filter.

Deleting Browsing History

Browsers store many traces of the sites users visit, including cached copies of pages and images, passwords, and cookies. If a user is accessing confidential information or authenticated Web sites from a shared computer, the user might be able to use the stored copies of the Web site to access private data. To simplify removing these traces, Internet Explorer 7 provides a Delete Browsing History option that allows users to initiate cleanup with one button, easily and instantly erasing personal data.

To delete your browsing history, follow these steps:

1. In your browser, open the Tools menu and select Internet Options.
2. In the Internet Options dialog box on the General tab, click Delete in the Browsing History group.
3. In the Delete Browsing History dialog box, shown in Figure 20-19, select only the objects you need to remove.

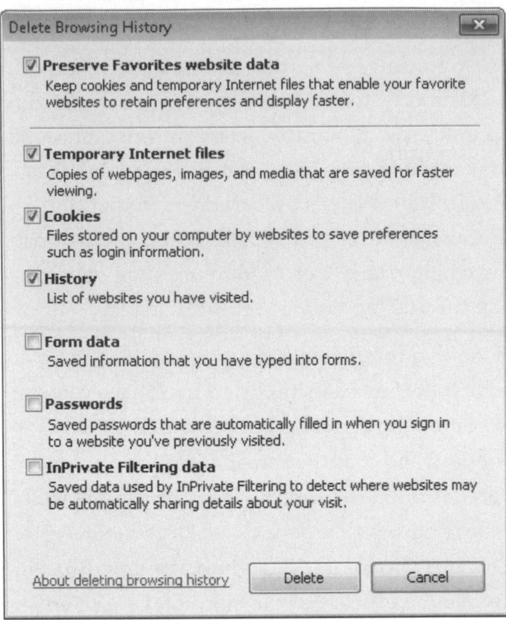

FIGURE 20-19 The Delete Browsing History dialog box provides a single interface for removing confidential remnants from browsing the Web.

If you don't want users to be able to delete their browsing history, form data, or passwords, you can enable the Group Policy settings located in both Computer Configuration \Administrative Templates\Windows Components\Internet Explorer\Delete Browsing History and User Configuration\Administrative Templates\Windows Components\Internet Explorer \Delete Browsing History.

Blocking IDN Spoofing

Look-alike attacks (sometimes called *homograph* attacks) are possible within the ASCII character set. For example, www.alpineskihouse.com would be a valid name for Alpine Ski House, but www.a1pineskihouse.com would be easily mistaken for the valid name—even though the lowercase L has been replaced with the number 1. However, with International Domain Name (IDN), the character repertoire expands from a few dozen characters to many thousands of characters from all the world's languages, thereby increasing the attack surface for spoofing attacks immensely.

The design of the anti-spoofing mitigation for IDN aims to:

- Reduce the attack surface.
- Treat Unicode domain names fairly.
- Offer a good user experience for users worldwide.
- Offer simple, logical options with which the user can fine-tune the IDN experience.

One of the ways Internet Explorer reduces this risk is by using Punycode. *Punycode*, as defined in RFC 3492, converts Unicode domain names into a limited character set. With Punycode, the domain name soüth.contoso.com (which might be used to impersonate south.contoso.com) becomes soth-kva.contoso.com. There is little doubt that showing the Punycode form leaves no ground for spoofing using the full range of Unicode characters. However, Punycode is not very user friendly.

Given these considerations, Internet Explorer 7 and later versions impose restrictions on the character sets allowed to be displayed inside the address bar. These restrictions are based on the user's configured browser-language settings. Using APIs from Idndl.dll, Internet Explorer will detect which character sets are used by the current domain name. If the domain name contains characters outside the user's chosen languages, it is displayed in Punycode form to help prevent spoofing.

A domain name is displayed in Punycode if any of the following are true:

- The domain name contains characters that are not a part of any language (such as www.☺.com).
- Any of the domain name's labels contains a mix of scripts that do not appear together within a single language. For instance, Greek characters cannot mix with Cyrillic within a single label.
- Any of the domain name's labels contain characters that appear only in languages other than the user's list of chosen languages. Note that ASCII-only labels are always permitted for compatibility with existing sites. A label is a segment of a domain name, delimited by dots. For example, www.microsoft.com contains three labels: www, microsoft, and com. Different languages are allowed to appear in different labels as long as all the languages are in the list chosen by the user. This approach is used to support domain names such as name.contoso.com, where contoso and name are composed of different languages.

Whenever Internet Explorer 7 and later versions prevent an IDN domain name from displaying in Unicode, an Information bar notifies the user that the domain name contains characters that Internet Explorer is not configured to display. It is easy to use the IDN Information bar to add additional languages to the allow list. By default, the user's list of languages will usually contain only the currently configured Microsoft Windows language.

The language-aware mitigation does two things:

- It disallows nonstandard combinations of scripts from being displayed inside a label. This takes care of attacks such as *http://bank.contoso.com*, which appears to use a single script but actually contains two scripts. That domain name will always be displayed as *http://xn--bnk-sgz.contoso.com* because two scripts (Cyrillic and Latin) are mixed inside a label. This reduces the attack surface to single-language attacks.
- It further reduces the surface attack for single-language attacks to only those users who have chosen to permit the target language.

Users who allow Greek in their language settings, for example, are as susceptible to Greek-only spoofs as the population using English is susceptible to pure ASCII-based spoofs. To protect against such occurrences, the Internet Explorer 7 Phishing Filter monitors both Unicode and ASCII URLs. If the user has opted in to the Phishing Filter, a real-time check is performed during navigation to see whether the target domain name is a reported phishing site. If so, navigation is blocked. For additional defense-in-depth, the Phishing Filter Web service can apply additional heuristics to determine whether the domain name is visually ambiguous. If so, the Phishing Filter will warn the user via the indicator in the Internet Explorer address bar.

Whenever a user is viewing a site addressed by an IDN, an indicator will appear in the Internet Explorer Address bar to notify the user that IDN is in use. The user can click the IDN indicator to view more information about the current domain name. Users who do not want to see Unicode addresses may select the Always Show Encoded Addresses check box on the Advanced tab of the Internet Options dialog box.

Security Zones

Web applications are capable of doing almost anything a standard Windows application can do, including interacting with the desktop, installing software, and changing your computer's settings. However, if Web browsers allowed Web sites to take these types of actions, some Web sites would abuse the capabilities to install malware or perform other malicious acts on computers.

To reduce this risk, Internet Explorer limits the actions that Web sites on the Internet can take. However, these limitations can cause problems for Web sites that legitimately need elevated privileges. For example, your users might need to visit an internal Web site that uses an unsigned ActiveX control. Enabling unsigned ActiveX controls for all Web sites is very dangerous, however.

Understanding Zones

To provide optimal security for untrusted Web sites while allowing elevated privileges for trusted Web sites, Internet Explorer provides multiple security zones:

- **Internet** All Web sites that are not listed in the trusted or restricted zones. Sites in this zone are restricted from viewing private information on your computer (including cookies or temporary files from other Web sites) and cannot make permanent changes to your computer.
- **Local Intranet** Web sites on your intranet. Internet Explorer can detect automatically whether a Web site is on your intranet. Additionally, you can add Web sites manually to this zone.
- **Trusted Sites** Web sites that administrators have added to the Trusted Sites list because they require elevated privileges. Trusted Sites do not use Protected Mode, which could introduce security weaknesses. Therefore, you need to select the Web sites added to the Trusted Sites zone carefully. You don't need to add all sites you trust

to this zone; instead, you should add only sites that you trust *and* that cannot work properly in the Internet or intranet zones. By default, this zone is empty.

- **Restricted Sites** Web sites that might be malicious and should be restricted from performing any potentially dangerous actions. You need to use this zone only if you plan to visit a potentially malicious Web site and you need to minimize the risk of a security compromise. By default, this zone is empty.

> ***NOTE*** **When moving from a trusted site to an untrusted site or vice versa, Internet Explorer warns the user and opens a new window. This reduces the risk of users accidentally trusting a malicious site.**

Configuring Zones on the Local Computer

You can configure the exact privileges assigned to each of these security zones by following these steps:

1. Select Internet Options from the Tools menu.
2. In the Internet Options dialog box, click the Security tab.
3. Click the zone you want to modify. In the Security Level For This Zone group, move the slider up to increase security and decrease risks, or move the slider down to increase privileges and increase security risks for Web sites in that zone. For more precise control over individual privileges, click Custom Level. To return to the default settings, click Default Level.
4. Click OK to apply your settings.

> ***NOTE*** **Application developers can use the *IInternetSecurityManager::SetZoneMapping()* method to add sites to specific security zones.**

To configure the Web sites that are part of the Local Intranet, Trusted Sites, or Restricted Sites zone, follow these steps:

1. In Internet Explorer, visit the Web page that you want to configure.
2. Select Internet Options from the Tools menu.
3. In the Internet Options dialog box, click the Security tab.
4. Click the zone you want to modify and then click Sites.
5. If you are adding sites to the Local Intranet zone, click Advanced.
6. If you are adding a site to the Trusted Sites zone and the Web site does not support HTTPS, clear the Require Server Verification (HTTPS:) For All Sites In This Zone check box.
7. Click Add to add the current Web site to the list of Trusted Sites. Then click Close.

8. Click OK to close the Internet Options dialog box. Then close Internet Explorer, reopen it, and visit the Web page again. If the problem persists, repeat these steps to remove the site from the Trusted Sites zone. Continue reading this section for more troubleshooting guidance.

You need to add sites to a zone only if they cause problems in their default zone. For more information, read the section titled "Troubleshooting Internet Explorer Problems" later in this chapter.

Configuring Zones Using Group Policy

To manage security zones in an enterprise, use the Group Policy settings located at \Administrative Templates\Windows Components\Internet Explorer\Internet Control Panel \Security Page under both Computer Configuration and User Configuration. Using these settings, you can configure the exact rights applied to each zone. To assign a standard security level (Low, Medium Low, Medium, Medium High, or High) to a zone, enable one of the following settings:

- Internet Zone Template
- Intranet Zone Template
- Local Machine Zone Template
- Restricted Sites Zone Template
- Trusted Sites Zone Template

If none of the standard security levels provides the exact security settings you need, you can edit the settings in the appropriate zone's node within the Security Page node. In particular, notice the Turn On Protected Mode setting located in each zone's node.

To specify that a URL is part of a specific zone, enable the Site To Zone Assignment List setting in the Security Page node. After you have enabled a URL, you can assign it (using the *Value Name* field, with an optional protocol) to a specific zone (using the *Value* field) using the zone's number:

- 1: Local Intranet zone
- 2: Trusted Sites zone
- 3: Internet zone
- 4: Restricted Sites zone

For example, Figure 20-20 shows the Group Policy setting configured to place any requests to *contoso.com* (regardless of the protocol) in the Restricted Sites zone (a value of 4). Requests to *www.fabrikam.com*, using either HTTP or HTTPS, are placed in the Intranet zone (a value of 1). HTTPS requests to *www.microsoft.com* are placed in the Trusted Sites zone (a value of 2). In addition to domain names, you can specify IP addresses, such as 192.168.1.1, or IP address ranges, such as 192.168.1.1-192.168.1.200.

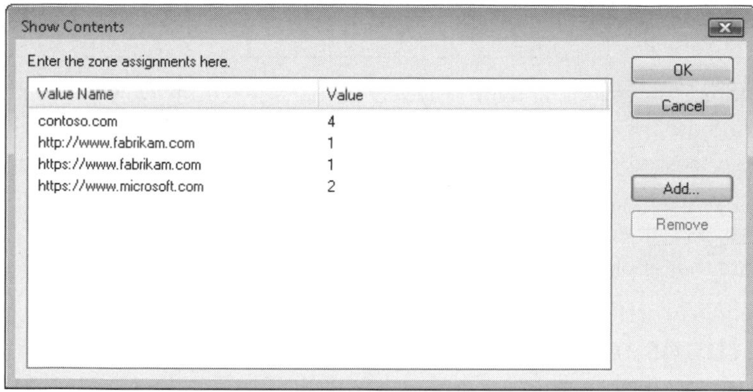

FIGURE 20-20 Use the Site To Zone Assignment List setting to override security zone assignment for specific URLs.

Network Protocol Lockdown

Sometimes you might want to apply different security settings to specific protocols within a zone. For example, you might want to configure Internet Explorer to lock down HTML content hosted on the Shell: protocol if it is in the Internet zone. Because the Shell: protocol's most common use is for local content and not Internet content, this mitigation can reduce the attack surface of the browser against possible vulnerabilities in protocols less commonly used than HTTP.

By default, Network Protocol Lockdown is not enabled, and this setting is sufficient for most environments. If you choose to create a highly restrictive desktop environment, you might want to use Network Protocol Lockdown to mitigate security risks. Configuring Network Protocol Lockdown is a two-phase process, as follows:

- **Configure the protocols that will be locked down for each zone** Enable the Group Policy setting for the appropriate zone and specify the protocols that you want to lock down. The Group Policy settings are located in both User Configuration and Computer Configuration under Administrative Templates\Windows Components\Internet Explorer\Security Features\Network Protocol Lockdown\Restricted Protocols Per Security Zone.
- **Configure the security settings for the locked-down zones** Enable the Group Policy setting for the zone and specify a restrictive template or configure individual security settings. The Group Policy settings are located in both User Configuration and Computer Configuration under Administrative Templates\Windows Components\Internet Explorer\Security Page\.

Managing Internet Explorer Using Group Policy

Internet Explorer has hundreds of settings, and the only way to manage it effectively in an enterprise environment is to use the more than 1,300 settings that Group Policy provides. Besides the security settings discussed earlier in this chapter, you can use dozens of other Group Policy settings to configure almost any aspect of Internet Explorer. The sections that follow describe Group Policy settings that apply to Internet Explorer 7 (which also apply to Internet Explorer 8), as well as those that apply only to Internet Explorer 8.

Group Policy Settings for Internet Explorer 7 and Internet Explorer 8

Table 20-2 shows some examples of the more useful settings that apply to both Internet Explorer 7 and Internet Explorer 8. Settings marked as CC can be found at Computer Configuration\Administrative Templates\Windows Components\Internet Explorer\. Settings marked as UC can be found at User Configuration\Administrative Templates \Windows Components\Internet Explorer\.

TABLE 20-2 Group Policy Settings for Internet Explorer 7 and Internet Explorer 8

SETTING	CC	UC	DESCRIPTION
Add A Specific List Of Search Providers To The User's Search Provider List	✓	✓	With the help of custom registry settings or a custom administrative template, you can configure custom search providers that will be accessible from the Search toolbar.
Turn Off Crash Detection	✓	✓	Allows you to disable Crash Detection, which automatically disables problematic add-ons. Enable this setting only if you have an internal add-on that is unreliable but still required.
Do Not Allow Users To Enable Or Disable Add-ons	✓	✓	Enable this setting to disable the Add-on Manager.
Turn On Menu Bar By Default	✓	✓	By default, Internet Explorer 7 does not display a menu bar. Users can display the menu bar by pressing the Alt key. Enable this setting to display the menu bar by default.
Disable Caching Of Auto-Proxy Scripts		✓	If you use scripts to configure proxy settings, you can use this setting if you experience problems with script caching.

SETTING	CC	UC	DESCRIPTION
Disable External Branding Of Internet Explorer		✓	Prevents the customization of logos and title bars in Internet Explorer and Microsoft Office Outlook Express. This custom branding often occurs when users install software from an Internet service provider.
Disable Changing Advanced Page Settings		✓	Enable this policy to prevent users from changing security, multimedia, and printing settings from the Internet Options Advanced tab.
Customize User Agent String	✓	✓	Changes the user-agent string, which browsers use to identify the specific browser type and version to Web servers.
Use Automatic Detection For Dial-Up Connections		✓	Disabled by default, you can enable this policy setting to allow Automatic Detection to use a Dynamic Host Configuration Protocol (DHCP) or Domain Name System (DNS) server to customize the browser the first time it starts.
Move The Menu Bar Above The Navigation Bar		✓	Enable this policy setting to control the placement of the menu bar. If you don't set this, users can configure the location of the menu bar relative to the navigation bar by dragging it.
Turn Off Managing Pop-Up Filter Level	✓	✓	Use this setting to configure whether users can set the Pop-up Filter level. You can't set the Pop-up Filter level directly with this setting; you can only define whether or not users can manage the setting.
Turn Off The Security Settings Check Feature	✓	✓	By default, Internet Explorer will warn users if settings put them at risk. If you configure settings in such a way that Internet Explorer would warn the users, enable this setting to prevent the warning from appearing.
Turn On Compatibility Logging	✓	✓	Enable this setting to log the details of requests that Internet Explorer blocks. Typically, you need to enable this setting only when actively troubleshooting a problem with a Web site.
Enforce Full Screen Mode	✓	✓	Enable this policy only if using a computer as a Web-browsing kiosk.

SETTING	CC	UC	DESCRIPTION
Configure Media Explorer Bar		✓	Enable this policy if you want to be able to disable the Media Explorer Bar. The Media Explorer Bar plays music and video content from the Internet. Keep in mind that multimedia content is used for legitimate, business-related Web sites more and more often, including replaying meetings and webcasts.
Prevent The Internet Explorer Search Box From Displaying		✓	Enable this policy to hide the search box.
Restrict Changing The Default Search Provider	✓	✓	Enable this policy to force users to use the search provider you configure.
Pop-Up Allow List	✓	✓	Enable this policy and specify a list of sites that should allow pop-ups if you have internal Web sites that require pop-up functionality.
Prevent Participation In The Customer Experience Improvement Program	✓	✓	Microsoft uses the Customer Experience Improvement Program (CEIP) to gather information about how users work with Internet Explorer. If you enable this policy, CEIP will not be used. In some organizations, you might need to disable CEIP to meet confidentiality requirements. If you disable this policy, CEIP will always be used. For more information about CEIP, visit *http://www.microsoft.com/products/ceip/.*

In addition to the settings in Table 20-2, several subnodes contain additional Internet Explorer–related settings. With the policy settings located in Administrative Templates \Windows Components\Internet Explorer\Administrator Approved Controls (within both User Configuration and Computer Configuration), you can enable or disable specific controls throughout your organization.

With the policy settings located in Administrative Templates\Windows Components \Internet Explorer\Application Compatibility (within both User Configuration and Computer Configuration), you can control cut, copy, and paste operations for Internet Explorer. Typically, you do not need to modify these settings.

With the policy settings located in Administrative Templates\Windows Components\Internet Explorer\Browser Menus (within both User Configuration and Computer Configuration), you can disable specific menu items.

With the policy settings located in Administrative Templates\Windows Components\Internet Explorer\Internet Control Panel (within both User Configuration and Computer Configuration), you can disable specific aspects of the Internet Options dialog box, including individual tabs and settings. Change these settings if you want to prevent users from easily modifying important Internet Explorer settings. This will disable the user interface only and will not prevent users from directly changing registry values.

With the policy settings located in Administrative Templates\Windows Components\Internet Explorer\Internet Settings (within both User Configuration and Computer Configuration), you can configure user interface elements, including AutoComplete, image resizing, smooth scrolling, link colors, and more. You need to change these settings only if one of the default settings proves problematic in your environment.

With the policy settings located in Administrative Templates\Windows Components\Internet Explorer\Offline Pages (within both User Configuration and Computer Configuration), you can disable different aspects of offline pages, which allows users to keep a copy of Web pages for use while disconnected from a network. Typically, you do not need to change these settings.

With the policy settings located in Administrative Templates\Windows Components\Internet Explorer\Persistence Behavior (within both User Configuration and Computer Configuration), you can configure maximum amounts for Dynamic HTML (DHTML) Persistence storage on a per-zone basis. Typically, you do not need to change these settings.

With the policy settings located in Administrative Templates\Windows Components\Internet Explorer\Security Features (within both User Configuration and Computer Configuration), you can configure all aspects of Internet Explorer security.

With the policy settings located in Administrative Templates\Windows Components\Internet Explorer\Toolbars (within both User Configuration and Computer Configuration), you can configure toolbar buttons and disable user customization of these buttons. Users will probably be most familiar with the default button configuration. However, you can modify the default settings to better suit your environment.

New Group Policy Settings for Internet Explorer 8

Table 20-3 shows some examples of the more useful settings that apply only to Internet Explorer 8. Settings marked as CC can be found at Computer Configuration\Administrative Templates\Windows Components\Internet Explorer\. Settings marked as UC can be found at User Configuration\Administrative Templates\Windows Components\Internet Explorer\.

TABLE 20-3 New Group Policy Settings for Internet Explorer 8

SETTING	CC	UC	DESCRIPTION
Accelerators\Turn Off Accelerators	✓	✓	Enable this policy setting to disable Accelerators.
Deploy Non-Default Accelerators	✓	✓	Enable this policy setting to deploy custom Accelerators.
Turn Off\Reopen Last Browsing Session	✓	✓	If Internet Explorer crashes, it prompts the user to reopen any tabs the next time the user opens it. Enable this policy to disable that behavior and always open with a single blank tab.
Compatibility View\Turn On Internet Explorer 7 Standards Mode and Turn On Internet Explorer 7 Standards Mode For Local Intranet	✓	✓	Use these two policies to enable Internet Explorer 7 Standards Mode on either the Internet or your intranet. Standards Mode configures Internet Explorer 8 to identify itself as Internet Explorer 7 to Web servers, and the policies cause Internet Explorer to render Web pages similar to pages in Internet Explorer 7.
Compatibility View\Turn Off Compatibility View	✓	✓	Turning on this policy prevents users from accessing Compatibility View.
Turn Off Data Execution Prevention	✓	✓	Data Execution Prevention (DEP) can cause problems with some Web applications. If you discover that DEP causes an important application to fail, you should attempt to fix the bug in the application. In the meantime, you can enable this policy to allow the application to function without being terminated by DEP.
Prevent Deleting Web Sites That The User Has Visited, Prevent Deleting Temporary Internet Files, Prevent Deleting Cookies, Prevent Deleting InPrivate Blocking Data, Configure Delete Browsing History On Exit	✓	✓	These policies give you control over the user's browsing history. You can configure these policies to prevent users from clearing their history to make it easier to monitor user activity. Alternatively, you can configure the history to be deleted automatically if you would rather not store browsing history.
Configure New Tab Default Behavior	✓	✓	Enable this policy to choose whether a new tab displays a blank page, the user's home page, or the standard new tab page.

SETTING	CC	UC	DESCRIPTION
Turn Off Windows Search AutoComplete	✓	✓	When a user begins typing in a search box, AutoComplete provides a list of the user's previous searches. While this can prevent the user from typing, it might inadvertently reveal something the user has searched for while a coworker is near or during a presentation.
InPrivate\Turn Off InPrivate Browsing	✓	✓	Enable this policy to prevent users from accessing InPrivate Browsing mode.

Using the Internet Explorer Administration Kit

Internet Explorer has dozens of settings. To simplify the process of configuring and customizing Internet Explorer for your organization and to add custom features, you can use the Internet Explorer Administration Kit (IEAK).

IEAK allows you to:

- Establish version control across your organization.
- Distribute and manage browser installations centrally.
- Configure automatic connection profiles for users' computers.
- Customize virtually any aspect of Internet Explorer, including home pages, search engines, RSS feeds, favorites, toolbar buttons, Accelerators, security, communications settings, and other important elements.

Naturally, you can also use Group Policy settings to configure each of these settings. In Active Directory Domain Services (AD DS) environments, configuring Group Policy is more efficient than using IEAK. IEAK is extremely useful for configuring workgroup computers, however, and nothing prevents you from using IEAK to help deploy Internet Explorer in AD DS environments.

You can download IEAK from Microsoft at *http://technet.microsoft.com/en-us/ie/bb219517.aspx*. After installing IEAK, start the Customization Wizard by clicking Start, pointing to All Programs, clicking Windows IEAK 8, and then clicking Internet Explorer Customization Wizard. The wizard prompts you for detailed information about your organization and how you want to configure Internet Explorer. Most of the wizard pages are self-explanatory. The following pages deserve some extra explanation:

- **Media Selection** On this page, if you are deploying the settings to only Windows Vista or later computers, you can create a Configuration-Only Package. Select CD-ROM or File if you need to deploy Internet Explorer 8 to earlier versions of Windows also.

- **Additional Settings** The Control Management settings do not apply to Windows Vista and later operating systems. Instead, you should use the Group Policy settings located in Administrative Templates\Windows Components\Internet Explorer \Administrator Approved Controls (within both User Configuration and Computer Configuration) to enable or disable specific controls throughout your organization.

After you complete the wizard, it saves your settings to the location you specify. You can edit them later using the IEAK 8 Profile Manager. This is useful if you need to make several slightly different variations of your Internet Explorer customizations.

Troubleshooting Internet Explorer Problems

Because Web pages are complex and change frequently, you might occasionally have problems using Internet Explorer. The sections that follow provide troubleshooting guidance for the following types of problems:

- Internet Explorer does not start.
- An add-on does not work properly.
- Some Web pages do not display properly.
- An unwanted toolbar appears.
- The home page or other settings have changed.

> ***NOTE*** **If you need to study the communications between Internet Explorer and a Web site, try Fiddler. Fiddler analyzes Web communications and is much easier to understand than Network Monitor. For more information about Fiddler (a free download), visit** ***http://www.fiddlertool.com/fiddler.***

Internet Explorer Does Not Start

If Internet Explorer does not start, or starts but appears to be frozen, the problem is likely caused by a problematic add-on. Often, you can simply terminate the Internet Explorer process (Iexplore.exe) with Task Manager and restart Internet Explorer. If restarting Internet Explorer does not solve the problem, start Internet Explorer in No Add-ons mode, as described in the section titled "Internet Explorer Add-ons Disabled Mode" earlier in this chapter.

An Add-on Does Not Work Properly

Occasionally, a Web page might require you to have a specific add-on. If the Web page displays a message indicating that you need to install the add-on, you should consider the security risks carefully before installing it.

If the page continues to display improperly after you install the add-on, the add-on might be disabled. Users can disable add-ons manually, or Internet Explorer might disable a problematic add-on automatically. To enable an add-on, follow these steps:

1. In your browser, open the Tools menu, select Manage Add-ons, and then click Enable Or Disable Add-ons.
2. Click the Show list and then click Add-ons That Have Been Used By Internet Explorer.
3. Select the add-on that you need to enable and then click Enable.
4. Click OK.

If the add-on later becomes disabled again, Internet Explorer probably disabled it because it is crashing. Visit the add-on developer's Web site and download the latest version—an update might be available that solves the problem. If no update is available or the problem persists, you can disable the ability of Internet Explorer to disable the plug-in automatically. To disable Crash Detection, enable the Turn Off Crash Detection Group Policy setting in either Computer Configuration\Administrative Templates\Windows Components\Internet Explorer\ or User Configuration\Administrative Templates\Windows Components\Internet Explorer\. If the problem occurs on a single computer, edit the setting in local Group Policy. If the problem occurs on all computers in a domain, edit the domain Group Policy settings.

Some Web Pages Do Not Display Properly

Most Web site developers test their Web pages using Internet Explorer's default settings. If you modify the default settings, you might cause pages to display incorrectly. In particular, enabling restrictive security settings or disabling features such as scripts can cause rendering problems.

If the problem occurs on a small number of trustworthy Web sites, your first troubleshooting step should be to enable Compatibility View, as described in the section titled "Internet Explorer 8 Improvements" at the beginning of this chapter. If that does not solve the problem, add the sites to the Trusted Sites zone by following these steps:

1. In Internet Explorer, visit the Web page.
2. Select Internet Options from the Tools menu.
3. In the Internet Options dialog box, click the Security tab.
4. Click Trusted Sites and then click Sites.
5. If the Web site does not support HTTPS, clear the Require Server Verification (HTTPS:) For All Sites In This Zone check box. Click Add to add the current Web site to the list of Trusted Sites and then click Close.
6. Click OK to close the Internet Options dialog box. Then close Internet Explorer, reopen it, and visit the Web page again. If the problem persists, repeat these steps to remove the site from the Trusted Sites zone. Continue reading this section for more troubleshooting guidance.

If many different Web sites have the same symptoms, it might be more effective to modify the browser security settings for all Web sites.

1. In Internet Explorer, select Internet Options from the Tools menu.
2. In the Internet Options dialog box, click the Security tab.
3. Click Internet. If the Default Level option is enabled, make note of the current security level for the Internet zone and then click Default Level.
4. Click OK to close the Internet Options dialog box. Close Internet Explorer, reopen it, and visit the Web page again. If the problem persists, repeat these steps to return the Internet security zone settings to their previous level. Continue reading this section for more troubleshooting guidance.

If changing zone security settings does not solve the problem, return your security settings to their previous state. Then, examine the advanced settings by following these steps:

1. Select Internet Options from the Tools menu.
2. In the Internet Options dialog box, click the Advanced tab.
3. Browse the Settings list and look for any settings that might cause your problem. Change one setting at a time and then test the Web page to determine whether the problem is solved. If the change does not solve the problem, return the setting to its original state and change another setting.

Because Web site developers tend to test pages using the browser's default settings, default settings will work correctly for most people. Before you restore settings, evaluate the risks—settings changes were probably made deliberately, and restoring the original settings might increase your security risks. If you determine that the risks are minimal, you can restore advanced settings by following these steps:

1. Select Internet Options from the Tools menu.
2. In the Internet Options dialog box, click the Advanced tab.
3. Click Restore Advanced Settings.
4. Click OK and then restart Internet Explorer.

If problems persist, you can reset all browser settings except for Favorites, Feed, Internet Connection Settings, Group Policy Settings, and Content Advisor Settings by following these steps:

1. Close all windows except for one Internet Explorer window.
2. Select Internet Options from the Tools menu.
3. In the Internet Options dialog box, click the Advanced tab.
4. Click Reset.
5. In the warning box that appears, click Reset.
6. Click Close and then click OK twice. Restart Internet Explorer.

If problems persist, you may have nonstandard settings defined by Group Policy. You can use the Resultant Set of Policy tool to determine whether any Internet Explorer Group Policy settings are overriding the defaults. To use this tool, follow these steps:

1. Click Start, type **Rsop.msc**, and then press Enter.
2. Check the following locations for Internet Explorer–related settings:
   - Computer Configuration\Administrative Templates\Windows Components \Internet Explorer\
   - User Configuration\Administrative Templates\Windows Components\Internet Explorer\
   - User Configuration\Windows Settings\Internet Explorer Maintenance

If you determine that Group Policy settings are causing problems, contact the administrator responsible for the effective Group Policy to discuss the problem.

As an alternative to changing Internet Explorer settings, you can contact the Web site administrator to discuss the problem. Most Web site administrators want the Web site to work well with as many browsers as possible and will be happy to work with you to troubleshoot any problems. When you contact the Web site administrator, send a screenshot of how the Web site appears in your browser. To e-mail a screenshot of a Web site, follow these steps:

1. Open the Web site in Internet Explorer.
2. Press Alt+Print Screen to capture the current window to the Clipboard.
3. Create an HTML e-mail to the Web site administrator.
4. In the body of the message, press Ctrl+V to paste the screenshot into the e-mail.

Preventing Unwanted Toolbars

Internet Explorer, together with Windows Vista and later operating systems, include several layers of defense to prevent unwanted software from modifying the Internet Explorer configuration. However, if an unwanted toolbar appears in Internet Explorer, you can disable it using the Add-on Manager. For more information, read the section titled "Add-on Manager Improvements" earlier in this chapter. If the problem persists, start Internet Explorer in No Add-ons mode, as described in the section titled "Internet Explorer Add-ons Disabled Mode" earlier in this chapter. Then use the Add-on Manager to disable all add-ons that you have not intentionally installed.

To prevent unwanted software, ensure that you have all Microsoft security updates installed and are using anti-malware software, such as Microsoft Forefront or Windows Defender. For more information about installing security updates, read Chapter 23, "Managing Software Updates." For more information about Microsoft Forefront and Windows Defender, read Chapter 24.

The Home Page or Other Settings Have Changed

If the home page or other settings have changed, you can reset all browser settings except for Favorites, Feed, Internet Connection Settings, Group Policy Settings, and Content Advisor Settings by following these steps:

1. Close all windows except for one Internet Explorer window.
2. Select Internet Options from the Tools menu.
3. In the Internet Options dialog box, click the Advanced tab.
4. Click Reset.
5. In the warning box that appears, click Reset.
6. Click Close and then click OK twice. Restart Internet Explorer.

To prevent unwanted changes in the future, ensure that you have all Microsoft security updates installed and are using anti-malware software, such as Microsoft Forefront or Windows Defender. For more information about installing security updates, read Chapter 23. For more information about Microsoft Forefront and Windows Defender, read Chapter 24.

Summary

To address the changing Web, Internet Explorer 8 includes significant improvements over earlier versions of the Web browser. The most important changes are not visible to the user, but the user benefits from improved security, privacy, and reliability. Compatibility View reverts to the Internet Explorer 7 rendering engine for Web sites that do not display properly in Internet Explorer 8. Tab Isolation prevents a Web page that crashes the browser from impacting more than one tab.

Users will notice InPrivate Browsing, InPrivate Filtering, SmartScreen, Domain Highlighting, and Accelerators. InPrivate Browsing allows users to browse the Web with no record of their activities on the local computer. InPrivate Filtering reduces the opportunity for third parties to monitor a user's activity across multiple Web sites. SmartScreen warns users before they visit known malicious Web sites, and Domain Highlighting helps users identify the Web site they are visiting. Finally, Accelerators improve user efficiency by allowing them to use Web services to cross-reference information quickly on a Web page.

Additional Resources

These resources contain additional information and tools related to this chapter.

Related Information

- Internet Explorer 8 home page at *http://www.microsoft.com/windows/internet-explorer/default.aspx*.

- "What's New in Internet Explorer 8" on MSDN at *http://msdn.microsoft.com/en-us/library/cc288472.aspx*.
- "Internet Explorer Administration Kit (IEAK) Information and Downloads" at *http://technet.microsoft.com/en-us/ie/bb219517.aspx*.
- Internet Explorer Team Blog at *http://blogs.msdn.com/ie/*.
- "How to Create Custom .adm or .admx Files to Add Search Providers to the Toolbar Search Box in Internet Explorer 7" at *http://support.microsoft.com/kb/918238*.
- "Understanding and Working in Protected Mode Internet Explorer" at *http://msdn.microsoft.com/library/bb250462.aspx*.
- "Introduction to the Protected Mode API" at *http://msdn.microsoft.com/en-us/library/ms537319.aspx* presents information about creating add-ons that work with Protected Mode.
- Chapter 23, "Managing Software Updates," includes information about deploying security updates in your organization.
- Chapter 24, "Managing Client Protection," includes more information about User Access Control and Windows Defender.

On the Companion Media

- Clean-IE.ps1
- Get-IEHomePage.ps1
- Get-IESearchPage.ps1
- Set-IEHomePage.ps1
- TroubleshootIEBrowseWeb.ps1
- TroubleshootIESecurity.ps1

PART IV

Desktop Maintenance

CHAPTER 21

Maintaining Desktop Health

Monitoring and maintaining desktop health is a key part of maintaining an IT infrastructure. This chapter describes some of the tools available for maintaining desktop health in the Windows 7 operating system, including Performance Monitor, Resource Monitor, Reliability Monitor, Windows Performance Tools (WPT) Kit, Event Viewer, the Windows System Assessment Tool, the Performance Information and Tools Control Panel item, Windows Error Reporting (WER), and Task Scheduler. Beginning with Windows 7, you can also use Windows PowerShell to collect performance data, read event logs, and perform other desktop maintenance tasks.

Performance Monitoring

Performance monitoring refers to the collecting, viewing, and analyzing of performance data such as processor usage, disk usage, memory usage, and other statistics for a computer. Performance monitoring can involve displaying performance data in real time or collecting performance data and saving it in log files that can be analyzed later.

Performance monitoring is based upon an always-present, always-on instrumentation infrastructure in Windows by which numeric information concerning operating system and application performance data is grouped into categories, counters, and instances. This performance data can be accessed in the following ways:

- Using the Performance Monitor snap-in in Microsoft Management Console (MMC)
- Using Windows PowerShell scripts
- Using native and managed application programming interfaces (APIs) programmatically

The Performance Monitor snap-in, shown in Figure 21-1, is typically used for baselining system behavior, monitoring resource utilization, and troubleshooting performance issues involving the operating system and applications. The Windows 7 version of Performance Monitor is essentially the same as that found in the Windows Vista operating system, which improved upon earlier versions of Windows by providing better visualizations, easier navigation, and more detailed control over the collection and display of performance data.

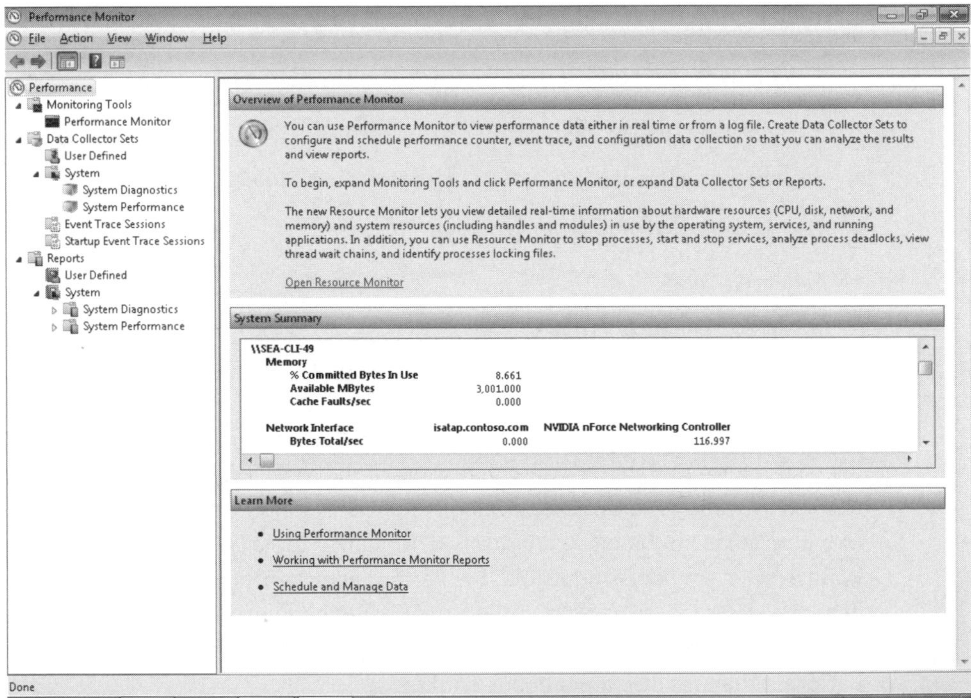

FIGURE 21-1 The Performance Monitor snap-in

Specifically, the following enhancements to Performance Monitor were introduced in Windows Vista:

- **Drag and drop** This feature allows a user to drag any Performance Monitor–related file into the display area to open the file. The Performance Monitor display changes to reflect the actions relevant to the opened file type. Supported file types include:
  - Templates (html, xml).
  - Logs (blg).

- Comma-separated or tab-separated value files (csv, tsv).

  You can also drag multiple binary log files (*.blg) into the Performance Monitor window. However, you cannot drag multiple .html, .xml, .csv, or .tsv files; attempting to do so will generate an error.

- **Time Range Control** Each performance counter data sample has a timestamp that identifies when the data was collected. In previous versions of Performance Monitor, users needed to view and change the properties of a loaded log file to adjust the log's visible timeframe (on the *x*-axis). When the graph is a line chart, time labels are now automatically displayed along the horizontal time axis in the main Performance Monitor view.

  The timestamps for the first and last samples are always displayed. Because of limited *x*-axis space, time labels cannot be displayed for all data points. The displayable time labels are determined based on the sample interval time and the currently visible time range. The actual number of time labels displayed varies as the size of the System Monitor graph window is resized or if the chart area scale is changed.

- **Legend Control** The Performance Monitor Legend Control added in Windows Vista provides two features that allow easier, more detailed control of the displayed performance counters:

  - Multiple counter selection
  - Show/Hide counters

  Previously, performance counter operations, such as changing the scale factor, could be performed only on a single counter, and the only way to hide a performance counter was to delete it from the System Monitor view. Now you can simultaneously select multiple counters for manipulation. The possible operations on multiple selected counters are Show Selected Counters, Hide Selected Counters, or Scale Selected Counters. You can select multiple counters in the legend, report, or chart window using standard keyboard or mouse functions (Ctrl+left-click or Shift+left-click). The selected counter items will be highlighted for ease of identification.

  You can also temporarily hide performance counters from a graph or report view using the menu options. This provides a convenient method for quickly hiding a counter to make a graph more readable. To hide or show counters, users can either select or clear the Show check box next to the desired counters, or they can select the counter (or counters) and use the shortcut menu to show or hide the selected counters. Note that the Show and Hide options do not apply to the report view. Previously, the only way to remove a performance counter from the current view was to delete it from the System Monitor legend.

- **Scale to Fit** Previously in the Windows XP operating system, because the values of some performance counters might have exceeded the current graph scale, not all of the data was visible and changing the graph or counter scales required several steps. The Scale to Fit feature added in Windows Vista allows the scaling of performance data to the current graph view on a counter-by-counter basis without changing the overall graph scale or performing numerous steps to change a particular counter's scale. The Scale to Fit feature is applicable to line and bar types of charts for both real-time and logged data sources.

When a user selects counters and applies the Scale to Fit feature to them, Performance Monitor automatically scales the selected counters to the current graph view based on the range of values for the counters. The view is updated to draw the graph with the new scale factor so that the values fall within the graph's current vertical minimum and maximum ranges. The Scale to Fit feature does not change the graph's vertical minimum or maximum ranges. You can determine the current scale factor for each counter from the Scale column in the counter list pane.

To use the Scale to Fit feature, select the counters you want to modify, right-click the counters at the bottom of Performance Monitor, and select Scale Selected Counters. When you use the Scale to Fit feature, you can select multiple counters by using Ctrl+left-click to individually select multiple counters or by using Shift+left-click to highlight a contiguous range of counters. Performance Monitor uses an algorithm to determine the best scale factor for each selected counter based on its current range of values and the graph scale. It then recalculates the data sample values and displays them in the graph, using the new scale factor.

Note that because the vertical minimum and maximum ranges are configurable and scaling uses a factor of 10, it is possible that the selected counter data still cannot be displayed within the configured vertical graph range, depending on the selected counter's values.

- **Add Counters dialog box** The Add Counters dialog box in Performance Monitor has been redesigned to improve usability based on user feedback. The design of the previous Add Counters dialog box made it difficult for users to confirm the performance counters that were being added. The new interface, shown in Figure 21-2, has a hierarchical design that allows you to instantly see the counters that are being added to a log.

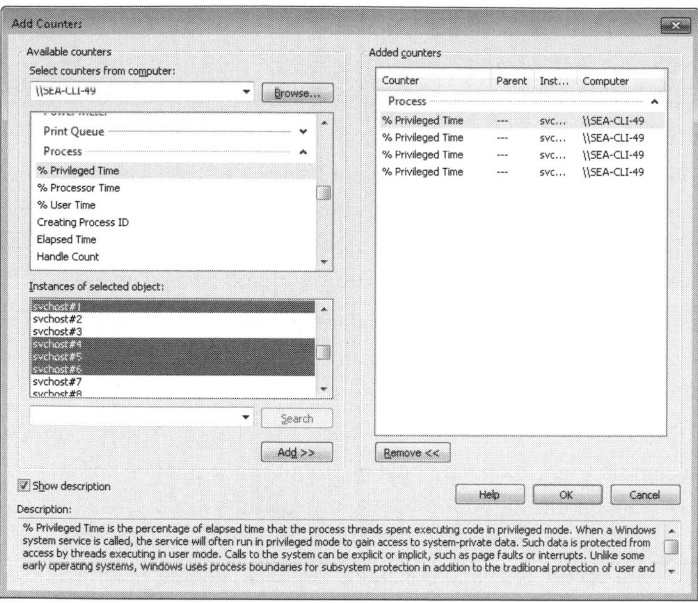

FIGURE 21-2 The new Add Counters dialog box

The Add Counters window contains a list of available objects on the left side just below the Computer Name field. You can view and select the counters for the selected object by clicking the down arrow to the right of the object name. The instances associated with the selected object are displayed in the Instances Of Selected Object list. You can add any combination of objects, counters, and instances by clicking Add with the desired elements highlighted. The added elements are immediately displayed in the Added Counters list. The Objects, Counters, and Instances windows support multi-select, so that you can select multiple items by using standard keyboard or mouse functions (Ctrl+left-click or Shift+left-click) and then adding to the log with one click of the Add button.

A search function is also available when the All Instances option is present for a performance object. The search feature provides you with the ability to search the available instances for the selected object. The search results will be grouped into the *<All searched instances>* instance item; you can add them to the log by clicking Add with the *<All searched instances>* item selected.

- **Zoom** The new zoom feature in Performance Monitor provides you with the ability to easily view logged data in more detail. (You cannot zoom in to real-time performance data.) Users can select a time range that they want to view in more detail and then use the new Zoom To shortcut menu item to clear the current log view and replace it with the zoomed time range. Fewer samples are displayed in the zoomed time range, but you can obtain more detail from the samples that are displayed. You can use the following methods to select a range of time to zoom in on:

- Using the left mouse button, click the graph to select the first time point, drag the mouse to the second time point, and then release the mouse button. The selected time range will be shadowed in the graph view. Click the right mouse button to open the shortcut menu and then select Zoom To.
- Use the time range slider control (visible under the graph) to select the desired time range. You can use each end of the slider control to change the time window you want to display. The selected time range will be shadowed in the graph view. Click the right mouse button to access the shortcut menu and then select Zoom To.

To zoom out, reset the time range using the slider control and then select Zoom To again to zoom to the currently selected time range. You can also use the left and right arrows on the slider control to scroll the time range in the graph.

- **Compare** By starting Performance Monitor using the *perfmon /comp* command, a Compare feature can be used to overlay multiple log files for relative comparison. An adjustable level of transparency is added to the logs being compared so that you can see through the logs that have been overlaid. This feature is useful if, for example, a user wants to compare server-resource utilization between 8:00 A.M. and 9:00 A.M. over a week-long period. The Compare feature is discussed in more detail in the section titled "Comparing Performance Monitor Logs" later in this chapter.
- **Tool tips** Tool tips are displayed when you pause the mouse on a data element in the Performance Monitor graph. The tool tips will show performance-counter data for the element nearest to the mouse pointer. This will be either the previous data point or the next data point, whichever is closest to the mouse pointer. Tool tips appear only for visible chart data elements.
- **Time-based algorithms** Time-based sample collection allows you to collect performance-counter data based on a given time range. Previously, if a logging session failed to collect data for some period of time, the assumption was that all of the data was continuously collected and showed no missing data points. This resulted in the display of inaccurate data. The new time-based algorithms display gaps in graphs when a log file has missing samples. This feature does not introduce any new chart type.
- **Transportable configuration files** In Microsoft Windows 2000, Windows XP, and Windows Server 2003 operating systems, the configuration of each performance log or alert can be saved to an Hypertext Markup Language (HTML) file, edited to change the computer name, and used as a template to create a log for another computer. Beginning with Windows Vista, the default configuration file format is changed to Extensible Markup Language (XML).
- **End of File command** Performance Monitor previously used CreateProcess to execute an *End of File* command to start the specified process when a log ended. To improve security and allow for flexibility of the execution context (credentials), this feature has been replaced by the ability to start an existing Task Scheduler job when a log file completes.

Improvements to Performance Monitoring in Windows 7

While the Performance Monitor snap-in is essentially unchanged in Windows 7, there are several other significant improvements to performance monitoring that have been added in Windows 7. These additional improvements include:

- Architectural improvements that provide enhanced performance, scalability, and robustness to the performance counter infrastructure.
- New version 2.0 Kernel Mode APIs that are declaratively defined using XML and leverage the version 2.0 infrastructure introduced in Windows Vista.
- New performance counters that expose additional aspects of Windows internals.
- Scriptable consumption of performance counters using Windows PowerShell. For more information on this new feature, see the section titled "Using Windows PowerShell for Performance Monitoring" later in this chapter.

Using Performance Monitor

You can open Performance Monitor by using any of the following methods:

- Select Computer Management, System Tools, Performance.
- Select Control Panel, Administrative Tools, Performance Monitor.
- Select Action Center, View Performance Information, Advanced Tools, Open Performance Monitor.
- Add the Performance Monitor snap-in to a new MMC console.
- Type **perf** in the Start menu search box and click Performance Monitor when it appears in the Programs group.
- Type **perfmon.exe** or **perfmon.msc** in the Start menu search box and press Enter.

The following command-line options are available for Perfmon.exe (but not for Perfmon.msc):

- **perfmon /rel** Lets you review your computer's reliability and problem history (the same result as right-clicking the Monitoring Tools node in Performance Monitor and selecting View System Reliability).
- **perfmon /report** Collects performance data for 60 seconds and then generates and displays a system diagnostics report.
- **perfmon /res** Opens the Resource Monitor (the same result as right-clicking the Monitoring Tools node in Performance Monitor and selecting Resource Monitor).
- **perfmon /sys** Opens the Performance Monitor in stand-alone mode (the Sysmon.ocx ActiveX control). An additional option, */comp,* allows for comparison overlay between two open Performance Monitor instances.

Performance monitoring concepts and procedures have changed little from Microsoft Windows NT 4.0. The sections that follow assume basic familiarity with using Performance Monitor on Windows XP and focus mainly on creating and using Data Collector Sets (DCSs) for logging and analyzing performance data. For general information on how to use Performance Monitor in Windows 7, see *http://technet.microsoft.com/en-us/library/cc749249.aspx.*

Real-Time Performance Monitoring

You can add and view real-time performance counters for the local computer or for a remote computer. You can add performance counters to a real-time line chart view using one of two methods:

- Click the Add Counter icon (+) on the toolbar.
- Right-click the chart anywhere and then select Add Counters from the shortcut menu.

You can open a saved Performance Monitor file for viewing by dragging the file into the Performance Monitor window or, as in previous versions, by clicking the View Log Data cylinder on the toolbar or pressing Ctrl+L. Another enhancement is the addition of the Save Image As shortcut menu item that allows you to save the current view as a GIF image file for later reference.

Performance Monitor Logging

In Windows XP, you created Performance Monitor logs or alerts by using the Report Type node under Performance Logs And Alerts in the Performance interface. You could configure each log to contain a single data collection entity (counter log, trace log, or alert). Beginning with Windows Vista, Performance Monitor uses the concept of data collector sets. In Windows Vista, a data collection entity is referred to as a *data collector* and must now be a member of a DCS. A DCS can contain any number of data collectors, allowing for greater control over performance monitoring and data organization tasks.

DCSs have been implemented to provide support for performance reports that require data from multiple log files of different types. These data collectors include counter, trace, alerts, and system configuration logs. You can add any number of data collectors to a single DCS. Before Windows Vista, each data collection entity contained its own scheduling properties to be used by the Performance Logs And Alerts service. Beginning with Windows Vista, all members of a DCS use the scheduling properties—and other common properties—that have been specified for the parent DCS. The DCS is implemented as a single Task Scheduler object, and you can specify a single task to execute after all the included data collectors have completed.

There are three types of DCSs:

- **User-defined** Most, if not all, user-configured DCSs fall into this category.
- **System** XML DCS templates that have been saved to Windows\PLA\System are displayed here. You cannot create these; they are included with Windows Vista.
- **Event trace sessions** These are DCSs configured for Event Tracing for Windows (ETW) tracing. (For more information, see the section titled "Understanding the Windows Event Architecture" later in this chapter.)

NOTE Log files created from DCSs in Windows Vista and later are not backward compatible with earlier versions of Windows. However, you can view logs created in earlier versions of Windows in Performance Monitor in Windows Vista and later.

Creating a Data Collector Set

You create a DCS by using a wizard or a preconfigured XML template. The data can be a single performance log, event trace, or system configuration data set, or any combination of the three. You can also configure Performance Counter Alerts from this interface.

To create a new DCS, follow these steps:

1. Open the Performance Monitor snap-in, shown here, and select the User Defined node beneath the Data Collector Sets node.

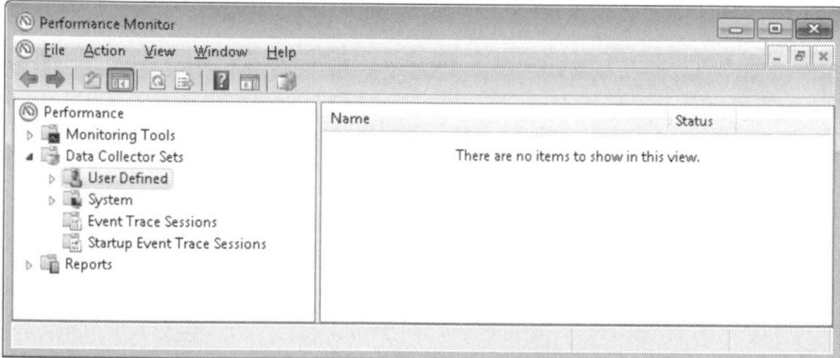

2. Right-click the User Defined node, select New, and then select Data Collector Set to start the Create New Data Collector Set wizard.
3. Provide a name for the data collector set and choose to create from a template or create manually by following the remaining steps of the wizard.

When you create a new DCS, it is simplest to use the Create From A Template option in the Create New Data Collector Set wizard. You can create templates for common monitoring scenarios and use them to quickly configure and start a new logging session using the template settings. The templates are in XML format; all settings for the DCS are specified in the template. There are three preconfigured templates for creating a new DCS:

- Basic
- System Diagnostics
- System Performance

You can also export a DCS as a template that can be modified and imported to create a new DCS. To export a DCS configuration XML file, right-click the DCS name under the Data Collector Sets node in Performance Monitor and select Save Template. The template files are not saved to a template store; you must import them each time you use them. You can save the XML template files to any folder to which you have access.

Generally, a template is exported from a manually configured DCS. After you export the DCS template, you can edit the template to customize it for particular scenarios (different computer, different folder, and so on). After you have exported the template, you can import it into the DCS by selecting Create From A Template in the Create New Data Collector Set wizard and browsing to the location of the XML file.

NOTE Performance Monitor no longer installs a default System Overview log as it did in Windows XP and earlier versions. However, it does provide a System Diagnostics Data Collector Set template.

To manually create a DCS, follow these steps:

1. In the Create New Data Collector Set wizard, select Create Manually and then click Next.
2. Select the desired data collector(s), as shown here, and then click Next.

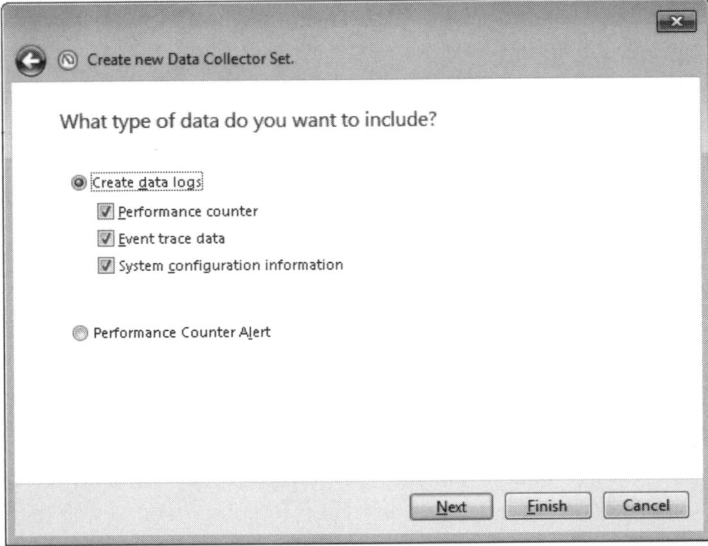

3. Select the performance counters, if any, that will be collected in the data collector and then click Next.
4. Select the event trace providers, if any, that will be used and then click Next.
5. Select registry keys to be monitored, if any, and then click Next.
6. Choose the path to the DCS and then click Next. All of the data files for the DCS will use this path and will share the parent folder that you specify. The default path for saving data collector sets is %SystemDrive%\PerfLogs\Admin*DCS_name*.
7. Click Change and then select the user account that will run this DCS.

8. Before completing the wizard, you can select options to open the properties of the data set when completing the wizard and start the data collection immediately after completing the wizard, as shown here.

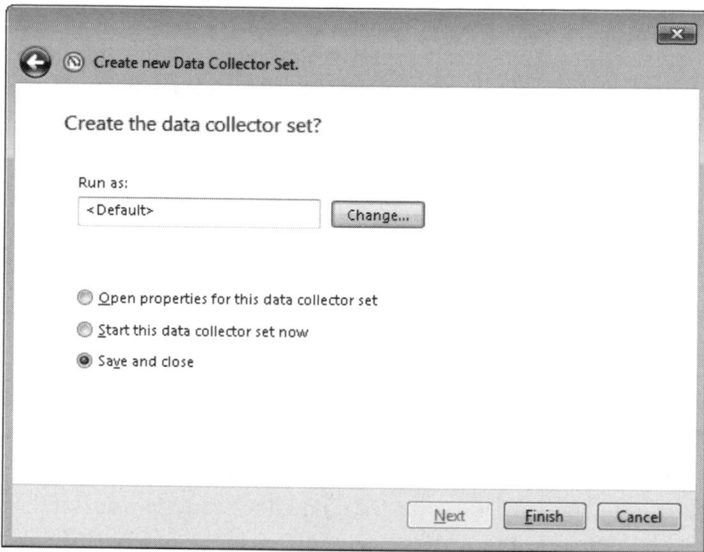

9. Click Finish to display the DCS in the Reliability And Performance Monitor. You can view the status of all of the configured DCSs by selecting the desired parent node under the Data Collector Sets node.

10. To view the data collector(s) contained within a DCS in the Reliability And Performance Monitor, expand the User Defined node in the left pane, as shown here. Then, either click the DCS name under the User Defined node or double-click the DCS name if it appears in the right pane.

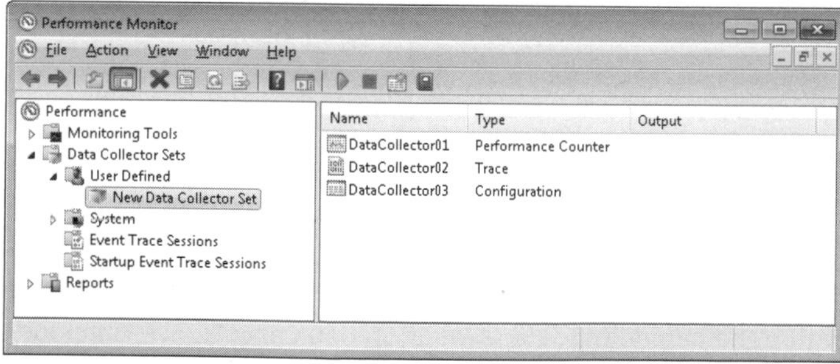

To start the DCS, click the DCS name to highlight it and either click the green arrow on the toolbar to start logging or right-click the DCS name and then select Start from the shortcut menu.

Configuring a Data Collector Set

To access the properties for a DCS, right-click the name of the DCS and select Properties from the shortcut menu. All of the properties for a data collector are configured from this interface. Properties available on each tab include the following:

- **General** Configure the data collector description, any keywords that are desired for search purposes, and the Run As properties that determine under what user context this DCS will run. Click Change to change the user context for the collector. The default is the Local System account.
- **Directory** Configure the root directory for the DCS and specify a separate subdirectory if desired. The default is %SystemDrive%\perflogs\<*Data Collector Set name*>. You can also specify the format of the subdirectory name based on the following options:
  - **Date and time** Choose from the available subdirectory name formatting options that are displayed.
  - **Computer name** You can also prefix the subdirectory with the computer name by selecting the Prefix Subdirectory With Computer Name check box.
  - **Serial Number** You can use the Serial Number format (N) to create a unique subfolder name each time the DCS is started. This allows multiple logs of the same data collectors to be saved within different subfolders in the parent DCS folder. You can edit the serial number only in the Data Collector Set Properties, but the serial number format may also be specified to be used by individual data collectors. The default DCS subdirectory naming convention is *NNNNNN*, which results in DCS subfolders named 00000*x* (where *x* is the serial number).

    For example, a DCS with a serial number of 8 that was run on January 31, 2003 at 4:20 A.M. would have the following results based on the selected subdirectory name format:

    Subdirectory name format: yyyyMMddNNNN; Actual subdirectory name: 200301310008

    Subdirectory name format: yyDDD NN; Actual subdirectory name: 03031 08

    Subdirectory name format: MMMM MM\, yyyy \a\t h mmtt \- N; Actual subdirectory name: January 31, 2003 at 4 20 AM – 8
- **Security** Specify security parameters on the DCS. Default permissions are granted to SYSTEM, Administrators, Performance Log Users, and the data collector creator/owner.
- **Schedule** Configure the beginning date, expiration date, and launch time and day. Click Add to configure a schedule.
- **Stop Condition** Define when the data collection will stop. Options available on this tab include the following:
  - **Overall Duration** Configures the log to stop after a defined duration in seconds, minutes, days, hours, or weeks.

- **Limits** Defines limits for the log size or duration and whether to restart the DCS when those limits are reached. You can set the time duration or maximum size limit.

- **Task** Configure a specific task to run when a DCS stops. The specified task must be an existing Task Scheduler task. You can also specify the task arguments and the working directory.

NOTE You can also view and edit the properties of each data collector within a DCS by using the shortcut menus for each data collector. The configuration settings for a data collector vary depending upon whether the data collector is used for collecting performance counter, event tracing, or registry information.

Using Data Manager to View Performance Data

The Data Manager was first introduced in Windows Vista as a central location to manage logged performance data files. Each DCS has an associated Data Manager that controls the data management tasks including report generation, data retention policy, conditions/actions, and data transfer for the data in all of the subfolders in the root path of the DCS.

By default, the Data Manager is disabled for a DCS. When you enable the Data Manager for a DCS, the Data Manager creates an overview report to summarize the data results when the data collection is complete. If you don't enable the Data Manager for a DCS, the DCS is still listed under the Reports node in the Diagnostic Console, but a report is not generated for the DCS.

To access the Data Manager Properties for a DCS, right-click the DCS name in the Data Collector Sets node in Performance Monitor and then select Data Manager from the shortcut menu. To enable the Data Manager for the DCS, select the Enable Data Management And Report Generation check box on the Data Manager tab (shown in Figure 21-3). Note that by default the Data Manager does not act on the selected options until the DCS has completed. To enforce the selected Data Manager options before the DCS starts, select the Apply Policy Before The Data Collector Set Starts check box. When you select this option, previous data is deleted based on the configured Data Manager conditions before the DCS creates the next log file.

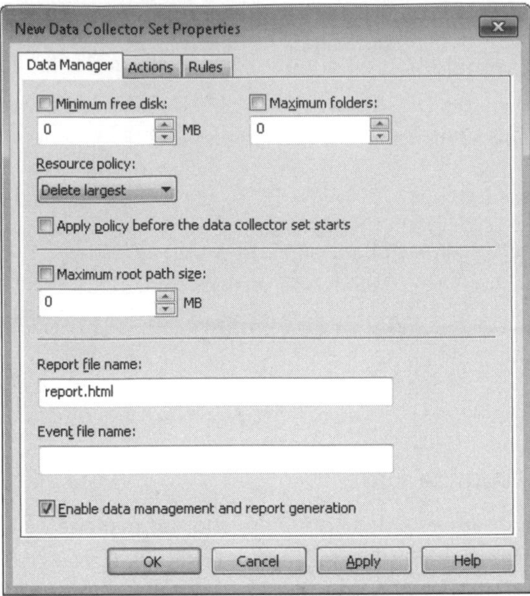

FIGURE 21-3 Data Manager properties

The available Data Manager conditions are:

- **Minimum Free Disk** The amount of disk space that must be available on the drive where log data is stored. If you select this condition, previous data is deleted according to the Resource Policy that you choose when the limit is reached.
- **Maximum Folders** The number of subfolders that can be in the DCS data directory. If you select this condition, previous data is deleted according to the Resource Policy that you choose when the limit is reached.
- **Maximum Root Path Size** The maximum size of the data directory for the DCS, including all subfolders. If you select this condition, this maximum path size overrides the Minimum Free Disk and Maximum Folders limits, and previous data will be deleted according to the Resource Policy that you choose when the limit is reached.

You can configure the Resource Policy to perform the following actions on the folders in the root folder of the DCS if one of the preceding limits is exceeded:

- **Delete Largest** The largest folder within the DCS root folder is deleted when one of the limits is exceeded
- **Delete Oldest** The oldest folder within the DCS root folder is deleted when one of the limits is exceeded

> ***NOTE*** **These Resource Policy actions are performed on a folder basis, rather than a file basis.**

You can use the Actions tab to define the folder actions to be performed when specified Data Manager conditions are met. The actions defined for the DCS are displayed in the Folder Actions section of the Actions tab window. Using this tab, you can add, edit, or remove folder actions for a DCS. Folder actions allow a user to choose how data is archived before it is permanently deleted according to the selected Resource Policy. You may also elect to not use the Data Manager limits in favor of managing all logged data according to the selected folder action rules. The following folder action options are available:

- **Age** The age of the data file in days or weeks. If the value is 0, the criterion is not used.
- **Folder size** The size, in megabytes, of the folder where log data is stored. If the value is 0, the criterion is not used.
- **Actions** Allows you to select which action to take when either the Resource Policy or Folder Action condition(s) are met. The actions include deletion of the raw data files and/or the report, as well as several cab file options. Cab files can be created, deleted, or sent (moved) to a local or shared folder.

Starting and Stopping Data Logging

The DCS will automatically start logging as soon as you create it if you select the Start This Data Collector Set Now option in the Create New Data Collector Set wizard. If you don't select the Start This Data Collector Set Now option, logging must be started manually.

After you create the DCS, use the following methods to start and stop logging:

- Right-click the DCS name in the User Defined Data Collector Sets node and select Start or Stop Action from the shortcut menu.
- Highlight the DCS name in the User Defined Data Collector Sets node and click the Start the Data Collector Set button or the Stop the Data Collector Set button on the Diagnostic Console toolbar.

> ***NOTE*** **To start performance counter logging automatically when the system reboots, create a scheduled task to run using System Startup as the condition and use Logman.exe to start the log.**

Viewing Performance Data

After you create the DCS, it is listed in the Reports section of Performance Monitor, as shown in Figure 21-4.

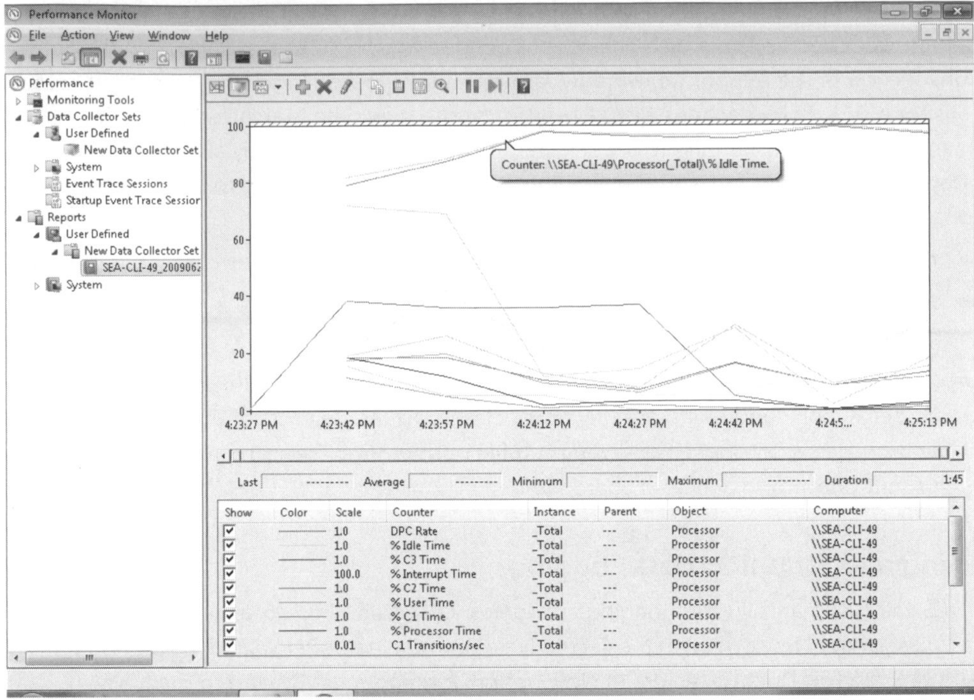

FIGURE 21-4 Using reports to view performance data

Additional methods for opening logged performance data include:

- Double-clicking a Performance Monitor log (.blg) file opens the log in Performance Monitor with all configured counters shown.
- Using the shortcut menu for the data collectors listed under Data Collector Sets in the Reports node in the Diagnostic Console.
- Right-clicking a data collector listed under the DCS name in the Reports node and selecting the desired view mode.

You can select the following three view modes from the Data Collector shortcut menu:

- **Performance Monitor View** If you select the Performance Monitor menu item, the Performance Monitor log file is displayed in the line chart with all configured counters.
- **Folder View** If you select the Folder menu item, the folder containing the selected data collector's files is displayed.
- **Report View** If you enabled the Data Manager for the DCS, the Report menu item is available when you right-click the data collector in the Reports node. If you did not enable the Data Manager, the Reports menu option will be inaccessible. The Data Manager report provides a summary of the logged performance data, as shown in Figure 21-5. The report is saved as an XML file in the DCS folder associated with the selected data collector.

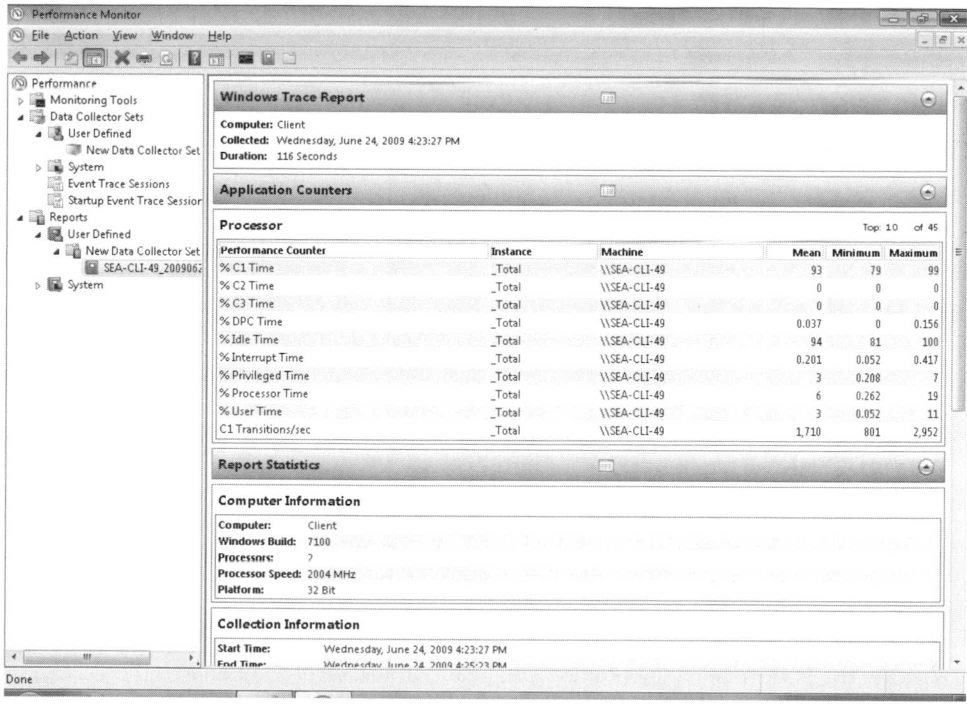

FIGURE 21-5 Example of a Data Manager report

If a user clicks a log that is currently started, the main Performance Monitor window displays a green status bar with a Collecting Data label. To view the log, you must first stop the DCS for the log. Log files are listed under the Data Collector Set node in the Reports node. File names follow a naming convention of

computer_name_YYYYMMDD_NNNNNN

The serial number *NNNNNN* is incremented each time the DCS is restarted.

Comparing Performance Monitor Logs

You can use Performance Monitor's Compare feature to overlay multiple log files for comparison. This feature is most useful for comparing multiple log files that have been configured to log the same data points for the same amount of time. To access the Compare feature, you must start Performance in stand-alone mode. After Performance Monitor is open, you can view and compare log files by performing the following steps:

1. Type **perfmon /sys /comp** to open Performance Monitor in stand-alone mode for comparison, and then click the View Log Data button on the toolbar to open the Performance Monitor properties with the focus on the Source tab, as shown here.

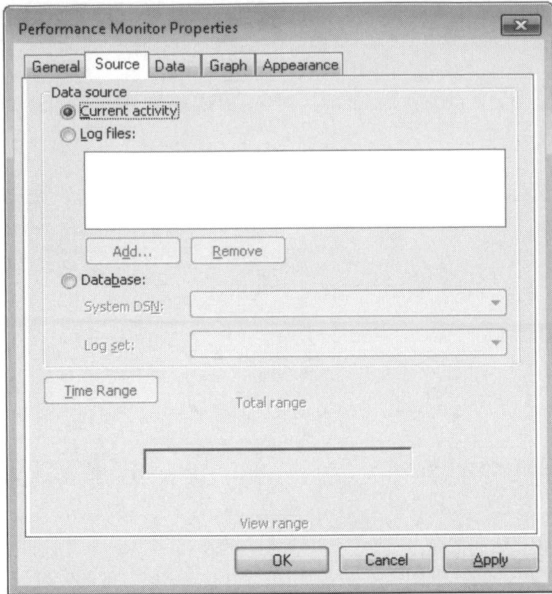

2. Click the Log Files option and click Add to open the Select Log File dialog box.
3. Locate the Performance Counter log (.blg) file that you want to open and then click Open. The log file will be added to the open Performance Monitor instance, but no counters will be added by default.
4. Click the Add button on the toolbar to open the Add Counters dialog box and add the counters that you want to display. The counter data will now be displayed in Performance Monitor.
5. Repeat steps 1 through 4 to open the second log file in a separate stand-alone Performance Monitor instance and display the desired counters.
6. After you open the logs for comparison, two opaque Performance Monitor windows will open on the desktop. Position the anchor window—which may be either one of the Performance Monitor windows—on your desktop and resize it as desired. This will be the Performance Monitor window upon which you overlay the other window.
7. Select the second Performance Monitor window—which will be overlaid on top of the first window—to bring it into focus, click the Compare menu, point to Set Transparency, and then select the desired transparency level. Note that transparency here is not related to the Windows Vista Aero Glass feature and will work on systems that are not capable of supporting Aero Glass.
8. The Set Transparency option sets the transparency of the window to be overlaid on the anchor window. The transparency options are No Transparency, 40% Transparency, and 70% Transparency. When you set the transparency to 40%, the desktop background remains visible through the second window.

9. Select the Compare menu item and then click the Snap To Compare option. The second window is resized to the same size as the anchor window and is overlaid on top of the anchor window, as shown here.

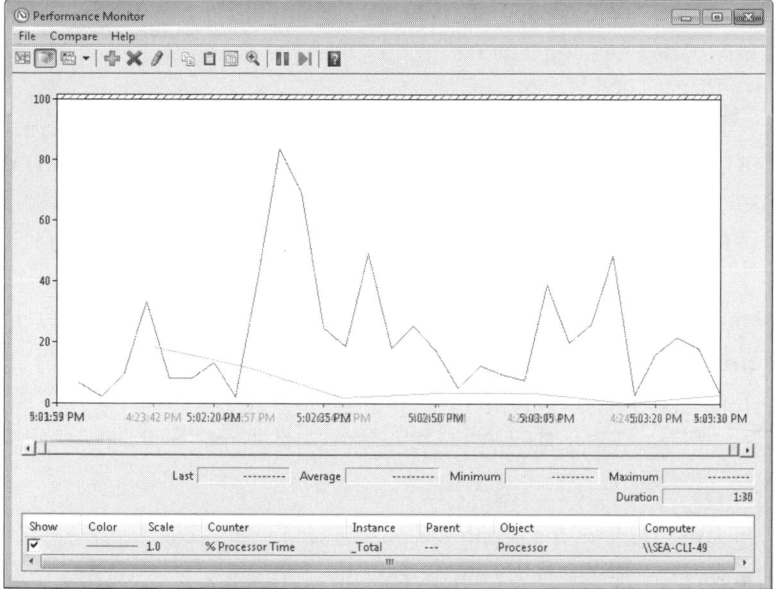

> **NOTE** You can still interact with both Performance Monitor windows individually to change properties; select menu items; and minimize, maximize, or close the windows.

Performance Monitor User Rights

Performance Monitor user rights are specified as follows:

- **Administrators** Members of this group have local and remote full control.
- **Performance Log Users** Members of this group can access and log performance counter data locally and remotely (create, manipulate, and view logs).
- **Performance Monitor Users** Members of this group can access performance counter data locally and remotely (view logs).

> **NOTE** On earlier versions of Windows, Performance Monitor can be used to monitor Windows Vista and later computers with options previously available on earlier versions of Windows but without support for new Windows Vista and later Performance Monitor features. The user of the earlier version of Windows must also be in the local Administrators group on the Windows Vista or later computer.

Remote Data Collection

To enable all remote performance logging and alerting, you must perform the following actions:

- Enable the Performance Logs And Alerts firewall exception on the user's computer.
- Add the user to the Event Log Readers group. (This applies only when the user belongs to the Performance Log Users group.)

Managing Performance Logs and Event Trace Sessions with Logman

Logman.exe creates and manages Event Trace Session and Performance logs and supports many functions of Performance Monitor from the command line. Logman commands include the following:

- **logman create** Creates a counter, trace, configuration data collector, or API
- **logman query** Queries data collector properties
- **logman start** Starts data collection
- **logman stop** Stops data collection
- **logman delete** Deletes an existing data collector
- **logman update** Updates the properties of an existing data collector
- **logman import** Imports a DCS from an XML file
- **logman export** Exports a DCS to an XML file
- **logman /?** Displays help for logman

The following usage examples illustrate logman syntax.

```
logman create counter perf_log -c "\Processor(_Total)\% Processor Time"
logman create trace trace_log -nb 16 256 -bs 64 -o c:\logfile
logman start perf_log
logman update perf_log -si 10 -f csv -v mmddhhmm
logman update trace_log -p "Windows Kernel Trace" (disk,net)
```

For detailed syntax of logman commands and more examples of usage, see *http://technet.microsoft.com/en-us/library/cc753820.aspx.*

Using Windows PowerShell for Performance Monitoring

New in Windows 7 is the capability of using Windows PowerShell for gathering performance data. Three new Windows PowerShell cmdlets provide functionality as follows:

- **Get-counter** Gets real-time performance counter data from local and remote computers
- **Import-counter** Exports PerformanceCounterSampleSet objects as performance counter log (.blg, .csv, .tsv) files
- **Export-counter** Imports performance counter log files and creates objects that represent each counter sample in the log

For example, the following Windows PowerShell command gets the current "% Processor Time" combined values for all processors on the local computer every 2 seconds until it has 100 values and displays the captured data.

```
PS C:\Users\mallen>Get-counter -Counter "\Processor(_Total)\% Processor Time"
-SampleInterval 2 -MaxSamples 100
```

The following command continuously gets the current "% Processor Time" combined values for all processors on the local computer every second (the default sampling interval) and displays the captured data until you press CTRL+C.

```
PS C:\Users\mallen>Get-counter -Counter "\Processor(_Total)\% Processor Time"
-Continuous
```

You can pipe the output of the *Get-counter* cmdlet into the *Export-counter* cmdlet. For example, the following command gets the current "% Processor Time" combined values for all processors on the local computer every 2 seconds until it has 100 values and exports the captured data as a performance counter log file named Data1.blg, which is saved in the current directory (here the root folder of user Michael Allen's user profile).

```
PS C:\Users\mallen>Get-counter "\Processor(*)\% Processor Time" -SampleInterval 2
-MaxSamples 100 | Export-counter -Path $home\data1.blg
```

You can also pipe the output of the *Import-counter* cmdlet into the *Export-counter* cmdlet. You might do this, for example, to convert a performance monitor log file from one format to another, such as from .csv to .blg format.

> ***MORE INFO*** **For more information on using Windows PowerShell for performance monitoring, see the help for the *Get-counter*, *Import-counter*, and *Export-counter* cmdlets in the Windows PowerShell Cmdlet Help Topics at *http://technet.microsoft.com/en-us/library/dd347701.aspx*.**

Resource Monitor

The Resource Overview screen of the Reliability and Performance Monitor Control Panel item in Windows Vista has become a separate tool in Windows 7 called Resource Monitor (see Figure 21-6). You can open Resource Monitor using any of the following methods:

- Type **resource** in the Start menu search box and click Resource Monitor when Resource Monitor appears in the Programs group.
- Type **perfmon /res** in the Start menu search box or at a command prompt and press Enter.
- Open Performance Monitor, right-click on the Monitoring Tools node, and select Resource Monitor.

■ Select Action Center, View Performance Information, Advanced Tools, Open Resource Monitor.

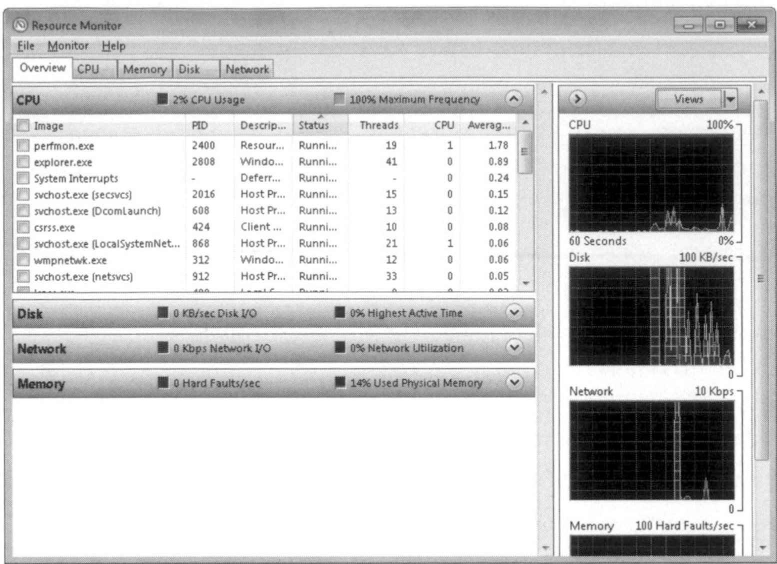

FIGURE 21-6 The Overview tab of Resource Monitor

Resource Monitor provides considerably more information in Windows 7 than the Resource Overview screen of the Reliability and Performance Monitor did in Windows Vista. The following sections summarize the information displayed on each tab of Resource Monitor.

> ***NOTE*** **Once you configure Resource Monitor to filter and display the information you want, you can save the configuration as an XML file by selecting Save Settings As from the File menu. You can save multiple configurations and then load each configuration as desired to display only the information you want to see.**

Overview Tab

The Overview tab (see Figure 21-6) displays graphs of CPU, disk, and network utilization, and a graph showing the rate of hard memory faults on the computer. These graphs can be resized using the Views button. The Overview tab also displays a summary of CPU, disk, network, and memory usage on the system as follows:

- **CPU** Displays the image name, Process Identifier (PID), description, status, number of threads, current percent of CPU consumption, and average CPU consumption for each process running on the computer. In addition, you can right-click a process and select any of the following options:
  - End Process
  - End Process Tree

- Analyze Wait Chain
- Suspend Process
- Resume Process
- Search Online

By selecting the check box for one or more processes, you can filter the information displayed in the Disk, Network, and Memory sections of this tab.

- **Disk** Displays the image name, PID, file name, average number of bytes per second read from the file, average number of bytes per second written to the file, average total number of bytes per second read from and written to the file, priority of I/O transfers, and disk response time in milliseconds for each process accessing the disk subsystem on the computer.
- **Network** Displays the image name, PID, address (IP, NetBIOS, or fully qualified domain name [FQDN]) to which the process is connected, average number of bytes per second sent, average number of bytes per second received, and average number of bytes per second transferred for each process accessing the network subsystem on the computer.
- **Memory** Displays the image name, PID, average number of hard page faults per second, kilobytes of virtual memory reserved by the operating system for the process, kilobytes of virtual memory currently in use by the process, kilobytes of virtual memory currently in use by the process that can be shared with other processes, and kilobytes of virtual memory currently in use by the process that cannot be shared with other processes for all processes on the system.

CPU Tab

The CPU tab displays graphs of percent total processor usage, percent processor usage used by services, and percent processor usage for each logical or physical CPU on the computer. The CPU tab also displays the following information concerning CPU utilization on the computer:

- **Processes** Displays the image name, PID, description, status, number of threads, current percent of CPU consumption, and average CPU consumption for each process running on the computer. In addition, you can right-click a process and select any of the following options:
  - End Process
  - End Process Tree
  - Analyze Wait Chain
  - Suspend Process
  - Resume Process
  - Search Online

- **Services**   Displays the image name, PID, description, status, service group name, current percent of CPU consumption, and average CPU consumption for each process running on the computer. In addition, you can right-click a process and perform any of the following options:
  - Start Service
  - Stop Service
  - Restart Service
  - Search Online
- **Associated Handles**   By selecting the check box for one or more processes in the Processes section of this tab, you can display the image name, PID, handle type, and handle name for each handle associated with the process. You can also search for the handles associated with a process by typing the name of the process in the Search Handles box.
- **Associated Modules**   By selecting the check box for one or more processes in the Processes section of this tab, you can display the image name, PID, module name, module version, and full path to the module file for each module associated with the process. You can also search for the modules associated with a process by typing the name of the process in the Search Modules box.

Memory Tab

The Memory tab (see Figure 21-7) displays percentage graphs of used physical memory, commit charge, and hard faults per second. The Memory tab also displays the following information concerning memory utilization on the computer:

- **Processes**   Displays the image name, PID, average number of hard page faults per second, kilobytes of virtual memory reserved by the operating system for the process, kilobytes of virtual memory currently in use by the process, kilobytes of virtual memory currently in use by the process that can be shared with other processes, and kilobytes of virtual memory currently in use by the process that cannot be shared with other processes for all processes on the system. In addition, you can right-click a process and select any of the following options:
  - End Process
  - End Process Tree
  - Analyze Wait Chain
  - Suspend Process
  - Resume Process
  - Search Online
- **Physical Memory**   Displays a map of how physical memory is being allocated on the computer.

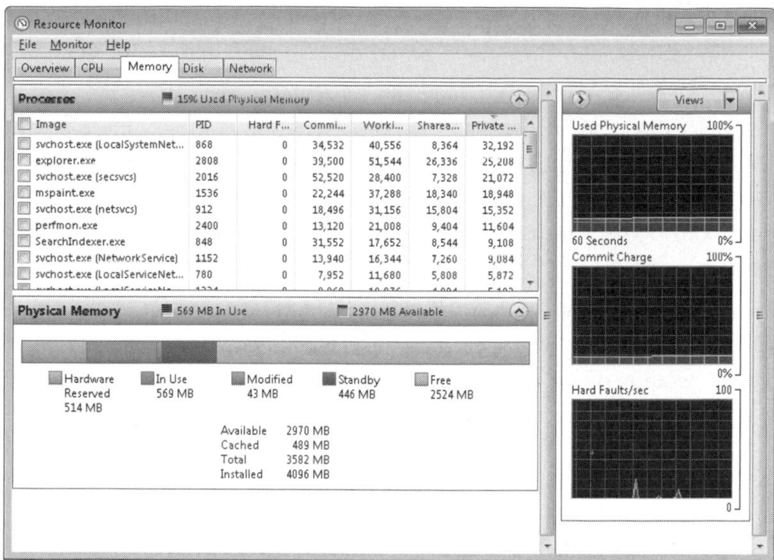

FIGURE 21-7 The Memory tab of Resource Monitor, showing the map of physical memory allocation

> ***NOTE*** **Hard page faults are a better indicator of memory starvation than soft page faults. A hard page fault occurs when the referenced memory page is no longer in physical memory and has been paged to the disk. A hard page fault is not an error, but it can indicate that more memory is needed to provide optimal performance.**

Disk Tab

The Disk tab displays a graph of total disk activity on the computer and graphs of disk queue length for each disk on the system. The Disk tab also displays the following information concerning disk utilization on the computer:

- **Processes With Disk Activity** Displays the image name, PID, average number of bytes per second read from the file, average number of bytes per second written to the file, and average total number of bytes per second read from and written to the file for each process accessing the disk subsystem on the computer. In addition, you can right-click a process and select any of the following options:
  - End Process
  - End Process Tree
  - Analyze Wait Chain
  - Suspend Process
  - Resume Process
  - Search Online

By selecting the check box for one or more processes in the Processes With Disk Activity section of this tab, you can filter the information displayed in the Disk Activity section of this tab.

- **Disk Activity** Displays the image name, PID, file name, average number of bytes per second read from the file, average number of bytes per second written to the file, average total number of bytes per second read from and written to the file, priority of I/O transfers, and disk response time in milliseconds for each process accessing the disk subsystem on the computer.
- **Storage** Displays the logical drive number, physical disk number, percentage of time the disk is not idle, free megabytes on the physical disk, total megabytes of space on the physical disk, and average disk queue length for each logical drive on the computer.

Network Tab

The Network tab displays graphs of average bytes transferred, number of Transmission Control Protocol (TCP) connections, and total network utilization for each network connection on the computer. The Network tab also displays the following information concerning network utilization on the computer:

- **Processes with Network Activity** Displays the image name, PID, average number of bytes per second sent, average number of bytes per second received, and average number of bytes per second transferred for each process accessing the network subsystem on the computer. In addition, you can right-click a process and select any of the following options:
  - End Process
  - End Process Tree
  - Analyze Wait Chain
  - Suspend Process
  - Resume Process
  - Search Online

  By selecting the check box for one or more processes in the Processes With Network Activity section of this tab, you can filter the information displayed in the Network Activity section of this tab.
- **Network Activity** Displays the image name, PID, address (IP, NetBIOS, or FQDN) to which the process is connected, average number of bytes per second sent, average number of bytes per second received, and average number of bytes per second transferred for each process accessing the network subsystem on the computer.
- **TCP Connections** Displays the image name, PID, local address and port number, remote address and port number, percentage of packet loss, and round-trip latency in milliseconds for each TCP connection on the computer.

- **Listening Ports** Displays the image name, PID, listening IP address, listening port number, network protocol, and firewall port status for each listening port on the computer.

Reliability Monitor

Reliability Monitor provides a graphical overview of the stability of a computer over time together with detailed information about individual events that may affect the overall stability of the system (see Figure 21-8). Reliability Monitor begins to collect data at the time of system installation. It then presents that data in a chart format that can be used to identify drivers, applications, or hardware that are causing stability issues or reliability problems on the computer. You can open Reliability Monitor using any of the following methods:

- Type **reliability** in the Start menu search box and click View Reliability History when it appears in the Programs group.
- Type **perfmon /rel** in the Start menu search box or at a command prompt and press Enter.
- Open Performance Monitor, right-click the Monitoring Tools node, and select View System Reliability.

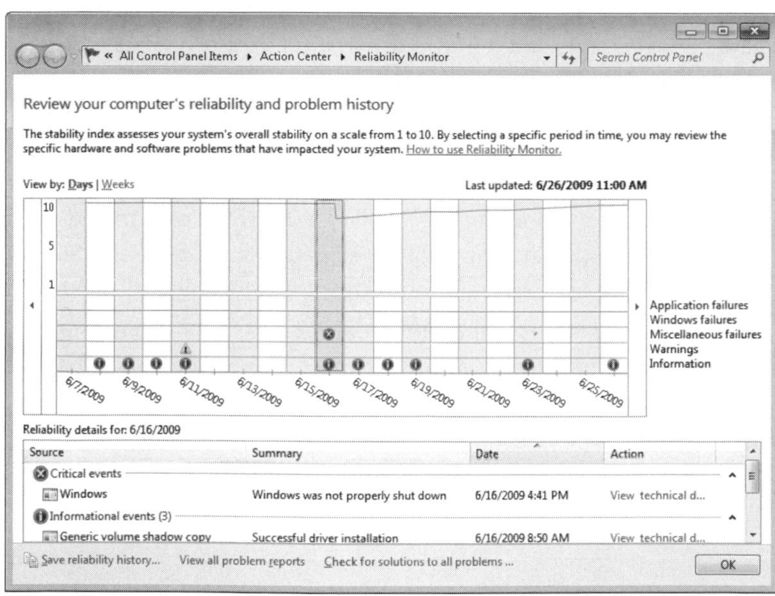

FIGURE 21-8 Reliability Monitor

Reliability Monitor tracks the following five categories of events:

- Application failures
- Windows failures

- Miscellaneous failures
- Warnings
- Information

How Reliability Monitor Works

Reliability Monitor gathers and processes data using the Reliability Analysis Component (RAC) of Windows 7. Data is automatically collected by the reliability analysis metrics calculation executable (RACAgent.exe), also known as the RACAgent process. The RACAgent analyzes, aggregates, and correlates user disruptions in the operating system, services, and programs and then processes the data into reliability metrics. The RACAgent runs as a hidden scheduled task named RACAgent to collect specific events from the event log. The RACAgent runs once every hour to collect relevant event log data and processes data once every 24 hours, so stability data will not be available immediately after installation.

After the data is collected, the RACAgent processes this information using a weighted algorithm. The result of the data processing is a stability index number that can vary on a scale from 0 to 10, with 0 being the least reliable and 10 being the most reliable. The stability index and the results of the event tracing are then displayed in graphical form over time.

System reliability information is displayed graphically as data points that represent the reliability index of the system for a specific day or week, depending upon the view selected. The horizontal axis displays the date range and the vertical axis displays the Stability Index number. The chart uses icons (red circles for critical events, yellow triangles for warnings, and blue circles for informational events) to indicate if an event of interest has occurred in one of the major categories on the indicated day or week. You can access the details of an event or failure by clicking the day or week the event occurred and then clicking View Technical Details for the event in the scrolling list box at the bottom. The Stability Index is the primary indicator of system stability over time based on the data that is gathered and processed by Reliability Monitor. The graph indicates the value of the stability index over the time range selected.

Reliability Monitor tracks the number of user disruptions per day over a 28-day rolling window of time, with the latest day of the rolling window being the current day. The Stability Index algorithm processes the information and calculates the stability index relative to the current day. Until the Reliability Monitor has collected 28 days of data, the Stability Index is displayed as a dotted line on the graph, indicating that it has not yet established a valid baseline for the measurement.

DIRECT FROM THE SOURCE

RACAgent Scheduled Task

CSS Global Technical Readiness (GTR) Team

The RACAgent is a hidden scheduled task (Microsoft\Windows\RAC\RacTask in Task Scheduler) that is automatically configured during system installation. This task is responsible for gathering reliability data and displaying it in chart view. The RACAgent task typically runs once every hour and will not wake the computer if it is sleeping. If the computer is a laptop on battery power, RACAgent.exe will immediately exit if the battery capacity is at less than 33 percent. To view the RACAgent task in Task Scheduler, select RAC in the Task Scheduler library and then right-click and select View – Show Hidden Tasks in the MMC action pane.

If you do not want to track system stability, you can disable the RACAgent task by selecting the Disable option, which is accessible in any of the following ways when the RACAgent task is highlighted in the main MMC pane:

- Via the action menu
- Via the action pane
- Via the shortcut menu for the task

Windows Performance Tools Kit

The Windows Performance Tools (WPT) Kit contains tools designed for analyzing a wide range of performance problems on Windows 7, Windows Vista, and Windows Server 2008. The types of performance problems that you can troubleshoot using the WPT Kit include application start times, boot issues, deferred procedure calls (DPCs), interrupt service routines (ISRs), system responsiveness issues, application resource usage, and interrupt storms. The WPT Kit is available as part of the Windows software development kit (SDK) for Windows Server 2008 or later and the Microsoft .NET Framework 3.5 or later. The WPT Kit is intended for use by system builders, hardware manufacturers, driver developers, and general application developers.

The WPT Kit is available as an MSI installer, one per architecture, and contains the Performance Analyzer tool suite, which consists of the following three tools:

- **Xperf.exe** Captures traces and post-processes them for use on any machine and supports command-line (action-based) trace analysis
- **Xperfview.exe** Displays trace content in the form of interactive graphs and summary tables

- **Xbootmgr.exe** Automates on/off state transitions and captures traces during such transitions

Typical scenarios where you might use Xperf include:

- Profiling applications or the system itself using sampling profiler mode.
- Capturing Event Tracing for Windows data for later analysis.
- Determining whether an application is I/O- or CPU-bound.

To use Xperf to capture a trace of a system, follow these steps:

1. Install the WPT Kit on the system.
2. Turn tracing on using the *xperf –on* provider command.
3. Perform the activities you want to profile on the system.
4. Capture a log file using the *xperf –d logfilename* command.
5. Analyze your log file using the *xperf logfilename* command.

> ***MORE INFO*** **For more information concerning the Windows Performance Tools, see *http://msdn.microsoft.com/en-us/performance/cc825801.aspx*. To obtain the latest Windows SDK, see *http://msdn.microsoft.com/en-us/windowsserver/bb980924.aspx*.**

Event Monitoring

Administrators, developers, and technical support personnel use event monitoring for gathering information about the state of the hardware, the software, and the system, as well as to monitor security events. To provide these users with useful information, you need to give an event the right level or severity, raise it to the appropriate log, provide it with the correct attributes, and give it a useful and actionable message.

Understanding the Windows Event Architecture

Prior to Windows Vista, the Windows Event Log API and ETW were separate components. The Windows Event Log API published events in event logs, such as the System and Application event logs, while ETW could be used to start event tracing sessions for detailed troubleshooting of system and application issues.

Beginning with Windows Vista, the Windows event logs and ETW are unified into a single architecture that provides an always-present, selectively-on logging infrastructure. While the Windows event logs and ETW integrated with each other in Windows Vista and later, event logs and ETW generally target two different types of users:

- **ETW** Used mainly by developers and for advanced troubleshooting by support professionals, ETW must be manually enabled on a computer and generates events at a higher rate (around 10,000 per second) than the event logs. ETW includes the following features:

- Defined declaratively in manifests
- Has localizable strings
- Has a flexible data model
- Uses programmatic consumption
- Has discoverability

- **Event logs** Used mainly by system administrators, event logs are always on and typically generate events at a lower rate (around 100 events per second) than ETW. Event logs include all the features of ETW, plus the following:
  - Admin-focused tools
  - Centralized event logs
  - Remote collection support
  - Data query support
  - Reduced logging rate

The Windows Event architecture consists of the following:

- **Event Providers** These define events and register with the ETW/Event Log infrastructure using XML manifest files that define the events that can be generated, logging levels, event templates, and other components.
- **Event Controllers** These are used to start and stop tracing sessions on the computer.
- **Event Consumers** These register to receive events in real time (from an event channel or ETW sessions) or from an existing log file (an event log file or trace file).

Channels

To publish an event, the event must be registered using the ETW API. An XML manifest then defines how the event is published. Windows events can be published to either a channel or an ETW session.

A *channel* is a named stream of events. Channels are used to transport events from an event publisher to an event log file so that an event consumer can get the event. Figure 21-9 shows the structure of the channels and event logs in Windows Vista and later versions. Windows Vista and later versions include the following types of channels:

- **System** System channels include the System, Application, and Security event log channels. These channels are created when Windows is installed on the computer.
- **Serviced** Serviced channels include the following:
  - **Admin** Events in this channel primarily target administrators, support technicians, and users. Admin events generally indicate problems that have well-defined solutions that you can act on.

- **Operational** Events in this channel are used for analyzing and diagnosing a problem with the computer. Operational events can be used to trigger tasks or tools for troubleshooting problems.

- **Direct** Direct channels include the following:
  - **Analytic** Events in this channel describe problems that cannot be resolved by user intervention. Analytic events are published in high volume and can be queried but cannot be subscribed to. Analytic channels are disabled by default.
  - **Debug** Events in this channel are used by developers or support technicians for debugging system and application issues. Debug channels are disabled by default.

> ***NOTE*** **Analytic and Debug channel event information should first be converted to the standard Event Log (.evtx) file format to make it easier to read in Event Viewer.**

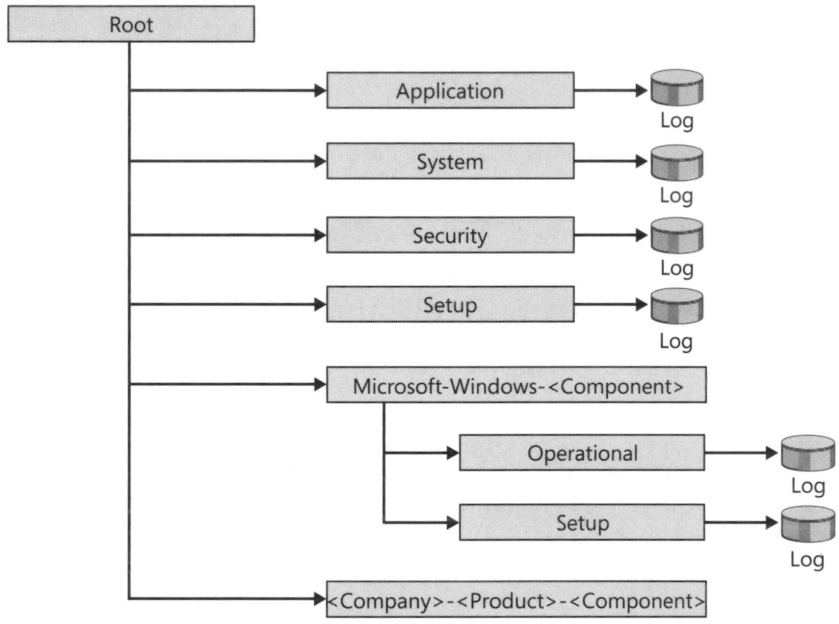

FIGURE 21-9 Event channel/event log structure

By default, an event log file is attached to each channel except the analytic and debug channels. The event logs for those channels are disabled by default and are hidden from view in Event Viewer. To make Analytic and Debug event logs visible in Event Viewer, select Show Analytic And Debug Logs from the View method. Once these logs are displayed, you can selectively enable them by right-clicking on them and selecting Enable Log.

Improvements to Event Monitoring in Windows 7

Previously in Windows Vista, event information (that is, event logs and ETW) could be accessed using the following methods:

- Using native and managed APIs programmatically.
- Using the Event Viewer MMC snap-in.
- Using the Wevtutil.exe command-line tool.
- Using the Tracerpt.exe command-line tool.

New in Windows 7 is the additional capability of using Windows PowerShell for scriptable consumption of event information on both local and remote computers. For more information concerning this topic, see the section titled "Using Windows PowerShell for Event Monitoring" later in this chapter.

Other improvements to ETW/Event Logs in Windows 7 include:

- New Windows events and event providers.
- Improved data formatting for event consumption.
- Enhanced performance, scalability, and robustness.
- Simplified event development for application developers using improved design-time validation and automatic generation of code from XML.

Using Event Viewer

You can open Event Viewer by using any of the following methods:

- In Control Panel, select Administrative Tools, Event Viewer.
- In Computer Management, select System Tools, Event Viewer.
- Type **event** in the Start menu search box and click Event Viewer when it appears in the Programs group.
- Type **eventvwr.exe** or **eventvwr.msc** at an elevated command prompt.

The sections that follow describe how to use the Event Viewer interface for viewing and managing event logs.

Understanding Views

When Event Viewer is opened, the Overview And Summary screen is displayed (see Figure 21-10), which summarizes all events across all Windows Logs. The total number of events for each type that have occurred are displayed, with additional columns that display the number of events of each type that have occurred over the last seven days, the last 24 hours, or the last hour. Clicking on the + (plus) sign allows you to browse to each event type and display the Event ID, Source, and Log in which the event occurred. Double-clicking a specific event summary takes you directly to that event in the log and automatically creates a filtered view showing all individual events with that event source and event ID, which can be accessed from the left pane.

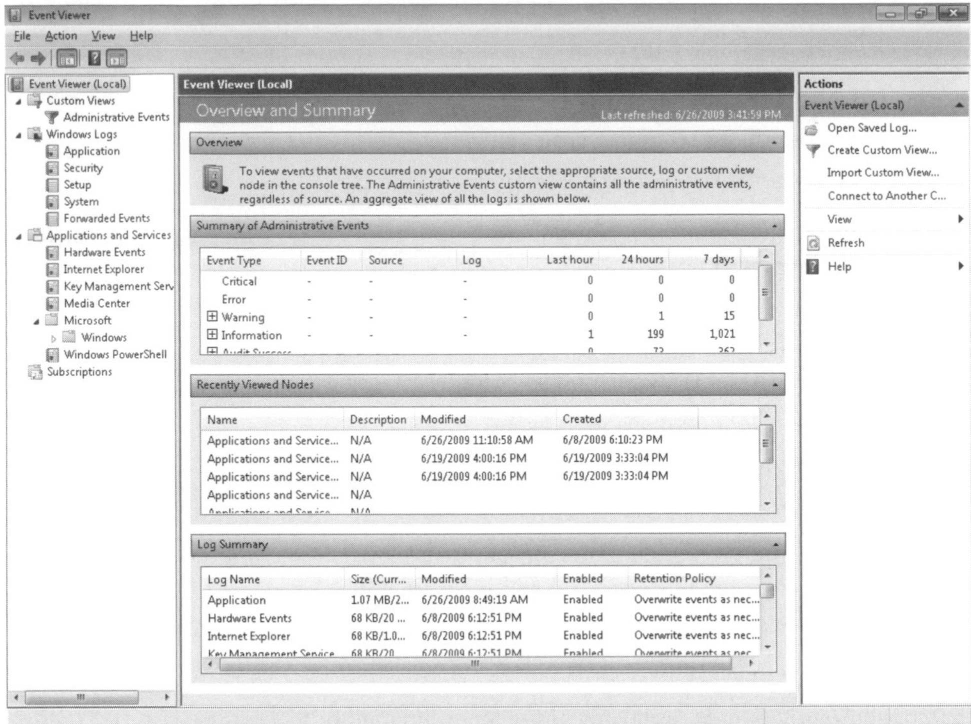

FIGURE 21-10 The Event Viewer snap-in

You can configure persistent event filters by using the Custom Views node in Event Viewer. You can create views automatically by double-clicking events in the summary view, or you can create views manually. A built-in custom view named Administrative Events shows all events on the system that may require administrative action by filtering errors and warnings across all admin logs on the system.

To create a view (filter) manually, follow these steps:

1. Right-click Custom Views and then select Create Custom View.
2. In the Create Custom View dialog box, shown here, enter the criteria for which you want events displayed.

   You can also click the XML tab and enter the XML filter directly. This may be useful if you are creating an advanced query for which the graphical user interface (GUI) options in the Filter tab are insufficient. Note that when you have edited a filter in the XML tab, you cannot return to the Filter tab for that filter.

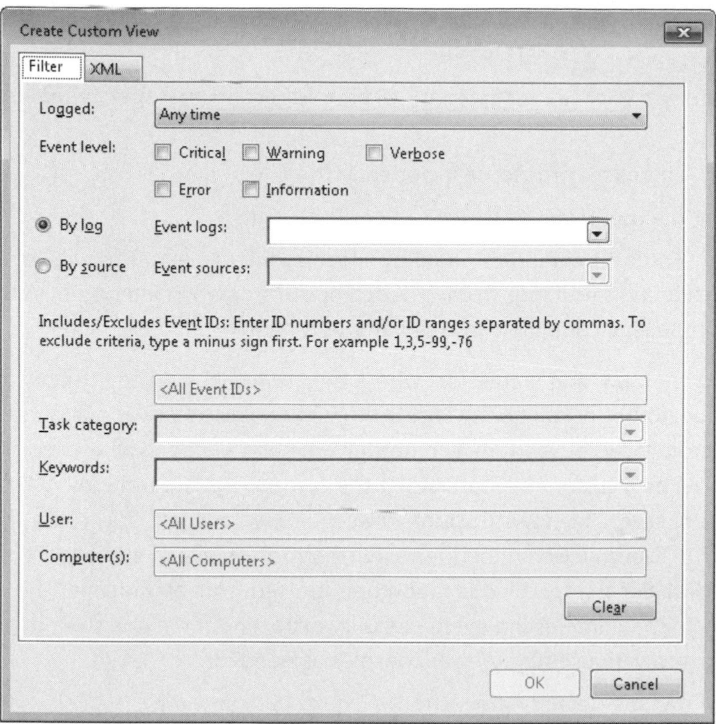

3. Select the fields used to filter events using the following criteria:

- **By Log** If you are filtering by log, first select the logs you are interested in. The Event Logs drop-down list adjusts to the list of logs relevant for those sources.
- **By Source** If you are filtering by source, pick the sources of interest first. The Sources drop-down list adjusts to just the sources available in those logs.
- **Logged** Last Hour, Last 12 Hours, Last 24 Hours, Last 7 Days, or Last 30 Days. Selecting Custom Range brings up the Custom Range dialog box, allowing you to select a much more specific date range, including when events start and when they stop.
- **Event Level** Select Critical, Warning, Verbose, Error, or Information.
- **Event Logs** Click the drop-down arrow to open the Event Log Selection window. Select the event log or event logs that you want to include in the view.
- **Event Sources** Click the drop-down arrow to display a list of available sources for the selected log so that you can specify which event source(s) to include in the view. In some cases, certain sources may not be listed (usually this can happen for event sources from older versions of Windows), in which case you can type in the source name manually.
- **Include/Exclude Event IDs** Enter Event ID numbers or ranges to be included or excluded, separated by commas. To exclude a number, include a minus sign in front

of it. For example, typing **1,3,5-99,-76** will include event IDs 1, 3, 5 through 99 and exclude 76.

- **Task Category** Select a task category to filter for events that specify that task category.
- **Keywords** Enter keywords to be included in the filter.
- **User** Enter the user name by which to filter the events.
- **Computer** Enter the computer name by which to filter events. This will likely be used when filtering saved logs from other computers or when filtering events forwarded from several computers on to a centralized log.

4. Click OK, name the view, and then select where the view will be saved. Create a new folder, if needed, to better categorize custom views you create for various purposes. By default, custom views defined on a computer will be available to all users on that computer. To define a custom view private to the current user, clear the All Users check box before saving the view. Custom views are saved and you may reuse them any time you run Event Viewer in the future. Furthermore, you can also export custom views into an XML file at a specified location or imported from an XML file. This allows administrators to share interesting event views by exporting them to a shared location and importing into various Event Viewer consoles as needed.

   Figure 21-11 shows the default Administrative Events custom view.

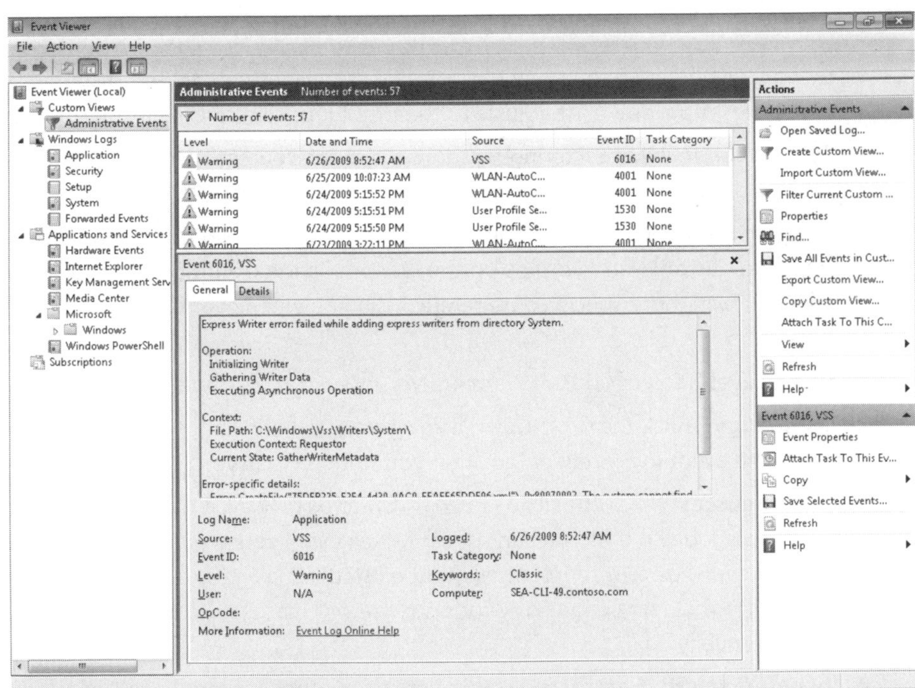

FIGURE 21-11 The default Administrative Events custom view

Viewing Event Logs

The Application, System, Security, and Setup logs are now located under the Windows Logs node in the Event Viewer tree view. An event summary view including the name, type, number of events, and size of each log is displayed when this node is selected. To view events in a log, select the log you want to view in the left pane.

Hardware Events, Windows Internet Explorer, and other Windows components and application events are accessible under the Applications And Services Logs node. Applications And Services Logs are a new category of event logs that store events from a single application or component rather than events that might have system-wide impact. Normally, available application or service logs will be listed in a hierarchy under the manufacturer and product name. (Some event providers that do not follow the naming convention that allows such categorization may show up directly under the Applications And Services node.) A summary view, including the name, type, number of events, and size of each log, is displayed when the Applications And Services node or any subnode that contains logs is selected in the Event Viewer tree view, as shown in Figure 21-12. If other applications are installed, such as Microsoft Office 2007 applications, additional Applications And Services Logs may be displayed.

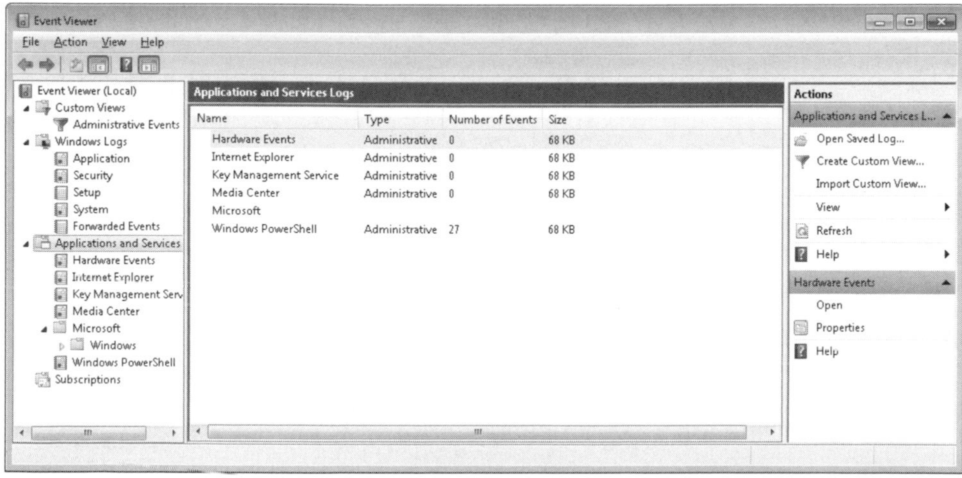

FIGURE 21-12 Summary view of Applications And Services Logs

As explained previously, Application and Services Logs include four log subtypes: Admin, Operational, Analytic (trace), and Debug logs. Events in Admin logs are of particular interest to IT professionals who use Event Viewer to troubleshoot problems, because events in the Admin log provide guidance on how to respond to the event. Events in the Operational log are also useful for IT professionals but sometimes require more interpretation.

Analytic and Debug logs are not as user friendly and are mostly designed to be used by advanced administrators and developers. Analytic logs store events that trace an issue, and often a high volume of events are logged. Debug logs are used by developers when debugging applications. Both Analytic and Debug logs are hidden by default. If you will be working with these types of logs and want to see them in the Event Viewer, select the Show Analytic And Debug Logs menu option from the View item on the Actions pane. Then, to turn logging into a particular Analytic or Debug log on or off, select the log of interest and click Enable Log or Disable Log on the Actions pane. Alternatively, you can also enable or disable Analytic and Debug logs by typing **wevtutil sl *log_name* /e:true** at an elevated command prompt. For more information concerning Wevtutil.exe, see the section titled "Using the Windows Events Command-Line Utility for Event Monitoring" later in this chapter.

> ***IMPORTANT*** **When you enable Analytic (trace) and Debug logs, they usually generate a large number of entries. For this reason, you should enable them only for a specified period to gather troubleshooting data and then turn them off to reduce the associated overhead.**

You can view the events in a log by highlighting the log you want to view in the left pane. Most Microsoft components that have their own channel are displayed under the Microsoft node, as shown in Figure 21-13.

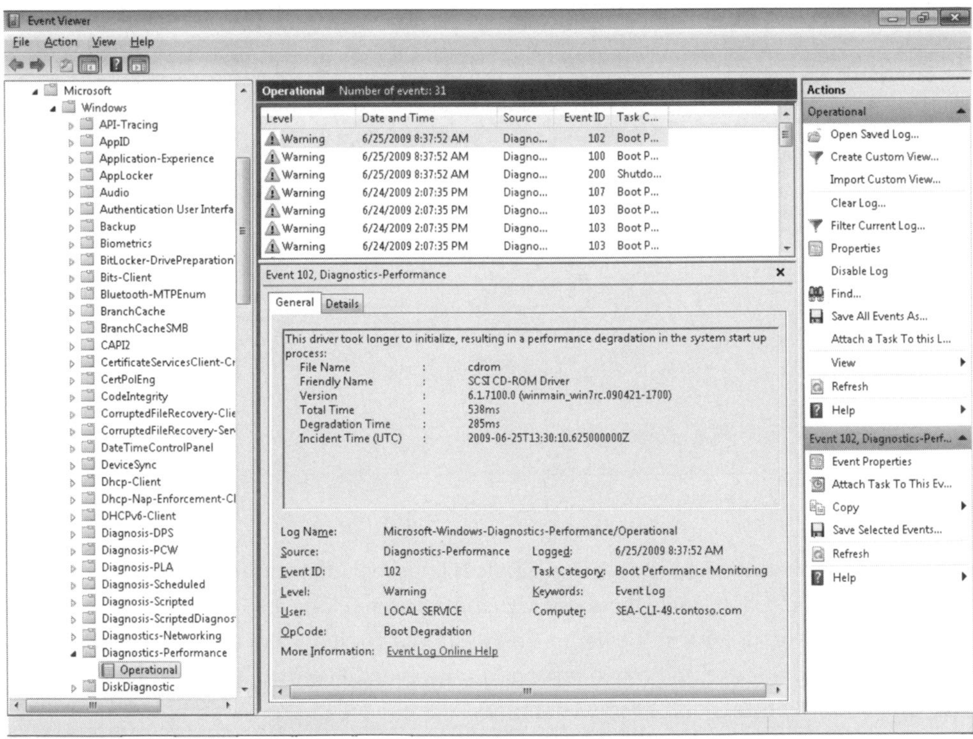

FIGURE 21-13 Events for different Microsoft components

NOTE By right-clicking an event and selecting Attach Task To This Event, you can open the Task Scheduler Wizard with the Event Log, Event Source, and Event ID fields automatically pre-populated. Doing this lets you attach any task to an event by using Task Scheduler. For more information, see the section titled "Using Task Scheduler" later in this chapter.

Saving Event Logs

You can use Event Viewer to save events and open saved event logs for archiving and analysis. You can save an event log using any of the following formats:

- Event log (.evtx) file (the default)
- XML (.xml) file
- Tab-delimited text (.txt) file
- Comma-separated text (.csv) file

Saved event logs can be viewed using Event Viewer. The supported formats include the following:

- Event log (.evtx) file
- Legacy event log (.evt) file
- Trace log (.etl) file

Configuring Event Subscriptions

Using Event Viewer, you can view events on a single remote computer. However, troubleshooting an issue might require you to examine a set of events stored in multiple logs on multiple computers.

Windows Vista and later versions include the ability to collect and forward event information from multiple remote computers and store them centrally on the local computer. To specify which events you want to collect, you create an *event subscription*. Among other details, the subscription specifies exactly which events will be collected and in which log they will be stored locally. When a subscription is active and events are being collected, you can view and manipulate these forwarded events as you would any other locally stored events.

To use subscriptions, you must first configure the forwarding computers and the collector computer. Event collecting functionality relies upon the Windows Remote Management (WinRM) and Windows Event Collector (Wecsvc) services. The WinRM service must be running on both the remote and local computers participating in the forwarding and collecting process. The Wecsvc service needs to be running only on the collector computer because the source computer has a forwarding plug-in that runs in-process to WinRM.

To define a subscription, you must be an administrator on the collector computer. As part of the subscription definition, you define what security context should be used when accessing the logs on the source computers. This can be either a specific user account or the collector computer account. The specified account must have Read access to the logs on the source computers that are participating in the subscription. One way to set this up is to use a new built-in group called Event Log Readers to which you can add any accounts you want to give access to reading logs.

To configure computers to forward and collect events, follow these steps:

1. Log on to all collector and source computers, which must be running Windows Vista or later versions. If the computers are members of a domain, it is best to use a domain account with administrative privileges.
2. On each source computer, type **winrm quickconfig** at an elevated command prompt. When prompted, confirm that the changes should be made. To skip the prompt (for example, if you are using this command in a script), add the *–q* parameter.
3. On the collector computer, type **wecutil qc** at an elevated command prompt. (If you use Event Viewer, this will be done automatically for you on the collector.) When prompted, confirm that the changes should be made. To skip the prompt, add the */q:true* parameter.
4. Add the computer account of the collector computer to the Event Log Readers group on each of the source computers if you will be using the computer account as the account to be used when collecting events. The advantage of using the collector computer account is that you don't need to deal with expiring passwords. However, if you do use a specific user account, you will need to add that account to the Event Log Readers instead of the collector computer account.

The computers are now configured to forward and collect events. Follow the steps described in the section titled "Creating a New Subscription" later in this chapter to specify the events you want to have forwarded to the collector.

> ***NOTE*** **By default, the Local Users And Groups MMC snap-in does not allow you to add computer accounts. In the Select Users, Computers, Or Groups dialog box, click Object Types and then select the Computers check box. You will now be able to add computer accounts.**

> ***NOTE*** **Beginning in Windows 7, you can now use the Set-WsManQuickConfig Windows PowerShell cmdlet to configure WinRM on the local computer. For more information, see *http://technet.microsoft.com/en-us/library/dd819520.aspx*.**

CONSIDERATIONS FOR WORKGROUP ENVIRONMENTS

In a workgroup environment, you can follow the same basic procedure described in the previous section to configure computers to forward and collect events. However, workgroups require some additional steps and considerations:

- You can use only Normal mode (Pull) subscriptions.
- You must add a Windows Firewall exception for Remote Event Log Management on each source computer.
- You must add an account with administrator privileges to the Event Log Readers group on each source computer. You must specify this account in the Configure Advanced Subscription Settings dialog box when you create a subscription on the collector computer.
- Type **winrm set winrm/config/client @{TrustedHosts="<*sources*>"}** at a command prompt on the collector computer to allow all of the source computers to use NTLM authentication when communicating with WinRM on the collector computer. Run this command only once. Where <*sources*> appears in the command, substitute a comma-separated list of the names of all of the participating source computers in the workgroup. Alternatively, you can use wildcards to match the names of all the source computers. For example, if you want to configure a set of source computers that each has a name that begins with *msft*, you could type the command **winrm set winrm/config/client @{TrustedHosts="msft*"}** on the collector computer. To learn more about this command, type **winrm help config** at a command prompt.
- If you configure a subscription to use the HTTPS protocol by using the HTTPS option in Advanced Subscription Settings, you must also set corresponding Windows Firewall exceptions for port 443. For a subscription that uses Normal (PULL mode) delivery optimization, you must set the exception only on the source computers. For a subscription that uses either Minimize Bandwidth or Minimize Latency (PUSH mode) delivery optimizations, you must set the exception on both the source and collector computers.
- If you intend to specify a user account by selecting the Specific User option in Advanced Subscription Settings when creating the subscription, you must ensure that the account is a member of the local Administrators group on each of the source computers in step 4 in the previous procedure instead of adding the machine account of the collector computer. Alternatively, you can use the Windows Event Log command-line utility to grant an account access to individual logs. To learn more about this command-line utility, type **wevtutil -?** at a command prompt.

CREATING A NEW SUBSCRIPTION

To configure a new subscription on the collector computer, follow these steps:

1. Right-click Subscriptions in the Event Viewer tree view and then select Create Subscription, or select the Subscriptions node and click the Create Subscription action in the Actions pane.
2. In the Subscription Properties dialog box, shown here, enter the Subscription Name.

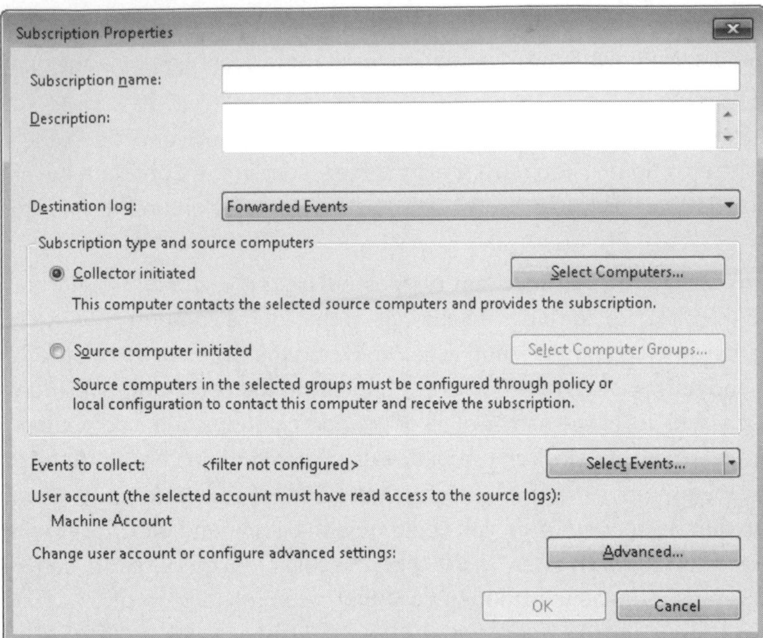

3. Select the Destination Log name to save the subscribed events to. By default, the event subscriptions will be collected in the ForwardedEvents log.
4. Click Select Computers to open the Computers dialog box, shown here.

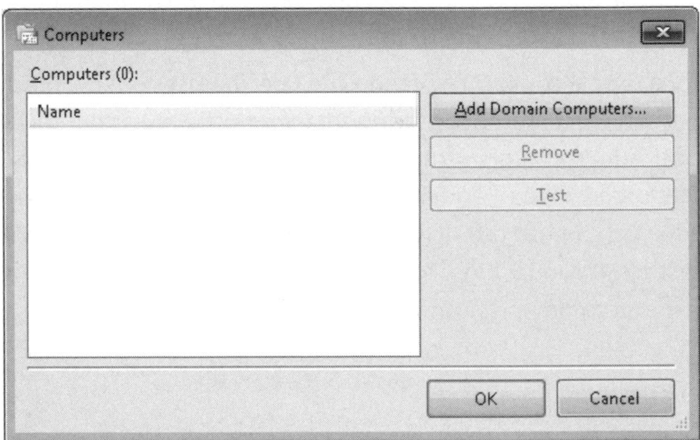

5. Click Add Domain Computers and add the source computers from which the subscription will pull data. The Test button can be used to test connectivity to the selected computer and ensure that the collector will have access to that computer to collect events. Click OK when finished adding source computers.
6. Click Select Events to configure the specific events that you want to collect. The Select Events button presents two options when you click the drop-down list:

   - **Edit** Opens the Query Filter dialog box to allow the creation of an event filter to be used for the subscription.

- **Copy From Existing Custom View** Allows the selection of an existing Custom View to be used for the subscription.

7. Click Advanced to configure the options shown in the following dialog box. The Advanced button lets you configure how collected events are delivered and also lets you specify the account used to manage the process of collecting events. Event Viewer provides three event delivery optimization options: Normal, Minimize Bandwidth, and Minimize Latency, as shown here (see Table 21-1 for more information).

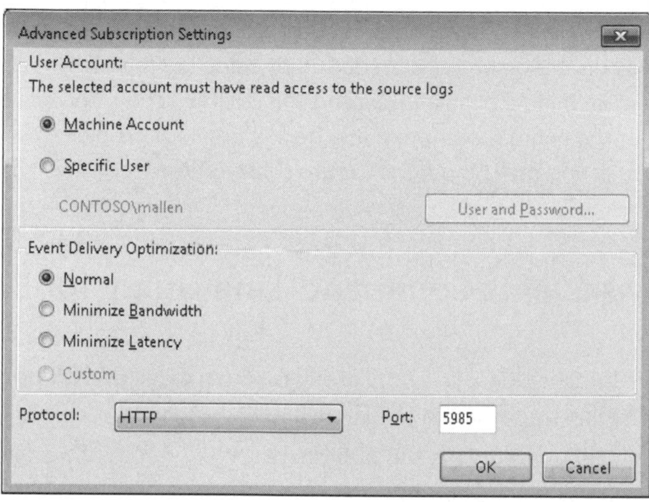

TABLE 21-1 Optimization Delivery Options for Configuring Event Collection

EVENT DELIVERY OPTIMIZATION METHOD	DESCRIPTION
Normal	Ensures reliable delivery of events and does not attempt to conserve bandwidth. This is the appropriate choice unless you need tighter control over bandwidth usage or need forwarded events delivered as quickly as possible. This method uses pull delivery mode, batches 5 items at a time, and sets a batch time-out of 15 minutes.
Minimize Bandwidth	Ensures that the use of network bandwidth for event delivery is strictly controlled. This is an appropriate choice if you want to limit the frequency of network connections made to deliver events. This method uses push delivery mode and sets a batch time-out of 6 hours. This method also uses a heartbeat interval of 6 hours.
Minimize Latency	Ensures that events are delivered with minimal delay. This is an appropriate choice if you are collecting alerts or critical events. This method uses push delivery mode and sets a batch time-out of 30 seconds.

After you create the subscription, you can view and configure it from the middle pane of Event Viewer. For each subscription, you can see its name, status, participating source computers, and description. To view detailed status for each source computer participating in a subscription, open the Subscription Properties dialog box for the subscription of interest. The Source Computers list displays the list of participating computers and the status for each. Selecting a specific computer in the list will display detailed status in the box underneath the computer list, and if there is a problem with that computer, the detailed status also includes possible causes and remedies. You can temporarily disable individual computers from participating in the subscription by selecting the computer in the list and clicking Disable. In addition, you can temporarily disable an entire subscription by selecting the subscription in the Subscriptions list in the main middle pane and clicking the Disable action. You can also retry individual computers or the entire subscription (to check if previous problems have been remedied, for example) by selecting the computer or entire subscription, respectively, and clicking Retry.

Using the Windows Events Command-Line Utility for Event Monitoring

The Windows Events Command-Line Utility (Wevtutil.exe) lets you manage event logs on a computer from the command line by performing tasks such as:

- Retrieving information about event logs and publishers.
- Installing and uninstalling event manifests.
- Executing queries for specific event.
- Exporting, archiving, and clearing event logs.

Wevtutil should be run from an elevated command prompt. The general syntax for Wevtutil is as follows.

```
wevtutil command [argument [argument] ...] [/option:value [/option:value] ...]
```

Here, `command` can be any of the following:

- **al (archive-log)** Archives an exported log
- **cl (clear-log)** Clears a log
- **el (enum-logs)** Lists log names
- **ep (enum-publishers)** Lists event publishers
- **epl (export-log)** Exports a log
- **gl (get-log)** Gets log configuration information
- **gli (get-log-info)** Gets log status information
- **gp (get-publisher)** Gets publisher configuration information
- **im (install-manifest)** Installs event publishers and logs from manifest
- **qe (query-events)** Queries events from a log or log file

- **sl (set-log)** Modifies configuration of a log
- **um (uninstall-manifest)** Uninstalls event publishers and logs from manifest

Common examples for `option` include:

- ***/r:value (remote)*** If specified, runs the command on a remote computer named value. Note that *im* (install-manifest) and *um* (uninstall-manifest) do not support remote operation.
- ***/u:value (username)*** Specifies a different user to log on to a remote computer. Here value is a user name in the form domain\user or user. This option is applicable only when option */r* (remote) is specified.
- ***/p:value (password)*** Specifies a password for the specified user. If not specified, or if the value is "*", the user will be prompted to enter a password. This option is applicable only when the */u* (user name) option is specified.
- ***/a:value (authentication)*** Specifies an authentication type for connecting to a remote computer. The value can be Default, Negotiate, Kerberos, or NTLM. The default is Negotiate.
- ***/uni:value (unicode)*** Displays output in Unicode. The value can be true or false (if true, output is in Unicode).

> ***NOTE*** **You can use either the short (ep /uni) or long (enum-publishers /unicode) version of the command and option names; and all commands, options, and option values are case-insensitive.**

> ***MORE INFO*** To learn more about a specific command, type **wevtutil command /?** at an elevated command prompt. For additional information concerning Wevtutil.exe, see *http://technet.microsoft.com/en-us/library/cc732848.aspx.*

Using Windows PowerShell for Event Monitoring

New in Windows 7 is the capability of using Windows PowerShell for managing event logs and gathering event information. A number of new Windows PowerShell cmdlets provide functionality, as follows:

- **Clear-EventLog** Deletes all entries from specified event logs on the local or remote computers
- **Get-Event** Gets the events in the event queue
- **Get-EventLog** Gets the events in a specified event log or a list of the event logs on a computer
- **Get-EventSubscriber** Gets the event subscribers in the current session

- **Get-WinEvent** Gets events from event logs and event tracing log files on local and remote computers
- **Limit-EventLog** Sets the event log properties that limit the size of the event log and the age of its entries
- **New-Event** Creates a new event
- **New-EventLog** Creates a new event log and a new event source on a local or remote computer
- **Register-EngineEvent** Subscribes to events that are generated by the Windows PowerShell engine and by the New-Event cmdlet
- **Register-ObjectEvent** Subscribes to the events that are generated by a .NET object
- **Register-WmiEvent** Subscribes to an event generated by a WMI object
- **Remove-Event** Deletes events from the event queue
- **Remove-EventLog** Deletes an event log or unregisters an event source
- **Show-Eventlog** Displays the event logs of the local or a remote computer in Event Viewer
- **Unregister-Event** Cancels an event subscription
- **Wait-Event** Waits until a particular event is raised before continuing to run
- **Write-EventLog** Writes an event to an event log

For example, to get information concerning the "classic" (Windows) event logs on the computer, use the **get-eventlog** cmdlet as follows.

```
PS C:\Windows\system32> get-eventlog -list

  Max(K) Retain OverflowAction        Entries Log
  ------ ------ --------------        ------- ---
  20,480      0 OverwriteAsNeeded         899 Application
  20,480      0 OverwriteAsNeeded           0 HardwareEvents
     512      7 OverwriteOlder              0 Internet Explorer
  20,480      0 OverwriteAsNeeded           0 Key Management Service
   8,192      0 OverwriteAsNeeded           0 Media Center
  20,480      0 OverwriteAsNeeded       1,473 Security
  20,480      0 OverwriteAsNeeded       3,125 System
  15,360      0 OverwriteAsNeeded          36 Windows PowerShell
```

To display the most recent three events from the System log, use the following command.

```
PS C:\Windows\system32> get-eventlog -newest 3 -logname System

   Index Time          EntryType   Source                 InstanceID Message
   ----- ----          ---------   ------                 ---------- -------
    3125 Jun 28 11:55  Information Service Control M...   1073748860 The Application
Information service entered the...
    3124 Jun 28 11:41  Information Service Control M...   1073748860 The Diagnostic
System Host service entered the ...
    3123 Jun 28 11:37  Information Service Control M...   1073748860 The Microsoft
Software Shadow Copy Provider ser...
```

To display all critical ("Error") events in the System log, use the following command.

```
PS C:\Windows\system32> get-eventlog -logname System -entrytype Error

   Index Time          EntryType   Source                 InstanceID Message
   ----- ----          ---------   ------                 ---------- -------
    1707 Jun 17 08:38  Error       EventLog               2147489656 The previous system
shutdown at 4:41:12 PM on ?...
    1688 Jun 16 16:22  Error       Server                 3221227977 The server could
not bind to the transport \Dev...
    1680 Jun 16 16:22  Error       Server                 3221227977 The server could
not bind to the transport \Dev...
    1675 Jun 16 16:16  Error       NETLOGON                     5783 The session setup
to the Windows NT or Windows ...
    1669 Jun 16 15:43  Error       RasSstp                         1 CoId={746056B2-
DA98-451B-BF59-6371A598B450}:The...
    1662 Jun 16 15:07  Error       Server                 3221227977 The server could
not bind to the transport \Dev...
    1659 Jun 16 15:06  Error       RasSstp                         1 CoId={40BE02A6-
FB36-4FC4-BA37-8F996CCEF143}:The...
    1656 Jun 16 15:06  Error       RasSstp                         1 CoId={600CDFFC-
90F9-4C85-990F-95F45582ADEE}:The...
```

To display detailed information concerning the NETLOGON event displayed above, specify the index number for that event in the following command.

```
PS C:\Windows\system32> get-eventlog -logname System -index 1675 | format-list -property *

EventID            : 5783
MachineName        : SEA-CLI-49.contoso.com
Data               : {}
Index              : 1675
Category           : (0)
CategoryNumber     : 0
EntryType          : Error
Message            : The session setup to the Windows NT or Windows 2000 Domain
Controller \\SEA-DC1.contoso.com for the
                     domain CONTOSO is not responsive.  The current RPC call from
Netlogon on \\SEA-CLI-49 to
                     \\SEA-DC1.contoso.com has been cancelled.
Source             : NETLOGON
ReplacementStrings : {\\SEA-DC1.contoso.com, CONTOSO, SEA-CLI-49}
InstanceId         : 5783
TimeGenerated      : 6/16/2009 4:16:45 PM
TimeWritten        : 6/16/2009 4:16:45 PM
UserName           :
Site               :
Container          :
```

The *get-winevent* cmdlet provides even more functionality for displaying event log and event information. For example, to view detailed information concerning the Application log on the computer, use the following command.

```
PS C:\Windows\system32> get-winevent -listlog Application | format-list -property *

FileSize                       : 1118208
IsLogFull                      : False
LastAccessTime                 : 6/8/2009 6:10:23 PM
LastWriteTime                  : 6/28/2009 11:01:10 AM
OldestRecordNumber             : 1
RecordCount                    : 899
LogName                        : Application
LogType                        : Administrative
LogIsolation                   : Application
IsEnabled                      : True
IsClassicLog                   : True
SecurityDescriptor             : O:BAG:SYD:(A;;0xf0007;;;SY)(A;;0x7;;;BA)(A;;0x7;;;SO)
(A;;0x3;;;IU)(A;;0x3;;;SU)(A;;0x3;;;S-1-5-3)(A;;0x3;;;S-1-5-33)(A;;0x1;;;S-1-5-32-573)
LogFilePath                    : %SystemRoot%\System32\Winevt\Logs\Application.evtx
MaximumSizeInBytes             : 20971520
LogMode                        : Circular
```

```
OwningProviderName            :
ProviderNames                 : {.NET Runtime, .NET Runtime Optimization Service,
Application, Application Error...}
ProviderLevel                 :
ProviderKeywords              :
ProviderBufferSize            : 64
ProviderMinimumNumberOfBuffers : 0
ProviderMaximumNumberOfBuffers : 64
ProviderLatency               : 1000
ProviderControlGuid           :
```

MORE INFO **For more information on using Windows PowerShell for event monitoring, see the help for these cmdlets in the Windows PowerShell Cmdlet Help Topics at *http://technet.microsoft.com/en-us/library/dd347701.aspx*.**

Using Task Scheduler

Task Scheduler is an MMC snap-in that lets you schedule automated tasks that perform actions according to scheduled times or when specific events occur. Task Scheduler maintains a library of all scheduled tasks and provides an organized view of these tasks and an interface for managing them. The Windows 7 version of Task Scheduler is essentially the same as that found in Windows Vista, which improved upon earlier versions of Windows by providing a better user interface, more flexible scheduling, enhanced security, and improved manageability. Specifically, the following enhancements to Task Scheduler were introduced in Windows Vista:

- **User interface improvements** The Windows Vista version of Task Scheduler introduced a completely new user interface based on the MMC. This interface includes a number of new conditions and filters to assist administrators in defining and managing scheduled tasks.
- **Scheduling improvements** Time-based task launch is improved, with more detailed control and enhanced scheduling options. One key improvement allows you to chain a series of actions together instead of having to create multiple scheduled tasks. You can schedule tasks on demand for execution when a specified event is logged to an event log. You can configure scheduled tasks to wake a computer from sleep or hibernation or to run only when the computer is idle. You can also run previously scheduled tasks when a powered-down computer is turned back on. Scalability has also been improved by removing limitations on the number of registered tasks and allowing multiple instances of a task to run in parallel or in sequence.

- **Security improvements** New security features include use of Credentials Manager (CredMan) to securely store passwords needed for running tasks, and also supporting Service for User (S4U) for many scenarios such that passwords do not need to be stored at all. Improved credentials management provided by S4U and Credentials Manager also increases reliability and reduces maintenance overhead. To further increase security, scheduled tasks are executed in their own session instead of the same session as system services or the current user:
  - Separate per-user credentials are required.
  - System tasks run in the system session (session 0), while user tasks run in the user's session.
- **Administrative improvements** The version of Task Scheduler in Windows Vista introduces features that enhance the administration experience for scheduled tasks. Scheduled tasks may be activated by Event Log events and may be synchronized using operational events fired by the service, which can be found under Applications And Services Logs/Microsoft/Windows/Task Scheduler/Operational log. Tasks may be configured to retry on failure and activated when resources become available, as in the case of mobile devices that may miss run times of scheduled tasks. Control and task status monitoring has been improved and now provides detailed failure reporting and task history. Status feedback has been significantly improved. For example, using the detailed events logged by the Task Scheduler about task operation, an administrator can set up an e-mail to be sent to her when a failure occurs, including a complete runtime history of the event. In addition, the complete history of executed scheduled tasks can be easily reviewed, and at any time the administrator can view the list of currently running tasks and run or stop tasks on demand. To assist administrators in scripting complex tasks, the Task Scheduler API is also fully available to scripting languages.
- **Platform and manageability improvements** The version of Task Scheduler in Windows Vista enables several new features that improve platform operations and manageability. Infrastructure features for application monitoring now allow hosting and activation of troubleshooters and other corrective actions. Periodic data collection has been implemented to improve event detection. Task process prioritization has been improved and quotas may be assigned. Computer resources are used more efficiently by activating tasks based on a true idle state, defined by a combination of the following criteria:
  - CPU, memory, and I/O usage
  - User presence
  - Nonpresentation mode

Improvements to Task Scheduler in Windows 7

While the Task Scheduler snap-in is essentially unchanged in Windows 7, there are several significant improvements to task scheduling that have been added in Windows 7. These additional improvements include:

- Additional security through task hardening (supported only for tasks running as LocalService or NetworkService).
- The ability to reject starting tasks in Remote Applications Integrated Locally (RAIL) sessions.
- The option of using the Unified Background Process Manager (UBPM) as a scheduling engine for tasks. UBPM is a new component of Windows 7 that drives the scheduling of both services and scheduled tasks and enables trigger-starting of services. Note that while using the unified scheduling engine is recommended, it does not support some Task Scheduler features including certain logon types, e-mail and message display task actions, task network settings, and certain types of task triggers. For more information on UBPM and trigger-start services, see the section titled "Understanding Services" in Chapter 17, "Managing Devices and Services."
- Various changes to Task Scheduler APIs.

Understanding Tasks

A *task* consists of a set of one or more triggers, execution conditions (named *settings*), and an execution body (named *actions*); specifically:

- **Task triggers** Conditions under which a task is started. A task trigger defines when a task will begin and can include conditions such as running a task when a system is started, when a user logs on to a computer, or when a specific event is logged in the event log. A task may have one or more triggers defined, so that the task will be started whenever one of the triggers' conditions is met.
- **Task settings** Additional conditions besides the trigger under which a task will execute; they also control the behavior of the task. Task settings include conditions such as running the task only if the computer is idle or running it only if the computer is connected to a specific network. Other task settings include allowing a task to run on demand, allowing a user to end a task forcefully, defining actions to take when a task fails, and deleting a task after it runs.
- **Task actions** Code that executes when the task is run. The body of a task can be a script, batch file, executable, or component written as a handler to the Task Scheduler interface. Execution hosts for task actions are called task scheduler engines. A task may define one or more actions to be run consecutively as part of the task execution.

Understanding the Task Scheduler Architecture

Task Scheduler supports an isolation model in which each set of tasks running in a specific security context is started in a separate session. Task Scheduler engines running in transient processes in the user or computer context process the execution defined to be started by a trigger. Tasks can be started in a computer account context such as LocalSystem, LocalService, or NetworkService, or they may be started in a specified user context. Task Scheduler also attempts to ensure task integrity even when a user's domain credentials are updated (applies to Windows Server 2003 domains only).

Tasks can be started either locally or remotely. Each task may contain multiple actions running in series. Multiple tasks can be started in parallel or serially to perform a series of synchronized operations using the events logged by the service. A set of predefined events in the System event log as well as the private Task Scheduler Operational event log are used to record each action's execution status for monitoring, synchronization, and health management.

The simplified block diagram shown in Figure 21-14 illustrates the high-level architecture implemented in Task Scheduler 2.0 (the version in Windows Vista and later).

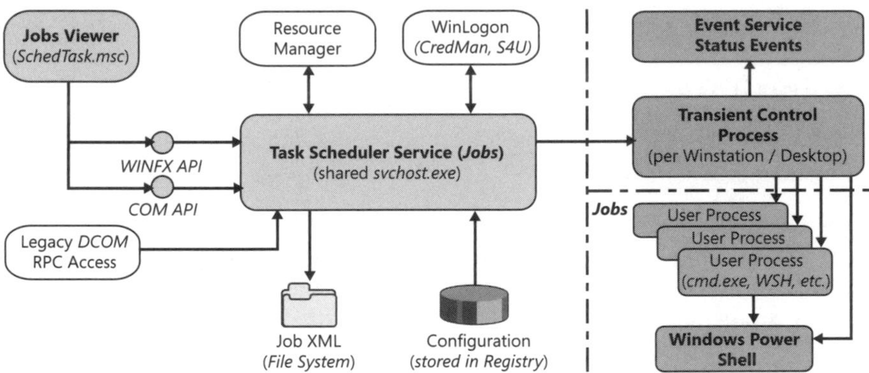

FIGURE 21-14 Task Scheduler architecture

Task Scheduler combines several components that work together to provide the Task Scheduler user interface, the task execution engine, and event tracking and management. Specifically:

- The Task Scheduler user interface has been redesigned in the MMC .NET snap-in SchedTask.msc. This GUI includes a wizard for creating and configuring tasks and property pages that accesses the Task Scheduler service through its COM API.
- A shared Svchost.exe loads the Task Scheduler Service DLL SchedSvc.dll using a LocalSystem account, uses the TaskSchd.dll component to interface with the Resource Manager, and uses S4U to obtain the required credentials. This service DLL also reads configuration information from the registry and writes job tasks to the disk in XML format.

- The Transient Control Process engine TaskEng.exe runs in the context of the task-defined user account, logs Event Log status events, and generates user processes that execute actions defined by the task.
- The TaskComp.dll component provides backward compatibility for management and execution of tasks that were created in previous versions of Windows.

Understanding Task Scheduler Security

Security in Task Scheduler 2.0 is greatly improved over the previous version Task Scheduler 1.0 (Windows XP and earlier versions). Task Scheduler now supports a security isolation model in which each set of tasks running in a specific security context starts in a separate session. Tasks executed for different users are started in separate window sessions, in complete isolation from one other and from tasks running in the machine (system) context. Passwords are stored (when needed) with the CredMan service. Using CredMan prevents malware from retrieving the stored password, tightening security further.

Beginning with Windows Vista, the burden of credentials management in Task Scheduler is lessened. Credentials are no longer stored locally for the majority of scenarios, so tasks do not "break" when a password changes. Administrators can configure security services such as S4U and CredMan, depending on whether the task requires remote or local resources. S4U relieves the need to store passwords locally on the computer; and CredMan, though it requires that passwords be updated once per computer, automatically updates all scheduled tasks configured to run for the specific user with the new password.

Credentials Management

CredMan stores the target/credentials pair locally in the user profile CredMan store. Upon registration, Task Scheduler impersonates the user and stores the target/credentials pair. This process is also used to access resources that require non-Windows credentials. CredMan also manages credentials for service accounts and extends credentials handling for computer accounts.

User Security

You can locally and remotely activate tasks and run them on behalf of a user who is not logged on. Credentials on distributed tasks can be updated when credentials are changed in the authentication authority. User security has been extended to function in a non-Microsoft Active Directory Domain Services (AD DS) environment across forests and across firewalls. These features allow tasks to be started even if the task accesses a resource that requires non-Windows credentials.

Security Concepts

Task Scheduler uses standard Windows security functions provided by S4U. Upon registration, Task Scheduler authenticates credentials as a trusted service and stores identity only in a *domain\user name* format. Upon execution, S4U provides restricted token access based on the identity provided by Task Scheduler. Service for User to Self (S4U2Self) implements the same functions as S4U for workgroups, stand-alone computers, and computers that belong to a domain but are not currently connected to that domain. For more information about S4U, see RFC 1510: "The Kerberos Network Authentication Service (V5)," at *http://www.ietf.org/rfc/rfc1510.txt*.

Securing Running Tasks

Task Scheduler supports an isolation model in which each set of tasks running in specific security contexts are started in separate Desktops. The execution defined and started by the trigger is handled by engines running in transient processes in a user or computer context. Tasks can be started in a system account context, such as LocalSystem, LocalService, or NetworkService, or in a specified user account context. Tasks started in a system account context will always run noninteractively in Session 0.

The *CreateProcess* function used to create tasks ensures that any Winstation created in a user context will run in a different session than Session 0. By default, all Winstations will be created in the same session.

Registration Permissions Matrix

The Task Scheduler service adheres to the following task registration permissions rules:

- Any user can schedule any task for herself.
- Any user can schedule any task for anyone whose password she supplies at registration.
- An administrator or system account can schedule tasks for other users or security groups without supplying a password, with the following restrictions:
  - Only with the Run Only If Logged On flag set, which is similar to a logon script and consistent with current behavior
  - Only running in interactive mode
- Tasks scheduled with *RunOnlyIfUserLoggedon* with no password will run only in interactive mode.
- Tasks scheduled to run in system contexts such as LocalSystem, LocalService, or NetworkService will not run in interactive mode.

Understanding AT and Task Scheduler v1.0 Compatibility Modes

Task Scheduler provides two backward-compatibility modes:

- **AT Compatibility Mode** Tasks registered through AT.exe are visible and can be modified by the Task Scheduler v1.0 GUI and the Task Scheduler command-line utility SchTasks.exe.
- **Task Scheduler v1.0 Compatibility Mode** Tasks created or modified in the Task Scheduler v1.0 user interface and the Task Scheduler command-line utility SchTasks.exe are *not* accessible or visible through AT.exe.

The Task Scheduler parser will determine at registration time if the task can be converted to either of these compatibility modes.

Understanding the Task Scheduler Snap-in

The Task Scheduler user interface is now an MMC snap-in, as shown in Figure 21-15.

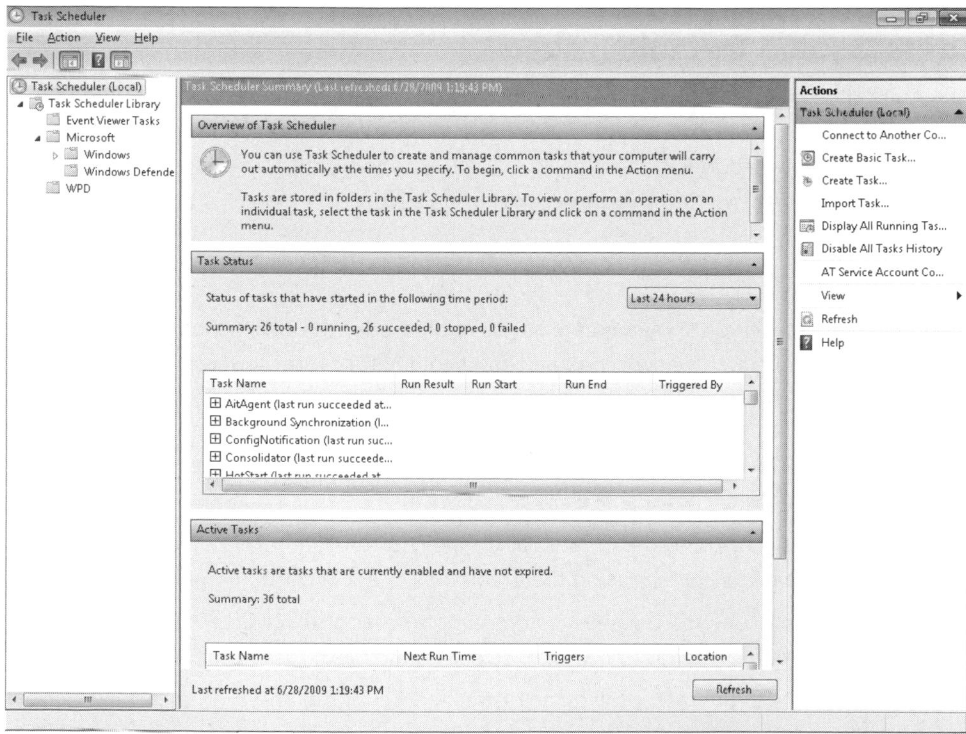

FIGURE 21-15 Task Scheduler user interface

The scope pane on the left contains the Task Scheduler Library subnode under the root Task Scheduler node by default. The Library subnode has all currently defined tasks listed under it, in a hierarchy of folders. The Microsoft subnode under the Task Scheduler Library contains a Windows subnode with default Windows system tasks used by operating system components, such as Reliability Analysis Component (RAC) and System Restore. Default system tasks are normally not modified.

The Results pane in the center shows the task name and other relevant information about the currently selected task. The bottom part of the center pane contains a preview pane showing the definition details of the currently selected task in the list at the top. You can modify task definitions by either double-clicking the task name in the list or by selecting and right-clicking the Properties action in the Actions Pane at right.

The Actions pane on the right shows relevant actions for a selected task or scope node. New tasks can be created using the Create Basic Task action for wizard-based simple tasks or using Create Task for full-featured tasks.

The Summary (home) page, which displays whenever you start Task Scheduler and have the top node selected, provides a summary of task status for the system that includes how many tasks ran, how many succeeded or failed, and a list of currently active tasks that are not disabled or expired.

Understanding Default Tasks

A default installation of Windows Vista and later versions creates a number of scheduled tasks used to maintain various aspects of your system. For more information concerning these default tasks, see Knowledge Base article 939039, "Description of the scheduled tasks in Windows Vista," at *http://support.microsoft.com/kb/939039*.

Creating Tasks

Before you create a task, you should create a new folder under the Task Scheduler Library to store the new task. To create a new Scheduled Tasks folder, follow these steps:

1. Select the Task Scheduler Library and then click New Folder in the Actions pane.
2. Enter the name of the new folder and click OK to complete creation of the new subnode.
3. Select the new folder to start creating a new task.

You can create tasks by using the Create Basic Task Wizard or manually by using the Create Task interface. To create a new task using the Create Basic Task Wizard, follow these steps:

1. Right-click the folder you created to store your tasks and select Create Basic Task to display the Create Basic Task Wizard, or select Create Basic Task in the Actions pane.
2. Enter the name of the task, provide an optional description, and then click Next.
3. On the Task Trigger page, specify when you want the task to start and then click Next. Some choices may require additional information to further define the trigger.
4. On the Action page, shown here, specify an action for your task to perform and then click Next to specify action details.

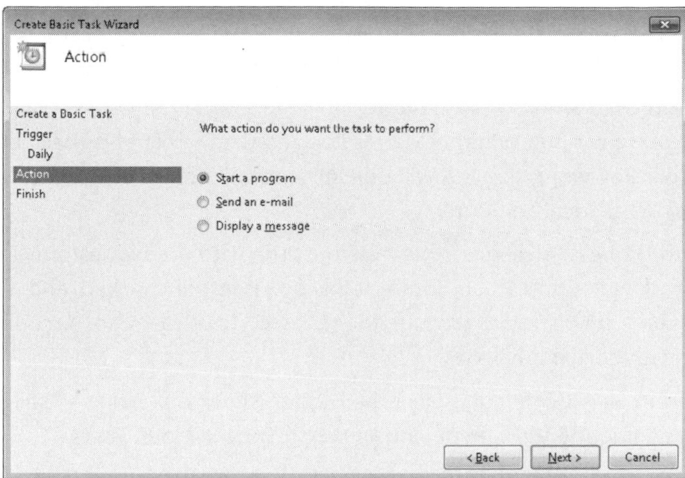

5. Options displayed on the next page depend on the action you selected in step 4.
6. After specifying the appropriate action details, click Finish to create the task and close the wizard.

To create a new task manually, follow these steps:

1. Select the folder that the task will reside in and either right-click the folder and select Create Task or select Create Task in the Actions pane. Either action will display the Create Task dialog box with several tabs for the different task details. The General tab, shown here, defines general information about the task.

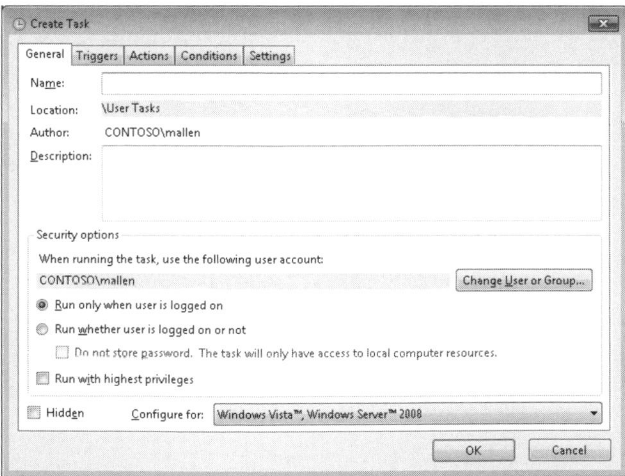

2. In the Name text box, enter a name for the task.
3. In the Description text box, you can enter an optional task description.
4. Under Security options, select the appropriate options for the task:

- By default, the task will run under the security context of the currently logged-on user. To select a different security context, click Change User Or Group.
- Select either Run Only When User Is Logged On or Run Whether User Is Logged On Or Not. If you select Run Whether User Is Logged On Or Not and check the box Do Not Store Password, the task will use S4U and will not be able to access any resources outside the local computer.
- Select Run With Highest Privileges if the task must run with the highest privileges that the specified user account can obtain. If this box is left unchecked, and if the user account is an administrative account, the task will run under User Account Control (UAC) with partial privileges.

5. To hide the task from view by default, select the Hidden check box. You can still view hidden tasks by opening the View menu and selecting Show Hidden Tasks.
6. By default, tasks are configured for Task Scheduler 2.0 (Windows Vista or later versions) compatibility. For backward compatibility, the list allows you to select Windows Server 2003, Windows XP, or Windows 2000 to define a task that is compatible with Task Scheduler v1.0.

Options on other tabs that are used to define task details are discussed in later sections of this chapter.

Defining Triggers

The Triggers tab allows users to view and configure one or more triggers that will start the task. To define a new trigger, click New to display the New Trigger dialog box (Figure 21-16). To edit an existing trigger, select the trigger in the list and click Edit. To delete an existing trigger, select the trigger and click Delete.

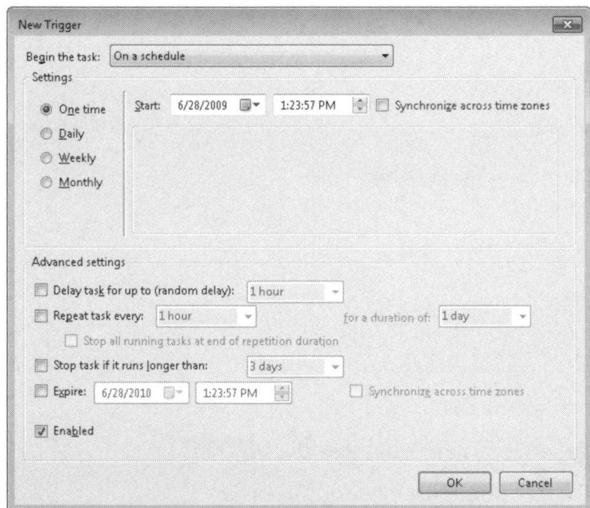

FIGURE 21-16 The Create New Trigger user interface

In the New Trigger dialog box, the Begin The Task drop-down list allows you to configure a task to begin based on the following trigger types:

- On A Schedule
- At Log On
- At Startup
- On Idle
- On An Event
- At Task Creation/Modification
- On Connection To And Disconnect From User Session
- On Workstation Lock And Unlock

The following sections explain trigger types and their corresponding settings in detail.

ON A SCHEDULE TRIGGER

The On A Schedule trigger configures the task to start on a defined schedule. Selecting the On A Schedule trigger type in the Begin The Task list displays the controls in the Settings group box to configure schedule parameters. Table 21-2 describes these controls.

TABLE 21-2 On A Schedule Trigger Settings

SETTING	DESCRIPTION
One Time	Configures the task to run once at the specified date and time
Daily	Configures the task to run on a schedule based on days
Weekly	Configures the task to run on a schedule based on weeks
Monthly	Configures the task to run on a schedule based on months
Synchronize Across Time Zones	Configures the task to run using Universal Time Coordinated (UTC) instead of local time

AT LOG ON TRIGGER

The At Log On trigger allows you to define a task to run when someone logs on to the computer. Selecting the At Log On trigger type in the Begin The Task list displays the controls in the Settings group box to configure schedule parameters. Table 21-3 describes these controls.

TABLE 21-3 At Logon Trigger Settings

SETTING	DESCRIPTION
Any User	Configures the task to start when any user logs on.
Specific User Or Group	Configures the task to start at logon of the specified user or group.
<domain\user>	Shows a read-only display of the currently selected user or group.
Change User Or Group	Opens the standard Windows Select User Or Group dialog box to allow the user to change the selected user or group. If the user makes a different selection in the dialog box and clicks OK to accept, the *<domain\user>* read-only text box should change to display the new selection.

AT STARTUP TRIGGER

This trigger causes the task to run when the computer starts up. The only settings for this trigger are the Advanced Settings shown at the bottom of Figure 21-16 previously.

ON IDLE TRIGGER

The On Idle trigger configures the task to run when the computer becomes idle. To complete configuration for this trigger, you must also select the Conditions tab and configure Idle settings; see the section titled "Defining Conditions" later in this chapter for more information about these settings.

ON AN EVENT TRIGGER

The On An Event trigger type allows a user to define a task to execute on a specified Event Log event. To define the event trigger, the Settings group box provides two options:

- **Basic** Allows for simple selection of a single event to be used as a trigger (by choosing the log, source, and event ID identifiers for the event).
- **Custom** Allows you to define a more complex event filter by providing the New Event Filter button. Click the button to open the Event Filter dialog box (same as in Event Viewer) and define a more detailed event filter by time, level, source, and so on.

AT TASK CREATION/MODIFICATION TRIGGER

Selecting the At Task Creation/Modification trigger type in the Begin The Task list configures the task to start immediately when it is created or modified. No other condition is required and no further settings are displayed for this trigger.

ON CONNECTION TO AND DISCONNECT FROM USER SESSION TRIGGERS

The user session triggers cause a task to run when a user session is connected to or disconnected from the local computer or from a remote desktop connection. For example, when you connect to a user session on the local computer by switching users on the computer, this trigger will cause the task to run. Another example that can trigger a task to run is when a user connects to a user session by using the Remote Desktop Connection program from a remote computer. The trigger's settings allow you to specify that the task should be triggered when any user connects to or disconnects from a user session or when a specific user or user group member connects or disconnects.

Selecting the On Connection To User Session or the On Disconnect From User Session trigger type in the Begin The Task list displays the controls listed in Table 21-4 in the Settings group box.

TABLE 21-4 On Connection To or Disconnect From User Session Trigger Settings

SETTING	DESCRIPTION
Any User	Configures the task to start when any user makes a connection to a user session.
Specific User Or Group	Configures the task to start when the specified user or group makes a connection to a user session.
<domain\user>	Shows a read-only display of the currently selected user or group.
Change User Or Group	Launches the standard Windows Select User Or Group dialog box to allow the user to change the selected user or group. If the user makes a different selection in the dialog box and clicks OK to accept, the *<domain\user>* read-only text box should change to display the new selection.
Connection From Local Computer	Configures the task to start when the specified user connects locally.
Connection From Remote Computer	Configures the task to start when the specified user connects remotely.

ON WORKSTATION LOCK AND UNLOCK TRIGGERS

Selecting the On Workstation Lock or the On Workstation Unlock trigger type in the Begin The Task list displays the controls listed in Table 21-5 in the Settings group box.

TABLE 21-5 On Workstation Lock and Unlock Trigger Settings

SETTING	DESCRIPTION
Any User	Configures the task to start when any user locks or unlocks the workstation.
Specific User Or Group	Configures the task to start when the specified user or member of the specified group locks or unlocks the workstation.
<domain\user>	Shows a read-only display of the currently selected user or group.
Change User Or Group	Opens the standard Windows Select User Or Group dialog box to allow the user to change the selected user or group. If the user makes a different selection in the dialog box and clicks OK to accept, the *<domain\user>* read-only text box should change to display the new selection.

Defining Actions

When you create a task, you must configure one or more actions to run a program, script, or batch file; send an e-mail; or pop up a message when your task starts. The Actions tab allows you to define, view, or modify actions for this task. To configure actions, click the Actions tab and then click New to display the New Action dialog box, as shown in Figure 21-17.

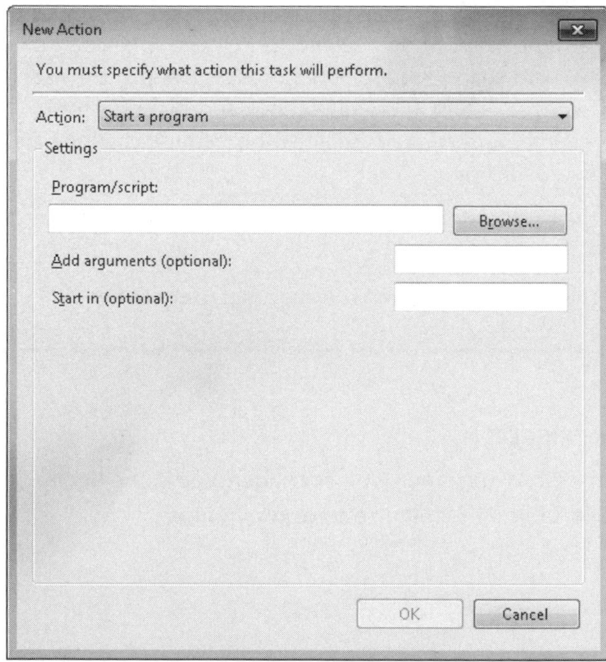

FIGURE 21-17 Create New Action – Start a Program

To configure an action to start a program, script, or batch file, follow these steps:

1. Click the Action list and select Start A Program to display the configuration options shown above.
2. In the Settings group box, under Program/Script, provide the path to the program or script or select Browse to choose a program, script, or batch file on the local computer.
3. If the directory that contains the program, script, or batch file is not included in the local computer path, enter the starting directory in the Start In text box.
4. If the program, script, or batch file requires additional arguments to be passed to it at launch, enter these arguments in the Add Arguments (Optional) text box.

To configure an action to send e-mail, follow these steps:

1. Open the Action list and select Send An E-mail to display the configuration options.
2. In the Settings group box, enter the required information listed in Table 21-6.

TABLE 21-6 Send E-Mail Settings

SETTING	DESCRIPTION
From	Specifies the e-mail address of the sender.
To	Specifies one or more e-mail addresses for recipients. When you enter multiple addresses, separate each address from the rest with a semicolon (;).
Subject	Specifies a subject for the e-mail.
Text	Allows the user to enter a formatted message to be included in the content of the e-mail.
Attachment	Displays a File Open dialog box that allows the user to select one or more files to attach to the e-mail.
SMTP Server	Allows the user to enter the Domain Name System (DNS) or NETBIOS name for the Simple Mail Transfer Protocol (SMTP) server to be used to send the e-mail.

> ***NOTE*** **To configure the task to pop up a message, choose Display A Message in the Action drop-down list and then enter a title and a message to be displayed when the task runs.**

Defining Conditions

The Conditions tab displays different conditions for running tasks and allows you to define settings for these conditions. If you do not specify condition settings, designated defaults will be applied to the task. Conditions on this page are optional unless you have selected the On Idle trigger type. If you have selected this trigger type, you must configure Idle settings as described in this section.

To configure task conditions, click the Conditions tab and configure the desired options as described in Table 21-7.

TABLE 21-7 Conditions Tab Options

SETTING	DESCRIPTION
Idle	Groups all conditions related to idle that affect the starting of the task.
Start The Task Only If The Computer Is Idle For	Configures the task to start only if the computer has been idle for a certain amount of time.

Wait For Idle	Enabled only by selecting the Start Only If Computer Is Idle For option; configures how long to wait for the idle condition to be satisfied.
	Options in the list include Indefinitely, 1 Minute, 5 Minutes, 10 Minutes, 15 Minutes, 30 Minutes, 1 Hour, and 2 Hours.
	Default value: 30 Minutes
	You can also enter other values using the following formats:
	`<ss> s[econds]`
	`<mm>[:<ss>] m[inutes]`
	`<hh>[:<mm>:<ss>] h[ours]`

Stop If The Computer Ceases To Be Idle	Configures the task to stop if the computer ceases to be idle. Default value: Selected
Restart If The Idle State Resumes	Enabled only by selecting the Stop If Computer Ceases To Be Idle option. Configures the task to restart if the computer re-enters the idle state. Default value: Cleared
Start The Task Only If The Computer Is On AC Power	Configures the task to start only if the computer is on AC power and not on battery power. Default value: Cleared
Stop If The Computer Switches To Battery Power	Configures the task to stop if the computer switches to battery power. Default value: Cleared
Wake The Computer To Run This Task	Specifies that the computer should be brought out of hibernation or standby to run this task. Default value: Cleared

SETTING	DESCRIPTION
Start Only If The Following Network Connection Is Available	Sets a condition to run the task only if a specific named network connection is available or if any network connection is available when the task's trigger is activated. Default value: Cleared

Defining Settings

The Settings tab displays additional global settings for the task and allows you to define these settings. All settings on this page are optional. If you do not specify these settings, designated default values will be applied to the task.

To configure global settings using the Settings tab, click the Settings tab and configure the desired settings as described in Table 21-8.

TABLE 21-8 Global Settings Defined on the Settings Tab

SETTING	DESCRIPTION
Allow Task To Be Run On Demand	Defines whether the task supports Run Now functionality that allows tasks to be run on demand from the user interface or command-line utilities. Default value: Selected
Run Task As Soon As Possible After A Scheduled Start Is Missed	Configures the task to run immediately if the service detects that a scheduled activation was missed; for example, the computer was turned off when the trigger condition occurred. Default value: Cleared
If The Task Is Already Running, Then The Following Rule Applies	Configures the action to be taken if the trigger for a task fires while an instance of that task is already running. Options include Do Not Start A New Instance, Stop The Existing Instance, Run A New Instance In Parallel, and Queue A New Instance. Default value: Do Not Start A New Instance
If The Task Fails	Use this setting to restart a task if the task fails to run. (The last run result of the task was not a success.) The user specifies the time interval that takes place between task restart attempts and the number of times to try to restart the task. Default value: Cleared

SETTING	DESCRIPTION
Restart Every	Enabled only by selecting the If The Task Fails option. Specifies how often a retry should be attempted. Options in the list include Indefinitely, 1 Minute, 5 Minutes, 10 Minutes, 15 Minutes, 30 Minutes, and 1 Hour. Default value: 1 Minute You can also enter other values using the following formats: <ss> s[econds] <mm>[:<ss>] m[inutes] <hh>[:<mm>:<ss>] h[ours]
Attempt To Restart Up To	Enabled only if you select the If The Task Fails option. Specifies the number of times to restart the task upon failure.
Stop The Task If It Runs Longer Than	Configures the task to stop if it has been running for longer than the specified time. Default value: Selected
<Execution Time Limit>	Enabled only if you select the Stop The Task If It Runs Longer Than check box. Configures the task to be stopped after the specified amount of time specified by Execution Time Limit. Options include 1 Hour, 2 Hours, 4 Hours, 8 Hours, 12 Hours, 1 Day, and 3 Days. Default value: 3 Days You can also enter other values using the following formats: <ss> s[econds] <mm>[:<ss>] m[inutes] <hh>[:<mm>:<ss>] h[ours]
If The Running Task Does Not End When Requested, Force It To Stop	If this setting is selected, the task will be forced to stop if the task does not respond to a request to stop. Default value: Selected
If The Task Is Not Scheduled To Run Again, Delete It	Configures the task to be deleted if it is not scheduled to run again. Default value: Cleared

SETTING	DESCRIPTION

After	Enabled only if you select the Delete Task option. Specifies the amount of time to wait, after the task completes its last run, before deleting it. Options include Immediately, 30 Days, 90 Days, 180 Days, or 365 Days.
	Default value: 30 Days
	You can also enter other values using the following formats:
	`<ss> s[econds]`
	`<mm>[:<ss>] m[inutes]`
	`<dd> d[ays]`
	`<mm> months`

Managing Tasks

The Task Scheduler snap-in simplifies task management and monitoring. This section focuses only on how to do the following:

- Display running tasks
- View task history
- Export tasks
- Import tasks

For additional information on how to manage tasks, see Task Scheduler Overview at *http://technet.microsoft.com/en-us/library/cc721871.aspx*.

Displaying Running Tasks

To display all tasks currently running on the system, open Task Scheduler and select Display All Running Tasks from the Action menu. This opens the All Running Tasks window, and you can click Refresh to manually refresh the display. You can also select one or more tasks and click End Task to stop tasks on demand.

Viewing History

The History tab of a task displays all the known events for that task and allows you to quickly see the last time the task ran and its status. Only events that relate to the currently selected task will be shown, eliminating the need to scour the Task Scheduler event log for individual events from specific tasks.

To view the history of a task, do the following:

1. If Task Scheduler is not open, start Task Scheduler.
2. Find and click the task folder in the console tree that contains the task you want to view.
3. In the console window, click the task that you want to view.
4. Click the History tab to view the task's history. Click an event from the list of events on the History tab to view the description of the event.

Exporting Tasks

You can export tasks to an .xml file and then import them at some later time on either the same computer or a different computer. This feature allows easy portability of tasks from computer to computer.

To export a task, follow these steps:

1. Right-click the task that you want to export and then select Export, or select Export in the Action pane.
2. Browse to where you want to save the file, enter the name of the file, and then click Save.
3. The task will be saved in .xml format. The following example shows the XML for a simple task.

```
<?xml version="1.0" encoding="UTF-16"?>
<Task version="1.2" xmlns="http://schemas.microsoft.com/windows/2004/02/mit/
task">
  <RegistrationInfo>
    <Date>2006-04-11T13:54:51</Date>
    <Author>USER1-VISTA\user1</Author>
    <Description>Test Task</Description>
  </RegistrationInfo>
  <Triggers>
    <TimeTrigger id="1a08ebe4-0527-4e7a-af76-84f2ef1dbfa0">
      <StartBoundary>2006-04-11T13:55:23</StartBoundary>
      <Enabled>true</Enabled>
    </TimeTrigger>
  </Triggers>
  <Principals>
    <Principal id="Author">
      <UserId>USER1-VISTA\user1</UserId>
      <LogonType>InteractiveToken</LogonType>
      <RunLevel>LeastPrivilege</RunLevel>
    </Principal>
  </Principals>
  <Settings>
```

```
      <IdleSettings>
        <Duration>PT10M</Duration>
        <WaitTimeout>PT1H</WaitTimeout>
        <StopOnIdleEnd>true</StopOnIdleEnd>
        <RestartOnIdle>false</RestartOnIdle>
      </IdleSettings>
      <MultipleInstancesPolicy>IgnoreNew</MultipleInstancesPolicy>
      <DisallowStartIfOnBatteries>true</DisallowStartIfOnBatteries>
      <StopIfGoingOnBatteries>true</StopIfGoingOnBatteries>
      <AllowHardTerminate>true</AllowHardTerminate>
      <StartWhenAvailable>false</StartWhenAvailable>
      <RunOnlyIfNetworkAvailable>false</RunOnlyIfNetworkAvailable>
      <AllowStartOnDemand>true</AllowStartOnDemand>
      <Enabled>true</Enabled>
      <Hidden>false</Hidden>
      <RunOnlyIfIdle>false</RunOnlyIfIdle>
      <WakeToRun>false</WakeToRun>
      <Priority>7</Priority>
    </Settings>
    <Actions Context="Author">
      <Exec>
        <Command>C:\Windows\System32\calc.exe</Command>
      </Exec>
    </Actions>
  </Task>
```

Importing Tasks

Tasks that have been exported can also be easily imported to another computer or the same computer.

To import a task, follow these steps:

1. Right-click a task folder under the Task Scheduler Library and then select Import Task, or select Import Task in the Action pane.
2. Browse to where the .xml file is located and click Open. The task will be automatically imported into the library using the settings contained in the .xml file.

> ***NOTE*** **To ensure that the task runs properly, it is recommended that you verify the properties of the task after you import it.**

Using SchTasks.exe for Creating and Managing Tasks

This section describes the SchTasks.exe command-line syntax and parameters. The Schtasks.exe command-line interface utility allows an administrator to create, delete, query, change, run, and end scheduled tasks on a local or remote system through the command shell.

Command Syntax

The SchTasks.exe command interface uses the following syntax:

SCHTASKS /<parameter> [arguments]

Command Parameters

The available parameters for SchTasks.exe are as follows:

- **/Create** Creates a new scheduled task
- **/Delete** Deletes the scheduled task(s)
- **/Query** Displays all scheduled tasks
- **/Change** Changes the properties of the scheduled task
- **/Run** Runs the scheduled task immediately
- **/End** Stops the currently running scheduled task
- **/?** Displays a help message

Creating Tasks

The general syntax for Schtasks.exe is as follows:

SCHTASKS /Create [/S system [/U <username> [/P [<password>]]]] [/RU <username> [/RP <password>]] /SC schedule [/MO <modifier>] [/D <day>] [/M <months>] [/I <idletime>] /TN <taskname> /TR <taskrun> [/ST <starttime>] [/RI <interval>] [{/ET <endtime> | /DU <duration>} [/K] [/XML <xmlfile>] [/V1]] [/SD <startdate>] [/ED <enddate>] [/IT] [/Z] [/F]

The following is an example command.

```
SCHTASKS /Create /S system /U user /P password /RU runasuser /RP runaspassword
   /SC HOURLY /TN rtest1 /TR notepad
```

Deleting Tasks

The general syntax for deleting a task is as follows:

SCHTASKS /Delete [/S <system> [/U <username> [/P [<password>]]]] /TN <taskname> [/F]

The following is an example command.

```
SCHTASKS /Delete /TN "Backup and Restore"
```

Running Tasks

The general syntax for running a task is as follows:

SCHTASKS /Run [/S <system> [/U <username> [/P [<password>]]]] /TN <taskname>

The following is an example command.

```
SCHTASKS /Run /TN "Start Backup"
```

Ending Tasks

The general syntax for ending a task is as follows:

SCHTASKS /End [/S <system> [/U <username> [/P [<password>]]]] /TN <taskname>

The following is an example command.

```
SCHTASKS /End /TN "Start Backup"
```

Querying Tasks

The general syntax for querying a task is as follows:

SCHTASKS /Query [/S <system> [/U <username> [/P [<password>]]]] [/FO <format>] [/NH] [/V] [/?]

The following is an example command.

```
SCHTASKS /Query /S system /U user /P password
SCHTASKS /Query /FO LIST /V
```

Changing Tasks

The general syntax for changing a task is as follows:

SCHTASKS /Change [/S <system> [/U <username> [/P [<password>]]]] /TN <taskname>
{ [/RU <runasuser>] [/RP <runaspassword>] [/TR <taskrun>] [/ST <starttime>]
[/RI <interval>]
[{/ET <endtime> | /DU <duration>} [/K]] [/SD <startdate>] [/ED <enddate>] [/ENABLE | /DISABLE] [/IT] [/Z] }

The following is an example command.

```
SCHTASKS /Change /RP password /TN "Backup and Restore"
```

Task Scheduler Events

In Windows Server 2003 and earlier versions, scheduled tasks used a Schedlgu.txt log file to track tasks and their status. Windows Vista implements all new event logs for applications, and Task Scheduler now logs all operational information about scheduled tasks into its own event log. The Scheduled Tasks event log Microsoft-Windows-TaskScheduler is located under Application Logs. Important errors or warnings about task or service failures are logged to the System log so that administrators can readily see them and take action.

Task Scheduler 2.0 will normally log an event on task registration (at creation), at task launch, and when the task instance has been sent to the engine. Events will also be logged on task failures and any task-related problems. This section provides examples of typical events that are logged by the Scheduled Tasks service.

Task Registration

An Event ID 106 is logged when a task is created. This event is also referred to as *task registration*.

Task Launch

Tasks can be started by either a user request or a trigger. An Event ID 110 is normally logged when a user manually starts a task. An Event ID 107 is normally logged when a task is started as the result of a trigger.

Task Execution

An Event ID 319 indicates that the Task Engine received a message from the Task Scheduler service requesting task launch, and it is the best indicator of a task launch. In these events, the Task Engine is identified by the user SID, and the task name is also logged.

Task Completion

An Event ID 102 is normally logged when a task completes successfully.

Troubleshooting Task Scheduler

Task or service failures are logged to the system event log. It is important to note that the events will vary and will be based on what failed. A user will see different events based on whether a task failed to start or if the task started successfully but the action failed.

The key to troubleshooting Task Scheduler is understanding specifically where the failure occurred in the process. A task is defined as an action, the trigger for the action, the conditions under which the task will run, and additional settings. The event log will show whether the failure is in the trigger, the task action, the conditions, or the settings of the task.

Tasks Won't Run If the Service Is Not Started

If you are having problems scheduling tasks or getting tasks to run correctly, first ensure that the Task Scheduler service is running. You can run Services.msc to verify that the Task Scheduler service status is Started.

The Task Did Not Run at the Expected Time

If a scheduled task does not run when you expect it to run, ensure that the task is enabled and also check the triggers on the task to ensure that they are set correctly. Also, check the history of the task, as shown in Figure 21-18, to see when the task was started and to check for errors.

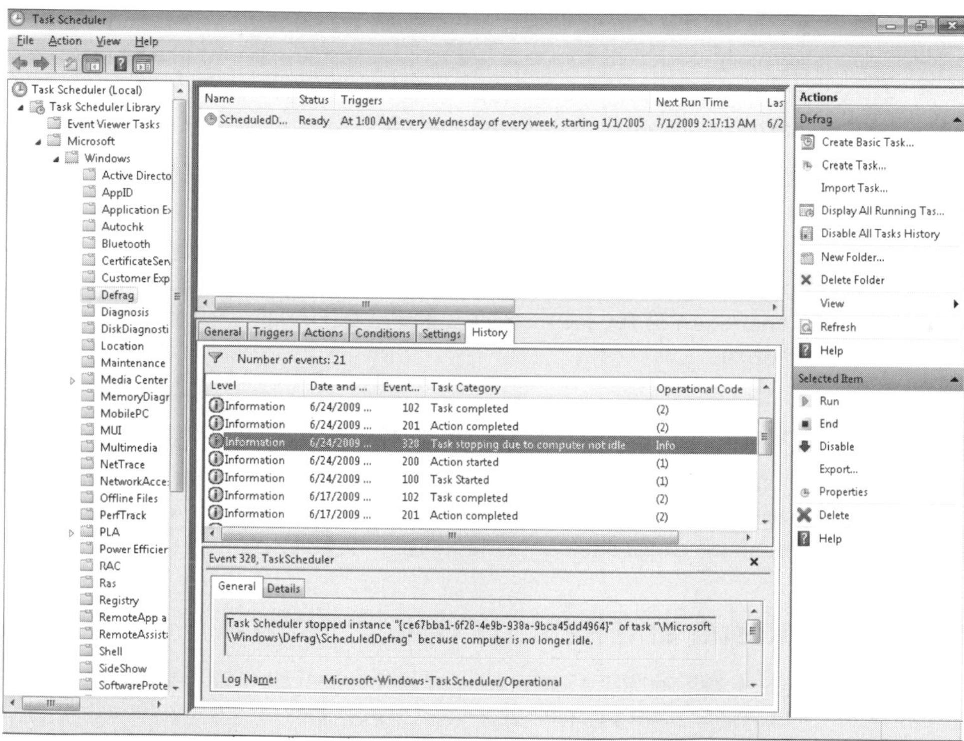

FIGURE 21-18 Task Scheduler History Tab

The Task Will Run Only If All Conditions Are Met

You can set task conditions on the Conditions tab of the Task Properties dialog box. If conditions are not met or are set up incorrectly, the task will not execute.

The Task Will Run Only When a Certain User Is Logged On

If a scheduled task does not run when you expect it to run, review the Security Options settings in the Task Properties dialog box on the General tab.

The Task Executed a Program But the Program Did Not Run Correctly

If a task attempts to execute a program, but the program does not run correctly, first try running the program manually (not from a task) to ensure that the program works correctly. You may need to add arguments to the program command or define the Start In path using the *Add Arguments* and *Start In* optional fields.

The Task Failed to Start

An Event ID 101 is normally logged when a task fails to start. In these events, the result code is also displayed. For more information about result and return codes, see the section titled "Interpreting Result and Return Codes" later in this chapter.

The Task Action Failed to Execute

When a task starts but the action configured for the task fails to execute, an Event ID 103 or an Event ID 203 is normally logged. These events also display the return code. For more information about result and return codes, see the section titled "Interpreting Result and Return Codes" later in this chapter.

The Program Specified in the Task Requires Elevated Privileges

If a task is running a program that requires elevated privileges, ensure that the task runs with the highest privileges. You can set a task to run with the highest privileges by changing the task's security options on the General tab of the Task Properties dialog box.

Interpreting Result and Return Codes

To interpret return codes, you can use a tool such as Err.exe, which you can obtain from the Microsoft Download Center. Err.exe parses source-code header files until it finds a match for the error. In this regard, the Scheduled Tasks service in Windows Vista still functions quite similarly to previous versions of Windows. Return codes from events that occur internally are always translated into hresult code. For example, the logon failed event will contain a result code that can be interpreted as a hresult. Task handler tasks also return result codes that you can interpret using the same tools.

However, when an executable is started and fails for an unknown reason, you have no way of knowing what the result code might mean. The hresult logged in the event log will typically indicate the value returned to the service from the executable itself, and additional research and documentation may be required for accurately interpreting the code.

NOTE You can download Err.exe from the Microsoft Download Center at *http://www.microsoft.com/downloads/details.aspx?familyid=be596899-7bb8-4208-b7fc-09e02a13696c*. Although this tool is called the Microsoft Exchange Server Error Code Look-up tool, it actually looks up any Windows operating system error codes.

Understanding the Windows System Assessment Tool

You can use the Windows System Assessment Tool (WinSAT) to assess the features and capabilities of a Windows PC. If the WinSAT scores have not been pre-populated by the original equipment manufacturer (OEM), then WinSAT will run the following tests:

1. The DWM test during initial install or Out-of-Box Experience (OOBE), to provide the Desktop Window Manager (DWM) with the video memory bandwidth data used in determining whether Aero can run on a system.
2. The remaining tests on system idle (as an idle task, to be kicked off by the Task Scheduler when the computer is not busy).

In addition, WinSAT checks once a week whether new hardware has been installed on this machine. If new hardware was installed and the current ratings are outdated, then WinSAT will run on idle to update the ratings. WinSAT can also be run on demand, when the Re-run The Assessment option is selected in the Performance Information And Tools Control Panel item.

DIRECT FROM THE SOURCE

WinSAT Data Files

CSS Global Technical Readiness (GTR) Team

Advanced users may want more information regarding the Windows Experience Index and system performance than is available in the Performance Information And Tools Control Panel item. The underlying technology that supports the Windows Experience Index is the WinSAT. This tool stores the 10 most recent assessments in a data store folder located at:

```
%WinDir%\Performance\WinSAT\DataStore
```

The data store consists of XML files that contain information regarding each assessment. These XML files contain details regarding system performance and the Windows Experience Index. The files are named by the date and time the assessments ran.

Understanding WinSAT Assessment Tests

WinSAT performs a variety of assessment tests on the hardware of a computer. These assessment tests include:

- **cpu** Measures the computation ability of the processor.
- **d3d** The Direct3D (D3D) assessment is targeted at assessing a system's ability to run 3D graphics; both business graphics and games.
- **disk** Measures the performance of disk drives for sequential and random reads, and for mixed read-write workloads.
- **dwm** The DWM assessment is targeted at assessing a system's ability to run a Windows–composited desktop, usually referred to as Aero Glass. Note that these are names of Aero themes. You can run this assessment only on computers with Windows Display Driver Model (WDDM) video drivers.
- **features** Enumerates relevant system information. This assessment is automatically run once for each invocation of WinSAT.
- **formal** Runs the full set of assessments and saves the results in the xml format needed to populate the Windows Experience Index score and subscores in the Performance Information And Tools Control Panel item.
- **media** Measures the performance of video encoding and decoding.
- **mem** Runs system memory bandwidth tests. This is intended to be reflective of large memory-to-memory buffer copies, like those used in multimedia processing (video, graphics, imaging, and so on).
- **mfmedia** Runs the Media Foundation–based assessment.

Examining the WinSAT Features Assessment

WinSAT automatically runs the Features assessment each time WinSAT runs, to gather the system information listed. This assessment enumerates system information relevant to the assessments, including:

- An optional globally unique identifier (GUID) if the *–iguid* command-line switch is used. This ensures that each XML file has a unique identifier.
- The iteration value from the *–iter N* command-line switch.
- The number of processors, cores, and CPUs.
- The presence of CPU threading technology.
- x64 capability.
- The processor signature.
- The size and other characteristics of the processor's L1 and L2 caches.
- The presence of MMX, SSE, and SSE2 instructions.
- Information on the memory subsystem. (Note that this is very system-dependent: Some systems will produce good detail here; others will not.)

- Graphics memory.
- Graphics resolution.
- Graphics refresh rate.
- Graphics names and device IDs.

Running WinSAT from the Command Line

Although in most cases, WinSAT will not need to be executed manually from a command prompt, the general format of the command line is as follows.

```
winsat <assessment_name> <assessment_parameters>
```

The WinSAT command-line options are not case sensitive. The command line does not require a dash or forward slash for the assessment name, but it does support either a leading dash (–) or a leading forward-slash (/) character to designate an assessment parameter. WinSAT can be run from a command shell with administrative privileges. An error may be reported if any options or switches are not supported.

The WinSAT tool also supports several command-line switches in addition to the assessment parameters. These are parsed by WinSAT before it passes control to one or more of the assessments. Some of these parameters are also supported by one or more assessments. The command-line parameters recognized by WinSAT include:

- ***–csv*** This causes WinSAT to save the top-level measured metrics to a Comma-Separated Value (CSV) file.
- ***–help or ?*** Displays the help content.
- ***–idiskinfo*** Information on the disk subsystem (logical volumes and physical disks) is not normally saved as part of the *<SystemConfig>* section in the XML output.
- ***–iguid*** Generates a GUID in the XML output file. Note that this is not valid with the formal assessment.
- ***–iter N*** Includes the iteration number *<n>* in the XML output file.
- ***–v*** This specifies that WinSAT should produce verbose output. This output includes progress and status information, and possibly error information. The default is for no verbose output. This switch is passed to all of the specified assessments.
- ***–xml file_name*** This specifies that the XML output from the assessment is to be saved in the specified file name. All assessments support the *–xml* command-line switch; a pre-existing file with the same name will be overwritten.

Understanding WinSAT Command Exit Values

WinSAT provides the following command exit values:

- **0** All requested assessments were completed successfully.
- **1** One or more assessments did not complete because of an error.

- **2** One or more assessments did not complete because of interference.
- **3** WinSAT was canceled by the user.
- **4** The command given to WinSAT was invalid.
- **5** WinSAT did not run with administrator privileges.
- **6** Another instance of WinSAT is already running.
- **7** WinSAT cannot run individual assessments (for example, D3D or DWM) on Remote Desktop server.
- **8** WinSAT cannot run a formal assessment on batteries.
- **9** WinSAT cannot run a formal assessment on Remote Desktop server.
- **10** No multimedia support was detected, so the WinSAT tests could not be run.
- **11** This version of WinSAT cannot run on Windows XP.
- **12** The WinSAT watchdog timer timed out, indicating something is causing the tests to run unusually slowly.
- **13** Can't run a formal assessment on a Virtual Machine.

DIRECT FROM THE SOURCE

When Does WinSAT Run?

Server Performance Group
Windows Fundamentals

In Windows Vista, all WinSAT tests were run during OOBE (the first-run install or out-of-box experience) in order to ensure that all systems had detailed ratings, but it took time (about 3-5 minutes).

In Windows 7, we've made the OOBE experience faster; only the DWM WinSAT test needs to run during OOBE. That test provides the video bandwidth data used by the DWM to determine whether Aero can be turned on. The remaining WinSAT tests (other than the DWM test) run as idle tasks.

After the initial scores are populated, WinSAT checks weekly to see whether hardware has changed sufficiently that the tests should be re-run. Customers can also choose to manually re-rate the system at any time using Performance Information And Tools in Control Panel. By default, WinSAT tracks the history of scores on a machine. If the hardware components have not changed, the highest score is maintained. This prevents temporary minor fluctuations in scoring; for example, if someone re-ran the assessment while a complex application was also running and competing for resources. To re-rate a system from scratch without taking history into account, Performance Information And Tools has an Advanced Tools option to "Clear all Windows Experience Index scores and re-rate the system."

In addition, WinSAT in Windows 7 now supports the new "prepop" syntax. Customers and partners who update images prior to rolling out installations can generate winsat.xml files containing scoring data for their particular systems. During OOBE, WinSAT looks for prepopulated files that match that system configuration. If the files are present, WinSAT will use them to supply the WinEI scores for Performance Information And Tools. Benefits of prepopulation include the following:

- The DWM test does not run during OOBE, because the corresponding winsat.xml file is already there.
- The customer has a complete set of WinEI scores from the start with no need to wait for the remaining WinSAT tests to run on idle.
- Components that make decisions based on WinSAT data will have the information as early as possible so they can modify their behavior based on prepopulated settings instead of using defaults. For example, SuperFetch is aware of advances in storage technology and will turn itself off automatically when the system disk has a WinEI Disk score greater than or equal to 6.5. (SuperFetch helps the common occurrence in which retrieving data from disk is relatively slow; when the system disk is extremely fast, SuperFetch gracefully backs off.)

Running WinSAT Using Performance Information and Tools

If WinSAT has not assessed the system at all, or if hardware has changed since the initial installation, the Windows Aero Glass features may not be available. If you have installed new video hardware or other hardware that might affect the system rating, you may need to run WinSAT from Performance Information And Tools in order to reassess the computer.

To run WinSAT again and reassess the hardware, perform these steps:

1. Click the Action Center icon in the system notification area to open the Action Center.
2. Click the View Performance Information link on the left to display the Performance Information and Tools Control Panel item, shown here.

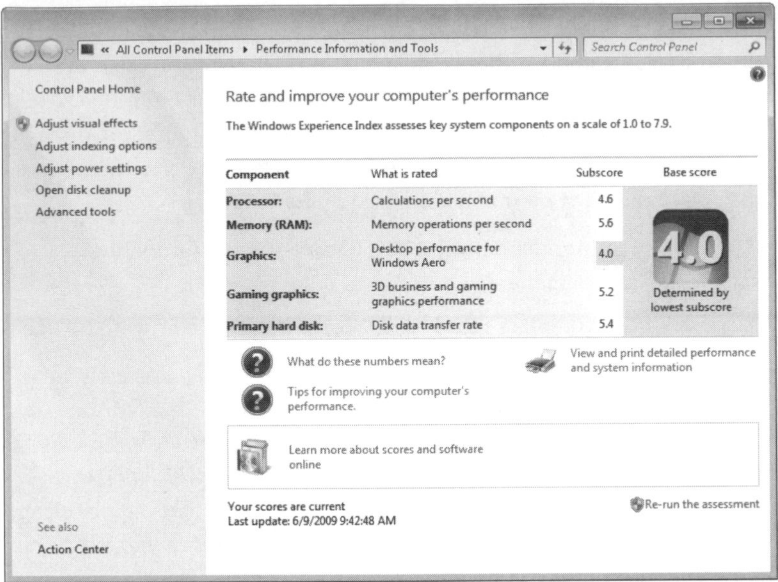

3. Click the Re-run The Assessment link at the bottom right. The Windows Experience Index dialog box will be displayed with a status bar. The reassessment process can take a few minutes and the screen may flash while the system is being assessed.

> ***NOTE*** **You cannot use Performance Information And Tools in Safe mode.**

The main screen of Performance Information and Tools includes the following sections, from top to bottom:

- System Capabilities
- Help links for more information
- A link to Print detailed system information
- OEM Upsell And Online Help

You can use Group Policy to configure what is displayed on the Performance Information And Tools Control Panel for targeted computers. The policy settings for doing this are found here:

Computer Configuration\Policies\Administrative Templates\System\Performance Control Panel

System Capabilities Section

The System Capability details section contains scores derived from the WinSAT data and provides the Windows Experience Index scores and subscores for each area. The Windows Experience consists of the base score (Index) and the subscores for the following areas:

- Processor
- Memory (RAM)
- Primary hard disk
- Desktop graphics
- 3D and gaming graphics

The base score is a positive integer that starts at 1 and can continue to grow as new technology comes out. For example, in Windows Vista, the maximum score was 5.9, while in Windows 7, the maximum score is 7.9. Each of the subscores also has a rating.

The System Capabilities section can be in one of three different states:

- **Unrated** The computer has not yet been rated.
- **Normal** The computer has been rated and the rating is up to date.
- **Outdated** Hardware configuration changed and the Windows Experience Index score and subscores should be updated.

OEM Upsell And Help Section

The OEM Upsell And Help section provides the following features:

- An area for OEM suppliers to place their logos and a link to a local page or their Web sites
- A link for additional information online

Accessing Advanced Performance Tools

Additional options available on the left side of Performance Information And Tools include:

- **Adjust Visual Effects** Opens the Performance Options dialog box
- **Adjust Indexing Options** Opens the Indexing Options dialog box
- **Adjust Power Settings** Opens the Power Options dialog box
- **Open Disk Cleanup** Opens the Disk Cleanup Options dialog box
- **Advanced Tools** Opens an Advanced Tools screen that provides access to other performance-related tools (see Figure 21-19)

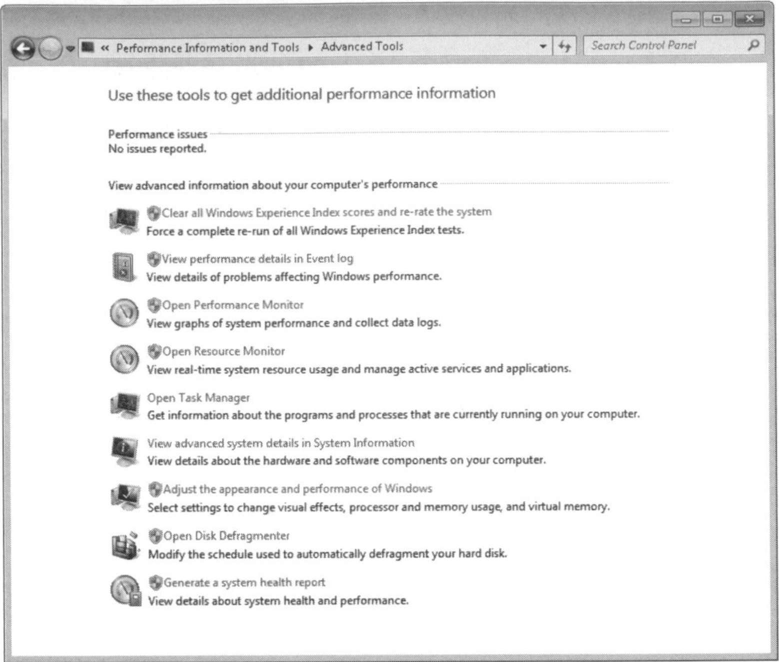

FIGURE 21-19 Advanced Tools

HOW IT WORKS

Understanding the System Performance Rating

Microsoft Global Technical Readiness Platforms Team

It is important to note that the System Performance Rating number indicates the general speed and power of a computer running Windows Vista. The rating pertains only to the performance aspects that affect how well features in Windows and other programs will run on this computer and does not reflect the overall quality of the computer. A higher performance rating means the computer will generally perform better and faster—especially when performing more advanced and resource-intensive tasks—than a computer with a lower performance rating.

The rating system is designed to accommodate future advances in computer technology. In general, the standards for each level of the rating system stay the same (within tenths). For example, a computer that is rated as a 4 should remain a 4 unless the computer's hardware changed. As technology continues to improve, additional higher-level Windows Experience scores will be introduced, and new tests added.

Understanding Windows Error Reporting

Windows Error Reporting (WER) is the client component for the overall Watson Feedback Platform (WFP), which allows Microsoft to collect reports about failure events that occur on a user's system, analyze the data contained in those reports, and respond to the user in a meaningful and actionable manner.

WER is the technology that reports user-mode freezes, user-mode faults, and kernel-mode faults to the back-end servers at Microsoft and replaces Dr. Watson as the default application exception handler.

> ***NOTE*** **WER in Windows Vista and later has support for any kind of problem event as defined by the developer, not just critical failures as in Windows XP.**

Overview of Windows Error Reporting

The WFP is illustrated in the high-level flow diagram in Figure 21-20, with WER labeled as the Watson Client.

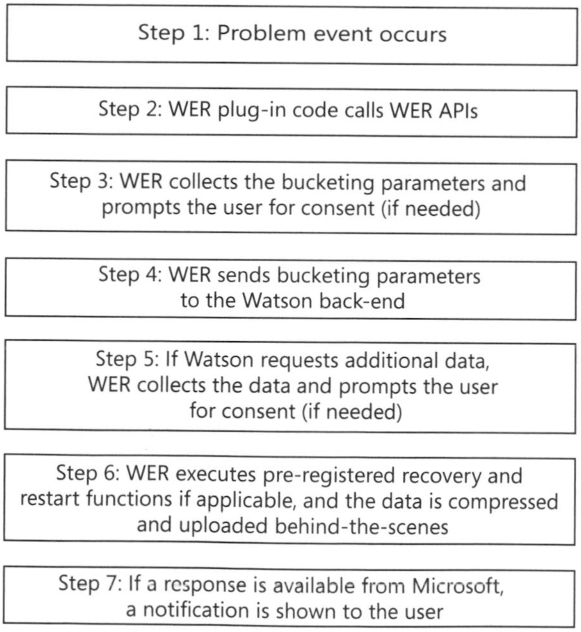

Step 1: Problem event occurs
Step 2: WER plug-in code calls WER APIs
Step 3: WER collects the bucketing parameters and prompts the user for consent (if needed)
Step 4: WER sends bucketing parameters to the Watson back-end
Step 5: If Watson requests additional data, WER collects the data and prompts the user for consent (if needed)
Step 6: WER executes pre-registered recovery and restart functions if applicable, and the data is compressed and uploaded behind-the-scenes
Step 7: If a response is available from Microsoft, a notification is shown to the user

FIGURE 21-20 Watson Feedback Platform flow diagram

A significant improvement of WER in Windows Vista and later versions is the concept of queuing. In Windows XP, WER reports could be sent only at the time the event occurred, with few exceptions. Beginning with Windows Vista, WER provides a flexible queuing architecture where users, administrators, and WER integrators can determine the queuing behavior of their WER events.

During the OOBE phase of installing Windows 7, the user can choose whether WER should automatically send basic problem reports to Microsoft. Basic problem reports include only the minimum amount of information necessary to search for a solution. Later you can choose to send additional information automatically as well.

How WER Works

WER consists of the following conceptual components:

- Report Processor
- Data Collection Module
- Transport System
- Store Management System

Client-side WER functionality is provided through the WER service.

Report Processor

The Report Processor is a conceptual component that is responsible for managing the state of a report after it has been sent to WER. Applications use WER APIs to create and submit reports. At that point, the Report Processor decides whether to queue the report or submit the report. The Report Processor will attempt to hand over the report to the Transport System if the following conditions are met: there is network connectivity, the report is for an interactive application, and a user interface can be shown. Otherwise, the Report Processor will hand over the report to the Queue Management System. The Report Processor will also invoke the user interface component if applicable.

Data Collection Module

The Data Collection Module is responsible for collecting the following data:

- Heap dump data
- WMI query results
- Registry key data
- Registry tree data
- Files
- File version information
- User documents
- Minidump
- Microdump (that is, a minidump that has been stripped of all other information except the faulting stack trace)

Transport System

WER uses two separate modes of transport:

- **Live Watson Mode** In this mode, WER uses a four-stage protocol based on top of HTTP to communicate with the live Watson back-end servers.
- **Agentless Exception Monitoring (AEM)** Support for the file share–based Corporate Error Reporting (CER) transport mode used in previous versions of Windows has been discontinued in Windows Vista. Instead, support for Agentless Exception Monitoring (AEM) has been added to Windows Vista for use in corporate environments. AEM is a component of the Client Monitoring feature in Microsoft System Center Operations Manager (SCOM) 2007 that lets you monitor operating systems and applications for errors within your organization. For more information about AEM, see *http://technet.microsoft.com/en-us/library/bb309493.aspx*.

Store Management System

The WER Store Management System component is responsible for maintaining the error report stores (folders) and for scheduling the prompts that a user will see when there are unsent queued error reports. WER uses user stores for user-level problems and machine stores for system-level problems. The type of store affects the WER prompts that a user sees and the location where the error report data is stored. In addition, user and machine stores contain two subfolders named ReportQueue and ReportArchive. These folders store the queued (unsent) and archived report contents, respectively. The actual data for each error report is stored in individual subfolders within the ReportQueue and ReportArchive folders, which are compressed by default using NTFS compression. When an error report is generated, the queue subsystem evaluates the WER configuration and connection status to determine the appropriate store to use. The WER queuing structure and behavior is discussed later in this section.

USER STORE

The WER user store is located in the following folder:

Users\<username>\AppData\Local\Microsoft\Windows\WER

The default WER behavior is to store error report data in user stores. Error reports are written to the current user's store if the following conditions are true:

- Reporting failed for any reason other than the user clicking Cancel.
- The application developer designed the application using WER APIs to specify queuing as the default behavior.
- The ForceAdminQueue policy is not enabled.

COMPUTER STORE

The WER computer store is located in the following folder:

ProgramData\Microsoft\Windows\WER

You can configure WER by using Group Policy or the registry to force all error report data to be written to the machine store. Reports are written to the machine store if either of the following conditions is true:

- The process submitting the report is not running in an interactive desktop (includes system services).
- The ForceAdminQueue policy is enabled.

REPORTQUEUE FOLDER

The ReportQueue folder contains reports that are queued for sending at a later time. These reports have either the necessary consent and are pending a network connection for upload, or they need consent from the user before they can be uploaded. When a report has been successfully uploaded, it is removed from the ReportQueue folder. This folder is referred to as the *Upload* or *Signoff queue*. After a report is successfully submitted, the report, along with any uploaded data, is copied into the ReportArchive folder.

The location of the ReportQueue folder is either of the following:

- Users\<*username*>\AppData\Local\Microsoft\Windows\WER\ReportQueue (for reports in the user store)
- ProgramData\Microsoft\Windows\WER\ReportQueue (for reports in the computer store)

Note that when the error data is collected initially and before it is queued in the Report-Queue folder, the collected error report files are stored in subfolders within the following folder:

Users\<username>\AppData\Local\Temp

REPORTARCHIVE FOLDER

The ReportArchive folder contains reports that have been uploaded or denied upload (via policy or explicit user action). This folder is referred to as the *Archive store*. Reports that are successfully submitted from the queue store(s) are automatically transferred to the archive store.

You also can create an Event Reporting Console (ERC) folder in the WER store folder(s). The subfolders in the ERC folder store response metadata and templates used for displaying the response data in the Problem Reports And Solutions Control Panel. You don't need to modify the data in the ERC folder, and modifying the data is not supported. The location of the ReportArchive folder is either of the following:

- Users\<*username*>\AppData\Local\Microsoft\Windows\WER\ReportArchive (for reports in the user store)
- ProgramData\Microsoft\Windows\WER\ReportArchive (for reports in the computer store)

QUEUE REPORTING

When a new error report is successfully submitted to any of the queues or directly to the Watson back-end servers, WER enters Queue Reporting mode. In Queue Reporting mode, WER will prompt you to send the queued report(s) if conditions permit. If conditions are not optimal for reporting, WER schedules itself to be started when a network connection is established (SENS) or when the current user logs on the next time (HKCU\Run). This ensures that at some point in the future when conditions are right for reporting, infrastructure will be able to show the queued reporting console.

In Queue Reporting mode, WER performs the following checks in the following order:

1. Is the failing process running in an interactive desktop? If not, WerMgr.exe terminates. This is necessary because WER dialog boxes should not be shown for noninteractive desktops, such as the ones that the service accounts own.
2. Does the current user have reports in her queue, or is the current user an administrator and is administrative queuing enabled? If neither of the conditions is true, the current user has no reports to report. In this case, WER will ensure that network and logon triggers for the current user are removed, and it will exit immediately. If either of the conditions is true, WER attempts to prompt you to report entries in the queue.
3. WER sets the network and logon triggers for the current user in case conditions are not optimal for reporting at this time.
4. WER checks network access to see if the last reporting time has expired. If either of these checks fails, WerMgr.exe terminates.
5. Open the Problem Reports And Solutions Control Panel to prompt you and update the last reporting time.

STORE MAINTENANCE

By default, the Queue Management System performs maintenance such as deleting stale data and trimming the size of the queue on a report store whenever 50 saved reports are in the store. When the total queued report count exceeds the number defined in the registry value MaxQueueCount or the registry value MaxArchiveCount for archive stores, the queue subsystem deletes the oldest .cab files from the queues in the following order until the size of the queue reaches MaxQueueCount or no more CABs remain to delete:

1. Archive Store
2. Signoff Queue
3. Upload Queue

The metadata for a report persists for one calendar year unless the user has disabled the archive via the DisableArchive setting.

WER queue data retention policies can be configured using Group Policy. If no queuing policies are configured, the Archive queue will retain 1,000 reports and the Upload/Signoff queue will retain 50 reports. If a queue becomes full and a new report is created, the new report will overwrite the oldest report in the respective queue.

QUEUE TRIGGERS

This section describes the launch triggers that WER uses to ensure that the queued reporting prompt is started for users when they have unsent reports in their queues. Triggers are persistent across reboots.

WER launch triggers include:

- **Network trigger** This trigger starts WerMgr.exe in Queue Reporting mode for a specific user when a network connection is established. The network trigger is implemented through the SENS API that senses the presence of a network connection.
- **Logon trigger** This trigger starts WerMgr.exe in Queue Reporting mode for a specific user when the user logs on. WerMgr.exe is responsible for WER error queue management.
- **Administrator trigger** The administrator trigger notifies an administrator of unsent entries in the machine queue. This trigger occurs only for administrators on the system.

WER Service

The WER service is responsible for obtaining the information that is provided to the back-end Watson servers when an application exception occurs. The service library, Wersvc.dll, is hosted in its own Svchost.exe process. When a process crashes, the WER service calls Werfault.exe (or Werfaultsecure.exe, discussed later in this section) to obtain all of the necessary data for the crashing/hanging process. Werfault.exe loads Dbgeng.dll and Dbghelp.dll to collect the application error data. It also loads Faultrep.dll to perform the reporting to the back-end Watson servers. If the WER service is not started when an application exception occurs, Werfault.exe and the dependent libraries will still be started to perform the data collection and reporting tasks for the fault.

WER in Windows Vista and later also supports error reporting for secure processes. Secure processes are processes that contain data encrypted with a private key and restricted permission. If a crash occurs in a secure process, the WER service uses Werfaultsecure.exe to obtain the necessary data for the crashing/hanging process. The report is encrypted when created and queued automatically to prevent any possibility of exploitation through the user interface. The encrypted data is then sent to the back-end Watson servers, where it is decrypted and analyzed.

DIRECT FROM THE SOURCE

WER and SCOM 2007

Dhananjay Mahajan, Senior Program Manager
Enterprise Management Division

All versions of Windows have a service called WER, which uses the WER client (on Windows Vista or later) or the Watson client (on earlier versions of Windows) to gather information about application and operating system crash. WER then forwards the crashes to Microsoft for analysis. SCOM 2007 allows WER to first forward those errors to a management server operated by the organization. The administrator can then decide if she wants to send the data to Microsoft for analysis and to see if a resolution to the problem exists. Having access to this information gives client administrators visibility into their system errors as they have never had before, through built-in reports that aggregate crash information from all WER clients. Using these reports, administrators can identify the top crashing applications, the top crashes, and any available solutions on WER service.

AEM, a feature of SCOM 2007, offers the flexibility of sending no information, error IDs only, or full crash information including memory images for analysis. If an error ID or full crash information is sent, Microsoft will search its knowledge base of errors and return a resolution if one exists. Microsoft uses crash information submitted by WER to improve the quality of its products. By having access to this crash data, administrators can use it to improve the quality of their own internal applications as well. AEM has very little overhead, and because crashes happen infrequently and it can easily be deployed across all of the client systems within an enterprise, without a large data storage burden. Typically, a single server can collect, aggregate, and analyze crashes from 100,000 desktops with "normal" crash rates.

Understanding the Error Reporting Cycle

The error reporting cycle for WER begins when a report is generated on a user's system and completes when a response is returned to the user. Overall, five primary steps are involved in this process: reporting, categorization, investigation, resolution, and response. The following sections explain what is involved in each of these steps.

Reporting

The first step is the creation and submission of the report. This can be triggered by a number of events, including an application crash, application freeze, or stop error (blue screen). Beginning with Windows Vista, applications can also be designed to define their own custom event types, allowing them to initiate the reporting process when any type of problem occurs.

Categorization

After the back-end servers at Microsoft receive the report, it is categorized by problem type. Categorization may be possible with only the event parameters (text descriptors of the event), or it may require additional data (dumps). The end result of categorization is that the event reported by the customer becomes a Watson Bucket ID. This allows the developers investigating the events to determine the most frequently reported problems and focus on the most common issues.

Investigation

After the problem is categorized, development teams may view the report data via the Watson portal. The Watson portal provides the data necessary to understand high-level trends and aggregate data, such as the top errors reported against an application. It also provides a mechanism to investigate the low-level data that was reported to debug the root cause of the problem.

Resolution

After a developer has determined the root cause of a problem, ideally a fix, workaround, or new version will be created that can be made available to the customer.

Response

The final step is to close the loop with the customer that reported the problem by responding to his report with information he can use to mitigate the issue. A customer may receive a response in two ways:

- If the issue is understood at the time an error report is submitted, the customer will see a response in the form of a dialog box immediately after the categorization step.
- If the issue is not understood at the time an error report is submitted but is resolved some time after the report, the customer can query for updated knowledge of the problem at a later time.

> ***NOTE*** **Resolutions found later are populated in Action Center.**

Understanding WER Data

To optimize the reporting process, the WER error data is divided into first- and second-level data. During first-level communication with the back-end servers, WER determines if more data is needed. If the server returns a request for more data, collection of the second-level data begins immediately. Simultaneously, a second-level consent dialog box is displayed.

First-Level Data

First-level data consists of up to 10 string parameters that identify a particular classification of the problem. This data is stored in the report manifest file, Report.wer, and is initially submitted to the Watson back-end servers. (The Report.wer file is not itself sent—only the parameters are sent.) The included parameters are used to identify a class of problems. For example, the parameters for a crash (Application Name, Application Version, Module Name, Module Version, Module Offset, AppTimeStamp, ModTimeStamp, and ExceptionCode) provide a unique way to accurately classify a crash. The parameters are the only data submitted to the Watson back-end during first-level communication.

Reports are stored in an archive as a folder structure on the system. Each report subfolder contains, at a minimum, the report manifest text file (Report.wer), which describes the contents of the error report. Although the Report.wer file is a simple text file, it is not meant to be human-readable or editable. Any files referenced by the report are also placed in this folder. The following major sections appear in most Report.wer files:

- Version
- Event Information
- Signature
- UI
- State
- Files
- Response

Second-Level Data

Second-level data is additional data that may be needed to diagnose and resolve a particular bucket. Because Microsoft usually needs only a small sample of this verbose data, the second-level data is submitted only if the back-end server requests it and the user consents to sharing the data. Second-level data is split into two categories:

- **Safe data** This is information that the developer feels is unlikely to contain any personal information, such as a small section of memory, a specific registry key, or a log file.
- **Other data** This encompasses everything that is not safe data, which may or may not contain personal information.

You have the option to always send safe data automatically. Second-level data is specified by the back-end Watson servers and can include, but is not limited to, the following items:

- Minidump file
- Contents of the heap
- Registry Keys
- WMI queries
- Miscellaneous files

MORE INFO For more information about what information can be sent with WER, see the Windows Vista WER Privacy Statement at *http://go.microsoft.com/fwlink/?linkid=50163*.

NOTE Beginning with Windows Vista, WER generates minidump files and heap dump files; it does not generate user-mode process dump files. For information about how to generate user-mode process dump files, see Knowledge Base article 931673, "How to create a user-mode process dump file in Windows Vista," at *http://support.microsoft.com/kb/931673*.

Configuring WER Using Group Policy

Administrators can use Group Policy to configure WER in AD DS environments. Table 21-9 describes the policy settings you can use for configuring WER on targeted computers running Windows Vista and later. WER policy settings can be found in two locations:

Computer Configuration\Policies\Administrative Templates\Windows Components\Windows Error Reporting

User Configuration\Policies\Administrative Templates\Windows Components\Windows Error Reporting

Note that all policy settings listed in this table are available as both per-computer and per-user policies except for the Configure Corporate Windows Error Reporting policy setting, which is available only as a per-computer policy.

TABLE 21-9 Group Policy Settings for Configuring WER

POLICY SETTING	DESCRIPTION
LOCATED UNDER \WINDOWS ERROR REPORTING	
Disable Windows Error Reporting	If this setting is enabled, WER will not send any problem information to Microsoft. Additionally, solution information will not be available in the Action Center Control Panel.
Prevent Display Of The User Interface For Critical Errors	This policy setting prevents the display of the user interface for critical errors. If you enable this policy setting, WER prevents the display of the user interface for critical errors. If you disable or do not configure this policy setting, WER displays the user interface for critical errors.
Disable Logging	If this setting is enabled WER events will not be logged to the system event log.
Do Not Send Additional Data	If this setting is enabled any additional data requests from Microsoft in response to a WER event will be automatically declined without notice to the user.
LOCATED UNDER \WINDOWS ERROR REPORTING\ADVANCED ERROR REPORTING SETTINGS	
Configure Report Archive	This setting controls the behavior of the WER archive. If Archive behavior is set to Store All, all data collected for each report will be stored in the appropriate location. If Archive behavior is set to Store Parameters Only, only the minimum information required to check for an existing solution will be stored. The setting for Maximum Number Of Reports To Store determines how many reports can be stored before old reports are automatically deleted. If this setting is disabled, no WER information will be stored.
Configure Corporate Windows Error Reporting	This setting determines the corporate server to which WER will send reports (instead of sending reports to Microsoft). Server port indicates the port to use on the target server. Connect using Secure Sockets Layer (SSL) determines whether Windows will send reports to the server using a secured connection.
List Of Applications To Be Excluded	This setting determines the behavior of the error reporting exclusion list. Windows will not send reports for any process added to this list. Click Show to display the exclusion list. In the Show Contents dialog box in the Value column, type a process name to add a process to the list. To remove a process from the list, click the process name to be removed and press the Delete key. Click OK to save the list.

POLICY SETTING	DESCRIPTION
Configure Report Queue	This setting determines the behavior of the WER queue. If Queuing behavior is set to Default, Windows will decide each time a problem occurs whether the report should be queued or the user should be prompted to send it immediately. If Queuing behavior is set to Always Queue, all reports will be queued until the user is notified to send them or until the user chooses to send them using the Solutions to Problems Control Panel. If Queuing behavior is set to Always Queue For Administrator, reports will be queued until an administrator is notified to send them or chooses to send them using the Solutions to Problems Control Panel. The setting for Maximum Number Of Reports To Queue determines how many reports can be queued before old reports are automatically deleted. The setting for Number Of Days Between Solution Check Reminders determines the interval time between the display of system notifications which remind the user to check for solutions to problems. A setting of 0 will disable the reminder. If the WER queue setting is disabled, no WER information will be queued and users will be able to send reports only at the time a problem occurs.
LOCATED UNDER \WINDOWS ERROR REPORTING\CONSENT	
Customize Consent Settings	This policy setting determines the consent behavior of WER for specific event types. If this policy setting is enabled and the consent level is set to 0 (Disable), WER will not send any data to Microsoft for this event. If the consent level is set to 1 (Always Ask Before Sending Data), Windows will prompt the user for consent to send reports. If the consent level is set to 2 (Send Parameters), the minimum data required to check for an existing solution will be sent automatically, and Windows will prompt the user for consent to send any additional data requested by Microsoft. If the consent level is set to 3 (Send Parameters And Safe Additional Data), the minimum data required to check for an existing solution as well as data that Windows has determined does not contain (within a high probability) personally identifiable data will be sent automatically, and Windows will prompt the user for consent to send any additional data requested by Microsoft. If the consent level is set to 4 (Send All Data), any data requested by Microsoft will be sent automatically. If this setting is disabled or not configured then consent will default to the default consent setting.

POLICY SETTING	DESCRIPTION
Ignore Custom Consent Settings	This setting determines the behavior of the default consent setting in relation to custom consent settings. If this setting is enabled, the default Consent level setting will always override any other consent setting. If this setting is disabled or not configured, each custom consent setting will determine the consent level for that event type and the default consent setting will determine the consent level of any other reports.
Advanced Error Reporting Settings\Configure Default Consent	This setting determines the consent behavior of WER. If the consent level is set to Always Ask Before Sending Data, Windows will prompt the user for consent to send reports. If the consent level is set to Send Parameters, the minimum data required to check for an existing solution will be sent automatically, and Windows will prompt the user for consent to send any additional data requested by Microsoft. If the consent level is set to "Send parameters and safe additional data", the minimum data required to check for an existing solution as well as data which Windows has determined does not contain (within a high probability) personally identifiable data will be sent automatically, and Windows will prompt the user for consent to send any additional data requested by Microsoft. If the consent level is set to Send All Data, any data requested by Microsoft will be sent automatically. If this setting is disabled or not configured, then the consent level will default to Always Ask Before Sending Data.

Configuring WER Using the Action Center

In Windows Vista, the user interface for WER was the Problem Reports And Solutions Control Panel. Beginning with Windows 7, however, the entry point for WER has been simplified and integrated into the new Action Center (see Figure 21-21), which is a central location where the user can deal with messages concerning the system's security, stability, reliability, and performance. The Action Center acts as a message queue that displays items needing the user's attention and consolidates 10 separate components in Windows Vista into a single tool.

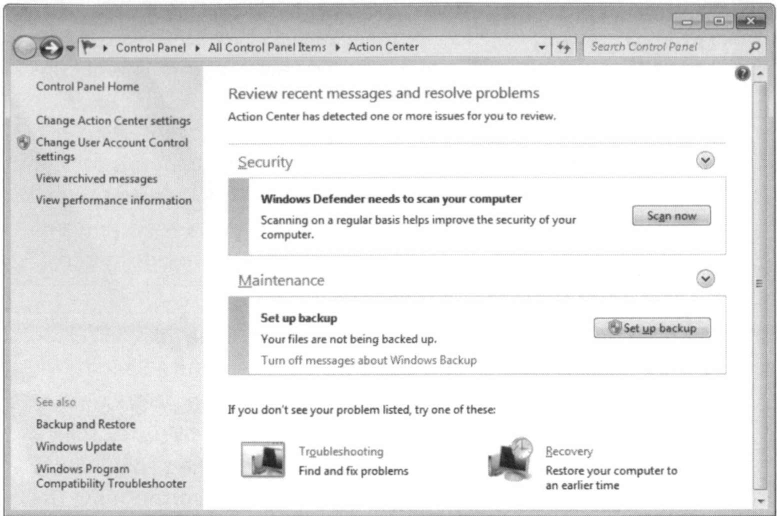

FIGURE 21-21 The new Action Center in Windows 7

To configure client-side WER settings using the Action Center, do the following:

1. Click the Change Action Center Settings link in the left side of the Action Center to display the Change Action Center Settings dialog box.
2. Click the Problem Reporting Settings link under Related Settings at the bottom of the Change Action Center Settings area to display the Problem Reporting Settings dialog box, shown here.

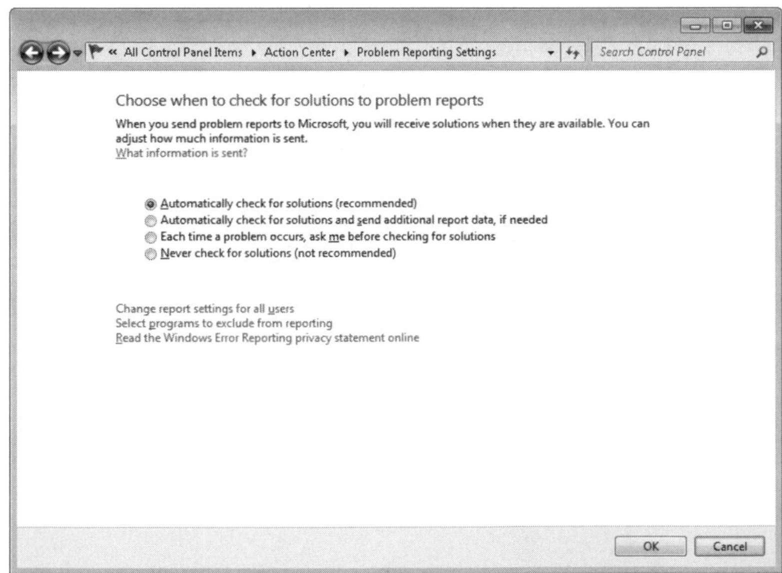

3. Use the Problem Reporting Settings dialog box to configure the error reporting method desired for all users on the computer.
4. To configure the error reporting method differently for each user on the computer, click the Change Reporting Settings For All Users link to display the Problem Reporting dialog box, shown here, which specifies the reporting method for the logged-on user.

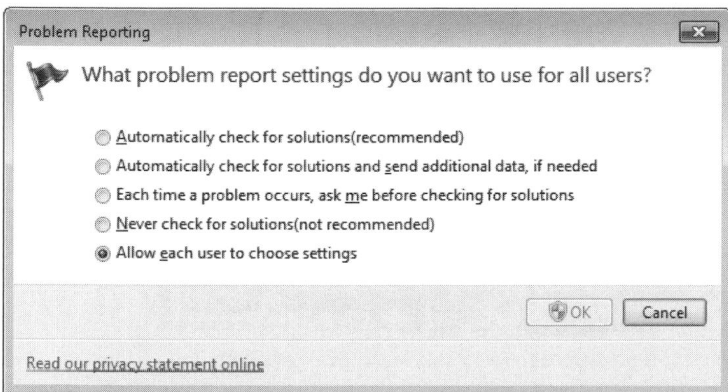

5. To exclude specific programs from reporting error data to Microsoft, click the Select Programs To Exclude From Reporting link in the Problem Reporting Settings dialog box and add the programs you want to the list, as shown here.

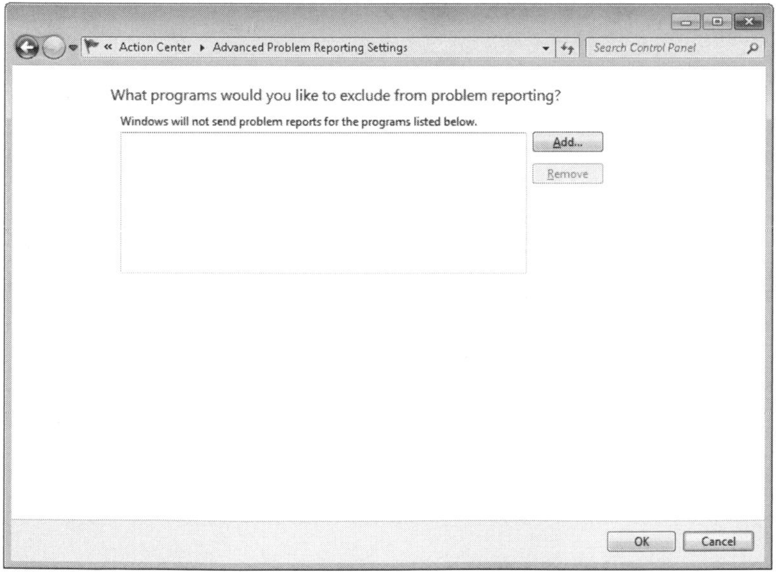

To review WER messages that have been sent to Microsoft from the computer, type **view all** in the Start menu search box, then click View All Problem Reports when this appears in the Control Panel group. This opens the Review Problem Reports dialog box (see Figure 21-22), which displays the source of each report sent, a summary of the issue that triggered the report, the date and time the report was sent, and the status of the issue.

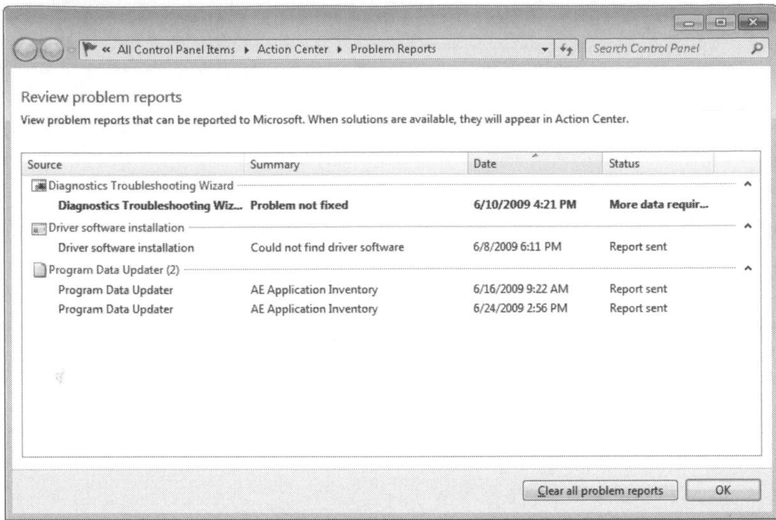

FIGURE 21-22 Reviewing error reports sent to Microsoft from the computer

Double-clicking a report will display detailed information concerning the problem and what was reported, including the Watson bucket ID (see Figure 21-23). You can use this information when trying to resolve outstanding issues with Microsoft product support specialists.

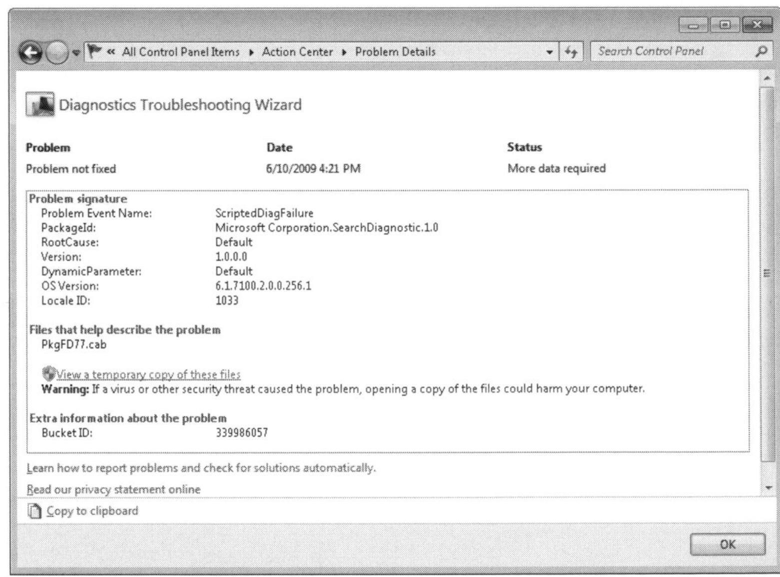

FIGURE 21-23 Detailed information for an error report

NOTE If you have a large number of reports that have been sent from the computer, you can click Clear All Problem Reports to delete them and make it easier to view newly generated reports.

Summary

This chapter has covered tools for monitoring and maintaining desktop health of Windows 7 computers. Using these tools, users can monitor event logs, manage tasks, monitor reliability, obtain performance information for their systems, configure WER, and perform other tasks that can help maintain the health of computers running Windows 7 in your organization.

Additional Resources

These resources contain additional information and tools related to this chapter.

Related Information

- For more information on how to use Performance Monitor in Windows 7, see *http://technet.microsoft.com/en-us/library/cc749249.aspx*.
- For more information concerning the Windows Performance Analysis Tools, see *http://msdn.microsoft.com/en-us/performance/cc825801.aspx*.
- For more information concerning Wevtutil.exe, see *http://technet.microsoft.com/en-us/library/cc732848.aspx*.
- For more information on how to manage tasks, see the Task Scheduler Overview at *http://technet.microsoft.com/en-us/library/cc721871.aspx*.

On the Companion Media

- CountErrors.ps1
- CreateScheduledTask.ps1
- DeleteScheduledTask.ps1
- FindUSBEvenets.ps1
- Get-DiagnosticEventLogs.ps1
- GetDetailedProcessInfo.ps1
- GetErrorsFromAllLogFiles.ps1
- GetEventLogErrors.ps1
- GetEventLogRetentionPolicy.ps1

- GetEventLogs.ps1
- GetFirstEntry.ps1
- GetLastEvent.ps1
- GetLogLastMinutes.ps1
- GetLogSources.ps1
- ListScheduledTask.ps1
- ListSystemRestorePoints.ps1
- MonitorCPU.ps1
- MonitorMemory.ps1
- MonitorNetwork.ps1
- QueryEventLog.ps1
- ReportWinSat.ps1

CHAPTER 22

Supporting Users with Remote Assistance

Remote Assistance (RA) in Windows Vista included improvements in connectivity, performance, usability, and security along with feature enhancements that make it even more useful than Remote Assistance in Windows XP was. The Windows 7 operating system builds on these earlier improvements with Easy Connect, a new feature of Remote Assistance that makes it easier than ever for novice users to request help from expert users and for experts to offer help to novices. With increased Group Policy support, command-line scripting capabilities, session logging, bandwidth optimization, and more, Remote Assistance is now an essential tool for enabling enterprises to support users in Help Desk scenarios. This chapter examines how Remote Assistance works in Windows 7, how to use it to support end users, and how to manage it using Group Policy and scripts.

Understanding Remote Assistance

Supporting end users is an essential function of IT departments and the corporate Help Desk. Unfortunately, conventional technical support provided over the telephone or using chat tools is generally cumbersome and inefficient. As a result, supporting users is often both time-consuming and costly for large enterprises to implement. For example, end users often have difficulty describing the exact nature of the problem they are having. Because of their general inexperience and lack of technical knowledge, end users may try to describe their problem using nontechnical, inexact language. As a result, Help Desk personnel are generally reduced to asking a series of simple questions to try to isolate the problem the user is having. The methodical nature of these questions sometimes causes users to feel as if Help Desk personnel are being condescending, and such misunderstandings can reduce the effectiveness of the support experience and can make users tend to avoid contacting support personnel when future problems arise.

End users also often have difficulty following instructions given to them by Help Desk personnel who are trying to assist them. Well-trained support personnel will try to avoid using technical jargon when communicating with end users, but although using plain language can improve the support experience, it may also mean that resolution steps become long and tiresome. For example, telling a user how to use Disk Cleanup from System Tools in Accessories can require several sentences or more, and this kind of communication can add time to support incidents, making them more costly to the company.

Remote Assistance solves these problems by enabling support personnel to view the user's desktop in real time. The user seeking assistance can demonstrate the nature of the problem to the support person. This is a quicker and more efficient way to communicate a problem than using words or e-mail. If necessary, the user can also give the support person permission to assume shared interactive control of the user's computer to show the user how to resolve the problem. The result of using Remote Assistance is faster problem resolution, an improved support experience, and a lower Total Cost of Ownership (TCO) for supporting end users in large, corporate environments.

Remote Assistance vs. Remote Desktop

Remote Assistance and Remote Desktop are different features of Windows 7 that have entirely different uses. Remote Desktop is based on Microsoft Terminal Services and is a tool for logging on to remote computers. When you use Remote Desktop to connect to a remote computer, a new user session is established. Remote Desktop can also establish sessions with computers that have no interactive sessions running (no users logged on locally), such as headless servers. For more information on Remote Desktop, see Chapter 27, "Connecting Remote Users and Networks."

Remote Assistance, on the other hand, is a tool for interactively helping users troubleshoot problems with their computers. To use Remote Assistance, both the User (also called the Novice) and the Helper must be present on their computers. Unlike Remote Desktop, Remote Assistance does not create a new session. Instead, Remote Assistance allows the Helper to work in the existing session of the User. The User's desktop gets remoted to the Helper, who can then view the User's desktop and, with the User's consent, share control of the desktop.

Here is another way to summarize the difference between these two features: In Remote Assistance, both users involved are looking at the same desktop using the same logon credentials (those of the interactively logged-on User) and can share control of that desktop; in Remote Desktop, when the remote person logs on, the interactively logged-on user (if one exists) is logged out.

Improvements to Remote Assistance in Windows 7

As mentioned previously, Remote Assistance in Windows 7 builds on the many enhancements introduced earlier for this feature in Windows Vista. These earlier enhancements improved upon the earlier Windows XP implementation of Remote Assistance and included the following:

- Connectivity improvements with transparent Network Address Translation (NAT) traversal using Teredo and IPv6
- An improved user interface (UI) that is easier to start and use
- A stand-alone executable (Msra.exe) that accepts command-line arguments and can easily be scripted
- Improved overall performance with a smaller footprint, quicker startup and connect times, and optimized bandwidth usage for screen updates
- Enhanced security with mandatory password and integration with User Account Control (UAC)
- New Offer RA via IM scenario and an open application programming interface (API) for integration with peer-to-peer (P2P) applications
- Additional Group Policy settings for improved manageability

In addition to these Windows Vista enhancements for Remote Assistance, Windows 7 adds the following new enhancements to Remote Assistance:

- Easy Connect, a method for soliciting Remote Assistance that uses the P2P collaboration infrastructure to simplify Remote Assistance user interactions
- An improved Windows Remote Assistance Wizard that makes it easier than ever for users to solicit or offer help
- New command-line arguments for the Remote Assistance executable (Msra.exe)

Remote Assistance in Windows 7 and Windows Vista deprecates the following features that were available on Windows XP:

- No more support for the MAILTO method of solicited Remote Assistance
- No more support for voice sessions

In addition, Remote Assistance in Windows 7 has deprecated the file transfer feature that was available in Windows XP and Windows Vista. Compatibility with earlier versions is still supported, however—for example, if a file transfer is initiated from a Windows XP or Windows Vista computer, Windows 7 will accept the transfer.

For information on interoperability between the Windows XP, Windows Vista, and Windows 7 versions of Remote Assistance, see the section titled "Interoperability with Remote Assistance in Windows XP" later in this chapter.

How Remote Assistance Works

In Remote Assistance, the person needing help is referred to as the *User* (or *Novice*), and the support person providing assistance is called the *Helper* (or *Expert*). You start Remote Assistance from the Start menu by navigating to All Programs, selecting Maintenance, and then selecting Windows Remote Assistance. You can also start Remote Assistance from a command prompt by typing **msra.exe**.

Remote Assistance has two basic modes of operation:

- **Solicited RA** In *Solicited RA* (also known as *Escalated RA*), the User requests assistance from the Helper by initiating the Remote Assistance session using e-mail, instant messaging (IM), Easy Connect, or by providing the Helper with a saved copy of an invitation file (*.MsRcIncident). Each of these methods uses a different underlying mechanism:
  - **Solicited RA using e-mail** This method requires that the e-mail clients being used by the User support Simple Mail Application Programming Interface (SMAPI). Examples of SMAPI-compliant e-mail clients include Windows Mail, which is included in Windows Vista, and Microsoft Office Outlook 2007. Windows 7 does not have a built-in e-mail SMAPI-compliant client, but you can install Windows Live Mail, which is available for download as part of the Windows Live Essentials suite of applications (at *http://get.live.com*). Web-based e-mail services, such as Windows Live Hotmail, are not SMAPI-compliant and cannot be used for soliciting or offering Remote Assistance using e-mail. In this approach, the User starts the Remote Assistance UI to create an e-mail message that has a Remote Assistance invitation file (*.MsRcIncident) attached to the message. The User must specify a password for the Remote Assistance session, which must be communicated to the Helper using an out-of-band (OOB) method such as calling the Helper on the telephone. When the Helper receives the User's Remote Assistance invitation, she opens the attached ticket, enters the password that was conveyed by the User, and the Remote Assistance session starts. The Helper must respond to the invitation from the User within a specified time limit (the default is 6 hours), or the invitation will expire and a new one will need to be sent. In a domain environment, this ticket lifetime can also be configured using Group Policy. See the section titled "Managing Remote Assistance Using Group Policy" later in this chapter.
  - **Solicited RA using file transfer** This method requires that both the User and Helper have access to a common folder (such as a network share on a file server), or that they use some other method for transferring the file (for example, by using a USB key to manually transfer the file or by uploading the file to an FTP site). The user creates a Remote Assistance invitation file and saves it in the shared folder. The User must provide a password that must be communicated to the Helper using an OOB method such as a telephone call. The Helper retrieves the ticket from the shared folder, opens it, enters the password, and the Remote Assistance session starts. Again, the Helper must respond to the invitation within a specified time, or the invitation will expire and a new one will be needed. (The expiration time is configurable through Group Policy.)

- **Solicited RA using instant messaging** This method for soliciting assistance requires that the IM applications being used by both the User and the Helper support the Microsoft Rendezvous API. An example of an IM application that supports the Rendezvous API is Windows Live Messenger, which is available for download as part of the Windows Live Essentials suite of applications (at *http://get.live.com*). In this approach, the User requests assistance from someone on his buddy list. To ensure that the remote person is really the User's buddy (and not someone masquerading as the buddy), Remote Assistance requires that a password be relayed from the User to the Helper by other means (such as a phone call) before the Helper can connect. For more information on the Rendezvous API, see the Windows Software Development Kit (SDK) on MSDN at *http://msdn.microsoft.com/en-us/library/aa359213.aspx*.
- **Solicited RA using Easy Connect** This method for soliciting assistance is new in Windows 7 and uses Peer Name Resolution Protocol (PNRP) to enable direct P2P transfer of the Remote Assistance invitation using the cloud. To establish the initial Remote Assistance session, the User only needs to communicate a password to the Helper using an OOB method such as by telephone. The Helper uses this password to obtain the Remote Assistance invitation from the cloud and initiate the session. When the initial Remote Assistance connection has been made, a trust relationship is established between the Helper and the User. This trust relationship is established through the exchange of contact and certificate information. Subsequent interactions are simplified because the contact information can be used to pick a Helper who is currently available. For more information on this method for soliciting assistance, see the section titled "Scenario 1: Soliciting Remote Assistance Using Easy Connect" later in this chapter. For information on how Easy Connect works, see the sidebar titled "Direct from the Source: How Easy Connect Works" later in this chapter. For information on how PNRP works, see the sidebar titled "How It Works: PNRP and Microsoft P2P Collaboration Services" later in this chapter.

- **Unsolicited RA** In Unsolicited RA (also known as Offer RA), the Helper offers help to the User by initiating the Remote Assistance session using Distributed Component Object Model (DCOM). Unsolicited RA is a typical corporate Help Desk scenario in which all the users are in a domain. The Helper enters either the fully qualified domain name (FQDN) or IP address of the User's computer to connect to the User's computer. This method requires that the Helper has been previously authorized as a domain administrator to be able to offer Remote Assistance to the Users. (For information on how to authorize Helpers for offering Remote Assistance, see the section titled "Managing Remote Assistance Using Group Policy" later in this chapter.) This method also requires that the Helper either knows the name (the host name on a local subnet; the fully qualified name otherwise) or address (IPv4 or IPv6) of the User's computer.

HOW IT WORKS

PNRP and Microsoft P2P Collaboration Services

Microsoft P2P network and collaboration technologies are designed to enable the next generation of peer-to-peer scenarios, including shared workspaces, distributed computing, and even load balancing. These P2P technologies allow users to securely communicate and share information with each other without requiring a central server to be involved. Because P2P technologies are designed to work in networking environments with transient connectivity—such as an ad hoc wireless network established between several laptops at a coffee shop—they cannot rely on the server-based Domain Name System (DNS) to perform name resolution between peers. Instead, P2P name resolution is based on the PNRP, a mechanism for distributed, serverless name resolution of peers in a P2P network.

PNRP works by utilizing multiple groupings of computers called clouds. These clouds correspond to two different scopes of IPv6 addresses:

- **Global cloud** Any given computer will be connected to a single Global cloud. For computers with IPv6 Internet connectivity, the Global cloud is Internet-wide. In networks where computers do not have IPv6 Internet connectivity but still have Global IPv6 addresses (such as firewalled corporate environments), the Global cloud is network-wide.
- **Link-local clouds** One or more clouds, each corresponding to nodes within the same subnet or network link (link-local addresses and the link-local address scope). Note that Remote Assistance only uses the Global (Internet-wide) cloud; link-local clouds are not used by Remote Assistance.

Peer names in PNRP are static identifiers of endpoints that can be resolved to changing IP addresses, enabling P2P communications. Peer names can be computers, users, devices, groups, services, or anything that can be identified by an IPv6 address and port. Peer names are represented by identifiers (IDs) that are 32 bytes long and can be either unsecured (names that can be spoofed) or secured (names that cannot be spoofed because they are derived from a public/private key pair owned by the publisher).

The underlying name resolution functions on PNRP IDs within a cloud are stored in a distributed fashion in a cache on each peer within the cloud, with each peer's cache containing only a portion of the names for all the peers in the cloud. When the issuing peer wants to resolve the name of the targeted peer to its published address and port number, it follows these steps:

1. The issuing peer first consults its own PNRP cache for this information. If it finds this information, it sends a PNRP Request message to the targeted peer and waits for a response. These Request messages serve the function of enabling peers to communicate to other peers their active involvement within the cloud.

2. If the issuing peer does not find this information, it sends the Request message to the peer whose ID most closely matches (that is, is closest numerically to) that of the targeted peer. The peer that receives this message then consults its own cache. If it finds a closer match or the match itself, it returns this information to the requesting peer. The requesting peer then goes to the returned peer and the process continues until the resolution succeeds or fails.
3. If the peer that receives this message does not find closer information in its cache, it returns the message to the issuing peer, indicating that it does not know the targeted peer. The issuing peer then repeats the previous step by sending a message to the peer whose ID next most closely matches that of the targeted peer. This process continues until the targeted peer is found (if present on the network) or not found (if no longer present within the cloud).

Looping is prevented by including in the Request message the list of peers that have already forwarded requests.

For more information on how PRNP and other Microsoft P2P technologies work, see *http://technet.microsoft.com/en-us/library/bb742623.aspx* on TechNet.

Remote Assistance Operational States

Remote Assistance has three operational states:

- **Waiting For Connect** This state occurs when either:
  - The Helper has offered Remote Assistance to the User, but the User has not yet agreed to allow the Helper to connect to his computer.
  - The User has sent the Helper an invitation but the Helper has not yet responded by opening the invitation, or the Helper has opened the invitation and the User has not yet agreed to allow the Helper to connect to his computer.

  In the Waiting For Connect state, the Helper cannot view or control the screen of the User's computer until a Remote Assistance connection has been established and both computers have entered the Screen Sharing state. After the Remote Assistance application has been started and is running in the Waiting For Connect state, the application should not be closed until the other party responds and establishes the connection. For example, if the User uses the Solicit RA Using E-mail method and sends an invitation file to a Helper, the Remote Assistance application opens on the User's computer and waits for the Helper to accept the invitation. If the User closes Remote Assistance on her computer before the Helper accepts the invitation, the Helper will not be able to connect to the User's computer and the User will need to send a new invitation.
- **Screen Sharing** This state occurs when the User has consented to allow the Helper to connect to his computer—either after the User has sent the Helper an invitation

or the Helper has offered Remote Assistance to the User. In the Screen Sharing state, a Remote Assistance session has been established and the Helper can view—but not control—the screen of the User's computer.

When the User is prompted for consent to allow the Helper to connect to his computer, a warning message appears on the User's computer saying that the Helper wants to connect to his computer. This warning message is customizable using Group Policy. See the section titled "Managing Remote Assistance Using Group Policy" later in this chapter for more information.

- **Control Sharing** This state occurs after the Screen Sharing state when the Helper has requested control of the User's computer and the User has consented to allow the Helper to have shared control of his computer. In the Control Sharing state, the Helper has the same level of access to the User's computer that the User has, and the Helper can use his own mouse and keyboard to remotely perform actions on the User's computer. Specifically:
  - If the User is a standard user on his computer, the Helper will be able to perform only those actions on the User's computer that can be performed by a standard user on that computer.
  - If the User is a local administrator on his computer, the Helper will be able to perform any actions on the User's computer that can be performed by a local administrator on that computer.

  For more information on the level of control that a Helper has on a User's computer, see the section titled "Remote Assistance and the Secure Desktop" later in this chapter.

User vs. Helper Functionality

After a Remote Assistance connection has been established and both computers have entered the Screen Sharing state, the User and Helper are able to perform the tasks listed in Table 22-1.

TABLE 22-1 Tasks That Can Be Performed by User and Helper During a Remote Assistance Session

DESCRIPTION OF TASK	USER?	HELPER?
Chat	Yes	Yes
Save a log of session activity	Yes (default)	Yes (default)
Configure bandwidth usage	Yes	No
Pause (temporarily hide screen)	Yes	No
Request shared control	No	Yes
Give up shared control	Yes	Yes
Disconnect	Yes	Yes

Remote Assistance and NAT Traversal

Remote Assistance works by establishing a P2P connection between the User's computer and the Helper's computer. One challenge this poses is that it can be difficult to establish P2P connections if one or both of the computers involved are behind a gateway or router that uses NAT. NAT is an IP routing technology described by RFC 1631 that is used to translate IP addresses and TCP/UDP port numbers of packets being forwarded. NAT is typically used to map a set of private IP addresses to a single public IP address (or to multiple public addresses). Home networks using a wireless or wired router also use NAT technology.

To overcome this difficulty, Windows 7 and Windows Vista include built-in support for Teredo, an IPv6 transition technology described in RFC 4380 that provides address assignment and automatic tunneling for unicast IPv6 connectivity across the IPv4 Internet. The NAT traversal capability provided by Teredo in Windows 7 and Windows Vista allows Remote Assistance connectivity when one or both of the users involved in a Remote Assistance session are hidden behind a NAT. The Remote Assistance experience is transparent from the perspective of the users involved, regardless of whether or not NAT is being used on either user's network. For most small business and home user environments, Remote Assistance in Windows 7 and Windows Vista will seamlessly traverse a NAT-enabled router with no additional router configuration required. For information on enterprises that need to remotely support users who work from home, see the section titled "Other Possible Remote Assistance Usage Scenarios" later in this chapter.

> ***NOTE*** **Offering Remote Assistance using DCOM is not usually a Teredo scenario because enterprise users are behind a corporate firewall and are not separated from each other by NATs.**

Remote Assistance can connect across restricted NATs and cone NATs, which generally comprise the large majority of deployed NATs. Beginning with Windows 7, Remote Assistance can also connect across certain types of symmetric NATs, but only if the other computer is not behind a symmetric NAT as well. For more information on NAT traversal support in Windows 7, see Chapter 28, "Deploying IPv6."

Remote Assistance will not connect in certain configurations. Specifically:

- Remote Assistance will not work if the NAT-enabled router is configured to block the specific ports used by Remote Assistance. See the section titled "Remote Assistance and Windows Firewall" later in this chapter for more information.
- Remote Assistance will not work if the User's NAT-enabled router is configured to block all UDP traffic.

> ***NOTE*** **To determine the type of NAT a network is using, open an elevated command prompt and type netsh interface teredo show state.**

For more information on IPv6 support in Windows 7, including built-in client support for Teredo and other IPv6 transition technologies, see Chapter 28.

To verify whether your NAT supports Remote Assistance, you can use the Internet Connectivity Evaluation Tool at *http://www.microsoft.com/windows/using/tools/igd/default.mspx*. If your NAT supports Universal Plug and Play (UPnP), then Remote Assistance should be able to get a global IPv4 address that allows anyone to connect to you. If your NAT supports Teredo/IPv6 and you are running Windows 7 or Windows Vista, then an RA Helper that is running Windows 7 or Windows Vista and is Teredo-enabled should be able to connect to you.

Remote Assistance and IP Ports Used

The ports used by a Remote Assistance session depend on which version of Windows is running on the two computers involved in the session. Specifically:

- **Windows 7 to Windows 7, Windows 7 to Windows Vista, or Windows Vista to Windows Vista** Dynamic ports allocated by the system in the range TCP/UDP 49152–65535
- **Windows 7 to Windows XP or Windows Vista to Windows XP** Port 3389 TCP (local/remote)

In addition, the Offer RA via DCOM scenario uses port 135 (TCP).

> ***NOTE*** **If you are concerned about opening the DCOM port (TCP port 135) on your corporate firewall and want to avoid doing this but still want to be able to offer Remote Assistance to remote users, you can do so by using Authenticated IPsec Bypass as described in *http://technet.microsoft.com/en-us/library/cc753463.aspx*.**

Remote Assistance and Windows Firewall

The Windows Firewall is configured with a group exception for Remote Assistance. This group exception has multiple properties that are grouped together as part of the Remote Assistance exception. The Remote Assistance exception properties will change depending on the network location of the computer (private, public, or domain). For example, the default Remote Assistance exception when the computer is in a public location is stricter than when the computer is in a private location. In a public location (such as an airport), the Remote Assistance exception is disabled by default and does not open ports for UPnP and Simple Service Discovery Protocol (SSDP) traffic. In a private network (a home or work network, for example) the Remote Assistance exception is enabled by default and UPnP and SSDP traffic is permitted. In a domain-based enterprise environment, the Remote Assistance exception is typically managed using Group Policy and is enabled by default in Windows 7; it was disabled by default in Windows Vista.

The default configuration of the Remote Assistance exception in Windows Firewall varies depending on the firewall profile. Specifically, note the following:

- **Private profile** The Remote Assistance exception in the Windows Firewall is enabled by default when the computer location is set to Private. It is configured for NAT traversal using Teredo by default so that users in a private networking environment (for example, the home environment) can solicit help from other users who may also be behind NATs. The private profile includes the appropriate exceptions needed to allow communication with UPnP NAT devices. If a UPnP NAT is in this environment, Remote Assistance will attempt to use the UPnP for NAT traversal. This profile also includes exceptions needed for PNRP. Offer RA via DCOM is not configured in this profile.

- **Public profile** The Remote Assistance exception is disabled by default and no inbound Remote Assistance traffic is permitted. Windows Firewall is configured this way by default to better protect users in a public networking environment (such as a coffee shop or airport terminal). When the Remote Assistance exception is enabled, NAT traversal using Teredo is enabled. However, traffic to UPnP devices is not enabled, and Offer RA via DCOM is not enabled.
- **Domain profile** The Remote Assistance exception when the computer is in a domain environment is geared toward the Offer RA scenario. This exception is enabled by default in Windows 7 and is typically managed via Group Policy.

Table 22-2 summarizes the state of the Remote Assistance firewall inbound exception for each type of network location. The Remote Assistance exception has outbound properties as well; however, outbound exceptions are not enabled in Windows Firewall by default.

TABLE 22-2 Default State of Remote Assistance Firewall Inbound Exception for Each Type of Network Location

NETWORK LOCATION	STATE OF REMOTE ASSISTANCE EXCEPTION	DEFAULT PROPERTIES OF THE REMOTE ASSISTANCE EXCEPTION
Private (Home or Work)	Enabled by default	■ Msra.exe application exception ■ UPnP enabled for communications with UPnP NATs ■ PNRP enabled ■ Edge traversal enabled to support Teredo
Public	Disabled by default; must be enabled by user with Admin credentials	■ Msra.exe application exception ■ Edge traversal enabled to support Teredo
Domain	Enabled by default in Windows 7; disabled by default in Windows Vista	■ Msra.exe application exception ■ RAServer.exe (the RA COM server) application exception ■ PNRP enabled ■ DCOM port 135 ■ UPnP enabled for communications with UPnP NATs

Remote Assistance and the Secure Desktop

When a User consents to having a Helper share control of her computer during a Remote Assistance session, the User has the option of allowing the Helper to respond to UAC prompts (Figure 22-1). Typically, UAC prompts appear on the Secure Desktop (which is not remoted), and consequently the Helper cannot see or respond to Secure Desktop prompts. The Secure Desktop mode is the same mode that a user sees when she logs on to her computer or presses the Secure Attention Sequence (SAS) keystroke (Ctrl+Alt+Delete). UAC elevation prompts are displayed on the Secure Desktop instead of the user's normal desktop to protect the user from unknowingly allowing malware to run with elevated privileges on her computer. The User must provide consent to a UAC prompt to return to her normal desktop and continue working. This consent requires either clicking Continue (if the user is a local administrator on her computer) or by entering local administrative credentials (if she is a standard user on her computer).

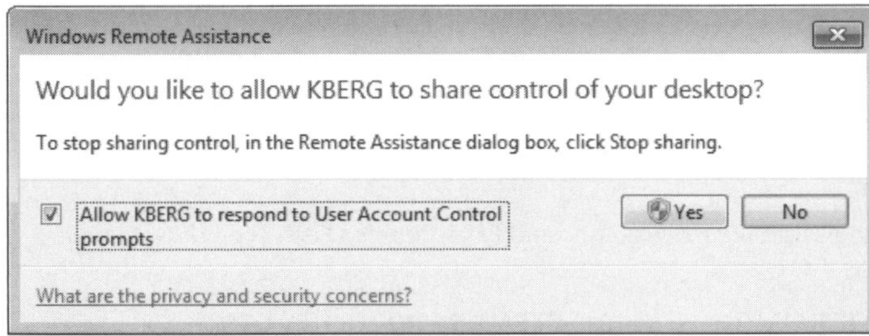

FIGURE 22-1 The User has the option of allowing the Helper to respond to UAC prompts when the Remote Assistance session is in the Control Sharing state.

It is important to understand that the Secure Desktop on the User's computer is not remoted to the Helper's computer. In other words, the Helper can respond only to UAC prompts on the User's computer using the User's own credentials. This means that if the User is a standard user on her computer and the Helper is a local administrator on the User's computer, the Helper can have only administrative privileges on the User's computer if the User can first supply those credentials.

Enforcing this limitation is essential to ensure the security of Windows 7 desktops. The reason behind this design decision is that, if Remote Assistance was architected to allow the Helper to remotely elevate the User's privileges, the User would be able to terminate the Remote Assistance session and thus steal local administrative credentials from the Helper.

Remote Assistance Logging

Remote Assistance can generate a session log of Remote Assistance-associated activity. Session logging is enabled by default and consists of timestamped records that identify Remote Assistance-related activities on each computer. Session logs only contain information about activities that specifically relate to Remote Assistance functionality, such as who initiated the session, if consent was given to a request for shared control, and so on.

Session logs do not contain information on actual tasks that the User or Helper performed during a session. For example, if the Helper is given Shared Control privileges, starts an Admin command prompt, and performs steps to reconfigure the TCP/IP configuration on the User's computer during a Remote Assistance session, the session logs will not contain a record of this action.

Session logs do include any chat activity performed during a Remote Assistance session. The log generated during a session is also displayed within the chat window so that both the User and the Helper can see what is being logged during the session. Session logs also include any file transfer activity that occurs during the session, and they also record when the session has been paused.

PURPOSE OF REMOTE ASSISTANCE SESSION LOGGING

Session logs for Remote Assistance are mainly intended for enterprises that are required to maintain records of system and user activity for record-keeping purposes. They are not intended as a way to record every action performed by Help Desk personnel when troubleshooting problems with users' computers. A typical environment in which session logging might be required would be in a banking environment, where a financial institution is required by law to maintain records of who accessed a computer and at what time.

Because the permissions on these session logs grant the User full control over logs stored on her own computer, by default, session logs are generated on both the User's computer and the Helper's computer so that the Helper can archive them and protect them from tampering. The logs created on each side of a Remote Assistance session are similar but not identical. This is because session logs are generated from the perspective of the computer involved—whether the User's computer or the Helper's computer—and therefore complement each other instead of being identical.

In an enterprise environment, Group Policy can be used to enable or disable session logging. If session logging is not configured using Group Policy, both the User and Helper are free to disable session logging on their own computers. For more information, see the section titled "Managing Remote Assistance Using Group Policy" later in this chapter.

SESSION LOG PATH AND NAMING CONVENTION

Session logs are XML-formatted documents so that they can be easily integrated into other data sets—for example, by importing them into a database managed by Microsoft SQL Server 2005. All session logs are stored in the following subfolder of the user's profile:

%UserProfile%\Documents\Remote Assistance Logs

A unique session log file is created for each Remote Assistance session on the computer. Log files stored within this folder are formatted using XML and are named using the convention *YYYYMMDDHHMMSS*.xml, where the time format is 24-hour. For example, a session log created at 3:45:20 P.M. on August 13, 2008, would be named 20080813154520.xml.

The XML content of a typical session log looks like the following:


```
<?xml version="1.0" ?>
<SESSION>
  <INVITATION_OPENED TIME="3:24 PM" DATE="Wednesday, May 07, 2008" EVENT="A Remote
Assistance invitation has been opened." />
  <INCOMING_IP_ADDRESS TIME="3:26 PM" DATE="Wednesday, May 07, 2008">fe80::2856:e5b0:
fc18:143b%10</INCOMING_IP_ADDRESS>
  <CONNECTION_ESTABLISHED TIME="3:26 PM" DATE="Wednesday, May 07, 2008" EVENT="A Remote
Assistance connection has been established.">jdow</CONNECTION_ESTABLISHED>
  <EXPERT_REQUEST_CONTROL TIME="3:27 PM" DATE="Wednesday, May 07, 2008" EVENT="jdow has
requested to share control of the computer." />
  <EXPERT_GRANTED_CONTROL TIME="3:27 PM" DATE="Wednesday, May 07, 2008" EVENT="jdow has
been granted permission to share control of the computer." />
  <EXPERT_CONTROL_STARTED TIME="3:27 PM" DATE="Wednesday, May 07, 2008" EVENT="jdow is
sharing control of the computer." />
  <EXPERT_CONTROL_ENDED TIME="3:27 PM" DATE="Wednesday, May 07, 2008" EVENT="jdow is not
sharing control of the computer." />
  <CHAT_MESSAGE TIME="3:30 PM" DATE="Wednesday, May 07, 2008">jdow: test</CHAT_MESSAGE>
  <CHAT_MESSAGE TIME="3:30 PM" DATE="Wednesday, May 07, 2008">jchen: ok</CHAT_MESSAGE>
  <CONNECTION_ENDED TIME="3:30 PM" DATE="Wednesday, May 07, 2008" EVENT="The Remote
Assistance connection has ended." />
  <INVITATION_CLOSED TIME="3:30 PM" DATE="Wednesday, May 07, 2008" EVENT="A Remote
Assistance invitation has been closed." />
</SESSION>
```


Using Remote Assistance in the Enterprise

The main Remote Assistance scenario within a corporate networking environment is supporting desktop computers that are on the corporate network and joined to a domain. Users' computers must be configured appropriately before they can be offered Remote Assistance. This is done via Group Policy, as explained in the section titled "Managing Remote Assistance Using Group Policy" later in this chapter. Additionally, the Remote Assistance exception in the Windows Firewall must be enabled. For more information, see the section titled "Remote Assistance and Windows Firewall" earlier in this chapter.

Because most corporate networks have a perimeter firewall blocking access from outside the internal network, supporting remote users who are connecting from outside the corporate network can be more difficult. However, most enterprises now use virtual private network (VPN) technologies to allow remote users to connect to their corporate networks over the Internet, and this kind of scenario generally poses no problem to Remote Assistance functionality.

Using Remote Assistance in the Corporate Help Desk Environment

The standard approach to using Remote Assistance in an enterprise environment is for Help Desk personnel to offer Remote Assistance to users who telephone to request assistance. A typical scenario might be as follows:

1. User Jane Dow (the User) is having problems configuring an application on her computer. She phones Help Desk, explains her problem briefly, and asks for help.
2. A Help Desk person named Jacky Chen (the Helper) asks Jane for the FQDN or IP address of her computer. She responds with the information, which she can get from computer properties or by running *ipconfig*.
3. Jacky starts Remote Assistance on his computer and uses the Offer RA feature to offer help to Jane. This causes a dialog box to appear on Jane's computer, asking her if she would like to allow Jacky to connect to her computer.
4. Jane accepts the offer, and at this point Jane's desktop may temporarily change to conserve network bandwidth used by the Remote Assistance session. The Remote Assistance window that opens on Jane's screen tells her that she is being helped by Jacky.
5. At this point, Jacky can see Jane's screen, but he can't control it. Jane then explains the problem she is having, either by using the Chat feature of Remote Assistance, or more likely over the telephone. Jacky asks Jane to perform a series of steps to correct the problem and watches her screen in his own Remote Assistance window as she does this.
6. If the instructions Jacky provides are too complex or if time is limited, Jacky can ask Jane if he can share control of her computer. If Jane agrees, Jacky clicks the Request Control button at the top of his Remote Assistance window. A dialog box appears on Jane's desktop asking her if she wants to allow Jacky to share control of her desktop. Jane accepts the prompt and also selects the option to allow Jacky to respond to UAC prompts on Jane's computer.
7. Jacky is now connected to Jane's computer using Jane's credentials, and he can both view her screen and interact with it using his own mouse and keyboard. Jacky then proceeds to perform the steps needed to resolve the problem, either correcting the issue or demonstrating to Jane how to fix the problem if it occurs again in the future. If at any time Jane wants to force Jacky to relinquish control of her computer, she can click the Stop Sharing button or the Disconnect button, or she can press the Panic key (Esc).

> ***NOTE*** **Offer RA needs preconfiguration of the User's computer via Group Policy. See the section titled "Managing Remote Assistance Using Group Policy" later in this chapter for more information.**

Other Possible Remote Assistance Usage Scenarios

Other types of Remote Assistance scenarios are also possible for businesses ranging from large enterprises to Small Office/Home Office (SOHO) environments. Examples of possible usage scenarios include:

- A user who is having a problem configuring an application on her computer can phone the Help Desk for assistance. A support person can then use Offer RA to connect to the user's computer, ask for control of her screen, and show the user how to configure her application. This scenario is the standard one for enterprise Help Desk environments and is described in more detail in the section titled "Using Remote Assistance in the Corporate Help Desk Environment" earlier in this chapter.
- A user who is having trouble installing a printer sends a Remote Assistance invitation to Help Desk using Windows Mail. A support person who is monitoring the Help Desk e-mail alias reads the message, opens the attached invitation file, and connects to the user's computer. The support person asks for control of the user's computer and walks him through the steps of installing the printer.
- A user is on the road and is connected to the internal corporate network using a VPN connection over the Internet. The user is having problems configuring Windows Mail on her computer, so she opens Windows Live Messenger and notices that someone she knows in Corporate Support is currently online. She sends a Remote Assistance invitation to the support person using Windows Live Messenger, and that person responds to the invitation, asks for control, and shows the user how to configure Windows Mail.
- A user who is having problems installing an application uses Easy Connect to request help from a support technician. Because this is the first time he has requested help from this particular support technician, the user must communicate the password for the session to the support technician using an OOB method such as making a telephone call. The next time the user needs help, however, he will not need to provide a password because of the trust relationship that was established during the first Remote Assistance session between them.

The preceding list is not intended to be complete—other corporate support scenarios using Remote Assistance are possible. Generally speaking, however, corporate environments will use Offer RA to provide assistance to users who phone Help Desk when they have problems. Some enterprises may also allow users to submit Remote Assistance invitations either via e-mail or by saving invitation files to network shares that are monitored by support personnel. Others might use IM applications that support Remote Assistance within the corpnet.

> ***NOTE*** **Helpers can have multiple Remote Assistance sessions open simultaneously—one session for each User they are supporting. However, Users can have only one Remote Assistance session in the Waiting For Connect state. The invitation that was created could be sent to multiple recipients—any of whom may connect. All subsequent connect attempts will be blocked until the first Helper disconnects, after which another Helper may connect. If the User disconnects the session, the Remote Assistance application terminates and no further connections will be allowed.**

Interoperability with Remote Assistance in Windows Vista

Remote Assistance in Windows 7 is fully backward-compatible with Remote Assistance in Windows Vista, except that Windows Vista does not support the new Easy Connect method for soliciting Remote Assistance found in Windows 7. This means that a User on a Windows Vista computer cannot use Easy Connect to solicit Remote Assistance from a Helper on a Windows 7 computer, and a User on a Windows 7 computer cannot use Easy Connect to solicit Remote Assistance from a Helper on a Windows Vista computer. In addition, a Windows 7 user cannot transfer a file with a Windows Vista user during a Remote Assistance session.

Interoperability with Remote Assistance in Windows XP

Remote Assistance in Windows 7 is backward-compatible with Remote Assistance in Windows XP, with the following limitations:

- Offer RA from Windows 7 to Windows XP is supported, but Offer RA from Windows XP to Windows 7 is not supported. This means that enterprises who want to implement Offer RA as a support solution for their Help Desk departments should ensure that computers used by support personnel who will help users running Windows 7 are themselves running Windows 7 (and not Windows XP).
- NAT traversal using Teredo and IPv6 is supported on Windows 7 to Windows 7 Remote Assistance only, and not on Windows 7 to Windows XP.
- Voice support for Remote Assistance in Windows XP is not supported by Remote Assistance in Windows 7, and any attempt by a User on a Windows XP computer to use this feature during a Remote Assistance session with a Helper on a Windows 7 computer will cause a notification message regarding this limitation to appear.
- The MAILTO method of soliciting assistance that is supported by Remote Assistance in Windows XP is not supported by Remote Assistance in Windows 7.
- Windows Messenger (which shipped with Windows XP) does not ship with Windows 7. Users of Remote Assistance with Windows Messenger in Windows XP will need to migrate to an IM application such as Windows Live Messenger that supports Windows 7 Remote Assistance.
- Offer RA via Windows Live Messenger is supported in Windows 7 but not in Windows XP.
- Windows XP does not support the new Easy Connect method for soliciting Remote Assistance found in Windows 7. This means that a User on a Windows XP computer cannot use Easy Connect to solicit Remote Assistance from a Helper on a Windows 7 computer, and a User on a Windows 7 computer cannot use Easy Connect to solicit Remote Assistance from a Helper on a Windows XP computer. A Windows 7 user cannot transfer a file with a Windows Vista user during a Remote Assistance session.

Implementing and Managing Remote Assistance

Remote Assistance is a powerful and flexible feature that can be used in many different ways to support users within large enterprises, medium-sized businesses, and SOHO environments. This section outlines how to initiate Remote Assistance sessions from both the UI and the command line. This section also demonstrates how to use Remote Assistance in an enterprise Help Desk environment involving two common scenarios:

- Helper offers Remote Assistance to a User who telephones the Help Desk with a problem.
- User creates a Remote Assistance invitation and saves it on a network share that is monitored by Help Desk personnel.

For information on other scenarios for implementing Remote Assistance, including sending invitations with Windows Mail and Windows Messenger, search for the topic "Remote Assistance" within Windows Help and Support.

Initiating Remote Assistance Sessions

Remote Assistance sessions can be initiated from either the UI or the command line. A significant usability enhancement, from the perspective of support personnel, is that Offer RA is no longer buried within Help And Support as it is in Windows XP, but instead is easily accessible now from the graphical user interface (GUI).

Initiating Remote Assistance from the GUI

Initiating Remote Assistance sessions from the GUI can be done using the following methods:

- From the Start menu, click Start, point to All Programs, select Maintenance, and then select Windows Remote Assistance.
- Click Start and type **assist** in the Start menu search box. When Windows Remote Assistance appears in the search results under Programs, click it.

Either of these actions will open the initial Remote Assistance screen, shown in Figure 22-2.

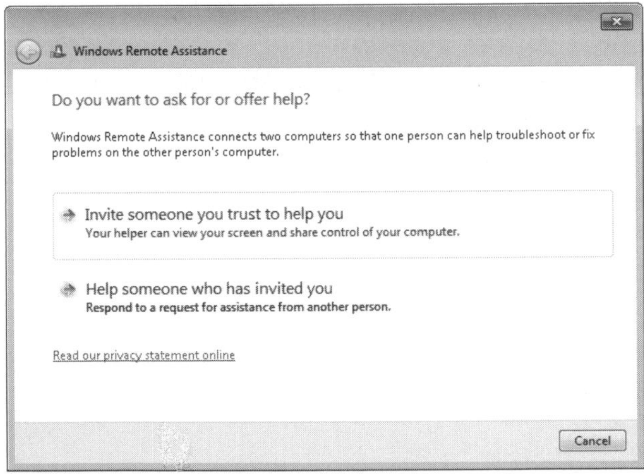

FIGURE 22-2 The initial screen of Windows Remote Assistance

When this initial screen appears, you can do either of the following:

- Solicit Remote Assistance from someone by clicking the Invite Someone You Trust To Help You option, which displays the How Do You Want To Invite Your Trusted Helper? screen, as shown in Figure 22-3.

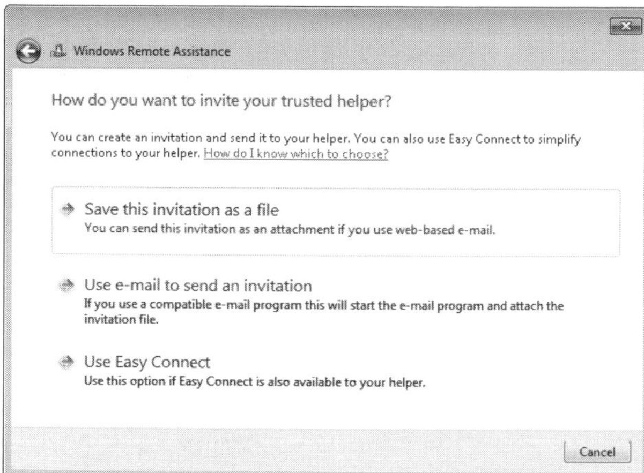

FIGURE 22-3 The screen for soliciting Remote Assistance from someone

- Accept a Remote Assistance invitation from someone or offer Remote Assistance to someone by clicking the Help Someone Who Has Invited You option, which displays the Choose A Way To Connect To The Other Person's Computer screen, as shown in Figure 22-4.

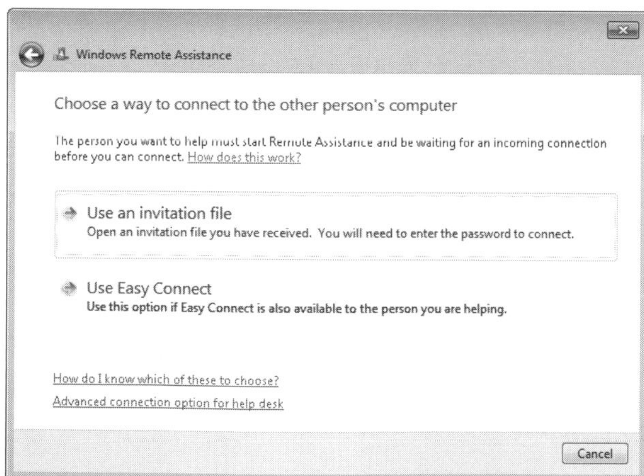

FIGURE 22-4 The screen for offering Remote Assistance to someone

The How Do You Want To Invite Your Trusted Helper? screen (see Figure 22-3) lets you select from the following methods for soliciting Remote Assistance:

- **Save This Invitation To A File** Selecting this option lets you save your Remote Assistance invitation file to a folder on your computer or to an available shared folder on the network.
- **Use E-mail To Send An Invitation** Selecting this option starts your e-mail client application, creates a new message, and attaches the invitation file to the message. Note that if you do not have an SMAPI-compatible e-mail client application on your computer, this option will be unavailable.
- **Use Easy Connect** Selecting this option creates and publishes your Remote Assistance invitation file to the cloud using PNRP and displays a 12-character password that you must communicate OOB to your Helper for him to accept your invitation. If, however, you previously used Easy Connect to establish a Remote Assistance session with the same Helper, the Helper can accept your invitation without any password required.

NOTE **If the computer has IPv6 disabled or is behind a NAT router that blocks Teredo traffic, the Easy Connect option will be unavailable.**

The Choose A Way To Connect To The Other Person's Computer screen (see Figure 22-4) lets you accept a Remote Assistance invitation from someone or offer Remote Assistance to someone. The following options are available on this screen for accepting a Remote Assistance invitation from someone:

- **Use An Invitation File** Selecting this option lets you browse your local file system or network share for the Remote Assistance invitation from someone who needs your help. You will need the password associated with the invitation, which must be provided OOB by the User who needs help.
- **Use Easy Connect** Selecting this option lets you browse the PNRP cloud for the Remote Assistance invitation from someone who needs your help. The first time you use Easy Connect to help this individual, you will need the password associated with the invitation, which must be provided OOB by the User who needs help. For subsequent times that you use Easy Connect to help this individual, the password is not required.

To offer Remote Assistance to someone, click the Advanced Connection Option For Help Desk link at the bottom of Figure 22-4. Additional steps for soliciting and offering Remote Assistance are described in the scenario sections later in this chapter.

HOW IT WORKS

RA Invitation Files

Remote Assistance invitation files (.MsRcIncident) are XML-formatted file documents that include information used by the Helper's computer that will attempt to connect. This ticket information is encrypted to prevent unauthorized users from accessing the information if e-mail or file transfer is used to send the invitation over an unsecured network.

If the e-mail method is used to send the invitation file to the Helper, the invitation file is sent as an e-mail attachment with a filename of RATicket.MsRcIncident. If the file transfer method is used instead, the invitation file is created by default on the desktop of the User's computer, and the filename of the invitation is Invitation.MsRcIncident.

Initiating Remote Assistance from the Command Line

Remote Assistance in Windows 7 and Windows Vista is implemented as a stand-alone executable called Msra.exe. You can initiate Remote Assistance sessions directly from the command line or by using scripts. The syntax and usage for this command is explained in Table 22-3.

TABLE 22-3 Syntax and Usage for Command-Line Remote Assistance (Msra.exe)

OPTION	SUPPORTED ON	DESCRIPTION
/novice	Windows 7 Windows Vista	Starts Remote Assistance as Novice (User) in Solicited RA mode and presents the user with the choice of either sending a Remote Assistance ticket using a SMAPI-enabled e-mail application such as Windows Mail or by saving the invitation as a file. After this choice has been made, Windows Remote Assistance opens on the User's computer in the Waiting For Connect state.
/expert	Windows 7 Windows Vista	Starts Remote Assistance in the Helper mode and presents the choice of either specifying the location of a Remote Assistance ticket to open or specifying the User's computer name or address (Offer RA). The computer name can be either a host name (if the User is on the local subnet) or an FQDN (DNS name), and the address can be either an IPv4 address or an IPv6 address. Unsolicited Remote Assistance without an invitation requires preconfiguration of the remote computer being helped.

OPTION	SUPPORTED ON	DESCRIPTION
/offerRA *computer*	Windows 7 Windows Vista	Starts Remote Assistance as Helper in Unsolicited (Offer) RA mode and uses DCOM to remotely open Remote Assistance on the User's computer and then connect to the User's computer to initiate a Remote Assistance session. The User's computer can be specified using either its computer name or address. The computer name can be either a host name (if the User is on the local subnet) or a FQDN (DNS name), and the address can be either an IPv4 address or an IPv6 address. This method is demonstrated in more detail in the section titled "Scenario 3: Offering Remote Assistance Using DCOM" later in this chapter.
/email *password*	Windows 7 Windows Vista	Starts Remote Assistance as Novice (User) in Solicited RA mode and creates a password-protected RA ticket that is attached to a new Remote Assistance invitation message opened by the default SMAPI-enabled e-mail client (which by default is Windows Mail). The password must be six characters or more and must be relayed separately to the Helper. The e-mail client application launches a window with the invitation file attached. The User must enter the e-mail address of the Helper in the To field to send the message to the Helper.
/saveasfile *path password*	Windows 7 Windows Vista	Starts Remote Assistance as Novice (User) in Solicited RA mode and creates a password-protected Remote Assistance ticket that is saved at the path specified. The path can be either a local folder or network share, and the User must have appropriate permissions on the destination folder to create the file. The path must include a file name for the ticket. (The .MsRcIncident file extension will be automatically added to the file name.) The password must be six characters or more. Use of this method is demonstrated in more detail in the section titled "Scenario 2: Soliciting Remote Assistance by Creating Remote Assistance Tickets and Saving Them on Monitored Network Shares" later in this chapter.

OPTION	SUPPORTED ON	DESCRIPTION
/openfile *path password*	Windows 7 Windows Vista	Starts Remote Assistance as Expert (Helper) in Solicited RA mode and opens a previously created Remote Assistance ticket that was saved within the path specified. The path may be either a local folder or network share, and the Helper must have appropriate permissions on the destination folder to open the file. The path must include the file name of a valid ticket that has the .MsRcIncident file extension. The password must be the same password that was used by the User to secure the ticket when it was created.
/geteasyhelp	Windows 7 only	Starts Remote Assistance as Novice (User) in Solicited RA mode and with the Easy Connect option already selected. After the Remote Assistance invitation has been posted to the PNRP cloud, the User is presented with a 12-character password that she must communicate OOB to the Expert (Helper), which the Helper can then use to accept the invitation and initiate the Remote Assistance session.
/offereasyhelp *address*	Windows 7 only	Starts Remote Assistance as Expert (Helper) in Offer RA mode and with the Easy Connect option already selected. The Helper is presented with a dialog box for entering the 12-character password that was communicated OOB to him by the Novice (User), which is needed by the Helper to accept the invitation and initiate the Remote Assistance session.
/getcontacthelp *address*	Windows 7 only	Starts Remote Assistance as Novice (User) in Solicited RA mode with the Easy Connect option already selected and with the Remote Assistance history contact specified by *address* already selected. You can find *address* for a contact in your Remote Assistance history by opening the RAContacthistory.xml file located in the \Users*Username*\Appdata\Local folder on your computer. The format for *address* is a 40-character hexadecimal string with .RAContact appended to it.

OPTION	SUPPORTED ON	DESCRIPTION
/offercontacthelp *address*	Windows 7 only	Starts Remote Assistance as Expert (Helper) in Offer RA mode with the Easy Connect option already selected and with the Remote Assistance history contact specified by *address* already selected. You can find *address* for a contact in your Remote Assistance history by opening the RAContacthistory.xml file located in the \Users*Username*\Appdata\Local folder on your computer. The format for *address* is a 40-character hexadecimal string with .RAContact appended to it.

> ***NOTE*** **There is no support for Windows Management Instrumentation (WMI) scripting of Msra.exe.**

Scenario 1: Soliciting Remote Assistance Using Easy Connect

In Windows 7, the simplest way for home users to request assistance from others is to use Easy Connect. (Easy Connect is not intended for enterprise environments because it requires global P2P connectivity to work.) In the following scenario, Tony Allen, a Novice user, requests help from Karen Berg, a friend who is an Expert user. Tony solicits Karen's help for the first time by starting Remote Assistance on his computer and selecting Invite Someone You Trust To Help You followed by Use Easy Connect. At this point, Windows Remote Assistance displays a password, as shown in Figure 22-5.

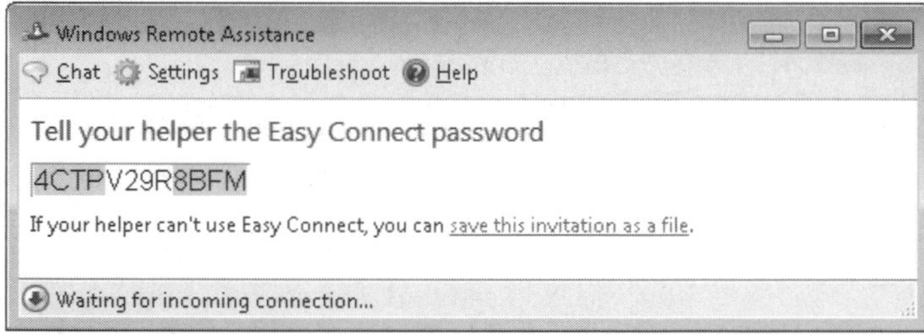

FIGURE 22-5 Tony's computer displays the password needed for Karen to connect using Remote Assistance.

Tony telephones Karen, indicates that he wants her to help him using Remote Assistance, and gives her the password. Karen now starts Remote Assistance on her own computer and selects Help Someone Who Has Invited You. Windows Remote Assistance opens and displays the dialog box shown in Figure 22-6.

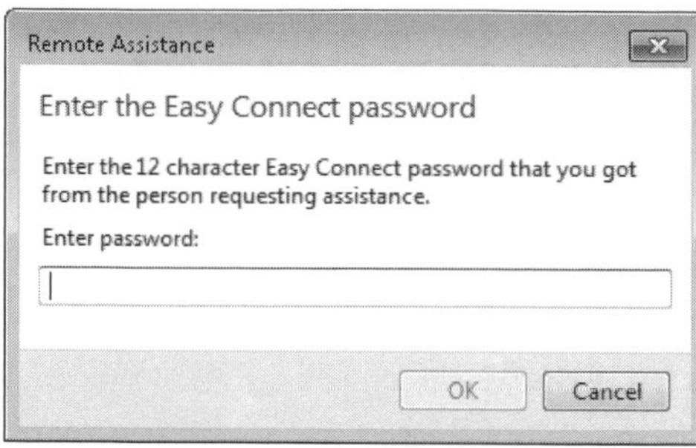

FIGURE 22-6 Karen needs Tony's password to connect to his computer using Remote Assistance.

Karen enters the password Tony has given her and clicks Enter. Karen's computer searches the PNRP cloud for Tony's Remote Assistance invitation and displays Attempting To Connect in the Remote Assistance status bar. When the invitation has been found, the status bar message changes to Waiting For Acceptance. At this point, a dialog box will appear on Tony's computer asking if he would like to allow Karen to connect to his computer and view his desktop (shown in Figure 22-7). Tony has two minutes to respond to this dialog box before the offer times out and the dialog box disappears, which will cause a message saying "The person you are trying to help isn't responding" to appear on Karen's computer.

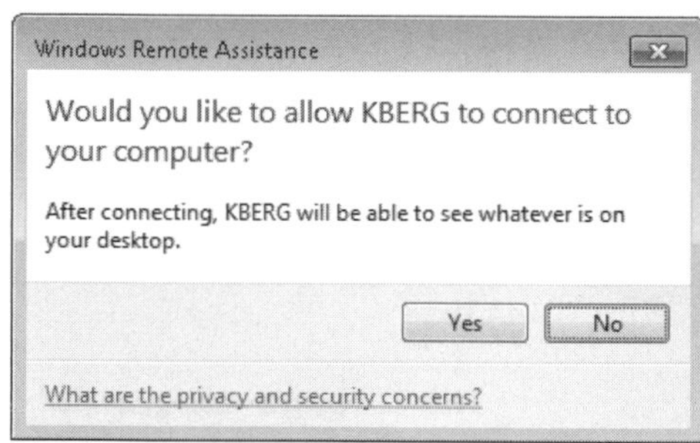

FIGURE 22-7 Tony must allow the Remote Assistance connection to occur.

Tony clicks Yes and the Remote Assistance session begins. At this point, the desktop properties of Tony's desktop may change (based on configurable settings) to optimize the network bandwidth used by Remote Assistance for screen updates on Karen's computer. Karen can now request control from Tony, send files to Tony or receive files from him, chat with Tony, or disconnect the session. Tony can send and receive files, chat, or pause or disconnect the session.

> ***NOTE*** **If you are a User and a Helper has shared control of your computer, you can immediately terminate shared control and return the session to Screen Sharing state by pressing the Panic key (Esc).**

If Tony needs help again from Karen on some future occasion, the steps involved are simpler. Tony starts Remote Assistance and selects Invite Someone You Trust To Help You. Remote Assistance displays the history list of recent contacts Tony has used before as Helpers, as shown in Figure 22-8.

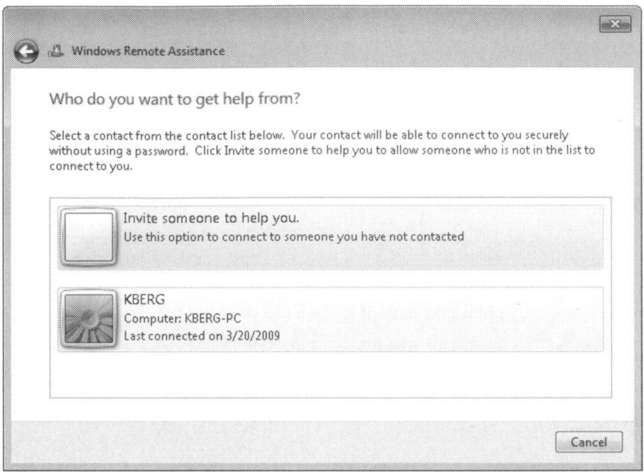

FIGURE 22-8 Karen is listed as a contact in Tony's history list.

Tony clicks Karen's contact info in his history list. This time, instead of a password being displayed, a message appears, indicating that Tony should tell Karen he needs her help (shown in Figure 22-9).

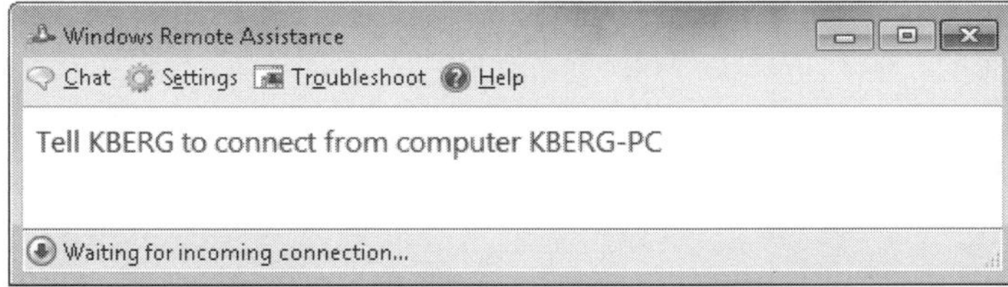

FIGURE 22-9 No password is needed on subsequent requests for help that use Easy Connect.

Tony telephones Karen and asks her to start Remote Assistance on her computer. Karen does this and selects Who Do You Want To Help (shown in Figure 22-10).

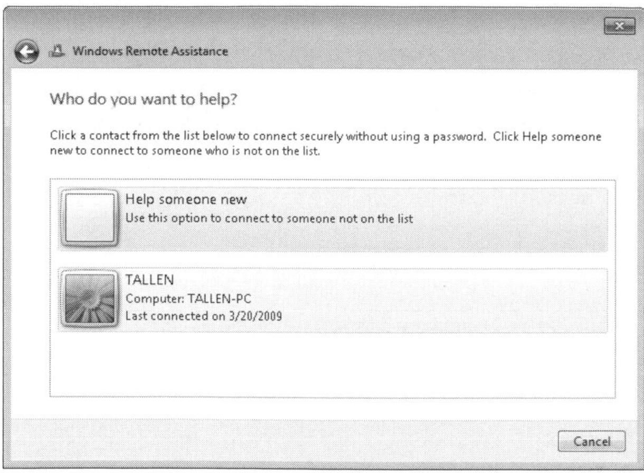

FIGURE 22-10 Tony is listed as a contact in Karen's history list.

Karen clicks Tony's contact info in her history list. Karen's computer searches the PNRP cloud for Tony's Remote Assistance invitation and displays Waiting For Acceptance in the Remote Assistance status bar when the invitation is found. Tony then clicks Yes, and the new Remote Assistance session begins.

You can also use the new command-line switches for Msra.exe in Windows 7 to simplify the Easy Connect experience even further. For example, if Tony frequently needs help from Karen, Karen (the Expert user) could create a shortcut on Tony's desktop that executes the following command:

```
msra.exe /getcontacthelp address
```

Here, *address* is the value of the ADDRESS attribute in Karen's Remote Assistance history contact information on Tony's computer, which is stored as an XML element in the RAContacthistory.xml file located in the \Users\TALLEN\Appdata\Local folder on Tony's computer. The contents of this file might look like the following:

```
<?xml version="1.0"?>
<RAINVITATIONCOLL>
<RAINVITATIONITEM NAME="KBERG" COMPUTERNAME="KBERG-PC" AVATAR="Qk1QgA…[lots of
characters]…"
PUBLICKEY="BgIAAAC…"
ADDRESS="5823b8d7b47af2c1cd94f32535a79d8f0569e7d0.RAContact"
TYPE="1"
TIME="20090320170235.779000"/>
</RAINVITATIONCOLL>
```

Using this example, the shortcut Karen creates on Tony's computer should execute the following command:

```
msra.exe /getcontacthelp 5823b8d7b47af2c1cd94f32535a79d8f0569e7d0.RAContact
```

Karen can then create a similar shortcut on her own computer using Tony's Remote Assistance history contact information, which is stored as an XML element in the RAContacthistory.xml file located in the \Users\KBERG\Appdata\Local folder on Karen's computer. After this is done, Tony can request assistance by simply double-clicking the shortcut on his desktop, and once he has informed Karen of this, Karen then double-clicks the corresponding shortcut on her own computer, and when Tony agrees to allow the connection, the session is started.

DIRECT FROM THE SOURCE

How Easy Connect Works

John Thekkethala, Program Manager
Remote Assistance Team

The new Easy Connect feature simplifies Remote Assistance by enabling a direct P2P transfer of the Remote Assistance invitation using PNRP. When the User starts Remote Assistance and selects Invite Someone You Trust To Help You and then Use Easy Connect, a Remote Assistance invitation is created, encrypted, and published as a payload on a node in the PNRP cloud. This invitation will be retrieved by the Helper from the PNRP cloud and the information is used to establish a Remote Assistance connection to the User.

When the invitation is created, a 12-character alphanumeric password is generated automatically and is displayed in the Tell Your Helper The Easy Connect Password dialog box. The first time the User uses any particular Helper, the password must be relayed OOB to the Helper before the Helper can connect to the User's computer. The password is case insensitive and avoids characters and numbers that could look similar (such as I and 1, 5 and S, and 0 and O).

After the PNRP node has been created in the PNRP cloud, the User's computer waits for an incoming connection from the Helper's computer. This node will exist for 30 minutes before expiring and invalidating the invitation.

The Helper starts Remote Assistance, selects Help Someone Who Has Invited You and then Use Easy Connect, and enters the password relayed OOB from the User. The Helper's computer uses the password to locate the PNRP node containing the User's invitation, grabs the payload (that is, the invitation), and decrypts it. Remote Assistance uses the invitation to connect to the User's computer. Of course, after the Remote Assistance connection has been established, the User must still provide explicit consent before his desktop is remoted.

When a Remote Assistance session has been established using Easy Connect, the User and the Helper become trusted contacts of each other. The Remote Assistance history store on each computer is used to maintain a list of records of trusted contacts that were established using Easy Connect. These records contain the following information for each trusted contact:

- User name
- Computer name
- User graphic (associated with the user logon account)
- Date and time of connection
- Public key of the connected user

Each history record identifies a specific user on a specific computer. A record is created only if each side of the connection has positive confirmation that the other side has received the user's entire contact info. Note that the Remote Assistance contact history does not include the user's role (User or Expert). This means that when trust is established between two user/computer pairs, either one of them may take the role of User and ask the other for assistance.

The next time the User tries to solicit assistance from the same Helper using Easy Connect, the User simply starts Remote Assistance and selects the Helper from the User's Remote Assistance contact list—no password is needed because the Helper is already trusted by the user. The Remote Assistance ticket is exchanged using Secure PNRP. All the User needs to do is notify the Helper that assistance is requested, and this can be done by telephone, IM, or any other OOB method.

After the User has notified the Helper that assistance is requested, the Helper starts Remote Assistance and selects the contact of the user. The Helper's computer uses Secure PNRP to retrieve the Remote Assistance invitation and the Remote Assistance session with the User is established without any password needing to be entered by the Helper.

Scenario 2: Soliciting Remote Assistance by Creating Remote Assistance Tickets and Saving Them on Monitored Network Shares

Another way that you can use Remote Assistance in an enterprise environment is by having users create invitation files and save them on a network share that is monitored by Help Desk personnel. This way, when Help Desk determines that a new ticket has been uploaded to the share, a support person can call the user on the telephone to obtain the password for the ticket and then use the ticket to establish a Remote Assistance session with the user who needs help.

To make the procedure easier, administrators can first deploy a script on users' desktops that uses command-line Remote Assistance (via Msra.exe) to create the invitation file and save it on the network share. For example, let's say that users' invitation files should be uploaded to \\FILESRV3.contoso.com\Support\IncomingTickets, a folder in the Support share on the file server named FILESRV3. The following script, named SubmitTicket.vbs, could be deployed on each user's desktop to accomplish this task.

```
dim strPassword
dim strUser
dim strTicketName

strPassword = InputBox("Enter a password for your ticket")
Set WshShell = Wscript.CreateObject("Wscript.Shell")
strUser = WshShell.ExpandEnvironmentStrings("%username%")
strTicketName = strUser & "-" & Year(Now) & "-" & Month(Now) & "-" & Day(Now) & _
   "-" & Hour(Now) & "-" & Minute(Now) & "-" & Second(Now)
strRA = "msra.exe /saveasfile \\FILESRV3\Support\IncomingTickets\" & _
   strTicketName & " " & strPassword
WshShell.Run strRA
```

When the user double-clicks this script to run it, an Input box appears asking the user to provide a password to be used to secure the invitation. After the user supplies a password, a new Remote Assistance ticket is created and saved in the target folder on the file server. The name of the ticket is unique and consists of the user's name followed by the date and time, such as *tallen-YYYY-MM-DD-HH-MM-SS.MsRcIncident*. When the support person monitoring the share has obtained the ticket's password using an OOB method such as a telephone call, the support person opens the ticket. After the user grants consent, the Remote Assistance connection is established.

To monitor the IncomingTickets folder in the network share, Help Desk personnel can use the file-screening capabilities of file servers running Windows Server 2008. To do this, perform the following steps to create a passive file screen that monitors the folder and sends an e-mail alert to a Help Desk alias whenever a new ticket is uploaded to the folder:

1. Install or upgrade the File Server role on the Windows Server 2008 computer where the Support folder is located.
2. Start the File Server Resource Manager console from Administrative Tools, right-click the root node, and select Configure Options.
3. Specify the DNS name of the IP address of a Simple Mail Transfer Protocol (SMTP) host that can be used to forward alert e-mails that are generated by the file screen you will create.
4. Click OK to close File Server Resource Manager Options and expand the console tree to select File Screens under File Screening Management.
5. In the Action pane, select the Create File Screen option.
6. Click Browse to select the Incoming folder for the File Screen Path.
7. Select the Define Custom File Screen Properties option and click Custom Properties.
8. Choose the Passive Screening option so that uploaded tickets will only be monitored and not blocked by the screen.
9. Click Create to create a new file group called RA Tickets, and click Add to add files of type *.MsRcIncident to the group.

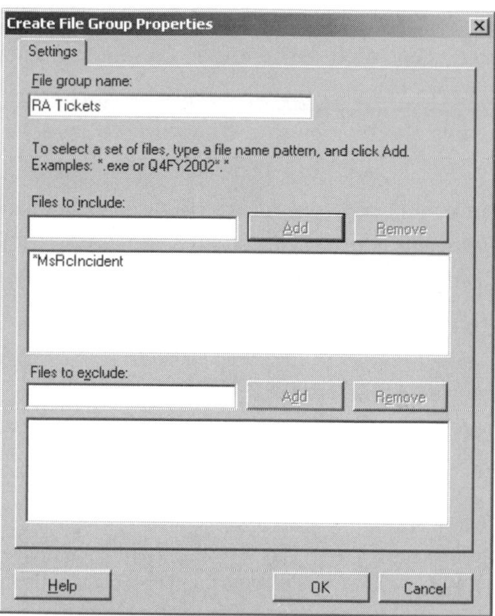

10. Click OK to return to the properties sheet for the new file screen and select the check box for the RA Tickets file group you just created.

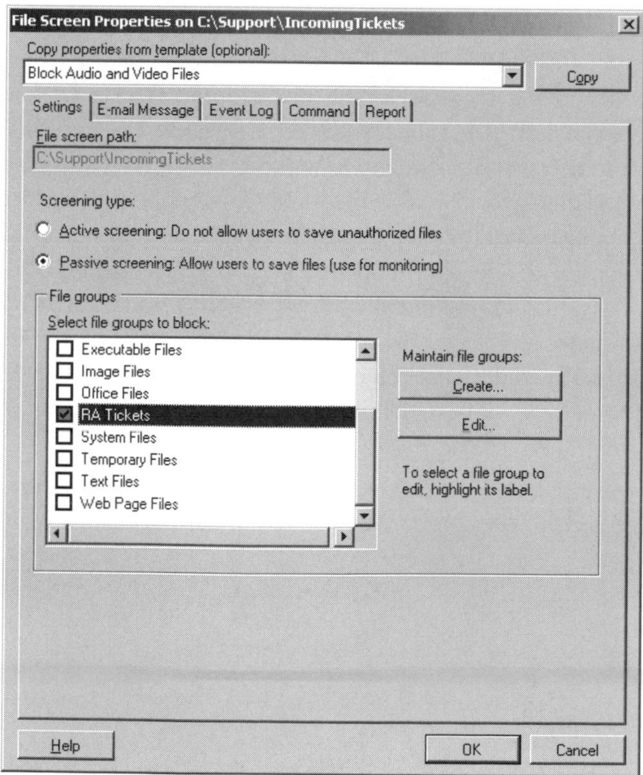

11. Click the E-mail tab and specify a support alias (such as support@contoso.com) that will be notified whenever a new ticket is uploaded to the folder. Configure a suitable subject and body for the message.
12. Click Create to create the new file screen and then choose the option to save the screen without creating a template.
13. Test the new file screen by opening a command prompt on a user's computer and then typing **msra.exe /saveasfile *path password*,** where *path* is the UNC path to the Incoming folder within the Support share on the file server, and *password* is any password of six or more characters that you specify.

> ***MORE INFO*** **For more information on how to implement file screening in Windows Server 2008, see the topic "Screening Files" in the Microsoft Windows Server TechCenter at *http://technet2.microsoft.com/windowsserver2008/en/library/c16070f8-25f6-4d22-8040-5299b08d6eea1033.mspx?mfr=true*.**

Scenario 3: Offering Remote Assistance Using DCOM

Before you can offer Remote Assistance to other users, your user account must be authorized as a Helper on the User's computer. You should use Group Policy to do this in an enterprise environment. (See the section titled "Managing Remote Assistance Using Group Policy" later in this chapter for information on how to do this.)

After a support person (or group of individuals) has been configured as a Helper for all Windows 7 computers in a domain or organizational unit (OU), the support person can offer Remote Assistance to users of those computers when they need assistance. For this scenario, let's say that Tony Allen (tallen@contoso.com) is a Windows 7 user who needs assistance with an issue on his computer. Tony telephones the Help Desk department, and the call is taken by Karen Berg (kberg@contoso.com), who asks Tony for the name or IP address of his computer. Tony provides Karen with his fully qualified computer name (TALLEN-PC.contoso.com) or IP address. Karen then offers assistance to Tony by starting Remote Assistance on her computer, selecting Help Someone Who Has Invited You, clicking Advanced Connection Option For Help Desk, and entering the name or IP address of Tony's computer (shown in Figure 22-11).

> ***NOTE*** **Karen could also type msra /offerRA TALLEN-PC.contoso.com at a command prompt to offer assistance quickly to Tony.**

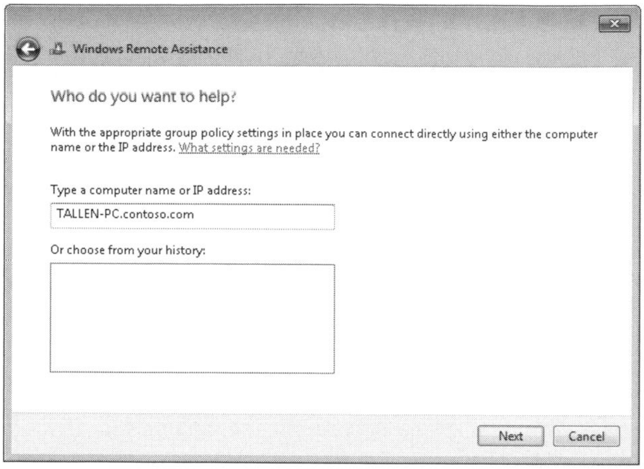

FIGURE 22-11 Karen offers help to Tony using an unsolicited RA.

The experience is even easier if Karen needs to offer help to Tony again on some future occasion. Karen simply starts Remote Assistance on her computer, selects Help Someone Who Has Invited You, and clicks Advanced Connection Option For Help Desk, and the name or IP address of Tony's computer is displayed in her Remote Assistance history list (shown in Figure 22-12).

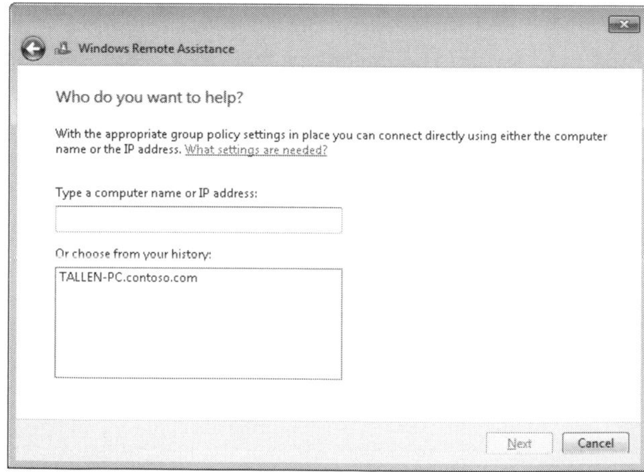

FIGURE 22-12 The history list makes it easy to start Remote Assistance sessions with users that were helped before.

> ***NOTE*** **Karen can also display the screen in Figure 22-12 quickly by typing msra /offerRA at the command prompt.**

Karen then clicks Tony's computer in her history list and clicks Next, and when Tony accepts the offer, the session begins.

Managing Remote Assistance Using Group Policy

In an enterprise environment, Remote Assistance can be managed using Group Policy. The policy settings for Remote Assistance are all machine settings and are found in the following policy location:

Computer Configuration\Policies\Administrative Templates\System\Remote Assistance

When these policy settings are written to the registry on targeted computers, they are stored under the following registry key:

HKLM\SOFTWARE\Policies\Microsoft\WindowsNT\Terminal Services

Remote Assistance policy settings are summarized in Table 22-4.

TABLE 22-4 Group Policy Settings for Remote Assistance

POLICY	DESCRIPTION
Solicited Remote Assistance	Enabling this policy allows users of targeted computers to use Solicited RA to request assistance using e-mail, file transfer, or IM. Disabling this policy prevents users from using Solicited RA. The default setting is Not Configured, which allows users to change their Remote Assistance settings using the Remote tab of the System item in Control Panel. If the policy is Enabled, you can further configure whether Helpers can be prevented from sharing control of the User's computer, the maximum ticket lifetime, and the method used for sending invitations by e-mail. (Windows 7 does not support the MAILTO method—select SMAPI instead if the targeted computers are running Windows 7.) Ticket lifetime applies only to Remote Assistance invitations sent by e-mail or file transfer. The default ticket lifetime when Group Policy is not being used is six hours. If this policy is Enabled, you must also enable the Remote Assistance exception in Windows Firewall to allow Solicited RA to work. In an unmanaged environment, this setting can also be configured using the Remote tab of the System CPL in Control Panel. This policy is also supported on Windows XP Professional and Windows Server 2003.

POLICY	DESCRIPTION
Offer Remote Assistance	Enabling this policy allows designated Helpers to use Offer RA to offer assistance to users of targeted computers. Disabling this policy or leaving it Not Configured prevents Offer RA from being used to offer assistance to users of targeted computers. If the policy is Enabled, you can further configure whether Helpers can view or control the Users' computers, and you must specify a list of Helpers who are allowed to Offer RA to the users of the targeted computers. Helpers can be either users or groups and must be specified in the form *domain_name\username or domain_name\groupname*. If this policy is Enabled, you must also enable the Remote Assistance exception in Windows Firewall to allow Offer RA to work. (In Windows 7, the Remote Assistance exception is open by default for the domain firewall profile.) This policy is also supported on Windows XP Professional and Windows Server 2003. See the Explain tab of this policy setting for more details.
Allow Only Vista Or Later Connections	The default Windows 7 invitation file includes an XP-specific node for backward compatibility. This node is not encrypted and allows Windows XP computers to connect to the Windows 7 computer that created the ticket. Enabling this policy causes all Remote Assistance invitations generated by users of targeted computers to *not* include the XP node, thereby providing an additional level of security and privacy. Disabling this policy or leaving it Not Configured leaves information such as IP address and port number unencrypted in Remote Assistance invitations This policy setting applies only to Remote Assistance invitations sent using e-mail or file transfer and has no effect on using IM to solicit assistance or on using Offer RA to offer assistance. In an unmanaged environment, this setting can also be configured by clicking Advanced from the Remote tab of the System Properties dialog box. This policy is supported only on Windows Vista and later platforms.
Customize Warning Messages	Enabling this policy causes a specified warning to be displayed on targeted computers when a Helper wants to enter Screen Sharing state or Control Sharing state during a Remote Assistance session. Disabling this policy or leaving it Not Configured causes the default warning to be displayed in each instance. If the policy is Enabled, you can further specify the warning message to be displayed in each instance. This policy is supported only on Windows Vista and later platforms.

POLICY	DESCRIPTION
Turn On Session Logging	Enabling this policy causes Remote Assistance session activity to be logged on the targeted computers. For more information, see the section titled "Remote Assistance Logging" earlier in this chapter. Disabling this policy causes Remote Assistance auditing to be disabled on the targeted computers. The default setting is Not Configured, in which case Remote Assistance auditing is automatically turned on. This policy is supported only on Windows Vista and later platforms.
Turn On Bandwidth Optimization	Enabling this policy causes the specified level of bandwidth optimization to be used to enhance the Remote Assistance experience over low-bandwidth network connections. Disabling this policy or leaving it Not Configured allows the system defaults to be used. If the policy is Enabled, you must specify the level of bandwidth optimization you want to use from the following options: ■ No Optimization ■ No Full Window Drag ■ Turn Off Background ■ Full Optimization If No Optimization is selected, the User's computer will use the Windows Basic theme with full background, and during a shared control session, the Helper will be able to drag full windows across the User's screen. Additional optimization turns off effects to allow a more responsive experience for the Helper. This policy is supported only on Windows Vista and later platforms.

> ***NOTE*** **In Windows XP, members of the Domain Admins group are granted Helper privileges implicitly even if they are not added to the Helpers list of the Offer Remote Assistance policy setting. This is no longer the case in Windows 7 and Windows Vista, where the Domain Admins group must now be added explicitly to the Helpers list to grant them Helper privileges for Offer RA.**

Configuring Remote Assistance in Unmanaged Environments

Users of unmanaged computers can enable and configure Remote Assistance using the Remote tab of the System CPL in Control Panel (shown in Figure 22-13). Enabling or disabling Remote Assistance and configuring its settings this way requires local administrator credentials on the computer, so a UAC prompt will appear when the user tries to do this.

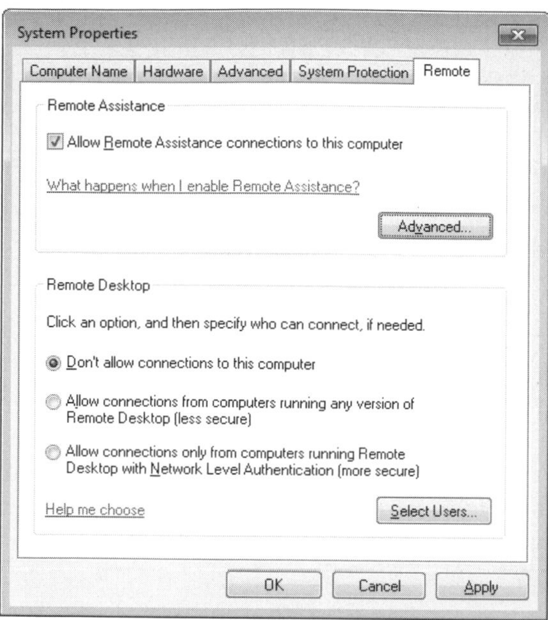

FIGURE 22-13 Configuring Remote Assistance from the Remote tab of System in Control Panel

Note that settings changes made this way will affect all users on the system. Clicking Advanced lets you specify whether remote control of the computer will be allowed during a Remote Assistance session, what the maximum lifetime of a Remote Assistance invitation can be before it times out (the default is six hours), and whether invitations supported only by Remote Assistance in Windows Vista or later versions will be created (see Figure 22-14).

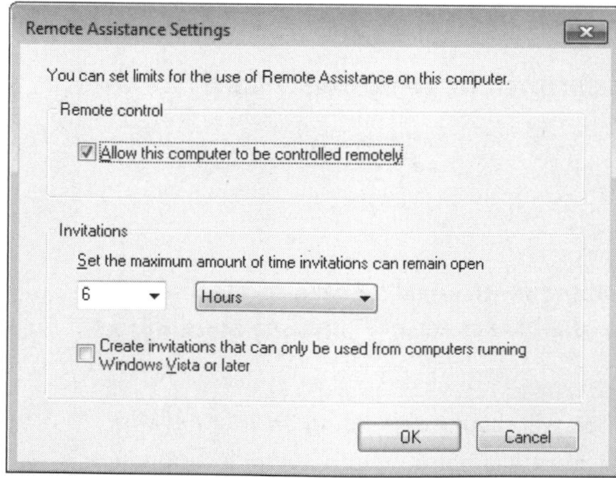

FIGURE 22-14 Advanced configuration settings for Remote Assistance

NOTE A PNRP invitation is valid for only 30 minutes and does not use this setting. This limitation does not apply to trusted contact-based invitations.

In managed environments, when the following Group Policy setting is Enabled, the Control Panel settings for configuring Remote Assistance become unavailable (appear dimmed):

Computer Configuration\Policies\Administrative Templates\System\Remote Assistance\Solicited Remote Assistance

Additional Registry Settings for Configuring Remote Assistance

Additional behavior for Remote Assistance can be configured by modifying certain registry settings. Specifically, per-user registry settings for Remote Assistance are found under the following key:

HKCU\Software\Microsoft\Remote Assistance

These settings are changeable when in the Waiting To Connect mode or when in the connected mode from the Settings button.

WARNING If Group Policy is used to manage Remote Assistance settings and any configured policy settings overlap these registry settings, the policy settings prevail.

DIRECT FROM THE SOURCE

Troubleshooting Remote Assistance in Windows 7 and Windows Vista

John Thekkethala, Program Manager
Remote Assistance Team

When I attempt to create an invitation with e-mail or save-to-file, I see a warning message stating that Windows Firewall is currently blocking Remote Assistance.

The Remote Assistance firewall exception will change depending on your network location (Private, Public, or Domain). If you are at home, your network location type should be set to Private, which enables the Remote Assistance firewall exception automatically. If your network location is set to Public, the Remote Assistance firewall exception is not enabled automatically for security purposes. It will need to be enabled by an administrator.

If you are connected to a managed network (for example, when you are within a corporate domain), the network location is categorized as Domain, and the Remote Assistance exception is not enabled automatically. It is expected to be configured by Group Policy by your system administrator.

I cannot use Remote Assistance to connect from my home computer to a work computer.

Remote Assistance uses Teredo (IPv6) to traverse NATs. However, Teredo cannot be used to traverse corporate edge firewalls that provide NAT for intranet clients and block dynamic ports or outbound UDP traffic. Because you do not have a globally reachable IPv4 address within the corpnet, Remote Assistance cannot make a connection to you from outside the corpnet.

If I disable the Windows Firewall, I cannot make a Remote Assistance connection in certain cases. This is counterintuitive, because I expect connectivity to be less restrictive with the firewall disabled.

In Windows 7 and Windows Vista, the Windows Firewall is IPv6 aware. The Remote Assistance exception in the Windows Firewall enables Teredo for edge traversal. If the Windows Firewall is disabled, the ability to use Teredo for NAT traversal is also disabled. The Windows Firewall must be running with the Remote Assistance exception enabled for Remote Assistance to be able to traverse NATs using Teredo.

I cannot use Remote Assistance to connect from my work computer to my home computer.

Your corporate firewall may be configured to block outbound P2P connections. In a managed environment (domain-joined computers), which is typically found in a corporate network, the Remote Assistance exception does not enable Teredo (edge traversal), because corporate firewalls typically block outbound UDP traffic. NAT traversal using Teredo is disabled by default in this scenario. If the person you are trying to help is behind a UPnP NAT or is connected directly to the Internet, you should be able to make a connection. Check with your network administrator to see whether outbound P2P connections through the corporate firewall can be enabled.

When I move my laptop (or change my home network location) from a private to a public location, I am not able to connect to certain computers.

If you have a laptop that moves between work and home, the properties of the Remote Assistance firewall exception in the Windows Firewall will change depending on whether your network location is classified as Private, Public, or Domain. In a Private location, the Remote Assistance exception is enabled by default. If you are using a UPnP NAT, the Remote Assistance exception will allow communications with the UPnP NAT to enable Remote Assistance connections that make use of UPnP. In a Public network, the Remote Assistance exception is not enabled by default and will need to be enabled using administrator credentials. In addition, the default

Public profile does not permit UPnP communication for security purposes, thereby restricting Remote Assistance connectivity in certain cases.

I am on a low-bandwidth connection, and the person helping me is experiencing slow screen refreshes.

Under Settings, set the Bandwidth Usage to Low to reduce the bandwidth used during a Remote Assistance connection. Keep in mind that display quality decreases as bandwidth usage is limited.

Why can't I connect to Windows XP computers that are behind a NAT as easily as I can connect to Windows 7 or Windows Vista computers?

Remote Assistance in Windows XP does not support Teredo for NAT traversal. Consequently, a Windows 7– or Windows Vista–to–Windows XP Remote Assistance connection may fail in cases in which both computers are behind non-UPnP NATs.

How does Remote Assistance make a connection?

When the Remote Assistance invitation is created, the User's computer will set itself as a listener on all of its IP addresses (IPv4 and IPv6), including its Teredo address. All of these listeners are waiting for a connection from the Helper's computer. The address and port information associated with these different listeners is relayed to the Helper's computer via the Remote Assistance invitation (which gets transported by Windows Messenger when Messenger is used to launch Remote Assistance). The Helper's computer then tries to connect concurrently on all the address/port pairs in the invitation. The first successful connection that is made is used for the Remote Assistance session and the rest of the connection attempts are terminated.

How do I troubleshoot a connection failure between two home-based Windows 7 or Windows Vista computers that are behind NATs?

Refer to the Remote Assistance Connectivity information in Tables 22-5 and 22-6 to verify that the network configuration you have is supported for Remote Assistance connectivity. Then confirm that the Windows Firewall on the computer of the person that is being helped is running and configured for Remote Assistance as follows:

- The Windows Firewall is IPv6 compatible and must be running to enable NAT traversal using Teredo.
- The network location of the computer must be set to Private or Public because Teredo is not enabled in Domain or Managed settings.
- The Remote Assistance exception in the firewall must be enabled to allow Remote Assistance connections.

Now check that there is no edge firewall between the User and Helper because it may block P2P applications like Remote Assistance.

Finally, confirm that the User and Helper are not behind a symmetric NAT and that Teredo is able to get to the Qualified state on both computers. To determine this, do the following:

1. First, initiate Teredo by forcing Remote Assistance into the Waiting To Connect state. You can do this by typing msra.exe /saveasfile myinvitation mypassword at a command prompt.
2. Next, check to see if Teredo can be activated on both computers and goes into the Qualified state. Open an elevated command prompt window and type netsh interface teredo show state at the command prompt. The output should show Teredo in the Qualified state. If Teredo does not go to the Qualified state on both computers, a Remote Assistance connection may not be possible between these two computers. Teredo will not go into the Qualified state if one of the following two conditions exists:
   - A global Teredo server could not be reached at teredo.ipv6.microsoft.com.
   - The computer is behind a symmetric NAT. To verify this, look at the output of netsh interface teredo show state and check the output on the NAT: line, which specifies NAT type.

When I am helping someone who is a standard user, I cannot run a program that needs administrator privileges even though I have administrator privileges to the User's computer.

Remote Assistance allows a User to share control of his computer with a remote Helper. If the User is a standard user, the remote Helper is given the same privileges as the standard user. If the Helper attempts to start a program that requires administrator credentials, by default these credentials must be entered locally (on the Secure Desktop) by the User and cannot be entered remotely by the Helper. This is required to prevent a security loophole where Admin programs started by a remote Helper could be hijacked by the local User simply by terminating the Remote Assistance session. In managed environments in which client computers are running Windows Vista Service Pack 1 (SP1) or later versions, however, a new Group Policy setting can be enabled that allows Remote Assistance to turn off the Secure Desktop during a Remote Assistance session even if the User is a standard user. As a result, the remote Helper can now enter administrator credentials when a UAC prompt appears during a Remote Assistance session to perform Admin-level tasks on the User's computer. To configure this behavior, enable the following policy setting:

> Computer Configuration\Policies\Windows Settings\Security Settings\Local Policies\Security Options\User Account Control: Allow UIAccess Applications To Prompt For Elevation Without Using The Secure Desktop

Cross-Platform Connectivity for Remote Assistance

For environments in which different versions of Windows are used, Tables 22-5 and 22-6 summarize the Remote Assistance connectivity between Expert and Novice users on computers running Windows XP, Windows Vista, and Windows 7.

TABLE 22-5 Remote Assistance Connectivity for Expert on Windows XP

		EXPERT ON WINDOWS XP			
		Directly Connected	**Behind UPnP NAT**	**Behind non-UPnP NAT**	**Behind Corporate Edge Firewall****
NOVICE (USER) ON WINDOWS XP	**Directly Connected**	Yes	Yes	Yes	Yes
	Behind UPnP NAT	Yes	Yes	Yes	Yes
	Behind non-UPnP NAT	Yes, using Msgr Only	Yes, using Msgr Only	No	No
	Behind Corporate Edge Firewall**	Yes, using Msgr Only	Yes, using Msgr Only	No	Yes, if both are behind same firewall No, if both are behind different firewalls
NOVICE (USER) ON WINDOWS 7 OR WINDOWS VISTA	**Directly Connected**	Yes	Yes	Yes	Yes
	Behind UPnP NAT	Yes	Yes	Yes	Yes
	Behind non-UPnP NAT	Yes, using Msgr Only	Yes, using Msgr Only	No	No
	Behind Corporate Edge Firewall**	Yes, using Msgr Only	Yes, using Msgr Only	No	Yes, if both are behind same firewall No, if both are behind different firewalls

TABLE 22-6 Remote Assistance Connectivity for Expert on Windows Vista and Windows 7

		EXPERT ON WINDOWS VISTA AND WINDOWS 7			
		Directly Connected	**Behind UPnP NAT**	**Behind non-UPnP NAT**	**Behind Corporate Edge Firewall****
NOVICE (USER) ON WINDOWS XP	**Directly Connected**	Yes	Yes	Yes	Yes
	Behind UPnP NAT	Yes	Yes	Yes	Yes
	Behind non-UPnP NAT	Yes, using Msgr Only	Yes, using Msgr Only	No	No
	Behind Corporate Edge Firewall**	Yes, using Msgr Only	Yes, using Msgr Only	No	Yes, if both are behind same firewall No, if both are behind different firewalls
NOVICE (USER) ON WINDOWS 7 OR WINDOWS VISTA	**Directly Connected**	Yes	Yes	Yes	Yes
	Behind UPnP NAT	Yes	Yes	Yes	Yes
	Behind non-UPnP NAT	Yes, using Teredo*	Yes, using Teredo*	Yes, using Teredo*	None
	Behind Corporate Edge Firewall**	No	No	No	Yes, if both are behind same firewall No, if both are behind different firewalls

**Teredo connectivity is not available if both computers are behind Symmetric NATs.*

***Edge Firewall must permit outbound connection (for example, using the Microsoft ISA Firewall Client).*

Summary

Remote Assistance has been enhanced in Windows 7 and Windows Vista to provide better performance, improved usability, NAT-traversal flexibility, and increased security. Best practices for implementing Remote Assistance in an enterprise environment include the following:

- Use Group Policy to enable users of targeted computers in a domain or OU to receive offers of Remote Assistance from Help Desk personnel.
- Use Group Policy to enable the Remote Assistance exception in the Windows Firewall.
- Use Group Policy to deploy scripts to enable users to run the Msra.exe executable if you want to customize how they launch Remote Assistance sessions—for example, to upload an invitation to a network share monitored by support personnel.
- If all of your support computers are running Windows 7 or Windows Vista, use Group Policy to encrypt Remote Assistance tickets to hide sensitive information such as users' IP addresses and computer names.
- If corporate policy requires Remote Assistance records for auditing purposes, use Group Policy to enable Remote Assistance logging on your company's desktop computers and run scripts to periodically move both Helper and User Remote Assistance logs to a safe storage.
- To meet corporate privacy and security requirements, use Group Policy to customize the text message that users see before they allow the Helper to view their screens or share control.

Additional Resources

These resources contain additional information and tools related to this chapter.

Related Information

- "Windows Remote Assistance: Frequently Asked Questions" at *http://windowshelp.microsoft.com/Windows/en-US/Help/398b5eda-aa7f-4078-94c5-1519b697bfa01033.mspx*.

On the Companion Media

- RemoteAssistanceDiag.ps1

CHAPTER 23

Managing Software Updates

Microsoft strives to make the Windows 7 operating system as secure and reliable as possible the day it is initially released. However, networked software will always require regular updates because security threats on networks change constantly. To minimize the risk of new security threats, you need to update Windows 7 regularly using updates provided by Microsoft.

This chapter discusses Windows 7 features that relate to software updates and describes how they will improve the efficiency of delivering updates in your organization. This chapter also explains the three primary ways to distribute Microsoft updates: the Windows Update client, Windows Server Update Services (WSUS), and Microsoft System Center Configuration Manager 2007 R2 (Configuration Manager 2007 R2). A detailed description of Background Intelligent Transfer Service (BITS) 3.0 and how you can manage BITS is also provided in this chapter.

Because you can use Group Policy settings to manage the Windows Update client in Windows 7, this chapter describes useful Group Policy settings. Organizations that use proxy servers might require an additional configuration step to allow the Windows Update client to work properly, and this chapter describes how to perform that configuration. To verify that updates are being deployed correctly, you can use auditing tools such as Microsoft Baseline Security Analyzer (MBSA) and Configuration Manager 2007 R2.

Occasionally, you might experience a problem with a Windows 7 client that fails to update properly. This chapter also provides troubleshooting information to allow you to diagnose and resolve the problem. Finally, the chapter provides a conceptual overview of the planning of the software update process and a description of the Microsoft approach to updates.

Methods for Deploying Updates

To meet the needs of various types of organizations, Microsoft provides several different methods for applying updates. For home users and small businesses, Windows 7 is configured to automatically retrieve updates directly from Microsoft. The preferred method for deploying updates in medium and many large organizations is WSUS, which provides better control and performance. Finally, enterprises that use Configuration Manager 2007 R2 can use that tool to deploy and manage updates.

Table 23-1 lists the advantages and disadvantages of each of the update distribution methods and the network size for which the method is effective. The sections that follow describe each of these methods in more detail.

TABLE 23-1 Comparison of Automated Update Distribution Methods

UPDATE DISTRIBUTION METHOD	NETWORK SIZE	ADVANTAGES	DISADVANTAGES
Windows Update client connecting directly to Microsoft	50 or fewer computers	Does not require that any infrastructure be deployed.	Does not allow administrators to centrally test or approve updates or manage installation errors. Wastes Internet bandwidth by downloading updates directly to each computer.
Windows Server Update Services	Any number of computers	Allows administrators to test, approve, and schedule updates. Reduces Internet bandwidth usage.	Requires an infrastructure server.

UPDATE DISTRIBUTION METHOD	NETWORK SIZE	ADVANTAGES	DISADVANTAGES
System Center Configuration Manager 2007 R2	Any number of computers	Provides highly customizable, centralized control over update deployment, with the ability to audit and inventory client systems. Can be used to distribute other types of software. Supports Microsoft Windows NT 4.0 and Windows 98.	Requires infrastructure servers and additional software licenses.

Windows Update Client

Whether a client computer is configured to retrieve updates directly from Microsoft or from a WSUS server on your intranet, the same client downloads and installs the updates: Windows Update. Windows Update can notify users automatically of critical updates and security updates available either at Microsoft or at a specified WSUS server.

The Windows Update client (implemented as both a service and a Control Panel application) in Windows 7 replaces the Automatic Updates client available in Windows 2000 Service Pack 3 (SP3), Windows XP Home Edition, Windows XP Professional, and Windows Server 2003. Both Windows Update in Windows 7 and Automatic Updates in previous platforms are proactive "pull" services that allow for automatic detection, notification, download, and installation of important updates. Both clients will even reboot a computer at a scheduled time to ensure that updates take effect as soon as possible.

The Windows Update client provides for a great deal of control over its behavior. You can configure individual computers by using the Control Panel\Security\Windows Update\Change Settings page. Networks that use Active Directory Domain Services (AD DS) can specify the configuration of each Windows Update client by using Group Policy. In non–AD DS environments, you also can configure computers by changing local Group Policy settings or by configuring a set of registry values.

Systems administrators can configure Windows Update to automatically download updates and schedule their installation for a specified time. If the computer is turned off at that time, the updates can be installed as soon as the computer is turned on. Alternatively, Windows Update can wake a computer from standby and install the update at the specified time if the computer hardware supports it. This will not work if a computer is shut down, however. Downloading updates will also not affect a user's network performance because the Windows Update agent downloads the updates by using BITS.

If complete automation is not acceptable, you can also give users control over when updates are downloaded and installed. The Windows Update client can be configured by using Group Policy to only notify the user that updates are available. The updates are not downloaded or applied until the user clicks the notification balloon and selects the desired updates. For more information, see the section titled "Windows Update Group Policy Settings" later in this chapter.

After the Windows Update client downloads updates, the client checks the digital signature and the Secure Hash Algorithm (SHA1) hash on the updates to verify that they have not been modified.

If Windows Update is configured to download or check for updates automatically and if WSUS or Configuration Manager 2007 R2 is not being used to manage updates, the Windows Update client will always update itself automatically. This ensures that the Windows Update client will continue to function correctly.

Windows Server Update Services

Windows Server Update Services (WSUS) is a version of the Microsoft Update service that you can host on your private network. WSUS connects to the Windows Update site, downloads information about available updates, and adds them to a list of updates that require administrative approval. To deploy updates to Windows 7 clients, you must use WSUS 3.0 with SP2 or later versions.

After an administrator approves and prioritizes these updates, WSUS automatically makes them available to any computer running Windows Update (or the Automatic Updates client on earlier versions of Windows). Windows Update (when properly configured) then checks the WSUS server and automatically downloads and installs updates as configured by the administrators. As shown in Figure 23-1, WSUS can be distributed across multiple servers and locations to scale to enterprise needs. WSUS meets the needs of medium-sized organizations and many enterprises.

WSUS requires at least one infrastructure server: a computer running Windows Server 2003 SP2 or later server operating systems with the Microsoft .NET Framework 2.0 SP1 or later versions. Additionally, the server must have Microsoft Internet Information Services (IIS) 6.0 or later versions installed. As shown in Figure 23-2, WSUS is managed using a Microsoft Management Console (MMC) console.

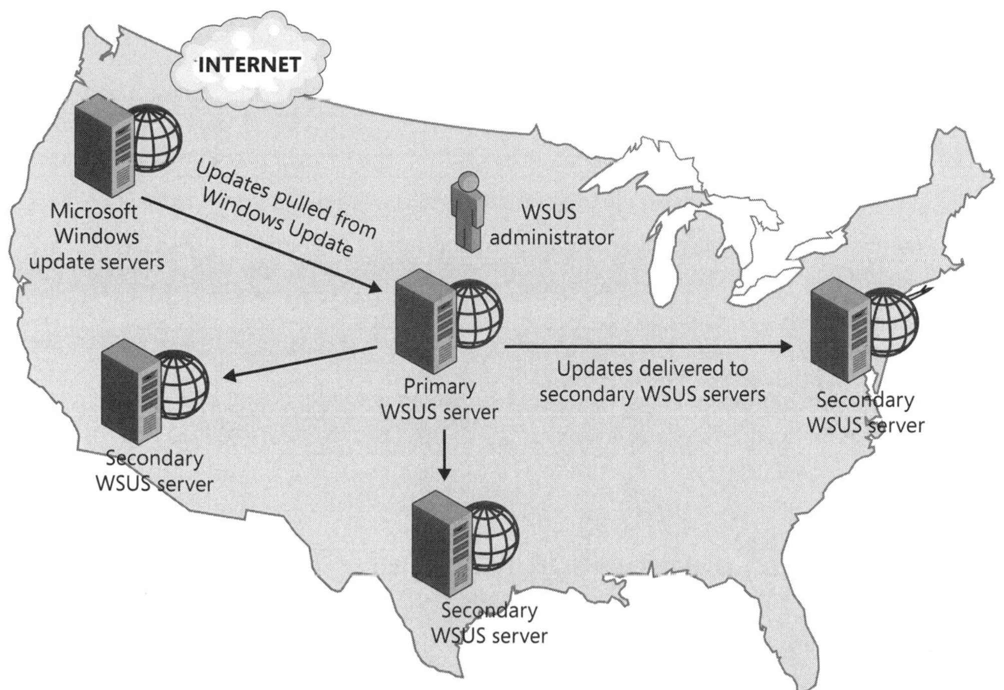

FIGURE 23-1 WSUS can scale for enterprises.

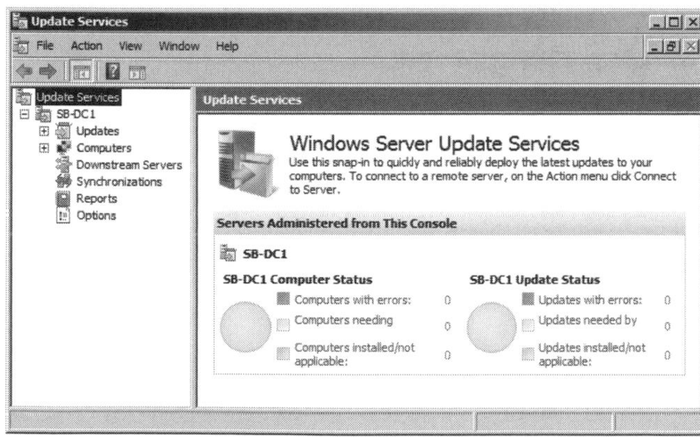

FIGURE 23-2 WSUS is managed using an MMC console.

IMPORTANT To deploy updates to Windows 7 computers, you must have WSUS 3.0 with SP2 or later versions.

The WSUS interface enables administrators to perform the following administrative tasks:

- Synchronize the WSUS server by downloading a list of updates from Microsoft.
- Approve updates for distribution to client computers.
- View a list of computers that successfully installed updates or experienced problems installing updates and determine exactly which updates have been installed.

NOTE For more information about update management with WSUS and to download WSUS, visit *http://www.microsoft.com/wsus*.

System Center Configuration Manager 2007 R2

Microsoft System Center Configuration Manager 2007 R2 (Configuration Manager 2007 R2) is software for enterprises to more efficiently manage their network infrastructure, including distributing software updates. The software update distribution mechanism of Configuration Manager 2007 R2 is based on WSUS. However, Configuration Manager 2007 R2 also supports:

- Custom software update catalogs that you can use to distribute updates for third-party and custom applications.
- Wake-on-LAN capability to start and update computers outside of normal business hours.
- Internet-based update distribution for clients that are disconnected from the internal network.
- Integration with Network Access Protection (NAP) to require client computers to apply updates before connecting to the internal network.
- Flexible reporting to simplify analyzing update distribution in your organization.

NOTE For more information about Configuration Manager 2007 R2, visit the Configuration Manager 2007 R2 Web site at *http://www.microsoft.com/sccm*. For information about using Configuration Manager 2007 R2 for update management, refer to "Software Updates in Configuration Manager" at *http://technet.microsoft.com/en-us/library/bb680701.aspx*.

Manually Installing, Scripting, and Removing Updates

Most updates in your organization should be installed using WSUS 3.0 SP2 or Configuration Manager 2007 R2. However, at times you might need to install, script, or remove updates manually. This section provides an overview of Windows Update files and describes how to work with updates.

Overview of Windows 7 Update Files

Windows 7 uses MSU files for installing updates, which are Microsoft Update Standalone Packages. MSU files are not executable as are updates for versions of Windows prior to Windows Vista. However, they function quite similarly to executable files because you can double-click them to install an update.

SECURITY ALERT **For security purposes, MSU files should be treated as executable files. Therefore, if you block executable files as e-mail attachments, you should also block MSU files.**

MSU filenames have the following format:

<WindowsVersion>-KB<ArticleNumber>-[v<VersionNumber>-]<Platform>.MSU

The version number is listed only if an update is re-released with a version number higher than 1. For example, version 1 of a 32-bit Windows 7 update can be named Windows6.1-KB961367-x86.MSU. The 64-bit version of the same release of that update would be named Windows6.1-KB961367-x64.MSU. The following list describes each of these placeholders:

- ***WindowsVersion*** The version of Windows to which the update applies. For Windows 7, this is Windows 6.1.
- ***ArticleNumber*** The Microsoft Knowledge Base article number that describes the update. You can look up the article at *http://support.microsoft.com/kb/<ArticleNumber>*. For example, if the update filename is Windows6.1-KB961367-v1-x86-ENU.MSU, you can look up the supporting Knowledge Base article at *http://support.microsoft.com/kb/961367*.
- ***VersionNumber*** Occasionally, Microsoft might release multiple versions of an update. Typically, the version number will be 1.
- ***Platform*** This value will be x86 for 32-bit operating systems, x64 for 64-bit versions of Windows, and ia64 for Itanium-based computers.

Standardized naming for updates simplifies update processing by allowing you to evaluate updates from a script using only the filename.

How to Script Update Installations

Windows 7 opens MSU files with the Windows Update Standalone Installer (Wusa.exe). To install an update from a script, run the script with administrative privileges, call Wusa, and provide the path to the MSU file. For example, you can install an update named Windows6.1-KB961367-x86.MSU in the current directory by running the following command.

```
wusa Windows6.1-KB961367-x86.MSU
```

Additionally, Wusa supports the following standard command-line options:

- ***/?, /h, or /help*** Displays the command-line options.
- ***/quiet*** Quiet mode. This is the same as unattended mode, but no status or error messages are displayed. Use quiet mode when installing an update as part of a script.
- ***/norestart*** Does not restart when installation has completed. Use this parameter when installing multiple updates simultaneously. All but the last update installed should have the */norestart* parameter.

Scripting is not usually the best way to install updates on an ongoing basis. Instead, you should use Automatic Updates, WSUS, or Configuration Manager 2007 R2. However, you might create a script to install updates on new computers or to install updates on computers that cannot participate in your standard update distribution method.

How to Remove Updates

Some updates can cause application compatibility problems. Although this is rare, if you suspect that an update has caused a problem, you can remove the update to alleviate the problem. Then you should work with Microsoft and any other software vendors to resolve the problem so that you can install the update.

SECURITY ALERT **Before you remove an update, view the update's Knowledge Base article to determine whether you can use a different countermeasure to remove the vulnerability that the update resolves. For example, you might be able to reduce the vulnerability by properly configuring your firewall. This will reduce the risk of being compromised while you work to resolve the problem with an update.**

You can remove an update in two different ways:

- **WSUS** You can remove some updates with WSUS, but many updates do not support being removed. To remove an update for a group of computers or all computers with WSUS, follow these steps:
  1. View the WSUS Updates page.
  2. Select the update and then click Change Approval under Update Tasks.
  3. Click the Approval list and then click Remove.
  4. Click OK.

- **Add/Remove Programs** Uninstall an update from a client computer manually by following these steps:
  1. Open Control Panel.
  2. Click Uninstall A Program under Programs.
  3. Click View Installed Updates under Tasks.
  4. Click an update and then click Uninstall.

Note that removing an update from a single computer in a networked environment can temporarily alleviate problems caused by the update. However, depending on the distribution mechanism used to install the update, it might reinstall automatically. Additionally, when you intentionally remove an update, you should inform the personnel responsible for auditing software updates that the missing update is intentional and that you have taken other measures to protect against the security vulnerability (if applicable).

Deploying Updates to New Computers

Microsoft will undoubtedly continue to release important updates for Windows 7. When you deploy a new computer, it might not have those updates installed. Therefore, the new computer can have known, but unprotected, vulnerabilities.

DIRECT FROM THE SOURCE

How Windows Update Behaves on New Computers

Gary Henderson, Lead Program Manager
Windows Update Agent

Windows 7 will not wait for the scheduled time to install the first batches of applicable updates; they will be downloaded and installed, and the user will be prompted to reboot if necessary.

Also, the WSUS administrator can deploy the most critical updates with a deadline. Thus, new computers connecting to that WSUS server will immediately download and install those very critical updates and force the immediate reboot to make sure the computer is secure.

To minimize the risk of attack against computers that haven't been updated, you can use the following techniques:

- **Integrate updates into the Windows 7 setup files** You can integrate service packs and other updates, including non-Microsoft updates, by installing Windows 7 and all updates on a lab computer and then using Windows PE and the XImage tool to create an operating system image (a .wim file) that you can deploy to new computers.

MORE INFO For more information about Windows PE and XImage, see Chapter 3, "Deployment Platform," and Chapter 6, "Developing Disk Images."

- **Include update files with your Windows 7 distribution and install them automatically during setup** If you cannot integrate updates into setup files, you should automate their installation after setup. You have several ways to run additional commands during installation:
  - Use the Windows System Image Manager to add a *RunSynchronous* command to an Unattend.xml answer file. *RunSynchronous* commands are available in the Microsoft-Windows-Setup and the Microsoft-Windows-Deployment features.

MORE INFO For more information about Windows System Image Manager, see Chapter 3 and Chapter 6.

  - Edit the %WinDir%\Setup\Scripts\SetupComplete.cmd file. This file runs after Windows Setup completes and any commands in this file are executed. Commands in the SetupComplete.cmd file are executed with local system privileges. You cannot reboot the system and resume running SetupComplete.cmd; therefore, you must install all updates in a single pass.
- **Deploy updates to client computers using removable media** If you cannot integrate updates into setup files, you should install them immediately after setup is complete. To minimize the risk of network attacks, set up Windows 7 computers without connecting them to a network. Then install all updates from removable media. When the computer has all critical updates, you can attach it to the network without unnecessary risk. The disadvantage to this technique is that it requires administrators to physically insert the removable media in each new computer.
- **Deploy updates to client computers across the network** As a more efficient alternative to installing updates from removable media, you can install updates across the network. However, connecting computers to a network exposes them to a risk of attack across that network. Even if the network is internal, other computers on your internal network might have malicious software, such as worms, that can launch attacks. Often, malicious software is extremely efficient at contacting new computers and can infect an unprotected computer within a few seconds after you connect it to a network. Therefore, you cannot necessarily update a networked computer fast enough to protect it. If you install updates for new computers across the network, create a private, nonrouted network for updates; keep the number of computers on the network extremely limited; and audit the computers regularly to ensure that they do not contain malicious software. This type of network is illustrated in Figure 23-3.

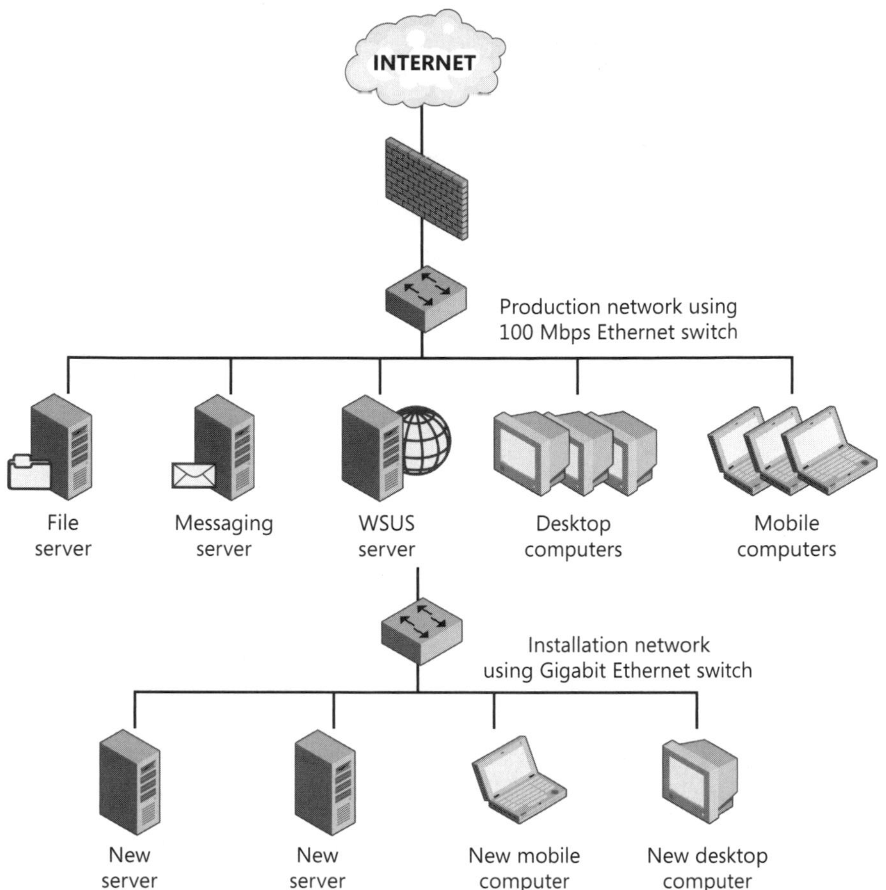

FIGURE 23-3 Create a separate subnet to protect new computers before installing updates.

Other Reasons to Use a Private Network for New Computers

Creating a separate network segment for installing new computers has benefits in addition to improved security. Installing an operating system across a network is extremely bandwidth intensive, and, depending on your network configuration, the bandwidth consumed while installing a computer can negatively affect the network performance of other computers on the network. Additionally, you can significantly reduce the time required to install a new computer by using a higher-speed network for installations. For example, if your production network segment is 100 Mbps Ethernet and you can't justify the cost of upgrading all computers to gigabit Ethernet, you might be able to justify the cost of a small gigabit Ethernet network switch and gigabit network interface cards to be used only during the installation process.

MORE INFO For more information about designing setup architectures, see Chapter 3.

Managing BITS

Windows 7 includes Background Intelligent Transfer Service (BITS) 3.5. BITS is a file-transfer service designed to transfer files across the Internet using only idle network bandwidth. Unlike standard Hypertext Transfer Protocol (HTTP), File Transfer Protocol (FTP), or shared-folder file transfers, BITS does not use all available bandwidth, so you can use BITS to download large files without affecting other network applications. BITS transfers are also very reliable and can continue when users change network connections or restart their computers.

BITS Network Protocol

BITS uses HTTP to transfer files in the same way as a Web browser. However, unlike standard HTTP transfers, BITS transfer speed is carefully throttled. Using the HTTP protocol enables BITS to work through proxy servers, to authenticate both clients and servers, and to provide encryption using Secure Sockets Layer (SSL) certificates. If you want to explicitly allow or block BITS transfers at your firewall, create filters for the HTTP or Hypertext Transfer Protocol Secure (HTTPS) protocol and the source or destination networks. For example, you can limit HTTP communications so that Windows 7 clients can connect only to your WSUS server.

HOW IT WORKS

BITS File Storage

Because updates can be very large and have the potential to affect network performance, Windows Update uses BITS to download updates from Microsoft Update or from a WSUS server. Additionally, custom applications can use BITS to transfer files. To use BITS, the Background Intelligent Transfer Service must be running.

In Windows 7, BITS can take advantage of BranchCache to reduce wide area network (WAN) bandwidth utilization. For more information, refer to Chapter 25, "Configuring Windows Networking."

BITS Behavior

BITS (and thus Windows Update) does not initiate a demand-dial network connection at times when it normally downloads updates. BITS will instead wait for the user or another application to initiate a network connection. If a computer stays disconnected or is otherwise unable to reach its update server for weeks or months at a time, the computer will not have recent updates and might be vulnerable to attack. To mitigate the risk of an unprotected computer spreading worms or viruses on your local network, use NAP.

> ***NOTE*** **For more information about Network Access Protection, see** ***http://www.microsoft.com/nap/.***

BITS stores the partially downloaded files in the destination folder under a temporary name; these files are marked as hidden. When the job is complete, BITS renames the file with its final name and removes the file's hidden attribute. BITS impersonates the job owner before writing these files to preserve the file system security and quotas for the user.

BITS Group Policy Settings

You can use Group Policy settings from the Bits.admx administrative template to configure several aspects of BITS and control how much bandwidth BITS uses. These policies are located in the Computer Configuration\Administrative Templates\Network\Background Intelligent Transfer Service node of the Group Policy Object Editor. For information about BranchCache-related policies, refer to Chapter 25.

- **Do Not Allow The Computer To Act As A BITS Peercaching Client** When this setting and the Allow BITS Peercaching setting are both enabled, Windows 7 client computers will not attempt to download files from peers. Instead, they will download files from the origin source directly. By default, a Windows 7 computer will act as a Peercaching client and thus will first attempt to download peer-enabled BITS jobs from peer computers before reverting to the origin server. This setting requires Windows Vista or Windows 7.
- **Do Not Allow The Computer To Act As A BITS Peercaching Server** When this setting and the Allow BITS Peercaching setting are both enabled, Windows 7 client computers will not attempt to share files with peers. However, they might still download files from other Windows 7 computers that are configured to act as Peercaching servers. By default, a Windows 7 computer will act as a Peercaching server. This setting requires Windows Vista or Windows 7.
- **Allow BITS Peercaching** By default, Windows 7 computers have Peercaching disabled, causing Windows 7 to always transfer files directly from the origin server. If you enable this setting, Windows 7 will also attempt to transfer files from other Windows 7 peers, potentially reducing bandwidth utilization on your Internet connection. This setting requires Windows Vista or Windows 7.

- **Timeout For Inactive BITS Jobs** The number of days without successful download action or job property changes, after which BITS will remove a pending job. After a job is considered abandoned, BITS deletes all downloaded files. This setting typically will not affect the Windows Update client, but it might affect other applications that use BITS. This setting is available for Microsoft Windows 2000, Windows XP, and Windows Server 2003 with BITS 1.5 in addition to Windows Vista and Windows 7.
- **Limit The Maximum Network Bandwidth For BITS Background Transfers** Enables you to limit the bandwidth that BITS uses. You can configure two different bandwidth limits for different times of the day. For example, you might limit the bandwidth to 10 kilobits per second (Kbps) per client computer during the day to minimize impact on the network during the busiest time but allow up to 20 Kbps per client computer after normal working hours. If you specify a value that is less than 2 Kbps, BITS will still use up to 2 Kbps. To prevent transfers from occurring, specify 0 Kbps. Because BITS is designed to make use of idle bandwidth, you do not usually need to define this setting. Instead, consult with your network engineering group to monitor BITS bandwidth usage and adjust this setting only if bandwidth utilization becomes a problem. Setting bandwidth restrictions too low can interfere with the ability of Windows Update to retrieve updates. This setting is available for Windows 2000, Windows XP, and Windows Server 2003 with BITS 2.0 in addition to Windows Vista and Windows 7.
- **Limit The Maximum Network Bandwidth Used For Peercaching** The maximum bandwidth used when transferring files to peers across the LAN. By default, BITS uses 8 megabits per second (Mbps) as the maximum bandwidth. If you have a LAN that is 10 Mbps or slower, you can decrease this setting to reduce the likelihood of BITS peer transfers affecting other network applications. This setting does not affect WAN or Internet bandwidth. This setting requires Windows Vista or Windows 7.
- **Limit The BITS Peercache Size** The minimum and maximum disk space to be used to cache BITS content. This setting requires Windows Vista or Windows 7.
- **Limit The Age Of Items In The BITS Peercache** The maximum number of days before BITS removes cached content. This setting requires Windows Vista or Windows 7.
- **Limit The Maximum BITS Job Download Time** The number of seconds an active BITS download can run. By default, this setting is 5,400 seconds, or 90 minutes. This setting requires Windows Vista or Windows 7.
- **Limit The Maximum Number Of Files Allowed In A BITS Job** The maximum number of files that can be added to a BITS job. Typically, you do not need to define this setting. This setting requires Windows Vista or Windows 7.
- **Limit The Maximum Number Of BITS Jobs For This Computer** The maximum number of BITS jobs allowed for all users except services and administrators. This setting requires Windows Vista or Windows 7.
- **Limit The Maximum Number Of BITS Jobs For Each User** The maximum number of BITS jobs allowed for each user except services and administrators. This setting requires Windows Vista or Windows 7.

- **Limit The Maximum Number Of Ranges That Can Be Added To The File In A BITS Job** The maximum number of ranges that can be added to a file. Ranges allow a portion of a file to be downloaded. This setting requires Windows Vista or Windows 7.
- **Set Up A Maintenance Schedule To Limit The Maximum Network Bandwidth Used For BITS Background Transfers** Restrict the bandwidth BITS uses at specific times of specific dates. This setting requires Windows 7.
- **Set Up A Work Schedule To Limit The Maximum Network Bandwidth Used For BITS Background Transfers** Restrict the bandwidth BITS uses at specific times of specific dates. This setting requires Windows 7.

Configuring the Maximum Bandwidth Served For Peer Client Requests Policy

The Maximum Bandwidth Served For Peer Client Requests policy is configured in bytes per second, which is a different measurement than the Maximum Network Bandwidth That Bits Uses setting, which uses kilobits per second (Kbps). There are 8 bits in a byte, so the default setting of 1048576 converts to about 8 megabits per second (Mbps), which is about 10 percent of the usable bandwidth of a standard 100-Mbps fast Ethernet network.

Managing BITS with Windows PowerShell

Previous versions of Windows provided command-line management of BITS using the BITSAdmin.exe tool. In Windows 7, BITSAdmin.exe is deprecated. Instead, you should use the Windows PowerShell cmdlets.

Within Windows PowerShell, begin by running the following command.

```
Import-Module BitsTransfer
```

After you import the BitsTransfer module, the following cmdlets are available:

- **Add-BitsFile** Adds files to a BITS transfer
- **Complete-BitsTransfer** Completes a BITS transfer
- **Get-BitsTransfer** Gets a BITS transfer
- **Remove-BitsTransfer** Stops a BITS transfer
- **Resume-BitsTransfer** Resumes a suspended BITS transfer
- **Set-BitsTransfer** Configures a BITS transfer job
- **Start-BitsTransfer** Creates and starts a BITS transfer job
- **Suspend-BitsTransfer** Pauses a BITS transfer job

For example, the following Windows PowerShell command begins a BITS transfer from the local computer to a computer named CLIENT.

```
Start-BitsTransfer -Source file.txt -Destination \\client\share -Priority normal
```

When running Windows PowerShell interactively, the PowerShell window displays the progress of the transfer. The following command uses an abbreviated notation to download a file from a Web site to the local computer.

```
Start-BitsTransfer http://server/dir/myfile.txt C:\docs\myfile.txt
```

For detailed information, run the following command within Windows PowerShell.

```
Help About_BITS_Cmdlets
```

Windows Update Group Policy Settings

You can configure Windows Update client settings using local or domain Group Policy settings. This is useful for the following tasks:

- Configuring computers to use a local WSUS server
- Configuring automatic installation of updates at a specific time of day
- Configuring how often to check for updates
- Configuring update notifications, including whether non-administrators receive update notifications
- Configuring client computers as part of a WSUS target group, which you can use to deploy different updates to different groups of computers

Windows Update settings are located at Computer Configuration\Administrative Templates\Windows Components\Windows Update. The Windows Update Group Policy settings are:

- **Configure Automatic Updates** Specifies whether this computer will receive security updates and other important downloads through the Windows automatic updating service. You also use this setting to configure whether the updates are installed automatically and what time of day the installation occurs.
- **Specify Intranet Microsoft Update Service Location** Specifies the location of your WSUS server.
- **Automatic Updates Detection Frequency** Specifies how frequently the Automatic Updates client checks for new updates. By default, this is a random time between 17 and 22 hours.
- **Allow Non-Administrators To Receive Update Notifications** Determines whether all users or only administrators will receive update notifications. Non-administrators can install updates using the Windows Update client.

- **Allow Automatic Updates Immediate Installation** Specifies whether Automatic Updates will install updates immediately that don't require the computer to be restarted.
- **Turn On Recommended Updates Via Automatic Updates** Determines whether client computers install both critical and recommended updates, which might include updated drivers.
- **No Auto-Restart For Scheduled Automatic Updates Installations** Specifies that to complete a scheduled installation, Automatic Updates will wait for the computer to be restarted by any user who is logged on instead of causing the computer to restart automatically.
- **Re-Prompt For Restart With Scheduled Installations** Specifies how often the Automatic Updates client prompts the user to restart. Depending on other configuration settings, users might have the option of delaying a scheduled restart. However, the Automatic Updates client will remind them automatically to restart based on the frequency configured in this setting.
- **Delay Restart For Scheduled Installations** Specifies how long the Automatic Updates client waits before automatically restarting.
- **Reschedule Automatic Updates Scheduled Installations** Specifies the amount of time for Automatic Updates to wait, following system startup, before proceeding with a scheduled installation that was missed previously. If you don't specify this amount of time, a missed scheduled installation will occur one minute after the computer is next started.
- **Enable Client-Side Targeting** Specifies the group to which the computer is a member. This option is useful only if you are using WSUS; you cannot use this option with SUS.
- **Enable Windows Update Power Management To Automatically Wake Up The System To Install Scheduled Updates** If people in your organization tend to shut down their computers when they leave the office, enable this setting to configure computers with supported hardware to start up automatically and install an update at the scheduled time. Computers will not wake up unless there is an update to be installed. If the computer is on battery power, the computer will return to Sleep automatically after 2 minutes.

Additionally, the following two settings are available at the same location under both Computer Configuration and User Configuration:

- **Do Not Display 'Install Updates And Shut Down' Option In Shut Down Windows Dialog Box** Specifies whether Windows XP with SP2 or later versions shows the Install Updates And Shut Down option.
- **Do Not Adjust Default Option To 'Install Updates And Shut Down' In Shut Down Windows Dialog Box** Specifies whether Windows XP with SP2 or later versions automatically changes the default shutdown option to Install Updates And Shut Down when Automatic Updates is waiting to install an update.

Finally, the last user setting is available at Administrative Templates\Windows Components\Windows Update:

- **Remove Access To Use All Windows Update Features** When enabled, prevents the user from accessing the Windows Update interface.

You should create separate Group Policy objects for groups of computers that have different update installation requirements. For example, if you deploy updates to the IT department first as part of a pilot deployment, IT computers should have their own Group Policy object with settings that place them in a specific WSUS target group for the pilot project.

Configuring Windows Update to Use a Proxy Server

Windows Update can use an HTTP proxy server. However, configuring Windows Internet Explorer is not sufficient to configure Windows Update because Windows Update uses Windows HTTP Services (WinHTTP) to scan for updates and BITS to download updates.

You can configure Windows Update to use a proxy server in two ways:

- Web Proxy Auto Detect (WPAD) settings are configured. The WPAD feature lets services locate an available proxy server by querying a Dynamic Host Configuration Protocol (DHCP) option or by locating a particular Domain Name System (DNS) record.
- Use the Netsh command-line tool, which replaces the Proxycfg.exe tool.

To use the Netsh command-line tool, first switch to the Netsh Winhttp context. Then, use the *show proxy* command to view settings or the *set proxy* command to define your proxy server configuration settings. For example, you can run the following command to view current proxy server settings.

```
Netsh winhttp show proxy
```

The following commands demonstrate how to configure proxy server settings.

```
Netsh winhttp set proxy myproxy
Netsh winhttp set proxy myproxy:80 "<local>;bar"
Netsh winhttp set proxy proxy-server="http=myproxy;https=sproxy:88" bypass-list="*.
contoso.com"
```

Alternatively, if you have configured Internet Explorer proxy server settings correctly, you can import settings from Internet Explorer into WinHTTP by using the following command.

```
Netsh winhttp import proxy source=ie
```

To reset your proxy server settings, run the following command.

```
Netsh winhttp reset proxy
```

Tools for Auditing Software Updates

One of the most important concepts in security is "Trust, but audit." Auditing provides a critical layer of protection against human error and omission. In the case of software update management, auditing enables you to verify that updates are distributed correctly and are not removed after distribution.

Microsoft provides the following tools for auditing software updates and the software update process:

- **WSUS** WSUS enables you to view which updates have been distributed to which computers. To detect updates that are removed after distribution and new computers that do not have the proper updates installed, use WSUS reporting in conjunction with one of the other tools in this list.
- **Configuration Manager 2007 R2** Configuration Manager 2007 R2 monitors installed updates and can generate reports showing whether updates are successful.
- **MBSA** The Microsoft Baseline Security Analyzer (MBSA) actively connects to computers on your network and, with proper credentials, generates reports displaying the installed updates and a list of other security vulnerabilities. MBSA is a graphical tool that simplifies manual, interactive auditing. MBSACLI and Configuration Manager 2007 R2, described next, use the MBSA engine.
- **MBSACLI** The MBSA command-line interface (MBSACLI) allows you to script MBSA auditing, enabling you to audit large numbers of computers in an automated fashion. You can generate Extensible Markup Language (XML)–based reports that you can view with the MBSA interface, or you can create tools that process the XML-based MBSACLI reports. MBSACLI is included with MBSA.

WSUS and Configuration Manager 2007 R2 were described earlier in this chapter. The sections that follow describe MBSA and MBSACLI.

The MBSA Console

MBSA is used to analyze one or more computers for vulnerabilities. MBSA scans for two categories of vulnerabilities: weak security configurations and missing security updates. This section focuses on using MBSA to scan for updates that should have been installed but have not been installed.

After installing MBSA, you can use it to scan all computers on your network or domain for which you have administrator access. To scan all computers on a specific subnet using your current user credentials, follow these steps:

1. Start MBSA by clicking Start, pointing to All Programs, and then clicking Microsoft Baseline Security Advisor.
2. On the Welcome To The Microsoft Baseline Security Analyzer page, click Scan Multiple Computers.

3. On the Which Computers Do You Want To Scan? page, type the domain or workgroup name or the IP address range you want to scan. To speed up the scanning process, clear all check boxes except for Check For Security Updates. If you have a WSUS server on your network, you can further speed up the process by selecting the Advanced Update Services Options check box and the Scan Using Assigned Update Services Servers Only option to prevent unmanaged computers from being scanned. Figure 23-4 shows MBSA configured to scan the contoso.com domain for security updates.

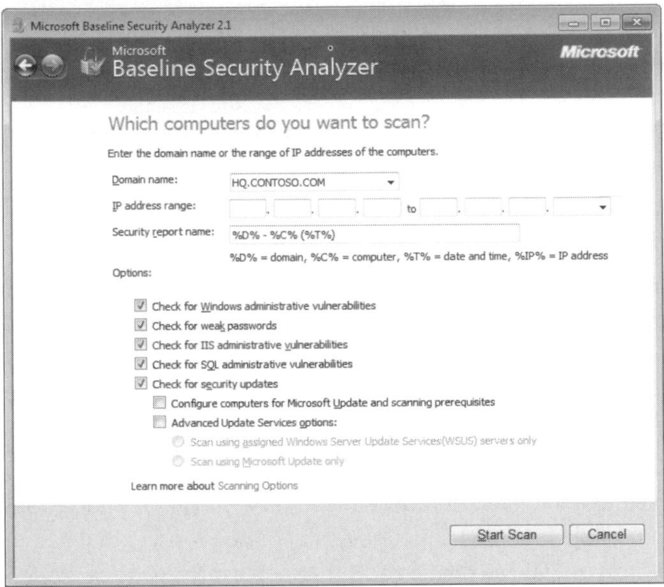

FIGURE 23-4 MBSA configured to scan a subnet

4. Click Start Scan. While MBSA performs the scan, it will keep you updated on the progress.
5. After the scan is completed, the View Security Report page appears, listing the computers that were scanned.

> ***NOTE*** **If you do not have sufficient credentials on a computer, MBSA will display the IP address of the computer with the following message: User Is Not An Administrator On The Scanned Machine.**

Missing security updates are marked by a red X, and missing service packs or update rollups are marked with a yellow X. A green check mark denotes a scan that was completed successfully with no missing updates found. Scan reports are stored on the computer from which you ran MBSA in the %UserProfile%\SecurityScans folder. An individual security report is created for each computer that is scanned.

During the scanning process, MBSA uses NetBIOS over Transmission Control Protocol/Internet Protocol (TCP/IP) and Common Internet File System (CIFS) protocols to connect to computers, which requires TCP ports 135, 139, and 445 and User Datagram Protocol (UDP) ports 137 and 139. If a firewall blocks these ports between you and the target computers or if the computers have Internet Connection Firewall enabled and these ports have not been opened, you will not be able to scan the computers.

At the beginning of the scan, MBSA must retrieve an updated MBSA detection catalog (Wsusscan.cab) that provides information about updates and security vulnerabilities. By default, this file is retrieved from the Microsoft Web site at *http://go.microsoft.com/fwlink/?LinkId=39043* and includes every current update available from Microsoft. If the computer is configured as a WSUS client, it will retrieve the file from your WSUS server instead.

MBSACLI

Scanning a large network should be done on a regular basis to find computers that have not been properly updated. However, scanning a large network is a time-consuming process. Although the MBSA console is the most efficient way to scan a network interactively, the MBSACLI command-line tool provides a way to script an analysis. By using scripts, you can schedule scanning to occur automatically, without your intervention. This way, you can have MBSACLI generate a report that you can refer to on demand.

Scheduling MBSA

It's convenient to schedule MBSACLI scans after business hours so that you don't consume network resources during working hours; however, if you do this, you won't be able to scan computers that users take home. It's a good idea to schedule scans at various times during the day.

Another good reason to schedule scans by using MBSACLI is that you can scan from multiple points on your network. For example, if your organization has five remote offices, it is more efficient to scan each remote office by using a computer located in that office. This improves performance, reduces the bandwidth used on your WAN, and allows you to scan computers even if a perimeter firewall blocks the ports that MBSACLI uses to scan.

As with the MBSA graphical console, you need administrative access to use MBSACLI to scan a computer. In a domain environment, simply log on to your computer using an account that has sufficient privileges. Otherwise, you can provide credentials at the command line by using the */u* and */p* parameters. However, you should avoid typing credentials in a script because the script can be compromised, allowing an attacker to gain privileges on remote computers.

Table 23-2 lists the parameters available in MBSACLI's MBSA mode.

TABLE 23-2 MBSA Mode Parameters in MBSACLI

PARAMETER	DESCRIPTION
/target *domain\computername* | *ipaddress*	Scans the host with the specified computer name or IP address.
/r *ipaddress1-ipaddress2*	Specifies an IP address range to be scanned, beginning with ipaddress1 and ending with ipaddress2, inclusive.
/listfile *filename*	Scans hosts specified in a text file.
/d *domain_name*	Scans all computers in a specified domain. Of course, your computer must be able to identify those computers. It uses the same mechanism as Network Neighborhood, so if you can browse computers in Network Neighborhood, this switch will work.
/u *username* /p *password*	Scans using the specified user name and password.
/n *scans*	Skips specific scans. You can choose OS, SQL, IIS, Updates, and Password. If you want to suppress multiple scans, separate them with a + sign. For example, to scan only for updates, use the command Mbsacli /n OS+SQL+IIS+Password.
/wa	Show only updates approved on the WSUS server.
/wi	Show all updates, even if they haven't been approved on the WSUS server.
/catalog *filename*	Specifies the MBSA detection catalog, Wsusscan.cab. You can download this file from *http://go.microsoft.com/fwlink/?LinkId=39043*.
/qp, /qe, /qr, /qt, /q	Does not display the scan progress, error list, and report list; the report following a single-computer scan; or any of these items, respectively.
/l, /ls	Lists all available reports or just the reports created in the latest scan, respectively.

PARAMETER	DESCRIPTION
/lr "*reportname*", /ld "*reportname*"	Displays an overview or detailed report summary when given the filename of the report. You do not need to specify the full filename—only the name of the report. For example, the following command shows a report for Computer1: mbsacli /ld "Cohowinery.com – Computer1 (11-11-2003 07-46 AM)"
/nai, nm, nd	Prevents MBSACLI from updating the Windows Update features, configuring computers to use the Microsoft Update Web site, or downloading files from the Microsoft Web site, respectively.
/nvc	Prevents MBSACLI from checking for a new version of MBSA.
/xmlout	Provides XML-based output, which is more difficult to read as a text file but easier to parse programmatically.
/o "*template*"	Uses a different template for the report filename. By default, the name is %domain% - %computername% (%date%). If you put one or more spaces in the template, be sure to enclose it in quotation marks.

When scanning a single computer, MBSACLI outputs information about vulnerabilities directly to the console. To save the output to a file, redirect it using the standard > notation. For example, this command saves the report output to a file named Output.txt.

```
Mbsacli > output.txt
```

When scanning multiple computers, MBSACLI displays only the computers scanned and the overall assessment. The details of the scan are stored in an XML report that is saved in your %UserProfile%\SecurityScans\ folder. By default, the filename for each report is set to *domain – computername* (*date*).mbsa.

You can view the reports by using the graphical MBSA console, however, by simply starting MBSA and then clicking View Existing Security Reports. MBSA will show the Pick A Security Report To View page, listing all of the available reports. You can also view them from the command line by using the */ld* parameter and specifying the report's filename.

For more information about creating scripts with MBSACLI to perform parallel scans and aggregate multiple scan reports, download the MBSA 2.0 Scripting Samples at *http://www.microsoft.com/downloads/details.aspx?familyid=3B64AC19-3C9E-480E-B0B3-6B87F2EE9042&displaylang=en*.

Troubleshooting the Windows Update Client

Occasionally, you might discover a client that isn't automatically installing updates correctly. Typically, such clients are identified during software update audits, as described in the section titled "Tools for Auditing Software Updates" earlier in this chapter. To identify the source of the problem, follow these steps:

1. Determine the last time the client was updated. This can be done in two different ways: by checking the client's registry (the most reliable technique) or, if you use WSUS, by checking the Reports page on the WSUS Web site.
   - To check the client's registry, open the HKEY_LOCAL_MACHINE\SOFTWARE\Microsoft\Windows\CurrentVersion\WindowsUpdate\Auto Update\Results registry key. In each of the Detect, Download, and Install subkeys, examine the LastSuccessTime entry to determine when updates were last detected, downloaded, and installed.
   - To check the WSUS server, open the Update Services console on the WSUS server. Click the Reports icon and then click Computer Detailed Status. Browse the computers to find the problematic computer and examine the updates that have been successfully installed, as well as those that have not yet been installed.
2. Examine any error messages returned by the Windows Update client by viewing the client's %SystemRoot%\WindowsUpdate.log file. This text file contains detailed output from the Windows Update client, including notifications for each attempt to find, download, and install updates. You can also use the WindowsUpdate.log file to verify that the client is attempting to access the correct update server. Search for any error messages in the Microsoft Knowledge Base for more troubleshooting information.

> ***NOTE*** **For detailed information about how to read the WindowsUpdate.log file, refer to Microsoft Knowledge Base article 902093 at *http://support.microsoft.com/kb/902093/*.**

3. If you are using WSUS, verify that the client can connect to the WSUS server. Open a Web browser on the client and go to *http://*<WSUSServerName>*/iuident.cab*. If you are prompted to download the file, this means that the client can reach the WSUS server and it is not a connectivity issue. Click Cancel. If you are not prompted to download the file, you might have a name resolution or connectivity issue, or WSUS is not configured correctly. Troubleshoot the problem further by identifying why the client cannot communicate with the WSUS server using HTTP.

4. If you can reach the WSUS server, verify that the client is configured correctly. If you are using Group Policy settings to configure Windows Update, use the Resultant Set of Policy (RSOP) tool (Rsop.msc) to check the computer's effective configuration. Within RSOP, browse to the Computer Configuration\Administrative Templates\Windows Components\Windows Update node and verify the configuration settings. Figure 23-5 shows the RSOP snap-in.

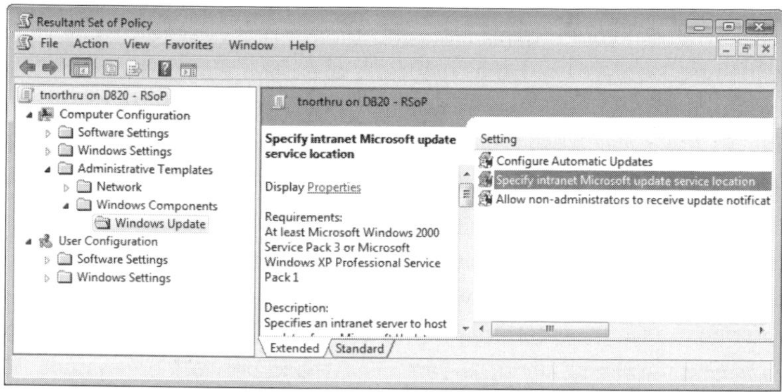

FIGURE 23-5 Use the RSOP snap-in to verify Windows Update configuration.

5. If you think WSUS is not configured correctly, verify the IIS configuration. WSUS uses IIS to update most client computers automatically to the WSUS-compatible Automatic Updates. To accomplish this, WSUS Setup creates a virtual directory named /Selfupdate under the Web site running on port 80 of the computer on which you install WSUS. This virtual directory, called the *self-update tree*, holds the latest WSUS client. For this reason, a Web site must be running on port 80, even if you put the WSUS Web site on a custom port. The Web site on port 80 does not have to be dedicated to WSUS. In fact, WSUS uses the site on port 80 only to host the self-update tree. To ensure that the self-update tree is working properly, first make sure a Web site is set up on port 80 of the WSUS server. Next, type the following at the command prompt of the WSUS server.

```
cscript <WSUSInstallationDrive>:\program files\microsoft windows server
update services\setup\InstallSelfupdateOnPort80.vbs
```

MORE INFO **For more information about troubleshooting WSUS, visit** ***http://technet.microsoft.com/en-us/library/cc708554.aspx.***

If you identify a problem and make a configuration change that you hope will resolve it, restart the Windows Update service on the client computer to make the change take effect and begin another update cycle. You can do this using the Services console or by running the following two commands.

```
net stop wuauserv
net start wuauserv
```

Within 6 to 10 minutes, Windows Update will attempt to contact your update server.

The Process of Updating Network Software

You must plan to update every network feature that uses software. This naturally includes client and server operating systems and applications, but it also includes routers, firewalls, wireless access points, and switches. To keep your systems up to date, follow these steps:

1. Assemble an update team.
2. Inventory all software in your organization, and then contact each software vendor and determine its process of notifying customers of software updates. Some vendors will notify you of updates directly via e-mail, but others require you to check a Web site regularly. Assign individuals to identify software updates on a regular basis. For example, someone on your team should be responsible for checking every software vendor's Web site for new updates on at least a weekly basis.
3. Create an update process for discovering, evaluating, retrieving, testing, installing, auditing, and removing updates. Although most of the process will be the same for all vendors, you might have to customize parts of the process to accommodate different uptime and testing requirements for servers, clients, and network equipment. As an example, this chapter will thoroughly document the update process to use for Microsoft operating system updates.

This resource kit focuses only on updating the Windows 7 operating system. However, your process should include the ability to manage updates for other operating systems, applications, and network devices. The sections that follow discuss these steps in more detail.

Assembling the Update Team

Identifying individuals with the right mix of technical and project management skills for deploying updates is one of the first decisions that you and your company's management will make. Even before staffing can begin, however, you need to identify the team roles, or areas of expertise, required for update management. Microsoft suggests using the Microsoft Solutions Framework (MSF) team model, which is based on six interdependent, multidisciplinary roles: product management, program management, development, testing, user experience, and release management. This model applies equally well to both Microsoft and non-Microsoft software.

- **Program management** The program management team's goal is to deliver updates within project constraints. Program management is responsible for managing the update schedule and budget, reporting status, managing project-related risk factors (such as staff illnesses), and managing the design of the update process.
- **Development** The development team builds the update infrastructure according to specification. The team's responsibilities include specifying the features of the update infrastructure, estimating the time and effort required to deploy the update infrastructure, and preparing the infrastructure for deployment.

- **Testing** The testing team ensures that updates are released into the production environment only after all quality issues are identified and resolved. The team's responsibilities include developing the testing strategy, designing and building the update lab, developing the test plan, and conducting tests.
- **User experience** The user experience team ensures that the update process meets the users' needs. The team gathers, analyzes, and prioritizes user requirements and complaints.
- **Release management** The release management team is responsible for deploying the updates. In large environments, the release management team also designs and manages a pilot deployment of an update to ensure that the update is sufficiently stable for deployment into the production environment.

The MSF team roles are flexible; they can be adapted to your organization's own processes and management philosophy. In a small organization or a limited deployment, one individual might play multiple roles. In larger organizations, a team might be required to perform all of the tasks assigned to each role.

> ***MORE INFO*** **For more information about the MSF team model, visit** ***http://www.microsoft.com/downloads/details.aspx?FamilyID=c54114a3-7cc6-4fa7-ab09-2083c768e9ab.***

Inventorying Software

After you create an update team, you must inventory the software on your network. Specifically, you need to know which operating systems and applications you have installed to identify updates that need to be deployed. You also need to understand the security requirements for each computer system, including which computers store highly confidential information, which are connected to the public Internet, and which will connect to exterior networks.

For each computer in your environment, gather the following information:

- **Operating system** Document the operating system version and update level. Remember that most routers, firewalls, and switches have operating systems. Also document which optional features, such as IIS, are installed.
- **Applications** Document every application installed on the computer, including versions and updates.
- **Network connectivity** Document the networks to which the computer is connected, including whether the computer is connected to the public Internet, whether it connects to other networks across a virtual private network (VPN) or dial-up connection, and whether it is a mobile computer that might connect to networks at other locations.

- **Existing countermeasures** Firewalls and virus checkers might already protect a computer against a particular vulnerability, making the update unnecessary. For firewalls, document the firewall configuration, including which ports are open.
- **Site** If your organization has multiple sites, you can choose to deploy updates to computers from a server located at each site to optimize bandwidth usage. Knowing at which site a computer or piece of network equipment is located allows you to deploy the updates efficiently.
- **Bandwidth** Computers connected across low-bandwidth links have special requirements. You can choose to transfer large updates during nonbusiness hours. For dial-up users, it might be more efficient to bypass the network link and transfer updates on removable media, such as CD-ROMs.
- **Administrator responsibility** You must understand who is responsible for deploying updates to a particular device and who will fix a problem if the device fails during the update process. If others are responsible for individual applications or services, make note of that as well.
- **Uptime requirements** Understand any service-level agreements or service-level guarantees that apply to a particular device and whether scheduled downtime counts against the total uptime. This will enable you to prioritize devices when troubleshooting and testing updates.
- **Scheduling dependencies** Applying updates requires planning systems to be offline. This can be a disruption for users, even if the device requires only a quick reboot. Understand who depends on a particular device so that you can clear downtime with that person ahead of time.

Some of this information, including operating system and installed applications, can be gathered in an automated fashion. Most network management tools have this capability, including Configuration Manager 2007 R2. You can also inventory Microsoft software on a computer by using Microsoft Software Inventory Analyzer (MSIA), a free download.

MORE INFO **For information about MSIA, visit *http://www.microsoft.com/resources/sam/msia.mspx*.**

Creating an Update Process

Deploying updates involves more than just choosing a technology to install the updates. An effective update process involves planning, discussion, and testing. Although you should use your organization's existing change-management process (if one exists), this section will describe the fundamental steps of an update process. The sections that follow describe each of these steps in more detail.

Discovering Updates

The security update process starts when Microsoft releases or updates a security bulletin. Reissued bulletins that have a higher severity rating should be evaluated again to determine whether an already-scheduled security release should be reprioritized and accelerated. You might also initiate the security update process when a new service pack is released.

You can be notified of Microsoft-related security issues and fixes by subscribing to the Microsoft Security Notification Services. You can register for this service from the following Web site: *http://www.microsoft.com/technet/security/bulletin/notify.mspx*. If you subscribe to this service, you will receive automatic notification of security issues by e-mail. Note that you will never receive the update as an attachment from Microsoft. E-mail is easy to spoof, so Microsoft includes a digital signature that can be verified. However, it's generally easier to simply check the Microsoft Web site to ensure that the bulletin is officially listed.

In addition, use non-Microsoft sources to receive an objective opinion of vulnerabilities. The following sources provide security alert information:

- Security alert lists, especially SecurityFocus (*http://www.securityfocus.com*)
- Security Web sites, such as *http://www.sans.org* and *http://www.cert.org*
- Alerts from antivirus software vendors

Evaluating Updates

After you learn of a security update, you need to evaluate the update to determine which computers at your organization, if any, should have the update applied. Read the information that accompanies the security bulletin and refer to the associated Knowledge Base article after it is released.

Next, look at the various parts of your environment to determine whether the vulnerability affects the computers on your network. You might not be using the software that is being updated, or you might be protected from the vulnerability by other means, such as a firewall. For example, if Microsoft releases a security update for Microsoft SQL Server and your company doesn't use SQL Server (and it's not a requirement for other installed applications), you don't need to act. If Microsoft releases a security update for the Server service but you have blocked the vulnerable ports by using Windows Firewall, you don't necessarily need to apply the update (although applying the update will provide an important additional layer of protection). As an alternative, you might decide that applying the update is not the best countermeasure for a security vulnerability. Instead, you might choose to add a firewall or adjust firewall filtering rules to limit the vulnerability's exposure.

Determining whether an update should be applied is not as straightforward as you might think. Microsoft updates are free downloads, but applying an update does have a cost: You will need to dedicate time to testing, packaging, and deploying the update. In larger organizations, applying a software update to a server requires that many hours be dedicated to justifying the update and scheduling the associated downtime with the groups who use the server.

Any type of update also carries the risk of something going wrong when the update is applied. In fact, any time you restart a computer, there is a small risk that the computer won't start up successfully. There's also the very real risk that the update will interfere with existing applications. This risk, fortunately, can be offset by extensively testing the update before applying it. Deciding not to apply a security update also has a cost: an increased risk of a security vulnerability being exploited.

Besides testing, you can offset the risk that an update will cause problems by having a plan to roll back the update. When evaluating an update, determine whether the release can be easily uninstalled if it causes a problem that isn't identified during testing. Functionality for uninstalling updates can vary from fully automated uninstall support, to manual uninstall procedures, to no uninstall. If an update cannot be uninstalled, your only option might be to restore the computer from a recent backup. Regardless of the uninstall method required for an update, ensure that you have a defined rollback plan in case the deployment doesn't match the success encountered in the test environment.

To be prepared for the worst, verify that you have recent backups of all computers that will be updated and that you are prepared to restore those systems if the update cannot be removed successfully. It's not likely that an update will cause your systems to fail completely and require them to be restored from backup, but it is a circumstance that you must be prepared to handle.

Choosing whether to apply an update is such a complicated, yet critical, decision that larger organizations should create a security committee that collectively determines which updates should be applied. The committee should consist of employees who are familiar with the update requirements of each different type of computer on your network. For example, if you have separate organizations that manage desktop and client computers, both organizations should have a representative on the committee. If separate individuals manage each of the Web, messaging, and infrastructure servers on your network, each person should have input into whether a particular update is applied. Ask members from your database teams, networking groups, and internal audit teams to play an active role—their experience and expertise can be an asset in determining risk. Depending on your needs, the committee can discuss each update as it is released, or it can meet on a weekly or biweekly basis.

If the committee determines that an update needs to be deployed, you then need to determine the urgency. In the event of an active attack, you must make every effort to apply the update immediately before your system is infected. If the attack is severe enough, it might even warrant removing vulnerable computers from the network until the update can be applied.

Speeding the Update Process

If it usually takes your organization more than a few days to deploy an update, create an accelerated process for critical updates. Use this process to speed or bypass time-consuming testing and approval processes. If a vulnerability is currently being exploited by a quickly spreading worm or virus, deploying the update immediately could save hundreds of hours of recovery time.

Retrieving Updates

After you decide to test and/or deploy an update, you must retrieve it from Microsoft. If you are using WSUS as your deployment mechanism, WSUS can download the update automatically. If you are deploying updates by using another mechanism, download the update from a trusted Microsoft server.

Testing Updates

After applying an update or group of updates to your test computers, test all applications and functionality. The amount of time and expense that you dedicate to testing the update should be determined by the potential damage that can be caused by a problematic update deployment. There are two primary ways you can test an update: in a test environment and in a pilot deployment. A test environment consists of a test lab or labs and includes test plans, which detail what you will test, and test cases, which describe how you will test each feature. Organizations that have the resources to test updates in a test environment should always do so because it will reduce the number of problems caused by update incompatibility with applications. Even if your organization does not have the resources to test critical updates and security updates, always test service packs before deploying them to production computers.

The test lab can be made up of a single lab or of several labs, each of which supports testing without presenting risk to your production environment. In the test lab, members of the testing team can verify their deployment design assumptions, discover deployment problems, and improve their understanding of the changes implemented by specific updates. Such activities reduce the risk of errors occurring during deployment and allow the members of the test team to rapidly resolve problems that might occur while deploying an update or after applying an update.

Many organizations divide their testing teams into two subteams: the design team and the deployment team. The design team collects information that is vital to the deployment process, identifies immediate and long-term testing needs, and proposes a test lab design (or recommends improvements to the existing test lab). The deployment team completes the process by implementing the design team's decisions and then testing new updates on an ongoing basis.

During the beginning of the lifetime of the update test environment, the deployment team will test the update deployment process to validate that the design is functional. Later, after your organization identifies an update to be deployed, the deployment will test the individual updates to ensure that all of the updates are compatible with the applications used in your environment.

An update test environment should have computers that represent each of the major computer roles in your organization, including desktop computers, mobile computers, and servers. If computers within each role have different operating systems, have each operating system available on either dedicated computers, a single computer with a multiboot configuration, or in a virtual desktop environment.

After you have a set of computers that represent each of the various types of computers in your organization, connect them to a private network. You will also need to connect test versions of your update infrastructure computers. For example, if you plan to deploy updates by using WSUS, connect a WSUS server to the lab network.

Load every application that users will use onto the lab computers and develop a procedure to test the functionality of each application. For example, to test the functionality of Internet Explorer, you can visit both the Microsoft Web site and an intranet Web site. Later, when testing updates, you will repeat this test. If one of the applications fails the test, the update you are currently testing might have caused a problem.

> ***NOTE*** **If you will be testing a large number of applications, identify ways to automate the testing of updates by using scripting.**

In addition to testing your implementation of an update, conducting a pilot deployment provides an opportunity to test your deployment plan and the deployment processes. It helps you to determine how much time is required to install the update as well as the personnel and tools needed to do so. It also provides an opportunity to train support staff and to gauge user reaction to the update process. For example, if a particular update takes an hour for a dial-up user to download, you might have to identify an alternative method for delivering the update to the user.

> ***NOTE*** **The more significant the update, the more important it is to use a pilot program. Service packs, in particular, require extensive testing both in and out of the lab.**

Besides testing the update yourself, subscribe to mailing lists and visit newsgroups frequented by your peers. People tend to report problems with updates to these forums before an official announcement is made by Microsoft. If you do discover a problem, report it to Microsoft. Historically, Microsoft has fixed and re-released security updates that have caused serious problems. On the other hand, Microsoft support might be able to suggest an alternative method for reducing or eliminating the vulnerability.

Installing Updates

After you are satisfied that you have sufficiently tested an update, you can deploy it to your production environment. During the installation process, be sure to have sufficient support staff to handle problems that might arise. Have a method in place to monitor the progress of the updates, and have an engineer ready to resolve any problems that occur in the update deployment mechanism. Notify network staff that an update deployment is taking place so that they are aware of the cause of the increased network utilization.

Removing Updates

Despite following proper planning and testing procedures, problems can arise when you deploy an update to production computers. Before you deploy updates, have a plan in place to roll back updates from one, many, or all of the target computers. The main steps for the rollback and redeployment of updates are as follows:

1. Stop the current deployment. Identify any steps necessary for deactivating release mechanisms used in your environment.
2. Identify and resolve any update deployment issues. Determine what is causing an update deployment to fail. The order in which updates are applied, the release mechanism used, and flaws in the update itself are all possible causes for a failed deployment.
3. Uninstall updates if necessary. Updates that introduce instabilities to your production environment should be removed if possible. For instructions, refer to the section titled "How to Remove Updates" earlier in this chapter.
4. Reactivate release mechanisms. After resolving update issues, reactivate the appropriate release mechanism to redeploy updates. Security bulletins issued by Microsoft will always indicate whether an update can be uninstalled. Because reverting computers to a previous state is not always possible, pay close attention to this detail before deploying an update that cannot be uninstalled.

When a simple uninstall process is not available for a security update, ensure that the necessary provisions are in place for reverting your critical computers back to their original states in the unlikely event that a security update deployment causes a computer to fail. These provisions might include having spare computers and data backup mechanisms in place so that a failed computer can be rebuilt quickly.

Auditing Updates

After you deploy an update, it is important to audit your work. Ideally, someone who is not responsible for deploying the update should perform the actual audit. This reduces the possibility that the person or group responsible for deploying the update would unintentionally overlook the same set of computers during both update deployment and auditing; it would also reduce the likelihood of someone deliberately covering up oversights or mistakes.

Auditing an update that resolves a security vulnerability can be done in one of two ways. The simplest way to audit is to use a tool, such as MBSA, to check for the presence of the update. This can also be done by checking the version of updated files and verifying that the version matches the version of the file included with the update.

Quarantine Control for Computers That Haven't Been Updated

You should require updates for remote computers connecting via dial-up and VPN solutions because they might miss your update and auditing. Windows 7 and Windows Server 2008 both support NAP, which you can use to restrict access to computers that do not meet specific security requirements, such as having the latest updates, and to distribute the updates to the client computer so that they can safely join the intranet. For more information about Network Access Protection, refer to Chapter 25. You can use NAP with a Windows Server 2008 infrastructure as described in *Windows Server 2008 Networking and Network Access Protection (NAP)* (Microsoft Press, 2008).

How Microsoft Distributes Updates

Microsoft continually works to reduce the risk of software vulnerabilities in its software, including Windows 7. This section describes the different types of updates released by Microsoft. It also describes the Microsoft product life cycle, which affects update management because Microsoft stops releasing security updates for a product at the end of its life cycle.

Security Updates

A security update is an update that the Microsoft Security Response Center (MSRC) releases to resolve a security vulnerability. Microsoft security updates are available for customers to download and are accompanied by two documents: a security bulletin and a Microsoft Knowledge Base article.

MORE INFO For more information about the MSRC, visit *http://www.microsoft.com/security/msrc/default.mspx*.

A Microsoft security bulletin notifies administrators of critical security issues and vulnerabilities and is associated with a security update that can be used to fix the vulnerability. Security bulletins generally provide detailed information about whom the bulletin concerns, the impact and severity of the vulnerability, and a recommended course of action for affected customers.

Security bulletins usually include the following pieces of information:

- **Title** The title of the security bulletin, in the format *MSyy-###*, where *yy* is the last two digits of the year and ### is the sequential bulletin number for that year.

- **Summary** Information about who should read the bulletin, the impact of the vulnerability and the software affected, the maximum severity rating, and the MSRC's recommendation on how to respond to the bulletin. The severity rating of a bulletin gauges the maximum risk posed by the vulnerability that the update fixes. This severity level can be Low, Moderate, Important, or Critical. The MSRC judges the severity of a vulnerability on behalf of the entire Microsoft customer base. The impact a vulnerability has on your organization might be more or less serious than this severity rating.
- **Executive summary** An overview of the individual vulnerabilities discussed in the security bulletin and their severity ratings. One security bulletin might address multiple, related vulnerabilities that are fixed with a single update.
- **Frequently asked questions** Discusses updates that are replaced, whether you can audit the presence of the update using MBSA or Configuration Manager 2007 R2, lifecycle information, and other relevant information.
- **Vulnerability details** The technical details of the vulnerabilities, a list of mitigating factors that might protect you from the vulnerability, and alternative workarounds that you can use to limit the risk if you cannot install the update immediately. One of the most important pieces of information in this section is whether there are known, active exploits that attackers can use to compromise computers that haven't been updated. If you are unable to install the update immediately, you should read this section carefully to understand the risk of managing a computer that hasn't been updated.
- **Security update information** Instructions on how to install the update and what files and configuration settings will be updated. Refer to this section if you need to deploy updated files manually or if you are configuring custom auditing to verify that the update has been applied to a computer.

> ***MORE INFO*** **If you are not familiar with the format of security bulletins, take some time to read current bulletins. You can browse and search bulletins at *http://www.microsoft.com/technet/security/current.aspx*.**

In addition to security bulletins, Microsoft also creates Knowledge Base articles about security vulnerabilities. Knowledge Base articles generally include more detailed information about the vulnerability and step-by-step instructions for updating affected computers.

From time to time, Microsoft releases security advisories. Security advisories are not associated with a security update. Instead, advisories communicate security guidance that might not be classified as a vulnerability to customers.

Update Rollups

At times, Microsoft has released a significant number of updates between service packs. It is cumbersome to install a large number of updates separately, so Microsoft releases an update rollup to reduce the labor involved in applying updates. An update rollup is a cumulative set of hotfixes, security updates, critical updates, and other updates all packaged together for easy deployment. An update rollup generally targets a specific area of a product, such as security, or a feature of a product, such as IIS. Update rollups are always released with a Knowledge Base article that describes the rollup in detail.

Update rollups receive more testing from Microsoft than individual security updates but less testing than service packs. In addition, because update rollups consist of updates that have been released previously and are being run by many other Microsoft customers, it is more likely that any incompatibilities associated with the update rollup have already been discovered. Therefore, the risk associated with deploying update rollups is typically lower overall than the risk of deploying security updates, despite the fact that rollups affect more code. However, you still need to test update rollups with critical applications before deploying them.

Service Packs

A service pack is a cumulative set of all of the updates that have been created for a Microsoft product. A service pack also includes fixes for other problems that have been found by Microsoft since the release of the product. In addition, a service pack can contain customer-requested design changes or features. Like security updates, service packs are available for download and are accompanied by Knowledge Base articles.

The chief difference between service packs and other types of updates is that service packs are strategic deliveries, whereas updates are tactical. That is, service packs are carefully planned and managed—the goal is to deliver a well-tested, comprehensive set of fixes that is suitable for use on any computer. In contrast, security updates are developed on an as-needed basis to combat specific problems that require an immediate response.

> ***NOTE*** **Service packs undergo extensive regression testing that Microsoft does not perform for other types of updates. However, because they can make significant changes to the operating system and add new features, they still require extensive testing within your environment.**

Microsoft does not release a service pack until it meets the same quality standards as the product itself. Service packs are constantly tested as they are built, undergoing weeks or months of rigorous final testing that includes testing in conjunction with hundreds or thousands of non-Microsoft products. Service packs also undergo a beta phase, during which customers participate in the testing. If the testing reveals bugs, Microsoft will delay the release of the service pack.

Even though Microsoft tests service packs extensively, they frequently have known application incompatibilities. However, they are less likely to have unknown application incompatibilities. It is critical that you review the service pack release notes to determine how the service pack might affect your applications.

Because service packs can make substantial changes to Windows 7, thorough testing and a staged deployment are essential. After Microsoft releases a service pack for beta, begin testing it in your environment. Specifically, test all applications, desktop configurations, and network connectivity scenarios. If you discover problems, work with Microsoft to identify the problem further so that Microsoft can resolve the issues before the service pack is released. After the service pack is released, you need to test the production service pack carefully before deploying it.

While testing a newly released service pack, stay in touch with the IT community to understand the experiences of organizations that deploy the service pack before you. Their experiences can be valuable for identifying potential problems and refining your deployment process to avoid delays and incompatibilities. Microsoft security updates can be applied to systems with the current or previous service pack so you can continue with your usual Microsoft update process until after you have deployed the new service pack.

> ***MORE INFO*** **For more information about the Microsoft TechNet IT Professional Community, visit *http://www.microsoft.com/technet/community/*.**

After testing, you should use staged deployments with service packs, just as you would for any major change. With a staged deployment, you install the service pack on a limited number of computers first. Then, you wait days or weeks for users to discover problems with the service pack. If a problem is discovered, you should be prepared to roll back the service pack by uninstalling it. Work to resolve all problems before distributing the service pack to a wider audience.

Microsoft Product Life Cycles

Every product has a life cycle, and, at the end of the product life cycle, Microsoft stops providing updates. However, this doesn't mean that no new vulnerabilities will be discovered in the product. To keep your network protected from the latest vulnerabilities, you will need to upgrade to a more recent operating system.

Microsoft offers a minimum of five years of mainstream support from the date of a product's general availability. When mainstream support ends, businesses have the option to purchase two years of extended support. In addition, online self-help support, such as the Knowledge Base, will still be available.

Security updates will be available through the end of the extended support phase at no additional cost for most products. You do not have to have an extended support contract to receive security updates during the extended support phase. For more information on the Windows 7 product life cycle, see *http://support.microsoft.com/gp/lifeselectwin*. When planning future operating system upgrades, you must keep the product life cycle in mind, particularly the period during which security updates will be released.

You have to stay reasonably current on updates to continue to receive Microsoft support because Microsoft provides support only for the current service pack and the one that immediately precedes it. This support policy allows you to receive existing hotfixes or to request new hotfixes for the currently shipping service pack, the service pack immediately preceding the current one, or both during the mainstream phase.

Summary

Networks and the Internet are constantly changing. In particular, network security threats continue to evolve, and new threats are introduced daily. Therefore, all software must change constantly to maintain high levels of security and reliability.

Microsoft provides tools for managing Windows 7 software updates for home users, small organizations, and large enterprises. Regardless of the organization, the Windows Update client in Windows 7 is responsible for downloading, sharing, and installing updates. Small organizations can download updates directly from Microsoft to a Windows 7 computer, which will then share the update with other computers on the same LAN. Larger organizations, as well as organizations that must test updates prior to installation, can use WSUS to identify, test, and distribute updates. Combined with AD DS Group Policy settings, you can manage updates centrally for an entire organization.

Additional Resources

These resources contain additional information and tools related to this chapter.

Related Information

- The Microsoft Update Management Web site at *http://technet.microsoft.com/updatemanagement.*
- See the MBSA 2.1 Web site at *https://www.microsoft.com/mbsa* for more information and to download MBSA.
- "MBSA 2.0 Scripting Samples" at *http://www.microsoft.com/downloads/details.aspx?familyid=3B64AC19-3C9E-480E-B0B3-6B87F2EE9042* includes examples of how to create complex auditing scripts using MBSA.
- The Configuration Manager 2007 R2 Web site at *https://www.microsoft.com/sccm* includes more information about using Configuration Manager 2007 R2.
- "Microsoft Update Product Team Blog" at *http://blogs.technet.com/mu* provides the latest Microsoft Update news direct from the Microsoft Update product team.
- "WSUS Product Team Blog" at *http://blogs.technet.com/wsus/* has the latest WSUS news.

On the Companion Media

- ConfigureSoftwareUpdatesSchedule.ps1
- DownloadAndInstallMicrosoftUpdate.ps1
- Get-MicrosoftUpdates.ps1
- Get-MissingSoftwareUpdates.ps1
- ScanForSpecificUpdate.ps1
- TroubleshootWindowsUpdate.ps1
- UninstallMicrosoftUpdate.ps1

CHAPTER 24

Managing Client Protection

Networked client computers are constantly under attack. In the past, repairing computers compromised by malware was a significant cost to IT departments. The Windows 7 operating system strives to reduce this cost by using a combination of technologies—including User Account Control (UAC), Windows AppLocker, and Windows Defender. Additionally, Microsoft offers Microsoft Forefront separately from Windows 7 to provide better manageability of client security.

Understanding the Risk of Malware

Malware (as described in Chapter 2, "Security in Windows 7") is commonly spread in several different ways:

- **Included with legitimate software** Malware is often bundled with legitimate software. For example, a peer-to-peer file transfer application might include potentially unwanted software that displays advertisements on a user's computer. Sometimes, the installation tool might make the user aware of the malware (although users often do not understand the most serious compromises, such as degraded performance and compromised privacy). Other times, the fact that unwanted software is being installed might be hidden from the user (an event known as a *non-consensual installation*). Windows Defender, as described later in this chapter, can help detect both the legitimate software that is likely to be bundled and the potentially unwanted software bundled with it, and it will notify the user about the software running on their system. Additionally, when UAC is active, standard user accounts will not have sufficient privileges to install most dangerous applications.

- **Social engineering** Users are often tricked into installing malware. A common technique is to attach a malware installer to an e-mail and provide instructions for installing the attached software in the e-mail. For example, the e-mail might appear to come from a valid contact and indicate that the attachment is an important security update. E-mail clients such as Microsoft Office Outlook now prevent the user from running executable attachments. Modern social engineering attacks abuse e-mail, instant messages, social networking, or peer-to-peer networks to instruct users to visit a Web site that installs the malware, either with or without the user's knowledge. The most effective way to limit the impact of social engineering attacks is to train users not to install software from untrustworthy sources and not to visit untrusted Web sites. Additionally, UAC reduces the user's ability to install software, AppLocker can prevent users from running untrusted software, and Windows Defender makes users more aware of when potentially unwanted software is being installed. For more information about social engineering, read "Behavioral Modeling of Social Engineering–Based Malicious Software" at *http://www.microsoft.com/downloads/details.aspx?FamilyID=e0f27260-58da-40db-8785-689cf6a05c73*.

> ***NOTE*** **Windows XP Service Pack 2 (SP2), Windows Vista, and Windows 7 support using Group Policy settings to configure attachment behavior. The relevant Group Policy settings are located in User Configuration\Administrative Templates\Windows Components\Attachment Manager.**

- **Exploiting browser vulnerabilities** Some malware has been known to install itself without the user's knowledge or consent when the user visits a Web site. To accomplish this, the malware needs to exploit a security vulnerability in the browser or a browser add-on to start a process with the user's or system's privileges, and then use those privileges to install the malware. The risk of this type of exploit is significantly reduced by Windows Internet Explorer Protected Mode in Windows Vista and Windows 7. Additionally, the new Internet Explorer 8 feature, SmartScreen, can warn users before they visit a malicious site. For more information about Internet Explorer, read Chapter 20, "Managing Windows Internet Explorer."
- **Exploiting operating system vulnerabilities** Some malware might install itself by exploiting operating system vulnerabilities. For example, many worms infect computers by exploiting a network service to start a process on the computer and then install the malware. The risks of this type of exploit are reduced by UAC, explained in this chapter, and Windows Service Hardening, described in Chapter 26, "Configuring Windows Firewall and IPsec."

User Account Control

Most administrators know that users should log on to their computers using accounts that are members of the Users group, but not the Administrators group. By limiting your user account's privileges, you also limit the privileges of any applications that you start—including software installed without full consent. Therefore, if you can't add a startup application, neither can a malicious process that you accidentally start.

With versions of Windows prior to Windows Vista, however, not being a member of the Administrators group could be very difficult, for a few reasons:

- Many applications would run only with administrative privileges.
- Running applications with elevated privileges required users to either right-click the icon and then click Run As or create a custom shortcut, which is inconvenient, requires training, and requires that the user has a local administrator account (largely defeating the purpose of limiting privileges).
- Many common operating system tasks, such as changing the time zone or adding a printer, required administrative privileges.

UAC is a feature of Windows Vista and Windows 7 that improves client security by making it much easier to use accounts without administrative privileges. At a high level, UAC offers the following benefits:

- **Most applications can now run without administrative privileges** Applications created for Windows Vista or Windows 7 should be designed to not require administrator credentials. Additionally, UAC virtualizes commonly accessed file and registry locations to provide backward compatibility for applications created for earlier versions of Windows that still require administrator credentials. For example, if an application attempts to write to a protected portion of the registry that will affect the entire computer, UAC virtualization will redirect the write attempt to a nonprotected area of the user registry that will affect only that single application.
- **Applications that require administrative privileges automatically prompt the user for administrator credentials** For example, if a standard user attempts to open the Computer Management console, a User Account Control dialog box appears and prompts for administrator credentials, as shown in Figure 24-1. If the current account has administrator credentials, the dialog box prompts to confirm the action before granting the process administrative privileges.

FIGURE 24-1 UAC prompts standard users for administrator credentials when necessary.

- **Users no longer require administrative privileges for common tasks** Windows Vista and Windows 7 have been improved so that users can make common types of configuration changes without administrator credentials. For example, in earlier versions of Windows, users needed administrator credentials to change the time zone. In Windows Vista and Windows 7, any user can change the time zone, which is important for users who travel. Changing the system time, which has the potential to be malicious, still requires administrator credentials, however.
- **Operating system features display an icon when administrator credentials are required** In earlier versions of Windows, users were often surprised when an aspect of the operating system required more privileges than they had. For example, users might attempt to adjust the date and time, only to see a dialog box informing them that they lack necessary privileges. In Windows Vista and Windows 7, any user can open the Date And Time properties dialog box. However, users need to click a button to change the time (which requires administrative privileges), and that button has a shield icon indicating that administrative privileges are required. Users will come to recognize this visual cue and not be surprised when they are prompted for credentials.
- **If you log on with administrative privileges, Windows Vista and Windows 7 will still run applications using standard user privileges by default** Most users should log on with only standard user credentials. If users do log on with an account that has Administrator privileges, however, UAC will still start all processes with only user privileges. Before a process can gain administrator privileges, the user must confirm the additional rights using a UAC prompt.

Table 24-1 illustrates the key differences in the behavior of Windows 7 with UAC installed when compared to Windows XP.

TABLE 24-1 Behavior Changes in Windows 7 with UAC When Compared to Windows XP

WINDOWS XP	WINDOWS 7 WITH UAC
When logged on as a standard user, administrators could run administrative tools by right-clicking the tool's icon, clicking Run As, and then providing administrative credentials.	Standard users open administrative tools without right-clicking. UAC then prompts the user for administrator credentials. All users can still explicitly start an application with administrator credentials by right-clicking, but it is rarely necessary.
Using a standard user account could be a nuisance, especially for technical or mobile users.	Standard accounts can perform many tasks that previously required elevation, and Windows 7 prompts users for administrator credentials when required.
When a user was logged on as a standard user, an application that needed to change a file or setting in a protected location would fail.	When a user is logged on as a standard user, UAC provides virtualization for important parts of the system, allowing the application to run successfully while protecting the operating system integrity.
If a specific Windows feature required administrative privileges, the entire tool required administrative privileges.	Windows 7 displays the UAC shield on buttons to warn users that the feature requires elevated privileges.
When a user was logged on as an administrator, all applications ran with administrative privileges.	When a user is logged on as an administrator, all applications run with standard user privileges. UAC confirms elevated privileges before starting a non-Windows tool that requires administrative privileges. Windows features that require administrative privileges automatically receive elevated privileges without prompting the user.

As described in Chapter 2, Windows 7 can reduce the number of UAC prompts when compared to Windows Vista. Instead of requiring multiple prompts for a file operation that performs multiple administrative tasks, all prompts are merged into a single prompt. Similarly, prompts from Internet Explorer are merged. When logged on as an administrator, you will no longer be prompted when Windows functions require administrator credentials. Additionally, there are now four levels of UAC notifications to choose from, as discussed later in the chapter.

The sections that follow describe UAC behavior in more detail.

UAC for Standard Users

Microsoft made many changes to the operating system so that standard users could perform almost any day-to-day task. Tasks that standard users can do without receiving a UAC prompt that requires administrative privileges in Windows XP include:

- Viewing the system clock and calendar
- Changing the time zone
- Connecting to wired or wireless networks
- Connecting to virtual private networks (VPNs)
- Changing display settings and the desktop background
- Changing their own passwords
- Installing critical Windows updates
- Installing device drivers that have been staged
- Scheduling tasks
- Adding printers and other devices that have the required drivers installed on the computer or that are allowed by an administrator in Group Policy
- Installing ActiveX Controls from sites approved by an administrator
- Playing or burning CDs and DVDs (configurable with Group Policy settings)
- Connecting to another computer with Remote Desktop
- Configuring battery power options on mobile computers
- Configuring accessibility settings
- Configuring and using synchronization with a mobile device
- Connecting and configuring a Bluetooth device
- Restoring backed-up files from the same user

Additionally, disk defragmentation is scheduled to happen automatically in the background, so users do not need privileges to initiate a defragmentation manually.

Some of the common tasks standard users *cannot* do include:

- Installing and uninstalling applications
- Installing device drivers that have not been staged
- Installing noncritical Windows updates
- Changing Windows Firewall settings, including enabling exceptions
- Configuring Remote Desktop access
- Restoring system files from a backup
- Installing ActiveX controls from sites not approved by an administrator

NOTE To install ActiveX controls in Internet Explorer, start Internet Explorer by right-clicking the icon and then clicking Run As Administrator. After installing the ActiveX control, close Internet Explorer and reopen it using standard privileges. After it is installed, the ActiveX control will be available to standard users.

The Power Users group still exists in Windows Vista and Windows 7. However, Windows Vista and Windows 7 remove the elevated privileges. Therefore, you should make users members of the Users group and not use the Power Users group at all. To use the Power Users group on Windows 7, you must change the default permissions on system folders and the registry to grant Power Users group permissions equivalent to Windows XP.

DIRECT FROM THE SOURCE

Bypassing UAC

Aaron Margosis, Senior Consultant
Microsoft Consulting Services

The frequently asked question, "Why can't I bypass the UAC prompt?" is often accompanied by statements like one or more of the following:

- "We want our application to run elevated automatically without prompting the user."
- "I don't get why I can't authorize an application once and be done with it."
- "UNIX has *setuid root*, which lets you run privileged programs securely."

The designers of UAC expressly decided not to incorporate functionality like setuid/suid or sudo found in UNIX and Mac OS X. I think they made the right decision.

As I'm sure everyone knows, large parts of the Windows ecosystem have a long legacy of assuming that the user has administrative permissions, and consequently a lot of programs work correctly only when they are run that way. As computer security has become increasingly important, breaking that cycle with Windows Vista became absolutely imperative. Indeed, the primary purpose of the technologies that comprise UAC is to enable standard user privileges to be the default for Windows, encouraging software developers to create applications that do not require administrative privileges.

If it were possible to mark an application to run with silently elevated privileges, what would become of all the existing applications that require administrative privileges? They'd all be marked to elevate silently. How would future software for Windows be written? To elevate silently. Few developers would fix their applications, and user applications would continue to require and run with full administrative permissions unnecessarily.

"Well, so what? We're only talking about applications I approved!" OK, let's say that's true, but how do you ensure that malware that has infected the user's session cannot drive an application programmatically to take over the system? Ensuring strict behavioral boundaries for complex software running with elevated privileges is incredibly difficult, and ensuring that it is free of exploitable design and implementation bugs is far beyond the capabilities of software engineering today. The complexity and risk compounds when you consider how many applications have extensibility points that load code that you or your IT administrator may not be aware of, or that can load code or consume data from user-writable areas with minimal if any validation.

We expect that in ordinary day-to-day usage, users should rarely, if ever, see elevation prompts, because most should rarely, if ever, have to perform administrative tasks—and never in a well-managed enterprise. Elevation prompts are to be expected when setting up a new system or installing new software. Beyond that, they should be infrequent enough that they catch your attention when they occur, and not simply trigger a reflexive approval response. This will increasingly be the case as more software conforms to least-privilege norms, and as improvements in the Windows user experience further reduces prompting.

Excerpted from *http://blogs.msdn.com/windowsvistasecurity/archive/2007/08/09/faq-why-can-t-i-bypass-the-uac-prompt.aspx.*

UAC for Administrators

UAC uses Admin Approval Mode to help protect administrators from malicious and potentially unwanted software. When an administrator logs on, Windows 7 generates two access tokens:

- **Standard user access token** This token is used to start the desktop (Explorer.exe). Because the desktop is the parent process for all user-initiated processes, any applications the user launches also use the standard user access token, which does not have privileges to install software or make important system changes.
- **Full administrator access token** This token has almost unlimited privileges to the local computer. This token is used only after the user confirms a UAC prompt.

NOTE As described in the section titled "How to Configure User Account Control" later in this chapter, you can change the default behavior to suit your needs.

To test this, open two command prompts: one with standard privileges and one with administrative privileges. In each command prompt, run the command **whoami /all**. The command prompt with administrative privileges will show a membership in the Administrators group. The standard command prompt will not show that group membership.

If the administrator attempts to start an application that requires administrative rights (as identified in the application's manifest, described later), UAC prompts the administrator to grant additional rights using the consent prompt, as shown in Figure 24-2. If the user chooses to grant elevated privileges to an application, the Application Information service creates the new process using the full administrator access token. The elevated privileges will also apply to any child processes that the application launches. Parent and child processes must have the same integrity level. For more information about integrity levels, read Chapter 20.

FIGURE 24-2 By default, Admin Approval Mode prompts administrators to confirm elevated privileges.

> ***NOTE*** **The Application Information service must be running to start processes with elevated privileges.**

By default, Windows 7 silently elevates privileges for Windows features that require administrator credentials when an administrator is logged on. Therefore, you can start the Computer Management console without responding to a UAC prompt if you are a member of the Administrators group. If you attempt to start a non-Windows application or if you manually start a Windows feature with administrator credentials that is not manifested for auto-elevation, such as Paint or a command prompt, you will still receive a UAC prompt.

Command prompts require special consideration, because UAC will not prompt you to elevate privileges if you attempt to run a command that requires administrative rights. To run a command with administrative rights, right-click Command Prompt on the Start menu and then click Run As Administrator. The command prompt that opens will include Administrator in the title, helping you identify the window on your taskbar.

Admin Approval Mode does not apply to the built-in Administrator account. To protect this account from attack, the built-in Administrator account is disabled by default. However, Microsoft Deployment Toolkit 2010 enables the Administrator account for use during the deployment process. For more information, refer to Chapter 3, "Deployment Platform."

UAC User Interface

Windows 7 uses a shield icon to indicate which features of an application require elevated rights. For example, standard users can run Task Manager (shown in Figure 24-3), but they will need administrator credentials if they click the Resource Monitor button. The shield icon serves to warn users before they attempt to access a feature for which they might not have sufficient privileges.

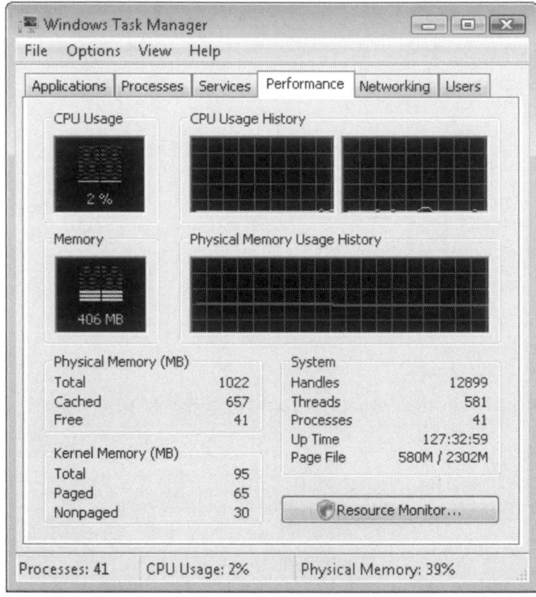

FIGURE 24-3 The shield icon on the Resource Monitor button indicates that this function requires elevation.

By default, the consent or credential prompt appears on the *secure desktop*. The secure desktop freezes and darkens the entire desktop except for the UAC prompt, making it very difficult for malware to trick you into providing consent.

HOW IT WORKS

Secure Desktop

The secure desktop actually makes a bitmap copy of the current screen and then alpha-blends it to darken it. To prove that it's a bitmap copy, open Task Manager, click the Performance tab, and notice how the CPU Usage History chart updates. Then, attempt to open Computer Manager. When the UAC prompt appears, Task Manager stops updating. Task Manager continues to draw the graph in the background, even though it's not visible—this will be apparent if you wait a few seconds and then close the UAC prompt.

How Windows Determines Whether an Application Needs Administrative Privileges

Windows examines several aspects of an executable to determine whether it should display a UAC prompt before running the application:

- **Application properties** Users can select the Run As Administrator check box for executable files.
- **Application manifest** A description of the application provided by the application developer, which can require Windows 7 to run the program as an administrator.
- **Application heuristics** Aspects of the application that might indicate it requires administrative privileges, such as being named Setup.exe.

The sections that follow describe each of these aspects and show you how to configure applications so that they always require elevated privileges. This can be important when an application does not work properly without elevated privileges but UAC does not prompt the user automatically for credentials.

How to Control UAC Using Application Properties

If the application does not run automatically with administrator credentials, you can right-click the application and then click Run As Administrator. If you deploy an application to users, however, you should configure the application to prompt the user automatically if it does not run automatically with administrator credentials. To mark an application to always run with administrator credentials, follow these steps:

1. Log on using administrator credentials but do not use the built-in Administrator account.
2. Right-click the application and then click Properties.
3. Click the Compatibility tab. If you want other users on the same computer to run the application with administrative privileges, click Change Settings For All Users.

4. Under Privilege Level, select the Run This Program As An Administrator check box, as shown in Figure 24-4. Click OK. If the check box is not available, it means that the application is blocked from always running elevated, the application does not require administrator credentials to run, the application is part of the current version of Windows 7, or you are not logged on to the computer as an administrator.

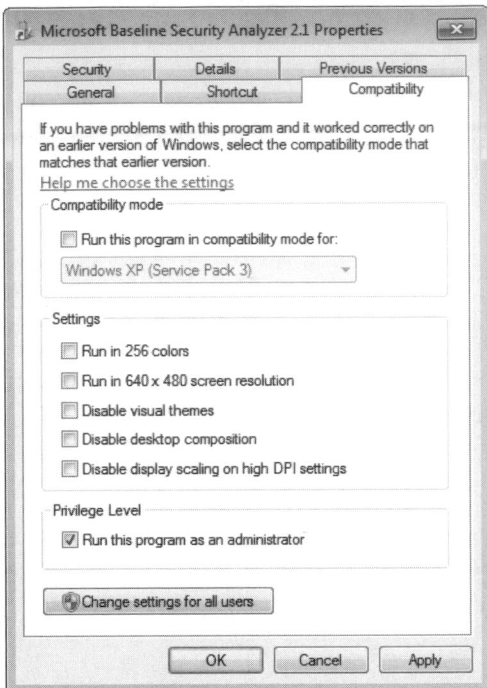

FIGURE 24-4 You can mark an application to always run with administrator credentials.

You need to mark only applications that require administrator credentials but do not cause UAC to automatically prompt the user. You cannot set a privilege level for Windows features, such as the command prompt. Instead, you should always right-click them and then click Run As Administrator. Alternatively, you can create a new shortcut to the application. Then, view the properties of the shortcut, click the Shortcut tab, click the Advanced button, and then select the Run As Administrator check box.

How UAC Examines the Application Manifest

For applications to receive a Certified For Windows Vista or Certified For Windows 7 logo, they must include an embedded *requested execution level manifest* that specifies the privileges required. The privilege level is one of the following:

- **asInvoker or RunAsInvoker** The application runs using the standard user privileges and will not initiate a UAC prompt.

- **highestAvailable or RunAsHighest** The application requests privileges higher than standard users and generates a UAC prompt. However, if the user does not provide additional credentials, the application will run anyway, using standard privileges. This is useful for applications that can adjust to either higher or lower privilege levels, or for applications that might need more privileges than a standard user, but fewer than a full administrator. For example, backup applications typically need the user to be a member of the Backup Operators group but do not require the user to be a member of the Administrators group.
- **requireAdministrator or RunAsAdmin** The application requires administrative privileges, generating a UAC prompt. The application will not run with standard privileges.

> ***NOTE*** **To add a manifest to existing applications, use the Application Compatibility Toolkit (ACT), which you can download at *http://go.microsoft.com/fwlink/?LinkId=23302*. The ACT also includes the Microsoft Standard User Analyzer tool, which allows you to diagnose issues that would prevent a program from running properly as a standard user. For more information about application compatibility, read Chapter 8, "Deploying Applications."**

UAC Heuristics

If you run an application setup file, UAC will prompt you for administrator credentials. This makes sense because most installation routines require elevated privileges. However, installers created before Windows Vista do not include a manifest, so Windows Vista and Windows 7 have to detect heuristically which executables are setup files. By contrast, 64-bit executables always have a requested execution manifest.

To do this, Windows examines 32-bit executables without a requested execution level manifest that would be run with standard privileges. If the executable meets those requirements and has a filename or metadata that includes keywords such as *install*, *setup*, or *update* (or several other indicators that it might be an installer), UAC prompts for elevated privileges before running the file. If UAC does not prompt you for administrator credentials for an install, right-click the setup file and then click Run As Administrator. Without administrative privileges, most installations will fail.

UAC Virtualization

By default, UAC virtualizes requests for protected resources to provide compatibility with applications not developed for UAC. This is important because many applications written for Windows XP and earlier operating systems assume that the user has administrative privileges and attempt to write to protected resources such as the Program Files or System folders.

UAC virtualization redirects requests for the following resources to safer, user-specific locations:

- %Program Files%

- %WinDir%
- %WinDir%\System32
- HKEY_LOCAL_MACHINE\Software

When a user process attempts to add a file to a protected folder, UAC redirects the request to the \AppData\Local\VirtualStore\ folder in the user's profile. For example, if a user named MyUser runs an application that stores a log file at C:\Program Files\MyApps\Logs\Log.txt, the file write attempt will succeed. However, UAC will actually store the file at C:\Users\MyUser\AppData\Local\VirtualStore\Program Files\MyApps\Logs\Log.txt. The application will be able to access the file at C:\Program Files\MyApps\Logs\Log.txt, but the user will need to browse to her profile to access the file directly, because virtualization affects only the application process itself. In other words, if the user browses to open the log file from within the application, it will appear to be under %Program Files%. If the user browses to open the log file using a Windows Explorer window, it will be under her profile.

The first time an application makes a change to a virtualized resource, Windows copies the folder or registry key to the location within the user's profile. Then, the change is made to the user's copy of that resource.

UAC virtualization is designed to allow already-installed applications to run successfully with standard user privileges, even if they store temporary files or logs in a protected folder. UAC virtualization does not allow users to install applications that make changes to these resources; users will still need to provide administrator credentials to do the installation.

When an executable has a requested execution level manifest, Windows automatically disables UAC virtualization. Therefore, virtualization should never be a factor for applications designed for Windows Vista or Windows 7. Native 64-bit applications are required to be UAC aware and to write data into the correct locations and thus are not affected. Virtualization also does not affect applications that administrators run with elevated privileges.

If you plan to run applications that would support virtualization, and you specifically want to prevent UAC from virtualizing requests from the application, you can disable virtualization by using the ACT to mark the application. Setting the NoVirtualization marking makes applications easier to debug (because you don't have to worry about file and registry requests being redirected), and it reduces the attack surface by making it more difficult for malware to infect an application (because that application's files would not be moved into the relatively unprotected user profile).

UAC and Startup Programs

By default, UAC blocks startup applications located in the Startup folder or identified in the Run registry key that require elevated privileges for both standard and administrative users. It would simply be too annoying to have multiple UAC prompts when logging on, and forcing users to confirm the prompts would require them to blindly elevate processes they did not explicitly start—a bad security practice. As an administrator, you should ensure that no startup programs require elevated privileges.

Startup applications started from the RunOnce registry key or specified in a Group Policy setting are unaffected by this feature; UAC will still prompt the user for administrator credentials. This allows applications that must make changes after restarting the computer to complete installation successfully.

Compatibility Problems with UAC

For applications to receive the Certified For Windows Vista or Certified For Windows 7 logo, the application must be designed to work well for standard users unless the tool is specifically intended for use by administrators. However, many applications were developed prior to Windows Vista and will not work correctly with UAC enabled. These might include some older antispyware, antivirus, firewall, CD/DVD-authoring, disk-defragmentation, and video-editing tools designed for Windows XP or earlier versions of Windows.

Typically, most features of an application will work correctly with UAC enabled, but specific features might fail. You have several ways to work around this:

- **Run the application with administrator credentials** As described in the section titled "How to Control UAC Using Application Properties" earlier in this chapter, you can specify that an application always requires administrator credentials.
- **Modify permissions on the computer** If an application requires access to a protected resource, you can change the permissions on that resource so that standard users have the necessary privileges. Instructions on how to isolate the protected resources are provided later in this section.
- **Run Windows XP (or an earlier version of Windows) in a virtual machine** If the application fails with administrative privileges or you do not want to grant the application administrative privileges to your computer, you can run the application within a virtual machine. Virtual machines provide an operating system within a sandbox environment, allowing you to run applications within Windows XP without requiring a separate computer. You can maximize virtual machines so that they display full screen, providing a similar experience to running the operating system natively. Virtual machines perform slightly slower than applications that run natively within Windows, however. Windows 7 Professional, Enterprise, and Ultimate operating systems include Windows Virtual PC and the Windows XP Mode environment. For more information about virtual machines, read Chapter 5, "Testing Application Compatibility."
- **Disable UAC** You can disable UAC to bypass most application compatibility problems related to the permission changes in Windows Vista. However, this increases the security risks of client computers when running any application, and therefore is not recommended. To disable UAC, read the section titled "How to Configure User Account Control" later in this chapter.

To isolate the protected resources accessed by an application, follow these steps:

1. On a computer running Windows 7 with UAC enabled, download and install the Microsoft Application Verifier from *http://www.microsoft.com/downloads/details.aspx?FamilyID=C4A25AB9-649D-4A1B-B4A7-C9D8B095DF18&displaylang=en*.
2. On the same computer, install the ACT, which you can download at *http://go.microsoft.com/fwlink/?LinkId=23302*.
3. Start the Standard User Analyzer (which is installed with the ACT). On the App Info tab, click Browse and then select the application's executable file.
4. Click Launch and then respond to any UAC prompts that appear. The Standard User Analyzer will start the application. Use the application, especially any aspects that might require elevated privileges, and then close the application.
5. Click the View menu and select Detailed Information.
6. Wait a few moments for the Standard User Analyzer to examine the application log file, as shown in Figure 24-5. Browse the different tabs to examine any errors. Errors indicate that the application attempted to perform an action that would have failed if it were not run with administrative privileges.

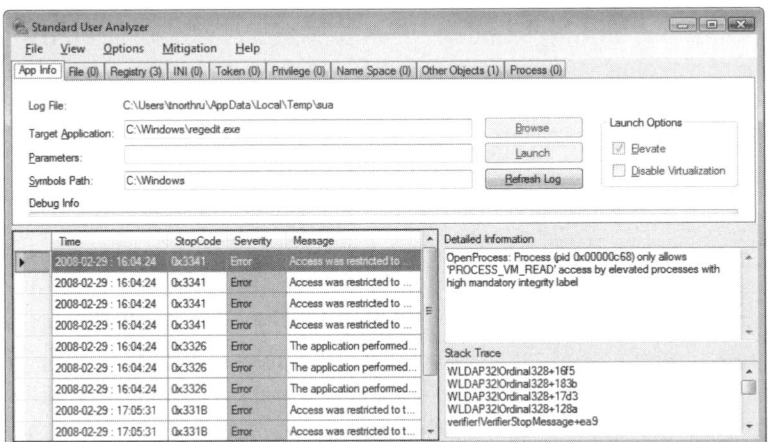

FIGURE 24-5 The Standard User Analyzer tool shows exactly which elevated privileges an application requires.

On the File tab and the Registry tab (shown in Figure 24-6), notice the Work With Virtualization column. If the entry in that column is Yes, that particular error will not cause a problem as long as UAC virtualization is enabled. If UAC virtualization is disabled, the error will still occur. If the entry in the column is No, it will always be a problem unless the application is run as an administrator.

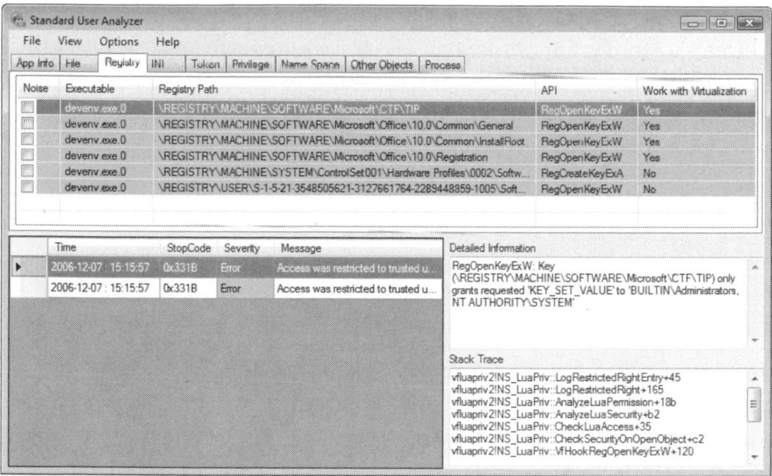

FIGURE 24-6 The Standard User Analyzer tool indicates which problems can be negated by UAC virtualization.

How to Configure UAC

You can use Group Policy settings to configure UAC behavior on targeted computers. Additionally, you can disable UAC by using Control Panel or Msconfig.exe or by editing registry settings directly. The sections that follow describe each of these techniques in more detail.

Group Policy Settings

You can configure UAC using local or Active Directory Domain Services (AD DS) Group Policy settings located in the following node:

Computer Configuration\Policies\Windows Settings\Security Settings\Local Policies\Security Options

You can configure the following settings:

- **User Account Control: Behavior Of The Elevation Prompt For Administrators In Admin Approval Mode** By default, this setting is set to Prompt For Consent For Non-Windows Binaries, which causes the UAC prompt to appear any time an application needs more than standard user privileges. Change this setting to Prompt For Credentials to cause Admin Approval Mode UAC prompts to behave like prompts for standard users, requiring the user to type an administrative password instead of simply clicking Continue. Change this setting to Elevate Without Prompting to provide administrative privileges automatically, effectively disabling UAC for administrative accounts. Choosing Elevate Without Prompting significantly reduces the security protection provided by Windows 7 and might allow malicious software to install itself or make changes to the system without the administrator's knowledge.

- **User Account Control: Behavior Of The Elevation Prompt For Standard Users** By default, this setting is Prompt For Credentials in workgroup environments and Automatically Deny Elevation Requests in domain environments. Prompt For Credentials causes UAC to prompt the user to enter an administrative user name and password. You can change this to Automatically Deny Elevation Requests to disable the UAC prompt. Disabling the prompt can improve security; however, the user might experience application failures because of denied privileges. If users do not have access to administrator credentials, you should disable the elevation prompt, because the user would not be able to provide credentials anyway. If you do not disable the prompt, users are likely to call the Support Center to ask for administrator credentials.
- **User Account Control: Admin Approval Mode For The Built-in Administrator Account** This policy applies only to the built-in Administrator account and not to other accounts that are members of the local Administrators group. When you enable this policy setting, the built-in Administrator account has UAC Admin Approval Mode enabled, just like other administrative accounts. When you disable the setting, the built-in Administrator account behaves just like it does in Windows XP, and all processes run using administrative privileges. This setting is disabled by default.
- **User Account Control: Detect Application Installations And Prompt For Elevation** By default, this setting is enabled in workgroup environments and disabled in domain environments. When enabled, UAC will prompt for administrator credentials when the user attempts to install an application that makes changes to protected aspects of the system. When disabled, the prompt won't appear. Domain environments that use delegated installation technologies such as Group Policy Software Installation (GPSI) or Microsoft Systems Management Server (SMS) can disable this feature safely because installation processes can escalate privileges automatically without user intervention.
- **User Account Control: Only Elevate Executables That Are Signed And Validated** If your environment requires all applications to be signed and validated with a trusted certificate, including internally developed applications, you can enable this policy to greatly increase security in your organization. When this policy is enabled, Windows Vista will refuse to run any executable that isn't signed with a trusted certificate, such as a certificate generated by an internal Public Key Infrastructure (PKI). All software with the Certified For Windows Vista logo must be signed with an Authenticode certificate, although you might have to configure your domain PKI to trust the certificate. This setting is disabled by default, which allows users to run any executable, including potentially malicious software.
- **User Account Control: Allow UIAccess Applications to Prompt For Elevation Without Using The Secure Desktop** This setting controls whether User Interface Accessibility (UIAccess) programs can automatically disable the secure desktop. By default, this setting is disabled. When enabled, UIAccess applications (such as Remote Assistance) automatically disable the secure desktop for elevation prompts. Disabling the secure desktop causes elevation prompts to appear in the standard desktop.

- **User Account Control: Only Elevate UIAccess Applications That Are Installed In Secure Locations** This setting, which is enabled by default, causes Windows Vista to grant user interface access (required for opening windows and doing almost anything useful) to only those applications started from Program Files, from \Windows\System32\, or from a subdirectory. Enabling this setting effectively prevents non-administrators from downloading and running an application because non-administrators won't have the privileges necessary to copy an executable file to one of those folders.
- **User Account Control: Run All Administrators In Admin Approval Mode** This setting, enabled by default, causes all accounts with administrator privileges *except* for the local Administrator account to use Admin Approval Mode. If you disable this setting, Admin Approval Mode is disabled for administrative accounts, and the Security Center will display a warning message.
- **User Account Control: Switch To The Secure Desktop When Prompting For Elevation** This setting, enabled by default, causes the screen to darken when a UAC prompt appears. If the appearance of the entire desktop changes, it is very difficult for malware that hasn't been previously installed to impersonate a UAC prompt. Some users might find the secure desktop annoying, and you can disable this setting to minimize that annoyance. However, disabling this setting decreases security by making it possible for other applications to impersonate a UAC prompt.
- **User Account Control: Virtualize File And Registry Write Failures To Per-User Locations** This setting, enabled by default, improves compatibility with applications not developed for UAC by redirecting requests for protected resources. For more information, read the section titled "UAC Virtualization" earlier in this chapter.

To disable UAC, set the User Account Control: Behavior Of The Elevation Prompt For Administrators In Admin Approval Mode setting to Elevate Without Prompting. Then, disable the User Account Control: Detect Application Installations And Prompt For Elevation and User Account Control: Run All Administrators In Admin Approval Mode settings. Finally, set User Account Control: Behavior Of The Elevation Prompt For Standard Users setting to Automatically Deny Elevation Requests. Then, restart the computer.

Additionally, you can configure the credential user interface using the following two Group Policy settings located at Computer Configuration\Policies\Administrative Templates\Windows Components\Credential User Interface:

- **Require Trusted Path For Credential Entry** If you enable this setting, Windows 7 requires the user to enter credentials using a trusted path, which requires the user to press Ctrl+Alt+Delete. This helps prevent a Trojan horse program or other types of malicious code from stealing the user's Windows credentials. This policy affects non-logon authentication tasks only. As a security best practice, you should enable this policy to reduce the risk of malware tricking the user into typing her password. However, users who need elevated privileges regularly will find it annoying and time consuming. Figures 24-7, 24-8, and 24-9 show the dialog boxes that appear each time a user must elevate privileges when this setting is enabled.

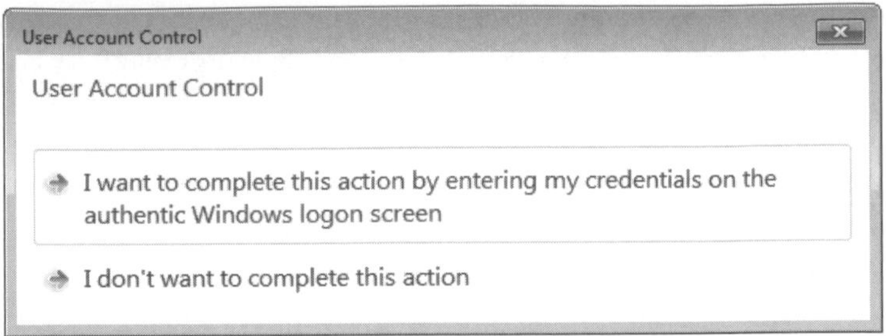

FIGURE 24-7 The first of three prompts to which the user must respond when you require a trusted path for administrator credentials

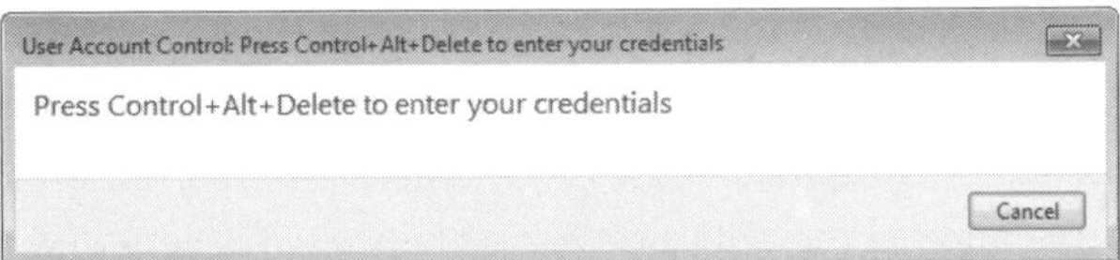

FIGURE 24-8 The second of three prompts to which the user must respond when you require a trusted path for administrator credentials

FIGURE 24-9 The third of three prompts to which the user must respond when you require a trusted path for administrator credentials

- **Enumerate Administrator Accounts On Elevation** By default, this setting is disabled, which causes the UAC prompt to list all Administrator accounts displayed when a user attempts to elevate a running application. If you enable this setting, users are required to type both a user name and password to elevate their privileges.

Control Panel

Group Policy is the best way to configure UAC in AD DS environments. In workgroup environments, administrators can configure UAC on a single computer by using Control Panel. Changes made while logged on as an administrator affect all administrators, and changes made while logged on as a user affect all users. To change the default setting, follow these steps:

1. In Control Panel, click System And Security.
2. Under Action Center, click Change User Account Control Settings.
3. Select one of the following four notification levels:
   - **Always Notify Me** Users are notified when they make changes to Windows settings and when programs attempt to make changes to the computer.
   - **Default-Notify Me Only When Programs Try To Make Changes To My Computer** Users are not notified when they make changes to Windows settings, but they do receive notification when a program attempts to make changes to the computer. This is the default setting.
   - **Notify Me Only When Programs Try To Make Changes To My Computer (Do Not Dim The Desktop)** Similar to the previous setting, but the secure desktop is not used. Disabling the secure desktop reduces security, but also reduces the impact of UAC on the user. This setting is available only to administrators.
   - **Never Notify Me** Users are not notified of any changes made to Windows settings or when software is installed. This causes all elevation-requests to be automatically accepted. This setting is available only to administrators.
4. Click OK.
5. When prompted, restart your computer.

Msconfig.exe

Msconfig.exe is a troubleshooting tool that can be useful for temporarily disabling UAC to determine whether UAC is causing an application compatibility problem. To make the change, Msconfig.exe simply modifies the registry value. To disable UAC with Msconfig.exe, follow these steps:

1. Click Start, type **msconfig**, and then press Enter. The System Configuration tool opens.
2. Click the Tools tab.
3. Click Change UAC Settings and then click Launch.
4. Select the desired notification level as described previously.
5. Click OK.
6. When prompted, restart your computer.

How to Configure Auditing for Privilege Elevation

You can enable auditing for privilege elevation so that every time a user provides administrator credentials or an administrator clicks Continue at a UAC prompt, an event is added to the Security Event Log. To enable privilege elevation auditing, enable success auditing for both the Audit Process Tracking and Audit Privilege Use settings in the Local Policies\Audit Policy node of Group Policy. Note that you should enable auditing only when testing applications or troubleshooting problems; enabling these types of auditing can generate an excessive number of events and negatively affect computer performance.

To enable auditing on a single computer, use the Local Security Policy console. To enable auditing on multiple computers within a domain, use Group Policy settings. In Group Policy, auditing settings are located within Computer Configuration\Policies\Windows Settings\Security Settings\Local Policies\Audit Policy node. After changing auditing settings, you must restart the computer for the change to take effect.

After enabling Audit Privilege Use, you can monitor Event IDs 4648 and 4624 in the Security Event Log to determine when users elevate privileges using the UAC consent dialog box. Event ID 4648 will always precede 4624 and will have a process name that includes Consent.exe, the UAC consent dialog box. These events will not appear if a user cancels the UAC consent dialog box. Events with Event ID 4673 will appear if the user cancels a consent dialog box; however, that same event will appear under different circumstances as well.

After enabling Audit Process Tracking, you can monitor Event ID 4688 to determine when administrators make use of Admin Approval Mode to provide full administrator privileges to processes. The description for this event includes several useful pieces of information:

- **Security ID** The user name and domain of the current user.
- **New Process Name** The path to the executable file being run. For more information about the new process, look for an event occurring at the same time as Event ID 4696.
- **Token Elevation Type** A number from 1 to 3 indicating the type of elevation being requested:
  - Type 1 (TokenElevationTypeDefault) is used only if UAC is disabled or if the user is the built-in Administrator account or a service account. This type does not generate a UAC prompt.
  - Type 2 (TokenElevationTypeFull) is used when the application requires (and is granted) elevated privileges. This is the only type that generates a UAC prompt. This type can also be generated if a user starts an application using RunAs, or if a previously elevated process creates a new process.
  - Type 3 (TokenElevationTypeLimited) is used when the application runs using standard privileges. This type does not require a UAC prompt.

Note that many events with Event ID 4688 won't be applications started by the user. Most of these events are generated by background processes and services that require no interaction with the user. To find the most interesting events, filter the Security Event Log using

Event ID 4688. Then, use the Find tool to search for the phrase "TokenElevationTypeFull." For information about using Event Viewer, read Chapter 21, "Maintaining Desktop Health."

Other UAC Event Logs

Besides security auditing (which is not enabled by default), UAC provides two additional logs within Event Viewer:

- **Applications and Services Logs\Microsoft\Windows\UAC\Operational** Logs UAC errors, such as processes that fail to handle elevation requirements correctly
- **Applications and Services Logs\Microsoft\Windows\UAC-FileVirtualization\Operational** Logs UAC virtualization details, such as virtualized files that are created or deleted

If you are experiencing a problem and you think it might be related to UAC, check these logs for any related information.

Best Practices for Using UAC

To receive the security benefits of UAC while minimizing the costs, follow these best practices:

- Leave UAC enabled for client computers in your organization.
- Have all users—especially IT staff—log on with standard user privileges.
- Each user should have a single account with only standard user privileges. Do not give users accounts with administrative privileges to their local computers. If you follow this guideline, you should also disable the UAC elevation prompts as described in the section titled "How to Configure User Account Control" earlier in this chapter.
- Domain administrators should have two accounts: a standard user account that they use to log on to their computers, and a second Administrator account that they can use to elevate privileges.
- Admin Approval Mode can slow down administrators by requiring them to frequently confirm elevation for administrative tools. If your administrators use a standard user account for day-to-day privileges and only log on with an Administrator account when managing a computer, your IT department might be more efficient if you disable the elevation prompt. To do this, configure the UAC policy setting Behavior Of The Elevation Prompt For Administrators In Admin Approval Mode to Elevate Without Prompting. However, changing this policy may increase the security risk in your environment, and the Windows Security Center will report it.
- Train users with local administrator credentials *not* to approve a UAC prompt if it appears unexpectedly. UAC prompts should appear only when the user is installing an application or starting a tool that requires elevated privileges. A UAC prompt that appears at any other time might have been initiated by malware. Rejecting the prompt will help prevent the malware from making permanent changes to the computer.

- Thoroughly test all applications with a standard user account in Windows Vista prior to deploying Windows Vista. If a third-party application does not work properly with a standard user account, contact the application developer and request an update for the application. If an internal application does not work properly, refer the developers to "Windows Vista Application Development Requirements for User Account Control Compatibility" at *http://msdn.microsoft.com/en-us/library/bb530410.aspx*. Although that document was written for Windows Vista, it also applies to Windows 7.
- Create Windows Firewall exceptions for users before deploying an application. For more information, read Chapter 26.
- Use GPSI, SMS, or another similar application-deployment technology to deploy applications. Disable application-installer detection using the User Account Control: Detect Application Installations And Prompt For Elevation setting, as described in the section titled "How to Configure User Account Control" earlier in this chapter.
- When users do require elevated privileges, administrators can provide the necessary credentials either by using Remote Assistance or by physically typing administrator credentials while at the user's computer.
- Use UAC as part of a defense-in-depth, client-security strategy that includes antispyware and antivirus applications, update management, and security auditing.

AppLocker

Some IT departments choose to control which applications users can run. Sometimes, administrators simply block specific applications that are known to be problematic. However, client security benefits more when administrators block all applications that IT has not approved.

The benefits of restricting users from running applications that are not approved can be immense. First, the risk of malware is significantly reduced, because Windows would prevent users from running the malware application because it had not been approved by IT. Second, compatibility problems are reduced, because users can only run approved versions of applications. Finally, user productivity is increased by eliminating the possibility that users could run games or other applications that might take time away from their work.

Restricting users from running applications does have significant costs, however, and for many organizations, those costs outweigh the benefits. IT has to test each application and create a rule that allows users to run it. Inevitably, users will be prevented from running legitimate applications, which can reduce their productivity while they wait for IT to approve a new application. Sometimes, users will choose to work around IT by running applications on non-IT computers. Each time an application is updated, IT needs to again test and approve the application.

Windows 7 includes AppLocker, which is an update to Software Restriction Policies, a feature in earlier versions of Windows. With Software Restriction Policies, IT professionals could create rules such as "Trust all content signed by Microsoft," "Trust this single executable file," or "Trust the file at this path." With AppLocker, IT professionals can create more refined rules based on an application's metadata, such as "Trust Microsoft Office if it is signed and the version is greater than 12.0.0.0." Additionally, AppLocker rules can be assigned on a per-group and per-user basis.

Table 24-2 lists the differences between Software Restriction Policies and AppLocker.

TABLE 24-2 Software Restriction Policies Compared to AppLocker

FEATURE	SOFTWARE RESTRICTION POLICIES	APPLOCKER
Conditions	Hash, path, certificate, registry path, and Internet zone	Hash, path, and publisher
Rule scope	All users	All users, or specific users and groups
Audit-only mode	No	Yes
Automatically generate rules	No	Yes
Policy import and export	No	Yes
Windows PowerShell support	No	Yes
Custom error messages	No	Yes

AppLocker is available only in Windows 7 Enterprise and Windows 7 Ultimate Editions. You can use Windows 7 Professional Edition to create AppLocker rules, but the rules will not be enforced on the computer running Windows 7 Professional. You must configure the Application Identity service to start for Windows 7 to apply AppLocker rules; by default, it is configured to start manually.

The sections that follow provide more detailed information about how to configure, test, and manage AppLocker.

AppLocker Rule Types

You can create three types of AppLocker rules:

- **Hash rules** Similar to the hash rules in Software Restriction Policies, this rule type creates a hash that uniquely identifies an executable. Before running an executable, Windows 7 calculates the hash of the file and compares it to the hash in each hash rule to determine whether the rule applies. The weakness of this rule type is that hash rules must be updated every time an executable file is updated. Therefore, every different version and every new version of an application requires its own hash rule.
- **Path Rules** Similar to the path rules in Software Restriction Policies, this rule type identifies executables based on the path. For example, you could create a path rule that allowed the executable at C:\Windows\Notepad.exe to run. This rule type allows an executable to be updated and still run, provided the path does not change.

However, a malicious user might be able to replace a legitimate executable with a different executable and run it successfully.

- **Publisher Rules** Although certificate rules in Software Restriction Policies provide some similar capabilities, publisher rules are more sophisticated because they allow you to create a rule for different combinations of the publisher, product name, file name, and version. Because this metadata is part of the cryptographic calculations used to create the digital signature, the metadata cannot be modified. This rule type identifies executables based on the digital signature and elements of the digital signature.

When creating AppLocker rules, you should always begin by creating the default rules. The default rules allow all files in the Windows folder and the Program Files folder to run, and they allow local administrators to run all programs. Because AppLocker blocks all applications that are not specifically allowed, not enabling the default rules would prevent Windows from running normally.

Use Group Policy settings to configure AppLocker rules. AppLocker is configured using the Computer Configuration\Windows Settings\Security Settings\Application Control Policies\AppLocker node. Within the AppLocker node, there are subnodes to configure Executable Rules, Windows Installer Rules, and Script Rules. To create the default rules, right-click each subnode within the AppLocker node in the Group Policy Editor and then click Create Default Rules.

The easiest way to generate rules for existing applications is to configure a Windows 7 reference computer with applications required by your organization. Start the Group Policy Editor on that computer (connecting to the domain using the Remote Server Administration Tools, available from the Microsoft Download Center at *http://www.microsoft.com/downloads/*). Then, follow these steps:

1. Right-click the Executable Rules node and click Automatically Generate Rules. The Automatically Generate Executable Rules page appears.
2. On the Folder And Permissions page, as shown in Figure 24-10, select the folder containing the executable files and the group to which the rules will apply, and assign a name to the rule. Then click Next.
3. On the Rule Preferences page (as shown in Figure 24-11), you typically can leave the default settings selected. The default settings create publisher rules for files that are digitally signed, because a digital signature is required for publisher rules. For files that are not digitally signed, the wizard generates hash rules that allow only the specific executable to run. Alternatively, you can choose to use less-secure path rules for files that do not have digital signatures, or you can choose to create hash rules for everything. Click Next.
4. On the Review Rules page, click Create.

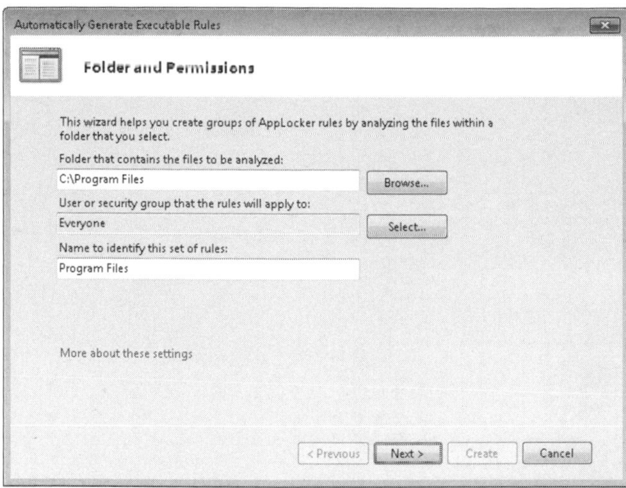

FIGURE 24-10 The Folder And Permissions page of the Automatically Generate Executable Rules page

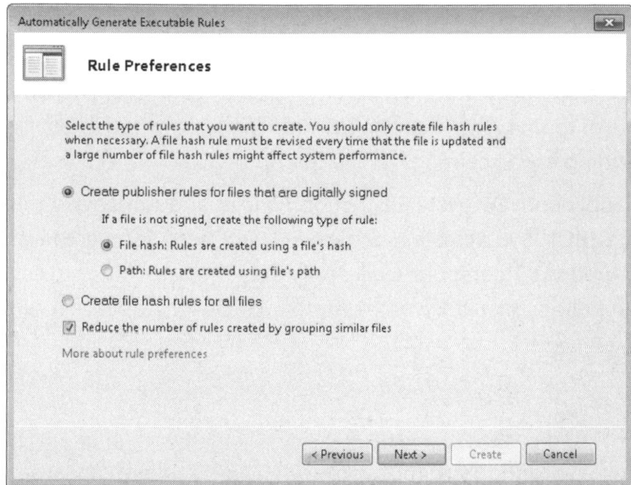

FIGURE 24-11 The Rule Preferences page of the Automatically Generate Executable Rules page

By default, all publisher rules are created to allow the application to run based on the product name and the current or later file version. Therefore, any application with a digital signature will be able to run, even if it is upgraded to a new version. For example, Figure 24-12 shows a rule automatically generated for the Microsoft Virtual Machine Additions, an executable file that includes a digital signature. Naturally, you can edit the automatically generated rules if you want to allow only the current version to run.

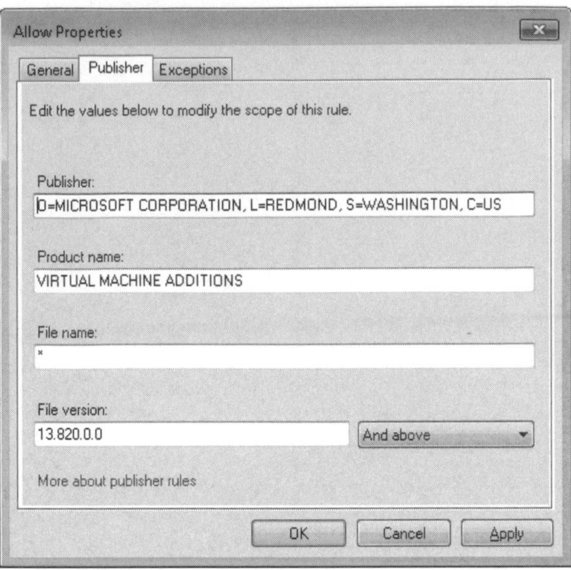

FIGURE 24-12 Automatically generated rules allow the current and later versions of a program to run.

You can create rules manually by right-clicking the Executable Rules, Windows Installer Rules, or Script Rules node in Group Policy and then clicking Create New Rule. The wizard walks you through the process of identifying your application, choosing whether to allow or block the application, and defining any exceptions to the rule.

Windows 7 clients will not apply both Software Restriction Policies and AppLocker rules within a single Group Policy object (GPO). If you create a single GPO with both Software Restriction Policies and AppLocker rules, Windows 7 computers will apply only the AppLocker rules and will ignore the Software Restriction Policies. Instead, create different GPOs for AppLocker rules and Software Restriction Policies.

Auditing AppLocker Rules

The consequences of an incorrectly configured AppLocker rule can be severe, because you can prevent a user from running a critical application or even logging on to Windows. When adding AppLocker rules to GPOs that are applied throughout your organization, a single mistake could stop productivity for thousands of users.

To allow you to test rules before applying them, AppLocker rules can be either enforced or audited. You should always configure new AppLocker rules as Audit Only and monitor the auditing results for users in a production environment to ensure there are no unwanted side effects, such as preventing users from running legitimate applications.

By default, AppLocker rules are enforced. To configure AppLocker rules to be audited only, follow these steps:

1. In the GPO Editor, right-click the Computer Configuration\Policies\Windows Settings\Security Settings\Application Control Policies\AppLocker node and then click Properties.
2. As shown in Figure 24-13, the AppLocker Properties dialog box appears. Select the Configured check box for each of the rule types that you have configured. Then, click the list and select Audit Only. If you have enabled DLL Rules, you will also see the option to audit or enforce dynamic-link library (DLL) rules on this tab.

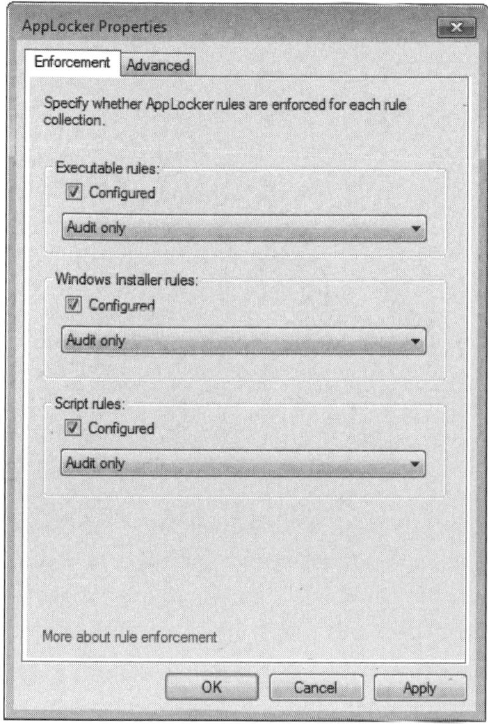

FIGURE 24-13 Configuring AppLocker rules for auditing only

3. Click OK.

With auditing enabled, AppLocker will add events to the AppLocker event logs (located within Application And Services Logs\Microsoft\Windows\AppLocker). After verifying that your AppLocker rules have the desired effect, you can repeat the previous steps and select Enforce Rules. Table 24-3 lists the events that AppLocker might add during either auditing or full rule enforcement.

TABLE 24-3 AppLocker Auditing Events

EVENT ID	EVENT LEVEL	EVENT TEXT	DESCRIPTION
8002	Informational	<*Filename*> was allowed to run.	Specifies that the .exe or .dll file is allowed by an AppLocker rule.
8003	Warning	<*Filename*> was allowed to run but would have been prevented from running if the AppLocker policy were enforced.	Specifies that the file would have been blocked if the Enforce Rules enforcement mode were enabled. You see this event level only when the enforcement mode is set to Audit Only.
8004	Error	<*Filename*> was not allowed to run.	The file cannot run. You see this event level only when the enforcement mode is set directly or indirectly through Group Policy inheritance to Enforce Rules.
8005	Information	<*Filename*> was allowed to run.	Specifies that the .msi file or script is allowed by an AppLocker rule.

DLL Rules

Dynamic-link libraries (DLLs) store executable code that multiple applications can use. For example, if a developer is creating an application that reads from a database, he might create a DLL that stores the functions that read from the database. Then he can use the same DLL to read from the database using both a Windows client and a Web interface for the database.

By default, AppLocker rules do not apply to DLLs—if an application is allowed to run, it can load any DLL. Typically, this level of security is sufficient. However, AppLocker can be configured to control access to individual DLLs. This makes configuration much more complex, however, and it can significantly reduce performance at run time.

To enforce DLL rules, follow these steps:

1. In the GPO Editor, right-click the Computer Configuration\Policies\Windows Settings\Security Settings\Application Control Policies\AppLocker node and then click Properties.

   The AppLocker Properties dialog box appears.
2. Click the Advanced tab and then select the Enforce DLL Rule Collection check box.
3. Click OK.

Now the DLL Rules node is visible within the AppLocker node in the GPO Editor. Use this node to define DLL rules. Additionally, you can choose to enforce or audit DLL rules from the Enforcement tab of the AppLocker Properties dialog box.

Custom Error Messages

You can specify a custom URL that Windows will display when AppLocker prevents an application from running. To specify the URL, enable the Administrative Templates\Windows Components\Windows Explorer\Set A Support Web Page Link policy.

Using AppLocker with Windows PowerShell

Windows PowerShell 2.0 includes the following cmdlets to enable you to create scripts that examine, create, and manage AppLocker:

- **Get-AppLockerFileInformation** Examines an executable or script and returns the information AppLocker might use to determine whether the application can run, including the file hash, file path, and publisher (for signed files).
- **Get-AppLockerPolicy** Examines either the effective AppLocker policy or the AppLocker policy from a GPO.
- **New-AppLockerPolicy** Creates a new AppLocker policy.
- **Set-AppLockerPolicy** After you create an AppLocker policy, use this cmdlet to define it for a GPO.
- **Test-AppLockerPolicy** Determines whether specified files will be allowed to run for a specific user and AppLocker policy.

For more information, open a Windows PowerShell prompt and run the command help *<module>*. You can also read the blog entry, "Getting Started with AppLocker Management Using Powershell," at *http://blogs.msdn.com/powershell/archive/2009/06/02/getting-started-with-applocker-management-using-powershell.aspx*.

Using Windows Defender

Windows Defender is a tool designed to reduce the risk of specific types of spyware and other potentially unwanted software for small office and home users. Although Windows Defender is not designed for use in large enterprises, it does provide some integration with AD DS Group Policy and can retrieve updates from an internal Windows Server Update Services (WSUS) server.

Windows Defender will interact with users if potentially unwanted software is detected. Therefore, users must be trained before Windows Defender is deployed so that they understand how to respond to the various prompts and can distinguish between genuine Windows Defender prompts and other software that might impersonate those prompts (a common social engineering technique).

For more information about Windows Defender, visit the Windows Defender Virtual Lab Express at *http://www.microsoftvirtuallabs.com/express/registration.aspx?LabId=92e04589-cdd9-4e69-8b1b-2d131d9037af*.

Understanding Windows Defender

Windows Defender provides two types of protection, both enabled by default:

- **Automatic scanning** Windows Defender scans the computer for potentially malicious software on a regular basis. By default, Windows Defender is configured to download updated definitions and then do a quick scan daily at 2 A.M. You can configure scanning frequency on the Windows Defender Options page.
- **Real-time protection** Windows Defender constantly monitors computer usage to notify you if potentially unwanted software might be attempting to make changes to your computer.

The sections that follow describe each type of protection in more detail.

Automatic Scanning

Windows Defender provides two different types of scanning:

- **Quick Scan** Scans the portions of a computer most likely to be infected by spyware or other potentially unwanted software, such as the computer's memory and portions of the registry that link to startup applications. This is sufficient to detect most malware applications.
- **Full Scan** Scans every file on the computer, including common types of file archives as well as applications already loaded in the computer's memory. A full scan typically takes several hours, but it may take more than a day, depending on the speed of the computer and the number of files to be scanned. The user can continue to work on the computer during a quick scan or a full scan; however, these scans do slow down the computer and will consume battery power on mobile computers very quickly.

By default, Windows Defender runs a quick scan daily. This is usually sufficient. If you think a user might have potentially unwanted software installed, you should run a full scan to increase the chances of removing every trace of the software. In addition to quick scans and full scans, you can configure a custom scan to scan specific portions of a computer. Custom scans always begin with a quick scan.

If Windows Defender finds potentially unwanted software, it will display a warning, as shown in Figure 24-14.

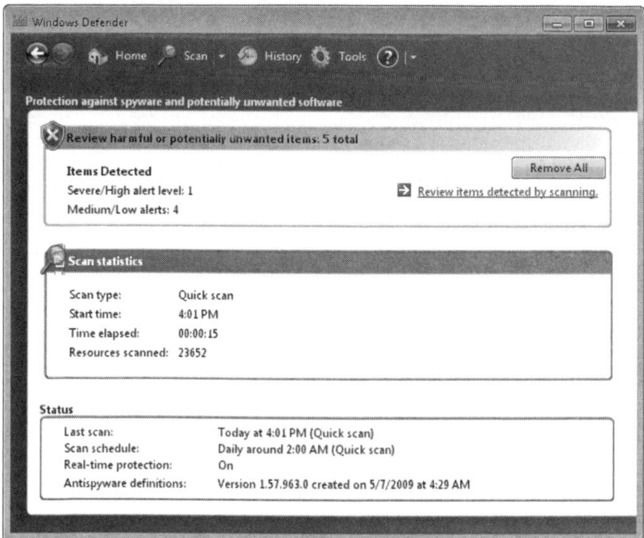

FIGURE 24-14 Windows Defender notifies the user of potentially unwanted software.

Most of the time, the user should simply choose to remove all the potentially unwanted software. However, Windows 7 will display four options for each item detected:

- **Ignore** Allows the software to be installed or run on your computer. If the software is still running during the next scan, or if the software tries to change security-related settings on your computer, Windows Defender will alert you about this software again.
- **Quarantine** When Windows Defender quarantines software, it moves it to another location on your computer, and then prevents the software from running until you choose to restore it or remove it from your computer.
- **Remove** Deletes the software from your computer.
- **Always Allow** Adds the software to the Windows Defender allowed list and allows it to run on your computer. Windows Defender will stop alerting you to actions taken by the program. Add software to the allowed list only if you trust the software and the software publisher.

For more information about malware infections, read the section titled "How to Troubleshoot Problems with Unwanted Software" later in this chapter.

Real-Time Protection

Windows Defender in Windows 7 includes real-time protection with greatly improved performance. Real-time protection can alert you when software attempts to install itself or run on your computer, as shown in Figure 24-15. Depending on the alert level, users can choose to remove, quarantine, ignore, or always allow the application, just as if the problem were encountered during a scan.

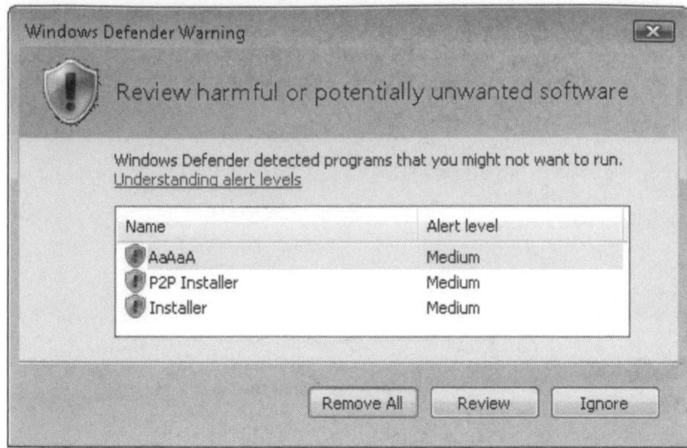

FIGURE 24-15 Windows Defender real-time protection warns the user if potentially unwanted software attempts to make changes to the computer.

If potentially unwanted software is allowed to run on your computer, it sometimes attempts to make changes to system settings so that it will run automatically the next time you start your computer. Of course, legitimate software also makes similar changes, so it's up to the user to determine whether the change should be allowed. If Windows Defender real-time protection detects software attempting to make a change to important Windows settings, the user will be prompted to Permit (allow the change) or Deny (block the change).

Whereas Windows Defender in Windows Vista included a large number of real-time security agents, Windows 7 reduces the number of agents to two. This improves performance while providing similar levels of security. The two agents are:

- **Downloaded Files And Attachments** Monitors files and programs that are designed to work with Web browsers, such as ActiveX controls and software installation programs. These files can be downloaded, installed, or run by the browser itself. Unwanted software is often included with these files and installed without the user's knowledge.
- **Programs That Run On Your Computer** Monitors when programs start and any operations they perform while running. Malware can use vulnerabilities in previously installed applications to run unwanted software without the user's knowledge. For example, spyware can run itself in the background when a user starts another frequently used application. Windows Defender monitors applications and alerts the user if suspicious activity is detected.

Windows Defender Alert Levels

When Windows Defender detects potentially malicious software, it assigns one of the following alert levels to it:

- **Severe** Assigned to potentially unwanted software that can severely affect your computer or compromise your privacy. You should always remove this software.

- **High** Similar to the severe rating, but slightly less damaging. You should always remove this software.
- **Medium** Assigned to potentially unwanted software that might compromise your privacy, affect your computer's performance, or display advertising. In some cases, software classified at a Medium alert level might have legitimate uses. Evaluate the software before allowing it to be installed.
- **Low** Assigned to potentially unwanted software that might collect information about you or your computer or change how your computer works but operates in agreement with licensing terms displayed when you installed the software. This software is typically benign, but it might be installed without the user's knowledge. For example, remote control software might be classified as a Low alert level because it could be used legitimately, or it might be used by an attacker to control a computer without the owner's knowledge.
- **Not yet classified** Programs that haven't yet been analyzed.

Understanding Microsoft SpyNet

Microsoft's goal is to create definitions for all qualifying software. However, thousands of new applications are created and distributed every day, some of which have behaviors unwanted by some people. Because of the rapid pace of newly released software, people can possibly encounter potentially unwanted software that Microsoft has not yet classified. In these cases, Windows Defender should still warn the user if the software takes a potentially undesirable action such as configuring itself to start automatically each time the computer is restarted.

To help users determine whether to allow application changes (detected by real-time protection) when prompted, Windows Defender contacts Microsoft SpyNet to determine how other users have responded when prompted about the same software. If the change is part of a desired software installation, most users will have approved the change, and Windows Defender can use the feedback from SpyNet when informing the user about the change. If the change is unexpected (as it would be for most unwanted software), most users will not approve the change.

Two levels of SpyNet participation are available:

- **Basic** Windows Defender sends only basic information to Microsoft, including where the software came from, such as the specific URL, and whether the user or Windows Defender allowed or blocked the item. With basic membership, Windows Defender does not alert users if it detects software or changes made by software that has not yet been analyzed for risks. Although personal information might possibly be sent to Microsoft with either basic or advanced SpyNet membership, Microsoft will not use this information to identify or contact the user.

NOTE For more information about what information might be transferred and how Microsoft might use it, view the Windows Defender privacy statement online at *http://go.microsoft.com/fwlink/?linkid=55418*.

- **Advanced** Advanced SpyNet membership is intended for users who have an understanding of the inner workings of the operating system and might be able to evaluate whether the changes an application is making are malicious. The key difference between basic and advanced membership is that with advanced membership, Windows Defender will alert users when it detects software or changes that have not yet been analyzed for risks. Also, advanced membership sends additional information to SpyNet, including the location of the software on the local computer, filenames, how the software operates, and how it has affected the computer.

You can configure your SpyNet level by clicking Microsoft SpyNet on the Windows Defender Tools page.

In addition to providing feedback to users about unknown software, SpyNet is also a valuable resource to Microsoft when identifying new malware. Microsoft analyzes information in SpyNet to create new definitions. In turn, this helps slow the spread of potentially unwanted software.

Configuring Windows Defender Group Policy

You can configure some aspects of Windows Defender Group Policy settings. Windows Defender Group Policy settings are located in Computer Configuration\Administrative Templates\Windows Components\Windows Defender. From that node, you can configure the following settings:

- **Turn On Definition Updates Through Both WSUS And Windows Update** Enabled by default, this setting configures Windows Defender to check Windows Update when a WSUS server is not available locally. This can help ensure that mobile clients, who might not regularly connect to your local network, can receive all new signature updates. If you disable this setting, Windows Defender checks for updates using only the setting defined for the Automatic Updates client—either an internal WSUS server or Windows Update. For more information about WSUS and distributing updates, read Chapter 23, "Managing Software Updates."

DIRECT FROM THE SOURCE

Analysis of Potentially Unwanted Software

Sterling Reasor, Program Manager
Windows Defender

Keeping up to date with the current malware definitions can help protect your computer from harmful or potentially unwanted software. Microsoft has taken several steps to create definition updates, including gathering new samples of suspicious files, observing and testing the samples, and performing a deep analysis. If we determine that the sample does not follow our criteria, its alert level is determined and the software is added to the software definitions and released to customers.

For more information, visit *http://www.microsoft.com/athome/security/spyware/software/msft/analysis.mspx.*

- **Turn On Definition Updates Through Both WSUS And The Microsoft Malware Protection Center** Provides similar functionality to the previous Group Policy setting, but clients download updates from a different site. You should set these two policies to the same value unless the computer has no access to the Internet and relies only on an internal WSUS server.
- **Check For New Signatures Before Scheduled Scans** Disabled by default, you can enable this setting to cause Windows Defender to always check for updates prior to a scan. This helps ensure that Windows Defender has the most up-to-date signatures. When you disable this setting, Windows Defender still downloads updates on a regular basis but will not necessarily check immediately prior to a scan.
- **Turn Off Windows Defender** Enable this setting to turn off Windows Defender real-time protection and to remove any scheduled scans. You should enable this setting only if you are using different anti-malware software. If Windows Defender is turned off, users can still run the tool manually to scan for potentially unwanted software.
- **Turn Off Real-Time Monitoring** If you enable this policy setting, Windows Defender does not prompt users to allow or block unknown activity. If you disable or do not configure this policy setting, by default Windows Defender prompts users to allow or block unknown activity on their computers.
- **Turn Off Routinely Taking Action** By default, Windows Defender will take action on all detected threats automatically after about ten minutes. Enable this policy to configure Windows Defender to prompt the user to choose how to respond to a threat.

- **Configure Microsoft SpyNet Reporting** SpyNet is the online community that helps users choose how to respond to potential spyware threats that Microsoft has not yet classified by showing users how other members have responded to an alert. When enabled and set to Basic or Advanced, Windows Defender will display information about how other users responded to a potential threat. When enabled and set to Basic, Windows Defender will also submit a small amount of information about the potentially malicious files on the user's computer. When set to Advanced, Windows Defender will send more detailed information. If you enable this setting and set it to No Membership, SpyNet will not be used, and the user will not be able to change the setting. If you leave this setting Disabled (the default), SpyNet will not be used unless the user changes the setting on his local computer. The Microsoft Malware Protection Center recommends that this setting be set to Advanced to provide their analysts with more complete information on potentially unwanted software.

Windows Defender Group Policy settings are defined in WindowsDefender.admx, which is included with Windows 7. For more information about using Group Policy administrative templates, read Chapter 14, "Managing the Desktop Environment."

Configuring Windows Defender on a Single Computer

Besides the settings that you can configure by using Group Policy, Windows Defender includes many settings that you can configure only by using the Windows Defender Options page on a local computer. To open the Options page, start Windows Defender by searching the Start menu, selecting Tools, and then selecting Options. Some of the settings you can configure from this page include:

- Frequency and time of automatic scans
- The security agents that are scanned automatically
- Specific files and folders to be excluded from scans
- Whether non-administrators can run Windows Defender

Because you cannot easily configure these settings with Group Policy settings, Windows Defender might not be the right choice for enterprise spyware control.

How to Determine Whether a Computer Is Infected with Spyware

Several signs indicate whether a computer is infected with spyware. You should train users in your environment to notice these changes and call your Support Center if they suspect a malware infection:

- A new, unexpected application appears.
- Unexpected icons appear in the system tray.
- Unexpected notifications appear near the system tray.

- The Web browser home page, default search engine, or favorites change.
- The mouse pointer changes.
- New toolbars appear, especially in Web browsers.
- The Web browser displays additional advertisements when visiting a Web page, or pop-up advertisements appear when the user is not using the Web.
- When the user attempts to visit a Web page, she is redirected to a completely different Web page.
- The computer runs more slowly than usual. This can be caused by many different problems, but spyware is one of the most common causes.

Some spyware might not have any noticeable symptoms, but it still might compromise private information. For best results, run Windows Defender real-time protection with daily quick scans.

Best Practices for Using Windows Defender

To receive the security benefits of Windows Defender while minimizing the costs, follow these best practices:

- Teach users how malware works and the problems that malware can cause. In particular, focus on teaching users to avoid being tricked into installing malware by social engineering attacks.
- Before deploying Windows 7, test all applications with Windows Defender enabled to ensure that Windows Defender does not alert users to normal changes the application might make. If a legitimate application does cause warnings, add the application to the Windows Defender allowed list.
- Change the scheduled scan time to meet the needs of your business. By default, Windows Defender scans at 2 A.M. If third-shift staff uses computers overnight, you might want to find a better time to perform the scan. If users turn off their computers when they are not in the office, you should schedule the scan to occur during the day. Although the automatic quick scan can slow computer performance, it typically takes fewer than 10 minutes, and users can continue working. Any performance cost typically is outweighed by the security benefits.
- Use WSUS to manage and distribute signature updates.
- Use antivirus software with Windows Defender. Alternatively, you might disable Windows Defender completely and use client security software that provides both antispyware and antivirus functionality.
- Do not deploy Windows Defender in enterprises. Instead, use Microsoft Forefront or a third-party client security suite that can be managed more easily in enterprise environments.

How to Troubleshoot Problems with Unwanted Software

A spyware infection is rarely a single application; most successful malware infections automatically install several, even dozens, of additional applications. Some of those applications might be straightforward to remove. However, if even a single malicious application remains, that remaining malware application might continue to install other malware applications.

If you detect a problem related to spyware and other potentially unwanted software, follow these steps to troubleshoot it:

1. Perform a quick scan and remove any potentially unwanted applications. Then, immediately perform a full scan and remove any additional potentially malicious software. The full scan can take many hours to run. Windows Defender will probably need to restart Windows.
2. If the software has made changes to Internet Explorer, such as adding unwanted add-ons or changing the home page, refer to Chapter 20 for troubleshooting information.
3. Run antivirus scans on your computer, such as that available from *http://safety.live.com*. Often, spyware might install software that is classified as a virus, or the vulnerability exploited by spyware might also be exploited by a virus. Windows Defender does not detect or remove viruses. Remove any viruses installed on the computer.
4. If you still see signs of malware, install an additional antispyware and antivirus application from a known and trusted vendor. With complicated infections, a single anti-malware tool might not be able to remove the infection completely. Your chances of removing all traces of malware increase by using multiple applications, but you should not configure multiple applications to provide real-time protection.
5. If problems persist, shut down the computer and use the Startup Repair tool to perform a System Restore. Restore the computer to a date prior to the malware infection. System Restore will typically remove any startup settings that cause malware applications to run, but it will not remove the executable files themselves. Use this only as a last resort: Although System Restore will not remove a user's personal files, it can cause problems with recently installed or configured applications. For more information, see Chapter 29, "Configuring Startup and Troubleshooting Startup Issues."

These steps will resolve the vast majority of malware problems. However, when malware has run on a computer, you can never be certain that the software is removed completely. In particular, malware known as *rootkits* can install themselves in such a way that they are difficult to detect on a computer. In these circumstances, if you cannot find a way to confidently remove the rootkit, you might be forced to reformat the hard disk, reinstall Windows, and then restore user files using a backup created prior to the infection.

Network Access Protection

Many organizations have been affected by viruses or worms that entered their private networks through a mobile PC and quickly infected computers throughout the organization. Windows Vista, when connecting to a Windows Server 2008 infrastructure, supports Network Access Protection (NAP) to reduce the risks of connecting unhealthy computers to private networks directly or across a VPN. If a NAP client computer lacks current security updates or virus signatures—or otherwise fails to meet your requirements for computer health—NAP blocks the computer from having unlimited access to your private network. If a computer fails to meet the health requirements, it will be connected to a restricted network to download and install the updates, antivirus signatures, or configuration settings that are required to comply with current health requirements. Within minutes, a potentially vulnerable computer can be updated, have its new health state validated, and then be granted unlimited access to your network.

NAP is not designed to secure a network from malicious users. It is designed to help administrators maintain the health of the computers on the network, which in turn helps maintain the network's overall integrity. For example, if a computer has all the software and configuration settings that the health requirement policy requires, the computer is considered compliant, and it will be granted unlimited access to the network. NAP does not prevent an authorized user with a compliant computer from uploading a malicious program to the network or engaging in other inappropriate behavior.

NAP has three important and distinct aspects:

- **Network policy validation** When a user attempts to connect to the network, the computer's health state is validated against the network access policies as defined by the administrator. Administrators can then choose what to do if a computer is not compliant. In a monitoring-only environment, all authorized computers are granted access to the network even if some do not comply with health requirement policies, but the compliance state of each computer is logged. In an isolation environment, computers that comply with the health requirement policies are allowed unlimited access to the network, but computers that do not comply with health requirement policies or are not compatible with NAP are placed on a restricted network. In both environments, administrators can define exceptions to the validation process. NAP also includes migration tools to make it easier for administrators to define exceptions that best suit their network needs.
- **Health requirement policy compliance** Administrators can help ensure compliance with health requirement policies by choosing to automatically update noncompliant computers with the required updates through management software, such as Microsoft System Center Configuration Manager. In a monitoring-only environment, computers will have access to the network even before they are updated with required software or configuration changes. In an isolation environment, computers that do not comply with health requirement policies have limited access until the software and

configuration updates are completed. Again, in both environments, the administrator can define policy exceptions.

- **Limited access for noncompliant computers** Administrators can protect network assets by limiting the access of computers that do not comply with health requirement policies. Computers that do not comply will have their network access limited as defined by the administrator. That access can be limited to a restricted network, to a single resource, or to no internal resources at all. If an administrator does not configure health update resources, the limited access will last for the duration of the connection. If an administrator configures health update resources, the limited access will last only until the computer is brought into compliance.

NAP is an extensible platform that provides an infrastructure and an application programming interface (API) set for adding features that verify and remediate a computer's health to comply with health requirement policies. By itself, NAP does not provide features to verify or correct a computer's health. Other features, known as system health agents (SHAs) and system health validators (SHVs), provide automated system health reporting, validation, and remediation. Windows Vista, Windows Server 2008, and Windows 7 include an SHA and an SHV that allow the network administrator to specify health requirements for the services monitored by the Windows Security Center.

When troubleshooting client-side problems related to NAP, open Event Viewer and browse the Applications And Services Logs\Microsoft\Windows\Network Access Protection Event Log. For more information about configuring a NAP infrastructure with Windows Server 2008, read Chapters 14 through 19 of *Windows Server 2008 Networking and Network Access Protection* by Joseph Davies and Tony Northrup (Microsoft Press, 2008).

Forefront

Forefront is enterprise security software that provides protection from malware in addition to many other threats. Whereas Windows Defender is designed for consumers and small businesses, Forefront is designed to be deployed and managed efficiently throughout large networks.

Forefront products are designed to provide defense-in-depth by protecting desktops, laptops, and server operating systems. Forefront currently consists of the following products:

- Microsoft Forefront Client Security (FCS)
- Microsoft Forefront Security for Exchange Server (formerly called Microsoft Antigen for Exchange)
- Microsoft Forefront Security for SharePoint (formerly called Antigen for SharePoint)
- Microsoft Forefront Security for Office Communications Server (formerly called Antigen for Instant Messaging)
- Microsoft Intelligent Application Gateway (IAG)
- Microsoft Forefront Threat Management Gateway (TMG)

Of these products, only FCS would be deployed to client computers. The other products typically would be deployed on servers to protect applications, networks, and infrastructure.

Enterprise management of anti-malware software is useful for:

- Centralized policy management.
- Alerting and reporting on malware threats in your environment.
- Comprehensive insight into the security state of your environment, including security update status and up-to-date signatures.

Forefront provides a simple user interface for creating policies that you can distribute automatically to organizational units and security groups by using GPOs. Clients also centrally report their status so that administrators can view the overall status of client security in the enterprise.

With Forefront, administrators can view statistics ranging from domain-wide to specific groups of computers or individual computers to understand the impact of specific threats. In other words, if malware does infect computers in your organization, you can easily discover the infection, isolate the affected computers, and then take steps to resolve the problems.

Forefront also provides a client-side user interface. Similar to Windows Defender, Forefront can warn users if an application attempts to make potentially malicious changes, or if it detects known malware attempting to run. The key differences between Defender and Forefront are:

- **Forefront is managed centrally** Forefront is designed for use in medium-sized and large networks. Administrators can use the central management console to view a summary of current threats and vulnerabilities, computers that need to be updated, and computers that are currently having security problems. Windows Defender is designed for home computers and small offices only, and threats must be managed on local computers.
- **Forefront is highly configurable** You can configure automated responses to alerts, and, for example, prevent users from running known malware instead of giving them the opportunity to override a warning as they can do with Windows Defender.
- **Forefront protects against all types of malware** Windows Defender is designed to protect against spyware. Forefront protects against spyware, viruses, rootkits, worms, and Trojan horses. If you use Windows Defender, you need another application to protect against the additional threats.
- **Forefront can protect a wider variety of Windows platforms** Forefront is designed to protect computers running Microsoft Windows 2000, Windows XP, Windows Server 2003, Windows Vista, Windows 7, and Windows Server 2008. Windows Defender can protect only computers running Windows XP, Windows Vista, and Windows 7.

Like Windows Defender, Forefront supports using Microsoft Update and WSUS to distribute updated signatures to client computers, but Forefront also supports using third-party software distribution systems. For more information about Forefront, visit *http://www.microsoft.com/forefront/*. Also, explore the Microsoft TechNet Virtual Labs at *http://technet.microsoft.com/bb499665.aspx*.

NOTE Microsoft offers a third client security solution: Windows Live OneCare. Windows Live OneCare is designed to help protect home computers and small businesses with antivirus protection, antispyware protection, improved firewall software, performance monitoring, and backup and restore assistance. For more information, visit *http://onecare.live.com/*.

Summary

Windows 7 is designed to be secure by default, but default settings don't meet everyone's needs. Additionally, the highly secure default settings can cause compatibility problems with applications not written specifically for Windows 7. For these reasons, it's important that you understand the client-security technologies built into Windows 7 and how to configure them.

One of the most significant security features is UAC. By default, both users and administrators are limited to standard user privileges, which reduces the damage that malware could do if it were to start a process successfully in the user context. If an application needs elevated privileges, UAC prompts the user to confirm the request or to provide administrator credentials. Because UAC changes the default privileges for applications, it can cause problems with applications that require administrative rights. To minimize these problems, UAC provides file and registry virtualization that redirects requests for protected resources to user-specific locations that won't impact the entire system.

AppLocker provides similar functionality to Software Restriction Policies available in earlier versions of Windows. However, AppLocker's publisher rules provide more flexible control and enable administrators to create a single rule that allows both current and future versions of an application without the risks of a path rule. Additionally, AppLocker includes auditing to enable administrators to identify applications that require rules and to test rules before enforcing them.

Microsoft also provides Windows Defender for additional protection from spyware and other potentially unwanted software. Windows Defender uses signature-based and heuristic antispyware detection. If it finds malware on a computer, it gives the user the opportunity to prevent it from installing or to remove it if it is already installed. Windows Defender isn't designed for enterprise use, however. For improved manageability and protection against other forms of malware (including viruses and rootkits), use Forefront or another similar enterprise client-security solution.

Additional Resources

These resources contain additional information and tools related to this chapter.

- Chapter 2, "Security in Windows 7," includes an overview of malware.

- Chapter 4, "Planning Deployment," includes more information about application compatibility.
- Chapter 20, "Managing Windows Internet Explorer," includes more information about protecting Internet Explorer.
- Chapter 23, "Managing Software Updates," includes information about deploying WSUS.
- Chapter 26, "Configuring Windows Firewall and IPsec," includes more information about Windows Service Hardening.
- Chapter 29, "Configuring Startup and Troubleshooting Startup Issues," includes information about running System Restore.
- "Behavioral Modeling of Social Engineering–Based Malicious Software" at *http://www.microsoft.com/downloads/details.aspx?FamilyID=e0f27260-58da-40db-8785-689cf6a05c73* includes information about social engineering attacks.
- "Windows 7 Security Compliance Management Toolkit" at *http://go.microsoft.com/fwlink/?LinkId=156033* provides detailed information about how to best configure Windows 7 security for your organization.
- "Microsoft Security Intelligence Report" at *http://www.microsoft.com/downloads/details.aspx?FamilyID=aa6e0660-dc24-4930-affd-e33572ccb91f* includes information about trends in the malicious and potentially unwanted software landscape.
- "Malware Removal Starter Kit" at *http://www.microsoft.com/downloads/details.aspx?FamilyID=6cd853ce-f349-4a18-a14f-c99b64adfbea.*
- "Applying the Principle of Least Privilege to User Accounts on Windows XP" at *http://technet.microsoft.com/en-us/library/bb456992.aspx.*
- "Fundamental Computer Investigation Guide for Windows" at *http://www.microsoft.com/downloads/details.aspx?FamilyId=71B986EC-B3F1-4C14-AC70-EC0EB8ED9D57.*
- "Security Compliance Management Toolkit Series" at *http://www.microsoft.com/downloads/details.aspx?FamilyID=5534bee1-3cad-4bf0-b92b-a8e545573a3e.*

On the Companion Media

- DeleteCertificate.ps1
- FindCertificatesAboutToExpire.ps1
- FindExpiredCertificates.ps1
- Get-Certificates.ps1
- Get-DefenderStatus.ps1
- Get-ForefrontStatus.ps1
- InspectCertificate.ps1
- ListCertificates.ps1

PART V

Networking

CHAPTER 25

Configuring Windows Networking

The Windows 7 operating system builds on the networking features introduced previously in Windows Vista and improves them. This chapter discusses how Windows 7 addresses the concerns of a modern network, how you can configure and manage these new features, and how you can deploy Windows 7 to take advantage of modern, flexible networking.

Usability Improvements

Improving the usability of Windows 7 helps both users and administrators. Users benefit because they can get more done in less time, and administrators benefit because users make fewer support calls.

The sections that follow describe important networking usability improvements first introduced in Windows Vista and improved in Windows 7, including Network And Sharing Center, Network Explorer, the Network Map, and the Set Up A Connection Or Network Wizard. Understanding these features will help you to use them effectively and guide you through many common network configuration and troubleshooting tasks.

Network And Sharing Center

Improved Network And Sharing Center in Windows 7, shown in Figure 25-1, provides a clear view of available wireless networks, a Network Map to show the surrounding network resources on a home or unmanaged network, and easy methods to create or join ad hoc wireless networks. Diagnostic tools built into Network And Sharing Center simplify troubleshooting connectivity problems. Users can also browse network resources with the new Network Explorer, which they can start by clicking the network.

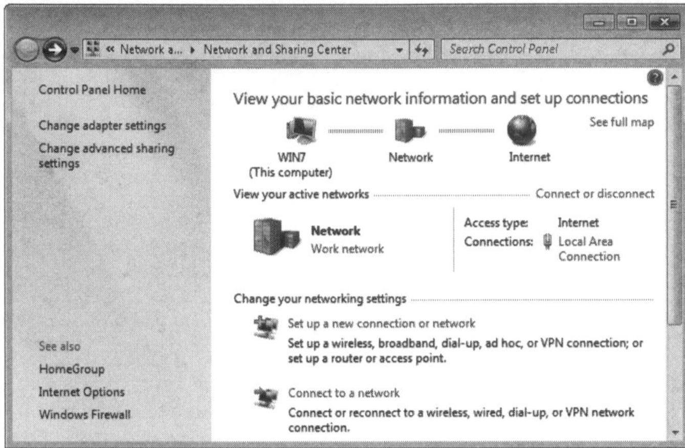

FIGURE 25-1 Network And Sharing Center simplifies network management for users.

If a network connection is not available, such as a failed Internet connection (even if the link connected to the computer is functioning), Network And Sharing Center detects this failure and displays it graphically on the abbreviated version of the Network Map, shown in Figure 25-2. Users can troubleshoot the problem simply by clicking the failed portion of the Network Map to start Windows Network Diagnostics. For more information, read Chapter 31, "Troubleshooting Network Issues."

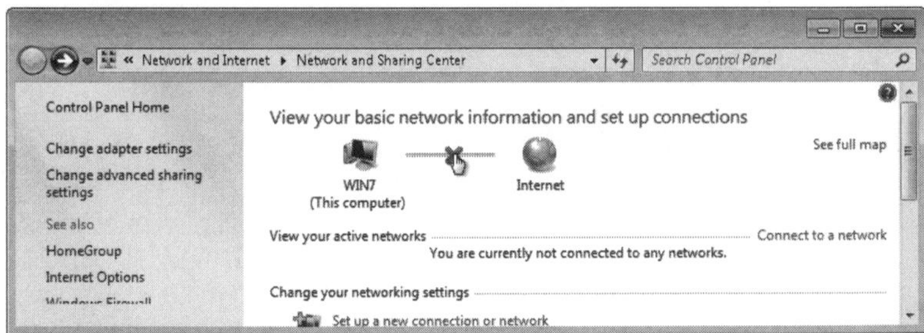

FIGURE 25-2 Network And Sharing Center automatically detects problems and can assist users with diagnosis and troubleshooting.

To open Network And Sharing Center, click the network icon in the notification area and then click Open Network And Sharing Center. Alternatively, you can open Control Panel, click Network And Internet, and then click Network And Sharing Center.

Network Explorer

Like My Network Places in Windows XP, Network Explorer (also known as the Network folder) allows users to browse resources on the local network. However, Network Explorer is more powerful than My Network Places, largely because of the Network Discovery support built into Windows Vista and Windows 7 (described later in this section).

To open Network Explorer, click a network from within Network And Sharing Center. As shown in Figure 25-3, Network Explorer displays other visible computers and network devices. Users can access network resources simply by double-clicking them.

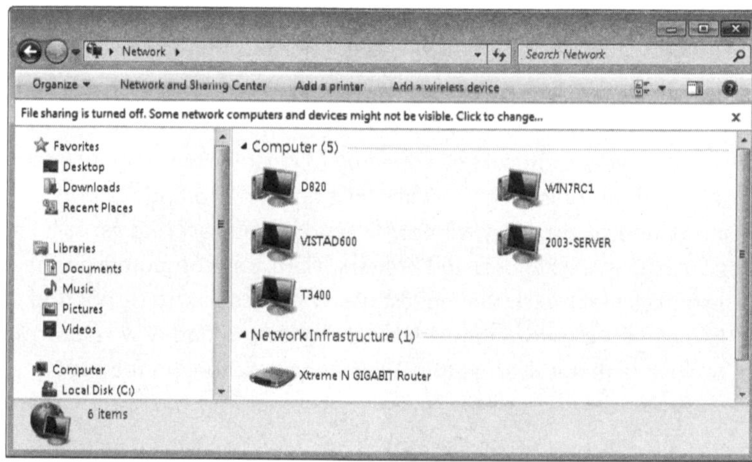

FIGURE 25-3 Network Explorer allows users to browse local resources.

The following sections discuss how different aspects of Network Explorer function, including Network Discovery and the Network Map.

How Windows Finds Network Resources

Versions of Windows prior to Windows Vista use NetBIOS broadcasts to announce their presence on the network to facilitate finding shared resources in workgroup environments. Windows Vista and Windows 7 expand this capability with a feature called Network Discovery, also known as Function Discovery (FD). Network Discovery's primary purpose is to simplify configuring and connecting network devices in home and small office environments. For example, Network Discovery can enable the Media Center feature to detect a Media Center Extender device (such as an Xbox 360) when it is connected to the network.

Network Discovery can be enabled or disabled separately for different network location types. For example, Network Discovery is enabled by default on networks with the private location type, but it is disabled on networks with the public or domain location types. By properly configuring network location types (described later in this chapter), computers running Windows Vista and Windows 7 in your environment can take advantage of Network Discovery when connected to your internal networks but minimize security risks by disabling Network Discovery when connected to other networks, such as the Internet. You might want to leave Network Discovery enabled for some network location types so that users can more easily find network resources on your intranet that aren't listed in Active Directory Domain Services (AD DS) and so that users with mobile PCs can configure network devices more easily on their home networks or when traveling.

Although Network Discovery is preferred, Windows Vista and Windows 7 continue to use the Computer Browser service and NetBIOS broadcasts to find earlier versions of Windows computers on the network. In addition, Windows Vista and Windows 7 use the Function Discovery Provider Host service and Web Services Dynamic Discovery (WS-Discovery) to find other Windows Vista and Windows 7 computers and use Universal Plug and Play (UPnP)/Simple Service Discovery Protocol (SSDP) to find networked devices that support the protocols. Therefore, enabling Network Discovery creates exceptions for each of these protocols through Windows Firewall.

WS-Discovery is a multicast discovery protocol developed by Microsoft, BEA, Canon, Intel, and webMethods to provide a method for locating services on a network. To find network resources, computers running Windows Vista and Windows 7 send a multicast request for one or more target services, such as shared folders and printers. Then, any computers on the local network with shared resources that match the request use WS-Discovery to respond to the message. To minimize the need for clients to regularly send requests to find new resources, newly published resources announce themselves on the network, as described in the next section.

WS-Discovery uses Simple Object Access Protocol (SOAP) over UDP port 3702. The multicast address is 239.255.255.250 for IPv4 and FF2::C for IPv6.

How Windows Publishes Network Resources

When you share a network resource, such as a folder or printer, Windows communicates using several protocols to make other computers on the network aware of the resource. To communicate with versions of Windows prior to Windows Vista, the Server service notifies the Computer Browser service when new shares are created or deleted, and the Computer Browser service sends the announcements over NetBIOS.

To announce resources to other computers running Windows Vista and Windows 7 using WS-Discovery, Windows 7 uses the Function Discovery Resource Publication (FDRP) service. Although FD is responsible for discovering shared resources on a network when the computer is acting as a client, FDRP is responsible for announcing resources when the computer is acting as a server. The primary functions are:

- Sends a HELLO message for each registered resource on service startup.

- Sends a HELLO message whenever a new resource is registered. Responds to network probes for resources matching one of the registered resources by type.
- Resolves network requests for resources matching one of the registered resources by name.
- Sends a BYE message whenever a resource is unregistered.
- Sends a BYE message for each registered resource on service shutdown.

The HELLO message includes the following information:

- Name
- Description
- Whether the computer is part of a workgroup or domain
- Computer type, such as desktop, laptop, tablet, Media Center, or server
- Whether Remote Desktop is enabled and allowed through Windows Firewall
- Folder and printer shares with at least Read access for Everyone if file sharing is enabled and allowed through Windows Firewall. Specifically, administrative shares are not announced. For each share, the following information is included:
  - Path
  - If applicable, the folder type (such as documents, pictures, music, or videos)
  - The share permissions assigned to the Everyone special group

FDRP is primarily intended for home networks, where ease of use is typically a requirement and networks are unmanaged. In corporate computing environments, where there can be a large number of computers on a single subnet and the network is managed, FDRP is not recommended because the traffic might become a nuisance. By default, FDRP is enabled in a workgroup and disabled in a domain environment.

How Windows Creates the Network Map

Windows creates the Network Map in part by using the Link Layer Topology Discovery (LLTD) protocol. As the name suggests, LLTD functions at Layer 2 (the layer devices use to communicate on a LAN) and enables network devices to identify each other, learn about the network (including bandwidth capabilities), and establish communications (even if devices are not yet configured with IP addresses). Typically, you do not need to manage LLTD directly. However, you can configure two Group Policy settings located within Computer Configuration\Policies\Administrative Templates\Network
\Link Layer Topology Discovery:

- **Turn on Responder (RSPNDR) Driver** This setting enables computers to be discovered on a network and to participate in Quality of Service (QoS) activities, such as bandwidth estimation and network health analysis. You can choose to enable the responder driver while connected to networks of the domain, public, or private location type. Windows enables the responder driver for all networks by default.

- **Turn on Mapper I/O (LLTDIO) Driver** This setting enables a computer to discover the topology of the local network and to initiate QoS requests. You can choose to enable the mapper driver while connected to networks of the domain, public, or private location type. This option is enabled for all networks by default. Windows enables the mapper driver for all networks by default.

Figure 25-4 illustrates how the LLTD responder and mapper relate to other networking components.

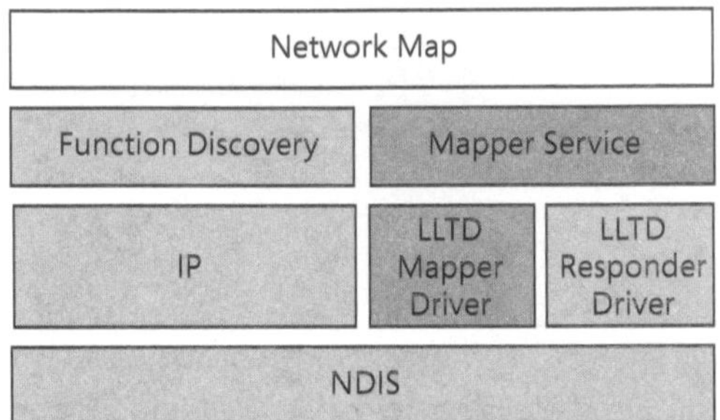

FIGURE 25-4 LLTD is implemented as a low-level mapper and responder.

> ***NOTE*** **Windows Vista and Windows 7 include an LLTD responder, but earlier versions of Windows do not. To find out how to download an LLTD responder that you can add to Windows XP, read Microsoft Knowledge Base article 992120 at *http://support.microsoft.com/kb/922120*. This will enable computers running Windows XP to appear on the Network Maps in Windows 7, but they still cannot generate the maps.**

LLTD is not a secure protocol, and there is no guarantee that the Network Map is accurate. It is possible for devices on the network to send false announcements, adding bogus items to the map.

Because each user can have his own set of network profiles, Windows creates Network Maps on a per-user basis. For each network profile that a user creates, Windows actually generates two maps: the current map and a copy of the last functional map (similar to the Last Known Good recovery option). When displaying the Network Map to the user, Windows combines these two maps.

Network Map

The Network Map, shown in Figure 25-5, makes it simpler to visually examine how a computer is connected to one or more networks and to other computers on your intranet. Although the tool is primarily intended to simplify networking for users, it is also a useful tool for administrators. A user can click the name of her computer to view her computer's properties, click a local network to view network resources with Network Explorer, or click the Internet icon to browse the Web.

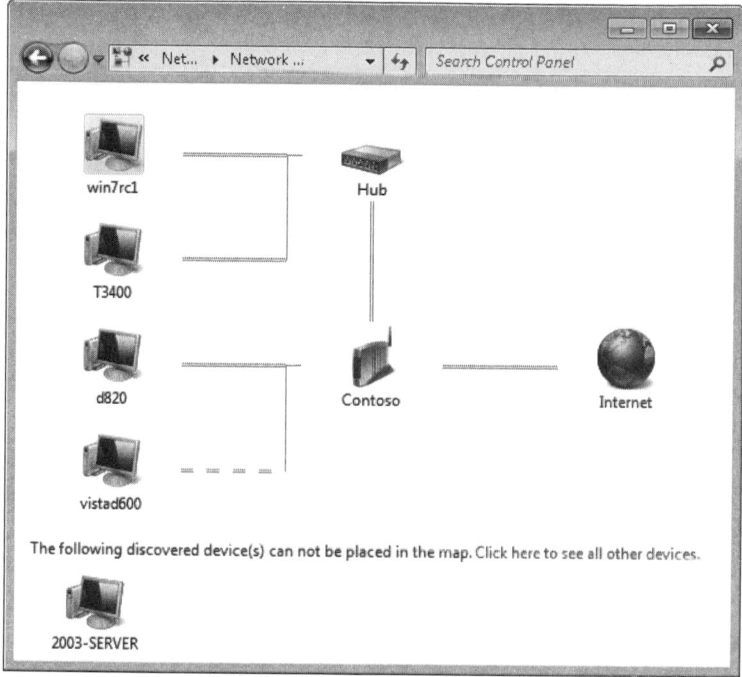

FIGURE 25-5 The Network Map visually represents all of a computer's connections.

For Windows to create a full Network Map, the Link Layer Topology Discovery Mapper service must be running and network mapping must be enabled. This service is set to start manually by default; the Network Map will start the service automatically when required. You should avoid disabling the Link Layer Topology Discovery Mapper service unless you also want to disable network mapping. Network maps might not always be accurate; Windows might not display devices that do not support LLTD.

Network mapping is disabled by default when a computer is connected to a domain. To enable Network Map, enable the Turn On Mapper I/O (LLTDIO) Driver Group Policy setting (described in the previous section) and select the Allow Operation While In Domain check box. To enable Windows client computers to appear on other computers' maps, enable the Turn On Responder (RSPNDR) Driver setting.

Set Up A Connection Or Network Wizard

Windows includes a network setup wizard to further simplify connecting to wired networks, wireless networks, dial-up connections, and virtual private networks (VPNs). Typically, administrators should configure all required network connections before deploying a computer. However, users often need to add wireless connections, VPN connections, and dial-up connections after a computer is deployed.

For more information about setting up wireless networks, read the section titled "Configuring Wireless Settings Manually" later in this chapter. For more information about setting up dial-up connections and VPNs, see Chapter 27, "Connecting Remote Users and Networks."

Manageability Improvements

Windows Vista networking includes several improvements in manageability that continue to be supported in Windows 7. First, network location types enable you to configure different security settings to better protect computers when connected to public networks but still enable required functionality when connected to private networks. Administrators can configure policy-based QoS to make better use of available networks and ensure that the most critical network applications have the bandwidth they need. Windows Firewall and Internet Protocol security (IPsec) continue to provide network filtering, authentication, and encryption, but you can now manage both features using a single tool. Windows Connect Now simplifies end-user configuration of computers and network devices.

The sections that follow describe these features in more detail.

Network Location Types

Different types of networks require different levels of protection. For example, when connected to your internal AD DS network, you might want computers to allow network management tools to establish incoming connections. However, you do not want to allow management connections if a user connects to a wireless hotspot at an airport or coffee shop.

Windows Vista and Windows 7 provide three different network location types:

- **Public** With public networks, such as wireless hotspots, protecting the computer from network attacks is vital. Network Discovery is disabled by default for public networks, and Windows Firewall blocks all unrequested, incoming traffic unless you specifically create exceptions.
- **Private (labeled as Home or Work)** Private networks are designed to be used for home or small office networks, where you may want to share resources with other computers on the LAN, but you do not have an AD DS domain controller. Network Discovery is enabled by default on private networks.
- **Domain** Any time the computer can connect to and authenticate with an AD DS domain controller of the domain for which it is a member, the network is considered a domain network. Network Discovery is disabled by default on domain networks unless overridden by domain Group Policy settings. Administrators should use Group Policy settings to create Windows Firewall exceptions for internal monitoring and management software.

It is important to understand network location types because any Windows Firewall exceptions you create apply only to the currently configured network location type. For example, if you want Microsoft Internet Information Services (IIS) to accept incoming connections when you are connected to your home network, you should specify that the home network is a private network prior to creating the exception. If your home network is configured as a public network when you create the exception, IIS will be available when you are connected to public networks such as wireless hotspots, thereby exposing IIS to attacks from the Internet.

Domain networks are configured automatically when a computer connects to a domain controller. All other networks are considered public networks by default. To specify a network as the private location type, follow these steps:

1. Connect your computer to the network you want to configure as private.
2. Open Network And Sharing Center. Click Public Network, located below your active network connection.
3. The Set Network Location dialog box appears. Click Home or Work.
4. Click Close.

Because Windows might connect to many different networks, it stores profiles of each network using the network's Domain Name System (DNS) suffix and gateway media access control (MAC) address. The gateway MAC address uniquely identifies a network adapter in your router.

Policy-Based QoS

The cost of bandwidth has fallen significantly in the last several years, but network congestion is still a problem. As more people and organizations begin to use real-time networking services, such as Voice over IP (VoIP), multimedia streaming, and video conferencing, it is obvious that increasing bandwidth alone cannot solve network quality problems.

> ***NOTE*** **Windows Vista and Windows 7 support Quality Windows Audio Video Experience (qWAVE), which provides QoS support for streaming audio and video across home networks. Because this resource kit focuses on enterprise networking, qWave is not discussed in detail. Instead, all references to QoS refer to enterprise QoS, also known as eQoS.**

Policy-based QoS in Windows Vista and Windows 7 enables domain-wide management of how computers on your network use bandwidth. This technology can solve network problems and make possible the following scenarios:

- Enable real-time traffic by prioritizing more important applications, such as VoIP, over lower-priority traffic, such as browsing the Web or downloading e-mail.
- Customize bandwidth requirements for groups of users and computers. For example, you can prioritize traffic for your IT Support Center over other users to increase responsiveness when managing and troubleshooting computers.
- Minimize the negative impact of high-bandwidth, low-priority traffic, such as backup data transfers, by using prioritization and throttling.

Network congestion problems occur because high-bandwidth applications tend to consume all available bandwidth, and applications are not written to give central bandwidth control to IT administrators. Adding more bandwidth does not usually solve these problems. Instead, adding more bandwidth only leads to applications consuming the newly available capacity. IT administrators need a central means to control and allocate bandwidth resources based on the needs of their business.

Policy-based QoS enables you to make the most of your current bandwidth by enabling flexible bandwidth management through Group Policy settings. With Policy-based QoS, you can prioritize and/or throttle outbound network traffic without requiring applications to be modified for QoS support. You can use Differentiated Services Code Point (DSCP) marking to configure QoS policies to outbound traffic so that network equipment can prioritize it or specify a maximum throttle rate. DSCP marking is useful only if prioritization is enabled in routers. Almost all enterprise-class routers support DSCP prioritization; however, it is usually disabled by default.

Each computer running Windows Vista and Windows 7 can prioritize or throttle outbound traffic based on a mix of any of the following conditions:

- Group of users or computers based on an AD DS container, such as a domain, a site, or an organizational unit
- Sending application
- Source or destination IPv4 or IPv6 address (including network prefix length notation, such as 192.168.1.0/24)
- Source or destination Transmission Control Protocol (TCP) or UDP port number
- For computers running Windows 7 only, the Uniform Resource Locator (URL) of a Web site being accessed with HTTP or Hypertext Transfer Protocol Secure (HTTPS)

Additionally, Windows 7 (when acting as a Web server) can now prioritize Web traffic based on the URL, allowing you to assign a lower priority to nonessential Web sites and a higher priority to critical Web sites. Because this is primarily a server feature, it is not discussed in detail here.

NOTE Windows Vista and Windows 7 include a new implementation of the QoS component in the Pacer.sys NDIS 6.0 lightweight filter driver, located in %SystemRoot%\System32\Drivers. Pacer.sys replaces Psched.sys, which is used in the Windows Server 2003 and Windows XP operating systems. It continues to support the Generic QoS (GQoS) and Traffic Control (TC) application programming interfaces (APIs) provided by Microsoft Windows 2000, Windows XP, and Windows Server 2003. Therefore, existing applications that use QoS will work with Windows Vista and Windows 7. For more information about these APIs, see "The MS QoS Components" at *http://technet.microsoft.com/en-us/library/bb742475.aspx*.

Selecting DSCP Values

When sending packets, computers add a DSCP value that your network infrastructure can examine to determine how the packet should be prioritized. Although DSCP values can be arbitrary depending on how your network infrastructure is configured, many organizations use a typical DSCP strategy with the following five queues:

- **Control traffic** Communications transmitted between routers. Typically, these communications require minimal bandwidth, but they should be assigned a high priority because quick transmission can reduce downtime in the event of a hardware failure. You should also use this priority for VoIP control traffic. Use DSCP values of 25 for control traffic.
- **Latency-sensitive traffic** Traffic, such as VoIP, that must be delivered as quickly as possible. Typically, you should assign this a DSCP value of 46, known as Expedited Forwarding (EF).
- **Business critical traffic, also known as Better than Best Effort (BBE)** Communications that should receive priority treatment, such as customer service database queries from a line-of-business (LOB) application or streaming video, but that are not highly sensitive to latency. Use a DSCP value of 34.
- **Best-effort (BE) traffic** Standard traffic, including any traffic not marked with a DSCP number, that should be handled after either of the preceding two queues. This traffic should have a DSCP value of 0, which is the default if no DSCP value is specified.
- **Scavenger traffic** Low-priority traffic, such as backups, downloading of updates, noncritical file synchronization, and non–work-related traffic that employees might generate. Use a DSCP value of 10 or 8.

> ***NOTE*** **If you mark traffic from too many applications as high priority, the high-priority queue on routers can grow long enough to add significant latency. This defeats the purpose of QoS. Therefore, you should reserve the highest-priority DSCP marking for real-time communications, such as VoIP.**

Table 25-1 summarizes these values.

TABLE 25-1 DSCP Interoperability Values

PURPOSE	COMMON USES	DSCP VALUE
VoIP	VoIP traffic, including signaling and control traffic	46
Interactive video	Two-way video conferencing	34
Mission-critical data	Database queries, LOB communications, video streaming	25
Best effort	All other traffic, including e-mail and Web browsing	0
Bulk data	Backups, nonbusiness applications, file transfers	10

Many networks use an even simpler structure with only two priorities: one for latency-sensitive traffic and another for BE traffic. However, if you have third-party tools that can use DSCP values to report on network performance for different types of traffic, it is advantageous to define a larger number of DSCP values even if your network infrastructure isn't configured to handle each DSCP value uniquely.

DSCP values might be lost when packets leave your network because most organizations do not trust priorities provided by computers outside the organization. Because sending traffic labeled as high priority can create a denial-of-service (DoS) attack, DSCP values from untrusted computers might be malicious.

Wireless Multimedia (WMM) includes four access categories for prioritizing traffic on 802.11 wireless networks. WMM uses DSCP values to set the priority, so you can take advantage of WMM automatically by specifying DSCP values. Table 25-2 shows how DSCP values correspond to WMM access categories.

TABLE 25-2 DSCP Values and WMM Access Categories

DSCP VALUE	WMM ACCESS CATEGORY
48–63	Voice (VO)
32–47	Video (VI)
24–31, 0–7	Best effort (BE)
8–23	Background (BK)

To support fully prioritizing traffic based on DSCP values, your network infrastructure must support the use of multiple queues as defined in RFC 2474.

Planning Traffic Throttling

Using DSCP values to prioritize traffic allows you to fully utilize your network's bandwidth while providing the best possible performance for your most important traffic. That's the ideal QoS scenario; however, not all network infrastructures support prioritizing traffic using DSCP values. If your network does not support traffic priorities, you can use traffic throttling to ensure that specific applications do not consume more than a specified amount of bandwidth.

Traffic throttling limits traffic on individual computers and cannot limit the aggregate bandwidth used by multiple computers. For example, if you have five Web servers and want to ensure that they never use more than half of your 1,000 Kbps (1 Mbps) link, you must configure the QoS policy to throttle traffic at 100 Kbps for each of the five computers, which will total 500 Kbps if all five servers are sending traffic at their throttled maximum. Do not attempt to use traffic throttling to limit the bandwidth of every application or protocol; instead, use traffic throttling to limit only traffic from low-priority applications, such as network backups or the downloading of large updates. Traffic throttling does not have any network infrastructure requirements.

Configuring QoS Policies

To configure QoS using Group Policy, edit the Computer Configuration\Windows Settings\Policy-based QoS node or the User Configuration\Windows Settings\Policy-based QoS node. Then, follow these steps:

1. Right-click the Policy-based QoS node and click Create New Policy.
2. The Policy-based QoS Wizard appears. On the Create A QoS Policy page, specify a name for the policy. Then, specify a DSCP value (which your network infrastructure can use to prioritize traffic) and a throttle rate (which Windows will use to restrict outgoing bandwidth usage) as needed. Click Next.

> ***NOTE*** **Notice that the throttle rate must be entered in kilobytes per second (KBps) or megabytes per second (MBps) rather than the more commonly used kilobits per second (Kbps) or megabits per second (Mbps)—notice the lowercase b. Eight bits equal one byte. Therefore, if you determine the Kbps or Mbps at which you want to throttle, divide that number by 8 when typing it into the Policy-based QoS Wizard. For example, if you want to throttle at 128 Kbps, you type 16 KBps.**

3. On the This QoS Policy Applies To page, select one of the following options: All Applications, Only Applications With This Executable Name, or Only HTTP Server Applications Responding To Requests For This URL. If you are specifying an application, Windows will apply the DSCP value or throttle rate to network traffic generated by that application. To identify the executable file used by a service, use the Services snap-in to check the service properties. If you are specifying a URL, keep in mind that you must specify the URL on the Web server, not on the client computer. Click Next.
4. On the Specify The Source And Destination IP Addresses page, you can configure the policy to apply to traffic between any two computers. Use network prefix length representation to specify networks—for example, specify 192.168.1.0/24 to indicate the entire 192.168.1.*x* network or 192.168.0.0/16 to indicate the entire 192.168.*x*.*x* network. For example, if you want to configure a QoS policy that applies a DSCP value for traffic sent to your e-mail server, you can select Only For The Following Destination IP Address Or Prefix and then type the e-mail server's IP address. (IPv4 and IPv6 addresses will both work.) Click Next.

> ***NOTE*** **QoS policies apply only to outgoing traffic, so the computer to which you're applying the policy will always be identified by the source address, and the remote computer or network will always be identified by the destination address.**

5. On the Specify The Protocol And Port Numbers page, you can prioritize traffic based on TCP or UDP port numbers. For example, if you want to throttle all outgoing Web requests, you can select TCP, select To This Destination Port Number Or Range, and then specify port 80. (The HTTP protocol uses TCP port 80.) Click Finish.

Windows applies QoS policies only for domain network location types. Therefore, if a user connects to a wireless network at a coffee shop (and your domain controller cannot be contacted), Windows will not apply your QoS policies. However, if the user then connects to your internal network using a VPN, Windows will apply QoS policies to that VPN connection.

HOW IT WORKS

Prioritizing QoS Policies

Much like applying Group Policy objects (GPOs), the most specific QoS policy applies when multiple policies conflict. For example, if you create policies for both a specific IP address and a network that includes that IP address, the IP address policy will be applied instead of the network policy. Windows uses the following rules when applying QoS policies:

1. **User-level QoS policies take precedence over computer-level QoS policies.**
2. **QoS policies that identify applications take precedence over QoS policies that identify networks or IP addresses.**
3. **QoS policies that specify IP addresses and more specific networks take precedence over QoS policies that specify less specific networks.**
4. **QoS policies that specify port numbers take precedence over QoS polices that specify port ranges, which take precedence over QoS policies that do not specify a port number.**
5. **If multiple QoS policies still conflict, policies that specify source IP addresses take precedence over policies that specify destination IP addresses, and policies that specify a source port take precedence over policies that specify a destination port.**

QoS policies are not cumulative; only one QoS policy can be applied to any given connection.

Configuring System-Wide QoS Settings

After creating a policy, you can edit it by right-clicking it in the details pane of the Group Policy Object Editor and then clicking Edit Existing Policy. You can configure system-wide QoS settings within the Computer Configuration\Policies\Administrative Templates\Network\QoS Packet Scheduler node of Group Policy. You must modify these settings only if you must limit the outstanding packets, limit the bandwidth that can be reserved, or change the Packet Scheduler timer resolution. The following policies are available in the QoS Packet Scheduler node:

- **Limit Outstanding Packets** Specifies the maximum number of outstanding packets that can be issued to the network adapter at any given time. When this limit is reached, new packets are queued until the network adapter completes a packet, at which point a previously queued packet is removed from the Pacer.sys queue and is sent to the network adapter. This setting is disabled by default, and you should never need to enable this setting.
- **Limit Reservable Bandwidth** Controls the percentage of the overall bandwidth that the application can reserve. By default, this is set to 20 percent, which provides 80 percent of bandwidth to processes that do not have reserved bandwidth.
- **Set Timer Resolution** This value is not supported and should not be set.

The QoS Packet Scheduler node also has the following three subnodes that you can use to manually configure the standard DSCP values:

- **DSCP Value Of Conforming Packets** These settings apply to packets that comply with flow specifications.
- **DSCP Value Of Non-Conforming Packets** These settings apply to packets that do not comply with flow specifications.
- **Layer-2 Priority Value** These settings specify default link-layer priority values for networks that support it.

You will need to change the values contained in these subnodes only if you have configured your network infrastructure to use nonstandard DSCP values.

Configuring Advanced QoS Settings

You can also configure advanced QoS settings for computers using Group Policy. Within the Group Policy Object Editor, right-click the Computer Configuration\Windows Settings\Policy-based QoS node and then click Advanced QoS Settings. You can use the Advanced QoS Settings dialog box to configure the following settings:

- **Specify The Inbound TCP Throughput Level** Most QoS policies relate to outbound traffic that the client computer sends. You can use this setting on the Inbound TCP Traffic tab to configure Windows so that it will attempt to throttle incoming traffic. Although Windows has direct control over the throughput of outbound traffic, it has indirect control only over the rate of incoming traffic. For TCP connections, you can configure a Windows client computer to limit incoming traffic by specifying the maximum size of the TCP receive window. The TCP receive window is the amount of data that a receiver allows a sender to send before having to wait for an acknowledgment. A larger maximum window size means that the sender can send more data at a time, increasing network utilization and throughput. By limiting the maximum size of the TCP receive window, a receiver can indirectly control the incoming throughput for a TCP connection. Level 3 (Maximum Throughput) is for a 16-megabyte (MB) TCP receive window. Level 2 is for a 1-MB TCP receive window. Level 1 is for a 256-kilobyte (KB) TCP receive window. Level 0 is for a 64-KB TCP receive window. Unlike Policy-based

QoS settings for outgoing traffic, this setting cannot control the rate of incoming traffic on a per-application, per-address, or per-port basis.

> ***NOTE*** **Because UDP traffic is not acknowledged, you cannot throttle UDP traffic from the receiving computer.**

- **Control DSCP Marking Requests From Applications** DSCP marking adds information to outgoing packets to identify the priority of the packet. If your network infrastructure supports DSCP-differentiated delivery, the infrastructure can use the DSCP value to select a priority for traffic. Use this setting to allow applications to specify their own DSCP values or to ignore application-specified values and only allow QoS policies to specify DSCP values.

For more information about Policy-based QoS, visit the "Quality Of Service" home page at *http://technet.microsoft.com/en-us/network/bb530836.aspx*. For detailed information, read Chapter 5, "Policy-Based Quality of Service," in *Windows Server 2008 Networking and Network Access Protection* by Joseph Davies and Tony Northrup (Microsoft Press, 2008).

Testing QoS

You can use the QoS Traffic Generator to test your QoS implementation by generating different types of traffic, at varying rates, with specific characteristics. The following example demonstrates using the QoS Traffic Generator to send UDP traffic to the IP address 10.12.1.1 at a rate of 5 Mbps for 5 seconds.

First, start the QoS Traffic Generator in sink mode on the destination computer.

```
qostraffic -sink -udp
```

Then, send traffic using the QoS Traffic Generator from the source computer to the destination computer.

```
qostraffic -source -udp -dest 10.12.1.1 -throttle 5000000 -duration 5
```

```
Parsing command line...
WSAStartup successful.
Time between each packet (microsec): 2400
Size of each packet: 1472
Statistics sampling interval (msec): 1000
Sending traffic at 5.00 Mbps to 192.168.1.100:9999
Date, Time, Packets received, Bytes received (headers included), Elapsed time (msec),
Throughput (Kbps), Bottleneck BW, Available BW, RTT, BBSet, ABSet, RTTSet, ErrorCode
05/15/2009, 10:51:54, 421, 631500, 1014, 4982.249,,,,,,,
05/15/2009, 10:51:55, 422, 633000, 1014, 4994.083,,,,,,,
05/15/2009, 10:51:56, 423, 634500, 1014, 5005.917,,,,,,,
05/15/2009, 10:51:57, 422, 633000, 1014, 4994.083,,,,,,,
```

```
05/15/2009, 10:51:58, 423, 634500, 1014, 5005.917,,,,,,,
05/15/2009, 10:51:59, 422, 633000, 1014, 4994.083,,,,,,,
05/15/2009, 10:52:00, 423, 634500, 1014, 5005.917,,,,,,,
05/15/2009, 10:52:01, 422, 633000, 1014, 4994.083,,,,,,,
05/15/2009, 10:52:02, 423, 634500, 1014, 5005.917,,,,,,,
Time has elapsed, or CTRL+C has been pressed.
Stopping Source traffic, waiting 5 sec.
SenderThread is exiting...
SenderThread exited successfully.
WSACleanup successful.
```

The sink computer will display confirmation of the datagrams received.

For detailed usage information, run the following command from a command prompt.

```
qostraffic -?
```

To download the QoS Traffic Generator, visit *http://connect.microsoft.com/wndp* and then click the Downloads link. The QoS Traffic Generator includes libraries and source code, allowing developers to integrate the capabilities into custom applications.

Windows Firewall and IPsec

As the need for enterprises to share data within and outside their organizations increases, so does the need for greater security. Windows 7 provides strong, easy-to-configure security features. For example, Windows Firewall with the Advanced Security Microsoft Management Console (MMC) snap-in combines inbound and outbound firewall port management with IPsec for authentication and/or encryption. This powerful layer of security can also be managed via Group Policy or command-line scripting to provide a simple way to deploy firewall filtering and traffic protection rules that can limit access by specific users, computers, or applications, providing the administrator with an extremely high level of control.

For more information about Windows Firewall and improvements to IPsec, see Chapter 26, "Configuring Windows Firewall and IPsec."

Windows Connect Now

To simplify the creation and configuration of wireless networks and their security settings, Windows 7 supports Windows Connect Now, with which users can store network configuration information on a universal serial bus (USB) flash drive (UFD). To configure a wireless network, users first step through a network setup wizard that gathers their wireless network preferences. Then, Windows configures the computer with authentication and encryption settings for a protected wireless network and stores the configuration on a UFD. Adding new computers (running Windows XP Service Pack 2 (SP2) or later, Windows Vista, or Windows 7) to the wireless network can be as simple as connecting the UFD to each computer. Although Group Policy is the preferred way to configure domain member computers for wireless networks, UFDs are an excellent way to grant guests access to an encrypted wireless network. Note, however, that the wireless network should be isolated from your internal networks to protect your intranet from your guests.

You can completely prevent users from accessing the Windows Connect Now Wizards by using the Prohibit Access Of The Windows Connect Now Wizards in either the Computer Configuration\Policies\Administrative Templates\Network\Windows Connect Now node or the User Configuration\Policies\Administrative Templates\Network\Windows Connect Now Group Policy node. In addition, the Computer Configuration\Policies\Administrative Templates\Network\Windows Connect Now node has the Configuration Of Wireless Settings Using Windows Connect Now setting, which provides the following options:

- **Turn Off Ability To Configure Using WCN Over Ethernet (UPnP)** Prevents Windows from being able to configure networked devices that support UPnP.
- **Turn Off Ability to Configure Using WCN Over In-band 802.11 Wi-Fi** Prevents Windows from being able to configure wireless networked devices.
- **Turn Off Ability To Configure Using A USB Flash Drive** Prevents Windows from being able to store a Windows Connect Now configuration to a UFD. Because the Windows Connect Now information stored on a UFD contains information that can allow computers to access your protected wireless network, you might choose to disable this setting to improve the security of your wireless networks.
- **Turn Off Ability To Configure Windows Portable Device (WPD)** Prevents Windows from being able to configure WPDs, which include portable media players, digital cameras, and mobile phones.
- **Maximum Number Of WCN Devices Allowed** Enables you to limit the number of Windows Connect Now devices that a computer running Windows can configure.
- **Higher Precedence Medium For Devices Discovered By Multiple Media** Determines which networking type is used when a device is available across both wired and wireless networks.

If you do not plan to use Windows Connect Now, you can disable it safely. The default setting for the Windows Connect Now–related Group Policy settings enables all Windows Connect Now capabilities.

Core Networking Improvements

Windows 7 networking features are designed to offer improved performance, security, and manageability. Most users will never notice many of the most important changes, however, because they function without user intervention. For example, BranchCache can reduce wide area network (WAN) utilization by caching content within branch offices, but users never need to be aware of its existence.

The sections that follow describe changes to the core networking functionality in Windows 7. Although many of these improvements are carried over from Windows Vista, BranchCache, DNS security (DNSsec) support, and GreenIT support are new to Windows 7. Chapter 27 describes DirectAccess and VPN Reconnect.

BranchCache

BranchCache uses peer-to-peer networking across LANs to reduce file sharing and HTTP traffic across the WAN. After you enable BranchCache, client computers running Windows 7 keep a local cached copy of data that they copy from a file or Web server running Windows Server 2008 R2. If another computer running Windows 7 on the same LAN or branch office needs the same data, it can copy it directly from the local cache, reducing WAN bandwidth usage and potentially improving performance.

BranchCache Architectures

BranchCache can function in one of two architectures: Hosted Cache and Distributed Cache. Hosted Cache is the preferred architecture, but it requires that a computer running Windows Server 2008 R2 be deployed to each regional office. Distributed Cache copies files directly between client computers running Windows 7 and thus does not require a server to be deployed to the regional offices. Hosted Cache provides caching for an entire branch office, even if it has multiple LANs, and allows cached data to be used even if the client that cached the data disconnects from the network. Distributed Cache caches only within a LAN, but it can be used for branch offices with clients running Windows 7 that cannot support a computer running Windows Server 2008 R2.

How Hosted Cache Works

At a detailed level, the Hosted Cache model follows this process to cache and retrieve data:

1. The client running Windows 7 connects to the content server (a file or Web server running Windows Server 2008 R2) and requests a file (or part of a file), exactly as it does if it retrieves the file without using BranchCache. After authorizing the user, the server returns an identifier that includes a signed hash of the data segment. The client uses the identifier to search for the file on the Hosted Cache, a local server running Windows Server 2008 R2. Because this is the first time any client has retrieved the file, it is not already cached. Therefore, the client retrieves the file directly from the content server.
2. The client stores a copy of the data in the Hosted Cache.
3. A second client running Windows 7 requests the same file from the content server. Again, the content server authorizes the user and returns an identifier.

4. The client uses the identifier to request the data from its Hosted Cache server. The Hosted Cache encrypts the data and returns it to the client. The client then validates the data using the hash provided as part of the identifier to verify that it has not been modified.

Figure 25-6 illustrates this process.

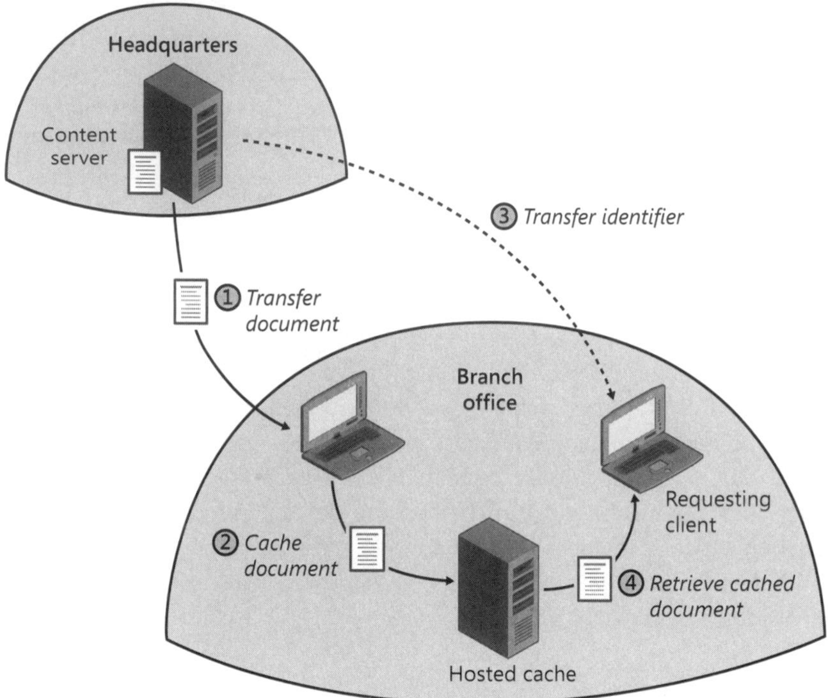

FIGURE 25-6 The Hosted Cache architecture

How Distributed Cache Works

The process is similar to that used by Hosted Cache mode, except requests for cached content are multicast to the local network and a Hosted Cache server is not required:

1. A client running Windows 7 connects to the content server and requests data. The server authorizes the user and returns an identifier. Because this is the first time any client has attempted to retrieve the file, it is not already cached on the local network. Therefore, the client retrieves the file directly from the content server and uses BranchCache to cache it on its hard disk.
2. A second requesting client running Windows 7 requests the same file from the content server. Again, the content server authorizes the user and returns an identifier.
3. The requesting client sends a request to its peers on the local network for the required file using the WS-Discovery multicast protocol.

4. The client that previously cached the file becomes the serving client and sends the file to the requesting client. The data is encrypted using an encryption key derived from the hashes. The client decrypts the data, validates it, and passes it to the application.

Figure 25-7 illustrates this process.

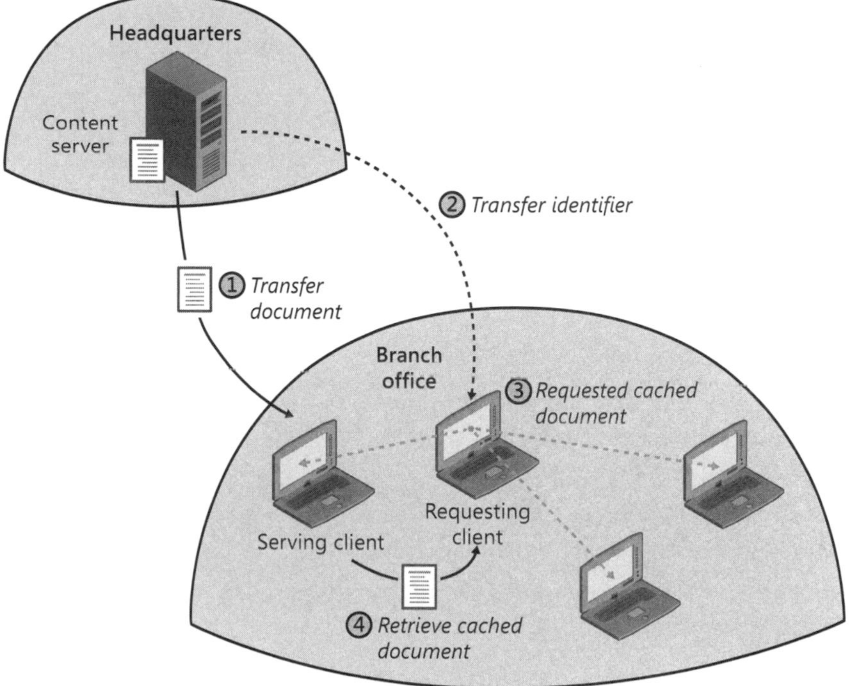

FIGURE 25-7 The Distributed Cache architecture

Configuring BranchCache

BranchCache clients can be managed using either Group Policy or the Netsh command-line tool. You can configure BranchCache using Group Policy settings located in Computer Configuration\Policies\Administrative Templates\Network\BranchCache. You can define the following settings:

- **Turn On BranchCache** Enable this setting to turn on BranchCache.
- **Set BranchCache Hosted Cache Mode** Enable this setting to turn on Hosted Cache mode and then specify the location of the Hosted Cache server. Because different branch offices should have different Hosted Caches, you will need to define different GPOs for different branch offices.
- **Set BranchCache Distributed Cache Mode** Enable this setting to turn on Distributed Cache mode when you cannot use Hosted Cache because a computer running Windows Server 2008 R2 is not available in the branch office.

- **Configure BranchCache For Network Files** Enable this setting to change the default latency required before BranchCache stores a copy of data retrieved from a file server. By default, BranchCache will cache data only if latency is greater than 80 milliseconds (ms). Typically, data travels across a LAN in less than 20 ms.
- **Set Percentage Of Disk Space Used For Client Computer Cache** Enable this setting to define the amount of space that Distributed Cache clients dedicate to the BranchCache data store. By default, BranchCache will use 5 percent of the total disk space.

  Additionally, you can prevent the Background Intelligent Transfer Service (BITS) from using BranchCache by enabling the Do Not Allow The BITS Client To Use Windows Branch Cache policy in the Computer Configuration\Policies\Administrative Templates \Network\Background Intelligent Transfer Service node of a GPO.

  You can use the Netsh command-line tool to view or change BranchCache settings. The following are the most useful Netsh commands:

- **Netsh BranchCache Show Status** Displays whether BranchCache is currently enabled.
- **Netsh BranchCache Show HostedCache** If Hosted Cache mode is enabled, displays the location of the Hosted Cache server.
- **Netsh BranchCache Show LocalCache** If Distributed Cache mode is enabled, displays the location and maximum size of the local cache.
- **Netsh BranchCache Set Service HostedClient** *<hosted_cache_server>* Configures a Hosted Cache client and defines the location (using a host name) of the Hosted Cache server.
- **Netsh BranchCache Set Service Distributed** Enables BranchCache in Distributed Cache mode.
- **Netsh BranchCache Set Service Disabled** Disables BranchCache on the client. BranchCache is disabled by default, so you only need to run this if you previously enabled it.

For more details, run the following command.

```
Netsh BranchCache
```

BranchCache Protocols

BranchCache supports file sharing using Server Message Block (SMB) and HTTP. As shown in Figure 25-8, applications do not need to communicate directly with BranchCache (although they can if they need to). Instead, applications will access the SMB and HTTP interfaces, exactly as they do in earlier versions of Windows.

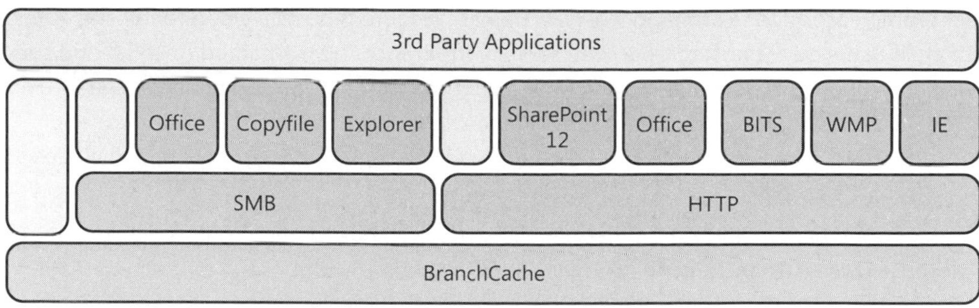

FIGURE 25-8 The BranchCache architecture

Because the BranchCache client is built into the SMB and HTTP stacks, any application that uses the Windows 7 SMB or HTTP stack will take advantage of BranchCache automatically. Applications that implement custom SMB or HTTP stacks, such as the Firefox Web browser, will not benefit from BranchCache.

The following sections describe how BranchCache can improve the efficiency of file sharing using SMB and Web browsing with HTTP.

File Sharing Using SMB

BranchCache supports SMB (including Signed SMB) and Common Internet File System (CIFS), the standard protocols for network file transfers when connecting to shared folders from Windows Explorer or when using command-line tools, such as Robocopy and Xcopy.

Naturally, the first request for a file can never be fulfilled from the cache. The first BranchCache client to retrieve a file must download it directly from the server and then store it in the cache. However, as long as the file is not updated, all subsequent read requests for the same file can be retrieved directly from the cache. If a user updates a file on a shared folder, clients will download the updated file directly from the server rather than the cache. Files smaller than 64 KB are never cached.

Web Browsing with HTTP (Including HTTPS)

HTTP and HTTPS are the standard protocols that Web browsers use. With HTTP or HTTPS and BranchCache, intranet Web pages can be cached in the branch office and retrieved by other clients on the local network. BranchCache provides a separate cache from the cache built into Windows Internet Explorer. The Internet Explorer cache is accessible only to the current user, whereas BranchCache is accessible to other users at the same branch.

BranchCache is not designed to be used with Internet Web pages. For HTTP caching to be supported, the Web server must be using Windows Server 2008 R2 with IIS. Only content marked as cacheable will be stored using BranchCache. Typically, this allows the most bandwidth-intensive Web content types to be cached, including static HTML pages, documents, images, sounds, and videos.

For example, consider a scenario in which Human Resources posts a video for all employees to watch. If that video is hosted on a Web server with BranchCache enabled, the first and second clients to view the video can download it from the intranet Web server across the WAN. The second client stores a copy of the video in the cache. Then, the third and subsequent clients download a small identifier from the intranet Web server and retrieve the full video directly from the cache.

Because each page might be different, most dynamically generated Web pages cannot be cached. However, BranchCache can still reduce WAN bandwidth usage by caching static images referenced in the page.

DNSsec

The DNS client in Windows 7 and Windows Server 2008 R2 and the DNS server in Windows Server 2080 R2 support DNS Security Extensions (DNSSECs) as per RFCs 4033, 4034, and 4035 to validate the integrity of DNS records. By validating that a DNS record was generated by the authoritative DNS server and that the DNS record has not been modified, Windows 7 and Windows Server 2008 R2 can validate the integrity of DNS responses.

With DNSsec, authoritative DNS servers running Windows Server 2008 R2 that support DNSSEC will sign a DNS zone cryptographically to generate digital signatures for all the resource records in the zone. Other DNS servers can verify that a DNS record was signed by the authoritative DNS server and that it has not been modified. The DNS client running Windows 7 is DNSSEC-aware and relies on its local DNS server for DNSSEC validation.

GreenIT

Users can save energy by putting computers into Sleep mode when they're not in use. With earlier versions of Windows, administrators could use Wake on LAN (WOL) to wake the computer so that it could be managed across the network. However, WOL only works when computers are connected to wired networks. Wireless computers in Sleep mode cannot be started or managed across the network, allowing them to fall behind on configuration changes, software updates, and other management tasks.

Windows 7 adds support for Wake on Wireless LAN (WoWLAN). With WoWLAN, Windows 7 can reduce electricity consumption by enabling users to remotely wake computers connected to wireless networks from Sleep mode. Because users can wake computers to access them across the network, IT can configure wireless computers to enter the low-power Sleep mode when not in use. This also benefits users who need to connect to their computer when working remotely.

Wired network connections use power when they're enabled, even if a network cable isn't connected. Although administrators could disable the wired network connections on mobile computers to save power and improve battery life, users would need to re-enable the network connection before connecting to a wired network. This might leave mobile users frustrated when they attempted to connect to a wired network—for example, in a hotel that did not offer a wireless network connection.

Windows 7 offers the power-saving benefits of disabling a wired network connection while still allowing users to connect to wired networks. Windows 7 can reduce energy consumption by turning off power to the network adapter when the cable is disconnected. When the user connects a cable, power is automatically restored.

Efficient Networking

Most network communications—including downloading files, browsing the Web, and reading e-mail—use the TCP Layer 3 protocol. TCP is considered a reliable network protocol because the recipient must confirm receipt of all transmissions. If a transmission isn't confirmed, it's considered lost and will be retransmitted.

However, confirming transmissions can prevent TCP transfers from using all available bandwidth. This happens because TCP breaks blocks of data into small pieces before transmitting them, and recipients must confirm receipt of each piece of the data. The number of pieces that can be sent before waiting to receive confirmation receipts is called the *TCP receive window size.*

When TCP was designed, network bandwidth was very low by today's standards, and communications were relatively unreliable. Therefore, waiting for confirmation for small pieces of a data block did not have a significant impact on performance. However, now that bandwidth is measured in Mbps instead of Kbps, a small TCP receive window size can slow communication significantly while the computer sending a data block waits for the receiving computer to send confirmation receipts.

Figure 25-9 demonstrates how TCP confirms portions of a data block.

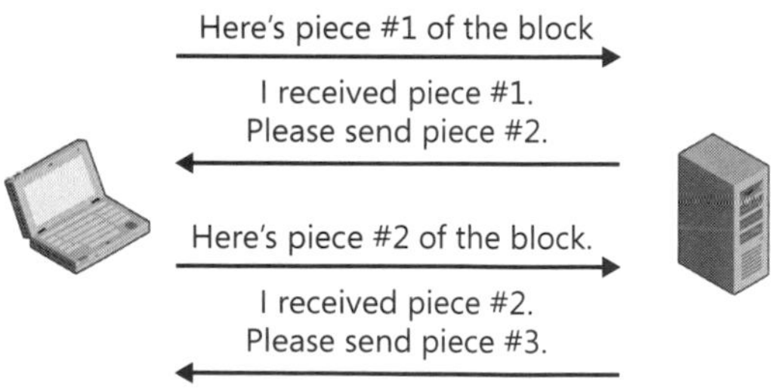

FIGURE 25-9 TCP requires data transfers to be confirmed.

TCP works well and does indeed provide reliable transfers over a variety of networks. However, waiting to confirm each portion of a data block causes a slight delay each time a confirmation is required. Just how much delay depends on two factors:

- **Network latency** Network latency is the delay, typically measured in ms, for a packet to be sent to a computer and for a response to be returned. Latency is also called the round-trip time (RTT). If latency is so high that the sending computer is waiting to receive confirmation receipts, latency has a direct impact on transfer speed because nothing is being transmitted while the sending computer waits for the confirmations.

- **How much of the file can be transferred before waiting for confirmation (TCP receive window size)** The smaller the TCP receive window size, the more frequently the sending computers might have to wait for confirmation. Therefore, smaller TCP receive window sizes can cause slower network performance because the sender has to wait for confirmations to be received. Larger TCP receive window sizes can improve performance by reducing the time spent waiting for confirmations.

What Causes Latency, How to Measure It, and How to Control It

Latency typically originates from two different sources: routers and distance.

Each router that a packet travels through has to copy the packet from one network interface to the next. This introduces a very slight delay—typically only a few milliseconds. However, traffic on the Internet might have to travel through more than fifty routers when making a round trip between two computers, so the delays do add up. Busy routers and networks that are near saturation can introduce more latency because the router might have to wait several milliseconds before it can place a packet onto a network interface.

Distance also introduces latency. Packets travel across networks at a speed slightly slower than the speed of light. A rough estimate of the speed packets travel would be about 100,000 miles per second. Although the speed is still very fast, a packet that has to travel to the other side of the Earth and back would have at least 250 ms of latency (before you calculate latency introduced by routers). Satellite connections add about 500 ms of latency sending the packet to and from the satellite. In addition, network paths are often very indirect, and packets often travel several times farther than the distance of a straight line between two computers. VPNs, in particular, can cause extremely indirect routing between computers.

The most common tool to measure latency is the command-line tool Ping. Ping can give you a rough idea of the latency between two points, but it is less than perfect because Ping does not transmit TCP-based data. Instead, Ping sends Internet Control Message Protocol (ICMP) messages that are designed for diagnostic purposes. Many routers give these ICMP messages a lower priority than other traffic, so Ping may report a higher latency than normal. In addition, many routers and computers are configured to completely block the ICMP messages used by Ping. A related command-line tool, PathPing, provides approximate latency information for all routers between two hosts. PathPing uses the same ICMP messages as Ping.

If latency is causing a problem on your network, first determine the source of the latency. If distance is causing the latency, find ways to shorten the distance. For example, you might replace a satellite link with a terrestrial link. Alternatively, if you determine that the path being taken between two points is inefficient, you might be able to reconfigure your network to shorten the distance that the packets need to travel between the two points. If you determine that busy networks or routers are introducing latency, you can upgrade your routers or increase the available bandwidth. Alternatively, you can use Policy-based QoS to prioritize the most important traffic to reduce latency for time-sensitive transmissions, such as streaming media and VOIP.

As you can see, high network latency can hurt performance, especially when combined with small TCP receive window sizes. Computers can reduce the negative impact of high-latency networks by increasing the TCP receive window size. However, versions of Windows prior to Windows Vista used a static, small, 64-KB receive window. This setting was fine for low-bandwidth and low-latency links, but it offered limited performance on high-bandwidth, high-latency links. Figure 25-10 shows the throughput that a TCP connection can get with various static values of the receive window over different latency conditions. As you can see, the maximum throughput of a TCP connection with the default receive window of 64 KB can be as low as 5 Mbps even within a single continent and can go all the way down to 1 Mbps on a satellite link.

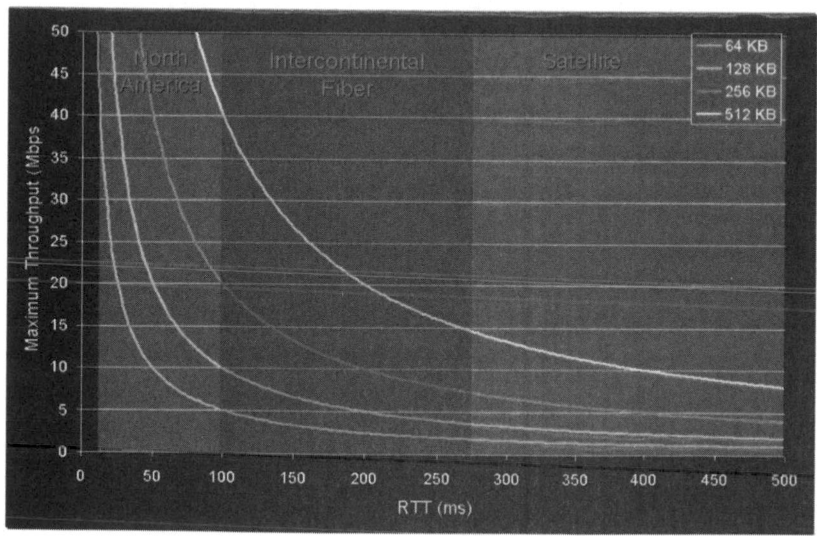

FIGURE 25-10 The TCP receive window size setting can significantly affect throughput.

Windows Vista and Windows 7 include an auto-tuning capability for TCP receive window size that is enabled by default. Every TCP connection can benefit in terms of increased throughput and decreased transfer times, but high-bandwidth, high-latency connections will benefit the most. Therefore, Receive Window Auto-Tuning can benefit network performance significantly across both satellite and WAN links. However, performance on high-speed LANs where latency is very low will benefit less.

Receive Window Auto-Tuning continually determines the optimal receive window size on a per-connection basis by measuring the bandwidth-delay product (the bandwidth multiplied by the latency of the connection) and the application retrieve rate, and it automatically adjusts the maximum receive window size on an ongoing basis. For auto-tuning to dramatically improve the throughput on a connection, all of the following conditions must be true:

- **High latency connection** For example, RTTs of greater than 100 ms.
- **High bandwidth connection** For example, greater than 5 Mbps.
- **Application does not specify a receive buffer size** Some applications may explicitly specify a receive buffer size, which would override the Windows default behavior. This can offer similar benefits on older versions of Windows, but changing the receive buffer size is uncommon.
- **Application consumes data quickly after receiving them** If an application does not immediately retrieve the received data, Receive Window Auto-Tuning may not increase overall performance. For example, if the application retrieves received data from TCP only periodically rather than continually, overall performance might not increase.

When TCP considers increasing the receive window size, it pays attention to the connection's past history and characteristics. TCP won't advertise more than the remote host's fair share of network bandwidth. This keeps the advertised receive window in line with the remote host's congestion window, discouraging network congestion while encouraging maximum utilization of the available bandwidth.

TCP Receive Window Scaling

The ability to increase the receive window would be meaningless without window scaling. On its own, TCP allows a window size of only 64 KB. Operating systems back through Windows XP use this as their default value on fast links. The window scaling option is a way for window sizes to scale to megabytes and beyond. Starting with Windows Vista, window scaling is used by default.

During connection establishment, use of the window scaling option is negotiated with the remote host. If supported by the remote side, window scaling is enabled on the connection. Windows Vista and Windows 7 use a scale factor of 8, which means that the advertised receive window value should be multiplied by 256. Therefore, Receive Window Auto-Tuning uses a maximum receive window size of 16 MB.

The Windows Vista and Windows 7 TCP/IP stacks support the following RFCs to optimize throughput in high-loss environments:

- **RFC 2582: The NewReno Modification to TCP's Fast Recovery Algorithm** The NewReno algorithm provides faster throughput by changing the way that a sender can increase the sending rate when multiple segments in a window of data are lost and the sender receives a partial acknowledgment (an acknowledgment for only part of the data that is successfully received). You can find this RFC at *http://www.ietf.org/rfc/rfc2582.txt*.

- **RFC 2883: An Extension to the Selective Acknowledgment (SACK) Option for TCP** SACK, defined in RFC 2018, allows a receiver to indicate up to four noncontiguous blocks of received data. RFC 2883 defines an additional use of the fields in the SACK TCP option to acknowledge duplicate packets. This allows the receiver of the TCP segment containing the SACK option to determine when it has retransmitted a segment unnecessarily and adjust its behavior to prevent future retransmissions. The fewer retransmissions sent, the better the overall throughput. You can find this RFC at *http://www.ietf.org/rfc/rfc2883.txt*.
- **RFC 3168: The Addition of Explicit Congestion Notification (ECN) to IP** If a packet is lost in a TCP session, TCP assumes that it is caused by network congestion. In an attempt to alleviate the source of the problem, TCP lowers the sender's transmission rate. With ECN support on both TCP peers and in the routing infrastructure, routers experiencing congestion mark the packets as they forward them. This enables computers to lower their transmission rate before packet loss occurs, increasing the throughput. Windows Vista and Windows 7 support ECN, but it is disabled by default. You can enable ECN support with the following command.

  ```
  netsh interface tcp set global ecncapability=enabled
  ```

  You can find this RFC at *http://www.ietf.org/rfc/rfc3168.txt*.
- **RFC 3517: A Conservative Selective Acknowledgment (SACK)–based Loss Recovery Algorithm for TCP** The implementation of TCP/IP in Windows Server 2003 and Windows XP uses SACK information only to determine which TCP segments have not arrived at the destination. RFC 3517 defines a method of using SACK information to perform loss recovery when duplicate acknowledgments are received, replacing the fast recovery algorithm when SACK is enabled on a connection. Windows Vista and Windows 7 keep track of SACK information on a per-connection basis and monitor incoming acknowledgments and duplicate acknowledgments to recover more quickly when multiple segments are not received at the destination. You can find this RFC at *http://www.ietf.org/rfc/rfc3517.txt*.
- **RFC 4138: Forward RTO-Recovery (F-RTO): An Algorithm for Detecting Spurious Retransmission Timeouts with TCP and the Stream Control Transmission Protocol (SCTP)** Spurious retransmissions of TCP segments can occur with a sudden and temporary increase in the RTT. The Forward Retransmission Timeout (F-RTO) algorithm prevents spurious retransmission of TCP segments. The result of the F-RTO algorithm is that for environments that have sudden and temporary increases in the RTT—such as when a wireless client roams from one wireless access point to another—F-RTO prevents unnecessary retransmission of segments and more quickly returns to its normal sending rate. You can find this RFC at *http://www.ietf.org/rfc/rfc4138.txt*.

Scalable Networking

As LAN bandwidth has increased beyond gigabit speeds, other components of a computer have become bottlenecks, limiting network performance. For example, a computer connected to a 10-gigabit network might not be able to saturate the link fully because the processor would be fully utilized processing network traffic.

Windows Vista, Windows 7, and Windows Server 2008 support the following scalable networking technologies (which require compatible hardware):

- **TCP Chimney Offload** The computer's processor must assemble data from multiple TCP packets into a single network segment. TCP Chimney Offload allows the network adapter to handle the task of segmenting TCP data for outgoing packets, reassembling data from incoming packets, and acknowledging sent and received data. TCP Chimney Offload is not compatible with QoS or adapter teaming drivers developed for earlier versions of Windows. TCP Chimney Offload does not change how non-TCP packets are handled, including Address Resolution Protocol (ARP), Dynamic Host Configuration Protocol (DHCP), ICMP, and UDP. TCP Chimney Offload still requires the operating system to process every application input/output (I/O). Therefore, it primarily benefits large transfers, and chatty applications that transmit small amounts of data will see little benefit. For example, file or streaming media servers can benefit significantly. However, a database server that is sending 100–500 bytes of data to and from the database might see little or no benefit.

> ***NOTE*** To examine TCP Chimney Offload performance testing data, read "Boosting Data Transfer with TCP Offload Engine Technology" at *http://www.dell.com/downloads/global/power/ps3q06-20060132-broadcom.pdf* and "Enabling Greater Scalability and Improved File Server Performance with the Windows Server 2003 Scalable Networking Pack and Alacritech Dynamic TCP Offload" at *http://www.alacritech.com/Resources/Files/File_Serving_White_Paper.pdf*. For more information about TCP Chimney Offload, read "Full TCP Offload" at *http://msdn.microsoft.com/en-us/library/aa503758.aspx*.

- **Receive-side scaling (RSS)** With NDIS 6.0 and in Windows Vista, Windows 7, and Windows Server 2008, incoming packets can be processed by multiple processors. In earlier versions of Windows, packets had to be processed by a single processor. Because more new computers have multiple cores and processors, this can alleviate an important bottleneck when used with a network adapter that supports RSS.

> ***NOTE*** For detailed information about RSS, read "Scalable Networking: Eliminating the Receive Processing Bottleneck—Introducing RSS" at *http://download.microsoft.com/download/5/D/6/5D6EAF2B-7DDF-476B-93DC-7CF0072878E6/NDIS_RSS.doc*.

- **NetDMA** NetDMA moves data directly from one location in the computer's main memory directly to another location without requiring the data to be moved through the processor, reducing the processor overhead. NetDMA requires the underlying hardware platform to support a technology such as Intel I/O Acceleration Technology (Intel I/OAT). NetDMA and TCP Chimney Offload are not compatible. If a network adapter supports both NetDMA and TCP Chimney Offload, Windows Vista and Windows 7 will use TCP Chimney Offload.
- **IPsec Offload** IPsec authentication and encryption requires some processor overhead. Although the IPsec generated by a typical workstation will not significantly affect processor utilization, a workstation that is transferring large amounts of data (typically at greater than gigabit speeds) can dedicate a significant amount of processing time to IPsec. IPsec Offload moves IPsec processing to the network adapter, which typically has a processor optimized for handling authentication and encryption tasks.

Improved Reliability

The Windows Vista and Windows 7 TCP/IP networking features also offer improvements designed to increase reliability when network conditions are less than optimal:

- **Neighbor Unreachability Detection for IPv4** Neighbor Unreachability Detection is a feature of IPv6 in which a node tracks whether a neighboring node is reachable, providing better error detection and recovery when nodes suddenly become unavailable. Windows also supports Neighbor Unreachability Detection for IPv4 traffic by tracking the reachable state of IPv4 neighbors in the IPv4 route cache. IPv4 Neighbor Unreachability Detection determines reachability through an exchange of unicast ARP Request and ARP Reply messages or by relying on upper-layer protocols such as TCP. With IPv4 Neighbor Unreachability Detection, IPv4-based communications benefit by determining when neighboring nodes, including routers, are no longer reachable and reporting the condition.
- **Changes in dead gateway detection** Dead gateway detection in TCP/IP for Windows Server 2003 and Windows XP provides a failover function, but it does not provide a failback function in which a dead gateway is tried again to determine whether it has become available. Windows Vista and Windows 7, however, also provide failback for dead gateways by periodically attempting to send TCP traffic through the previously detected dead gateway. If the TCP traffic sent through the dead gateway is successful, Windows switches the default gateway to the previously detected dead gateway. Support for failback to primary default gateways can provide faster throughput by sending traffic through the primary default gateway on the subnet.
- **Changes in PMTU black-hole router detection** Path maximum transmission unit (PMTU) discovery, defined in RFC 1191, relies on the receipt of ICMP Destination Unreachable-Fragmentation Needed and Don't Fragment (DF) Set messages from routers containing the MTU of the next link. However, in some cases, intermediate routers silently discard packets that cannot be fragmented. These types of routers

are known as black-hole PMTU routers. In addition, intermediate routers might drop ICMP messages because of configured firewall rules. As a result, TCP connections can time out and terminate because intermediate routers silently discard large TCP segments, their retransmissions, and the ICMP error messages for PMTU discovery. PTMU black-hole router detection senses when large TCP segments are being retransmitted and automatically adjusts the PMTU for the connection rather than relying on the receipt of the ICMP Destination Unreachable-Fragmentation Needed and DF Set messages. With TCP/IP in Windows Server 2003 and Windows XP, PMTU black-hole router detection is disabled by default because enabling it increases the maximum number of retransmissions that are performed for a given segment. However, with increasing use of firewall rules on routers to drop ICMP traffic, Windows Vista and Windows 7 enable PMTU black-hole router detection by default to prevent TCP connections from terminating. PMTU black-hole router detection is triggered on a TCP connection when it begins retransmitting full-sized segments with the DF flag set. TCP resets the PMTU for the connection to 536 bytes and retransmits its segments with the DF flag cleared. This maintains the TCP connection, although possibly at a lower PMTU size than actually exists for the connection.

IPv6 Support

To solve problems with limited public IPv4 addresses, many governments, Internet service providers (ISPs), and other organizations are transitioning to IPv6, the next version of the Network layer protocol that drives the Internet. Windows Vista and Windows 7 support the following enhancements to IPv6 when compared to Windows XP:

- **Dual IP layer stack enabled by default** Windows Vista and Windows 7 support a dual IP layer architecture in which the IPv4 and IPv6 implementations share common transport (including TCP and UDP) and framing layers, as Figure 25-11 illustrates. Windows Vista and Windows 7 both enable IPv4 and IPv6 by default. You don't need to install a separate feature to obtain IPv6 support. You can disable either IPv4 or IPv6 for a network adapter, however.

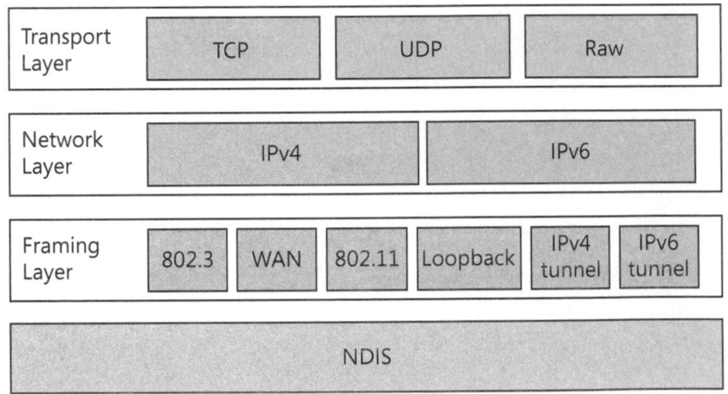

FIGURE 25-11 IPv4 and IPv6 work side by side in Windows 7.

- **Graphical user interface–based configuration** In Windows Vista and Windows 7, you can now configure IPv6 settings manually through a set of dialog boxes in the Network Connections folder (similar to the way you manually configure IPv4 settings). In addition, you can configure both IPv4 and IPv6 using the Netsh command.
- **Integrated IPsec support** In Windows Vista and Windows 7, IPsec support for IPv6 traffic is the same as that for IPv4, including support for Internet Key Exchange (IKE) and data encryption. The Windows Firewall with Advanced Security and IP Security Policies snap-ins now support the configuration of IPsec policies for IPv6 traffic in the same way as for IPv4 traffic. For example, when you configure an IP filter as part of an IP filter list in the IP Security Policies snap-in, you can now specify IPv6 addresses and address prefixes when specifying a specific source or destination IP address.
- **MLDv2** Multicast Listener Discovery version 2 (MLDv2), specified in RFC 3810, provides support for source-specific multicast traffic. MLDv2 is equivalent to Internet Group Management Protocol version 3 (IGMPv3) for IPv4.
- **LLMNR** Link-Local Multicast Name Resolution (LLMNR) allows IPv6 hosts on a single subnet without a DNS server to resolve each other's names. This capability is useful for single-subnet home networks and ad hoc wireless networks.
- **IPv6 over PPP** The built-in remote access client now supports IPv6 over the Point-to-Point Protocol (PPP) (PPPv6), as defined in RFC 2472. Native IPv6 traffic can now be sent over PPP-based connections. For example, PPPv6 support allows you to connect with an IPv6-based ISP through dial-up or PPP over Ethernet (PPPoE)–based connections that might be used for broadband Internet access.
- **Random interface IDs for IPv6 addresses** To prevent address scans of IPv6 addresses based on the known company IDs of network adapter manufacturers, Windows Vista, Windows 7, and Windows Server 2008 by default generate random interface IDs for non-temporary, autoconfigured IPv6 addresses, including public and link-local addresses.
- **DHCPv6 support** Windows Vista, Windows 7, and Windows Server 2008 include a DHCPv6-capable DHCP client that will perform stateful address autoconfiguration with a DHCPv6 server. Windows Server 2008 includes a DHCPv6-capable DHCP Server service.

For more information about IPv6, see Chapter 28, "Deploying IPv6."

802.1X Network Authentication

802.1X is a protocol for authenticating computers to your network infrastructure before allowing them access. 802.1X is commonly used to protect IEEE 802.11 wireless networks. If a client computer cannot provide a set of valid credentials for a wireless network, the wireless access point will not allow the client to join the network.

802.1X can also be used to protect wired networks. For example, if you physically connect a computer to an Ethernet network, the Ethernet switch can use 802.1X to require the client computer to authenticate to the network infrastructure. If the computer passes the authentication requirements, the network infrastructure will forward network traffic freely to and from the client computer. If the client computer does not provide valid credentials or otherwise cannot meet specified requirements, it can be denied access or placed onto a restricted network.

Windows Vista and Windows 7 support 802.1X authentication for both wired and wireless networks. Clients can authenticate themselves using a user name and password or a certificate, which can be stored locally on the computer or on a smart card. With compatible network hardware and a Remote Authentication Dial-in User Service (RADIUS) authentication server (such as a computer running Windows Server 2003 or Windows Server 2008), you can control both wired and wireless access to your intranet centrally. This means that an attacker with physical access to your facilities cannot simply plug a computer into an available Ethernet port and gain access to your intranet. When you combine 802.1X authentication with Network Access Protection (NAP), you can ensure that computers have required security updates and meet other system health requirements before allowing them unlimited access to your intranet.

Although almost all wireless access points support 802.1X, only newer wired network switches support the authentication protocol. When a computer is connected to your network, the switch must detect this connection, initiate the authentication process with the connected computer, send an authentication request to the RADIUS server you have configured, and then use the server's response to determine whether the client computer should be connected to your private intranet, a restricted network, another virtual LAN (VLAN), or whether other restrictions should be applied. Figure 25-12 illustrates this process. In addition to restricting network access, 802.1X can be used to apply user-specific bandwidth or QoS policies.

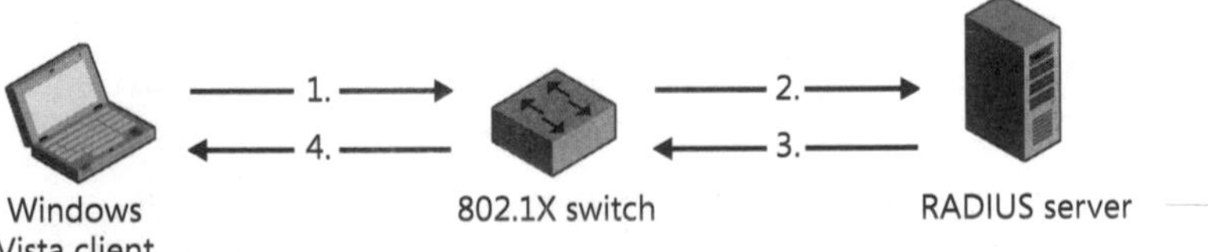

1. User connects a computer to a wired Ethernet port.
2. 802.1X switch notices the connection and initiates authentication by passing the request to the RADIUS server.
3. The RADIUS server authenticates the computer and sends a message to the switch.
4. The switch opens the Ethernet port to allow intranet access and enforces any restrictions or QoS policies.

FIGURE 25-12 You can use 802.1X to protect both your wired and wireless networks.

To configure 802.1X for a network adapter on a single computer, use the Authentication tab on the network adapter's properties. This tab enables you to configure the authentication type and the certificate to use for authentication. In addition, you can configure 802.1X from the command line using the *Netsh Lan* command. The Authentication tab appears only if the

Wired AutoConfig service is started, and the *Netsh Lan* command also requires this service to be running.

> ***WARNING*** **802.1X improves security, but it is not foolproof. An attacker with both physical access to your network and a computer configured to authenticate successfully with 802.1X can insert a hub (or even a wireless access point) between the legitimate computer and the network. When the computer authenticates the network port, the network infrastructure will allow all communications through that port, whether they originate from an unauthenticated computer connected to the hub or from the legitimate computer. For better security, require both 802.1X and IPsec.**

To configure computers in an AD DS domain to use 802.1X authentication, follow these high-level steps:

1. Configure AD DS for accounts and groups. Set the remote access permission on the Dial-up tab of the user or computer account properties dialog box to either Allow Access or Control Access Through Remote Access Policy.
2. Configure primary and redundant Network Policy Server (NPS) servers. Then, create a wired remote access policy on the NPS server. (For more information about NPS, visit *http://technet.microsoft.com/network/bb545879.aspx*.)
3. Deploy and configure your authenticating switches. You will need to configure the switches with the IP addresses of your primary and secondary IAS servers.
4. Configure client computers. If necessary, configure a certificate infrastructure to issue certificates that client computers and users will use for authentication. In addition, you should start the Wired AutoConfig service and configure it to start automatically.

For more information about configuring 802.1X, see "NAP Enforcement for 802.1X" at *http://technet.microsoft.com/en-us/library/cc770861.aspx*.

802.1X Improvements in Windows Vista and Windows 7

In wired 802.1X networks running Windows XP and Windows 2000 with SP4, a known problem can occur if all the following conditions are true:

- **You've configured 802.1X only for computer (not computer and user) authentication.**
- **You're using PEAP-MS-CHAP v2 (not EAP-TLS).**
- **Your computer's computer account password has expired.**

If a computer meets all these conditions, the computer won't be able to log on to the domain. However, this shortcoming is fixed in Windows Vista and Windows 7, and you will be able to log on to the domain.

NOTE Requiring 802.1X will eliminate your ability to use PXE boot, in which a client computer loads the operating system directly from the network, because Pre-Boot Execution Environment (PXE) clients can't provide the necessary credentials—another good reason to have a separate network for deployment.

To manage 802.1X using Group Policy, extend the AD DS schema as described in "Active Directory Schema Extensions for Windows Vista Wireless and Wired Group Policy Enhancements" at *http://technet.microsoft.com/en-us/library/bb727029.aspx*.

In addition, Windows Vista and Windows 7 also support the new EAPHost architecture to enable easier development of 802.1X authentication mechanisms. For more information, see the section titled "EAPHost Architecture" later in this chapter.

Server Message Block (SMB) 2.0

Server Message Block (SMB), also known as the Common Internet File System (CIFS), is the file sharing protocol used by default on Windows-based computers. Windows includes an SMB client (the Client For Microsoft Windows feature installed through the properties of a network connection) and an SMB server (the File And Printer Sharing For Microsoft Windows feature installed through the properties of a network connection). SMB in versions of Windows prior to Windows Server 2008 and Windows Vista, known as SMB 1.0, was originally designed in the early 1990s for early Windows-based network operating systems, such as Microsoft LAN Manager and Windows for Workgroups, and carries with it the limitations of its initial design.

Windows Server 2008, Windows Vista, and Windows 7 also support SMB 2.0, a new version of SMB that has been redesigned for today's networking environments and the needs of the next generation of file servers. SMB 2.0 has the following enhancements:

- Supports sending multiple SMB commands within the same packet. This reduces the number of packets sent between an SMB client and server, a common complaint against SMB 1.0.
- Supports much larger buffer sizes compared to SMB 1.0.
- Increases the restrictive constants within the protocol design to allow for scalability. Examples include an increase in the number of concurrent open file handles on the server and the number of file shares that a server can have.
- Supports durable handles that can withstand short interruptions in network availability.
- Supports symbolic links.

Computers running Windows Server 2008, Windows Vista, or Windows 7 support both SMB 1.0 and SMB 2.0. SMB 2.0 can be used only if both the client and server support it, however. Therefore, both the client and the server must be using SMB 2.0 to benefit from the improvements. Windows Vista and Windows 7 support complete backward compatibility with SMB 1.0 and earlier versions of Windows.

As with other versions of Windows, server-side support for SMB (sharing files and printers) is provided by the Server service, and client-side support (connecting to shared resources) is provided by the Workstation service. Both services are configured to start automatically, and you can safely disable either service if you don't require it. The security risks presented by having the Server service running are minimized because Windows Firewall will block incoming requests to the Server service on public networks by default.

Strong Host Model

When a unicast packet arrives at a host, IP must determine whether the packet is locally destined (its destination matches an address that is assigned to an interface of the host). IP implementations that follow a weak host model accept any locally destined packet, regardless of the interface on which the packet was received. IP implementations that follow the strong host model accept locally destined packets only if the destination address in the packet matches an address assigned to the interface on which the packet was received.

The current IPv4 implementation in Windows XP and Windows Server 2003 uses the weak host model. Windows Vista and Windows 7 support the strong host model for both IPv4 and IPv6 and are configured to use it by default. However, you can revert to the weak host model using Netsh. The weak host model provides better network connectivity, but it also makes hosts susceptible to multihome-based network attacks.

To change the host model being used, use the following Netsh commands (and specify the name of the network adapter).

```
Netsh interface IPv4 set interface "Local Area Connection" WeakHostSend=enabled
Ok.
Netsh interface IPv4 set interface "Local Area Connection" WeakHostReceive=enabled
Ok.
```

To return to the default settings, use the same command format but disable the *WeakHostSend* and *WeakHostReceive* parameters.

Wireless Networking

In Windows Server 2003 and Windows XP, the software infrastructure that supports wireless connections was built to emulate an Ethernet connection and can be extended only by supporting additional Extensible Authentication Protocol (EAP) types for 802.1X authentication. In Windows Vista and Windows 7, the software infrastructure for 802.11 wireless connections, called the Native Wi-Fi Architecture (also referred to as Revised Native Wi-Fi MSM, or RMSM), has been redesigned for the following:

- IEEE 802.11 is now represented inside of Windows as a media type separate from IEEE 802.3. This allows hardware vendors more flexibility in supporting advanced features of IEEE 802.11 networks, such as a larger frame size than Ethernet.

- New features in the Native Wi-Fi Architecture perform authentication, authorization, and management of 802.11 connections, reducing the burden on hardware vendors to incorporate these functions into their wireless network adapter drivers. This makes the development of wireless network adapter drivers much easier.
- The Native Wi-Fi Architecture supports APIs to allow hardware vendors the ability to extend the built-in wireless client for additional wireless services and custom capabilities. Extensible components written by hardware vendors can also provide customized configuration dialog boxes and wizards.

In addition, Windows Vista and Windows 7 include several important changes to the behavior of wireless auto configuration. Wireless auto configuration is now implemented in the WLAN AutoConfig service, which dynamically selects the wireless network to which the computer will connect automatically, based either on your preferences or on default settings. This includes automatically selecting and connecting to a more preferred wireless network when it becomes available. The changes include:

- **Single sign-on** To enable users to connect to protected wireless networks before logon (and thus, allow wireless users to authenticate to a domain), administrators can use Group Policy settings or the new Netsh wireless commands to configure single sign-on profiles on wireless client computers. After a single sign-on profile is configured, 802.1X authentication will precede the computer logon to the domain and users are prompted for credential information only if needed. This feature ensures that the wireless connection is placed prior to the computer domain logon, which enables scenarios that require network connectivity prior to user logon, such as Group Policy updates, execution of login scripts, and wireless client domain joins.
- **Behavior when no preferred wireless networks are available** In earlier versions of Windows, Windows created a random wireless network name and placed the network adapter in infrastructure mode if no preferred network was available and automatically connecting to nonpreferred networks was disabled. Windows would then scan for preferred wireless networks every 60 seconds. Windows Vista and Windows 7 no longer creates a randomly named network; instead, Windows "parks" the wireless network adapter while periodically scanning for networks, preventing the randomly generated wireless network name from matching an existing network name.
- **Support for hidden wireless networks** Earlier versions of Windows would always connect to preferred wireless networks that broadcast a Service Set Identifier (SSID) before connecting to preferred wireless networks that did not broadcast that identifier, even if the hidden network had a higher priority. Windows Vista and Windows 7 connect to preferred wireless networks based on their priority, regardless of whether they broadcast an SSID.
- **WPA2 support** Windows Vista and Windows 7 support Wi-Fi Protected Access 2 (WPA2) authentication options, configurable by either the user (to configure the standard profile) or by AD DS domain administrators using Group Policy settings. Windows Vista and Windows 7 support both Enterprise (IEEE 802.1X authentication) and Personal

(preshared key authentication) modes of operation for WPA2 and can connect to ad hoc wireless networks protected by WPA2.

- **Integration with NAP** WPA2-Enterprise, WPA-Enterprise, and dynamic WEP connections that use 802.1X authentication can use the NAP platform to prevent wireless clients that do not comply with system health requirements from gaining unlimited access to a private network.

In addition, troubleshooting wireless connection problems is now easier because wireless connections do the following:

- Support the Network Diagnostics Framework, which attempts to diagnose and fix common problems
- Record detailed information in the event log if a wireless connection attempt fails
- Prompt the user to send diagnostic information to Microsoft for analysis and improvement

For more information about troubleshooting wireless networks, see Chapter 31. For more information about configuring wireless networks, see the section titled "How to Configure Wireless Settings" later in this chapter.

Improved APIs

Windows Vista and Windows 7 also include improved APIs that will enable more powerful networked applications. Systems administrators will not realize immediate benefits from these improved APIs; however, developers can use these APIs to create applications that are more robust when running on Windows Vista and Windows 7. This enables developers to create applications faster and to add more powerful features to those applications.

Network Awareness

More applications are connecting to the Internet to look for updates, download real-time information, and facilitate collaboration between users. However, creating applications that can adapt to changing network conditions has been difficult for developers. Network Awareness enables applications to sense changes to the network to which the computer is connected, such as closing a mobile PC at work and then opening it at a coffee shop wireless hotspot. This enables Windows Vista and Windows 7 to alert applications of network changes. The application can then behave differently, providing a seamless experience.

For example, Windows Firewall with Advanced Security can take advantage of Network Awareness to automatically allow incoming traffic from network management tools when the computer is on the corporate network but block the same traffic when the computer is on a home network or wireless hotspot. Network Awareness can therefore provide flexibility on your internal network without sacrificing security when mobile users travel.

Applications can also take advantage of Network Awareness. For example, if a user disconnects from a corporate internal network and then connects to his or her home network, an application could adjust security settings and request that the user establish a VPN connection to maintain connectivity to an intranet server. New applications can go offline or online automatically as mobile users move between environments. In addition, software vendors can integrate their software into the network logon process more easily because Windows Vista and Windows 7 enable access providers to add custom connections for use during logon.

Network Awareness benefits only applications that take advantage of the new API and does not require any management or configuration. For Network Awareness to function, the Network Location Awareness and Network List Service services must be running.

Improved Peer Networking

Windows Peer-to-Peer Networking, originally introduced with the Advanced Networking Pack for Windows XP and later included in Windows XP SP2, is an operating system platform and API in Windows Vista and Windows 7 that allow the development of peer-to-peer (P2P) applications that do not require a server. Windows Vista and Windows 7 include the following enhancements to Windows Peer-to-Peer Networking:

- **New, easy-to-use API** APIs to access Windows Peer-to-Peer Networking capabilities such as name resolution, group creation, and security have been highly simplified in Windows Vista and Windows 7, making it easier for developers to create P2P applications.
- **New version of PNRP** Peer Name Resolution Protocol (PNRP) is a name resolution protocol, like DNS, that functions without a server. PNRP uniquely identifies computers within a peer *cloud*. Windows Vista and Windows 7 include a new version of PNRP (PNRP v2) that is more scalable and uses less network bandwidth. For PNRP v2 in Windows Vista and Windows 7, Windows Peer-to-Peer Networking applications can access PNRP name publication and resolution functions through a simplified PNRP API that supports the standard name resolution methods used by applications. For IPv6 addresses, applications can use the *getaddrinfo()* function to resolve the fully qualified domain name (FQDN) *name*.prnp.net, in which *name* is the peer name being resolved. The *pnrp.net* domain is a reserved domain for PNRP name resolution. The PNRP v2 protocol is incompatible with the PNRP protocol used by computers running Windows XP. Microsoft is investigating the development and release of an update to the Windows Peer-to-Peer Networking features in Windows XP to support PNRP v2.
- **People Near Me** People Near Me is a new capability of Windows Peer-to-Peer Networking that allows users to dynamically discover other users on the local subnet and their registered People Near Me–capable applications, as well as to invite users into a collaboration activity easily. The invitation and its acceptance start an application on the invited user's computer, and the two applications can begin participating in a collaboration activity such as chatting, photo sharing, or game playing.

PNRP v2 is not backward compatible with earlier versions of the protocol. Although PNRP v2 can coexist on a network with earlier versions, it cannot communicate with PNRP v1 clients.

Services Used by Peer-to-Peer Networking

Windows Peer-to-Peer Networking uses the following services, which by default start manually (Windows will start services automatically as required):

- Peer Name Resolution Protocol (PNRP)
- Peer Networking Grouping
- Peer Networking Identity Manager
- PNRP Machine Name Publication Service

If these services are disabled, some P2P and collaborative applications might not function.

Managing Peer-to-Peer Networking

Windows Peer-to-Peer Networking is a set of tools for applications to use, so they don't provide capabilities without an application. You can manage Windows Peer-to-Peer Networking using the Netsh tool or by using Group Policy settings:

- **Netsh tool** Commands in the *Netsh p2p* context will be used primarily by developers creating P2P applications. Systems administrators should not need to troubleshoot or manage Windows Peer-to-Peer Networking directly, so that aspect of the Netsh tool is not discussed further here.
- **Group Policy settings** You can configure or completely disable Windows Peer-to-Peer Networking by using the Group Policy settings in Computer Configuration \Policies\Administrative Templates\Network\Microsoft Peer-to-Peer Networking Services. You should need to modify the configuration only if an application has specific, nondefault requirements.

HOW IT WORKS

Peer-to-Peer Name Resolution

In P2P networking, peers use PNRP names to identify computers, users, groups, services, and anything else that should be resolved to an IP address. Peer names can be registered as unsecured or secured. Unsecured names are just automatically generated text strings that are subject to spoofing by a malicious computer that registers the same name. Unsecured names are therefore best used in private or otherwise secure networks. Secured names are signed digitally with a certificate and thus can be registered only by the owner.

PNRP IDs are 256 bits long and are composed of the following:

- The high-order 128 bits, known as the peer-to-peer ID, are a hash of a peer name assigned to the endpoint.
- The low-order 128 bits are used for the service location, which is a generated number that uniquely identifies different instances of the same ID in a cloud.

The 256-bit combination of peer-to-peer ID and service location allows multiple PNRP IDs to be registered from a single computer. For each cloud, each peer node manages a cache of PNRP IDs that includes both its own registered PNRP IDs and the entries cached over time.

When a peer needs to resolve a PNRP ID to the address, protocol, and port number, it first examines its own cache for entries with a matching peer ID (in case the client has resolved a PNRP ID for a different service location on the same peer). If that peer is found, the resolving client sends a request directly to the peer.

If the resolving client does not have an entry for the peer ID, it sends requests to other peers in the same cloud, one at a time. If one of those peers has an entry cached, that peer first verifies that the requested peer is connected to the network before resolving the name for the requesting client. While the PNRP request message is being forwarded, its contents are used to populate caches of nodes that are forwarding it. When the response is sent back through the return path, its contents are also used to populate node caches. This name resolution mechanism allows clients to identify each other without a server infrastructure.

EAPHost Architecture

For easier development of EAP authentication methods for IEEE 802.1X-authenticated wireless connections, Windows Vista and Windows 7 support a new EAP architecture called EAPHost. EAPHost provides the following features that are not supported by the EAP implementation in earlier versions of Windows:

- **Network Discovery** EAPHost supports Network Discovery as defined in the "Identity selection hints for Extensible Authentication Protocol (EAP)" Internet draft.
- **RFC 3748 compliance** EAPHost will conform to the EAP State Machine and address a number of security vulnerabilities that are specified in RFC 3748. In addition, EAPHost will support additional capabilities such as Expanded EAP Types (including vendor-specific EAP methods).
- **EAP method coexistence** EAPHost allows multiple implementations of the same EAP method to coexist simultaneously. For example, the Microsoft version of Protected EAP (PEAP) and the Cisco Systems, Inc. version of PEAP can be installed and selected.
- **Modular supplicant architecture** In addition to supporting modular EAP methods, EAPHost also supports a modular supplicant architecture in which new supplicants can be added easily without having to replace the entire EAP implementation.

For EAP method vendors, EAPHost provides support for EAP methods already developed for Windows Server 2003 and Windows XP, as well as an easier method of developing new EAP methods. Certified EAP methods can be distributed with Windows Update. EAPHost also allows better classification of EAP types so that the built-in 802.1X- and PPP-based Windows supplicants can use them.

For supplicant method vendors, EAPHost provides support for modular and pluggable supplicants for new link layers. Because EAPHost is integrated with NAP, new supplicants do not have to be NAP aware. To participate in NAP, new supplicants only need to register a connection identifier and a callback function that informs the supplicant to re-authenticate.

For more information, read "EAPHost in Windows" at *http://technet.microsoft.com/en-us/magazine/cc162364.aspx*.

Layered Service Provider (LSP)

The Windows Sockets (Winsock) Layered Service Provider (LSP) architecture resides between the Winsock dynamic-link library (DLL), which applications use to communicate on the network, and the Winsock kernel-mode driver (Afd.sys), which communicates with network adapter drivers. LSPs are used in several categories of applications, including:

- Proxy and firewalls.
- Content filtering.
- Virus scanning.
- Adware and other network data manipulators.
- Spyware and other data-monitoring applications.
- Security, authentication, and encryption.

Windows Vista and Windows 7 include several improvements to LSPs to enable more powerful network applications and better security:

- Adding and removing LSPs is logged to the System Event Log. Administrators can use these events to determine which application installed an LSP and to troubleshoot failed LSP installations.
- A new installation API (*WSCInstallProviderAndChains*) provides simpler, more reliable LSP installations.
- New facilities categorize LSPs and allow critical system services to bypass LSPs. This can improve reliability when working with flawed LSPs.
- A diagnostics module for the Network Diagnostics Framework allows users to selectively remove LSPs that are causing problems.

Windows Sockets Direct Path for System Area Networks

Windows Sockets Direct (WSD) enables Winsock applications that use TCP/IP to obtain the performance benefits of system area networks (SANs) without application modifications. SANs are a type of high-performance network often used for computer clusters.

WSD allows communications across a SAN to bypass the TCP/IP protocol stack, taking advantage of the reliable, direct communications provided by a SAN. In Windows Vista and Windows 7, this is implemented by adding a virtual switch between Winsock and the TCP/IP stack. This switch has the ability to examine traffic and pass communications to a SAN Winsock provider, bypassing TCP/IP entirely. Figure 25-13 illustrates this architecture.

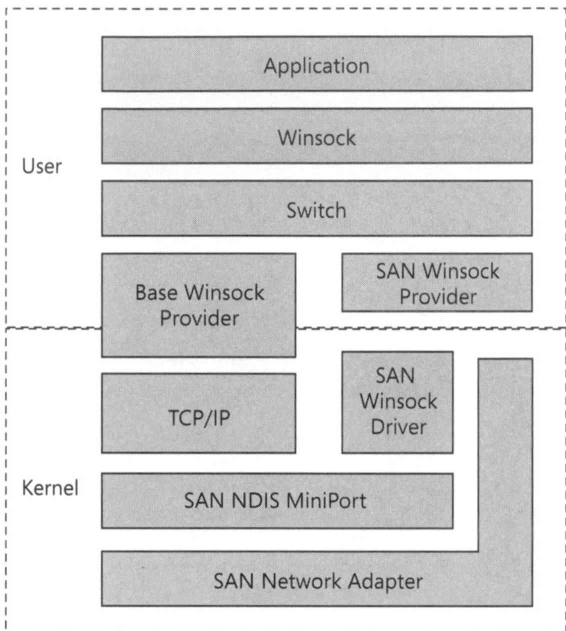

FIGURE 25-13 WSD enables improved performance across SANs by selectively bypassing TCP/IP using a virtual switch.

How to Configure Wireless Settings

Users want to stay constantly connected to their networks, and wireless LANs and wireless WANs are beginning to make that possible. However, managing multiple network connections can be challenging, and users often have difficulty resolving connectivity problems. As a result, users place more calls to support centers, increasing support cost and user frustration. You can reduce this by configuring client computers to connect to preferred wireless networks.

Windows will connect automatically to most wired networks. Wireless networks, however, require configuration before Windows will connect to them. You can connect Windows computers to wireless networks in three different ways:

- **Manually** Windows 7 includes a new user interface that makes it simple to connect to wireless networks. You can use this interface to manually configure intranet-based computers running Windows 7; users can use this method to connect to public networks when they travel.

- **Using Group Policy** Group Policy settings are the most efficient way to configure any number of computers running Windows in your organization to connect to your internal wireless networks.
- **From the command line or by using scripts** Using the Netsh tool and commands in the *netsh wlan* context, you can export existing wireless network profiles, import them into other computers, connect to available wireless networks, or disconnect a wireless network.

After a wireless network is configured, the Wireless Single Sign-On feature executes 802.1X authentication at the appropriate time based on the network security configuration, while simply and seamlessly integrating with the user's Windows logon experience. The following sections describe each of these configuration techniques.

Configuring Wireless Settings Manually

Windows 7 makes it very easy to connect to a wireless network using the enhanced View Available Networks (VAN) feature included in the platform. For example, to configure a wireless network that is currently available, follow these steps:

1. Click the networking icon in the notification area.

> ***NOTE*** **The WLAN AutoConfig service must be started for wireless networks to be available. This service by default is set to start automatically.**

2. Click the network to which you want to connect and then click Connect, as shown in Figure 25-14.

FIGURE 25-14 The Network Connection Details dialog box provides graphical access to IP configuration settings.

NOTE A network that is configured not to broadcast an SSID will appear as an Unnamed Network, allowing you to connect to the network.

3. If the network is encrypted, provide the encryption key.

Why Disabling SSID Broadcasting Doesn't Improve Security

Wireless networks broadcast an SSID that specifies the network name to help users who have not connected to the network previously find it. However, disabling the SSID broadcast does not increase security, because the tools that a malicious attacker might use to find and connect to your wireless network do not rely on SSID broadcasts. The SSID broadcast does make it easier for legitimate users to find and connect to your wireless networks. So by disabling the broadcast of the SSID, you can negatively affect the people whom you do want to be able to connect.

Using Group Policy to Configure Wireless Settings

In AD DS environments, you can use Group Policy settings to configure wireless network policies. For best results, you should have Windows Server 2003 SP1 or later installed on your domain controllers because Microsoft extended support for wireless Group Policy settings when they released SP1.

Before you can use Group Policy to configure wireless networks, you need to extend the AD DS schema using the 802.11Schema.ldf file included on this book's companion media. If you do not have access to the companion media, you can copy the schema file from *http://technet.microsoft.com/en-us/library/bb727029.aspx*. To extend the schema, follow these steps:

1. Copy the 802.11Schema.ldf file to a folder on a domain controller.
2. Log on to the domain controller with Domain Admin privileges and open a command prompt.
3. Select the folder containing the 802.11Schema.ldf file and run the following command (where *Dist_Name_of_AD_Domain* is the distinguished name of the AD DS domain whose schema is being modified; an example of a distinguished name is DC=wcoast,DC=microsoft,DC=com for the wcoast.microsoft.com AD DS domain).

   ```
   ldifde -i -v -k -f 802.11Schema.ldf -c DC=X Dist_Name_of_AD_Domain
   ```

4. Restart the domain controller.

After you extend the schema, you can configure a wireless network policy by following these steps:

1. Open the Active Directory GPO in the Group Policy Object Editor.

2. Expand Computer Configuration, Windows Settings, Security Settings, and then click Wireless Network (IEEE 802.11) Policies.
3. Right-click Wireless Network (IEEE 802.11) Policies and then click Create A New Windows Vista Policy. The Wireless Network Properties dialog box appears.
4. To add an infrastructure network, click Add and then click Infrastructure to open the Connection tab of the New Profile Properties dialog box. In the Network Names list, click NEWSSID and then click Remove. Then, type a valid internal SSID in the Network Names box and click Add. Repeat this to configure multiple SSIDs for a single profile. If the network is hidden, select the Connect Even If The Network Is Not Broadcasting check box.
5. On the New Profile Properties dialog box, click the Security tab. Use this tab to configure the wireless network authentication and encryption settings. Click OK.

NOTE This resource kit does not cover how to design wireless networks. However, you should avoid using Wired Equivalent Privacy (WEP) whenever possible. WEP is vulnerable to several different types of attack, and WEP keys can be difficult to change. Whenever possible, use WPA or WPA2, which both use strong authentication and dynamic encryption keys.

The settings described in the previous process will configure client computers to connect automatically to your internal wireless networks and to not connect to other wireless networks.

Configuring Wireless Settings from the Command Line or a Script

You can also configure wireless settings using commands in the *netsh wlan* context of the Netsh command-line tool, which enables you to create scripts that connect to different wireless networks (whether encrypted or not). To list available wireless networks, run the following command.

```
Netsh wlan show networks
```

```
Interface Name : Wireless Network Connection
There are 2 networks currently visible

SSID 1 : Litware
    Network Type            : Infrastructure
    Authentication          : Open
    Encryption              : None

SSID 1 : Contoso
    Network Type            : Infrastructure
    Authentication          : Open
    Encryption              : WEP
```

Before you can connect to a wireless network using Netsh, you must have a profile saved for that network. Profiles contain the SSID and security information required to connect to a network. If you have previously connected to a network, the computer will have a profile for that network saved. If a computer has never connected to a wireless network, you need to save a profile before you can use Netsh to connect to it. You can save a profile from one computer to an Extensible Markup Language (XML) file and then distribute the XML file to other computers in your network. To save a profile, run the following command after manually connecting to a network.

```
Netsh wlan export profile name="SSID"
```

```
Interface profile "SSID" is saved in file ".\Wireless Network
Connection-SSID.xml" successfully.
```

Before you can connect to a new wireless network, you can load a profile from a file. The following example demonstrates how to create a wireless profile (which is saved as an XML file) from a script or the command line.

```
Netsh wlan add profile filename="C:\profiles\contoso1.xml"
```

```
Profile contoso1 is added on interface Wireless Network Connection
```

To connect to a wireless network quickly, use the *netsh wlan connect* command and specify a wireless profile name (which must be configured or added previously). The following examples demonstrate different but equivalent syntaxes for connecting to a wireless network with the Contoso1 SSID.

```
Netsh wlan connect Contoso1
```

```
Connection request is received successfully
```

```
Netsh wlan connect Contoso1 interface="Wireless Network Connection"
```

```
Connection request is received successfully
```

Note that you need to specify the interface name only if you have multiple wireless network adapters—an uncommon situation. You can use the following command to disconnect from all wireless networks.

```
Netsh wlan disconnect
```

```
Disconnection request is received successfully
```

You can use scripts and profiles to simplify the process of connecting to private wireless networks for your users. Ideally, you should use scripts and profiles to save users from ever needing to type wireless security keys.

You can also use Netsh to allow or block access to wireless networks based on their SSIDs. For example, the following command allows access to a wireless network with the Contoso1 SSID.

```
Netsh wlan add filter permission=allow ssid=Contoso networktype=infrastructure
```

Similarly, the following command blocks access to the Fabrikam wireless network.

```
Netsh wlan add filter permission=block ssid=Fabrikam networktype=adhoc
```

To block all ad hoc networks, use the Denyall permission, as the following example demonstrates.

```
Netsh wlan add filter permission=denyall networktype=adhoc
```

To prevent Windows from automatically connecting to wireless networks, run the following command.

```
Netsh wlan set autoconfig enabled=no interface="Wireless Network Connection"
```

You can also use Netsh to define the priority of user profiles (but not Group Policy profiles). Group Policy profiles always have precedence over user profiles. The following example demonstrates how to configure Windows to connect automatically to the wireless network defined by the Contoso profile before connecting to the wireless network defined by the Fabrikam profile.

```
Netsh wlan set profileorder name=Contoso interface="Wireless Network Connection"
priority=1
Netsh wlan set profileorder name=Fabrikam interface="Wireless Network Connection"
priority=2
```

Netsh has many other commands for configuring wireless networking. For more information, run the following at a command prompt.

```
Netsh wlan help
```

> ***NOTE*** **When troubleshooting problems connecting to wireless networks, open Event Viewer and browse the Applications And Services Logs\Microsoft\Windows\WLAN-AutoConfig event log. You can also use this log to determine the wireless networks to which a client is connected, which might be useful when identifying the source of a security compromise. For more information, see Chapter 31.**

How to Configure TCP/IP

You can use several different techniques to configure TCP/IP. Most environments use DHCP to provide basic settings. Alternatively, you can configure TCP/IP settings manually using graphical tools. Finally, some settings are configured most easily using scripts that call command-line tools such as Netsh. You can use logon scripts to automate command-line configuration. The following sections describe each of these configuration techniques.

> ***NOTE*** **For wireless networks, you will need to first connect the wireless adapter to the wireless network and then configure the TCP/IP settings. However, wireless networks almost always have a DHCP server available.**

DHCP

Almost all client computers should be configured using DHCP. With DHCP, you configure a DHCP server (such as a computer running Windows Server 2003) to provide IP addresses and network configuration settings to client computers when they start up. Windows 7 and all recent Windows operating systems are configured to use DHCP by default, so you can configure network settings by simply setting up a DHCP server and connecting a computer to the network.

As the number of mobile computers, traveling users, and wireless networks has increased, so has the importance of DHCP. Because computers may have to connect to several different networks, manually configuring network settings would require users to make changes each time they connected to a network. With DHCP, the DHCP server on the local network provides the correct settings when the client connects.

Some of the configuration settings you can configure with DHCP include the following:

- **IP address** Identifies a computer on the network
- **Default gateway** Identifies the router that the client computer will use to send traffic to other networks
- **DNS servers** Internet name that servers use to resolve host names of other computers
- **WINS servers** Microsoft name that servers use for identifying specific computers on the network
- **Boot server** Used for loading an operating system across the network when configuring new computers or starting diskless workstations

Clients use the following process to retrieve DHCP settings:

1. The client computers transmit a DHCPDiscover broadcast packet on the local network.

2. DHCP servers receive this broadcast packet and send a DHCPOffer broadcast packet back to the client computer. This packet includes the IP address configuration information. If more than one DHCP server is on the local network, the client computer might receive multiple DHCPOffer packets.
3. The client computer sends a DHCPRequest packet to a single DHCP server requesting the use of those configuration settings. Other DHCP servers that might have sent a DHCPOffer broadcast will see this response and know that they no longer need to reserve an IP address for the client.
4. Finally, the DHCP server sends a DHCPACK packet to acknowledge that the IP address has been leased to the client for a specific amount of time. The client can now begin using the IP address settings.

In addition, client computers will attempt to renew their IP addresses after half the DHCP lease time has expired. By default, computers running Windows Server 2003 have a lease time of eight days. Therefore, client computers running Windows attempt to renew their DHCP settings after four days and will retrieve updated settings if you have made any changes to the DHCP server.

Because client computers retrieve new DHCP settings each time they start up, connect to a new network, or a DHCP lease expires, you have the opportunity to change configuration settings with only a few days' notice. Therefore, if you need to replace a DNS server and you want to use a new IP address, you can add the new address to your DHCP server settings, wait eight days for client computers to renew their DHCP leases and acquire the new settings, and then have a high level of confidence that client computers will have the new server's IP address before shutting down the old DNS server.

If a client computer does not receive a DHCP address and an alternate IP address configuration has not been manually configured, Windows client computers automatically configure themselves with a randomly selected Automatic Private IP Addressing (APIPA) address in the range of 169.254.0.1 to 169.254.255.255. If more than one computer running Windows on a network has an APIPA address, the computers will be able to communicate. However, APIPA has no default gateway, so client computers will not be able to connect to the Internet, to other networks, or to computers with non-APIPA addresses. For information about IPv6, refer to Chapter 28.

You can use the following techniques to determine whether a client has been assigned an IP address and to troubleshoot DHCP-related problems:

- **IPConfig** From a command line, run *IPConfig /all* to view the current IP configuration. If the client has a DHCP-assigned IP address, the DHCP *Enabled* property will be set to Yes, and the DHCP *Server* property will have an IP address assigned, as the following example demonstrates.

```
Ipconfig /all
```

```
Windows IP Configuration
   Host Name . . . . . . . . . . . . : Win7
   Primary Dns Suffix  . . . . . . . : hq.contoso.com
   Node Type . . . . . . . . . . . . : Hybrid
   IP Routing Enabled. . . . . . . . : No
   WINS Proxy Enabled. . . . . . . . : No
   DNS Suffix Search List. . . . . . : contoso.com

Ethernet adapter Local Area Connection:

   Connection-specific DNS Suffix  . : contoso.com
   Description . . . . . . . . . . . : Broadcom NetXtreme 57xx Gigabit
Controller
   Physical Address. . . . . . . . . : 00-15-C5-08-82-F3
   DHCP Enabled. . . . . . . . . . . : Yes
   Autoconfiguration Enabled . . . . : Yes
   Link-local IPv6 Address . . . . . :
fe80::a1f2:3425:87f6:49c2%10(Preferred)
   IPv4 Address. . . . . . . . . . . : 192.168.1.242(Preferred)
   Subnet Mask . . . . . . . . . . . : 255.255.255.0
   Lease Obtained. . . . . . . . . . : Sunday, August 20, 2006 11:12:44 PM
   Lease Expires . . . . . . . . . . : Monday, August 28, 2006 11:12:44 PM
   Default Gateway . . . . . . . . . : 192.168.1.1
   DHCP Server . . . . . . . . . . . : 192.168.1.210
   DNS Servers . . . . . . . . . . . : 192.168.1.210
   NetBIOS over Tcpip . . . . . . . . . . : Enabled
```

NOTE If you are troubleshooting a client connectivity problem and notice that the IP address begins with 169.254, the DHCP server was not available when the client computer started. Verify that the DHCP server is available and the client computer is properly connected to the network. Then, issue the *ipconfig /release* and *ipconfig /renew* commands to acquire a new IP address. For more information about troubleshooting network connections, see Chapter 31.

- **Network And Sharing Center** In Network And Sharing Center, click the name of the connection (such as Local Area Connection) to open the connection status. Then, click Details to open the Network Connection Details dialog box, as shown in Figure 25-15. This dialog box provides similar information to that displayed by the *IPConfig /all* command.

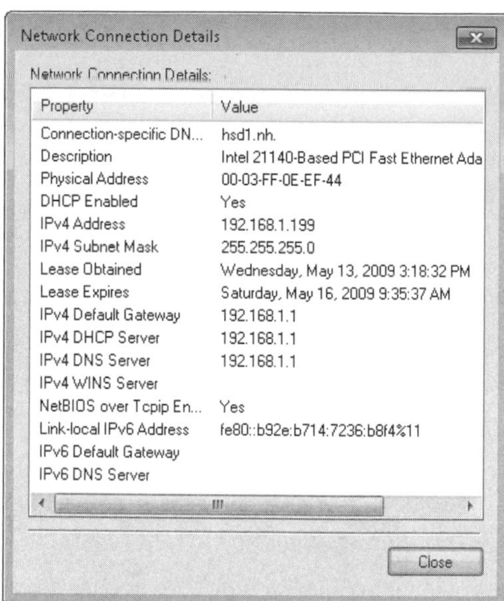

FIGURE 25-15 The Network Connection Details dialog box provides graphical access to IP configuration settings.

- **Event Viewer** Open Event Viewer and browse the Windows Logs\System Event Log. Look for events with a source of Dhcp-Client for IPv4 addresses or DHCPv6-Client for IPv6 addresses. Although this technique is not useful for determining the active configuration, it can reveal problems that occurred in the past.

Configuring IP Addresses Manually

The alternative to using DHCP is to configure IP address settings manually. However, because of the time required to configure settings, the likelihood of making a configuration error, and the challenge of connecting new computers to a network, manually configuring IP addresses is rarely the best choice for client computers.

To configure an IPv4 address manually, follow these steps:

1. Click the network icon in the notification area and then click Open Network And Sharing Center.
2. Click Change Adapter Settings.
3. Right-click the network adapter and then click Properties.
4. In the Properties dialog box, click Internet Protocol Version 4 (TCP/IPv4) and then click Properties.

5. If you always want to use manually configured network settings, click the General tab and then click Use The Following IP Address. If you want to use manually configured network settings only when a DHCP server is not available, click the Alternate Configuration tab and then click User Configured. Then, configure the computer's IP address, default gateway, and DNS servers.
6. Click OK twice. The configuration changes will take effect immediately, without requiring you to restart the computer.

You should rarely need to configure an IPv6 address manually because IPv6 is designed to configure itself automatically. For more information about IPv6 autoconfiguration, refer to Chapter 28. To configure an IPv6 address manually, follow these steps:

1. Click the network icon in the notification area and then click Open Network And Sharing Center.
2. Click Change Adapter Settings.
3. Right-click the network adapter and then click Properties.
4. In the Properties dialog box, click Internet Protocol Version 6 (TCP/IPv6) and then click Properties.
5. Click Use The Following IPv6 Address and configure the computer's IP address, subnet prefix length, default gateway, and DNS servers. TCP/IPv6 does not support an alternate configuration, as TCP/IPv4 does.
6. Click OK twice. The configuration changes will take effect immediately, without requiring you to restart the computer.

You can prevent users from accessing these graphical tools. Most important settings require administrative credentials, so simply not giving users local administrator access to their computers will prevent them from making most important changes. You can also use the Group Policy settings located in User Configuration\Policies\Administrative Templates \Network\Network Connections to restrict the user interface further (but this will not necessarily prevent a user from using other tools to make changes).

Command Line and Scripts

You can also configure network settings from the command line or from a script using the Netsh tool and commands in the *Netsh interface ipv4* or *Netsh interface ipv6* contexts. For example, to configure the standard network interface to use DHCP and to use the DNS servers provided by DHCP, you could issue the following commands.

```
Netsh interface ipv4 set address "Local Area Connection" dhcp
Netsh interface ipv4 set dnsserver "Local Area Connection" dhcp
```

NOTE Windows XP also included the Netsh tool. However, the Windows XP version of Netsh uses different commands. For example, you would use *Netsh interface ip set dns* to configure DNS settings for a computer running Windows XP instead of *Netsh interface ipv4 set dnsserver,* which you use to configure DNS settings for a computer running Windows Vista or Windows 7. However, Netsh in Windows Vista and Windows 7 is backward compatible and will accept the older, Windows XP–compatible syntax.

Because DHCP is the default setting for network adapters, it is more likely that you will need to use Netsh commands to configure a static IP address. The following command demonstrates how to do this for IPv4.

```
Netsh interface ipv4 set address "Local Area Connection" source=static
address=192.168.1.10 mask=255.255.255.0 gateway=192.168.1.1
Netsh interface ipv4 set dnsserver "Local Area Connection" source=static
address=192.168.1.2 register=primary
```

The following commands demonstrate configuring a static IP address and DNS server configuration for IPv6.

```
Netsh interface ipv6 set address "Local Area Connection" address=2001:db8:3fa8:102a::2
anycast
Netsh interface ipv6 set dnsserver "Local Area Connection" source=static
address=2001:db8:
3fa8:1719::1 register=primary
```

You should avoid using scripts to configure production client computers because they are not tolerant of varying hardware configurations and because DHCP provides most of the configuration capabilities required for production networks. However, scripts can be useful for quickly changing the network configuration of computers in lab environments. Instead of manually writing Netsh commands, you can configure a computer using graphical tools and use the Netsh tool to generate a configuration script.

NOTE You can generate a configuration script that can be run from within Netsh by running the command *Netsh interface dump* > script_filename. You can then apply that script using the command *Netsh –f* script_filename.

Netsh provides the ability to configure almost any aspect of Windows 7 networking. For detailed instructions, refer to Windows Help And Support or run the following command from a command prompt.

```
Netsh ?
```

DIRECT FROM THE SOURCE

Automate Network Interface Card Configuration Using Netsh

Don Baker, Premier Field Engineer

Windows Platform

During the years I worked as a consultant, it was not uncommon to connect my laptop to several different networks in the same day. In some cases, they were DHCP-enabled, so connection was easy. For others, I would have to configure the network adapter manually. Ugh!

Enter the Netsh commands. You can use the Netsh command to modify the network configuration on computers running Windows 2000 and later versions. It's not the friendliest syntax to use, but it is a real time-saver once you learn to use it. The following sample scripts use Netsh to set STATIC IP entries on an adapter and to set the adapter back to DHCP mode so the settings can be obtained automatically. To use the code, type it into a batch file, modify "name=" to the name of the adapter in quotation marks, and change the IP addresses.

Static IP

```
netsh interface ipv4 set address name="Wireless Network Connection"
source=static addr=192.168.0.100 mask=255.255.255.0 gateway=192.168.0.250
gwmetric=0
netsh interface ipv4 set dnsserver name="Wireless Network Connection"
source=static addr=192.168.0.2 register=NONE
REM netsh interface ipv4 set wins name="Wireless Network Connection"
source=static addr=10.217.27.9
REM  OR if no WINS server
netsh interface ipv4 set winsserver name="Wireless Network Connection"
source=dhcp
ipconfig /all
```

DHCP

```
netsh interface ipv4 set address name="Wireless Network Connection"
source=dhcp
netsh interface ipv4 set dnsserver name="Wireless Network Connection"
source=dhcp
netsh interface ipv4 set winsserver name="Wireless Network Connection"
source=dhcp
ipconfig /renew "Wireless Network Connection"
ipconfig /all
```

How to Connect to AD DS Domains

Most organizations with more than a few client computers running Windows should use an AD DS domain to simplify managing the computers. Typically, joining clients to a domain is one of the first steps in configuring a computer. The process you should use is slightly different if you have 802.1X authentication enabled.

How to Connect to a Domain When 802.1X Authentication Is Not Enabled

For networks without 802.1X authentication, follow these steps to join a domain:

1. Click Start. Right-click Computer and then click Properties.
2. Under Computer Name, Domain, And Workgroup Settings, click Change Settings.
3. From the System Properties dialog box, click Network ID.
4. The Join A Domain Or Workgroup Wizard appears. Select This Computer Is Part Of A Business Network; I Use It To Connect To Other Computers At Work. Click Next.
5. On the Is Your Company Network On A Domain? page, click My Company Uses A Network With A Domain. Click Next.
6. On the You Will Need The Following Information page, verify that you have domain credentials available and that you know the domain name. Click Next.
7. On the Type Your User Name, Password, And Domain Name For Your Domain Account page, provide your domain credentials. Click Next.
8. If the Type The Computer Name And Computer Domain Name page appears, type the computer and domain name. Then click Next.
9. If prompted, type a user name, password, and domain. Click OK.
10. On the Do You Want To Enable A Domain User Account On This Computer? page, click Do Not Add A Domain User Account. Click Next.
11. Click Finish.
12. Click OK and then restart the computer when prompted.

If you experience problems joining a domain, see Chapter 31.

How to Connect to a Domain When 802.1X Authentication Is Enabled

For networks with 802.1X authentication, joining a domain is slightly more complicated. During 802.1X authentication, the client authenticates the server's identity by ensuring that the server certificate is valid and was issued by a trusted certification authority (CA). However, if you used an internal CA (such as one hosted by Windows Server 2003 certificate services) to issue the server certificate, the CA will not be trusted by default until the computer joins a domain. Therefore, to join the domain, you must temporarily configure the client computer to ignore the 802.1X authentication server's certificate.

> ***NOTE*** **If you have configured your 802.1X authentication servers with a server certificate issued by a public CA that is trusted by Windows by default, you can leave the Validate Server Certificate check box selected.**

To join a domain with 802.1X authentication enabled, follow these steps:

1. Start the Services console, start the Wired AutoConfig service, and set the Wired AutoConfig service to start automatically.
2. Open Network And Sharing Center and then click Manage Adapter Settings.
3. Right-click the network adapter and then click Properties.
4. In the Properties dialog box, click the Authentication Tab. Click the Choose A Network Authentication Method list and then click Microsoft: Protected EAP (PEAP).
5. Click Settings. In the Protected EAP (PEAP) Properties dialog box, clear the Validate Server Certificate check box. Click OK twice.
6. Follow the standard instructions for joining the computer to a domain, as described in the previous section.
7. After the computer has joined the domain and is restarted, perform steps 2 though 5 again. This time, in step 5, select the Validate Server Certificate check box.

To automate this process partially, configure a computer running Windows 7 to not validate the server certificate. Then use the *Netsh lan export profile* command to export a profile for the configured network adapter. You can create a script to import that profile on other client computers to allow them to join a domain without validating a server certificate. For more information about exporting and importing profiles, see the section titled "Configuring Wireless Settings from the Command Line or a Script" earlier in this chapter.

Summary

Windows Vista represented the most significant update to Windows networking since 1995. Windows 7 provides incremental improvements and several key new features. Most significantly, you can use the new BranchCache feature to reduce WAN utilization between branch offices and your central office. Support for DNSsec can reduce the risk of man-in-the-middle attacks that might take advantage of weaknesses in your name resolution infrastructure. Support for GreenIT can reduce power utilization while still allowing remote manageability. These changes let you do more with your network infrastructure while minimizing administration time and maximizing end-user productivity.

Additional Resources

These resources contain additional information and tools related to this chapter.

Related Information

- Chapter 24, "Managing Client Protection," includes information about configuring the desktop.
- Chapter 26, "Configuring Windows Firewall and IPsec," includes information about Windows Firewall and improvements to IPsec.
- Chapter 27, "Connecting Remote Users and Networks," includes information about setting up dial-up connections and VPNs.
- Chapter 28, "Deploying IPv6," includes information about IPv6.
- Chapter 31, "Troubleshooting Network Issues," includes information about solving networking problems.
- "Active Directory Schema Extensions for Windows Vista Wireless and Wired Group Policy Enhancements" at *http://technet.microsoft.com/en-ca/library/bb727029.aspx* includes instructions on extending the AD DS schema to support configuring wireless Windows Vista clients.
- "Deployment of IEEE 802.1X for Wired Networks Using Microsoft Windows" at *http://www.microsoft.com/downloads/details.aspx?familyid=05951071-6b20-4cef-9939-47c397ffd3dd* includes more information about 802.1X authentication.
- RFC 1191: *http://www.ietf.org/rfc/rfc1191.txt*
- RFC 2581: *http://www.ietf.org/rfc/rfc2581.txt*
- RFC 2582: *http://www.ietf.org/rfc/rfc2582.txt*
- RFC 2883: *http://www.ietf.org/rfc/rfc2883.txt*
- RFC 3517: *http://www.ietf.org/rfc/rfc3517.txt*
- RFC 4138: *http://www.ietf.org/rfc/rfc4138.txt*

On the Companion Media

- AssociatedAdaptersAndSettings.ps1
- ConfigureDNSSettings.ps1
- DetectNetworkAdapterConnection.ps1
- EnableDisableNetworkAdapters.ps1
- Get-DNSLookup.ps1
- GetActiveNicAndConfig.ps1
- GetConfigurationOfConnectedAdapters.ps1
- GetHalfDuplex.ps1

- GetNetAdapterConfig.ps1
- GetNetAdapterStatus.ps1
- GetNetID.ps1
- ManageDHCP.ps1
- ReportBandwidth.ps1
- SetStaticIP.ps1
- TroubleshootNetworking.ps1

CHAPTER 26

Configuring Windows Firewall and IPsec

Host-based firewalls and Internet Protocol security (IPsec) are two important ways of ensuring your network is protected. Windows Firewall with Advanced Security has been enhanced in the Windows 7 operating system with improvements in configurability, manageability, and diagnostics. This chapter examines how Windows Firewall with Advanced Security works in Windows 7 and how to configure, manage, monitor, and troubleshoot firewall and IPsec connectivity issues.

Understanding Windows Firewall with Advanced Security

Windows Firewall with Advanced Security (also referred to as "Windows Firewall" in this chapter) is a host-based, stateful firewall included in the Windows Vista operating system and later versions that can be used to specify which types of network traffic are allowed to pass between the local computer and the rest of the network. Specifically, Windows Firewall with Advanced Security is:

- A host-based firewall designed to protect the local computer, as opposed to a perimeter firewall designed to protect the entire internal network.
- A stateful firewall that can inspect and filter both inbound and outbound packets for both IPv4 and IPv6.

Windows Firewall with Advanced Security can also be used to protect network traffic as it passes between the local computer and other computers on the network. To accomplish this, Windows Firewall with Advanced Security uses IPsec.

Windows 7 builds upon the foundation of Windows Vista by adding new features and enhancements to Windows Firewall with Advanced Security. This section begins by outlining the improvements introduced previously in Windows Vista followed by a summary of the new improvements added in Windows 7. The section then continues by describing the underlying architecture of Windows Firewall with Advanced Security and how it works. Unless otherwise indicated, Windows Firewall and IPsec features available in Windows 7 are also available in Windows Server 2008 R2.

Improvements to Windows Firewall Introduced Previously in Windows Vista

The introduction of Windows Firewall with Advanced Security in Windows Vista represented a significant advance over the Windows Firewall introduced earlier in Windows XP Service Pack 2 (SP2). The following new or enhanced features were added to Windows Firewall with Advanced Security in Windows Vista:

- **Windows Filtering Platform** Windows Filtering Platform (WFP) is the engine that implements packet-filtering logic for Windows Firewall. WFP is accessible through a collection of public application programming interfaces (APIs) that allow Windows Firewall and third-party firewall applications to hook into the networking stack and the same filtering logic used by Windows Firewall. For more information concerning this feature, see the section titled "Understanding the Windows Filtering Platform" later in this chapter.
- **Windows Service Hardening** Windows Service Hardening (WSH) helps prevent misuse of Windows services by detecting and blocking abnormal behavior. For more information concerning this feature, see the section titled "Understanding Windows Service Hardening" later in this chapter.
- **Location-aware profiles** Windows Firewall in Windows XP supported only two types of firewall profiles: domain and standard. Windows Vista expanded the number of firewall profiles to three (domain, private, and public) and uses Network Location Awareness (NLA) to determine whether the computer is joined to an Active Directory Domain Services (AD DS) domain or is connected to a private network behind a gateway, a Network Address Translation (NAT) router, or a security device such as a firewall.
- **Configurable firewall rules** Firewall rules in Windows Vista are much more configurable than in Windows XP and allow filtering of any protocol number.
- **Outbound filtering** Beginning with Windows Vista, you can create firewall rules for filtering outbound traffic. This allows administrators to control which applications can send traffic onto the network.
- **Full IPv6 support** Windows Firewall with Advanced Security in Windows Vista fully supports filtering IPv6 network traffic.
- **IPsec integration** Windows Firewall with Advanced Security in Windows Vista integrates IPsec protection with firewall filtering through the use of connection security

rules and global IPsec settings for key exchange (main mode), data protection (quick mode), and authentication methods. For more information concerning IPsec integration with Windows Firewall, see the section titled "Understanding Connection Security Rules" later in this chapter.

- **Authenticated bypass rules** In Windows Vista, you can create authenticated bypass rules for specific computers to enable connections from those computers to bypass other firewall rules. This allows you to block certain types of traffic while allowing authenticated computers to bypass the block. You can also create firewall rules that filter by computer, user, or group in AD DS. For more information concerning this feature, see the section titled "Authenticated Bypass Rules" later in this chapter.

Additional Improvements to Windows Firewall in Windows 7

Beginning with Windows 7, Windows Firewall with Advanced Security has been further improved with the addition of the following new and enhanced features:

- **Multiple Active Firewall Profiles** In Windows Vista, only one firewall profile could be active at any one time. This means that if the computer is simultaneously connected to multiple networks, the firewall profile that has the most restrictive rules is applied to all the network connections. Beginning with Windows 7, however, each network connection is assigned its own firewall profile independently of all other connections on the computer. For more information concerning this feature, see the section titled "Understanding Multiple Active Firewall Profiles" later in this chapter.
- **Authorization exceptions** In Windows 7, when you create inbound firewall rules that specify which computers or users are authorized to access the local computer over the network, you can now also specify exceptions that should be denied access to the local computer. This enables you to create rules of the form "everyone except a, b, and c," which block network traffic from the users or computers you specify while allowing traffic from other users or computers. For more information, see the section titled "Configuring Firewall Profiles and IPsec Settings by Using Group Policy" later in this chapter.
- **Support for specifying port ranges for rules** Firewall and connection security rules in Windows 7 can now specify ranges of port numbers, making it easier to create rules for applications who need access to a range of ports.
- **User interface support for specifying port numbers and protocols for connection security rules** In Windows Vista, you had to use the Netsh command if you wanted to specify port numbers and protocols for connection security rules. In Windows 7, however, you can now use the New Connection Security Rule Wizard to do this.
- **Support for dynamic encryption** Connection security rules in Windows 7 now support dynamic encryption, which allows a computer to receive inbound packets from another computer that are authenticated but not encrypted. Once the connection

is established, a new quick mode security association is then negotiated to require encryption.

- **Dynamic tunnel endpoints** Tunnel connection security rules in Windows 7 now support having an address specified for only one endpoint of the tunnel. This helps simplify policy creation for scenarios in which there are multiple IPsec gateways and clients on multiple remote networks.
- **Tunnel mode authorization** In Windows 7, you can now specify groups of users or computers that are authorized to establish a tunnel to the IPsec gateway tunnel termination point. This is important when used in conjunction with dynamic tunnel endpoints to ensure that only authorized users can establish a connection with the computer. Windows 7 also supports exceptions to tunnel mode authorization similar to the authentication exceptions described previously.
- **New edge traversal options** In Windows Vista, you could only block or allow edge traversal. Beginning with Windows 7, however, two new options have been added for configuring edge traversal that can be used to allow users or applications to decide whether they can receive unsolicited traffic. For more information, see *http://msdn.microsoft.com/en-us/library/dd775221.aspx*.
- **Easier configuration of Suite B algorithms** In Windows Vista, you had to use the Netsh command if you wanted to create connection security rules that used the Suite B set of algorithms specified in RFC 4869. In Windows 7, however, you can now use the New Connection Security Rule Wizard to do this. For more information concerning Suite B algorithms support in Windows, see *http://support.microsoft.com/kb/949856/*.
- **Support for certificates issued by intermediate CAs** In Windows Vista, connection security rules could only use certificates issued by root certification authorities (CAs). In Windows 7, however, these rules can now use certificates issued by intermediate CAs as well.
- **Support for multiple main mode configurations** In Windows Vista, you could create only one global main mode configuration for IPsec communications involving the local computer. While the Windows Firewall with Advanced Security Microsoft Management Console (MMC) snap-in in Windows 7 still allows you to configure only a single main mode configuration for the computer, you can now use the Netsh command-line tool in Windows 7 and Windows Server 2008 R2 to create additional main mode configurations that you can use for secure connections to different computers on the network based on the security requirements associated with those endpoints.
- **New tunnel rule types** In Windows 7, you now have two additional tunnel rule types that you can configure: Gateway-to-Client and Client-to-Gateway.
- **Force Diffie-Hellman** In Windows 7, you now have the option of forcing the use of Diffie-Hellman for key exchange.

DIRECT FROM THE SOURCE

Dynamic Tunnel Endpoints

Sharad Kylasam, Program Manager
Core Networking

Dynamic tunnel endpoints refers to the ability of IPsec to dynamically determine the local and remote tunnel endpoint IP addresses that should be used for packets.

Previously, in scenarios in which the client's IP address is not static (that is, nomadic scenarios like home, hotel, meeting rooms, and so on), the policy configuration was such that the client's IP address had to be specified in a separate tunnel rule for each possible location from which the client could originate. This resulted in a proliferation of policies based on the client's origination and destinations and, given the nomadic nature of clients today, this complicates deployment, configuration, and management.

Dynamic tunnel endpoints simplify the specification of tunnel mode policies; the administrator can simply specify a single rule that applies to the client by specifying ANY for the tunnel endpoints. What actually happens is that IPsec figures out the actual tunnel endpoint address based on the application traffic that needs to be tunneled. In domain-based Group Policy scenarios, a single policy can therefore be applied to all clients, making it an even simpler deployment. This is a common deployment scenario for IPsec and has applicability in the following scenarios:

- DirectAccess
- Communication between IPsec-capable and non–IPsec-capable peers

Understanding the Windows Filtering Platform

The Windows Filtering Platform (WFP) is an architectural feature of Windows Vista and later versions that allows access to Transmission Control Protocol/Internet Protocol (TCP/IP) packets as they are being processed by the TCP/IP networking stack. WFP is the engine that implements packet-filtering logic, and it is accessible through a collection of public APIs which provide hooks into the networking stack and the underlying filtering logic upon which Windows Firewall is built. Independent Software Vendors (ISVs) can also use WFP to develop third-party firewalls, network diagnostic software, antivirus software, and other types of network applications. Using these APIs, a WFP-aware filtering application can access a packet anywhere in the processing path to view or modify its contents. Third-party vendors and network application developers should utilize the WFP APIs only for filtering applications or security applications.

As shown in Figure 26-1, the main features of the WFP are as follows:

- **Base Filter Engine** The Base Filter Engine (BFE) runs in user mode and receives filtering requests made by Windows Firewall, third-party applications, and the legacy IPsec policy service. The BFE then plumbs the filters created by these requests into the Kernel Mode Generic Filter Engine. The BFE (Bfe.dll) runs within a generic SvcHost.exe process.
- **Generic Filter Engine** The GFE receives the filters plumbed from the BFE and stores them so that the different layers of the TCP/IP stack can access them. As the stack processes a packet, each layer the packet encounters calls the GFE to determine whether the packet should be passed or dropped. The GFE also calls the various callout modules (defined next) to determine whether the packet should be passed or dropped. (Some callouts may perform an identical function, especially if multiple third-party firewalls are running concurrently.) The GFE (Wfp.lib) is part of the Kernel Mode Next Generation TCP/IP Stack (NetioTcpip.sys) first introduced in Windows Vista. The GFE is actually the Kernel Mode enforcement engine portion of the BFE and is not a separate feature.
- **Callout modules** These features are used for performing deep inspection or data modification of packets being processed by the pack. Callout modules store additional filtering criteria that the GFE uses to determine whether a packet should be passed or dropped.

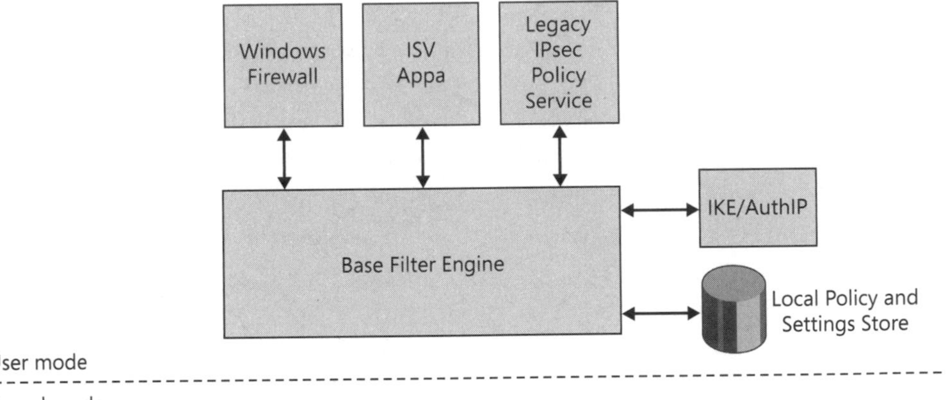

Kernel mode

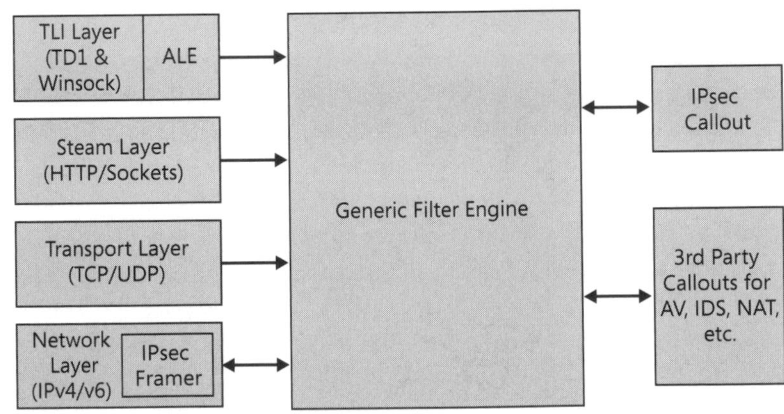

FIGURE 26-1 Simplified architecture of the WFP

NOTE The BFE can support multiple clients simultaneously. This means that a third-party, WFP-aware application can interact with and even override Windows Firewall with Advanced Security if so designed.

The APIs of the BFE are all publicly documented so that ISVs can create applications that hook into the advanced filtering capabilities of the Next Generation TCP/IP Stack in Windows Vista and later versions. Some of the filtering features of the WFP are implemented using callouts, but most filtering is performed using static filters created by the BFE as it interacts with Windows Firewall. The Windows Firewall service monitors the system to make sure the filters passed to BFE reflect the environment of the system at any given time. These public WFP APIs are scriptable and expose the full configurability of Windows Firewall, but they have some limitations, such as no support for IPsec integration.

MORE INFO For more information about the WFP, see *http://msdn.microsoft.com/en-us/library/aa366510.aspx*. You can find the "Windows Filtering Platform API Reference" at *http://msdn.microsoft.com/en-us/library/aa364947.aspx*.

Windows Firewall and the Startup Process

When a computer running Windows 7 starts, boot-time filters are applied to all network interfaces to reduce the attack surface prior to the Windows Firewall service (MpsSvc) starting. The boot-time filters perform the following actions:

- Block all unsolicited inbound traffic to the computer.
- Allow all inbound Dynamic Host Configuration Protocol (DHCP) traffic.
- Allow inbound Internet Control Message Protocol 6 (ICMPv6) Type 135:* Neighbor Discovery traffic.
- Allow all outbound traffic.
- Block outbound TCP Resets.
- Block outbound ICMPv6 Type 1:3 and ICMPv4 Type 3:3 Destination Unreachable / Port Unreachable error messages.

Once the BFE has initialized, Windows switches to using persistent filters until MpsSvc starts. These persistent filters are identical in policy to the boot-time filters. Once MpsSvc starts, Windows Firewall policy is processed and applied to the computer. For more information on persistent filters, see the sidebar titled "Direct from the Source: Windows Firewall and Boot-Time Filtering" in this chapter.

DIRECT FROM THE SOURCE

Windows Firewall and Boot-Time Filtering

Eran Yariv
Principal Development Manager

Windows Vista introduced the WFP, which performs filtering for Windows Firewall with Advanced Security. Firewall rules and settings are implemented via three types of WFP filters:

- **Boot-time filters** These filters are in effect from the time the TCP/IP stack starts until the BFE service starts. Once the BFE starts, these filters are removed.
- **Persistent filters** These filters are stored persistently in the BFE service (in the registry) and applied while the BFE is running.
- **Dynamic filters** These filters are not persistent and are associated with an active API session. Once the session ends, these filters are automatically removed.

This is what happens during startup:

1. The computer starts. There's no networking yet.
2. The TCP/IP stack starts and starts the WFP driver (Netio.sys).
3. Networking starts and the WFP boot-time filters are in effect.
4. The BFE service starts. Persistent filters replace the boot-time filters.
5. The Firewall Service starts, adding the current policy rules and settings (as filters) based on the current profile.

The boot-time filters (step 3) and the persistent filters (step 4) are identical and contain the following:

- Block All Unsolicited Inbound Traffic
- Allow Inbound Loopback Traffic
- Allow Inbound ICMPv6 Neighbor Discovery (also known as Neighbor Solicitation), which is used for mapping IPv6 addresses to the media access control (MAC) address (equivalent of Address Resolution Protocol [ARP] in IPv4)

These filters are present at all times and are low priority. Higher-priority filters mask out these filters when Windows Firewall policy is in effect (step 5). When Windows Firewall is disabled, the WFP boot-time and persistent filters are removed. If Windows Firewall is enabled but the Windows Firewall service is stopped or killed, the dynamic filters are automatically removed and you end up with the persistent filters, which in effect block all inbound traffic.

Understanding Windows Service Hardening

Windows Service Hardening (WSH) is a feature of Windows Vista and later versions that is designed to protect critical network services running on a system. If a service is compromised, WSH reduces the potential damage that can occur by reducing the attack surface that could be potentially exploited by some forms of malicious code. Because network services (both those built into the operating system and those installed by third-party applications) are by their nature exposed to the network (which itself is usually connected to the Internet), they provide a vector by which attackers can try to compromise a system. WSH implements the following protection improvements over previous versions of Windows:

- Configuring services to run whenever possible within the lower-privileged LocalService or NetworkService context instead of the LocalSystem context favored by many services in previous versions of Windows.
- Implementing a new type of per-service security identifier (service SID) that extends the Windows access control model to services and the system resources they access. When a service is started by the Service Control Manager (SCM), the SID is added to the secondary SIDs list of the process token if the service opted for doing this.
- Applying a write-restricted access token to the process for each service so that any attempt to access a system resource that does not have an explicit allow access control entry (ACE) for the service SID will fail.
- Tightening control over the generic SvcHost.exe grouping and distribution of services.
- Reducing the number of privileges assigned to services to only those needed by the service.

Understanding Service SIDs

Service SIDs are of the form S-1-5-80-{SHA1 hash of short service name} and complement the existing set of user, group, machine, and special SIDs used by previous versions of Windows. Service SIDs are secondary SIDs that are added to the SIDs list of the service process token when the SCM starts the service. The primary SID for a service is the built-in identity (LocalService, NetworkService, or LocalSystem) under which the service runs.

To have a service SID added to its token, the service must first opt in to doing so. Opt in is normally done by the operating system or application when the service is started. Administrators can manually opt in user-mode services by using the *sc sidtype* command, which can configure the service SID as either RESTRICTED, UNRESTRICTED, or NONE. For example, *sc sidtype service_name restricted* will add the service SID for the service to its service process token and also make it a write-restricted token. This means, for example, that any registry key used by the service must be explicitly assigned permissions to allow the service to access it. On the other hand, *sc sidtype service_name unrestricted* adds the SID of the service so that access check operations requesting that SID on the service token will succeed. Finally, *sc sidtype service_name none* does not include any SID in the token. For more information, type **sc sidtype ?** at a command prompt.

NOTE To query the SID type of a service, you can use the *sc qsidtype* command.

Some services in Windows Vista and later versions ship out of box as UNRESTRICTED, and most services will fail to start if changed to RESTRICTED. Third-party applications, such as antivirus software, can be designed to opt in to having service SIDs and can be designed to run either RESTRICTED or UNRESTRICTED. If the local administrator changes an existing service SID type from NONE to UNRESTRICTED, she gets the service having SID type with probably zero regression or issues with this service. (A SID type of UNRESTRICTED is sufficient for network traffic filtering.)

NOTE The service SIDs of all the configured services per process are always present in the process. Only the running services have their SIDs enabled; the SIDS of non-running services are there, but in a disabled state. However, the filtering platform considers all SIDs to be activated, regardless of whether the service is in a disabled state.

Windows Firewall and WSH

You can use service SIDs to restrict ways that services can interact with system objects, the file system, the registry, and events. For example, by changing the permissions of the firewall driver object using the Windows Firewall service SID, this driver will accept communication only from the Windows Firewall service.

WSH also protects services by using rules similar to those used by Windows Firewall. These rules are called service restriction rules, and they are built into Windows and can specify things such as which ports the service should listen on or which ports the service should send data over. An example of a built-in WSH rule might be "The DNS client service should send data only over port UDP/53 and should never listen on any port." These rules add additional protection to network services because network objects, such as ports, do not support ACLs. ISVs can extend this protection to third-party services they develop by using the public Component Object Model (COM) APIs for WSH found at *http://msdn.microsoft.com/en-us/library/aa365489.aspx*. However, WSH rules don't actually allow traffic (assuming Windows Firewall is turned on); instead, they define the restricted traffic that can be allowed to/from a service, regardless of the administrator-created firewall rules. WSH rules are thus a sandbox for the service.

WSH rules are also merged into the filtering process performed when Windows Firewall with Advanced Security decides whether to pass or drop a packet. In other words, when making decisions about traffic destined to or originating from services, Windows Firewall rules and WSH rules work closely together to decide whether to allow or drop traffic. For more information on how service restriction rules merge with Windows Firewall rules, see the section titled "Understanding Windows Firewall Policy Storage and Rule Merge Logic" later in this chapter.

NOTE An assumption behind WSH is that the services being protected are running under either the NetworkService or LocalService accounts. Services running under the LocalSystem account are omnipotent. In other words, they can turn off Windows Firewall with Advanced Security or ignore its rules; and therefore, they are not protected.

DIRECT FROM THE SOURCE

Windows Firewall Stealth

Eran Yariv

Principal Development Manager

Windows Firewall comes with an always-on, non-configurable stealth feature. The purpose of this feature is to prevent fingerprinting attacks that remotely attempt to figure out which ports are open on the computer, which services are running, the update state of the computer, and so on.

When a remote computer tries to connect to a non-listening TCP port (a TCP port that is not used on the local computer), the TCP/IP stack sends back a special TCP packet called TCP Reset (RST). However, if an application is listening on that port but a firewall is blocking it from receiving traffic, the remote computer will simply time out. This is a common technique to fingerprint the computer and see which ports are unused and which are used but blocked by the firewall. With the stealth feature of Windows Firewall, all TCP RST outbound packets are blocked so that the remote computer will time out when it connects to a port that is not allowed through the firewall, regardless of whether this port is in use.

For UDP ports and non-TCP/UDP sockets, a similar mechanism is used. Unlike TCP, these are not session-based protocols, so when a remote computer tries to connect to a non-listening UDP port (or a non-TCP/UDP socket), the stack replies back with an ICMP packet saying "nobody's home." For IPv4 traffic, the response is ICMPv4 (protocol 1)/type 3/code 3 (Destination Unreachable/Port Unreachable) or ICMPv4 (protocol 1)/type 3/code 2 (Destination Unreachable/Protocol Unreachable). For IPv6 UDP traffic, the response is ICMPv6 (protocol 58)/type 1.

With the stealth feature on, Windows Firewall blocks these outbound responses so that the remote computer can't tell the difference between a non-listening UDP port (or non-TCP/UDP socket) and one that is listening but is blocked by the firewall.

Windows Firewall and Service Triggers

Windows 7 now allows services to register to be started or stopped whenever a trigger event occurs, a new feature known as *Trigger Start services*. This eliminates the need for services to start when the system starts, which can improve boot performance. It also eliminates the need for services to poll or actively wait for an event to occur. In other words, services can now start when they are needed instead of having to starting automatically regardless of whether there is work for the service to do.

Beginning with Windows 7, the WFP and Windows Firewall with Advanced Security now work together to implement service triggers based on WFP filters. This helps stop unneeded services on the computer and only start them when Windows Firewall with Advanced Security has been configured to allow traffic for such services. For more information on how Windows Firewall uses service triggers, see the sidebar titled "Direct from the Source: Service Demand-Start on Firewall Triggers" in this chapter. For additional information concerning Trigger Start services, see the section titled "Services Enhancements in Windows 7" in Chapter 17, "Managing Devices and Services."

DIRECT FROM THE SOURCE

Service Demand-Start on Firewall Triggers

CSS Global Technical Readiness (GTR) Team

Before Windows 7, a number of services like Peer Name Resolution Protocol (PNRP), Simple Service Discovery Protocol (SSDP) Discovery Service (SSDPSRV), and other services, start up on initial boot and continue to run regardless of whether there are any consumers of their functionality and traffic is blocked through Windows Firewall with Advanced Security. The consuming applications are using a platform that is supposed to be always available; therefore, the services must always be running to be ready for the application.

The new Demand-Start service on Windows Firewall is designed to provide a way to reduce the number of services that are running at any given time and thereby improve performance. This service has a system-wide impact including improvement to boot-time, increase in battery life, lessened memory usage, and so on. Services configured with appropriate firewall triggers will only start when a consuming application starts and requests to open ports in the firewall to allow its traffic. Services can also be started and stopped (or notified) by the changes in profiles.

For example, remote management of Windows Firewall is only possible when the policy agent is running. Accordingly, there is a trigger related to the Windows Firewall Remote Management rules so that if you enable the Windows Firewall group, "Windows Firewall Remote Management," the policy agent service is started (see the following examples). This feature also works with third-party firewalls if they are designed correspondingly.

IMPORTANT If the BFE service is stopped, all registered services are started.

How It Works

Every service can register its Windows Firewall Demand-Start Parameters with the SCM. When the BFE is starting, it will enumerate all installed services and query each of them for firewall trigger information. After starting up, BFE will monitor all filter additions and deletions and fire appropriate events to the Unified Background Process Manager (UBPM) via its ETW channel. For more information about this topic, see *http://msdn.microsoft.com/en-us/library/dd405512.aspx*.

The Firewall Trigger

A firewall trigger consists of at least two and up to four of the following elements:

- Port number (or a Remote Procedure Call [RPC] token for dynamic port allocation)
- Protocol number
- Application that listens on the port (optional)
- Service name (optional; for SvcHost.exe, the service name can be specified to scope only the trigger to the service)

To determine whether a service has registered a firewall trigger you can use the *sc* command as follows.

```
c:\>sc qtriggerinfo policyagent

[SC] QueryServiceConfig2 SUCCESS
SERVICE_NAME: policyagent
START SERVICE
FIREWALL PORT EVENT : b7569e07-8421-4ee0-ad10-86915afdad09 [PORT OPEN]
DATA : RPC;TCP;%windir%\system32\svchost.exe;policyagent;
```

The DATA section describes the firewall trigger as follows:

- **RPC** The dynamic port (can be a fixed number)
- **TCP** The protocol
- **%Windir%\System32\SvcHost.exe** The listening application
- **policyagent** The service name

Here is another example.

```
c:\>sc qtriggerinfo Browser

[SC] QueryServiceConfig2 SUCCESS
SERVICE_NAME: Browser
START SERVICE
 FIREWALL PORT EVENT  : b7569e07-8421-4ee0-ad10-86915afdad09
```

```
[PORT OPEN]
 DATA                         : 139;TCP;System;
 DATA                         : 137;UDP;System;
 DATA                         : 138;UDP;System;
STOP SERVICE
 FIREWALL PORT EVENT  : a144ed38-8e12-4de4-9d96-e64740b1a524
[PORT CLOSE]
 DATA                         : 139;TCP;System;
 DATA                         : 137;UDP;System;
 DATA                         : 138;UDP;System;
```

Firewall triggers can be found in the registry under the service entry at

HKLM\SYSTEM\CurrentControlSet*services**service_name*\TriggerInfo

The subkeys are sorted in ascending order (0,1,2, and so on), and within the subkeys, only the values *Action* and *Type* are human readable. Appropriate values for *Action* are:

- 1 Service Start
- 2 Service Stop

A value of 4 for Type indicates SERVICE_TRIGGER_TYPE_FIREWALL_PORT_EVENT.

Understanding Multiple Active Firewall Profiles

Windows Vista and later versions support Network Location Awareness (NLA), a feature that enables Windows to detect changes in network connectivity so that applications can continue to operate seamlessly when network changes occur. The Network Location Awareness service (NLASVC) monitors the local computer for changes in its connectivity to connected networks. When Windows connects to a new network for the first time, the Network List Service assigns a globally unique identifier (GUID) to the new network. If the NLASVC later detects a change in network connectivity on the computer, it notifies the Network List Service, which then notifies Windows Firewall.

The NLA APIs in Windows can be used by applications to determine whether a network is in a connected or disconnected state. The APIs can also be used to determine which type of connection (such as wired connections, remote access connections, or wireless connections) Windows is currently using to access a specific network. Each network identified by Windows is assigned a location based on the type of network to which the computer is connected. The three types of network locations supported in Windows Vista and later versions are:

- **Domain network** A network on which Windows can authenticate access to a domain controller for the domain to which the computer is joined.

- **Private network** A network that has been specifically designated by the user or by an application as being a private network located behind a gateway device such as a NAT router, with the typical scenario being a Small Office/Home Office (SOHO).
- **Public network** A network that provides a direct connection with the Internet or is in a public place such as a coffee shop or airport. All non-domain networks are identified as public by default.

Windows Firewall is an example of such a network-aware application and uses the NLA APIs to identify the type of each connected network. Windows Firewall automatically associates a firewall profile with each identified network connection and configures the profile appropriately for that type of network. For example, if a network connection on the computer is a wireless connection to a WiFi hotspot at a coffee shop, Windows identifies the network as a public network and associates the appropriate firewall profile (public) with the connection. The firewall settings for a network connection are determined by the firewall profile assigned to that location. For example, if Windows Firewall with Advanced Security identifies a connected network as a public network, the firewall rules for File and Printer Sharing will be disabled by default to prevent other users on the network from accessing shared folders or printers on your computer. By contrast, if Windows Firewall with Advanced Security identifies the connected network as private, the File and Printer Sharing rules will be enabled because the network has been specified by the computer's administrator as a work/home environment where other trusted users and/or computers may reside.

Corresponding to these three types of network locations, the three types of firewall profiles are:

- **Domain profile** Applies to network connections whose network location type has been identified as domain network.
- **Private profile** Applies to network connections whose network location type has been identified as private network.
- **Public profile** Applies to network connections whose network location type has been identified as public network.

By default, the public profile is the most restrictive firewall profile, and the domain profile is the least restrictive in terms of the number of different types of traffic each profile allows.

In Windows Vista, only one firewall profile could be active at any one time even if your computer is connected to more than one network. In addition, the active profile would always be the most restrictive profile of all the networks to which the computer is connected. This caused problems for virtual private network (VPN) scenarios. For example, consider a user with a laptop running Windows Vista who is sitting at a coffee shop where free Internet access is provided via a wireless hotspot. The wireless connection is identified by Windows as a public network, and so the public firewall profile is the active firewall profile. The user then establishes a VPN connection via the Internet with her company's internal network using her domain credentials. Because there can be only one active firewall profile in Windows Vista, the firewall profile that is applied to the VPN connection is the same public profile being used for filtering Internet access. This causes some corporate applications to break when used over the VPN connection because these applications expect to use the less-restrictive domain profile, not the more-restrictive public profile.

Windows 7 solves this problem by allowing multiple firewall profiles to be active on the computer simultaneously. In this scenario, the user with a laptop running Windows 7 uses the wireless hotspot to connect to the Internet. The wireless connection is identified as a public network and the public firewall profile is assigned to the network and is active. The user now establishes a VPN connection with corpnet using her domain credentials, and in this case the domain profile is assigned to the VPN connection since authentication with a domain controller has been achieved. Both firewall profiles—the public profile for the wireless Internet connection and the domain profile for the VPN connection—are active in Windows 7. The public profile filters traffic that does not go through the VPN tunnel, while the domain profile filters traffic passing through the tunnel. The result is that corporate applications now work as intended over the VPN connection. Both networks are connected (see Figure 26-2) and the firewall profile for each network is active (see Figure 26-3).

> ***NOTE*** **If a computer running Windows 7 has a network adapter that is not connected to any network, the network location type will be Unidentified and the public firewall profile will automatically be assigned.**

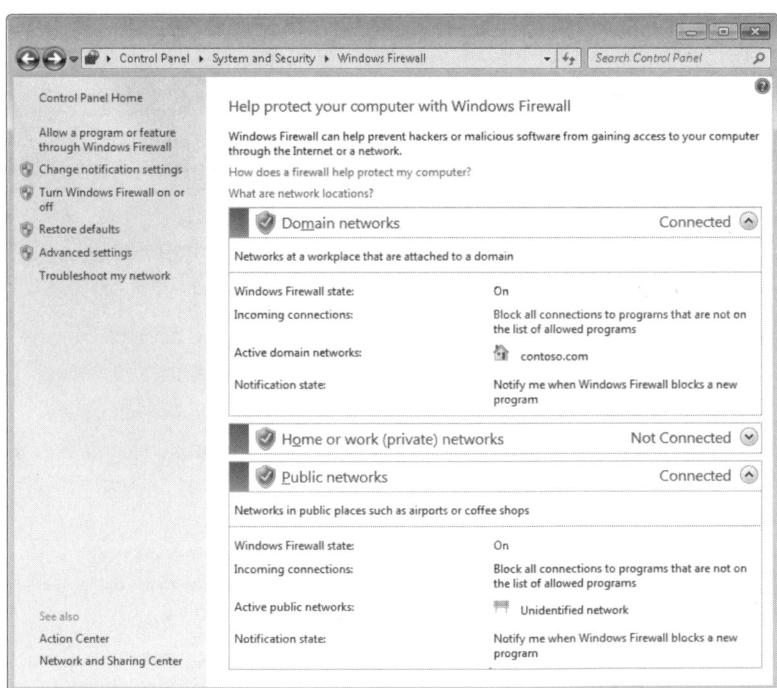

FIGURE 26-2 This computer running Windows 7 is connected to both a wired domain network and a wireless public network, and the Windows Firewall state is On for both network connections.

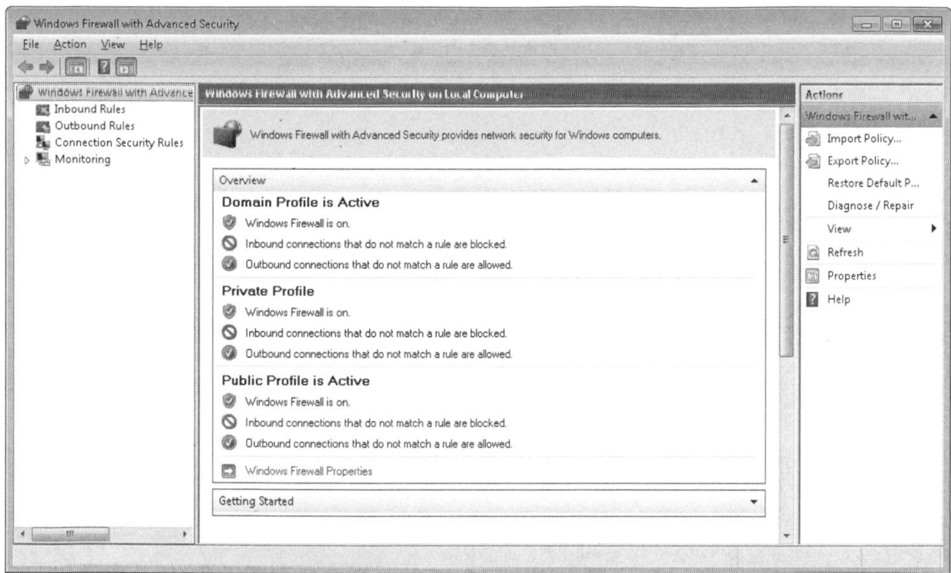

FIGURE 26-3 The Windows Firewall with Advanced Security MMC snap-in shows that both the domain profile and public profile are simultaneously active on this computer running Windows 7.

DIRECT FROM THE SOURCE

Multiple Active Firewall Profiles at Work

Sharad Kylasam, Program Manager
Core Networking

In Windows 7, more than one firewall profile can be active at any given time, with the firewall rules applicable to that profile enforced appropriately on the network interfaces that are classified under that profile.

The following example illustrates Multiple Active Firewall Profiles at work: I connect to my home network that I previously classified as Private, and I then fire up my VPN client and connect to my corporate network. The VPN connection gets classified as a domain network, and network traffic over this interface is subject to the firewall rules for the Domain profile; traffic over the home network is subject to the firewall rules of the Private profile.

In Windows Vista, only one firewall profile is active at any particular time, and that profile is the "most restrictive" (the order is: Public is more restrictive than Private, and Private is more restrictive than Domain). Therefore, from the previous example, the rules that are enforced on the VPN connection are the rules for the Private profile. As a result, there could be applications whose network traffic a domain administrator wanted to allow through the firewall when connected to the corporate network, but the applications are not allowed through because the firewall rules that are being enforced on all network interfaces are those for the Private profile. To work around this, a domain administrator can deploy firewall rules for the same applications scoped to Public and Private profiles while restricting them to the remote access interface type.

As mentioned previously, this limitation in Windows Vista has been resolved by introduction of the Multiple Active Firewall Profiles feature in Windows 7. So in this example, the Domain profile rules would be applied to the VPN connection and the Public profile rules would be applied to the home network connection.

DIRECT FROM THE SOURCE

Windows Firewall and Unidentified Networks

Dave Bishop, Senior Technical Writer
WSUA Networking

Multiple Active Firewall Profiles help to prevent a situation that can occur in Windows Vista and Windows Server 2008, when multiple network adapters are installed and one of them is connected to an "unidentified" network. If Windows cannot identify the network, it assigns the Public profile to that connection, which means that the Public profile is assigned to the entire computer, affecting all network connections. This likely disrupts the operation of some network programs or services because the Public profile has more restrictive rules by default than the Private or Domain profiles. Because of this scenario, on servers running Windows Server 2008 that are not expected to ever change profiles, it is recommended that you configure all profiles the same. This way, if the profile unexpectedly changes for any reason, the server continues to operate normally. It becomes more problematic on a laptop running Windows Vista because you really need separate profiles for different networks. However, on computers that are running Windows 7 or Windows Server 2008 R2, only the unidentified network is assigned the Public profile; all other adapters continue to use the profile that is appropriate to the currently connected network. You might still want to configure all profiles the same on a server so that if one network connection switches profiles unexpectedly, then services provided on that connection continue to operate as expected.

Understanding Rules

Windows Firewall with Advanced Security uses rules to control the behavior of network traffic passing between the local computer and the network. A *rule* is basically a collection of settings that controls the behavior of a specific type of network traffic. Windows Firewall with Advanced Security allows you to create two types of rules:

- **Firewall rules** These rules control whether network traffic passing between the local computer and the rest of the network should be allowed or blocked. Firewall rules can be configured locally using the Windows Firewall with Advanced Security snap-in or on targeted computers by using Group Policy.
- **Connection security rules** These rules determine how network traffic passing between the local computer and other computers on the network should be protected using IPsec. Unlike firewall rules, which function unilaterally, connection security rules require that both computers involved have either a connection security rule or a compatible IPsec policy configured. Connection security rules can be configured locally using the Windows Firewall with Advanced Security snap-in or on targeted computers by using Group Policy.

Additional types of rules used by Windows Firewall with Advanced Security include:

- **Default rules** These rules define what action should be taken when a connection does not match any other rule. Default rules can be configured locally using the Windows Firewall with Advanced Security snap-in or on targeted computers by using Group Policy.
- **WSH rules** These built-in rules prevent services from establishing connections in ways other than those to which they were designed. WSH rules can be configured locally using APIs only; they cannot be configured using Group Policy.

The sections that follow explain these various types of rules in more detail and also describe other types of rules used by Windows Firewall with Advanced Security.

Understanding Firewall Rules

Firewall rules are used to filter network traffic between the local computer and the network. To filter traffic means to allow or block traffic based on the filtering conditions specified in the rule. These filtering conditions can include protocol; local or remote port; local or remote IP address scope; user, computer or group; interface type; program or service; and ICMP Type Code. For more information concerning filtering conditions, see the section titled "Filtering Conditions for Firewall Rules" later in this chapter.

Firewall rules in Windows Firewall with Advanced Security can be classified in various ways:

- **Inbound vs. outbound rules** Determines the direction of the rule; that is, whether the rule applies to traffic passing from the network to the local computer or vice versa.
- **Allow vs. block rules** Determines the action the rule takes; that is, whether the traffic specified by the rule will be permitted or not.

- **Allow if secure rules** Indicates another action that a rule can take; namely, that only traffic protected using IPsec will be permitted.
- **Authenticated bypass rules** Overrides blocking rules for properly authenticated traffic (an optional subtype of allow if secure rules).

The sections that follow provide more detail concerning these different types of rules.

In addition to the above types of rules, any particular firewall rule you create (such as an inbound allow rule) can be configured as follows:

- **Program rule** This type of rule is used to allow traffic for a specific program (executable file) on the computer.
- **Port rule** This type of rule is used to allow traffic over a specific TCP or UDP port number or range of port numbers.
- **Predefined rule** Windows Firewall with Advanced Security includes a number of predefined firewall rules for specific Windows functionality. Examples of predefined rules include File and Printer Sharing and Remote Assistance. Each predefined rule is actually a group of rules that allow the particular Windows experience or feature to access the network in the way needed.
- **Custom rule** Create this type of rule when the other types of firewall rules don't meet the needs of your environment.

For more information, see the section titled "Creating and Configuring Firewall Rules" later in this chapter.

INBOUND VS. OUTBOUND RULES

Inbound rules filter traffic passing from the network to the local computer based on the filtering conditions specified in the rule. Conversely, outbound rules filter traffic passing from the local computer to the network based on the filtering conditions specified in the rule. Both inbound and outbound rules can be configured to allow or block traffic as needed.

Windows Firewall with Advanced Security includes a number of predefined inbound and outbound rules for filtering traffic typically associated with different Windows features. These rules are organized into rule groups, which identify a collection of rules designed to enable a particular Windows experience or feature. For example, the Remote Assistance rule group is a set of firewall rules designed to enable users of the local computer to use Remote Assistance to help other users on the network or to receive help from them. The Remote Assistance rule group includes the following rules:

- **Remote Assistance (DCOM-In)** Inbound rule to allow offering Remote Assistance using Distributed Component Object Model (DCOM)
- **Remote Assistance (PNRP-In) and Remote Assistance (PNRP-Out)** Inbound and outbound rules to allow use of the PNRP
- **Remote Assistance (RA Server TCP-In) and Remote Assistance (RA Server TCP-Out)** Inbound and outbound rules to allow offering Remote Assistance to other users

- **Remote Assistance (SSDP TCP-In) and Remote Assistance (SSDP TCP-Out)** Inbound and outbound rules to allow use of Universal Plug and Play (UPnP) over TCP port 2869
- **Remote Assistance (SSDP UDP-In) and Remote Assistance (SSDP UDP-Out)** Inbound and outbound rules to allow use of UPnP over UDP port 1900
- **Remote Assistance (TCP-In) and Remote Assistance (TCP-Out)** Inbound and outbound rules to allow Remote Assistance traffic

In addition, some of these rules exist in separate form for different firewall profiles. For example, there are two separate Remote Assistance (TCP-In) rules, one for the domain and private firewall profiles and the other for the public firewall profile. Firewall rules can also be either enabled or disabled. Rules that are enabled actively filter traffic; rules that are disabled exist but are not used for filtering traffic unless they are enabled. For example, by default the Remote Assistance (TCP-In) rule for the domain and private firewall profiles is enabled, while the Remote Assistance (TCP-In) rule for the public firewall profile is disabled. This means that by default, Remote Assistance can be used in domain-based scenarios and on work/home networks, but not at a coffee shop when connecting to the public Internet using a wireless hotspot connection.

Figure 26-4 shows the inbound rules for Remote Assistance as displayed in the Windows Firewall with Advanced Security MMC snap-in. Rules that are enabled are indicated by a green check mark before them; rules that are disabled are indicated by a red X before them. Filtering conditions for all rules can be viewed by scrolling horizontally in the central pane of the snap-in. Alternatively, you can display the filtering conditions of a specific rule by double-clicking the rule. Additional predefined rules may also be displayed if certain Windows features are turned on or off. For example, installing the Telnet Server feature adds a new predefined inbound rule named Telnet Server.

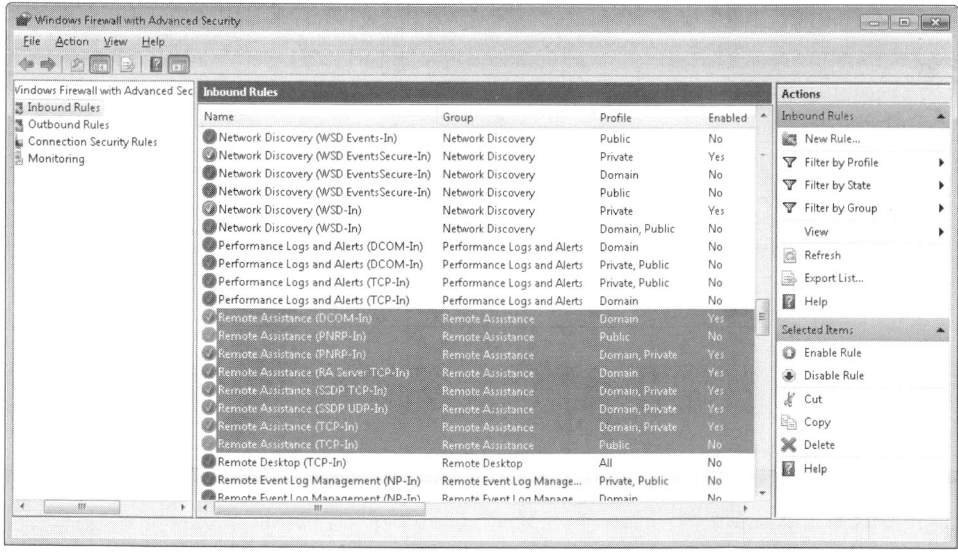

FIGURE 26-4 Inbound firewall rules in the rule group for Remote Assistance

ALLOW VS. BLOCK RULES

Both inbound and outbound firewall rules can be configured to either allow or block traffic that matches the filtering conditions specified in the rule. For example, Figure 26-5 shows the properties of the Remote Assistance (TCP-In) rule for the domain and private firewall profiles. By default, this predefined rule is configured to Allow The Connection, making it an allow rule. This means that if Windows Firewall with Advanced Security is processing an incoming packet and determines that this rule applies to the traffic, the packet will be permitted to enter the TCP/IP networking stack of the local computer. By contrast, if you change this rule by selecting Block The Connection, then when Windows Firewall with Advanced Security is processing an incoming packet and determines that the rule applies, the packet is prevented from entering the networking stack of the computer.

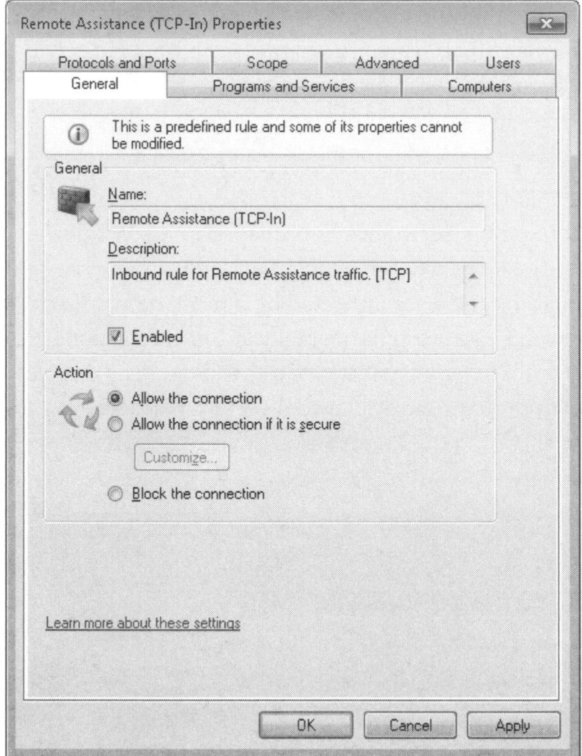

FIGURE 26-5 An allow rule permits the network traffic that matches the filtering conditions specified in the rule.

ALLOW IF SECURE RULES

A third action (apart from allow or block) that can be configured for a firewall rule is to Allow The Connection If It Is Secure. Selecting this option causes the rule to only permit the traffic to pass if it is being protected by IPsec. By default, selecting this option requires the traffic to be both authenticated and integrity protected but does not require that the traffic be encrypted (see Figure 26-6). Note that the actual IPsec settings for allowing secure traffic must be defined using separately created connection security rules.

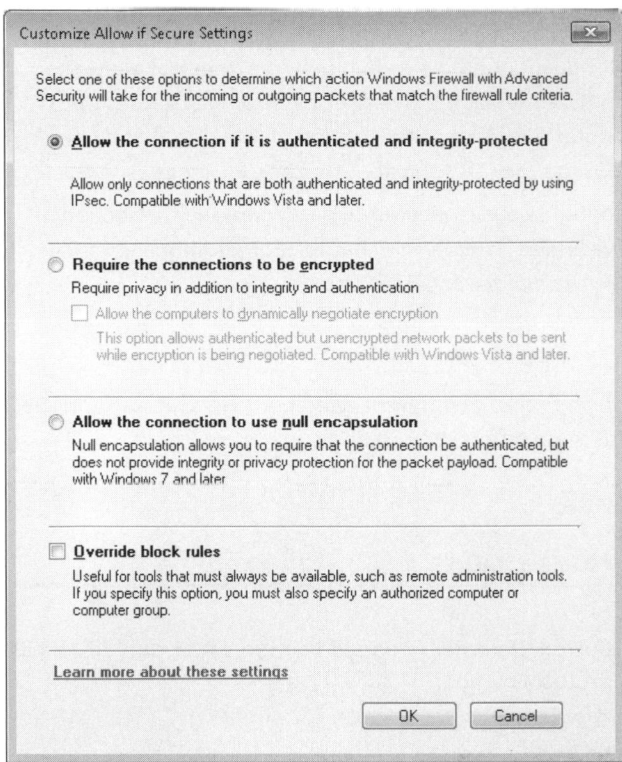

FIGURE 26-6 Default conditions for allowing traffic that must be protected using IPsec

AUTHENTICATED BYPASS RULES

Authenticated bypass rules are firewall rules that will allow a connection even though the existing firewall rules in Windows Firewall with Advanced Security would block the connection. Specifically, authenticated bypass rules let you block a particular type of traffic using firewall rules while allowing authenticated users or computers to bypass the block. A typical use for authenticated bypass rules is to allow network scanners and intrusion-detection systems to run on computers running Windows and to not have Windows Firewall with Advanced Security block their functionality.

Authenticated bypass rules require that the network traffic from the authorized computers be authenticated using IPsec so that identity can be confirmed. Authenticated bypass can be configured for inbound firewall rules, not outbound rules. However, you can specify override block rules in conjunction with authenticated outbound rules. The difference is that for the outbound rules, you don't have to specify remote machines, while for inbound rules you have to specify either remote machines or users.

For example, to enable authenticated bypass for the example rule discussed previously, select Override Block Rules in Figure 26-6 and then modify the filtering conditions for the rule to specify an authorized computer, user, or group of computers or users. Note that specifying users or user groups does not suffice—you must specify a computer or a computer group. Specifying only a user or user group for an inbound override block rule does not allow the rule to be configured and displays the error message "Rules that override block rules must specify at least one computer or computer group for authorization." Note also that if you do specify a computer or computer group, you may also specify users or user groups.

For more information on how to configure authenticated bypass rules, see the section titled "Creating and Configuring Firewall Rules" later in this chapter. For additional information, see *http://technet.microsoft.com/en-us/library/cc753463.aspx*.

FILTERING CONDITIONS FOR FIREWALL RULES

Firewall rules can filter traffic based on a number of different conditions (see Table 26-1). The effect of a rule is the logical AND of all these different conditions.

TABLE 26-1 Filtering Conditions for Firewall Rules

CONDITION	POSSIBLE VALUES
Protocol	Any Custom (Internet Assigned Numbers Authority [IANA] IP protocol number) TCP or UDP ICMPv4 or ICMPv6 Other protocols, including Internet Group Management Protocol [IGMP], HOPOPT, Generic Route Encapsulation [GRE], IPv6-NoNxt, IPv6-Opts, Virtual Router Redundancy Protocol [VRRP], Pragmatic General Multicast [PGM], Layer 2 Tunneling Protocol [L2TP], IPv6-Route, IPv6-Frag
Local port (inbound TCP only)	All ports Specific ports RPC dynamic ports RPC end-point mapper IP over Hypertext Transfer Protocol Secure (HTTPS) (IP-HTTPS)
Local port (inbound UDP only)	All ports Specific ports Edge traversal

CONDITION	POSSIBLE VALUES
Local port (outbound TCP only)	All ports Specific ports
Local port (outbound UDP only)	All ports Specific ports
Remote port (inbound TCP only)	All ports Specific ports
Remote port (inbound UDP only)	All ports Specific ports
Remote port (outbound TCP only)	All ports Specific ports IP-HTTPS
Remote port (outbound UDP only)	All ports Specific ports
ICMP Type Code (for ICMPv4 and ICMPv6)	All ICMP Types Specific types of ICMP traffic
Local IP address scope*	A specific IPv4 or IPv6 address or list of addresses A range of IPv4 or IPv6 addresses or list of ranges An entire IPv4 or IPv6 subnet or list of subnets
Remote IP address scope*	A specific IPv4 or IPv6 address or list of addresses A range of IPv4 or IPv6 addresses or list of ranges An entire IPv4 or IPv6 subnet or list of subnets A predefined set of computers—including local subnet, default gateway, DNS servers, WINS servers, or DHCP servers—or a list of such items
Profiles	Specify the profile(s) to which the rule applies; for example, Domain, Private, and/or Public
Interface type	All interface types Local area network Remote access Wireless
Edge traversal	Allow edge traversal Block edge traversal Defer to user Defer to application

CONDITION	POSSIBLE VALUES
Programs	All programs System, a special keyword that if used will restrict traffic to the System Process (useful for scoping traffic to any Kernel Mode driver such as Http.sys, Smb.sys, and so on) Specify path and .exe name to program executable (path can include environment variables)
Services**	Apply to all programs and services Apply to services only Apply to a specified service or to a service with the specified short name
User	Only allows connections from the specified users or groups of users (optionally with specified exceptions); this filtering condition can only be used when Allow This Connection If It Is Secure has been selected on the General tab of the rule's properties
Computer	Only allows connections from the specified computers or groups of computers (optionally with specified exceptions); this filtering condition can only be used when Allow This Connection If It Is Secure has been selected on the General tab of the rule's properties

**When creating and configuring firewall rules, use the scope filtering condition wherever possible. For example, if you do network backup and need to allow incoming connections from the backup service, configure the scope so that Windows Firewall allows connections only from the backup server's IP address or network. Similarly, refine the scope for network management and remote administration tools to just those networks that require it.*

***Firewall rules can allow or block services regardless of where their executables are located on the computer. Services can be specified by their service name, even if the service is implemented as a dynamic-link library (DLL). Programs are identified by specifying the application path. (Specifying DLLs is not supported.) In addition, the service needs to have an associated service SID for this scoping to work correctly. To verify this, use the* sc qsidtype serviceshortname *command to verify that the service SID is not set to NONE.*

Understanding Connection Security Rules

Connection security rules specify how and when Windows Firewall with Advanced Security uses IPsec to protect traffic passing between the local computer and other computers on the network. Connection security rules force two peer computers to authenticate before a connection can be established between them. Connection security rules can also ensure that communications between the computers is secure by encrypting all traffic passed between them. Connection security rules are typically used in the following types of scenarios:

- **Server isolation** Server isolation involves configuring connection security rules on a server so that connection attempts from other computers on the network must be authenticated (and optionally, encrypted) before the server accepts these connection attempts. For example, a back-end database server might be configured to accept only authenticated connections from a front-end Web application server. For more information on how server isolation works and how to implement it, see *http://technet.microsoft.com/en-us/network/bb545651.aspx*. See also the *Step-by-Step Guide: Deploying Windows Firewall and IPsec Policies* at *http://technet.microsoft.com/en-us/library/cc732400.aspx* for a walkthrough of how to implement a basic server isolation scenario.

- **Domain isolation** Domain isolation involves configuring connection security rules on both clients and servers so that domain members accept only authenticated (and optionally, encrypted) connection attempts from other domain members. By default, connection attempts from non-domain members are not accepted, but you can configure exception rules that allow unauthenticated connections from specific non-domain members. For more information on how domain isolation works and how to implement it, see *http://technet.microsoft.com/en-us/network/bb545651.aspx*. See also the *Step-by-Step Guide: Deploying Windows Firewall and IPsec Policies* at *http://technet.microsoft.com/en-us/library/cc732400.aspx* for a walkthrough of how to implement a basic domain isolation scenario.
- **Network Access Protection** Network Access Protection (NAP) is a technology available in Windows 7, Windows Vista, Windows Server 2008, and Windows Server 2008 R2 that enforces health requirements by monitoring and assessing the health of client computers when they try to connect or communicate on a network. Client computers that are found to be out of compliance with the health policy can then be provided with restricted network access until their configuration has been updated and brought into compliance with policy. Windows Firewall with Advanced Security can be used as part of a NAP implementation by creating connection security rules that require computer certificates for authentication. Specifically, client computers that are determined to be in compliance with health policy are provisioned with the computer certificate needed to authenticate. For more information on how NAP works and how to implement it, see *http://www.microsoft.com/nap/*.
- **DirectAccess** DirectAccess is a new feature of Windows 7 and Windows Server 2008 R2 that provides users with the experience of being seamlessly connected to their corporate network any time they have Internet access. Using DirectAccess, users can securely access internal resources such as e-mail servers and intranet sites without the need of first establishing a VPN connection with their corporate network. DirectAccess uses IPv6 together with IPsec tunnels to establish secure, bidirectional communications between the client computer and the corporate network over the public Internet. DirectAccess also seamlessly integrates with server and domain isolation scenarios and NAP implementations enabling enterprises to create comprehensive end-to-end security, access, and health requirement solutions. For more information on how DirectAccess works and how to implement it, see *http://www.microsoft.com/directaccess/*.

DIRECT FROM THE SOURCE

Combining Domain Isolation with Server Isolation

Dave Bishop, Senior Technical Writer
WSUA Networking

You can easily combine both Domain Isolation and Server Isolation on the same network. The Domain Isolation rules that configure your computers to authenticate before connecting can also serve as the basis for identifying computers and users to restrict access to sensitive servers. By default, only computer authentication is performed, but on computers that are running Windows 7, Windows Vista, Windows Server 2008, or Windows Server 2008 R2, you can configure the rules to also require user authentication.

The client rules that support Domain Isolation support Server Isolation as well. To isolate a server, you configure the server to permit connections from authorized users and computers only. To do this, add a firewall rule to the isolated server that uses the Allow The Connection If It Is Secure action. This enables the Users and Computers tabs, where you can identify the user and computer accounts that are authorized to connect to the isolated server. No further configuration on the client computers is required; the user and computer credentials used for authentication for Domain Isolation are also used for the authorization on the isolated server.

Server Isolation is an important defense-in-depth layer that helps to protect your sensitive servers, such as Payroll, Personnel, and other servers that must be carefully guarded.

TYPES OF CONNECTION SECURITY RULES

Depending on the scenario you want to implement or the business need you are trying to meet, different types of connection security rules may be needed for your environment. Windows Firewall with Advanced Security allows you to create the following types of connection security rules:

- **Isolation rules** These rules are used to isolate computers by restricting inbound connections based on credentials such as domain membership. Isolation rules are typically used when implementing a server or domain isolation strategy for your network.
- **Authentication exemption rules** These rules are used to identify computers that do not require authentication when attempting to connect to a domain member when implementing a domain isolation strategy.
- **Server-to-server rules** These rules are used to protect communications between specific computers. This is basically the same as an isolation rule except that you can specify the endpoints.

- **Tunnel rules** These rules are used to protect communications between gateways on the public Internet. In Windows 7, you can create dynamic tunnel endpoint rules that enable Client-to-Gateway and Gateway-to-Client tunnel configurations.
- **Custom rules** These rules can be created when the other types of connection security rules don't meet the needs of your environment.

SUPPORTED IPSEC SETTINGS FOR CONNECTION SECURITY RULES

Connection security rules use IPsec to protect traffic between the local computer and other computers on the network. IPsec is an industry-standard set of protocols for protecting communications over IP networks using cryptographic security services. IPsec can provide network-level peer authentication, data origin authentication, data integrity, data confidentiality (encryption), and replay protection to ensure the security of traffic as it passes across a network. For general information concerning IPsec concepts and how IPsec can be used to protect a network, see the resources available at *http://www.microsoft.com/IPsec/*.

The range of IPsec features supported previously in the Windows Vista RTM has been expanded, first in Windows Vista SP1 and later versions in Windows 7 to include new security methods, data integrity algorithms, data encryption algorithms, and authentication protocols. Tables 26-2 through 26-6 summarize the key exchange algorithms, data protection (integrity or encryption) algorithms, and authentication methods now supported for IPsec communications in Windows 7. Note that some algorithms are supported only for main mode or quick mode, and different authentication methods are supported for first and second authentication. For more information on how to configure IPsec settings in Windows 7, see the section titled "Creating and Configuring Connection Security Rules" later in this chapter.

TABLE 26-2 Supported Key Exchange Algorithms for IPsec Communications in Windows 7

KEY EXCHANGE ALGORITHM	NOTES
Diffie-Hellman Group 1 (DH Group 1)	Not recommended. Provided for backward compatibility only.
DH Group 2	Stronger than DH Group 1.
DH Group 14	Stronger than DH Group 2.
Elliptic Curve Diffie-Hellman P-256	Stronger than DH Group 2. Medium resource usage. Compatible only with Windows Vista and later versions.
Elliptic Curve Diffie-Hellman P-384	Strongest security. Highest resource usage. Compatible only with Windows Vista and later versions.

TABLE 26-3 Supported Data Integrity Algorithms for IPsec Communications in Windows 7

DATA INTEGRITY ALGORITHM	NOTES
Message-Digest algorithm 5 (MD5)	Not recommended. Provided for backward compatibility only.
Secure Hash Algorithm 1 (SHA-1)	Stronger than MD5 but uses more resources.
SHA 256-bit (SHA-256)	Main mode only. Supported on Windows Vista SP1 and later versions.
SHA-384	Main mode only. Supported on Windows Vista SP1 and later versions.
Advanced Encryption Standard-Galois Message Authentication Code 128 bit (AES-GMAC 128)	Quick mode only. Supported on Windows Vista SP1 and later versions. Equivalent to AES-GCM 128 for integrity.
AES-GMAC 192	Quick mode only. Supported on Windows Vista SP1 and later versions. Equivalent to AES-GCM 192 for integrity.
AES-GMAC 256	Quick mode only. Supported on Windows Vista SP1 and later versions. Equivalent to AES-GCM 256 for integrity.
AES-GCM 128	Quick mode only. Supported on Windows Vista SP1 and later versions. Equivalent to AES-GMAC 128 for integrity.
AES-GCM 192	Quick mode only. Supported on Windows Vista SP1 and later versions. Equivalent to AES-GMAC 192 for integrity.
AES-GCM 256	Quick mode only. Supported on Windows Vista SP1 and later versions. Equivalent to AES-GMAC 256 for integrity.

TABLE 26-4 Supported Data Encryption Algorithms for IPsec Communications in Windows 7

DATA ENCRYPTION ALGORITHM	NOTES
Data Encryption Standard (DES)	Not recommended. Provided for backward compatibility only.
Triple-DES (3DES)	Higher resource usage than DES.
Advanced Encryption Standard-Cipher Block Chaining 128-bit (AES-CBC 128)	Faster and stronger than DES. Supported on Windows Vista and later versions.
AES-CBC 192	Stronger than AES-CBC 128. Medium resource usage. Supported on Windows Vista and later versions.
AES-CBC 256	Strongest security. Highest resource usage. Supported on Windows Vista and later versions.
AES-GCM 128	Quick mode only. Faster and stronger than DES. Supported on Windows Vista and later versions. The same AES-GCM algorithm must be specified for both data integrity and encryption.
AES-GCM 192	Quick mode only. Medium resource usage. Supported on Windows Vista and later versions. The same AES-GCM algorithm must be specified for both data integrity and encryption.
AES-GCM 256	Quick mode only. Faster and stronger than DES. Supported on Windows Vista and later versions. The same AES-GCM algorithm must be specified for both data integrity and encryption.

TABLE 26-5 Supported First Authentication Methods for IPsec Communications in Windows 7

FIRST AUTHENTICATION METHOD	NOTES
Computer (Kerberos V5)	Compatible with Microsoft Windows 2000 or later versions.
Computer (NTLMv2)	Use on networks that include systems running an earlier version of Windows and on stand-alone systems.
Computer certificate	The default signing algorithm is RSA, but Elliptic Curve Digital Signature Algorithm (ECDSA)–P256 and ECDSA-P384 are also supported signing algorithms. New in Windows 7 is added support for using an intermediate CA as a certificate store in addition to using a root CA as was previously supported in Windows Vista. Certificate to account mapping is also supported. First authentication can also be configured to accept only health certificates when using a NAP infrastructure.
Pre-shared key	Not recommended.

TABLE 26-6 Supported Second Authentication Methods for IPsec Communications in Windows 7

SECOND AUTHENTICATION METHOD	NOTES
User (Kerberos V5)	Compatible with Windows 2000 or later versions.
User (NTLMv2)	Use on networks that include systems running an earlier version of Windows and on stand-alone systems.
User certificate	The default signing algorithm is RSA, but ECDSA-P256 and ECDSA-P384 are also supported signing algorithms. New in Windows 7 is added support for using an intermediate CA as a certificate store in addition to using a root CA as was previously supported in Windows Vista. Certificate to account mapping is also supported.

SECOND AUTHENTICATION METHOD	NOTES
Computer health certificate	The default signing algorithm is RSA, but ECDSA-P256 and ECDSA-P384 are also supported signing algorithms. New in Windows 7 is added support for using an intermediate CA as a certificate store in addition to using a root CA as was previously supported in Windows Vista. Certificate to account mapping is also supported.

DEFAULT IPSEC SETTINGS FOR CONNECTION SECURITY RULES

The default IPsec settings for Windows Firewall with Advanced Security are as follows:

- Default key exchange settings (main mode):
  - Key exchange algorithm: DH Group 2
  - Data integrity algorithm: SHA-1
  - Primary data encryption algorithm: AES-CBC 128
  - Secondary data encryption algorithm: 3DES
  - Key lifetime: 480 minutes/0 sessions
- Default data integrity settings (quick mode):
  - Primary protocol: Encapsulating Security Payload (ESP)
  - Secondary protocol: Authentication Header (AH)
  - Data integrity algorithm: SHA-1
  - Key lifetime: 60 minutes/100,000 KB
- Default data encryption settings (quick mode):
  - Primary protocol: ESP
  - Secondary protocol: ESP
  - Data integrity algorithm: SHA-1
  - Primary data encryption algorithm: AES-CBC 128
  - Secondary data encryption algorithm: 3DES
  - Key lifetime: 60 minutes/100,000 KB

The default authentication method used for first authentication of IPsec connections is Computer (Kerberos V5). By default, no second authentication method is configured for IPsec connections.

By default, these settings are used when creating new connection security rules unless you select different settings when using the New Connection Security Rule Wizard. For more information, see the section titled "Creating and Configuring Connection Security Rules" later in this chapter.

Windows Firewall and Windows PE

Beginning with Windows 7 and Windows Server 2008 R2, you can now configure IPsec in Windows Preinstallation Environment (Windows PE) for added security during desktop and server deployment. While Windows PE 3.0 now supports IPsec by default, the computer you want to connect to may require additional configuration to allow a connection. The default IPsec settings for Windows PE 3.0 are as follows:

- **MM Security Offer: AES128-SHA1-ECDHP256, where MM is main mode.**
- **MM Authentication Method: Anonymous**
- **QM Policy: 3DES-SHA1; AES128-SHA1, where QM is quick mode.**
- **QM Authentication Method: NTLMv2**

Understanding Default Rules

Default rules specify the default behavior of Windows Firewall with Advanced Security when traffic does not match any other type of rule. Default rules can be configured on a per-profile basis. The possible default rules for inbound traffic are:

- Block (the default for all profiles)
- Block all connections
- Allow

The possible default rules for outbound traffic are:

- Allow (the default for all profiles)
- Block

From a practical standpoint, the block all connections default rule for inbound traffic can be interpreted as "shields up" or "ignore all allow and allow-bypass rules." For information on configuring default rules, see the section titled "Configuring Firewall Profiles and IPsec Settings by Using Group Policy" later in this chapter.

Understanding WSH Rules

WSH rules are built-in rules that protect Windows services (and thereby also the applications that use these services) by restricting services from establishing connections in ways other than they were designed. WSH rules are not exposed to management using the Windows Firewall with Advanced Security MMC snap-in, the Netsh command, or Group Policy.

Third-party ISVs who create services for Windows can also create WSH rules to protect those services. For more information on this, see *http://msdn.microsoft.com/en-us/library/aa365491.aspx*.

Understanding Rules Processing

If more than one rule matches a particular packet being examined, Windows Firewall with Advanced Security must decide which of these rules to apply to the packet so as to decide what action to take. The order in which Windows Firewall with Advanced Security processes rules is as follows:

1. WSH rules (this is not configurable by the user)
2. Connection security rules
3. Authenticated bypass rules
4. Block rules
5. Allow rules
6. Default rules

When a packet is being examined by Windows Firewall with Advanced Security, the packet is compared to each of these types of rules in the order they are listed. If the packet matches a particular rule, that rule is applied, and rule processing stops. In addition, if two rules in the same group match, then the rule that is more specific (that is, has more matching criteria) is the one that is applied. For example, if rule A matches traffic to 192.168.0.1 and rule B matches traffic to 192.168.0.1 TCP port 80, then traffic to port 80 on that server matches rule B, and its action is the one taken.

By default, the rule processing described previously includes both local rules (firewall and/or connection security rules configured by the local administrator of the computer) and rules applied to the computer by Group Policy. If more than one Group Policy object (GPO) applies to a particular computer, the default rules come from the GPO with the highest precedence. Merging of local rules can be enabled or disabled using Group Policy. For more information, see the section titled "Considerations When Managing Windows Firewall Using Group Policy" later in this chapter.

Managing Windows Firewall with Advanced Security

Windows 7 and Windows Server 2008 R2 include tools for configuring and managing Windows Firewall with Advanced Security in both stand-alone and domain environments. These tools can be used to perform common tasks such as creating firewall rules to block or allow traffic, creating connection security rules to protect network traffic using IPsec, monitoring firewall and connection security activity, and more. The sections that follow examine the tools that you can use to manage Windows Firewall with Advanced Security and describe some common management tasks.

Tools for Managing Windows Firewall with Advanced Security

The following tools can be used for managing Windows Firewall with Advanced Security:

- Windows Firewall Control Panel item
- Windows Firewall with Advanced Security MMC snap-in
- Windows Firewall with Advanced Security Group Policy node
- *Netsh advfirewall* command context

The sections that follow summarize the differences in functionality between using these various tools.

Managing Windows Firewall Using Control Panel

The Windows Firewall utility in Control Panel exposes only a small subset of Windows Firewall with Advanced Security functionality and is primarily intended for consumers and for users working in SOHO environments. Using this utility, a user on the local computer can perform the following tasks:

- Turning Windows Firewall on or off for each type of network location (domain, private, or public)
- Enabling or disabling firewall notifications for each type of network location
- Verifying which firewall profiles apply to which network connections on the computer
- Allowing a program or feature to communicate through Windows Firewall for a particular firewall profile (see Figure 26-7)
- Restoring the default settings for Windows Firewall

Note that most actions involving Windows Firewall require local administrator credentials on the computer.

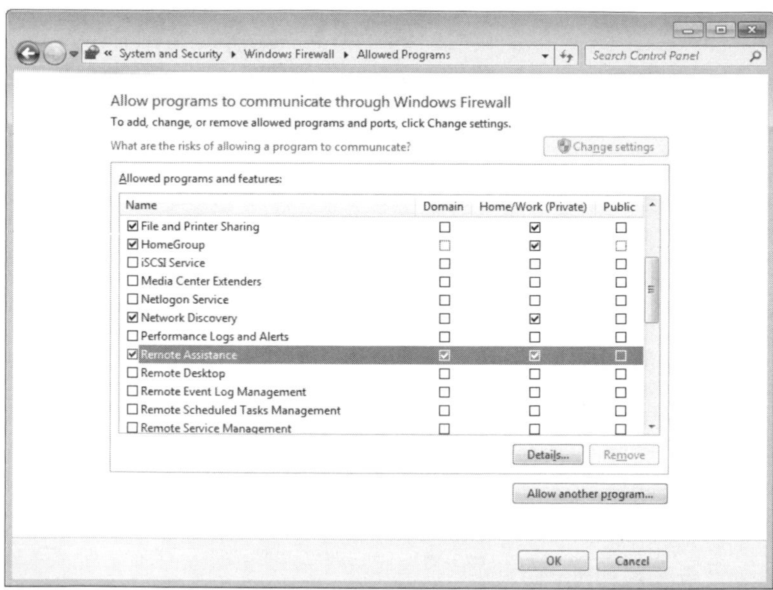

FIGURE 26-7 Viewing which firewall profiles allow Remote Assistance to communicate through Windows Firewall

Managing Windows Firewall Using the Windows Firewall with Advanced Security Snap-in

The Windows Firewall with Advanced Security MMC snap-in exposes most of the functionality of Windows Firewall for advanced users and administrators of the local computer (main mode rules and some advanced global IPsec settings are configurable only by Netsh). To start this snap-in, do any of the following:

- From the Start menu, select Control Panel, System And Security, Windows Firewall, Advanced Settings.
- Type **fire** in the Start menu Search box, and then click Windows Firewall With Advanced Security in the Programs group.
- Type **wf.msc** in the Start menu Search box and press Enter.
- Type **mmc** in the Start menu Search box and press Enter to open a new MMC console, and then add the Windows Firewall with Advanced Security snap-in to the console in the usual way.

The first three methods listed here can be used only to manage Windows Firewall on the local computer. The last method can be used to manage Windows Firewall on either the local computer or a specified remote computer. You must have local administrator credentials on the computer on which you want to manage Windows Firewall when using this snap-in.

NOTE The Windows 7 version of the Windows Firewall with Advanced Security snap-in can be used to manage Windows Firewall on Windows 7, Windows Vista, Windows Server 2008, and Windows Server 2008 R2.

Using the Windows Firewall with Advanced Security snap-in, you can perform a wide variety of administrative tasks, including the following:

- Configuring default settings for each firewall profile
- Enabling and disabling firewall rules
- Creating and configuring firewall rules
- Configuring default IPsec settings
- Enabling and disabling connection security rules
- Creating and configuring connection security rules
- Exporting and importing firewall policy for the computer
- Restoring the default firewall settings for the computer
- Configuring firewall logging settings
- Monitoring the state of the firewall and its configuration
- Monitoring active firewall rules
- Monitoring active connection security rules
- Monitoring security associations for both main mode and quick mode
- Monitoring event logs associated with Windows Firewall

Many of these management tasks are described in more detail in the section titled "Common Management Tasks" later in this chapter.

To make it easier to manage large numbers of rules on a computer, the Windows Firewall with Advanced Security snap-in lets you filter firewall and connection security rules by profile (domain, private or public) and/or by state (enabled or disabled). In addition, firewall rules (but not connection rules) can also be filtered by rule group. Figure 26-8 shows all inbound rules that match the following filtering criteria:

- Profile: domain
- State: enabled
- Group: Remote Assistance

To remove applied filters, select Clear All Filters from the shortcut menu.

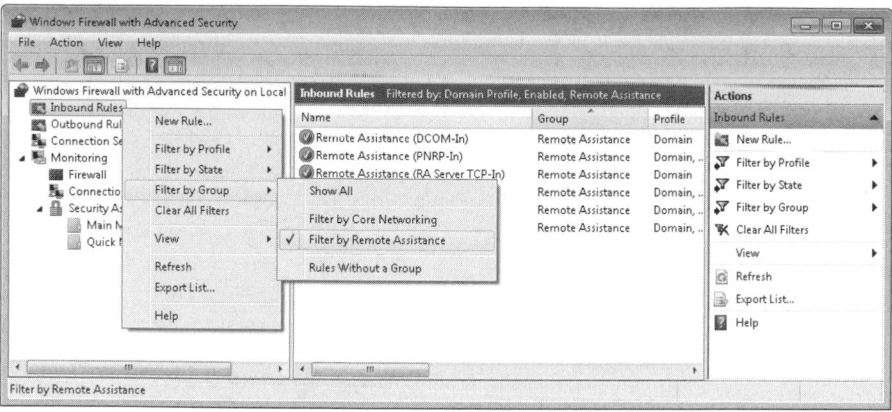

FIGURE 26-8 You can filter firewall rules by profile, state, and group to make it easier to manage large numbers of rules.

Managing Windows Firewall Using Group Policy

In enterprise environments, the primary method for managing Windows Firewall on remote computers (both clients and servers) is to use Group Policy. To manage Windows Firewall on a collection of computers on your network using Group Policy, do the following:

1. Create a new GPO and link the GPO to the organizational unit (OU) where the computer accounts for these computers reside.
2. Open the GPO using the Group Policy Management Editor from the Group Policy Management Console (GPMC) and navigate to the following location:

   Computer Configuration\Policies\Windows Settings\Security Settings\Windows Firewall With Advanced Security\
3. Select the policy node under this location, which should look like this:

   Windows Firewall with Advanced Security - LDAP://CN={GUID},CN=POLICIES,CN=SYSTEM,DC=domain_name,DC=COM

   Here GUID is the globally unique identifier for the Group Policy Container (GPC) associated with the GPO you have opened.

Once you have selected this node, you can configure Group Policy settings for Windows Firewall using the same graphical user interface for the Windows Firewall with Advanced Security snap-in described previously (see Figure 26-9).

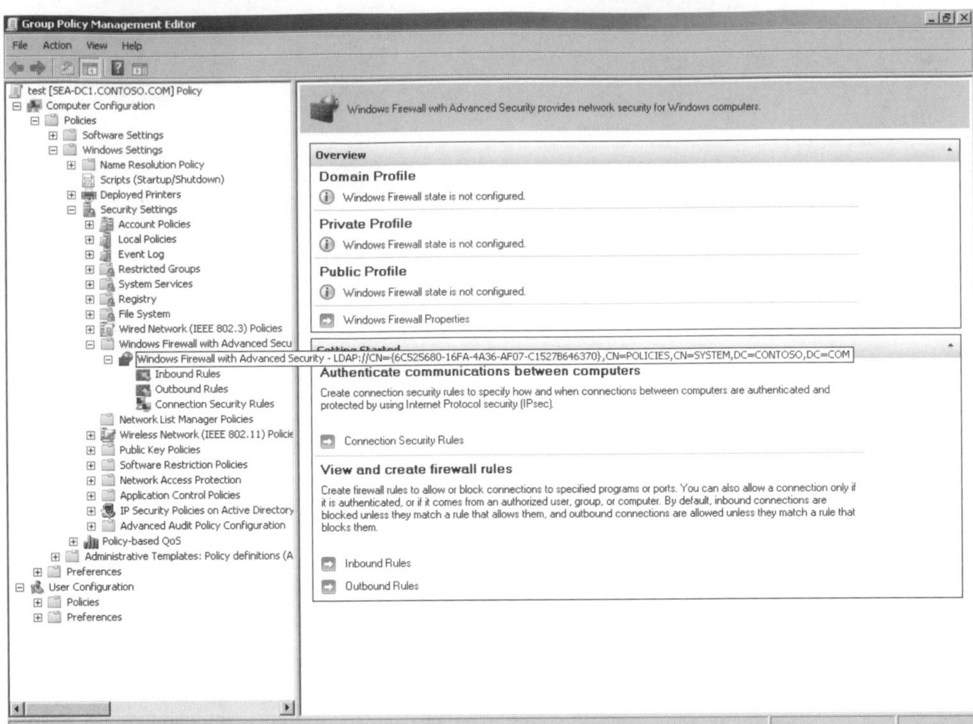

FIGURE 26-9 Using Group Policy to configure Windows Firewall with Advanced Security on targeted computers

CONSIDERATIONS WHEN MANAGING WINDOWS FIREWALL USING GROUP POLICY

The following considerations should be kept in mind when managing Windows Firewall using Group Policy:

- The state of each firewall profile in the firewall policy of a GPO is initially Not Configured. This means that firewall policy applied to computers targeted by the GPO will have no effect. For example, if the domain profile of Windows Firewall on a targeted computer is enabled, it will remain enabled after Group Policy processing has occurred. Similarly, if the domain profile of Windows Firewall on a targeted computer is disabled, it will remain disabled after Group Policy processing has taken place on the computer. So if a local administrator on the targeted computer turns off Windows Firewall on his computer, it will remain turned off even after Group Policy processing has taken place on the computer. Therefore, if you want to ensure that the firewall policy in the GPO applies to targeted computers, you must enable the firewall profiles in the policy. To do this, right-click the following policy node in the GPO:

  Windows Firewall with Advanced Security - LDAP://CN={GUID},CN=POLICIES,CN=SYSTEM,DC=*domain_name*,DC=COM

Select Properties from the context menu, and on each profile tab (Domain Profile, Private Profile, and Public Profile), change the Firewall State policy setting from Not Configured to On (Recommended).

- The default inbound and outbound rules for each firewall profile in the firewall policy of a GPO are also initially Not Configured. Therefore, if you want to ensure that firewall rules are processed as expected when the GPO is processed by targeted computers, you should configure the desired default inbound and outbound rules in the policy. To do this, right-click on the policy node described above and select Properties from the context menu. Then on each profile tab (Domain Profile, Private Profile, and Public Profile), change the Inbound Connections and Outbound Connections policy settings to the values you want to use, which are typically the following.

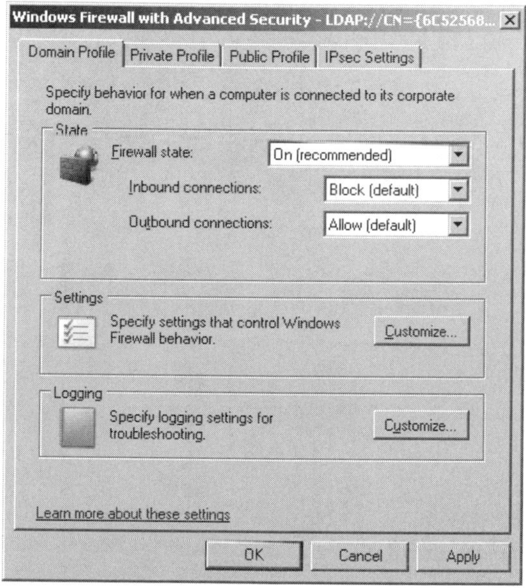

Note that if multiple GPOs for firewall policy target the same computer and each GPO has different default rules configured, the default rules for the GPO that has the highest precedence apply. Note also that if you set outbound connections to Block and then deploy the firewall policy by using a GPO, computers that receive it will not receive subsequent Group Policy updates unless you first create and deploy an outbound rule that enables Group Policy to work. Predefined rules for Core Networking include outbound rules that enable Group Policy to work. Ensure that these outbound rules are active, and thoroughly test firewall profiles before deploying the policy

- By default, rule merging is enabled between local firewall policy on Windows 7 computers and firewall policy specified in GPOs that target those computers. This means that local administrators can create their own firewall and connection security rules on their computers, and these rules will be merged with the rules obtained through Group Policy targeting the computers. Rule merging can be enabled or disabled on a per-GPO, per-profile basis by opening the Properties of the policy node described previously, selecting a firewall profile, and clicking Customize under Settings. Then under Rule Merging in the Customize Settings For The *firewall_profile* dialog box, change the Apply Local Firewall Rules and/or Apply Local Connection Security Rules policy settings from Not Configured to Yes (Default) or No, as shown here.

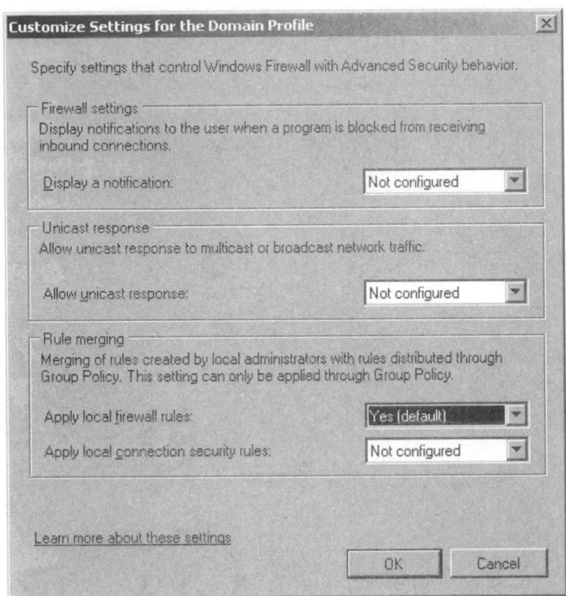

To ensure that only GPO-supplied rules are applied to computers targeted by the GPO and that locally defined rules on the computers are ignored, change these two policy settings from Not Configured to No. If you decide to leave rule merging enabled in the firewall policy of a GPO by configuring these two policy settings as either Yes (Default) or Not Configured, you should explicitly configure all firewall policy settings that may be needed by the targeted computers including firewall and IPsec settings, firewall rules, and connection security rules. Otherwise, any policy settings that you leave unconfigured in the GPO can be overridden by the local administrator on the targeted computer by using the Windows Firewall with Advanced Security snap-in or the Netsh command.

MORE INFO See also the ***Step-by-Step Guide: Deploying Windows Firewall and IPsec Policies*** **at** ***http://technet.microsoft.com/en-us/library/cc732400.aspx,*** **for a walkthrough of how to deploy firewall and connection security rules using Group Policy.**

NOTE For faster processing of GPOs that are used only for applying firewall policy to targeted computers, disable the User portion of the GPO using the GPMC.

Managing Windows Firewall Using the Netsh Command

The *Netsh* command can be used to manage Windows Firewall either interactively from the command line or by using scripts. The *Netsh* command also has been enhanced in Windows 7 to expose almost all aspects of Windows Firewall to viewing and configuration (some settings, such as global quick mode, can only be configured using the Windows Firewall with Advanced Security snap-in. By using the *netsh advfirewall* context of this command, you can display the status and configuration of Windows Firewall, configure firewall and IPsec settings, create and configure both firewall and connection security rules, monitor active connections, and perform other management tasks.

> ***NOTE*** **You must run the *netsh advfirewall* command from an elevated command prompt to set (configure) Windows Firewall settings. You do not need to run it from an elevated command prompt if you only want to show (view) Windows Firewall settings.**

To enter the *netsh advfirewall* context from the command line, type **netsh** and press Enter, then type **advfirewall** and press Enter.

```
C:\Windows\System32>netsh
netsh>advfirewall
netsh advfirewall>
```

The prompt indicates the current context of the command. Typing help at the *netsh advfirewall* prompt displays the following additional commands available for this context:

- **consec** Changes to the *netsh advfirewall consec* context, which lets you view and configure connection security rules.
- **export** Exports the current firewall policy to a .wfw file.
- **firewall** Changes to the *netsh advfirewall firewall* context, which lets you view and configure firewall rules.
- **import** Imports a .wfw policy file into the current policy store.
- **mainmode** New in Windows 7, this changes to the *netsh advfirewall mainmode* context, which lets you view and configure main mode configuration rules.
- **monitor** Enhanced with added functionality in Windows 7, this changes to the *netsh advfirewall monitor* context, which lets you view the current IPsec, firewall, and main mode states, and the current quick mode and main mode security associates established on the local computer.
- **reset** Resets the firewall policy to the default out-of-box policy.
- **set** Sets per-firewall profile and global firewall settings.
- **show** Displays firewall profiles and global firewall settings.

For example, you can use the *show domainprofile* command to view the firewall settings for the domain profile as follows.

```
netsh advfirewall>show domainprofile

Domain Profile Settings:
----------------------------------------------------------------------
State                                 ON
Firewall Policy                       BlockInbound,AllowOutbound
LocalFirewallRules                    N/A (GPO-store only)
LocalConSecRules                      N/A (GPO-store only)
InboundUserNotification               Enable
RemoteManagement                      Disable
UnicastResponseToMulticast            Enable

Logging:
LogAllowedConnections                 Disable
LogDroppedConnections                 Disable
FileName                              %systemroot%\system32\LogFiles\Firewall\pfirewall.log
MaxFileSize                           4096
```

To view the global firewall and IPsec settings on the local computer, use the *show global* command as follows.

```
netsh advfirewall>show global

Global Settings:
----------------------------------------------------------------------
IPsec:
StrongCRLCheck                        0:Disabled
SAIdleTimeMin                         5min
DefaultExemptions                     NeighborDiscovery,DHCP
IPsecThroughNAT                       Never
AuthzUserGrp                          None
AuthzComputerGrp                      None

StatefulFTP                           Enable
StatefulPPTP                          Enable

Main Mode:
KeyLifetime                           480min,0sess
SecMethods                            DHGroup2-AES128-SHA1,DHGroup2-3DES-SHA1
ForceDH                               No

Categories:
BootTimeRuleCategory                  Windows Firewall
FirewallRuleCategory                  Windows Firewall
StealthRuleCategory                   Windows Firewall
ConSecRuleRuleCategory                Windows Firewall
```

To view full details concerning a particular firewall rule such as the Remote Assistance (TCP-In) rule, first type **firewall** and press Enter to change to the *netsh advfirwall firewall* context, then use the *show rule* command as follows.

```
netsh advfirewall firewall>show rule name="Remote Assistance (TCP-In)"
profile=domain,private verbose

Rule Name:                            Remote Assistance (TCP-In)
----------------------------------------------------------------------
Description:                          Inbound rule for Remote Assistance traffic.
[TCP]
Enabled:                              Yes
Direction:                            In
Profiles:                             Domain,Private
Grouping:                             Remote Assistance
LocalIP:                              Any
RemoteIP:                             Any
Protocol:                             TCP
LocalPort:                            Any
RemotePort:                           Any
Edge traversal:                       Defer to application
Program:                              C:\Windows\system32\msra.exe
InterfaceTypes:                       Any
Security:                             NotRequired
Rule source:                          Local Setting
Action:                               Allow
```

You can also pipe Netsh to Findstr to display the names of all inbound rules belonging to a specific rule group. For example, to display all inbound rules for the Remote Assistance rule group, use this command.

```
C:\Windows\system32>netsh advfirewall firewall show rule name=all dir=in |
findstr /I /C:"remote assistance"
Rule Name:                            Remote Assistance (PNRP-In)
Grouping:                             Remote Assistance
Rule Name:                            Remote Assistance (SSDP TCP-In)
Grouping:                             Remote Assistance
Rule Name:                            Remote Assistance (SSDP UDP-In)
Grouping:                             Remote Assistance
Rule Name:                            Remote Assistance (TCP-In)
Grouping:                             Remote Assistance
Rule Name:                            Remote Assistance (DCOM-In)
Grouping:                             Remote Assistance
Rule Name:                            Remote Assistance (RA Server TCP-In)
Grouping:                             Remote Assistance
Rule Name:                            Remote Assistance (PNRP-In)
Grouping:                             Remote Assistance
Rule Name:                            Remote Assistance (TCP-In)
Grouping:                             Remote Assistance
```

To show all connection security rules configured on the local computer, type **consec** to change to the *netsh advfirewall consec* context. Then use the *show rule* command as follows.

```
netsh advfirewall consec>show rule name=all

Rule Name:                           Lab Server
----------------------------------------------------------------------
Enabled:                             Yes
Profiles:                            Domain
Type:                                Static
Mode:                                Transport
Endpoint1:                           172.16.11.131/32
Endpoint2:                           172.16.11.163/32
Protocol:                            Any
Action:                              RequestInRequestOut
Auth1:                               ComputerPSK
Auth1PSK:                            test
MainModeSecMethods:                  DHGroup2-AES128-SHA1,DHGroup2-3DES-SHA1
QuickModeSecMethods:                 ESP:SHA1-None+60min+100000kb,ESP:SHA1-
                                     AES128+60min+100000kb,ESP:SHA1-3DES+60min+
                                     100000kb,AH:SHA1+60min+100000kb
```

> ***NOTE*** To view all firewall settings including global settings, per-firewall profile settings, and all active firewall rules on the computer, type **netsh advfirewall monitor show firewall verbose** at a command prompt.

Also new in Windows 7 are the following two Netsh contexts:

- **netsh trace** Enables ETW tracing and/or Network Diagnostics Framework (NDF) diagnostics for various features and scenarios including Windows Firewall and IPsec.
- **netsh wfp** Enables WFP and Internet Key Exchange (IKE)/AuthIP tracing.

> ***MORE INFO*** For more information concerning Netsh syntax and examples of usage, see "Netsh Commands for Windows Firewall with Advanced Security" at *http://technet.microsoft.com/en-us/library/cc771920.aspx*.

Common Management Tasks

The sections that follow briefly describe some common management tasks for administering Windows Firewall with Advanced Security on Windows 7 and Windows Server 2008 R2. For additional information concerning managing Windows Firewall with Advanced Security, see the references in the section titled "Related Information" at the end of this chapter.

IMPORTANT When using Group Policy to perform these tasks, be sure to refer to the section titled "Considerations When Managing Windows Firewall Using Group Policy" earlier in this chapter.

Enabling or Disabling Windows Firewall

Windows Firewall with Advanced Security should be turned on to ensure maximum protection for computers running Windows 7 and Windows Server 2008 R2. However, should you need to enable or disable Windows Firewall with Advanced Security for some reason on a computer, you can do one of the following:

- Open Windows Firewall from Control Panel and click Turn Windows Firewall On Or Off. Then select Turn Off Windows Firewall (Not Recommended) for each firewall profile for which you want to disable the firewall.
- Open the Windows Firewall with Advanced Security snap-in. Right-click on the root node and select Properties, then change the Firewall State to Off on the tab for each firewall profile for which you want to disable the firewall.
- Open a command prompt and type **netsh advfirewall set *profile_name* state off,** where *profile_name* can be *domainprofile, privateprofile,* or *publicprofile.* You can also type **netsh advfirewall set allprofiles state off** to completely turn off Windows Firewall on the computer.

IMPORTANT Turning off Windows Firewall by disabling the Windows Firewall service is not supported by Microsoft.

DIRECT FROM THE SOURCE

Firewall Coexistence (aka Categories) in Windows 7

Sharad Kylasam, Program Manager
Core Networking

Windows Firewall with Advanced Security enforces security policy for core firewall, IPsec, Stealth mode, boot time, and service hardening. In Windows Vista, when Windows Firewall is turned off (typically when another host firewall is installed), this meant that functionality associated with IPsec, Stealth mode, and boot time were no longer enforced. This has been changed in Windows 7 such that additional switches are provided for third parties to take over only parts of the functionality that they intend to control (like Core firewall policy) while allowing Windows Firewall to continue enforcement of the rest of the functionality (like IPsec policy). This functionality eases the adoption and deployment of scenarios like Server and Isolation.

For a host firewall to use this functionality, a new API has been created so that the firewall can register to selectively replace the functionalities of Windows Firewall. See *http://msdn.microsoft.com/en-us/library/aa366415.aspx* for guidance on these APIs.

The Windows Firewall functions (aka Categories) that a host firewall can register to replace via the APIs discussed previously are as follows:

1. Firewall
2. Connection Security
3. Boot Time
4. Stealth

The following is a description of the each of the Categories:

- **Firewall** Firewall policy is configured based on the security needs as identified by the administrator. If ownership of the Firewall category is taken, ownership of the Boot Time category (described next) must also be taken. Failure to do so would leave the operating system in an unknown firewall state.
- **Connection Security (IPsec)** Connection Security policy enables secure networking by ensuring that communications can be authenticated and encrypted with IPsec. If Connection Security ownership is taken, ownership of the Firewall and Boot Time categories must be taken as well.
- **Boot Time** Boot Time policy is present when Windows is starting up and is used to prevent unsolicited inbound connections.
- **Stealth Mode** Stealth Mode policy makes a computer running Windows invisible on a network and is used to prevent port scanning discoverability.

Configuring Firewall Profiles and IPsec Settings by Using Group Policy

To configure firewall profiles on targeted computers using Group Policy, right-click the firewall policy node in your GPO and select Properties to display the properties for the firewall policy (shown in Figure 26-10). For each firewall profile (domain, private, and public), you can use the tab for the profile to perform the following tasks:

- Enable or disable the firewall state for that profile.
- Configure default rules for inbound and outbound connections.
- Configure whether users should receive notifications when firewall rules for that profile block inbound connections.
- Configure whether a unicast response should be allowed for broadcast or multicast traffic.

- Configure whether rule merging should be enabled or disabled for firewall and/or connection security rules (this can only be configured using Group Policy).
- Configure firewall logging for traffic filtered by that profile.

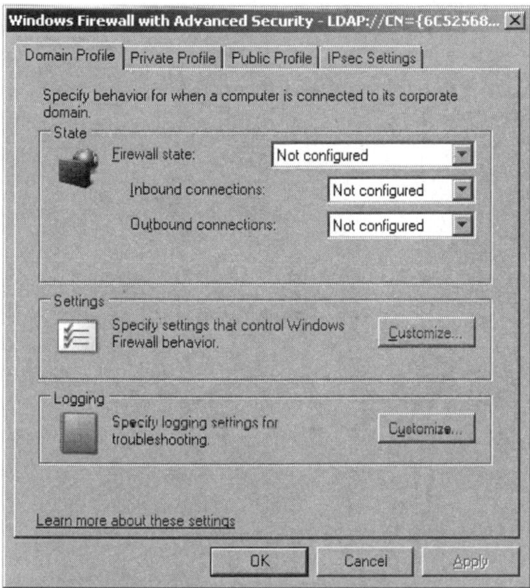

FIGURE 26-10 Configuring firewall profiles

> ***NOTE*** **You can use the *netsh advfirewall monitor show currentprofile* command in Windows 7 to display all currently active firewall profiles on the computer and also the networks assigned to each active profile.**

The IPsec tab of this properties sheet (shown in Figure 26-11) can be used to configure default and system-wide IPsec settings on the targeted computers. Examples of settings you can configure here include:

- **IPsec Defaults** Clicking Customize opens other dialog boxes that allow you to configure the default key exchange methods, data protection algorithms, and authentication methods used by IPsec. These default settings are used for new connection security rules that you create. However, when you create a connection security rule, you can also override the default authentication methods specified here.
- **IPsec Exemptions** This option determines whether ICMP traffic should be protected by IPsec. Because ICMP is used by many network troubleshooting tools, exempting such traffic from IPsec can ensure that such troubleshooting tools function as intended.
- **IPsec Tunnel Authorization** New in Windows 7, this option determines whether you can specify authorized and exempted users and computers for IPsec tunnel connections

to the computer. Selecting Advanced and clicking Customize opens a dialog box that lets you specify two types of information:

- Authorized computers, users, or groups of computers or users
- Exempted computers, users, or groups of computers or users

Note that any authorizations and exemptions you specify here apply only to tunnel rules for which the Apply IPsec Tunnel Authorization option is selected when the tunnel rule is created.

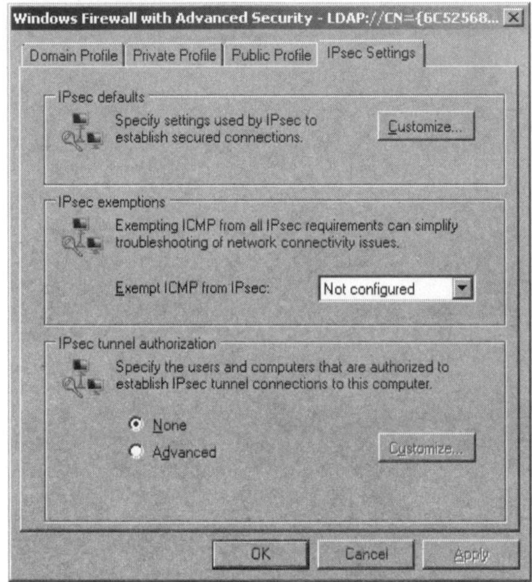

FIGURE 26-11 Configuring default and system-wide IPsec settings

For more information on configuring firewall profiles and IPsec settings, see the following sections of the TechNet Library:

- "Configuring a Profile" at *http://technet.microsoft.com/en-us/library/cc754139.aspx*
- "Configuring IPsec Settings" at *http://technet.microsoft.com/en-us/library/cc733077.aspx*
- "Windows Firewall with Advanced Security Properties Page" at *http://technet.microsoft.com/en-us/library/cc753002.aspx*

Creating and Configuring Firewall Rules

You can create and configure firewall rules on targeted computers using Group Policy. Firewall rules filter traffic passing between the computer and the network. For information concerning the types of firewall rules that you can create and the different rule conditions you can specify, see the section titled "Understanding Rules" earlier in this chapter.

To create an inbound firewall rule on targeted computers using Group Policy, right-click the Inbound Rules node under the firewall policy node in your GPO and select New Rule.

Doing this starts the New Inbound Rule Wizard, shown in Figure 26-12, which walks you through the steps of creating an inbound firewall rule by selecting the type of rule you want to create and specifying the conditions needed for the rule. Note that different pages may be displayed in the wizard depending upon the options you select on each page. For example, if you select Allow The Connection If It Is Secure on the Action page, a Users page and a Computers page is displayed so you can specify the user and computer accounts allowed to access the computer using the rule. (This also requires creating a separate connection security rule that requires traffic that matches the rule to be authenticated.)

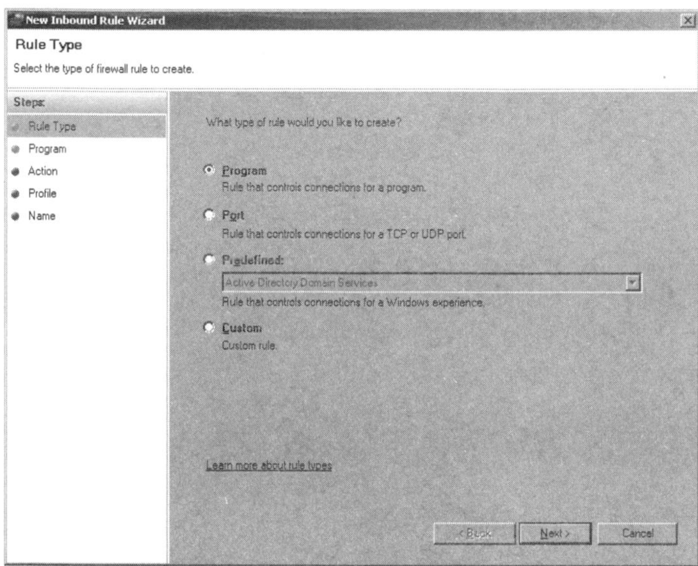

FIGURE 26-12 Creating a new firewall rule using the New Inbound Rule Wizard

Similarly, to create an outbound firewall rule using Group Policy, right-click the Outbound Rules node and select New Rule to start the New Outbound Rules Wizard. Again, different pages may be displayed in the wizard depending upon the options you select on each page. For example, if you select the Allow The Connection If It Is Secure option on the Action page, a Computers page is displayed so that you can specify the computer account allowed to access the computer using the rule. (Again, this also requires creating a separate connection security rule that requires traffic that matches the rule to be authenticated.)

Best practices for creating firewall rules include the following:

- When possible, select Predefined as the rule type because this enables a group of rules to enable a specific Windows experience or feature to access the network.
- If a predefined rule doesn't meet your needs, the next best rule type to use is Program, which will allow a specified application (executable) to access the network. Program rules are enabled when the underlying application is running and disabled when the application is terminated. This allows Windows Firewall to keep the minimum number of ports open at any time, which reduces the attack surface of the computer. Note

that program rules can be created only if the application uses Winsock to access the network.

- If a program rule doesn't meet your needs, select Port as the rule type. Port rules allow traffic on a specified TCP or UDP port or range of ports. Note that port rules cause their specified ports to always remain open regardless of whether they are needed by the application or service using them.

NOTE **If you configure a program rule to meet your needs, you should also configure a port rule. In this way, a port is open only when the program is running (instead of being open all the time, as when a port rule is configured alone) and only the ports approved for use by the program can be used (instead of all ports being available for the program rule).**

For more information on creating firewall rules, see the following sections of the TechNet Library:

- "Creating New Rules" at *http://technet.microsoft.com/en-us/library/cc771477.aspx*
- "Firewall Rule Wizard" at *http://technet.microsoft.com/en-us/library/dd448516.aspx*

Once you finish creating a new firewall rule, the rule is automatically enabled. To disable the rule, right-click it and select Disable Rule.

After you have created a firewall rule, you can further configure it if needed. To do this, double-click the rule to display its properties sheet, which exposes all configurable rule conditions for viewing and modification (as shown in Figure 26-13).

For more information on configuring firewall rules, see the following sections of the TechNet Library:

- "Understanding Firewall Rules" at *http://technet.microsoft.com/en-us/library/dd421709.aspx*
- "Configuring Firewall Rules" at *http://technet.microsoft.com/en-us/library/dd448559.aspx*
- "Firewall Rule Properties Page" at *http://technet.microsoft.com/en-us/library/dd421727.aspx*

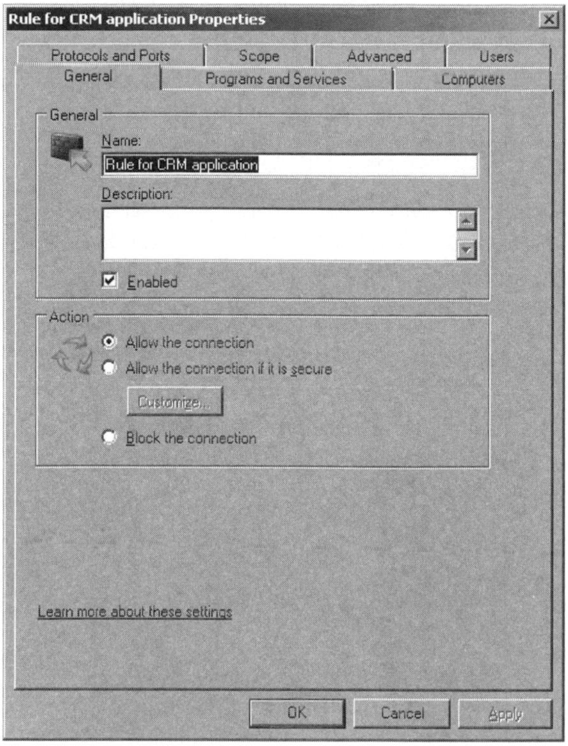

FIGURE 26-13 Configuring a firewall rule

DIRECT FROM THE SOURCE

Using RPC with Windows Firewall

Eran Yariv
Principal Development Manager

Remote Procedure Call (RPC) is a common method for applications to receive traffic from the network, process it, and respond. RPC is very common in servers, whose role in part is to provide a service over the network for clients. Some primary examples are the Microsoft Exchange Server, Microsoft Internet Security and Acceleration (ISA) server (for remote administration purposes), the Windows Fax service, and so on. RPC is even used in various scenarios for client computers. For example, the Windows Firewall Remote Management feature, when enabled, works by having the PolicyAgent service use an RPC over TCP (RPC/TCP) interface to answer remote management requests and proxy it locally to the Windows Firewall service. The purpose of this proxy approach is to keep the Windows Firewall service from directly accessing the network so that it can keep running in a secure, can't-touch-the-network account.

There are two methods for RPC/TCP:

- **A fixed TCP port** In this case, the port is usually known in advance to both the RPC server and client(s). The clients simply connect to the server using TCP with that port number. If you have an RPC server that uses RPC/TCP with a fixed port, all you need to do to allow traffic is add an allow firewall rule to that application/service for that specific local TCP port. Using a fixed TCP port is not recommended because it lacks the flexibility of avoiding port collisions with other networking applications. As a result, it's a less common method for RPC/TCP; only a few services actually use it (such as the RPCSS service).
- **A dynamic TCP port** In this case, the actual port that the RPC server uses to expose its RPC/TCP interface is determined at run time from a pool of available ports. Because the RPC clients can't tell in advance to which TCP port they need to connect, they need to use a mediator in the form of the RPC end-point mapper.

The second method works like this:

1. Application App1 (the RPC server) starts running and registers its RPC interface with the RPC subsystem for dynamic RPC/TCP.
2. The RPC subsystem assigns a dynamic TCP port (denote port X) to that application and starts listening on port X from the process context of application App1.
3. The RPCSS service, which acts as an end-point mapper, listens for RPC end-point mapping requests on a fixed port: TCP/135.
4. The RPC client, from another computer, connects to TCP/135 and talks to the RPCSS service (the end-point mapper).
5. The RPC client asks for a specific RPC interface. The end-point-mapper, being part of the RPC subsystem, knows about steps (a) and (b) and replies with port X.
6. The RPC client connects to port TCP/X and starts the interface activation with the RPC server.

As you can see, two firewall rules are necessary to enable dynamic RPC/TCP:

- Allow the RPCSS service to receive traffic over TCP/135 for end-point mapping purposes.
- Allow application App1 to receive traffic over TCP/X.

Two problems come to mind:

1. You want to enable the RPCSS service inbound traffic only if RPC servers are registered on the computer. If none are registered, TCP/135 should not be open in the firewall—this might expose the computer to unnecessary attacks.
2. You can't tell in advance what port X is, and you can't create a firewall rule to allow it.

To address the first problem, Windows Firewall uses a special local port keyword called RPC endpoint mapper. You can use this local port keyword when creating the Allow The RPCSS Service To Receive Traffic Over TCP/135 For End-Point Mapping Purposes rule, replacing TCP/135 with the RPC endpoint mapper keyword. The Windows Firewall service keeps a special and secure interface with the RPCSS service. The RPCSS service notifies the Windows Firewall service whenever RPC servers are registered, and the Windows Firewall service dynamically replaces the keyword with the actual port value (in this case, TCP/135, but it could also be TCP/593 for RPC/HTTP cases). If no RPC servers are registered with the RPC subsystem, the Windows Firewall service does not open port TCP/135.

To address the second problem, Windows Firewall uses a special local port keyword called Dynamic RPC. When this keyword is used, Windows Firewall makes sure that the socket receiving the TCP traffic (port X, in this example) was actually acquired by the RPC subsystem and is used for RPC purposes. Instead of a firewall rule that says Allow Application App1 To Receive TCP Traffic Over Any Port, you use the Dynamic RPC local port keyword to create this rule: Allow application App1 to receive TCP traffic for RPC purposes only.

Creating and Configuring Connection Security Rules

You can create and configure connection security rules on targeted computers using Group Policy. Connection security rules force computers to authenticate before they are allowed to establish a connection, and they use IPsec to protect the data passed between the computers once a connection has been established between them. For information concerning the types of connection security rules you can create, see the section titled "Understanding Connection Security Rules" earlier in this chapter.

To create a connection security rule on targeted computers using Group Policy, right-click the Connection Security Rules node under the firewall policy node in your GPO and select New Rule. Doing this starts the New Connection Security Rule Wizard, shown in Figure 26-14, which walks you through the steps of creating a connection security rule by selecting the type of rule you want to create and specifying the rule conditions needed for the rule. Note that different pages may be displayed in the wizard depending upon the options you select on each page.

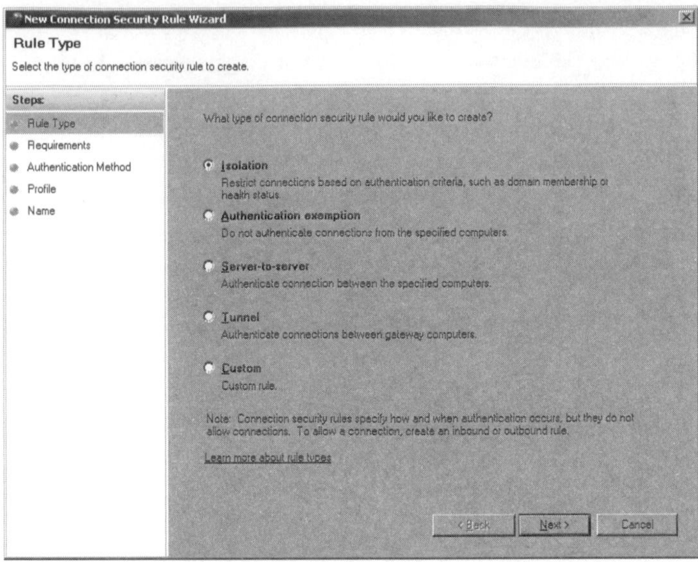

FIGURE 26-14 Creating a new connection security rule using the New Connection Security Rule Wizard

For more information on creating connection security rules, see the following sections of the TechNet Library:

- "Understanding Connection Security Rules" at *http://technet.microsoft.com/en-ca/library/dd448591.aspx*
- "Creating Connection Security Rules" at *http://technet.microsoft.com/en-us/library/cc725940.aspx*
- "Connection Security Rule Wizard" at *http://technet.microsoft.com/en-us/library/dd759064.aspx*

Once you finish creating a new connection security rule, the rule is automatically enabled. To disable the rule, right-click it and select Disable Rule.

After you have created a connection security rule, you can further configure it if needed. To do this, double-click the rule to display its properties sheet, which exposes all configurable rule conditions for viewing and modification (as shown in Figure 26-15).

For more information on configuring connection security rules, see the following sections of the TechNet Library:

- "Understanding Connection Security Rules" at *http://technet.microsoft.com/en-us/library/dd448591.aspx*
- "Connection Security Rule Properties Page" at *http://technet.microsoft.com/en-ca/library/dd421705.aspx*

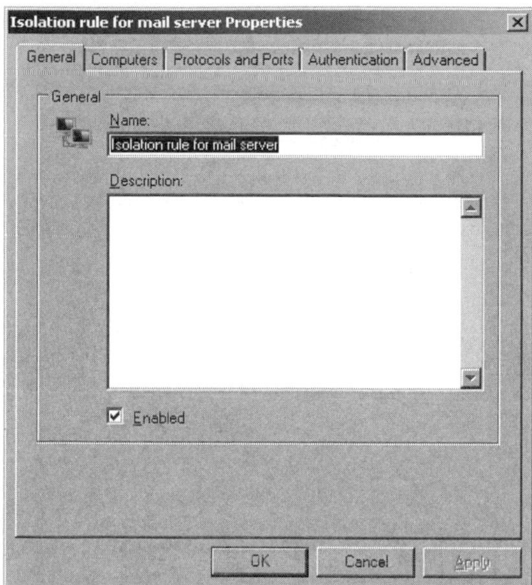

FIGURE 26-15 Configuring a connection security rule

Monitoring Windows Firewall

The Monitoring node in the Windows Firewall with Advanced Security snap-in can be used for monitoring the following (see Figure 26-16):

- Active (enabled) firewall rules on the computer. Note that active outbound allow rules are not displayed because the default outbound rule is set to Allow for all profiles; only active outbound block rules are displayed.
- Active connection security rules on the computer and detailed information concerning their settings.
- Active main mode and quick mode security associations for the computer, including detailed information concerning their settings and endpoints.

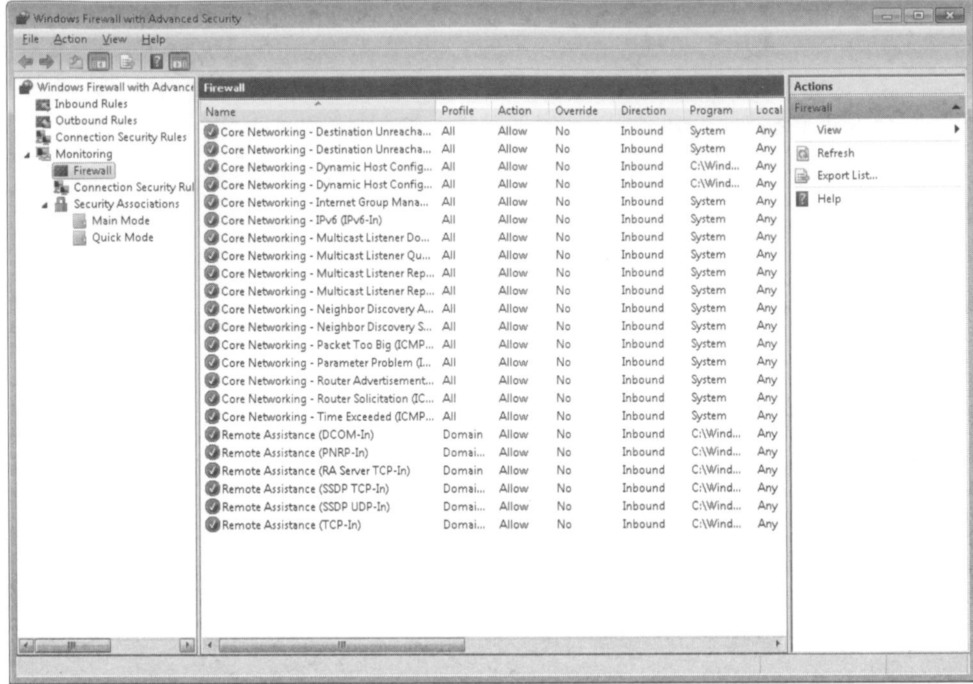

FIGURE 26-16 Monitoring active firewall rules on the computer

You can also monitor Windows Firewall activity using:

- Windows Firewall logs
- Windows event logs

For more information, see the next section, "Troubleshooting Windows Firewall." For additional information on monitoring Windows Firewall with Advanced Security, see "Monitoring Windows Firewall with Advanced Security" at *http://technet.microsoft.com/en-us/library/dd421717.aspx* in the TechNet Library.

> ***NOTE*** **The Monitoring node is not available under the firewall policy node in Group Policy.**

Troubleshooting Windows Firewall

Tools for troubleshooting Windows Firewall with Advanced Security include the following:

- Firewall logs
- Windows event logs
- Auditing

- netsh wfp
- netsh trace

TROUBLESHOOTING WINDOWS FIREWALL USING FIREWALL LOGS

You can enable and configure firewall logging in Windows Firewall with Advanced Security to log success and failure events for firewall activity. Firewall logging can be configured on targeted computers using Group Policy and can be configured separately for each firewall profile on the targeted computers. To configure firewall logging on targeted computers using Group Policy, right-click the Connection Security Rules node under the firewall policy node in your GPO and select Properties. Then select the tab for the firewall profile for which you want to configure logging and click Customize under the Logging section. This opens the Customize Logging Settings For *profile_name* dialog box, shown in Figure 26-17, which lets you configure:

- Where the log file will be created and how big the file can grow.
- Whether you want the log file to record information about dropped packets, successful connections, or both.

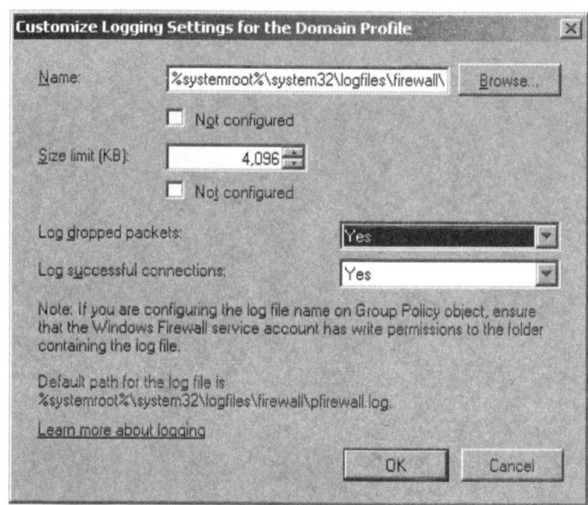

FIGURE 26-17 Enabling firewall logging on targeted computers using Group Policy

For more information concerning firewall logging, see the sidebar titled "Direct from the Source: Understanding the Firewall Log."

DIRECT FROM THE SOURCE

Understanding the Firewall Log

CSS Global Technical Readiness (GTR) Team

The Pfirewall.log shows what packets were dropped by the firewall and/or what connection attempts were allowed. This is useful to check if the firewall is involved in a connection problem.

The following snippet from a Pfirewall.log file shows that the log contains all necessary information to determine whether a packet was dropped by the firewall such as IP addresses, ports, TCP flags, ICMP types and codes, and the direction.

```
2009-03-29 12:40:52 ALLOW UDP fe80::8413:5c0:13e9:79bc ff02::1:2 546
547 0 - - - - - - - SEND
2009-03-29 12:40:53 DROP TCP 192.168.1.176 192.168.1.175 49653 23 52 S
3161718899 0 8192 - - - RECEIVE
2009-03-29 12:40:53 ALLOW UDP 192.168.1.176 192.168.1.175 500 500 0 -
- - - - - - RECEIVE
2009-03-29 12:40:53 DROP TCP 192.168.1.176 192.168.1.175 49653 23 52 S
3161718899 0 8192 - - - RECEIVE
2009-03-29 12:40:56 DROP TCP 192.168.1.176 192.168.1.175 49653 23 52 S
3161718899 0 8192 - - - RECEIVE
2009-03-29 12:41:02 DROP TCP 192.168.1.176 192.168.1.175 49653 23 48 S
3161718899 0 65535 - - - RECEIVE
2009-03-29 12:41:24 ALLOW UDP fe80::8413:5c0:13e9:79bc ff02::1:2 546
547 0 - - - - - - - SEND
2009-03-29 12:41:36 ALLOW TCP 192.168.1.175 192.168.1.170 49871 389 0
- 0 0 0 - - - SEND
2009-03-29 12:41:36 ALLOW TCP 192.168.1.175 192.168.1.170 49872 445 0
- 0 0 0 - - - SEND
```

Logging for each profile can be configured in the user interface or via netsh.

When using the *netsh advfirewall* set, only one option can be set per command. To set several parameters, you must issue a sequence of *netsh advfirewall* set commands to build up the desired settings; for example,

```
Netsh advfirewall set %profile% logging droppedconnections enable
Netsh advfirewall set %profile% logging allowedconnections enable
Netsh advfirewall set %profile% logging filename %path\filename%
Netsh advfirewall set %profile% logging maxfilesize %value in kb
between 1 - 32767%
```

The Pfirewall.log file is stored by default at %Windir%\System32\Logfiles\Firewall\Pfirewall.log, but this location is configurable. Note, however, that if you specify a location other than the default, you must ensure that the Windows Firewall service has permissions to write to that location. To grant Write permissions for the log folder to the Windows Firewall service, perform the following steps:

1. Locate the folder that you specified for the logging file, right-click it, and then click Properties.
2. Click the Security tab, and then click Edit.
3. Click Add, and then, in Enter Object Names To Select, type **NT SERVICE\mpssvc** and click OK.
4. In the Permissions dialog box, verify that MpsSvc has Write access, and then click OK.

TROUBLESHOOTING WINDOWS FIREWALL USING EVENT LOGS

You can use the Windows event logs to monitor Windows Firewall and IPsec activity and to troubleshoot issues that may arise. The event logs for Windows Firewall are found under the following location in Event Viewer:

Applications and Services Logs\Microsoft\Windows\Windows Firewall With Advanced Security

As shown in Figure 26-18, there are four event logs you can use for monitoring and troubleshooting Windows Firewall activity:

- ConnectionSecurity
- ConnectionSecurityVerbose
- Firewall
- FirewallVerbose

The two verbose logs are disabled by default because of the large amounts of information they collect. To enable these logs, right-click them and select Enable Log.

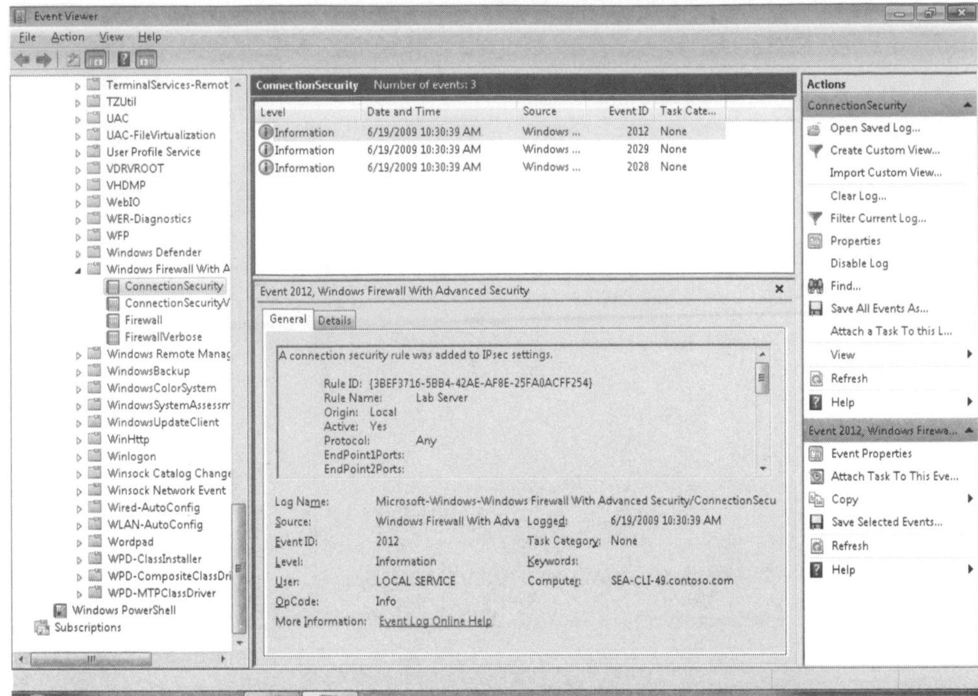

FIGURE 26-18 Using the event logs for Windows Firewall with Advanced Security

For more information on working with event logs, see Chapter 21, "Maintaining Desktop Health." See also *Windows Firewall with Advanced Security Troubleshooting Guide: Diagnostics and Tools* in the TechNet Library at *http://technet.microsoft.com/en-us/library/cc722062.aspx*.

TROUBLESHOOTING WINDOWS FIREWALL USING AUDITING

You can use auditing to monitor Windows Firewall and IPsec activity and to troubleshoot issues that may arise. Auditing events for Windows Firewall and IPsec activity are written to the Security Event Log and have Event IDs in the range 4600 to 5500.

Auditing for Windows Firewall and IPsec activity can be enabled on targeted computers in two ways:

- Using Group Policy
- Using the Auditpol.exe command

To configure auditing for Windows Firewall and IPsec activity using Group Policy, use the audit policy subcategories found under the following location:

Computer Configuration\Policies\Windows Settings\Security Settings\Advanced Audit Policy Configuration\Audit Policies

Figure 26-19 shows the audit policy subcategories available under this policy node. The audit policy subcategories relevant for Advanced Audit Policy Configuration are as follows:

- Logon/Logoff
  - IPsec Main Mode
  - IPsec Quick Mode
  - IPsec Extended Mode
- Object Access
  - Filtering Platform packet drop
  - Filtering Platform connection
- Policy Change
  - MPSSVC rule-level policy change
  - Filtering Platform policy change
- System
  - IPsec Driver
  - Other system events

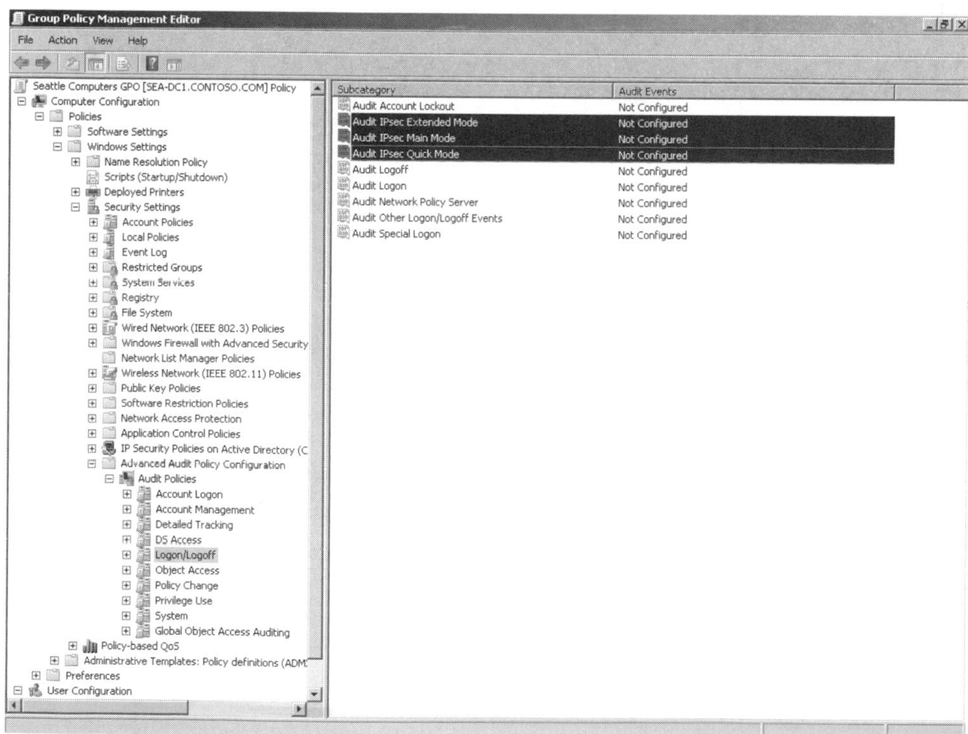

FIGURE 26-19 Using Group Policy to audit Windows Firewall and IPsec activity

To list all audit policy subcategories from the command line, type **auditpol /list /subcategory:*** at an administrative-level command prompt. To use Auditpol.exe to enable auditing for Windows Firewall activity, type the following command.

```
auditpol.exe /set /SubCategory:"MPSSVC rule-level Policy Change","Filtering Platform
policy change","Other System Events","Filtering Platform Packet Drop","Filtering
Platform Connection" /success:enable /failure:enable
```

To use Auditpol.exe to enable auditing for IPsec activity, type the following command.

```
auditpol.exe /set /SubCategory:"MPSSVC rule-level Policy Change","Filtering Platform
policy change","IPsec Main Mode","IPsec Quick Mode","IPsec Extended Mode","IPsec
Driver","Other System Events","Filtering Platform Packet Drop","Filtering Platform
Connection" /success:enable /failure:enable
```

> ***IMPORTANT*** **Enabling auditing for Windows Firewall and IPsec activity can generate a large number of events in the Security Event Log, so be sure to enable it only when actively collecting troubleshooting information.**

TROUBLESHOOTING IPSEC ISSUES USING NETSH WFP

New in Windows 7 is the *netsh wfp* command context, which can be used for advanced troubleshooting of IPsec issues in conjunction with Microsoft Customer Support Services (CSS). This new *Netsh* context replaces the Microsoft IPsec Diagnostic Tool (Wfputil.exe), which can be obtained for previous versions of Windows from the Microsoft Download Center. To use *netsh wfp* for troubleshooting an IPsec communications issue that you are experiencing on a computer, follow these steps:

1. Type **netsh wfp capture start** at a command prompt to begin capturing real-time IPsec diagnostic information on the computer.
2. Reproduce the IPsec communications problem you have been experiencing on the computer.
3. Type **netsh wfp capture stop** to stop tracing.

The result of performing these steps is a WfpDiag.cab file located in the current directory from which the command was run. This .cab file contains an Event Trace Log (ETL) file named WfpDiag.etl and a corresponding Extensible Markup Language (XML) file named WfpDiag.xml, which contain detailed information collected during the trace. Once you have collected this information, you can send it to Microsoft support personnel, who can decode the information and help you troubleshoot your issue.

> ***NOTE*** **You can use the *netsh trace convert wfpdiag.etl file_name.txt* command to convert a binary ETL file into human-readable plain-text format after you have extracted the ETL file from the .cab file.**

TROUBLESHOOTING WINDOWS FILTERING PLATFORM AND IPSEC ISSUES USING NETSH TRACE

New in Windows 7 is the *netsh trace* command context, which can be used to activate logging and tracing on the computer for advanced troubleshooting of Windows Firewall and IPsec issues in conjunction with CSS. This new *Netsh* context replaces the Logman.exe command used in previous versions of Windows. To use *netsh trace* for troubleshooting a Windows Firewall or IPsec communications issue that you are experiencing on a computer, follow these steps:

1. Start a trace session using one of the following commands:
   - **netsh trace start scenario=WFP-IPsec** Starts a trace session for the predefined Windows Filtering Platform and IPsec scenario.
   - **netsh trace start provider="Microsoft-Windows-Windows Firewall With Advanced Security"** Starts a trace session for troubleshooting issues involving firewall rules using the Microsoft-Windows-Windows Firewall With Advanced Security provider.
   - **netsh trace start provider="Microsoft-Windows-WFP"** Starts a trace session for troubleshooting IPsec communications issues using the Microsoft-Windows-WFP provider.
2. Reproduce the Windows Firewall or IPsec communications problem that you have been experiencing on the computer.
3. Type **netsh trace stop** to stop tracing.

The result of performing these steps is a NetTrace.etl file and a NetTrace.cab file located at %UserProfile%\AppData\Local\Temp\NetTraces.

The .cab file contains a number of different files that contain information collected during the trace. Once you have collected this information, you can send it to Microsoft support personnel, who can decode the information and help you troubleshoot your issue. You can also view this information yourself by extracting the files contained in the .cab file and then opening the Report.html file, one of the extracted files.

> ***MORE INFO*** **More information on troubleshooting Windows Firewall and IPsec issues can be found in the TechNet Library at *http://technet.microsoft.com/en-us/library/cc771597.aspx*.**

Summary

Windows Firewall with Advanced Security has been enhanced in Windows 7 with support for multiple active firewall profiles; support for authorization exemptions; support for specifying port ranges for rules; support for dynamic encryption, dynamic tunnel endpoints, and tunnel mode authorization; support for specifying port numbers and protocols for connection security rules; new edge traversal options; easier configuration of Suite B algorithms; support for multiple main mode configurations; and support for certificates issued by intermediate CAs. This chapter has examined how Windows Firewall with Advanced Security works and how to configure, manage, monitor, and troubleshoot firewall and IPsec connectivity issues.

Additional Resources

These resources contain additional information and tools related to this chapter.

Related Information

- *Step-by-Step Guide: Deploying Windows Firewall and IPsec Policies* at *http://technet.microsoft.com/en-us/library/cc732400.aspx.*
- *Windows Firewall with Advanced Security Design Guide* at *http://technet.microsoft.com/en-us/library/cc732024.aspx.*
- *Windows Firewall with Advanced Security Deployment Guide* at *http://technet.microsoft.com/en-us/library/cc972925.aspx.*
- Windows Firewall with Advanced Security Operations guidance at *http://technet.microsoft.com/en-us/library/cc771611.aspx.*
- Windows Firewall with Advanced Security Technical Reference at *http://technet.microsoft.com/en-us/library/dd125354.aspx.*
- "Windows Firewall with Advanced Security" product help at *http://technet.microsoft.com/en-us/library/dd448511.aspx.*
- IPsec Technologies and Solutions TechCenter at *http://technet.microsoft.com/en-us/network/bb531150.aspx.*

On the Companion Media

- ConfigureFWLogging.ps1
- EnableDisableRemoteAdmin.ps1

CHAPTER 27

Connecting Remote Users and Networks

Remote connectivity is an important aspect of enterprise networking, and the Windows 7 operating system includes several features for making such connectivity faster, easier to use, and simpler to manage. This chapter examines the remote access capabilities of Windows 7, including virtual private networks (VPNs), DirectAccess, BranchCache, and Remote Desktop.

Enhancements for Connecting Remote Users and Networks in Windows 7

Windows 7 builds on the foundation of Windows Vista by adding new features and enhancing existing features used for connecting remote users and networks. These improvements include the following:

- Support for a new tunneling protocol called Internet Key Exchange version 2 (IKEv2)
- Support for Mobility and Multihoming Protocol for Internet Key Exchange (MOBIKE), an extension of IKEv2 that allows VPN connections to change their reachable addresses without reestablishing security associations (SAs)

- VPN Reconnect, a new feature of Windows 7 and Windows Server 2008 R2 that uses IKEv2 and MOBIKE to provide automatic and seamless switchover of an active VPN connection whenever the underlying Internet connection changes
- Automatic fallback to Secure Socket Tunneling Protocol (SSTP) when an IKEv2 connection is attempted and fails
- Integration of remote access and VPN connections into the View Available Networks user interface (UI) to provide an improved connection dialing experience
- Support for allowing administrators to select the certificate to use for server authentication in SSTP
- DirectAccess, a new feature of Windows 7 and Windows Server 2008 R2 that provides users with the experience of being seamlessly connected to the corporate network from any location where they have Internet access
- BranchCache, a new feature of Windows 7 and Windows Server 2008 R2 that allows content from file servers and Web servers at a central office to be cached on computers at a local branch office, thus improving application response time and reducing wide area network (WAN) traffic
- Enhancements to the Remote Desktop Protocol (RDP) that improve the performance and quality of user experience for Remote Desktop sessions
- Mobile Broadband, which makes it easy to connect Windows 7 computers to the Internet using a wireless data card regardless of the cellular provider being used.

The sections that follow provide more information concerning some of these new features and enhancements, and information on some of the other improvements can be found in later sections of this chapter.

Understanding IKEv2

Internet Key Exchange (IKE) is a key protocol within the Internet Protocol security (IPsec) protocol suite. IKEv1 can be used to set up SAs that enable secure, encrypted communications over a VPN connection. To do this, IKE uses a Diffie-Hellman key exchange to set up a shared session secret from which cryptographic keys are then derived. Public or pre-shared keys can then be used to mutually authenticate the endpoints of the VPN connection. IKEv1 is supported on Windows Vista, Windows Server 2003, and earlier versions of Windows.

IKEv2 is a newer version of IKE that is supported on Windows 7 and Windows Server 2008 R2. IKEv2 includes a number of improvements over IKEv1, including the following:

- A simplified initial exchange of messages that reduces latency and increases connection establishment speed
- Improved reliability through the use of sequence numbers, acknowledgements, and error correction
- Support for Extensible Authentication Protocol (EAP) as a method for authenticating VPN endpoints

- Backward compatibility with the ports used by IKEv1 to ensure Network Address Translation (NAT) traversal
- VPN mobility support using the MOBIKE extension
- Support for the IPv6 protocol
- Other features that provide improved speed, security, and ease of configuration when compared with IKEv1

Support for IKEv2 as a VPN tunneling protocol is new in Windows 7 and Windows Server 2008 R2, and IKEv2 is a key enabler of the new VPN Reconnect feature of these platforms. For more information on VPN Reconnect, see the section titled "Understanding VPN Reconnect" later in this chapter. For more information about IPsec protocols and how IPsec is implemented in Windows 7, see Chapter 26, "Configuring Windows Firewall and IPsec."

> ***MORE INFO*** **For more information concerning IKEv2, see RFC 4306 at *http://www.ietf.org/rfc/rfc4306.txt*.**

Understanding MOBIKE

MOBIKE is an extension to the IKEv2 protocol that provides mobility for VPN connections. Specifically, MOBIKE provides:

- The ability for a VPN client to change its reachable (Internet) address without having to reestablish its SAs with the VPN server.
- The ability for a VPN client and server to select pairs of reachable addresses when they each have access to more than one reachable address.

MOBIKE thus prevents disconnected VPN clients from having to perform IKEv2 renegotiation when Internet connectivity with the VPN server has been reestablished. Because IKEv2 negotiations typically require that between 4,000 and 8,000 bytes of traffic be exchanged, while MOBIKE negotiations only exchange about 500 bytes, MOBIKE enables interrupted VPN connections to be reestablished quickly, minimizing user impact.

Support for MOBIKE is new in Windows 7 and Windows Server 2008 R2 and is a key enabler of the new VPN Reconnect feature of these platforms. For more information on VPN Reconnect, see the next section.

> ***MORE INFO*** **For more information concerning MOBIKE, see RFC 4555 at *http://www.ietf.org/rfc/rfc4555.txt*.**

Understanding VPN Reconnect

VPN Reconnect is a new feature of Windows 7 and Windows Server 2008 R2 that allows VPN connections to remain alive even when the underlying Internet connectivity for the connection is temporarily lost. VPN Reconnect is designed to make VPN connections more reliable by eliminating the need for users to manually reestablish their connection when it has been interrupted.

In previous versions of Windows, when Internet connectivity is lost, the VPN connection is also lost. This means that if the user was working with an application or had a document open when the interruption occurred, the user's work would be lost. This issue occurred with any of the tunneling protocols supported on previous versions of Windows, including Point-to-Point Tunneling Protocol (PPTP), Layer 2 Tunneling Protocol over IPsec (L2TP/IPsec), and SSTP.

With VPN Reconnect, however, which uses the new IKEv2 tunneling protocol with the MOBIKE extension, when the user's Internet connectivity is interrupted, the user's VPN connection remains alive, and when Internet connectivity is restored, the user can continue using her application or working with her open document. VPN Reconnect thus eliminates the need to manually reconnect mobile computers to the corporate network after Internet connectivity is interrupted, thus making it easier for mobile users to access the corporate network and perform their work over a VPN connection.

VPN Reconnect also enables new types of mobile worker scenarios. For example, consider a mobile user who is traveling on a train and using a wireless mobile broadband card to connect her laptop to the Internet and establish a VPN connection to her company's internal network. As the train leaves the station, the user moves out of range of the train station's wireless access point, and the user's Internet connectivity is temporarily lost. The train comes into range of an access point at the next stop a few minutes later, and using VPN Reconnect, the user's VPN connection is automatically and seamlessly restored and she can continue doing her work.

Other scenarios in which VPN Reconnect can benefit mobile users can include maintaining a VPN connection when the user transitions between any of the following:

- A costly, slow wireless WAN (WWAN) to a cheaper, faster wireless local area network (WLAN), such as when a user is traveling and then arrives at a customer location or at her own home
- A public wireless network and the corporate wired LAN, such as when a traveling user arrives at work

> ***NOTE*** **DirectAccess can replace the VPN as the preferred remote access method for many organizations. However, some organizations will continue to use VPNs side by side with DirectAccess, and Microsoft has improved VPN usability in Windows 7 with VPN Reconnect to meet the needs of these organizations. For more information about DirectAccess, see the section titled "Understanding DirectAccess" later in this chapter.**

Protocols and Features of VPN Reconnect

VPN Reconnect works by using the following protocols:

- IPsec tunnel mode using Encapsulating Security Payload (ESP) for secure transmission
- IKEv2 for key negotiation and MOBIKE for switching the tunnel endpoints when interfaces change

On the server side, VPN Reconnect is implemented within the Routing and Remote Access service (RRAS) mainly by the addition of two new features:

- A new Kernel Mode miniport driver for creating IKEv2 tunnels
- A new VPN IKE Protocol Engine that plugs into the Remote Access Connection Manager service (Rasman)

On the client side, Rasman loads the VPN IKE Protocol Engine, which controls IKEv2 protocol negotiation and provides interfaces for IPsec for authentication and IP parameter configuration. A new Network Driver Interface Specification (NDIS) miniport driver called the VPN Reconnect driver then performs the necessary encapsulation for IKEv2-based tunnels.

In addition, a feature called Mobility Manager is involved in making VPN Reconnect possible. Mobility Manager provides support for the switching of mobility-enabled VPN connections when the underlying interface fails. Mobility Manager is implemented as a scheduled task having LocalService privileges. This task gets triggered when the first mobility-enabled IKEv2 tunnel is established, and it continues running until there is no longer any mobility-enabled IKEv2 tunnels present on the system.

IKEv2 tunnels support two types of client-side authentication:

- Using EAP to enable authentication based on the user's credentials
- Using a machine certificate that has been installed on the VPN server

For more information on how IKEv2 tunnels are authenticated, see the sidebar titled "Direct from the Source: IKEv2 Authentication" later in this chapter.

How VPN Reconnect Works

VPN Reconnect (IKEv2) is available only on Windows 7 and Windows Server 2008 R2. This means that mobile computers must be running Windows 7 and the VPN server at the corporate network must be running Windows Server 2008 R2 to use VPN Reconnect.

A typical example of how VPN Reconnect works is as follows:

1. A user's Windows 7 mobile computer at remote location A establishes Internet connectivity using a wireless access point at the location. This Internet connectivity provides the user's computer with a reachable IP address.
2. The user initiates a VPN connection to a VPN server running Windows Server 2008 R2 on the corporate network. The user's VPN connection has been configured to attempt IKEv2 first as a tunneling protocol for the connection.

3. The VPN client exchanges IKEv2 messages with the VPN server and uses EAP to negotiate an authentication protocol.
4. The VPN server uses Remote Authentication Dial-in User Service (RADIUS) to authenticate and authorize the remote client.
5. An SA is negotiated for tunnel mode ESP.
6. The VPN client obtains an internal IP address for the duration of the session.
7. Data is now exchanged between the VPN client and server. This data is encapsulated in an IP packet that uses the internal address, which is then encapsulated by ESP, which is finally encapsulated in an IP packet that uses the reachable address.
8. Then, at some point, the user's computer is moved away from location A so that Internet connectivity is lost.
9. VPN Reconnect ensures that the SA remains valid, keeping the VPN session alive even though the VPN connection is temporarily broken.
10. The user's computer is now moved to a new location B, where Internet connectivity is reestablished using a different wireless access point.
11. The user's computer acquires a new reachable IP address that is different from the one used previously.
12. The VPN client exchanges MOBIKE messages with the VPN server to update the existing VPN tunnel and SA with the newly acquired reachable address.
13. The VPN connection is now automatically restored with no action required on the part of the user.

For information on how to configure VPN Reconnect on the client and server side, see the section titled "Configuring Mobility for IKEv2 Connections" later in this chapter.

NOTE **Unlike other VPN tunneling protocols such as PPTP, L2TP/IPsec, and SSTP, VPN Reconnect (IKEv2) does not run a Point-to-Point Protocol (PPP)–based handshake on top of the tunnel.**

DIRECT FROM THE SOURCE

IKEv2 Authentication

CSS Global Technical Readiness (GTR) Team

VPN client connections configured to use IKEv2 as their tunneling protocol can use one of two methods for authentication with the VPN server: EAP or machine certificates. If the client connection has been configured to use EAP and the VPN server allows this type of authentication, the authentication process on the client side is as follows:

1. Netman invokes Ras UI or Connection Manager (CM) UI to make an RRAS connection. The UI internally uses RAS application programming interfaces (APIs) to make this connection.
2. RAS APIs internally read the connection properties from the phonebook file.
3. RAS APIs then call the Next Generation RASMAN (RAS Connection Manager) to establish the connection. RAS APIs pass the RRAS server's IP address, authentication type (machine or user—in this case, it is user authentication), and other information to the RASMAN.
4. RASMAN configures the SA policy, MOBIKE-supported flag, and authentication type (as EAP with Base Filter Engine [BFE]) and initiates IKEv2 negotiation with the RRAS server.
5. BFE starts the IKEv2 negotiation (IKE_SA_INIT) with the RRAS server.
6. BFE requests RASMAN to provide the client identity (because EAP is used for authentication).
7. RASMAN starts an EAPHost session and requests the user's identity.
8. RASMAN passes the information to BFE.
9. BFE starts the IKE_AUTH exchange. It validates the Server Certificate and AUTH information.
10. Because EAP authentication is used, it requests RRAS to provide an EAP blob.
11. RRAS requests EAPHost to provide authentication information.
12. RRAS passes the EAP blob to IKEv2.

    Steps 10 to 12 are repeated until EAP authentication is completed. On authentication completion, EAP may pass the shared key to the RRAS to pass it to BFE. BFE will use this information to construct the AUTH information.
13. BFE notifies RRAS that connection is successful and passes the configuration information, such as the IP address, Domain Name System (DNS) server list, and Windows Internet Naming Service (WINS) server list, to the RRAS. It also passes the IPsec driver context to the VPN Reconnect driver.
14. RASMAN creates the interface by calling the RRAS kernel driver and also plumbs the IP address, DNS list, and WINS server list on the interface.

If the client connection has been configured to use machine certificates and the VPN server has a machine certificate installed and allows this type of authentication, the authentication process on the client side is as follows:

1. NETMAN invokes the RAS UI or CM UI to make an RRAS connection. The UI internally uses RAS APIs to make this connection.
2. RAS APIs internally read the connection properties from the phonebook file.

3. RAS APIs then call the Next Generation RASMAN to establish the connection. RAS APIs pass the RRAS server's IP address, authentication type (machine or user—in this case, it is machine authentication), and other information to the RASMAN.
4. RASMAN configures the SA policy, MOBIKE-supported flag, and authentication type (as machine with BFE) and initiates IKEv2 negotiation with the RRAS server.
5. BFE starts the IKEv2 negotiation (IKE_SA_INIT) with the RRAS server. BFE extracts the client identity from the machine certificate. BFE starts the IKE_AUTH exchange and validates the Server Certificate and AUTH information.
6. BFE notifies RRAS that connection is successful and passes the configuration information (IP address, DNS server list, and WINS server list) to the RRAS. It also passes the IPsec driver context to the VPN Reconnect driver.
7. RASMAN creates the interface by calling WANARP and also plumbs the IP address, DNS list, and WINS server list on the interface.

In addition, the connection process on the server side for authentication using machine certificates is as follows:

1. BFE receives the incoming IKEv2 tunnel mode (IKE_SA_INIT) request. It sends the response for the request.
2. On receiving an IKE_AUTH message, it checks whether the EAP authentication is enabled by Demand-Dial Manager (DDM). If yes, it invokes DDM, passing the received identity information to DDM. (BFE should ensure that it calls back the DDM only once for each incoming connection request; i.e., in case of retransmission of a request, DDM should not be invoked multiple times.)
3. DDM passes the identity information, along with any additional parameters, to the RADIUS server using the RADIUS protocol.
4. RADIUS server responds with the EAP blob.
5. DDM passes the EAP blob to the BFE, which sends this information along with other information in the IKE_AUTH response.
6. BFE, on receiving the EAP blob from the peer, passes it to the DDM.
7. DDM passes this information along with any additional parameters to the RADIUS server using the RADIUS protocol.
8. Steps 4 to 7 are repeated until DDM receives an ACCESS_ACCEPT (or REJECT) from the RADIUS server. In the case of ACCESS_ACCEPT, the RADIUS server also sends the session keys to the DDM.
9. DDM passes the EAP blob, session keys, and success/failure information to BFE. It stores other information (such as IP filters) within itself.

10. BFE passes the EAP blob to the peer.
11. On receiving AUTH information from the peer, BFE validates the AUTH information using the session keys and, if valid, it notifies DDM to pass configuration information (IP address, DNS server list, WINS server list, and optionally, any routes) along with IPsec context (for use by the VPN Reconnect driver).
12. DDM allocates an IP address (or an interface identifier in the case of IPv6), creates a subinterface (and the incoming interface if it is not already created), adds a host route on the interface, and adds the allocated IP address to the WANARP Address Resolution Protocol (ARP) table. It also applies the IP filters (and any other attributes) received from the RADIUS server on the connection.
13. DDM passes the configuration information to BFE, which passes it in the IKE_AUTH response and successfully creates a tunnel.

Understanding DirectAccess

DirectAccess is a new feature of Windows 7 and Windows Server 2008 R2 that provides users with the experience of being seamlessly connected to the corporate network from any location where they have Internet access. This section provides an overview of the benefits of DirectAccess, how it works, and how it can be implemented.

Benefits of DirectAccess

DirectAccess provides users with transparent access to internal network resources whenever they are connected to the Internet. Traditionally, remote users connect to internal network resources using a VPN. This can often be cumbersome, however, because:

- Connecting to a VPN typically takes several steps, and the user needs to wait for authentication before he can access the internal network. And for organizations that perform a health check of a VPN client before allowing the connection, establishing a VPN can often take several minutes.
- Any time users lose their Internet connection, they must reestablish their VPN connection, which can create additional delays.
- Internet access, such as browsing Web pages, is slowed when all network traffic is routed through the VPN.

Because of these issues, many remote users avoid connecting to a VPN. Instead, they use technologies such as Microsoft Office Outlook Web Access (OWA) to connect to internal resources, for example to retrieve internal e-mail without establishing a VPN connection. However, if a user tries to open a document linked to an e-mail message and that document resides on the internal network, the user is denied access, because internal resources are not accessible from the Internet.

When users avoid using VPNs like this, it also causes issues for network administrators because they can only manage mobile computers when they connect to the internal network. So when users avoid establishing an internal connection, mobile computers can miss critical updates and updated Group Policy settings.

DirectAccess solves these problems by enabling users to have the same experience working at home or at a wireless hotspot as they would in the office. Using DirectAccess, authorized users on Windows 7 computers can access corporate shares, view intranet Web sites, and work with intranet applications without going through a VPN. DirectAccess therefore provides the following benefits to enterprises and their users:

- **Seamless connectivity** DirectAccess is operative whenever the user has an Internet connection, giving users access to intranet resources whether they are traveling, at the local coffee shop, or at home.
- **Remote management** IT administrators can connect directly to DirectAccess client computers to monitor them, manage them, and deploy updates, even when the user is not logged on. This can reduce the cost of managing remote computers by keeping them up to date with critical updates and configuration changes.
- **Improved security** DirectAccess uses IPsec for authentication and encryption. Optionally, you can require smart cards for user authentication. DirectAccess integrates with Network Access Protection (NAP) to require that DirectAccess clients must be compliant with system health requirements before allowing a connection to the DirectAccess server. IT administrators can configure the DirectAccess server to restrict the servers that users and individual applications can access.

In a typical DirectAccess scenario, a user with a laptop computer in her office starts with a wired connection to the corporate LAN. The user can run both local and network applications, access documents stored in file and Web servers, and otherwise perform her daily work. She then shuts down and undocks her laptop to go on the road to a remote location, which could be a customer site or a coffee shop—it doesn't matter as long as Internet access is available there. Once she reaches the remote site, she boots up her laptop and accesses the Internet using a wireless connection to an access point at the site. Without having to initiate a VPN connection or perform any action whatsoever, her laptop is automatically connected to the corporate network after Internet connectivity is established. While at the remote site, she can run many of the same network applications and access the same documents as if she were still in her office at work (resource availability is subject to IPv6 reachability, as described later in this section). In addition, her laptop, though physically disconnected from the corporate network, remains in a managed state. This means that Group Policy is still being applied to her laptop, patches can still be applied when they become available, support personnel can use Remote Assistance to connect to her computer when help is needed, and so on. Also, when she needs to download something from the Internet, she can do so (depending on how DirectAccess is configured) using her local Internet access at the remote site instead of having to access the Internet through her connection to the corporate network.

How DirectAccess Works

DirectAccess is built on several different technologies as described in the next sections.

ACTIVE DIRECTORY DOMAIN SERVICES

An Active Directory Domain Services (AD DS) infrastructure is required for DirectAccess, with at least one domain controller in the domain running Windows Server 2008 or later versions. DirectAccess clients and servers must be domain members.

WINDOWS 7 AND WINDOWS SERVER 2008 R2

Client computers must be running Windows 7 Enterprise or Ultimate operating systems or Windows Server 2008 R2 to use DirectAccess. In addition, at least one server on the corporate network must be running Windows Server 2008 R2 so it can act as the DirectAccess server. This server typically resides on your perimeter network and acts as both a relay for IPv6 traffic and also an IPsec gateway.

IPv6

DirectAccess uses IPv6 to enable client computers to maintain constant end-to-end connectivity with remote intranet resources over a public Internet connection. Because most of the public Internet currently uses IPv4, however, DirectAccess can use IPv6 transition technologies such as Teredo and 6to4 to provide IPv6 connectivity over the IPv4 Internet. The preferred connectivity method for the client computer depends on the type of IP address assigned to the client. Specifically:

- If the client is assigned a globally routable IPv6 address, the preferred connectivity method is to use this address.
- If the client is assigned a public IPv4 address, the preferred connectivity method is to use 6to4.
- If the client is assigned a private (NAT) IPv4 address, the preferred connectivity method is to use Teredo.
- If the client is assigned a private (NAT) IPv4 address and the NAT device also provides 6to4 gateway functionality, 6to4 will be used.

If none of these connectivity methods can be used in a particular scenario, DirectAccess can also use IP-HTTPS, a new protocol developed by Microsoft for Windows 7 and Windows Server 2008 R2, which enables hosts located behind a Web proxy server or firewall to establish connectivity by tunneling IPv6 packets inside an IPv4-based HTTPS session. For more information about IPv6 transition technologies and about IP-HTTPS, see Chapter 28, "Deploying IPv6."

For remote client computers to use DirectAccess to connect to computers on the internal corporate network, these computers and their applications must be reachable over IPv6. This means the following:

- The internal computers and the applications running on them support IPv6. Computers running Windows 7, Windows Vista, Windows Server 2008, or Windows Server 2008 R2 support IPv6 and have IPv6 enabled by default.
- You have deployed native IPv6 connectivity or Intra-Site Automatic Tunnel Addressing Protocol (ISATAP) on your intranet. ISATAP allows your internal servers and applications to be reachable by tunneling IPv6 traffic over your IPv4-only intranet.

For computers and applications that do not support IPv6, you can use a Network Address Translation-Protocol Translation (NAT-PT) device to translate IPv6 and IPv4 traffic. Microsoft recommends using IPv6-capable computers and applications and native IPv6 or ISATAP-based connectivity over the use of NAT-PT devices.

IPSEC

DirectAccess uses IPsec to provide protection for DirectAccess traffic across the Internet. IPsec policies are used for authentication and encryption of all DirectAccess traffic across the Internet. These policies can also be used to provide end-to-end traffic protection between DirectAccess clients and intranet resources. These policies are configured and applied to client computers using Group Policy. For more information on IPsec and how to configure it, see Chapter 26.

PUBLIC KEY INFRASTRUCTURE

A Public Key Infrastructure (PKI) is required to issue computer certificates for authentication, issue health certificates when NAP has been implemented, and providing certificate revocation checking services. These certificates can be issued by a certification authority (CA) on the internal network—they do not need to be issued by a public CA.

PERIMETER FIREWALL EXCEPTIONS

If your corporate network has a perimeter firewall, the following traffic to and from the DirectAccess server over the IPv4 Internet must be allowed:

- UDP port 3544 for Teredo traffic
- IPv4 protocol 41 for 6to4 traffic
- TCP port 443 for IP-HTTPS traffic

If you need to support client computers that connect over the IPv6 Internet, the following traffic to and from the DirectAccess server must be allowed:

- Internet Control Message Protocol version 6 (ICMPv6)
- UDP port 500
- IPv4 protocol 50

SMART CARDS

DirectAccess also supports the optional use of smart cards for authenticating remote users.

Implementing DirectAccess

To implement DirectAccess on the server side, you need a computer running Windows Server 2008 R2 with two physical network adapters and at least two consecutive public IPv4 addresses that can be externally resolved through the Internet DNS. You can add the DirectAccess Management Console feature using Server Manager and then use the DirectAccess Setup Wizard in the DirectAccess Management Console to configure DirectAccess on your network. For more information on setting up the server side of DirectAccess, click the Help links in the DirectAccess Management Console.

To implement DirectAccess on the client side, your client computers must be running Windows 7 Enterprise or Ultimate Edition, be domain joined, and be a member of a security group for DirectAccess clients. Initial configuration is done automatically by the DirectAccess Setup Wizard for the members of the specified security groups for DirectAccess clients. Additional client configuration can be done using Group Policy settings or with scripts.

> ***MORE INFO*** **For more information on deploying a DirectAccess solution for your organization, see the technical documentation found on the DirectAccess page on TechNet at *http://technet.microsoft.com/en-us/network/dd420463.aspx*. See also the product documentation at *http://www.microsoft.com/directaccess/*.**

Understanding BranchCache

BranchCache is a new feature of Windows 7 and Windows Server 2008 R2 that allows content from file servers and Web servers at a central office to be cached on computers at a local branch office, thus improving application response time and reducing WAN traffic. This section provides an overview of the benefits of BranchCache, how it works, and how it can be implemented.

Benefits of BranchCache

BranchCache can provide the following benefits to enterprises and their users:

- **Reduces WAN link utilization** By enabling branch office clients to use locally cached copies of files instead of having to download them from the central office over the WAN, BranchCache reduces WAN link utilization, thus freeing up bandwidth for other applications that need to use the WAN.
- **Improves user productivity and reduces application response time** Opening a file located on a remote file server from a locally cached version of the file is typically much faster than downloading the file over a slow WAN link. BranchCache thus

increases user productivity when accessing content over the WAN for applications that use Server Message Block (SMB; for example, using Microsoft Office Word to open a document stored in a shared folder on a file server) or HTTP/HTTPS (for example, using Windows Internet Explorer to open a page on an intranet Web site or using Windows Media Player [WMP] to play a video embedded in an intranet Web page).

BranchCache adds significant value to Windows 7 and Windows Server 2008 R2 with little overhead by providing significant bandwidth savings and an improved user experience. BranchCache doesn't require additional equipment in the branch offices, is easy to deploy, supports your existing security requirements, and can be easily managed using Group Policy.

How BranchCache Works

Depending on how you implement it, BranchCache can function in one of two modes:

- **Hosted Cache** This scenario uses a client/server architecture in which clients running Windows 7 at a branch office site cache the content they've downloaded over the WAN from the central office to a Windows Server 2008 R2 computer (called the Hosted Cache) located at the same branch office site. Other clients that need this content can then retrieve it directly from the Hosted Cache without needing to use the WAN link.

  Hosted Cache mode does not require a dedicated server. The BranchCache feature can be enabled on a server that is running Windows Server 2008 R2, which is located in a branch that is also running other workloads. In addition, BranchCache can be set up as a virtual workload and can run on a server with other workloads, such as File and Print.

- **Distributed Cache** This scenario uses a peer-to-peer architecture in which Windows 7 clients cache content that they retrieve by using the WAN, and then they send that content directly to other authorized Windows 7 clients on request.

  Distributed Cache mode allows IT professionals to take advantage of BranchCache with minimal hardware deployments in the branch office. However, if the branch has deployed other infrastructure (for example, servers running workloads such as File or Print), using Hosted Cache mode may be beneficial for the following reasons:

  - **Increased cache availability** Hosted Cache mode increases the cache efficiency, because content is available even if the client that originally requested the data is offline.
  - **Caching for the entire branch office** Distributed Cache mode operates on a single subnet. If a branch office that is using Distributed Cache mode has multiple subnets, a client on each subnet needs to download a separate copy of each requested file. With Hosted Cache mode, all clients in a branch office can access a single cache, even if they are on different subnets.

Protocols Supported by BranchCache

BranchCache supports the SMB 2 and HTTP 1.1 protocols. Applications do not need to directly communicate with BranchCache, although they can if they need to. However, applications accessing SMB and HTTP interfaces in the Windows 7 and Windows Server 2008 R2 operating systems automatically benefit from BranchCache.

Consequently, applications like Windows Explorer, Robocopy CopyFile, WMP, Internet Explorer, and Silverlight automatically benefit. These benefits are also realized when using HTTPS, IPsec, or SMB signing. However, applications that implement SMB or HTTP stacks will not benefit from BranchCache, because BranchCache optimizations are leveraged directly by the SMB and HTTP protocol stack implementations in the Windows 7 and Windows Server 2008 R2 operating systems.

Implementing BranchCache

To implement BranchCache for a file server located at your central site, the file server must be running Windows Server 2008 R2 and you must install the BranchCache For Network Files role service of the File Services role on the server using the Add Roles Wizard. After doing this, you must also configure the shares on your file server to use BranchCache. Using Group Policy, you can enable or disable BranchCache on all your file server's shares, or you can mark specific shares to use BranchCache.

To implement BranchCache for a Web or application server located at your central site, the Web or application server must be running Windows Server 2008 R2, and you must install the BranchCache feature on the server using the Add Features Wizard. After doing this, you must also start the BranchCache service on your Web or application server by typing **netsh BranchCache set service mode=local** at an administrative-level command prompt.

To configure a computer running Windows Server 2008 R2 located at a branch office as a Hosted Cache server, you must install the BranchCache feature on the server, enable the feature and configure it to use Hosted Cache server mode, and install a certificate that is trusted by your client computers on the server.

To configure clients running Windows 7 located at a branch office to use BranchCache, you must enable BranchCache on the computers, configure the computers to use either Distributed Cache mode or Hosted Cache mode as needed, and open the necessary exceptions in Windows Firewall to allow the computers to access the cache on other computers at the site. BranchCache can be enabled and configured on computers running Windows 7 either by using Group Policy or by using the *netsh branchcache* context of the Netsh command.

> ***MORE INFO*** **For more information on deploying a BranchCache solution for your organization, see the documentation found on the BranchCache section of the Networking and Access Technologies TechCenter on Microsoft TechNet at *http://technet.microsoft.com/en-us/network/dd425028.aspx.***

Supported Connection Types

Windows 7 supports both outgoing and incoming network connections. For outgoing connections, the computer running Windows 7 acts as a client that connects to a remote computer, server, or network to access remote resources. For incoming connections, Windows 7 acts as a server to allow other computers to connect to the computer and access resources on it.

Outgoing Connection Types

As Windows Vista did before it, Windows 7 supports a number of different types of outgoing (client-side) network connections:

- **LAN or high-speed Internet connections** Connections to an Ethernet LAN or broadband router providing high-speed access to the Internet. LAN connections are computer-to-network connections that Windows creates automatically when it detects the presence of an installed network interface card (NIC). Internet connections are computer-to-network connections that you can create and configure manually using the Set Up A Connection Or Network wizard to provide Internet access using a broadband Digital Subscriber Line (DSL) adapter or cable modem, an Integrated Services Digital Network (ISDN) modem, or an analog (dial-up) modem. Broadband Internet connections use Point-to-Point Protocol over Ethernet (PPPoE); dial-up Internet connections use Point-to-Point Protocol (PPP).
- **Wireless network connections** Connections to a WLAN through a wireless access point or wireless router. Wireless network connections are computer-to-network connections that you can create and configure manually using the Set Up A Connection Or Network wizard, provided that the computer has a wireless network adapter installed. Wireless network connections may be either secured or unsecured, depending on how the access point has been configured.
- **Wireless ad hoc connections** Connections to another computer that is enabled for wireless networking. Wireless ad hoc connections are temporary computer-to-computer connections that you can use to share files between users.
- **Wireless routers or access points** Devices used to network wireless-enabled computers primarily for Small Office/Home Office (SOHO) environments so that users can share files and printers and connectivity to the Internet. Setting up this type of connection in Windows Vista using the Connect To A Network wizard requires that the computer has a wireless network adapter installed or attached to the computer and the presence of an external wireless router or wireless access point device that can be configured.
- **Dial-up connections** Connections to a remote access server (RAS server) or modem pool at a remote location. Dial-up connections are computer-to-server or computer-to-network connections that you can create and configure manually using the Set Up

A Connection Or Network wizard, provided that the computer has an analog or ISDN modem installed or connected to it. Dial-up connections either provide remote access to corporate networks or dial-up access to the Internet using the services of an Internet service provider (ISP).

- **VPN connections** Connections to a remote workplace by tunneling over the Internet. VPN connections work by creating a secure tunnel that encapsulates and encrypts all traffic between the client computer and the remote corporate network. This tunnel creates a secure private link over a shared public infrastructure such as the Internet. After the user is connected, her experience on the client computer is similar to what it would be if her computer were directly attached to the remote LAN (with performance limitations depending on the speed of the remote connection), with the exception of any restrictions imposed on remote connections by the network administrator. VPN connections are computer-to-server or computer-to-network connections that you can create and configure manually using the Set Up A Connection Or Network wizard. VPN connections can use Internet connectivity, or they can establish an existing broadband Internet connection or an existing analog or ISDN dial-up connection to obtain the Internet connectivity they require.

The rest of this chapter describes how to create and manage VPN and dial-up connections. For information about LAN and wireless connections in Windows 7, see Chapter 25, "Configuring Windows Networking."

Incoming Connection Types

As Windows Vista did before it, Windows 7 supports the following types of incoming (server-side) network connections:

- **Incoming VPN connections** Connections from a remote computer by tunneling over the Internet, using either a broadband Internet connection or a dial-up connection to an ISP
- **Incoming dial-up connections** Connections from a remote computer using an analog or ISDN modem

For more information on how to create and configure incoming connections, see the section titled "Configuring Incoming Connections" later in this chapter.

Deprecated Connection Types

The following connection technologies supported in Windows XP were deprecated in Windows Vista and are no longer available in Windows 7:

- X.25
- Microsoft Ethernet permanent virtual circuit (PVC)
- Direct cable connection using a serial, parallel, universal serial bus (USB), or IEEE 1394 cable

NOTE Most types of network connections available in Windows 7 support IPv6 out of the box and can be used to establish pure-IPv6 connectivity with remote servers or networks (provided they support incoming IPv6 connections). More information concerning IPv6 support for network connections in Windows 7 is provided throughout this chapter where appropriate.

Configuring VPN Connections

Windows 7 supports both outgoing and incoming VPN connections. For outgoing connections, Windows 7 is the client and connects to a VPN server on a remote network, usually the corporate intranet. For incoming connections, Windows 7 acts as a server and allows a remote client computer to establish a VPN connection between the two computers. In enterprise environments, outgoing VPN connections are commonly used to allow mobile users to securely access resources on the corporate intranet from remote locations. Incoming VPN connections to client computers are rarely used in enterprise environments, so most of this discussion deals with outbound connections only. For information on how to create and configure an inbound connection on Windows 7, see the section titled "Configuring Incoming Connections" later in this chapter.

Supported Tunneling Protocols

Windows 7 supports four different tunneling protocols for creating secure VPN connections to remote corporate networks:

- **Internet Key Exchange version 2** New in Windows 7, IKEv2 is an updated version of the IKE protocol that uses the IPsec tunnel mode over UDP port 500. IKEv2 enables VPN connections to be maintained when the VPN client moves between wireless hotspots or switches from a wireless to a wired connection. Using IKEv2 and IPsec together enables support for strong authentication and encryption methods. IKEv2 is documented in RFC 4306.
- **Secure Socket Tunneling Protocol** Supported in Windows Vista Service Pack 1 (SP1) and later versions, SSTP encapsulates PPP frames over HTTPS (HTTP over Secure Sockets Layer [SSL]) to facilitate VPN connectivity when a client is behind a firewall, NAT, or Web proxy that allows outgoing TCP connection over port 443. The SSL layer provides data integrity and encryption while PPP provides user authentication. SSTP was introduced in Windows Vista SP1 and Windows Server 2008. SSTP was developed by Microsoft and the SSTP protocol specification can be found on MSDN at *http://msdn.microsoft.com/en-us/library/cc247338.aspx*.
- **Layer Two Tunneling Protocol** An industry-standard Internet tunneling protocol designed to run natively over IP networks and which encapsulates PPP frames like

PPTP does. Security for L2TP VPN connections is provided by IPsec, which provides the authentication, data integrity, and encryption needed to ensure that L2TP tunnels are protected. The combination of L2TP with IPsec for tunneling purposes is usually referred to as L2TP over IPsec or L2TP/IPsec. L2TP/IPsec is documented in RFC 3193, while L2TP is documented in RFC 2661.

- **Point-to-Point Tunneling Protocol** An open industry standard developed by Microsoft and others, PPTP provides tunneling over PPP frames (which themselves encapsulate other network protocols such as IP) and uses PPP authentication, compression, and encryption schemes. PPTP was first introduced in Microsoft Windows NT 4.0 and is simpler to set up than L2TP, but it does not provide the same level of security as L2TP. PPTP is documented in RFC 2637.

Comparing the Different Tunneling Protocols

Table 27-1 compares the four different tunneling protocols that are available in Windows 7 and Windows Server 2008 R2.

TABLE 27-1 Comparison of VPN Tunneling Protocols Supported by Windows 7 and Windows Server 2008 R2

PROTOCOL	PROVIDES DATA CONFIDENTIALITY	PROVIDES DATA INTEGRITY	PROVIDES DATA AUTHENTICATION	REQUIRES A PUBLIC KEY INFRASTRUCTURE	SUPPORTED VERSIONS
IKEv2	Yes	Yes	Yes	Yes	Windows 7, Windows Server 2008 R2, and later versions
SSTP	Yes	Yes	Yes	Yes for issuing computer certificates	Windows Vista SP1, Windows Server 2008, and later versions
L2TP/IPsec	Yes	Yes	Yes	Recommended for issuing computer certificates; an alternative is using a pre-shared key	Microsoft Windows 2000 and later versions
PPTP	Yes	No	No	No	Windows 2000 and later versions

Microsoft recommendations for choosing the right tunneling protocol for providing VPN access to your corporate network are as follows:

- For client computers running Windows 7 and VPN servers running Windows Server 2008 R2, implement IKEv2 as your tunneling protocol. In addition to providing data confidentiality, data integrity, and data origin authentication (to confirm that the data was sent by the authorized user), IKEv2 provides resiliency to VPN connections using MOBIKE, which enables VPN connections to be maintained when the underlying Layer 2 network connectivity changes.
- For client computers running Windows 7 and VPN servers running Windows Server 2008 RTM or SP2, use SSTP as a fallback tunneling protocol. This way, whenever an IKEv2 tunnel connection is blocked due to a firewall configuration or some other issue, the client can use SSTP to achieve VPN connectivity to the corporate network. For more information about the order in which different tunneling protocols are used during a VPN connection attempt, see the section titled "Understanding the VPN Connection Negotiation Process" later in this chapter.
- For client computers running Windows 7 that need to connect to VPN servers running older versions of Windows, use L2TP/IPsec if a PKI is available; otherwise use PPTP.

NOTE **Microsoft may remove support for L2TP/IPsec and PPTP in future versions of Windows, so enterprises deploying Windows 7 should implement IKEv2 with SSTP fallback as their VPN solution wherever possible.**

Understanding Cryptographic Enhancements

Beginning with Windows Vista, support for cryptographic algorithms and protocols used for data integrity, encryption, and authentication is now updated to increase VPN security. These updates include:

- Addition of support for the Advanced Encryption Standard (AES).
- Removal of support for weak cryptographic algorithms.
- Removal of support for less secure authentication protocols.

The sections that follow provide more details concerning these security enhancements.

Support for AES

Support for the AES was first added in Windows Vista. AES is a Federal Information Processing Standard (FIPS) encryption standard developed by the National Institute of Standards and Technology (NIST) that supports variable key lengths and that replaces Data Encryption Standard (DES) as the standard encryption algorithm for government and industry. For L2TP/IPsec–based VPN connections, the following AES encryption levels are supported in Windows Vista and later versions:

- **Main mode** IPsec main mode supports AES 256- and 128-bit encryption using Elliptical Curve Diffie-Hellman (ECDH) with 384- and 256-bit encryption, respectively.
- **Quick mode** IPsec quick mode supports AES 128-bit and 3DES encryption when the encryption setting in the Advanced Security Settings properties of the VPN connection is either Optional Encryption or Require Encryption. IPsec quick mode supports AES 256-bit and 3DES encryption when the encryption setting inside the Advanced Security Settings properties is Maximum Strength Encryption.

NOTE **Using AES is a requirement for many U.S. government agencies.**

Weak Cryptography Removal from PPTP/L2TP

Support for weak or nonstandard cryptographic algorithms has been removed beginning with Windows Vista. This initiative was based on a desire by Microsoft to move customers toward stronger crypto algorithms to increase VPN security, based on recommendations by the NIST and the Internet Engineering Task Force (IETF) as well as mandates toward stronger crypto algorithms from different industry standards bodies and regulators.

The following crypto algorithms are no longer supported on Windows Vista or later versions:

- 40- and 56-bit RC4 encryption, formerly used by the Microsoft Point-to-Point Encryption (MPPE) Protocol for PPTP-based VPN connections
- DES encryption, formerly used by IPsec policy within L2TP/IPsec-based VPN connections
- MD5 integrity checking, formerly used by IPsec policy within L2TP/IPsec-based VPN connections

The removal of support from the default configuration for 40- and 56-bit RC4 encryption means that PPTP-based VPN connections now support only 128-bit RC4 for data encryption and integrity checking. This means the encryption strength remains the same as 128-bit RC4—that is, independent of the encryption settings (Optional Encryption, Require Encryption, or Maximum Strength Encryption) specified by the Advanced Security Settings properties of the VPN connections. This also means that if your existing VPN server does not support 128-bit encryption and supports only incoming PPTP-based VPN connections, clients will not be able to connect. If you are unable to upgrade your existing VPN servers to support 128-bit encryption for PPTP or if 128-bit encryption is unavailable to you because of export restrictions, you can enable weak crypto for PPTP by editing the following registry value:

HKLM\System\CurrentControlSet\Services\Rasman\Parameters\AllowPPTPWeakCrypto

The default value of this DWORD registry value is 0, and by changing it to 1, you can enable 40- and 56-bit RC4 encryption on the computer for both outgoing and incoming PPTP-based VPN connections. You must restart the computer for this registry change to take effect. As an alternative to restarting the computer, you can restart the Remote Access

Connection Manager service by opening a command prompt and typing **net stop rasman** followed by **net start rasman**.

The removal of support for DES encryption and MD5 integrity checking for L2TP/IPsec-based VPN connections means that L2TP/IPsec-based VPN connections now support the following data encryption and data integrity algorithms by default:

- 128-bit AES, 256-bit AES, and 3DES for data encryption using IPsec
- Secure Hash Algorithm (SHA1) for data integrity using IPsec

The removal of support for DES and MD5 from the default configuration means that L2TP/IPsec-based VPN connections will not work if your existing VPN server supports only DES for data encryption and/or MD5 for data integrity checking. If you are unable to upgrade your existing VPN servers to support AES or 3DES for data encryption and/or SHA1 for integrity checking or if these crypto algorithms are unavailable to you because of export restrictions, you can disable weak crypto for L2TP by editing the following registry value:

HKLM\System\CurrentControlSet\Services\Rasman\Parameters\AllowL2TPWeakCrypto

The default value of this DWORD registry value is 0, and by changing it to 1, you can enable DES encryption and MD5 integrity checking on the computer for both outgoing and incoming L2TP/IPsec-based VPN connections. You must restart the computer for this registry change to take effect. As an alternative to restarting the computer, you can restart the Remote Access Connection Manager service by opening a command prompt and typing **net stop rasman** followed by **net start rasman**.

> ***NOTE*** **Microsoft recommends that you upgrade your VPN server to support 128-bit RC4 for PPTP and/or AES and SHA1 for L2TP instead of disabling weak crypto support on your VPN clients.**

Table 27-2 summarizes the differences between Windows 7, Windows Vista, and Windows XP with regard to crypto support for data integrity and encryption for VPN connections.

TABLE 27-2 Data Integrity and Encryption Support for VPN Connections in Windows 7, Windows Vista, and Windows XP

CRYPTO ALGORITHM	USE	WINDOWS 7	WINDOWS VISTA	WINDOWS XP
40-bit RC4	Data encryption and integrity checking for PPTP only			✓
56-bit RC4	Data encryption and integrity checking for PPTP only			✓

CRYPTO ALGORITHM	USE	WINDOWS 7	WINDOWS VISTA	WINDOWS XP
128-bit RC4	Data encryption and integrity checking for PPTP only	✓	✓	✓
DES	Data encryption			✓
3DES	Data encryption	✓	✓	✓
128-bit AES	Data encryption	✓	*	
196-bit AES	Data encryption	✓	*	
256-bit AES	Data encryption	✓	*	
MD5	Integrity checking			✓
SHA1	Integrity checking	✓	✓	✓
256-bit SHA	Integrity checking (main mode only)	✓	*	
384-bit SHA	Integrity checking (main mode only)	✓	*	

An asterisk (*) in Table 27-2 means that configuration is possible, but only by using the Netsh command.

Supported Authentication Protocols

The following authentication protocols are supported for logon security for VPN connections in Windows 7:

- **PAP** Stands for Password Authentication Protocol; uses plaintext (unencrypted) passwords.
- **CHAP** Stands for Challenge Handshake Authentication Protocol; uses one-way MD5 hashing with challenge-response authentication.
- **MSCHAPv2** Stands for Microsoft Challenge Handshake Authentication Protocol version 2; an extension by Microsoft of the CHAP authentication protocol that provides mutual authentication of Windows-based computers and stronger data encryption. MSCHAPv2 is an enhancement of the earlier MS-CHAP protocol that provided only one-way authentication of the client by the server.
- **EAP** Stands for Extensible Authentication Protocol; extends PPP by adding support for additional authentication methods including using smart cards and certificates.
- **PEAP** Stands for Protected Extensible Authentication Protocol, or Protected EAP; enhances the protection provided by EAP by using Transport Layer Security (TLS) to provide a secure channel for EAP negotiation. PEAP is also used in Windows 7 to support NAP scenarios.

Starting with Windows Vista, the following authentication protocols have been deprecated for use by VPN connections:

- SPAP (Shiva Password Authentication Protocol)
- MS-CHAP
- EAP using MD5

Note that by default PAP and CHAP are not enabled as authentication protocols on new VPN connections you create using the Set Up A Connection Or Network wizard. This is because PAP and CHAP are not considered secure; use them only when connecting to ISPs whose network access devices support only these older authentication schemes. And although PPTP in Windows 7 no longer supports MD5 for data integrity checking using L2TP/IPsec-based VPN connections, support for MD5 usage in CHAP has been maintained because of the continuing popularity of this authentication protocol with many broadband- and dial-up–based ISPs.

Table 27-3 summarizes the differences between Windows 7, Windows Vista, and Windows XP with regard to user authentication protocols used for VPN connections.

> ***NOTE*** **In addition to the user authentication protocols listed in Table 27-3, L2TP/IPsec also supports machine-level authentication (using either pre-shared keys or machine certificates), and SSTP supports the client validating the server (using the certificate sent by the server to the client during the SSL negotiation phase).**

TABLE 27-3 Authentication Protocols Supported for VPN Connections in Windows 7, Windows Vista, and Windows XP

AUTHENTICATION PROTOCOL	WINDOWS 7	WINDOWS VISTA	WINDOWS XP
PAP	✓	✓	✓
SPAP			✓
CHAP	✓	✓	✓
MS-CHAP			✓
MS-CHAPv2	✓	✓	✓
EAP with MD5 challenge			✓
EAP with smart card	✓	✓	✓
EAP with other certificate	✓	✓	✓
PEAP	✓	✓	

DIRECT FROM THE SOURCE

VPN Security Enhancements

Samir Jain and Santosh Chandwai, Lead Program Managers
Windows Enterprise Networking

Beginning with Windows Vista, many extensions have been made regarding VPN security. First, all the weak crypto algorithms have been removed and new stronger crypto algorithms have been added to VPN tunnels. For PPTP, 40/56-bit RC4 encryption has been removed by default. This means PPTP now supports only 128-bit RC4 encryption by default. So if your VPN server or VPN client doesn't support 128-bit encryption, your calls may fail. You can still get 40/56-bit RC4 encryption back by changing a registry key, but this is not recommended. It is better to upgrade your client or server to one that supports the more secure 128-bit RC4 encryption method.

For L2TP/IPsec, DES (for encryption) and MD5 (for integrity check) have been removed, but AES support has been added. This means that Windows Vista and later versions support AES 128-bit, AES 256-bit, and 3DES for encryption, and SHA1 for integrity check. (AES is more CPU efficient than 3DES.) So if your VPN server or VPN client doesn't support either DES or MD5, your connectivity may fail. You can still get DES and MD5 back by changing a registry key, but this is not recommended. It is better to upgrade your client or server to one that supports the more secure AES/3DES and SHA1 encryption methods.

Second, many new authentication algorithms have been added; EAP-MD5, SPAP, and MSCHAPv1 are now deprecated. Windows Vista and later versions support (in increasing order of strength) PAP, CHAP, MSCHAPv2, EAP-MSCHAPv2, EAP-smart card/certificate, PEAP-MSCHAPv2, and PEAP-smart card/certificate. Using PAP or CHAP as an authentication algorithm over a VPN tunnel is not recommended because it is weaker than other authentication algorithms. Arguably, it might be safe to use PAP/CHAP over a L2TP/IPsec VPN connection because IPsec provides a secure session before PPP authentication begins. But always remember this subtle security point: IPsec provides you with machine-level authentication, whereas PPP authentication provides you with user-level authentication, and both are important.

Finally, the L2TP/IPsec client in Windows Vista and later versions has added more verification of specific fields inside the server certificate used for IPsec negotiation to avoid the trusted man-in-the-middle (TMITM) attack. The L2TP/IPsec client checks for the Subject Alternative Name (SAN) field in the server's X.509 certificate to verify that the server you are connecting to is the same as the server that was issued the certificate. It also checks for the Extended Key Usage (EKU) field to validate that the certificate issued to the server is for the purpose of server authentication. For older deployments, Windows Vista and later versions provide a registry key that if enabled will allow the VPN client to override the verification of the SAN and EKU fields of the server's certificate. However, it is recommended that you not override these checks. Instead, if your VPN server offering L2TP/IPsec connectivity is issued X.509 certificates that do not have the DNS name of the server in the SAN field, it is recommended that you reissue appropriately configured certificates to the server.

Understanding the VPN Connection Negotiation Process

When a client running Windows 7 tries to establish a connection with a remote VPN server, the tunneling protocol, authentication protocol, data encryption algorithm, and integrity-checking algorithm used depend on several factors:

- The enabled authentication protocols and crypto algorithms on the client side
- The remote access policy on the server side
- The available network transports (IPv4 and/or IPv6)

By default, if Type Of VPN is set to Automatic on the client side, the client running Windows 7 attempts to establish a connection with the remote VPN server in the following order:

1. IKEv2
2. SSTP
3. PPTP
4. L2TP

The VPN client typically resolves the name of the VPN server using DNS. If the DNS lookup provides only an IPv4 or IPv6 address to the client, the connection attempts using the various tunneling protocols use only IPv4 or IPv6. If the DNS lookup provides the client with both the IPv4 and IPv6 addresses of the server, then IPv6 is preferred and the following tunnel connections are attempted, in this order:

1. IKEv2 over IPv6
2. SSTP over IPv6
3. PPTP over IPv4 (because PPTP doesn't support IPv6)
4. L2TP over IPv6

After a tunneling protocol has been selected for the connection, the authentication and crypto algorithms are then negotiated between the client and the server.

NOTE You can reduce connection time by explicitly specifying the tunneling protocol you want your client to use (provided that the remote server also supports this protocol) instead of selecting the Automatic type of VPN on the Networking tab of the connection's properties. Note that doing so means that if the connection attempt using the specified tunneling protocol fails then VPN connectivity cannot be established.

HOW IT WORKS

VPN Connections and IPv4/IPv6

Samir Jain, Lead Program Manager
Enterprise Networking (RRAS)

First, a little background: After you establish VPN connectivity, you have two interfaces on your client computer. One is your Internet interface (that is, Ethernet, wireless, PPPoE, PPP over dial-up, and so on); the other is your corporate or WAN interface (that is, a VPN tunnel). This really means that you have two sets of IP addresses, and each of these can be IPv4 and/or IPv6.

How Do We Support IPv4 and IPv6 for VPN Connections?

In Windows 7, we support SSTP, L2TP, and IKEv2 VPN tunnels over IPv6 (in other words, when your ISP connectivity is IPv6) and SSTP/L2TP/PPTP/IKEv2 VPN tunnels over IPv4. In all scenarios, IPv4 and/or IPv6 packets can be sent on top of a VPN tunnel. (Packets going to/from your corporate network can be IPv4/IPv6.)

- If you are confused about the difference between "over" and "on top of," here's a rule of thumb: Look at the connectivity between the VPN client and the VPN server (your ISP connectivity). This determines how the tunnel packets flow over the Internet and indirectly determines which type of VPN tunnel to be used.
- Look at the connectivity between the VPN server and your corporate network (your corporate connectivity). This determines what flows on top of (or inside) the tunnel, and indirectly determines which network inside your corporate network you can access (IPv4 and/or IPv6).

How Can I Identify This While Configuring a VPN Connection?

Open the Properties dialog box of your VPN connection and click the General tab. Here is where you specify the IP address (v4 or v6) or host name of the VPN server—the IP address that you are going to use to connect to the VPN server or the IP address over which the VPN tunnel will be established. In other words, this determines your ISP connectivity. If you enter an IPv6 address here, L2TP, IKEv2, and SSTP tunnels are supported. If you enter an IPv4 address, all tunnel types are supported. But if you enter a host name, the type of tunnel selection is deferred until you actually connect and a name lookup is performed. The DNS server could return to you both IPv4 and IPv6 addresses. In this scenario, IPv4 and IPv6 are tried in the order in which the addresses were returned by the DNS server inside the DNS response. The result also depends on the type of VPN tunnel type selection (PPTP, L2TP/IPsec, SSTP, IKEv2, or Automatic).

Switch to the Networking tab and look at This Connection Uses The Following Items. The protocols listed here include both IPv4 and IPv6, and this protocol will be the one that gets negotiated "on top of" (or "inside") the VPN tunnel. In other words, this determines your corporate connectivity—whether you will be sending IPv4 and/or IPv6 packets to the corporate network on top of the tunnel. You can typically get both IPv4 and IPv6 addresses from your corporate VPN server if your VPN server is configured accordingly. Depending on the name lookups, the appropriate address will be taken.

What Happens When I Select Automatic as My Type of VPN?

Automatic VPN tunnel logic is very simple:

- First try IKEv2, and if that fails, try SSTP. If that fails, try PPTP. And if that fails, try L2TP.
- Let's say you have configured an IPv4 address as the destination VPN server. The logic remains the same: first IKEv2, then SSTP, then PPTP, and finally L2TP.
- Let's say instead that you have configured an IPv6 address as the destination VPN server. Try IKEv2. If that fails, try SSTP. And if that fails, try L2TP.
- Finally, let's say that you have configured a host name as the destination VPN server. Now if your DNS server returns only IPv4 addresses (A records), go to bullet 2 above. If your DNS server returns only IPv6 addresses (AAAA records), go to bullet 3. If your DNS server returns both IPv4 and IPv6 addresses, the logic will be to go through each IP address returned and then go to either bullet 2 or 3 depending upon the IP address.

What Happens When I Select My Type of VPN Using Connection Manager Administration Kit?

Connection Manager Administration Kit (CMAK), a tool for network administrators on Windows Server 2008 R2, also supports the following tunnel order strategies:

- Use PPTP only.
- Try PPTP first, which means PPTP, IKEv2, SSTP, and then L2TP.
- Use L2TP.
- Try L2TP first, which means L2TP, IKEv2, PPTP, and then SSTP.
- Use SSTP only.
- Try SSTP first, which means SSTP, IKEv2, PPTP, and then L2TP.
- Use IKEv2 only.
- Try IKEv2 first, which means IKEv2, PPTP, SSTP, and then L2TP.

Note that you must use a computer running a version of Windows with the same processor architecture as the clients on which you want to install the profile. A 32-bit connection profile can be created and installed on a 32-bit version of

Windows only. A 64-bit connection profile can be created and installed on a 64-bit version of Windows only. To create 64-bit connection profiles, use the Add Features Wizard to install the CMAK feature on a computer running Windows Server 2008 R2. To create 42-bit connection profiles, use the Turn Windows Features On Or Off option to install the RAS CMAK feature on a computer running a 32-bit version of Windows 7.

What Will Happen if I Connect a Windows 7 Client to a VPN Server That Doesn't Support IPv6?

You won't be able to use the VPN server "over" IPv6 (you can only have IPv4 connectivity to an ISP), which means your tunnel can be SSTP, L2TP, IKEv2, or PPTP. Then, "on top of" the VPN tunnel, the client running Windows 7 will try to get an IPv4 as well as an IPv6 address from the VPN server, but it will get only an IPv4 address. Hence the connection will still go through. In other words, the connection fails only if you cannot get both IPv4 and IPv6 addresses on top of the VPN tunnel.

What Will Happen if I Connect a Windows 7 Client to a VPN Server That Doesn't Support SSTP?

The SSTP connection will fail (and then you should remove SSTP from the preceding tunnel order).

Creating and Configuring VPN Connections

The Set Up A Connection Or Network wizard simplifies the task of creating VPN connections. The screens displayed when you use this wizard vary depending on the choices you make as you proceed through the wizard.

MORE INFO This chapter covers only configuring client connections for establishing VPN connectivity. For information about configuring Windows Server 2008 VPN servers including Network Policy Server (NPS) servers, see the "Windows Server 2008 Networking and Network Access Protection (NAP)" volume in the "Windows Server 2008 Resource Kit" from Microsoft Press at *http://www.microsoft.com/learning/en/us/books/11160.aspx.*

In addition to creating and configuring new connections on clients running Windows 7, administrators can use the new version of the CMAK included with Windows Server 2008. CMAK is a set of tools that you can use to tailor the appearance and behavior of connections made using Connection Manager, the built-in remote access client dialer included in Windows Vista. Using CMAK, administrators can create and deploy custom connections for client computers to simplify the user experience of connecting to remote networks. For instance, you could create a client connection that tries only a single specified tunneling protocol when attempting to establish a connection, or you could create a connection that tries each tunneling protocol in a specified order.

> **NOTE** You must use the new Windows Server 2008 R2 version of CMAK to create and configure connections for clients running Windows 7.

Creating a VPN Connection

To create a new VPN connection on a computer if you already have a broadband (PPPoE) or dial-up connection to the Internet, follow these steps:

1. Open Network And Sharing Center either from Control Panel or by clicking the networking icon in the system notification area followed by clicking Open Network And Sharing Center.
2. After Network And Sharing Center is displayed, click Set Up A New Connection Or Network to start the Set Up A New Connection Or Network wizard.
3. On the Choose A Connection Option page, select Connect To A Workplace and then click Next.
4. If this is the first connection you have created on the computer, proceed to step 5. Otherwise, select Yes, I'll Choose An Existing Connection and then select one of the existing connections displayed on the Do You Want To Use A Connection That You Already Have? page. For example, if you want to use an existing dial-up connection (analog or ISDN modem) to provide Internet access for your new VPN connection, select that connection and then click Dial when the Connect dialog box is displayed for that connection. After you've used your existing connection to connect to the Internet, you can continue setting up your new VPN connection.
5. Click Use My Internet Connection (VPN).
6. Specify the IPv4 or IPv6 address or fully qualified domain name (FQDN) of the remote VPN server you want to connect to, as shown here. You can also give the connection a descriptive name to distinguish it from other connections on the computer. Typically, this will be the name of your remote network or remote VPN server.

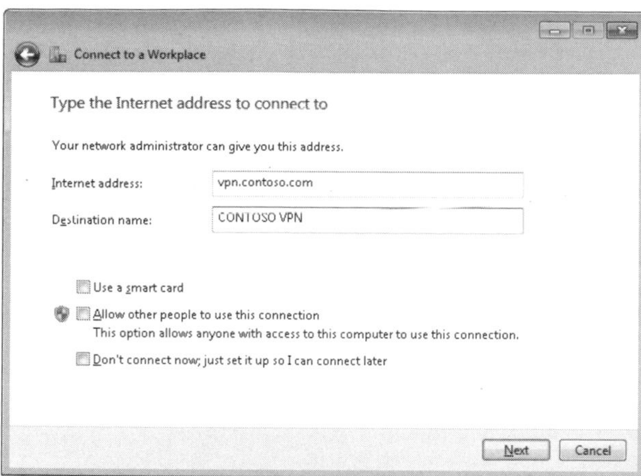

7. To use a smart card for authentication, select Use A Smart Card. You must have a smart card reader installed on the computer to use this option. If you select this option, proceed to step 10.
8. To allow other users of the computer to use the connection, select Allow Other People To Use This Connection. Selecting this option configures your connection to be of the All Users type rather than a Private connection, which can be used only by the user who created it. The All Users connection type is also used for Windows logon over your VPN connection.
9. To create a new connection that needs further configuration before you can use it, select Don't Connect Now Just Set It Up So I Can Connect Later.
10. Click Next and specify the credentials (user name, password, and optionally the domain) you will use to be authenticated by the remote VPN server. (This option is available only if you left the Use A Smart Card option cleared earlier in the wizard.)
11. If you chose to create a connection that needs further configuring before being used, click Create and then either click Close to create the connection or click Connect Now to initiate the connection.

NOTE **You can also start the Connect To A Network wizard by adding a Connect To option to your Start menu. To do this, right-click the Start menu and select Properties, click Customize, and select the check box labeled Connect To.**

Initiating a Connection

To initiate a previously created connection, perform the following steps:

1. Click the networking icon in the system tray to display the View Available Networks (VAN) UI. Any VPN client connections configured on the computer will be displayed in the Dial-up And VPN section of the VAN UI, as shown here.

2. Click the VPN client connection you want to initiate, as shown here, and then click Connect.

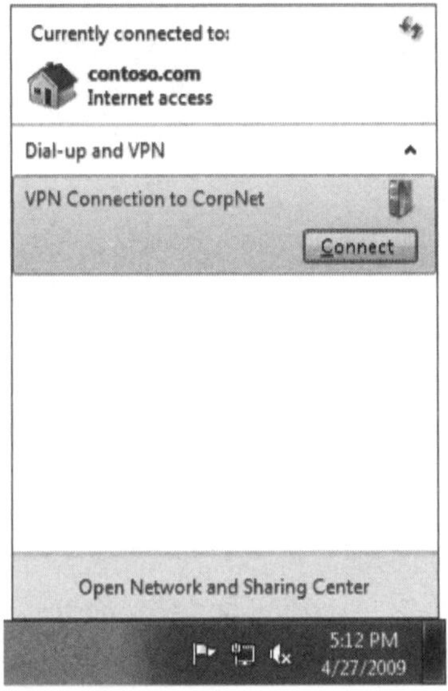

3. In the Connect <*connection name*> dialog box that appears, specify the credentials to be used for the connection, as shown here, and then click Connect.

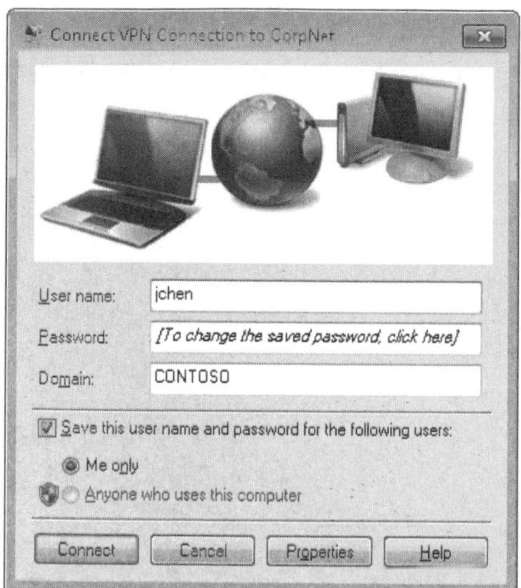

4. When the connection has been established, the connection is displayed as Connected in the VAN UI, as shown here.

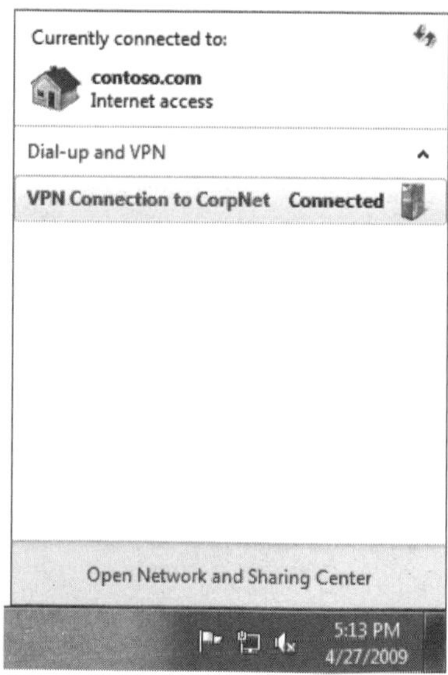

NOTE You can also initiate a connection by opening the Network Connections folder, double-clicking the connection, and clicking Connect. You can also drag a connection to the desktop from the Network Connections folder to create a desktop shortcut to your connection, which allows you to initiate your connection by double-clicking the shortcut and clicking Connect.

Terminating a Connection

To disconnect an active connection, click the connection in the VAN UI and then click Disconnect (see Figure 27-1). You can also right-click a connection to view its status, open its properties, or to connect or disconnect the connection.

FIGURE 27-1 You can connect or disconnect a connection, view its properties, or display its status using the VAN user interface.

> ***NOTE*** Windows 7 supports Fast User Switching (FUS) on both domain-joined and workgroup computers. Active VPN connections of the All Users variety are not terminated when you switch your computer to another user.

DIRECT FROM THE SOURCE

Using a VPN Connection at Logon

Santosh Chandwani, Lead Program Manager
Windows Enterprise Networking

To establish a RAS (VPN or dial-up) connection during logon, or to log on to a domain over a RAS connection, the user must have a connection for use by all users on the computer (called an All User connection). To log on to a domain over a RAS connection, follow these steps:

1. On the Logon screen, click the Network Logon icon in the lower-right corner. This will display tiles representing each of the All User connections that can be dialed during logon.
2. Click the tile representing the connection you want to dial. This will display the UI for entering the connection credentials.
3. If the RAS connection requires a smart card and you want to use user name/password for logging on to Windows, select the Use Password For Logon To Windows check box below the RAS credential user interface. This will display the UI for entering the user name and password that will be used for Winlogon.
4. Similarly, if the RAS connection requires user name/password and you want to use a smart card for logging on to Windows, select the Use Smart Card For Logon To Windows check box below the RAS credential to display the smart card UI.

   If the RAS connection and the logon to Windows require the same type of credentials, Windows will by default attempt to use the same credentials for establishing the RAS connection and for Winlogon. If the credentials required are different, you will establish a successful RAS connection, but logon to Windows will fail and the following error message will be displayed: "The network connection has been established successfully, but the logon to the local machine has failed using the credentials provided. Please click OK to retry logon to Windows." Clicking OK will give you the opportunity to enter the appropriate credentials for logging on to Windows.
5. If the RAS connection has been successfully established but the logon to Windows has failed, and you want to disconnect the RAS connection instead, click Disconnect Network Connection on the logon screen.

Viewing Connection Details

You can view the details of connections on your computer by using the Network Connections folder and selecting Details using the More Options toolbar item. Using this method, you can view the connection status, device name, connectivity, network category, owner, type, and phone number of the host address of the remote server (see Figure 27-2).

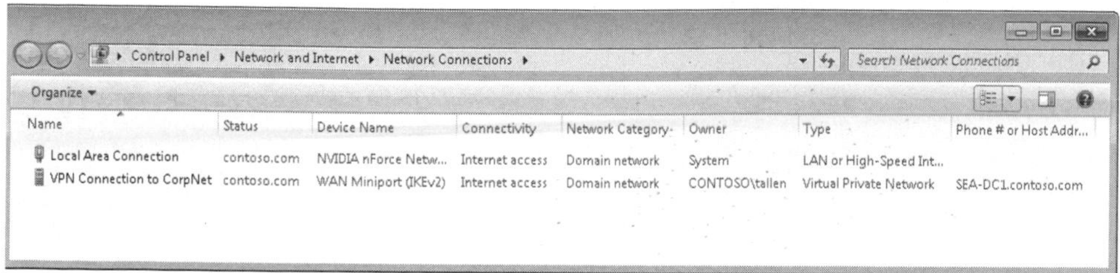

FIGURE 27-2 Use the Network Connections folder to view detailed information about connections.

NOTE You can view additional information for a connection including media state (connected or disconnected), duration (uptime), bytes sent and received, IP address details, and other data by right-clicking a connection in the Network Connections folder and selecting Status. This information can also be viewed by displaying the VAN, right-clicking the connection, and selecting Status.

Configuring a VPN Connection

To configure the settings of a connection that you have already created, open its Properties dialog box by doing one of the following:

- Click the networking icon in the system tray to display the View Available Networks (VAN) UI and then right-click the connection and select Properties.
- Open Network And Sharing Center, click Change Adapter Settings, and then right-click the connection and select Properties.
- At a command prompt or in the Search box on the Start menu, type **ncpa.cpl**, press Enter, and then right-click the connection and select Properties.

The properties sheet for configuring a VPN connection has five tabs, as shown in Figure 27-3:

- **General** Specifies the host name or IP address (IPv4 or IPv6) of the remote VPN server and whether to use another connection first to establish Internet connectivity before initiating the VPN connection.
- **Options** Specifies dialing options, redialing options, and PPP settings.
- **Security** Specifies authentication and data encryption settings.
- **Networking** Specifies the tunneling protocol(s) used (PPTP, L2TP/IPsec, SSTP, or Automatic), IP address settings (static or Dynamic Host Configuration Protocol [DHCP]), and IPsec settings (for L2TP/IPsec-based connections only).
- **Sharing** Enables Internet Connection Sharing for the connection and specifies whether to dial another connection to establish Internet connectivity before initiating this connection.

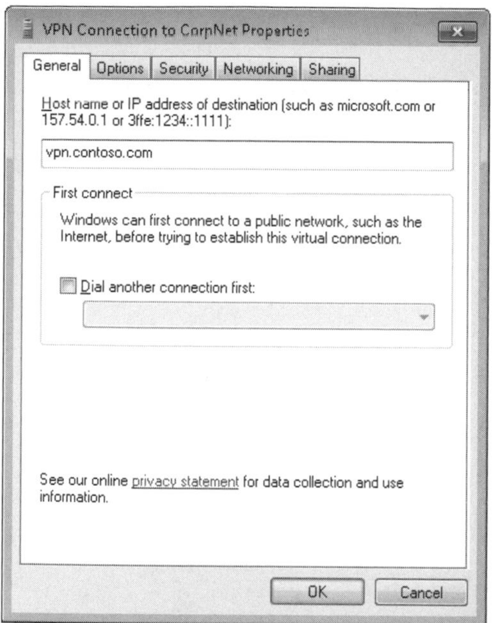

FIGURE 27-3 Configure the properties of a connection.

For more information about configuring connection properties, use Help And Support. Some specific configuration options, focusing on differences with connection properties in Windows Vista, are discussed in the next section.

Configuring Security Settings for a VPN Connection

For administrators familiar with configuring connections in Windows Vista, there have been several changes to how this is done in Windows 7. Most obviously, the option for selecting the tunneling protocol(s) the connection will use has been moved from the Networking tab to the Security tab. In addition, the settings for configuring data encryption and authentication have been reorganized to make them easier to configure. Finally, the settings available to configure on this tab now depend upon the tunneling protocol(s) selected.

CONFIGURING THE TUNNELING PROTOCOL(S) USED

Figure 27-4 shows the default settings on the Security tab when a new VPN connection is created in Windows 7. Clicking the Type Of VPN control lets you select the tunneling protocol(s) that the connection can use when attempting to connect to a VPN server. The following options are available:

- **Automatic** The connection tries different tunneling protocols in the following order: IKEv2, SSTP, PPTP, and L2TP/IPsec. For example, if you want the connection to use IKEv2 with fallback to SSTP, choose this type of VPN for your connection. This is the default type of VPN for a newly created connection in Windows 7.

- **PPTP** The connection will try PPTP only when attempting to establish a connection with the VPN server.
- **L2TP/IPsec** The connection will try L2TP/IPsec only when attempting to establish a connection with the VPN server.
- **SSTP** The connection will try SSTP only when attempting to establish a connection with the VPN server.
- **IKEv2** The connection will try IKEv2 only when attempting to establish a connection with the VPN server.

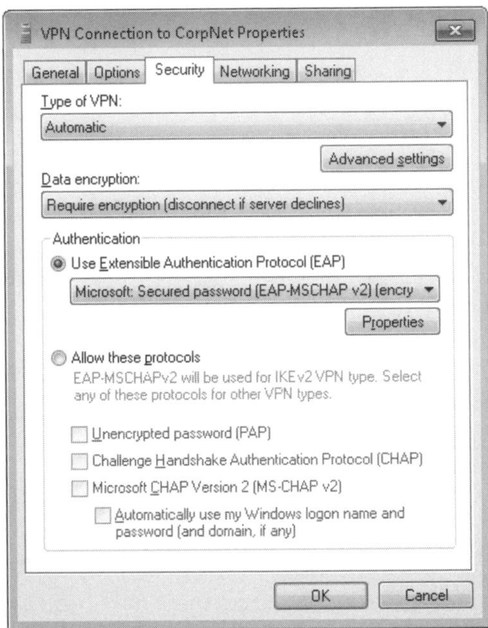

FIGURE 27-4 Specifying the type of VPN determines which tunneling protocol(s) can be used by the connection.

> ***NOTE*** **A best practice when client computers are running Windows 7 and the VPN server is running Windows Server 2008 R2 is to leave Type Of VPN set at its default value of Automatic.**

You can reduce the time that it takes to establish a VPN connection by specifying the tunneling protocol you want your client to use (provided that the remote server also supports this protocol). To specify a tunneling protocol for a connection, follow these steps:

1. Open the properties of your VPN connection and then select the Security tab.
2. Under Type Of VPN, change the setting from Automatic to either PPTP, L2TP/IPsec, SSTP, or IKEv2 as desired.

The default setting of Automatic means that Windows negotiates the tunneling protocol to use based on the algorithm outlined earlier in this chapter in the section titled "Understanding the VPN Connection Negotiation Process."

NOTE Using FUS during a RAS/VPN session can affect your connectivity. For more information, see Knowledge Base article 289669 at *http://support.microsoft.com/kb/289669*.

CONFIGURING ADVANCED CONNECTION SETTINGS

If the Type Of VPN is set to Automatic, clicking Advanced Settings displays a properties sheet with two tabs (see Figure 27-5). These tabs expose the following settings:

- **L2TP tab** Used to specify whether a certificate (the default) or a pre-shared key will be used for authentication of the server by the client.
- **IKEv2 tab** Used to enable or disable connection mobility—for more information, see the section titled "Configuring Mobility for IKEv2 Connections" later in this chapter.

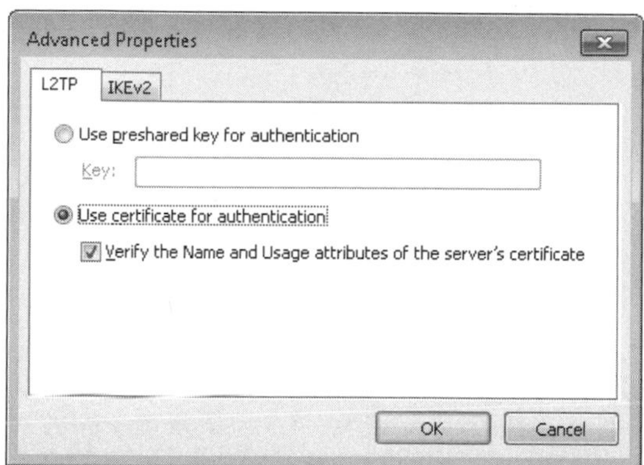

FIGURE 27-5 Configure advanced settings for an Automatic tunnel-type connection.

CONFIGURING THE DATA ENCRYPTION LEVEL

Selecting the control under Data Encryption on the Security tab lets you specify the level of data encryption used by the connection. The available options are self explanatory and include the following:

- No Encryption Allowed (server will disconnect if it requires encryption)
- Optional Encryption (connect even if no encryption)
- Require Encryption (disconnect if server declines)
- Maximum Strength Encryption (disconnect if server declines)

The default value for this setting in a newly created connection is Require Encryption.

CONFIGURING THE AUTHENTICATION METHOD USED

Under Authentication on the Security tab are two authentication methods that your connection can use:

- **Use Extensible Authentication Protocol (EAP)** Selecting this authentication method lets you choose from one of the following three protocols for authenticating the VPN connection:
    - Protected EAP (PEAP)
    - EAP-MSCHAPv2
    - Smart Card Or Other Certificate

  All three of these options ensure the security and data integrity of the EAP conversation by using encryption. The default setting here for a new connection is EAP-MSCHAPv2, which is also known as Secure Password.

  Additional authentication settings for EAP can be configured by clicking Properties. These additional settings depend on which EAP authentication method you have selected. Specifically:

    - If PEAP is selected, clicking Properties lets you configure various authentication settings including client-side NAP settings. For more information on implementing NAP in enterprise environments, see the "Windows Server 2008 Networking and Network Access Protection (NAP)" volume in the "Windows Server 2008 Resource Kit" from Microsoft Press at *http://www.microsoft.com/learning/en/us/books/11160.aspx.*
    - If EAP-MSCHAPv2 is selected, clicking Properties lets you configure the connection to automatically use your Windows logon credentials for authenticating the connection.
    - If Smart Card Or Other Certificate is selected, clicking Properties lets you specify whether to use a smart card or other digital certificate for authenticating the connection. For example, if you are using certificates stored on the local computer rather than smart cards, you can select the Use A Certificate On This Computer option to enable certificates to be used for authenticating VPN connections. Selecting the Use Simple Certificate Selection (Recommended) option enables Windows Vista to determine which certificate on the computer should be used for VPN authentication. Selecting the Valid Server Certificate option forces the client computer to verify that the certificate of the remote VPN server is valid (this option is selected by default). You should also specify the trusted root authorities you want the client computer to trust, and you can optionally specify the IP address or FQDN of your CA in the Connect To These Servers text box.

- **Allow These Protocols** Selecting this authentication method lets you choose one or more of the following authentication protocols to be used by your connection:
    - PAP
    - CHAP
    - MS-CHAP v2

In addition, you can choose whether to configure the connection to automatically use your Windows logon credentials. Note that the choice of using PAP, CHAP, or MSCHAPv2 applies only to PPTP, L2TP/IPsec, and SSTP tunnels; IKEv2 tunnels can only use EAP-MSCHAPv2 or certificates (see the next section for details).

CONFIGURING AUTHENTICATION FOR IKEv2 CONNECTIONS

When you force a connection to use IKEv2 as its tunnel type, you have a choice of two authentication methods from which to select for authenticating the client to the server (see Figure 27-6):

- Use EAP to authenticate the remote user to the VPN server.
- Use a machine certificate installed on the client computer to authenticate the client computer to the VPN server.

The default setting here is to use EAP, which doesn't require a machine certificate to be installed on the client computer. For IKEv2 to work, however, a machine certificate must be installed on the VPN server so that the server's identity can be authenticated by the client.

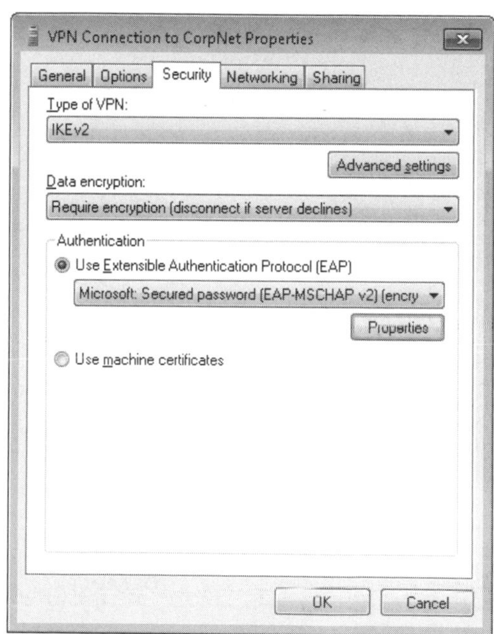

FIGURE 27-6 Forcing IKEv2 as the tunnel type provides two authentication methods from which to choose.

Note that if you select the Use Machine Certificates option on your client computers running Windows 7, you must also configure your VPN server running Windows Server 2008 R2 to support this configuration. To do this, follow these steps on the server:

1. Open the Properties dialog box of the VPN server in the RRAS console.
2. Select the Security tab and click Authentication Methods.
3. Select the check box labeled Allow Machine Certificate Authentication Using IKEv2.

CONFIGURING MOBILITY FOR IKEv2 CONNECTIONS

When you force a connection to use IKEv2 as its tunnel type, you also have a choice of enabling or disabling mobility (VPN Reconnect) for the VPN connection. To enable mobility for the connection, click Advanced Settings and make sure the check box is selected (see Figure 27-7). To disable mobility for the connection, clear the check box. The default setting for an IKEv2 connection is for mobility to be enabled.

You can also use this dialog box to configure the maximum allowed network outage time for the VPN connection, which can range from 5 minutes to 8 hours (the default is 30 minutes). If the underlying Layer 2 network connectivity is interrupted and not restored within the configured network outage time, the VPN connection will be terminated (that is, mobility will fail).

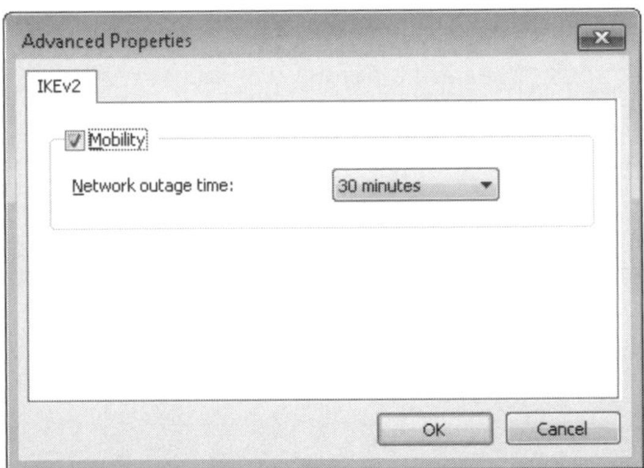

FIGURE 27-7 Configure mobility for IKEv2 VPN connections.

Additional mobility settings for IKEv2 VPN connections can be configured on the server side. To see these settings, begin by opening Routing And Remote Access from Administrative Tools on a VPN server running Windows Server 2008 R2. Then right-click the VPN server node and select Properties, select the IKEv2 tab, and configure the settings on this tab as shown in Table 27-4.

TABLE 27-4 Server-Side Settings for Configuring IKEv2 Mobility

SETTING	EXPLANATION	DEFAULT
Idle Time-out (Minutes)	The time (in minutes) that an IKEv2 client connection can be idle before it is terminated.	5 minutes
Network Outage Time (Minutes)	The time (in minutes) that IKEv2 packets are retransmitted without a response before the connection is considered lost. Higher values support connection persistence through network outages.	30 minutes

SETTING	EXPLANATION	DEFAULT
SA Expiration Time (Minutes)	The time (in minutes) after which an IKEv2 client SA expires. An SA expires either at the expiration time or when the SA data size limit is reached, whichever occurs first; a new quick mode negotiation must succeed before the two computers can continue to exchange data.	480 minutes
SA Data Size Limit (MB)	The amount of network traffic (in megabytes) that can be sent through an IKEv2 SA before the SA expires; a new quick mode negotiation must succeed before the two computers can continue to exchange data.	100 MB

In Windows 7 and Windows Server 2008 R2, you can also configure IKEv2 settings (including mobility settings) from the command line by using the Netsh command. The following examples show some of the *netsh ras set* commands that are available for configuring IKEv2 mobility.

```
netsh ras set ikev2connection [[idletimeout=] <idle_timeout>] [[nwoutagetime=]
<nw_outage_time>]
```

This command sets the idle time-out and network outage time values for IKEv2 client connections by using the following parameters:

- **idletimeout** Specifies the idle time-out in minutes for IKEv2 client connections. This value is used to disconnect IKEv2 connections in case the client machine is idle.
- **nwoutagetime** Specifies the network outage time value in minutes for IKEv2 client connections.

```
netsh ras set ikev2saexpiry [[saexpirytime=] <sa_expiry_time>] [[sadatasizelimit=]
<sa_datasize_limit>]
```

This command sets the IKEv2 SA expiration controls by using the following parameters:

- **saexpirytime** Specifies the SA expiry value in minutes for IKEv2 client connections.
- **sadatasizelimit** Specifies the SA data size limit in megabytes.

The next examples show commands for reviewing IKEv2 connections.

- **netsh ras show ikev2connections** This command shows the idle time-out and network outage time values for IKEv2 client connections.
- **netsh ras show ikev2saexpirycontrols** This command shows the IKEv2 SA expiration controls, specifically the SA expiry value in minutes for IKEv2 client connections and the SA datasize limit in megabytes.

- **netsh ras show portstatus** This command displays the IKEv2 port status as well as the status for L2TP, PPTP, and SSTP ports. By default, this command shows all ports, but it can also show settings for individual ports or ports in a particular status.
- **netsh ras dump** This command exports the configuration script for all supported RAS features, including (in Windows 7 and Windows Server 2008 R2) the IKEv2 configuration details.

DIRECT FROM THE SOURCE

The Three States of an IKEv2-based VPN Connection

CSS Global Technical Readiness (GTR) Team

Because of VPN Reconnect, an IKEv2-based connection can be in one of three possible states:

- **Connected** This state is self explanatory.
- **Dormant: Server Unavailable** When the underlying interface through which IKEv2 is connected to the corporate network goes down or the access point is changing (connectivity is not available).
- **Dormant: Waiting To Reconnect** When the Mobility Manager is trying to switch the connection to the next available interface or access point.

As an example, consider a user is at home connected to the corporate network via an IKEv2-based VPN over a broadband (PPPoE) connection. The user has a disabled wireless network that can also provide Internet connectivity. Here's what typically happens, in order:

1. Initially the VPN connection is connected as shown here in the VAN user interface.

2. The broadband connection becomes disconnected (and the wireless network is still disabled), so the VPN connection goes into a dormant state, as shown here.

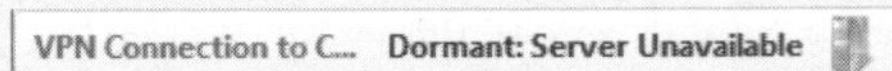

3. The user enables the wireless network, and the Mobility Manager attempts to switch the VPN connection. While the switch over to the wireless network is in progress, the VPN connection shows Dormant: Waiting To Reconnect. (If the reconnection happens fast enough, this mode may not be displayed.)
4. After a successful switchover, the user's VPN connection is reconnected.

Configuring Dial-Up Connections

Windows 7 supports both outgoing and incoming dial-up connections. For outgoing connections, Windows 7 is the client and connects to either a remote access server (RAS server) on a remote network (usually the corporate intranet) or a network access device (typically a modem bank) at an ISP. For incoming connections, Windows 7 acts as a mini-RAS server and allows a remote client computer to establish a dial-up connection between the two computers. Some enterprise environments still use RAS servers to provide mobile users with remote connectivity to the corporate network, but most enterprises now use VPN servers instead to save on long-distance telephone costs and the cost of maintaining multiple phone lines for RAS access. This section deals briefly with how to set up a dial-up connection to enable clients running Windows 7 to connect directly to a RAS server.

> ***NOTE*** **Incoming dial-up connections to client computers are rarely used in enterprise environments, so most of this discussion deals with outbound connections only. For information on how to create and configure an inbound connection on Windows 7, see the section titled "Configuring Incoming Connections" later in this chapter.**

Creating a Dial-Up Connection

To create a new dial-up connection to a server at your workplace, perform the following steps:

1. Open Network And Sharing Center, either from Control Panel or by clicking the networking icon in the system notification area and then clicking Open Network And Sharing Center.
2. After Network And Sharing Center is displayed, click Set Up A New Connection Or Network to start the Set Up A New Connection Or Network wizard.
3. On the Choose A Connection Option page, select Connect To A Workplace and then click Next.
4. If this is the first connection you have created on the computer, proceed to step 5. Otherwise, select No, Create A New Connection and then click Next.
5. Click Dial Directly and specify a telephone number for the RAS server to which you want to connect, as shown here. (You can also give the connection a descriptive name to distinguish it from other connections on the computer. Typically, this will be the name of your remote network or RAS server.)

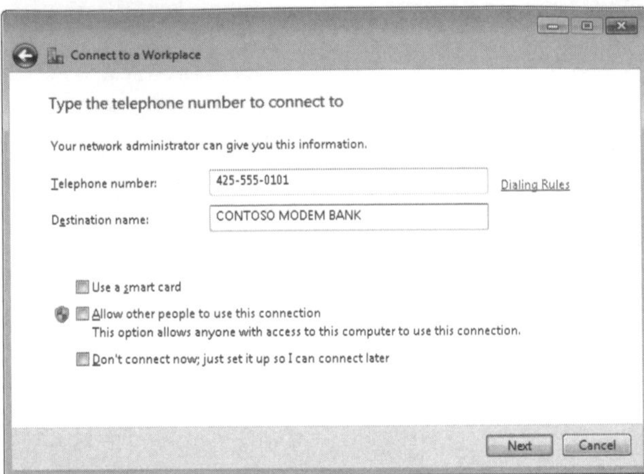

6. If dialing rules have not been configured for your computer, click Dialing Rules and then configure them as required.
7. To use a smart card for authentication, select Use A Smart Card. You must have a smart card reader installed on the computer to use this option. If you select this option, proceed to step 11.
8. To allow other users of the computer to use the connection, select Allow Other People To Use This Connection. Selecting this option requires that you have local administrative credentials for the computer so that you can respond to the User Account Control (UAC) prompt that appears.
9. To create a new connection that needs further configuration before you can use it, select Don't Connect Now; Just Set It Up So I Can Connect Later.
10. Click Next and specify the credentials (user name, password, and optionally the domain) you will use to be authenticated by the RAS server. (This option is available only if you left the option to Use A Smart Card cleared earlier in the wizard.)
11. If you chose to create a connection that needs further configuring before being used, click Create and then either click Close to create the connection or click Connect Now to initiate the connection.

NOTE **Administrators can also use the new version of the CMAK included with Windows Server 2008 R2 to tailor the appearance and behavior of connections made using Connection Manager, the built-in remote access client dialer included in Windows 7. Using CMAK, administrators can create and deploy custom connections for client computers to simplify the user experience of connecting to remote networks. You must use the new Windows Server 2008 R2 version of CMAK to create and configure connections for clients running Windows 7 because the new CMAK includes multiple-locale support that lets you create Connection Manager profiles on a server of any locale for installation on a client of any other locale.**

Configuring a Dial-Up Connection

Configuring a dial-up connection is similar in many respects to configuring a VPN connection and supports the same authentication and data encryption features as VPN connections. See the section titled "Configuring VPN Connections" earlier in this chapter for more information on VPN connection settings.

The same five tabs are displayed in the Properties dialog box for both dial-up and VPN connections, with the following changes for dial-up connections:

- **General** Select and configure modem (analog or ISDN), specify phone number(s) for RAS server, and enable and configure dialing rules
- **Options** An additional setting to prompt for phone number when connecting
- **Security** Additional settings to optionally display a terminal window and run a connection script
- **Networking** Same options as for VPN connections
- **Sharing** Same options as for VPN connections

> ***NOTE*** **If your computer running Windows 7 has file sharing enabled on it, the File And Printer Sharing For Microsoft Networks option on the Networking tab is enabled on VPN connections but is disabled on dial-up connections.**

Advanced Connection Settings

Configure advanced connection settings for all connections on the computer by following these steps:

1. Open the Network Connections folder from Network And Sharing Center or by clicking Change Adapter Settings in the upper-left side of Network And Sharing Center.
2. Press the Alt key to make the menu bar visible.
3. Select Advanced Settings under the Advanced menu option.
4. Rearrange the order of the network adapters, network bindings, and network providers on the computer as desired.

> ***NOTE*** **You can also open the Network Connections folder by typing Connections in the Search box on the Start menu and clicking View Network Connections in the Control Panel area of the search results. Still another way of opening the Network Connections folder is by typing Ncpa.cpl in the Search box on the Start menu and pressing Enter.**

Configuring Incoming Connections

Windows 7 also supports incoming connections of both the dial-up and the VPN types. In this scenario, Windows 7 is acting as a mini-VPN or RAS server to other client computers on the network.

Creating an incoming connection on a computer running Windows 7 requires administrator credentials on the computer and is supported only in workgroup environments. To create a new incoming connection, follow these steps:

1. Open the Network Connections folder.
2. Press the Alt key to make the menu bar visible.
3. Select New Incoming Connection under the File menu option.
4. Select the users you want to allow to connect to the computer, as shown here. You can also click Add Someone to add additional users to the local user database on the computer.

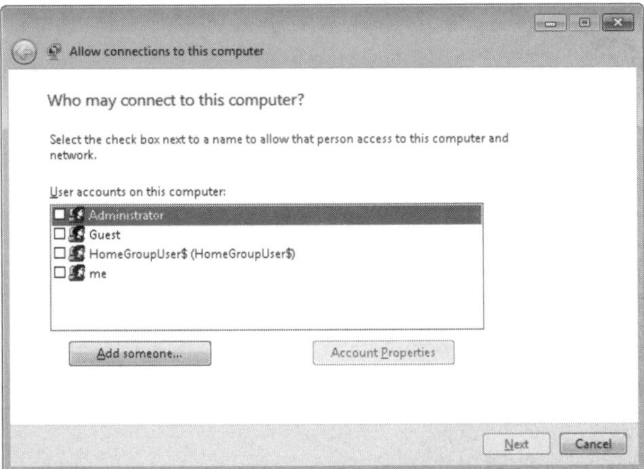

5. Click Next and then specify whether the selected users will connect to the computer through the Internet (using a VPN connection) or directly (using a dial-up modem). For this scenario, we will assume that the VPN option has been selected.
6. Click Next and then specify which networking features to enable for the incoming connection. By default, IPv4 and File And Printer Sharing are enabled, and IPv6 is disabled.
7. Select Internet Protocol Version 4 (TCP/IPv4) and click Properties to configure the following:
   - Whether the calling (connecting) computer can have access to your LAN using your computer as a gateway
   - Whether the calling computer is assigned an IP address for its tunnel endpoint from a DHCP server on the network or is assigned an IP address from a range of addresses that you specify

- Whether the calling computer can specify its own IP address for its tunnel endpoint

8. Click OK and then click Allow Access to enable the incoming connection.
9. The new incoming connection will be displayed in the Network Connections folder. Note that incoming connections are not displayed in the View Available Networks (VAN) UI.
10. To further configure an incoming connection, open the Network Connections folder, right-click the connection, and then select Properties.

> **NOTE** You can also view and configure some properties of incoming connections from the command line by using the Netsh command. For example, to show which users are allowed to connect to the computer, type **netsh ras show user** at a command prompt. For more help, type **netsh ras ?** at a command prompt.

Managing Connections Using Group Policy

In previous Windows platforms, you could use Group Policy to lock down or manage certain aspects of network connections on the computer. The Group Policy settings for doing this are located at:

User Configuration\Policies\Administrative Templates\Network\Network Connections

For example, by enabling the Prohibit Access To The Advanced Settings Item On The Advanced Menu policy setting, you could prevent users from opening Advanced Settings under the Advanced menu option in the Network Connections folder. If you also enable the Enable Windows 2000 Network Connections Settings For Administrators policy setting, even local administrators on the computer would not have access to Advanced Settings.

Beginning with Windows Vista, however, because of UAC and how it is implemented, some of these Group Policy settings are no longer supported. For example:

- If a user is a local administrator on a computer running Windows Vista or later versions, none of the restrictions from these Group Policy settings found under User Configuration\Policies\Administrative Templates\Network\Network Connections applies. Also, the Enable Windows 2000 Network Connections Settings For Administrators policy setting is no longer supported. This policy was used in older Windows platforms to enable Group Policy restrictions for Network Connections to apply to administrators and not just ordinary users.
- If a user is a standard user on a computer running Windows Vista or later versions, some but not all of the Group Policy settings found under User Configuration\Policies \Administrative Templates\Network\Network Connections still apply. The exception is policies for actions that now require administrative privileges to perform them. An

example of this exception is accessing Advanced Settings under the Advanced menu option in the Network Connections folder, which in Windows Vista and later versions requires administrative privileges to perform. As a result, the Prohibit Access To The Advanced Settings Item On The Advanced Menu policy setting in Windows Vista and later versions does not apply to standard users, because they cannot perform this action anyway without administrator credentials; therefore, this Group Policy setting is superfluous. Another example is installing or removing network features for a connection, which requires administrative privileges. As a result, the Prohibit TCP/IP Advanced Configuration policy setting does not apply to standard users because this policy setting is superfluous for them.

Table 27-5 summarizes support for Network Connection user policy settings in Windows Vista and later versions.

TABLE 27-5 Support for Group Policy User Settings for Network Connections for Standard Users in Windows Vista and Later Versions

POLICY SETTING	SUPPORTED IN WINDOWS VISTA AND LATER VERSIONS
Prohibit Adding And Removing Components For A LAN Or Remote Access Connection	
Prohibit Access To The Advanced Settings Item On The Advanced Menu	
Prohibit TCP/IP Advanced Configuration	
Prohibit Enabling/Disabling Components Of A LAN Connection	
Ability To Delete All User Remote Access Connections	
Prohibit Deletion Of Remote Access Connections	✓
Prohibit Access To The Remote Access Preferences Item On The Advanced Menu	✓
Enable Windows 2000 Network Connections Settings For Administrators	
Turn Off Notifications When A Connection Has Only Limited Or No Connectivity	
Prohibit Access To Properties Of Components Of A LAN Connection	
Ability To Enable/Disable A LAN Connection	
Prohibit Access To Properties Of A LAN Connection	✓

POLICY SETTING	SUPPORTED IN WINDOWS VISTA AND LATER VERSIONS
Prohibit Access To The New Connection Wizard	
Ability To Change Properties Of An All-User Remote Access Connection	✓
Prohibit Access To Properties Of Components Of A Remote Access Connection	
Prohibit Connecting And Disconnecting A Remote Access Connection	✓
Prohibit Changing Properties Of A Private Remote Access Connection	✓
Ability To Rename All User Remote Access Connections	
Ability To Rename LAN Connections Or Remote Access Connections Available To All Users	
Ability To Rename LAN Connections	
Prohibit Renaming Private Remote Access Connections	✓
Prohibit Viewing Of Status For An Active Connection	

DIRECT FROM THE SOURCE

Troubleshooting Connections

Samir Jain and Santosh Chandwani, Lead Program Managers
Windows Enterprise Networking

The error codes returned by the built-in remote access client have been improved in Windows Vista and later versions to help you troubleshoot your connections. Table 27-6 describes some common error codes.

TABLE 27-6 Common Error Codes Returned by the Built-In Remote Access Client in Windows Vista and Later Versions

ERROR CODE	CAUSE	RESOLUTION
806	Generic Route Encapsulation (GRE) packets are getting dropped	Look for any firewall between VPN client and server and enable GRE (IP protocol 47) to pass through it.

ERROR CODE	CAUSE	RESOLUTION
812	Policy mismatch between client and server	Check the encryption and authentication settings between the client and server.
741, 742	Encryption type mismatch between client and server	Check the encryption settings between client and server.
807	VPN connection is disconnected after getting established	VPN server reaching capacity or latency has increased and your VPN server is no longer reachable. Troubleshoot server- or connectivity-related problems.
868	The remote connection was not made because the name of the remote access server did not resolve.	Check DNS name resolution, and also check underlying Layer 2 network connectivity.

In Windows Vista and later versions, a failure to connect in a VPN connection will also provide a Diagnose option in addition to the error message describing the cause of failure. When you select the Diagnose option, Windows Network Diagnostics is used to try to diagnose the cause of the VPN connection failure. Note that Windows may not always be able to successfully diagnose the root cause of the problem, given the complexity of Internet architecture and lack of access to the network infrastructure along the path between the VPN client and the VPN server.

In addition to PPP logging, which is still available in Windows Vista and later versions, Netsh-based logging is available, which can assist Microsoft support services in resolving your problem. To use Netsh for diagnosing connection failures, perform the following steps from a command prompt. (Note that Administrator privileges are required to execute the following commands.)

1. Click Start, click All Programs, click Accessories, and then right-click Command Prompt to start an elevated command prompt. Select Run As Administrator and respond to the UAC prompt that appears.
2. Type the command netsh ras set tracing * disable in the elevated command prompt.
3. Delete all files (if any) in the %WinDir%\Tracing folder.
4. Type the command netsh ras set tracing * enable in the elevated command prompt.

5. Reproduce the error condition (for example, launch the VPN connection and click Connect) and wait for failure to happen.
6. Type the command netsh ras set tracing * disable in the elevated command prompt.
7. Put all the files from the %WinDir%\Tracing folder in a compressed (.zip) file and send it to your Microsoft representative for analysis. This tracing will help Microsoft representatives to find a resolution for your problem more quickly.

Using Remote Desktop

Remote Desktop is an extension of Remote Desktop Services, a Windows technology that provides users with the flexibility of working on their computers from anywhere, at any time. Using Remote Desktop, users can run applications on a remote computer running Windows 7 or Windows Server 2008 R2 from any other computer running a supported Windows operating system. Additionally, Remote Desktop can allow administrators to remotely manage both desktop computers and servers as if they were interactively logged on at the local console of these computers.

NOTE In previous versions of Windows, Remote Desktop Services was called Terminal Services. See the section titled "Understanding Remote Desktop Services Terminology" later in this chapter for more information about terminology changes in Windows Server 2008 R2 and Windows 7.

NOTE Remote Desktop is different from Remote Assistance, which is also based on Remote Desktop Services technology. For more information about Remote Assistance, see Chapter 22, "Supporting Users with Remote Assistance."

Understanding Remote Desktop

Remote Desktop consists of the following features:

- Remote Desktop Protocol (RDP)
- Remote Desktop client software—that is, Remote Desktop Connection (RDC)

Understanding Remote Desktop Protocol

Remote Desktop Protocol (RDP) is a protocol that transmits keyboard input, mouse input, and display output information between a remote computer and a host computer—that is, a Remote Desktop Session Host or a computer running Windows that has Remote Desktop enabled (see Figure 27-8). The network connection between the computers can be any TCP/IP network connection, including LAN, WAN, VPN, or dial-up.

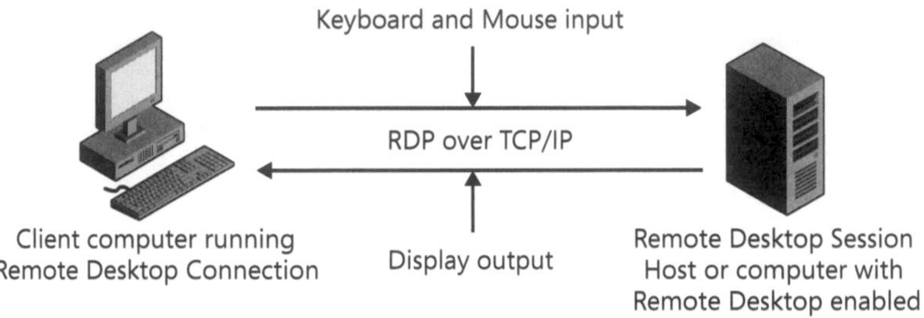

FIGURE 27-8 How RDP works

In addition to transmitting keyboard and mouse input and display output between the two computers, RDP also enables the local computer (the computer running Remote Desktop client software) to access various resources on the remote computer (a Remote Desktop Session Host or a computer running Windows with Remote Desktop enabled) by redirecting these resources to the local computer. These resources can include disks, printers, serial ports, smart cards, audio sources, and Plug and Play (PnP) devices. RDP also enables the computers to share a clipboard, allowing the interchange of data between applications running on the two computers.

VERSIONS OF RDP

RDP has evolved through several versions since it was first introduced in Windows NT Server 4.0, Terminal Server Edition. Table 27-7 summarizes the different versions of the protocol used by each version of Windows.

TABLE 27-7 Versions of RDP

WINDOWS VERSION	RDP VERSION
Windows NT 4.0	4.0
Windows 2000	5.0
Windows XP and Windows Server 2003	5.1
Windows XP SP2 and Windows Server 2003 SP1	5.2
Windows Vista RTM	6.0
Windows Vista SP1 and Windows Server 2008	6.1
Windows 7 and Windows Server 2008 R2	7.0

RDP 6.1 FEATURES AND ENHANCEMENTS

RDP was previously enhanced in Windows Vista RTM and again in Windows Vista SP1 to provide more robust remote access capabilities for users in enterprise environments. Additional services were also added on the server side in Windows Server 2008 to provide new capabilities for remote clients. See the section titled "Understanding Remote Desktop Services Terminology" later in this chapter for more information about these services.

On the Windows Vista SP1 and Windows Server 2008 platforms, RDP 6.1 provided the following features and enhancements:

- **PnP device redirection for media players and digital cameras** Users can redirect supported Windows Portable Devices, such as certain media players and digital cameras that use the Media Transfer Protocol (MTP) or Picture Transfer Protocol (PTP). PnP device redirection over cascaded Remote Desktop connections is not supported, however.
- **Windows Embedded for Point of Service device redirection** Users can redirect Windows Embedded for Point of Service devices that use Microsoft Point of Service (POS) for .NET 1.1, a class library that provides Microsoft .NET Framework applications with an interface for communicating with POS peripheral devices from Windows Server 2008 Remote Desktop Session Hosts. You can download Microsoft POS for .NET 1.1 from the Microsoft Download Center at *http://www.microsoft.com/downloads/details.aspx?FamilyID=6025b728-ec06-48f9-bc80-c38b2a27a242&displaylang=en*. It requires the .NET Framework Redistributable Package version 1.1 or higher.
- **Custom display ratios and resolutions** Users can customize RDC to support monitors with resolution as high as 4096 × 2048 with display resolution ratios as large as 16:9 or 16:10. The previous version RDP 5.2 supports only a 4:3 display resolution ratio at a maximum resolution of 1600 × 1050.
- **Multiple monitor spanning** Users can span multiple monitors placed together to form a single, large desktop that can enhance productivity. Monitors must use the same resolution and can be spanned only side by side, not vertically. The maximum resolution across all spanned monitors cannot exceed 4096 × 2048. Repositioning of dialog boxes is not supported, including the Winlogon dialog box.
- **Desktop Experience** By installing the Desktop Experience feature on a Windows Server 2008 R2 Remote Desktop Session Host, users of remote computers can use Windows Vista features such as new desktop themes and Windows Media Player 11, within a Remote Desktop session.
- **Desktop composition and font smoothing** Lets users use desktop composition and ClearType font smoothing within a Remote Desktop session to enhance readability on liquid crystal display (LCD) monitors.
- **Display data prioritization** Users can customize RDC to prioritize keyboard, mouse, and display traffic so that the Remote Desktop experience is not adversely affected when bandwidth-intensive tasks are being performed on the remote computer, such as

copying large files or submitting large print jobs. For more information, see the section titled "Improving Remote Desktop Performance" later in this chapter.

- **Network Level Authentication Support** Users can configure Remote Desktop to enable a connection from only clients that support Network Level Authentication. With Network Level Authentication, the user/client and server can negotiate a secure channel for exchanging data prior to allocating resources for sessions.
- **Server authentication** Allows users to verify that their RDC client is connecting to the correct remote computer or Remote Desktop Session Host. This provides increased security and protection of confidential information by ensuring that you are connecting to the computer to which you intend to connect.

RDP 7.0 NEW FEATURES AND ENHANCEMENTS

Beginning with Windows 7 and Windows Server 2008 R2, additional features have been added to RDP to provide improved performance in certain scenarios and an enhanced user experience within a Remote Desktop session. The improvements made in RDP 7.0 include the following:

- **Audio and video playback redirection** RDP can now redirect audio and video content from the Remote Desktop Session Host to the client computer in its original format and render it using the client computer's resources.
- **Improved multiple monitor support** RDP now supports using up to 10 monitors simultaneously on the client computer.
- **Audio recording redirection** RDP can now redirect audio recording devices such as microphones from the client computer to the Remote Desktop session, which can be useful for Voice over IP (VoIP) and speech recognition scenarios.
- **Desktop composition** RDP now fully supports Windows Aero within a remote desktop session.
- **DirectX redirection** Applications that use DirectX versions 9 and 10 are rendered on the Remote Desktop Session Host and have their graphic output redirected to the client computer as bitmap images.
- **Language bar redirection** RDP lets users use the language bar on the client computer to control language settings for RemoteApp programs.

> ***NOTE*** **Desktop Connection is not supported on a Remote Desktop session that uses multiple monitors.**

REMOTEAPP AND DESKTOP CONNECTION

Another enhancement in Windows 7 is RemoteApp and Desktop Connection, which allows a user to access programs and desktops (remote computers and virtual computers) published for the user by the workplace network administrator using Windows Server 2008 R2 Remote

Desktop Services. Windows Server 2008 introduced RemoteApp programs, which are programs that are accessed remotely through Remote Desktop Services and appear as if they are running locally on the user's client computer. Remote Desktop Services in Windows Server 2008 R2 has been enhanced to provide administrators with the ability to group RemoteApp programs and virtual desktops and make them available on the Start menu of users whose computers are running Windows 7. This new feature is called RemoteApp and Desktop Connection.

In Windows 7 and Windows Server 2008 R2, users can configure a RemoteApp and Desktop Connection by using the RemoteApp and Desktop Connections item in Control Panel. After a RemoteApp and Desktop Connection has been configured, RemoteApp programs and virtual desktops that are part of this connection are available to users in the Start menu on their computers. Any changes made to the RemoteApp and Desktop Connection, such as adding or removing RemoteApp programs or virtual desktops, are automatically updated on the client and in the Start menu. Users can also use the new RemoteApp and Desktop Connection system tray icon to identify when they are connected to a RemoteApp and Desktop Connection. They can also use this system tray icon to disconnect from a RemoteApp and Desktop Connection if the connection is no longer needed.

For more information on RemoteApp and Desktop Connection, see the section titled "Configuring and Using RemoteApp and Desktop Connection" later in this chapter.

NOTE **Users can also connect to a RemoteApp and Desktop Connection using a Web browser by signing in to the Web site provided by Remote Desktop Web Access. In this case, the user's client computer does not need to be running Windows 7.**

Understanding RDC

Previously known as Terminal Services Client or TS Client, RDC is a client application that runs on a computer that enables the computer to establish a Remote Desktop session with either a Remote Desktop Session Host or a computer running Windows that has Remote Desktop enabled. The RDC client is a feature that is installed by default and can be accessed either from the Start menu or by running Mstsc.exe.

In typical usage, a user at a remote location must connect to a private network before she can start a Remote Desktop session with a computer within the private network—typically by using a VPN connection to the target computer. When end-to-end network connectivity has been established between the user's computer and the host computer, the user can use the RDC client to open a Remote Desktop session that will provide an experience comparable to being interactively logged on at the local console of the host computer (depending on the available bandwidth of the network connection).

For more information on configuring and using the RDC client, see the section titled "Configuring and Deploying Remote Desktop Connection" later in this chapter.

> **NOTE** Newer versions of RDC have also been backported to earlier Windows platforms. For example, the RDC 6.1 client, which supports RDP 6.1, has been backported to Windows XP SP2. You can download selected versions of RDC for older Windows versions by searching for "Remote Desktop Connection" on the Microsoft Download Center at *http://www.microsoft.com/downloads/*.

Understanding Remote Desktop Services Terminology

Beginning with Windows 7 and Windows Server 2008 R2, Terminal Services has been renamed Remote Desktop Services, and the various Terminal Services role services have been renamed as well. Table 27-8 summarizes the old and new names for these different role services.

TABLE 27-8 New Names for Role Services

OLD NAME	NEW NAME
Terminal Services	Remote Desktop Services
Terminal Server	Remote Desktop Session Host
Terminal Services Licensing (TS Licensing)	Remote Desktop Licensing (RD Licensing)
Terminal Services Gateway (TS Gateway)	Remote Desktop Gateway (RD Gateway)
Terminal Services Session Broker (TS Session Broker)	Remote Desktop Connection Broker (RD Connection Broker)
Terminal Services Web Access (TS Web Access)	Remote Desktop Web Access (RD Web Access)

> **MORE INFO** For detailed information on what each of these role services can be used for and how they can enhance a remote user's experience and make them more productive, see the "Windows Server 2008 Terminal Services Resource Kit" from Microsoft Press at *http://www.microsoft.com/learning/en/us/Books/12716.aspx*.

Configuring and Using Remote Desktop

To configure and use the Remote Desktop feature to establish a Remote Desktop session with another computer, complete the following steps:

1. Enable Remote Desktop on the remote (host) computer.
2. Authorize users to access the host computer.

3. Configure Remote Desktop client software on the local (client) computer.
4. Establish network connectivity between the client and host computers.
5. Establish the Remote Desktop session from the client to the host.

The following sections describe these steps in detail.

Enabling Remote Desktop and Authorizing Users on a Single Computer

By default, Remote Desktop is not enabled on host computers running Windows 7. To enable Remote Desktop on a single host computer, follow these steps:

1. Click Start, right-click Computer, and then click Properties.
2. Click the Remote Settings link to open the Remote tab of System Properties.
3. Choose either the second or third option under Remote Desktop, as shown here.

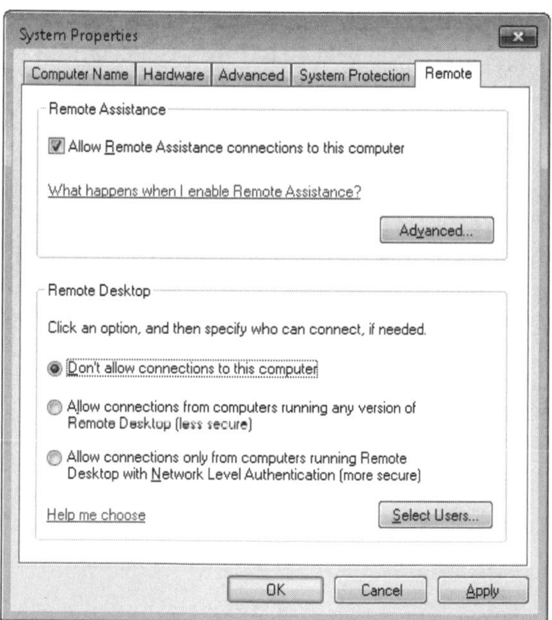

NOTE **Enabling Remote Desktop on a computer requires administrative credentials because inbound rules must be enabled in Windows Firewall to allow the host computer to listen for incoming connection attempts from RDC clients over TCP port 3389. You can change the port that RDC uses by modifying the HKLM\System\CurrentControlSet\Control \TerminalServer\WinStations\RDP-Tcp registry value, but if you do this, you must create and enable an inbound firewall rule on the host computer to allow it to listen for incoming RDP traffic. You also have to configure the RDP client to use the changed port. For more information about configuring Windows Firewall, see Chapter 26.**

The two options for enabling Remote Desktop are:

- **Allow Connections From Computers Running Any Version Of Remote Desktop (Less Secure)** Choosing this option enables computers running a previous version of Windows to use a version of RDP earlier than 6.0 to connect to the host computer.
- **Allow Connections Only From Computers Running Remote Desktop With Network Level Authentication (More Secure)** Choosing this option only allows RDP connections from client computers running Windows Vista or later versions. (Computers running Windows XP SP2 or Windows Server 2003 SP1 that have version 6.0 of RDC installed can also connect when this option is selected.)

In previous versions of Windows, Remote Desktop authenticated users late in the connection sequence after the Remote Desktop session had started and Winlogon came up in the session. As a result, Remote Desktop sessions were susceptible to spoofing and man-in-the-middle attacks. With the new Network Level Authentication in RDP 6.0, however, the client and host computers negotiate a mutually authenticated, secure channel for exchanging data using the Security Service Provider Interface (SSPI). In an AD DS environment, by default this mutual authentication is performed using the Kerberos v5 protocol and TLS 1.0.

If you try to establish a Remote Desktop session from a client computer running Windows 7 to a host computer running a version of Windows that supports only a version of RDP earlier than 6.0, the dialog box shown in Figure 27-9 will be displayed, warning that the identity of the host computer cannot be verified. When the client computer running Windows connects to the host computer and establishes a Remote Desktop session, the absence of the lock icon indicates that Network Level Authentication has not been used to mutually authenticate the client and host computers.

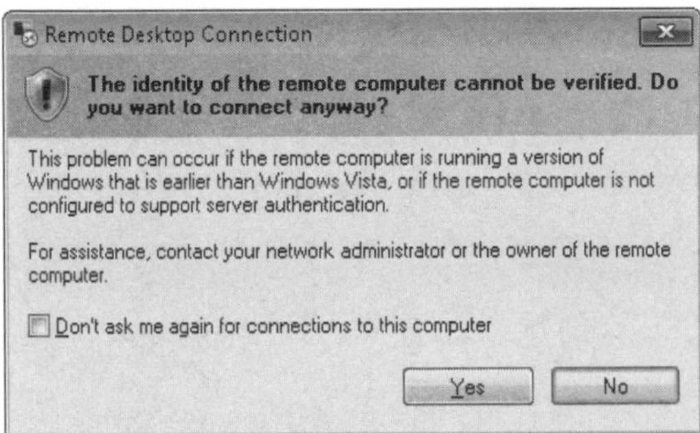

FIGURE 27-9 The identity of a host computer on which an earlier version of Remote Desktop has been enabled cannot be verified.

> ***NOTE*** **The authentication response displayed while attempting to establish a Remote Desktop session depends on the configuration of the RDC client. For more information, see Table 27-9 later in this chapter.**

When enabling Remote Desktop on a computer, you must also authorize which users will be allowed to remotely connect to that computer using RDC. By default, only administrators are authorized to remotely connect to the host computer. Authorize additional users by following these steps:

1. Click the Select Users button to open the Remote Desktop Users dialog box.
2. Click Add and then either specify or find user accounts in AD DS (or on the local computer on stand-alone host computers) and add them to the list of Remote Desktop Users authorized to access the host computer using Remote Desktop. This adds the selected users to the Remote Desktop Users local group on the host computer.

Enabling Remote Desktop Using Group Policy

You can also use Group Policy to enable Remote Desktop on host computers. To enable Remote Desktop on all computers in a specified organizational unit (OU), open the Group Policy object (GPO) linked to the OU using Group Policy Object Editor, enable the following policy setting and add users to the Remote Desktop Users group:

Computer Configuration\Policies\Administrative Templates\Windows Components \Remote Desktop Services\Remote Desktop Session Host\Connections\Allow Users To Connect Remotely Using Remote Desktop Services

Enabling Remote Desktop on computers using Group Policy also enables the Allow Connections From Computers Running Any Version Of Remote Desktop (Less Secure) option on the computers targeted by the GPO. To enable Remote Desktop using the Allow Connections Only From Computers Running Remote Desktop With Network Level Authentication (More Secure) option instead, you must enable the following policy setting in addition to the preceding one:

Computer Configuration\Policies\Administrative Templates\Windows Components \Remote Desktop Services\Remote Desktop Session Host\Security\Require User Authentication For Remote Connections By Using Network Level Authentication

NOTE By default, when the first policy setting is enabled but the second setting is not configured, local administrators on the targeted computers have the ability to change the Remote Desktop security level on their computers to Allow Connections Only From Computers Running Remote Desktop With Network Level Authentication (More Secure) if desired. When the second policy setting is enabled, the option Allow Connections From Computers Running Any Version Of Remote Desktop (Less Secure) on the Remote tab is unavailable and appears dimmed.

Configuring and Deploying Remote Desktop Connection

After you have enabled Remote Desktop on the host computer, you must configure the RDC client software on the client computer. You can configure RDC in several ways:

- Click Start, click All Programs, click Accessories, and then click Remote Desktop Connection. This opens the Remote Desktop Connection UI, shown in Figure 27-10.
- Type **mstsc** at a command prompt or in the Search box to open the Remote Desktop Connection UI, or type **mstsc** followed by various parameters to customize how the RDC client software will run. For help with Mstsc.exe parameters, type **mstsc /?** at a command prompt.
- Use Notepad to manually edit an *.rdp file previously saved from the Remote Desktop Connection UI. For more information, read the section titled "Configuring Remote Desktop Connection Using Notepad" later in this chapter.
- Configure those Remote Desktop Services Group Policy settings that apply to Remote Desktop.

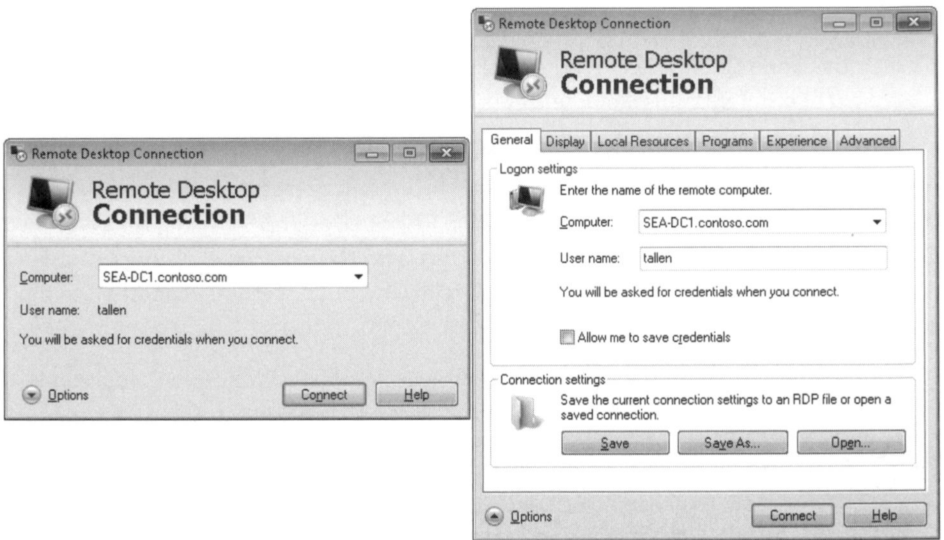

FIGURE 27-10 The Remote Desktop Connection client UI shows configuration options both hidden and displayed.

Table 27-9 summarizes the configuration options available on the different tabs of the Remote Desktop Connection client UI.

TABLE 27-9 Configuration Options for Remote Desktop Connection Client

TAB	SETTING	NOTES
General	Logon Settings: Computer	Specifies the FQDN or IP address (can be IPv4 or IPv6) of the host computer.
	Logon Settings: User Name	Specifies the user account to be used to establish the Remote Desktop session. This is displayed only when credentials from previous Remote Desktop sessions have been saved.
	Logon Settings: Always Ask For Credentials	Select this check box to require the user to always supply credentials. This is displayed only when credentials from previous Remote Desktop sessions have been saved.
	Connection Settings	Saves the current configuration of RDC client as an *.rdp file or opens a previously saved *.rdp file.
Display	Display Configuration	Changes the size of your remote desktop.
	Use All My Monitors For The Remote Session	Configures the Remote Desktop session monitor layout to match the current client-side configuration.
	Colors	Specifies color depth for your remote desktop.
	Display The Connection Bar When In Full-Screen Mode	Makes it easier to use Remote Desktop in full-screen mode without needing to remember keyboard shortcuts.
Local Resources	Remote Audio	Controls where remote audio is played back and whether it should be recorded.
	Keyboard	Specifies how Windows key combinations, such as Alt+Tab, behave when used from within a Remote Desktop session.
	Local Devices And Resources: Printers	Prints to network computers connected to the host computer from within the Remote Desktop session without having to install additional drivers.
	Local Devices And Resources: Clipboard	Shares a clipboard between the client and host computers.
	Local Devices And Resources: More	Redirects additional devices local to the host computer to the remote client including serial ports, smart cards, disk drives, and supported PnP devices such as media players and digital cameras.

TAB	SETTING	NOTES
Programs	Start A Program	Specifies a program that should automatically start when your Remote Desktop session is established.
Experience	Performance: Choose Your Connection Speed To Optimize Performance	Specifies the connection speed closest to actual available network bandwidth to obtain the optimal mix of functionality and performance for your Remote Desktop session.
	Desktop Background Font Smoothing Desktop Composition Show Window Contents While Dragging Menu And Window Animation Visual Styles Persistent Bitmap Caching	Enables or disables each desktop user interface feature that is indicated.
	Reconnect If Connection Is Dropped	Specifies that the RDC client should attempt to re-establish a connection with the remote host if the connection between them is unexpectedly terminated.
Advanced	Server Authentication: Authentication Options	Specifies whether unauthenticated Remote Desktop sessions should be allowed; if they are allowed, specify whether a warning message should be displayed. For more information, see the sidebar titled "Remote Desktop Connection Server Authentication" later in this chapter.
	Connect From Anywhere: Settings	Configures Remote Desktop Gateway (RD Gateway) settings to allow RDC clients to connect to remote computers behind corporate firewalls.

NOTE In enterprise environments, administrators can also preconfigure RDC client configurations and save them as Remote Desktop files (*.rdp files). These *.rdp files can then be deployed to users as e-mail attachments or copied from a network share using a logon script.

Remote Desktop Connection Server Authentication

RDC includes a Server Authentication setting that ensures that you are connecting to the remote computer or server that you intend to connect to. To configure Server Authentication for an RDC, open the Properties dialog box of your connection, click the Advanced tab, and click Settings. Then select one of the following three options:

- **Connect And Don't Warn Me (Least Secure)** Lets you connect even if RDC can't verify the identity of the remote computer.
- **Warn Me (More Secure)** Lets you choose whether to continue with the connection when RDC can't verify the identity of the remote computer.
- **Do Not Connect (Most Secure)** Prevents you from connecting to the remote computer when RDC can't verify the remote computer's identity.

The default setting for Server Authentication is Warn Me.

Configuring Remote Desktop Connection from the Command Line

To use the RDC client from the command line or custom shortcut, type **mstsc** followed by the appropriate command-line switches. For example, to initiate a Remote Desktop session using a custom display resolution of 1680 × 1050, type **mstsc /w:1680 /h:1050** at a command prompt.

You can use the */span* switch to initiate a Remote Desktop session that spans across multiple monitors. Note that when both the */span* and */h: /w:* switches are present, the */span* switch takes precedence. In addition, when the */span* option is selected, the slider for adjusting remote desktop size is unavailable on the Display tab so that users cannot change their initial settings, which can cause confusion.

New in Windows 7 is the */multimon* switch, which configures the Remote Desktop session monitor layout to match the current client-side configuration.

Using the */public* switch runs Remote Desktop in public mode. When an RDC client is running in public mode, it does not persist any private user data (such as user name, password, domain, and so on) either to disk or to the registry on the computer on which the client is running, nor does the client make use of any saved private data that may exist on the computer (a trusted sites list, the persistent bitmap cache, and so on). This means that the client essentially functions as if there were no registry or secondary storage present for storing private data. A client running in public mode still honors Group Policy settings, however. Finally, the */console* switch used in previous versions of Mstsc.exe was removed in Windows Vista SP1 and has been replaced with the */admin* switch. For more information about this, see the following sidebar, titled "Direct from the Source: Replacement of */console* by */admin*."

NOTE For more help with Mstsc.exe parameters, type **mstsc /?** at a command prompt.

DIRECT FROM THE SOURCE

Replacement of */console* by */admin*

Mahesh Lotlikar, SDE II
Remote Desktop Services Team

In Windows Server 2003, the */console* option for Mstsc.exe was used for several purposes. With the introduction of the */admin* option in Windows Vista SP1 and Windows Server 2008, the */console* option has now been deprecated. The following examples illustrate the */console* switch's significance in previous versions of Windows and why the scenario does not apply for Windows 7, Windows Vista SP1 or later versions, Windows Server 2008, and Windows Server 2008 R2.

First, in earlier versions of Windows such as Windows XP and Windows Server 2003, the */console* option was used to connect to the session on the physical console (session 0), because some applications could not install and run in any session other than session 0. In Windows Vista and Windows Server 2008, the Windows features are re-architected, so that only services run in session 0 and applications do not need to run in session 0. Therefore, the administrator does not need the */console* option for this purpose.

Second, in earlier versions of Windows, the */console* option was also used for the purpose of reconnecting to and resuming work in the user session on the physical console. In Windows Vista and Windows Server 2008, this option is not required to reconnect to the existing session on the physical console. (The blog post referenced at the end of this sidebar includes details on console behavior differences.)

Third, in Windows Server 2003, the */console* option was used for administering the Remote Desktop Session Host remotely without consuming a client access license (CAL). In Windows Server 2008, */admin* option serves this purpose.

Thus, you do not need the */console* option while connecting to Windows Vista or Windows Server 2008, and you can now use the */admin* switch to connect to the physical console of Windows Vista or Windows Server 2003.

For more information, see the following post on the Remote Desktop Services Team Blog: ***http://blogs.msdn.com/ts/archive/2007/12/17/changes-to-remote-administration-in-windows-server-2008.aspx***.

Configuring Remote Desktop Connection Using Notepad

You can also configure a saved RDC client by opening its *.rdp file in Notepad and editing it. For example, to configure a saved RDC client to use a custom display resolution of 1680 × 1050, change the lines specifying screen resolution to read as follows.

```
desktopwidth:i:1680
desktopheight:i:1050
```

As a second example, to configure a saved RDC client to span a Remote Desktop session across multiple monitors, add or change the following line:

```
span:i:0
```

to

```
span:i:1
```

Configuring Remote Desktop Using Group Policy

You can also use Group Policy to manage some aspects of how Remote Desktop works. You can find the policy settings for managing Remote Desktop in two locations:

- Per-computer policy settings can be found under Computer Configuration\Policies \Administrative Templates\Windows Components\Remote Desktop Services
- Per-user policy settings can be found under User Configuration\Policies\Administrative Templates\Windows Components\Remote Desktop Services

Table 27-10 lists Group Policy settings that affect Remote Desktop. Policies that were introduced earlier in Windows Vista are marked with an asterisk (*), and policies that are new in Windows 7 are marked with two asterisks (**). (Additional policy settings found in these locations apply only to Remote Desktop Session Hosts or only when an RDC client is used to connect to a Remote Desktop Session Host.) If a computer and user policy setting are identical, the computer setting takes precedence if configured.

To use the Group Policy settings in this table, configure them in a GPO linked to an OU where the host computers (the computers that have Remote Desktop enabled) are located. For additional Group Policy settings that affect Remote Desktop, see the section titled "Enabling Remote Desktop Using Group Policy" earlier in this chapter.

> ***NOTE*** **The folder layout of the Group Policy settings for Remote Desktop Services—under Computer Configuration\Policies\Administrative Templates\Windows Components\Remote Desktop Services and User Configuration\Policies\Administrative Templates\Windows Components\Remote Desktop Services—has been reorganized in Windows 7 for ease of discoverability, but the registry keys are still the same. All policy settings common to both Windows Vista and Windows XP, even if located under different folders, will still be applied to all computers in the targeted OU.**

TABLE 27-10 Group Policy Settings That Affect Remote Desktop

FOLDER	POLICY SETTING	NOTES
Remote Desktop Connection Client	Do Not Allow Passwords To Be Saved	Prevents users from saving their credentials in the RDC client. Windows Vista saves the password using Credential Manager instead of saving it within the *.rdp file as in earlier versions of Windows.
Remote Desktop Session Host\Connections	Automatic Reconnection	Enables RDC clients to attempt to automatically reconnect when underlying network connectivity is lost.
	Allow Users To Connect Remotely Using Remote Desktop Services	Enables Remote Desktop on the targeted computer.
	Deny Logoff Of An Administrator Logged In To The Console Session	Prevents an administrator on the client computer from bumping an administrator off of the host computer.
Remote Desktop Session Host\Device and Resource Redirection	Allow Audio And Video Playback Redirection	Enables redirection of the remote computer's audio and video output in a Remote Desktop session. (This policy was named Allow Audio Redirection in Windows Vista and earlier versions.)
	Allow Audio Recording Redirection	Enables recording of audio to the remote computer during a Remote Desktop session.
	**Limit Audio Playback Quality	Enables limiting of audio quality to improve the performance of a Remote Desktop session over a slow link.
	Do Not Allow Clipboard Redirection	Prevents sharing of a clipboard.
	Do Not Allow COM Port Redirection	Prevents redirection of serial port devices.
	Do Not Allow Drive Redirection	Prevents redirection of disk drive resources.
	Do Not Allow LPT Port Redirection	Prevents redirection of parallel port devices.
	*Do Not Allow Supported Plug And Play Device Redirection	Prevents redirection of supported PnP media players and digital cameras.

FOLDER	POLICY SETTING	NOTES
	Do Not Allow Smart Card Device Redirection	Prevents redirection of smart card readers.
Remote Desktop Session Host\Printer Redirection	Do Not Set Default Client Printer To Be Default Printer In A Session	Prevents users from redirecting print jobs from the remote computer to a printer attached to their local (client) computer.
	Do Not Allow Client Printer Redirection	Prevents the client default printer from automatically being set as the default printer for the Remote Desktop session.
Remote Desktop Session Host\Remote Session Environment	Limit Maximum Color Depth	Enables specifying a maximum color depth to improve performance of a Remote Desktop session over a slow link.
	**Limit Maximum Display Resolution	Enables specifying a maximum display resolution to improve performance of a Remote Desktop session over a slow link.
	**Limit Maximum Number Of Monitors	Enables specifying a maximum number of monitors to improve performance of a Remote Desktop session over a slow link.
	**Optimize Visual Experience For Remote Desktop Services Sessions	Enables optimizing the Remote Desktop session for either multimedia or text.
	Enforce Removal Of Remote Desktop Wallpaper	Prevents wallpaper from being displayed in the Remote Desktop session.
	Remove "Disconnect" Option From Shut Down Dialog	Removes the Disconnect button from the Start menu but doesn't prevent the remote user from disconnecting the session using other methods.
Remote Desktop Session Host\Security	Set Client Connection Encryption Level	Specifies the level of encryption used to protect RDP traffic between the client and host computers. The options available are High (128-bit), Low (56-bit), and Client Compatible (highest encryption level supported by the client). When this policy setting is Not Configured, the default encryption level used is Client Compatible.

FOLDER	POLICY SETTING	NOTES
	Always Prompt For Password Upon Connection	Requires remote users to always enter a password to establish a Remote Desktop session with the targeted computer.
	*Require Use Of Specific Security Layer For Remote (RDP) Connections	Specifies whether the client should attempt to authenticate the host computer during establishment of the Remote Desktop session. The options available are: ■ DP, which means that no computer-level authentication is required. ■ SSL (TLS 1.0), which means that the client tries to use Kerberos or certificates to authenticate the host computer; if this fails, the session is not established. ■ Negotiate, which first attempts to authenticate the host using Kerberos or certificates; if this fails, the session is still established. When this policy setting is Not Configured, the default authentication method used is Negotiate.
	*Require User Authentication For Remote Connections By Using Network Level Authentication	Requires client computers to be running Windows Vista or Windows XP SP2 with the downloadable RDC 6.0 client installed. (This policy was named Require User Authentication Using RDP 6.0 For Remote Connections in Windows Vista and earlier versions.)
	*Server Authentication Certificate Template	Lets you specify a certificate template to be used for authenticating the host computer.
Remote Desktop Session Host\Session Time Limits	Terminate Session When Time Limits Are Reached	Forcibly logs the remote user off of the Remote Desktop session when the session time limit has been reached.
	Set Time Limit For Disconnected Sessions	Forcibly logs the remote user off of the Remote Desktop session when the session time limit for disconnected sessions has been reached.

FOLDER	POLICY SETTING	NOTES
	Set Time Limit For Active But Idle Remote Desktop Services Sessions	Specifies a time limit for no activity in Remote Desktop sessions. When the time limit is reached, the session is disconnected, but the remote user is not logged off. If, however, the Terminate Session When Time Limits Are Reached policy is enabled, the user is disconnected and then forcibly logged off.
	Set Time Limit For Active Remote Desktop Services Sessions	Specifies a time limit for Remote Desktop sessions. When the time limit is reached, the session is disconnected, but the remote user is not logged off. If, however, the Terminate Session When Time Limits Are Reached policy is enabled, the user is disconnected and then forcibly logged off.

Establishing a Remote Desktop Session

After the host computer has been configured to enable Remote Desktop for authorized users and the RDP client software has been configured and deployed on the client computer, the user can initiate establishment of a Remote Desktop session with the remote host computer by using one of the following methods:

- Double-click the desired *.rdp file (or a shortcut to this file) and (if required) click Yes. Then specify your credentials for connecting to the host computer (if required).
- Open a command prompt and type **mstsc *rdp_file*,** where *rdp_file* is the name of the desired *.rdp file (specifying the path may be required) and (if required) click Yes. Then specify your credentials for connecting to the host computer, if required.

When a Remote Desktop session has been established, the client can end the session in two ways:

- **By disconnecting** This ends the Remote Desktop experience on the client computer but leaves the session running on the host computer so that the client can reconnect later if desired. Any applications running in the session on the host continue to run until this session is terminated, either by the user on the client (who must reconnect and then log off) or by a user logging on interactively to the host.
- **By logging off** This ends the Remote Desktop experience on the client computer and terminates the session on the host computer as well.

NOTE You can also remotely shut down the host computer to which you are remotely connected, or you can put it into Sleep mode. To do this from within a Remote Desktop session, click the taskbar, press Alt+F4, and then choose the option you want to select. You can also open a command prompt in your Remote Desktop session and type **shutdown -s -t 0** to immediately shut down the host computer or **shutdown -r -t 0** to immediately restart it. (Be sure to save any open files first.)

Improving Remote Desktop Performance

If available network bandwidth between a client computer and the remote host computer is limited, you can improve a Remote Desktop experience by reducing the color depth on the Display tab of the RDC client from its default 32-bit value. You can also selectively disable desktop experiences on the Experience tab to further improve Remote Desktop performance.

If you routinely transfer large files, submit large print jobs, or perform other bandwidth-intensive actions over a Remote Desktop connection, you may be able to improve the performance of a Remote Desktop experience by configuring display data prioritization on the host computer. Display data prioritization is designed to ensure that the screen performance aspect of a Remote Desktop experience is not adversely affected by such bandwidth-intensive actions. Display data prioritization works by automatically controlling virtual channel traffic between the client and host computer by giving display, keyboard, and mouse data higher priority than other forms of traffic.

The default setting for display data prioritization is to allocate 70 percent of available bandwidth for input (keyboard and mouse) and output (display) data. All other traffic, including use of a shared clipboard, file transfers, print jobs, and so on, is allocated by default only 30 percent of the available bandwidth of the network connection.

You can manually configure display data prioritization settings by editing the registry on a host computer running Windows Vista or later versions. The registry entries for display data prioritization are the following values, which are found under HKLM\SYSTEM\CurrentControlSet \Services\TermDD. (If these DWORD values are not present, you can create them.)

- **FlowControlDisable** Set this value to 1 to disable all display data prioritization and handle all requests on a first-in-first-out (FIFO) basis. The default value of this setting is 0.
- **FlowControlDisplayBandwidth** Specify a relative bandwidth priority for display and input data up to an allowed value of 255. The default value of this setting is 70.
- **FlowControlChannelBandwidth** Specify a relative bandwidth priority for all other virtual channels up to an allowed value of 255. The default value of this setting is 30.
- **FlowControlChargePostCompression** Determine whether flow control will calculate bandwidth allocation based on pre-compression bytes (if the value is 0) or post-compression bytes (if the value is 1). The default value for this setting is 0.

By default, the ratio of *FlowControlDisplayBandwidth* to *FlowControlChannelBandwidth* is 70 to 30 or 70:30. This means that 70 percent of available bandwidth is reserved for display and input traffic, and the remaining 30 percent will be used for other types of traffic. If your Remote Desktop experience is being degraded during large file transfers and other bandwidth-intensive activity, you might change *FlowControlDisplayBandwidth* to 85 and *FlowControlChannelBandwidth* to 15, which allocates 85 percent of available bandwidth for display and input traffic while reserving only 15 percent for other traffic.

NOTE **You must reboot your host computer for these registry changes to take effect.**

Troubleshooting Remote Desktop Sessions

If you have trouble establishing a Remote Desktop session with the host computer, do the following:

- Verify that Remote Desktop has been enabled on the host computer.
- Verify that you are using credentials that have been authorized for remotely connecting to the host computer.
- Verify that you have the correct FQDN or IP address of the remote computer.
- Verify network connectivity with the remote computer by using the *ping* command.

If you are missing expected functionality during a Remote Desktop session, do the following:

- Check whether the host computer is running an older version of Windows such as Windows XP Professional Edition or Windows Server 2003.
- Verify that you have the latest version of Remote Desktop Connection client software installed on your computer.
- Verify that Group Policy is not locking down some aspect of Remote Desktop functionality that you expected to experience.

NOTE **For additional troubleshooting guidance, read Chapter 31, "Troubleshooting Network Issues." When working through the troubleshooting processes in this chapter, keep in mind that RDP uses TCP port 3389.**

Configuring and Using RemoteApp and Desktop Connection

RemoteApp and Desktop Connection requires configuration on both the server and client side. On the server side, you need a Windows Server 2008 R2 server that has the Remote Desktop Services role installed together with the following role services:

- Remote Desktop Session Host
- Remote Desktop Web Access
- Remote Desktop Connection Broker

In addition, if you want users on client computers to also be able to connect to virtual machines using RemoteApp and Desktop Connection, you must install the Remote Desktop Virtualization Host role service, which also requires installing the Hyper-V role to the server.

For guidance on configuring RemoteApp and Desktop Connection on the server side, refer to steps 1 and 2 in the "Deploying RemoteApp Programs to the Start Menu by Using RemoteApp and Desktop Connection Step-by-Step Guide" found at *http://technet.microsoft.com/en-us/library/dd772639.aspx*. You will also need to import the SSL certificate for the Remote Desktop Web Access server to your client computers before the users of these computers can use RemoteApp and Desktop Connection. For information on how to import certificates, see step 3 of the above guide.

After you have configured your servers and have installed certificates on your clients, you can configure RemoteApp and Desktop Connection on the client side by following these steps:

1. Open RemoteApp and Desktop Connection from Control Panel.
2. Click Set Up A New Connection With RemoteApp And Desktop Connections to launch the New Connection wizard.
3. Type the URL to the Remote Desktop Web Access server in the Connection URL box:

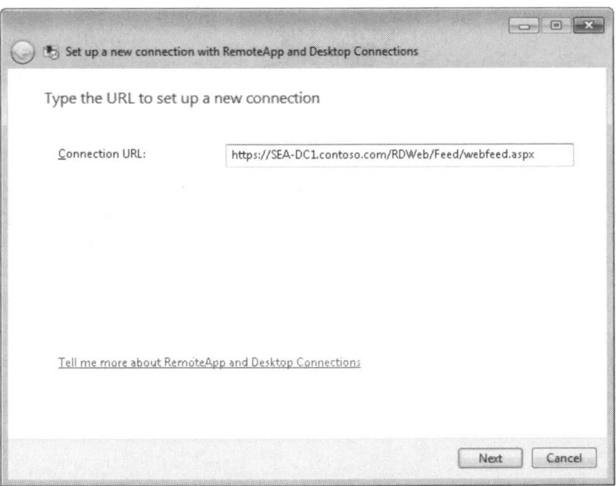

4. Click Next to add connection resources for the RemoteApp And Desktop Connection (be sure to enter your credentials if prompted to do so). When the connection resources have been added, the details of the RemoteApp And Desktop Connection will be displayed.

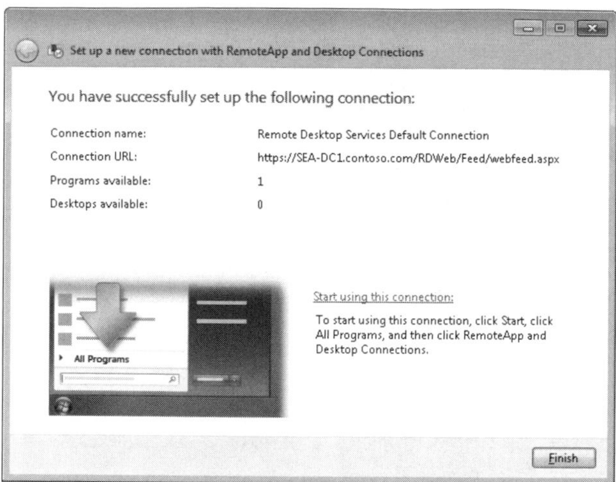

5. Click Finish to complete the wizard.
6. To view all RemoteApp And Desktop Connections that have been added to the client, open RemoteApp And Desktop Connections again from Control Panel.

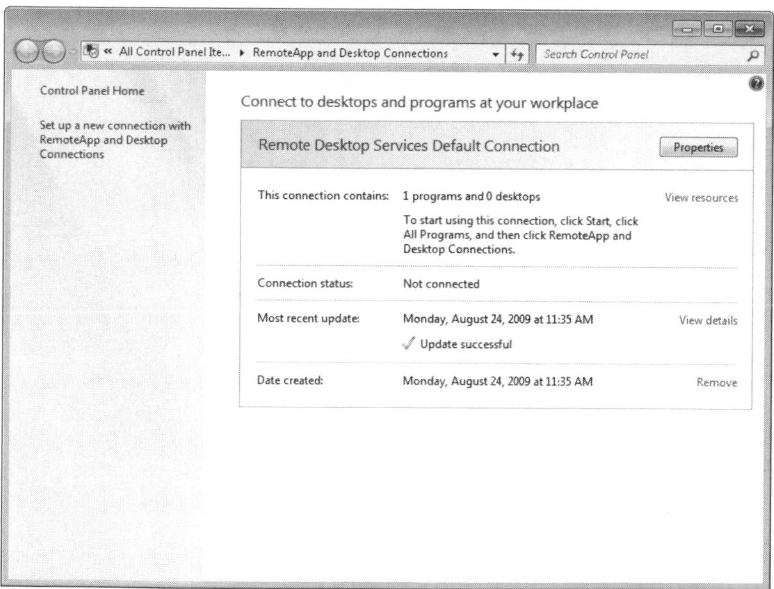

7. You can now access your RemoteApp programs from the RemoteApp and Desktop Connections folder of your Start menu.

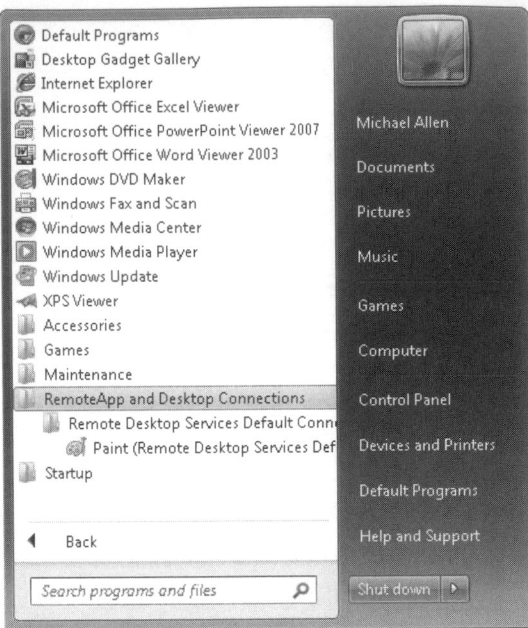

8. You can even access them by searching for them using Start menu search.

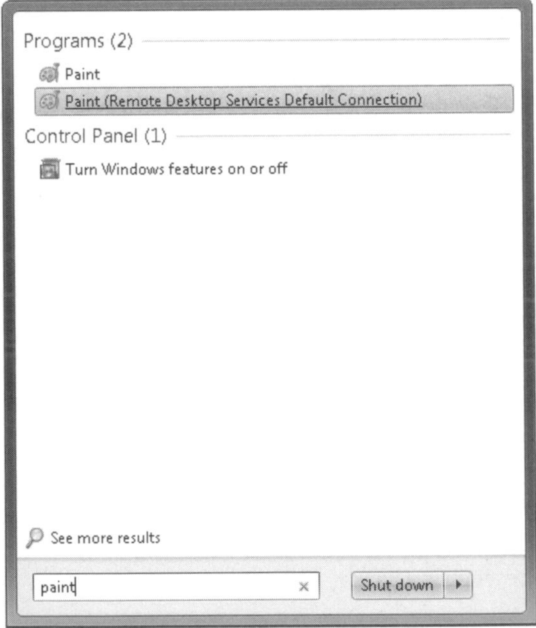

9. When you start a RemoteApp program, a balloon notification above the system tray icon indicates that a RemoteApp program is being used.

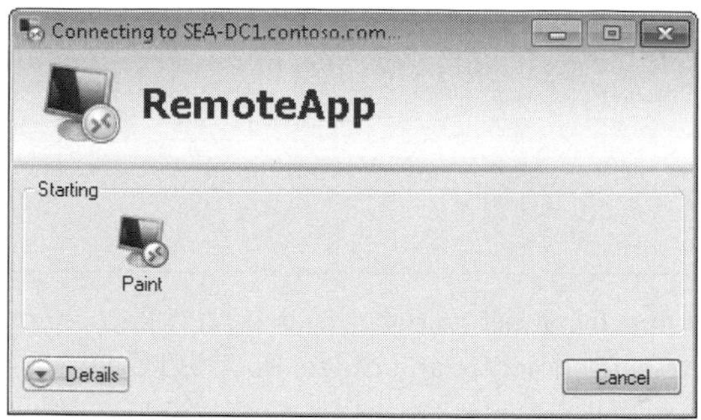

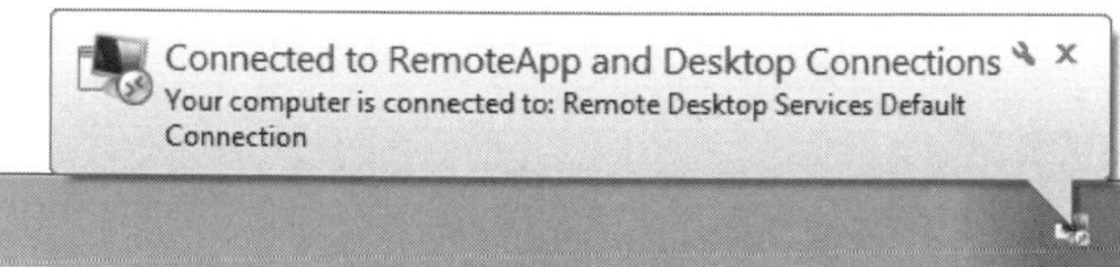

Administrators can create a RemoteApp and Desktop Connection client configuration file (.wcx) and distribute it to users so they can automatically configure the RemoteApp and Desktop Connection. Administrators can also use scripts to run the client configuration file silently on the client so that the RemoteApp and Desktop Connection is set up automatically when the user logs on to her Windows 7 computer.

To create a .wcx configuration file, follow these steps:

1. Open Remote Desktop Connection Manager on your Remote Desktop Connection Broker server.
2. Right-click on the root node in the console tree and select Create Configuration File.
3. In the Create Configuration File dialog box, type the URL to the Remote Desktop Web Access server in the RAD Connection Feed URL box.

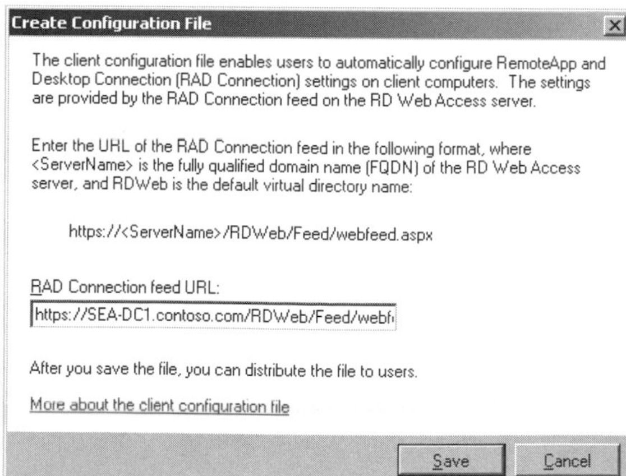

4. Click Save, then distribute the configuration file to users as e-mail attachments, by placing them on a network share, or by using scripts.

For more information on RemoteApp and Desktop Connection, see the Remote Desktop Services section of Microsoft TechNet at *http://technet.microsoft.com/en-us/library/cc770412.aspx*.

Summary

Windows 7 includes new remote connectivity technologies, such as VPN Reconnect, DirectAccess, and BranchCache. These technologies and others, such as Remote Desktop, have been enhanced in Windows 7 to make them more reliable, more secure, and easier to use and manage.

Additional Resources

These resources contain additional information and tools related to this chapter.

Related Information

- General information concerning virtual private networks on Microsoft platforms can be found at *http://technet.microsoft.com/en-us/network/bb545442.aspx*.
- General information concerning DirectAccess can be found at *http://www.microsoft.com/directaccess/*.
- General information concerning BranchCache can be found at *http://technet.microsoft.com/en-us/network/dd425028.aspx*.
- General information concerning Remote Desktop Services in Windows Server 2008 R2 and Windows 7 can be found at *http://technet.microsoft.com/en-us/library/cc770412.aspx*.
- The white paper, "Networking Enhancements for Enterprises," at *http://www.microsoft.com/downloads/details.aspx?FamilyID=38fd1d96-3c6e-43ca-b083-3334ddd1ef86&DisplayLang=en*.
- The Routing and Remote Access Blog can be found at *http://blogs.technet.com/rrasblog/*.
- The Remote Desktop Services Team Blog can be found at *http://blogs.msdn.com/ts/*.
- The white paper, "Step-by-Step Guide: Deploying SSTP Remote Access" can be found at *http://download.microsoft.com/download/b/1/0/b106fc39-936c-4857-a6ea-3fb9d1f37063/Deploying%20SSTP%20Remote%20Access%20Step%20by%20Step%20Guide.doc*.

On the Companion Media

- Get-Modem.ps1

CHAPTER 28

Deploying IPv6

Like the Windows Vista operating system before it, the Windows 7 operating system has a new Next Generation Transmission Control Protocol/Internet Protocol (TCP/IP) stack with enhanced support for Internet Protocol version 6 (IPv6). This chapter provides you with an understanding of why IPv6 is necessary and how it works. The chapter describes the IPv6 capabilities in Windows 7, Windows Vista, and Windows Server 2008 and outlines how to migrate the IPv4 network infrastructure of your enterprise to IPv6 using IPv6 transition technologies, such as Intra-Site Automatic Tunnel Addressing Protocol (ISATAP). Finally, the chapter describes how to configure and manage IPv6 settings in Windows 7 and how to troubleshoot IPv6 networking problems.

Understanding IPv6

The need for migrating enterprise networks from IPv4 to IPv6 is driven by a number of different technological, business, and social factors. The most important of these are:

- The exponential growth of the Internet is rapidly exhausting the existing IPv4 public address space. A temporary solution to this problem has been found in Network Address Translation (NAT), a technology that maps multiple private (intranet) addresses to a (usually) single, public (Internet) address. Unfortunately, using NAT-enabled routers can introduce additional problems, such as breaking end-to-end connectivity and security for some network applications. In addition, the rapid proliferation of mobile IP devices is accelerating the depletion of the IPv4 public address space.

- The growing use of real-time communications (RTC) on the Internet, such as Voice over IP (VoIP) telephony, instant messaging (IM), and audio/video conferencing, exposes the limited support for Quality of Service (QoS) currently provided in IPv4. These new RTC technologies need improved QoS on IP networks to ensure reliable end-to-end communications. The design of IPv4 limits possible improvements.
- The growing threats faced by hosts on IPv4 networks connected to the Internet can be mitigated considerably by deploying Internet Protocol security (IPsec), both on private intranets and on tunneled connections across the public Internet. However, IPsec was designed as an afterthought to IPv4 and is complex and difficult to implement in many scenarios.

IPv6, developed by the Internet Engineering Task Force (IETF) to solve these problems, includes the following improvements and additions:

- IPv6 increases the theoretical address space of the Internet from 4.3×10^{9} addresses (based on 32-bit IPv4 addresses) to 3.4×10^{38} possible addresses (based on 128-bit IPv6 addresses), which most experts agree should be more than sufficient for the foreseeable future.
- The IPv6 address space is designed to be hierarchical rather than flat in structure, which means that routing tables for IPv6 routers can be smaller and more efficient than for IPv4 routers.
- IPv6 has enhanced support for QoS that includes a Traffic Class field in the header to specify how traffic should be handled and a new Flow Label field in the header that enables routers to identify packets that belong to a traffic flow and handle them appropriately.
- IPv6 now requires IPsec support for standards-based, end-to-end security across the Internet. The new QoS enhancements work even when IPv6 traffic is encrypted using IPsec.

Understanding how IPv6 works is essential if you plan to benefit from IPv6 by deploying it in your enterprise. The following sections provide an overview of key IPv6 concepts, features, and terminology.

> **NOTE** For more detailed information on IP concepts, features, and terminology, see the white paper titled "Introduction to IP Version 6" at *http://www.microsoft.com/downloads/details.aspx?FamilyID=CBC0B8A3-B6A4-4952-BBE6-D976624C257C&displaylang=en*. Another good reference for learning IPv6 is the book, *Understanding IPv6, 2nd Edition*, by Joseph Davies (Microsoft Press, 2008).

Understanding IPv6 Terminology

The following terminology is used to define IPv6 concepts and describe IPv6 features:

- **Node** An IPv6-enabled network device that includes both hosts and routers.
- **Host** An IPv6-enabled network device that cannot forward IPv6 packets that are not explicitly addressed to itself. A host is an endpoint for IPv6 communications (either the source or destination) and drops all traffic not explicitly addressed to it.
- **Router** An IPv6-enabled network device that can forward IPv6 packets that are not explicitly addressed to itself. IPv6 routers also typically advertise their presence to IPv6 hosts on their attached links.
- **Link** One or more LAN (such as Ethernet) or wide area network (WAN, such as Point-to-Point Protocol [PPP]) network segments bounded by routers. Like interfaces, links may be either physical or logical.
- **Neighbors** Nodes that are connected to the same physical or logical link.
- **Subnet** One or more links having the same 64-bit IPv6 address prefix.
- **Interface** A representation of a node's attachment to a link. This can be a physical interface (such as a network adapter) or a logical interface (such as a tunnel interface).

> ***NOTE*** **An IPv6 address identifies an interface, not a node. A node is identified by having one or more unicast IPv6 addresses assigned to one of its interfaces.**

Understanding IPv6 Addressing

IPv6 uses 128-bit (16-byte) addresses that are expressed in colon-hexadecimal form. For example, in the address 2001:DB8:3FA9:0000:0000:0000:00D3:9C5A, each block of 4-digit hexadecimal numbers represents a 16-bit digit binary number. The eight blocks of four-digit hexadecimal numbers thus equal 8 × 16 = 128 bits in total.

You can shorten colon-hexadecimal addresses by suppressing leading zeros for each block. Using this technique, the representation for the preceding address now becomes 2001:DB8:3FA9:0:0:0:D3:9C5A.

You can shorten colon-hexadecimal addresses even further by compressing contiguous 0 (hex) blocks as double colons ("::"). The address in this example thus shortens to 2001:DB8:3FA9::D3:9C5A. Note that only one double colon can be used per IPv6 address to ensure unambiguous representation.

Understanding IPv6 Prefixes

An IPv6 prefix indicates the portion of the address used for routing (a subnet or a set of subnets as a summarized route) or for identifying an address range. IPv6 prefixes are expressed in a manner similar to the Classless Inter-Domain Routing (CIDR) notation used by IPv4. For example, 2001:DB8:3FA9::/48 might represent a route prefix in an IPv6 routing table.

In IPv4, CIDR notation can be used to represent individual unicast addresses in addition to routes and subnets. IPv6 prefixes, however, are used only to represent routes and address ranges, not unicast addresses. Unlike IPv4, IPv6 does not support variable-length subnet identifiers, and the number of high-order bits used to identify a subnet in IPv6 is almost always 64. It is thus redundant to represent the address in our example as 2001:DB8:3FA9::D3:9C5A/64; the /64 portion of the representation is understood.

Understanding IPv6 Address Types

IPv6 supports three different address types:

- **Unicast** Identifies a single interface within the scope of the address. (The scope of an IPv6 address is that portion of your network over which this address is unique.) IPv6 packets with unicast destination addresses are delivered to a single interface.
- **Multicast** Identifies zero or more interfaces. IPv6 packets with multicast destination addresses are delivered to all interfaces listening on the address. (Generally speaking, multicasting works the same way in IPv6 as it does in IPv4.)
- **Anycast** Identifies multiple interfaces. IPv6 packets with anycast destination addresses are delivered to the nearest interface (measured by routing distance) specified by the address. Currently, anycast addresses are assigned only to routers and can only represent destination addresses.

> ***NOTE*** **IPv6 address types do not include broadcast addresses as used by IPv4. In IPv6, all broadcast communications are performed using multicast addresses. See Table 28-2 for more information on multicast addresses.**

Understanding Unicast Addresses

Unicast addresses are addresses that identify a single interface. IPv6 has several types of unicast addresses:

- **Global unicast address** An address that is globally routable over the IPv6-enabled portion of the Internet. Therefore, the scope of a global address is the entire Internet, and global addresses in IPv6 correspond to public (non-RFC 1918) addresses used in IPv4. The address prefix currently used for global addresses as defined in RFC 3587 is 2000::/3, and a global address has the following structure:
  - The first 48 bits of the address are the global routing prefix specifying your organization's site. (The first three bits of this prefix must be 001 in binary notation.) These 48 bits represent the public topology portion of the address, which represents the collection of large and small Internet service providers (ISPs) on the IPv6 Internet and which is controlled by these ISPs through assignment by the Internet Assigned Numbers Authority (IANA).
  - The next 16 bits are the subnet ID. Your organization can use this portion to specify up to 65,536 unique subnets for routing purposes inside your organization's site. These 16 bits represent the site topology portion of the address, which your organization has control over.

- The final 64 bits are the interface ID and specify a unique interface within each subnet.

- **Link-local unicast address** An address that can be used by a node for communicating with neighboring nodes on the same link. Therefore, the scope of a link-local address is the local link on the network; link-local addresses are never forwarded beyond the local link by IPv6 routers. Because link-local addresses are assigned to interfaces using IPv6 address autoconfiguration, link-local addresses in IPv6 correspond to Automatic Private IP Addressing (APIPA) addresses used in IPv4 (which are assigned from the address range 169.254.0.0/16). The address prefix used for link-local addresses is FE80::/64, and a link-local address has the following structure:
  - The first 64 bits of the address are always FE80:0:0:0 (which will be shown as FE80::).
  - The last 64 bits are the interface ID and specify a unique interface on the local link.

  Link-local addresses can be reused—in other words, two interfaces on different links can have the same address. This makes link-local addresses ambiguous; an additional identifier called the zone ID (or scope ID) indicates to which link the address is either assigned or destined. In Windows 7, the zone ID for a link-local address corresponds to the interface index for that interface. You can view a list of interface indexes on a computer by typing **netsh interface ipv6 show interface** at a command prompt. For more information on the zone ID, see the section titled "Displaying IPv6 Address Settings" later in this chapter.

- **Unique local unicast address** Because a site-local address prefix can represent multiple sites within an organization, it is ambiguous and not well suited for intraorganizational routing purposes. Therefore, RFC 4193 currently proposes a new type of address called a unique local unicast address. The scope of this address is global to all sites within the organization, and using this address type simplifies the configuration of an organization's internal IPv6 routing infrastructure. A unique local address has the following structure:
  - The first seven bits of the address are always 1111 110 (binary) and the eighth bit is set to 1, indicating a unique local address. This means that the address prefix is always FD00::/8 for this type of address.
  - The next 40 bits represent the global ID, a randomly generated value that identifies a specific site within your organization.
  - The next 16 bits represent the subnet ID and can be used for further subdividing the internal network of your site for routing purposes.
  - The last 64 bits are the interface ID and specify a unique interface within each subnet.

NOTE Site-local addresses have been deprecated by RFC 3879 and are replaced by unique local addresses.

Identifying IPv6 Address Types

As Table 28-1 shows, you can quickly determine which type of IPv6 address you are dealing with by looking at the beginning part of the address—that is, the high-order bits of the address. Tables 28-2 and 28-3 also show examples of common IPv6 addresses that you can recognize directly from their colon-hexadecimal representation.

TABLE 28-1 Identifying IPv6 Address Types Using High-Order Bits and Address Prefix

ADDRESS TYPE	HIGH-ORDER BITS	ADDRESS PREFIX
Global unicast	001	2000::/3
Link-local unicast	1111 1110 10	FE80::/64
Unique local unicast	1111 1101	FD00::/8
Multicast	1111 1111	FF00::/8

TABLE 28-2 Identifying Common IPv6 Multicast Addresses

FUNCTION	SCOPE	REPRESENTATION
All-nodes multicast	Interface-local	FF01::1
All-nodes multicast	Link-local	FF02::1
All-routers multicast	Interface-local	FF01::2
All-routers multicast	Link-local	FF02::2
All-routers multicast	Site-local	FF05::2

TABLE 28-3 Identifying Loopback and Unspecified IPv6 Addresses

FUNCTION	REPRESENTATION
Unspecified address (no address)	::
Loopback address	::1

> ***NOTE*** **For information on IPv6 address types used by different IPv6 transition technologies, see the section titled "Planning for IPv6 Migration" later in this chapter.**

Understanding Interface Identifiers

For all the types of unicast IPv6 addresses described in the preceding sections, the last 64 bits of the address represent the interface ID and are used to specify a unique interface on a local link or subnet. In previous versions of Windows, the interface ID is uniquely determined as follows:

- For link-local addresses, such as a network adapter on an Ethernet segment, the interface ID is derived from either the unique 48-bit media access control (MAC)–layer address of the interface or the unique Extended Unique Identifier (EUI)–64 address of the interface as defined by the Institute of Electrical and Electronics Engineers (IEEE).
- For global address prefixes, an EIU-64–based interface ID creates a public IPv6 address.
- For global address prefixes, a temporary random interface ID creates a temporary address. This approach is described in RFC 3041; you can use it to help provide anonymity for client-based usage of the IPv6 Internet.

In Windows 7, however, the interface ID by default is randomly generated for all types of unicast IPv6 addresses assigned to LAN interfaces.

> **NOTE** Windows 7 randomly generates the interface ID by default. You can also disable this behavior by typing **netsh interface ipv6 set global randomizedidentifiers=disabled** at a command prompt.

Comparing IPv6 with IPv4

Table 28-4 compares and contrasts the IPv4 and IPv6 addressing schemes.

TABLE 28-4 IPv4 vs. IPv6 Addressing

FEATURE	IPv4	IPv6
Number of bits (bytes)	32 (4)	128 (16)
Expressed form	Dotted-decimal	Colon-hexadecimal
Variable-length subnets	Yes	No
Public addresses	Yes	Yes (global addresses)
Private addresses	Yes (RFC 1918 addresses)	Yes (unique local addresses)
Autoconfigured addresses for the local link	Yes (APIPA)	Yes (link-local addresses)
Support for address classes	Yes, but deprecated by CIDR	No
Broadcast addresses	Yes	Multicast used instead
Subnet mask	Required	Implicit 64-bit address prefix length for addresses assigned to interfaces

NOTE For detailed specifications concerning IPv6 addressing, see RFC 4291 at *http://www.ietf.org/rfc/rfc4291.txt*. There are also other differences between IPv4 and IPv6, such as how the headers are structured for IPv4 versus IPv6 packets. For more information, see the white paper, "Introduction to IP Version 6," at *http://www.microsoft.com/downloads/details.aspx?FamilyID=CBC0B8A3-B6A4-4952-BBE6-D976624C257C&displaylang=en*.

Understanding IPv6 Routing

Routing is the process of forwarding packets between connected network segments and is the primary function of IPv6. An IPv6 network consists of one or more network segments, also called *links* or *subnets*. These links are connected by IPv6 routers, devices that forward IPv6 packets from one link to another. These IPv6 routers are typically third-party hardware devices, but you can also configure a multihomed computer running Windows Server 2008 as an IPv6 router if needed.

How IPv6 Routing Works

The header of an IPv6 packet contains both the source address of the sending host and the destination address of the receiving host. When an IPv6 packet arrives at a host, the host uses its local IPv6 routing table to determine whether to accept the packet or forward it to another host or network.

Each IPv6 node (host or router) has its own IPv6 routing table. A *routing table* is a collection of routes that store information about IPv6 network prefixes and how they can be reached, either directly or indirectly. On IPv6 hosts, such as computers running Windows 7, Windows Vista, or Windows Server 2008, the IPv6 routing table is generated automatically when IPv6 initializes on the system. Local administrators can use the *netsh interface ipv6* commands to manage these tables by viewing them and by manually adding or removing routes. The use of this command is discussed further later in this section.

When an IPv6 packet arrives at a physical or logical network interface on an IPv6 host, such as a multihomed computer running Windows Server 2008, the host uses the following process to determine how to forward the packet to its intended destination:

1. The host checks its destination cache to see whether there is an entry that matches the destination address in the packet header. If such an entry is found, the host forwards the packet directly to the address specified in the destination cache entry and the routing process ends.
2. If the destination cache does not contain an entry that matches the destination address in the packet header, the host uses its local routing table to determine how to forward the packet. Using the routing table, the host determines the following:
   - **Next-hop address** If the destination address is on the local link, the next-hop address is simply the destination address in the packet header. If the destination

address is on a remote link, the next-hop address is the address of a router connected to the local link.

- **Next-hop interface** This is the physical or logical network interface on the host that should be used to forward the packet to the next-hop address.

3. The host then forwards the packet to the next-hop address using the next-hop interface. The host also updates its destination cache with this information so that subsequent packets sent to the same destination address can be forwarded using the destination cache entry instead of using its local routing table.

IPv6 Route Determination Process

In step 2 of the preceding procedure, the host determines the next-hop address and next-hop interface by using its local routing table. The details of this process are as follows:

1. For each routing table entry, the first *N* bits in the route's network prefix are compared with the same bits in the destination address in the packet header, where *N* is the number of bits in the route's prefix length. If these bits match, the route is determined to be a match for the destination.
2. The list of all matching routes is compiled. If only one matching route is found, this route is chosen and the route determination process is ended.
3. If multiple matching routes are found, the matching route having the largest prefix length is chosen and the route determination process is ended.
4. If multiple matching routes having the largest prefix length are found, the matching route having the lowest metric is chosen and the route determination process is ended.
5. If multiple matching routes having the largest prefix length and lowest metric are found, one of these routes is selected and the route determination process is ended.

The effective result of this IPv6 route determination process is as follows:

1. If a route can be found that matches the entire destination address in the packet header, then the next-hop address and interface specified in this route are used to forward the packet.
2. If a route of the type described in step 1 is not found, the most efficient (that is, lowest-metric) route that has the longest prefix length matching the destination address is used to forward the packet.
3. If a route of the type described in step 2 is not found, the packet is forwarded using the default route (with network prefix ::/0).

IPv6 Routing Table Structure

IPv6 routing tables can contain four different types of routing table entries (that is, routes):

- **Directly attached network routes** These typically have 64-bit prefixes and identify adjacent links (network segments connected to the local segment via one router).

- **Remote network routes** These have varying prefixes and identify remote links (network segments connected to the local segment via several routers).
- **Host routes** These have 128-bit prefixes and identify a specific IPv6 node.
- **Default route** This uses the network prefix ::/0 and is used to forward packets when a network or host route cannot be determined.

On a computer running Windows 7, Windows Vista, or Windows Server 2008, you can use the *netsh interface ipv6 show route* command to display the IPv6 routing table entries. The following is a sample routing table from a domain-joined computer running Windows 7 that has a single LAN network adapter, no IPv6 routers on the attached subnet, and no other configured network connections.

```
Publish  Type      Met  Prefix                         Idx  Gateway/Interface Name
-------  --------  ---  ------------------------       ---  ------------------------
No       Manual    256  ::1/128                          1  Loopback Pseudo-Interface 1
No       Manual    256  fe80::/64                       15  Teredo Tunneling Pseudo-
                                                            Interface
No       Manual    256  fe80::/64                       12  Local Area Connection
No       Manual    256  fe80::100:7f:fffe/128           15  Teredo Tunneling Pseudo-
                                                            Interface
No       Manual    256  fe80::5efe:172.16.11.131/128    14  isatap.{9D607D7D-0703-4E67-
                                                            82ED-9A8206377C5C}
No       Manual    256  fe80::5da9:fa1d:2575:c766/128  12  Local Area Connection
No       Manual    256  ff00::/8                         1  Loopback Pseudo-Interface 1
No       Manual    256  ff00::/8                        15  Teredo Tunneling Pseudo-
                                                            Interface
No       Manual    256  ff00::/8                        12  Local Area Connection
```

Each route in this table is specified using the following fields:

- **Publish** If set to Yes, the route is advertised in a routing Advertisement message; otherwise No.
- **Type** If set to Autoconf, the route was configured automatically using the IPv6 routing protocol; if Manual, the route has been configured by the operating system or an application.
- **Met** Indicates the metric for the route. For multiple routes having the same prefix, the lower the metric, the better the match.
- **Prefix** Specifies the address prefix for the route.
- **Idx** Specifies the index of the network interface over which packets matching the route's address prefix are reachable. To display a list of interfaces and their indices, use the *netsh interface ipv6 show interface* command.
- **Gateway/Interface Name** For directly attached network routes, specifies the name of the interface; for remote network routes, specifies the next-hop address of the route.

NOTE For more information about IPv6 routing and routing tables, see The Cable Guy article titled "Understanding the IPv6 Routing Table" at *http://technet.microsoft.com/en-ca/library/bb878115.aspx*.

Understanding ICMPv6 Messages

Internet Control Message Protocol (ICMP) for IPv4 (ICMPv4) is used in IPv4 networks to allow nodes to send and respond to error messages and informational messages. For example, when a source node uses the *ping* command to send ICMP Echo Request messages (ICMP type 8 messages) to a destination node, the destination node can respond with ICMP Echo messages (ICMP type 0 messages) indicating its presence on the network.

On IPv6 networks, ICMP for IPv6 (ICMPv6) fulfills the same functions as ICMPv4 on IPv4 networks—namely, to provide a mechanism for exchanging error messages and informational messages. ICMPv6 also provides informational messages for the following:

- **Neighbor Discovery (ND)** The process by which hosts and routers discover each other on the network so that they can communicate at the data-link layer. (ND serves the same purpose as Address Resolution Protocol [ARP] does in IPv4 networks.)
- **Multicast Listener Discovery (MLD)** The process by which membership in multicast groups is determined and maintained.

NOTE For more information about ND, see the next section titled "Understanding Neighbor Discovery." For more information about ICMPv6 message types and header formats and about MLD, see the white paper, "Introduction to IP Version 6," at *http://www.microsoft.com/downloads/details.aspx?FamilyID=CBC0B8A3-B6A4-4952-BBE6-D976624C257C&displaylang=en*.

Understanding Neighbor Discovery

ND is the process by which nodes on an IPv6 network can communicate with each other by exchanging frames at the data-link layer. ND performs the following functions on an IPv6 network:

- Enables IPv6 nodes (IPv6 hosts and IPv6 routers) to resolve the link-layer address of a neighboring node (a node on the same physical or logical link)
- Enables IPv6 nodes to determine when the link-layer address of a neighboring node has changed
- Enables IPv6 nodes to determine whether neighboring nodes are still reachable
- Enables IPv6 routers to advertise their presence, on-link prefixes, and host configuration settings

- Enables IPv6 routers to redirect hosts to more optimal routers for a specific destination
- Enables IPv6 hosts to discover addresses, address prefixes, and other configuration settings
- Enables IPv6 hosts to discover routers attached to the local link

To understand how ND works, it helps to first compare it with the similar processes used in IPv4. In IPv4, you use three separate mechanisms to manage node-to-node communication:

- **Address Resolution Protocol** A data link-layer protocol that resolves IPv4 addresses assigned to interfaces to their corresponding MAC-layer addresses. This enables network adapters to receive frames addressed to them and send response frames to their source. For example, before a host can send a packet to a destination host whose IPv4 address is 172.16.25.3, the sending host first needs to use ARP to resolve this destination address (if the host is on the same LAN) or the IP address of the local gateway (if the host is on a different LAN) to its corresponding 48-bit MAC address (such as 00-13-20-08-A0-D1).
- **ICMPv4 router discovery** These ICMPv4 messages enable routers to advertise their presence on IPv4 networks and enable hosts to discover the presence of these routers. When router discovery is enabled on a router, the router periodically sends router advertisements to the all-hosts multicast address (224.0.0.1) to indicate to hosts on the network that the router is available. When router discovery is enabled on hosts, the hosts can send router solicitations to the all-routers multicast address (224.0.0.2) to obtain the address of the router and assign this address as the host's default gateway.
- **ICMPv4 Redirect** Routers use these ICMPv4 messages to inform hosts of more optimal routers to use for specific destinations. ICMPv4 Redirect messages are needed because hosts typically cannot determine the best router on their subnet to send remote traffic for a given destination.

On IPv4 networks, these three mechanisms enable nodes on a network segment to communicate on a link. On IPv6 networks, these three mechanisms are replaced by the five ICMPv6 message types shown in Table 28-5.

> ***NOTE*** **The solicited-node multicast address, which is used as the destination address for ICMPv4 Neighbor Solicitation messages (ICMPv6 type 135 messages) when address resolution is being performed, is a special type of multicast address composed of the prefix FF02::1:FF00:0/104 followed by the last 24 bits of the IPv6 address that is being resolved. IPv6 nodes listen on their solicited-node multicast addresses. The advantage of using this multicast address for address resolution in IPv6 is that typically only the targeted host is disturbed on the local link. By contrast, the ARP messages used in IPv4 for address resolution queries are sent to the MAC-layer broadcast address, which disturbs all hosts on the local segment.**

TABLE 28-5 ICMPv6 Message Types Used for ND

MESSAGE TYPE	ICMPV6 TYPE	DESCRIPTION
Router Solicitation	133	Sent by IPv6 hosts to the link-local scope all-routers multicast address (FF02::2) to discover IPv6 routers present on the local link.
Router Advertisement	134	Sent periodically by IPv6 routers to the link-local scope all-nodes multicast address (FF02::1), or sent to the unicast address of a host in response to receiving a Router Solicitation message from that host. (Windows Vista and later versions use multicast for optimization.) Router Advertisement messages provide hosts with the information needed to determine link prefixes, link maximum transmission unit (MTU), whether to use DHCPv6 for address autoconfiguration, and lifetime for autoconfigured addresses.
Neighbor Solicitation	135	Sent by IPv6 nodes to the solicited-node multicast address of a host to discover the link-layer address of an IPv6 node, or sent to the unicast address of the host to verify the reachability of the host.
Neighbor Advertisement	136	Sent by an IPv6 node to the unicast address of a host in response to receiving a Neighbor Solicitation message from the host, or sent to the link-local scope all-nodes multicast address (FF02::1) to inform neighboring nodes of changes to the host's link-layer addresses.
Redirect	137	Sent by an IPv6 router to the unicast address of a host to inform the host of a more optimal first-hop address for a specific destination.

Understanding Address Autoconfiguration

On IPv4 networks, addresses can be assigned to hosts in three ways:

- Manually, using static address assignment
- Automatically, using Dynamic Host Configuration Protocol (DHCP) if a DHCP server is present on the subnet (or a DHCP relay agent is configured on the subnet)
- Automatically, using APIPA, which randomly assigns the host an address from the range 169.254.0.0 to 169.254.255.255 with subnet mask 255.255.0.0

On IPv6 networks, static addresses are generally assigned only to routers and (sometimes) servers, but hardly ever to client computers. Instead, IPv6 addresses are almost always assigned automatically using a process called *address autoconfiguration.* Address autoconfiguration can work in three ways: stateless, stateful, or both. Stateless address autoconfiguration is based on the receipt of ICMPv6 Router Advertisement messages. Stateful address autoconfiguration, on the other hand, uses DHCP for IPv6 (DHCPv6) to obtain address information and other configuration settings from a DHCPv6 server.

NOTE **The DHCP Server service of Windows Server 2008 supports DHCPv6. The DHCP Server service of Windows Server 2003 does not support DHCPv6.**

All IPv6 nodes (hosts and routers) automatically assign themselves link-local addresses (addresses having the address prefix FE80::/64); this is done for every interface (both physical and logical) on the node. (6to4 interfaces are an exception—they might not have link-local addresses automatically assigned.) These autoconfigured link-local addresses can be used only to reach neighboring nodes (nodes on the same link). When specifying one of these addresses as a destination address, you might need to specify the zone ID for the destination. In addition, link-local addresses are never registered in DNS servers.

NOTE **Manual assignment of IPv6 addresses is generally needed only for IPv6 routers and for some servers. You can configure a computer running Windows 7 with multiple interfaces to be used as a router. For more information on configuring IPv6 routers, see the Cable Guy article titled "Manual Configuration for IPv6" at *http://technet.microsoft.com/en-us/library/bb878102.aspx*. For a description of the IPv6 routing table, see the Cable Guy article titled "Understanding the IPv6 Routing Table" at *http://technet.microsoft.com/en-us/library/bb878115.aspx*.**

An autoconfigured IPv6 address can be in one or more of the states shown in Table 28-6.

TABLE 28-6 Possible States for an Autoconfigured IPv6 Address

STATE	DESCRIPTION
Tentative	The uniqueness of the address is still being verified using duplicate address detection.
Valid	The address is unique and can now send and receive unicast IPv6 traffic until the Valid Lifetime expires.
Preferred	The address can be used for unicast traffic until the Preferred Lifetime expires.
Deprecated	The address can still be used for unicast traffic during existing communication sessions, but its use is discouraged for new communication sessions.
Invalid	The Valid Lifetime for the address has expired and it can no longer be used for unicast traffic.

NOTE The Valid and Preferred Lifetime for stateless autoconfigured IPv6 addresses is included in the Router Solicitation message.

For detailed descriptions of how address autoconfiguration, address resolution, router discovery, redirect, duplicate address detection, and neighbor unreachability detection processes are performed, see the white paper, "Introduction to IP Version 6," at *http://www.microsoft.com/downloads/details.aspx?FamilyID=CBC0B8A3-B6A4-4952-BBE6-D976624C257C&displaylang=en.*

NOTE To display the state for each autoconfigured IPv6 address on a Windows 7 computer, open a command prompt and type **netsh interface ipv6 show addresses** at a command prompt.

Understanding Name Resolution

The Domain Name System (DNS) is fundamental to how name resolution works on both IPv4 and IPv6 networks. On an IPv4 network, host (A) records are used by name servers (DNS servers) to resolve fully qualified domain names (FQDNs) like *server1.contoso.com* into their associated IP addresses in response to name lookups (name queries) from DNS clients. In addition, reverse lookups—in which IP addresses are resolved into FQDNs—are supported by using pointer (PTR) records in the *in-addr.arpa* domain.

Name resolution works fundamentally the same way with IPv6, with the following differences:

- Host records for IPv6 hosts are AAAA ("quad-A") records, not A records.
- The domain used for reverse lookups of IPv6 addresses is *ip6.arpa,* not *in-addr.arpa.*

NOTE The enhancements to DNS that make IPv6 support possible are described in the draft standard RFC 3596 at *http://www.ietf.org/rfc/rfc3596.txt.*

Understanding Name Queries

Because the dual-layer TCP/IP stack in Windows 7 means that both IPv4 and IPv6 are enabled by default, DNS name lookups by clients running Windows 7 can involve the use of both A and AAAA records. (This is true only if your name servers support IPv6, which is the case with the DNS Server role for Windows Server 2008 and Windows Server 2003.) By default, the DNS client in Windows 7 uses the following procedure when performing a name lookup using a particular interface:

1. The client computer checks to see whether it has a non–link-local IPv6 address assigned to the interface. If it has no non–link-local addresses assigned, the client sends a single name lookup to the name server to query for A records and does not query for AAAA records. If the only non–link-local address assigned to the interface is a Teredo address, the client again does not query for AAAA records. (The Teredo client in Windows Vista and later versions is explicitly built not to automatically perform AAAA lookups or register with DNS to prevent overloading of DNS servers.)
2. If the client computer has a non–link-local address assigned to the interface, the client sends a name lookup to query for A records.
   - If the client then receives a response to its query (not an error message), it follows with a second lookup to query for AAAA records.
   - If the client receives no response or receives any error message (except for Name Not Found), it does not send a second lookup to query for AAAA records.

NOTE **Because an interface on an IPv6 host typically has multiple IPv6 addresses, the process by which source and address selection works during a name query is more complex than when DNS names are resolved by IPv4 hosts. For a detailed description of how source and address selection works for IPv6 hosts, see the Cable Guy article titled "Source and Destination Address Selection for IPv6" at *http://technet.microsoft.com/en-us/library/bb877985.aspx*. For additional information on DNS behavior in Windows 7 and Windows Vista, see "Domain Name System Client Behavior in Windows Vista" at *http://technet.microsoft.com/en-us/library/bb727035.aspx*. For information about the different types of IPv6 addresses usually assigned to an interface, see the section titled "Configuring and Troubleshooting IPv6 in Windows 7" later in this chapter.**

NOTE **Issues have arisen with poorly configured DNS name servers on the Internet. These issues, which are described in RFC 4074 (*http://www.ietf.org/rfc/rfc4074.txt*), do not cause problems on Windows Vista or later versions because Microsoft has altered the DNS client behavior specifically to compensate for them. However, administrators of DNS servers should make sure these issues are fixed, because they can cause problems with DNS name resolution for most IPv6 networking stacks, including stacks found in earlier Windows platforms such as Windows XP.**

Understanding Name Registration

DNS servers running Windows Server 2003 can dynamically register both A and AAAA records for clients running Windows 7. Dynamic registration of DNS records simplifies the job of maintaining name resolution on networks running the Active Directory Directory Service.

When a client running Windows 7 starts up on a network, the DNS Client service tries to register the following records for the client:

- A records for all IPv4 addresses assigned to all interfaces configured with the address of a DNS server
- AAAA records for all IPv6 addresses assigned to all interfaces configured with the address of a DNS server
- PTR records for all IPv4 addresses assigned to all interfaces configured with the address of a DNS server

NOTE **AAAA records are not registered for link-local IPv6 addresses that have been assigned to interfaces using address autoconfiguration.**

PTR Records and IPv6

Clients running Windows 7 do not try to register PTR records for IPv6 addresses assigned to interfaces on the computer. If you want to enable clients to perform reverse lookups for Windows 7 computers using IPv6, you must manually create a reverse lookup zone for the ip6.arpa domain on your DNS servers and then manually add PTR records to this zone. For detailed steps on how to do this, see "IPv6 for Microsoft Windows: Frequently Asked Questions" at *http://www.microsoft.com/technet/network/ipv6/ipv6faq.mspx*.

However, PTR records for reverse lookups using IPv6 are not often used, because the namespace for reverse queries is formed by using each hexadecimal digit in the colon-hexadecimal representation of an IPv6 address as a separate level in the reverse domain hierarchy. For example, the PTR record associated with the IPv6 address 2001:DB8::D3:00FF:FE28:9C5A, whose full representation is 2001:0DB8:0000:0000:00D3:00FF:FE28:9C5A, would be expressed as A.5.C.9.8.2.E.F.F.F.0.0.3.D.0.0.0.0.0.0.0.0.0.0.8.B.D.0.1.0.0.2.IP6.ARPA. The performance cost of resolving such a representation is generally too high for most DNS server implementations.

By default, DNS servers running Windows Server 2003 do not listen for DNS traffic sent over IPv6. To enable these DNS servers to listen for IPv6 name registrations and name lookups, you must first configure the servers using the **dnscmd /config /EnableIPv6 1** command. By default, DNS servers running Windows Server 2008 listen for DNS traffic sent over IPv6. You must then configure each client running Windows 7 with the unicast IPv6 addresses of your DNS servers using DHCPv6, the properties of IPv6 (TCP/IPv6) in the Network Connections folder, or the *netsh interface ipv6 add dns interface=NameOrIndex address=IPv6Address index=*PreferenceLevel command where *PreferenceLevel* specifies the index for the specified

DNS server address. (DHCP servers running Windows Server 2003 do not support stateful address assignment using DHCPv6.)

> ***NOTE*** **For more information on enabling Windows Server 2003 DNS server support for IPv6, see Chapter 9, "Windows Support for DNS," in the online book *TCP/IP Fundamentals for Microsoft Windows,* which you can download from *http://www.microsoft.com/downloads/details.aspx?FamilyID=c76296fd-61c9-4079-a0bb-582bca4a846f &displaylang=en.* For further details on the DNS name query and registration behavior in Windows 7 and Windows Vista, see the article titled "Domain Name System Client Behavior in Windows Vista" on Microsoft TechNet at *http://technet.microsoft.com/en-us/library/bb727035.aspx.***

IPv6 Enhancements in Windows 7

The TCP/IP networking stack in the Windows XP and Windows Server 2003 platforms had a dual-stack architecture that used separate network and framing layers for IPv4 and IPv6 based on separate drivers: Tcpip.sys and Tcpip6.sys. Only the transport and framing layers for IPv4 were installed by default, and adding support for IPv6 involved installing an additional IPv6 protocol feature through the Network Connections folder.

By contrast, in Windows 7, Windows Vista, and Windows Server 2008, the TCP/IP stack has been completely redesigned and now uses a dual–IP-layer architecture in which both IPv4 and IPv6 share common transport and framing layers. In addition, IPv6 is installed and enabled by default in these new platforms to provide out-of-the-box support for new features such as the Windows Meeting Space application, which uses only IPv6. Finally, the dual IP layer architecture means that all of the performance enhancements of the Next Generation TCP/IP stack that apply to IPv4 also apply to IPv6. These performance enhancements include Compound TCP, Receive Window Auto-Tuning, and other enhancements that can dramatically improve performance in high-latency, high-delay, and high-loss networking environments.

> ***NOTE*** **For more information about the performance enhancements in the Next Generation TCP/IP stack, see Chapter 25, "Configuring Windows Networking."**

Summary of IPv6 Enhancements in Windows 7

Windows 7 builds on the many IPv6 enhancements introduced earlier in Windows Vista and Windows Server 2008. These earlier enhancements include the following:

- **Dual–IP-layer architecture** A new TCP/IP stack architecture that uses the same transport and framing layers for both IPv4 and IPv6.
- **Enabled by default** Both IPv4 and IPv6 are installed and enabled by default, with the stack giving preference to IPv6 when appropriate without impairing the perfor-

mance of IPv4 communications on the network. For example, if a DNS name query returns both an IPv4 and IPv6 address for a host, the client will try to use IPv6 first for communicating with the host. This preference also results in better network performance for IPv6-enabled applications.

- **User interface configuration support** In addition to being able to configure IPv6 settings from the command line using the *netsh interface ipv6* command context, you can also configure them in Windows 7 using the user interface. For more information, see the section titled "Configuring IPv6 in Windows 7 Using the User Interface" later in this chapter.
- **Full IPsec support** IPv6 support in previous versions of Windows offered only limited support for IPsec protection of network traffic. In Windows 7 and Windows Vista, however, IPsec support for IPv6 is the same as for IPv4, and you can configure IPsec connection security rules for IPv6 in the same way as IPv4 by using the Windows Firewall With Advanced Security console. For more information on configuring IPsec in Windows 7, see Chapter 26, "Configuring Windows Firewall and IPsec."
- **LLMNR support** The implementation of IPv6 in Windows 7 and Windows Vista supports Link-Local Multicast Name Resolution (LLMNR), a mechanism that enables IPv6 nodes on a single subnet to resolve each other's names in the absence of a DNS server. LLMNR works by having nodes send multicast DNS name queries instead of unicast queries. Computers running Windows 7 and Windows Vista listen by default for multicast LLMNR traffic, which eliminates the need to perform local subnet name resolution using NetBIOS over TCP/IP when no DNS server is available. LLMNR is defined in RFC 4795.
- **MLDv2 support** The implementation of IPv6 in Windows 7 and Windows Vista supports MLD version 2 (MLDv2), a mechanism described in RFC 3810 that enables IPv6 hosts to register interest in source-specific multicast traffic with local multicast routers by specifying an include list (to indicate specific source addresses of interest) or an exclude list (to exclude unwanted source addresses).
- **DHCPv6 support** The DHCP Client service in Windows 7 and Windows Vista supports DHCPv6 as defined in RFCs 3736 and 4361. This means that computers running Windows 7 and Windows Vista can perform both stateful and stateless DHCPv6 configuration on a native IPv6 network.
- **IPv6CP support** The built-in remote access client functionality in Windows 7 and Windows Vista supports IPv6 Control Protocol (IPv6CP) (RFC 5072) to configure IPv6 nodes on a PPP link. This means that native IPv6 traffic can be sent over PPP-based network connections, such as dial-up connections or broadband PPP over Ethernet (PPPoE) connections, to an ISP. IPv6CP also supports Layer 2 Tunneling Protocol (L2TP), and for Windows Vista with Service Pack 1 (SP1) or later, Secure Socket Tunneling Protocol (SSTP)–based virtual private network (VPN) connections. For more information on IPv6CP support in Windows 7, see Chapter 27, "Connecting Remote Users and Networks."

- **Random interface IDs** By default, Windows 7 and Windows Vista generate random interface IDs for non-temporary autoconfigured IPv6 addresses, including both public addresses (global addresses registered in DNS) and link-local addresses. For more information, see the section titled "Disabling Random Interface IDs" later in this chapter.
- **Literal IPv6 addresses in URLs** Windows 7 and Windows Vista support RFC 2732–compliant literal IPv6 addresses in URLs by using the WinINet application programming interface (API) support in Windows Internet Explorer 8.0. This can be a useful feature for troubleshooting Internet connectivity with IPv6-enabled Web servers.
- **New Teredo behavior** The Teredo client in Windows 7 and Windows Vista remains dormant (inactive) until it spins up (is activated by) an IPv6-enabled application that tries to use Teredo. In Windows 7 and Windows Vista, three things can bring up Teredo: an application trying to communicate using a Teredo address (the outbound instantiated scenario), a listening application that has the Edge Traversal rule enabled in Windows Firewall (any IPv6-enabled applications that need to use Teredo can easily do so by setting the *Edge Traversal* flag using the Windows Firewall APIs), and the *NotifyStableUnicastIpAddressTable* IP Helper API. For more information about Windows Firewall rules, see Chapter 26.

In addition to these earlier enhancements, Windows 7 and Windows Server 2008 R2 introduce the following new IPv6 improvements:

- **IP-HTTPS** This stands for Internet Protocol over Hypertext Transfer Protocol Secure (IP over HTTPS), a new protocol that enables hosts located behind a proxy or firewall to establish connectivity by tunneling IP traffic inside an HTTPS tunnel. HTTPS is used instead of HTTP so that proxy servers will be prevented from looking inside the data stream and terminating the connection if traffic seems anomalous. Note that HTTPS does not provide data security—you must use IPsec to provide data security for an IP-HTTPS connection.

  In the Windows 7 implementation of DirectAccess described in the following More Info box, IT-HTTPS is used whenever a firewall or proxy server blocks a client computer from using 6to4 or Teredo to establish an IPv6-over-IPv4 tunnel with an IPv6-enabled DirectAccess server on the corporate intranet.

> ***MORE INFO*** **For more information about IP-HTTPS, see the article, "IP over HTTPS (IP-HTTPS) Tunneling Protocol Specification," on MSDN at *http://msdn.microsoft.com/en-us/library/dd358571.aspx*.**

- **DirectAccess** This is a new feature of Windows 7 and Windows Server 2008 R2 that provides users with the experience of being seamlessly connected to the corporate network whenever they have Internet access. Using DirectAccess, remote users who attempt to access corporate intranet resources, such as e-mail servers, shared folders, or intranet Web sites, can access these resources without the need to connect to a VPN.

By providing users with the same connectivity experience both inside and outside the office, DirectAccess can increase the productivity of your mobile users. DirectAccess also enables administrators to keep the computers of mobile uses in a managed state even when they are off-site by allowing Group Policy changes to be propagated over the Internet.

DirectAccess is implemented as a client/server architecture in which remote IPv6-enabled client computers communicate with IPv6-enabled servers located on the corporate network. DirectAccess can work over existing IPv4 networks, such as the public IPv4 Internet, by using IPv4/IPv6 transition technologies such as 6to4, Teredo, and ISATAP. DirectAccess also supports native IPv6 connectivity for clients that have been assigned native IPv6 addresses.

DirectAccess uses IPsec tunneling to provide security for authentication and resource access. DirectAccess can be implemented in different ways ranging from providing client computers with secure access to intranet resources via an IPv6-enabled IPsec gateway to providing them with secure end-to-end connectivity with each IPv6-enabled application server located on the intranet. DirectAccess requires the use of IPv6 so that client computers can have globally routable addresses.

MORE INFO For more information about DirectAccess, see Chapter 27 in this resource kit. Also see the article, "DirectAccess Technical Overview for Windows 7 and Windows Server 2008 R2," at *http://technet.microsoft.com/en-us/library/dd637827.aspx.*

HOW IT WORKS

Teredo Behavior in Windows 7 and Windows Vista

Michael Surkan
Program Manager for TCP and IPv6

Teredo is default-enabled but inactive in both workgroup and domain scenarios. Teredo becomes active in two main scenarios:

- An application tries to communicate with a Teredo address (for example, by using a URL with a Teredo address in a Web browser). This is outbound-initiated traffic, and Teredo will go dormant again after 60 minutes of inactivity. The host firewall will allow only incoming Teredo traffic corresponding to the specific outbound request, ensuring that system security isn't compromised. This is really no different than the way in which any outbound-initiated traffic works with the host firewall with IPv4. (In other words, all outbound traffic is allowed by default, and a state table allows responses that match the outgoing requests.)

- An application or service is authorized to use Teredo with the advanced Windows Firewall *Edge Traversal* flag. If an application has the Edge Traversal option, it is allowed to receive any incoming traffic over Teredo from any source (such as unsolicited traffic). Windows Meeting Space and Remote Assistance automatically set this flag for themselves, but users can do it manually for other Windows services if they prefer, such as with a Web service.

Configuring and Troubleshooting IPv6 in Windows 7

Although IPv6 is designed to allow IPv6-enabled nodes, such as computers running Windows 7, to automatically configure their interfaces with link-local addresses, these autoconfigured addresses are not registered in DNS servers and can be used only for communicating with other nodes on the local link. Alternatively, by using a DHCPv6 server, you can automatically assign global, site-local, or unique local IPv6 addresses to IPv6-enabled interfaces of link-attached nodes. This is the preferred scenario for end-to-end IPv6 connectivity in enterprises that have a native IPv6-only network infrastructure.

However, you can also use two methods to configure IPv6 settings manually on computers running Windows 7:

- Using the new IPv6 graphical user interface
- Using the *netsh interface ipv6* command context

In addition, it is important to understand the different kinds of IPv6 addresses assigned to computers running Windows 7 so that you can troubleshoot IPv6 connectivity when problems arise.

Displaying IPv6 Address Settings

To display the IPv4 and IPv6 address configuration of the local computer, open a command prompt window and type **ipconfig /all**. The following is an example of the information displayed by running this command on a managed (domain-joined) computer running Windows 7 with a single LAN network adapter, no IPv6 routers on the attached subnet, and no other configured network connections.

```
Windows IP Configuration

   Host Name . . . . . . . . . . . . : KBERG-PC
   Primary Dns Suffix  . . . . . . . : contoso.com
   Node Type . . . . . . . . . . . . : Hybrid
   IP Routing Enabled. . . . . . . . : No
   WINS Proxy Enabled. . . . . . . . : No
   DNS Suffix Search List. . . . . . : contoso.com
```

```
Ethernet adapter Local Area Connection:

   Connection-specific DNS Suffix  . : contoso.com
   Description . . . . . . . . . . . : Broadcom NetXtreme 57xx Gigabit Controller
   Physical Address. . . . . . . . . : 00-13-D4-C2-50-F5
   DHCP Enabled. . . . . . . . . . . : Yes
   Autoconfiguration Enabled . . . . : Yes
   Link-local IPv6 Address . . . . . : fe80::3530:6107:45a2:a92c%8(Preferred)
   IPv4 Address. . . . . . . . . . . : 172.16.11.13(Preferred)
   Subnet Mask . . . . . . . . . . . : 255.255.255.0
   Lease Obtained. . . . . . . . . . : Tuesday, March 17, 2009 9:01:24 AM
   Lease Expires . . . . . . . . . . : Wednesday, March 25, 2009 9:01:29 AM
   Default Gateway . . . . . . . . . : 172.16.11.1
   DHCP Server . . . . . . . . . . . : 172.16.11.32
   DHCPv6 IAID . . . . . . . . . . . : 201331668
   DHCPv6 Client DUID. . . . . . . . : 00-01-00-01-11-50-8C-A7-00-17-31-C5-D2-8E
   DNS Servers . . . . . . . . . . . : 172.16.11.32
   NetBIOS over Tcpip. . . . . . . . : Enabled

Tunnel adapter isatap.contoso.com:

   Media State . . . . . . . . . . . : Media Disconnected
   Connection-specific DNS Suffix  . : contoso.com
   Description . . . . . . . . . . . : Microsoft ISATAP Adapter
   Physical Address. . . . . . . . . : 00-00-00-00-00-00-00-E0
   DHCP Enabled. . . . . . . . . . . : No
   Autoconfiguration Enabled . . . . : Yes
```

The preceding command output displays two interfaces on this computer:

- Local Area Connection (the installed network adapter)
- ISATAP tunneling interface

The Local Area Connection interface is an Ethernet network adapter and has both an IPv4 address (172.16.11.13) assigned by DHCP and a link-local IPv6 address (fe80::3530:6107:45a2:a92c) that has been automatically assigned using IPv6 address autoconfiguration. (You can recognize the link-local address by its address prefix, FE80::/64.)

The *%8* appended to this address is the zone ID (or scope ID) that indicates the connected portion of the network on which the computer resides. This zone ID corresponds with the interface index for the Local Area Connection interface. To view a list of interface indexes on a computer, type **netsh interface ipv6 show interface** at a command prompt. For the example computer, the output of this command is the following code.

```
Idx  Met   MTU          State         Name
---  ---  -----         -----------   -------------------
  1   50  4294967295    connected     Loopback Pseudo-Interface 1
  9   25  1280          connected     isatap.contoso.com
  8   20  1500          connected     Local Area Connection
```

Here the Idx column indicates the interface index. The zone ID might be needed when testing network connectivity with this computer from other computers using the *ping* and *tracert* commands. See the section titled "Troubleshooting IPv6 Connectivity" later in this chapter for more information.

Returning to the output of the *ipconfig /all* command, the state of the link-local address assigned to the LAN connection is Preferred, which indicates a valid IPv6 address that you can use to send and receive unicast IPv6 traffic.

The media state of the ISATAP tunneling interface isatap.contoso.com is Media Disconnected. You can enable the ISATAP tunneling interface by opening an elevated command prompt and typing the **netsh interface isatap set state enabled** command. After you have enabled the ISATAP interface, the ISATAP portion of the *ipconfig /all* output will look something like this.

```
Tunnel adapter isatap.contoso.com:

   Connection-specific DNS Suffix  . : contoso.com
   Description . . . . . . . . . . . : Microsoft ISATAP Adapter
   Physical Address. . . . . . . . . : 00-00-00-00-00-00-00-E0
   DHCP Enabled. . . . . . . . . . . : No
   Autoconfiguration Enabled . . . . : Yes
   Link-local IPv6 Address . . . . . : fe80::5efe:172.16.11.13%9(Preferred)
   Default Gateway . . . . . . . . . :
   DNS Servers . . . . . . . . . . . : 172.16.11.32
   NetBIOS over Tcpip. . . . . . . . : Disabled
```

> ***NOTE*** **If the computer is unmanaged (not domain-joined), the ISATAP adapter will be enabled automatically and will be displayed with a GUID, for example isatap.{9D607D7D-0703-4E67-82ED-9A8206377C5C}.**

The above ISATAP adapter has an autoconfigured link-local address of fe80::5efe:172.16.11.13. The format for an ISATAP address is:

- The first 64 bits are a unicast prefix that can be a link-local, global, or unique local unicast IPv6 address prefix. This example uses the link-local address prefix because no ISATAP router is present on the network. This means that the resulting ISATAP address can be used only for communicating with other ISATAP hosts on the IPv4 network, and this ISATAP address is not registered in DNS servers.
- The next 32 bits are either 0:5EFE (for a private IPv4 address) or 200:5EFE (for a public IPv4 address) in an ISATAP address. (RFC 4214 also allows 100:5EFE and 300:5EFE in this portion of an ISATAP address.)
- The final 32 bits consist of the 32-bit IPv4 address of the host in dotted-decimal form (172.16.11.13 in this example).

MORE INFO For more information on ISATAP addressing, see the white paper, "IPv6 Transition Technologies," at *http://www.microsoft.com/downloads/details.aspx?FamilyID=afe56282-2903-40f3-a5ba-a87bf92c096d&displaylang=en*, and the white paper, "Intra-site Automatic Tunnel Addressing Protocol Deployment Guide," at *http://www.microsoft.com/downloads/details.aspx?FamilyID=0f3a8868-e337-43d1-b271-b8c8702344cd&displaylang=en*. Also see the section titled "Understanding ISATAP" later in this chapter.

The output of the *ipconfig /all* and *netsh interface ipv6 show interface* commands does not show a Teredo adapter on the computer because the computer is managed (domain joined). On an unmanaged computer, the Teredo adapter is enabled (in online mode) by default and the *ipconfig /all* output will look something like this.

```
Tunnel adapter Teredo Tunneling Pseudo-Interface:

   Connection-specific DNS Suffix  . :
   Description . . . . . . . . . . . : Microsoft Teredo Tunneling Adapter
   Physical Address. . . . . . . . . : 02-00-54-55-4E-01
   DHCP Enabled. . . . . . . . . . . : No
   Autoconfiguration Enabled . . . . : Yes
   IPv6 Address. . . . . . . . . . . : 2001:0:4136:e37c:4e8:3426:7c94:fffe(Preferred)
   Link-local IPv6 Address . . . . . : fe80::4e8:3426:53ef:f4f2%10(Preferred)
   Default Gateway . . . . . . . . . : ::
   NetBIOS over Tcpip. . . . . . . . : Disabled
```

The above Teredo tunneling pseudo-interface displays the IPv6 address of the Teredo client as 2001:0:4136:e37c:4e8:3426:53ef:f4f2. The format for a Teredo client address is:

- The first 32 bits are always the Teredo prefix, which is 2001::/32.
- The next 32 bits contain the public IPv4 address of the Teredo server that helped in the configuration of this Teredo address (here 4136:E37C hexadecimal, which converts to 65.54.227.124 in dotted-decimal format). By default, the Teredo client in Windows 7, Windows Vista, and Windows Server 2008 automatically tries to determine the IPv4 addresses of Teredo servers by resolving the name *teredo.ipv6.microsoft.com*.
- The next 16 bits are reserved for various Teredo flags.
- The next 16 bits contain an obscured version of the external UDP port number that corresponds to all Teredo traffic for this Teredo client. (The external UDP port number is obscured, XORing it with 0xFFFF, and, in this example, is 0x3426 XOR 0xFFFF = 0xCBD9 or decimal 52185, meaning UDP port 52185.)
- The final 32 bits contain an obscured version of the external IPv4 address that corresponds to all Teredo traffic for this Teredo client. (The external IPv4 address is obscured, XORing it with 0xFFFF FFFF, and, in this example, is 0x7C94 FFFE XOR 0xFFFF FFFF = 0x836B 0001 or dotted-decimal 131.107.0.1.)

NOTE IANA has allocated the IPv6 address prefix 2001::/32 for Teredo as of January 2006. (See RFC 4830 at *http://www.rfc-editor.org/rfc/rfc4380.txt* for details.) Windows XP–based clients originally used the 3FFE:831F::/32 Teredo prefix. Windows XP–based clients with the Microsoft Security Bulletin MS06-064 at *http://www.microsoft.com/technet/security/Bulletin/MS06-064.mspx* now use the 2001::/32 prefix.

Another way to display the IPv6 settings on a computer running Windows 7 is to type the **netsh interface ipv6 show address** command. The results for the computer in the preceding example are as follows.

```
Interface 1: Loopback Pseudo-Interface 1

Addr Type  DAD State   Valid Life Pref. Life Address
---------  ----------- ---------- ---------- ------------------------
Other      Preferred     infinite   infinite ::1

Interface 9: isatap.{9D607D7D-0703-4E67-82ED-9A8206377C5C}

Addr Type  DAD State   Valid Life Pref. Life Address
---------  ----------- ---------- ---------- ------------------------
Other      Preferred     infinite   infinite fe80::5efe:172.16.11.13%9

Interface 10: Teredo Tunneling Pseudo-Interface

Addr Type  DAD State   Valid Life Pref. Life Address
---------  ----------- ---------- ---------- ------------------------
Public     Preferred     infinite   infinite 2001:0:4136:e37c:1071:3426:31d2:bfce
Other      Preferred     infinite   infinite fe80::1071:3426:31d2:bfce%10

Interface 8: Local Area Connection

Addr Type  DAD State   Valid Life Pref. Life Address
---------  ----------- ---------- ---------- ------------------------
Other      Preferred     infinite   infinite fe80::3530:6107:45a2:a92c%8
```

NOTE An advantage of displaying IPv6 address settings using the *netsh interface ipv6 show address* command instead of *ipconfig* is that you can execute Netsh.exe commands remotely against a targeted computer by using the *–r RemoteComputerName* option.

MORE INFO For more information on how to use *ipconfig,* Netsh.exe, and other tools to display IPv6 configuration information, see the article, "Using Windows Tools to Obtain IPv6 Configuration Information," on Microsoft TechNet at *http://technet.microsoft.com/en-us/library/bb726952.aspx*.

DIRECT FROM THE SOURCE

Explanation of Teredo States

Kalven Wu, Software Design Engineer in Test
Windows Core Networking

With netsh int teredo show state, you can see the current state of Teredo, which can be one of the following:

- **Offline state** In this state, something has failed and Teredo cannot be activated (cannot be in the Qualified state) to be used by applications. Teredo enters this state in three ways:
  - When the Administrator disables it via netsh int teredo set state disabled.
  - When Teredo detects that the computer is on a managed network (detects the presence of a domain controller on the network—see the section in this sidebar titled "Teredo in Enterprise Networks" for more information), it will go offline if its type is not set to "enterpriseclient".
  - When some internal mechanism has failed in Teredo, such as suddenly being unable to reach the Teredo server or being unable to resolve teredo.ipv6.microsoft.com. In only this case, Teredo will attempt to move into the Dormant state using an exponential back-off time-out as follows: wait 5 seconds, try again; wait 10 seconds, try again; wait 20 seconds, try again; and continue until it tries every 15 minutes.
- **Dormant state** This is the state when Teredo is "enabled but not active." IPv6 traffic cannot flow over Teredo, but applications can trigger to activate Teredo. No edge traversal will occur in this state. No traffic is sent to the Teredo servers.
- **Probe state** This is the transition state from Dormant to Qualified. In this state, Teredo will try to establish communication with the Teredo server. If this succeeds, Teredo moves to the Qualified state. If this fails, Teredo will go to the Offline state.
- **Qualified state** In this state, IPv6 traffic can flow into and out of the system over Teredo and possibly traverse the edge firewall/NAT.

Teredo in Enterprise Networks

Whether a computer is domain joined or in a workgroup doesn't matter to Teredo. Teredo looks only at the environment that the computer is in. If Teredo detects the presence of a domain controller, it will assume that the network is managed. In this case, Teredo will go offline and stay offline unless it was administratively set to "enterpriseclient" using the command *netsh interface teredo set state enterpriseclient*. Hence, Teredo will go to the Offline state on a workgroup computer that is connected to a network with a domain controller to avoid traversing the edge of a corporate network. Conversely, if you take a domain-joined laptop home, Teredo will detect that it is no longer in a managed network and will go to the Dormant state.

Note that if you disable Teredo via the DisabledComponents registry key, it will override all the Teredo netsh settings.

Configuring IPv6 in Windows 7 Using the User Interface

To configure the IPv6 settings for a network connection in Windows 7 using the user interface, follow these steps:

1. In Control Panel, open Network And Sharing Center.
2. Click Manage Network Connections and then double-click the connection you want to configure.
3. Click Properties and respond to the User Account Control (UAC) prompt.
4. Select Internet Protocol Version 6 (TCP/IPv6) and click Properties to open the Internet Protocol Version 6 (TCP/IPv6) properties sheet (see Figure 28-1).

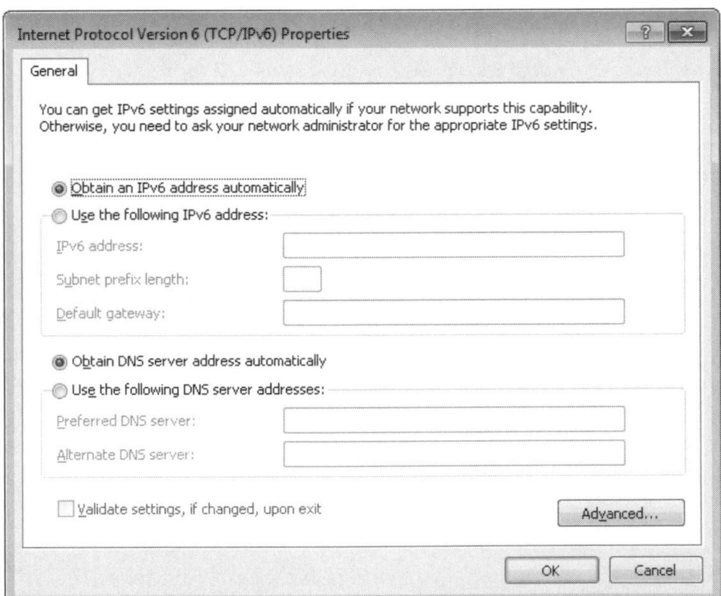

FIGURE 28-1 IPv6 properties of a network connection

5. Configure the IPv6 settings for the network connection as desired.
6. If you want, validate the new TCP/IP settings using the Windows Network Diagnostics Troubleshooter.

By default, the IPv6 settings for a network connection are configured as follows:

- **Obtain An IPv6 Address Automatically** This specifies that the physical or logical interface associated with this connection uses stateful or stateless address autoconfiguration to obtain its IPv6 address.
- **Obtain DNS Server Address Automatically** This specifies that the physical or logical interface associated with this connection uses stateful address autoconfiguration (DHCPv6) to obtain the IPv6 addresses of preferred and alternate DNS servers.

By selecting Use The Following IPv6 Address, you can manually configure the IPv6 address settings for a network connection by specifying the following:

- **IPv6 Address** Type the unicast IPv6 address you want to assign to the physical or logical interface associated with this connection in colon-hexadecimal form. If you need to assign additional unicast IPv6 addresses to the interface, click Advanced and then click the IP Settings tab.
- **Subnet Prefix Length** Type the subnet prefix length for the IPv6 address you assigned to the physical or logical interface associated with this connection. For unicast IPv6 addresses, the subnet prefix length should almost always be specified as 64.
- **Default Gateway** Type the unicast IPv6 address of the default gateway for the local IPv6 subnet in colon-hexadecimal form. If you need to specify additional default gateways, click Advanced and then click the IP Settings tab.

By selecting Use The Following DNS Server Addresses, you can manually specify IPv6 addresses for a preferred and an alternate DNS server to be used by your connection. If you need to specify additional alternate DNS servers, click Advanced and then click the DNS tab. The remaining settings on the DNS tab have similar functionality to those used for configuring IPv4 address settings.

> ***NOTE*** **The Advanced TCP/IP Settings dialog box does not have a WINS tab because IPv6 does not use NetBIOS for name resolution.**

Configuring IPv6 in Windows 7 Using Netsh

To configure the IPv6 settings for a network connection in Windows 7 using the Netsh.exe command, open a Command Prompt window with local administrator credentials and type the appropriate Netsh.exe command from the *netsh interface ipv6* context. Some examples of IPv6 configuration tasks that can be performed from this context include:

- To add the unicast IPv6 address 2001:DB8::8:800:20C4:0 to the interface named Local Area Connection as a persistent IPv6 address with infinite Valid and Preferred Lifetimes, type the following command.

  ```
  netsh interface ipv6 add address "Local Area Connection" 2001:DB8::8:800:20C4:0
  ```

- To configure a default gateway with unicast IPv6 address 2001:DB8:0:2F3B:2AA:FF:FE28:9C5A for the interface named Local Area Connection, add a default route with this address specified as a next-hop address by typing the following command.

  ```
  netsh interface ipv6 add route ::/0 "Local Area Connection" 2001:DB8:0:2F3B:2AA:F
  F:FE28:9C5A
  ```

- To configure a DNS server with unicast IPv6 address 2001:DB8:0:1::1 as the second (alternate) DNS server on the list of DNS servers for the interface named Local Area Connection, type the following command.

  ```
  netsh interface ipv6 add dnsserver "Local Area Connection" 2001:DB8:0:1::1 index=2
  ```

For more information on using the *netsh interface ipv6* context, type **netsh interface ipv6 ?** at a command prompt.

Other IPv6 Configuration Tasks

The following section describes some additional IPv6 configuration tasks that network administrators may need to know how to perform with computers running Windows 7.

Enabling or Disabling IPv6

You cannot uninstall IPv6 in Windows 7, but you can disable IPv6 on a per-adapter basis. To do this, follow these steps:

1. In Control Panel, open Network And Sharing Center.
2. Click Manage Network Connections and then double-click the connection you want to configure.
3. Clear the check box labeled Internet Protocol Version 6 (TCP/IPv6), and then click OK (see Figure 28-2).

Note that if you disable IPv6 on all your network connections using the user interface method described in the preceding steps, IPv6 will still remain enabled on all tunnel interfaces and on the loopback interface.

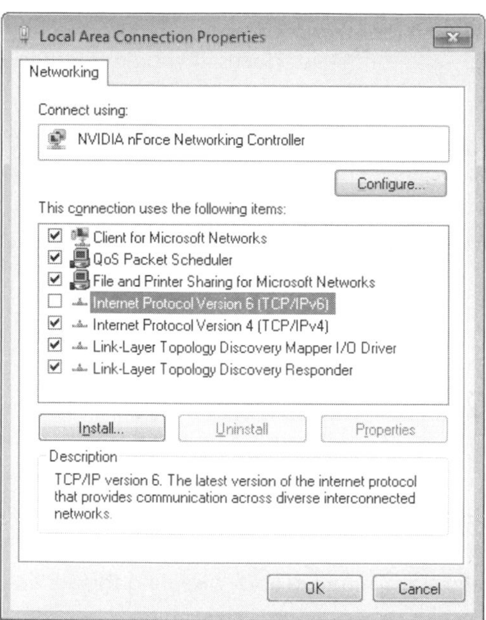

FIGURE 28-2 Disabling IPv6 for a network connection

As an alternative to using the user interface to disable IPv6 on a per-adapter basis, you can selectively disable certain features of IPv6 by creating and configuring the following DWORD registry value:

HKLM\SYSTEM\CurrentControlSet\Services\tcpip6\Parameters\DisabledComponents

Table 28-7 describes the flag values that control each IPv6 feature. By combining these flag values together into a bitmask, you can disable more than one feature at once. (By default, DisabledComponents has the value 0.)

TABLE 28-7 Bitmask Values for Disabling IPv6 Features in Windows 7

FLAG LOW-ORDER BIT	RESULT OF SETTING THIS BIT TO A VALUE OF 1
0	Disables all IPv6 tunnel interfaces, including ISATAP, 6to4, and Teredo tunnels
1	Disables all 6to4-based interfaces
2	Disables all ISATAP-based interfaces
3	Disables all Teredo-based interfaces
4	Disables IPv6 over all non-tunnel interfaces, including LAN and PPP interfaces
5	Modifies the default prefix policy table* to prefer IPv4 over IPv6 when attempting connections

**For more information concerning the IPv6 prefix policy table, see the Cable Guy article, "Source and Destination Address Selection for IPv6," at http://technet.microsoft.com/en-us/library/bb877985.aspx.*

For example, by setting the value of DisabledComponents to 0xFF, you can simultaneously disable IPv6 on all your network connections and tunnel interfaces. If you do this, IPv6 still remains enabled on the loopback interface, however.

> ***NOTE*** **For some examples of common flag combinations that can be used to enable or disable different aspects of IPv6 functionality in Windows 7 and Windows Vista, see the Cable Guy article, "Configuring IPv6 with Windows Vista," at *http://technet.microsoft.com/en-us/library/bb878057.aspx*.**

Depending on your scenario, there are other ways of effectively disabling IPv6 on computers running Windows 7, including the following:

- **Disable the IP Helper service** This service must be running for IPv6 transition technologies such as ISATAP, Teredo, and 6to4 to function on the computer. This service provides automatic IPv6 connectivity over an IPv4 network, and if the service is stopped, the computer will have only IPv6 connectivity if it is connected to a native IPv6 network. Therefore, if your network is not native IPv6, disabling this service on Windows 7 computers effectively disables IPv6 on them. You can use Group Policy to disable this service on targeted Windows 7 computers.
- **Use *netsh* to disable all IPv6 interfaces** For example, the following commands will disable all IPv6 transition technologies (Teredo, 6to4, and ISATAP).

  ```
  netsh interface teredo set state disabled

  netsh interface ipv6 6to4 set state state=disabled undoonstop=disabled

  netsh interface ipv6 isatap set state state=disabled
  ```

  You can include these commands in a script and send them inside a Microsoft System Center Configuration Manager (SCCM) package to disable transition technologies on targeted computers.
- **Configure Windows Firewall to block IPv6 traffic** You could block incoming and outgoing IPv6 protocol 41 (for ISATAP and 6to4) and UDP 3544 (for Teredo) traffic using the Windows Firewall, and you can use Group Policy to push this out to targeted computers. Businesses that implement perimeter firewalls may want to do this as a best practice for safeguarding their networks.

Disabling Random Interface IDs

You can disable the default behavior of generating random interface IDs for non-temporary autoconfigured public addresses (global addresses registered in DNS) and link-local addresses by using the following command.

```
netsh interface ipv6 set global randomizeidentifiers=disabled
```

To re-enable the generating of random interface IDs, use the following command.

```
netsh interface ipv6 set global randomizeidentifiers=enabled
```

NOTE Disabling random interface IDs causes link-local addresses to revert to using 48-bit MAC-layer (or 64-bit EUI) addresses for generating the interface ID portion of the address. In Windows, this happens immediately and does not require a reboot.

Resetting IPv6 Configuration

To remove all user-configured IPv6 settings and restore the IPv6 configuration of a computer to its default state, type the following command.

```
netsh interface ipv6 reset
```

You must reboot the computer for this command to take effect.

Displaying Teredo Client Status

To verify the current state of the Teredo client on your computer, open a Command Prompt window using local administrator credentials, and then type the following command.

```
netsh interface teredo show state
```

For a computer running Windows 7 on which Teredo is currently inactive, the typical output for this command looks like this.

```
Teredo Parameters
---------------------------------------------
Type                    : default
Server Name             : teredo.ipv6.microsoft.com.
Client Refresh Interval : 30 seconds
Client Port             : unspecified
State                   : dormant
Client Type             : teredo client
Network                 : managed
NAT                     : none (global connectivity)
```

NOTE If your command output doesn't contain all the preceding information, you probably started your command prompt session using standard credentials instead of administrator credentials.

If you now start an IPv6-enabled application that uses Teredo, such as Windows Meeting Space or Windows Remote Assistance, and then type the same *Netsh* command, the command output typically now looks like this.

```
Teredo Parameters
---------------------------------------------
Type                   : default
Server Name            : teredo.ipv6.microsoft.com.
Client Refresh Interval : 30 seconds
Client Port            : unspecified
State                  : qualified
Client Type            : teredo client
Network                : managed
NAT                    : restricted
```

Comparing these two command outputs shows that starting an application that uses Teredo changes the Teredo client state from Dormant (inactive) to Qualified (active).

> **NOTE** The output of the *netsh interface teredo show state* command also tells you the type of NAT your computer is behind (if any). In the preceding example, the computer is behind a restricted NAT. Teredo works well behind restricted and cone NATs and can even work behind symmetric NATs, but communication between certain types of NATs doesn't work. If you plan to purchase a Small Office/Home Office (SOHO) router for broadband Internet connectivity, the best choice is a router that supports 6to4. For more information on how Teredo works and on the different types of NATs, see "Teredo Overview" at *http://technet.microsoft.com/en-us/network/cc917486.aspx*.

Troubleshooting IPv6 Connectivity

The standard approach for troubleshooting TCP/IP network connectivity issues on IPv4 networks is to follow these steps:

1. Type **ipconfig /all** at a command prompt to verify the IPv4 configuration of the computer that is experiencing the problem.
2. If verifying the computer's IPv4 configuration doesn't resolve the issue, try using the *ping* command to test for network connectivity, beginning with the local computer and working outward until the cause of the problem is determined. Specifically, follow these steps in the order listed:
   a. Ping the IPv4 loopback address 127.0.0.1 to verify that TCP/IP is installed and configured properly on the computer.
   b. Ping the IPv4 address of the local computer.
   c. Ping the IPv4 address of the default gateway.
   d. Ping the IPv4 address of an IPv4 host on a remote subnet.

Other TCP/IP troubleshooting steps you can use on IPv4 networks include:

- Use the **route print** command to verify the configuration of the local computer's routing table.

- Use *tracert* to verify that intermediate routers are configured properly.
- Use the *pathping* command to identify packet loss over multihop paths.
- Clear the ARP cache by typing **netsh interface ip delete arpcache** at a command prompt.
- Verify the computer's DNS configuration, clear the DNS client resolver cache, and verify DNS name resolution.

NOTE For more information on how to systematically troubleshoot IPv4 connectivity problems, read Chapter 31, "Troubleshooting Network Issues."

Troubleshooting IPv6 network connectivity issues requires many of the same tools you use when troubleshooting IPv4. However, you use some of these tools in a different way because of the nature of IPv6 addressing and the way IPv6 is implemented in Windows 7 and Windows Vista. The differences include:

- You might need to specify a zone ID when attempting to verify IPv6 network connectivity with a target host using the *ping* command. The syntax for using *ping* with IPv6 is **ping *IPv6Address%ZoneID***, where *ZoneID* is the zone ID (or scope ID) of the sending interface. For example, if the target host has the link-local unicast IPv6 address FE80::D3:00FF:FE28:9C5A and the sending interface has a zone ID of 12, to verify IPv6 connectivity with this host, you type **ping FE80::D3:00FF:FE28:9C5A%12** at a command prompt. To determine the zone ID for an interface, you can either use the *ipconfig /all* command or type **netsh interface ipv6 show interface** at a command prompt. Note that because the zone ID is locally defined, a sending host and a receiving host on the same link may have different zone IDs. (Global and unique local unicast IPv6 addresses do not need a zone ID.)
- You should view and clear the neighbor cache on your computer before attempting to use ping to verify IPv6 network connectivity. The neighbor cache contains recently resolved link-layer IPv6 addresses; you can view it by typing **netsh interface ipv6 show neighbors** and flush it by typing **netsh interface ipv6 delete neighbors** at an elevated command prompt.
- You should also view and clear the destination cache on your computer before attempting to verify IPv6 network connectivity using *ping*. The destination cache contains next-hop IPv6 addresses for destinations. You can view the cache by typing **netsh interface ipv6 show destinationcache**; you can flush it by typing **netsh interface ipv6 delete destinationcache** at an elevated command prompt.
- You should use the *–d* option when attempting to trace the route to a remote IPv6 host using *tracert* or the *–n* option when using *pathping*. These options prevent these commands from performing DNS reverse queries on every near-side router interface along the routing path. Using these options can help speed up the display of the routing path.

NOTE For more help on troubleshooting IPv6 network connectivity issues, see the Cable Guy article, "Troubleshooting IPv6," at *http://technet.microsoft.com/en-us/library/bb878005.aspx*. See also Chapter 12, "Troubleshooting TCP/IP," in the online book *TCP/IP Fundamentals for Microsoft Windows,* which you can download from *http://www.microsoft.com/downloads/details.aspx?FamilyID=c76296fd-61c9-4079-a0bb-582bca4a846f&displaylang=en.*

NOTE Disabling IPv4 can also be a useful troubleshooting technique for developers who need to verify that their applications are IPv6-capable.

Planning for IPv6 Migration

Migrating your existing IPv4-based network infrastructure to IPv6 requires an understanding of different IPv6 transition technologies that you can use to achieve your goal. Windows 7, Windows Vista, and Windows Server 2008 support three transition technologies in particular:

- **ISATAP** An address assignment and automatic tunneling technology defined in RFC 4214 that you can use to provide unicast IPv6 connectivity between IPv6/IPv4 hosts (hosts that support both IPv6 and IPv4) across an IPv4-based intranet (a private network whose infrastructure hardware, such as routers, supports only IPv4, not IPv6).
- **6to4** An address assignment and automatic tunneling technology defined in RFC 3056 that you can use to provide unicast IPv6 connectivity between IPv6/IPv4 hosts and sites across the IPv4-based public Internet. 6to4 enables you to assign global IPv6 addresses within your private network so that your hosts can reach locations on the IPv6 Internet without needing a direct connection to the IPv6 Internet or an IPv6 global address prefix obtained from an IPv6-supporting ISP. (Communication between a 6to4 site and a node on the IPv6 Internet requires the use of a 6to4 relay, however.)
- **Teredo** An address assignment and automatic tunneling technology defined in RFC 4380 that you can use to provide unicast IPv6 connectivity between IPv6/IPv4 hosts across the IPv4 public Internet, even when the IPv6/IPv4 hosts are located behind zero or more NATs. Teredo provides similar functionality to 6to4 but without needing edge devices that support 6to4 tunneling.

NOTE For more information on IPv4/IPv6 transition technologies, see the white paper, "IPv6 Transition Technologies," at *http://www.microsoft.com/downloads/details.aspx?FamilyID=afe56282-2903-40f3-a5ba-a87bf92c096d&DisplayLang=en.*

These three IPv6 transition technologies are supported by Windows 7, Windows Vista, Windows Server 2008, Windows XP SP2, and Windows Server 2003 SP1. Of the three, ISATAP is the primary transition technology that you should use for migrating an existing IPv4-based intranet to IPv6; it is discussed further in the following sections. Teredo is primarily useful in SOHO networking environments, where NAT-enabled broadband routers provide Internet connectivity for users. (Think of Teredo as a transition technology of last resort, because as IPv6 connectivity becomes ubiquitous, the need for NAT traversal will decline until Teredo is no longer needed.)

HOW IT WORKS

Blocking Teredo

Teredo is intended to be a consumer technology and has generally not been recommended for enterprises because Teredo requires the edge device to allow all outbound UDP traffic. For example, because of security reasons, many enterprise administrators do not want client computers on the corporate network to be directly accessible from the Internet, and in that case turning off Teredo is a good idea.

If administrators want to disable Teredo on their client computers or simply prevent it from working, they can do so in one of three ways:

- Block all outbound UDP traffic by default. (This is the only reliable "external" method.)
- Block name resolution of the Teredo DNS host name, which by default on computers running Windows 7 is teredo.ipv6.microsoft.com. (This method, however, leaves an easy workaround, because the user can hard-code IP addresses.)
- Use Group Policy or a script to create the following DWORD registry value, which turns off Teredo on targeted computers running Windows 7. (This registry setting is not exposed by default in Group Policy but can be pushed down using a custom ADMX file.)

  HKLM\SYSTEM\CurrentControlSet\Services\Tcpip6\Parameters\DisabledComponents

  You can specify the following settings for this value:

  - **0x10** Setting this value will disable Teredo only on the computer.
  - **0x01** Setting this value will disable all tunnel interfaces on the computer.

If administrators want to support only native IPv6 in their networks or if they don't want to support any IPv6 traffic until they deploy native IPv6, they can choose to turn off all tunneling technologies using the second choice in the preceding list.

Understanding ISATAP

By default, the IPv6 protocol in Windows 7 automatically configures a link-local unicast IPv6 address of the form FE80::5EFE:*w.x.y.z* (for private IPv4 addresses) or FE80::200:5EFE:*w.x.y.z* (for public IPv4 addresses). This address is a link-local ISATAP address, and it is assigned to the ISATAP tunneling interface. Using their link-local ISATAP addresses, two ISATAP hosts (such as computers running Windows 7) can communicate using IPv6 by tunneling across an IPv4-only network infrastructure (such as a network whose routers forward only IPv4 packets and not IPv6 packets).

> **NOTE** In Windows 7 and in Windows Vista SP1 or later versions, link-local ISATAP addresses are automatically configured only if the name "ISATAP" (the ISATAP router name) can be resolved. Otherwise, the ISATAP interface will be media disconnected. However, if you administratively enable ISATAP by using the *netsh interface isatap set state enabled* command, the link-local address will be configured regardless of whether the ISATAP router name can be resolved.

With the addition of one or more ISATAP routers (IPv6-enabled routers that advertise address prefixes, forward packets between ISATAP hosts and other ISATAP routers, and act as default routers for ISATAP hosts), a variety of transition topologies become possible, including:

- Connecting ISATAP hosts on an IPv4-only intranet to an IPv6-capable network.
- Connecting multiple "islands" of ISATAP hosts through an IPv6-capable backbone.

These configurations are possible because ISATAP routers advertise address prefixes that enable ISATAP hosts (such as computers running Windows 7) to autoconfigure global or unique local unicast IPv6 addresses.

> **NOTE** Without the presence of an ISATAP router, ISATAP hosts running Windows Vista RTM could only autoconfigure link-local unicast IPv6 addresses, which limited IPv6 communications to those between hosts on the IPv4-only intranet. This was changed in Windows Vista SP1 so that without an ISATAP router, the interface will show media disconnected. In other words, Windows Vista SP1 won't configure a link-local ISATAP address when no ISATAP router is configured. The behavior in Windows 7 is the same as in Windows Vista SP1.

> **NOTE** For more information on how ISATAP works, see the white paper, "IPv6 Transition Technologies," at *http://www.microsoft.com/downloads/details.aspx?FamilyID=afe56282-2903-40f3-a5ba-a87bf92c096d &displaylang=en.*

DIRECT FROM THE SOURCE

ISATAP Interface Name

Xinyan Zan, Technical Lead
IPv6 Transition Technology

The ISATAP interface name is based on the DNS setting of the primary IPv4 interface of this ISATAP interface. For example, if the DNS suffix assigned to the primary IPv4 interface of this ISATAP interface is contoso.com, the ISATAP interface name will be isatap.contoso.com.

An alternate form of the ISATAP interface name is isatap.{GUID}, where GUID is a globally unique identifier. However, this GUID form is used to name the ISATAP interface only if there is no DNS suffix setting on the primary IPv4 interface.

Migrating an Intranet to IPv6

Best practices for migrating existing IPv4-based network infrastructures to IPv6 are still evolving. Therefore, this section presents a general outline on how to migrate an intranet to IPv6 and provides references to more detailed information on the subject for interested readers.

The ultimate goal of IPv4 to IPv6 migration is to achieve an IPv6-only network infrastructure that has IPv6-only hosts. From a practical standpoint, however, the lesser goal of achieving a network infrastructure that supports both IPv6 and IPv4—and where hosts also support both IPv6 and IPv4 but use mainly IPv6—is a more reasonable goal for which to aim. Achieving this goal is a lengthy process that involves seven main steps:

1. Upgrading your applications and services
2. Preparing your DNS infrastructure
3. Upgrading your hosts
4. Migrating from IPv4-only to ISATAP
5. Upgrading your routing infrastructure
6. Upgrading your DHCP infrastructure
7. Migrating from ISATAP to native IPv6

Step 1: Upgrading Your Applications and Services

To prepare your applications and services for migration, you will need to upgrade existing applications and services to support IPv6 in addition to IPv4. This may require upgrades from ISVs and third-party vendors or custom coding on your part. Although the ultimate goal is for all your applications and services to run native IPv6, a more appropriate target is to ensure that they work with both IPv4 and IPv6.

For further guidance, see the MSDN topic "IPv6 Guide for Windows Sockets Applications" at *http://msdn2.microsoft.com/en-us/library/ms738649.aspx*.

Step 2: Preparing Your DNS Infrastructure

You must prepare your DNS infrastructure to support the AAAA records used to resolve DNS names to IPv6 addresses. This might require upgrading your existing DNS servers. The DNS Server service of Windows Server 2008 and Windows Server 2003 supports dynamic registration of AAAA records for unicast IPv6 addresses (excluding link-local addresses).

> ***MORE INFO*** **For more information on configuring Windows Server 2003 DNS servers to support IPv6 hosts, see Chapter 9, "Windows Support for DNS," in the online book *TCP/IP Fundamentals for Microsoft Windows*, which can be found at *http://technet.microsoft.com/en-us/library/bb727009.aspx*.**

Step 3: Upgrading Your Hosts

You may need to upgrade some of your hosts until all your hosts support both IPv6 and IPv4. Windows platforms from Windows XP SP2 onward support both IPv4 and IPv6, although full support for IPv6 functionality for built-in programs and services is provided only in Windows Vista and later versions.

Step 4: Migrating from IPv4-only to ISATAP

After you prepare your applications, services, hosts, and DNS/DHCP infrastructure, you can begin deploying ISATAP routers to create islands of IPv6 connectivity within your IPv4-based intranet. You will need to add A records to the appropriate DNS zones so that your ISATAP hosts can determine the IPv4 addresses of your ISATAP routers.

You may decide to deploy zero or more ISATAP routers for inter-ISATAP subnet routing within your intranet, depending on the size of your intranet and the geographical distribution of its sites. You may decide to deploy redundant ISATAP routers to provide consistent availability of IPv6 address prefixes and other configuration settings for your ISATAP hosts. You will also likely deploy one or more ISATAP routers to provide IPv6 connectivity between your IPv4-based network infrastructure and the public IPv6 Internet as this evolves.

For more information on deploying ISATAP routers using different migration scenarios, see the white paper, "Intra-site Automatic Tunnel Addressing Protocol Deployment Guide," at *http://www.microsoft.com/downloads/details.aspx?FamilyID=0f3a8868-e337-43d1-b271-b8c8702344cd &displaylang=en*.

Step 5: Upgrading Your Routing Infrastructure

After you have deployed ISATAP to enable IPv6 hosts to communicate over your IPv4 network infrastructure, you should begin upgrading your network infrastructure (including routers, gateways, and other access devices) to support IPv6. Rather than upgrading your infrastructure to support only IPv6, a more reasonable upgrade goal is dual IPv4/IPv6 support. In many cases, actual replacement of router hardware is not necessary. Because many modern hardware routers support both IPv4 and IPv6 routing, the task of upgrading your routing infrastructure to support IPv6 becomes configuration, not replacement. As you enable IPv6 routing support for a subnet, also enable the DHCPv6 relay agent for the subnet.

Typically, you will begin upgrading your routing infrastructure early in your ISATAP deployment by upgrading the core routers on your network backbone to support IPv6. This will create islands of ISATAP hosts that connect to this backbone to communicate with other IPv6 hosts anywhere in your intranet.

Step 6: Upgrading Your DHCP Infrastructure

You can optionally upgrade your routing and DHCP infrastructure to support DHCPv6 for automatic assignment of global or unique local unicast IPv6 addresses or configuration settings for IPv4/IPv6 nodes on your network. By using DHCPv6, an IPv6 host can obtain subnet prefixes and other IPv6 configuration settings. A common use of DHCPv6 is to configure Windows 7–based client computers with the IPv6 addresses of DNS servers on the network. (DNS servers are not configured through IPv6 router discovery.)

The DHCP Server service in Windows Server 2003 does not support stateful address autoconfiguration or the DHCPv6 protocol. The DHCP Server role in Windows Server 2008, however, supports both stateful and stateless IPv6 address autoconfiguration using DHCPv6. The DHCP Client service in Windows 7, Windows Vista, and Windows Server 2008 supports address autoconfiguration using DHCPv6.

Just as with DHCP with IPv4, you also need to deploy and configure DHCPv6 relay agents for each subnet containing Windows 7 clients. Many hardware routers already support a DHCPv6 relay agent. You must configure relay agents with the IPv6 addresses of the DHCPv6 servers on your network. Relay agents can be configured but should not be enabled until you deploy IPv6 routing on your subnets.

When you are ready to enable DHCPv6 on subnets, configure your IPv6 routers to set the *Managed Address Configuration* and *Other Stateful Configuration* flags to the appropriate values for stateful or stateless DHCPv6 operation. For more information, see the Cable Guy article titled "The DHCPv6 Protocol" at *http://www.microsoft.com/technet/technetmag/issues/2007/03/CableGuy/default.aspx*.

Step 7: Migrating from ISATAP to Native IPv6

Finally, when all your network infrastructure devices support IPv6, you can begin to decommission your ISATAP routers because you no longer need them. Whether you will also migrate your infrastructure and hosts to support only pure-IPv6 is a decision best left for the distant future.

DIRECT FROM THE SOURCE

Tips and Tricks for Transitioning from IPv4 to IPv6

Mike Owen, Network Engineer
Data and Storage Platform Division

When transitioning a network from IPv4-only to dual stack, there are several areas that need special attention.

Addressing

This is actually one area that gets easier with IPv6 due to the huge address space that it offers. In general, you will want to add to each individual network segment a single IPv6 /64 prefix, even in cases in which you have more than one IPv4 subnet assigned to the same network (for example, by using the secondary keyword on Cisco routers). You should not need to use unique local addresses, even for lab networks. One exception might be that you do not want to use a routable /64 prefix for a segment that is not connected to your organization's globally routable space (that is, it is physically separate).

Firewalls

Deploying IPv6 can present issues for an organization's security team. Because IPsec services are available in all IPv6 stacks, it is more common to see end-to-end security implemented with IPv6-enabled desktops. When faced with end-to-end encryption, a firewall administrator has one of two choices: Either deny the traffic and drop it at the perimeter or allow it through unchecked, thus bypassing the access control lists (ACLs) and other security enabled on the firewall. Note that this problem exists even with IPv6-enabled firewalls.

Tunneling Technologies

Many transition technologies, such as ISATAP, 6to4, and manually configured IPv6-in-IPv4 tunnels, encapsulate IPv6 packets inside IPv4 to transport them across an IPv4-only part of your network. These packets are identified by the use of IP protocol 41 in the encapsulating packet. If firewalls, ACLs, or other devices in your network are not configured to forward these packets, then communications using these technologies will break. Many home routers, for example, are configured by default to only forward UDP and TCP protocols.

Here's a real-life example: After configuring a router to provide IPv6 services at an IANA meeting in Florida, IPv6 connectivity was not working. After some troubleshooting with the service provider, I determined that their router was dropping IP protocol 41, thus preventing IPv6 connectivity across the service provider's IPv4-only network.

Network Applications

When deciding to IPv6-enable an existing workflow or application, make sure to consider all parts of the process. For example, while upgrading a Web front end to support IPv6, don't forget to enable the separate file store and back-end database servers as well, otherwise the workflow may appear to support IPv6 from the front end but actually will not be completely tested.

DNS

Many DNS products today support the AAAA records which are used to store name-to-address mappings for IPv6 end systems. However, that does not mean that they support IPv6 lookups against the database—in some cases, this functionality must be enabled through a configuration setting or an upgrade to the product itself. This is another part of an end-to-end IPv6 workflow that needs to be considered.

Address Management

A simple way to enable IPv6 autoconfiguration on your hosts is to configure your edge routers to advertise an IPv6 prefix via Router Advertisements. This enables IPv6-enabled operating systems, including Windows Vista, Windows Server 2008, and Windows 7, to configure themselves with an IPv6 address. This method of configuration is considered stateless because the router will not track which IPv6 addresses are configured on which end system. When performing address auditing against these systems (to investigate a security incident, for example), it is impossible to determine which host was assigned a given IPv6 address at a particular time. At best, if you are lucky, the router's ARP tables will contain the necessary information, but more often than not, you will be unable to track a specific IPv6 address to the host on which it was configured.

Here's a real-life example: At a previous job, I was contacted by the local office of the U.S. Secret Service to investigate a threat made against a government official. I was able to track the IPv4 address that they provided to a high school in the school district where I worked and to a specific classroom at a certain time, based on DHCP logs and switch CAM tables. A student was subsequently identified as being in the classroom alone at the time and admitted to sending the messages, which turned out to be a hoax. Tracking down autoconfigured IPv6 addresses at this level of detail is nearly impossible.

Summary

This chapter described the features of IPv6 in Windows 7, provided an overview of how IPv6 works, and outlined best practices for migrating an existing IPv4-only network to IPv6. An IPv6 migration requires careful planning and a thorough understanding of how IPv6 works, and both Windows 7 and Windows Server 2008 R2 provide the features and tools you need to migrate your network successfully.

Additional Resources

These resources contain additional information and tools related to this chapter.

Related Information

- *Understanding IPv6, Second Edition,* by Joseph Davies (Microsoft Press, 2008). See *http://www.microsoft.com/MSPress/books/11607.aspx.*
- The IPv6 home page on Microsoft TechNet at *http://www.microsoft.com/ipv6/.*
- The IPv6 blog of Sean Siler, IPv6 Program Manager, at *http://blogs.technet.com/ipv6.*
- "IPv6 for Microsoft Windows: Frequently Asked Questions" at *http://technet.microsoft.com/en-us/network/cc987595.aspx.*
- The white paper, "Introduction to IP Version 6," at *http://www.microsoft.com/downloads/details.aspx?FamilyID=CBC0B8A3-B6A4-4952-BBE6-D976624C257C&displaylang=en.*
- The white paper, "IPv6 Transition Technologies," at *http://www.microsoft.com/downloads/details.aspx?FamilyID=afe56282-2903-40f3-a5ba-a87bf92c096d&displaylang=en.*
- The white paper, "Intra-site Automatic Tunnel Addressing Protocol Deployment Guide," at *http://www.microsoft.com/downloads/details.aspx?FamilyID=0f3a8868-e337-43d1-b271-b8c8702344cd &displaylang=en.*
- The Cable Guy article, "Understanding the IPv6 Routing Table," at *http://technet.microsoft.com/en-us/library/bb878115.aspx.*
- The Cable Guy article, "Manual Configuration for IPv6," at *http://technet.microsoft.com/en-us/library/bb878102.aspx.*
- The Cable Guy article, "Troubleshooting IPv6," at *http://technet.microsoft.com/en-us/library/bb878005.aspx.*
- The Cable Guy article, "Source and Destination Address Selection for IPv6," found on Microsoft TechNet at *http://technet.microsoft.com/en-us/library/bb877985.aspx.*
- "Domain Name System Client Behavior in Windows Vista" on Microsoft TechNet at *http://technet.microsoft.com/en-us/library/bb727035.aspx.*

- Knowledge Base article 929852, "How to Disable Certain Internet Protocol Version 6 (IPv6) Components in Windows Vista, Windows 7 and Windows Server 2008," at *http://support.microsoft.com/kb/929852*.
- Knowledge Base article 929851, "The Default Dynamic Port Range for TCP/IP Has Changed in Windows Vista and in Windows Server 2008," at *http://support.microsoft.com/kb/929851*.
- Chapter 9, "Windows Support for DNS," and Chapter 12, "Troubleshooting TCP/IP," in the online book *TCP/IP Fundamentals for Microsoft Windows*, which you can download from *http://www.microsoft.com/downloads/details.aspx?FamilyID=c76296fd-61c9-4079-a0bb-582bca4a846f &displaylang=en*.

On the Companion Media

- Get-IPV6.ps1

PART VI

Troubleshooting

CHAPTER 29

Configuring Startup and Troubleshooting Startup Issues

Diagnosing and correcting hardware and software problems that affect the startup process require different tools and techniques than troubleshooting problems that occur after the system starts because the person troubleshooting the startup problem does not have access to the full suite of the Windows 7 operating system troubleshooting tools. Resolving startup issues requires a clear understanding of the startup process, the core operating system features, and the tools used to isolate and resolve problems.

This chapter covers changes to the Windows 7 startup process, how to configure startup settings, and how to troubleshoot problems that stop Windows 7 from starting and allowing a user to complete the interactive logon process successfully.

What's New with Windows Startup

Windows 7 includes a few improvements to startup. Most significantly, setup now automatically installs Windows Recovery Environment (WinRE). WinRE, which includes the Startup Repair tool, was available for Windows Vista, but it was not automatically installed. IT professionals could configure the required partition and install the tools to the computer's hard disk, but this was not done by default. Therefore, most users started WinRE from the Windows Vista setup DVD. With Windows 7, users can start WinRE directly from the hard disk if Windows cannot start, and Windows startup will automatically open WinRE if Windows fails to start. If the hard disk is damaged, users can still start WinRE from the Windows 7 DVD.

Other than the automatic installation of WinRE, Windows 7 also reduces the time to start up, shut down, and resume from sleep. Because the changes to startup are minimal with Windows 7, most of this chapter focuses on changes introduced since Windows XP. These changes are all available in both Windows 7 and Windows Vista.

Several aspects of the Windows Vista and Windows 7 startup process have changed when compared to Windows XP. Most significantly, Ntldr (the feature of Windows XP that displayed the boot menu and loaded the Windows XP kernel) has been replaced by the Windows Boot Manager and the Windows Boot Loader. The Boot.ini file (a file that contains entries describing the available boot options) has been replaced by the boot configuration data (BCD) registry file. Ntdetect.com functionality has been merged into the kernel, and Windows Vista no longer supports hardware profiles. In fact, hardware profiles are no longer required: Windows will automatically detect different hardware configurations without requiring administrators to explicitly configure profiles. Finally, the command-line recovery console has been replaced by the graphical WinRE, which simplifies troubleshooting. This chapter discusses these changes in more detail.

Boot Configuration Data

The BCD registry file replaces the Boot.ini files used in Windows XP and earlier versions of Windows to track operating system locations, and it allows for a variety of new Windows Vista and Windows 7 features, including the Startup Repair tool and the Multi-User Install shortcuts. The BCD is stored in a data file that uses the same format as the registry and is located on either the Extensible Firmware Interface (EFI) system partition (for computers that support EFI) or on the system volume. On BIOS-based operating systems, the BCD registry file is located at \Boot\Bcd on the active partition. On EFI-based operating systems, the BCD registry file is located in the \EFI\Microsoft\Boot\ folder on the EFI system partition.

The BCD registry file can contain the following types of information:

- Entries that describe Windows Boot Manager (\Bootmgr) settings
- Entries to start the Windows Boot Loader (\Windows\System32\WinLoad.exe), which can then load Windows Vista
- Entries to start Windows Resume Application (\Windows\System32\WinResume.exe), which can then restore Windows Vista from hibernation
- Entries to start Windows Memory Diagnostic (\Boot\MemTest.exe)
- Entries to start Ntldr to load previous versions of Windows
- Entries to load and execute a Volume Boot Record, which typically starts a non-Microsoft boot loader

Additionally, you can add more entries to load custom applications, such as recovery tools.

You can modify the BCD registry file in several different ways:

- **Startup And Recovery** With the Startup And Recovery dialog box (available on the Advanced tab of the System Properties dialog box), you can select the default operating system to start if you have multiple operating systems installed on your computer. You can also change the time-out value. This dialog box has changed very little when compared to Windows XP; however, it now changes the BCD registry file instead of the Boot.ini file.
- **System Configuration utility (Msconfig.exe)** Msconfig.exe is a troubleshooting tool that you can use to configure startup options. The Boot tab in Windows 7 provides similar functionality to the Boot.ini tab in Windows XP, such as starting in safe mode, enabling a boot log, or disabling the graphical user interface (GUI).
- **BCD Windows Management Instrumentation provider** The BCD Windows Management Instrumentation (WMI) provider is a management interface that you can use to script utilities that modify BCD. This is the only programmatic interface available for BCD; you should always use this interface rather than attempting to access the BCD registry file directly. For more information, see "BCD WMI Provider Classes" at *http://msdn2.microsoft.com/en-us/library/aa362675.aspx*.
- **BCDEdit.exe** BCDEdit.exe is a command-line utility that replaces Bootcfg.exe in Windows XP. BCDEdit can be run from within Windows 7 at an administrative command prompt, from within Windows RE or even from within earlier versions of Windows (if the BCDEdit.exe file is available). BCDEdit provides more configuration options than the Startup And Recovery dialog box.
- **Non-Microsoft tools** Third-party software vendors have released tools to simplify editing the BCD registry file, including:
  - BootPRO, available at *http://www.vistabootpro.org*
  - EasyBCD, available at *http://neosmart.net*

You cannot use Bootcfg.exe to modify BCD. However, Bootcfg.exe will remain in the operating system to support configuring older operating systems that might be installed on the same computer.

For EFI computers, BCDEdit also replaces NvrBoot. In previous versions of Windows, you could use NvrBoot to edit the EFI boot manager menu items.

HOW IT WORKS

BCD Stores

Physically, a BCD store is a binary file in the registry hive format. A computer has a system BCD store that describes all installed Windows Vista and Windows 7 operating systems and installed Windows boot applications. A computer can optionally have many non-system BCD stores. Figure 29-1 shows an example of how the BCD hierarchy is implemented in a typical BCD store.

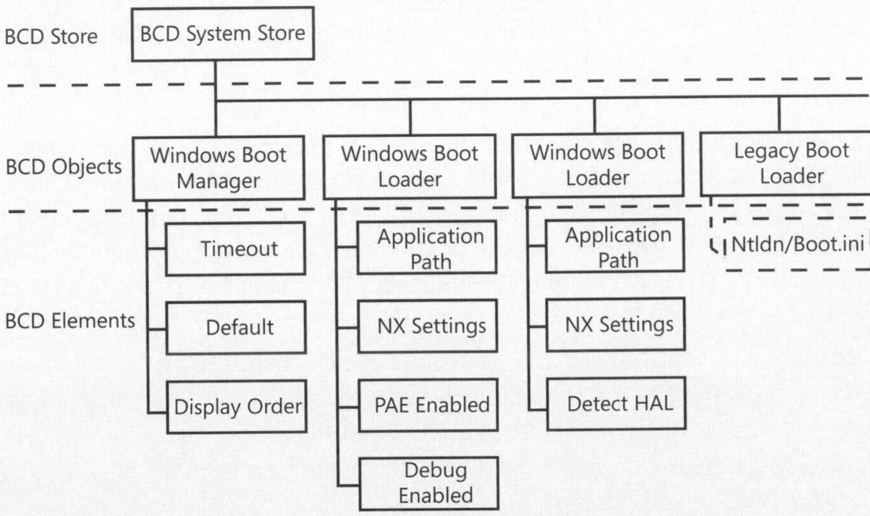

FIGURE 29-1 The BCD hierarchy allows for multiple boot options.

A BCD store normally has at least two (and optionally, many) BCD objects:

- **A Windows Boot Manager object** This object contains BCD elements that pertain to the Windows Boot Manager, such as the entries to display in an operating system selection menu, boot tool selection menu, and time-out for the selection menus. The Windows Boot Manager object and its associated elements serve essentially the same purpose as the *[boot loader]* section of a Boot.ini file. A store can optionally have multiple instances of the Windows Boot Manager. However, only one of them can be represented by the Windows Boot Manager well-known globally unique identifier (GUID). You can use the GUID's alias, *{bootmgr}*, to manipulate a store with BCDEdit.
- **At least one and optionally several Windows Boot Loader objects** Stores contain one instance of this object for each version or configuration of Windows Vista, Windows Server 2008, or Windows 7 that is installed on the system. These objects contain BCD elements that are used when loading Windows or during Windows initialization such as no-execute (NX) page protection policy, physical address extension (PAE) policy, and kernel debugger settings. Each object and its

associated elements serve essentially the same purpose as one of the lines in the *[operating systems]* section of Boot.ini. When a computer is booted into Windows, the alias *{current}* represents the associated boot loader object. When manipulating a store with BCDEdit, the default boot loader object has the alias *{default}*.

- **An optional Windows {ntldr} object** The *{ntldr}* object describes the location of Ntldr, which you can execute to boot Windows XP or earlier versions of Windows. This object is required only if the system includes versions of Windows that are earlier than Windows Vista. It is possible to have multiple instances of objects that describe Ntldr. However, as with the Windows Boot Manager, only one instance can be represented by the *{ntldr}* well-known GUID alias. You can use the GUID's alias, *{ntldr}*, to manipulate a store with BCDEdit.
- **Optional boot applications** Stores can optionally have BCD objects that perform other boot-related operations. One example is the Windows Memory Tester, which runs memory diagnostics.

MORE INFO For detailed information about BCD, see "Boot Configuration Data in Windows Vista" at *http://www.microsoft.com/whdc/system/platform/firmware/bcd.mspx*, and read "Boot Configuration Data Editor Frequently Asked Questions" at *http://technet.microsoft.com/en-us/library/cc721886.aspx*.

System Recovery

Windows Vista and Windows 7 replace the Recovery Console troubleshooting tool with the new System Recovery tool (part of WinRE). Typically, you will start the tool by pressing F8 before starting Windows and then choosing Repair Your Computer from the Advanced Boot Options screen. If that choice is not available because the hard disk has failed, you can start the tool by starting from the Windows 7 DVD and then clicking Repair Your Computer (after configuring the language options). This loads a specialized version of Windows Preinstallation Environment (Windows PE) and then displays the System Recovery tool. For step-by-step instructions on how to load the System Recovery tools, see the section titled "How to Start the System Recovery Tools" later in this chapter.

The System Recovery tools provide access to the following tools:

- **Startup Repair** The Startup Repair tool can solve many common startup problems automatically. Startup Repair performs an exhaustive analysis to diagnose your startup problems, including analyzing boot sectors, the Boot Manager, disk configuration, disk integrity, BCD registry file integrity, system file integrity, registry integrity, boot logs, and event logs. It will then attempt to solve the problem, which may involve repairing configuration files, solving simple disk problems, replacing missing system files, or running System Restore to return the computer to an earlier state. Because Startup Repair performs these tasks automatically, you can solve startup problems much faster than performing the analysis and repair manually.

- **System Restore** Windows automatically captures system state before installing new applications or drivers. You can later use the System Restore tool to return to this system if you experience problems. Because System Restore is available from the System Recovery tools, you can use System Restore to repair problems that prevent Windows Vista or Windows 7 from booting. Startup Repair can prompt you to initiate a System Restore, so you might never need to access this tool directly. For more information about System Restore, read Chapter 16, "Managing Disks and File Systems."
- **System Image Recovery** You use this tool to initiate a complete restore of the system hard disk. However, because any files saved since the last backup will be lost, you should use this only as a last resort. For information about backups and restores, see Chapter 16.
- **Windows Memory Diagnostic** The Windows Memory Diagnostics tool performs an automated test of the reliability of your computer's memory. For more information, see Chapter 30, "Troubleshooting Hardware, Driver, and Disk Issues."
- **Command Prompt** From the Command Prompt tool, you have access to many standard command-line tools. Some tools will not work properly, however, because Windows Vista is not currently running. For example, because WinRE does not include networking capabilities, network tools will not function correctly. However, several tools in WinRE are useful:
  - BCDEdit.exe for making changes to the BCD registry file
  - Diskpart.exe for viewing and changing disk partitioning
  - Format.exe for formatting partitions
  - Chkdsk.exe for finding and resolving some disk problems (note that Chkdsk cannot add events to the event log when started from System Recovery tools)
  - Notepad.exe for viewing log files or editing configuration files
  - Bootsect.exe (available on the Windows 7 DVD in the \Boot\ folder) for updating the master boot code for hard disk partitions to switch between the Windows 7 Boot Manager and Ntldr, used by Windows XP and earlier versions of Windows
  - Bootrec.exe for manually repairing disk problems if Startup Repair cannot fix them

Windows Boot Performance Diagnostics

Sometimes, Windows might start correctly but might take an unusually long time to do so. Such a problem can be difficult to troubleshoot because there's no straightforward way to monitor processes while Windows is starting. To help administrators identify the source of startup performance problems and to automatically fix some problems, Windows 7 includes Windows Boot Performance Diagnostics.

You can use the Group Policy settings to manage Windows Boot Performance Diagnostics in an Active Directory Domain Services (AD DS) environment. In the Computer Configuration \Policies\Administrative Templates\System\Troubleshooting and Diagnostics\Windows Boot

Performance Diagnostics node, edit the Configure Scenario Execution Level policy. When this policy is enabled, you can choose from the following two settings:

- **Detection And Troubleshooting Only** Windows Boot Performance Diagnostics will identify startup performance problems and will add an event to the event log, allowing administrators to detect the problems and manually troubleshoot them. Windows Boot Performance Diagnostics will not attempt to fix the problems, however.
- **Detection, Troubleshooting, And Resolution** Windows Boot Performance Diagnostics will identify startup performance problems and automatically take steps to attempt to alleviate the problems.

If you disable the setting, Windows Boot Performance Diagnostics will neither identify nor attempt to resolve startup performance problems. For Windows Boot Performance Diagnostics to function, the Diagnostic Policy Service must be running.

Settings for Windows Shutdown Performance Diagnostics, which function similarly to the Windows Boot Performance Diagnostics, are located in the Computer Configuration\Policies\Administrative Templates\System\Troubleshooting And Diagnostics\Windows Shutdown Performance Diagnostics node.

Understanding the Startup Process

To diagnose and correct a startup problem, you need to understand what occurs during startup. Figure 29-2 provides a high-level overview of the different paths startup can take.

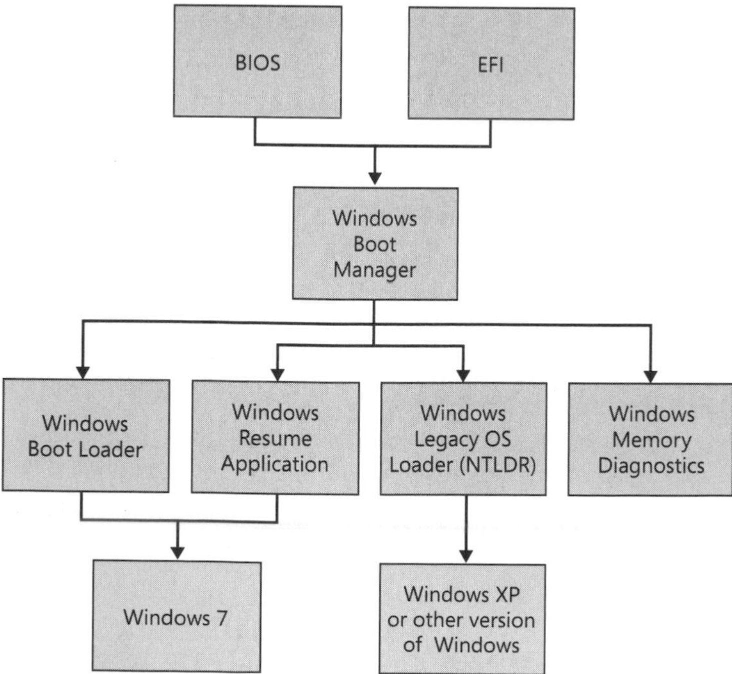

FIGURE 29-2 The Windows Boot Manager provides several different startup paths.

The normal startup sequence for Windows 7 is:

1. Power-on self test (POST) phase.
2. Initial startup phase.
3. Windows Boot Manager phase.
4. Windows Boot Loader phase.
5. Kernel loading phase.
6. Logon phase.

This sequence will vary if the computer is resuming from hibernation or if a non–Windows 7 option is selected during the Windows Boot Manager phase. The following sections describe the phases of a normal startup process in more detail.

Power-on Self Test Phase

As soon as you turn on a computer, its processor begins to carry out the programming instructions contained in the BIOS or EFI. The BIOS and EFI, which are types of firmware, contain the processor-dependent code that starts the computer regardless of the operating system installed. The first set of startup instructions is the POST, which is responsible for the following system and diagnostic functions:

- Performs initial hardware checks, such as determining the amount of memory present
- Verifies that the devices needed to start an operating system, such as a hard disk, are present
- Retrieves system configuration settings from nonvolatile memory, which is located on the motherboard

The contents of the nonvolatile memory remain even after you shut down the computer. Examples of hardware settings stored in the nonvolatile memory include device boot order and Plug and Play (PnP) information.

After the motherboard POST completes, add-on adapters that have their own firmware (for example, video and hard drive controllers) carry out internal diagnostic tests.

If startup fails before or during POST, your computer is experiencing a hardware failure. Generally, the BIOS or EFI displays an error message that indicates the nature of the problem. If video is not functioning correctly, the BIOS or EFI usually indicates the nature of the failure with a series of beeps.

To access and change system and peripheral firmware settings, consult the system documentation provided by the manufacturer. For more information, refer to your computer's documentation and see the section titled "How to Diagnose Hardware Problems" later in this chapter.

Initial Startup Phase

After the POST, computers must find and load the Windows Boot Manager. Older BIOS computers and newer EFI computers do this slightly differently, as the following sections describe.

Initial Startup Phase for BIOS Computers

After the POST, the settings that are stored in the nonvolatile memory, such as boot order, determine the devices that the computer can use to start an operating system. In addition to floppy disks or hard disks attached to Advanced Technology Attachment (ATA), Serial ATA, and small computer system interface (SCSI) controllers, computers can typically start an operating system from other devices, such as the following:

- CDs or DVDs
- Network adapters
- Universal serial bus (USB) flash drives
- Removable disks
- Secondary storage devices installed in docking stations for portable computers

It is possible to specify a custom boot order, such as CDROM, Floppy, Hard Disk. When you specify CDROM, Floppy, Hard Disk as a boot order, the following events occur at startup:

1. The computer searches the CD-ROM for bootable media. If a bootable CD or DVD is present, the computer uses the media as the startup device. Otherwise, the computer searches the next device in the boot order. You cannot use a non-bootable CD or DVD to start your system. The presence of a non-bootable CD or DVD in the CD-ROM drive can add to the time the system requires to start. If you do not intend to start the computer from CD, remove all CDs from the CD-ROM drive before restarting.
2. The computer searches the floppy disk for bootable media. If a bootable floppy is present, the computer uses the floppy disk as the startup device and loads the first sector (sector 0, the floppy disk boot sector) into memory. Otherwise, the computer searches the next device in the boot order or displays an error message.
3. The computer uses the hard disk as the startup device. The computer typically uses the hard disk as the startup device only when the CD-ROM drive and the floppy disk drive are empty.

There are exceptions in which code on bootable media transfers control to the hard disk. For example, when you start your system by using the bootable Windows DVD, Windows Setup checks the hard disk for Windows installations. If one is found, you have the option of bypassing DVD startup by not responding to the Press Any Key To Boot From CD Or DVD prompt that appears. This prompt is actually displayed by the startup program located on the Windows DVD, not by your computer's hardware.

If startup fails during the initial startup phase, you are experiencing a problem with the BIOS configuration, the disk subsystem, or the file system. The following error message is common during this phase. It indicates that none of the configured bootable media types was available.

```
Non-system disk or disk error
Replace and press any key when ready
```

If you changed the disk configuration recently, verify that all cables are properly connected and jumpers are correctly configured. If booting from the hard disk, verify that all removable media have been removed. If booting from a CD or DVD, verify that the BIOS is configured to start from the CD or DVD and that the Windows medium is present. If the disk subsystem and BIOS are configured correctly, the problem may be related to the file system. For instructions on repairing the Master Boot Record (MBR) and the boot sector, see the section titled "How to Run Startup Repair" later in this chapter. For detailed information about troubleshooting problems with the file system, see Chapter 16. For more information about configuring the boot order, consult your computer's documentation.

If you boot from the hard disk, the computer reads the boot code instructions located on the MBR. The MBR is the first sector of data on the startup hard disk. The MBR contains instructions (called *boot code*) and a table (called a *partition table*) that identify primary and extended partitions. The BIOS reads the MBR into memory and transfers control to the code in the MBR.

The computer then searches the partition table for the active partition, also known as a *bootable partition*. The first sector of the active partition contains boot code that enables the computer to do the following:

- Read the contents of the file system used.
- Locate and start a 16-bit stub program (Bootmgr) in the root directory of the boot volume. This stub program switches the processor into 32- or 64-bit Protected mode and loads the 32- or 64-bit Windows Boot Manager, which is stored in the same Bootmgr file. After the Windows Boot Manager loads, startup is identical for both BIOS and EFI computers.

> ***NOTE*** **The stub program is necessary because 32-bit and 64-bit computers first start in Real mode. In Real mode, the processor disables certain features to allow compatibility with software designed to run on 8-bit and 16-bit processors. The Windows Boot Manager is 32-bit or 64-bit, however, so the stub program sets up the BIOS computer to run the 32-bit or 64-bit software properly.**

If an active partition does not exist or if boot sector information is missing or corrupt, a message similar to any of the following might appear:

- Invalid partition table
- Error loading operating system
- Missing operating system

If an active partition is successfully located, the code in the boot sector locates and starts Windows Boot Loader (WinLoad) and the BIOS transfers execution to it.

Initial Startup Phase for EFI Computers

Startup for EFI computers initially differs from startup for BIOS computers. EFI computers have a built-in boot manager that enables the computer's hardware to choose from multiple operating systems based on user input. When you install Windows 7 on an EFI computer, Windows adds a single entry to the EFI boot manager with the title Windows Boot Manager. This entry points to the \Efi\Microsoft\Boot\Bootmgfw.efi 32-bit or 64-bit EFI executable program—the Windows Boot Manager. This is the same Windows Boot Manager that is eventually loaded on BIOS-based computers. Windows configures the EFI boot manager to display the EFI startup menu for only 2 seconds and then load the Windows Boot Manager by default to minimize complexity and startup time.

If you install a different operating system or manually change the EFI boot manager settings, EFI might no longer load the Windows Boot Manager. To resolve this problem, use the Startup Repair tool, as described in the section titled "The Process of Troubleshooting Startup" later in this chapter. Alternatively, you might be able to update the EFI boot manager settings manually using your computer's built-in EFI tools. For more information about configuring EFI, consult your computer's documentation.

Windows Boot Manager Phase

The Windows Boot Manager is capable of natively reading supported file systems, and it uses that capability to parse the BCD registry file without fully loading the file system.

For computers that have a single operating system, Windows Boot Manager never displays a user interface. It does, however, wait for a few moments to allow the user to press a key to display the standard boot menu, as shown in Figure 29-3, or to press F8 to choose Advanced Boot Options, as shown in Figure 29-4. If the user does not press a key within a few seconds of POST completing, Windows Boot Manager starts the Windows Boot Loader, which in turn starts Windows 7.

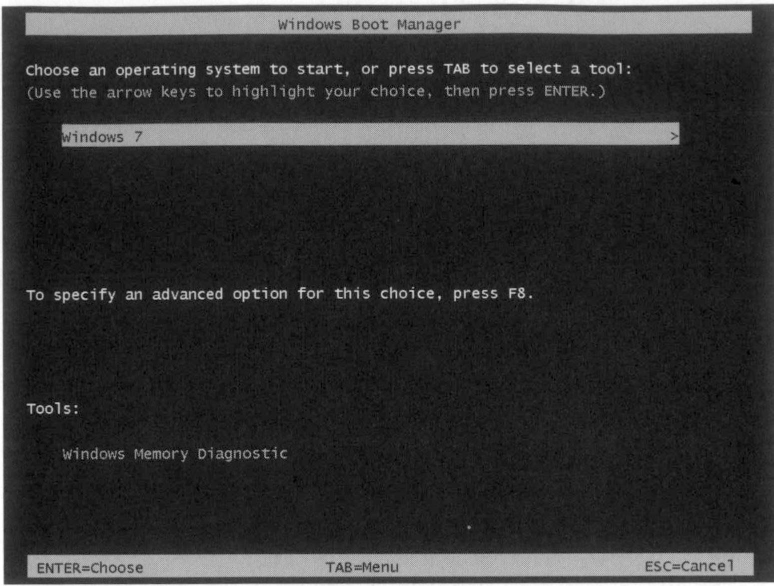

FIGURE 29-3 Windows Boot Manager enables you to choose from multiple operating systems or start Windows Memory Diagnostics.

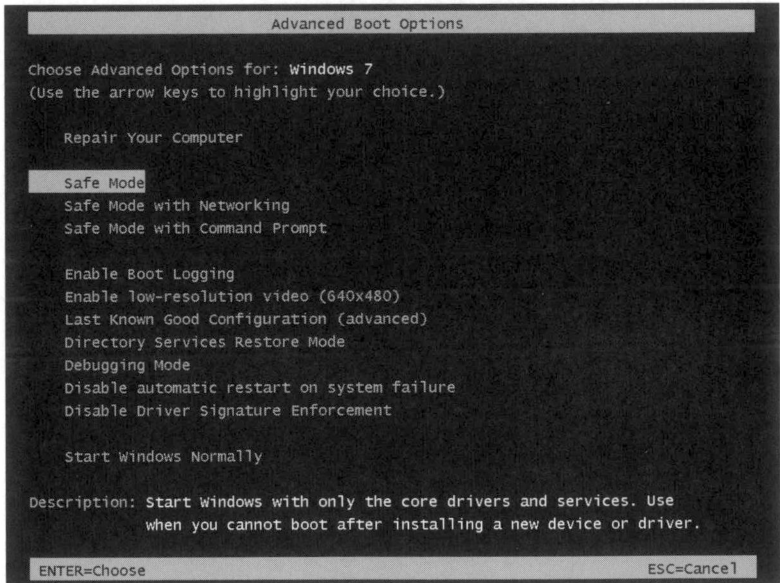

FIGURE 29-4 During startup, you can interrupt the default behavior of Windows Boot Manager to view the Advanced Boot Options.

For computers with multiple operating systems installed (such as both Windows 7 and Windows XP), Windows Boot Manager displays a menu of operating system choices at startup. Depending on what you choose, Windows Boot Manager will start a different process:

- If you choose Windows Vista or Windows 7, Windows Boot Manager starts the Windows Boot Loader to open Windows.
- If you choose Earlier Version Of Windows or another entry for Windows Server 2003, Windows XP Professional, Microsoft Windows 2000, or Microsoft Windows NT 4.0, Windows Boot Manager starts Ntldr, which then proceeds with the hardware detection phase.
- If you select another operating system, control is passed to the boot sector for the other operating system.
- If you choose Windows Memory Diagnostic by pressing the Tab key, Windows Boot Manager starts the diagnostic tool without first opening Windows.

Windows Boot Loader Phase

The Windows Boot Manager starts the Windows Boot Loader phase when the user chooses to load Windows Vista or Windows 7. The Windows Boot Loader does the following:

1. Loads the operating system kernel, Ntoskrnl.exe, but does not yet run it.
2. Loads the Hardware Abstraction Layer (HAL), Hal.dll. This will not be used until the kernel is run.
3. Loads the system registry hive (System32\Config\System) into memory.
4. Scans the HKEY_LOCAL_MACHINE\SYSTEM\Services key for device drivers and loads all drivers that are configured for the boot class into memory. The Windows Boot Loader does not, however, initiate the drivers. Drivers are not initiated until the kernel loading phase.
5. Enables paging.
6. Passes control to the operating system kernel, which starts the next phase.

Kernel Loading Phase

The Windows Boot Loader is responsible for loading the Windows kernel (Ntoskrnl.exe) and the HAL into memory. Together, the kernel and the HAL initialize a group of software features that are called the *Windows executive*. The Windows executive processes the configuration information stored in the registry in HKLM\SYSTEM\CurrentControlSet and starts services and drivers. The following sections provide more detail about the kernel loading phase.

Control Sets

The Windows Boot Loader reads control set information from the registry key HKEY_LOCAL_MACHINE\SYSTEM, which is stored in the file %SystemRoot%\System32\Config\System, so that the kernel can determine which device drivers need to be loaded during startup. Typically, several control sets exist, with the actual number depending on how often system configuration settings change.

The HKEY_LOCAL_MACHINE\SYSTEM subkeys used during startup are:

- \CurrentControlSet, a pointer to a ControlSet*xxx* subkey (where *xxx* represents a control set number, such as 001) designated in the \Select\Current value.
- \Select, which contains the following entries:
    - **Default** Points to the control set number (for example, 001=ControlSet001) that the system has specified for use at the next startup. If no error or manual invocation of the LastKnownGood startup option occurs, this control set number is designated as the value of the Default, Current, and LastKnownGood entries (assuming that a user is able to log on successfully).
    - **Current** Points to the last control set that was used to start the system.
    - **Failed** Points to a control set that did not start Windows Vista successfully. This value is updated when the LastKnownGood option is used to start the system.
    - **LastKnownGood** Points to the control set that was used during the last user session. When a user logs on, the LastKnownGood control set is updated with configuration information from the previous user session.

The Windows Boot Loader uses the control set identified by the \Select\Default value unless you choose the Last Known Good Configuration from the Advanced Boot Options menu.

The kernel creates the registry key HKEY_LOCAL_MACHINE\HARDWARE, which contains the hardware data collected at system startup. Windows supports an extensive set of devices, with additional drivers not on the Windows operating system DVD provided by hardware manufacturers. Drivers are kernel-mode features required by devices to function within an operating system. Services are features that support operating system and application functions and act as network servers. Services can run in a different context than user applications and typically do not offer many user-configurable options.

For example, the Print Spooler service does not require a user to be logged on to run and functions independently of the user who is logged on to the system. Drivers generally communicate directly with hardware devices, whereas services usually communicate with hardware through drivers. Driver and service files are typically stored in the %SystemRoot%\System32 and %SystemRoot%\System32\Drivers folders and use .exe, .sys, or .dll file name extensions.

Drivers are also services. Therefore, during kernel initialization, the Windows Boot Loader and Ntoskrnl use the information stored in the HKEY_LOCAL_MACHINE\SYSTEM\CurrentControlSet\Services*Servicename* registry subkeys to determine both the drivers and services to load. In the *Servicename* subkeys, the Start entry specifies when to start the service. For example, the Windows Boot Loader loads all drivers for which Start is 0, such as device drivers for hard disk controllers. After execution is transferred to the kernel, the kernel loads drivers and services for which Start is 1.

Table 29-1 lists the values (in decimal) for the registry entry Start. Boot drivers (those for which Start is 0) and file system drivers are always loaded regardless of the value of Start because they are required to start Windows.

TABLE 29-1 Values for the Start Registry Entry

VALUE	START TYPE	VALUE DESCRIPTIONS FOR START ENTRIES
0	Boot	Specifies a driver that is loaded (but not started) by the boot loader. If no errors occur, the driver is started during kernel initialization prior to any non-boot drivers being loaded.
1	System	Specifies a driver that loads and starts during kernel initialization after drivers with a Start value of 0 have been started.
2	Auto load	Specifies a driver or service that is initialized at system startup by Session Manager (Smss.exe) or the Services Controller (Services.exe).
3	Load on demand	Specifies a driver or service that the Service Control Manager (SCM) will start only on demand. These drivers have to be started manually by calling a Win32 SCM application programming interface (API), such as the Services snap-in.
4	Disabled	Specifies a disabled (not started) driver or service.
5	Delayed start	Specifies that less-critical services will start shortly after startup to allow the operating system to be responsive to the user sooner. This start type was first introduced in Windows Vista.

Table 29-2 lists some of the values (in decimal) for the Type registry entry.

TABLE 29-2 Type Registry Values

VALUE	VALUE DESCRIPTIONS FOR TYPE ENTRIES
1	Specifies a kernel device driver
2	Specifies a kernel-mode file system driver (also a kernel device driver)
4	Specifies arguments passed to an adapter
8	Specifies a file system driver, such as a file system recognizer driver
16	Specifies a service that obeys the service control protocol, runs within a process that hosts only one service, and can be started by the Services Controller
32	Specifies a service that runs in a process that hosts multiple services
256	Specifies a service that is allowed to display windows on the console and receive user input

Some drivers and services require that conditions, also known as *dependencies*, be met. You can find dependencies listed under the DependOnGroup and DependOnService entries in the HKEY_LOCAL_MACHINE\SYSTEM\CurrentControlSet\Services*Servicename* subkey for each service or driver. For more information about using dependencies to prevent or delay a driver or service from starting, see the section titled "How to Temporarily Disable a Service" later in this chapter. The Services subkey also contains information that affects how drivers and services are loaded. Table 29-3 lists some of these other entries.

TABLE 29-3 Other Registry Entries in the *Servicename* Subkeys

ENTRY	DESCRIPTION
DependOnGroup	At least one item from this group must start before this service is loaded.
DependOnService	Lists the specific services that must load before this service loads.
DisplayName	Describes the feature.
ErrorControl	Controls whether a driver error requires the system to use the LastKnownGood control set or to display a Stop message. If the value is 0x0 (Ignore, No Error Is Reported), it does not display a warning and proceeds with startup. If the value is 0x1 (Normal, Error Reported), it records the event to the System Event Log and displays a warning message but proceeds with startup. If the value is 0x2 (Severe), it records the event to the System Event Log, uses the LastKnownGood settings, restarts the system, and proceeds with startup. If the value is 0x3 (Critical), it records the event to the System Event Log, uses the LastKnownGood settings, and restarts the system. If the LastKnownGood settings are already in use, it displays a Stop message.
Group	Designates the group that the driver or service belongs to. This allows related drivers or services to start together (for example, file system drivers). The registry entry List in the subkey HKEY_LOCAL_MACHINE\SYSTEM \CurrentControlSet\Control \ServiceGroupOrder specifies the group startup order.
ImagePath	Identifies the path and file name of the driver or service if the ImagePath entry is present.
ObjectName	Specifies an object name. If the Type entry specifies a service, it represents the account name that the service uses to log on when it runs.
Tag	Designates the order in which a driver starts within a driver group.

Session Manager

After all entries that have Boot and Startup data types are processed, the kernel starts the Session Manager (Smss.exe), a user process that continues to run until the operating system is shut down. The Session Manager performs important initialization functions, such as:

- Creating system environment variables.
- Starting the kernel-mode portion of the Win32 subsystem (implemented by %SystemRoot%\System32\Win32k.sys), which causes Windows to switch from text mode (used to display the Windows Boot Manager menu) to graphics mode (used to display the Starting Windows logo). Windows-based applications run in the Windows subsystem. This environment allows applications to access operating system functions, such as displaying information to the screen.
- Starting the user-mode portion of the Win32 subsystem (implemented by %SystemRoot%\System32\Csrss.exe). The applications that use the Windows subsystem are user-mode processes; they do not have direct access to hardware or device drivers. Instead, they have to access Windows APIs to gain indirect access to hardware. This allows Windows to control direct hardware access, improving security and reliability. User-mode processes run at a lower priority than kernel-mode processes. When the operating system needs more memory, it can page to disk the memory used by user-mode processes.
- Starting the Logon Manager (%SystemRoot%\System32\Winlogon.exe).
- Creating additional virtual memory paging files.
- Performing delayed rename operations for files specified by the registry entry HKEY_LOCAL_MACHINE\SYSTEM\CurrentControlSet\Control\Session Manager \PendingFileRenameOperations. For example, you might be prompted to restart the computer after installing a new driver or application so that Windows can replace files that are currently in use.

Session Manager searches the registry for service information contained in the following subkeys:

- HKEY_LOCAL_MACHINE\SYSTEM\CurrentControlSet\Control\Session Manager contains a list of commands to run before loading services. The Autochk.exe tool is specified by the value of the registry entry BootExecute and virtual memory (paging file) settings stored in the Memory Management subkey. Autochk, which is a version of the Chkdsk tool, runs at startup if the operating system detects a file system problem that requires repair before completing the startup process.
- HKEY_LOCAL_MACHINE\SYSTEM\CurrentControlSet\Control\Session Manager \SubSystems stores a list of available subsystems. For example, Csrss.exe contains the user-mode portion of the Windows subsystem.

If startup fails during the kernel loading phase after another operating system was installed on the computer, the cause of the problem is likely an incompatible boot loader. Boot loaders installed by versions of Windows prior to Windows Vista cannot be used to start

Windows Vista or Windows 7. Use System Recovery to replace startup files with Windows startup files.

Otherwise, if startup fails during the kernel loading phase, use boot logging to isolate the failing feature. Then use safe mode to disable problematic features (if possible) or use System Recovery to replace problematic files. For more information, see the section titled "Startup Troubleshooting Before the Starting Windows Logo Appears" later in this chapter. If you experience a Stop error during this phase, use the information provided by the Stop message to isolate the failing feature. For more information about troubleshooting Stop errors, see Chapter 32, "Troubleshooting Stop Messages."

Logon Phase

The Windows subsystem starts Winlogon.exe, a system service that enables you to log on and log off. Winlogon.exe then does the following:

- Starts the Services subsystem (Services.exe), also known as the SCM. The SCM initializes services that the registry entry Start designates as Autoload in the registry subkey HKEY_LOCAL_MACHINE\SYSTEM\CurrentControlSet\Services*Servicename*.
- Starts the Local Security Authority (LSA) process (Lsass.exe).
- Parses the Ctrl+Alt+Delete key combination at the Begin Logon prompt (if the computer is part of an AD DS domain).

The logon user interface (LogonUI) feature and the credential provider (which can be the standard credential provider or a third-party credential provider) collect the user name and password (or other credentials) and pass this information securely to the LSA for authentication. If the user supplied valid credentials, access is granted by using either the default Kerberos V 5 authentication protocol or Windows NT LAN Manager (NTLM).

Winlogon initializes security and authentication features while PnP initializes auto-load services and drivers. After the user logs on, the control set referenced by the registry entry LastKnownGood (located in HKLM\SYSTEM\Select) is updated with the contents in the CurrentControlSet subkey. By default, Winlogon then starts Userinit.exe and the Windows Explorer shell. Userinit may then start other processes, including:

- **Group Policy settings take effect** Group Policy settings that apply to the user and computer take effect.
- **Startup programs run** When not overridden by Group Policy settings, Windows starts logon scripts, startup programs, and services referenced in the following registry subkeys and file system folders:
  - HKEY_LOCAL_MACHINE\SOFTWARE\Microsoft\Windows\CurrentVersion\Runonce
  - HKEY_LOCAL_MACHINE\SOFTWARE\Microsoft\Windows\CurrentVersion\Policies\Explorer\Run
  - HKEY_LOCAL_MACHINE\SOFTWARE\Microsoft\Windows\CurrentVersion\Run

- HKEY_CURRENT_USER\Software\Microsoft\Windows NT\CurrentVersion\Windows\Run
- HKEY_CURRENT_USER\Software\Microsoft\Windows\CurrentVersion\Run
- HKEY_CURRENT_USER\Software\Microsoft\Windows\CurrentVersion\RunOnce
- *SystemDrive*\Documents and Settings\All Users\Start Menu\Programs\Startup
- *SystemDrive*\Documents and Settings*username*\Start Menu\Programs\Startup

Several applications might be configured to start by default after you install Windows, including Windows Defender. Computer manufacturers or IT departments might configure other startup applications.

Windows startup is not complete until a user successfully logs on to the computer. If startup fails during the logon phase, you have a problem with a service or application configured to start automatically. For troubleshooting information, see the section titled "How to Temporarily Disable Startup Applications and Processes" later in this chapter. If you experience a Stop error during this phase, use the information provided by the Stop message to isolate the failing feature. For more information about troubleshooting Stop errors, see Chapter 32.

Important Startup Files

For Windows to start, the system and boot partitions must contain the files listed in Table 29-4.

TABLE 29-4 Windows Startup Files

FILE NAME	DISK LOCATION	DESCRIPTION
BootMgr	Root of the system partition	The Windows Boot Manager.
WinLoad	%SystemRoot%\System32	The Windows Boot Loader.
BCD	\Boot	A file that specifies the paths to operating system installations and other information required for Windows to start.
Ntoskrnl.exe	%SystemRoot%\System32	The core (also called the *kernel*) of the Windows operating system. Code that runs as part of the kernel does so in privileged processor mode and has direct access to system data and hardware.
Hal.dll	%SystemRoot%\System32	The HAL dynamic-link library (DLL) file. The HAL abstracts low-level hardware details from the operating system and provides a common programming interface to devices of the same type (such as video adapters).

FILE NAME	DISK LOCATION	DESCRIPTION
Smss.exe	%SystemRoot%\System32	The Session Manager file. Session Manager is a user-mode process created by the kernel during startup. It handles critical startup tasks including creating page files and performing delayed file rename and delete operations.
Csrss.exe	%SystemRoot%\System32	The Win32 Subsystem file. The Win32 Subsystem is started by Session Manager and is required by Windows to function.
Winlogon.exe	%SystemRoot%\System32	The Logon Process file, which handles user logon requests and intercepts the Ctrl+Alt+Delete logon key sequence. The Logon Process is started by Session Manager. This is a required feature.
Services.exe	%SystemRoot%\System32	The Service Control Manager is responsible for starting and stopping services and is a required feature of Windows.
Lsass.exe	%SystemRoot%\System32	The Local Security Authentication Server process is called by the Logon Process when authenticating users and is a required feature.
System registry file	%SystemRoot%\System32 \Config\System	The file that contains data used to create the registry key HKEY_LOCAL_MACHINE\SYSTEM. This key contains information that the operating system requires to start devices and system services.
Device drivers	%SystemRoot%\System32 \Drivers	Driver files in this folder are for hardware devices, such as keyboard, mouse, and video.

In Table 29-4, the term *%SystemRoot%* is one of many *environment variables* used to associate string values, such as folder or file paths, to variables that Windows applications and services use. For example, by using environment variables, scripts can run without modification on computers that have different configurations. To obtain a list of environment variables that you can use for troubleshooting, type **set** at the Windows command prompt.

How to Configure Startup Settings

Windows Vista and Windows 7 enable administrators to configure startup settings using many of the same graphical tools that Windows XP provides. Command-line tools for configuring startup tools have been replaced with new tools, however, and you can no longer directly edit the startup configuration file (formerly the Boot.ini file). The following sections describe several techniques for configuring startup settings.

How to Use the Startup And Recovery Dialog Box

The simplest way to edit the BCD registry file is to use the Startup And Recovery dialog box. To use the Startup And Recovery dialog box to change the default operating system, follow these steps:

1. Click Start, right-click Computer, and then click Properties.
2. Click Advanced System Settings.
3. In Startup And Recovery, click Settings.
4. Click the Default Operating System list and then click the operating system that you want to boot by default.
5. Click OK twice.

The default operating system will automatically load the next time you start the computer.

How to Use the System Configuration Tool

The System Configuration tool offers more advanced control over startup settings, including some ability to configure the BCD registry file. This tool is specifically designed for troubleshooting, and you can use it to easily undo changes that you have made to the computer's configuration (even after restarting the computer). If you make changes with the System Configuration tool, it will remind users logging on that settings have been temporarily changed—thus reducing the likelihood that settings will not be reset after the troubleshooting process has been completed.

Some common tasks for the System Configuration tool include:

- Temporarily disabling startup applications to isolate the cause of a post-logon problem.
- Temporarily disabling automatic services to isolate the cause of a pre-logon or post-logon problem.
- Permanently or temporarily configuring the BCD registry file.
- Configuring a normal, diagnostic, or selective startup for Windows Vista.

To use the System Configuration tool, click Start, type **Msconfig**, and then press Enter. The System Configuration tool provides five tabs:

- **General** Use this tab to change the next startup mode. Normal Startup loads all device drivers and services. Diagnostic Startup is useful for troubleshooting startup problems, and it loads only basic devices and services. Use Selective Startup to specify whether you want to load system services or startup items.
- **Boot** Use this tab to configure the BCD registry file and startup settings. You can remove startup operating system options, set the default operating system, configure

advanced settings for an operating system (including number of processors, maximum memory, and debug settings), and configure Windows for Safe Boot or to boot without a graphical interface.

- **Services** Use this tab to change the startup settings for a service temporarily. This is an excellent way to determine whether an automatic service is causing startup problems. After you disable a service, restart your computer and determine whether the problem still exists. If it does, you have eliminated one potential cause of the problem. You can then use this tab to re-enable the service, disable another service, and repeat the process. To disable services permanently, use the Services console.
- **Startup** Lists applications that are configured to start automatically. This is the best way to disable applications temporarily during troubleshooting because you can easily re-enable them later using the same tool. You should not use the System Configuration tool to permanently remove startup applications, however, because the System Configuration tool is designed to enable you to easily undo changes. Instead, you should manually remove the application.
- **Tools** Provides links to other tools that you can start.

> ***NOTE*** **The Win.ini, System.ini, and Boot.ini tabs do not appear in the System Configuration tool because those files have not been used since Windows XP.**

Because the System Configuration tool is a graphical tool, it is primarily useful when Windows is booting successfully.

How to Use BCDEdit

The BCDEdit command-line tool provides you with almost unlimited control over the BCD registry file and configuration settings.

> ***NOTE*** **If you have a computer with both Windows XP and Windows 7 installed and you want to modify the BCD registry file from Windows XP, you can run BCDEdit from Windows XP by starting it directly from the Windows\System32 folder of your Windows 7 installation. Although this might be useful in some multiboot configurations, typically, you should run BCDEdit from the System Recovery command prompt if you cannot load Windows 7.**

You must use administrative credentials to run BCDEdit from within Windows 7. To do this, follow these steps:

1. Click Start, click All Programs, and then click Accessories.
2. Right-click Command Prompt and then click Run As Administrator.

To view detailed information about using BCDEdit, run **BCDEdit /?** from a command prompt. The following sections describe how to perform specific tasks with BCDEdit.

How to Interpret BCDEdit Output

You can view settings currently defined in your BCD registry file by using the *bcdedit /enum* command. Optionally, you can follow the command with one of the following parameters to change which entries are displayed:

- **Active** The default setting that is displayed if you run *bcdedit /enum* without any additional parameters. Displays all entries in the Boot Manager display order.
- **Firmware** Displays all firmware applications.
- **Bootapp** Displays all boot environment applications.
- **Osloader** Displays all operating system entries.
- **Resume** Displays all resume from hibernation entries.
- **Inherit** Displays all inherit entries.
- **All** Displays all entries.

For example, to view the startup entry used to resume from hibernation, run the following command at an administrative command prompt.

```
bcdedit /enum resume
```

Similarly, to view all startup entries, use the following command.

```
bcdedit /enum all
```

How to Back Up and Restore Settings

Making changes to your BCD registry file can render your computer unbootable. Therefore, before making changes to your BCD registry file, you should make a backup copy, have a bootable Windows DVD available, and be prepared to restore the original BCD registry file.

To make a backup of your current BCD registry, call the *BCDEdit /export* command, as shown here.

```
bcdedit /export backupbcd.bcd
```

Later, you can restore your original BCD registry file by calling the *BCDEdit /import* command, as shown here.

```
bcdedit /import backupbcd.bcd
```

NOTE **The file name and extension you use are not significant.**

If Windows is unbootable, follow the instructions in the section titled "The Process of Troubleshooting Startup" later in this chapter.

How to Change the Default Operating System Entry

To view the current default operating system entry, run the following command and look for the *default* line.

```
bcdedit /enum {bootmgr}
```

```
Windows Boot Manager
--------------------
identifier              {bootmgr}
device                  partition=\Device\HarddiskVolume1
description             Windows Boot Manager
locale                  en-US
inherit                 {globalsettings}
default                 {current}
resumeobject            {24a500f3-12ea-11db-a536-b7db70c06ac2}
displayorder            {current}
toolsdisplayorder       {memdiag}
timeout                 30
```

To change the default operating system entry, first run the following command to view the existing entries and make note of the identifier for the entry that you want to be the default.

```
bcdedit /enum
```

Then run the following command to set a new default (where *<id>* is the identifier for the new entry).

```
bcdedit /default <id>
```

For example, to configure the Windows Boot Manager to start the previous installation of Windows XP by default (which is identified as *{ntldr}*), run the following command.

```
bcdedit /default {ntldr}
```

To configure the currently running instance of Windows 7 as the default, run the following command.

```
bcdedit /default {current}
```

How to Change the Boot Menu Time-Out

The boot menu, by default, is displayed for 30 seconds if you have more than one boot menu entry. If you have only one boot menu entry, the menu is not displayed at all (although the Boot Manager does wait several seconds so that you can press a key to view the menu).

To change the time-out for the boot menu, use the *bcdedit /timeout seconds* command, as shown here.

```
bcdedit /timeout 15
```

How to Change the Order of Boot Manager Menu Items

To change the order of Boot Manager menu items, use the *bcdedit /display* command, and then list the menu item identifiers in the desired sequence, as shown in the following example.

```
bcdedit /display {current} {ntldr} {cbd971bf-b7b8-4885-951a-fa0344f5d71}
```

How to Create an Entry for Another Operating System

You can use BCDEdit to create an entry for an operating system other than Windows 7. You may need to add boot entries to the BCD registry file if you want to be able to load different operating systems on a single computer. Although Windows automatically creates boot entries for existing operating systems when installed, you might need to add a boot entry manually if you install another operating system after Windows 7 or if you want to load an operating system from a newly attached hard disk.

By default, the BCD registry file contains an entry called *{ntldr}* that is configured to start an older version of Windows from your C:\ partition. If you have only one older operating system and Earlier Version Of Windows does not currently appear on the computer's boot menu, you can use this existing entry to start the older operating system. To do this, call *BCDEdit /set* to configure the boot volume. Then add the entry to the Windows Boot Manager operating system menu by calling the *BCDEdit /displayorder* command. The following code demonstrates how to do this.

```
REM Modify the following line to identify the other OS' partition
REM The following line could also be, "bcdedit /set {ntldr} device boot"
bcdedit /set {ntldr} device partition=C:

REM The following line makes the entry bootable by adding it to the menu
bcdedit /displayorder {ntldr} /addlast
```

You can verify that the new entry will appear on the boot menu by running the command *bcdedit /enum ACTIVE* and looking for the Windows Legacy OS Loader entry.

If you need to be able to choose from multiple older Windows operating systems, you should choose the *{ntldr}* entry from the boot menu. The Windows Boot Manager will then pass control to Ntldr, which will display a menu based on the Boot.ini file that you can use to choose from all Windows operating systems.

If you want to create an entry for a non-Microsoft operating system, you can either create an entry using the *bcdedit /create* command, or you can copy the existing *{ntldr}* entry and update it for the operating system. To base a new entry on *{ntldr}*, copy the entry, update the boot loader path, and then add it to the boot menu by running these commands.

```
bcdedit /copy {ntldr} /d "Other operating system (or other description)"

REM The previous command will display a new GUID that identifies the copy.
REM Use the GUID in the following command, and modify the partition identifier as
needed.
bcdedit /set {NEW-GUID} device partition=C:
```

> **NOTE** Don't retype the GUID by hand—you're likely to make a mistake. Instead, copy it to the Clipboard as follows: Click the command menu in the upper-left corner of the command prompt window, click Edit, and then click Mark. Select the GUID text (including the brackets) and then press Enter on your keyboard. To paste the GUID to the command prompt, click the command menu, click Edit, and then click Paste.

Now run the following command to identify the operating system's boot loader.

```
REM Replace the last parameter with the boot loader filename
bcdedit /set {NEW-GUID} path \boot-loader
```

If *{ntldr}* was not part of the boot menu when you copied it, you also need to run the following command to add the copied entry to the boot menu.

```
bcdedit /displayorder {NEW-GUID} /addlast
```

Additionally, you might need to configure the operating system's own boot loader.

How to Remove a Boot Entry

Typically, you do not need to remove entries from the BCD registry file. Instead, you should simply remove entries from the Windows Boot Manager menu. To remove an entry from the menu, first run *bcdedit /enum* and note the boot entry's identifier. Then run the following command, substituting the identifier.

```
bcdedit /displayorder {GUID} /remove
```

For example, to remove the entry to load the previous version of Windows from the boot menu, you would run this command.

```
bcdedit /displayorder {ntldr} /remove
```

You can later re-add the entry to the boot menu by calling the following command.

```
bcdedit /displayorder {GUID} /addlast
```

To permanently remove an entry from the BCD registry, run the following command.

```
bcdedit /delete {GUID} /remove
```

You should permanently remove an entry only if you have removed the operating system files from the computer.

How to View and Update Global Debugger Settings

To view debugger settings for startup entries, run the following command.

```
bcdedit /enum
```

For more information about viewing entries, see the section titled "How to Interpret BCDEdit Output" earlier in this chapter. To change debugger settings for a startup entry, run the following command.

```
bcdedit /dbgsettings DebugType [debugport:Port] [baudrate:Baud]
[channel:Channel] [targetname:TargetName]
```

Replace the parameters with your custom settings, as described in the following list:

- **DebugType** Specifies the type of debugger. DebugType can be SERIAL, 1394, or USB. The remaining options depend on the debugger type selected.
- **Port** For SERIAL debugging, specifies the serial port to use as the debugging port.
- **Baud** For SERIAL debugging, specifies the baud rate to be used for debugging.
- **Channel** For 1394 debugging, specifies the 1394 channel to be used for debugging.
- **Target Name** For USB debugging, specifies the USB target name to be used for debugging.

For example, the following command sets the global debugger settings to SERIAL debugging over com1 at 115,200 baud.

```
bcdedit /dbgsettings serial debugport:1 baudrate:115200
```

The following command sets the global debugger settings to 1394 debugging using channel 23.

```
bcdedit /dbgsettings 1394 CHANNEL:32
```

The following command sets the global debugger settings to USB debugging using target name *debugging*.

```
bcdedit /dbgsettings USB targetname:debugging
```

How to Remove the Windows 7 Boot Loader

If you want to remove Windows 7 from a dual-boot environment that includes Windows XP or an earlier version of Windows, follow these steps:

1. Use Bootsect.exe to restore the Ntldr.exe program. To do this, type the following command, where *D:* is the drive containing the Windows installation media.

   ```
   D:\Boot\Bootsect.exe -NT52 All
   ```

   After the computer restarts, it does not load the Windows Boot Manager program. Instead, Ntldr.exe loads and processes the Boot.ini file to start an earlier version of Windows.

2. If Windows 7 is not installed on the active partition, you can now delete or remove the partition where Windows 7 is installed.

> **NOTE** You can follow these steps in any version of Windows. If you follow these steps in Windows Vista or Windows 7, run the commands from a command prompt that has elevated user rights. To do this, click Start, click Accessories, right-click the command prompt shortcut, and then click Run As Administrator.

How to Configure a User Account to Automatically Log On

Requiring users to enter credentials when their computers start is an important part of Windows security. If a user account automatically logs on, anyone who has physical access to the computer can restart it and access the user's files. Nonetheless, in scenarios in which a computer is physically secure, automatic logon might be preferred. To configure a workgroup computer (you cannot perform these steps on a domain member) to automatically log on, follow these steps:

1. Click Start, type **netplwiz**, and then press Enter.
2. In the User Accounts dialog box, click the account you want to automatically log on to. If it is available, clear the Users Must Enter A User Name And Password To Use This Computer check box.
3. Click OK.
4. In the Automatically Log On dialog box, enter the user's password twice. Click OK.

The next time you restart the computer, it will automatically log on with the local user account you selected. Configuring automatic logon stores the user's password in the registry unencrypted, where someone might be able to retrieve it.

How to Disable the Windows Startup Sound

By default, Windows plays a sound as part of the startup process. This sound can be useful for troubleshooting startup problems because it indicates whether you have reached a specific startup phase. If you prefer, you can disable the startup sound by following these steps:

1. Click Start and then click Control Panel.
2. In Control Panel, click Hardware And Sound.
3. Click Change System Sounds.
4. On the Sounds tab, clear the Play Windows Startup Sound check box. Click OK.

How to Speed Up the Startup Process

Although startup is a complex process and the time required varies from computer to computer, you can often reduce the startup time. To optimize settings that might improve startup time, follow these steps:

1. In the computer's BIOS settings, set the computer to boot first from the Windows boot drive. If you need to boot from removable media in the future, you will first need to change this setting.
2. In the computer's BIOS settings, enable Fast Boot, if available, to disable time-consuming and often unnecessary hardware checks.
3. If you have more than one boot menu item, reduce the boot menu time-out value using the Boot tab of the Msconfig tool. Alternatively, you can use BCDEdit to reduce the time-out value, as described in the section titled "How to Change the Boot Menu Time-Out" earlier in this chapter.
4. Clear disk space if free disk space is below 15 percent and then defragment the hard disk, as described in Chapter 16. Although defragmentation happens automatically by default, defragmentation is less effective if free disk space is low.
5. Disable unnecessary hardware using Windows Device Manager, as described in Chapter 17, "Managing Devices and Services."
6. Use Windows ReadyBoost, as described in Chapter 16, to cache some files used in the startup process to a USB flash drive.
7. Remove unnecessary startup applications.
8. For services (other than those included with Windows) that need to start automatically but do not need to start immediately, use the Services console to change the startup type to Automatic (Delayed Start). If services are set to start automatically but are not required, change the startup type to Manual. For more information, refer to Chapter 16.

For detailed startup performance troubleshooting, examine the Applications And Services Logs\Microsoft\Windows\Diagnostics-Performance\Operational Event Log. Events with IDs from 100 to 199 provide startup performance detail in the event of long startup times. In particular, event ID 100 indicates the startup time in milliseconds. Other events identify applications or services that are causing a startup performance degradation.

The Process of Troubleshooting Startup

Startup problems can be divided into three distinct categories:

- **Problems that occur before the Starting Windows logo appears** These problems are typically caused by missing startup files (often as a result of installing a different operating system over Windows 7), corrupted files, or hardware problems. For information about troubleshooting problems that occur after logon, read the next section, "Startup Troubleshooting Before the Starting Windows Logo Appears."

- **Problems that occur after the Starting Windows logo appears but before the logon prompt is displayed** These problems are typically caused by faulty or misconfigured drivers and services. Hardware problems can also cause failure during this phase of startup. For information about troubleshooting problems that occur after the Starting Windows logo appears but before logon, read the section titled "Startup Troubleshooting After the Starting Windows Logo Appears" later in this chapter.
- **Problems that occur after logon** These problems are typically caused by startup applications. For information about troubleshooting problems that occur after logon, read the section titled "Troubleshooting Startup Problems After Logon" later in this chapter.

Startup Troubleshooting Before the Starting Windows Logo Appears

Troubleshooting startup problems is more challenging than troubleshooting problems that occur while Windows is running, because you cannot access the full suite of troubleshooting tools included with Windows. However, Windows does provide several tools that you can use to identify the cause and resolve the problem if you cannot start the operating system. Most important, you can start WinRE by booting from the Windows Vista DVD or directly from the computer's hard disk. WinRE can start automatically if Windows cannot start correctly. The WinRE tools include the Startup Repair tool, which can automatically fix many common startup problems.

Follow the process illustrated in Figure 29-5 to troubleshoot startup problems that occur before the Starting Windows logo appears. After each troubleshooting step, you should attempt to start the computer. If the computer starts successfully or if startup progresses far enough to display the Starting Windows logo, you can stop troubleshooting.

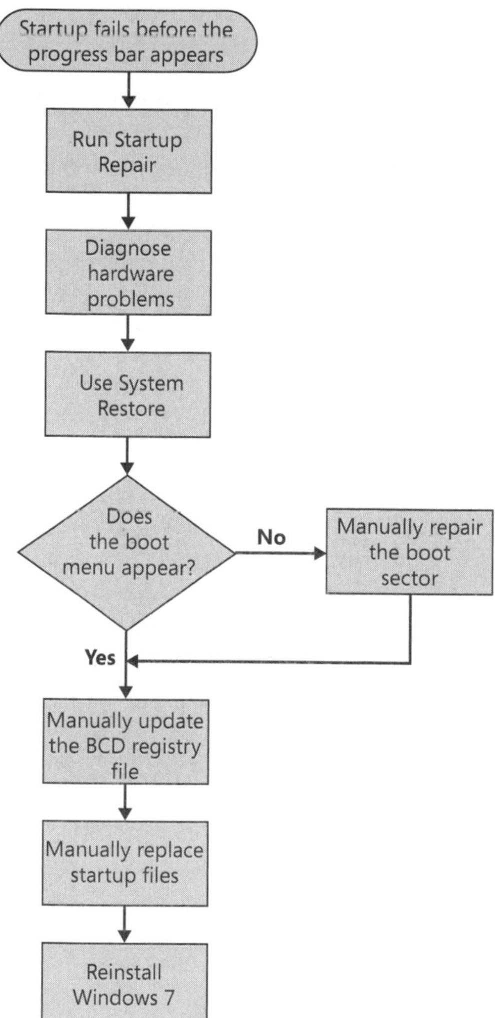

FIGURE 29-5 Follow this process to troubleshoot startup problems before logon.

The following sections describe each of these troubleshooting steps in more detail.

> ***NOTE*** **After you enable Windows BitLocker, a lost encryption key can result in an unbootable computer. For information about BitLocker, see Chapter 16.**

How to Run Startup Repair

To run Startup Repair, open the System Recovery tools and then start Startup Repair, as described in the following sections.

HOW TO START THE SYSTEM RECOVERY TOOLS

Windows 7 automatically installs the System Recovery tools, which are capable of fixing almost any startup problem related to boot sectors, MBRs, or the BCD registry file. The Startup Repair tool can fix most startup problems automatically, without requiring you to understand the details of how an operating system loads. The tool is so straightforward that you could easily talk end users through the troubleshooting process remotely.

To start the System Recovery tools, follow these steps:

1. Restart the computer. If the System Recovery tools do not automatically start, restart the computer again, press F8 before the Starting Windows logo appears, and then choose Repair Your Computer from the Advanced Boot Options screen.
2. Select your language and keyboard input method and then click Next.
3. Select your user name and type your password. Then, click OK.

> ***NOTE*** **Most Windows 7 computers have the System Recovery tools preinstalled by the computer manufacturer. On these computers, you can start the System Recovery tools faster by pressing F8 before the Starting Windows logo appears and then choosing Repair Your Computer from the Advanced Boot Options screen. These computers can also automatically detect startup failure (by noticing that the last startup failed) and start Startup Repair.**

If you cannot start the System Recovery tools from the hard drive, insert the Windows DVD and configure the computer to start from the DVD. Then, follow these steps:

1. Insert the Windows DVD in your computer
2. Restart your computer. When prompted to boot from the DVD, press any key. If you are not prompted to boot from the DVD, you may have to configure your computer's startup sequence. For more information, see the section titled "Initial Startup Phase" earlier in this chapter.
3. Wait while Windows 7 setup loads.
4. When prompted, select your regional preferences and keyboard layout and then click Next.
5. Click Repair Your Computer to start RecEnv.exe.
6. When the System Recovery tools start, System Recovery scans your hard disks for Windows installations.
7. If the standard Windows drivers do not detect a hard disk because it requires drivers that were not included with Windows 7, click Load Drivers to load the driver and then select an operating system to repair. Click Next.

From this point, the steps are the same whether you loaded the System Recovery tools from the hard disk or the Windows DVD. If Windows failed to start during its last attempt, the Startup Repair tool will be started automatically. Otherwise, the Choose A Recovery Tool page appears, as shown in Figure 29-6.

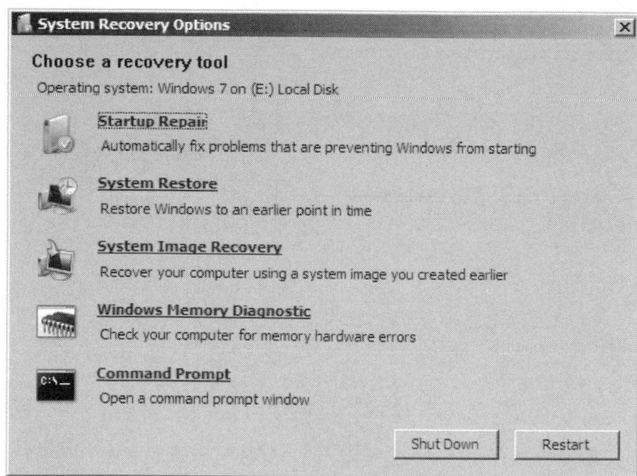

FIGURE 29-6 System Recovery provides a variety of different troubleshooting tools.

HOW TO RUN STARTUP REPAIR

The simplest way to solve startup problems is to load the System Recovery tools, as described in the previous section, and then click Startup Repair and follow the prompts that appear. To run Startup Repair, follow these steps:

1. Click Startup Repair and then follow the prompts that appear. The prompts may vary depending on the problem that Startup Repair identifies. You might be prompted to restore your computer using System Restore or to restart your computer and continue troubleshooting.
2. After the Startup Repair tool has completed diagnosis and repair, click Click Here For Diagnostic And Repair Details. At the bottom of the report, Startup Repair lists a root cause, if found, and any steps taken to repair the problem. Log files are stored at %WinDir%\System32\LogFiles\SRT\SRTTrail.txt.
3. Restart the computer and allow Windows to start normally.

How to Use BootRec.exe

Startup Repair can automatically recover from most BCD problems. If you prefer to manually analyze and repair problems, you can use the command-line tool BootRec.exe by starting the System Recovery tools and then clicking Command Prompt in the System Recovery Options dialog box.

BootRec.exe supports the following command-line parameters:

- **/FIXMBR** The /FIXMBR switch writes an MBR to the system partition.
- **/FIXBOOT** The /FIXBOOT switch writes a new boot sector onto the system partition.
- **/SCANOS** The /SCANOS switch scans all disks for Windows installations and displays entries currently not in the BCD store.

- **/REBUILDBCD** The /REBUILDBCD switch scans all disks for Windows installations and provides a choice of which entries to add to the BCD store.

DIRECT FROM THE SOURCE

Windows XP Recovery Console Equivalents

Parveen Patel, Developer
Windows Reliability

The recovery console has been deprecated in Windows Vista and Windows 7, so what happened to all those wonderful commands that were available in recovery console? Well, we were hoping that you wouldn't need them anymore. But if you do, you'll be glad to know that most of them are available via the command line in WinRE. The recovery console commands listed in the following table are different or unavailable in WinRE.

RECOVERY CONSOLE COMMAND	WINRE EQUIVALENT(S)
BootCfg	BOOTREC /SCANOS BOOTREC /REBUILDBCD bcdedit
FIXBOOT	BOOTREC /FIXBOOT
FIXMBR	BOOTREC /FIXMBR
Map	DiskPart
Logon	Not needed
LISTSVC	Not available
ENABLE	Not available
DISABLE	Not available
SYSTEMROOT	Not available

All the remaining commands have the same name in WinRE. You can work around the unavailable services-related commands (LISTSVC, ENABLE, AND DISABLE) by using regedit to manually load the registry hive.

How to Diagnose Hardware Problems

If Startup Repair cannot solve the problem or if you cannot start Windows Setup, you might have a hardware problem. Although most hardware-related problems will not stop Windows Vista from successfully starting, hardware-related problems may appear early in the startup process; symptoms include warning messages, startup failures, and Stop messages. The causes are typically improper device configuration, incorrect driver settings, or hardware malfunction and failure. For detailed information about troubleshooting hardware problems, read Chapter 30.

How to Use System Restore

Windows automatically captures system state before installing new applications or drivers. You can later use the System Restore tool to return to this system if you experience problems.

To start System Restore from within Windows (including safe mode), click Start, click All Programs, click Accessories, click System Tools, and then click System Restore.

To start System Restore when you cannot open Windows, follow these steps:

1. Start System Recovery tools, as described in the section titled "How to Start the System Recovery Tools" earlier in this chapter.
2. Click System Restore.

The System Restore Wizard appears. Follow these steps to restore Windows to an earlier state:

1. On the Restore System Files And Settings page of the System Restore Wizard, click Next.
2. On the Choose A Restore Point page, click a restore point. Typically, you should choose the most recent restore point when the computer functioned correctly. If the computer has not functioned correctly for more than five days, select the Show More Restore Points check box (as shown in Figure 29-7) and then select a restore point. Click Next.

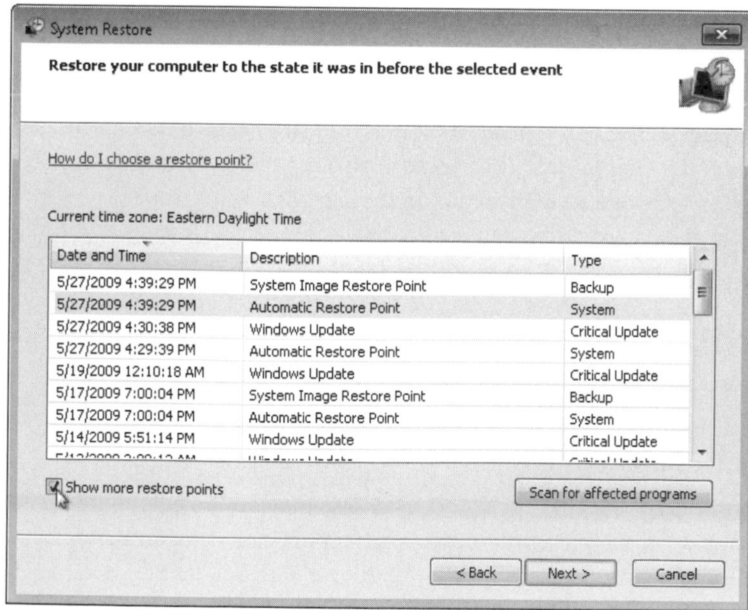

FIGURE 29-7 You can solve some startup problems by using System Restore.

3. On the Confirm Disks To Restore page, click Next.
4. On the Confirm Your Restore Point page, click Finish.
5. Click Yes to confirm the system restore. System Restore modifies system files and settings to return Windows to the state it was in at the time the restore point was captured.
6. When System Restore is done, click Restart. You should now attempt to start the computer and identify whether the problem was resolved.
7. When the computer restarts, Windows will display a System Restore notification. Click Close.

How to Manually Repair the Boot Sector

Startup Repair is by far the quickest and easiest way to solve most startup problems. However, if you are familiar with troubleshooting startup problems and simply need to fix a boot sector problem after installing another operating system, you can run the following command from a command prompt (including the Command Prompt tool in the System Recovery tools).

```
bootsect /NT60 ALL
```

Bootsect.exe is available from the \Boot\ folder of the Windows DVD and can be run from within WinRE or Windows 7.

After running Bootsect, you should be able to load Windows, but you may not be able to load earlier versions of Windows that are installed on the same computer. To load other operating systems, add entries to the BCD registry file, as described in the section titled "How to Create an Entry for Another Operating System" earlier in this chapter.

How to Manually Update the BCD Registry File

The simplest way to solve problems related to the BCD registry file is to run Startup Repair, as described earlier in this chapter. However, you can also use the System Recovery tools to update the BCD registry file manually by following these steps:

1. Load the System Recovery tools, as described in the previous section.
2. Click Command Prompt.
3. Use BCDEdit to update the BCD registry file.

For detailed information, read the section titled "How to Use BCDEdit" earlier in this chapter.

How to Manually Replace Files

If startup files are missing or become corrupted, Windows may not be able to boot successfully. Often, Windows will display an error message that shows the name of the missing file, as shown in Figure 29-8.

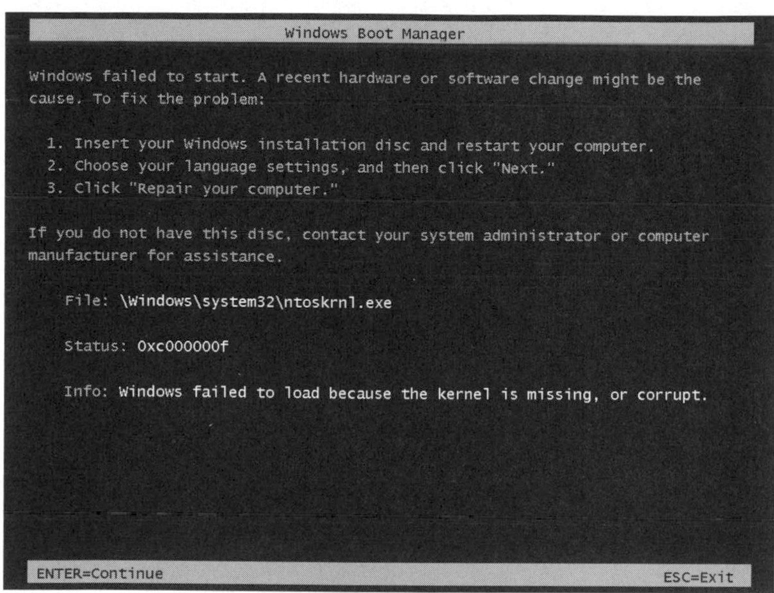

Windows Boot Manager
Windows failed to start. A recent hardware or software change might be the cause. To fix the problem:
1. Insert your Windows installation disc and restart your computer.
2. Choose your language settings, and then click "Next."
3. Click "Repair your computer."
If you do not have this disc, contact your system administrator or computer manufacturer for assistance.
File: \Windows\system32\ntoskrnl.exe
Status: 0xc000000f
Info: Windows failed to load because the kernel is missing, or corrupt.
ENTER=Continue
ESC=Exit

FIGURE 29-8 Windows can display the names of missing startup files, which you can then manually replace.

Startup Repair can automatically replace missing system files, but it may not detect corrupted files. However, you can manually replace files using the System Recovery command-line tool.

To replace files, follow these steps:

1. From another computer, copy the new files to removable media such as a CD-ROM or a USB flash drive. You cannot access Windows system files from the Windows DVD because they are stored within a Windows Imaging (WIM) file that is not accessible from within System Recovery.
2. Start System Recovery tools, as described in the section titled "How to Start the System Recovery Tools" earlier in this chapter.
3. After the System Recovery tools start, click Command Prompt.
4. Your removable media will have a drive letter, just like a hard disk. System Recovery tools assign hard disk letters starting with C and then assign letters to removable media. To identify the drive letter of your removable media, run the following commands.

```
C:\>diskpart
DISKPART> list volume

  Volume ###  Ltr  Label        Fs     Type        Size     Status     Info
  ----------  ---  -----------  -----  ----------  -------  ---------  --------
  Volume 0     C   Win7         NTFS   Partition     63 GB  Healthy
  Volume 1     E   Windows XP   NTFS   Partition     91 GB  Healthy
  Volume 2     D                NTFS   Partition     69 GB  Healthy
  Volume 3     I                       Removable      0 B  No Media
  Volume 4     H                       Removable      0 B  No Media
  Volume 5     F   LR1CFRE_EN_  UDF    Partition   2584 MB  Healthy
  Volume 6     G   USBDRIVE     FAT32  Partition    991 MB  Healthy
```

5. Use the *Copy* command to transfer files from your removable media to the computer's hard disk.

How to Reinstall Windows

Infrequently, startup files and critical areas on the hard disk can become corrupted. If you are mainly concerned with salvaging readable data files and using the Backup And Restore Center to copy them to backup media or a network location, you can perform a parallel installation of Windows. Although this may provide access to the file system, it will permanently damage your existing operating system and applications.

If you cannot start Windows after following the troubleshooting steps in this guide, you can reinstall Windows for the purpose of data recovery by following these steps:

1. Insert the Windows DVD in your computer.
2. Restart your computer. When prompted to boot from the CD/DVD, press any key.
3. Windows Setup loads. When prompted, select your regional preferences and then click Next.
4. Click Install Now.
5. When prompted, enter your product key.
6. Select the I Accept The License Terms check box and then click Next.
7. Click Custom.
8. On the Where Do You Want to Install Windows? page, select the partition containing your Windows installation and then click Next.
9. When prompted, click OK.

Setup will install a new instance of Windows and will move all files from your previous installation into the \Windows.Old folder (including the \Program Files, \Windows, and \Users folders). You now have two choices for returning the computer to its original state:

- **Reformat the system partition** If you have an automated deployment solution in place (as described in Part II of this book, "Deployment"), the quickest solution is to back up important files and redeploy Windows. If you need to manually reinstall Windows, you can follow this process:

1. Back up all important files by writing them to removable media, copying them to an external hard disk, or copying them to a shared folder on the network.
2. Reinstall Windows. This time, choose to reformat the system partition.
3. Reinstall all applications and reconfigure all custom settings.
4. Restore important files.

- **Continue working with the current system partition** You can move important files to the proper locations within the new instance of Windows. Then, reinstall all applications and reconfigure any custom settings. Finally, you can delete the original Windows instance by removing the \Windows.Old folder using Disk Cleanup.

Startup Troubleshooting After the Starting Windows Logo Appears

If your computer displays the graphical Starting Windows logo before failing, as shown in Figure 29-9, the Windows kernel was successfully loaded. Most likely, the startup failure is caused by a faulty driver or service.

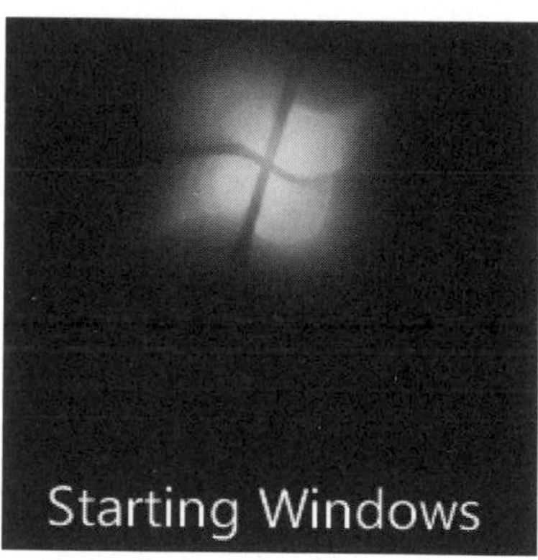

FIGURE 29-9 Displaying the Starting Windows logo indicates that Windows 7 has successfully loaded the kernel.

Use the process illustrated in Figure 29-10 to identify and disable the failing software feature to allow Windows to start successfully. After Windows starts, you can perform further troubleshooting to resolve the problem with the feature if necessary. If the startup problem occurs immediately after updating or installing a startup application, try troubleshooting the startup application. For information about troubleshooting startup applications, see the section titled "How to Temporarily Disable Startup Applications and Processes" later in this chapter.

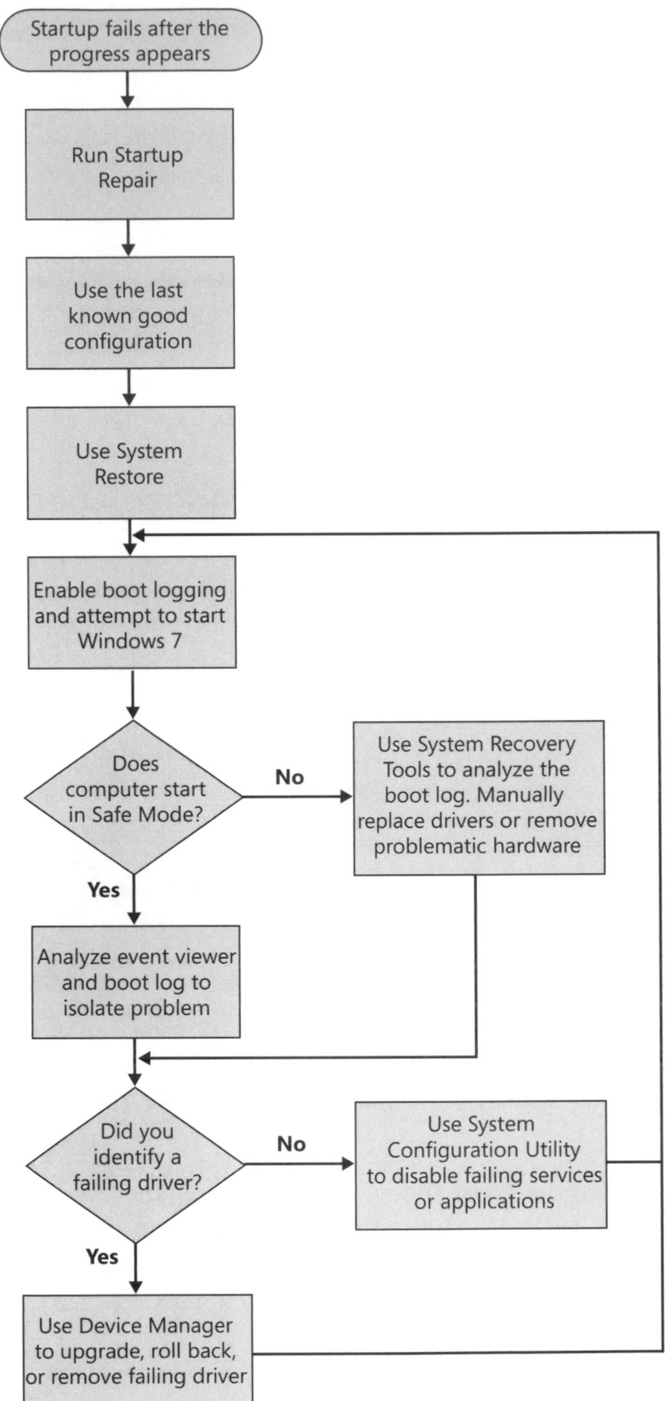

FIGURE 29-10 Follow this process to troubleshoot startup problems after the Starting Windows logo appears but before logon.

The sections that follow describe each of these steps in more detail.

How to Run Startup Repair

Startup Repair can automatically fix many common startup problems, even if the problem occurs after the Starting Windows logo is displayed. Because Startup Repair is easy to use and has a very low likelihood of causing additional problems, it should be your first troubleshooting step. For detailed instructions, refer to the section titled "How to Run Startup Repair" earlier in this chapter.

After running Startup Repair, attempt to start your computer normally and continue with the troubleshooting process only if Windows fails to start.

How to Restore the Last Known Good Configuration

Last Known Good Configuration is usually used to enable the operating system to start if it fails after the Starting Windows logo is displayed. Using Last Known Good Configuration helps to correct instability or startup problems by reversing the most recent system, driver, and registry changes within a hardware profile. When you use this feature, you lose all configuration changes that were made since you last successfully started your computer.

Using the Last Known Good Configuration restores previous drivers and also restores registry settings for the subkey HKEY_LOCAL_MACHINE\SYSTEM\CurrentControlSet. Windows Vista does not update the LastKnownGood control set until you successfully start the operating system in normal mode and log on.

When you are troubleshooting, it is recommended that you use Last Known Good Configuration before you try other startup options, such as safe mode. However, if you decide to use safe mode first, logging on to the computer in safe mode does not update the LastKnownGood control set. Therefore, Last Known Good Configuration remains an option if you cannot resolve your problem by using safe mode.

To access the Last Known Good Configuration startup option, follow these steps:

1. Remove all floppy disks, CDs, DVDs, and other bootable media from your computer and then restart your computer.
2. Press F8 at the operating system menu. If the operating system menu does not appear, press F8 repeatedly after the firmware POST process completes but before the Starting Windows logo appears. The Advanced Boot Options menu appears.
3. On the Advanced Boot Options menu, select Last Known Good Configuration (Advanced), as shown in Figure 29-11.

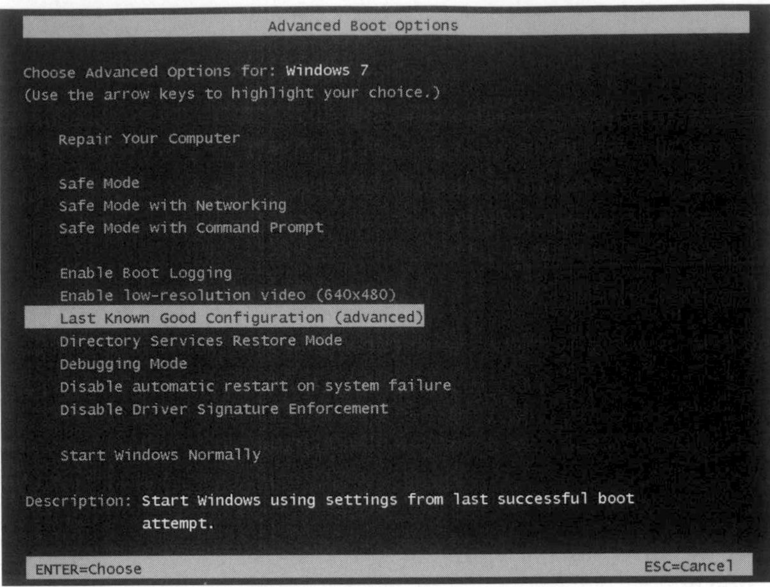

FIGURE 29-11 Use Last Known Good Configuration to restore some settings to their state during the last time a user successfully logged on.

When Windows starts, it reads status information from the file %WinDir%\Bootstat.dat. If Windows detects that the last startup attempt was unsuccessful, it automatically displays the startup recovery menu, which provides startup options similar to the Advanced Boot Options menu, without requiring you to press F8.

> ***NOTE*** **If you suspect that changes made since you last successfully restarted the computer are causing problems, do not start Windows and log on normally—logging on overwrites the LastKnownGood control set. Instead, restart the computer and use the Last Known Good Configuration. You can also log on in safe mode without overwriting the Last Known Good Configuration. For more information about control sets, see the section titled "Kernel Loading Phase" earlier in this chapter.**

How to Use System Restore

If Last Known Good Configuration fails to resolve the problem, you can manually perform a system restore if Startup Repair did not initiate it. However, Startup Repair would typically have taken this step already if it might have solved the problem. For information on how to use System Restore, see the section titled "How to Use System Restore" earlier in this chapter.

How to Enable Boot Logging

Boot logging is useful for isolating the cause of a startup problem that occurs after the operating system menu appears. You can enable boot logging by following these steps:

1. Remove all floppy disks, CDs, DVDs, and other bootable media from your computer and then restart your computer.
2. Press F8 at the operating system menu. If the operating system menu does not appear, press F8 repeatedly after the firmware POST process completes but before the Starting Windows logo appears. The Advanced Boot Options menu appears.
3. On the Advanced Boot Options menu, select Enable Boot Logging, as shown in Figure 29-12.

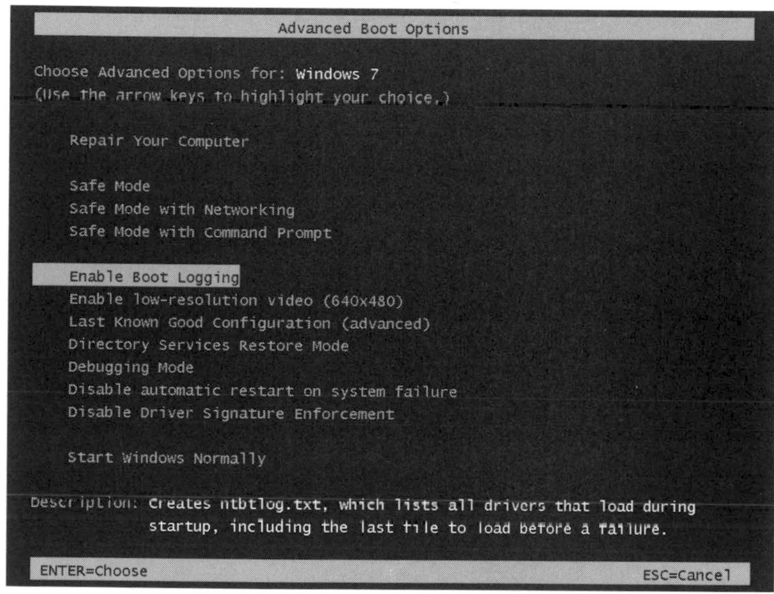

FIGURE 29-12 Enabling boot logging can help you identify the cause of startup problems.

Windows starts and creates a log file at %WinDir%\Ntbtlog.txt. The log file starts with the time and version information and then lists every file that is successfully loaded, as shown here.

```
Microsoft (R) Windows (R) Version 6.1 (Build 7100)
 5 27 2009 17:57:37.500
Loaded driver \SystemRoot\system32\ntoskrnl.exe
Loaded driver \SystemRoot\system32\hal.dll
Loaded driver \SystemRoot\system32\kdcom.dll
Loaded driver \SystemRoot\system32\mcupdate_GenuineIntel.dll
Loaded driver \SystemRoot\system32\PSHED.dll
Loaded driver \SystemRoot\system32\BOOTVID.dll
Loaded driver \SystemRoot\system32\CLFS.SYS
```

```
Loaded driver \SystemRoot\system32\CI.dll
Loaded driver \SystemRoot\system32\drivers\wdf0100.sys
Loaded driver \SystemRoot\system32\drivers\WDFLDR.SYS
Did not load driver \SystemRoot\system32\drivers\serial.sys
Loaded driver \SystemRoot\system32\drivers\acpi.sys
```

The following sections will provide additional information about viewing and analyzing the boot log file.

How to Start in Safe Mode

Safe mode is a diagnostic environment that runs only a subset of the drivers and services that are configured to start in normal mode. Safe mode is useful when you install software or a device driver that causes instability or problems with starting in normal mode. Often, Windows can start in safe mode even if hardware failure prevents it from starting in normal mode. In most cases, safe mode allows you to start Windows and then troubleshoot problems that prevent startup.

Logging on to the computer in safe mode does not update the LastKnownGood control set. Therefore, if you log on to your computer in safe mode and then decide you want to try Last Known Good Configuration, this option is still available to you.

In safe mode, Windows uses the minimum set required to start the GUI. The following registry subkeys list the drivers and services that start in safe mode:

- Safe mode: HKEY_LOCAL_MACHINE\SYSTEM\CurrentControlSet\Control\SafeBoot\Minimal
- Safe mode with networking: HKEY_LOCAL_MACHINE\SYSTEM\CurrentControlSet\Control\SafeBoot\Network

To access safe mode, follow these steps:

1. Remove all floppy disks and CDs from your computer and then restart your computer.
2. Press F8 at the operating system menu. If the operating system menu does not appear, press F8 repeatedly after the firmware POST process completes but before the Starting Windows logo appears. The Advanced Boot Options menu appears.
3. On the Advanced Boot Options menu, select Safe Mode, Safe Mode With Networking, or Safe Mode With Command Prompt. Select Safe Mode if you do not require networking support. Select Safe Mode With Networking if you require access to the network for your troubleshooting—for example, if you must download an updated driver. Select Safe Mode With Command Prompt if you want to work at a command prompt.

When Windows starts, it reads status information from the file %SystemRoot%\Bootstat.dat. If Windows detects that the last startup attempt was unsuccessful, it automatically displays the startup recovery menu, which provides startup options similar to the Advanced Boot Options menu, without requiring you to press F8.

How to Identify Failing Drivers and Services

When you are troubleshooting, the method for determining which services and processes to temporarily disable varies from one computer to the next. The most reliable way to determine what you can disable is to gather more information about the services and processes enabled on your computer.

The following Windows tools and features generate a variety of logs that can provide you with valuable troubleshooting information:

- Event Viewer
- Sc.exe
- System Information
- Error reporting service
- Boot logs

Of these tools, only the boot logs are available when using System Recovery tools. All tools are available when using safe mode, however.

HOW TO ANALYZE STARTUP PROBLEMS IN SAFE MODE

Safe mode gives you access to all standard graphical troubleshooting tools, including those described in the following sections.

Event Viewer (Eventvwr.msc)

You can use Event Viewer (Eventvwr.msc) to view logs that can help you to identify system problems when you are able to start the system in safe or normal mode. When you are troubleshooting, use these logs to isolate problems by application, driver, or service and to identify frequently occurring issues. You can save these logs to a file and specify filtering criteria.

Event Viewer provides a minimum of three logs, as follows:

- **Application logs** The Application log contains events logged by applications or programs. For example, a database program might record read or write errors here.
- **Security logs** The security log holds security event records, such as logon attempts and actions related to creating, opening, or deleting files. An administrator can specify what events to record in the security log.
- **System logs** The system log contains information about system features. Event Viewer logs an entry when a driver or other system feature does not load during startup. Therefore, you can use Event Viewer to search for information about drivers or services that did not load.

To use Event Viewer to obtain driver and service error information from the system log, follow these steps:

1. Click Start, right-click Computer, and then click Manage.

2. Under System Tools, expand Event Viewer, expand Windows Logs, and then click System.
3. Click the Action menu and then click Filter Current Log.
4. Under Event Level, select the Critical and Error check boxes.
5. In the Event source list, click Service Control Manager and then click OK.
6. Double-click an event entry to view details.

Not all startup problems result in an entry being added to the event log. Therefore, you might not find any related information. For more information about the Event Viewer, read Chapter 21, "Maintaining Desktop Health."

System Information

If a startup problem occurs inconsistently and if you can start Windows in safe or normal mode, you can use System Information to view driver and service name, status, and startup information.

Using System Information, you can create lists of drivers that were processed during safe and normal mode startups. By comparing the differences between the two lists, you can determine which features are not required to start Windows. For diagnostic purposes, you can use this list of differences to help you determine which services to disable. In safe mode, disable a service and then try to restart the operating system in normal mode. Repeat this process for each service until you are able to start in normal mode.

To view service or driver information, follow these steps:

1. Click Start, type **msinfo32**, and then press Enter.
2. Depending on the information you want, do one or more of the following:
   - To view service information, expand Software Environment and then click Services.
   - To view the state of a driver, expand Software Environment and then click System Drivers. Information for each driver is in the right pane.
   - To view driver information arranged by category, expand Components and then select a category, such as Display.
   - To view problem devices, expand Components and then click Problem Devices. Examine the Error Code column for information relating to the source of the problem.
   - To view shared and conflicting resources (which do not always indicate a critical problem), expand Hardware Resources and then click Conflicts/Sharing. Examine the Resource and Device columns for devices that are incorrectly assigned overlapping resources. Remove or disable one of the devices or use Device Manager to change the resources assigned to the devices.

Error Reporting Service

The Windows error reporting service monitors your computer for problems that affect services and applications. When a problem occurs, you can send a problem report to Microsoft and receive an automated response with more information, such as news about an update for an application or device driver. For more information about the Event Viewer, read Chapter 21.

HOW TO USE DEVICE MANAGER TO VIEW OR CHANGE RESOURCES

Installing new hardware or updating drivers can create conflicts, causing devices to become inaccessible. You can use Device Manager to review resources used by these devices to identify conflicts manually.

To use Device Manager (Devmgmt.msc) to view or change system resource usage information, follow these steps:

1. Click Start, right-click Computer, and then click Manage.
2. Click Device Manager and then double-click a device.
3. Click the Resources tab to view the resources used by that device.
4. Clear the Use Automatic Settings check box.
5. Click Change Setting and specify the resources assigned to the device.

For more information about managing devices, see Chapter 17.

HOW TO ANALYZE BOOT LOGS

Boot logging lists the files that successfully and unsuccessfully processed during startup. You use boot logging to log the Windows features that are processed when you start your computer in safe mode and also in normal mode. By comparing the differences between the two logs, you can determine which features are not required to start.

Windows records the name and path of each file that runs during startup in a log, %WinDir%\Ntbtlog.txt. The log marks each file as successful ("Loaded Driver...") or unsuccessful ("Did Not Load Driver..."). Boot logging appends entries to Ntbtlog.txt when you start Windows in safe mode. Comparing normal mode and safe mode entries enables you to determine which services run in normal mode only—one of which must be the cause of the startup problem if Windows is able to start in safe mode successfully. The following lines are sample Ntbtlog.txt entries.

```
Loaded driver \SystemRoot\System32\DRIVERS\flpydisk.sys
Did not load driver \SystemRoot\System32\DRIVERS\sflpydisk.SYS
```

Note that not every "Did Not Load Driver" message necessarily indicates an error that would prevent Windows from booting, because many drivers are not required for Windows to start. To repair problems caused by problematic drivers when you can start safe mode, follow these steps:

1. Restart the computer and enable boot logging.
2. Restart the computer after it fails and then start safe mode.
3. Click Start and then type **%WinDir%\ntbtlog.txt**. The boot log file opens in Notepad.
4. Compare the list of drivers loaded in normal mode to the list of drivers loaded in safe mode. The driver that is causing the system to fail is one of the drivers listed with

"Loaded Driver..." in the normal mode boot log, but listed with "Did Not Load Driver..." in the safe mode boot log.

5. In safe mode, use Device Manager to replace or roll back potentially problematic drivers, as described in the next section, "How to Roll Back Drivers." Start by replacing drivers that have been recently installed or updated. After replacing a driver, repeat this process until the system starts successfully in normal mode.

For the services that run only in normal mode, disable those services one at a time, trying to restart your computer in normal mode after you disable each service. Continue to disable services individually until your computer starts in normal mode.

To repair problems caused by problematic drivers when the computer does not start in safe mode, follow these steps:

1. Restart the computer and then load System Recovery tools.
2. Click Command Prompt. At the command prompt, type **Notepad %WinDir%\ntbtlog.txt**. Notepad opens and displays the boot log.
3. Compare the boot log created when the system failed to start in safe mode to a boot log created when the system started successfully in safe mode. If you do not have a boot log that was created when the system started successfully in safe mode, create a boot log on a similarly configured computer by starting it in safe mode. The driver that is causing safe mode to fail is one of the drivers that is not listed in the boot log that was created when the system failed but is listed with "Loaded Driver..." in the boot log created when safe mode started successfully.
4. Replace the driver file with a working version, using the Copy command at the command prompt. Start by replacing or deleting drivers that have been recently installed or updated. After replacing a driver, repeat this process until the system starts successfully in normal mode.

How to Roll Back Drivers

When you update a device driver, your computer might have problems that it did not have with the previous version. For example, installing an unsigned device driver might cause the device to malfunction or cause resource conflicts with other installed hardware. Installing faulty drivers might cause Stop errors that prevent the operating system from starting in normal mode. Typically, the Stop message text displays the file name of the driver that causes the error.

Windows provides a feature called Device Driver Roll Back that might help you restore system stability by rolling back a driver update.

> ***NOTE*** **You can use System Information or the Sigverif tool to determine whether a driver on your computer is signed and to obtain other information about the driver, such as version, date, time, and manufacturer. This data, combined with information from the manufacturer's Web site, can help you decide whether to roll back or update a device driver.**

To roll back a driver, follow these steps:

1. Click Start, right-click Computer, and then click Manage.
2. Under System Tools, click Device Manager.
3. Expand a category (Network Adapters, for example) and then double-click a device.
4. Click the Driver tab and then click Roll Back Driver. You are prompted to confirm that you want to overwrite the current driver. Click Yes to roll back the driver. The rollback process proceeds, or else you are notified that an older driver is not available.

How to Temporarily Disable a Service

Many services automatically run at startup, but others are started only by users or by another process. When you troubleshoot startup issues that are related to system services, a useful technique is to simplify your computer configuration so that you can reduce system complexity and isolate operating system services. To decrease the number of variables, temporarily disable startup applications or services and re-enable them one at a time until you reproduce the problem. Always disable applications first before attempting to disable system services.

The System Configuration utility allows you to disable system services individually or several at a time. To disable a service by using the System Configuration utility, follow these steps:

1. Click Start, type **msconfig**, and then press Enter.
2. Do one of the following:
   - To disable all services, on the General tab, click Selective Startup and then clear the Load System Services check box.
   - To disable specific services, on the Services tab, click to clear the check boxes that correspond to the items you want to disable. You can also click Disable All to disable all items.

If you change any startup setting by using the System Configuration utility, Windows prompts you to return to normal operations the next time you log on. The System Configuration Utility prompt will appear each time you log on until you restore the original startup settings by clicking Normal Startup under Startup Selection on the General tab. To change a startup setting permanently, use the Services console, change a Group Policy setting, or uninstall the software that added the service.

Troubleshooting Startup Problems After Logon

If your computer fails immediately after a user logs on, use the process illustrated in Figure 29-13 to identify and disable the failing startup application to allow the user to log on successfully. If the problem occurs immediately after updating or installing an application, try uninstalling that application.

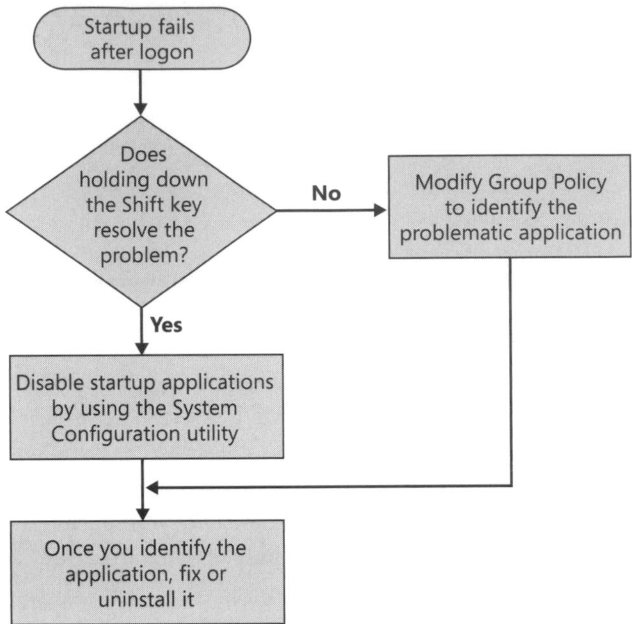

FIGURE 29-13 Follow this process to troubleshoot startup problems that occur after logon.

How to Temporarily Disable Startup Applications and Processes

If a problem occurs after installing new software, you can temporarily disable or uninstall the application to verify that the application is the source of the problem.

Problems with applications that run at startup can cause logon delays or even prevent you from completing Windows startup in normal mode. The following subsections provide techniques for temporarily disabling startup applications.

HOW TO DISABLE STARTUP APPLICATIONS USING THE SHIFT KEY

One way you can simplify your configuration is to disable startup applications. By holding down the Shift key during the logon process, you can prevent the operating system from running startup programs or shortcuts in the following folders:

- %SystemDrive%\Users*username*\AppData\Roaming\Microsoft\Windows\Start Menu \Programs\Startup
- %SystemDrive%\ProgramData\Microsoft\Windows\Start Menu\Programs\Startup

To disable the applications or shortcuts in the preceding folders, you must hold down the Shift key until the desktop icons appear. Holding down the Shift key is a better alternative than temporarily deleting or moving programs and shortcuts, because this procedure affects only the current user session.

To use the Shift key to disable applications and shortcuts in startup folders, log off the computer and then log on again. Immediately press and hold down the Shift key. Continue to hold down the Shift key until the desktop icons appear. If you can log on successfully, you have isolated the cause of the problem to your startup applications. Next, you should use the System Configuration utility to temporarily disable applications one by one until you identify the cause of the problem. With the cause of the problem identified, you can fix the application or permanently remove it from your startup programs.

HOW TO DISABLE STARTUP PROGRAMS USING THE SYSTEM CONFIGURATION UTILITY

The System Configuration utility allows you to disable startup applications individually or several at a time. To disable a startup program by using the System Configuration utility, follow these steps:

1. Click Start, type **msconfig**, and then press Enter.
2. You can disable all or selective startup applications:
   - To disable all startup applications, click the General tab, click Selective Startup, and then clear the Load Startup Items check box.
   - To disable specific startup items, click the Startup tab and then clear the check boxes that correspond to the items you want to disable temporarily. You can also click Disable All on the Startup tab to disable all items.

To change a startup setting permanently, you must move or delete startup shortcuts, change a Group Policy setting, or uninstall the application that added the startup application.

HOW TO DISABLE STARTUP APPLICATIONS CONFIGURED USING GROUP POLICY OR LOGON SCRIPTS

You can use the Group Policy snap-in to disable applications that run at startup. Local Group Policy can be applied to computers, in which case you need to edit the Group Policy settings on the computer that you are troubleshooting. Group Policy objects (GPOs) are frequently applied within AD DS domains, in which case you need to connect to the domain to edit the appropriate policy. Before modifying domain Group Policy settings, you should follow the steps described later in this section to disconnect the computer you are troubleshooting from the network to determine whether the problem is related to domain Group Policy settings.

To disable startup applications by using the Group Policy Management Editor snap-in, follow these steps:

1. Click Start, type **gpedit.msc**, and then click OK.
2. Within either Computer Configuration (for computer-wide startup applications) or User Configuration (for user-specific startup applications), expand Policies, expand Administrative Templates, expand System, and then click Logon.
3. Double-click Run These Programs At User Logon, which is a Group Policy setting. Next, do one of the following:

- To disable all startup applications configured by that policy, click Disabled.
- To selectively disable individual programs that are listed in the computer-specific or user-specific policy, click Show. In the Show Contents dialog box, select a program to disable and then click Remove.

You can change additional Group Policy settings that might help you simplify your computer configuration when you are troubleshooting startup problems by enabling the Do Not Process The Run Once List policy. If you enable this Group Policy setting, the computer ignores the programs listed in the following RunOnce subkeys the next time a user logs on to the computer:

- HKEY_LOCAL_MACHINE\SOFTWARE\Microsoft\Windows\CurrentVersion\RunOnce
- HKEY_CURRENT_USER\Software\Microsoft\Windows\CurrentVersion\RunOnce

Additionally, you can enable the Group Policy setting Do Not Process The Legacy Run List to disable the HKEY_LOCAL_MACHINE\SOFTWARE\Microsoft\Windows\CurrentVersion\Run subkey that startup applications might use. The programs listed in this subkey are a customized list of programs that were configured by using the System Policy Editor for Windows NT 4.0 or earlier versions. If you enable this Group Policy setting, Windows ignores the programs listed in this subkey when you start your computer. If you disable or do not configure this Group Policy setting, Windows processes the customized run list that is contained in this registry subkey when you start the computer.

Group Policy changes do not always take effect immediately. You can use the Gpupdate (Gpupdate.exe) tool to refresh local Group Policy changes to computer and user policies. After you refresh the policy, you can use the Group Policy Result (Gpresult.exe) tool to verify that the updated settings are in effect.

Group Policy settings can be applied locally or to an entire domain. To determine how settings are applied to a specific computer, use the Resultant Set Of Policy (Rsop.msc) tool. Then, edit those Group Policy objects to apply a change. For the purpose of isolating the source of the problem, you can prevent Group Policy, logon scripts, roaming user profiles, scheduled tasks, and network-related issues from affecting your troubleshooting by temporarily disabling the network adapter and then logging on by using a local computer account.

If local and domain Group Policy settings do not reveal the source of the startup problem, the application may be started by a logon script. Logon scripts are configured in the local or domain user properties. To view the logon script, open Computer Management and then view the user's properties. Then click the Profile tab. Make note of the path to the logon script and edit it in a tool such as Notepad to determine whether any startup applications are configured. For more detailed information about Group Policy, read Chapter 14, "Managing the Desktop Environment."

How to Permanently Disable Startup Applications and Processes

You can permanently disable a startup application in several ways, explained in the following sections.

UNINSTALL THE APPLICATION

If you find that recently installed software causes system instability or if error messages consistently point to a specific application, you can use Uninstall A Program under Programs in Control Panel to uninstall the software. If the application is required, you can install it in a lab environment and perform additional testing before reinstalling it on production computers.

MANUALLY REMOVE THE ENTRY

You can manually delete shortcuts from the Startup folder, remove startup entries from the registry, remove entries from Group Policy or logon scripts, or disable a service. For a list of registry subkeys that contain entries for service and startup programs, see the section titled "Logon Phase" earlier in this chapter.

Summary

Windows 7 automatically installs WinRE and improves startup, shutdown, and sleep recovery times. Although the startup improvements over Windows Vista are minimal, Windows Vista introduced many improvements over Windows XP that Windows 7 continues to support. These features include:

- Windows Boot Manager
- Windows Boot Loader
- The BCD registry file and the BCDEdit command-line tool
- System Recovery tools
- Startup Repair

If you are familiar with earlier versions of Windows, you will be comfortable troubleshooting most problems that occur in the kernel loading phase of startup or later. Fortunately, you (or any user) can resolve many common startup problems simply by running the Startup Repair tool from the Windows DVD.

Additional Resources

These resources contain additional information and tools related to this chapter.

Related Information

- Chapter 16, "Managing Disks and File Systems," includes more information about startup problems related to disk configuration.
- Chapter 17, "Managing Devices and Services," includes information about configuring hardware and services.

- Chapter 30, "Troubleshooting Hardware, Driver, and Disk Issues" includes more information about hardware-related startup problems.
- Chapter 32, "Troubleshooting Stop Messages" includes more information about Stop errors that might occur during startup.
- "Boot Configuration Data in Windows Vista," which includes detailed information about the BCD registry file, is found at *http://www.microsoft.com/whdc/system/platform/firmware/bcd.mspx*.
- "BCD WMI Provider Classes" on MSDN is found at *http://msdn.microsoft.com/en-us/library/aa362675.aspx*.
- Article 92765 in the Microsoft Knowledge Base, "Terminating a SCSI Device," is found at *http://support.microsoft.com/?kbid=92765*.
- Article 154690 in the Microsoft Knowledge Base, "How to Troubleshoot Event ID 9, Event ID 11, and Event ID 15 Error Messages," is found at *http://support.microsoft.com/?kbid=154690*.
- Article 224826 in the Microsoft Knowledge Base, "Troubleshooting Text-Mode Setup Problems on ACPI Computers," is found at *http://support.microsoft.com/?kbid=224826*.

On the Companion Media

- ConfigureCrashSettings.ps1
- DetectStartUpPrograms.ps1
- DisplayBootConfig.ps1
- Get-SystemDisk.ps1

CHAPTER 30

Troubleshooting Hardware, Driver, and Disk Issues

This chapter describes how to use the Windows 7 operating system to troubleshoot common hardware problems. This chapter is not intended to be a comprehensive guide to troubleshooting hardware; instead, it focuses on using Windows diagnostic and troubleshooting tools to solve hardware problems. First, this chapter describes improvements to Windows 7 that simplify the process of troubleshooting hardware problems. Then the chapter describes the process of using Windows tools for troubleshooting hardware problems.

For hardware problems that prevent Windows from starting, see Chapter 29, "Configuring Startup and Troubleshooting Startup Issues." For network problems, see Chapter 31, "Troubleshooting Network Issues." For problems that result in Stop errors (also known as *blue screens*), see Chapter 32, "Troubleshooting Stop Messages."

Windows 7 Improvements for Hardware and Driver Troubleshooting

Windows 7 includes Reliability Monitor and Resource Monitor to simplify how you isolate the source of hardware problems, allowing you to reduce client computer downtime. Additionally, Windows 7 includes several troubleshooting features first introduced with Windows Vista. The following sections describe these improvements.

Windows Troubleshooting Platform

The Windows Troubleshooting Platform, new to Windows 7, is an extensible infrastructure for automated diagnosis of software and hardware problems. If you used Windows Network Diagnostics in Windows Vista, you're familiar with how Windows Troubleshooting Platform works.

To the user performing the troubleshooting, the Windows Troubleshooting Platform is a wizard that attempts to identify the source of the problem and might provide instructions to the user for solving the problem or might solve the problem directly. Users can launch a troubleshooting pack from several different locations. For example, if Windows Internet Explorer cannot open a Web site, the user can click the Diagnose Connection Problems button to launch Windows Network Diagnostics (implemented using the Windows Troubleshooting Platform). Users can also launch troubleshooting packs from Control Panel (located at Control Panel\All Control Panel Items\Troubleshooting) or Help And Support.

Built-in Troubleshooting Packs

Windows 7 includes built-in troubleshooting packs to correlate to the top 10 categories of Microsoft support calls, including power efficiency, application compatibility, networking, and sound. Table 30-1 describes the troubleshooting packs that are built into Windows 7 or are currently available using the Windows Online Troubleshooting Service (WOTS). WOTS is a free online service that Windows 7 can use to download new or updated troubleshooting packs.

TABLE 30-1 Windows 7 Troubleshooting Packs

TROUBLESHOOTING PACK	DESCRIPTION
Aero	Troubleshoot problems that prevent your computer from displaying Aero animations and effects
Playing Audio	Troubleshoot problems that prevent your computer from playing sound
Recording Audio	Troubleshoot problems that prevent your computer from recording sound
Printer	Troubleshoot problems that prevent you from using a printer

TROUBLESHOOTING PACK	DESCRIPTION
Performance	Adjust settings in Windows that can help improve overall speed and performance
System Maintenance	Clean up unused files and shortcuts and perform other maintenance tasks
Power	Adjust power settings to improve battery life and reduce power consumption
HomeGroup	Troubleshoot problems that prevent you from viewing computer or shared files in a HomeGroup
Hardware And Devices	Troubleshoot problems with hardware and devices
Internet Explorer Performance	Troubleshoot problems that prevent you from browsing the Web with Internet Explorer
Internet Explorer Safety	Adjust settings to improve browser safety in Internet Explorer
Windows Media Player Library	Troubleshoot problems that prevent music and movies from being shown in the Windows Media Player Library
Windows Media Player Settings	Reset Windows Media Player back to default settings
Windows Media Player DVD	Troubleshoot problems that prevent playing a DVD in Windows Media Player
Connection to a Workplace Using DirectAccess	Connect to your workplace network over the Internet
Shared Folders	Access shared files and folders on other computers
Incoming Connections	Allow other computers to connect to your computer
Network Adapter	Troubleshoot Ethernet, wireless, or other network adapters
Internet Connections	Connect to the Internet or to a particular Web site
Program Compatibility	Troubleshoot a program that doesn't work in this version of Windows
Search And Indexing	Troubleshoot problems finding items with Windows Search
Windows Update	Troubleshoot problems preventing Windows Update from working correctly

Windows Troubleshooting Platform Components

The Windows Troubleshooting Platform consists of three main components:

- **Windows troubleshooting packs** A collection of Windows PowerShell 2.0 scripts that diagnose and resolve problems. Because they are based on Windows PowerShell, administrators with scripting experience can create their own troubleshooting packs.

You can use this capability to automate troubleshooting of problems unique to your environment, such as those relating to your internal applications or network.

- **Windows troubleshooting engine** The tool that runs the troubleshooting pack's Windows PowerShell scripts. The Windows PowerShell scripts within a troubleshooting pack use a set of developer interfaces provided by the troubleshooting engine to identify root causes, prompt the user for information, and mark problems as resolved.
- **The troubleshooting wizard** The primary user interface for the troubleshooting packs. The wizard first displays the publisher and description of the troubleshooting pack to the user. The Windows PowerShell scripts within the troubleshooting pack can prompt the user through the wizard interface. After the troubleshooting pack has completed, the wizard displays the troubleshooting results in a report. You can bypass the wizard interface to run the troubleshooting pack from a command line or use Extensible Markup Language (XML)–based answer files to run a troubleshooting pack automatically.

Creating Custom Troubleshooting Packs

The Windows 7 Software Development Kit (SDK), a free download from *http://download.microsoft.com*, includes the Windows Troubleshooting Pack Designer in the \Bin\TSPDesigner folder. You can use the Windows Troubleshooting Pack Designer to create your own troubleshooting packs to troubleshoot common problems not covered by the built-in troubleshooting packs. Troubleshooting packs are also a convenient way to maintain computers; by scheduling them to run in an automated way, you can use troubleshooting packs to detect and resolve common problems without user intervention.

Users can run stand-alone troubleshooting packs packaged as .diagcab files. The .diagcab file format is a specialized archive that contains each of the troubleshooting pack scripts. When packaged as a .diagcab file, troubleshooting packs can be distributed using Group Policy preferences, Microsoft System Center Configuration Manager (either during or after deployment), or non-Microsoft software distribution tools. For external customers, you could post the .diagcab files to a Web site and direct your users to open the Uniform Resource Locator (URL) when they experience a problem.

Running Troubleshooting Packs Remotely

You can run a troubleshooting pack across the network on a remote computer, which can allow you to diagnose common problems quickly and possibly solve them without walking the user through the troubleshooting process. The following Windows PowerShell commands, when run on a Windows 7 computer (either locally or remotely using Invoke-Command or the *-PSession cmdlets), will run the built-in Windows Aero troubleshooting pack, automatically attempt to resolve any problems, and store the results to the C:\DiagResult folder.

```
Import-Module TroubleshootingPack
$aero = Get-TroubleshootingPack $env:SystemRoot\Diagnostics\System\Aero
Invoke-TroubleshootingPack -Pack $aero -Result C:\DiagResult -unattend
```

You could also use this technique in a script to run a troubleshooting pack on multiple computers across the network; in combination with a custom troubleshooting pack, you could quickly determine which computers suffered from a specific problem or misconfiguration. Because troubleshooting packs can make configuration changes to solve problems, you could use this approach to detect and resolve a common problem without contacting users or manually connecting to computers.

Reliability Monitor

Two of the biggest challenges of troubleshooting hardware problems are determining when the problem began occurring and what might have changed on the computer to introduce the problem. Windows Vista introduced the Reliability Monitor snap-in (as part of the Computer Management console) so that you can easily view application installations, driver installations, and significant failures over several weeks or months.

With Windows 7, Reliability Monitor is now integrated with the Action Center to better correlate system changes and events. Figure 30-1 shows Reliability Monitor providing details about events on a specific day, including a failed application installation and security updates.

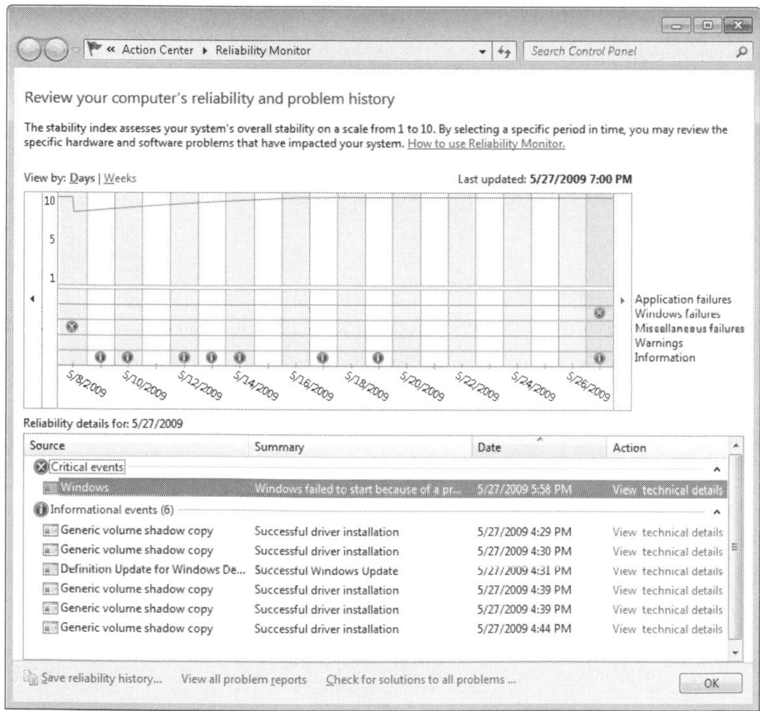

FIGURE 30-1 Reliability Monitor provides you with a history of changes and problems.

Beyond the improved user interface, Windows 7 extends Reliability Monitor by exposing reliability data via the Windows Management Instrumentation (WMI). Using WMI, you can gather reliability data remotely and process it using Windows PowerShell scripts and WMI-related cmdlets (pronounced *command-lets*). Now, you can use WMI to centrally monitor the reliability of computers running Windows 7 throughout the network.

Management tools such as Microsoft System Center Configuration Manager and Microsoft System Center Operations Manager can centrally monitor the reliability data from all computers running Windows 7, or you can create your own Windows PowerShell scripts to monitor reliability. By centrally monitoring reliability data, you can identify unreliable computers that are affecting user productivity even if the users don't take the time to call the Support Center.

Reliability Monitor is discussed in more detail later in this chapter and in Chapter 21, "Maintaining Desktop Health."

Resource Monitor

IT professionals need deep insight into a computer's inner workings to efficiently troubleshoot problems. The more complex the problem is, the more detailed the information must be. For example, although Task Manager is sufficient to identify the process that is using the most processor time, IT professionals need a more powerful tool to identify which process is generating the most disk or network input/output (I/O).

To give IT professionals detailed information about resource utilization on a process-by-process basis, Windows 7 includes an improved version of Resource Monitor. As shown in Figure 30-2, Resource Monitor displays this data in a format that provides rapid access to a great deal of information that you can use to easily explore process-specific details.

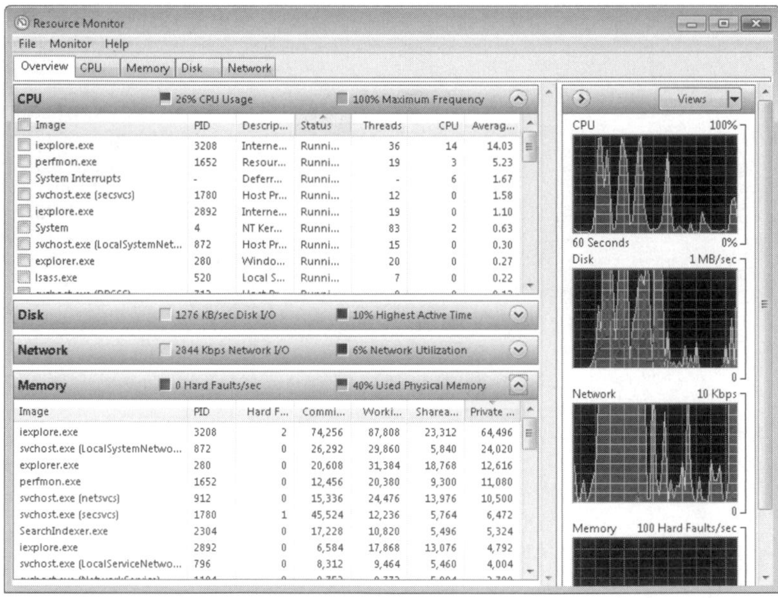

FIGURE 30-2 Resource Monitor shows detailed, real-time performance data

Within seconds, you can use Resource Monitor to view:

- Which processes are using the most processor time and memory.
- Which processes are reading and writing the most data to the disk.
- How much network data each process is sending and receiving.
- How much memory each process is using.
- Why a process is nonresponsive.
- Which services are hosted within a SvcHost.exe process.
- Which handles, including devices, registry keys, and files, a process is accessing.
- Which modules, including dynamic-link libraries (DLLs) and other libraries, a process is accessing.
- Which processes are listening for incoming network connections or have network connections open.

Additionally, you can end processes and search online for information about a process. With Resource Monitor, IT professionals can quickly identify the source of performance and resource utilization problems, reducing the time required to troubleshoot complex issues. Resource Monitor is discussed in more detail in Chapter 21.

Windows Memory Diagnostics

Application failures, operating system faults, and Stop errors are often caused by failing memory. Failing memory chips return different data than the operating system originally stored. Failing memory can be difficult to identify: Problems can be intermittent and might occur only under very rare circumstances. For example, a memory chip might function perfectly when tested in a controlled environment but begin to fail when the internal temperature of the computer becomes too high. Failing memory can also cause secondary problems, such as corrupted files. Often, administrators take drastic steps to repair the problem, such as reinstalling applications or the operating system, only to have the failures persist.

Windows includes Windows Memory Diagnostics to help administrators track down problems with unreliable memory. If Windows Error Reporting (WER) or Microsoft Online Crash Analysis (MOCA) determines that failing memory might be the cause of an error, the software can prompt the user to perform memory diagnostics without requiring an additional download or separate boot disk. Additionally, you can run Windows Memory Diagnostics by choosing a special boot menu option or by loading the Windows Recovery Environment.

If memory diagnostics identify a memory problem, Windows can avoid using the affected portion of physical memory so that the operating system can start successfully and avoid application crashes. Upon startup, Windows provides an easy-to-understand report detailing the problem and instructing the user on how to replace the memory. For detailed information, see the section titled "How to Use Windows Memory Diagnostics" later in this chapter.

Disk Failure Diagnostics

Disk reliability problems can vary in severity. Minor problems can cause seemingly random application failures. For example, if a user connects a new camera and the operating system fails to load the driver, disk corruption may be causing the problem. More severe problems can result in the total loss of data stored on the hard disk.

Windows can eliminate much of the impact of a disk failure by detecting disk problems proactively, before total failure occurs. Hard disks often show warning signs before failure, but earlier Windows operating systems did not record the warning signs. Windows now checks for evidence that a hard disk is beginning to fail and warns the user or the Support Center of the problem. The IT department can then back up the data and replace the hard disk before the problem becomes an emergency. For administrators, Windows acts as a guide through the process of backing up their data so that they can replace the drive without data loss.

Most new hard disks include Self-Monitoring Analysis and Reporting Technology (SMART) and Disk Self Tests (DSTs). SMART monitors the health of the disk using a set of degradable attributes, such as head-flying height and bad block reallocation count. DSTs actively check for failures by performing read, write, and servo tests.

Windows queries for SMART status on an hourly basis and regularly schedules DSTs. If Windows detects impending disk failure, Windows can start disk diagnostics to guide the user or IT professionals through the process of backing up the data and replacing the disk before total failure occurs. Windows can also detect problems related to a dirty or scratched CD or DVD and instruct the user to clean the media.

You can configure disk diagnostics using two Group Policy settings. Both are located in Computer Configuration\Policies\Administrative Templates\System\Troubleshooting And Diagnostics\Disk Diagnostic.

- **Disk Diagnostic: Configure Execution Level** Use this policy to enable or disable disk diagnostic warnings. Disabling this policy does not disable disk diagnostics; it simply blocks disk diagnostics from displaying a message to the user and taking any corrective action. If you have configured a monitoring infrastructure to collect disk diagnostic events recorded to the event log and prefer to manually respond to events, you can disable this policy.
- **Disk Diagnostic: Configure Custom Alert Text** Enable this property to define custom alert text (up to 512 characters) in the disk diagnostic message that appears when a disk reports a SMART fault.

For disk diagnostics to work, the Diagnostic Policy Service must be running. Note that disk diagnostics cannot detect all impending failures. Additionally, because SMART attribute definitions are vendor specific, different vendor implementations can vary. SMART will not function if hard disks are attached to a hardware redundant array of independent disks (RAID) controller.

> ***NOTE*** **Many hardware vendors use SMART failures as a warranty replacement indicator.**

Self-Healing NTFS

Windows Vista and Windows 7 include self-healing NTFS File System (NTFS), which can detect and repair file system corruption while the operating system is running. In most cases, Windows will repair file corruption without disrupting the user. Essentially, self-healing NTFS functions similarly to ChkDsk (described in the section titled "How to Use ChkDsk" later in this chapter), but it works in the background, without locking an entire volume. Specifically, if Windows detects corrupted metadata on the file system, it invokes the self-healing capabilities of NTFS to rebuild the metadata. Some data may still be lost, but Windows can limit the damage and repair the problem without taking the entire system offline for a lengthy check-and-repair cycle.

Self-healing NTFS is enabled by default and requires no management. Instead, it will serve to reduce the number of disk-related problems that require administrative intervention. If self-healing fails, the volume will be marked "dirty," and Windows will run ChkDsk on the next startup.

Improved Driver Reliability

Drivers should be more reliable in Windows Vista and Windows 7 than they are in previous versions of Windows. Improved I/O cancellation support is built into Windows Vista and Windows 7 to enable drivers that might become blocked when attempting to perform I/O to gracefully recover. Windows Vista and Windows 7 also have new application programming interfaces (APIs) to allow applications to cancel I/O operations, such as opening a file.

To help developers create more stable drivers, Microsoft provides the Driver Verifier. Developers can use the Driver Verifier to verify that their drivers remain responsive and to ensure that they correctly support I/O cancellation. Because driver response failures can affect multiple applications or the entire operating system, these improvements will have a significant impact on Windows stability. This improvement requires no effort from administrators; you will simply benefit from a more reliable operating system.

Improved Error Reporting

Windows 7 offers improved application reliability, and the new error reporting capabilities allow applications to continue to become more reliable over time. In earlier versions of Windows, application response failures were very hard for developers to troubleshoot, because error reporting provided limited or no information about them. Windows Vista and Windows 7 improve error reporting to give developers the information they need to permanently resolve the root cause of the problems, thus providing continuous improvements in reliability.

The Process of Troubleshooting Hardware Issues

Hardware problems can take several different forms:

- Hardware problems that prevent Windows from starting

- A newly installed hardware accessory that does not work as expected
- A hardware accessory that did work correctly, but now fails
- Unpredictable symptoms, such as failing applications and services, Stop errors, system resets, and accessories that behave unreliably

You should use a different process to troubleshoot each of these broad problem categories. The following sections discuss each of these suggested processes.

How to Troubleshoot Problems That Prevent Windows from Starting

Some hardware problems—especially those related to hard disks or core features such as the motherboard or processor—can prevent Windows from starting. For information about troubleshooting startup problems, see Chapter 29.

How to Troubleshoot Problems Installing New Hardware

Often, you might have difficulty installing a new hardware feature, or an existing hardware feature might suddenly fail. If you are having trouble installing a new hardware feature, follow these steps:

1. If Windows will not start, see Chapter 29.
2. Install any updates available from Windows Update. For more information, see Chapter 23, "Managing Software Updates."
3. Download and install updated software and drivers for your hardware. Hardware manufacturers often release updated software for hardware features after they release the hardware. You can typically download software updates from the manufacturer's Web site.
4. Remove and reinstall any newly installed hardware by strictly following the manufacturer's instructions. You often need to install the software before connecting the hardware. For more information, see the sections titled "How to Diagnose Hardware Problems" and "How to Troubleshoot Driver Problems" later in this chapter. For detailed information about troubleshooting universal serial bus (USB) devices, see the section titled "How to Troubleshoot USB Problems" later in this chapter. For information about troubleshooting devices that connect using Bluetooth, see the section titled "How to Troubleshoot Bluetooth Problems" later in this chapter.
5. Use Event Viewer to find any related events that might provide useful information for diagnosing the problem. Typically, drivers will add events to the System Event Log. However, drivers could add events to any log. For information about using Event Viewer, see the section titled "How to Use Event Viewer" later in this chapter.
6. Install updated drivers for other hardware features, including basic input/output system (BIOS) and firmware updates for all hardware accessories and your computer.

Updated drivers for other hardware features can sometimes solve incompatibility problems with new hardware.

7. If possible, move hardware to different connectors on your computer. For example, move internal cards to different slots, or connect USB devices to different USB ports. If this solves the problem, the original connector on your computer has failed or the device was not connected correctly.
8. Replace any cables used to connect the new hardware to your computer. If this solves the problem, the cable was faulty.
9. Connect the new hardware to a different computer. If the hardware fails on multiple computers, you might have faulty hardware.
10. Contact the failed hardware manufacturer for support. You might have a hardware or software failure; the hardware manufacturer can assist with additional troubleshooting.

How to Troubleshoot Problems with Existing Hardware

If a hardware feature that previously worked suddenly fails, follow these troubleshooting steps:

1. If Windows will not start, see Chapter 29.
2. Use Reliability Monitor to determine how long the problem has been occurring and what related symptoms might be occurring. For more information, see the section titled "How to Use Reliability Monitor" later in this chapter. Then use Event Viewer to find any related events that might provide useful information for diagnosing the problem. For information about using Event Viewer, see the section titled "How to Use Event Viewer" later in this chapter.
3. Install any updates available from Windows Update. For more information, see Chapter 23.
4. Roll back any recently updated drivers, even if they are for other devices. Driver problems might cause incompatibilities with different devices. For more information, see the section titled "How to Roll Back Drivers" later in this chapter.
5. Download and install updated software and drivers for your hardware. Hardware manufacturers often release updated software for hardware features after they release the hardware. You can typically download software updates from the manufacturer's Web site.
6. Remove and reinstall any newly installed hardware. For more information, see the sections titled "How to Diagnose Hardware Problems" and "How to Troubleshoot Driver Problems" later in this chapter. For detailed information about troubleshooting USB devices, see the section titled "How to Troubleshoot USB Problems" later in this chapter.

7. Install updated drivers for other hardware features, including BIOS and firmware updates for all hardware accessories and your computer. Updated drivers for other hardware features can sometimes solve incompatibility problems with hardware.
8. Troubleshoot disk problems by using ChkDsk to identify and possibly fix disk-related problems. Disk problem can corrupt drivers, which might cause hardware to stop functioning. For more information, see the section titled "How to Troubleshoot Disk Problems" later in this chapter.
9. If possible, move hardware to different connectors on your computer. For example, move internal cards to different slots and connect USB devices to different USB ports. If this solves the problem, the original connector on your computer has failed or the device was not connected correctly.
10. Replace any cables used to connect the new hardware to your computer. If this solves the problem, the cable was faulty.
11. Connect problematic hardware to a different computer. If the hardware fails on multiple computers, you might have a hardware malfunction. Contact the hardware manufacturer for technical support.
12. Perform a system restore to attempt to return the computer to the latest state when it was functioning correctly. To use System Restore, see the section titled "How to Use System Restore" later in this chapter.
13. Contact the hardware manufacturer for support. You might have a hardware or software failure, and the hardware manufacturer can assist with additional troubleshooting.

How to Troubleshoot Unpredictable Symptoms

Hardware, driver, and disk problems can cause unpredictable symptoms when Windows is running, including:

- Failing applications and services
- Stop errors
- System resets
- Accessories that behave unreliably

Many different types of problems can cause these symptoms. To identify the source of these problems and possibly fix the issue, follow these steps. After each step, determine whether the problem continues.

1. If Windows will not start, see Chapter 29.
2. Use Reliability Monitor to determine how long the problem has been occurring and what other related symptoms might be occurring. For more information, read the section titled "How to Use Reliability Monitor" later in this chapter. Then use Event Viewer to find any related events that might provide useful information for diagnosing the problem. Typically, drivers will add events to the System Event Log. However, drivers

could add events to any log. For information about using Event Viewer, see the section titled "How to Use Event Viewer" later in this chapter.

3. Install any updates available from Windows Update. For more information, see Chapter 23.
4. Install updated drivers available directly from the hardware manufacturer, including BIOS and firmware updates for all hardware accessories and your computer.
5. Roll back any recently updated drivers. For more information, see the section titled "How to Roll Back Drivers" later in this chapter.
6. Troubleshoot disk problems by using ChkDsk to identify and possibly fix disk-related problems. To resolve problems related to low free disk space, run the Disk Cleanup Wizard. For more information, see the section titled "How to Troubleshoot Disk Problems" later in this chapter.
7. Test your memory for problems by using Windows Memory Diagnostics. For more information, see the section titled "How to Use Windows Memory Diagnostics" later in this chapter.
8. Remove unnecessary hardware features one by one. If the problem disappears after removing a hardware feature, that feature likely is causing the problem. Continue troubleshooting that specific feature by following the steps listed in the section titled "How to Troubleshoot Problems with Existing Hardware" earlier in this chapter.
9. Perform a system restore to attempt to return the computer to the latest state when it was functioning correctly. To use System Restore, see the section titled "How to Use System Restore" later in this chapter.
10. Contact your computer manufacturer for support. You might have a hardware or software failure, and your computer manufacturer can assist with additional troubleshooting.

How to Diagnose Hardware Problems

Always remember to check basic issues before attempting to remove and replace parts. Before installing new peripherals, refer to your motherboard and device manuals for helpful information, including safety precautions, firmware configuration, and expansion slot or memory slot locations. Some peripheral manufacturers recommend that you use a bus-mastering PCI slot and advise that installing their adapter in a secondary slot might cause it to function improperly.

How to Use Device Manager to Identify Failed Devices

Windows 7 can detect hardware that is not working properly. View failed hardware by following these steps to use Windows Device Manager:

1. Click Start, right-click Computer, and then select Manage.

2. Under System Tools, click Device Manager.
3. Device Manager displays all devices. Problem devices (including any devices with which Windows 7 is unable to successfully communicate) are displayed with a warning sign. If no categories are expanded and no devices are visible, Windows did not detect a problem with any device.

How to Check the Physical Setup of Your Computer

If you have recently opened the computer case or the computer has been moved or shipped, connectors may have loosened. You should perform the following tasks to verify that connections are solid:

- **Confirm that the power cords for all devices are firmly plugged in and that the computer power supply meets hardware specifications** Computer power supplies are available in different sizes and are typically rated between 200 and 400 watts. Installing too many devices into a computer with an inadequate amount of power can cause reliability problems or even damage the power supply. See the manufacturer's power specifications when installing new devices and verify that your computer can handle the increased electrical load.
- **Disconnect external accessories** External accessories—such as those that connect using USB or IEEE 1394, PC cards, and ExpressCards—can malfunction and interfere with the startup process. You can identify the cause of the problem either by disconnecting devices one by one and attempting to start the computer after disconnecting each device or by disconnecting all the devices, restarting the computer, and then reconnecting the devices one by one.
- **Verify that you correctly installed and firmly seated all internal adapters** Peripherals such as keyboards and video cards often must be installed and functioning to complete the initial startup phase without generating error messages. Adapters might become loose if the computer is moved or bumped or if the computer vibrates from moving parts such as hard disks.
- **Verify that you correctly attached cables** Check that you have firmly seated all cable connectors by disconnecting and reconnecting cables. Search for damaged or worn cables and replace them as required. To ensure that contacts are solid, use a pencil eraser to clean dirty connectors.
- **Check the system temperature** High temperatures inside a computer can cause unpredictable failures. Many computers will display internal temperatures for the processor, hard disk, graphics card, or other features if you start the Firmware menu. Graphical third-party tools also run within Windows for displaying temperature diagnostic information. If the temperature is high, verify that all fans are working properly and the vents are not blocked. Verify that the computer's case is completely assembled. Leaving panels open might seem like it would improve airflow, but it can actually misdirect air that should be cooling hot features. Verify that air can flow freely around the

outside of the computer. Particularly with mobile PCs, verify that the computer is not resting on a soft surface that can prevent heat dissipation, such as a couch or carpet. Finally, reset processor and memory speeds to their default settings to verify that the computer has not been overclocked.

How to Check the Configuration of Your Hardware

If you have recently changed the hardware configuration of your computer, or you are configuring a new computer, you should check the configuration to identify the cause of a startup problem.

- **Verify that you correctly configured any jumpers or dual in-line package (DIP) switches** Jumpers and DIP switches close or open electric contacts on circuit boards. For hard disks, jumper settings are especially important, because they can adversely affect the startup process if not correctly set. For example, configuring two master Advanced Technology Attachment (ATA) disks that are installed on the same channel or assigning duplicate small computer system interface (SCSI) ID numbers to devices in the same SCSI chain might cause a Stop error or error messages about hard disk failure.
- **Configure boot configuration data (BCD) references correctly when a hard disk is added** Installing an additional hard disk or changing the disk configuration in a computer can prevent Windows from starting. In this case, use the Startup Repair tool within System Recovery tools to automatically resolve the problem. For more information, see Chapter 29.
- **Verify SCSI configuration** If your computer uses or starts from SCSI devices and you suspect that these devices are causing startup problems, you need to check the items listed in Table 30-2.

TABLE 30-2 Checklist for Troubleshooting SCSI Devices

ITEM	DESCRIPTION
All devices are correctly terminated.	Verify that devices are correctly terminated. You must follow specific rules for termination to avoid problems with the computer not recognizing an SCSI device. Although these rules can vary slightly from one type of adapter to another, the basic principle is that you must terminate an SCSI chain at both ends.
All devices use unique SCSI ID numbers.	Verify that each device located on a particular SCSI chain has a unique identification number. Duplicate identification numbers can cause intermittent failures or even data corruption. For newer devices, you can use the SCSI Configured AutoMagically (SCAM) standard. The host adapter and all devices must support the SCAM standard. Otherwise you must set ID numbers manually.

ITEM	DESCRIPTION
The BIOS on the startup SCSI controller is enabled.	Verify that the SCSI BIOS is enabled for the primary SCSI controller and that the BIOS on secondary controllers is disabled. SCSI firmware contains programming instructions that allow the computer to communicate with SCSI disks before Windows 7 starts. Disabling this feature for all host adapters causes a startup failure. For information about disabling or enabling the BIOS, refer to the documentation provided with your SCSI controller.
You are using the correct cables.	Verify that the connecting cables are the correct type and length and are compliant with SCSI requirements. Different SCSI standards exist, each with specific cabling requirements. Consult the product documentation for more information.
The firmware settings for the host SCSI adapter match device capabilities.	Verify that host adapter BIOS settings for each SCSI device are set correctly. (The BIOS for the SCSI adapter is separate from the computer motherboard firmware.) For each SCSI device, you can specify settings—such as Sync Negotiation, Maximum Transfer Rate, and Send Start Command—that can affect performance and compatibility. Certain SCSI devices might not function correctly if settings are set beyond the capabilities of the hardware. Consult the documentation for your SCSI adapter and device before changing default settings.
SCSI adapters are installed in a master PCI slot.	Verify that you installed the host adapter in the correct motherboard slot. The documentation for some PCI SCSI adapters recommends using busmaster PCI slots to avoid problems on 32-bit computers. Refer to the manufacturer's documentation for your motherboard or computer to locate these busmaster PCI slots. If your SCSI adapter is installed in a non-busmaster PCI slot, move it to a master slot to see whether the change improves operation and stability.

WARNING **As a precaution, always shut down the computer and remove the power connector before troubleshooting hardware. Never attempt to install or remove internal devices if you are unfamiliar with hardware.**

MORE INFO **For more information about SCSI termination, see Microsoft Knowledge Base article 92765, "Terminating a SCSI Device," at _http://support.microsoft.com/?kbid=92765_ and Microsoft Knowledge Base article 154690, "How to Troubleshoot Event ID 9, Event ID 11, and Event ID 15 Error Messages," at _http://support.microsoft.com/?kbid=154690_.**

How to Verify That System Firmware and Peripheral Firmware Are Up to Date

You can sometimes trace instability and compatibility problems to outdated firmware. Whenever possible, use the latest firmware version. If Setup does not respond when you are installing the operating system, the cause might be the firmware for your DVD drive. Try upgrading the DVD firmware to the latest version.

How to Test Your Hardware by Running Diagnostic Tools

If the problem occurs after the power-on self test (POST) routine finishes but before Windows fully loads, run any diagnostic software that the manufacturer of the hardware adapter provides. This software typically includes self-test programs that allow you to quickly verify proper operation of a device and might help you to obtain additional information about the device, such as model number, hardware, and device firmware version.

Additionally, you can use Windows to run a memory test on your computer. For detailed instructions, see the section titled "How to Use Windows Memory Diagnostics" later in this chapter.

How to Simplify Your Hardware Configuration

Hardware problems can occur when you have both newer and older devices installed on your computer. If you cannot resolve problems by using safe mode and other options such as rolling back drivers, temporarily disable or remove Microsoft Internet Security and Acceleration (ISA) devices that do not support Plug and Play. If you can start Windows with these older devices removed, these devices are causing resource conflicts, and you need to manually reconfigure the resources assigned to them. For more information about rolling back drivers, see the section titled "How to Roll Back Drivers" later in this chapter.

While you are diagnosing startup problems related to hardware, it is recommended that you simplify your configuration. By simplifying your computer configuration, you might be able to start Windows. You can then gradually increase the computer's hardware configuration complexity until you reproduce the problem, which allows you to diagnose and resolve the problem.

Avoid troubleshooting when you have several adapters and external peripherals installed. Starting with external and ISA devices, disable or remove hardware devices one at a time until you are able to start your computer. Reinstall devices by following the manufacturer's instructions, verifying that each is functioning properly before checking the next device. For example, installing a PCI network adapter and a SCSI adapter at the same time can complicate troubleshooting, because either adapter might cause a problem.

ISA devices cause a large share of startup problems related to hardware because the PCI bus does not have a reliable method for determining ISA resource settings. Device conflicts might occur because of miscommunication between the two bus types. To avoid ISA and PCI conflicts, try temporarily removing ISA devices. After you install a new PCI device, you can use Device Manager to determine which system resources are available to ISA devices. Then reconfigure the ISA devices that do not support Plug and Play to eliminate any conflicts. If the problems continue after you reinstall ISA devices and you cannot resolve them with assistance from technical support, consider upgrading to newer hardware.

Simplifying your computer configuration also helps when problems prevent you from installing Windows. For more information about simplifying your hardware configuration to resolve setup problems, see Microsoft Knowledge Base article 224826, "Troubleshooting Text-Mode Setup Problems on ACPI Computers," at *http://support.microsoft.com/?kbid=224826*.

How to Diagnose Disk-Related Problems

Disk-related problems typically occur before Windows starts or shortly afterward. Refer to Table 30-3 for a list of symptoms, possible causes, and sources of information about disk-related startup problems.

TABLE 30-3 Diagnosing Disk-Related Startup Problems

SYMPTOM, MESSAGE, OR PROBLEM	POSSIBLE CAUSE	FOR MORE INFORMATION

The POST routine displays messages similar to the following.
`Hard disk error.`
`Hard disk absent/failed.`
	The system self-test routines halt because of improperly installed devices.	Verify that hardware is connected properly, as described earlier in this section.

The system displays MBR-related or boot sector–related messages similar to the following.
`Missing operating system.`
`Insert a system diskette and restart the system.`
	The Master Boot Record (MBR) or partition boot sector is corrupt because of problems with hardware or viruses.	Run Startup Repair, as described in Chapter 29.

The system displays messages about the partition table similar to the following.
`Invalid partition table.`
`A disk-read error occurred.`
	The partition table is invalid because of incorrect configuration of newly added disks.	Run Startup Repair, as described in Chapter 29. If Windows still fails to start, use the System Recovery command prompt to configure your disks.

You cannot access Windows after installing another operating system.	The boot sector is overwritten by another operating system's setup program.	Run Startup Repair, as described in Chapter 29.

SYMPTOM, MESSAGE, OR PROBLEM	POSSIBLE CAUSE	FOR MORE INFORMATION
System files are missing.	Required startup files are missing or damaged, or entries in the BCD registry file are pointing to the wrong partition.	Run Startup Repair, as described in Chapter 29.

The EFI boot manager or Windows Boot Manager displays messages similar to the following.
`Couldn't find loader.`
`Please insert another disk.`
	System files are missing.	Run Startup Repair, as described in Chapter 29.

CMOS or NVRAM disk configuration settings are not retained.	The CMOS memory or NVRAM is faulty, data is corrupted, or the battery that retains these settings needs replacing.	Follow the manufacturer's instructions for replacing or recharging the system battery.

Infrequently, disk-related issues such as corrupted files, file system problems, or insufficient free space might cause Stop messages to appear. For more information about maintaining disks and troubleshooting disk-related problems, see Chapter 16, "Managing Disks and File Systems."

How to Use Built-In Diagnostics

Windows 7 includes several different tools to assist you in diagnosing the source of hardware problems. The following sections describe the most important tools.

How to Use Reliability Monitor

To view Reliability Monitor, click Start, type **Reliability** and then click View Reliability History. The chart provides a day-by-day report of any problems or significant changes. To view events that occurred on a specific day, click the day in the chart and then view the reliability details for more information. You can also click the drop-down list in the upper-right corner and then click Select All to view a report that contains all events that Windows has recorded. For more information, read Chapter 21.

From Reliability Monitor, you can access capabilities that were part of Problem Reports And Solutions in Windows Vista. At the bottom of the page, click View All Problem Reports or Check For Solutions To All Problems.

How to Use Event Viewer

Event Viewer provides a central location for operating system and application event logging. On most computers, Event Viewer contains thousands of events generated by Windows, drivers, and applications. Most of these events can be safely ignored. However, when troubleshooting problems, you should examine the event log to find events that might be related to your problem. It is entirely possible that no events will be related to your problem, however, because not all problems may initiate an event.

To open Event Viewer and view hardware-related events, follow these steps:

1. Click Start, right-click Computer, and then click Manage.
2. Under System Tools, expand Event Viewer.
3. Under Event Viewer, expand Windows Logs and then click System.
4. In the Actions pane, click Filter Current Log.
5. In the Filter Current Log dialog box, select the Critical, Warning, and Error check boxes. Click OK.

Browse through the displayed events. Most of the events will not be related to your problem, but it is important to evaluate each event to determine any potential impact. In particular, pay close attention to events with a source of Advanced Configuration and Power Interface (ACPI), PlugPlayManager, or another source related to the hardware feature that is experiencing problems. For more information, read Chapter 21.

How to Use Data Collector Sets

The Performance snap-in includes data collector sets and corresponding reports that perform detailed analysis of different aspects of a computer's configuration and performance.

To use data collector sets and reports, follow these steps:

1. Click Start, right-click Computer, and then select Manage.
2. Expand Performance, expand Data Collector Sets, and then click System.
3. In the middle pane, right-click the data collector set you want to analyze and then click Start. For example, to analyze the computer's hardware, right-click System Diagnostics and then click Start. Windows 7 will begin collecting data.
4. Right-click the data collector set and then click Latest Report. Windows shows the report status while data is being collected (this might take several minutes). After enough data has been collected, the report is displayed. Figure 30-3 shows a System Diagnostics report.

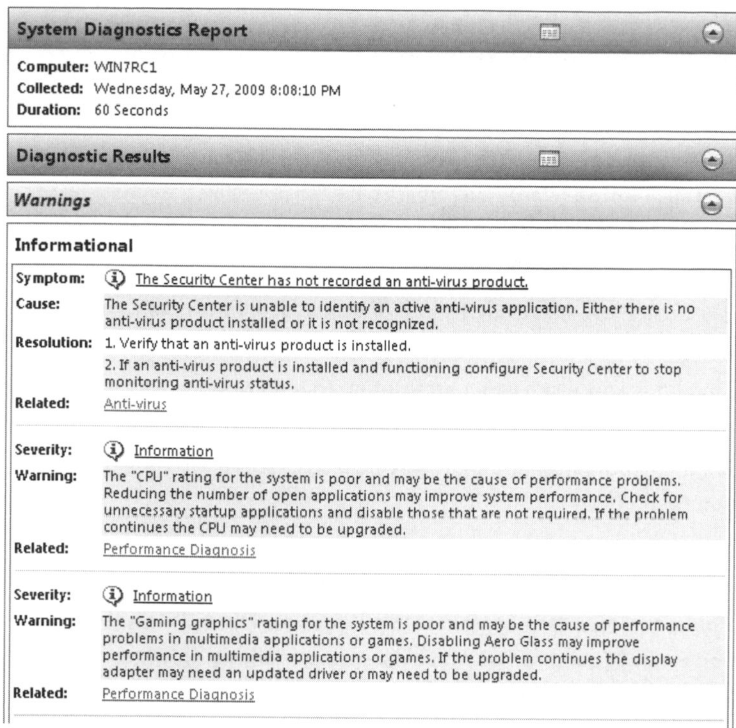
System Diagnostics Report
Computer: WIN7RC1
Collected: Wednesday, May 27, 2009 8:08:10 PM
Duration: 60 Seconds
Diagnostic Results
Warnings
Informational
Symptom: The Security Center has not recorded an anti-virus product.
Cause: The Security Center is unable to identify an active anti-virus application. Either there is no anti-virus product installed or it is not recognized.
Resolution: 1. Verify that an anti-virus product is installed.
2. If an anti-virus product is installed and functioning configure Security Center to stop monitoring anti-virus status.
Related: Anti-virus
Severity: Information
Warning: The "CPU" rating for the system is poor and may be the cause of performance problems. Reducing the number of open applications may improve system performance. Check for unnecessary startup applications and disable those that are not required. If the problem continues the CPU may need to be upgraded.
Related: Performance Diagnosis
Severity: Information
Warning: The "Gaming graphics" rating for the system is poor and may be the cause of performance problems in multimedia applications or games. Disabling Aero Glass may improve performance in multimedia applications or games. If the problem continues the display adapter may need an updated driver or may need to be upgraded.
Related: Performance Diagnosis

FIGURE 30-3 The System Diagnostics report includes detailed information about the computer, including possible sources of hardware problems.

Examine the report to determine whether any of the causes might be related to the problem you are troubleshooting.

How to Use Windows Memory Diagnostics

Memory problems are one of the most common types of hardware problem. Memory problems can prevent Windows from starting and cause unpredictable Stop errors when Windows has started. Because memory-related problems can cause intermittent failures, they can be difficult to identify.

HOW IT WORKS

Memory Failures

Because of the massive number of memory chips that hardware manufacturers produce and the high standards customers have for reliability, memory testing is a highly refined science. Different memory tests are designed to detect specific types of common failures, including the following:

- A bit may always return 1, even if set to 0. Similarly, a bit may always return 0, even if set to 1. This is known as a Stuck-At Fault (SAF).
- The wrong bit is addressed when attempting to read or write a specific bit. This is known as an Address Decoder Fault (AF).
- A section of memory may not allow values to change. This is known as a Transition Fault (TF).
- A section of memory changes when being read. This is called a Read Disturb Fault (RDF).
- One or more bits lose their contents after a period of time. This is known as a Retention Fault (RF) and can be one of the more challenging types of failures to detect.
- A change to one bit affects another bit. This is known as a Coupling Fault (CF) if the faulty bit changes to the same value as the modified bit, an Inversion Coupling Fault (CFin) if the faulty bit changes to the opposite value as the modified bit, or an Idempotent Coupling Fault (CFid) if the faulty bit always becomes a certain value (1 or 0) after any transition in the modified bit. This behavior can also occur because of a short between two cells, known as a Bridging Fault (BF).

Given these types of failures, it's clear that no single test could properly diagnose all the problems. For example, a test that wrote all 1s to memory and then verified that the memory returned all 1s would properly diagnose an SAF fault in which memory is stuck at 0. However, it would fail to diagnose an SAF fault in which memory is stuck at 1, and it would not be complex enough to find many BFs or CFs. Therefore, to properly diagnose all types of memory failures, Windows Memory Diagnostics provides several different types of tests.

Fortunately, Windows includes Windows Memory Diagnostics, an offline diagnostic tool that automatically tests your computer's memory. Windows Memory Diagnostics tests your computer's memory by repeatedly writing values to memory and then reading those values from memory to verify that they have not changed. To identify the widest range of memory failures, Windows Memory Diagnostics includes three different testing levels:

- **Basic** Basic tests include:
  - MATS+
  - INVC
  - SCHCKR (which enables the cache)
- **Standard** All basic tests, plus:
  - LRAND
  - Stride6 (which enables the cache)
  - CHCKR3
  - WMATS+
  - WINVC
- **Extended** All standard tests, plus:
  - MATS+ (which disables the cache)
  - Stride38
  - WSCHCKR
  - WStride-6
  - CHKCKR4
  - WCHCKR3
  - ERAND
  - Stride6 (which disables the cache)
  - CHCKR8

Although the specifics of each of these tests are not important for administrators to understand, it is important to understand that memory testing is never perfect. Failures are often intermittent and may occur only once every several days or weeks in regular usage. Automated tests such as those done by Windows Memory Diagnostics increase the likelihood that a failure can be detected; however, you can still have faulty memory while Windows Memory Diagnostics indicates that no problems were detected. To minimize this risk, run the Extended tests and increase the number of repetitions. The more tests you run, the more confident you can be in the result. If you have even a single failure, it indicates faulty memory.

After Windows Memory Diagnostics completes testing, the computer will automatically restart. Windows will display a notification bubble with the test results, as shown in Figure 30-4, and you can view events in the System Event Log with the source MemoryDiagnosticsResults (Event ID 1201).

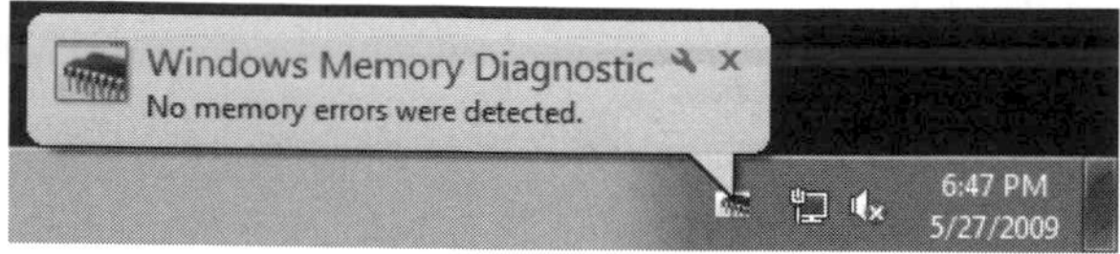

FIGURE 30-4 Windows Memory Diagnostics displays a notification bubble after logon.

If you do identify a memory failure, it is typically not worthwhile to attempt to repair the memory. Instead, you should replace unreliable memory. If the computer has multiple memory cards and you are unsure which card is causing the problem, replace each card and then rerun Windows Memory Diagnostics until the computer is reliable.

If problems persist even after replacing the memory, the problem is caused by an outside source. For example, high temperatures (often found in mobile PCs) can cause memory to be unreliable. Although computer manufacturers typically choose memory specifically designed to withstand high temperatures, adding third-party memory that does not meet the same specifications can cause failure. Besides heat, other devices inside the computer can cause electrical interference. Finally, motherboard or processor problems may occasionally cause memory communication errors that resemble failing memory.

How Windows Automatically Detects Memory Problems

When Windows analyzes problem reports, it can determine that memory problems might be a source of the problem. If this happens, the Action Center prompts the user to run Windows Memory Diagnostics. Users can click a link to either restart Windows and test for memory errors immediately or wait until the next time the computer is restarted.

How to Schedule Windows Memory Diagnostics

If Windows is running, you can schedule Windows Memory Diagnostics for the next startup by following these steps:

1. Click Start, type **mdsched.exe**, and then press Enter.
2. Choose to restart the computer and run the tool immediately or schedule the tool to run at the next restart, as shown in Figure 30-5.

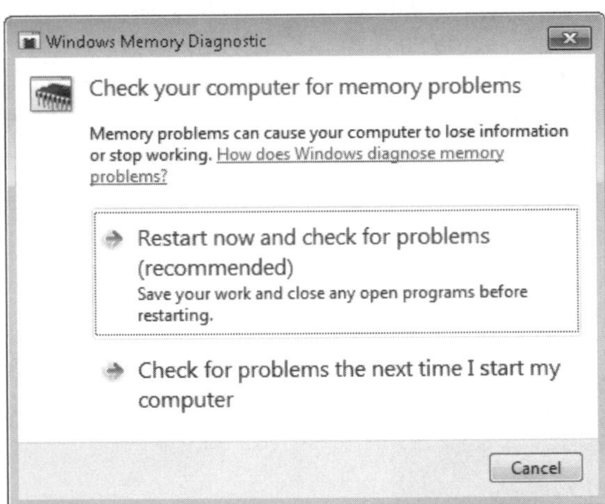

FIGURE 30-5 You can schedule Windows Memory Diagnostics to run when you next restart your computer.

Windows Memory Diagnostics runs automatically after the computer restarts.

How to Start Windows Memory Diagnostics When Windows Is Installed

If Windows is already installed, you can start Windows Memory Diagnostics from the Windows Boot Manager menu. To do this, follow these steps:

1. Remove all floppy disks and CDs from your computer and then restart your computer.
2. If the Windows Boot Manager menu does not normally appear, press the spacebar repeatedly as the computer starts. If you are successful, the Windows Boot Manager menu will appear. If the progress bar appears, restart your computer and try again to interrupt the startup process by pressing the spacebar.
3. On the Windows Boot Manager menu, press the Tab button on your keyboard to select Windows Memory Diagnostics, as shown in Figure 30-6, and then press Enter.

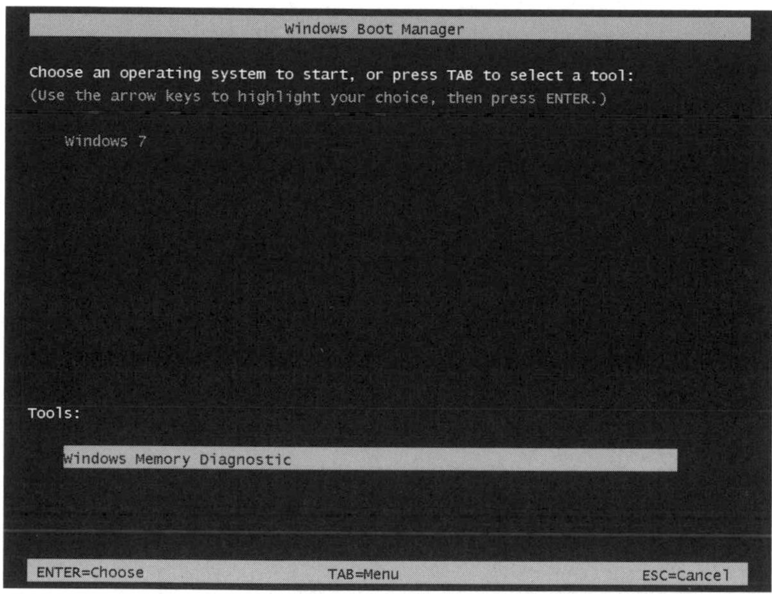

FIGURE 30-6 You can start Windows Memory Diagnostics from the Windows Boot Manager menu.

Windows Memory Diagnostics will start and automatically begin testing your computer's memory. For information on how to configure the automated tests, see the section titled "How to Configure Windows Memory Diagnostics" later in this chapter.

How to Start Windows Memory Diagnostics from the Windows DVD

If Windows is not installed, you can run Windows Memory Diagnostics from the Windows DVD by following these steps:

> ***NOTE*** **If Windows 7 is installed but will not start, you can start System Recovery tools faster by pressing F8 before the Starting Windows logo appears and then choosing Repair Your Computer from the Advanced Boot Options screen.**

1. Insert the Windows DVD into your computer.
2. Restart your computer. When prompted to boot from the DVD, press any key. If you are not prompted to boot from the DVD, you may have to configure your computer's startup sequence. For more information, see the section titled "Initial Startup Phase" in Chapter 29.
3. Windows Setup loads. When prompted, select your regional preferences and then click Next.
4. Click Repair Your Computer.
5. Select your keyboard layout and then click Next.
6. System Recovery scans your hard disks for Windows installations. If the standard drivers do not detect a hard disk because the drivers were not included with Windows, click the Load Drivers button to load the driver. Select an operating system to repair and then click Next.
7. The Choose A Recovery Tool page appears. Click Windows Memory Diagnostic Tool.

Windows Memory Diagnostics will start and automatically begin testing your computer's memory. For information on how to configure the automated tests, read the next section. For more information about System Recovery tools, see Chapter 29.

How to Configure Windows Memory Diagnostics

As shown in Figure 30-7, you can configure different options for Windows Memory Diagnostics. You can use these options to configure more thorough (and more time-consuming) diagnostics.

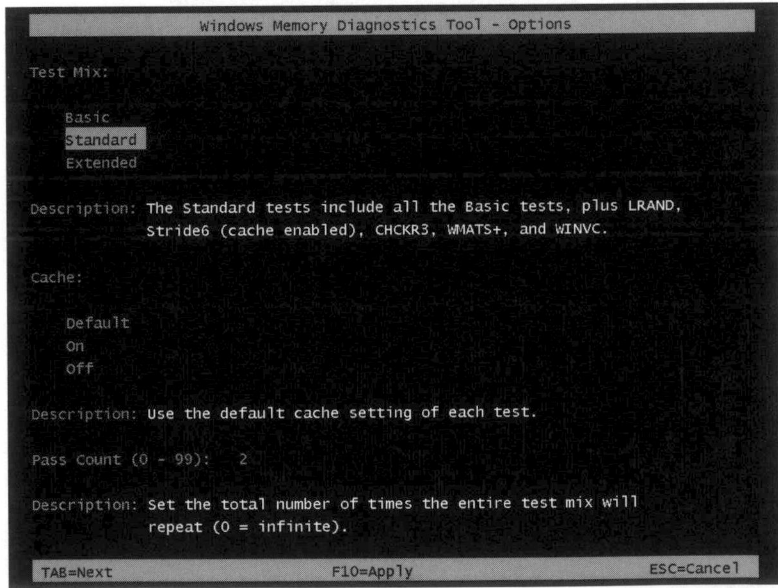

FIGURE 30-7 You can configure Windows Memory Diagnostics to use more thorough testing procedures.

To view Windows Memory Diagnostics options, start Windows Memory Diagnostics and then press F1. You can configure three different settings, which you select by pressing the Tab key:

- **Test Mix** The default set of tests, Standard, provides efficient testing while catching most common types of memory failures. To reduce testing time (and the types of failures that might be caught), choose Basic. To increase the types of failures that might be caught (as well as testing time), choose Extended.
- **Cache** Some tests use the cache, while others disable the cache. Tests are specifically designed to use or disable the cache to identify problems with different memory features. Therefore, you should typically leave this as the default setting.
- **Pass Count** This defines the number of iterations. Increase this number to provide more thorough testing and to increase the likelihood that you will identify any existing problems. The higher the Pass Count, the more likely you are to find problems.

After you have configured settings, press F10 to apply your changes. Windows Memory Diagnostics will then restart the tests.

How to Troubleshoot Disk Problems

Disk problems can cause unpredictable behavior in Windows. First, disk problems can lead to corrupted files because important system files and drivers are stored on your hard disk. Second, disk problems can lead to corruption in the page file or temporary files. Third, low disk space can lead to failed attempts to allocate disk space for temporary files. Any of these types of problems can cause unpredictable behavior. As a result, one step in troubleshooting hardware problems should be to check for disk problems and free up available disk space. Additionally, if you have a hard disk with nonvolatile caching, you can disable nonvolatile caching to determine whether the cache is causing problems.

The following sections provide information about troubleshooting disk-related problems. For general information concerning disks, see Chapter 16.

How to Prepare for Disk Failures

You can take several steps to prepare yourself—and your computers—for troubleshooting disk problems before the problems occur. First, familiarize yourself with recovery and troubleshooting tools. Use of disk redundancy lessens the impact of hardware failures. Backups ensure minimized data loss when failures occur. Protect yourself from malicious attacks by using antivirus software. Finally, perform regular maintenance on your storage devices.

You should familiarize yourself with the System Recovery tools and have a Windows DVD available to start the tools if the hard disks are not available. For more information, see Chapter 29.

Run ChkDsk /f /r regularly to fix file system problems that may appear because of faulty hardware, power failures, or software errors. Schedule downtime to reboot the computer and allow Autochk to resolve problems on boot and system volumes. Regularly review the ChkDsk output and the event log to identify problems that ChkDsk cannot fix.

For desktop computers that store critical, constantly updated data, use hardware disk redundancy (also known as RAID) to allow computers to continue to function if a hard disk fails. Keep replacement disks on hand.

At a minimum, back up critical files nightly. Redundancy does not eliminate the need for backups. Even redundant file systems can fail, and disk redundancy cannot protect against files that are corrupted by an application. You must restore corrupted files from an archival backup created before the corruption occurred.

Viruses, spyware, and other types of malware are a significant source of disk and file system problems. Follow these guidelines to avoid infecting computers with viruses:

- Install a virus detection program. Configure the virus detection program to automatically retrieve updated virus signatures.
- Use Windows Update to ensure that operating system files stay up to date.
- Keep applications up to date, especially Web browsers, which malware often abuses to install unwanted software. Windows Update distributes updates for Internet Explorer.
- Never run untrusted scripts or applications.
- Use Windows AppLocker to prevent users from running nonapproved software. For more information, refer to Chapter 24, "Managing Client Protection."

Although fragmentation will not cause a hard disk to fail, it will cause performance problems. To avoid performance problems, schedule the Defrag command-line tool to run regularly during off-peak hours. Store the output of the Defrag tool to a text file and review that text file regularly to ensure that defragmentation is performing as expected. To further minimize problems caused by fragmentation, ensure that all volumes have at least 15 percent free space available. For more information about using Defrag, see Chapter 16.

How to Use ChkDsk

ChkDsk (ChkDsk.exe) is a command-line tool that checks disk volumes for problems and attempts to repair any that it finds. For example, ChkDsk can repair problems related to bad sectors, lost clusters, cross-linked files, and directory errors. Disk errors are a common source of difficult-to-track problems, and ChkDsk should be one of the first tools you use when troubleshooting problems that do not appear to be the result of a recent system change. You must be logged on as an administrator or a member of the Administrators group to use ChkDsk.

Before running ChkDsk, be aware of the following:

- ChkDsk requires exclusive access to a volume while it is running. ChkDsk might display a prompt asking whether you want to check the disk the next time you restart your computer.

- ChkDsk might take a long time to run, depending on the number of files and folders, the size of the volume, disk performance, and available system resources (such as processor and memory).
- ChkDsk might not accurately report information in read-only mode.

ChkDsk Examples

To correct disk errors from a command line, open an administrative command prompt and type

Chkdsk *DriveLetter*: /f /r

For example, to check drive C for errors, type

Chkdsk C: /f /r

If you need to run ChkDsk on a large D volume and you want ChkDsk to complete as quickly as possible, type

Chkdsk D: /f /c /i

ChkDsk Syntax

The command-line syntax for ChkDsk is

```
Chkdsk [volume[[path] filename]] [/f] [/v] [/r] [/x] [/i] [/c] [/b] [/l[:size]]
```

Table 30-4 lists all ChkDsk command-line parameters. Unless otherwise noted, parameters apply to any file system type.

TABLE 30-4 ChkDsk Parameters

PARAMETER	DESCRIPTION

volume	Specifies the volume that you want ChkDsk to check. You can specify the volume by using any of the formats in the following examples:
	To run ChkDsk on the C volume, specify
	`c:`
	To run ChkDsk on a mounted volume called data that is mounted on the C volume, specify
	`c:\data`
	To run ChkDsk on a volume, you can specify the symbolic link name for a volume, such as
	`\\?\Volume{109d05a2-6914-11d7-a037-806e6f6e6963}\`
	You can determine a symbolic link name for a volume by using the *mountvol* command.

PARAMETER	DESCRIPTION
path	FAT/FAT32 only. Specifies the location of a file or set of files within the folder structure of the volume.
filename	FAT/FAT32 only. Specifies the file or set of files to check for `<a ID="wPopUp" HREF="HELP=glossary.hlp TOPIC=gls_fragmentation"> fragmentation </a>`. Wildcard characters (* and ?) are allowed.
/f	Fixes errors on the disk. The volume must be locked. If ChkDsk cannot lock the volume, ChkDsk offers to check it the next time the computer restarts.
/v	On FAT/FAT32: Displays the full path and name of every file on the disk. On NTFS: Displays additional information or cleanup messages, if any.
/r	Locates `<a ID="wPopUp" HREF="HELP=glossary.hlp TOPIC=glos_glo_cigj">` bad sectors </a> and recovers readable information (implies */f*). If ChkDsk cannot lock the volume, it offers to check it the next time the computer starts. Because NTFS also identifies and remaps bad sectors during the course of normal operations, it is usually not necessary to use the */r* parameter unless you suspect that a disk has bad sectors.
/x	Forces the volume to dismount first, if necessary. All opened handles to the volume are then invalid (implies */f*). This parameter does not work on the boot volume. You must restart the computer to dismount the boot volume.
/i	NTFS only. Performs a less-detailed check of index entries, reducing the amount of time needed to run ChkDsk.
/c	NTFS only. Skips the checking of cycles within the folder structure, reducing the amount of time needed to run ChkDsk.
/l:*size*	NTFS only. Changes the size of the log file to the specified number of kilobytes. Displays the current size if you do not enter a new size. If the system loses power, stops responding, or is restarted unexpectedly, NTFS runs a recovery procedure when Windows restarts. This procedure accesses information stored in this log file. The size of the log file depends on the size of the volume. In most conditions, you do not need to change the size of the log file. However, if the number of changes to the volume is so great that NTFS fills the log before all metadata is written to disk, then NTFS must force the metadata to disk and free the log space. When this condition occurs, you might notice that Windows stops responding for 5 seconds or longer. You can eliminate the performance impact of forcing the metadata to disk by increasing the size of the log file.
/b	NTFS only. Re-evaluates bad clusters on the volume. This is typically not necessary, but it might allow you to reclaim some lost disk space on a hard disk with a large number of bad clusters. However, these clusters might experience problems in the future, decreasing reliability.
/?	Displays information about using ChkDsk.

How to Use the Graphical ChkDsk Interface

In addition to using the command-line version of ChkDsk, you can run ChkDsk from My Computer or Windows Explorer by following these steps:

1. Click Start and then click Computer.
2. Right-click the volume you want to check and then click Properties.
3. Click the Tools tab and then click Check Now.
4. Do one of the following:
   - To run ChkDsk in read-only mode, clear all check boxes and then click Start.
   - To repair errors without scanning the volume for bad sectors, select the Automatically Fix File System Errors check box and then click Start.
   - To repair errors, locate bad sectors, and recover readable information, select both the Automatically Fix File System Errors and Scan For And Attempt Recovery Of Bad Sectors check boxes and then click Start.

ChkDsk will run immediately if the volume is not in use and then display the results in a dialog box. If the volume is in use, ChkDsk will request that you schedule a disk check for the next time the computer is restarted.

How to Determine Whether ChkDsk Is Scheduled to Run

Windows might also configure ChkDsk to run automatically at startup if it detects problems with a volume. Volumes that Windows determines need to be checked are considered dirty. To determine whether a volume is considered dirty, run the following command at a command prompt.

```
Chkntfs volume:
```

For example, to determine whether drive C is considered dirty, run the following.

```
Chkntfs C:
```

You can also use the Chkntfs tool to prevent a dirty volume from being checked at startup, which is useful if you want to avoid the time-consuming ChkDsk process and will not be at the computer during startup to bypass ChkDsk. For more information, run the following at a command prompt.

```
Chkntfs /?
```

ChkDsk Process on NTFS Volumes

When you run ChkDsk on NTFS volumes, the ChkDsk process consists of three major stages and two optional stages. ChkDsk displays its progress for each stage with the following messages.

```
Windows is verifying files (stage 1 of 5)...
File verification completed.
CHKDSK is verifying indexes (stage 2 of 5)...
Index verification completed.
CHKDSK is verifying security descriptors (stage 3 of 5)...
Security descriptor verification completed.
CHKDSK is verifying file data (stage 4 of 5)...
File data verification completed.
CHKDSK is verifying free space (stage 5 of 5)...
Free space verification completed.
```

The following list describes each of the ChkDsk stages.

- **Stage 1: ChkDsk verifies each file record segment in the Master File Table** During stage 1, ChkDsk examines each file record segment in the volume's Master File Table (MFT). A specific file record segment in the MFT uniquely identifies every file and directory on an NTFS volume. The percentage complete that ChkDsk displays during this phase is the percentage of the MFT that has been verified.

  The percentage complete indicator advances relatively smoothly throughout this phase, although some unevenness might occur. For example, file record segments that are not in use require less time to process than do those that are in use, and larger security descriptors take more time to process than do smaller ones. Overall, the percentage complete indicator is a fairly accurate representation of the actual time required for that phase.

- **Stage 2: ChkDsk checks the directories in the volume** During stage 2, ChkDsk examines each of the indexes (directories) on the volume for internal consistency and verifies that every file and directory represented by a file record segment in the MFT is referenced by at least one directory. ChkDsk also confirms that every file or subdirectory referenced in each directory actually exists as a valid file record segment in the MFT and checks for circular directory references. ChkDsk then confirms that the timestamps and the file size information associated with files are up to date in the directory listings for those files.

  The percentage complete that ChkDsk displays during this phase is the percentage of the total number of files on the volume that are checked. For volumes with many thousands of files and folders, the time required to complete this stage can be significant.

  The duration of stage 2 varies because the amount of time required to process a directory is closely tied to the number of files or subdirectories listed in that directory. Because of this dependency, the percentage complete indicator might not advance smoothly during stage 2, though the indicator continues to advance even for large directories. Therefore, do not use the percentage complete indicator as a reliable representation of the actual time remaining for this phase.

- **Stage 3: ChkDsk verifies the security descriptors for each volume** During stage 3, ChkDsk examines each of the security descriptors associated with each file and directory on the volume by verifying that each security descriptor structure is well formed and internally consistent. The percentage complete that ChkDsk displays during this phase is the percentage of the number of files and directories on the volume that are checked.

  The percentage complete indicator advances relatively smoothly throughout this phase, although some unevenness might occur.

- **Stage 4: ChkDsk verifies file data** During stage 4 (which is optional), ChkDsk verifies all clusters in use. ChkDsk performs stages 4 and 5 if you specify the */r* parameter when you run ChkDsk. The */r* parameter confirms that the sectors in each cluster are usable. Specifying the */r* parameter is usually not necessary, because NTFS identifies and remaps bad sectors during the course of normal operations, but you can use the */r* parameter if you suspect the disk has bad sectors.

  The percentage complete that ChkDsk displays during stage 4 is based on the percentage of used clusters that are checked. Used clusters typically take longer to check than unused clusters, so stage 4 lasts longer than stage 5 on a volume with equal numbers of used and unused clusters. For a volume with mostly unused clusters, stage 5 takes longer than stage 4.

- **Stage 5: ChkDsk verifies free space** During stage 5 (which is optional), ChkDsk verifies unused clusters. ChkDsk performs stage 5 only if you specify the */r* parameter when you run ChkDsk. The percentage complete that ChkDsk displays during stage 5 is the percentage of unused clusters that are checked.

How to Use the Disk Cleanup Wizard

With Disk Cleanup (Cleanmgr.exe), you can delete unneeded files and compress infrequently accessed files. This tool is primarily useful for resolving problems that might be related to a shortage of disk space. Insufficient free disk space can cause many problems, ranging from Stop errors to file corruption. To increase free space, you can do the following:

- Move files to another volume or archive them to backup media.
- Compress files or disks to reduce the space required to store data.
- Delete unneeded files.

To run Disk Cleanup, follow these steps:

1. Click Start and then click Computer.
2. Right-click the drive you want to clean and then select Properties. On the General tab of the Properties dialog box, click Disk Cleanup.
3. If prompted, click either My Files Only or Files From All Users On This Computer.
4. On the Disk Cleanup tab, select the files to delete and then click OK.

How to Disable Nonvolatile Caching

Windows Vista is the first Windows operating system to support caching hard disk data to a nonvolatile cache on hard disks with the required cache. Windows Vista and Windows 7 can use the cache to improve startup performance, improve the performance of frequently modified system data, and reduce utilization. In rare circumstances, the failing nonvolatile cache might cause problems. To eliminate the possibility that the nonvolatile cache is causing problems, you can disable different cache functionality using the following Group Policy settings (located in Computer Configuration\Administrative Templates\System\Disk NV Cache):

- **Turn Off Boot And Resume Optimizations** Enable this policy to prevent Windows from using the nonvolatile cache to speed startup times.
- **Turn Off Cache Power Mode** Enable this policy to prevent Windows from putting disks into a nonvolatile cache power-saving mode, which enables the hard disk to spin down while continuing to use the nonvolatile cache.
- **Turn Off Non Volatile Cache Feature** Enable this policy to completely disable all use of the nonvolatile cache.
- **Turn Off Solid State Mode** Enable this policy to prevent frequently written files such as the system metadata and registry from being stored in the nonvolatile cache.

How to Troubleshoot Driver Problems

Drivers are software features that Windows uses to communicate with hardware accessories. Windows typically has dozens of drivers active at any given point, allowing it to communicate with your graphics card, hard disks, sound card, USB devices, and other hardware. Without a driver, hardware cannot function properly. Additionally, you might have problems with hardware if a driver is outdated or unreliable.

The following sections describe how to work with drivers to solve hardware problems.

How to Find Updated Drivers

Microsoft or hardware vendors occasionally release updated drivers to improve hardware performance and reliability. Many updates are available directly from Windows Update. To find and download any updates available for a computer, follow these steps:

1. Click Start, click All Programs, and then click Windows Update.
2. If available, click Check For Updates.
3. If Windows Update displays any optional updates, click View Available Updates.
4. Windows displays any driver updates if available. Select the update and then click Install.
5. Windows Update downloads any selected updates, creates a system restore point, and then installs the updates.

Additionally, hardware manufacturers might release updated drivers directly to users before they are available on Windows Update. Check manufacturer Web sites for updated drivers.

How to Roll Back Drivers

When you update a device driver, your computer might have problems that it did not have with the previous version. For example, installing an unsigned device driver might cause the device to malfunction or cause resource conflicts with other installed hardware. Installing faulty drivers might cause Stop errors that prevent the operating system from starting in normal mode. Typically, Stop message text displays the file name of the driver that causes the error.

Windows provides a feature called Device Driver Roll Back that might help you restore system stability by rolling back a driver update.

> ***NOTE*** **You can use System Information or the Sigverif tool to determine whether a driver on your computer is signed and to obtain other information about the driver, such as version, date, time, and manufacturer. This data, combined with information from the manufacturer's Web site, can help you decide whether to roll back or update a device driver.**

To roll back a driver, follow these steps:

1. Click Start, right-click Computer, and then select Manage.
2. Under System Tools, click Device Manager.
3. Expand a category (Network Adapters, for example) and then double-click a device.
4. Click the Driver tab and then click Roll Back Driver.
5. You are prompted to confirm that you want to overwrite the current driver. Click Yes to roll back the driver. The rollback process proceeds, or you are notified that an older driver is not available.

How to Use Driver Verifier

Windows 7 (and all versions of Windows since Microsoft Windows 2000) includes the Driver Verifier (Verifier.exe). You can run either graphical or command-line versions of the Driver Verifier. To run a command-line version, open a command prompt and then type **Verifier.exe**. To run the graphical version, click Start, type **Verifier.exe**, and then press Enter.

Driver Verifier is useful for isolating a problematic driver that is causing a computer running Windows to intermittently fail, because you can use the tool to configure Windows to actively test potentially problematic drivers. After driver verification has been configured for a driver, Windows puts additional stress on the driver during normal operations by simulating conditions that include low memory and verification of I/O. Enabling driver verification for a problematic driver is highly likely to initiate a Stop error that identifies the driver.

To use Driver Verifier Manager to troubleshoot problems that might be related to a driver, enable driver verification for all drivers that might potentially be causing the problems. Restart the system and then wait. Driver verification happens in the background while the system performs normal tasks and might not yield immediate results. If a verified driver returns an inappropriate response, Driver Verifier will initiate a Stop error. If a Stop error has not occurred after several days, the verified drivers might not be the source of the problem you are troubleshooting. After you have completed the troubleshooting process, use Driver Verifier to delete the settings and disable driver verification.

> ***NOTE*** **Use Driver Verifier only on nonproduction systems to identify a problematic driver. Using Driver Verifier greatly increases the likelihood of a Stop error occurring and decreases system performance.**

To verify unsigned drivers, follow these steps:

1. Click Start, type **Verifier**, and then press Enter.
2. Click Create Standard Settings and then click Next.
3. Click Automatically Select Unsigned Drivers and then click Next.

   As shown in Figure 30-8, Driver Verifier Manager finds unsigned drivers, enables verification of those drivers, and then displays the list of unsigned drivers.

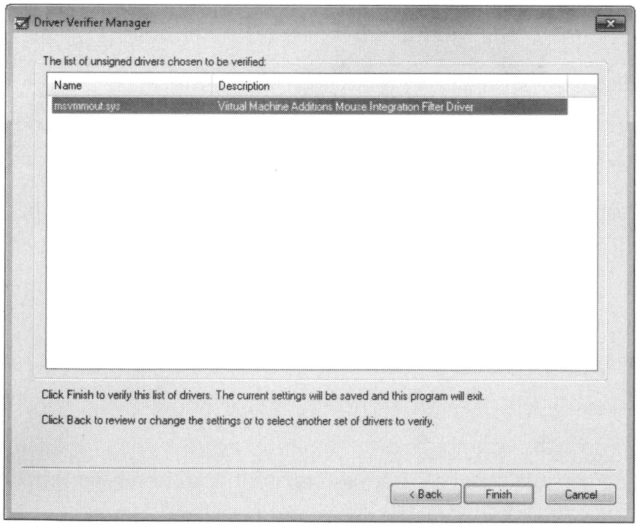

   FIGURE 30-8 Driver Verifier Manager can help you identify problematic drivers.

4. Click Finish.
5. Click OK and then restart the computer.

To verify all drivers, follow these steps:

1. Click Start, type **Verifier**, and then press Enter.
2. Click Create Standard Settings and then click Next.
3. Click Automatically Select All Drivers Installed On This Computer and then click Finish.
4. Click OK and then restart the computer.

To disable driver verification, follow these steps:

1. Click Start, type **Verifier**, and then press Enter.
2. Click Delete Existing Settings and then click Finish.
3. Click Yes.
4. Click OK and then restart the computer.

How to Use the File Signature Verification

File Signature Verification (Sigverif.exe) detects signed files and allows you to

- View the certificates of signed files to verify that the file has not been tampered with after being certified.
- Search for signed files.
- Search for unsigned files.

NOTE **Unsigned or altered drivers cannot be installed on x64-based versions of Windows.**

Driver signing is a multistage process in which device drivers are verified. For a driver to earn this certification, it must pass a series of compatibility tests administered by the Windows Hardware Quality Labs (WHQL). Because of stringent WHQL standards, using signed drivers typically results in a more stable system. When troubleshooting a problem that might be caused by a driver, you might choose to remove unsigned drivers to eliminate the possibility that the unsigned driver is causing the problem. Although most unsigned drivers will not cause problems, they have not been verified by Microsoft and therefore have a higher risk of causing problems than signed drivers. Microsoft digitally signs drivers that pass the WHQL tests, and Windows performs signature detection for device categories such as:

- Keyboards
- Hard disk controllers
- Modems
- Mouse devices
- Multimedia devices
- Network adapters
- Printers
- SCSI adapters

- Smart card readers
- Video adapters

A Microsoft Corporation digital signature indicates that a driver file is an original, unaltered system file that Microsoft has approved for use with Windows. Windows can warn or prevent users from installing unsigned drivers. If a driver is not digitally signed, the user receives a message that requests confirmation to continue. Microsoft digitally signs all drivers included with Windows or distributed by Windows Update. When you download updated drivers from a manufacturer's Web page, always select drivers that are signed by Microsoft.

The following tools are useful for troubleshooting problems caused by unsigned files:

- File Signature Verification
- Device Manager
- Driver Verifier Manager

To identify unsigned drivers, follow these steps:

1. Click Start and then type **Sigverif**. Press Enter.
2. In the File Signature Verification window, click Start.
3. After several minutes, the Signature Verification Results page displays unsigned drivers. Unsigned drivers can be reliable, but they have not undergone the same testing that is required of signed drivers. If you are experiencing reliability problems, you should replace unsigned drivers with signed versions from Microsoft.
4. Click Close to return to the File Signature Verification window.
5. Click Close again.

How to Use Device Manager to View and Change Resource Usage

Installing new hardware or updating drivers can create conflicts, causing devices to become inaccessible. You can use Device Manager to review resources used by these devices to manually identify conflicts. Typically, however, you should let Windows automatically allocate resources. With modern hardware, there is almost never a valid reason to adjust resource usage manually, and you might cause more problems than you resolve.

To use Device Manager (Devmgmt.msc) to view or change system resource usage information, follow these steps:

1. Click Start, right-click Computer, and then click Manage.
2. Click Device Manager and then double-click a device.
3. Click the Resources tab to view the resources used by that device.
4. Click a resource and then clear the Use Automatic Settings check box.
5. Click Change Setting and then specify the resources assigned to the device.

For more information about managing devices, see Chapter 17, "Managing Devices and Services."

How to Use System Restore

System Restore regularly captures system settings so that you can restore them later if you experience a problem. Using System Restore to return your computer to an earlier state should be one of your last troubleshooting steps, however, because it might cause problems with recently installed applications and hardware.

You can run System Restore from within either the System Recovery tools or from within Windows. To use System Restore from System Recovery tools (which is necessary only if Windows will not start), see Chapter 29. To use System Restore from within Windows, follow these steps:

1. Click Start, click All Programs, click Accessories, click System Tools, and then click System Restore. The System Restore Wizard appears.
2. If this is the first time you are running the System Restore Wizard, click Next to accept the default restore point. Then, skip to step 4.
3. If you have run System Restore previously and it did not solve the problem, click Choose A Different Restore Point and then click Next.
4. On the Restore Your Computer To The State It Was In Before The Selected Event page, select the most recent restore point when the computer was functioning correctly. Click Next.
5. On the Confirm Your Restore Point page, click Finish. When prompted, click Yes.
6. System Restore restarts your computer. When the restart has completed, System Restore displays a dialog box to confirm that the restoration was successful. Click Close.

If System Restore does not solve your problem, you can do one of two things:

- **Undo the system restore** The problem might not be the result of changes to your computer at all, but rather a hardware failure. Therefore, using System Restore might not solve your problem. Because restoring the computer to an earlier state might remove important changes to your system configuration, you should undo any restorations that do not solve your problem. To undo a system restore, simply rerun System Restore using the steps in this section and choose the default settings.
- **Restore an earlier restore point** Your problem may be caused by recent changes to your computer, but the negative changes occurred before the most recent system restore. Therefore, restoring an earlier restore point might solve your problem. Repeat the steps in this section to restore to an earlier restore point.

How to Troubleshoot USB Problems

The most common way to connect external devices to a computer is USB. USB provides expandability without the complexity of connecting internal devices such as PCI cards. Connecting USB devices is so simple that most users can connect and configure USB devices without help from the Support Center (provided that they have sufficient privileges). However, users do occasionally experience problems with USB devices. The following sections provide guidance for troubleshooting USB problems.

How to Solve USB Driver and Hardware Problems

If you do experience problems, following these steps might solve them:

1. Restart the computer. Some software might require the computer to be restarted before functioning properly. Additionally, restarting the computer forces Windows to detect the USB hardware again.
2. Install updated driver software, if available. Check Windows Update and the hardware manufacturer's Web site for updates.
3. Uninstall the device's driver and software, disconnect the USB device, restart the computer, and then follow the manufacturer's instructions to reinstall the software. Many USB devices require a driver. Typically, the driver should be installed before connecting the USB device. If you are experiencing problems with a USB device, the most likely cause is a driver problem. For information on how to troubleshoot the driver problem, see the section titled "How to Troubleshoot Driver Problems" earlier in this chapter. External storage devices such as USB flash drives and external hard drives typically do not require a driver, because the required software is built into Windows.
4. Disconnect the USB device and reconnect it to a different USB port. This can cause Windows to detect the device as new and reinstall required drivers. Additionally, this will solve problems related to a specific USB port, such as a failed port or power limitations.
5. Replace the USB cable with a new cable or a different cable that you know works properly.

Understanding USB Limitations

If you installed the USB device's software correctly and you are using the most up-to-date version of the driver, you still might have problems because of USB's physical limitations. Limitations that can cause problems include:

- **Insufficient power** Many USB devices receive power from the USB port. Connecting too many unpowered devices to a USB hub can result in a power shortage, which can cause a USB device to not respond properly. This is particularly common when using an unpowered external USB hub. To quickly determine whether a problem is power related, disconnect other USB devices and connect each USB device directly to the computer one by one. If devices work when connected separately but fail when connected simultaneously, the problem is probably power related. Decrease the number of devices or add a powered USB hub.
- **Excessive length** USB devices can be no more than 5 meters (16 feet) away from the USB hub to which they are connected. Although USB devices will never ship with cables

longer than 5 meters (16 feet), some users connect USB extenders to allow longer distances. Depending on the quality of the cable and possible sources of interference, you might experience problems with shorter distances. To determine whether length is the source of problems, remove any USB extenders and connect the USB device directly to the computer.

- **Too many devices** USB can support up to a maximum of 127 devices connected to a single USB host controller, which is more than enough for the vast majority of client computer scenarios. You can have a maximum of seven layers of USB hubs connected to the computer's USB host controller, and no more than five external hubs.
- **Insufficient bandwidth** Most USB devices are designed to work within USB bandwidth limitations. However, video cameras in particular might need more bandwidth than USB is capable of providing. If you receive a "Bandwidth Exceeded" message, first try disconnecting other USB devices. If the message continues to appear, attempt to reduce the bandwidth used by the device by lowering the resolution of the camera. For best results with a video camera, connect it to an IEEE 1394 (also known as Firewire or iLink) port.

> ***NOTE*** **If you see the message, "Hi-speed USB device is plugged into non-hi-speed USB hub," the USB device is USB 2.0, but the USB port is an earlier version. The device will probably work, but it will work slowly. You can improve performance by adding a USB 2.0 port to the computer.**

How to Identify USB Problems Using Performance Monitor

If you are concerned that you may have a USB bandwidth or performance problem, you can identify the problem by using the Performance snap-in:

1. If the problem you need to identify occurs when you are actively using a USB device, connect the USB device that you want to troubleshoot and turn it on. If the problem occurs when you first connect the USB device, do not connect the device until after you have begun logging.
2. Click Start, right-click Computer, and then select Manage.
3. Expand System Tools, Performance, Monitoring Tools, and then click Performance Monitor.
4. On the Performance Monitor toolbar, click the green Add button.
5. In the Add Counters dialog box, in the Available Counters group, expand USB. If you are troubleshooting the failure of a USB device, add the following counters for the <All Instances> instance:
   - Iso Packet Errors/Sec
   - Transfer Errors/Sec

If you are troubleshooting a USB performance problem, add the following counters for the <All Instances> instance:

- Bulk Bytes/Sec
- Avg. Bytes/Transfer

6. Click OK to add the counters to Performance Monitor.

Performance Monitor begins collecting data about your USB devices and connections. Attempt to reproduce the problem (for example, by copying a file to a USB hard disk or connecting a video camera). If you are troubleshooting performance problems, right-click the Performance Monitor display and click Clear immediately after you begin using the device to ensure the counters include only data created during your test. The longer you allow the test to run, the more accurate it will be. You should stop Performance Monitor before your test ends.

After reproducing the problem, pause Performance Monitor by clicking the Freeze Display button on the toolbar or by pressing Ctrl+F. Because you added performance counters for all instances, you probably have a large number of counters. To browse individual counters to identify the specific source of your problems, press Ctrl+H to enable highlighting.

Click the first counter in the list. After you select a counter, the graph related to that counter will be shown in bold. Examine the values for that particular counter. If the counter shows an error, make note of the USB controller and device causing the problem. Press the down arrow on your keyboard to select the next counter and continue analyzing USB performance values.

USB errors should not occur under normal circumstances; however, Windows can automatically recover from many USB errors without affecting the user. After you identify the source of the USB problems, follow the steps in the section titled "How to Solve USB Driver and Hardware Problems" earlier in this chapter.

If you are troubleshooting USB performance problems, examine the Bulk Bytes/Sec counter to identify the instance that relates to the device you are using. Then select the counter and make note of the Average value. Theoretically, USB 2.0 can transfer a maximum of 60,000,000 bytes/sec. However, this theoretical maximum will never be realized. More realistically, you might be able to achieve half that value. USB storage devices are often much slower, and performance will vary depending on the performance of the device itself. USB hard disks typically average less than 10,000,000 bytes/sec but can peak over 20,000,000 bytes/sec. Performance of hard disks will also vary depending on the portion of the disk being written to or read from, the size of the files being accessed, and the disk fragmentation. For more information on using Performance Monitor, see Chapter 21.

How to Examine USB Hubs

Connecting a USB device to a computer can include several different layers:

- **A USB host controller, which is connected directly to your computer** USB host controllers are often built into the computer's motherboard, but you can add them by using an internal adapter or a PC card. If the name of the controller includes the word "Enhanced," the controller supports USB 2.0.

- **A USB root hub, which is connected directly to the USB host controller** Typically, USB root hubs are built into the same device that contains the USB host controller—your computer's motherboard or an adapter card.
- **Optionally, additional USB hubs that connect to the USB root hub to create additional USB ports** USB hubs can be external devices that you add, they can be an internal device within a computer, or they can be built into a docking station.

You can use Device Manager to examine the USB controllers and hubs in a computer, determine their power capabilities, and examine the power requirements of the connected devices. This can help you to identify the source of a USB problem. To examine USB devices, follow these steps:

1. Click Start, right-click Computer, and then select Manage.
2. In the Computer Management console, click Device Manager (under System Tools).
3. In the right pane, expand Universal Serial Bus Controllers.
4. Right-click an instance of USB Root Hub (there might be several) and then click Properties.
5. Click the Power tab, as shown in Figure 30-9. This tab displays the power capabilities of the hub and the power requirements of every connected device. To determine the requirements of any specific device, disconnect the devices and connect them again one by one.

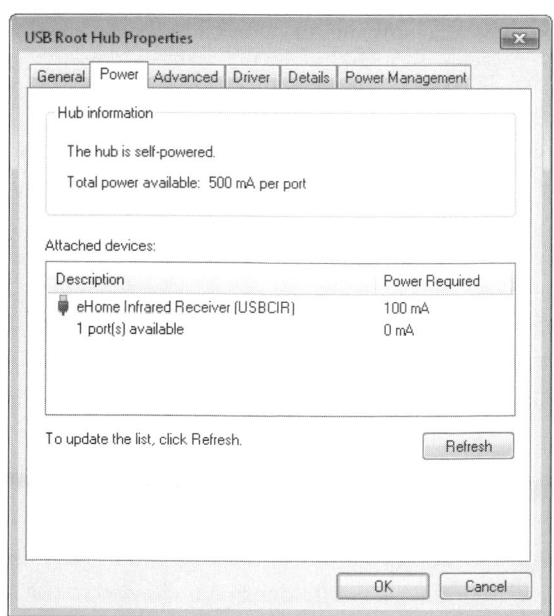

FIGURE 30-9 View USB root hub properties to determine power capabilities and requirements.

How to Troubleshoot Bluetooth Problems

Bluetooth is a wireless protocol for connecting accessories to computers. Bluetooth is commonly used to connect keyboards, mice, handheld devices, mobile phones, and global positioning system (GPS) receivers.

Bluetooth is simple enough to configure that most users can connect Bluetooth devices without help from the Support Center. However, users may occasionally have problems initiating a Bluetooth connection. Other times, a connection that previously worked may stop working for no apparent reason.

If you cannot successfully connect a Bluetooth device, try these troubleshooting steps:

1. Verify that the device is turned on and that the batteries are charged.
2. Place the device within a few feet of your computer (but not too close to your Bluetooth adapter). Additionally, verify that the device is not near other devices that use radio frequencies, such as microwave ovens, cordless phones, remote controls, or 802.11 wireless networks.
3. Verify that the device has Bluetooth enabled and that it is configured as discoverable. For security reasons, many devices are not discoverable by default. For more information, refer to the instructions that came with the device.
4. Install any updates available from Windows Update. For more information, see Chapter 23.
5. Download and install updated software and drivers for your hardware. Hardware manufacturers often release updated software for hardware features after they release the hardware. You can typically download software updates from the manufacturer's Web site.
6. Verify that Windows is configured to accept incoming Bluetooth connections.
7. Verify that security is configured correctly. You might have configured a nondefault passkey for your device. By default, many devices use 0000 or 0001 as a passkey.
8. Remove and reinstall the Bluetooth device.

Troubleshooting Tools

The sections that follow describe free Microsoft tools that can be useful for advanced troubleshooting.

DiskView

DiskView shows how files are physically laid out on your disk and allows you to view where specific files are stored. To run DiskView, save the file to a folder that is allowed to run executable files, such as C:\Program Files\. Specifically, you cannot save it to a Temporary Files folder. Then, right-click DiskView.exe and click Run As Administrator. Click the Volume list and select the volume you want to analyze. Then, click Refresh. DiskView will spend several minutes examining the contents of the disk.

As shown in Figure 30-10, the main window displays how files are laid out on a section of your disk. Below the main window is a map that shows your entire disk. The black overlay shows which portion of the disk is displayed in the main window.

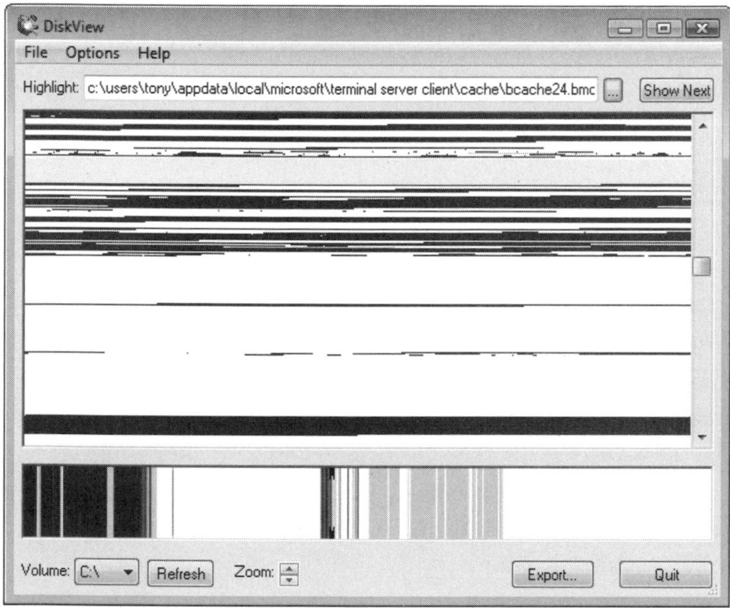

FIGURE 30-10 DiskView shows the physical layout of files on your disk.

Click any file in the main window to display the name of the file in the Highlight box. To view a specific file, click the "..." button and select the file. You can download DiskView from *http://technet.microsoft.com/sysinternals/bb896650.aspx*.

Handle

Handle allows you to determine which process has a file or folder open. Handle is useful any time you need to update or delete a file or folder, but access is denied because the object is in use.

To run Handle, save the file to a folder that is allowed to run executable files, such as C:\Program Files\. Specifically, you cannot save it to a Temporary Files folder. Then, open an administrative command prompt and select the folder containing the Handle executable.

To view all open handles, run Handle without any parameters. To view which process has a particular file or folder open, run Handle with a portion of the file's name. For example, if the sample music file Amanda.wma is locked, you can identify which process has it open by running the following command.

```
Handle amanda
```

The following output demonstrates that Windows Media Player (Wmplayer.exe) has the file locked.

```
Handle v3.3
Copyright (C) 1997-2007 Mark Russinovich
Sysinternals - www.sysinternals.com

wmplayer.exe       pid: 3236    2C0: C:\Users\Public\Music\Sample Music\Amanda.wma
```

Because the output lists the process name and Process Identifier (PID), you can use Task Manager to kill the process, allowing you to access the locked file. You can download Handle from *http://technet.microsoft.com/en-us/sysinternals/bb896655.aspx*.

Process Monitor

Process Monitor is an extremely powerful troubleshooting tool that monitors file and registry accesses by an application. With Process Monitor, you can see exactly what an application is doing, allowing you to isolate the resources to which an application requires access. If an application fails because a resource is unavailable or access is denied, Process Monitor can allow you to identify the resource. Often, you can use that information to resolve the problem.

To run Process Monitor, save the file to a folder that is allowed to run executable files, such as C:\Program Files\. Specifically, you cannot save it to a Temporary Files folder. Then, right-click ProcMon.exe and click Run As Administrator.

When run, Process Monitor immediately begins capturing events. To stop or restart capturing events, press Ctrl+E or click Capture Events from the File menu.

To use Process Monitor, enable event capturing and then run the application that you want to monitor. After you perform the task that you need to analyze, stop event capturing.

Process Monitor displays all disk and file accesses that occurred while capturing was enabled, as shown in Figure 30-11. To view events for just a specific process, right-click any event generated by the process and then click Include. Process Monitor will filter the displayed event so that only events generated by the selected process are visible. You can create more complex filters using the Filter menu.

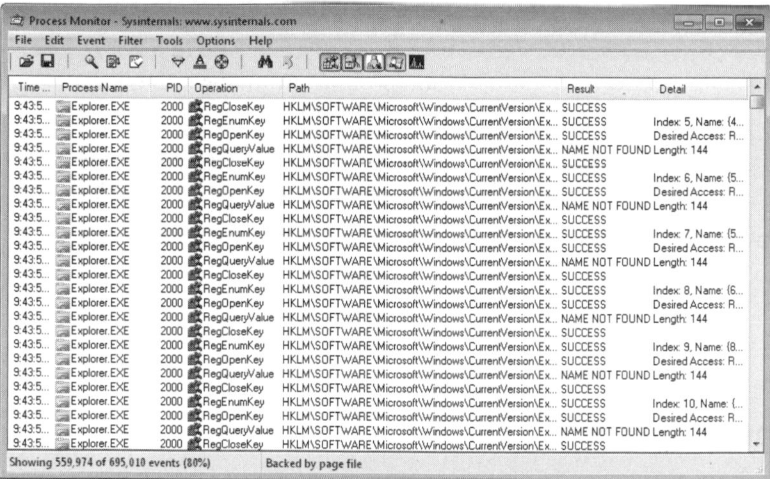

FIGURE 30-11 Process Monitor displays every file and registry access by an application.

When examining the captured events, pay close attention to events with a result other than Success. Although non-Success events are common and normal, they are more likely to indicate the cause of an error.

You can download Process Monitor from *http://technet.microsoft.com/en-ca/sysinternals/bb896645.aspx*. For an example of how Process Monitor can be used, read "The Case of the Failed File Copy" at *http://blogs.technet.com/markrussinovich/archive/2007/10/01/2087460.aspx* and "The Case of the Missing AutoPlay" at *http://blogs.technet.com/markrussinovich/archive/2008/01/02/2696753.aspx.*

Summary

Problems can arise when connecting hardware to a computer. Fortunately, Windows 7 provides many different tools for diagnosing the source of the problem. In many cases, Windows 7 also provides the tools required to resolve the problem by updating software or reconfiguring the hardware. If the cause of the problem is failed hardware, the device will need to be repaired or replaced before it can be used with Windows 7.

Additional Resources

These resources contain additional information and tools related to this chapter.

Related Information

- Chapter 16, "Managing Disks and File Systems," includes information about configuring disks and volumes.

- Chapter 17, "Managing Devices and Services," includes information about configuring hardware and drivers.
- Chapter 23, "Managing Software Updates," includes more information about updating device drivers.
- Chapter 29, "Configuring Startup and Troubleshooting Startup Issues," includes information about troubleshooting problems that prevent Windows from starting.
- Chapter 31, "Troubleshooting Network Issues," includes information about network connectivity problems.
- Chapter 32, "Troubleshooting Stop Messages," includes information concerning Stop errors.

On the Companion Media

- CheckDeviceDrivers.ps1
- CheckSignedDeviceDrivers.ps1
- FindMaxPageFaults.ps1
- Get-DiskUtilization.ps1
- Get-IRQResources.ps1
- Get-PageFileUtilization.ps1
- Get-PowerPlan.ps1
- Get-ProcessorInformation.ps1
- Get-ProcessorUtilization.ps1
- GetTopMemory.ps1
- ListComputerSystem.ps1
- ListVideoController.ps1
- ReportAvailableDrivers.ps1
- SetPowerConfig.ps1
- ShutdownRebootComputer.ps1
- SystemDriversAndDevices.ps1

CHAPTER 31

Troubleshooting Network Issues

Users often rely on network connectivity to do their jobs, and network failures can dramatically affect an organization's productivity. When failures occur, you need to quickly diagnose the problem. You will often need to escalate the troubleshooting to a network specialist. However, you can diagnose and resolve many common networking problems from a computer running the Windows 7 operating system.

This chapter describes how to use important network troubleshooting tools and provides step-by-step instructions for troubleshooting common network problems.

Tools for Troubleshooting

The following common network problems are listed with the tools most likely to be useful in isolating, diagnosing, and resolving them. These tools are described in the appropriate sections in this chapter unless otherwise noted.

- **Some clients cannot connect to a server** Arp, IPConfig, Nbtstat, Netstat, Network Monitor, Nslookup, PathPing, PortQry, Telnet Client, Windows Network Diagnostics
- **No clients can connect to a server** IPConfig, Network Monitor, PortQry, Telnet Client, Windows Network Diagnostics
- **Clients cannot connect to shared resources** IPConfig, Nbtstat, Net, Nslookup, Network Monitor, PortQry, Telnet Client, Windows Network Diagnostics
- **Clients cannot connect to the network** IPConfig, Windows Network Diagnostics

- **Network performance is poor or unpredictable** Network Monitor, Performance Monitor, PathPing, Resource Monitor, Task Manager

Many factors affect network performance and reliability, including remote connections, hardware configuration (network adapters or the physical network connection), and device drivers. Quite often, network difficulties are related to protocol configuration errors. For example, using incorrect settings in networks based on Transmission Control Protocol/Internet Protocol (TCP/IP) can affect IP addressing, routing, and IP security.

Windows 7 provides a collection of useful troubleshooting tools with which you can monitor and test network performance. Table 31-1 lists the most important tools for troubleshooting network problems.

TABLE 31-1 Network Troubleshooting Tools

TOOL	PURPOSE	MEMBERSHIP REQUIRED	DESCRIPTION
Arp	Displays and clears the Address Resolution Protocol (ARP) cache, which affects communications with hosts on the local network.	Users or Administrators, depending on the commands used	Operating system, command line
IPConfig	Displays network configuration information about the local computer, requests new dynamically assigned IP addresses, manages the Domain Name System (DNS) client resolver cache, and registers new DNS records.	Users or Administrators, depending on the commands used	Operating system, command line
Nblookup	Tests Windows Internet Naming Service (WINS) name resolution.	Users	Free download, command line
Nbtstat	Displays and clears network basic input/output system (NetBIOS) names.	Users	Operating system, command line
Net	Displays information about shared resources and connects to shared resources.	Users	Operating system, command line
Netsh	Views and modifies network configuration settings.	Users or Administrators, depending on the commands used	Operating system, command line

TOOL	PURPOSE	MEMBERSHIP REQUIRED	DESCRIPTION
Netstat	Displays detailed information about open connections.	Users	Operating system, command line
Network Monitor	Captures and displays network traffic sent to and from the local computer.	Administrators	Free download, graphical user interface (GUI)
Nslookup	Diagnoses DNS name resolution problems.	Users	Operating system, command line
PathPing	Diagnoses network connectivity, routing, and performance problems.	Users	Operating system, command line
Performance Monitor	Displays detailed information about hundreds of network performance counters.	Administrators	Operating system, GUI
PortQry	Identifies the availability of network services from a client that has the tool installed.	Users	Free download, command line
Resource Monitor	Displays information about network utilization.	Administrators	Operating system, GUI
Route	Displays and modifies the local computer's IP routing tables, which is primarily useful when multiple gateways are on the local network.	Users or Administrators, depending on the commands used	Operating system, command line
Task Manager	Quickly determines current network utilization, identifies processes that are using the network, and identifies processes that are consuming processor time.	Users or Administrators, depending on the commands used	Operating system, GUI
Telnet Client	Identifies the availability of network services from a client that does not have PortQry installed. This tool is an optional feature and is not installed by default.	Users	Operating system, command line

TOOL	PURPOSE	MEMBERSHIP REQUIRED	DESCRIPTION
Test TCP	Tests TCP connectivity between two computers.	Users	Operating system, command line
Windows Network Diagnostics	Automatically diagnoses some network problems and provides a user-friendly interface for resolving them.	Users	Operating system, GUI

NOTE In Windows 7, troubleshooting IPv6 is identical to troubleshooting IPv4. Most of the same tools work, including Ping, PathPing, Nslookup, IPConfig, Route, Netstat, Tracert, and Netsh. To use them, simply specify IPv6 addresses instead of IPv4 addresses. Unfortunately, PortQry does not currently support IPv6. However, you can use Telnet instead. Additionally, you cannot use the Route tool to add or delete IPv6 addresses. Instead, you should use the ***netsh interface ipv6 add route*** and ***netsh interface ipv6 delete route*** commands.

Arp

Arp (Arp.exe) is a useful command-line tool for diagnosing problems in connecting to systems on a LAN where communications between computers do not travel through a router. Arp is also useful for diagnosing problems related to the client communicating with the default gateway. When a client contacts a server on the same subnet, it must address the frame with both the media access control (MAC) address and the IPv4 address. The MAC address is a 48-bit number that uniquely identifies a network adapter.

Arp is the name of a tool; it is also the acronym for the Address Resolution Protocol (ARP), which is used to find the MAC address corresponding to an IPv4 address. When a client communicates with a system on the same LAN, ARP broadcasts a message to all systems on the LAN asking for a response from the system that has the requested IPv4 address. That system responds to the broadcast by sending its MAC address, and ARP stores the MAC address in the ARP cache.

NOTE IPv4 addresses are used to identify computers on different networks. However, computers communicating across a LAN use MAC addresses to identify each other. ARP lets a computer look up a MAC address based on an IPv4 address so that two computers on the same LAN can communicate.

Problems with ARP occur only occasionally. For example, if a system changes its network adapter, clients might store the incorrect MAC address in the ARP cache. You can also manually place MAC addresses into the ARP cache, but if a manually added MAC address is incorrect, communications sent to that IPv4 address will not succeed.

How to Identify a Problem with the ARP Cache

To identify an incorrect entry in the ARP cache, first determine the MAC addresses and IPv4 addresses of hosts or gateways on the LAN with which the computer cannot communicate (as shown in the *ipconfig /all* example in this section). View the ARP cache on the computer that is experiencing the problem. Compare the output with the correct IPv4 address and MAC address combinations. If an entry is incorrect, clear the ARP cache to resolve the problem.

To determine the MAC address of a computer, open a command prompt and run the following command. Then find the Physical Address line in the output for your network adapter (which appears in bold in the code shown here).

`ipconfig /all`

```
Ethernet adapter Local Area Connection:

   Connection-specific DNS Suffix  . : contoso.com
   Description . . . . . . . . . . . : NVIDIA nForce Networking Controller
   Physical Address. . . . . . . . . : 00-13-D3-3B-50-8F
   DHCP Enabled. . . . . . . . . . . : Yes
```

After you use IPConfig to determine the correct MAC address, you can view the ARP cache on the problematic computer to determine whether the cached address is incorrect. To view the ARP cache, open a command prompt and run the following command.

`arp -a`

```
Interface: 192.168.1.132 --- 0xa
  Internet Address      Physical Address      Type
  192.168.1.1           00-11-95-bb-e2-c7     dynamic
  192.168.1.210         00-03-ff-cf-38-2f     dynamic
  192.168.1.241         00-13-02-1e-e6-59     dynamic
  192.168.1.255         ff-ff-ff-ff-ff-ff     static
  224.0.0.22            01-00-5e-00-00-16     static
```

How to Clear the ARP Cache

If you determine that one of the entries in the ARP cache is incorrect, resolve the problem by clearing the ARP cache. Clearing the ARP cache isn't harmful, even if all entries appear correct. Therefore, it's a safe step to take during troubleshooting.

To clear the ARP cache, open a command prompt and run the following command.

`arp -d`

Alternatively, you can clear the ARP cache by disabling and re-enabling a network adapter or by choosing the automated Repair option. For more information about the Arp tool, run **Arp -?** at a command prompt.

Event Viewer

The Windows Troubleshooting Platform records extremely detailed information in the System Event Log, both when problems occur and when network connections are successful. Additionally, administrators can use Wireless Diagnostics tracing to capture and analyze diagnostic information by using graphical tools.

You can find network diagnostic information in two places in Event Viewer:

- **Windows Logs\System** Look for events with a Source of Diagnostics-Networking. These events detail troubleshooting options that were presented to the user (Event ID 4000), the results of the user's choice (Event ID 5000), and detailed information gathered during the diagnosis process (Event ID 6100). When troubleshooting wireless networks, events also include the name of the wireless network adapter and whether it is a native Windows 7 driver or an older driver; a list of visible wireless networks with the signal strength, channel, and protocol (such as 802.11b or 802.11g) for each; and the list of preferred wireless networks and each network's configuration settings. Event descriptions resemble the following.

  ```
  The Network Diagnostics Framework has completed the repair phase of operation.
  The following repair option or work-around was executed:
  Helper Class Name: AddressAcquisition
  Repair option: Reset the network adapter "Local Area Connection"
  Resetting the adapter can sometimes resolve an intermittent problem.
  RepairGuid: {07D37F7B-FA5E-4443-BDA7-AB107B29AFB9}
  The repair option appears to have successfully fixed the diagnosed problem.
  ```

- **Applications and Services Logs\Microsoft\Windows\Diagnostics-Networking \Operational** This event log details the inner workings of the Windows Troubleshooting Platform and will be useful primarily when escalating problems to Microsoft support.

IPConfig

IPConfig (Ipconfig.exe) is a useful command-line tool for troubleshooting problems with automatic configuration such as Dynamic Host Configuration Protocol (DHCP). You can use IPConfig to display the current IP configuration, identify whether DHCP or Automatic Private IP Addressing (APIPA) is being used, and release and renew an automatic IP configuration.

To view detailed IP configuration information, open a command prompt and run the following command.

```
ipconfig /all
```

This command displays the current IP configuration and produces output similar to the following.

```
Windows IP Configuration

   Host Name . . . . . . . . . . . . : Win7
   Primary Dns Suffix  . . . . . . . : hq.contoso.com
   Node Type . . . . . . . . . . . . : Hybrid
   IP Routing Enabled. . . . . . . . : No
   WINS Proxy Enabled. . . . . . . . : No
   DNS Suffix Search List. . . . . . : hq.contoso.com
                                       contoso.com

Ethernet adapter Local Area Connection:

   Connection-specific DNS Suffix  . : contoso.com
   Description . . . . . . . . . . . : NVIDIA nForce Networking Controller
   Physical Address. . . . . . . . . : 00-13-D3-3B-50-8F
   DHCP Enabled. . . . . . . . . . . : Yes
   Autoconfiguration Enabled . . . . : Yes
   Link-local IPv6 Address . . . . . : fe80::a54b:d9d7:1a10:c1eb%10(Preferred)
   IPv4 Address. . . . . . . . . . . : 192.168.1.132(Preferred)
   Subnet Mask . . . . . . . . . . . : 255.255.255.0
   Lease Obtained. . . . . . . . . . : Wednesday, September 27, 2009 2:08:58 PM
   Lease Expires . . . . . . . . . . : Friday, September 29, 2009 2:08:56 PM
   Default Gateway . . . . . . . . . : 192.168.1.1
   DHCP Server . . . . . . . . . . . : 192.168.1.1
   DHCPv6 IAID . . . . . . . . . . . : 234886099
   DNS Servers . . . . . . . . . . . : 192.168.1.210
   NetBIOS over Tcpip. . . . . . . . : Enabled
```

To determine whether DHCP addressing was successful, open a command prompt and run the following command.

```
ipconfig
```

This command produces output similar to the following.

```
Windows IP Configuration

Ethernet adapter Local Area Connection:

   Connection-specific DNS Suffix  . :
   Autoconfiguration IP Address. . . : 169.254.187.237
   Subnet Mask . . . . . . . . . . . : 255.255.0.0
   Default Gateway . . . . . . . . . :
```

If the IP address shown is in the range from 169.254.0.0 through 169.254.255.255, Windows used APIPA because the operating system was unable to retrieve an IP configuration from a DHCP server upon startup, and there was no alternate configuration. To confirm this, examine the IPConfig output for the DHCP Enabled setting without a DHCP server address.

To release and renew a DHCP-assigned IPv4 address, open a command prompt with administrative credentials and run the following commands.

```
ipconfig /release
ipconfig /renew
```

Windows will stop using the current IPv4 address and attempt to contact a DHCP server for a new IPv4 address. If a DHCP server is not available, Windows will either use the alternate configuration or automatically assign an APIPA address in the range of 169.254.0.0 through 169.254.255.255.

To release and renew an automatically assigned IPv6 address, open a command prompt and run the following commands.

```
ipconfig /release6
ipconfig /renew6
```

Nblookup

Windows Internet Naming Service (WINS) is a NetBIOS name resolution protocol. WINS performs a function for NetBIOS names similar to the function that DNS performs for host names. For many years, WINS name resolution was the most common way for computers running Windows to identify each other on networks. However, in Active Directory Domain Services (AD DS) domain environments, DNS is used by default, and WINS is primarily used to support older clients and applications.

For environments that still rely on WINS servers, Nblookup is a valuable tool for diagnosing WINS name resolution problems. Nblookup is not included with Windows but is available as a free download from *http://support.microsoft.com/kb/830578*. After saving Nblookup.exe to a computer, you can double-click the file to run it in interactive mode within a command prompt. Alternatively, command-line mode allows you to run it from any command prompt. The following examples demonstrate the use of command-line mode.

To look up a NetBIOS name using the computer's configured WINS server, run the following command.

```
nblookup computer_name
```

To look up a NetBIOS name using a specific WINS server, add the */s server_ip* parameter, as the following example demonstrates.

```
nblookup /s server_ip computer_name
```

For example, to look up the name COMPUTER1 using the WINS server located at 192.168.1.222, you would run the following command.

```
nblookup /s 192.168.1.222 COMPUTER1
```

NetBIOS names actually identify services, not computers. If you want to attempt to resolve a NetBIOS name for a specific service, use the */x* parameter and specify the service's NetBIOS suffix. For example, the following command would look up domain controllers (which use a NetBIOS suffix of 1C) in a domain named DOMAIN.

```
nblookup /x 1C DOMAIN
```

Because WINS is not typically relied on for name resolution by Windows 7 in AD DS environments, troubleshooting WINS name resolution is not discussed further in this chapter. For more information, refer to Chapter 8 of *Windows Server 2008 Networking and Network Access Protection* by Joseph Davies and Tony Northrup (Microsoft Press, 2008).

Nbtstat

Nbtstat (Nbtstat.exe) is a command-line tool for troubleshooting NetBIOS name resolution problems. NetBIOS is a session-layer protocol that formed the foundation of Microsoft network applications for several years. NetBIOS applications identify services on the network by using 16-character NetBIOS names. Each computer on a network might have several different NetBIOS names to identify NetBIOS services on that system.

Today, NetBIOS is implemented on TCP/IP networks by using NetBIOS over TCP/IP (NetBT). NetBT includes its own form of name resolution to resolve NetBIOS names to IP addresses. Names might be resolved by broadcast queries to the local network segment or by queries to a WINS server.

Unfortunately, NetBIOS name resolution is a common source of problems. You can use Nbtstat to reveal the NetBIOS names available on the local computer or remote computers. In troubleshooting scenarios, this helps you to verify that a NetBIOS service is available and its name is being correctly resolved.

To view the NetBIOS name cache, open a command prompt and run the following command.

```
nbtstat -c
```

This command produces output similar to the following.

```
Local Area Connection:
Node IpAddress: [192.168.1.132] Scope Id: []

                  NetBIOS Remote Cache Name Table

        Name              Type       Host Address    Life [sec]
    ------------------------------------------------------------
    WIN71          <00>  UNIQUE          192.168.1.196        602
    WIN72          <00>  UNIQUE          192.168.1.200        585
```

To view the local NetBIOS service names, open a command prompt and run the following command.

```
nbtstat -n
```

This command produces output similar to the following.

```
Local Area Connection:
Node IpAddress: [192.168.1.132] Scope Id: []

                NetBIOS Local Name Table

       Name               Type         Status
    ---------------------------------------------
    WIN71          <00>  UNIQUE      Registered
    HQ             <00>  GROUP       Registered
    HQ             <1E>  GROUP       Registered
    HQ             <1D>  UNIQUE      Registered
    ..__MSBROWSE__.<01>  GROUP       Registered
```

To view the NetBIOS names on a remote system by using the computer name, open a command prompt and run the following command.

```
nbtstat -a computername
```

For example:

```
nbtstat -a win71
```

This command produces output similar to the following.

```
Local Area Connection:
Node IpAddress: [192.168.1.132] Scope Id: []

           NetBIOS Remote Machine Name Table

       Name               Type         Status
    ---------------------------------------------
    WIN71          <00>  UNIQUE      Registered
    WIN71          <20>  UNIQUE      Registered
    MSHOME         <00>  GROUP       Registered
    MSHOME         <1E>  GROUP       Registered

    MAC Address = 00-15-C5-08-82-F3
```

Notice that the output is similar to the output when running *nbtstat –n* locally. However, this output also displays the remote computer's MAC address. To view the NetBIOS names on a remote system by using the IP address, open a command prompt and run the following command.

```
nbtstat -A IP_Address
```

Windows 7 (and all recent versions of Windows) prefers to use DNS host names instead of NetBIOS names. Therefore, if you have an AD DS domain with a DNS server configured, you will rarely need to troubleshoot NetBIOS names. However, Windows might still use NetBIOS names to communicate with computers on the local network and will use NetBIOS names if a host name cannot be resolved with DNS and you have configured a WINS server. To troubleshoot NetBIOS name resolution with WINS servers, use Nblookup, described earlier in this chapter.

Net

Net (Net.exe) is a command-line tool that is useful for changing network configuration settings, starting and stopping services, and viewing shared resources. Although other tools provide friendlier interfaces for much of the functionality provided by Net, Net is very useful for quickly determining the available shared resources on local or remote computers. When you are troubleshooting connections to resources, this tool is useful for verifying that shared resources are available and for verifying the names of those shared resources.

How to View Shared Folders on the Local Computer

Use the *net share* command to view shared resources located on the local computer. If the Server service is started, Net will return a list of shared resources names and locations. To view shared resources, open a command prompt and run the following command.

```
net share
```

This command produces output similar to the following.

```
Share name   Resource                        Remark


-------------------------------------------------------------------------------
C$           C:\                             Default share
D$           D:\                             Default share
E$           E:\                             Default share
print$       C:\Windows\system32\spool\drivers
                                             Printer Drivers
IPC$                                         Remote IPC
ADMIN$       C:\Windows                      Remote Admin
MyShare      C:\PortQryUI
HP DeskJet 930C932C935C
             LPT1:                  Spooled  HP DeskJet 930C/932C/935C
The command completed successfully.
```

How to View Shared Folders on Another Computer

Use the *net view* command to view shared resources located on another computer. To view shared folders on another computer, open a command prompt and run the following command.

```
net view computer
```

For example:

```
net view d820
```

This command produces output similar to the following.

```
Shared resources at d820

Share name   Type   Used as  Comment
-------------------------------------------------------------------------------
In Progress  Disk
Printer      Print           Microsoft Office Document Image Writer
publish      Disk
SharedDocs   Disk
Software     Disk
The command completed successfully.
```

You can identify *Computer* by using the computer name, host name, or IP address. If you receive an "Access is denied" error message when attempting to view shares on a remote computer, establish a NetBIOS connection to the remote computer. For example, you could use *Net use* to establish a connection and then use *Net view*, as the following example demonstrates.

```
net use \\win7 /user:username
net view \\win7
```

Netstat

For a network service to receive incoming communications, it must listen for communications on a specific TCP or UDP port. When troubleshooting network problems, you might want to view the ports on which your computer listens for incoming connections to verify that a service is properly configured and that the port number has not changed from the default.

Netstat (Netstat.exe) is a useful command-line tool for identifying network services and the ports they listen on. Listing the ports a computer listens on is useful for verifying that a network service is using the expected port. It is common practice to change the port numbers that services listen on, and Netstat can quickly identify nonstandard listening ports.

To view open ports and active incoming connections, open a command prompt and run the following command.

```
netstat -a -n -o
```

Netstat will display a list of listening ports as well as outgoing connections and the Process Identifiers (PIDs) associated with each listener or connection. The following edited output from Netstat shows the listening ports on a computer running Windows that has Remote Desktop enabled.

```
Active Connections

  Proto  Local Address          Foreign Address        State           PID
  TCP    0.0.0.0:135            0.0.0.0:0              LISTENING       884
  TCP    0.0.0.0:3389           0.0.0.0:0              LISTENING       1512
  TCP    0.0.0.0:49152          0.0.0.0:0              LISTENING       592
  TCP    192.168.1.132:139      0.0.0.0:0              LISTENING       4
  TCP    192.168.1.132:3389     192.168.1.196:1732     ESTABLISHED     1512
  TCP    [::]:135               [::]:0                 LISTENING       884
  TCP    [::]:445               [::]:0                 LISTENING       4
  TCP    [::]:2869              [::]:0                 LISTENING       4
  TCP    [::]:3389              [::]:0                 LISTENING       1512
  UDP    [fe80::28db:d21:3f57:fe7b%11]:1900  *:*                       1360
  UDP    [fe80::28db:d21:3f57:fe7b%11]:49643  *:*                      1360
  UDP    [fe80::a54b:d9d7:1a10:c1eb%10]:1900  *:*                      1360
  UDP    [fe80::a54b:d9d7:1a10:c1eb%10]:49641  *:*                     1360
```

Notice that the line in bold is listening for incoming connections on TCP port 3389, which Remote Desktop uses. Because the Foreign Address column shows an IPv4 address, you can tell that a user is connected to the computer using Remote Desktop from a computer with the IP address of 192.168.1.196. If you notice that a computer is listening for incoming connections on unexpected ports, you can use the value in the PID column to identify the process. Tools such as the Processes tab in Task Manager can reveal which process is associated with a PID.

> ***NOTE*** **To identify processes by PID in Task Manager, select the Processes tab. On the View menu, click Select Columns. Select the PID (Process Identifier) check box and then click OK.**

Alternatively, if you can open a command prompt with elevated privileges, you can use the *–b* parameter to resolve applications associated with active connections. The following example demonstrates that using the *–b* parameter shows the associated process in brackets before each connection.

```
netstat -a -n -o -b
```

```
Active Connections

  Proto  Local Address          Foreign Address        State           PID
  TCP    0.0.0.0:135            0.0.0.0:0              LISTENING       828
  RpcSs
 [svchost.exe]
  TCP    0.0.0.0:3389           0.0.0.0:0              LISTENING       1444
  Dnscache
 [svchost.exe]
  TCP    0.0.0.0:49152          0.0.0.0:0              LISTENING       508
 [wininit.exe]
  TCP    0.0.0.0:49153          0.0.0.0:0              LISTENING       972
  Eventlog
 [svchost.exe]
  TCP    0.0.0.0:49154          0.0.0.0:0              LISTENING       1236
  nsi
 [svchost.exe]
  TCP    0.0.0.0:49155          0.0.0.0:0              LISTENING       1076
  Schedule
 [svchost.exe]
  TCP    0.0.0.0:49156          0.0.0.0:0              LISTENING       564
 [lsass.exe]
  TCP    0.0.0.0:49157          0.0.0.0:0              LISTENING       552
 [services.exe]
  TCP    169.254.166.248:139    0.0.0.0:0              LISTENING       4
```

TCPView, a free download from Microsoft, provides similar functionality with a graphical interface. TCPView is described later in this chapter.

Network Monitor

Network Monitor 3.3, a free download from *http://www.microsoft.com/downloads/*, is the most capable—and complicated—tool for analyzing network communications. Network Monitor is a protocol analyzer (commonly known as a *sniffer*) capable of capturing every byte transferred to and from a computer running Windows 7. An experienced system administrator can use Network Monitor to troubleshoot a wide variety of problems, including:

- Network performance problems.
- TCP connection problems.
- IP protocol stack configuration problems.
- Problems caused by network filtering.
- Application-layer problems with text-based protocols, including Hypertext Transfer Protocol (HTTP), Post Office Protocol (POP), and Simple Mail Transfer Protocol (SMTP).

Network Monitor performs a significant amount of interpretation of captured information by separating the different protocols involved in network communications. Network Monitor can even interpret most common application-layer protocols. For example, when analyzing HTTP traffic, Network Monitor automatically identifies the packet containing the HTTP request and lists the request method, Uniform Resource Locator (URL), referrer, user agent, and other parameters included in the request. This information is extremely useful when troubleshooting compatibility problems with a specific browser.

To analyze network traffic by using Network Monitor, follow these steps:

1. Download and install Network Monitor and then restart the computer to enable the Network Monitor driver for your network adapters.
2. Click Start, click All Programs, click Microsoft Network Monitor 3.3, and then click Microsoft Network Monitor 3.3.
3. Click New Capture.
4. With the New Capture tab selected, click the Select Networks tab and select one or more network adapters.
5. Click Start to begin capturing communications.
6. Switch to the application from which you want to capture the network traffic and then perform the steps to generate the traffic. For example, if you want to capture a request to a Web server, switch to Windows Internet Explorer and enter the Web address. After you have generated the traffic that you want to capture, return to Network Monitor.
7. On the Capture menu in Network Monitor, click Stop.
8. On the Network Conversations page, click the application you want to monitor.
9. In the Frame Summary pane, browse the captured frames. Click a frame to view its contents.

Figure 31-1 shows a capture of a TCP connection and an HTTP request created by visiting a Web site with a browser. Because Iexplore.exe is selected in the Network Conversations pane, only frames sent to or from Internet Explorer are displayed. The Frame Summary pane lists the captured packets. The first three frames show the three-way TCP handshake. As you can see from the Frame Details pane, the selected frame shows Internet Explorer requesting / from the Web server. The following frame is the response, which is an HTTP 302 redirection to a different page. Frame 35 is Internet Explorer requesting the page to which it was directed, */en/us/default.aspx*.

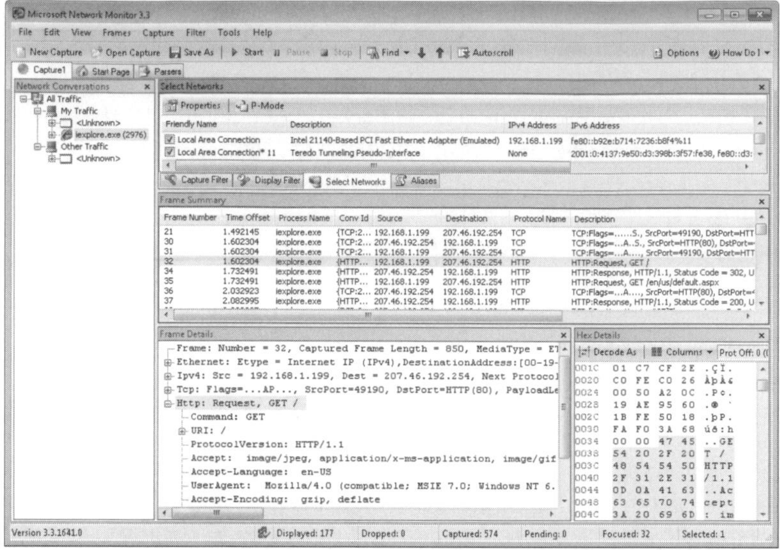

FIGURE 31-1 Use Network Monitor to capture and analyze traffic.

> ***MORE INFO*** **For additional information about Network Monitor and to keep up with the latest improvements, read the Network Monitor Team blog at *http://blogs.technet.com/netmon/*.**

Nslookup

Nslookup (Nslookup.exe) is the primary tool for isolating DNS name resolution problems when connected to the client experiencing the problems. Nslookup is a command-line tool capable of performing DNS lookups and reporting on the results. Other tools, such as PathPing, are capable of resolving host names to IP addresses and displaying the results, but only Nslookup displays the DNS server used to resolve the request. Additionally, Nslookup displays all the results returned by the DNS server and allows you to choose a specific DNS server rather than using the server automatically chosen by Windows.

Nslookup is the correct tool to use when troubleshooting the following types of problems:

- Clients take several seconds to establish an initial connection.
- Some clients can establish a connection to a server, but other clients experience problems.
- The DNS server is configured correctly, but clients are resolving host names incorrectly.

NOTE The Hosts file, located in the %WinDir%\System32\Drivers\Etc folder, might contain static entries that override DNS lookups for most applications. Nslookup ignores this file, however. If applications resolve a host name differently than Nslookup, verify that the Hosts file does not contain an entry for the host name.

Verifying that the Default DNS Server Resolves Correctly

To verify that a client is able to resolve a host name to the correct IP address, open a command prompt and type the command **nslookup *hostname*.** Nslookup reports the server used to resolve the request and the response from the DNS server. If the client has been configured to use multiple DNS servers, this action might reveal that the client is not issuing requests to the primary DNS server.

To resolve a DNS host name to an IP address, open a command prompt and run the following command.

```
nslookup hostname
```

To resolve an IP address to a DNS host name by performing a reverse DNS lookup, open a command prompt and run the following command.

```
nslookup ipaddress
```

If the DNS server returns multiple IP addresses, Nslookup displays all addresses. Generally, applications use the first IP address returned by the DNS server. Some applications, including Internet Explorer, try each IP address returned by the DNS server until a response is received.

Verifying that a Specific DNS Server Resolves Correctly

One of the most common sources of DNS resolution problems is the caching of an outdated DNS address. Particularly on the Internet, DNS servers might continue to return an outdated IP address several hours after a change has been made to the DNS server containing the record. If some clients are unable to correctly resolve an IP address but other systems resolve it correctly, one or more DNS servers have probably cached the incorrect address. To identify the problematic DNS servers, use Nslookup to manually query each server.

To verify that a specific DNS server is able to resolve a host name to the correct IP address, open a command prompt and run the following command.

```
nslookup hostname server_name_or_address
```

Nslookup will query the specified server only, regardless of the DNS servers configured on the client. If a specific server returns an incorrect IP address, that server is the source of the problem. Generally, this problem will resolve itself after the incorrect entry expires in the DNS server's cache. However, you can also resolve the problem by manually clearing the DNS server's cache.

DIRECT FROM THE SOURCE

Looking Up Lists of DNS Records

Tim Rains, Program Manager
Windows Networking

If you need to frequently check whether numerous DNS records correctly resolve on numerous DNS servers, consider using DNSLint with the *–ql* parameter instead of Nslookup. This command can test name resolution for specific DNS records across many DNS servers very quickly. DNSLint can also help troubleshoot some DNS issues related to AD DS. DNSLint is a free download available from *http://support.microsoft.com/kb/321045/*.

Verifying Specific Types of Addresses

You can also use Nslookup to verify specific types of addresses, including Mail eXchange (MX) addresses used to identify the mail servers for a domain.

To identify the mail server for a domain, open a command prompt and run the following command.

```
nslookup "-set type=mx" domainname
```

For example, to use Nslookup to view all MX servers listed for the domain microsoft.com using the client's default DNS servers, type the following command.

```
nslookup "-set type=mx" microsoft.com
```

Additionally, you can query a specific DNS server by listing the server name or IP address after the domain name in the following form.

```
nslookup "-set type=type" hostname server_name_or_address
```

DIRECT FROM THE SOURCE

Using TCP for DNS Lookups

Tim Rains, Program Manager
Windows Networking

When a DNS server returns a response to a DNS query but the response contains more DNS records than can fit into a single UDP packet, the client may decide to send the query again, this time using TCP instead of UDP. With TCP, multiple packets can deliver all the DNS records in the response. You can use Nslookup to test whether a DNS server can respond using either UDP or TCP. Use the following command to submit a UDP query to the DNS server.

```
nslookup microsoft.com
```

The following command uses TCP to query the DNS server.

```
nslookup "-set vc" microsoft.com
```

The *"–set vc"* parameter configures Nslookup to use a virtual circuit. This test can be especially useful when you are expecting a large number of DNS records in response to a query.

PathPing

Perhaps the most useful tool for isolating connectivity problems from the client, PathPing (PathPing.exe) can help diagnose problems with name resolution, network connectivity, routing, and network performance. For this reason, PathPing should be one of the first tools you use to troubleshoot network problems. PathPing is a command-line tool whose syntax is similar to that of the Tracert and Ping tools.

> ***NOTE*** **Ping's usefulness has become very limited in recent years, and it is no longer an effective tool for determining the state of network services. Ping often reports that it cannot reach an available server because a firewall, such as Windows Firewall, is configured to drop Internet Control Message Protocol (ICMP) requests. If a host is still capable of responding to ICMP requests, Ping might report that the remote host is available even if critical services on the remote host have failed. To determine whether a remote host is responding, use the PortQry support tool instead of Ping.**

To test connectivity to an endpoint, open a command prompt and run the following command.

```
pathping destination
```

The destination can be a host name, a computer name, or an IP address.

PathPing Output

PathPing displays its output in two sections. The first section is immediately displayed and shows a numbered list of all devices that responded between the source and the destination. The first device, numbered 0, is the host on which PathPing is running. PathPing will attempt to look up the name of each device, as shown here.

```
Tracing route to support.go.microsoft.contoso.com [10.46.196.103]over a maximum of
30 hops:  0  contoso-test [192.168.1.207]   1  10.211.240.1   2  10.128.191.245
3  10.128.191.73   4  10.125.39.213   5  gbr1-p70.cb1ma.ip.contoso.com [10.123.40.98]
6  tbr2-p013501.cb1ma.ip.contoso.com [10.122.11.201]
7  tbr2-p012101.cgcil.ip.contoso.com [10.122.10.106]
8  gbr4-p50.st6wa.ip.contoso.com [10.122.2.54]
9  gar1-p370.stwwa.ip.contoso.com [10.123.203.177]
10  10.127.70.6  11  10.46.33.225  12  10.46.36.210
13  10.46.155.17  14  10.46.129.51  15  10.46.196.103
```

To speed up the display of PathPing, use the *–d* command option to keep PathPing from attempting to resolve the name of each intermediate router address.

The second section of the PathPing output begins with the message "Computing statistics for *xxx* seconds." The amount of time for which PathPing computes statistics will vary from a few seconds to a few minutes, depending on the number of devices that PathPing found. During this time, PathPing is querying each of the devices and calculating performance statistics based on whether—and how quickly—each device responds. This section will resemble the following.

```
Computing statistics for 375 seconds...           Source to Here
This Node/LinkHop  RTT    Lost/Sent = Pct  Lost/Sent = Pct  Address  0
                                           contoso-test [192.168.1.207]
                               0/ 100 =  0%    |  1   50ms
     1/ 100 =  1%     1/ 100 =  1%  10.211.24.1
                               0/ 100 =  0%    |  2   50ms
     0/ 100 =  0%     0/ 100 =  0%  10.128.19.245
                               0/ 100 =  0%    |  3   50ms
     2/ 100 =  2%     2/ 100 =  2%  10.128.19.73
                               0/ 100 =  0%    |  4   44ms
     0/ 100 =  0%     0/ 100 =  0%  10.12.39.213
                               0/ 100 =  0%    |  5   46ms
     0/ 100 =  0%     0/ 100 =  0%  gbr1-p70.cb1ma.ip.contoso.com [10.12.40.98]
                               0/ 100 =  0%    |  6   40ms
     2/ 100 =  2%     2/ 100 =  2%  tbr2-p013501.cb1ma.ip.contoso.com [10.12.11.201]
                               0/ 100 =  0%    |  7   62ms
     1/ 100 =  1%     1/ 100 =  1%  tbr2-p012101.cgcil.ip.contoso.com [10.12.10.106]
                               0/ 100 =  0%    |  8  107ms
     2/ 100 =  2%     2/ 100 =  2%  gbr4-p50.st6wa.ip.contoso.com [10.12.2.54]
                               0/ 100 =  0%    |  9  111ms
     0/ 100 =  0%     0/ 100 =  0%  gar1-p370.stwwa.ip.contoso.com [10.12.203.177]
                               0/ 100 =  0%    | 10  118ms
     0/ 100 =  0%     0/ 100 =  0%  10.12.70.6
                               0/ 100 =  0%    | 11  ---
     100/ 100 =100%   100/ 100 =100%  10.46.33.225
```

```
                                0/ 100 =  0%    | 12  ---
    100/ 100 =100%   100/ 100 =100%  10.46.36.210
                                0/ 100 =  0%    | 13  123ms
    0/ 100 =  0%     0/ 100 =  0%  10.46.155.17
                                0/ 100 =  0%    | 14  127ms
    0/ 100 =  0%     0/ 100 =  0%  10.46.129.51
                                1/ 100 =  1%    | 15  125ms
    1/ 100 =  1%     0/ 100 =  0%  10.46.196.103 Trace complete.
```

Based on PathPing's output, you can often quickly identify the source of your connectivity problems as a name resolution problem, a routing problem, a performance problem, or a possible connectivity issue. By using PathPing, you can also rule out active connectivity issues at the network layer or below.

Routing Loops

You can use PathPing to detect routing loops. Routing loops—a situation in which traffic is forwarded back to a router that has already forwarded a particular packet—are evident because the output from PathPing will show a set of routers repeated multiple times. For example, the following output indicates a routing loop between the routers at 10.128.191.245, 10.128.191.73, and 10.125.39.213.

```
Tracing route to support.go.microsoft.contoso.com [10.46.196.103]over a maximum of 30
hops:  0  contoso-test [192.168.1.207]   1  10.211.240.1   2  10.128.191.245
3  10.128.191.73   4  10.125.39.213   5  10.128.191.245
6  10.128.191.73   7  10.125.39.213   8  10.128.191.245   9  10.128.191.73
10  10.125.39.213 (...continued...)
```

Routing loops are generally caused by router or routing protocol misconfiguration, and further troubleshooting must be performed on the network routing equipment.

Performance Problems

The RTT column of the Performance section of the PathPing output might identify a performance problem. This column shows round-trip time (RTT) in milliseconds, which is the two-way latency of communications with that particular device. Although all networks will show gradually increasing latency as the hop count increases, a large latency increase from one hop to the next identifies performance problems.

Performance problems might also be evident from a high percentage shown in the Lost/Sent = Pct column. This column measures packet loss. Although packet loss in the single digits generally does not indicate a problem that would cause performance or connectivity problems, packet loss of greater than 30 percent generally indicates that the network node is experiencing problems.

NOTE If a network device shows packet loss of 100 percent but packets are processed at later hops, the network device has been configured to not answer PathPing queries, which does not necessarily indicate a problem.

Possible Connectivity Issues

If the last item shown in the first section of PathPing output resembles the following example, PathPing was unable to communicate directly to the destination.

```
14     *     *     *
```

This might or might not indicate a possible connectivity problem, however. Although the device might be offline or unreachable, it is also likely that the destination—or a network node in the path to the destination—has been configured to drop the ICMP packets that PathPing uses to query devices. ICMP is disabled by default in many modern operating systems. Additionally, administrators often manually disable ICMP on other operating systems as a security measure to make it more difficult for malicious attackers to identify nodes on the network and to reduce the effects of some denial-of-service attacks.

NOTE Windows Firewall drops ICMP packets by default on public networks. Therefore, unless you connect to a domain controller or configure a network as private, Windows will not respond to ICMP requests by default.

If PathPing is unable to reach the destination, you should attempt to communicate directly with the application by using Telnet, as described in the section titled "Telnet Client" later in this chapter.

No Connectivity Issues

If the PathPing output indicates that PathPing was able to communicate successfully with the destination and the RTT time shown for the destination is less than 1,000 milliseconds, there are probably no name resolution or IP connectivity problems between the source and destination. However, PathPing will not show problems with a specific service or application. For example, PathPing might successfully communicate with a Web server even if the Web server services are stopped. For more information about troubleshooting application issues, see the section titled "How to Troubleshoot Application Connectivity Problems" later in this chapter.

Performance Monitor

You can use Performance Monitor, shown in Figure 31-2, to view thousands of real-time counters containing information about your computer or a remote computer. When troubleshooting network performance problems, you can use Performance Monitor to view current bandwidth utilization in a more detailed way than provided by Task Manager or Resource Monitor. Additionally, Performance Monitor provides access to counters measuring retries, errors, and much more.

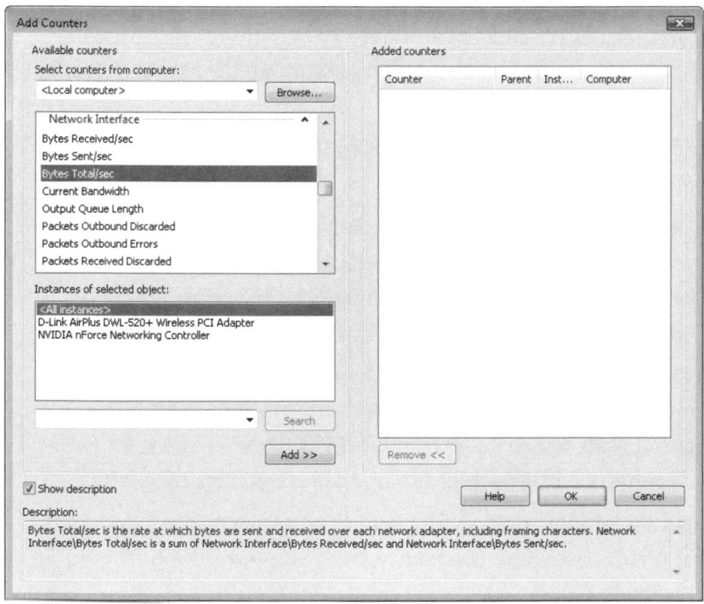

FIGURE 31-2 Performance Monitor provides real-time, detailed network statistics.

Performance Monitor provides access to the following categories, which contain counters that might be useful for troubleshooting network problems:

- **.NET CLR Networking** Examines network statistics for specific Microsoft .NET Framework applications. Use these counters if you are experiencing application-specific networking problems and the application is based on the .NET Framework.
- **BITS Net Utilization** Provides statistics related to Background Intelligent Transfer Service (BITS), which is used to transfer files in the background. Windows Update, among other applications, uses BITS to transfer files. Use these counters if you think a network performance problem might be related to BITS transfers or if BITS transfers do not perform as expected. For more information about BITS, see Chapter 25, "Configuring Windows Networking."
- **Browser** Provides statistics related to the Computer Browser service, which is used to browse network resources. Use these counters only if you are troubleshooting problems with browsing local networks, specifically for resources such as Windows XP

or earlier versions of Windows. For more information about the Computer Browser service, see Chapter 25.

- **ICMP and ICMPv6** Provide ICMP statistics. ICMP is used by tools such as Ping, Tracert, and PathPing. Use these counters only if you are actively using ICMP to test network connectivity.
- **IPsec AuthIPv4, IPsec AuthIPv6, IPsec Driver, IPsec IKEv4, and IPsec IKEv6** Provide Internet Protocol security (IPsec) statistics. Use these counters if you are experiencing networking problems and IPsec is enabled in your environment.
- **IPv4 and IPv6** These categories provide Layer 3 networking information, such as fragmentation statistics. If you need to monitor total network utilization, you should use the Network Interface counters instead.
- **NBT Connection** Provides information about bytes sent and received for NetBIOS networking, such as file and printer sharing.
- **Network Interface** The most useful category for troubleshooting, this provides counters for all network traffic sent to and from a single network adapter. These counters are the most reliable way to measure total network utilization. Network Interface counters also provide information about errors.
- **Redirector** Provides statistics gathered from the Windows redirector, which helps direct traffic to and from different networking features. Interpreting most of these counters requires a detailed understanding of the Windows network stack. However, the Network Errors/sec counter can be useful for diagnosing network problems.
- **Server** Provides statistics related to sharing files and printers, including bandwidth used and the number of errors. Use these counters when troubleshooting file and printer sharing from the server.
- **TCPv4 and TCPv6** Provide information about TCP connections. Of particular interest for troubleshooting are the Connection Failures, Connections Active, and Connections Established counters.
- **UDPv4 and UDPv6** Provide information about UDP communications. Use these counters to determine whether a computer is sending or receiving UDP data, such as DNS requests. Monitor the Datagrams No Port/sec and Datagrams Received Errors counters to determine whether a computer is receiving unwanted UDP traffic.

To access Performance Monitor, follow these steps:

1. Click Start, right-click Computer, and then click Manage.
2. Expand System Tools, expand Performance, and then expand Monitoring Tools. Click Performance Monitor.
3. Add counters to the real-time graph by clicking the green plus sign on the toolbar.

> ***MORE INFO*** **For additional information on using Performance Monitor, refer to Chapter 21, "Maintaining Desktop Health."**

Data Collector Sets

While you can use Performance Monitor to gather a custom set of information, it's generally quicker to start one of the built-in data collector sets. Both the System Diagnostics and System Performance data collector sets gather network performance counters that might reveal the cause of network problems.

To use a data collector set, follow these steps:

1. Click Start, right-click Computer, and then click Manage.
2. Expand Performance, Data Collector Sets, and System.
3. Under System, right-click System Diagnostics, and then click Start.
4. Starting diagnostics tracing causes Windows to collect detailed information about network adapters and overall operating system performance.
5. Now that you have started tracing, you should reproduce the networking problem. The data collector set will gather data for 60 seconds.
6. Windows takes a few seconds to generate a report after you stop tracing. Then, you can view the collected information in a report, as shown in Figure 31-3. To view the report, under Performance, expand Reports. Then, expand System Diagnostics and click the latest report.

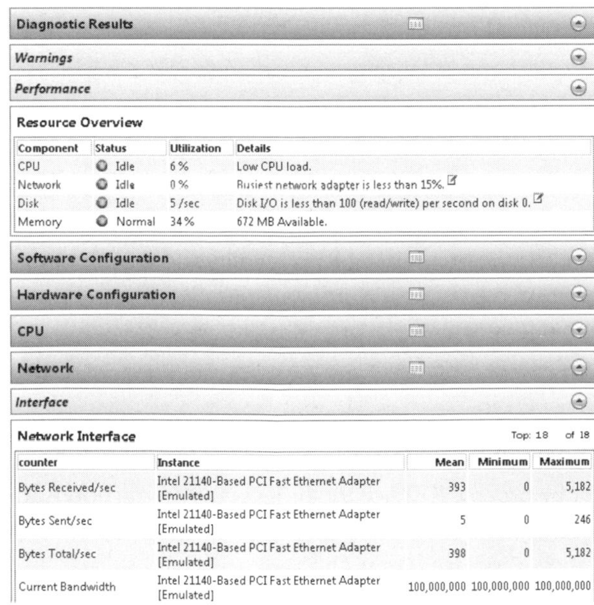

FIGURE 31-3 Data collector sets show detailed information.

Depending on the type of report, it can include the following information:

- Computer make and model
- Operating system version

- A list of all services, their current states, and their PIDs
- Network adapter driver information and networking system files and versions
- Processor, disk, network, and memory utilization
- Total bandwidth of each network adapter
- Packets sent and received
- Active TCPv4 and TCPv6 connections

Resource Monitor

Windows 7 provides Resource Monitor so that you can view processor, disk, network, and memory utilization. Open Resource Monitor in one of two primary ways:

- Click Start, All Programs, Accessories, System Tools, and Resource Monitor.
- Open Task Manager, click the Performance tab, and then click Resource Monitor.

In the context of troubleshooting network issues, the Network section is the most interesting section of the Resource Monitor. The Network section displays bytes per minute that each process on your computer is using. With this information, you can identify a process that is transmitting large amounts of data and stop it if it should not be communicating on the network. To identify and terminate a process that is using the network, follow these steps:

1. Open Resource Monitor.
2. Expand the Network section. Click the Total column heading to sort the process list by bandwidth utilization.
3. The topmost process is sending and receiving the most data. Make note of the process name (in the Image column), the PID, and the remote computer (in the Address column). If this is enough information to identify the process, you can close the application now.
4. If the process is SvcHost.exe, you might not be able to identify the specific application generating the network traffic, because it is a Windows feature (or it is using a feature for communications). If it is a different process, open Task Manager.
5. In Task Manager, click the Processes tab, click the View menu, and then click Select Columns.
6. In the Select Process Page Columns dialog box, select the PID check box. Click OK.
7. Click the PID column to sort by process ID. Click the process that corresponds to the PID you identified as generating the network traffic using the Resource Monitor. If the PID does not appear, click Show Processes From All Users.
8. To identify the service, right-click the service and then click Go To Service. To stop the process, click End Process.

In most cases, an application that is sending or transmitting a large amount of data has a legitimate need for that data, and you should not terminate it. However, in some cases, the process may be associated with malware. Verify that the computer has Windows Defender enabled and that Windows Defender is up to date.

MORE INFO For additional information on using Resource Monitor, refer to Chapter 21.

Ping

Ping is of limited usefulness today because most new computers drop Ping requests (which use ICMP). Therefore, you might ping a computer that is connected to the network but not receive any response. Additionally, a computer might respond to Ping requests even if a firewall is dropping all other traffic—misleading you into thinking that you had connectivity.

However, Ping is still the best tool to easily monitor network connectivity on an ongoing basis. After using PathPing to identify network hosts that respond to ICMP requests, you can use Ping to constantly submit Ping requests and thereby easily determine whether you currently have connectivity to the host. If you are experiencing intermittent connectivity problems, a Ping loop will indicate whether your connection is active at any given time.

To start a Ping loop, run the following command.

```
ping -t hostname
```

Replies indicate that the packet was sent successfully, while Request Timed Out messages indicate that the computer did not receive a response from the remote host. The following example indicates how to monitor the connection to a host at the IP address 192.168.1.1.

```
ping -t 192.168.1.1
```

```
Pinging 192.168.1.1 with 32 bytes of data:

Reply from 192.168.1.1: bytes=32 time=1ms TTL=64
Reply from 192.168.1.1: bytes=32 time<1ms TTL=64
Reply from 192.168.1.1: bytes=32 time<1ms TTL=64
Reply from 192.168.1.1: bytes=32 time<1ms TTL=64
Request timed out.
Request timed out.
Request timed out.
Request timed out.
Request timed out.
Reply from 192.168.1.1: bytes=32 time<1ms TTL=64
Request timed out.
Request timed out.
Reply from 192.168.1.1: bytes=32 time<1ms TTL=64
```

Note that Ping loops provide only an approximate estimation of connectivity. Ping packets will occasionally be dropped even if connectivity is constant. Additionally, because Ping sends requests sooner if a reply is received than if the reply times out, you cannot use the ratio of replies to time-out errors as a useful indication of network uptime.

DIRECT FROM THE SOURCE

Finding Blackhole Routers

Tim Rains, Program Manager
Windows Networking

Ping can be useful in determining whether upstream routers are black hole routers, which drop datagrams larger than a specific size. For more information, see *http://support.microsoft.com/kb/314825.*

If you want to use Ping from a Windows PowerShell script, use the Test-Connection cmdlet. The functionality is almost identical to Ping, with the added benefit of being able to specify the –*Source* parameter to initiate the ICMP requests from a remote computer.

PortQry

Directly query critical services on the remote host to determine whether it is available and accessible. You can use two troubleshooting tools to query services on a remote host: PortQry (Portqry.exe) and Telnet Client. PortQry is more flexible and simpler to use than Telnet Client; however, because it is not included with Windows (but can be downloaded from the Microsoft Web site), it might not be installed on all systems. Use Telnet Client to query remote services only when PortQry is not available.

PortQry version 1.22 is a TCP/IP connectivity testing utility that is included with the Windows Server 2003 Support Tools. For information on how to download these tools, see *http://support.microsoft.com/kb/892777.* PortqryV2.exe is a new version of PortQry that includes all the features and functionality of the earlier version and has new features and functionality. For information concerning PortqryV2.exe and how to download it, see *http://support.microsoft.com/kb/832919.* The following examples can be performed using either version.

NOTE **Information concerning PortQryUI, a user Interface for the original Portqry.exe command-line port scanner, can be found at *http://support.microsoft.com/kb/310099,* which includes a link for downloading this tool.**

Identifying the TCP Port for a Service

A single computer can host many network services. These services distinguish their traffic from each other by using port numbers. When testing connectivity to an application by using Telnet, you must provide Telnet with the port number that the destination application is using.

NOTE Most services allow the administrator to specify a port number other than the default. If the service does not respond to the default port number, verify that the service has not been configured to use a different port number. You can run Netstat on the server to list listening ports. For more information, see the section titled "Netstat" earlier in this chapter.

For a list of common port numbers, see the section titled "How to Troubleshoot Network Connectivity Problems" later in this chapter.

Testing Service Connectivity

After you have identified the port number for the service, you can use PortQry to test connectivity to that service. To test connectivity to a service, open a command prompt and run the following command.

portqry -n *destination* -e *portnumber*

For example, to test HTTP connectivity to *www.microsoft.com*, type the following command at the command line.

portqry -n www.microsoft.com -e 80

This command produces output similar to the following.

```
Querying target system called:
www.microsoft.com
Attempting to resolve name to IP address...
Name resolved to 10.209.68.190
TCP port 80 (http service): LISTENING
```

The destination might be a host name, computer name, or IP address. If the response includes LISTENING, the host responded on the specified port number. If the response includes NOT LISTENING or FILTERED, the service you are testing is not available.

NOTE Netcat is a great non-Microsoft tool for testing connectivity to specific ports or determining on which ports a computer is listening for connections. Netcat is an open-source tool freely available from *http://netcat.sourceforge.net/*.

Determining Available Remote Management Protocols

When troubleshooting a computer remotely, you might need to determine which remote management protocols are available. PortQry can test the default port numbers for common remote management protocols and identify which protocols are available.

To determine which management protocols are available on a remote host, open a command prompt and run the following command.

portqry -n *destination* -o 32,139,445,3389

This command queries the remote host to determine whether Telnet Server, NetBIOS, Common Internet File System (CIFS), and the Remote Desktop are available.

DIRECT FROM THE SOURCE

Specifying the Source Port

Tim Rains, Program Manager
Windows Networking

The Portqry *–sp* option allows you to specify which source port you want to use for the connectivity test. Use this parameter to specify the initial source port to use when you connect to the specified TCP and UDP ports on the destination computer. This functionality is useful to help you test firewall or router rules that filter ports based on their source ports.

The following PortQry output indicates that the remote system will respond to NetBIOS, CIFS, and Remote Desktop requests, but not to Telnet requests.

```
Querying target system called:
192.168.1.200
Attempting to resolve IP address to a name...
IP address resolved to CONTOSO-SERVER
TCP port 32 (unknown service): NOT LISTENING
TCP port 139 (netbios-ssn service): LISTENING
TCP port 445 (microsoft-ds service): LISTENING
TCP port 3389 (unknown service): LISTENING
```

DIRECT FROM THE SOURCE

Why PortQry Is Great

Tim Rains, Program Manager
Windows Networking

The real advantage that PortQry has over Telnet Client and other such tools is the support for UDP-based services. Telnet Client can help test connectivity only on TCP ports, but you can use PortQry to test UDP ports as well as TCP ports. The UDP ports that PortQry can test include Lightweight Directory Access Protocol (LDAP), Remote Procedure Calls (RPCs), DNS, NetBIOS Name Service, Simple Network Management Protocol (SNMP), Microsoft Internet Security and Acceleration (ISA) Server, Microsoft SQL Server 2000 Named Instances, Trivial File Transfer Protocol (TFTP), and Layer Two Tunneling Protocol (L2TP).

Route

All IP-based networked devices, including computers, have *routing tables*. Routing tables describe the local network, remote networks, and gateways that you can use to forward traffic between networks. In networks with a single gateway, the routing table is very simple and indicates that local traffic should be sent directly to the local network, whereas traffic for any network other than the LAN should be sent through the gateway.

However, some networks have multiple gateways. For example, you might have two gateways on a LAN: one that leads to the Internet and another that leads to a private network. In that case, the local computer's routing table must describe that specific networks are available through the internal gateway and all other networks are available through the Internet gateway.

> ***NOTE*** **A client computer is most often configured with multiple routes in remote access scenarios. Specifically, if a client is using a virtual private network (VPN) connection, there might be separate routes for the networks accessible through the VPN connection, and all other traffic will be sent directly to the Internet.**

Typically, computers running Windows will be automatically configured with the correct routing table. For example, network administrators will configure the DHCP server to assign a default gateway. When making a VPN connection, the VPN server will provide routing information that Windows will use to update the routing tables. Therefore, you rarely need to use the Route command to view or update the routing table.

However, if you are having connectivity problems and you are connected to a remote network or if your local network has multiple gateways, you can use Route to diagnose routing problems and even test different routing configurations. To view the local computer's IPv4 and IPv6 routing tables, open a command prompt and run the following command.

```
C:\>route print
```

This command produces output similar to the following.

```
===========================================================================
Interface List
 11 ...00 80 c8 ac 0d 9e ...... D-Link AirPlus DWL-520+ Wireless PCI Adapter
  8 ...00 13 d3 3b 50 8f ...... NVIDIA nForce Networking Controller
  1 ........................... Software Loopback Interface 1
  9 ...02 00 54 55 4e 01 ...... Teredo Tunneling Pseudo-Interface
 12 ...00 00 00 00 00 00 00 e0  isatap.{B1A1A1DE-A1E5-4ED6-B597-7667C85F8999}
 13 ...00 00 00 00 00 00 00 e0  isatap.hsd1.nh.comcast.net.
===========================================================================

IPv4 Route Table
===========================================================================
```

```
Active Routes:
Network Destination        Netmask          Gateway       Interface  Metric
          0.0.0.0          0.0.0.0      192.168.1.1    192.168.1.132     20
        127.0.0.0        255.0.0.0         On-link         127.0.0.1    306
        127.0.0.1  255.255.255.255         On-link         127.0.0.1    306
  127.255.255.255  255.255.255.255         On-link         127.0.0.1    306
      169.254.0.0      255.255.0.0         On-link   169.254.166.248    286
  169.254.166.248  255.255.255.255         On-link   169.254.166.248    286
  169.254.255.255  255.255.255.255         On-link   169.254.166.248    286
      192.168.1.0    255.255.255.0         On-link     192.168.1.132    276
    192.168.1.132  255.255.255.255         On-link     192.168.1.132    276
    192.168.1.255  255.255.255.255         On-link     192.168.1.132    276
        224.0.0.0        240.0.0.0         On-link         127.0.0.1    306
        224.0.0.0        240.0.0.0         On-link     192.168.1.132    276
        224.0.0.0        240.0.0.0         On-link   169.254.166.248    286
  255.255.255.255  255.255.255.255         On-link         127.0.0.1    306
  255.255.255.255  255.255.255.255         On-link     192.168.1.132    276
  255.255.255.255  255.255.255.255         On-link   169.254.166.248    286
===========================================================================
Persistent Routes:
  None

IPv6 Route Table
===========================================================================
Active Routes:
 If Metric Network Destination      Gateway
  9     18 ::/0                     On-link
  1    306 ::1/128                  On-link
  9     18 2001::/32                On-link
  9    266 2001:0:4136:e37a:14fc:39dc:3f57:fe7b/128
                                    On-link
  8    276 fe80::/64                On-link
 11    286 fe80::/64                On-link
  9    266 fe80::/64                On-link
 12    296 fe80::5efe:169.254.166.248/128
                                    On-link
 13    281 fe80::5efe:192.168.1.132/128
                                    On-link
  9    266 fe80::14fc:39dc:3f57:fe7b/128
                                    On-link
  8    276 fe80::41e9:c80b:416d:717c/128
                                    On-link
 11    286 fe80::c038:ad1f:3cc6:a6f8/128
                                    On-link
  1    306 ff00::/8                 On-link
```

```
  9    266 ff00::/8                     On-link
  8    276 ff00::/8                     On-link
 11    286 ff00::/8                     On-link
===========================================================================
Persistent Routes:
  None
```

Fully interpreting the routing configuration requires a detailed understanding of IP networking; however, you can quickly identify default routes for traffic being sent to your default gateway by locating the Active Route with a Network Destination and Network Mask of 0.0.0.0 for IPv4 routes and an Active Route with the prefix *::/0* for IPv6 routes. Other Active Routes with a Gateway assigned cause traffic for the specific Network Destination and Network Mask to be sent through that gateway, with a preference for the route with the lowest metric.

> ***MORE INFO*** **For additional information on IPv6 networking, read Chapter 28, "Deploying IPv6."**

If you must manually update the IPv4 routing table (you should typically make changes to the network infrastructure that assigned the routes to the client), you can use the *route add, route change,* and *route delete* commands. For more information, type **route –?** at a command prompt.

To update the IPv6 routing table, you must use the *netsh interface ipv6 add|set|delete route* commands.

Task Manager

Task Manager (Taskmgr.exe) is a GUI tool that you can use to view or end a process or an unresponsive application. You can also use Task Manager to gather other information, such as CPU statistics. To start Task Manager, click Start, type **Taskmgr**, and then press Enter. Alternatively, you can right-click the taskbar and then click Task Manager.

The Windows Task Manager window contains six tabs: Applications, Processes, Services, Performance, Networking, and Users.

- The Applications and Processes tabs provide a list of applications or processes that are currently active on your system. These lists are valuable because active tasks do not always display a user interface, which can make it difficult to detect activity. Task Manager displays active processes and lets you end most items by clicking End Process. You cannot end some processes immediately; you might need to use the Services snap-in or Taskkill to end them. You can also customize Task Manager to increase or decrease the level of detail shown on the Processes tab.
- The Services tab displays running services and their PID. If you determine that a specific PID is using network resources and you find the PID on this tab, you know that a service

is causing the network utilization. To stop a service, right-click it and then click Stop Service, as shown in Figure 31-4.

FIGURE 31-4 Use the Services tab to identify services by PID and stop them.

- The Performance tab graphically displays process and memory utilization. Viewing this tab quickly reveals the total utilization of all programs and services on the computer. The Performance tab also shows key performance counters including the number of processes, the number of threads, and the total physical memory installed in the system.
- The Networking tab shows the utilization of all network interfaces.
- With the Users tab, you can disconnect and log off active users.

To view detailed information about processes, follow these steps:

1. Start Task Manager and then click the Processes tab.
2. Optionally, click Show Processes From All Users.
3. On the View menu, click Select Columns.
4. Select or clear the columns that you want to add to, or remove from, the Processes tab.
5. Click OK to return to Task Manager.

To identify the cause of high processor utilization, follow these steps:

1. Start Task Manager and then click the Performance tab.
2. Click the View menu and then select Show Kernel Times (if it is not already selected).
3. Examine the CPU Usage History graph. If the graph shows values close to 100 percent, one process or multiple processes are consuming the bulk of the computer's process-

ing capability. The red line shows the percentage of the processor consumed by the kernel, which includes drivers. If the bulk of the processing time is consumed by the kernel, verify that you are using signed drivers and have the latest version of all drivers installed. If the kernel is not responsible for the majority of the processor usage, continue following these steps to identify the process.

4. Click the Processes tab.
5. Click the CPU column heading twice to sort the processes by processor utilization with the highest utilization at the top of the list.

The process or processes consuming the processor will show high CPU utilization values. When the processor is not being used heavily, the System Idle Process shows high CPU utilization.

To find the PID of an application, follow these steps:

1. Start Task Manager and verify that the Process ID (PID) column is displayed on the Processes tab. If it is not displayed, open the View menu, click Select Columns, and then select PID. Click OK.
2. Click the Applications tab.
3. Right-click the application and then click Go To Process.

Task Manager will display the Processes tab. The process associated with the application will be highlighted. The PID is shown in the PID column.

To stop a process, follow these steps:

1. Start Task Manager and then click the Processes tab.
2. Right-click the process you want to stop and then click End Process.

Task Manager will attempt to end the process. If Task Manager fails, use Taskkill.

To identify the network utilization, start Task Manager and then click the Networking tab. Task Manager shows the utilization of each network adapter. The percentage of utilization is measured in relation to the reported Link Speed of the adapter. In most cases, network adapters are not capable of 100 percent utilization; peak utilization is approximately 60 percent to 70 percent.

MORE INFO **For additional information on using Task Manager, refer to Chapter 21.**

TCPView

TCPView, shown in Figure 31-5, monitors both incoming and outgoing connections, as well as listening applications, in real time. You can use TCPView to identify exactly which servers a client connects to, including the port numbers, or identify the clients connecting to a server.

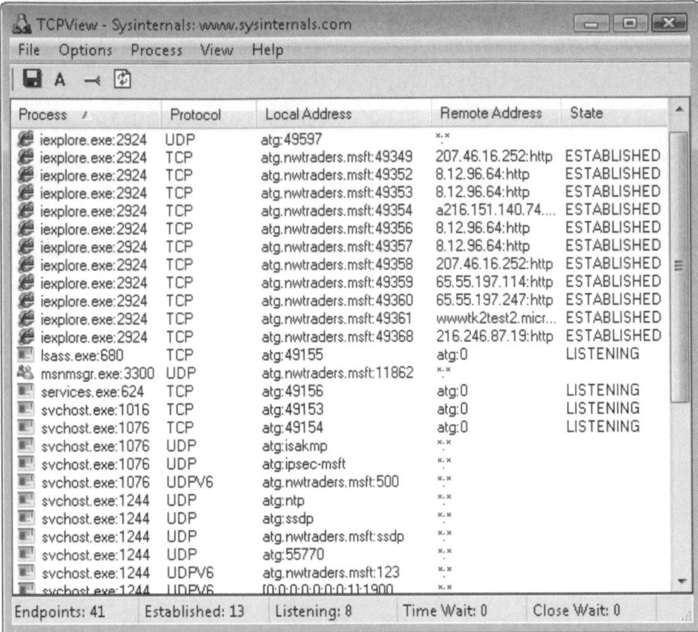

FIGURE 31-5 TCPView allows you to monitor network connections in real time.

To download TCPView, visit *http://technet.microsoft.com/en-us/sysinternals/bb897437.aspx*. You do not need to install TCPView; simply copy the executable file to a folder that allows applications to be run (such as C:\Program Files\) and then double-click Tcpview.exe. TCPView also includes Tcpvcon.exe, a command-line tool that provides similar functionality.

Telnet Client

Although it is not primarily a troubleshooting tool, Telnet Client is extremely useful for determining whether TCP-based network services are reachable from a client. Most commonly used network services are TCP based, including Web services, mail services, and file transfer services. Telnet Client is not useful for troubleshooting UDP-based network services such as DNS and many streaming media communications.

Telnet Client is not installed by default in Windows 7. To install it, run the following command from a command prompt with administrative privileges.

```
start /w pkgmgr /iu:"TelnetClient"
```

Alternatively, you can install it by following these steps:

1. Click Start and then click Control Panel.
2. Click Programs.
3. Click Turn Windows Features On Or Off.
4. In the Windows Features dialog box, select the Telnet Client check box. Click OK.

Telnet Client is useful only for determining whether a service is reachable, and it will not provide information that you can use for troubleshooting name resolution, network performance, or network connectivity problems. Use Telnet Client only after you have used Ping to eliminate the possibility of name resolution problems. For more information about Ping, see the section titled "Ping" earlier in this chapter.

Testing Service Connectivity

After you have identified the port number for the service, you can use Telnet Client to test connectivity to that service. To test connectivity to a service, open a command prompt and run the following command.

```
telnet destination portnumber
```

For example, to test HTTP connectivity to *www.microsoft.com*, type the following command at the command line.

```
telnet www.microsoft.com 80
```

The destination might be a host name, computer name, or IP address. The response you receive will indicate whether a connection was established. If you receive the message "Could not open connection to the host," the host did not respond to the request for a connection on the port number you specified, and the service you are testing is unreachable.

If you receive any other response, including all text disappearing from the command window, the connection was successfully established. This eliminates the possibility that the problem you are troubleshooting is caused by a connectivity issue between the client and the server. Depending on the service you are testing, Telnet Client can be automatically disconnected, or the session might remain open. Either circumstance indicates a successful connection. If the Telnet Client session remains open, you should disconnect Telnet Client to close the connection.

To disconnect Telnet Client, follow these steps:

1. Press Ctrl+].
2. When the Microsoft Telnet> prompt appears, type **quit**.

Test TCP

With Test TCP, you can both initiate TCP connections and listen for TCP connections. You can also use the Test TCP tool for UDP traffic. With Test TCP, you can configure a computer to listen on a specific TCP or UDP port without having to install the application or service on the computer. This allows you to test network connectivity for specific traffic before the services are in place.

Test TCP (Ttcp.exe) is a tool that you can use to listen for and send TCP segment data or UDP messages between two nodes. Ttcp.exe is provided with Windows Server 2003 in the Valueadd\Msft\Net\Tools folder of the Windows Server 2003 or Windows XP Service Pack 2 (SP2) product CD-ROM.

Test TCP differs from Port Query in the following ways:

- With Test TCP, you can configure a computer to listen on a specific TCP or UDP port without having to install the application or service on the computer. This allows you to test network connectivity for specific traffic before the services are in place. For example, you could use Test TCP to test for domain replication traffic to a computer before you make the computer a domain controller.
- Test TCP also supports IPv6 traffic.

When you are using a TCP port, the following code shows the basic syntax for Ttcp.exe on the listening node (the receiver):

```
ttcp -r -pPort
```

When using a UDP port, use the following syntax.

```
ttcp -r -pPort -u
```

After starting Test TCP in receive mode, the tool will wait indefinitely for a transmission before returning you to the command prompt. The first time you use Test TCP to listen from a computer running Windows 7, you might be prompted to create a Windows Firewall exception. You must create the exception for Test TCP to work. If you choose to unblock the application, Windows Firewall will allow all traffic for that computer on the specified port in the future. Therefore, you will not need to create a new exception for that network type, even if you listen on a different port. In Windows Firewall, the exception is named Protocol Independent Perf Test Command.

When you are using a TCP port, the following code shows the basic syntax for Ttcp.exe on the sending node (the transmitter):

```
ttcp -t -pPort hostname
```

When using a UDP port, use the following syntax.

```
ttcp -t -pPort -u hostname
```

If the two computers are able to communicate, the transmitting computer will display output such as the following.

```
ttcp-t: Win7 -> 192.168.1.132
ttcp-t: local 192.168.1.196 -> remote 192.168.1.132
ttcp-t: buflen=8192, nbuf=2048, align=16384/+0, port=81  tcp  -> Win7
ttcp-t: done sending, nbuf = -1
ttcp-t: 16777216 bytes in 1423 real milliseconds = 11513 KB/sec
ttcp-t: 2048 I/O calls, msec/call = 0, calls/sec = 1439, bytes/call = 8192
```

Meanwhile, the receiving computer will display output similar to the following.

```
ttcp-r: local 192.168.1.132 <- remote 192.168.1.196
ttcp-r: buflen=8192, nbuf=2048, align=16384/+0, port=81  tcp
ttcp-r: 16777216 bytes in 1416 real milliseconds = 11570 KB/sec
ttcp-r: 3492 I/O calls, msec/call = 0, calls/sec = 2466, bytes/call = 4804
```

You can use Test TCP to connect to any computer listening for incoming TCP connections, even if that computer is not running Test TCP. However, to accurately test UDP connectivity, Test TCP must be running on both the receiver and transmitter. For example, to attempt a connection to *www.microsoft.com* on TCP port 80, you would run the following command.

```
ttcp -t -p80 www.microsoft.com
```

```
ttcp-t: local 192.168.1.196 -> remote 10.46.20.60
ttcp-t: buflen=8192, nbuf=2048, align=16384/+0, port=80  tcp  -> www.microsoft.com
send(to) failed: 10053
ttcp-t: done sending, nbuf = 2037
ttcp-t: 81920 bytes in 16488 real milliseconds = 4 KB/sec
ttcp-t: 11 I/O calls, msec/call = 1498, calls/sec = 0, bytes/call = 7447
```

In this example, the TCP connection was successful, even though the output includes the line "send(to) failed." If the connection was unsuccessful, the output would have included the phrase "connection refused." Alternatively, some servers will simply not respond to invalid communications, which will cause the Test TCP transmitter to pause indefinitely while it awaits a response from the server. To cancel Test TCP, press Ctrl+C.

Each instance of Test TCP can listen on or send to only a single port. However, you can run it in multiple command prompts to listen or send on multiple ports. For additional command-line options, type **Ttcp** at the command prompt.

Windows Network Diagnostics

Troubleshooting network problems is complicated, especially for users. Many users discover network problems when they attempt to visit a Web page with Internet Explorer. If the Web page is not available, Internet Explorer returns the message "Internet Explorer cannot display the webpage." The problem could be any one of the following, however:

- The user mistyped the address of the Web page.
- The Web server is not available.
- The user's Internet connection is not available.
- The user's LAN is not available.
- The user's network adapter is misconfigured.
- The user's network adapter has failed.

The cause of the problem is important for the user to understand. For example, if the Web server is not available, the user does not need to take any action—the user should simply wait for the Web server to become available. If the Internet connection has failed, the user might need to call her Internet service provider (ISP) to troubleshoot the problem. If the user's network adapter has failed, she should attempt to reset it and contact her computer manufacturer's technical support for additional assistance.

Windows Network Diagnostics and the underlying Windows Troubleshooting Platform assist users in diagnosing and, when possible, resolving network connectivity issues. When Windows 7 detects network problems, it will prompt the user to diagnose them. For example, Internet Explorer displays a link to start Windows Network Diagnostics if a Web server is unavailable, and the Network And Sharing Center will display a diagnostic link if a network is unavailable.

Applications might prompt users to open Windows Network Diagnostics in response to connectivity problems. To start Windows Network Diagnostics manually, open Network And Sharing Center, click Troubleshoot Problems, and follow the prompts that appear. Unlike many of the tools described in this chapter, Windows Network Diagnostics is designed to be useful without a deep understanding of network technologies. For more information about Windows Network Diagnostics, see Chapter 25.

The Process of Troubleshooting Network Problems

To most users, the term *connectivity problems* describes a wide range of problems, including a failed network connection, an application that cannot connect because of firewall filtering, and serious performance problems. Therefore, the first step in troubleshooting connectivity problems is to identify the scope of the connectivity problem.

To identify the source of a connectivity problem, follow these steps and answer the questions until you are directed to a different section:

1. Open the Network And Sharing Center by clicking the network icon in the system tray and then clicking Open Network And Sharing Center. At the bottom of the page, click Troubleshoot Problems and follow the prompts that appear. If Windows Network Diagnostics does not identify or resolve the problem, please choose to send the information to Microsoft to help improve Windows Network Diagnostics. Then, continue following these steps.
2. Are you attempting to connect to a wireless network, but your connection attempt is rejected? If so, see the section titled "How to Troubleshoot Wireless Networks" later in this chapter.
3. Are you attempting to connect to a remote network using a VPN connection, but your connection attempt is rejected? If so, see Chapter 27, "Connecting Remote Users and Networks."

4. Can you occasionally access the network resource, but it is unreliable or slow? If so, see the section titled "How to Troubleshoot Performance Problems and Intermittent Connectivity Issues" later in this chapter.
5. Can you access other network resources using different applications, such as e-mail or different Web sites? If not, you have a network connectivity problem or a name resolution problem. If you can contact servers using the IP address instead of the host name, see the section titled "How to Troubleshoot Name Resolution Problems" later in this chapter. If servers are not accessible when you specify an IP address or if you do not know an IP address, see the next section, "How to Troubleshoot Network Connectivity Problems."
6. Are you trying to join a domain or log on to your computer using a domain account but are receiving an error message that the domain controller is unavailable? If so, see the section titled "How to Troubleshoot Joining or Logging on to a Domain" later in this chapter.
7. Open a command prompt and run the command **Nslookup *servername*.** If Nslookup does not display an answer similar to the following, you have a name resolution problem. See the section titled "How to Troubleshoot Name Resolution Problems" later in this chapter for information on solving these problems.

```
C:\>nslookup contoso.com

Non-authoritative answer:
Name:    contoso.com
Addresses:  10.46.232.182, 10.46.130.117
```

8. Are you trying to connect to a shared folder? If so, see the section titled "How to Troubleshoot File and Printer Sharing" later in this chapter.
9. If other network applications work and name resolution succeeds, you might have a firewall problem. See the section titled "How to Troubleshoot Application Connectivity Problems" later in this chapter.

How to Troubleshoot Network Connectivity Problems

If you have a network connectivity problem, you will be unable to reach any network resource that can normally be accessed using the failed network. For example, if your Internet connection has failed, you will be unable to access Internet resources, but you might still be able to access resources on your LAN. If your LAN fails, however, nothing will be accessible. Most network connectivity problems result from one of the following issues:

- Failed network adapter
- Failed network hardware
- Failed network connection
- Faulty network cables

- Misconfigured network hardware
- Misconfigured network adapter

NOTE **Often, people jump to the conclusion that the network has failed when only a single network resource has failed. For example, a failed DNS server will stop your computer from resolving host names, which would prevent the computer from finding resources on the network by name. Similarly, if the only network resource a user accesses is her e-mail server and that server has failed, the failure might appear to that user to be a total loss of connectivity. To avoid spending time troubleshooting the wrong problem, the processes in this chapter always start by isolating the cause of the problem.**

After you isolate the failed feature, you can work to resolve that specific problem or you can escalate the problem to the correct support team. For example, if you determine that the network adapter has failed, you will need to contact the hardware manufacturer for a replacement part. If you determine that the Internet connection has failed, you will need to contact your ISP. To isolate the cause of a network connectivity problem, follow these steps:

1. Open the Network And Sharing Center by clicking the network icon in the system tray and then clicking Open Network And Sharing Center. At the bottom of the page, click Troubleshoot Problems and follow the prompts that appear. If Windows Network Diagnostics does not identify or resolve the problem, continue following these steps.
2. Open a command prompt on the computer experiencing the problems. Run the command *ipconfig /all*. Examine the output as follows:
    - If no network adapters are listed, the computer either lacks a network adapter or (more likely) it does not have a valid driver installed. Refer to Chapter 30, "Troubleshooting Hardware, Driver, and Disk Issues," for more information.
    - If all network adapters show a Media State of Media Disconnected, the computer is not physically connected to a network. If you are using a wireless network, see the section titled "How to Troubleshoot Wireless Networks" later in this chapter. If you are using a wired network, disconnect and reconnect both ends of the network cable. If the problem continues, replace the network cable. Attempt to connect a different computer to the same network cable; if the new computer can connect successfully, the original computer has a failed network adapter. If neither computer can connect successfully, the problem is with the network wiring, the network switch, or the network hub. Replace the network hardware as necessary.
    - If the network adapter has an IPv4 address in the range of 169.254.0.1 through 169.254.255.254, the computer has an APIPA address. This indicates that the computer is configured to use a DHCP server, but no DHCP server is available. With administrative credentials, run the following commands at a command prompt.

      ```
      ipconfig /release
      ipconfig /renew
      ipconfig /all
      ```

If the network adapter still has an APIPA address, the DHCP server is offline. Bring a DHCP server online and restart the computer. If the network does not use a DHCP server, configure a static or alternate IPv4 address provided by your network administration team or your ISP. For information about configuring static IP addresses, see Chapter 25. For more information about IPConfig, read the section titled "IPConfig" earlier in this chapter.

- If all network adapters show DHCP Enabled: No in the display of the *ipconfig /all* command, the network adapter might be misconfigured. If DHCP is disabled, the computer has a static IPv4 address, which is an unusual configuration for client computers. Update the network adapter IPv4 configuration to Obtain An IP Address Automatically and Obtain DNS Server Address Automatically, as shown in Figure 31-6. Then configure the Alternate Configuration tab of the IP Properties dialog box with your current, static IP configuration. For information about configuring IP addresses, see Chapter 25.

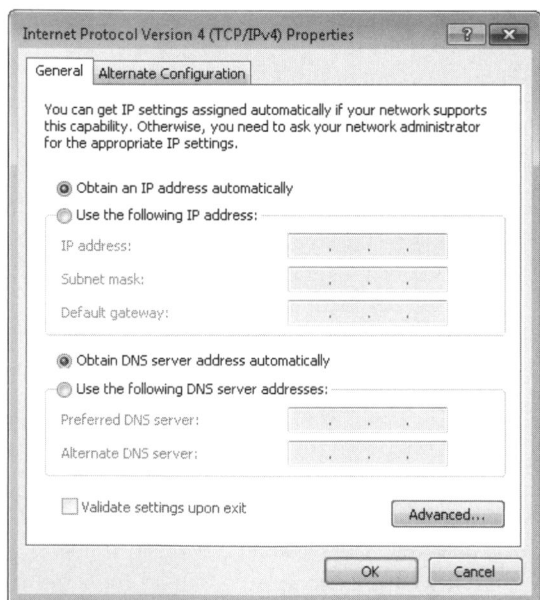

FIGURE 31-6 Enable DCHP for most client computers.

For most networks, set client configuration to Obtain An IP Address Automatically.

3. Having arrived at this step, you know that your computer has a valid, DHCP-assigned IPv4 address and can communicate on the LAN. Therefore, any connectivity problems are caused by failed or misconfigured network hardware. Although you cannot solve the problem from a client running Windows, you can still diagnose the problem. View the output from the *ipconfig* command and identify the IPv4 address of your default gateway. Verify that the IPv4 address of the default gateway is on the same subnet as the network adapter's IP address. If they are not on the same subnet, the default

gateway address is incorrect—the default gateway must be on the same subnet as the client computer's IPv4 address.

> ***NOTE*** **To determine whether an IPv4 address is on the same subnet as your computer's IPv4 address, first look at your subnet mask. If your subnet mask is 255.255.255.0, compare the first three sets of numbers (called octets) in the IPv4 addresses (for example, 192.168.1 or 10.25.2). If they match exactly, the two IPv4 addresses are on the same subnet. If your subnet mask is 255.255.0.0, compare the first two octets. If your subnet mask is 255.0.0.0, compare only the first octet (the first grouping of numbers before the period in the IP address). If any of the numbers in the subnet mask are between 0 and 255, you will need to use binary math and the AND operation to determine whether they are on the same subnet.**

4. Attempt to ping the default gateway using the following command.

   ping ***default_gateway_ip_address***

   For example, given the following IPConfig output:

```
Ethernet adapter Local Area Connection:

   Connection-specific DNS Suffix  . : hsd1.nh.contoso.com.
   Link-local IPv6 Address . . . . . : fe80::1ccc:d0f4:3959:7d74%10
   IPv4 Address. . . . . . . . . . . : 192.168.1.132
   Subnet Mask . . . . . . . . . . . : 255.255.255.0
   Default Gateway . . . . . . . . . : 192.168.1.1
```

   you would run the following command.

   ping 192.168.1.1

   If the Ping results show "Request timed out," your computer has the incorrect IP address configured for your default gateway, your default gateway is offline, or your default gateway is blocking ICMP requests. If the Ping results show "Reply from ...," your default gateway is correctly configured, and the problem is occurring elsewhere on the network.

> ***NOTE*** **Ping is not a reliable tool for determining whether computers or network equipment are available on the network. Today, to reduce security risks, many administrators configure devices not to respond to Ping requests. However, Ping is still the most reliable tool for testing routers, and most administrators configure routers to respond to Ping requests from the local network. It's a good idea to ping your network equipment when everything is working properly just to determine whether it responds under normal conditions.**

5. Use the *Tracert* command to test whether you can communicate with devices outside your LAN. You can reference any server on a remote network; however, this example uses the host *www.microsoft.com*.

```
C:\>tracert www.microsoft.com
```

```
Tracing route to www.microsoft.com [10.46.19.30]
over a maximum of 30 hops:
  0  win7.hsd1.nh.contoso.com. [192.168.1.132]
  1  192.168.1.1
  2  c-3-0-ubr01.winchendon.ma.boston.contoso.com [10.165.8.1]
  3  ge-3-37-ur01.winchendon.ma.boston.contoso.com [10.87.148.129]
  4  ge-1-1-ur01.gardner.ma.boston.contoso.com [10.87.144.225]
  5  10g-9-1-ur01.sterling.ma.boston.contoso.com [10.87.144.217]
```

The 0 line is your client computer. The 1 line is the default gateway. Lines 2 and above are routers outside your local area network.

- If you see the message "Unable to resolve target system name," your DNS server is unreachable because the DNS server is offline, your client computer is misconfigured, or the network has failed. If your DNS server is on your LAN (as displayed by the *ipconfig /all* command) and you can still ping your router, the DNS server has failed or is misconfigured; see the section titled "How to Troubleshoot Name Resolution Problems" later in this chapter for more information on these issues. If your DNS server is on a different network, the problem could be either a network infrastructure problem or a name resolution problem. Repeat this step, but use Ping to contact your DNS server IP address (as displayed by the *ipconfig /all* command). Then, follow the steps outlined in the section titled "How to Troubleshoot Name Resolution Problems" later in this chapter to further isolate the issue.
- If nothing responds after line 1, your default gateway cannot communicate with external networks. Try restarting the default gateway. If the default gateway is connected directly to the Internet, the Internet connection or the device that connects you to the Internet (such as a cable or DSL modem) might have failed. Contact your ISP for additional troubleshooting.
- If the same gateway appears multiple times in the Tracert route, the network is experiencing a routing loop. Routing loops can cause performance problems or cause communications to fail entirely. Networks typically fix routing loops automatically; however, you should contact your network support team to make sure they are aware of the problem. The following Tracert output demonstrates a routing loop, because nodes 5, 6, and 7 repeat.

```
C:\>tracert www.contoso.com
```

```
Tracing route to www.contoso.com [10.73.186.238]
over a maximum of 30 hops:
  0  d820.hsd1.nh.contoso.com. [192.168.1.196]
  1  192.168.1.1
  2  c-3-0-ubr01.winchendon.ma.boston.contoso.com [10.165.8.1]
  3  ge-3-37-ur01.winchendon.ma.boston.contoso.com [10.87.148.129]
  4  ge-1-1-ur01.gardner.ma.boston.contoso.com [10.87.144.225]
  5  10g-9-1-ur01.sterling.ma.boston.contoso.com [10.87.144.217]
  6  te-9-2-ur01.marlboro.ma.boston.contoso.com [10.87.144.77]
  7  10g-8-1-ur01.natick.ma.boston.contoso.com [10.87.144.197]
  8  10g-9-1-ur01.sterling.ma.boston.contoso.com [10.87.144.217]
  9  te-9-2-ur01.marlboro.ma.boston.contoso.com [10.87.144.77]
 10  10g-8-1-ur01.natick.ma.boston.contoso.com [10.87.144.197]
 11  10g-9-1-ur01.sterling.ma.boston.contoso.com [10.87.144.217]
 12  te-9-2-ur01.marlboro.ma.boston.contoso.com [10.87.144.77]
 13  10g-8-1-ur01.natick.ma.boston.contoso.com [10.87.144.197]
```

- If any routers on line 2 or above respond (it doesn't matter if the final host responds), the client computer and the default gateway are configured correctly. The problem exists with the network infrastructure, or your Internet connection may have failed. Follow the troubleshooting steps described in the next section, "How to Troubleshoot Application Connectivity Problems," or contact network support to troubleshoot the problem.

To double-check your results, repeat these steps from another client computer on the same network. If the second client computer exhibits the same symptoms, you can be confident that part of the network infrastructure has failed. If the second client can successfully communicate on the network, compare the IPConfig /all output from the two computers. If the Default Gateway or DNS Server addresses differ, try configuring the problematic computer with the other computer's settings. If this does not resolve the problem, the problem is unique to the problematic computer and may indicate a hardware or driver problem (see Chapter 30).

How to Troubleshoot Application Connectivity Problems

Sometimes, you might be able to access the network with some applications but not others. For example, you might be able to download your e-mail but not access Web servers. Or, you might be able to view pages on a remote Web server but not connect to the computer with Remote Desktop.

Several issues might cause these symptoms (in rough order of likelihood):

- The remote service is not running. For example, Remote Desktop might not be enabled on the remote computer.

- The remote server has a firewall configured that is blocking that application's communications from your client computer.
- A firewall between the client and server computer is blocking that application's communications.
- Windows Firewall on the local computer might be configured to block the application's traffic.
- The remote service has been configured to use a non-default port number. For example, Web servers typically use TCP port 80, but some administrators might configure TCP port 81 or a different port.

To troubleshoot an application connectivity problem, follow these steps:

1. Before you begin troubleshooting application connectivity, first verify that you do not have a name resolution problem. To do this, open a command prompt and run the command **Nslookup *servername***. If Nslookup does not display an answer similar to the following example, you have a name resolution problem. See the section titled "How to Troubleshoot Name Resolution Problems" later in this chapter.

```
C:\>nslookup contoso.com
```

```
Non-authoritative answer:
Name:    contoso.com
Addresses:  10.46.232.182, 10.46.130.117
```

2. Identify the port number used by the application. Table 31-2 lists port numbers for common applications. If you are not sure which port numbers your application uses, consult the application's manual or contact the technical support team. Alternatively, you can use a protocol analyzer, such as Network Monitor, to examine network traffic to determine the port numbers used.

TABLE 31-2 Default Port Assignments for Common Services and Tasks

SERVICE NAME OR TASK	UDP	TCP
Web servers, HTTP, and Internet Information Services (IIS)		80
HTTP- Secure Sockets Layer (SSL)		443
DNS client-to-server lookup (varies)	53	53
DHCP client		67
File and printer sharing	137	139, 445
FTP-control		21
FTP-data		20
Internet Relay Chat (IRC)		6667

SERVICE NAME OR TASK	UDP	TCP
Microsoft Office Outlook (see POP3, IMAP, and SMTP for ports)		
Internet Mail Access Protocol (IMAP)		143
IMAP (SSL)		993
LDAP		389
LDAP (SSL)		636
Message Transfer Agent (MTA) – X.400 over TCP/IP		102
POP3		110
POP3 (SSL)		995
RPC endpoint mapper		135
SMTP		25
Network News Transfer Protocol (NNTP)		119
NNTP (SSL)		563
POP3		110
POP3 (SSL)		995
SNMP	161	
SNMP Trap	162	
SQL Server		1433
Telnet		23
Terminal Server and Remote Desktop		3389
Point-to-Point Tunneling Protocol (PPTP) (See Chapter 27 for more information.)		1723
Joining an AD DS domain (See the section titled "How to Troubleshoot Joining or Logging on to a Domain" later in this chapter for more information.)		

After identifying the port number, the first step in troubleshooting the application connectivity problem is to determine whether communications are successful using that port. If it is a TCP port, you can use PortQry, Test TCP, or Telnet. Of those three tools, Telnet is the least flexible, but it is the only tool included with Windows (but note that it is not installed by default). For more information about Telnet, including how to install it, see the section titled "Telnet Client" earlier in this chapter.

To test a TCP port with Telnet, run the following command.

```
Telnet hostname_or_address TCP_port
```

For example, to determine whether you can connect to the Web server at *www.microsoft.com* (which uses port 80), you would run the following command.

```
Telnet www.microsoft.com 80
```

If the command prompt clears or if you receive text from the remote service, you have successfully established a connection. Close the command prompt to cancel Telnet. This indicates that you can connect to the server; therefore, the server application is listening for incoming connections and no firewall is blocking your traffic. Instead of troubleshooting the problem as a connectivity issue, you should consider application-level issues, including:

- **Authentication issues** View the server's Security Event Log or the application's log to determine whether it is rejecting your client connections because of invalid credentials.
- **Failed service** Restart the server. Test whether other client computers can connect to the server.
- **Invalid client software** Verify that the client software running on your computer is the correct version and is configured properly.

If Telnet displays "Could not open connection to the host," this indicates an application connectivity issue, such as a misconfigured firewall. Follow these steps to continue troubleshooting the problem:

1. If possible, verify that the server is online. If the server is online, attempt to connect to a different service running on the same server. For example, if you are attempting to connect to a Web server and you know that the server has file sharing enabled, attempt to connect to a shared folder. If you can connect to a different service, the problem is almost certainly a firewall configuration problem on the server.
2. Attempt to connect from different client computers on the same and different subnets. If you can connect from a client computer on the same subnet, you might have an application configuration problem on the client computer. If you can connect from a client computer on a different subnet but not from the same subnet, a firewall on the network or on the server might be filtering traffic from your client network.
3. If possible, connect a client computer to the same subnet as the server. If you can connect from the same subnet but not from different subnets, a router-based firewall is blocking traffic. If you cannot connect from the same subnet, the server has a firewall that is blocking traffic. Alternatively, the server application might not be running or might be configured to use a different port.
4. Log on to the server and use Telnet to attempt to connect to the server application port. If you can connect to the server from the server but not from other computers, the server definitely has firewall software configured. Add an exception for the application to the firewall software. If you cannot connect to the server application from the server, the application is not listening for connections or is configured to listen

for incoming connections on a different port. Refer to the application documentation for information on how to start and configure the application. If the server is running Windows, you can use Netstat to identify on which ports the server is listening for incoming connections. For more information, read the section titled "Netstat" earlier in this chapter.

Sometimes, specific applications might require additional troubleshooting steps:

- For more information about troubleshooting printing, see Chapter 18, "Managing Printing."
- For more information about troubleshooting Web and e-mail access, see Chapter 20, "Managing Windows Internet Explorer."

How to Troubleshoot Name Resolution Problems

Computers use numeric IP addresses (such as 192.168.10.233 or 2001:db8::1) to identify each other on networks. However, IP addresses are difficult for people to remember, so we use more friendly host names (such as *www.contoso.com*). *Name resolution* is the process of converting a host name to an IP address, and DNS is by far the most common name resolution technique.

Many apparent connectivity problems are actually name resolution problems. If any of the following problems occur, the client will be unable to contact a server using its host name:

- DNS servers have failed.
- The network connecting the client to the DNS server has failed.
- A host name is missing from the DNS database.
- A host name is associated with an incorrect IP address. Often, this happens because a host has recently changed IP addresses and the DNS database has not been updated.
- The client does not have DNS servers configured or is configured with the incorrect DNS server IP addresses.

To diagnose a name resolution problem, follow these steps:

1. Open the Network And Sharing Center by clicking Start, clicking Network, and then clicking Network And Sharing Center. If a red X is displayed over a network link, click the link to start Windows Network Diagnostics and follow the prompts that appear. Windows Network Diagnostics can solve many common configuration problems. If Windows Network Diagnostics does not identify or resolve the problem, continue following these steps.
2. Verify that you can connect to other computers using IP addresses. If you cannot connect to servers by using their IP address, the source of your problem is network connectivity rather than name resolution. See the section titled "How to Troubleshoot Network Connectivity Problems" earlier in this chapter. If you can connect to servers by using their IP address but not by using their host names, continue following these steps.

NOTE When your network is working properly, look up the IP addresses of several different computers, including computers on your subnet, other subnets on your intranet, and computers on the Internet. Test the IP addresses to verify that they respond to Ping requests. Keep this list available so that you can use the IP addresses to test for network connectivity without relying on name resolution.

3. Open a command prompt and use Nslookup to look up the host name you are attempting to contact, as the following example shows.

   ```
   Nslookup www.microsoft.com
   ```

   Examine the output.

   - If Nslookup displays addresses or aliases for the host name, name resolution was successful. Most likely, the server you are trying to reach is offline, you have a connectivity problem preventing you from reaching the server, the application you are using is misconfigured, or the DNS server database is incorrect. See the sections titled "How to Troubleshoot Network Connectivity Problems" and "How to Troubleshoot Application Connectivity Problems" earlier in this chapter. If you believe the DNS server database is incorrect, contact your DNS server administrator.
   - If Nslookup displays only "DNS request timed out," the DNS server is not responding. First, repeat the test several times to determine whether it is an intermittent problem. Then, use the *ipconfig* command to verify that the client computer has the correct DNS servers configured. If necessary, update the client computer's DNS server configuration. If the DNS server's IP addresses are correct, the DNS servers or the network to which they are connected are offline. Contact the server or network administrator for additional assistance.
   - If Nslookup displays the message "Default servers are not available," the computer does not have a DNS server configured. Update the client network configuration with DNS server IP addresses or configure the computer to acquire an address automatically.

4. If you can connect to the server from a different client computer, run **ipconfig /all** from a command prompt to determine which DNS servers the client computer is configured to use. If the IP addresses are different, consider changing the problematic client computer to use those IP addresses.

How to Verify Connectivity to a DNS Server

Although DNS traffic can use either TCP port 53 or UDP port 53, UDP is almost always used because it is more efficient for short communications. Because Telnet always uses TCP, it is not useful for testing UDP DNS connectivity. Instead, you can install and use the PortQry tool, as described earlier in this chapter.

To test for connectivity to DNS traffic, install PortQry, and then run the following command.

```
portqry -n DNS_server_name_or_IP_address -p UDP -e 53
```

If PortQry can connect to the specified DNS server, it will respond with "LISTENING." If PortQry cannot connect, it will respond with "LISTENING OR FILTERED." After displaying "LISTENING OR FILTERED," PortQry will attempt to issue a DNS request to the remote computer and then will display whether the server responded to the request.

If you prefer graphical tools, you can use the PortQueryUI tool to query for UDP port 53, as shown in Figure 31-7.

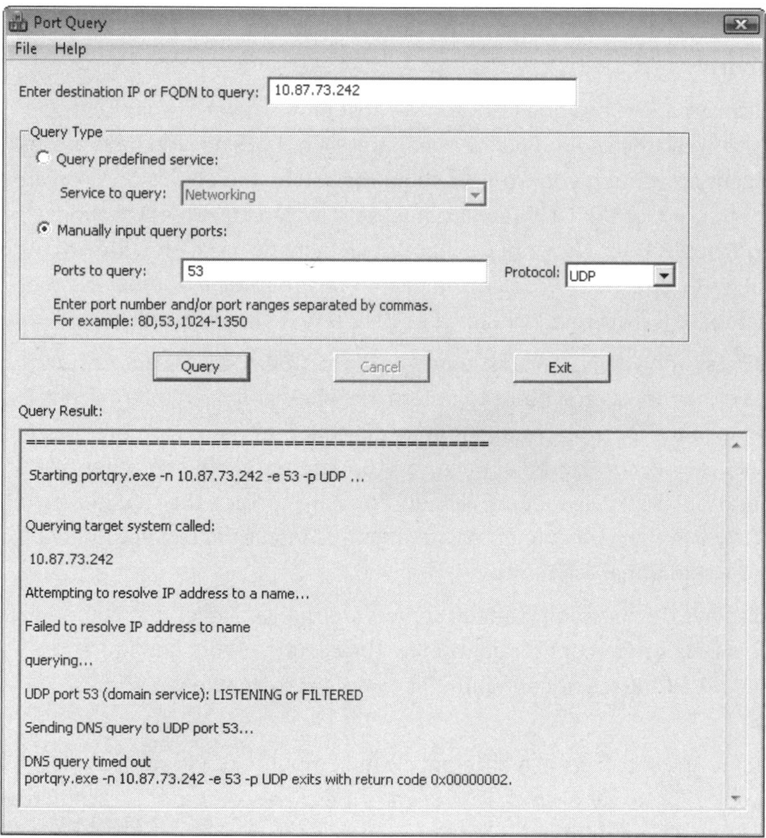

FIGURE 31-7 PortqryUI provides a GUI that you can use to test DNS connectivity.

How to Use the Hosts File

You can use the Hosts file as another name resolution method. You might do this if you know that your DNS server is unavailable or the database is out of date, you need to access a server, and you know the server's IP address. It's also useful when you've recently installed a new server and you want to contact it using a host name before the DNS database is updated.

Although you can typically contact servers using their IP addresses, Web sites often need to be reached using the correct host name, and IP addresses might not work.

Your Hosts file is located at %WinDir%\System32\Drivers\Etc\Hosts. It is a text file, and you can edit it using Notepad. To open the Hosts file, run Notepad using administrative permissions. Then, open the Notepad %WinDir%\System32\Drivers\Etc\Hosts file (it does not have a file extension). To add an entry to the Hosts file to enable name resolution without using DNS, add lines to the bottom of the Hosts file, as demonstrated here for IPv4 and IPv6 addresses.

```
192.168.1.10 www.microsoft.com
10.15.33.25 www.contoso.com
2001:db8::1   www.microsoft.com
```

After updating the Hosts file, you can contact servers by using the host name. When an entry is in the Hosts file, Windows will use the associated IP address without contacting a DNS server. In fact, the only application that bypasses the Hosts file is Nslookup, which always contacts DNS servers directly. Remember to remove entries from the Hosts file after you finish using them; otherwise, you might have name resolution problems later if the server's IP address changes.

How to Troubleshoot Performance Problems and Intermittent Connectivity Issues

Often, network problems don't result in total loss of connectivity. Network problems also can be file transfers that take longer than they should for your network bandwidth, jumpy streaming audio and video, or extremely unresponsive network applications.

To troubleshoot network performance problems, you must first identify the source of the problem. Several different components can cause performance problems:

- **The local computer** Your local computer might have an application that is using all of the processor's time, thus slowing down everything on your computer, including networking. Alternatively, failing hardware or problematic drivers can cause performance problems or intermittent failures. To solve these problems, you can stop or reduce the impact of problematic applications, replace hardware, or upgrade drivers.
- **The network infrastructure** Overutilized routers cause increased latency and dropped packets, both of which can cause performance problems and intermittent failures. Routing problems, such as routing loops, can cause traffic to be routed through an unnecessarily long path, increasing network latency. Sometimes, such as when you are using a satellite link, latency and the performance problems caused by latency are unavoidable. Although solving network infrastructure problems is outside the scope of this book, you can identify the source of the problem so that you can escalate the problem to the correct support team. For information about how Windows adapts to provide the best possible performance over different types of links, see Chapter 25.

- **The server** If the server is overutilized, all network communication to that server will suffer performance problems. Solving server performance problems is outside the scope of this book. However, when you have identified the source of the problem, you can escalate it to the correct support team.

To identify the source of a network performance problem, follow these steps. After each step, test your network performance to determine whether the problem still exists.

1. Start Task Manager by right-clicking the taskbar, clicking Task Manager, and then clicking the Performance tab. If processor utilization is near 100 percent, that might cause the perceived network performance problem. Click the Processes tab, find the process that is using the processor time, and close it.
2. In Task Manager, click the Networking tab. This tab shows a chart for each network adapter installed in the computer. If network utilization is near the practical capacity of the network link, that is the cause of your performance problem. For wired Ethernet networks (such as 10 megabits-per-second [Mbps], 100-Mbps, or 1,000-Mbps links), utilization cannot typically exceed about 60 to 70 percent of the link speed. For wireless networks, utilization cannot exceed about 50 percent of the link speed. However, wireless utilization often peaks at much lower than 50 percent of the link speed, so even 15 or 20 percent utilization may indicate that your performance problems are caused by insufficient bandwidth on the wireless network. To identify the source of the bandwidth, click the Performance tab in Task Manager and then click Resource Monitor. In Resource Monitor, expand the Network section, as shown in Figure 31-8. Identify the process that is creating the most bandwidth, the PID, and the destination server. You can then return to Task Manager to identify the specific process creating the network bandwidth. Stop the process to determine whether it is the cause of your performance problems.

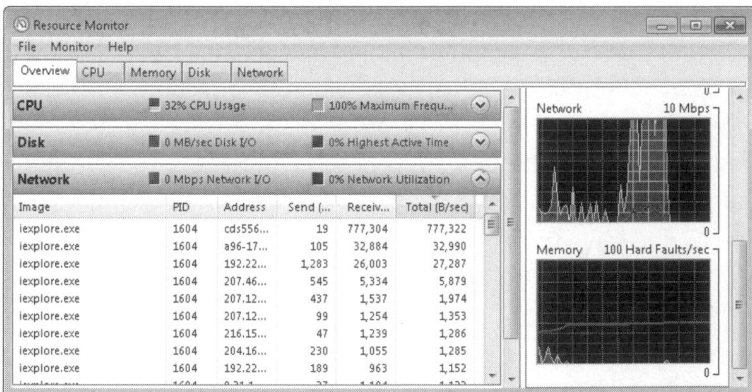

FIGURE 31-8 Use Resource Monitor to help identify the source of network bandwidth.

> ***NOTE*** **The network utilization displayed in Task Manager and Resource Monitor only accounts for traffic sent to or from your computer. If another computer on your network is using bandwidth, that bandwidth won't be available to you—but neither Task Manager nor Resource Monitor can show you bandwidth used by other hosts.**

3. If possible, use the same application to connect to a different server. If the performance problem occurs when connecting to different servers, the problem is probably local host or network related. Performing the following steps will help you further isolate the problem. If the problem occurs only when connecting to a single server, the problem might be related to the server's performance or performance problems with the network to which the server is attached. Contact the server administrator for assistance.
4. If possible, run the same application from a different computer on the same network. If both computers experience the same problem, the problem is probably related to network performance. The following steps will help you further isolate that problem. If other computers on the same network do not experience the same problem, it is probably related to your local computer. First, apply any updates and restart the computer. Then, install any network adapter driver updates. If problems persist, replace network cables and replace the network adapter. For more information, see Chapter 30.

At this point in the troubleshooting process, you have identified the network infrastructure as the most likely source of your problem. Open a command prompt and then run the PathPing tool, using your server's host name. PathPing will identify the route between your computer and the server and then spend several minutes calculating the latency of each router and network link in the path.

Ideally, each network link will add only a few milliseconds of latency (displayed in the RTT column) onto the time measured for the prior link. If latency increases more than 100 milliseconds for a single link and stays at that level for following links, that link may be the cause of your performance problems. If the link is a satellite or intercontinental link, that latency is to be expected and probably cannot be improved.

If, however, the link is your Internet connection or another network that is part of your intranet, your performance problems may be caused by overutilized network infrastructure. For example, if several computers are backing up their disk content to a folder on the network, a link can become overutilized, which can cause performance problems. Similarly, if several users are transferring large files across your Internet connection, other applications (especially real-time video or audio streaming, such as Voice over IP [VoIP]), may suffer. Contact network support for assistance. You might also be able to use Quality of Service (QoS) to prioritize time-sensitive traffic over file transfers. For more information about QoS, see Chapter 25.

> ***NOTE*** **If you are an administrator on a Small Office/Home Office (SOHO) network, you can quickly determine whether other computers on the network are causing Internet performance problems by connecting your computer directly to your Internet connection and disconnecting all other computers. If the problems disappear, another computer on your network is causing the problem.**

If the same gateway appears multiple times in the PathPing route, the network is experiencing a routing loop. Routing loops can cause performance problems or cause communications to fail entirely. Networks that use routing protocols typically fix routing loops automatically; however, you should contact your network support team to make sure they are aware of the problem. The following PathPing output demonstrates a routing loop, because nodes 5, 6, and 7 repeat.

```
C:\>pathping www.contoso.com
```

```
Tracing route to www.contoso.com [10.73.186.238]
over a maximum of 30 hops:
  0  d820.hsd1.nh.contoso.com. [192.168.1.196]
  1  192.168.1.1
  2  c-3-0-ubr01.winchendon.ma.boston.contoso.com [10.165.8.1]
  3  ge-3-37-ur01.winchendon.ma.boston.contoso.com [10.87.148.129]
  4  ge-1-1-ur01.gardner.ma.boston.contoso.com [10.87.144.225]
  5  10g-9-1-ur01.sterling.ma.boston.contoso.com [10.87.144.217]
  6  te-9-2-ur01.marlboro.ma.boston.contoso.com [10.87.144.77]
  7  10g-8-1-ur01.natick.ma.boston.contoso.com [10.87.144.197]
  8  10g-9-1-ur01.sterling.ma.boston.contoso.com [10.87.144.217]
  9  te-9-2-ur01.marlboro.ma.boston.contoso.com [10.87.144.77]
 10  10g-8-1-ur01.natick.ma.boston.contoso.com [10.87.144.197]
 11  10g-9-1-ur01.sterling.ma.boston.contoso.com [10.87.144.217]
 12  te-9-2-ur01.marlboro.ma.boston.contoso.com [10.87.144.77]
 13  10g-8-1-ur01.natick.ma.boston.contoso.com [10.87.144.197]
```

How to Troubleshoot Joining or Logging on to a Domain

Administrators often encounter problems when joining a computer running Windows to an AD DS domain. Additionally, users might receive error messages about domain controllers being unavailable when trying to log on to their computer with a domain account.

The first step in troubleshooting domain join problems is to click Details in the Computer Name/Domain Changes dialog box to view the error information. For example, the error shown in Figure 31-9 indicates that the DNS server does not have a DNS entry for the domain controller. If you want to view this error information after closing the Computer Name/Domain Changes dialog box, open the %WinDir%\Debug\Dcdiag.txt log file.

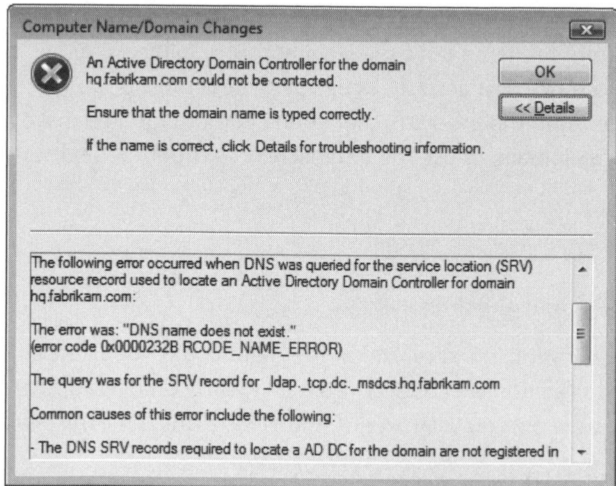

FIGURE 31-9 In most cases, Windows will reveal the source of the problem in the detailed error message.

How to Analyze the NetSetup.Log file

If the Computer Name/Domain Changes dialog box does not reveal the source of the problem, view the %WinDir%\Debug\Netsetup.log file. This log details the process of joining a domain as well as the details of any problems encountered. For best results, compare a log file generated on a computer that successfully joined your domain to a computer that failed to join the domain. For example, the following entry indicates that the computer successfully located the *hq.contoso.com* domain controller (note the return value of 0x0).

```
-----------------------------------------------------------------
NetpValidateName: checking to see if 'HQ.CONTOSO.COM' is valid as type 3 name
NetpCheckDomainNameIsValid [ Exists ] for 'HQ.CONTOSO.COM' returned 0x0
NetpValidateName: name 'HQ.CONTOSO.COM' is valid for type 3
-----------------------------------------------------------------
```

The following entry indicates that the computer failed to locate the *hq.fabrikam.com* domain controller (note the return value of 0x54b).

```
-----------------------------------------------------------------
NetpValidateName: checking to see if 'hq.fabrikam.com' is valid as type 3 name
NetpCheckDomainNameIsValid for hq.fabrikam.com returned 0x54b, last error is 0x3e5
NetpCheckDomainNameIsValid [ Exists ] for 'hq.fabrikam.com' returned 0x54b
-----------------------------------------------------------------
```

If you see this type of name resolution failure during an unattended setup but you are able to manually join a domain, verify that clients are receiving a valid DHCP configuration. Specifically, verify that the DNS server addresses are correct and that the identified DNS servers contain service location (SRV) resource records for your domain controllers in the format `_ldap._tcp.dc._msdcs.`*`DNSDomainName`*.

If you see an error resembling the following, it indicates that the computer was previously joined to a domain using the same computer name but a different account. Joining the domain might fail because the administrative user account does not have permission to modify the existing account. To work around the problem, change the computer name, have the computer account deleted from the domain, or use the original user account to join the computer to the domain.

```
NetpManageMachineAccountWithSid: NetUserAdd on '\\hq.contoso.com' for
'43L2251A2-55$' failed: 0x8b0
04/06 06:36:20 SamOpenUser on 3386585 failed with 0xc0000022
```

If you see an error resembling the following, it indicates that the client could not establish a Server Message Block (SMB) session to the domain controller to manage the client computer account. One possible cause of this issue is missing WINS registrations for a domain controller.

```
NetUseAdd to \\ntdev-dc-02.ntdev.corp.microsoft.com\IPC$ returned 53
```

To reproduce this problem (and test whether you have fixed it), open a command prompt and run the following command.

```
net use \\<server from above>\ipc$ /u:<account used for join> <password>
```

To determine whether the edition of Windows supports joining a domain, search for the keyword *NetpDomainJoinLicensingCheck* (most recent entries are at the bottom of the log file). If the *ulLicenseValue* is anything other than 1, it indicates that the edition of Windows cannot join a domain. To join a domain, a computer must be running the Windows 7 Professional, Windows 7 Enterprise, or Windows 7 Ultimate operating systems. The following shows a log file entry for a computer running a supported version of Windows (as indicated by *ulLicenseValue=1*).

```
NetpDomainJoinLicensingCheck: ulLicenseValue=1, Status: 0x0
```

How to Verify Requirements for Joining a Domain

To join or log on to a domain successfully, you must meet several different requirements. When troubleshooting a problem joining a domain, verify each of these requirements:

- **The client computer must be able to resolve the IP address for a domain controller** In most enterprise networks, client computers receive an IP address assignment from a DHCP server, and the DHCP server provides addresses for AD DS–enabled DNS servers that can resolve the domain controller IP address. If another DNS server is configured, you should update the client computer's IP configuration to use an AD DS–enabled DNS server. If this is not possible, you can add two records to your existing DNS server that resolve to a domain controller's IP address:
    - The _ldap._tcp.dc._msdcs.*DNSDomainName* SRV resource record, which identifies the name of the domain controller that hosts the AD DS domain. *DNSDomainName* is the DNS name of the AD DS domain the computer is attempting to join.

    - A corresponding address (A) resource record that identifies the IP address for the domain controller listed in the _ldap._tcp.dc._msdcs.*DNSDomainName* SRV resource record.
- **The client computer must be able to exchange traffic with the domain controller on several different TCP and UDP ports** These ports include:
    - TCP port 135 for RPC traffic
    - TCP port 389 and UDP port 389 for LDAP traffic
    - TCP port 636 for LDAP over SSL traffic
    - TCP port 3268 for LDAP Global Catalog (GC) traffic
    - TCP port 3269 for LDAP GC SSL traffic
    - TCP port 53 and UDP port 53 for DNS traffic
    - TCP port 88 and UDP port 88 for Kerberos traffic
    - TCP port 445 for SMB (also known as CIFS) traffic

> ***NOTE*** **For information about determining whether specific ports are available, see the section titled "How to Troubleshoot Application Connectivity Problems" earlier in this chapter. The easiest way to test for all of these ports at one time is to use Portqueryui.exe and the "Domains and Trusts" predefined service.**

- **The administrator must have privileges to add a computer to a domain** Administrators who add a computer to a domain must have the Add Workstations To Domain user right.
- **The computer must be running Windows 7 Professional, Windows 7 Enterprise, or Windows 7 Ultimate** Windows 7 Starter, Windows 7 Home Basic, and Windows 7 Home Premium operating systems cannot join a domain.

How to Troubleshoot Network Discovery

With Network Discovery, users can browse shared network resources from the Network window. On private networks, this is convenient because users can connect to resources without knowing the names of other computers on the network. On public networks, however, Network Discovery is a security concern because it will announce the presence of the computer on the public network and users might use it to connect to a potentially malicious computer.

For these reasons, Network Discovery is enabled on private networks but disabled on public networks by default. When connected to an AD DS domain, Network Discovery is controlled by Group Policy settings but is disabled by default. Therefore, if the Network window does not display shared resources on the local network, it is almost certainly because Network

Discovery is disabled. To remedy this, follow these steps (all of which require administrator privileges and can increase your computer's exposure to security attacks):

1. Verify that the Function Discovery Provider Host service is running.
2. Verify that Windows Firewall has exceptions enabled for Network Discovery.
3. Change the type of network from public to private. Alternatively, you can manually enable Network Discovery by opening the Network And Sharing Center window and enabling Network Discovery.

For more information about Network Discovery, see Chapter 25.

How to Troubleshoot File and Printer Sharing

Several different factors can cause problems with connecting to shared files and printers (which use the same communications protocols):

- Windows Firewall or another software firewall is blocking traffic at the client or server.
- A network firewall between the client and server is blocking traffic.
- The client is providing invalid credentials, and the server is rejecting the client's connection attempt.
- Name resolution problems prevent the client from obtaining the server's IP address.

First, start troubleshooting from the client computer. If the server is a computer running Windows 7 and you have administrator access to it, you can also troubleshoot from the server. The two sections that follow assume that the client and server belong to a domain.

How to Troubleshoot File and Printer Sharing from the Client

Follow these steps to troubleshoot problems connecting to shared files and printers:

1. If you can connect to the shared folder but receive an Access Is Denied message when attempting to open the folder, your user account has permission to access the share but lacks NTFS File System (NTFS) permissions for the folder. Contact the server administrator to grant the necessary NTFS file permissions. If the server is a computer running Windows 7, see the section titled "How to Troubleshoot File and Printer Sharing from the Server" later in this chapter.
2. Verify that you can resolve the server's name correctly. At a command prompt, type **ping *hostname***. If Ping displays an IP address, as shown here, you can resolve the server's name correctly. It does not matter whether the server replies to the pings. If this step fails, it indicates a name resolution problem. Contact your AD DS or DNS administrator.

   ```
   ping server

   Pinging server [10.1.42.22] with 32 bytes of data:
   ```

3. Attempt to connect using the server's IP address, as identified in the previous step, rather than the server's host name. For example, instead of connecting to *server*\printer, you might connect to \\10.1.42.22\printer.
4. From a command prompt, attempt to establish a connection to a server using the *net use* \\ip_address command. If it succeeds, you have sufficient network connectivity, but your user account lacks privileges to connect to the folder or printer share. Have the server administrator grant your account the necessary share permissions. Share permissions are separate from NTFS file permissions.
5. Use Telnet or PortQry to test whether your computer can connect to TCP port 445 of the remote computer. If you cannot connect using TCP port 445, test TCP port 139. For instructions on how to test for connectivity using a specific port, see the section titled "How to Troubleshoot Application Connectivity Problems" earlier in this chapter. If you cannot connect using either TCP port 139 or TCP port 445, verify that File And Printer Sharing is enabled on the server. Then, verify that the server has a firewall exception for TCP ports 139 and 445 or that an exception in Windows Firewall is enabled for File And Printer Sharing. For more information about configuring Windows Firewall, see Chapter 26, "Configuring Windows Firewall and IPsec."
6. Attempt to connect to the server using an account with administrative credentials on the server. If you can connect with a different account, your normal account lacks sufficient credentials. Have the server administrator grant your account the necessary privileges. Depending on the server configuration, you might be able to identify authentication problems by viewing the Security Event Log. However, logon failure auditing must be enabled on the server for the events to be available.

If you are still unable to connect, continue troubleshooting from the server. If you do not have access to the server, contact the server administrator for assistance.

How to Troubleshoot File and Printer Sharing from the Server

To troubleshoot file and printer sharing from a server running Windows 7 that is sharing the folder or printer, follow these steps:

1. Verify that the folder or printer is shared. Right-click the object and then click Sharing. If it does not indicate that the object is already shared, share the object and then attempt to connect from the client.
2. If you are sharing a folder and it is not already shared, right-click the folder and click Share. In the File Sharing Wizard, click Change Sharing Permissions. If the File Sharing Wizard does not appear, the Server service is not running. Continue with the next step. Otherwise, verify that the user account attempting to connect to the share appears on the list or that the user account is a member of a group that appears on the list. If the account is not on the list, add it to the list. Click Share and then click Done.

3. Verify that the Server service is running. The Server service should be started and set to start automatically for file and printer sharing to work. For more information about configuring services, see Chapter 17, "Managing Devices and Services."
4. Verify that users have the necessary permission to access the resources. Right-click the object and then click Properties. In the Properties dialog box, click the Security tab. Verify that the user account attempting to connect to the share appears on the list, or that the user account is a member of a group that appears on the list. If the account is not on the list, add it to the list.
5. Check the Windows Firewall exceptions to verify that it is configured properly by following these steps:
   a. Click Start and then click Control Panel.
   b. Click Security and then click Windows Firewall.
   c. In the Windows Firewall dialog box, note the Network Location. Click Change Settings.
   d. In the Windows Firewall Settings dialog box, click the Exceptions tab. Verify that the File And Printer Sharing check box is selected.
   e. If the File And Printer Sharing exception is enabled, it applies only for the current network profile. For example, if Windows Firewall indicated your Network Location was Domain Network, you might not have the File And Printer Sharing exception enabled when connected to private or public networks. Additionally, Windows Firewall will, by default, allow file and printer sharing traffic from the local network only when connected to a private or public network. For more information about configuring Windows Firewall, see Chapter 26.

How to Troubleshoot Wireless Networks

Wireless networks are now very common. However, users often have problems connecting to wireless networks, because these networks are more complex than wired networks. To troubleshoot problems connecting to a wireless network, follow these steps. For information about configuring a wireless network connection, see Chapter 26.

1. Verify that the wireless network adapter is installed and has an active driver. From Network And Sharing Center, click Change Adapter Settings. If your wireless network connection does not appear as shown in Figure 31-10, your network adapter or driver is not installed. See Chapter 32, "Troubleshooting Stop Messages," for more information.

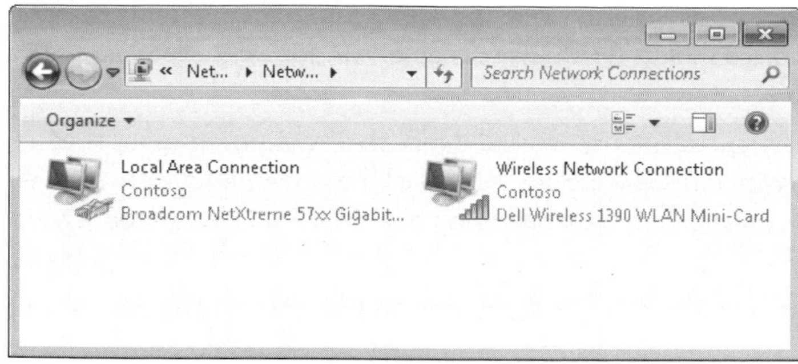

FIGURE 31-10 Network Connections will display the adapter if your wireless network adapter and driver are properly installed.

2. If a wireless network adapter is installed, right-click it in Network Connections and then click Diagnose. Follow the prompts that appear. Windows might be able to diagnose the problem.

DIRECT FROM THE SOURCE

Network Diagnostics

Tim Rains, Program Manager
Windows Networking

Network Diagnostics is capable of diagnosing more than 180 different issues related to wireless networking. To get the most from network diagnostics for wireless networks, ensure that you are using native WiFi drivers instead of legacy WiFi drivers. To determine which type of driver(s) is installed on a system, run the following command at a command prompt.

```
netsh wlan show drivers
```

In the resulting output, look for the line labeled "Type." It should be either legacy WiFi Driver or Native Wi-Fi Driver. If a legacy WiFi driver is installed, contact the manufacturer of the wireless network adapter to see whether a native WiFi driver for the adapter is available.

3. Open Event Viewer and view the System Event Log. Filter events to view only those events with a Source of Diagnostics-Networking. Examine recent events and analyze the information provided by the Windows Troubleshooting Platform for the possible source of the problem.
4. Verify that wireless networking is enabled on your computer. To save power, most portable computers have the ability to disable the wireless network radio. Often, this is controlled by a physical switch on the computer. Other times, you must press a special,

computer-specific key combination (such as Fn+F2) to enable or disable the radio. If the wireless radio is disabled, the network adapter will appear in Network Connections but it will not be able to view any wireless networks.

5. If the wireless network adapter shows Not Connected, attempt to connect to a wireless network. Within Network Connections, right-click the Network Adapter and then click Connect. In the Connect To A Network dialog box, click a wireless network and then click Connect.
6. If the wireless network is security enabled and you are prompted for the passcode but cannot connect (or the wireless adapter indefinitely shows a status of Identifying or Connected With Limited Access), verify that you typed the passcode correctly. Disconnect from the network and reconnect using the correct passcode.
7. If you are still unable to connect to a wireless network, perform a wireless network trace and examine the details of the report for a possible cause of the problem, as described in the section titled "How to Troubleshoot Performance Problems and Intermittent Connectivity Issues" earlier in this chapter.

If the wireless network adapter shows the name of a wireless network (rather than Not Connected), you are currently connected to a wireless network. This does not, however, necessarily assign you an IP address configuration, grant you access to other computers on the network, or grant you access to the Internet. First, disable and re-enable the network adapter by right-clicking it, clicking Disable, right-clicking it again, and then clicking Enable. Then, reconnect to your wireless network. If problems persist, move the computer closer to the wireless access point to determine whether the problem is related to signal strength. Wireless networks have limited range, and different computers can have different types of antennas and therefore different ranges. If the problem is not related to the wireless connection itself, read the section titled "How to Troubleshoot Network Connectivity Problems" earlier in this chapter.

> ***NOTE*** **This section focuses only on configuring a wireless client running Windows 7; it does not discuss how to configure a wireless network infrastructure. For more information, refer to Chapter 10 of *Windows Server 2008 Networking and Network Access Protection* by Joseph Davies and Tony Northrup (Microsoft Press, 2008).**

How to Troubleshoot Firewall Problems

Many attacks are initiated across network connections. To reduce the impact of those attacks, Windows Firewall by default blocks unrequested, unapproved incoming traffic and unapproved outgoing traffic. Although Windows Firewall will not typically cause application problems, it has the potential to block legitimate traffic if not properly configured. When troubleshooting application connectivity issues, you will often need to examine and possibly modify the client's or server's Windows Firewall configuration.

Misconfiguring Windows Firewall can cause several different types of connectivity problems. On a computer running Windows 7 that is acting as the client, Windows Firewall might block outgoing communications for the application (though blocking outgoing communications is not enabled by default). On a computer running Windows 7 that is acting as the server (for example, a computer that is sharing a folder), Windows Firewall misconfiguration might cause any of the following problems:

- Windows Firewall blocks all incoming traffic for the application.
- Windows Firewall allows incoming traffic for the LAN but blocks incoming traffic for other networks.
- Windows Firewall allows incoming traffic when connected to a domain network but blocks incoming traffic when connected to a public or private network.

The symptoms of client- or server-side firewall misconfiguration are the same: application communication fails. To make troubleshooting more complex, network firewalls can cause the same symptoms. Answer the following questions to help identify the source of the problem:

1. Can you connect to the server from other clients on the same network? If the answer is yes, you have a server-side firewall configuration problem that is probably related to the configured scope of a firewall exception. See Chapter 26 for information about adjusting the scope of an exception. If adjusting the scope of the firewall exception does not solve the problem, it is probably caused by a network firewall, and you should contact your network administrators for further assistance.
2. Can you connect to the server when the client is connected to one type of network location (such as a home network or a domain network), but not when it is connected to a different type of network location? If the answer is yes, you have a client-side firewall configuration problem that is probably caused by having an exception configured for only one network location type. See Chapter 26 for information about how to add exceptions for different network location types.
3. Can other clients on the same network connect to the server using the same application? If the answer is yes, you have a client-side firewall configuration problem that is probably caused by having a rule that blocks outgoing traffic for the application. See Chapter 26 for information about how to adjust outgoing firewall rules.
4. Can the client connect to other servers using the same application? If the answer is yes, you have a server-side firewall configuration problem, and the server needs a firewall exception added. See Chapter 26 for information about how to add a firewall exception. If adding an exception does not solve the problem, it is probably caused by a network firewall, and you should contact your network administrators for further assistance.

Summary

Windows 7 can automatically diagnose many common network problems. Other problems are more complicated and require you as an administrator to perform additional troubleshooting to isolate the source of the problem. When you have isolated the source of the problem, you may be able to fix the problem yourself. If the problem is related to a failed network circuit or another factor outside of your control, isolating the problem allows you to escalate the issue to the correct support team and allow the support team to resolve the problem as quickly as possible.

Additional Resources

These resources contain additional information and tools related to this chapter.

Related Information

- Chapter 17, "Managing Devices and Services," includes information about configuring services to start automatically.
- Chapter 18, "Managing Printing," includes information about configuring and troubleshooting shared printers.
- Chapter 20, "Managing Windows Internet Explorer," includes information about configuring and troubleshooting Internet Explorer and Windows Mail.
- Chapter 25, "Configuring Windows Networking," includes information about configuring network settings.
- Chapter 26, "Configuring Windows Firewall and IPsec," includes information about configuring Windows Firewall.
- Chapter 27, "Connecting Remote Users and Networks," includes information about virtual private networks.
- Chapter 30, "Troubleshooting Hardware, Driver, and Disk Issues," includes information about troubleshooting hardware- and driver-related network adapter problems.

On the Companion Media

- ConfigureTimeSource.ps1
- DisplayComputerRoles.ps1
- Get-DcSiteInfo.ps1
- Get-LocalTime.ps1
- Get-UserPrivileges.ps1

CHAPTER 32

Troubleshooting Stop Messages

When Windows detects an unexpected problem from which it cannot recover, a Stop error occurs. A Stop error serves to protect the integrity of the system by immediately stopping all processing. Although it is theoretically possible for Windows to continue functioning when it detects that a core feature has experienced a serious problem, the integrity of the system would be questionable, which could lead to security violations, system corruption, and invalid transaction processing.

When a Stop error occurs, Windows displays a *Stop message,* sometimes referred to as a *blue screen*, which is a text-mode error message that reports information about the condition. A basic understanding of Stop errors and their underlying causes improves your ability to locate and understand technical information or perform diagnostic procedures requested of you by technical support personnel.

Stop Message Overview

Stop errors occur only when a problem cannot be handled by using the higher-level error-handling mechanisms in Windows. Normally, when an error occurs in an application, the application interprets the error message and provides detailed information to the system administrator. However, Stop errors are handled by the kernel, and Windows is only able to display basic information about the error, write the contents of memory to the disk (if memory dumps are enabled), and halt the system. This basic information is described in more detail in the section titled "Stop Messages" later in this chapter.

As a result of the minimal information provided in a Stop message and the fact that the operating system stops all processing, Stop errors can be difficult to troubleshoot. Fortunately, they tend to occur very rarely. When they do occur, they are almost always caused by driver problems, hardware problems, or file inconsistencies.

Identifying the Stop Error

Many different types of Stop errors occur. Each has its own possible causes and requires a unique troubleshooting process. Therefore, the first step in troubleshooting a Stop error is to identify the Stop error. You need the following information about the Stop error to begin troubleshooting:

- **Stop error number** This number uniquely identifies the Stop error.
- **Stop error parameters** These parameters provide additional information about the Stop error. Their meaning is specific to the Stop error number.
- **Driver information** When available, the driver information identifies the most likely source of the problem. Not all Stop errors are caused by drivers, however.

This information is often displayed as part of the Stop message. If possible, write it down to use as a reference during the troubleshooting process. If the operating system restarts before you can write down the information, you can often retrieve the information from the System Event Log in Event Viewer.

If you are unable to gather the Stop error number from the Stop message and the System Log, you can retrieve it from a memory dump file. By default, Windows is configured to create a memory dump whenever a Stop error occurs. If no memory dump file was created, configure the system to create a memory dump file. Then, if the Stop error reoccurs, you will be able to extract the necessary information from the memory dump file.

Finding Troubleshooting Information

Each Stop error requires a different troubleshooting technique. Therefore, after you identify the Stop error and gather the associated information, use the following sources for troubleshooting information specific to that Stop error:

- **The section titled "Common Stop Messages" later in this chapter** This section is intended as a reference for troubleshooting Stop errors; however, it does not include every possible Stop error. If the Stop error number you are troubleshooting is not listed in "Common Stop Messages," refer to the Debugging Tools For Windows Help.
- **Microsoft Debugging Tools For Windows Help** Install Microsoft Debugging Tools For Windows and consult Help for that tool. This Help contains the definitive list of Stop messages, including many not covered in this chapter, and explains how to troubleshoot a wide variety of Stop errors. To install Debugging Tools For Windows, visit *http://www.microsoft.com/whdc/devtools/debugging/*.

- **Microsoft Knowledge Base** The Knowledge Base includes timely articles about a limited subset of Stop errors. Stop error information in the Knowledge Base is often specific to a particular driver or hardware feature and generally includes step-by-step instructions for resolving the problem.
- **Microsoft Help and Support** For related information, see Microsoft Help and Support at *http://support.microsoft.com*.
- **Microsoft Product Support Services** If you cannot isolate the cause of the Stop error, obtain assistance from trained Microsoft Product Support Services personnel. You might need to furnish specific information and perform certain procedures to help technical support investigate your problem. For more information about Microsoft product support, visit *http://www.microsoft.com/services/microsoftservices/srv_enterprise.mspx*.

Stop Messages

Stop messages report information about Stop errors. The intention of the Stop message is to assist the system administrator in isolating and eventually resolving the problem that caused the Stop error. Stop messages provide a great deal of useful information to administrators who understand how to interpret the information in the Stop message. In addition to other information, the Stop message includes the Stop error number, or bugcheck code, that you can use to find or reference troubleshooting information about the specific Stop error in the section titled "Common Stop Messages" later in this chapter.

When examining a Stop message, you need to have a basic understanding of the problem so that you can plan a course of action. Always review the Stop message and record as much information about the problem as possible before searching through technical sources. Stop messages use a full-screen character mode format, as shown in Figure 32-1.

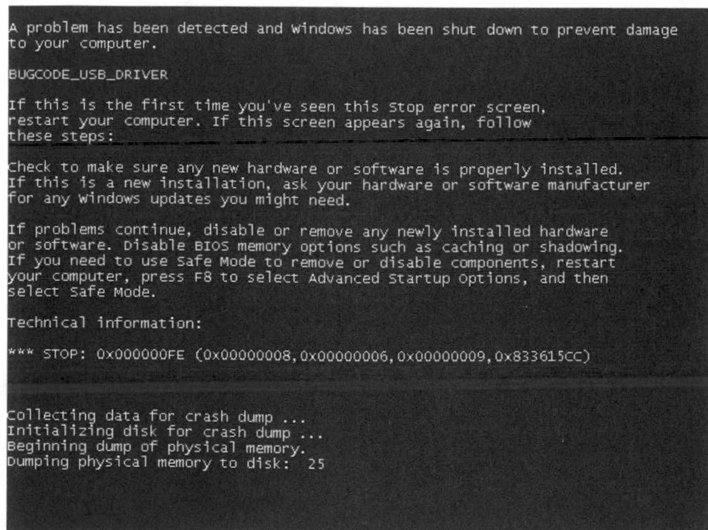

FIGURE 32-1 Stop messages display information to help you troubleshoot the Stop error.

As shown in Figure 32-1, a Stop message screen has several major sections, which display the following information:

- Bugcheck Information
- Recommended User Action
- Technical Information
- Driver Information (if available)
- Debug Port and Dump Status Information

NOTE **If the video display drivers have stopped functioning, the kernel might not be able to fully display the entire Stop message. In such a case, only the first line may be visible, or the screen may be black. Wait several minutes to allow the memory dump file to be created and then use the standard troubleshooting techniques described in this chapter.**

Bugcheck Information

The Bugcheck Information section lists the Stop error descriptive name. Descriptive names are directly related to the Stop error number listed in the Technical Information section.

Recommended User Action

The Recommended User Action section informs the user that a problem has occurred and that Windows was shut down. It also provides the symbolic name of the Stop error. In Figure 32-1, the symbolic name is BUGCODE_USB_DRIVER. It also attempts to describe the problem and lists suggestions for recovery. In some cases, restarting the computer might be sufficient because the problem is not likely to recur. But if the Stop error persists after you restart the operating system, you must determine the root cause to return the operating system to an operable state. This process might involve undoing recent changes, replacing hardware, or updating drivers to eliminate the source of the problem.

Technical Information

The Technical Information section lists the Stop error number, also known as the bugcheck code, followed by up to four Stop error–specific codes (displayed as hexadecimal numbers enclosed in parentheses), which identify related parameters. Stop error codes contain a *0x* prefix, which indicates that the number is in hexadecimal format. For example, in Figure 32-1, the Stop error hexadecimal code is 0x000000FE (often written as 0xFE).

Driver Information

The Driver Information section identifies the driver associated with the Stop error. If a file is specified by name, you can use safe mode to verify that the driver is signed or has a date stamp that coincides with other drivers. If necessary, you can replace the file manually (in Startup Repair or in safe mode) or use Roll Back Driver to revert to a previous version. For more information about Startup Repair and safe mode, see Chapter 29, "Configuring Startup and Troubleshooting Startup Issues." For more information about troubleshooting drivers, see Chapter 30, "Troubleshooting Hardware, Driver, and Disk Issues." Figure 32-1 does not display a driver name.

Debug Port and Dump Status Information

The Debug Port and Dump Status Information section lists Component Object Model (COM) port parameters that a kernel debugger uses, if enabled. If you have enabled memory dump file saves, this section also indicates whether one was successfully written. As a dump file is being written to the disk, the percentage shown after *Dumping physical memory to disk* is incremented to 100. A value of 100 indicates that the memory dump was successfully saved.

For more information about installing and using kernel debuggers, see the section titled "Using Symbol Files and Debuggers" later in this chapter.

Types of Stop Errors

A hardware or software problem can cause a Stop error, which causes a Stop message to appear. Stop messages typically fit into one of the following categories:

- **Stop errors caused by faulty software** A Stop error can occur when a driver, service, or system feature running in Kernel mode introduces an exception. For example, a driver attempts to perform an operation above its assigned interrupt request level (IRQL) or tries to write to an invalid memory address. A Stop message might seem to appear randomly, but through careful observation, you might be able to associate the problem with a specific activity. Verify that all installed software (especially drivers) in question is fully Windows 7–compatible and that you are running the latest versions. Windows 7 compatibility is especially important for applications that might install drivers.
- **Stop errors caused by hardware issues** This problem occurs as an unplanned event resulting from defective, malfunctioning, or incorrectly configured hardware. If you suspect a Stop error is caused by hardware, first install the latest drivers for that hardware. Failing hardware can cause Stop errors regardless of the stability of the driver, however. For more information about how to troubleshoot hardware issues, see Chapter 30.
- **Executive initialization Stop errors** Executive initialization Stop errors occur only during the relatively short Windows executive initialization sequence. Typically, these Stop errors are caused by corrupted system files or faulty hardware. To resolve them,

run Startup Repair as described in Chapter 29. If problems persist, verify that all hardware features have the latest firmware and then continue troubleshooting as described in Chapter 30.

- **Installation Stop errors that occur during setup** For new installations, installation Stop errors typically occur because of incompatible hardware, defective hardware, or outdated firmware. During an operating system upgrade, Stop errors can occur when incompatible applications and drivers exist on the system. Update the computer's firmware to the version recommended by the computer manufacturer before installing Windows. Consult your system documentation for information about checking and upgrading your computer's firmware.

Memory Dump Files

When a Stop error occurs, Windows displays information that can help you analyze the root cause of the problem. Windows writes the information to the paging file (Pagefile.sys) on the %SystemDrive% root by default. When you restart the computer in normal or safe mode after a Stop error occurs, Windows uses the paging file information to create a memory dump file in the %SystemRoot% folder. Analyzing dump files can provide more information about the root cause of a problem and lets you perform offline analysis by running analysis tools on another computer.

You can configure your system to generate three types of dump file:

- **Small memory dump files** Sometimes referred to as *minidump files*, these dump files contain the least amount of information but are very small. Small memory dump files can be written to disk quickly, which minimizes downtime by allowing the operating system to restart sooner. Windows stores small memory dump files (unlike kernel and complete memory dump files) in the %SystemRoot%\Minidump folder, instead of using the %SystemRoot%\Memory.dmp file name.
- **Kernel memory dump files** These dump files record the contents of kernel memory. Kernel memory dump files require a larger paging file on the boot device than small memory dump files and take longer to create when a failure has occurred. However, they record significantly more information and are more useful when you need to perform in-depth analysis. When you choose to create a kernel memory dump file, Windows also creates a small memory dump file.
- **Complete memory dump files** These dump files record the entire contents of physical memory when the Stop error occurred. A complete memory dump file's size will be slightly larger than the amount of physical memory installed at the time of the error. When you choose to create a complete memory dump file, Windows also creates a small memory dump file.

By default, Windows is configured to create kernel memory dump files. By default, small memory dump files are saved in the %SystemRoot%\Minidump folder, and kernel and complete memory dump files are saved to a file named %SystemRoot%\Memory.dmp. To change the type of dump file Windows creates or to change their location, follow these steps:

1. Click Start, right-click Computer, and then select Properties.
2. Click Advanced System Settings.
3. In the System Properties dialog box, click the Advanced tab. Under Startup And Recovery, click Settings.
4. Use the drop-down Write Debugging Information list and then select the debugging type.
5. If desired, change the path shown in the Dump File box. Figure 32-2 shows the Startup And Recovery dialog box.

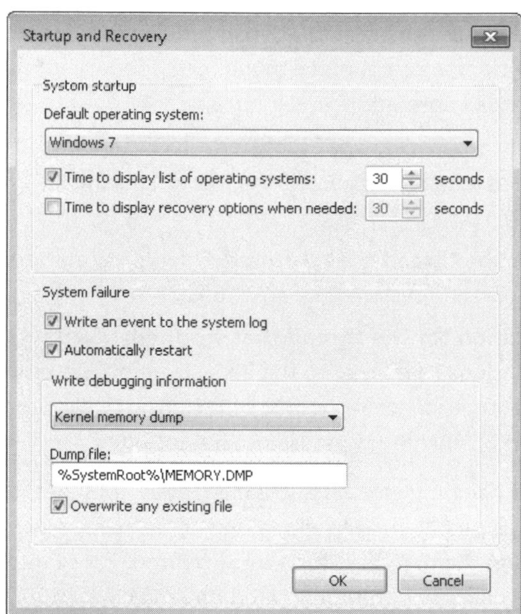

FIGURE 32-2 Use the Startup And Recovery dialog box to change dump types and locations.

6. Click OK twice and then restart the operating system if prompted.

The sections that follow describe the different types of dump files in more detail.

Configuring Small Memory Dump Files

Small memory dump files contain the least amount of information, but they also consume the least amount of disk space. By default, Windows stores small memory dump files in the %SystemRoot%\Minidump folder.

Windows always creates a small memory dump file when a Stop error occurs, even when you choose the kernel dump file or complete memory dump file options. Small memory dump files can be used by both Windows Error Reporting (WER) and debuggers. These tools read the contents of a small memory dump file to help diagnose problems that cause Stop errors. For more information, see the sections titled "Using Memory Dump Files to Analyze Stop Errors" and "Using Windows Error Reporting" later in this chapter.

A small memory dump file records the smallest set of information that might identify the cause of the system stopping unexpectedly. For example, the small memory dump includes the following information:

- **Stop error information** Includes the error number and additional parameters that describe the Stop error.
- **A list of drivers running on the system** Identifies the modules in memory when the Stop error occurred. This device driver information includes the file name, date, version, size, and manufacturer.
- **Processor context information for the process that stopped** Includes the processor and hardware state, performance counters, multiprocessor packet information, deferred procedure call information, and interrupts.
- **Kernel context information for the process that stopped** Includes offset of the directory table and the page frame number database, which describes the state of every physical page in memory.
- **Kernel context information for the thread that stopped** Identifies registers and IRQLs and includes pointers to operating system data structures.
- **Kernel-mode call stack information for the thread that stopped** Consists of a series of memory locations and includes a pointer to the initial location. Developers might be able to use this information to track the source of the error. If this information is greater than 16 kilobytes (KB), only the topmost 16 KB is included.

A small memory dump file requires a paging file of at least 2 megabytes (MB) on the boot volume. The operating system saves each dump file with a unique file name every time a Stop error occurs. The file name includes the date the Stop error occurred. For example, Mini011007-02.dmp is the second small memory dump generated on January 10, 2007.

Small memory dump files are useful when space is limited or when you are using a slow connection to send information to technical support personnel. Because of the limited amount of information that can be included, these dump files do not include errors that were not directly caused by the thread that was running when the problem occurred.

Configuring Kernel Memory Dump Files

By default, Windows systems create kernel memory dump files. The kernel memory dump file is an intermediate-size dump file that records only kernel memory and can occupy several megabytes of disk space. A kernel memory dump file takes longer to create than a small dump file and thus increases the downtime associated with a system failure. On most systems, the increase in downtime is minimal.

Kernel memory dumps contain additional information that might assist troubleshooting. When a Stop error occurs, Windows saves a kernel memory dump file to a file named %SystemRoot%\Memory.dmp and creates a small memory dump file in the %SystemRoot%\Minidump folder.

A kernel memory dump file records only kernel memory information, which expedites the dump file creation process. The kernel memory dump file does not include unallocated memory or any memory allocated to user-mode programs. It includes only memory allocated to the Executive, kernel, Hardware Abstraction Layer (HAL), and file system cache, in addition to nonpaged pool memory allocated to kernel-mode drivers and other kernel-mode routines.

The size of the kernel memory dump file will vary, but it is always less than the size of the system memory. When Windows creates the dump file, it first writes the information to the paging file. Therefore, the paging file might grow to the size of the physical memory. Later, the dump file information is extracted from the paging file to the actual memory dump file. To ensure that you have sufficient free space, verify that the system drive would have free space greater than the size of physical memory if the paging file were extended to the size of physical memory. Although you cannot exactly predict the size of a kernel memory dump file, a good rule of thumb is that roughly 50 MB to 800 MB, or one-third the size of physical memory, must be available on the boot volume for the paging file.

For most purposes, a kernel memory dump file is sufficient for troubleshooting Stop errors. It contains more information than a small memory dump file and is smaller than a complete memory dump file. It omits those portions of memory that are unlikely to have been involved in the problem. However, some problems do require a complete memory dump file for troubleshooting.

NOTE **By default, a new kernel memory dump file overwrites an existing one. To change the default setting, clear the Overwrite Any Existing File check box. You can also rename or move an existing dump file prior to troubleshooting.**

Configuring Complete Memory Dump Files

A complete memory dump file, sometimes referred to as a *full dump file,* contains everything that was in physical memory when the Stop error occurred. This includes all the information included in a kernel memory dump file, plus user-mode memory. Therefore, you can examine complete memory dump files to find the contents of memory contained within applications, although this is rarely necessary or feasible when troubleshooting application problems.

If you choose to use complete memory dump files, you must have available space on the *systemdrive* partition large enough to hold the contents of the physical RAM. Additionally, you must have a paging file equal to the size of your physical RAM.

When a Stop error occurs, the operating system saves a complete memory dump file to a file named %SystemRoot%\Memory.dmp and creates a small memory dump file in the

%SystemRoot%\Minidump folder. A Microsoft technical support engineer might ask you to change this setting to facilitate data uploads over slow connections. Depending on the speed of your Internet connection, uploading the data might not be practical, and you might be asked to provide the memory dump file on removable media.

> ***NOTE*** **By default, new complete memory dump files overwrite existing files. To change this, clear the Overwrite Any Existing File check box. You can also choose to archive or move a dump file prior to troubleshooting.**

How to Manually Initiate a Stop Error and Create a Dump File

To be absolutely certain that a dump file will be created when a Stop error occurs, you can manually initiate a Stop error by creating a registry value and pressing a special sequence of characters. After Windows restarts, you can verify that the dump file was correctly created.

To initiate a crash dump manually, follow these steps:

1. Click Start and type **Regedit**. On the Start menu, right-click Regedit and click Run As Administrator. Respond to the User Account Control (UAC) prompt that appears.
2. In the Registry Editor, navigate to HKEY_LOCAL_MACHINE\SYSTEM\CurrentControlSet\Services\i8042prt\Parameters.
3. On the Edit menu, click New, DWORD (32-bit) Value, and then add the following registry value:
   - Value Name: CrashOnCtrlScroll
   - Value: 1
4. Close the Registry Editor and then restart the computer.
5. Log on to Windows. While holding down the right Ctrl key, press the Scroll Lock key twice to initiate a Stop error.

You cannot manually initiate a Stop error on a virtual machine that has virtual machine extensions installed.

Using Memory Dump Files to Analyze Stop Errors

Memory dump files record detailed information about the state of your operating system when the Stop error occurred. You can analyze memory dump files manually by using debugging tools or by using automated processes provided by Microsoft. The information you obtain can help you understand more about the root cause of the problem.

You can use WER to upload your memory dump file information to Microsoft. You can also use the following debugging tools to analyze your memory dump files manually:

- Microsoft Kernel Debugger (Kd.exe)
- Microsoft WinDbg Debugger (WinDbg.exe)

You can view information about the Stop error in the System Log after a Stop error occurs. For example, the following information event (with a source of Bugcheck and an Event ID of 1001) indicates that a 0xFE Stop error occurred.

```
The computer has rebooted from a bugcheck.  The bugcheck was: 0x000000fe (0x00000008,
0x00000006, 0x00000001, 0x87b1e000). A dump was saved in: C:\Windows\MEMORY.DMP.
```

Using Windows Error Reporting

When enabled, the WER service monitors your operating system for faults related to operating system features and applications. By using the WER service, you can obtain more information about the problem or condition that caused the Stop error.

When a Stop error occurs, Windows displays a Stop message and writes diagnostic information to the memory dump file. For reporting purposes, the operating system also saves a small memory dump file. The next time you start your system and log on to Windows as Administrator, WER gathers information about the problem and performs the following actions:

1. Windows displays the Windows Has Recovered From An Unexpected Shutdown dialog box, as shown in Figure 32-3. To view the Stop error code, operating system information, and dump file locations, click View Problem Details. Click Check For Solution to submit the minidump file information and possibly several other temporary files to Microsoft.

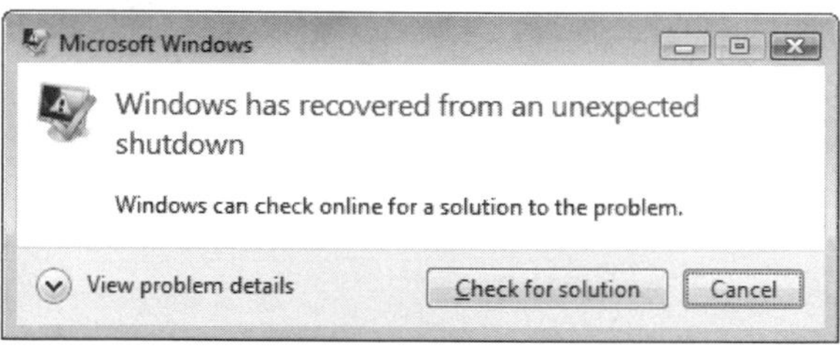

FIGURE 32-3 Windows prompts you to check for a solution after recovering from a Stop error.

2. You might be prompted to collect additional information for future errors. If prompted, click Enable Collection, as shown in Figure 32-4.

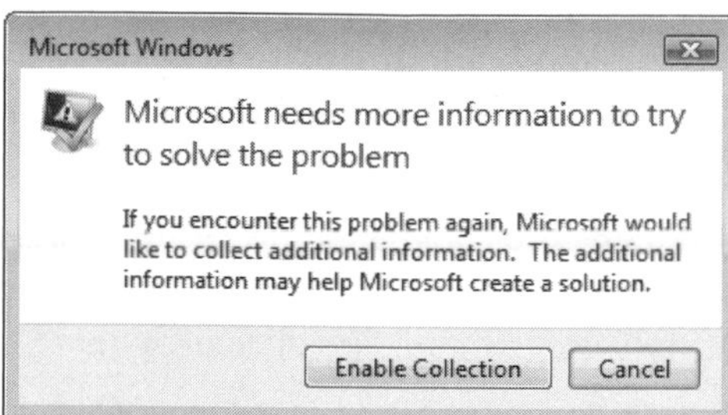

FIGURE 32-4 Windows might prompt you to collect additional information for future error reports.

3. You might also be prompted to enable diagnostics. If prompted, click Turn On Diagnostics, as shown in Figure 32-5.

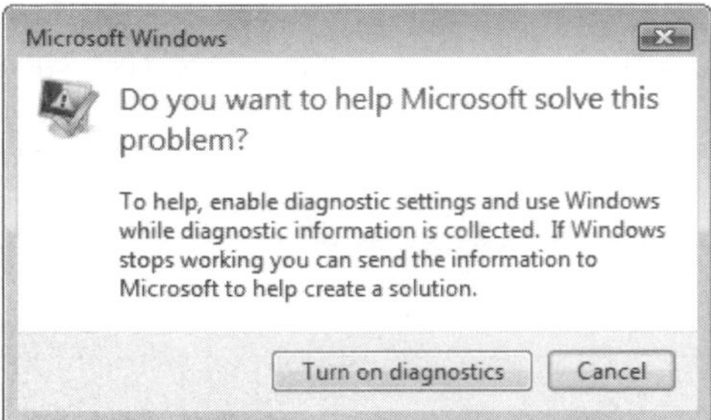

FIGURE 32-5 Windows might prompt you to enable diagnostics to gather more troubleshooting information.

4. If prompted to send additional details, click View Details to review the additional information being sent. Then, click Send Information.
5. If prompted to automatically send more information about future problems, choose Yes or No.
6. When a possible solution is available, Action Center displays an icon in the system tray with a notification message.
7. Open Action Center to view the solution. Alternatively, you can search for View All Problem Reports in Control Panel.

If WER does not identify the source of an error, you might be able to determine that a specific driver caused the error by using a debugger, as described in the next section.

Using Symbol Files and Debuggers

You can also analyze memory dump files by using a kernel debugger. Kernel debuggers are primarily intended to be used by developers for in-depth analysis of application behavior. However, kernel debuggers are also useful tools for administrators troubleshooting Stop errors. In particular, kernel debuggers can be used to analyze memory dump files after a Stop error has occurred.

A *debugger* is a program that users with the Debug Programs user right (by default, only the Administrators group) can use to step through software instructions, examine data, and check for certain conditions. The following two examples of kernel debuggers are installed by installing Debugging Tools For Windows:

- **Kernel Debugger** Kernel Debugger (Kd.exe) is a command-line debugging tool that you can use to analyze a memory dump file written to disk when a Stop message occurs. Kernel Debugger requires that you install symbol files on your system.
- **WinDbg Debugger** WinDbg Debugger (WinDbg.exe) provides functionality similar to Kernel Debugger, but it uses a graphical user interface (GUI).

Both tools allow users with the Debug Programs user right to analyze the contents of a memory dump file and debug kernel-mode and user-mode programs and drivers. Kernel Debugger and WinDbg Debugger are just a few of the many tools included in the Debugging Tools For Windows installation. For more information about these and other debugging tools included with Debugging Tools For Windows, see Help in Debugging Tools For Windows.

To use WinDbg to analyze a crash dump, first install the debugging tools available at *http://www.microsoft.com/whdc/devtools/debugging/*.

To gather the most information from a memory dump file, provide the debugger access to symbol files. The debugger uses symbol files to match memory addresses to human-friendly module and function names. The simplest way to provide the debugger access to symbol files is to configure the debugger to access the Microsoft Internet-connected symbol server.

To configure the debugger to use the Microsoft symbol server, follow these steps:

1. Click Start, point to All Programs, point to Debugging Tools For Windows, right-click WinDbg, and then click Run As Administrator.
2. Select Symbol File Path from the File menu.
3. In the Symbol Path box, type

   SRV**localpath****http://msdl.microsoft.com/download/symbols**

   where *localpath* is a path on the hard disk that the debugger will use to store the downloaded symbol files. The debugger will automatically create *localpath* when you analyze a dump file.

   For example, to store the symbol files in C:\Websymbols, set the symbol file path to **"SRV*c:\websymbols*http://msdl.microsoft.com/download/symbols"**.
4. Click OK.

   Debuggers do not require access to symbol files to extract the Stop error number and parameters from a memory dump file. Often, the debugger can also identify the source of the Stop error without access to symbols.

NOTE **You can also download symbol files for offline use from** ***http://www.microsoft.com/whdc/devtools/debugging/*****.**

To analyze a memory dump file, follow these steps:

1. Click Start, point to All Programs, point to Debugging Tools For Windows, right-click WinDbg, and then click Run As Administrator.
2. Select Open Crash Dump from the File menu.
3. Type the location of the memory dump file and then click Open. By default, this location is %SystemRoot%\Memory.dmp.
4. In the Save Workspace Information dialog box, click No.
5. Select the Command window.

As shown in Figure 32-6, the Bugcheck line tells you the Stop error number. The Probably Caused By line indicates the file that was being processed at the time of the Stop error.

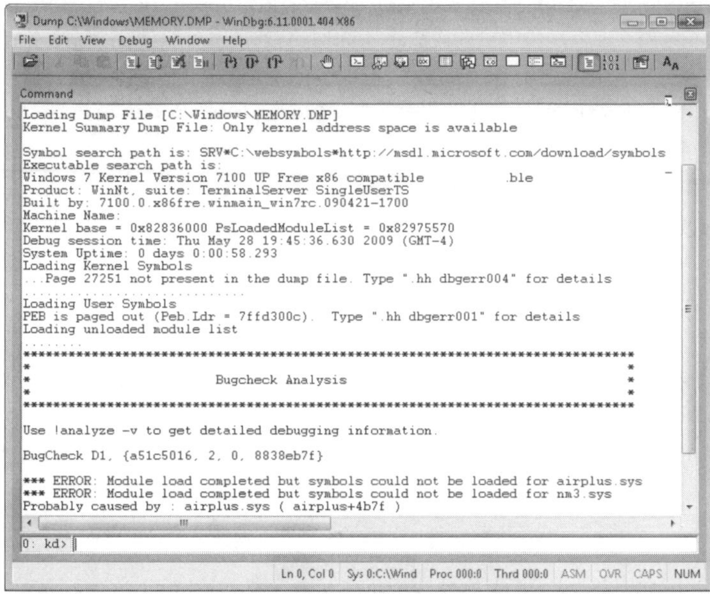

FIGURE 32-6 WinDbg displays the Stop error code and the driver that caused the Stop error.

The Command window displays feedback from the debugger and allows you to issue additional commands. When a crash dump is opened, the Command window automatically displays the output of the *!analyze* command. In many cases, this default information is sufficient to isolate the cause of the Stop error.

If the default analysis does not provide all the information you need for troubleshooting, run the following command in the Command window.

```
!analyze -v
```

This command will display the *stack*, which contains a list of method calls preceding the Stop error. This might give clues to the source of a Stop error. For example, the following stack trace output, created by calling *!analyze –v,* correctly indicates that the Stop error was related to the removal of a universal serial bus (USB) device, as shown by the bold text.

```
STACK_TEXT:
WARNING: Frame IP not in any known module. Following frames may be wrong.
ba4ffb2c ba26c6ff 89467df0 68627375 70646f52 0x8924ed33
ba4ffb5c ba273661 88ffade8 8924eae0 89394e48 usbhub!USBH_PdoRemoveDevice+0x41
ba4ffb7c ba26c952 88ffaea0 89394e48 00000002 usbhub!USBH_PdoPnP+0x5b
ba4ffba0 ba26a1d8 01ffaea0 89394e48 ba4ffbd4 usbhub!USBH_PdoDispatch+0x5a
ba4ffbb0 804eef95 88ffade8 89394e48 88eac2e0 usbhub!USBH_HubDispatch+0x48
ba4ffbc0 ba3f2db4 88eac228 88eac2e0 00000000 nt!IopfCallDriver+0x31
ba4ffbd4 ba3f4980 88eac228 89394e48 89394e48 USBSTOR!USBSTOR_FdoRemoveDevice+0xac
ba4ffbec b9eed58c 88eac228 89394e48 89394f48 USBSTOR!USBSTOR_Pnp+0x4e
```

Being Prepared for Stop Errors

Some useful software- and hardware-related techniques can help you prepare for Stop errors when they occur. Stop messages do not always pinpoint the root of the problem, but they do provide important clues that you or a trained support technician can use to identify and troubleshoot the cause.

Prevent System Restarts After a Stop Error

When a Stop error occurs, Windows displays a Stop message related to the problem. By default, Windows automatically restarts after a Stop error occurs unless the system becomes unresponsive. If Windows restarts your system immediately after a Stop error occurs, you might not have enough time to record Stop message information that can help you analyze the cause of a problem. Additionally, you might miss the opportunity to change startup options or start the operating system in safe mode.

Disabling the default restart behavior allows you to record Stop message text, information that can help you analyze the root cause of a problem if memory dump files are not accessible. To disable the Automatically Restart option, follow these steps:

1. Click Start, right-click Computer, and then select Properties.
2. Click Advanced System Settings.
3. In the System Properties dialog box, click the Advanced tab. Then, under Startup And Recovery, click Settings.
4. In the System Failure box, clear the Automatically Restart check box.

If you cannot start your computer in normal mode, you can perform the preceding steps in safe mode.

Record and Save Stop Message Information

With the automatic restart behavior disabled, you must restart your computer manually after a Stop message appears. Stop messages provide diagnostic information, such as Stop error numbers and driver names, which you can use to resolve the problem. However, this information disappears from the screen when you restart your computer. Generally, you can retrieve this information after the system is restarted by examining the memory dump file, as described in the section titled "Using Memory Dump Files to Analyze Stop Errors" earlier in this chapter. In some situations, Stop error information is not successfully logged; therefore, it is important to record the information displayed in the Stop message for future reference. Before restarting the system, take the following actions to ensure that you have saved important information, which you can refer to when using the resources listed in this chapter.

To record and save Stop message information, follow these steps:

1. Record data that is displayed in the Technical Information and Driver Information sections of the Stop message for later reference. These sections are described in the section titled "Stop Messages" earlier in this chapter.
2. Record and evaluate suggestions in the Recommended User Action section. Stop messages typically provide troubleshooting tips relevant to the error.
3. Check the Debug Port and Dump File Status sections to verify that Windows successfully created a memory dump file.
4. If a memory dump file does exist, copy the file to removable media, another disk volume, or a network location for safekeeping. You can use Startup Repair to copy the dump file if you are not able to start Windows in normal mode or safe mode.

Analyzing memory dump files can assist you with identifying root causes by providing you with detailed information about the system state when the Stop error occurred. By following the preceding steps, you can save important information that you can refer to when using the resources listed in the section titled "Stop Messages" earlier in this chapter. For more information about creating and analyzing memory dump files, see the section titled "Memory Dump Files" earlier in this chapter.

Check Software Disk Space Requirements

Verify that adequate free space exists on your disk volumes for virtual memory paging files and application data files. Insufficient free space might cause Stop errors and other symptoms, including disk corruption. To determine the amount allocated to paging files, see the section titled "Memory Dump Files" earlier in this chapter.

You can move, delete, or compress unused files manually or by using Disk Cleanup to increase free space on disk volumes.

To run Disk Cleanup, click Start, type **Cleanmgr**, and then press Enter. Follow the prompts to increase free disk space on your system drive. Note that Disk Cleanup provides you with the option to delete memory dump files. For more information about managing disks, see Chapter 16, "Managing Disks and File Systems."

Install a Kernel Debugger and Symbol Files

You can use a kernel debugger to gather more information about the problem. For more information about installing and using debugging tools, see the section titled "Using Memory Dump Files to Analyze Stop Errors" earlier in this chapter.

Common Stop Messages

The following Stop error descriptions can help you to troubleshoot problems that cause Stop errors. The section titled "Stop Message Checklist" at the end of this chapter also provides suggestions useful for resolving all types of Stop errors. If errors persist after you have followed the recommendations given, request assistance from your hardware manufacturer or a Microsoft support engineer.

Stop 0xA or IRQL_NOT_LESS_OR_EQUAL

The Stop 0xA message indicates that a kernel-mode process or driver attempted to access a memory location to which it did not have permission or at a kernel IRQL that was too high. A kernel-mode process can access only other processes that have an IRQL lower than or equal to its own. This Stop message is typically the result of faulty or incompatible hardware or software.

Interpreting the Message

This Stop message has four parameters:

1. Memory address that was improperly referenced
2. IRQL that was required to access the memory
3. Type of access (0x00 = read operation, 0x01 = write operation)
4. Address of the instruction that attempted to reference memory specified in parameter 1

If the last parameter is within the address range of a device driver used on your system, you can determine which device driver was running when the memory access occurred. You can typically determine the driver name by reading the line that begins with

```
**Address 0xZZZZZZZZ has base at <address>- <driver name>
```

If the third parameter is the same as the first parameter, a special condition exists in which a system worker routine—carried out by a worker thread to handle background tasks known as *work items*—returned at a higher IRQL. In that case, some of the four parameters take on new meanings:

1. Address of the worker routine
2. Kernel IRQL
3. Address of the worker routine
4. Address of the work item

Resolving the Problem

The following suggestions are specific to Stop 0xA errors. For additional troubleshooting suggestions that apply to all Stop errors, see the section titled "Stop Message Checklist" later in this chapter.

- To resolve an error caused by a faulty device driver, system service, or basic input/output system (BIOS), follow these steps:
  1. Restart your computer.
  2. Press F8 at the character-based menu that displays the operating system choices.

3. Select the Last Known Good Configuration option from the Windows Advanced Options menu. This option is most effective when only one driver or service is added at a time.

- To resolve an error caused by an incompatible device driver, system service, virus scanner, or backup tool, follow these steps:
  1. Check the System Log in Event Viewer for error messages that might identify the device or driver that caused the error.
  2. Try disabling memory caching of the BIOS.
  3. Run the hardware diagnostics supplied by the system manufacturer, especially the memory scanner. For details on these procedures, see the owner's manual for your computer.
  4. Make sure the latest Service Pack is installed.
  5. If your system has small computer system interface (SCSI) adapters, contact the adapter manufacturer to obtain updated Windows drivers. Try disabling sync negotiation in the SCSI BIOS, checking the cabling and the SCSI IDs of each device, and confirming proper termination.
  6. For integrated device electronics (IDE) devices, define the onboard IDE port as Primary only. Also, check each IDE device for the proper master/subordinate/stand-alone setting. Try removing all IDE devices except for hard disks.
- If you encounter a Stop 0xA message while upgrading to Windows 7, the problem might be due to an incompatible driver, system service, virus scanner, or backup. To avoid problems while upgrading, simplify your hardware configuration and remove all third-party device drivers and system services (including virus scanners) prior to running setup. After you have successfully installed Windows, contact the hardware manufacturer to obtain compatible updates. For more information about simplifying your system for troubleshooting purposes, see Chapter 30.
- If the Stop error occurs when resuming from hibernation or suspend, read Knowledge Base articles 941492 at *http://support.microsoft.com/kb/941492* and 945577 at *http://support.microsoft.com/kb/945577*.
- If the Stop error occurs when starting a mobile computer that has the lid closed, refer to Knowledge Base article 941507 at *http://support.microsoft.com/kb/941507*.

MORE INFO For more information about Stop 0xA messages, see the Knowledge Base at *http://support.microsoft.com/*. Search the Knowledge Base using the keywords *0x0000000A* and *0xA*.

Stop 0x1E or KMODE_EXCEPTION_NOT_HANDLED

The Stop 0x1E message indicates that the Windows kernel detected an illegal or unknown processor instruction. The problems that cause Stop 0x1E messages share similarities with those that generate Stop 0xA errors in that they can be due to invalid memory and access violations. This default Windows error handler typically intercepts these problems if error-handling routines are not present in the code itself.

Interpreting the Message

This Stop message has four parameters:

1. Exception code that was not handled
2. Address at which the exception occurred
3. Parameter 0 of the exception
4. Parameter 1 of the exception

The first parameter identifies the exception generated. Common exception codes include:

- **0x80000002: STATUS_DATATYPE_MISALIGNMENT** An unaligned data reference was encountered. The trap frame supplies additional information.
- **0x80000003: STATUS_BREAKPOINT** A breakpoint or ASSERT was encountered when no kernel debugger was attached to the system.
- **0xC0000005: STATUS_ACCESS_VIOLATION** A memory access violation occurred. Parameter 4 of the Stop error (which is Parameter 1 of the exception) is the address that the driver attempted to access.
- **0xC0000044: STATUS_QUOTA_EXCEEDED** The text Insufficient Quota Exists To Complete The Operation indicates a pool memory leak. A quota allocation attempt necessary for the system to continue operating normally was unsuccessful because of a program or driver memory leak.

The second parameter identifies the address of the module in which the error occurred. Frequently, the address points to an individual driver or faulty hardware named on the third parameter of the Stop message. Make a note of this address and the link date of the driver or image that contains it.

The last two Stop message parameters vary, depending on the exception that has occurred. If the error code has no parameters, the last two parameters of the Stop message are listed as 0x00.

Resolving the Problem

The following suggestions are specific to Stop 0x1E errors. For additional troubleshooting suggestions that apply to all Stop errors, see the section titled "Stop Message Checklist" later in this chapter.

- Stop 0x1E messages typically occur after you install faulty drivers or system services, or they can indicate hardware problems, such as memory and interrupt request (IRQ) conflicts. If a Stop message lists a driver by name, disable, remove, or roll back that driver to correct the problem. If disabling or removing applications and drivers resolves the issue, contact the hardware manufacturer about a possible update. Using updated software is especially important for multimedia applications, antivirus scanners, and CD mastering tools.
- If the Stop message mentions the file Win32k.sys, the source of the error might be a third-party remote control program. If such software is installed, you might be able to disable it by starting the system in safe mode. If not, use Startup Repair to manually delete the system service file that is causing the problem. For more information about safe mode and Startup Repair, see Chapter 29.
- Problems can result from system firmware incompatibilities. You can resolve many Advanced Configuration and Power Interface (ACPI) issues by updating to the latest firmware.
- Other possible causes include insufficient disk space while installing applications or performing certain functions that require more memory. You can free up space by deleting unneeded files. Use Disk Cleanup to increase available disk space. For more information about Disk Cleanup, see Chapter 30.
- The problem might be due to a memory leak caused by an application or service that is not releasing memory correctly. Poolmon (Poolmon.exe) helps you to isolate the features that are causing kernel memory leaks. For more information about troubleshooting memory leaks, see Knowledge Base articles 177415, "How to Use Memory Pool Monitor (Poolmon.exe) to Troubleshoot Kernel Mode Memory Leaks," at *http://support.microsoft.com/kb/177415* and 298102, "How to Find Pool Tags That Are Used by Third-Party Drivers," at *http://support.microsoft.com/kb/298102*.

MORE INFO **To find additional articles, search using the keywords *poolmon*, *pool tag*, *pooltag*, and *memory leak*. For more information about Stop 0x1E messages, see the Knowledge Base at *http://support.microsoft.com/*. Search the Knowledge Base using the keyword *0x1E*.**

DIRECT FROM THE SOURCE

Understanding Kernel Stack Overflows

Omer Amin, Escalation Engineer
Microsoft Global Escalation Services Team

Kernel stack overflows are a common error in many cases reported to us by customers. These are caused by drivers taking up too much space on the kernel stack. This results in a kernel stack overflow, which will then crash the system with one of the following bugchecks:

- STOP 0x7F: UNEXPECTED_KERNEL_MODE_TRAP with Parameter 1 set to EXCEPTION_DOUBLE_FAULT, which is caused by running off the end of a kernel stack.
- STOP 0x1E: KMODE_EXCEPTION_NOT_HANDLED, 0x7E: SYSTEM_THREAD_EXCEPTION_NOT_HANDLED, or 0x8E: KERNEL_MODE_EXCEPTION_NOT_HANDLED, with an exception code of STATUS_ACCESS_VIOLATION, which indicates a memory access violation.
- STOP 0x2B: PANIC_STACK_SWITCH, which usually occurs when a kernel-mode driver uses too much stack space.

Each thread in the system is allocated with a kernel mode stack. Code running on any kernel-mode thread (whether it is a system thread or a thread created by a driver) uses that thread's kernel-mode stack unless the code is a deferred procedure call (DPC), in which case it uses the processor's DPC stack on certain platforms.

The stack grows negatively. This means that the beginning (bottom) of the stack has a higher address than the end (top) of the stack. For example, let's say the beginning of your stack is 0x80f1000, and this is where your stack pointer (ESP) is pointing. If you push a DWORD value onto the stack, its address would be 0x80f0ffc. The next DWORD value would be stored at 0x80f0ff8 and so on up to the limit (top) of the allocated stack. The top of the stack is bordered by a guard page to detect overruns.

The size of the kernel-mode stack varies among different hardware platforms. For example, on 32-bit platforms, the kernel-mode stack is 12 KB, and on 64-bit platforms, the kernel-mode stack is 24 KB. The stack sizes are hard limits that are imposed by the system, and all drivers need to use space conservatively so that they can coexist. When we reach the top of the stack, one more push instruction is going to cause an exception, which in turn can lead to a Stop error. This could be either a simple push instruction or something along the lines of a call instruction that also pushes the return address onto the stack.

Stop 0x24 or NTFS_FILE_SYSTEM

The Stop 0x24 message indicates that a problem occurred within Ntfs.sys, the driver file that allows the system to read and write to NTFS File System (NTFS) drives. A similar Stop message, 0x23, exists for the file allocation table (FAT16 or FAT32) file system.

Interpreting the Message

This Stop message has four parameters:

1. Source file and line number
2. A non-zero value that contains the address of the exception record (optional)
3. A non-zero value that contains the address of the context record (optional)
4. A non-zero value that contains the address where the original exception occurred (optional)

Parameters for this Stop message are useful only to Microsoft technical support with access to Windows source code. Stop messages resulting from file system issues have the source file and the line number within the source file that generated the error encoded in their first parameter. The first four hexadecimal digits (also known as the high 16 bits) after the 0x identify the source file number, and the last four hexadecimal digits (the low 16 bits) identify the source line in the file where the stop occurred.

Resolving the Problem

The following suggestions are specific to Stop 0x24 errors. For additional troubleshooting suggestions that apply to all Stop errors, see the section titled "Stop Message Checklist" later in this chapter.

- Malfunctioning SCSI and Advanced Technology Attachment (ATA) hardware or drivers can also adversely affect the system's ability to read and write to disk, causing errors. If using SCSI hard disks, check for cabling and termination problems between the SCSI controller and the disks. Periodically check Event Viewer for error messages related to SCSI or FASTFAT in the System Log or any messages in the Applications And Services Logs\Microsoft\Windows\DiskDiagnostic\Operational log. For more information about troubleshooting SCSI adapters and disks, see Chapter 30.
- Verify that the tools you use to continually monitor your system—such as virus scanners, backup programs, or disk defragmenters—are compatible with Windows. Some disks and adapters come packaged with diagnostic software that you can use to run hardware tests. For more information, see the documentation for your computer, hard disk, or controller.
- Check your hard disk for problems. For more information, see Chapter 30.
- Nonpaged pool memory might be depleted, which can cause the system to stop. You can resolve this situation by adding more RAM, which increases the quantity of nonpaged pool memory available to the kernel.

MORE INFO For more information about Stop 0x24 messages, see the Knowledge Base at *http://support.microsoft.com/*. Search the Knowledge Base using the keywords *0x00000024* and *0x24*.

Stop 0x2E or DATA_BUS_ERROR

The Stop 0x2E message indicates a system memory parity error. The cause is typically failed or defective RAM (including motherboard, Level 2 (L2) cache, or video memory), incompatible or mismatched memory hardware, or a device driver attempting to access an address in the 0x8*xxxxxxx* range that does not exist (meaning that it does not map to a physical address). A Stop 0x2E message can also indicate hard disk damage caused by viruses or other problems.

Interpreting the Message

This Stop message has four parameters:

1. Virtual address that caused the fault
2. Physical address that caused the fault
3. Processor status register
4. Faulting instruction register

Resolving the Problem

The following suggestions are specific to Stop 0x2E errors. For additional troubleshooting suggestions that apply to all Stop errors, see the section titled "Stop Message Checklist" later in this chapter.

- Stop 0x2E is typically the result of defective, malfunctioning, or failed memory hardware, such as memory modules, L2 SRAM cache, or video adapter RAM. If you added new hardware recently, remove the hardware and replace it to determine whether it is causing or contributing to the problem. Run Windows Memory Diagnostics as described in Chapter 30 to determine whether the feature has failed.
- Stop 0x2E messages can also occur after you install faulty drivers or system services. If a driver file name is given, you need to disable, remove, or roll back that driver. Disable the service or application and confirm that this resolves the error. If so, contact the hardware manufacturer about a possible update. Using updated software is especially important for backup programs, multimedia applications, antivirus scanners, and CD mastering tools.
- Hard disk corruption can also cause this Stop message. For more information about checking hard disk integrity, see Chapter 30.

- The problem might also be due to cracks, scratched traces, or defective features on the motherboard. If all else fails, take the system motherboard to a repair facility for diagnostic testing.

MORE INFO For more information about Stop 0x2E messages, see the Knowledge Base at *http://support.microsoft.com/*. Search the Knowledge Base using the keywords *0x0000002E* and *0x2E*.

Stop 0x3B or SYSTEM_SERVICE_EXCEPTION

The Stop 0x3B message indicates that an exception happened while executing a routine that transitions from nonprivileged code to privileged code.

Interpreting the Message

This Stop message has three parameters:

1. The exception that caused the bugcheck
2. The address of the exception record for the exception that caused the bugcheck
3. The address of the context record for the exception that caused the bugcheck

Resolving the Problem

This error has been linked to excessive paged pool usage and may occur due to user-mode graphics drivers crossing over and passing bad data to the kernel code. To resolve the problem, update to the latest driver for your video card. If you currently have the latest version installed, try rolling back to an earlier version.

MORE INFO For more information about Stop 0x3B messages, see the Knowledge Base at *http://support.microsoft.com/*. Search the Knowledge Base using the keywords *0x0000003B* and *0x3B*.

Stop 0x3F or NO_MORE_SYSTEM_PTES

The Stop 0x3F message indicates one or more of the following problems:

- The system Page Table Entries (PTEs) are depleted or fragmented because the system is performing a large number of input/output (I/O) actions.
- A faulty device driver is not managing memory properly.
- An application, such as a backup program, is improperly allocating large amounts of kernel memory.

Interpreting the Message

Depending on the configuration of your system, the value of the first parameter might vary. The following are possible values for the first parameter and the information returned:

- **0x0A** PTE type: 0x00 = system expansion, 0x01 = nonpaged pool expansion
- **0x0B** Requested size
- **0x0C** Total free system PTEs
- **0x0D** Total system PTEs

Resolving the Problem

The following suggestions are specific to Stop 0x3F errors. For additional troubleshooting suggestions that apply to all Stop errors, see the section titled "Stop Message Checklist" later in this chapter.

- Stop 0x3F messages can occur after you install faulty drivers or system services. If a driver file name is given, you need to disable, remove, or roll back that driver. Disable the service or application and confirm that this resolves the error. If so, contact the hardware manufacturer about a possible update. Using updated software is especially important for backup programs, multimedia applications, antivirus scanners, and CD mastering tools.
- The system might not actually be out of PTEs, but a contiguous memory block of sufficient size may not be available to satisfy a driver or application request. Check for the availability of updated driver or application files and consult the hardware or program documentation for minimum system requirements.

A related Stop message, 0xD8: DRIVER_USED_EXCESSIVE_PTES, is described in the section titled "Stop 0xD8 or DRIVER_USED_EXCESSIVE_PTES" later in this chapter.

> ***MORE INFO*** **For more information about Stop 0x3F messages, see the Knowledge Base at *http://support.microsoft.com/*. Search the Knowledge Base using the keywords *0x0000003F* and *0x3F*.**

Stop 0x50 or PAGE_FAULT_IN_NONPAGED_AREA

The Stop 0x50 message indicates that requested data was not in memory. The system generates an exception error when using a reference to an invalid system memory address. Defective memory (including main memory, L2 RAM cache, and video RAM) or incompatible software (including remote control and antivirus software) might cause Stop 0x50 messages.

Interpreting the Message

This Stop message has four parameters:

1. Memory address that caused the fault
2. Type of access (0x00 = read operation, 0x01 = write operation)
3. If not zero, the instruction address that referenced the address in parameter 0x01
4. This parameter is reserved (set aside for future use)

Resolving the Problem

The following suggestions are specific to Stop 0x50 errors. For additional troubleshooting suggestions that apply to all Stop errors, see the section titled "Stop Message Checklist" later in this chapter.

- If you added new hardware recently, remove and replace the hardware to determine whether it is causing or contributing to the problem. Run Windows Memory Diagnostics as described in Chapter 30 to determine whether the feature has failed.
- Stop 0x50 messages can also occur after you install faulty drivers or system services. If the driver file name is listed, you need to disable, remove, or roll back that driver. If not, disable the recently installed service or application to determine whether this resolves the error. If this does not resolve the problem, contact the hardware manufacturer for updates. Using updated drivers and software is especially important for network interface cards, video adapters, backup programs, multimedia applications, antivirus scanners, and CD mastering tools. If an updated driver is not available, attempt to use a driver from a similar device in the same family. For example, if printing to a Model 1100C printer causes Stop 0x50 errors, using a printer driver meant for a Model 1100A or Model 1000 might temporarily resolve the problem.
- Check your hard disk for problems. For more information, see Chapter 30.

MORE INFO **For more information about Stop 0x50 messages, see the Knowledge Base at *http://support.microsoft.com/*. Search the Knowledge Base using the keywords *0x00000050* and *0x50*. Specifically, refer to Knowledge Base article 938239.**

Stop 0x77 or KERNEL_STACK_INPAGE_ERROR

The Stop 0x77 message indicates that a page of kernel data requested from the paging (virtual memory) file could not be found or read into memory. This Stop message can also indicate disk hardware failure, disk data corruption, or possible virus infection.

Interpreting the Message

This Stop message has four parameters. The following set of definitions applies only if the first and third parameters are both zero:

1. This value is 0x00 (zero).

2. Value found in the stack.
3. This value is 0x00 (zero).
4. Address of signature on kernel stack.

Otherwise, the following definitions apply:

1. Status code
2. I/O status code
3. Page file number
4. Offset into page file

Frequently, you can determine the cause of this error from the second parameter, the I/O status code. Some common status codes include the following:

- 0xC000009A, or STATUS_INSUFFICIENT_RESOURCES, indicates a lack of nonpaged pool resources.
- 0xC000009C, or STATUS_DEVICE_DATA_ERROR, generally indicates bad blocks (sectors) on the hard disk.
- 0xC000009D, or STATUS_DEVICE_NOT_CONNECTED, indicates defective or loose data or power cables, a problem with SCSI termination, or improper controller or hard disk configuration.
- 0xC000016A, or STATUS_DISK_OPERATION_FAILED, also indicates bad blocks (sectors) on the hard disk.
- 0xC0000185, or STATUS_IO_DEVICE_ERROR, indicates improper termination, defective storage controller hardware, defective disk cabling, or two devices attempting to use the same system resources.

Resolving the Problem

The following suggestions are specific to Stop 0x77 errors. For additional troubleshooting suggestions that apply to all Stop errors, see the section titled "Stop Message Checklist" later in this chapter.

- Stop 0x77 messages can be caused by bad sectors in the virtual memory paging file or a disk controller error. In extremely rare cases, depleted nonpaged pool resources can cause this error. If the first and third parameters are zero, the stack signature in the kernel stack is missing, an error that is typically caused by defective hardware. If the I/O status is 0xC0000185 and the paging file is on a SCSI disk, check for cabling and termination issues. An I/O status code of 0xC000009C or 0xC000016A indicates that the requested data could not be found. You can try to correct this by restarting the computer. Additionally, use ChkDsk to check the disk for problems. For more information about ChkDsk, see Chapter 30.
- Another cause of Stop 0x77 messages is defective, malfunctioning, or failed memory hardware, such as memory modules, L2 SRAM cache, or video adapter RAM. If you

added new hardware recently, remove and replace the hardware to determine whether it is causing or contributing to the problem. Run Windows Memory Diagnostics as described in Chapter 30 to determine whether the feature has failed.

- The problem might also be due to cracks, scratched traces, or defective features on the motherboard. If all else fails, take the system motherboard to a repair facility for diagnostic testing.
- Problems that cause Stop 0x77 messages can also cause Stop 0x7A messages. For more information about Stop 0x7A messages, see the following section, "Stop 0x7A or KERNEL_DATA_INPAGE_ERROR."

> ***MORE INFO*** **For more information about Stop 0x77 messages, see the Knowledge Base at *http://support.microsoft.com/*. Search the Knowledge Base using the keywords *0x00000077* and *0x77*.**

Stop 0x7A or KERNEL_DATA_INPAGE_ERROR

The Stop 0x7A message indicates that a page of kernel data was not found in the paging (virtual memory) file and could not be read into memory. This might be due to incompatible disk or controller drivers, firmware, or hardware.

Interpreting the Message

This Stop message has four parameters:

1. Lock type value (0x01, 0x02, 0x03, or PTE address).
2. I/O status code.
3. If the lock type is 0x01, this parameter represents the current process; if the lock type is 0x03, this parameter represents the virtual address.
4. The virtual address that could not be read into memory.

Frequently, the cause of this error can be determined from the second parameter, the I/O status code. Some common status codes are the following:

- 0xC000009A, or STATUS_INSUFFICIENT_RESOURCES, indicates a lack of nonpaged pool resources.
- 0xC000009C, or STATUS_DEVICE_DATA_ERROR, indicates bad blocks (sectors) on the hard disk.
- 0xC000009D, or STATUS_DEVICE_NOT_CONNECTED, indicates defective or loose data or power cables, a problem with SCSI termination, or improper controller or disk configuration.
- 0xC000016A, or STATUS_DISK_OPERATION_FAILED, indicates bad blocks (sectors) on the hard disk.

- 0xC0000185, or STATUS_IO_DEVICE_ERROR, indicates improper termination, defective storage controller hardware, defective disk cabling, or two devices attempting to use the same resources.

Resolving the Problem

The following suggestions are specific to Stop 0x7A errors. For additional troubleshooting suggestions that apply to all Stop errors, see the section titled "Stop Message Checklist" later in this chapter.

- Stop 0x7A can be caused by bad sectors in the virtual memory paging file, disk controller error, virus infection, or memory hardware problems. In extremely rare cases, depleted nonpaged pool resources can cause this error. If the first and third parameters are zero, the stack signature in the kernel stack is missing, an error typically caused by defective hardware. If the I/O status is 0xC0000185 and the paging file is on a SCSI disk, check for cabling and termination issues. An I/O status code of 0xC000009C or 0xC000016A indicates that the requested data could not be found. You can try to correct this by restarting the computer. If a problem with disk integrity exists, Autochk—a program that attempts to mark bad disk sectors as defective so that they are not used in the future—starts automatically. If Autochk fails to run, you can manually perform the integrity check yourself by following the instructions to run ChkDsk provided in the section titled "Stop 0x24 or NTFS_FILE_SYSTEM" earlier in this chapter. For more information about ChkDsk, see Chapter 30.
- Another cause of Stop 0x7A messages is defective, malfunctioning, or failed memory hardware, such as memory modules, L2 SRAM cache, or video adapter RAM. If you added new hardware recently, remove and replace the hardware to determine whether it is causing or contributing to the problem. Run Windows Memory Diagnostics as described in Chapter 30 to determine whether the feature has failed.
- Check the hardware manufacturer's Web site for updates to disk adapter firmware or drivers that improve compatibility. Verify that your disks and controller support the same set of advanced features, such as higher transfer rates. If necessary, select a slower transfer rate if an update is not yet available. Consult your hardware or device documentation for more information.
- The problem might also be due to cracks, scratched traces, or defective features on the motherboard. If all else fails, take the system motherboard to a repair facility for diagnostic testing.
- Problems that cause Stop 0x7A messages can also cause Stop 0x77 messages. For more information about Stop 0x77 messages, see the section titled "Stop 0x77 or KERNEL_STACK_INPAGE_ERROR" earlier in this chapter.

MORE INFO **For more information about Stop 0x7A messages, see the Knowledge Base at *http://support.microsoft.com/.* Search the Knowledge Base using the keywords *0x0000007A* and *0x7A*.**

Stop 0x7B or INACCESSIBLE_BOOT_DEVICE

The Stop 0x7B message indicates that Windows has lost access to the system partition or boot volume during the startup process. Installing incorrect device drivers when installing or upgrading storage adapter hardware typically causes Stop 0x7B errors. Stop 0x7B errors could also indicate a possible virus infection.

Interpreting the Message

This Stop message has four parameters:

1. The address of a Unicode string data structure representing the Advanced RISC Computing (ARC) specification name of the device at which you attempted startup.
2. Pointer to ARC name string in memory.
3. This value is 0x00 (zero).
4. This value is 0x00 (zero).

The first parameter typically contains two separate pieces of data. For example, if the parameter is 0x00800020, 0x0020 is the actual length of the Unicode string and 0x0080 is the maximum ARC name string length. The next parameter contains the address of the buffer. This address is in system space, so the high-order bit is set.

If the file system is unable to mount the boot device or simply does not recognize the data on the boot device as a file system structure, the following parameter definition applies:

1. The address of the device object that could not be mounted.
2. Error code value or 0x00 (zero).
3. This value is 0x00 (zero).
4. This value is 0x00 (zero).

The value of the first parameter determines whether the parameter is a pointer to an ARC name string (ARC names are a generic method of identifying devices within the ARC environment) or a device object because a Unicode string never has an odd number of bytes, and a device object always has a Type code of 0003.

The second parameter is very important, because it can indicate whether the Stop 0x7B message was caused by file system issues or problems with storage hardware and drivers. Values of 0xC000034 or 0xC000000E typically indicate:

- Disks or storage controllers that are failing, defective, or improperly configured.
- Storage-related drivers or programs (tape management software, for example) that are not fully compatible with Windows.

Resolving the Problem

The following suggestions are specific to Stop 0x7B errors. For additional troubleshooting suggestions that apply to all Stop errors, see the section titled "Stop Message Checklist" later in this chapter.

- During I/O system initialization, the controller or driver for the startup device (typically the hard disk) might have failed to initialize the necessary hardware. File system initialization might have failed because of disk or controller failure or because the file system did not recognize the data on the boot device.
- Repartitioning disks, adding new disks, or upgrading to a new disk controller might cause the information in the Windows Boot Manager or boot configuration data (BCD) file to become outdated. If this Stop message occurs after you install new disks to your system, edit the BCD file or adjust the Boot Manager parameters to allow the system to start. If the error occurs after upgrading the disk controller, verify that the new hardware is functioning and correctly configured. For more information about Windows Boot Manager, the BCD file, and automatically correcting configuration problems, see Chapter 29.
- Verify that the system firmware and disk controller BIOS settings are correct and that the storage device was properly installed. If you are unsure, consult your computer's documentation about restoring default firmware settings or configuring your system to auto-detect settings. If the error occurs during Windows setup, the problem might be due to unsupported disk controller hardware. In some cases, drivers for new hardware are not in the Driver.cab library, and you need to provide additional drivers to complete Windows setup successfully. If this is the case, follow the hardware manufacturer's instructions when installing drivers. Periodically check for driver and firmware updates.
- Hard disk corruption can also cause this Stop message. For more information about checking hard disk integrity, see the instructions provided in the section titled "Stop 0x24 or NTFS_FILE_SYSTEM" earlier in this chapter.
- Problems that cause 0x7B errors might also cause Stop 0xED errors. For more information about Stop 0xED messages, see the section titled "Stop 0xED or UNMOUNTABLE_BOOT_VOLUME" later in this chapter.

MORE INFO For more information about Stop 0x7B messages, see the Knowledge Base at *http://support.microsoft.com/*. Search the Knowledge Base using the keywords *0x0000007B*, *0x7B*, and *Txtsetup.oem*. Specifically, refer to Knowledge Base article 935806.

Stop 0x7F or UNEXPECTED_KERNEL_MODE_TRAP

The Stop 0x7F message indicates that one of three types of problems occurred in kernel mode:

- A condition that the kernel is not allowed to have or intercept (also known as a *bound trap*)
- Software problems
- Hardware failures

Interpreting the Message

This Stop message has four parameters:

1. Processor exception code.
2. This value is 0x00 (zero).
3. This value is 0x00 (zero).
4. This value is 0x00 (zero).

The first parameter is the most important and can have several different values, indicating different causes of this error. You can find all conditions that cause a Stop 0x7F in any x86 microprocessor reference manual because they are specific to the x86 platform. Some of the most common exception codes are the following:

- 0x00, or a divide-by-zero error, occurs when a divide (DIV) instruction is run and the divisor is 0. Memory corruption, other hardware failures, or software problems can cause this message.
- 0x04, or Overflow, occurs when the processor carries out a call to an interrupt handler when the overflow (OF) flag is set.
- 0x05, or Bounds Check Fault, indicates that the processor, while carrying out a BOUND instruction, found that the operand exceeded the specified limits. BOUND instructions are used to ensure that a signed array index is within a certain range.
- 0x06, or Invalid Opcode, is generated when the processor attempts to run an invalid instruction. This typically occurs when the instruction pointer is corrupted as a result of a hardware memory problem and is pointing to a wrong location.
- 0x08, or Double Fault, indicates an exception while trying to call the handler for a prior exception. Normally, two exceptions can be handled serially, but certain exceptions (almost always caused by hardware problems) cause the processor to signal a double fault.

Less common codes include the following:

- **0x01** A system-debugger call
- **0x03** A debugger breakpoint
- **0x0A** A corrupted Task State Segment
- **0x0B** An access to a memory segment that was not present
- **0x0C** An access to memory beyond the limits of a stack
- **0x0D** An exception not covered by some other exception; a protection fault that pertains to access violations for applications

Resolving the Problem

The following suggestions are specific to Stop 0x7F errors. For additional troubleshooting suggestions that apply to all Stop errors, see the section titled "Stop Message Checklist" later in this chapter.

- Stop 0x7F messages are typically the result of defective, malfunctioning, or failed memory hardware. If you added new hardware recently, remove and replace the hardware to determine whether it is causing or contributing to the problem. Run Windows Memory Diagnostics as described in Chapter 30 to determine whether the feature has failed.
- Running the CPU beyond the rated specification, known as *overclocking*, can cause Stop 0x7F or other error messages because of heat buildup. When diagnosing problems on overclocked systems, first restore all clock and bus speed settings to the manufacturer-recommended values to determine whether this resolves the issues.
- The problem might also be due to cracks, scratched traces, or defective features on the motherboard. If all else fails, take the system motherboard to a repair facility for diagnostic testing.
- Stop 0x7F messages can occur after you install incompatible applications, drivers, or system services. Contact the software manufacturer about possible Windows 7–specific updates. Using updated software is especially important for backup programs, multimedia applications, antivirus scanners, and CD mastering tools.

> ***MORE INFO*** **For more information about Stop 0x7F messages, see the Knowledge Base at *http://support.microsoft.com/*. Search the Knowledge Base using the keywords *0x0000007F* and *0x7F*.**

Stop 0x9F or DRIVER_POWER_STATE_FAILURE

The Stop 0x9F message indicates that a driver is in an inconsistent or invalid power state.

Interpreting the Message

Table 32-1 describes the information provided by Stop 0x9F messages. The value of the first parameter indicates the type of violation (see the Description column) and determines the meaning of the next three parameters.

TABLE 32-1 Parameter Listings for Stop Message 0x9F

PARAMETER 1	PARAMETER 2	PARAMETER 3	PARAMETER 4	DESCRIPTION
0x01	Pointer to the device object	Reserved	Reserved	The device object being freed still has an incomplete power request pending.
0x02	Pointer to the target device object	Pointer to the device object	Reserved	The device object completed the I/O request packet for the system power state request but failed to call PoStartNextPowerIrp.
0x03	Pointer to the target device object	Pointer to the device object	The I/O request packet	The device driver did not properly set the I/O request packets pending or complete the I/O request packet.
0x00000100	Pointer to the nonpaged device object	Pointer to the target device object	Pointer to the device object to notify	The device objects in the devnode were inconsistent in their use of DO_POWER_PAGABLE.
0x00000101	Child device object	Child device object	Parent device object	A parent device object has detected that a child device has not set the DO_POWER_PAGABLE bit.

This Stop error typically occurs during events that involve power state transitions, such as shutting down, suspending, or resuming from sleep.

Resolving the Problem

The following suggestions are specific to Stop 0x9F errors. For additional troubleshooting suggestions that apply to all Stop errors, see the section titled "Stop Message Checklist" later in this chapter.

- Stop 0x9F messages can occur after you install faulty applications, drivers, or system services. If a file is listed by name and you can associate it with an application, uninstall the application. For drivers, disable, remove, or roll back that driver to determine whether this resolves the error. If it does, contact the hardware manufacturer for a possible update. Using updated software is especially important for backup programs, multimedia applications, antivirus scanners, and CD mastering tools.
- Stop 0x9F messages can occur when you perform one of the following operations:
  - Connect to a shared printer on the network, and then run the "Common Scenario Stress with IO" test in Driver Test Manager (DTM).
  - Print to a shared printer on the network.

- Perform a power management operation. For example, put the computer to sleep or into hibernation. Or wake the computer from sleep or from hibernation.

MORE INFO For more information about Stop 0x9F messages, see the Knowledge Base at *http://support.microsoft.com/*. Search the Knowledge Base using the keywords *0x0000009F* and *0x9F*. Specifically, refer to Knowledge Base articles 937322, 941858, 937322, 937500, and 931671.

Stop 0xBE or ATTEMPTED_WRITE_TO_READONLY_MEMORY

The Stop 0xBE message indicates that a driver attempted to write to read-only memory.

Interpreting the Message

This Stop message has four parameters:

1. Virtual address of attempted write
2. PTE contents
3. Reserved
4. Reserved

Resolving the Problem

A Stop 0xBE message might occur after you install a faulty device driver, system service, or firmware. If a Stop message lists a driver by name, disable, remove, or roll back that driver to correct the problem. If disabling or removing drivers resolves the issues, contact the manufacturer about a possible update. Using updated software is especially important for multimedia applications, antivirus scanners, DVD playback, and CD mastering tools.

MORE INFO For more information about Stop 0xBE messages, see the Knowledge Base at *http://support.microsoft.com/*. Search the Knowledge Base using the keywords *0x000000BE* and *0xBE*.

Stop 0xC2 or BAD_POOL_CALLER

The Stop 0xC2 message indicates that a kernel-mode process or driver incorrectly attempted to perform memory operations in the following ways:

- By allocating a memory pool size of zero bytes
- By allocating a memory pool that does not exist
- By attempting to free a memory pool that is already free
- By allocating or freeing a memory pool at an IRQL that was too high

This Stop message is typically the result of a faulty driver or software.

Interpreting the Message

Table 32-2 describes the information provided by Stop 0xC2 messages. The value of the first parameter indicates the type of violation (see the Description column) and determines the meaning of the next three parameters.

TABLE 32-2 Parameter Listings for Stop Message 0xC2

PARAMETER 1	PARAMETER 2	PARAMETER 3	PARAMETER 4	DESCRIPTION
0x00	This value is always 0	The pool type being allocated	The pool tag being used	The caller is requesting a zero-byte pool allocation
0x01, 0x02, or 0x04	Pointer to pool header	First part of pool header contents	This value is always zero	Pool header has been corrupted
0x06	Reserved	Pointer to pool header	Pool header contents	Attempt to free a memory pool that was already freed
0x07	Reserved	Pointer to pool header	This value is always zero	Attempt to free a memory pool that was already freed
0x08	Current IRQL	Pool type	Size of allocation	Attempt to allocate pool at invalid IRQL
0x09	Current IRQL	Pool type	Address of pool	Attempt to free pool at invalid IRQL
0x40	Starting address	Start of system ad-dress space	This value is always zero	Attempt to free usermode address to kernel pool
0x41	Starting address	Physical page frame	Highest physical page frame	Attempt to free a nonallocated nonpaged pool address
0x42 or 0x43	Address being freed	This value is always zero	This value is always zero	Attempt to free a virtual address that was never in any pool
0x50	Starting address	Start offset in pages from beginning of paged pool	Size in bytes of paged pool	Attempt to free a nonallocated paged pool address
0x99	Address being freed	This value is always zero	This value is always zero	Attempt to free pool with invalid address or corruption in pool header
0x9A	Pool type	Size of allocation in bytes	Allocation's pool tag	Attempt to allocate must succeed

Resolving the Problem

The following suggestions are specific to Stop 0xC2 errors. For additional troubleshooting suggestions that apply to all Stop errors, see the section titled "Stop Message Checklist" later in this chapter.

- A Stop 0xC2 message might occur after you install a faulty device driver, system service, or firmware. If a Stop message lists a driver by name, disable, remove, or roll back that driver to correct the problem. If disabling or removing drivers resolves the issues, contact the manufacturer about a possible update. Using updated software is especially important for multimedia applications, antivirus scanners, DVD playback, and CD mastering tools.
- A Stop 0xC2 message might also be due to failing or defective hardware. If a Stop message points to a category of devices (such as disk controllers, for example), try removing or replacing the hardware to determine whether it is causing the problem. For more information, see Chapter 30.
- If you encounter a Stop 0xC2 message while upgrading to Windows, the problem might be due to an incompatible driver, system service, virus scanner, or backup. To avoid problems while upgrading, simplify your hardware configuration and remove all third-party device drivers and system services (including virus scanners) prior to running setup. After you have successfully installed Windows, contact the hardware manufacturer to obtain compatible updates.

> ***MORE INFO*** **For more information about Stop 0xC2 messages, see the Knowledge Base at *http://support.microsoft.com/*. Search the Knowledge Base using the keywords *0x000000C2* and *0xC2*.**

Stop 0xCE or DRIVER_UNLOADED_WITHOUT_CANCELLING_PENDING_OPERATIONS

This Stop message indicates that a driver failed to cancel pending operations before exiting.

Interpreting the Message

This Stop message has four parameters:

1. Memory address referenced
2. Type of access (0x00 = read operation, 0x01 = write operation)
3. If non-zero, the address of the instruction that referenced the incorrect memory location
4. Reserved

Resolving the Problem

Stop 0xCE messages can occur after you install faulty drivers or system services. If a driver is listed by name, disable, remove, or roll back that driver to resolve the error. If disabling or removing drivers resolves the error, contact the manufacturer about a possible update. Using updated software is especially important for backup programs, multimedia applications, antivirus scanners, DVD playback, and CD mastering tools.

> ***MORE INFO*** **For more information about Stop 0xCE messages, see the Knowledge Base at** ***http://support.microsoft.com/.*** **Search the Knowledge Base using the keywords** ***0x000000CE*** **and** ***0xCE.***

Stop 0xD1 or IRQL_NOT_LESS_OR_EQUAL

The Stop 0xD1 message indicates that the system attempted to access pageable memory using a kernel process IRQL that was too high. Drivers that have used improper addresses typically cause this error.

Interpreting the Message

This Stop message has four parameters:

1. Memory referenced
2. IRQL at time of reference
3. Type of access (0x00 = read operation, 0x01 = write operation)
4. Address that referenced memory

Resolving the Problem

Stop 0xD1 messages can occur after you install faulty drivers or system services. If a driver is listed by name, disable, remove, or roll back that driver to resolve the error. If disabling or removing drivers resolves the error, contact the manufacturer about a possible update. Using updated software is especially important for backup programs, multimedia applications, antivirus scanners, DVD playback, and CD mastering tools.

> ***MORE INFO*** **For more information about Stop 0xD1 messages, see the Knowledge Base at** ***http://support.microsoft.com/.*** **Search the Knowledge Base using the keywords** ***0x000000D1*** **and** ***0xD1.***

Stop 0xD8 or DRIVER_USED_EXCESSIVE_PTES

The Stop 0xD8 message typically occurs if your computer runs out of PTEs because a driver requests large amounts of kernel memory.

Interpreting the Message

Depending on the configuration of your system, the number of parameters returned might vary. The four possible values are:

1. If this parameter has a non-null value, it contains the name of the driver that caused the Stop error.
2. If the first parameter has a non-null value, this parameter contains the number of PTEs used by the driver that is causing the error.
3. This parameter represents the total number of free system PTEs.
4. This parameter represents the total number of system PTEs.

Resolving the Problem

For suggestions about resolving problems related to inadequate PTEs, see the section titled "Stop 0x3F or NO_MORE_SYSTEM_PTES" earlier in this chapter.

MORE INFO For more information about Stop 0xD8 messages, see the Knowledge Base at *http://support.microsoft.com/*. Search the Knowledge Base using the keywords *0x000000D8* and *0xD8*.

Stop 0xEA or THREAD_STUCK_IN_DEVICE_DRIVER

In Stop 0xEA errors, a device driver problem is causing the system to pause indefinitely. Typically, this problem is caused by a display driver waiting for the video hardware to enter an idle state. This might indicate a hardware problem with the video adapter or a faulty video driver.

Interpreting the Message

This Stop message has four parameters:

1. Pointer to the thread object that is caught in an infinite loop
2. Pointer to a DEFERRED_WATCHDOG object, which is useful when using a kernel debugger to find out more information about this problem
3. Pointer to Graphics Device Interface (GDI)–supplied context
4. Additional debugging information

Resolving the Problem

Stop 0xEA messages can occur after you install faulty drivers (especially video drivers) or system services. If a driver is listed by name, disable, remove, or roll back that driver to resolve the error. If disabling or removing drivers resolves the error, contact the manufacturer about a possible update. Using updated software is especially important for backup programs, multimedia applications, antivirus scanners, DVD playback, and CD mastering tools.

> ***MORE INFO*** **For more information about Stop 0xEA messages, see the Knowledge Base at *http://support.microsoft.com/*. Search the Knowledge Base using the keywords *0x000000EA* and *0xEA*.**

Stop 0xED or UNMOUNTABLE_BOOT_VOLUME

The kernel-mode I/O subsystem attempted to mount the boot volume and failed. This error might also occur during an upgrade to Windows 7 on systems that use higher-throughput ATA disks or controllers with incorrect cabling. In some cases, your system might appear to work normally after you restart.

Interpreting the Message

This Stop message has two parameters:

1. Device object of the boot volume
2. Status code from the file system on why it failed to mount the volume

Resolving the Problem

The following suggestions are specific to Stop 0xED errors. For additional troubleshooting suggestions that apply to all Stop errors, see the section titled "Stop Message Checklist" later in this chapter.

- If you are using higher-throughput ATA disks and controllers, which are those capable of data transfer rates above 33.3 MB/sec, replace the standard 40-pin cable with an 80-pin cable. Using an 80-pin cable is optional for transfer rates up to and including 33.3 MB/sec, but it is mandatory for higher transfer rates. The additional grounded pins are required to avoid data loss.
- Some firmware allows you to force higher transfer rates even when you are using the incorrect cable type. Your firmware might issue a warning but allow the startup process to proceed. Restore the default firmware setting for ATA cable detection.
- Problems that cause 0xED errors might also cause Stop 0x7B errors. For more information about 0x7B Stop messages, see the section titled "Stop 0x7B or INACCESSIBLE_BOOT_DEVICE" earlier in this chapter.

MORE INFO For more information about Stop 0xED messages, see the Knowledge Base at *http://support.microsoft.com/*. Search the Knowledge Base using the keywords *0x000000ED* and *0xED*.

Stop 0xFE or BUGCODE_USB_DRIVER

The Stop 0xFE message occurs if the kernel detects an error in a USB driver.

Interpreting the Message

This Stop message has four parameters. Parameter 1 indicates the type of violation, whereas parameters 2 through 4 provide more information specific to that error type. Typically, only parameter 1 is useful to system administrators, although parameters 2 through 4 might be useful to Microsoft developers, who will be able to extract that information from the memory dump.

Parameter 1 can have a value of 0x1 to 0x5, as described here:

1. An internal error has occurred in the USB stack.
2. The USB client driver has submitted a USB request block (URB) that is still attached to another I/O request packet (IRP) that is pending in the bus driver.
3. The USB miniport driver has generated a Stop error. This usually happens in response to a catastrophic hardware failure.
4. The caller has submitted an IRP that is already pending in the USB driver.
5. A hardware failure has occurred because of a bad physical address found in a hardware data structure. This is not due to a driver bug.

Resolving the Problem

The following suggestions are specific to Stop 0xFE errors. For additional troubleshooting suggestions that apply to all Stop errors, see the section titled "Stop Message Checklist" later in this chapter.

To resolve this problem, follow these procedures:

1. Check the computer or motherboard manufacturer's Web site for updated system firmware.
2. Upgrade the firmware and drivers of all USB devices attached to the computer.
3. Verify that all hardware is compatible with Windows 7.
4. Remove USB devices and external hubs one by one and determine whether the Stop error reoccurs. If the Stop error does not reoccur when a specific device is not attached, that device might be malfunctioning, or it might not be compatible with Windows. Contact the device manufacturer for additional support.
5. If problems persist, you might have a computer hardware failure. Contact your computer manufacturer for additional assistance.

MORE INFO For more information about Stop 0xFE messages, see the Knowledge Base at *http://support.microsoft.com/*. Search the Knowledge Base using the keywords *0x000000FE* and *0xFE*. Specifically, refer to Knowledge Base article 934374.

Stop 0x00000124

The Stop 0x00000124 message occurs when Windows has a problem handling a PCI-Express device. Most often, this occurs when adding or removing a hot-pluggable PCI-Express card; however, it can occur with driver- or hardware-related problems for PCI-Express cards.

Resolving the Problem

To troubleshoot 0x00000124 stop errors, first make sure you have applied all Windows updates and driver updates. If you recently updated a driver, roll back the change. If the stop error continues to occur, remove PCI-Express cards one by one to identify the problematic hardware. When you have identified the card causing the problem, contact the hardware manufacturer for further troubleshooting assistance. The driver might need to be updated, or the card itself could be faulty.

MORE INFO For more information about Stop 0x00000124 messages, see the Knowledge Base at *http://support.microsoft.com/*. Search using the keyword *0x00000124*.

Stop 0xC000021A or STATUS_SYSTEM_PROCESS_TERMINATED

The Stop 0xC000021A message occurs when Windows switches into kernel mode and a user-mode subsystem, such as Winlogon or the Client Server Runtime Subsystem (CSRSS), is compromised and security can no longer be guaranteed. Because Windows cannot run without Winlogon or CSRSS, this is one of the few situations in which the failure of a user-mode service can cause the system to stop responding. You cannot use the kernel debugger in this situation because the error occurred in a user-mode process.

A Stop 0xC000021A message can also occur when the computer is restarted after a system administrator has modified permissions in such a way that the System account no longer has adequate permissions to access system files and folders.

Interpreting the Message

This Stop message has three parameters:

1. Status code.
2. This value is 0x00 (zero).
3. This value is 0x00 (zero).

Resolving the Problem

The following suggestions are specific to Stop 0x21A errors. For additional troubleshooting suggestions that apply to all Stop errors, see the section titled "Stop Message Checklist" later in this chapter.

- Stop 0xC000021A messages occur in a user-mode process. The most common causes are third-party applications. If the error occurs after you install a new or updated device driver, system service, or third-party application, you need to remove, disable, or roll back the driver or uninstall the new software. Contact the software manufacturer about a possible update.
- A system file mismatch caused by partially restoring the system from backup media might cause this error. (Some backup programs do not restore files that they determine are in use.) Always use backup software that is Windows 7 compatible.

> ***MORE INFO*** **For more information about Stop 0xC000021A messages, see the Knowledge Base at *http://support.microsoft.com/.* Search using the keyword *0xC000021A*.**

Stop 0xC0000221 or STATUS_IMAGE_CHECKSUM_ MISMATCH

The Stop 0xC0000221 message indicates driver, system file, or disk corruption problems (such as a damaged paging file). Faulty memory hardware can also cause this Stop message to appear.

Interpreting the Message

This Stop message typically displays the name of the damaged file as follows.

```
STOP: 0xC0000221 STATUS_IMAGE_CHECKSUM_MISMATCH <path>\<file name>
- or -
Unable to load device driver <driver_name>
```

Resolving the Problem

The following suggestions are specific to Stop 0xC0000221 errors. For additional trouble-shooting suggestions that apply to all Stop errors, see the section titled "Stop Message Checklist" later in this chapter.

- You can use Driver Rollback or System Restore from safe mode to restore a previous driver. You can also use Windows 7 recovery features, such as the Last Known Good Configuration startup option, Backup, or Automated System Recovery, to restore a previous working configuration. For more information, see Chapter 29. After restoring from backup media, you might need to reapply service packs or hotfixes, depending on when the backups were made.

- If the Stop message names the specific file, try replacing it manually with a fresh copy from another Windows computer using safe mode or Startup Repair. For more information, see Chapter 30.
- Stop message 0xC000026C, caused by similar conditions, provides the name of the system file. You can also use the preceding suggestions to resolve this error.

> ***MORE INFO*** **For more information about Stop 0xC0000221 messages, see the Knowledge Base at *http://support.microsoft.com/*. Search using the keyword *0xC0000221*.**

Hardware Malfunction Messages

Stop messages also take the form of hardware malfunction messages. Like all Stop messages, they are displayed in non-windowed text mode. These Stop messages occur after the processor detects a hardware malfunction; the first one or two lines of the message contain a description. The error description typically points to a hardware problem, as shown in this example.

```
Hardware malfunction.
Call your hardware vendor for support.
```

Prior to proceeding with the recommendation provided by the message, it is best to contact the manufacturer for technical support. Record the information displayed after the first two lines of the message, which might prove useful to the support technician.

Under certain circumstances, driver problems can generate Stop messages that appear to be related to a hardware malfunction. For example, if a driver writes to the wrong I/O port, the device at the destination port might respond by generating a hardware malfunction message. Errors of this kind, which are typically detected and debugged in advance of public release, underscore the need to periodically check for updated drivers.

Stop Message Checklist

Stop messages provide diagnostic information, such as Stop codes and driver names, that you can use to resolve the problem. However, this information disappears when you restart your computer. Therefore, for future reference, it is important to record the information displayed. When a Stop message appears, follow these steps before restarting the system:

1. Record any data found in the Bugcheck Information and Driver Information sections for future reference.
2. Record and evaluate suggestions found in the Recommended User Action section. Stop messages typically provide troubleshooting tips relevant to the error.

3. Check the Stop message Debug Port and Dump Status Information section to verify that Windows successfully dumped memory contents to the paging file. Then proceed with your troubleshooting efforts.
4. After you resolve the problem or can at least start the computer, you can copy the memory dump file to another location, such as removable media, for further evaluation. Analyzing memory dump files can assist you with identifying root causes by providing you with detailed information about the system state when the Stop message occurred. For more information about creating and analyzing memory dump files, see the section titled "Memory Dump Files" earlier in this chapter.

By following the preceding steps, you can save important information to which you can refer when using the resources listed in the section titled "Stop Message Overview" earlier in this chapter. Stop messages do not always point to the root of the problem, but they do provide important clues that you or a trained support technician can use to identify and troubleshoot a problem.

Check Your Software

The following are useful software-related techniques that you can use to recover from problems that cause Stop messages.

Check Software Disk Space Requirements

Verify that adequate free space exists on your disk volumes for virtual memory paging files and application data files. Insufficient free space might cause Stop messages and other symptoms, including disk corruption. Always check the minimum system requirements recommended by the software publisher before installing an application. To determine the amount allocated to paging files, see the section titled "Memory Dump Files" earlier in this chapter. You can move, delete, or compress unused files manually or by using Disk Cleanup (Cleanmgr.exe) to increase free space on disk volumes.

Use the Last Known Good Configuration

If a Stop message occurs immediately after you install new software or drivers, use the Last Known Good Configuration startup option to undo the registry and driver changes. To use this option, restart your computer and then press F8 when prompted to activate the Windows Advanced Options menu. Last Known Good Configuration is one of the available options. For more information about Windows startup and recovery options, see Chapter 29.

Use Disaster Recovery Features

Disaster recovery features such as System Restore and Driver Rollback can undo recent changes. For more information about recovery options, see Chapter 29.

Restart the System in Safe Mode

Safe mode is a diagnostic environment that loads a minimum set of drivers and system services, increasing your chances of successfully starting the operating system. After Windows has started, you can enable or disable drivers and make the necessary changes to restore stability. To enter safe mode, restart your computer and then press F8 when prompted to activate the Windows Advanced Options menu. Safe mode is one of the available options. For more information about startup and recovery options, see Chapter 29.

Use Startup Repair

You can use Startup Repair to perform advanced operations, such as replacing corrupted files. You can also disable a service by renaming the file specified in a Stop message. For more information about using Startup Repair to recover from startup problems, see Chapter 29.

Check Event Viewer Logs

Check the Event Viewer System and Application logs for warnings or error message patterns that point to an application or service. Record this information and refer to it when searching for more information or when contacting technical support.

Check Application and Driver Compatibility

Categories of software known to cause Stop messages if they are not fully compatible with Windows 7 (such as those meant for previous versions of Windows) include backup, remote control, multimedia, CD mastering, Internet firewall, and antivirus tools. If temporarily disabling a driver or uninstalling software resolves the problem, contact the manufacturer for information about an update or workaround. You need to disable a service that is causing Stop errors or other problems rather than stop or pause it. A stopped or paused service runs after you restart the computer. For more information about disabling services for diagnostic or troubleshooting purposes, see Chapter 29.

Install Compatible Antivirus Tools

Virus infection can cause problems such as Stop errors (for example, Stop 0x7B) and data loss. Before running antivirus software, verify that you are using updated virus signature files. Signature files provide information that allows the antivirus scanning software to identify viruses. Using current signature files increases the chances of detecting the most recent viruses. Verify that your virus scanner product checks the Master Boot Record (MBR) and the boot sector. For more information about MBR and boot sector viruses, see Chapter 30.

Check for and Install Service Pack Updates

Microsoft periodically releases service packs containing updated system files, security enhancements, and other improvements that can resolve problems. You can use Windows Update to check for and install the latest versions as they become available. To check the service pack revision installed on your system, click Start, right-click Computer, and then click Properties. For more information about Windows Update, see Chapter 23, "Managing Software Updates."

Report Your Errors

You can find out more information about the conditions that caused the Stop message by using WER. For more information about options for analyzing memory dump files, see the section titled "Using Memory Dump Files to Analyze Stop Errors" earlier in this chapter.

Install Operating System and Driver Updates

Occasionally, Microsoft and third parties release software updates to fix known problems. For more information about software updates, read Chapter 23.

Check Information Sources

You might find information about a workaround or solution to the problem. Information sources include the Knowledge Base and the manufacturer's technical support Web page.

Install and Use a Kernel Debugger

You can use a kernel debugger to gather more information about the problem. The Debugging Tools Help file contains instructions and examples that can help you find additional information about the Stop error affecting you. For more information about installing and using debugging tools, see the sections titled "Stop Message Overview" and "Using Memory Dump Files to Analyze Stop Errors" earlier in this chapter.

Check Your Hardware

You can use the following hardware-related techniques to recover from problems that cause Stop messages.

Restore a Previous Configuration

If a Stop message appears immediately after you add new hardware, see if removing or replacing the part and restoring a previous configuration resolves the problem. You can use recovery features such as Last Known Good Configuration, Driver Rollback, and System Restore to restore the system to the previous configuration or to remove a specific driver. For more information about startup and recovery options, see Chapter 29.

Check for Nondefault Firmware Settings

Some computers have firmware that you can use to change hardware settings such as power management parameters, video configuration, memory timing, and memory shadowing. Do not alter these settings unless you have a specific requirement to do so. If you are experiencing hardware problems, verify that the firmware values are set to the default values. To restore the default firmware values, follow the instructions provided by the computer or motherboard manufacturer.

Check for Non-Default Hardware Clock Speeds

Verify that the hardware is running at the correct speed. Do not set clock speeds for features such as the processor, video adapter, or memory above the rated specification (overclocking). This can cause random errors that are difficult to diagnose. If you are experiencing problems with overclocked hardware, restore default clock speed and CPU voltage settings according to the instructions provided by the hardware manufacturer.

Check for Hardware-Related Updates

Check the manufacturer's Web site to see if updated firmware is available for your system or individual peripherals.

Check by Running Hardware Diagnostic Tools

Run hardware diagnostic software to verify that your hardware is not defective. These tools are typically built into or bundled with your hardware.

Check ATA Disk and Controller Settings

If your system uses ATA storage devices such as hard disks, determine whether the firmware setting Primary IDE Only is available. If the setting is available, enable it if the second ATA channel is unused. Verify that primary and secondary device jumper settings are set correctly. Storage devices (including CD and DVD-ROM drives) use their own firmware, so check the manufacturer's Web site periodically for updates. Verify that you are using a cable that is compatible with your device—certain ATA standards require that you use a different cable type.

Check for SCSI Disk and Controller Settings

If your system uses an SCSI adapter, check for updates to device drivers and adapter firmware. Try disabling advanced SCSI firmware options, such as sync negotiation for low-bandwidth devices (tape drives and CD-ROM drives). Verify that you are using cables that meet the SCSI adapter's requirements for termination and maximum cable length. Check SCSI ID settings and termination to ensure that they are correct for all devices. For more information, see Chapter 30.

Check for Proper Hardware Installation and Connections

Verify that internal expansion boards and external devices are firmly seated and properly installed and that connecting cables are properly fastened. If necessary, clean adapter card electrical contacts using supplies available at electronics stores. For more information about troubleshooting hardware, see Chapter 30.

Check Memory Compatibility

If a Stop message appears immediately after you add new memory, verify that the new part is compatible with your system. Do not rely solely on physical characteristics (such as chip count or module dimensions) when purchasing new or replacement memory. Always adhere to the manufacturer's specifications when purchasing memory modules. For example, you can fit a memory module rated for 66-megahertz (MHz) or 100-MHz operation (PC66 or PC100 RAM, respectively) into a system using a 132-Mhz memory bus speed, and it might initially appear to work. However, using the slower memory results in system instability. To test memory, use Windows Memory Diagnostics, as described in Chapter 30.

Check by Temporarily Removing Devices

Installing a new device can sometimes cause resource conflicts with existing devices. You might recover from this problem by temporarily removing devices not needed to start the operating system. For example, temporarily removing a CD-ROM or audio adapter might allow you to start Windows. You can then examine the device and operating system settings separately to determine what changes you need to make. For more information about simplifying your hardware configuration for troubleshooting purposes, see Chapter 29.

Check by Replacing a Device

If you are unable to obtain diagnostic software for the problem device, install a replacement to verify that this action resolves the problem. If the problem disappears, the original hardware might be defective or incorrectly configured.

Check Information Sources

You might be able to find information about a workaround or solution to the problem. Information sources include the Knowledge Base and the manufacturer's technical support Web page.

Contact Technical Support

As a last resort, Microsoft technical support can assist you with troubleshooting. For more information about Microsoft technical support options, see the Support link on the Microsoft Web site at *http://www.microsoft.com*.

Summary

Stop errors can be frustrating to troubleshoot. However, by following the procedures outlined in this chapter, you can identify the source of Stop errors and begin working to resolve them. Most of the time, Stop errors are caused by drivers or faulty hardware. If Stop errors are caused by drivers, you need to work with the hardware manufacturer to develop an improved driver. If a Stop error is caused by faulty hardware, you should repair or replace the hardware.

Additional Resources

These resources contain additional information and tools related to this chapter.

Related Information

- Chapter 16, "Managing Disks and File Systems," includes information about configuring disks.
- Chapter 17, "Managing Devices and Services," includes information about configuring services to start automatically.
- Chapter 29, "Configuring Startup and Troubleshooting Startup Issues," includes information about using safe mode and Startup Repair.
- Chapter 30, "Troubleshooting Hardware, Driver, and Disk Issues," includes information about troubleshooting hardware- and driver-related network adapter problems.
- The Microsoft Global Escalation Services team blog, at *http://blogs.msdn.com/ntdebugging/*, includes useful articles about troubleshooting stop errors and other complex problems.
- The Windows Driver Kit (WDK) includes information about Stop errors not listed here. To download the WDK, visit *http://www.microsoft.com/whdc/DevTools/WDK/WDKpkg.mspx*.

On the Companion Media

- Get-MiniDump.ps1
- Get-MiniDumpCount.ps1
- Set-MiniDumpCount.ps1

Appendix

Accessibility in Windows 7

THE WINDOWS 7 OPERATING system improves the accessibility features and programs that were included in the Windows Vista operating system, making it easier than ever for individuals with physical and cognitive difficulties to see, hear, and use their computers. These accessibility settings and programs are particularly helpful to people with visual difficulties, hearing loss, pain in their hands or arms, or reasoning and cognitive issues.

- **Visual difficulties** Include poor lighting conditions, individuals who have low vision, or individuals who are blind.
- **Dexterity difficulties** Include pain in the hands, arms, or wrists, or difficulty using a keyboard, mouse, other pointing device, or pen.
- **Hearing difficulties** Include environments with high background noise and individuals who are hard of hearing or deaf.
- **Reasoning and cognitive issues** Include difficulty concentrating and focusing on tasks, difficulty remembering things, and learning disabilities such as dyslexia.

Ease of Access Center

The Ease of Access Center (shown in Figure A-1) provides a convenient, central location where the user can quickly adjust accessibility settings and manage assistive technology (AT) programs. The Ease of Access Center replaces the Accessibility Wizard and the Utilities Manager found in Microsoft Windows XP and earlier versions.

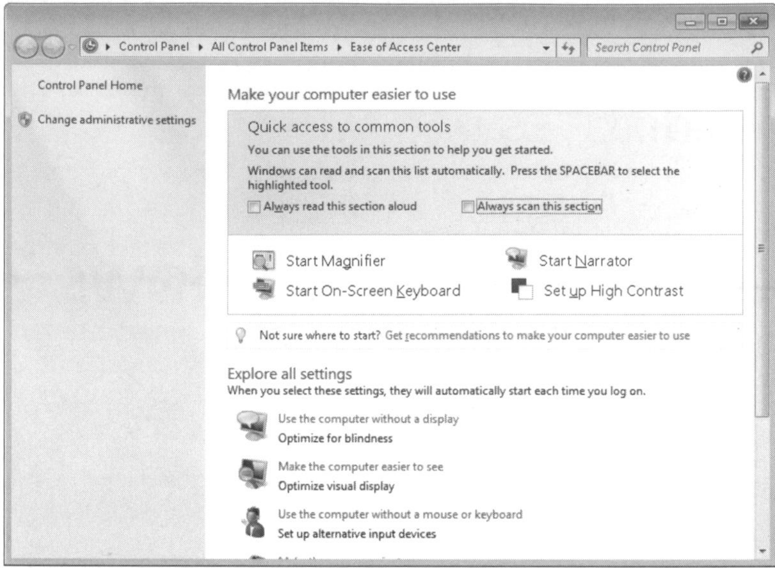

FIGURE A-1 The Ease of Access Center

With the Ease of Access Center, the user can enable and configure the following accessibility settings:

- **Start Narrator** Opens Microsoft Narrator, a text-to-speech program that reads on-screen text aloud and describes some events (such as error messages appearing) that happen while you are using the computer.
- **Start Magnifier** Enlarges a portion of the screen where the user is working. You can choose magnification levels from 2 to 16 times the original, as well as whether to track the mouse, the keyboard, and/or text editing. You can also choose between three modes: docked (existed in Windows XP), full screen, and lens mode (new in Windows 7).
- **Start On-Screen Keyboard** Opens a visual, on-screen keyboard with all the standard keys that you can use instead of a physical keyboard. On-Screen Keyboard lets you type using an alternative input device. On-Screen Keyboard also features text prediction (only on the Windows 7 Home Premium Edition operating system and higher editions) as well as Hover mode (so no clicking is necessary) and Scan mode (for single-click input).
- **High Contrast** Heightens the color contrast of some text and images on your computer screen, making those items more distinct and easier to identify.
- **Make The Focus Rectangle Thicker** Thickens the rectangle around the currently selected item in a dialog box.
- **Turn On Sticky Keys** Instead of having to press multiple keys at once (such as pressing the Ctrl, Alt, and Del keys simultaneously to log on to Windows), you can press one key at a time when Sticky Keys is turned on.

- **Turn On Toggle Keys** Causes Windows to play an alert when Caps Lock, Num Lock, or Scroll Lock is pressed.
- **Turn On Filter Keys** Causes Windows to ignore keystrokes that occur in rapid succession or keystrokes caused by unintentionally holding down keys for several seconds.
- **Underline Keyboard Shortcuts And Access Keys** Makes using the keyboard to access controls in dialog boxes easier.
- **Change The Color And Size Of Mouse Pointers** Makes the mouse pointer larger or a different color.
- **Activate A Window By Hovering Over It With A Mouse** Lets the user select and activate a window by pointing at it instead of clicking it.
- **Prevent windows from being automatically arranged when moved to the edge of the screen** Windows 7 introduces "snapping" of windows when moved to the edges of the screen to maximize the window or utilize exactly half of the screen. This option turns off this feature.
- **Turn On Mouse Keys** Lets users move the mouse pointer using the arrow keys on the keyboard or on the numeric keypad.
- **Turn On Audio Description** Causes Windows to use videos to describe what is happening on the computer.
- **Turn Off All Unnecessary Animations (Where Possible)** Turns off animation, such as fading effects when windows are closed.
- **Remove Background Images (Where Available)** Turns off all unimportant images, overlapping background content, and all background images.
- **Turn On Or Off High Contrast When Left Alt+Left Shift+Print Screen Is Pressed** Sets the screen to display using a high-contrast color scheme.
- **How Long Should Windows Notification Dialog Boxes Stay Open?** Specifies the time Windows notification dialog boxes are displayed before disappearing.
- **Turn On Visual Notifications For Sounds (Sound Sentry)** Replaces system sounds with visual cues such as a flashing caption bar, flashing window, or flashing desktop.
- **Turn On Text Captions For Spoken Dialog (When Available)** Displays text captions instead of sounds to indicate that activity is happening on your computer.

Additional Accessibility Features

Additional accessibility features not managed by the Ease of Access Center include the following:

- **Keyboard Shortcuts** Allows the user to control actions that programs perform using the keyboard instead of the mouse.
- **Windows Speech Recognition** Allows the user to interact with the computer using voice as an input device.

Table A-1 maps Windows 7 accessibility features with the types of challenges they can help to address.

TABLE A-1 Windows 7 Accessibility Features

ACCESSIBILITY FEATURE	VISUAL DIFFICULTIES	DEXTERITY PROBLEMS	HEARING DIFFICULTIES	REASONING AND COGNITIVE ISSUES
Use Narrator	✔			✔
Use Magnifier	✔			
Make The Focus Rectangle Thicker	✔			✔
Turn On Sticky Keys		✔		✔
Turn On Toggle Keys		✔		✔
Turn On Filter Keys		✔		✔
Underline Keyboard Shortcuts And Access Keys	✔	✔		
Change The Color And Size Of Mouse Pointers	✔	✔		✔
Activate A Window By Hovering Over It With A Mouse		✔		
Prevent windows from being automatically arranged when moved to the edge of the screen	✔	✔		✔
Turn On Mouse Keys		✔		✔
Turn On Audio Description	✔			
Turn Off All Unnecessary Animations (Where Possible)	✔			✔
Remove Background Images (Where Available)	✔			✔
Turn On Or Off High Contrast When Left Alt+Left Shift+Print Screen Is Pressed	✔			

ACCESSIBILITY FEATURE	VISUAL DIFFICULTIES	DEXTERITY PROBLEMS	HEARING DIFFICULTIES	REASONING AND COGNITIVE ISSUES
How Long Should Windows Notification Dialog Boxes Stay Open?	✔	✔		✔
Turn On Visual Notifications For Sounds (Sound Sentry)			✔	
Turn On Text Captions For Spoken Dialog (When Available)			✔	
Use On-Screen Keyboard		✔		
Keyboard Shortcuts		✔		
Windows Speech Recognition		✔		

Using the Ease of Access Center

To open the Ease of Access Center, do one of the following:

- Click Start, click Control Panel, click Ease Of Access, and then click Ease Of Access Center.
- Press the Windows logo key+U.

In addition, you can enable the following subset of Ease of Access features directly from the logon screen by clicking the Ease Of Access icon at the lower-left area of the logon screen:

- Narrator
- Magnifier
- High Contrast
- On-Screen Keyboard
- Sticky Keys
- Filter Keys

The Ease of Access Center includes the following:

- **Quick Access** Start Magnifier, Narrator, On-Screen Keyboard, and High Contrast.
- **Recommended Settings** Based on answers to questions about performing routine tasks, such as whether you have difficulty seeing faces or text on TV, hearing conversations, or using a pen or pencil, Windows 7 provides a personalized recommendation of the accessibility settings and programs that are likely to improve your ability to see, hear, and use your computer.

- **Explore available settings by category** The Ease of Access Center also lets you explore settings options by categories, including making the computer easier to see, using the computer without a display, changing mouse or keyboard settings, using the computer without a mouse or keyboard, using alternatives for sounds, and making it easier to focus on tasks.

When you enable accessibility features by using Quick Access To Common Tools, the features are available only during the current logon session; when you log off, the enabled features are disabled. To enable accessibility features and have them persist across logon sessions, use either Get Recommendations To Make Your Computer Easier To Use or Explore All Settings.

To ensure that Magnifier, On-Screen Keyboard, and Narrator are also available at the logon screen, enable them in the Ease of Access Center and click Change Administrative Settings, then select the Apply All Settings To The Logon Desktop checkbox and click OK.

Using Magnifier

Magnifier enlarges a portion of the computer screen in a separate window to make it easier to see. By default, Magnifier enlarges the screen by a factor of 2, but you can configure Magnifier to enlarge up to 16 times compared to only 9 times in Windows XP and earlier versions. You can also invert colors in the Magnifier window to increase screen legibility.

Magnifier can track any or all of the following user actions:

- Mouse pointer
- Keyboard focus
- Text editing

Magnifier has three modes:

- **Full-screen mode** The entire screen is magnified, and you can have Magnifier follow the mouse pointer.
- **Lens mode** The area around the mouse pointer is magnified. When you move the mouse pointer, the area of the screen that is magnified moves with it.
- **Docked mode** Only a portion of the screen is magnified, leaving the rest of your desktop displayed in normal size. You can control which area of the screen is magnified.

> ***NOTE*** **Full-screen mode and lens mode are available only when the Windows Aero theme is enabled.**

When Magnifier is running, a magnifier glass icon is displayed on the desktop, as shown here.

Clicking the icon shown here displays the Magnifier toolbar.

Clicking the plus and minus toolbar buttons increases and deceases magnification by 100 percent, but you can change this zoom increment and other Magnifier settings by clicking Options to display the Magnifier Options dialog box, shown here.

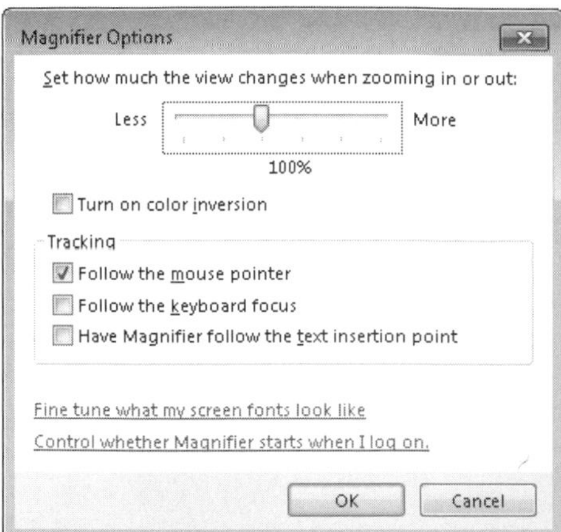

The lens can be resized by going to the Options dialog box when the user is in lens mode and using the sliders to adjust the width and height of the lens.

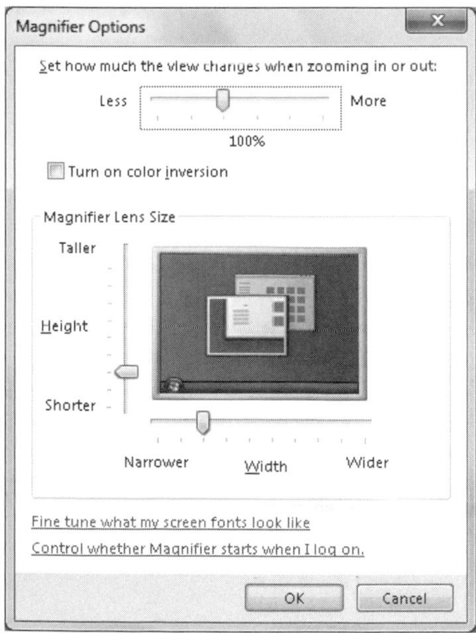

Using Narrator

Narrator is a text-to-speech program that reads the contents of the active window, menu options, or text that the user has typed. Narrator in Windows 7 has the following improvements over Narrator in Windows XP:

- The tool has a more pleasant, natural-sounding voice called Microsoft Anna, which replaces the Microsoft Sam voice.
- The user can move around the desktop with the number keys using virtual focus, and Narrator will read aloud any contents that each desktop window or object contains.
- The user can use bookmarks to find commonly used programs.

In addition, Narrator is compatible with any Speech Application Programming Interface (SAPI)–compliant voice. Figure A-2 shows the configuration options available for Narrator.

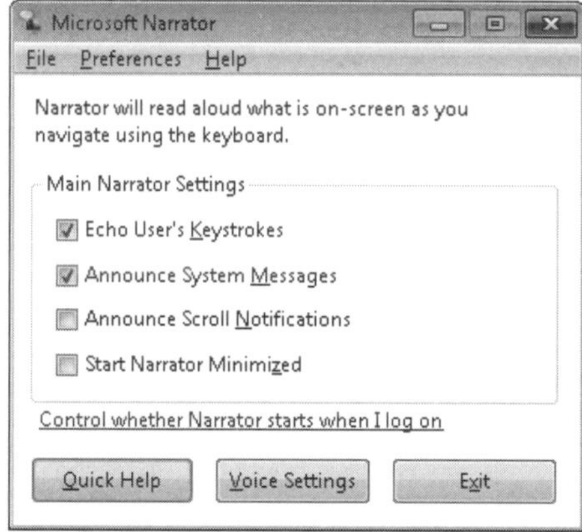

FIGURE A-2 Configuring Narrator options

Using the On-Screen Keyboard

The On-Screen Keyboard (shown in Figure A-3) displays a visual keyboard with which the user can type without relying on a physical keyboard. The functionality of the On-Screen Keyboard has been greatly enhanced in Windows 7. First, users are able to resize the On-Screen Keyboard to any height and width. Also new in Windows 7 is the text prediction feature, which is included on Windows 7 Home Premium Edition operating systems and higher editions. Hover mode and Scan mode have also been enhanced to work under new conditions. For example, if you are in Hover mode and accidentally minimize the On-Screen Keyboard, you can hover your mouse over the icon on the Start menu to return it to its last position. And in Scan mode the user can recover an accidentally minimized On-Screen Keyboard just by pressing the Scan key. Finally, scan and hover intervals of 0.75 seconds have been added to give users more flexibility.

FIGURE A-3 The On-Screen Keyboard

The On-Screen Keyboard options can be accessed by clicking the Options key in the lower right corner of the keyboard next to the Fn and Help keys. The Options dialog box allows users to configure all of the modes and options described above (see Figure A-4).

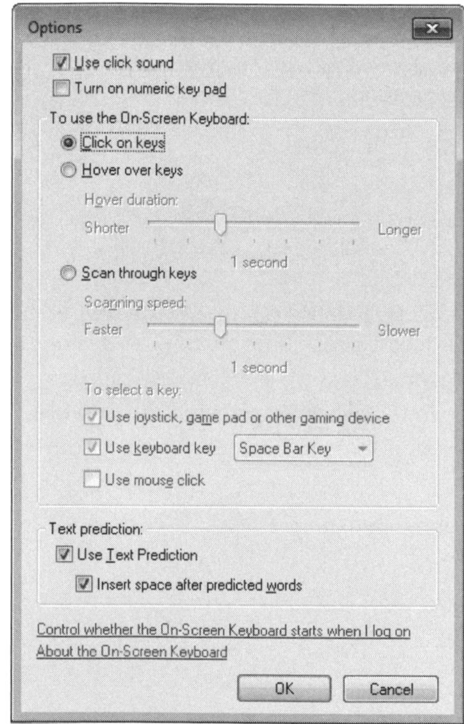

FIGURE A-4 The Options dialog box for the On-Screen Keyboard

Ease of Access Keyboard Shortcuts

As shown in Table A-2, you can enable and disable common accessibility features by using keyboard shortcuts.

TABLE A-2 Keyboard Shortcuts for Ease of Access Features

PRESS THIS KEY	TO DO THIS
Right Shift for 8 seconds	Turn Filter Keys on and off
Left Alt+Left Shift+Print Screen (or Prtscrn)	Turn High Contrast on or off
Left Alt+Left Shift+Num Lock	Turn Mouse Keys on or off
Shift five times	Turn Sticky Keys on or off
Num Lock for 5 seconds	Turn Toggle Keys on or off
Windows logo key+U	Open the Ease of Access Center
Windows logo key+Esc	Exit Magnifier

MORE INFO **You can find additional accessibility keyboard shortcuts for Microsoft products at *http://www.microsoft.com/enable/products/keyboard.aspx.***

Windows Speech Recognition

Windows Speech Recognition was first introduced in Windows Vista and allows the user to interact with the computer using his or her voice. Windows Speech Recognition was designed for the individual who wants to use the mouse and keyboard less while still maintaining (or even increasing) overall productivity. In addition, Windows Speech Recognition can provide benefits to individuals with physical disabilities by allowing them to interact with their computers without a keyboard or mouse.

Windows Speech Recognition supports the following languages:

- English (United States)
- English (United Kingdom)
- German (Germany)
- French (France)
- Spanish (Spain)
- Japanese
- Traditional Chinese
- Simplified Chinese

By using Windows Speech Recognition, you can control your computer with your voice. For example, you can say commands to which your computer will respond, and you can dictate text to your computer. Before you begin using Windows Speech Recognition, you must perform these steps:

1. Make sure a microphone and speakers are properly connected to your computer.
2. Open Windows Speech Recognition by opening the Ease of Access Center and clicking Speech Recognition.
3. Click Use The Computer Without A Mouse Or Keyboard.
4. Click Start Speech Recognition. The wizard will take you through setting up your microphone as well as a speech tutorial to train your voice and teach you how to use Windows Speech Recognition.

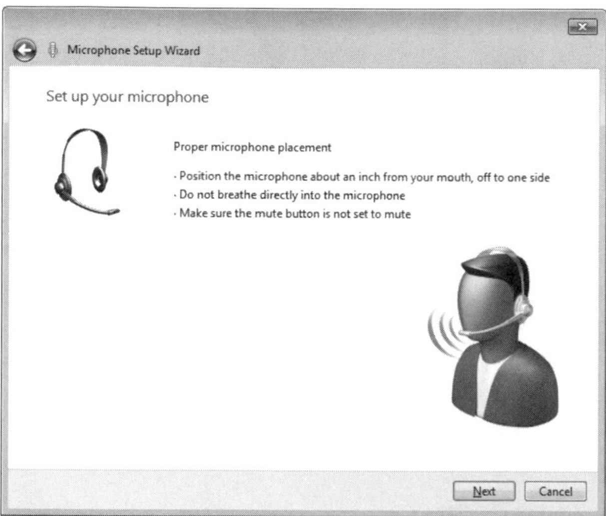

5. (Optional) If you want to further improve Speech Recognition accuracy, click Train Your Computer To Better Understand You in the Speech Recognition Control Panel. The Speech Recognition Voice Training window opens, as shown here, with which you can create a voice profile that your computer can use to recognize your voice and spoken commands.

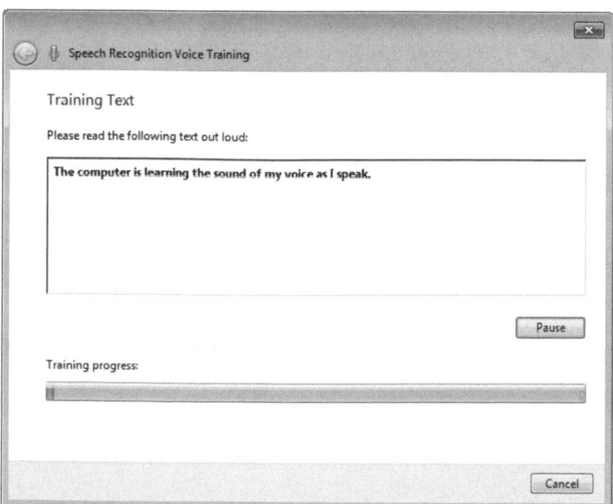

Once you have your microphone and voice profile set up, you can use Speech Recognition to do the following:

- **Control your computer** Windows Speech Recognition can listen to and respond to your spoken commands so that you can run programs and interact with Windows.
- **Dictate and edit text** You can use Windows Speech Recognition to dictate words into Microsoft Office Word, fill out online forms in Windows Internet Explorer, and perform similar tasks. You can also use Windows Speech Recognition to edit text you have entered into these programs.

MORE INFO For more information on how to use Windows Speech Recognition, search Help And Support for the keyword "speech recognition."

Assistive Technology Products

Individuals with physical and cognitive difficulties can use third-party AT products to use computers more easily and effectively. Many AT products are available on Windows 7. Be sure to check with your AT manufacturer before upgrading if you have concerns. AT products include:

- Alternative input devices.
- Speech and voice recognition software.
- Screen readers.
- Screen magnifiers and screen enlargers.
- On-screen keyboards.
- Other types of hardware and software.

There are hundreds of AT products compatible with different versions of Windows. To learn whether a specific AT product is compatible with Windows 7, go to *http://www.microsoft.com/enable/at/*.

Microsoft Accessibility Resource Centers

Microsoft has developed a network of Microsoft Accessibility Resource Centers where users can learn more about technology solutions that meet their needs, including how to effectively use the accessibility features found in Windows 7.

MORE INFO For more information and to locate a Microsoft Accessibility Resource Center near you, go to *http://www.microsoft.com/enable/centers/*.

Additional Resources

These resources contain additional information and tools related to this chapter.

- "Accessibility in Windows 7" on the Windows 7 Engineering blog at *http://blogs.msdn.com/e7/archive/2008/11/30/accessibility-in-windows-7.aspx.*
- Microsoft Accessibility site at *http://www.microsoft.com/enable/.*

Glossary

802.1X A standard that defines port-based, network access control used to provide authenticated network access for Ethernet networks. This standard uses the physical characteristics of the switched LAN infrastructure to authenticate devices attached to a LAN port.

802.11 An industry standard for a shared WLAN that defines the physical layer and MAC sublayer for wireless communications.

A

ABE *See* Access-Based Enumeration (ABE).

Accelerator A feature of Windows Internet Explorer 8 that lets you select text on a Web page to perform such tasks as opening a street address in a mapping Web site or looking up the dictionary definition of a word.

Access-Based Enumeration (ABE) Allows a user to see only those files and folders within a network share that that user actually has permission to access. When using ABE, an administrator can share C:\Budgets and assign ACLs as before, but ordinary users who browse the BUDGETS share see only the Public.doc file. The Secret.doc file is not visible to them—in fact, they won't even know of its existence. ABE thus increases the security of shared data and also helps protect its privacy.

Action Center The central place to view alerts and take actions that can help keep Windows running smoothly. Action Center lists important messages about security and maintenance settings that need your attention. Red items in Action Center are labeled Important and indicate significant issues that should be addressed right away, such as an outdated antivirus program that needs updating. Yellow items are suggested tasks that you should consider addressing, like recommended maintenance tasks.

Adaptive Display Brightness With this feature, Windows 7 automatically dims the display brightness after a period of inactivity. This enables Windows 7 to reduce battery consumption without the full impact of going into Sleep mode.

activation The process of registering an instance of Windows with Microsoft to confirm the legitimacy of the product key and license.

Address Resolution Protocol (ARP) A Layer 2 protocol that TCP/IP clients use to resolve local IP addresses to MAC addresses.

Address Space Layout Randomization (ASLR) A feature of Windows that randomly assigns executable images (.dll and .exe files) included as part of the operating system to one of 256 possible locations in memory. This makes it harder for exploitative code to locate and therefore take advantage of the functionality inside the executables by using a buffer overrun attack.

Admin Approval mode A feature of Windows that prompts administrators to confirm actions that require more than Standard privileges.

admin broker A feature of Protected mode that allows Windows Internet Explorer to install ActiveX controls.

ADML template file One of a set of files used to add custom registry-based Group Policy settings. ADML files provide language-specific translations of Group Policy setting names and descriptions.

ADMX template file One of a set of files used to add custom registry-based Group Policy settings. ADMX files specify the registry location and possible values.

Aero Peek Lets you quickly preview the desktop without minimizing all your windows or preview an open window by pointing at its button on the taskbar.

Aero Shake Lets you quickly minimize all open windows on the desktop except the one on which you want to focus. Just click the title bar of the window you want to keep open and drag (or shake) the window back and forth quickly, and the other open windows are minimized.

Aero Snap Lets you arrange and resize windows on the desktop with a simple mouse movement. You can quickly align windows at the side of the desktop, expand them vertically to the entire height of the screen, or maximize them to completely fill the desktop. Aero Snap can be especially helpful when comparing two documents, copying or moving files between two windows, maximizing the window you're currently working on, or expanding long documents so they're easier to read and require less scrolling.

answer file An XML-based file that contains settings to use during a Windows installation.

AppLocker A new feature in Windows 7 and Windows Server 2008 R2 that replaces the Software Restriction Policies feature in previous versions of Windows. AppLocker contains new capabilities and extensions that reduce administrative overhead and help administrators control how users can access and use files such as .exe files, scripts, Windows Installer files (.msi and .msp files), and DLLs.

ARP *See* Address Resolution Protocol (ARP).

ASLR *See* Address Space Layout Randomization (ASLR).

Authorization Manager (AzMan) An MMC user interface that administrators can use to configure RBAC settings for supported applications.

AzMan *See* Authorization Manager (AzMan).

B

Background Intelligent Transfer Service (BITS) A file-transfer service designed to transfer files across the Internet using only idle network bandwidth. Unlike standard HTTP, FTP, or shared-folder file transfers, BITS does not use all available bandwidth, so you can use it to download large files without affecting other network applications. BITS transfers are also very reliable and can continue when users change network connections or restart their computers. BITS is used to transfer data between the Software Update Services or the Windows Update server to the Automatic Updates client.

bench deployment A deployment process in which a technician deploys and configures a computer in a lab environment before physically moving it to the user's desk.

BitLocker Drive Encryption A feature of Windows capable of encrypting the entire system volume, thus protecting the computer in the event of attacks that bypass the operating system security.

BitLocker To Go A new feature of Windows BitLocker Drive Encryption in Windows 7 that gives administrators control over how removable storage devices can be utilized within their environment and the strength of protection that they require. Administrators can require data protection for any removable storage device that users want to write data upon, while still allowing unprotected storage devices to be utilized in a read-only mode. Policies are also available to require appropriate passwords, smart cards, or domain user credentials to utilize a protected removable storage device.

BITS *See* Background Intelligent Transfer Service (BITS).

Bluetooth A short-range radio technology for device networking that is most commonly used by mobile phones and handheld devices, such as PDAs and Pocket PCs.

boot image An operating system image that is directly bootable without being installed. For example, Windows PE can be run from a boot image.

BranchCache A new feature of Windows 7 and Windows Server 2008 R2 that improves the responsiveness of intranet applications for remote offices while simultaneously reducing WAN utilization. BranchCache keeps a local copy of data that clients access from remote Web and file servers. The cache can be placed on a hosted server located in the branch office, or it can reside on users' individual computers. If another client requests the same file, the client downloads it across the LAN without having to retrieve it over the WAN. BranchCache ensures that only authorized clients can access requested data, and it is compatible with secure data retrieval over SSL or IPsec.

buffer overflow An attack that submits larger or longer values than an application or API is designed to process.

build In the context of MDT 2010, the association of source files from the distribution share with a configuration. *See also* Microsoft Deployment Toolkit 2010 (MDT 2010).

C

catalog The system index together with the property cache.

catalog file A binary file that contains the state of all settings and packages in a Windows image.

central store In the context of Group Policy, a location for storing administrative templates for use throughout an organization. Only Windows Vista and later versions support using a central store.

channel In Meeting Space, the basis for communication between participants in a meeting. There are three kinds of Meeting Space channels: metadata, file, and streaming. The term *channel* can also refer to an application-specific event log.

Clear key A key stored unencrypted on the disk volume. This key is used to freely access the VMK and, in turn, the FVEK if BitLocker protection is disabled but disk volume remains encrypted.

client-side cache (CSC) A Microsoft internal term referring to Offline Files.

cloud In peer-to-peer networks, a grouping of computers that uses addresses of a specific scope. A *scope* is an area of the network over which the address is unique.

CNG services *See* Crypto Next Generation (CNG) services.

Code Integrity A feature of Windows that detects changes to system files and drivers.

compatibility layer A feature of Protected mode in Windows Internet Explorer that redirects requests for protected resources (such as the user's Documents folder) to safe locations (such as the Temporary Internet Files folder).

component store A portion of an operating system image that stores one or more operating system features or language packs.

configuration pass A phase of Windows installation in which different parts of the operating system are installed and configured. You can specify unattended installation settings to be applied in one or more configuration passes.

configuration set A file and folder structure containing files that control the preinstallation process and define customizations for the Windows installation.

Confirmation Identifier A digitally signed value returned by a Microsoft clearinghouse to activate a system.

core application An application that is common to most computers in your organization, such as a virus scanner or a management agent.

Crypto Next Generation (CNG) services An extensible cryptographic configuration system that replaces the CryptoAPI of Windows XP and earlier versions.

Cryptographic Service Provider (CSP) An infrastructure that developers can use to create applications that use cryptographic functions such as encryption, hashes, and digital signatures.

CSC *See* client-side cache (CSC).

CSP *See* Cryptographic Service Provider (CSP).

D

data store In deployment, the location in which the USMT stores a user state between the time it is read from the original computer and the time it is deployed to the target computer.

defense-in-depth A proven technique of layered protection that reduces the exposure of vulnerabilities. For example, you might design a network with three layers of packet filtering: a packet-filtering router, a hardware firewall, and software firewalls on each of the hosts (such as Internet Connection Firewall). If an attacker manages to bypass one or two of the layers of protection, the hosts are still protected.

Deploying Phase In deployment, this is the phase in which computers are actually set up and configured. Additionally, in this phase the deployment team verifies that deployed computers are stable and usable.

Deployment Image Servicing and Management (DISM) A new command-line tool introduced in Windows 7 that can be used to service a Windows image or to prepare a Windows PE image. It replaces Package Manager (Pkgmgr.exe), PEImg, and Intlcfg, which were included in Windows Vista. The functionality that was included in these tools is now consolidated in DISM, and new functionalities have been added to improve the experience for offline servicing.

Desktop Windows Manager (DWM) A feature of Windows that performs desktop composition to enable visual effects such as glass window frames, three-dimensional window transition animations, Windows Flip and Windows Flip3D, and high-resolution support.

destination computer The computer on which you install Windows during deployment. You can either run Windows Setup on the destination computer or copy a master installation onto the destination computer.

developing phase In deployment, the period during which the team builds and unit-tests the solution.

DirectAccess A new feature of Windows 7 and Windows Server 2008 R2 that increases the productivity of remote users by enabling them to seamlessly and securely access the corporate network any time they have an Internet connection, without requiring a VPN connection. DirectAccess also enhances the security and flexibility of the corporate network infrastructure, enabling IT professionals to remotely manage and update corporate computers whenever they connect to the Internet—even when users are not logged in.

directory junction A technique for redirecting requests for a specific folder to a different location. Directory junctions are used to provide backward compatibility for folder locations used in earlier versions of Windows.

discoverable A state in which a Bluetooth-enabled device sends out radio signals to advertise its location to other devices and computers.

DLL *See* dynamic-link library (DLL).

DNS Security Extensions (DNSSEC) An Internet standard supported by Windows 7 and Windows Server 2008 R2 that enables computers to authenticate DNS servers, which mitigates man-in-the-middle attacks. A *man-in-the-middle attack* redirects clients to a malicious server, which can allow an attacker to intercept passwords or confidential data.

DNSSEC *See* DNS Security Extensions (DNSSEC).

DWM *See* Desktop Windows Manager (DWM).

Dynamic Driver Provisioning A new feature of Windows Deployment Services in Windows Server 2008 R2 that stores drivers in a central location, which saves IT professionals time by not requiring operating system images to be updated when new drivers are required (for example, when the IT department buys different hardware). Drivers can be installed dynamically based on the Plug and Play IDs of a PC's hardware or as predetermined sets based on information contained in the BIOS.

dynamic-link library (DLL) A file containing executable code that programs can run. Multiple programs can reference a single DLL, and a single program might use many different DLLs.

E

envisioning phase The phase in a MDT 2010 deployment in which management creates teams, performs an assessment of existing systems and applications, defines business goals, creates a vision statement, defines scope, creates user profiles, develops a solution concept, creates risk-assessment documents, writes a project structure, and approves milestones. *See also* Microsoft Deployment Toolkit 2010 (MDT 2010).

escalated Remote Assistance (RA) *See* solicited Remote Assistance (RA).

expert In a Remote Assistance scenario, the user who provides help. Also known as a *helper*.

F

feature team In the context of MDT 2010, a cross-organizational team that focuses on solving a particular problem such as security. *See also* Microsoft Deployment Toolkit 2010 (MDT 2010).

feature team guide In the context of MDT 2010, a document that addresses the tasks required of a specific feature team. *See also* Microsoft Deployment Toolkit 2010 (MDT 2010).

Federated Search A new feature of Windows 7 and Windows Server 2008 R2, based on the OpenSearch protocol, which enables users to search remote data sources from within Windows Explorer. The goal of Federated Search is not to replace server repositories, like Microsoft Office SharePoint Server, but to enable these repositories to expose their search capabilities through Windows and thus get more value out of the repositories for users.

file sharing The process of making files or folders available to more than one user.

folder redirection A technique for configuring computers to access user profile data from an alternate location. Folder redirection is commonly used to store user documents and data files on a shared folder.

forced guest *See* ForceGuest.

ForceGuest A common term for one of the network access models used by Windows XP that requires all network users to be treated as guests. Beginning with Windows Vista, however, ForceGuest is no longer a supported setting; turning this setting on is not recommended.

Full Volume Encryption Key (FVEK) The algorithm-specific key used to encrypt (and optionally, diffuse) data on disk sectors. Currently, this key can vary from 128 bits through 512 bits. The default encryption algorithm used on disk volumes is AES 128 bit with Diffuser.

FVEK *See* Full Volume Encryption Key (FVEK).

G

gadget A mini-application that can do almost anything, including show news updates, display a picture slideshow, or show weather reports.

GPT *See* GUID Partition Table (GPT).

Group Policy preferences Lets you manage drive mappings, registry settings, local users and groups, services, files, and folders without the need to learn a scripting language. You can use preference items to reduce scripting and the number of custom system images needed, standardize management, and help secure your networks. By using preference item-level targeting, you can streamline desktop management by reducing the number of GPOs needed.

GUID Partition Table (GPT) A new disk-partitioning technology that offers several advantages over MBR, including support for larger partitions and up to 128 partitions on a single disk.

H

HAL *See* Hardware Abstraction Layer (HAL).

Hard-Link Migration A new feature of the USMT for Windows 7 that enables customers to install Windows Vista or Windows 7 on an existing computer while retaining data locally on that computer during operating system installation.

Hardware Abstraction Layer (HAL) A feature of Windows that simplifies how the operating system accesses hardware by providing a single interface that behaves identically across different platforms.

helper *See* expert.

high-volume deployment A deployment project that involves a large number of computers.

HomeGroup A new networking feature of Windows 7 that makes it easier to share files and printers on a home network. You can share pictures, music, videos, documents, and printers with other people in your HomeGroup. Other people can't change the files that you share unless you give them permission to do so.

hybrid image An imaging strategy that combines thick and thin images. In a hybrid image, you configure the disk image to install applications on first run, giving the illusion of a thick image but installing the applications from a network source. Hybrid images have most of the advantages of thin images. However, they aren't as complex to develop and do not require a software distribution infrastructure. They do require longer installation times, however, which can raise initial deployment costs.

I

ICMP *See* Internet Control Message Protocol (ICMP).

IFilter A feature of the Windows search engine that is used to convert documents in different formats into plain text so they can be indexed. IFilters are also responsible for extracting a number of format-dependent properties such as Subject, Author, and Locale. Microsoft provides IFilters for many common document formats by default, while third-party vendors such as Adobe provide their own IFilters for indexing other forms of content.

IID *See* Installation Identifier (IID).

image-based setup A setup process based on applying a disk image of an operating system to the computer.

in place sharing *See* in profile sharing.

in profile sharing Sharing a file or folder from within your user profile. Also known as *in place sharing*.

InPrivate Browsing Prevents Windows Internet Explorer from storing data about your browsing session.

InPrivate Filtering Helps prevent Web site content providers from collecting information about sites you visit.

Installation Identifier (IID) A code generated by combining a system's hardware ID (created by scanning the system hardware) and the product ID (derived from the Windows installation). This code is transmitted to a Microsoft activation clearinghouse during system activation.

installation image An operating system image that can be installed on a computer. Unlike boot images, installation images cannot be booted directly from the image and must be deployed to a computer before running.

IntelliMirror A set of change and configuration management features based on Active Directory Domain Services that enables management of user and computer data and settings, including security data. IntelliMirror also provides a limited ability to deploy software to workstations or servers running Microsoft Windows 2000 and later versions.

Internet Control Message Protocol (ICMP) A Layer 3 protocol that IP applications use to test connectivity and communicate routing changes. ICMP is most commonly used by the Ping tool.

IPConfig A command-line tool that displays the current network configuration.

J

Jump List A list of recent items, such as files, folders, or Web sites, organized by the program that you use to open them. In addition to being able to open recent items using a Jump List, you can also pin favorites to a Jump List so that you can quickly get to the items that you use every day.

K

Kernel mode A processing mode provided by x86-based processors that provides processes with unrestricted access to memory and other system resources. Beginning with Windows Vista, only system features and trusted drivers should run in Kernel mode.

Key Management Service (KMS) An infrastructure that simplifies tracking product keys in enterprise environments.

KMS *See* Key Management Service (KMS).

known folders Windows user profile folders that can be redirected with Folder Redirection.

L

legacy mode A Windows Deployment Services mode that uses OSChooser and Riprep (sector-based) images. This mode is compatible with RIS. Moving from RIS-only functionality to legacy mode happens when you install the Windows Deployment Services update on a server that is running RIS.

library A virtual container for users' content. A library can contain files and folders stored on the local computer or in a remote storage location. In Windows Explorer, users interact with libraries in a way similar to the way they would interact with other folders. Libraries are built upon the known folders (such as My Documents, My Pictures, and My Music) that users are familiar with, and these known folders are automatically included in the default libraries and set as the default save location.

Lite Touch Installation (LTI) A deployment option in MDT 2010 that deploys client computers with little human interaction. An alternative deployment option, ZTI, deploys client computers with no human interaction, but that requires more preparation and engineering time beforehand. Therefore, LTI is more appropriate for environments that deploy fewer computers. *See also* Microsoft Deployment Toolkit 2010 (MDT 2010), Zero Touch Installation (ZTI).

local sharing The process of making files and folders available to other users on the same computer. Also known as *same computer sharing*.

local user profile The default approach for storing user profiles in Windows in which the user profile is stored on the computer's hard disk.

location-aware printing A new feature of Windows 7 and Windows Server 2008 R2 that makes the Default Printer setting location aware. Mobile and laptop users can set a different default printer for each network to which they connect. They may have a default printer set for home use and a different default printer set for the office. Their computers can now automatically select the correct default printer depending on where the users are currently located.

LTI *See* Lite Touch Installation (LTI).

M

MAK *See* Multiple Activation Key (MAK).

malware A term that describes a broad range of malicious software, including viruses, worms, Trojan horses, spyware, and adware.

managed service account A new feature of Windows 7 and Windows Server 2008 R2 that allows administrators to create a class of domain accounts that can be used to manage and maintain services on local computers.

Mandatory Integrity Control (MIC) A model in which lower-integrity processes cannot access higher-integrity processes. The primary integrity levels are Low, Medium, High, and System. Windows assigns to each process an integrity level in its access token. Securable objects such as files and registry keys have a new mandatory ACE in the system ACL.

mandatory label An ACE used by MIC.

mandatory user profile A user profile that cannot be modified by the user. Mandatory user profiles are useful for ensuring consistent desktop environments.

Master Boot Record (MBR) The most common disk partition system, MBR is supported by every version of Windows. Gradually, MBRs are being replaced by GPTs. *See also* GUID Partition Table (GPT).

master computer A fully assembled computer containing a master installation of Windows.

master image A collection of files and folders (sometimes compressed into one file) captured from a master installation. This image contains the base operating system as well as additional configurations and files.

master index A single index formed by combining shadow indexes by using a process called the master merge. *See also* master merge.

master installation A Windows installation on a master computer to be captured as a master image. You create the master installation by using automation to ensure a consistent and repeatable configuration each time. *See also* master computer, master image.

master merge The process of combining index fragments (shadow indexes) into a single content index called the master index. *See also* master index.

MBR *See* Master Boot Record (MBR).

MBSA *See* Microsoft Baseline Security Analyzer (MBSA).

MBSACLI *See* Microsoft Baseline Security Analyzer Command Line Interface (MBSACLI).

MIC *See* Mandatory Integrity Control (MIC).

Microsoft Baseline Security Analyzer (MBSA) A free tool available for download from Microsoft.com that administrators can use to scan computers for security vulnerabilities and missing security updates.

Microsoft Baseline Security Analyzer Command Line Interface (MBSACLI) A command-line interface for MBSA, which administrators can use to scan computers for security vulnerabilities and missing security updates from scripts. *See also* Microsoft Baseline Security Analyzer (MBSA).

Microsoft Deployment Toolkit 2010 (MDT 2010) An SA that enables rapid deployment of Windows 7, Windows Server 2008 R2, Windows Vista SP1, Windows Server 2008, Windows XP SP3, and Windows 2003 SP2. MDT 2010 provides unified tools, scripts, and documentation for desktop and server deployment using an integrated deployment console called the Deployment Workbench.

mixed mode A Windows Deployment Services mode that supports both OSChooser and Windows PE for boot environments and Riprep and ImageX imaging. Moving from legacy mode to mixed mode happens when you configure Windows Deployment Services and add .wim image files to it.

Multicast Multiple Stream Transfer A new feature of Windows Deployment Services in Windows Server 2008 R2 that enables you to more efficiently deploy images to multiple computers across a network. Instead of requiring separate direct connections between deployment servers and each client, it enables deployment servers to send image data to multiple clients simultaneously. Windows 7 includes an improvement that allows servers to group clients with similar network bandwidth and stream at different rates to each group so that total throughput is not limited by the slowest client.

Multiple Activation Key (MAK) A limited-use product key that can be used to activate Windows on multiple computers.

N

name resolution The process of converting a host name to an IP address.

NAP *See* Network Access Protection (NAP).

native mode A Windows Deployment Services mode that supports only the Windows PE boot environment and ImageX image files. The final move to native mode occurs after you have converted all legacy images to the .wim image file format and disabled the OSChooser functionality.

Nbtstat A command-line tool used to display NetBIOS networking information including cached NetBIOS computer names.

Net A command-line tool used to perform a variety of networking tasks including starting and stopping services, sharing resources, and connecting to shared resources.

Netstat A command-line tool used to display networking statistics.

Network Access Protection (NAP) A feature supported by Windows Vista and later versions that uses network authentication to validate the identity and integrity of client computers before they are allowed to connect to the network.

Network Monitor A graphical tool that administrators can use to capture and analyze network communications.

Network Sharing The process of making a folder available across the network.

New Computer scenario In MDT 2010, a deployment scenario that deploys the operating system and applications to a computer that has not been previously configured and therefore contains no user data. *See also* Microsoft Deployment Toolkit 2010 (MDT 2010).

nondestructive imaging A deployment technique supported by ImageX and Windows Setup in which an operating system image is deployed without destroying the existing data.

novice In a Remote Assistance (RA) scenario, the user seeking assistance.

Nslookup A command-line tool used to test DNS name resolution.

O

OEM *See* Original Equipment Manufacturer (OEM).

offered Remote Assistance (RA) *See* unsolicited Remote Assistance (RA).

Office Genuine Advantage (OGA) An initiative that tracks the product keys from licensed versions of Microsoft Office programs to ensure that they are not reused on other computers. Users who validate their copies of Microsoft Office products gain access to add-ins and updates to those products.

offline In the context of preparing an image for deployment, when the operating system is not started and changes or updates are made directly to the image.

Offline Files A feature of Windows that locally stores a copy of a file located on a shared folder. Windows can then access the local copy of the file if the user needs it while disconnected from the network. Windows includes technology for synchronizing Offline Files that have been modified and resolving synchronization conflicts.

OGA *See* Office Genuine Advantage (OGA).

online In the context of preparing an image for deployment, when the operating system is started and changes or updates are made while Windows is running.

Original Equipment Manufacturer (OEM) An organization that designs and manufactures computer hardware.

P

P2P *See* peer-to-peer (P2P).

package A group of files that Microsoft provides to modify Windows features. Package types include service packs, security updates, language packs, and hotfixes.

panning hand A specialized cursor that enables dragging a page.

PatchGuard Microsoft's kernel patch protection technology for 64-bit versions of Windows that is designed to prevent unauthorized and unsupported access to the kernel. It prohibits all software from performing unsupported patches.

PathPing A command-line tool used to test connectivity to an endpoint. PathPing collects connectivity statistics for every gateway between the client and the tested endpoint and displays latency and availability statistics for every node.

PCR *See* platform configuration register (PCR).

Peer Name Resolution Protocol (PNRP) A mechanism for distributed, serverless name resolution of peers in a P2P network. *See also* peer-to-peer (P2P).

peer-to-peer (P2P) A method for communicating directly between client computers without involving a separate server. In Windows Vista and later versions, P2P refers to a set of networking and collaboration technologies that are used by Windows Meeting Space and other applications.

pen flick A Tablet PC pen technique that enables users to call menu commands by moving the pen using various gestures.

People Near Me A subnet-level system that enables users who are signed on to this service to automatically publish their availability onto the local subnet and discover other users using the Web Services Dynamic Discovery (WS-Discovery) protocol. Once users are published using People Near Me, they can be invited to start activities such as Windows Meeting Space.

personal identification number (PIN) This is an administrator-specified secret value that must be entered each time the computer starts (or resumes from hibernation). The PIN can have 4 to 20 digits and internally is stored as a 256-bit hash of the entered Unicode characters. This value is never displayed to the user in any form or for any reason. The PIN is used to provide another factor of protection in conjunction with TPM authentication. *See also* Trusted Platform Module (TPM).

phishing A form of Internet fraud that aims to steal valuable information such as credit cards, Social Security numbers, user IDs, and passwords. A fake Web site is created that is similar to that of a legitimate organization, typically a financial institution such as a bank or insurance company. An e-mail is sent requesting that the recipient access the fake Web site and enter personal details including security access codes. The page looks genuine because it is easy to fake a valid Web site. Any HTML page on the Web can be modified to suit a phishing scheme.

PIN *See* personal identification number (PIN).

Ping A command-line tool used to test connectivity to an endpoint.

Planning Phase A phase in a MDT 2010 deployment in which the deployment team lays the groundwork for the deployment. *See also* Microsoft Deployment Toolkit 2010 (MDT 2010).

platform configuration register (PCR) A register of a TPM. This register is sufficiently large to contain a hash (currently only SHA-1). A register can normally only be extended, which means that its content is a running hash of all values that are loaded to it. To learn when these registers are reset, refer to the TCG specification document. *See also* Trusted Platform Module (TPM).

PNRP *See* Peer Name Resolution Protocol (PNRP).

Point-to-Point Tunneling Protocol (PPTP) A networking technology that supports multiprotocol VPNs. This enables remote users to securely access corporate or other networks across the Internet, to dial into an ISP, or to connect directly to the Internet. PPTP tunnels, or encapsulates, IP or IPX banter traffic inside IP packets. This means that users can remotely run applications that depend on particular network protocols. PPTP is described in RFC 2637.

PortQry A command-line tool that tests connectivity to a network service by attempting to establish a TCP connection to an endpoint.

PPTP *See* Point-to-Point Tunneling Protocol (PPTP).

Pre-Boot Execution Environment (PXE) A DHCP-based remote boot technology used to boot or install an operating system on a client computer from a remote server. A Windows Deployment Services server is an example of a PXE server.

Print Management An MMC snap-in that administrators can use to manage printers, print servers, and print jobs across an enterprise.

printer driver isolation A new feature of Windows 7 and Windows Server 2008 R2 that lets you configure printer driver features to run in an isolated process separate from the print spooler process. By isolating the printer driver, you can prevent a faulty printer driver from stopping all print operations on a print server, which results in a significant increase in server reliability.

Printer Migrator A tool for backing up printer configurations on print servers so that the configuration can be moved between print servers or consolidated from multiple servers onto a single server. A command-line version (Printbrm.exe) is also available.

product key A code used to validate installation media such as CDs during installation. Product keys, also known as CD keys, do not prove licensing for a product, but they do discourage casual copying of software. All

Windows product keys use five groups of five characters, with the format *XXXXX-XXXXX-XXXXX-XXXXX-XXXXX*.

protocol handler A feature of the Windows search engine that is used to communicate with and enumerate the contents of stores such as the file system, MAPI e-mail database, and the CSC or offline files database. *See also* client-side cache (CSC).

proximity A measurement of the network latency between two computers. For Windows Media Sharing to work, the network latency between two computers must be 7 milliseconds or less.

Punycode The self-proclaimed "bootstring encoding" of Unicode strings into the limited character set supported by DNS, as defined in RFC 3492. The encoding is used as part of IDNA, which is a system enabling the use of internationalized domain names in all languages that are supported by Unicode where the burden of translation lies entirely with the user application (such as a Web browser).

PXE *See* Pre-Boot Execution Environment (PXE).

R

RAC *See* Reliability Analysis Component (RAC).

Reliability Analysis Component (RAC) A Windows feature that gathers and processes reliability data.

Replace Computer scenario In MDT 2010, a deployment scenario that involves giving a new computer to an existing user. In this scenario, the user receives a new computer, and the user's data is migrated to the replacement computer to minimize impact on the user. *See also* Microsoft Deployment Toolkit 2010 (MDT 2010).

requested execution level manifest An application marking that indicates the privileges required by the application. Windows uses the requested execution level manifest, among other factors, to determine whether to provide a UAC prompt to the user to elevate privileges when the application is run.

Roaming User Profile An alternative approach for storing user profiles that involves storing them on a shared folder on the network. Roaming user profiles provide simplified backup and enable users to use the same profile on different computers.

S

SAM *See* Software Asset Management (SAM).

same computer sharing *See* local sharing.

screen scraping A technique for automating applications by simulating keystrokes as if a human were sitting at the keyboard. Screen scraping is the least reliable automation technique and should be used only when no other automation option is available.

Server Message Block (SMB) A network protocol used for file and printer sharing.

Server Performance Advisor (SPA) A report that provides a summary of logged performance data.

shadow index A temporary index created during the indexing process. The shadow indexes created during indexing are later combined into a single index called the *master index*.

sharing The process of making files, folders, printers, or other resources available to other users.

shatter attack An attack in which a process attempts to use Windows messages to elevate privileges by injecting code into another process.

Simple Service Discovery Protocol (SSDP) This protocol forms the basis of the discovery protocol used by UPnP and PNRP.

single instance storage A technique for storing multiple Windows images efficiently and in a single location. The deployment engineer configuring a computer has the option to select one of the images for deployment from the client computer.

Sleep A new power state that combines the quick resume time of Standby with the data-protection benefits of Hibernate.

slipstreaming The process of integrating a service pack into operating system setup files so that new computers immediately have the service pack installed.

SMB *See* Server Message Block (SMB).

SME *See* subject matter expert (SME).

SMS *See* Systems Management Server (SMS).

sniffer A tool such as Network Monitor that collects network communications. Sniffers are also known as protocol analyzers.

Software Asset Management (SAM) An initiative promoted by Microsoft as a way to maintain accurate inventories of installed and licensed software. This practice helps organizations maintain legally licensed versions of all the software they need.

solicited Remote Assistance (RA) A Remote Assistance request initiated by the novice (the user seeking help). Also known as escalated Remote Assistance (RA).

SPA *See* Server Performance Advisor (SPA).

SSDP *See* Simple Service Discovery Protocol (SSDP).

stabilizing phase In deployment, the phase that addresses the testing of a solution that is feature complete. This phase typically occurs when pilots are conducted, with an emphasis on real-world testing and with the goal of identifying, prioritizing, and fixing bugs.

stack A list of memory locations that identify the calling methods of return locations. Windows uses the stack to remember the location to return to when a called method has finished running.

start address A URL that points to the starting location for indexed content. When indexing is performed, each configured starting address is enumerated by a protocol handler to find the content to be indexed.

Starter GPO Collections of preconfigured administrative templates in Windows 7 that IT professionals can use as standard baseline configurations to create a live GPO. They encapsulate Microsoft best practices, containing recommended policy settings and values for key enterprise scenarios. IT professionals also can create and share their own Starter GPOs based on internal or industry regulatory requirements.

startup key A key stored on a USB flash drive that must be inserted every time the computer starts. The startup key is used to provide another factor of protection in conjunction with TPM authentication. *See also* Trusted Platform Module (TPM).

Stop error An error that Windows raises when a Kernel mode process has been compromised or has experienced an unhandled exception.

subject matter expert (SME) A person who is skilled in a particular topic. During deployment, you should use SMEs to help in the planning, development, and stabilizing processes. SMEs are users who are most familiar with the applications and data to migrate (though despite their name, they are not necessarily experts), and they're usually stakeholders in seeing that the process is properly performed.

subscription Provides the ability to collect copies of events from multiple remote computers and store them locally.

supplemental application An application installed on a select few computers in your environment, such as specialized applications used by individual groups. Supplemental applications are in contrast to core applications, which are installed on most computers.

Sync Center A tool that provides a user interface for managing content synchronization activities including redirected folders and other folders marked for offline use.

System Starter GPO A read-only GPO that provides a baseline of settings for a specific scenario. Like Starter GPOs, System Starter GPOs derive from a GPO, let you store a collection of Administrative template policy settings in a single object, and can be imported. *See also* Starter GPO.

Systems Management Server (SMS) A Microsoft computer management infrastructure used to improve administrative efficiency and help distribute and manage software.

T

task sequence A series of actions to run on a destination computer to install Windows and applications and then configure the destination computer. In MDT 2010, the task sequence is part of a build, and the feature responsible for executing the task sequence is the Task Sequencer. *See also* Microsoft Deployment Toolkit 2010 (MDT 2010).

Task Sequencer The MDT 2010 feature that runs the task sequence when installing a build. *See also* Microsoft Deployment Toolkit 2010 (MDT 2010).

TCP receive window size The number of bytes that a TCP/IP host can transmit without receiving a response from the remote computer. The TCP receive window size can have a significant impact on performance. If the size is too large and the network is unreliable, a great deal of data might need to be retransmitted if data is lost. If the size is too small, utilization is unnecessarily low while the sending computer waits for confirmations from the receiving computer.

technician computer The computer on which you install MDT 2010 or Windows SIM. This computer is typically in a lab environment, separated from the production network. In MDT 2010, this computer is usually called the *build server. See also* Microsoft Deployment Toolkit 2010 (MDT 2010).

Telnet A protocol and tool for remotely managing computers using a text-based interface similar to a command prompt.

Test TCP A network troubleshooting tool for testing TCP connectivity between two computers.

thick image An operating system installation image that contains core, and possibly supplemental, applications. Thick images simplify deployment by installation applications alongside the operating system. However, because they are more specialized, you typically require more thick images than thin images.

thin image An operating system installation image that contains few if any core applications. Thin images have the advantage of being applicable to a larger number of computers in your organization than a thick image, which is more specialized.

TPM *See* Trusted Platform Module (TPM).

Trusted Platform Module (TPM) The Trusted Platform Module is a hardware device defined by the Trusted Computing Group (TCG). A TPM provides a hardware-based root of trust and can be used to provide a variety of cryptographic services. Version 1.2 TPMs with TCG-compliant BIOS upgrades allow BitLocker to provide drive encryption as well as integrity checking of early boot features, which helps prevent tampering and provides a transparent startup experience.

U

UIPI *See* User Interface Privilege Isolation (UIPI).

Unattend.xml The generic name for the Windows answer file. Unattend.xml replaces all the answer files in earlier versions of Windows, including Unattend.txt and Winbom.ini.

unhandled exception An error that is not processed by an application. When a User mode process has an unhandled exception, the process is closed and Windows can present the user with an opportunity to send an error notification to Microsoft. When a Kernel mode process has an unhandled exception, a Stop error occurs.

unsolicited Remote Assistance (RA) A Remote Assistance request initiated by the expert (the user offering help). Also known as *offered Remote Assistance (RA).*

Upgrade Computer scenario In MDT 2010, a deployment scenario that deploys a new version of Windows to an existing computer that has an earlier version of Windows installed. The Upgrade Computer scenario preserves user data. *See also* Microsoft Deployment Toolkit 2010 (MDT 2010).

URL-based Quality of Service A new feature of Windows 7 and Windows Server 2008 R2 that enables IT administrators to use Group Policy settings to prioritize Web traffic based on a URL. With URL-based QoS, IT administrators can ensure critical Web traffic receives appropriate prioritization, improving performance on busy networks.

User Broker A feature of Protected mode in Windows Internet Explorer that provides a set of functions that lets the user save files to areas outside low-integrity areas.

User Interface Privilege Isolation (UIPI) A feature of Windows that blocks lower-integrity processes from accessing higher-integrity processes. This helps protect against shatter attacks. *See also* shatter attack.

User mode A processing mode provided by x86-based processors that provides only limited access to memory and other system resources. Processes that run in User mode can access memory allocated to the process, but must be elevated to Kernel mode by calling system APIs before the process can access protected resources.

user profile The set of user documents and settings that make up a user's desktop environment.

user profile namespace The hierarchy of folders within a user's profile folder.

user state The data files and settings associated with a user profile.

user state migration The process of transferring user files and settings from one computer to another or from an older version of Windows to a newer version of Windows installed on the same computer.

V

VHD Boot The Windows 7 bootloader can be configured to start Windows from a VHD file exactly as though the VHD file were a standard partition. Simply copy the VHD file to the local computer and then use BCDEdit.exe to add an entry to the boot menu for the VHD file. Windows 7 can also mount VHD files in the Disk Management console as if they were native partitions.

View Available Networks A new feature of wireless networking in Windows 7 that lets users display available wireless networks and quickly choose one to connect to.

VMK *See* Volume Master Key (VMK).

Volume License A license purchased from Microsoft or another software vendor to use multiple copies of an operating system or program.

Volume Master Key (VMK) The key used to encrypt the FVEK.

VPN Reconnect A new feature of Windows 7 that provides seamless and consistent VPN connectivity by automatically re-establishing a VPN connection if users temporarily lose their Internet connection. For example, if a user connected over mobile broadband passes through an area without reception, Windows 7 automatically reconnects any active VPN connections once Internet connectivity is reestablished.

W

Wake on Wireless LAN (WoWLAN) A new feature of Windows 7 that can reduce electricity consumption by enabling users and IT professionals to wake computers connected to wireless networks from Sleep mode remotely. Because users can wake computers to access them across the network, IT professionals can configure them to enter the low-power Sleep mode when not in use.

WAU *See* Windows Anytime Upgrade (WAU).

WCS *See* Windows Color System (WCS).

Web Services for Devices (WSD) A new type of network connectivity supported by Windows Vista and later versions. WSD enables users to have a Plug and Play experience similar to that of USB devices, except over the network instead of for locally connected devices.

WER *See* Windows Error Reporting (WER).

WGA *See* Windows Genuine Advantage (WGA).

.wim A file name extension that identifies Windows image files created by ImageX.

Windows AIK *See* Windows Automated Installation Kit (Windows AIK).

Windows Anytime Upgrade (WAU) An upgrade service primarily intended for home users that allows upgrades from one edition of Windows to a more advanced edition.

Windows Automated Installation Kit (Windows AIK) A collection of tools and documentation that you can use to automate the deployment of the Windows operating system. Windows AIK is one of several resources that you can use to deploy Windows; for example, tools and software such as MDT 2010 and Microsoft System Center Configuration Manager use features of Windows AIK to create system images and automate operating system installations.

Windows Color System (WCS) A feature that works with the Windows print subsystem to provide a richer color printing experience that supports wide-gamut printers (inkjet printers that use more than four ink colors) for lifelike printing of color photos and graphic-rich documents.

Windows Defender A feature of Windows that provides protection from spyware and other potentially unwanted software.

Windows Easy Transfer The feature in Windows 7 and Windows Vista that replaces the Windows XP Files And Settings Transfer Wizard. This tool leads the user through a series of pages to determine how much data to migrate and which migration method (disc or removable media, direct cable connection, or network) to use.

Windows Error Reporting (WER) The client feature for the overall Watson Feedback Platform (WFP), which allows Microsoft to collect reports about failure events that occur on a user's system, analyze the data contained in those reports, and respond to the user in a meaningful and actionable manner. WER is the technology that reports user-mode hangs, user-mode faults, and kernel-mode faults to the servers at Microsoft or to an internal error-reporting server.

Windows Genuine Advantage (WGA) A Microsoft initiative to ensure that users of copied Windows operating systems become aware of their counterfeit versions. By recording the product key and a signature from the computer's BIOS, Microsoft can effectively determine when retail versions of Windows have been copied and when volume-activated versions of Windows have been excessively distributed.

Windows Imaging A single compressed file containing a collection of files and folders that duplicates a Windows installation on a disk volume.

Windows PowerShell Integrated Scripting Environment (ISE) A GUI for Windows PowerShell that lets you run commands and write, edit, run, test, and debug scripts in the same window. It offers up to eight independent execution environments and includes a built-in debugger, multiline editing, selective execution, syntax colors, line and column numbers, and context-sensitive Help.

Windows PowerShell Modules Windows PowerShell modules let you organize your Windows PowerShell scripts and functions into independent, self-contained units. You can package your cmdlets, providers, scripts, functions, and other files into modules that you can distribute to other users. Modules are easier for users to install and use than Windows PowerShell snap-ins.

Windows PowerShell Remoting A feature introduced in Windows PowerShell 2.0 that lets you run Windows PowerShell commands for automated or interactive remote management.

Windows Product Activation (WPA) A way to ensure that customers are using genuine Windows operating systems purchased from Microsoft resellers. This tool, which began with Windows XP, defeated casual copying of Windows XP by ensuring that other systems had not recently been activated with the same product key.

Windows Server Update Services (WSUS) A free server tool available for download from Microsoft.com that administrators can use to manage which updates are distributed to computers running Windows on their internal network.

Windows System Assessment Tool (WinSAT) A command-line tool included with Windows for assessing the features, capabilities, and attributes of computer hardware.

Windows Troubleshooting Packs Collections of Windows PowerShell scripts that attempt to diagnose a problem and, if possible, solve the problem with the user's approval. Windows 7 includes 20 built-in Troubleshooting Packs that address more than 100 root causes of problems. Troubleshooting Packs can also perform ongoing maintenance of a specific feature.

Windows Virtual PC A new optional feature that you can use to evaluate and migrate to Windows 7 while maintaining compatibility with applications that run on older versions of Windows. This feature is available as a downloadable update package for Windows 7.

WinSAT *See* Windows System Assessment Tool (WinSAT).

WPA *See* Windows Product Activation (WPA).

WSD *See* Web Services for Devices (WSD).

WSUS *See* Windows Server Update Services (WSUS).

X

XML Paper Specification (XPS) A set of conventions for using XML to describe the content and appearance of paginated documents.

XPS *See* XML Paper Specification (XPS).

Z

Zero Touch Installation (ZTI) A MDT 2010 deployment option that fully automates the deployment of client computers. During a ZTI installation, the Windows operating system and all applications are automatically deployed the first time a computer is connected to the network and turned on. *See also* Microsoft Deployment Toolkit 2010 (MDT 2010).

ZTI *See* Zero Touch Installation (ZTI).

Index

Symbols and Numbers

A

B

C

D

E

G

H

I

J

K

N

O

P

S

T

U

V

W

Z

About the Authors

MITCH TULLOCH, lead author for the *Windows 7 Resource Kit*, is a widely recognized expert on Windows administration, networking, and security and has been repeatedly awarded Most Valuable Professional (MVP) status by Microsoft for his outstanding contributions in supporting users who deploy Microsoft platforms, products, and solutions. Mitch has written or contributed to almost two dozen books on computing and networking topics, including the *Microsoft Encyclopedia of Networking*, the *Microsoft Encyclopedia of Security*, *Introducing Windows Server 2008*, *Microsoft Office Communications Server 2007 Resource Kit*, *Windows Vista Resource Kit*, and *Understanding Microsoft Virtualization Solutions: From the Desktop to the Datacenter*, all published by Microsoft Press.

Mitch has published hundreds of articles on WindowsNetworking.com, WindowsDevCenter.com, ITworld.com, and other IT professional Web sites. Mitch has also written feature articles for leading industry magazines such as *BizTech Magazine*, *FedTech Magazine*, and *NetworkWorld*. Mitch's articles have been widely syndicated on sites ranging from TechTarget.com to CNN.com. In addition, Mitch has developed e-learning courses on Windows 7 for Microsoft Learning, and he has developed graduate-level courses in Information Security Management for the Masters of Business Administration (MBA) program of Jones International University.

Mitch currently resides in Winnipeg, Canada, where he runs an IT content development business. Prior to starting his own business in 1998, Mitch worked as a Microsoft Certified Trainer (MCT) for Productivity Point International. For more information about Mitch, visit his Web site at *http://www.mtit.com*.

TONY NORTHRUP, MVP, MCSE, MCTS, and CISSP, is a Windows consultant and author living near Boston, Massachusetts. Tony started programming before Windows 1.0 was released, but he has focused on Windows administration and development for the last 15 years. He has written more than 20 books covering Windows networking, security, and development. Among other titles, Tony is coauthor of the *Windows Server 2003 Resource Kit* and the *Windows Vista Resource Kit*.

When he's not writing, Tony enjoys photography, travel, and exercise. Tony lives with his dog, Sandi. You can learn more about Tony by visiting his technical blog at *http://www.windows7clues.com* or his personal Web site at *http://www.northrup.org*.

JERRY HONEYCUTT empowers people to work more productively by helping them deploy and use popular technologies, including the Windows and Microsoft Office suite product families. He reaches out to the community through his frequent writings, talks, and consulting practice.

Jerry is intimately involved in Microsoft's desktop-deployment initiatives. He was the documentation lead for Microsoft Deployment and frequently writes white papers and articles for Microsoft about desktop deployment.

Jerry owns and operates Deployment Forum at *http://www.deploymentforum.com/*. This Web site is a member-driven community for IT professionals who deploy the Windows operating system.

Jerry has written more than 30 books. His most recent titles include the *Microsoft Windows Desktop Deployment Resource Kit* (Microsoft Press, 2004) and the *Microsoft Windows XP Registry Guide* (Microsoft Press, 2002), which is part of the *Windows Server 2003 Resource Kit*. See Jerry's Web site at *www.honeycutt.com* or send mail to *jerry@honeycutt.com*.

ED WILSON is one of the Microsoft Scripting Guys (see *http://www.ScriptingGuys.com*) and is a well-known scripting expert. He writes the daily "Hey Scripting Guy!" blog, a weekly blog posting for Microsoft Press, and a monthly "Hey Scripting Guy!" article for *Technet Magazine*. He has also spoken at TechEd and at the Microsoft internal TechReady conferences. He is a Microsoft-certified trainer who has delivered a popular Microsoft Windows PowerShell workshop to Microsoft Premier Customers worldwide. He has written 8 books, including 5 on Windows scripting that were published by Microsoft Press. He has also contributed to nearly a dozen other books as well, and he is currently working on a Windows PowerShell Best Practices book for Microsoft Press. Ed holds more than 20 industry certifications, including Microsoft Certified Systems Engineer (MCSE) and Certified Information Systems Security Professional (CISSP). Prior to coming to work for Microsoft, he was a senior consultant for a Microsoft Gold Certified Partner, where he specialized in Active Directory Domain Services design and Microsoft Exchange Server implementation. In his spare time, he enjoys woodworking, underwater photography, and scuba diving. Find out more about Ed at *http://www.edwilson.com*.

JAMES BRUNDAGE is a software tester on the Windows PowerShell team. He has tested parts of the Windows PowerShell Engine and Scripting Language throughout the development of version 2 of Windows PowerShell. He won the Gold Star Award for work in scripted user interfaces in June 2008 following the "Week of WPF" series on the Windows PowerShell team blog at *http://blogs.msdn.com/powershell/*. When he's not testing software, James can often be found pursuing his curiosity about programming and gadgets throughout the rest of Microsoft. If he's not pursuing any form of programming, James can be found spending time with his girlfriend or playing games on his Xbox.

System Requirements

You can access the contents of the companion media using a computer running Windows XP operating system or later. The computer should meet the minimum hardware requirements for the version of Windows being used.

To access the eBook and sample chapters, use an application that can display PDF files, such as Adobe Acrobat Reader, which can be downloaded for free from *http://get.adobe.com/reader/*.

To read the Volume Activation guides for Chapter 11, use either Microsoft Office Word 2007 or download the latest Microsoft Word Viewer from the Microsoft Download Center at *http://www.microsoft.com/downloads/*.

The Windows 7 Resource Kit PowerShell Pack and the sample Windows PowerShell scripts on the companion media require Windows PowerShell 2.0. The Windows PowerShell Pack and sample scripts have been tested only on Windows 7. See the Introduction to this book for more information on how to install and use these items.